To the Student

This modern text is designed to prepare you for your future professional career. While theories, ideas, techniques, and data are dynamic, the information contained in this volume will provide you a quick and useful reference as well as a guide for future learning for many years to come. Your familiarity with the contents of this book will make it an important volume in your professional library.

A Study Guide for this textbook is available through your college bookstore. It has been written to enhance your understanding of the process of human resource management. Ask the bookstore manager to order a copy for you if it is not in stock.

FOUNDATIONS
OF PERSONNEL
HUMAN RESOURCE
MANAGEMENT

FOUNDATIONS OF PERSONNEL

HUMAN RESOURCE MANAGEMENT

JOHN M. IVANCEVICH

Cullen Professor of Organizational
Behavior and Management
University of Houston

WILLIAM F. GLUECK

Late Professor of
University of Georgia

FOURTH EDITION
1989

Homewood, IL 60430
Boston, MA 02116

Executive editor: Gary L. Nelson
Project editor: Suzanne Ivester
Production manager: Carma W. Fazio
Design: Image House, Inc.
Compositor: Better Graphics, Inc.
Typeface: 10/12 Century Schoolbook
Printer: R. R. Donnelley & Sons Company

LIBRARY OF CONGRESS
Library of Congress Cataloging-in-Publication Data

Ivancevich, John M.
    Foundations of personnel/human resource management/John M.
Ivancevich, William F. Glueck.—4th ed.
        p.   cm.
    Includes bibliographical references and indexes.
    ISBN 0-256-06670-1
    1. Personnel management.   2. Personnel management—Case studies.
I. Glueck, William F.   II. Title.
HF5549.I88 1989
658.3—dc19   88–15528
                                                              CIP

Printed in the United States of America
    3 4 5 6 7 8 9 0 DO 6 5 4 3 2 1 0

PREFACE

The first edition of this text was published a decade ago. Bill Glueck was the author of the first edition, which was entitled *Foundations of Personnel*. It was Bill's belief that many faculty members wanted an uncluttered, straightforward, practically oriented text to use in their personnel courses. He provided a text that appealed to both instructors and students, and this accomplishment is a tribute to his ability to communicate his knowledge in a clear, intelligible way.

Bill's untimely passing prevented his further development and refinement of the text through the three revised editions. This edition still incorporates many of Bill Glueck's ideas, orientation, and basic text structure in its examination of personnel/human resource management (P/HRM). His original crafting of a high-quality and teachable text remains noticeable in this fourth edition.

Personnel/human resource management is a necessary activity in all organizations. Its focal point is *people*. People are the lifeblood of organizations. Without them, there is no need for P/HRM systems, programs, or procedures. Because they involve people, P/HRM activities have to be fine-tuned and properly implemented in order to achieve desired outcomes. The uniqueness of P/HRM lies in its emphasis on people in work settings and its concern for the well-being and comfort of the human resources in an organization. This edition focuses on people who work directly in P/HRM as specialists, and those who, as employees (e.g., engineers, clerks, typists, machinists, chemists, teachers, nurses) are influenced by it.

In order to make the book interesting, scholarly, and practical, a number of pedagogical procedures were adopted:

1. Each chapter begins with a brief list of behavioral learning objectives, key terms that will be covered, and an outline of the chapter.
2. Each chapter is introduced by a short situation called P/HRM In Action, which emphasizes applied P/HRM techniques and issues. At various points in the chapter, and at its conclusion, the situation is further developed. The P/HRM In Action element highlights the chapter's content.
3. Most chapters use the diagnostic model that serves as the integrative framework of this book.
4. In most chapters, the role played by a P/HRM manager, specialist, or operating manager is described.
5. Most chapters include a P/HRM Manager Close-Up. These real-life personal viewpoints of P/HRM managers or specialists answer the question: "What does someone actually working in the P/HRM field do?"
6. Most chapters conclude with recommendations for the most effective use of P/HRM in seven kinds of organizations, which differ on the basis of size (number of employees), complexity of products or services, and degree to which products or services change over time.

7. Each chapter summary provides students with a handy, concise reference to the chapter's main points of interest.
8. Cases and experiential exercises at the end of various chapters reflect P/HRM issues, concerns, and problems faced in organizations such as Domino's Pizza, Dunkin' Donuts, GTE, Goldman, Sachs & Co., General Foods, IBM, Nucor, Levi Strauss, Ameritrust Bank, Bechtel Power, and Firestone Tire and Rubber. The realism offered by the cases and exercises illustrates the vital role played by P/HRM in organizations of all sizes.
9. A comprehensive glossary of key terms is provided at the end of each chapter and the book.

The Parts and Appendixes

The revised edition consists of six parts. Part One, Introduction to Personnel/Human Resource Management and the Environment, contains three chapters. Chapter 1 defines the role of P/HRM in organizations. Chapter 2 provides the integrative model that is used throughout the book. Chapter 3 is a comprehensive treatment of equal employment opportunity laws and programs.

Part Two, Analysis, Planning, and Staffing, contains four chapters covering: job analysis and design, Chapter 4; human resource planning, Chapter 5; recruitment, Chapter 6; and selection, Chapter 7.

Part Three examines performance evaluation and compensation. Chapter 8 covers performance evaluation; Chapter 9, an overview of compensation; Chapter 10, compensation methods and policies of personnel; and Chapter 11, employee benefits and services.

Part Four, Training and Development for Better Performance, contains four chapters. Chapter 12 discusses orientation and training. Management and organizational development are covered in Chapter 13. Career planning and development is presented in Chapter 14. Discipline and the difficult employee is covered in Chapter 15.

Part Five, Labor Relations and Safety and Health, includes Chapters 16 and 17, on labor unions, and Chapter 18, on employee safety and health.

Part Six, Work Scheduling and Evaluation of Personnel/Human Resource Management includes two chapters. Chapter 19 covers work schedules and the quality of work life. Chapter 20 discusses procedures for evaluating the P/HRM function.

Three main appendixes were added to the last edition and are included in the fourth edition. Appendix A—Sources of Personnel/Human Resource Management Information, Facts, and Figures—was prepared by Paul N. Keaton of the University of Wisconsin, LaCrosse. This provides valuable sources of information that are useful in P/HRM.

Appendix B—Designing a P/HRM Measurement System—was prepared by Jac Fitz-enz, Ph.D., president of the Saratoga Institute. This appendix spells out the reasons why measurement is important and how a measurement system for the P/HRM unit can be developed and styled.

Appendix C—Career Planning—was prepared by the author of the text. It examines the important steps involved in career planning that each person must accept responsibility for and initiate at the appropriate time. Each reader of the book must become actively involved in his or her own career plan.

New and Strengthened Features

The dynamic changes in personnel/human resource management required some alteration, deletion, and expansion of material presented in the previous edition. Instructor and student comments were reviewed and carefully considered in the course of the revision. In addition, numerous personnel/human resource experts in organizations have been interviewed in the past decade. These endeavors resulted in some new features which add to Bill Glueck's original ideas and views about P/HRM:

- A slightly revised diagnostic framework used throughout the book. The model is first presented in Exhibit 2–1.
- An updated and revised Chapter 3, The Law and Personnel/Human Resource Management. The increasing importance of laws, regulations, and court rulings to P/HRM activities continues to grow and needs to be constantly updated. This edition has more coverage of sexual harassment, the economic status of women, and EEO than previous editions.
- Computers play a growing role in P/HRM programs and activities. In many chapters, computer use in P/HRM practices is discussed.
- The P/HRM Manager Close-Up, sections started in the last edition are continued. Many of the managers discuss actual problems that they have or are working on in performing their P/HRM activities.
- Again, actual company forms, materials, and charts are used throughout this book. They were furnished and updated by P/HRM managers who wanted to share them with students and instructors.
- Coverage of the Immigration and Control Act of 1986 is introduced in the discussion of recruitment responsibilities of organizations.
- A much more focused and detailed coverage of comparable worth is provided. Different viewpoints of this issue are presented.
- Examples and some analysis of gainsharing programs are covered.
- The concerns about maternity/paternity leave and child care are expanded in this edition.
- The Consolidated Omnibus Budget Reconciliation Act (COBRA) and the potential impact of noncompliance is covered.
- Changes in benefit programs brought about by the tax reform act of 1986 are considered and introduced.
- Mentoring and the impact it can have on the personal development of employees is discussed.
- Instead of examining discipline programs only in negative terms, we introduce the idea of positive discipline. Also, the notion of termination-at-will is discussed in Chapter 15.
- Union-management cooperation and the consequences of such interactions and arrangements is discussed in more detail in Chapter 17.
- Although the number of AIDS victims is escalating, very few American and Canadian firms are addressing the issue. The role that employers must play

to address AIDS in the workplace are spelled out in detail in Chapter 18. The coverage here is factual, thorough, and important.

Each of these new features was designed to (1) stimulate student interest in P/HRM as a field of study and as a set of programs and procedures that influence people within organizations; (2) clearly illustrate that P/HRM is a dynamic, changing field; (3) show by example that what is being discussed has both a theoretical rationale (often a research base) and offers practical useful applications in the "real world"—the organization; and (4) provide instructors with material, statistics, and illustrations that can help make the classroom experience more exciting. In essence, the third edition was written for students and instructors alike.

Acknowledgments

The fourth edition in its final form is the result of the efforts of numerous people. Special thanks are due to the following P/HRM managers and specialists who willingly provided ideas, information, and data:

David M. Aultfather
Manager–Personnel Services
Miller-Dwan Hospital and Medical Center

Herbert J. Ayers
EEO Administrator
J.A. Jones Construction Services Co.

John F. Baggaley
Director of Personnel
Doctors Medical Center

John F. Barrows
Director–Training and Development
Packaging Corporation of America

Christian K. Bement
Vice President
Director of Industrial Relations
Thrifty Corporation

Paul S. Bernius
Director, Manpower
Planning and Development
Hilti Corporation

Robert L. Berra
Vice President–Personnel
Monsanto Company

Betty Bessler
Director of Personnel
Mary Kay Cosmetics

Louis J. Bibri
Vice President and Director of Employee Relations
Armstrong World Industries, Inc.

John D. Blodger
Group Director of Employee Relations
Bendix Corporation

William J. Danos
Safety Engineer
New Wales Chemicals, Inc.

Eileen M. DeCoursey
Vice President–Employee Relations
Johns-Manville

Howard Falberg
Vice President–Personnel
Associated Dry Goods Corporation

Naomi Garner
Vice President and Director–Human Resources
First National Bank of Hot Springs

Adrianne H. Geiger
Manager–Human Resource Systems
Owens-Illinois, Inc.

Ernest J. E. Griffes
Director of Employee Benefits
Levi Strauss & Co.

Richard W. Hucke
Vice President–Human Resources
Weston Company

Audrey Johnson
Manager–Employee Relations
Gillette Company

Mary Kale
Senior College Relations Representative
Bethlehem Steel Company

John C. Midler
Director of Personnel and Labor Relations
Archer Daniels Midland

David A. Miron
Director of Management Development and Human Resource Systems
Owens-Illinois, Inc.

Henry Oliver
Manager of Compensation and Benefits
University Computing Company

Andrew J. Porter
Manager–Communications and Development
Honeywell Information Systems

James H. Pou
Staff Vice President–Employee Relations
University Computing Company

John Quigley
Vice President–Human Resources
Dr Pepper

William M. Read
Senior Vice President
Atlantic Richfield Company

William J. Streidl
Director of Management Education and Development
Tenneco, Inc.

Kenneth W. Tynes
Manager–Professional Employment
Cessna Aircraft Company

Gregory M. Watts
Personnel Director
Chicago Switch

Helpful comments were provided for each edition by outstanding reviewers, many of whose ideas and recommendations were used. Their promptness, tactfulness, and knowledge about P/HRM were certainly appreciated. The lead reviewers for the fourth edition were:

Richard Leventhal
Metropolitan State College

John Samaras
Central State University

Bruce Johnson
Gustav Adolphus College

Henry Houser
Auburn University at Montgomery

Kim Stewart developed a number of new, exciting, and teachable cases for this edition. These cases when integrated with the chapter content should provide many opportunities for some challenging classroom debates. Kim's dedication to effective teaching is appreciated and is certainly reflected in her cases.

I also want to personally recognize my secretary, Anne Highfill, who pleasantly worked and worked to perfect this book. Without Anne's efforts and tolerance for working on repeated revisions this book would not be ready. An author needs to have a solid work support team and Anne is the entire team.

Finally, I want to dedicate this fourth edition to Bill Glueck. Bill was a hard worker whose contributions will endure long beyond his passing. The continued success of *Foundations of Personnel/Human Resource Management* was made possible only because he took the necessary, pioneering step of developing an idea and converting it into an educationally sound text.

John M. Ivancevich

SHORT CONTENTS

DETAILED CONTENTS

XV

PART V   LABOR RELATIONS AND SAFETY AND HEALTH   686

INTRODUCTION TO PERSONNEL/ HUMAN RESOURCE MANAGEMENT AND THE ENVIRONMENT

Personnel/human resource management (P/HRM) is concerned with the effective management of people at work. P/HRM examines what can or should be done to make people both more productive and more satisfied with their working life.

This book has been written for all those interested in people working within organizations. Its goal is to help develop more effective managers and staff specialists who work directly with the human resources of organizations. The function is called personnel, employee relations, or human resource management. In this book, however, the term *personnel/human resource management* (P/HRM) will be used.

Part One consists of three chapters. Chapter 1, Personnel/Human Resource Management, is an introduction to P/HRM. The diagnostic approach to P/HRM is introduced in Chapter 2, A Diagnostic Approach to Personnel/ Human Resource Management, which also reviews behavioral science perspectives on people and how this knowledge affects employee effectiveness at work. The ways managers use knowledge of environmental factors—such as the work setting, government regulations, and union requirements—to influence the performance of people at work are also discussed in Chapter 2. Chapter 3, The Law and Personnel/Human Resource Management, describes the legal environmental influences on P/HRM. A number of major laws and regulations are discussed in this chapter, as well as throughout the book.

1

PERSONNEL/HUMAN RESOURCE MANAGEMENT

LEARNING OBJECTIVES

After studying this chapter, you should be able to:

- **Define** the term *personnel/human resource management.*
- **Describe** the personnel/human resource management activities performed in organizations.
- **Explain** why human resources are a key ingredient in the strategic plans of organizations.
- **Discuss** the role that specialists and operating managers play in performing personnel/human resource management activities.
- **List** at least three of the main objectives pursued by P/HRM units in organizations.

KEY TERMS

Personnel/Human Resource Management (P/HRM)
P/HRM Objectives
P/HRM Policy
P/HRM Procedure

CHAPTER OUTLINE

P/HRM · IN · ACTION

Don Brokop

Don Brokop has, over the past nine years, proved himself to be an outstanding shift supervisor at the Melody Machine Products Corp. plant in South Chicago. He has worked every shift, likes people, and recently was the winner of the Outstanding Plant Manager award. Don is now 34 years old and is beginning to look closely at his career plans. He believes that he needs to gain some experience in jobs other than production.

Last week a position opened at the plant for an assistant director of personnel/human resources. At first, Don gave no thought to the position; but later he asked his boss, Marty Fogestrom, about it. Marty encouraged Don to think his plans through and to consider whether he wanted to work in the personnel/human resource management area.

Don talked with plant colleagues about the new position, looked over the want ads in the *Chicago Tribune,* read *The Wall Street Journal,* and found a number of interesting news items concerning personnel/human resource management. He found that many different careers existed in the personnel/human resource management area. He realized that he had not really under-

stood the job being done by Melody's department of personnel/human resources. What struck him the most was that issues, problems, and challenges concerning people are what personnel/human resources are about.

Here are a few of the news items that caught his eye:[1]

- The use of microcomputers in P/HRM is mushrooming in organizations. Today uses of P/HRM microsystems can be found for building personnel databases, human resource planning, benefits planning and administration, compliance reporting, and monitoring the effectiveness of P/HRM departments. More and more P/HRM department employees are using microcomputers to help them deal with day-to-day problems.
- Approximately 2,500 U.S. companies help with their employees' child-care needs. That is about a fourfold increase between 1983 and 1987. The push in these companies comes from personnel/human resource management executives who believe that

---

[1] Eric G. Flamholtz, Yvonne Randle, and Sonja Sackmann, "Personnel Management: The Tone of Tomorrow," *Personnel Journal,* July 1987, pp. 42–48.

(continued)

getting involved in child care helps increase recruiting effectiveness, morale, and productivity, and decreases accident rates, absenteeism, tardiness, and turnover. Companies that help in child care are getting involved by providing services where the community supply is lacking, offering information about parenting and selecting quality care, giving financial assistance for purchasing community services, and freeing up time to help employees balance the responsibilities of family and work.

- A personnel/human resource manager observed cafeteria workers whispering in the hallway. When she asked what the trouble was, they angrily replied that they were afraid a co-worker had AIDS. The manager attempted to reassure them, but in the following days rumors spread. Suddenly absenteeism among the workers increased, four employees quit, and other employees boycotted the cafeteria. The manager expressed the view that this type of problem is becoming more common as the AIDS epidemic becomes more widespread.

- More and more organizations are thinking globally about their employees. There is a definite trend toward thinking and planning for the effective use of human resources. In most U.S. companies, the top human resource person reports directly to the top operating officer.

- One leading technologist predicted that within five years, there will be over 500,000 robots at work in Japan's industrial community. U.S. robotics experts predict that by 2005 robots will possess human equivalence. That is, robots will have awareness of their existence, intelligence, and common sense similar to human beings.

- The number of employed women reached 50 million in 1987. Increases in women's participation in the workforce have been most noticeable in professional occupations (e.g., law, medicine, engineering) and computer systems analysis.

- A 10-year-old bias case involving General Motors was settled at a cost to the company of $42.5 million. Blacks, women, and Hispanics will benefit from the agreement, which calls for the largest ever out-of-court settlement of job bias charges.

Don thought about his recent conversations, his career plans, the news stories, and the challenges of moving from production to personnel/human resource management. He thought his experience in supervisory management would be helpful if he was fortunate enough to land the job, but he wondered if he was qualified for this kind of job. He was confident, and considered his college education and experience invaluable. He wanted new challenges. Then he learned through the grapevine that the job was his if he wanted to make the move. (If you were Don, would you be likely to make this kind of career shift? Don's decision will be presented at the end of this chapter.)

People; human resources; making organizations more aware of human resources; being in the people business—these words and thoughts are common in our modern society. Today bromides and panaceas for solving people-problems are being replaced by a total, professional approach to **personnel/human resource management (P/HRM).** Don Brokop is considering the challenges associated with this new wave of professional treatment and concern for people within organizations. Organizations are definitely in the people business—Don certainly saw this after only a quick review of a few news stories.

This book will focus on people in organizational settings. The entire book will be concerned with the employees of organizations—the clerks, technicians, supervisors, managers, and executives. Large, medium, and small organizations, such as IBM, Procter & Gamble, Victoreen, Medco, Greensway Pharmacies, Tenneco, and TRW Systems understand clearly that to grow, prosper, and remain healthy, they must optimize the return on investment of all resources, financial and human.

When an organization is really concerned about people, its total philosophy, climate, and tone will reflect this belief. In this book personnel/human resource management is used to describe the function that is concerned with people—the employees.

> Personnel/human resource management is the function performed in organizations that facilitates the most effective use of people (employees) to achieve organizational and individual goals.

Terms such as *personnel, human resource management, industrial relations,* and *employee development* are used by different individuals to describe the unit, department, or group concerned about people. The term *human resource management* is now widely used, though many people still refer to a *personnel department.* In order to keep contact with history, the more modern term, *personnel/human resource management (P/HRM)* will be used throughout the book. It is a term that reflects the increased concern both society and organizations have in people. Today employees—the human resource—demand more of their jobs and respond favorably to management activities that give them greater control of their lives.

Personnel/human resource management consists of numerous activities, including:

- Equal employment opportunity programs.
- Job analysis.
- Human resource planning.
- Employee recruitment, selection, and orientation.
- Career development and counseling, performance evaluation, and training and development.
- Compensation and benefits.
- Safety and health.

- Labor relations.
- Discipline, control, and evaluation of the personnel function.
- Work scheduling.
- Quality of work life.

These activities are topics of the various chapters in this book. They also appear as elements in the diagnostic model of the P/HRM function that is used throughout the text. (This model is described in Chapter 2.)

The following three things should be stressed about P/HRM at the outset:

It is action oriented—Effective P/HRM focuses on action, rather than on record-keeping, written procedure, or rules. Certainly, P/HRM uses rules, records, and policies, but it stresses action. P/HRM emphasizes the solution of employment problems to help achieve organizational objectives and facilitate employee development and satisfaction.

It is individually oriented—Whenever possible, P/HRM treats each employee as an *individual* and offers services and programs to meet the individual's needs. McDonald's, the fast-food chain, has gone so far as to give its chief personnel executive the title of vice president of individuality.

It is future oriented—Effective P/HRM is concerned with helping an organization achieve its objectives in the future by providing for competent, well-motivated employees. Thus, human resources need to be incorporated into an organization's long-term strategies.

A BRIEF HISTORY OF PERSONNEL/ HUMAN RESOURCE MANAGEMENT (P/HRM)

The history of personnel/human resource management can be traced to England, where masons, carpenters, leather workers, and other craftspeople organized themselves into guilds. They used their unity to improve their work conditions.[2] These guilds became the forerunners of trade unions.

The field further developed with the arrival of the Industrial Revolution in the latter part of the 18th century, which laid the basis for a new and complex industrial society. In simple terms, the Industrial Revolution began with the substitution of steam power and machinery for time-consuming hand labor. Working conditions, social patterns, and the division of labor were significantly altered. A new kind of employee, a boss, who wasn't necessarily the owner as had usually been the case in the past, became a power broker in the new factory system. With these changes also came a widening gap between workers and owners.

The drastic changes in technology, the growth of organizations, the rise of unions, and government concern and intervention concerning working people resulted in the development of personnel departments. There is no specific date assigned to the appearance of the first personnel department, but around the

---

[2] Henry S. Gilbertson, *Personnel Policies and Unionism* (Boston: Ginn and Co., 1950), p. 17.

1920s more and more organizations seemed to take note of and do something about the conflict between employees and management.[3] Early personnel administrators were called *welfare secretaries*. Their job was to bridge the gap between management and operator (worker); in other words, they were to speak to workers in their own language and then recommend to management what had to be done to get the best results from employees.

The early history of personnel still obscures the importance of the P/HRM function to management. Until the 1960s, the personnel function was considered to be concerned only with blue-collar or operating employees. It was viewed as a record-keeping unit that handed out 25-year tenure pins and coordinated the annual company picnic. Peter Drucker, a respected management scholar and consultant, made a statement about personnel management that reflected its blue-collar orientation. Drucker stated that the job of personnel was "partly a file clerk's job, partly a housekeeping job, partly a social worker's job, and partly fire fighting, heading off union trouble."[4]

The P/HRM function today is concerned with much more than simple filing, housekeeping, and record-keeping.[5] When P/HRM strategies are integrated within the organization, P/HRM plays a major role in clarifying the firm's human resource problems and develops solutions to them. It is oriented toward action, the individual, and the future. Today it would be difficult to imagine any organization achieving and sustaining effectiveness without efficient P/HRM programs and activities. The strategic importance of P/HRM to the survival of an organization will become clearer as we move into the book.

ORGANIZATIONAL EFFECTIVENESS

Survival is the major long-run objective of any organization. Personnel/human resource management activities play a major role in ensuring that an organization will survive and prosper. Organizational effectiveness and the lack of it are described in this book in terms of such criteria and components as performance, legal compliance, employee satisfaction, absenteeism, turnover, scrap rates, grievance rates, and accident rates. In order for a firm to survive and prosper, reasonable goals in each of these components must be achieved.[6] In most organizations, effectiveness is measured by the balance of such complementary characteristics as reaching goals, employing the skills and abilities of employees efficiently, and ensuring the influx and retention of well-trained and motivated employees.

---

[3] Henry Eilbert, "The Development of Personnel Management in the United States," *Business History Review*, Autumn 1959, pp. 345–64.

[4] Fred K. Foulkes, "The Expanding Role of the Personnel Function," *Harvard Business Review*, March-April 1975, pp. 71–72.

[5] Randall S. Schuler, "Personnel and Human Resource Management Choices and Organizational Strategy," *Human Resource Planning*, Spring 1987, pp. 1–17.

[6] Joseph R. Toto, "Eight Characteristics of Organizational Effectiveness," *Personnel Journal*, May 1986, pp. 35–41.

Successful managers recognize that human resources deserve attention because they are a significant factor in top-management strategic decisions that guide the organization's future operations. Three crucial elements are needed for firms to be effective: mission and strategy, organizational structure, and human resource management.[7] However, it is important to remember that people do the work and create the ideas that allow the organization to survive. Even the most capital-intensive, well-structured organizations need people to run them.

People limit or enhance the strengths and weaknesses of an organization. Current changes in the environment are often related to changes in human resources, such as shifts in the composition, education, and work attitudes of employees. The P/HRM function should provide for or respond to these changes.

One problem top management has in making strategic planning decisions regarding people is that all other resources are evaluated in terms of money, and at present, in most organizations, people are not. There has been a push toward human resource accounting, which would place dollar values on the human assets of organizations.[8] Professional sports teams, such as the New York Yankees, Boston Celtics, and Washington Redskins place a dollar value on athletes. They then depreciate these values over the course of time.

If the objectives of P/HRM are to be accomplished, top managers will have to treat the human resources of the organization as the *key* to effectiveness. To do this—to accomplish the important objectives of P/HRM—management must regard the development of superior human resources as an essential competitive requirement that needs careful planning, hard work, and evaluation.

OBJECTIVES OF THE P/HRM FUNCTION

The contributions P/HRM makes to organizational effectiveness include the following:

- Helping the organization reach its goals.
- Employing the skills and abilities of the work force efficiently.
- Providing the organization with well-trained and well-motivated employees.
- Increasing to the fullest the employee's job satisfaction and self-actualization.
- Developing and maintaining a quality of work life that makes employment in the organization desirable.
- Communicating P/HRM policies to all employees.

---

[7] Noel M. Tichy, Charles J. Fornbrun, and Mary Anne Devanna, "Strategic Human Resource Management," *Sloan Management Review,* Fall 1982, pp. 47–61.

[8] Jac Fitz-enz, *How to Measure Human Resources Management* (New York: McGraw-Hill, 1984).

- Helping to maintain ethical policies and behavior.
- Managing change to the mutual advantage of individuals, groups, the enterprise, and the public.

Helping the Organization Reach Its Goals

David Babcock, chairman of the board and chief executive officer of the May Company and formerly its personnel vice president, expresses the purpose of personnel: "Personnel, like other subunits of the enterprise, exists to achieve the goals of the enterprise first and foremost. If it does not serve that purpose, personnel (or any other subunit) will wither and die."

Employing the Skills and Abilities of the Work Force Efficiently

Clyde Benedict, the chief personnel officer for Integon Corporation, stated this purpose somewhat differently. He said the purpose is "to make people's strengths productive, and to benefit customers, stockholders, and employees. I believe this is the purpose Walt Disney had in mind when he said his greatest accomplishment was to build the Disney organization with its own people."

Providing the Organization with Well-Trained and Well-Motivated Employees

This is an effectiveness measure for P/HRM. Babcock phrases this purpose as "building and protecting the most valuable asset of the enterprise: people." Andrew Grove is the president of Intel, a high-technology company, who considers training and motivation to be extremely important for accomplishing performance objectives. He stated:

> The single most important task of a manager is to elicit peak performance from his subordinates. So if two things limit high output, a manager has two ways to tackle the issue: through training and motivation. . . . How does a manager motivate his subordinates? For most of us, the word implies doing something to another person. But I don't think that can happen, because motivation has to come from within somebody. Accordingly, all a manager can do is create an environment in which motivated people can flourish.[9]

So P/HRM's effectiveness measure—its chief effectiveness measure, anyway—is to provide the right people at the right phase of performing a job, at the right time for the organization.

---

[9] Andrew S. Grove, *High Output Management* (New York: Random House, 1983), p. 158.

Increasing to the Fullest the Employees's Job Satisfaction and Self-Actualization

Thus far, the emphasis has been on the organization's needs. But unlike computers or cash balances, employees have feelings of their own. For employees to be productive, they must feel that the job is right for their abilities and that they are being treated equitably. For many employees the job is a major source of personal identity. Most of us spend the majority of our waking hours at work and getting to and from work. Thus, our identity is tied closely to our job.

Satisfied employees are not *automatically* more productive. However, unsatisfied employees do tend to quit more often, to be absent more frequently, and to produce lower quality work than satisfied workers. Nevertheless, both satisfied and dissatisfied employees may perform equally in quantitative terms, such as processing the same number of insurance claims per hour.

Developing and Maintaining a Quality of Work Life that Makes Employment in the Organization a Desirable Personal and Social Situation

This purpose is closely related to the previous one. Quality of work life is a somewhat general concept, referring to several aspects of the job experience. These include such factors as management and supervisory style, freedom and autonomy to make decisions on the job, satisfactory physical surroundings, job safety, satisfactory working hours, and meaningful tasks. Basically, a sound quality of work life (QWL) program assumes that a job and the work environment should be structured to meet as many of the worker's needs as possible. Former General Motors Chairperson Thomas Murphy captured the QWL philosophy when he stated:

> We should try to treat our people the way we would like to be treated. That in my judgment will be good for the individual and good for business.[10]

Roy F. Bennett, the Chief Executive Officer of Ford Motor Company, added that:

> Employee involvement is not a substitute for good management or labor practices. . . . . The 60s were probably the MBO decade. The 80s are likely to be the decade of employee involvement in QWL.[11]

---

[10] Michael LeBoeuf, *The Productivity Challenge* (New York: McGraw-Hill, 1982), pp. 125–26.

[11] Deborah Shaw Cohen, "Why Quality of Work Life Doesn't Always Mean Quality," *Training: The Magazine of Human Resources Development,* October 1981, p. 57.

Communicating P/HRM Policies to All Employees

Clyde Benedict explains this objective. P/HRM's responsibility is "to communicate in the fullest possible sense both in tapping ideas, opinions, and feelings of customers, noncustomers, regulators, and other external publics, as well as in understanding the views of internal human resources. The other facet of this responsibility is communicating managerial decisions to relevant publics in their own language."

Closely related to communication within the organization is representation of the organization to those outside. The outside units in contact with an organization include trade unions and local, state, and federal government bodies that pass laws and issue regulations affecting P/HRM. The P/HRM department must also communicate effectively with other top-management people (e.g., marketing, production, research and development) to illustrate what it can offer these areas in the form of support, counsel, and techniques, and increase its contribution to the overall strategic mission and goals of the organization.

Helping to Maintain Ethical Policies and Behavior

David Babcock believes it is vital for P/HRM to help communicate and monitor the firm's ethical code so that it is more than a piece of paper. P/HRM should develop incentives that reward ethical practices, not the opposite. "Personnel's purpose is to practice morality in management in preparing people for change, dealing with dissent and conflict, holding high standards of productivity, building acceptance of standards that determine progression, and adhering to the spirit and letter of high professional conduct," Clyde Benedict said. Babcock calls this "keeping attuned to the times"—the social and economic changes affecting working conditions. This relates to both employee satisfaction and organizational efficiency and effectiveness.

Managing Change to the Mutual Advantage of Individuals, Groups, the Organization, and the Public

In the past decade, there has been rapid, turbulent, and often strained development in the relationship between employers and employees. New trends and changes have occurred in telecommuting, paternity leave, QWL programs, spouse-relocation assistance, gain-sharing, benefit cost-sharing, union-management negotiations, testing, and many other P/HRM areas of interest. Nearly all of these trends and changes can be traced to the emergence of new lifestyles and an aging population.[12]

---

[12] John K. Ortman, "Human Resources 1984: The State of the Profession," *Personnel Administrator,* June 1984, pp. 35–48.

What these changes mean to P/HRM managers is that new, flexible approaches must be initiated and used effectively without jeopardizing the survival of the organization. P/HRM managers must cope with trends and changes, while still contributing to the organization. Jerry Holder, senior vice president for Marion Laboratories, makes a crucial point about P/HRM managers when he says: "Those who fail to measure up will suffer the same fate as technical staff who become obsolete—downgrades, reassignment, and even replacement."[13]

Robert B. Kurtz, chairman of Manufacturing Studies Group, in the following statement called specific attention to the need for managing change:

Relatively few domestic manufacturers have devised effective responses to ensure success in the new manufacturing environment. . . . Without changes in corporate culture, organizational structure, and human resource management, new technologies will not produce the results needed for competitive manufacturing. These changes are far more difficult than plugging in a new machine—they require creative thinking, new attitudes and a willingness to embrace change.[14]

These are the most significant and widely accepted P/HRM objectives. There are, of course, other objectives and different ways of stating them. But these can serve as guidelines for the P/HRM function in organizations. Effective P/HRM departments set specific, measurable objectives to be accomplished within specified time limits. Chapter 20 shows how this is done. Other chapters discuss cost/benefit analyses to determine whether measurable objectives have been met.

WHO PERFORMS P/HRM ACTIVITIES

Certain facts are known about the professional in personnel work. In 1987, there were over 430,000 people employed in P/HRM work in the United States. About 60 percent of them work in the private sector, 30 percent in the public sector, and the remaining 10 percent in the third sector (health, education, the arts, libraries, voluntary organizations, and so on). There has been about a 5 percent growth in personnel positions each year since 1970.[15]

Delegation of P/HRM duties has changed over time. In most organizations two groups perform P/HRM activities: P/HRM managers/specialists and operating managers. Operating managers (supervisors, department heads, vice presidents) are involved in P/HRM activities, since they are responsible for effective utilization of *all* the resources at their disposal. The human resource

---

[13] Ibid., p. 40

[14] Jeffrey J. Hallett, "Worklife Visions," *Personnel Administrator*, May 1987, p. 62.

[15] These are estimates based on data obtained from the *Occupational Outlook Handbook: 1985–86* (Washington, DC: U.S. Department of Labor, 1987).

is a very special kind of resource. If it is improperly managed, effectiveness declines more quickly than with other resources. And in all but the most capital-intensive organizations, the people investment has more effect on organizational effectiveness than resources such as money, materials, and equipment.

Therefore, operating managers spend considerable time managing people. In the same way an operating manager is personally responsible if a machine breaks down and production drops, he or she must see to the training, performance, and satisfaction of employees. Research indicates that a large part of an operating manager's day is spent in unscheduled and scheduled meetings, telephone conversations, and solving problems that directly impact people. The manager, through constant contact with many different people, attempts to solve problems, reach decisions, and prevent future difficulties.[16]

Smaller organizations usually have no P/HRM unit, so the operating managers have many P/HRM responsibilities, such as scheduling work, recruitment and selection, and compensating people. As the organization increases in size, the operating manager's work is divided up, and some of it becomes specialized. P/HRM is one such specialized function. Usually the manager of a unit first assigns an assistant to coordinate certain P/HRM matters. P/HRM specialists are employed in organizations with about 100–150 employees, and a P/HRM department is typically created when the number of employees reaches 200–500, depending on the nature of the organization.

The Interaction of Operating and P/HRM Managers

With two sets of employees (operating managers and P/HRM specialists) making P/HRM decisions, there can be conflict.[17] Conflict occurs because operating and P/HRM managers sometimes differ on who has authority for what decisions, or there may be other differences between operating and P/HRM managers. They have different orientations, called *line* and *staff,* which have different objectives. A *staff* person/manager/specialist typically supports the primary functions such as marketing and production by providing advice, counsel, and information. The picture of organizational life portrayed by a textbook assumes that the staff does not wield direct authority over the line manager. *Line* managers have the authority to make final decisions concerning their operations. However, the specific distinction between line and staff is not as clear-cut in organizations. More often than not, members of the P/HRM unit have much to say about various programs and activities. Consider recruitment and selection practices and the crucial role played by P/HRM specialists. Line managers are generally not familiar with the legal requirements concerning recruitment and selection. Therefore, they welcome the

---

[16] Henry Mintzberg, *The Nature of Management Work* (Englewood Cliffs, N.J.: Prentice-Hall, 1980), p. 52.

[17] Barry D. Leskin, "Two Different Worlds," *Personnel Administrator,* December 1986, pp. 58–60.

P/HRM experts' involvement and direct decision-making authority in final decisions.

John Miner and Mary Miner, two researchers, argue that operating and P/HRM managers and specialists also have different motivations, if not personalities. In a research study they conducted, it was determined that personnel managers are less assertive, less competitive, less interested in administrative detail, and less receptive to authority than are operating managers.[18]

The conflict between P/HRM employees and operating managers is most pressing when the decisions must be joint efforts on such issues as discipline, physical working conditions, termination, transfer, promotion, and employment planning. Research indicates that operating managers and P/HRM specialists differ on how much authority personnel should have over job design; labor relations; organization planning; and certain rewards, such as bonuses and promotions.[19]

One way to minimize the conflict between operating managers and P/HRM employees is to show the operating manager that it is beneficial to use P/HRM techniques and programs. Daniel Ewing of Boston Gas Company urges P/HRM managers to involve operating managers in the design of human resource systems. "It's amazing how their attitudes change when they are asked to help create a system—that will serve them," he said, then added jokingly, "You start talking to them about their problems, and you can't shut them up."[20]

John W. O'Brien of Digital Equipment Corporation (DEC) also believes that working together can reduce unproductive conflict between operating managers and P/HRM employees. He said that at DEC, "They determine what human resources will be required to attain their objectives, taking environmental factors in consideration."[21]

Another way to work out actual or potential conflicts of this type so that the employee is not caught in the middle is to try to assign the responsibility for some P/HRM decisions exclusively to operating managers and others exclusively to P/HRM specialists. Some observers feel that this is what is happening, and P/HRM is gaining more power at the expense of the operating managers.[22]

Another approach is to train both sets of managers in how to get along together and how to make better joint decisions. This training is more effective if the organization has a career pattern that rotates its managers through both operating and staff positions, such as those in P/HRM. This rotation helps each group understand the other's problems.

---

[18] John Miner and Mary Miner, "Managerial Characteristics of Personnel Managers," *Industrial Relations,* May 1976, pp. 225–34.

[19] T. F. Cawsey, "Why Line Managers Don't Listen to Their Personnel Department," *Personnel,* January-February 1980, p. 4.

[20] "How the Human Resources Function Contributes to Corporate Goals," *Management Review,* June 1984, p. 31.

[21] Ibid., pp. 31–32.

[22] Wickham Skinner, "Big Hat, No Cattle: Managing Human Resources," *Harvard Business Review,* September-October 1981, p. 107.

The Role of the P/HRM Manager or Specialist

When an organization creates specialized positions for the P/HRM function, the primary responsibility for accomplishing the P/HRM objectives previously described is assigned to the P/HRM managers. But the chief executive is still responsible for the accomplishment of P/HRM objectives. At all levels in the organization, P/HRM and operating executives must work together to help achieve objectives. The chief P/HRM executive promotes the P/HRM function within the organization to employees and operating executives both.

The ideal P/HRM executive understands the objectives and activities of P/HRM. Ideally, he or she has had some experience as an operating manager, as well as experience in P/HRM. The ideal P/HRM manager has superior interpersonal skills and is creative. It is vital that operating management perceives the P/HRM manager as a manager first, interested in achieving organizational goals, and as a specialist adviser in P/HRM matters secondarily. This makes the P/HRM executive a member of the management team and gives the function a better chance to be effective.

P/HRM's Place in Management

How important is P/HRM in the top-management hierarchy? In the past, the answer clearly was not very important. As in Drucker's statement, personnel, as it was called, was "work suitable for a file clerk." This view has changed. Articles have proclaimed that personnel is the fast track to the top and personnel directors are the new corporate heroes.[23] In fact, personnel is advancing rapidly as a vital force in top management. At some firms, such as RCA, United Parcel Service, and Brown and Williamson Tobacco, the top personnel executive is on the board of directors.

A number of presidents and chief operating officers of large firms were promoted to these positions after substantial personnel experience. Examples include the top executives of Colonial Stores, Cummins Engine Company, Delta Airlines, Eli Lilly, and the May Company.

This is not a groundswell trend found in all organizations. However, it does indicate that those who work in the P/HRM function do and can find their way to the top. In the long run, opportunities for P/HRM executives in the top jobs are likely to increase.[24]

What appears to be occurring in an increasing number of firms is recognition that the P/HRM department has a responsibility to be a proactive, integral component of management and the strategic planning process.[25] This new emphasis does not replace the competence required in counseling, consulting,

---

[23] M. Beer, B. Spector, P. R. Lawrence, D. Q. Mills, and R. Walton, *Managing Human Assets* (New York: Free Press, 1984).

[24] R. Foltz, R. Rosenberg, and J. Foehrenback, "Senior Management Views the Human Resource Function," *Personnel Administrator*, September 1982, pp. 37–54.

[25] Janet R. Andrews, "Is There a Crisis in the Personnel Department's Identity?" *Personnel Journal*, June 1986, pp. 86–93.

industrial relations, or managerial control systems. Instead, it is an orientation that states that P/HRM departments must do more than simply sit and listen when strategic management plans are nurtured and developed. The department must determine a strategic direction for its own activities that will make it a proactive arm of the management team.[26] To accomplish this new strategic involvement role, P/HRM must ascertain organizational needs for its competence, evaluate the use and satisfaction among other departments, and educate management and employees about the availability and use of P/HRM department services.

As P/HRM executives play a more dominant role at the organization's strategic planning table they must lead and/or challenge the members of other departments or units about the human resource implications of various decisions.[27] Thus, the P/HRM executive must be familiar with other aspects of the organization—investments, advertising, marketing, production control, computer utilization, research, and development.

P/HRM DEPARTMENT OPERATIONS

Both the makeup and procedures of P/HRM departments have changed over time. P/HRM units vary by size and sector, but most organizations keep them small. One study found that in the largest headquarters unit there were 150 people.[28]

The number of P/HRM specialists in relation to the number of operating employees, or the *personnel ratio,* varies in different industries. According to one study, the national average is one P/HRM specialist per 200 employees. Some industries—construction, agriculture, retail and wholesale trade, and services—have fewer personnel specialists than the average. Others—public utilities, durable goods manufacturing, banking, insurance, and government—have an above-average ratio.

In a detailed study of the personnel function, the American Society of Personnel Administration, with Prentice-Hall, surveyed 1,400 P/HRM executives and found both P/HRM staffs and budgets to be growing. Based on this study, Exhibit 1-1 indicates current size of P/HRM ratio variations. A 1985 survey indicated little significant change in the personnel-staff ratios shown in Exhibit 1-1. In 1985 as in 1976, it appears that there is 1 P/HRM employee for about every 200 employees.

You will see how P/HRM departments allocate their time in the chapters to follow; however, here is an idea of what proportions are devoted to what types of activities. The greatest amount of time, 33 percent, is spent in staffing

[26] John A. Hooper, Ralph F. Catalanello, and Patrick L. Murray, "Shoring Up the Weakest Link," *Personnel Administrator,* April 1987, pp. 49–55, 134.

[27] George G. Gordon, "Getting in Step," *Personnel Administrator,* April 1987, pp. 45–48, 134.

[28] David Babcock and John Boyd, "PAIR Department Policy and Organization," in *PAIR Policy and Program Management,* ed. Dale Yoder and Herbert Heneman, Jr. (Washington, DC: Bureau of National Affairs, 1978).

(recruiting, selection, orientation, evaluation, discipline). Next comes compensation and benefits, 28.5 percent; then training and development, 11 percent; and labor relations, 10 percent. The other activities consume 5 percent or less of a P/HRM department's time.[29]

Clarifying Meaningful P/HRM Objectives

The objectives of an organization or department are the ends it seeks to achieve—its reason for existence. Eight objectives of the P/HRM function have already been pointed out, but most of these objectives were stated in very general terms.

---

[29] Harriet Gorlin, "An Overview of Corporate Personnel Practices," *Personnel Journal,* February 1982, pp. 125–30.

EXHIBIT 1–1   Size of P/HRM Staff

Industry—Number Reporting	P/HRM Staff Ratio*	Number on P/HRM Staff†
Manufacturing (under 500 persons)—217	1:96	1–12 (300)
Manufacturing (500–999)—136	1:116	1–20 (800)
Manufacturing (1,000–4,999)—142	1:130	2–90 (4,900)
Manufacturing (over 5,000)—26	1:352	7–126 (22,000)
Research and development—15	1:102	1–60 (5,000)
Public utilities—30	1:154	1–110 (22,339)
Hospitals—108	1:180	1–28 (4,000)
Retail stores—47	1:228	1–31 (5,800)
Banks—104	1:98	1–72 (9,000)
Insurance companies—101	1:101	1–142 (30,000)
Transportation and distribution—24	1:272	1–75 (26,000)
Government agencies—41	1:272	2–104 (68,000)
Education—34	1:161	1–46 (11,300)
Nonprofit organizations—28	1:76	1–12 (1,955)
Other firms—328	1:194	1–120 (35,000)

* Average number of employees on payroll for each person on personnel staff.
† Smallest and largest P/HRM staff reported for each industry; numbers in parentheses refer to number of employees on payroll for firms reporting largest personnel staffs. (Firms represented here do not necessarily have the lowest or highest *ratio* of personnel staffers, relative to total work force.)

Source: "The Personnel Executive's Job," *Personnel Management: Policies and Practices,* December 14, 1976, published by Prentice-Hall, Inc., Englewood Cliffs, N.J. Reprinted with permission.

To help the organization achieve these objectives, more specific statements are developed in larger, most middle-sized, and some smaller organizations. Often, a general objective is made more specific. For example, suppose that one of a number of P/HRM objectives is: To increase our employees' job satisfaction with advancement opportunities.

How can this objective be achieved? First, management must measure employee satisfaction with advancement opportunities. Management could design an attitude survey to ask employees how satisfied they are with facets of their jobs. The key issue is to determine the degree of job satisfaction associated with advancement opportunities. Next, the organization could use the survey information to develop plans to correct any deficiencies in advancement opportunity satisfaction. These plans are called *policies* and *procedures/ rules*. Exhibit 1–2, which illustrates the relationship between the objectives, policies, and rules, indicates that objectives are the most general factor. For example, job satisfaction for employees is an objective. An organization makes an objective more specific by developing policies.

P/HRM Policy

A *policy* is a general guide to decision making. Policies are developed for past problem areas or for potential problem areas that management considers important enough to warrant policy development. Policies free managers from having to make decisions in areas in which they have less competence or on matters with which they do not wish to become involved. Policies ensure some consistency in behavior and allows managers to concentrate on decisions in which they have the most experience and knowledge.

After the broadest policies are developed, some organizations develop *procedures* and *rules*. These are more specific plans that limit the choices of managers and employees, as Exhibit 1–2 shows. Procedures and rules are developed for the same reason as policies.

P/HRM Procedure

A *procedure* or *rule* is a specific direction to action. It tells a manager how to do a particular activity. In large organizations, procedures are collected and put into manuals, usually called standard operating procedures (SOPs).

Organizations must be careful to have consistent decision making that flows from a well-developed, but not excessive, set of policies and procedures. Some organizations in effect eliminate managerial initiative by trying to develop policies and procedures for everything. Procedures should be developed only for the most vital areas.

Organization of the P/HRM Department

In most organizations, the chief P/HRM executive reports to the top manager; in the larger firms, perhaps to an executive vice president. Exhibit 1–3 shows one way P/HRM is organized in a large insurance business. The vice president of personnel has responsibility and authority for all P/HRM activities within the firm. Specific attention is given to the insurance firm's employee relations organization and job duties in Exhibit 1–4. Notice the wide range of P/HRM activities carried out in this unit. The activities range from developing attitude surveys to preparing a report of the number of maternity leaves taken. In some other organizations, P/HRM is divided into two departments, personnel and labor relations.

In medium-sized (500 to 5,000 employees) and smaller organizations (under 500 employees), however, personnel and other functions, such as public relations, may be part of a single department.

Thirty percent of all P/HRM managers work for local, state, and federal governments. Exhibit 1–5 is an example of P/HRM organization in a typical state government. The legislature and the governor set policy for departments, subject to review by the courts, and appoint a P/HRM commission which is headed by a P/HRM officer. This central P/HRM unit is a policymaking body that serves a policy, advisory, and regulatory purpose similar to that of the home office P/HRM unit of a business. At the federal government level, this personnel commission is called the Office of Personnel Management.

In third-sector organizations, such as hospitals and universities, P/HRM typically is a unit in the business office, as shown in Exhibit 1–6. More will be said about differences in P/HRM work in these three settings in Chapter 2.

P/HRM specialists are usually located at the headquarters of an organization, but larger organizations may divide the P/HRM function. Usually the

EXHIBIT 1–2   **Relationship among Objectives, Policies, and Rules**

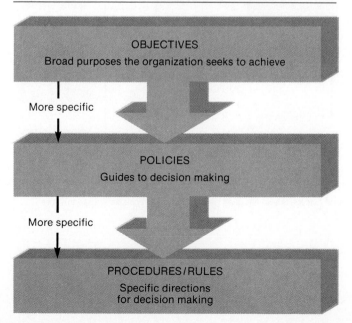

EXHIBIT 1–3 **Organization of Large Insurance Company**

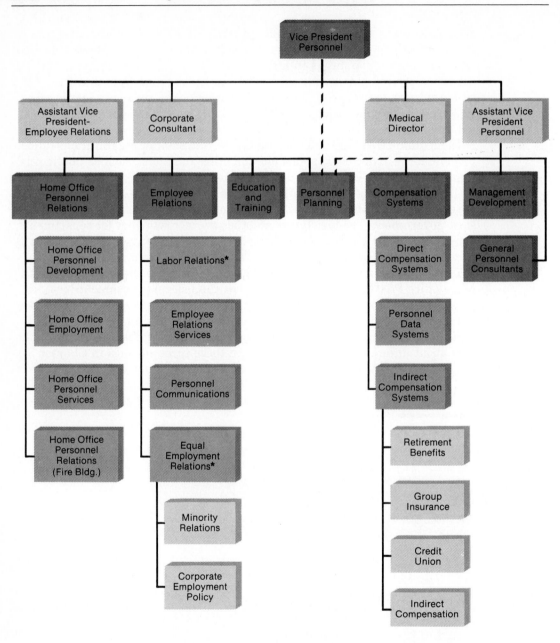

* Manager of function is also assigned general personnel consultant responsibilities.

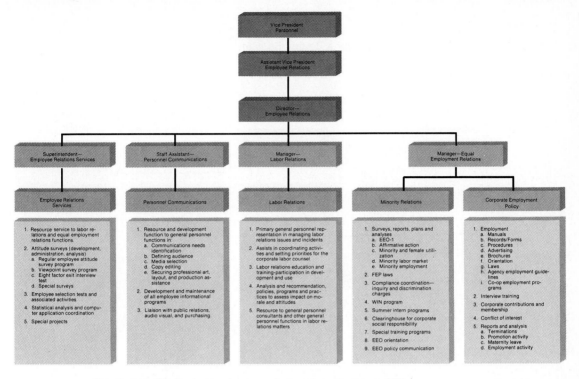

Note: Manager of function is also assigned general personnel consultant responsibilities.

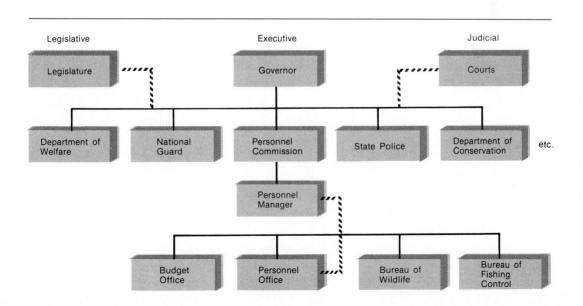

EXHIBIT 1–6   Organization of a County Hospital

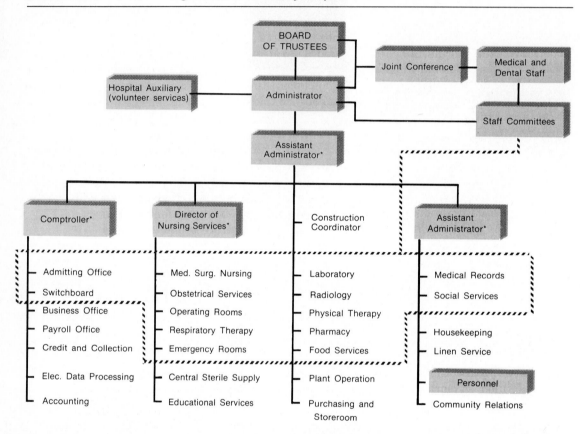

* Area directors.

This chart reflects the "line" responsibility and authority in the hospital organization. It should be understood, however, that a great part of the work of the hospital is accomplished through informal interaction between the identified services and functions. These "functional" working relationships are encouraged. Where there is difference in understanding or when changes in procedure are required, the line organization should be carefully observed.

largest group is at headquarters, but P/HRM advisers may be stationed at unit levels and divisional levels. In this case, the headquarters unit consists of specialists or experts on certain topics and advisers to top management, while the unit-level P/HRM people are generalists who serve as advisers to operating managers at their level.

PLAN OF THE BOOK

This book is designed to show how P/HRM departments work, to study the importance of P/HRM activities in organizations of any size, and to describe the challenges that exist for P/HRM department employees. The chapters (and many of the sections) begin with a P/HRM In Action vignette, an example from a real organization that describes a P/HRM problem or issue being confronted.

The method by which the problem or issue is solved is a P/HRM activity. This activity is explained, then the type of personnel staff who performs this activity is discussed. The interrelationship between operating and P/HRM managers and the role of top management in the activity is described and analyzed.

In each chapter (or group of chapters), the extent to which the activity has been developed is analyzed. Some P/HRM activities are quite well established, while others are just emerging. The activity being considered is assigned to one of four stages through which P/HRM activities seem to evolve (see Exhibit 1–7). The stage of activity can be assessed by examining the literature on the topic.

It is most likely that the P/HRM activities of career pathing, two-tier compensation, outplacement, and preventive health are currently included in Stage I. Stage II includes systematic evaluation of the total P/HRM function and formal orientation. Typical activities in Stage III are performance evaluation and informal management development. Stage IV functions include many employment and compensation activities.

EXHIBIT 1–7   **Stages of Development of a P/HRM Activity**

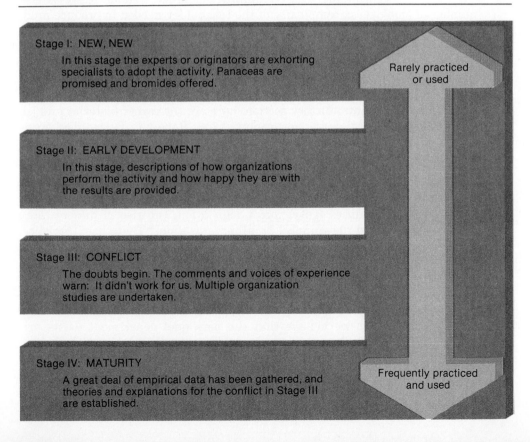

Stage I: NEW, NEW
In this stage the experts or originators are exhorting specialists to adopt the activity. Panaceas are promised and bromides offered.

Rarely practiced or used

Stage II: EARLY DEVELOPMENT
In this stage, descriptions of how organizations perform the activity and how happy they are with the results are provided.

Stage III: CONFLICT
The doubts begin. The comments and voices of experience warn: It didn't work for us. Multiple organization studies are undertaken.

Stage IV: MATURITY
A great deal of empirical data has been gathered, and theories and explanations for the conflict in Stage III are established.

Frequently practiced and used

The chapters also include a diagnostic analysis of the activity being discussed. It is assumed that P/HRM activities are affected by many different factors, such as the types of people employed, organized labor, and government. The solution of P/HRM problems depends on consideration of all these factors. The diagnostic theme will be thoroughly examined in Chapter 2.

For each P/HRM activity, suggestions are given for the techniques, tools, and approaches available to solve the problem, with an evaluation of when each tool is most useful and tips on how to use it well. The various P/HRM activities are evaluated when feasible with a cost/benefit approach. Since P/HRM must compete with requests for other resources (machinery, advertising, buildings, and so on), the expenditures and investments in the organization's people must be justified in cost/benefit terms.

The chapter summary sections review the major points in each chapter. The organization of the book's chapters is presented in Exhibit 1–8. The 6 sections and 20 chapters cover P/HRM activities that need to be performed to achieve acceptable levels of organization effectiveness and employee development.

The recommendations for applications of the activity are presented as suggestions for the activities used in various types of organizations. Since P/HRM functions are not performed the same way in all organizations, recommendations are given for the most effective way to handle each problem in seven model organizations. These organizations differ systematically by size (number of employees), complexity of the technology needed to produce products or services (equipment, resources, expertise), and stability or volatility (degree to which the organization's products or services change over time). If you place your focal organization (where you have worked or want to work) on this scale you can get an idea of how the P/HRM challenge would be handled there. The seven model organizations are defined in Exhibit 1–9.

To conclude this introductory section, here are the career histories and job descriptions of several personnel leaders. First, Robert L. Berra, vice president–personnel for the Monsanto Company, gives these views of the personnel department at Monsanto:

> The scope of the personnel function has expanded considerably in recent years, due both to greater understanding of its contribution internally and to externalities (government legislation, the rise of dissent, etc.) which have had their impact on all organizations. There has, therefore, been an increase in the amount of specialized services rendered to the line. At the same time, the basic personnel contribution of helping the line do its job better has also increased measurably because of the increasing complexity of interpersonal relationships in our present environment.
>
> At Monsanto we believe that the personnel department exists primarily to enable those who create, make and sell to do their jobs better. We try very hard to keep from doing it for them. At Monsanto, nothing has higher priority than the creation of an environment in which each individual has the maximum opportunity to realize his full potential.
>
> We are blessed with exceptional personnel people at Monsanto. We

EXHIBIT 1–8   **The Organization of *Foundations of Personnel/Human Resource Management***

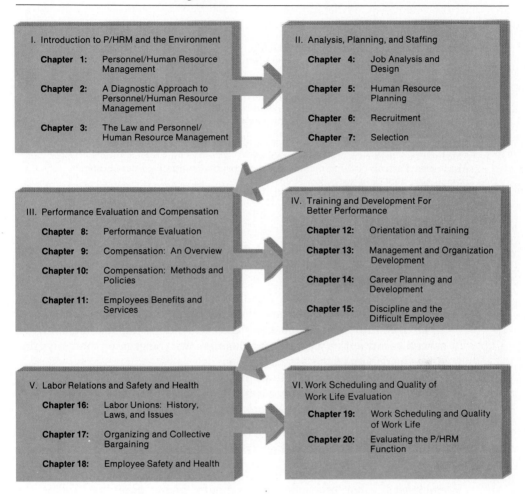

I. Introduction to P/HRM and the Environment

Chapter 1: Personnel/Human Resource Management

Chapter 2: A Diagnostic Approach to Personnel/Human Resource Management

Chapter 3: The Law and Personnel/Human Resource Management

II. Analysis, Planning, and Staffing

Chapter 4: Job Analysis and Design

Chapter 5: Human Resource Planning

Chapter 6: Recruitment

Chapter 7: Selection

III. Performance Evaluation and Compensation

Chapter 8: Performance Evaluation

Chapter 9: Compensation: An Overview

Chapter 10: Compensation: Methods and Policies

Chapter 11: Employees Benefits and Services

IV. Training and Development For Better Performance

Chapter 12: Orientation and Training

Chapter 13: Management and Organization Development

Chapter 14: Career Planning and Development

Chapter 15: Discipline and the Difficult Employee

V. Labor Relations and Safety and Health

Chapter 16: Labor Unions: History, Laws, and Issues

Chapter 17: Organizing and Collective Bargaining

Chapter 18: Employee Safety and Health

VI. Work Scheduling and Quality of Work Life Evaluation

Chapter 19: Work Scheduling and Quality of Work Life

Chapter 20: Evaluating the P/HRM Function

have an excellent mix of seasoned professionals and bright, enthusiastic young people who are honing their professional skills. We are also fortunate to have a significant number of exceptional beginners in the feeder system. Monsanto has traditionally given much attention to its people and, consequently, has considered the personnel department as a working partner. However, to whom much is given, much is expected, and we are constantly challenged to provide policies which anticipate rather than respond to opportunities.

Eileen DeCoursey, vice president, employee relations, for Johns-Manville Corporation says:

EXHIBIT 1–9   **Seven Model Organizations in Which Various P/HRM Practices Might Be Used**

---

1. Large size, low complexity, high stability.
   Examples: Social security agencies, copper smelter, tuberculosis hospital.
2. Medium size, low complexity, high stability.
   Examples: Running and sport shoe manufacturer, Department of Commerce, state of Indiana.
3. Small size, low complexity, high stability.
   Examples: wooden pencil manufacturer, small insect exterminator.
4. Medium size, moderate complexity, moderate stability.
   Examples: food manufacturer, Memphis city welfare agency.
5. Large size, high complexity, low stability.
   Examples, Mattel Toy Corporation, innovative community general hospital.
6. Medium size, high complexity, low stability.
   Examples: Fashion clothing manufacturer, innovative multiple-purpose hospital.
7. Small size, high complexity, low stability.
   Examples: Solar energy producer, computer manufacturer, elite psychiatric hospital, small media conglomerate.

> The future of personnel is secure. I think it's going to be the most exciting game in town. And hopefully we are going to attract the best and brightest talent available.
>
> I expect it will become a regular stepping stone to general management such as sales and finance. We are going through enormous changes as we head into "a post-industrial" society. And the impact on employees, as well as our entire way of doing business, will be greater than anything since the design of the assembly line.
>
> Knowledgeable, prepared employee relations professionals must be able to anticipate the changes before they occur so we are in a position to support and assist the transition—not merely to record its happening.

John Blodger, director of employee relations for Bendix Corporation's Electronics and Engine Control Systems Group, says:

> Personnel has come a long way from its initial responsibilities of hiring employees, labor relations, and company picnic planning. Today, the corporation and its employees have high expectations of the personnel professional. This expectation level carries with it a new requirement for individuals occupying positions in the personnel function. Problems of a changing work ethic and the ever-increasing statutory requirements place today's personnel professional at the apex of the management team. EEO, ERISA, OSHA, organizational development, and management development require specialization and a professional approach to problem solving. Understanding the profit-and-loss concept and the contribution that personnel can make to the bottom line will be the key to bringing these expectations to reality.

SUMMARY

This chapter (and all others in the text) concludes with a list of statements summarizing the most important concepts covered in the chapter. You can use this list to review your understanding of the P/HRM process and the P/HRM manager's job.

In your introduction to this field, P/HRM has been defined as the function, in all organizations, which facilitates the most effective utilization of human resources to achieve both the objectives of the organization and the employees. It has described some of the characteristics of today's P/HRM managers and a number of approaches to the organization and operation of P/HRM units. The chapter concludes with a brief description of how the material in this book is organized and the devices we have used to present it. A special appendix to the chapter describes careers in P/HRM and P/HRM professionalism, including a brief description of accreditation procedures.

To summarize the major points covered in this chapter:

1. P/HRM is action and future oriented and focuses on satisfying the needs of individuals at work.

2. P/HRM is a necessary function. Effectively performed, it can make the crucial difference between successful and unsuccessful organizations.

3. One of the challenges faced in P/HRM is that many decisions require input from both operating managers and P/HRM specialists.

4. This dual purpose can lead to conflict, or it can result in more effective P/HRM decisions.

P/HRM is one of the most challenging and exciting functions in an organization. This book has been written to help you face these challenges more effectively.

P/HRM Manager Close-Up

Robert L. Berra
Monsanto Company

Biography

Robert L. Berra, whose title is vice president–personnel for the Monsanto Company, joined that organization as assistant training manager at the former Plastics Division in 1951. Berra was graduated from St. Louis University with a B.S. in commerce and finance. Subsequently he received his M.B.A. degree from the Harvard Graduate School of Business. He has done graduate work in psychology at Washington University, St. Louis.

After holding various positions with Monsanto, Berra became assistant director of the corporate personnel department in June 1967. From October 1970 until June 1974, Berra held the title of corporate vice president of personnel and public relations at Foremost-McKesson, Inc. He rejoined Monsanto Company as vice president–personnel in June 1974 and was named senior vice president of administration in 1983.

Berra is the author of several articles in the area of management and motivation. He has served as guest lecturer at Harvard Graduate School of Business, Washington University, St. Louis University, Southern Illinois University, and the University of South Carolina.

Job Description

Robert L. Berra is responsible for the worldwide direction of the corporate personnel function for Monsanto Company. He describes his job as that of the chief morale officer for over 60,000 employees. His areas of responsibility include labor force planning and development, labor and employee relations, salary administration and benefits, professional recruitment and university relations, and corporate headquarters site administration. Berra exercises functional direction of the personnel relations activities in all companies, divisions, and departments of the corporation. He reports to the vice chairperson and directly supervises four directors with a total group size of about 350 employees.

P/HRM Manager Close-Up

Eileen M. DeCoursey
Johns-Manville Corporation

Biography

Eileen M. DeCoursey was named to the position of vice president, employee relations for Johns-Manville Corporation upon joining J-M in 1975. Before that, she served as vice president and executive assistant to the chairman of Squibb Corporation, a position that included extensive work in personnel planning, employee benefits, compensation, and personnel policies. DeCoursey has served as a personnel assistant (Warner-Lambert), a research associate (Handy Associate), junior account executive (Johnson & Higgins), employee relations supervisor (Time, Inc.), and manager of employee benefits (Bristol-Myers). She is a native of Livingston, New Jersey, and received her B.S. degree from New Jersey State.

Job Description

As vice president, employee relations, of Johns-Manville Corporation, Eileen DeCoursey's responsibilities involve the design and development of corporate-wide personnel policies, procedures, and programs. These include recruiting, compensation, benefits, affirmative action, management development, and training.

P/HRM Manager Close-Up

John D. Blodger
Bendix Corporation

Biography

John D. Blodger's title is group director of employee relations for the Bendix Corporation, Electronics and Engine Control Systems Group, located at Newport News, Virginia. Prior to moving to Newport News, he was director of employee relations for the Communications Division of the Bendix Corporation in Baltimore. Blodger is a graduate of Wayne State University and has acquired B.S. and M.B.A. degrees. Before joining Bendix, he held a broad range of personnel assignments for several major corporations.

Blodger has been active with the American Society of Personnel Administrators for many years and has held the offices of district director, board member at large, and national treasurer. He was president-elect for 1978 and president in 1979. He is active in the Industrial Relations Research Association and was formerly a member of the Personnel Association of Greater Baltimore, Inc.

Job Description

John Blodger, the group director of employee relations for Bendix (Electronics and Engine Control Systems Group, Newport News, Virginia), is responsible for total employee relations, the safety and security of a two-plant division with employment of 900 salaried and hourly employees, grievance processing through arbitration, wage and salary administration, employee benefits, management development and training programs, and recruitment for both hourly and salaried employees.

APPENDIX A

CAREERS IN P/HRM

This appendix discusses what a P/HRM career is like, describes some typical personnel specialists' positions, and suggests ways personnel specialists can achieve greater professionalism.

P/HRM Careers

Let us begin this section by discussing what current P/HRM professionals are like. When this edition was published in 1989, about 70 percent of P/HRM managers were men. Women P/HRM managers were usually found in medium-sized and smaller organizations. Most P/HRM managers have college degrees. Those who attended college in recent years usually majored in business, economics, or psychology. Their experience has been primarily in P/HRM work, especially the younger managers.

A study of the 300 largest employing firms in the United States was conducted to determine the key skills and backgrounds organizations are looking for in staffing entry level positions in P/HRM units.[30] The P/HRM managers were asked to rank order their choice of academic preparations for those interested in entry level positions. They ranked business administration first, followed in order by social sciences, humanities, and science and education tied for fourth and fifth positions.

P/HRM specialists have been moving toward greater specialization, if not actual professionalism. College training includes courses such as P/HRM, compensation administration, P/HRM problems, labor law and legislation, and collective bargaining. Those who want to become more specialized can join associations such as the American Society for Personnel Administrators (ASPA), attend meetings, read professional journals, or seek ASPA accreditation. There are 33,500 members of ASPA, and more than 390 local chapters.[31]

P/HRM specialists generally are paid comparably to other graduates of business schools at the supervisory and middle-management levels. At top-management levels, they sometimes are paid slightly less than operating vice presidents. Current salaries of P/HRM specialists and executives are published

---

[30] Thomas J. Bergmann and M. John Close, "Preparing for Entry Level Human Resource Management Positions," *Personnel Administrator*, April 1984, pp. 95–98.

[31] Ibid.

yearly by the ASPA in its *Salary Survey*. In 1987 the median salaries for P/HRM type jobs were reported as follows:

Median Incomes By Job Function

Top labor relations executive	$50,500
Top employee and community relations executive	$50,000
Top compensation and benefits executive	$46,750
Top personnel executive	$45,406
Top training and O.D. manager	$44,914
Training and O.D. manager	$41,613
Employee services manager	$40,400
EEO/affirmative action manager	$40,270
Job evaluation manager	$40,000
Personnel/industrial relations manager	$39,130
Safety manager	$38,700
Personnel information systems manager	$38,640
Training manager (plant)	$37,725
Recruitment/selection/employment manager	$35,780
Employment Interviewer (professional/managerial employees)	$33,175
Training specialist (managerial)	$32,697
Safety specialist	$32,394
Recruiter (college)	$31,100
Employee counselor	$30,106
Benefits planning analyst	$29,326
Compensation analyst (salaried personnel)	$28,788
Personnel records manager	$28,630
EEO/affirmative action specialist	$28,600
Personnel information systems specialist	$28,500
House organ editor	$27,638
Personnel assistant/personnel generalist	$26,500
Employee health nurse/plant nurse	$25,688

Source: Steven Langer, "Where the Dollars Are: Annual Salary Survey Results," *Personnel Journal*, December 1987, p. 112.

Career ladder opportunities for a P/HRM professional are given in Exhibit 1A-1. A P/HRM professional can enter the field through different types of positions. One way is to become a P/HRM manager for a small unit of a large organization. Remember Don Brokop at the beginning of this chapter? This is what he would be doing if he accepted the Melody Machine Products plant position. When a person enters the small unit of a large organization, he or she implements headquarter's P/HRM policies at that level and works with local operating managers to help achieve unit goals, as well as personnel objectives. The other route is to become a specialized P/HRM professional. Typically, this position is found in a large organization, and the duties are associated with a single P/HRM function—interviewing, recruiting, compensation, labor relations, or training and development.

As positions open up, the P/HRM professional can usually move up in the

EXHIBIT 1A–1   Sample Career Patterns of Personnel Professionals

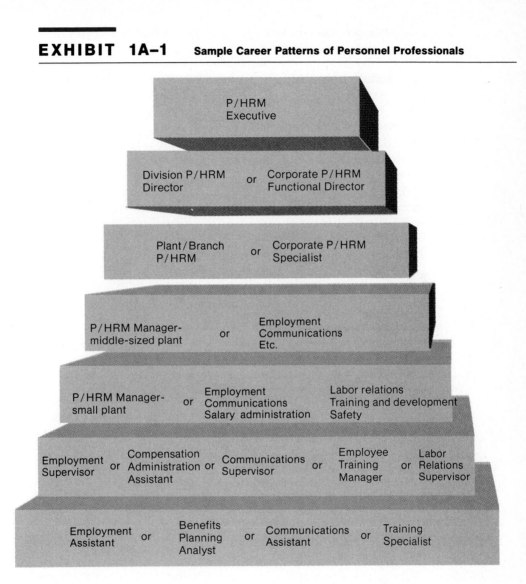

P/HRM
Executive

Division P/HRM   or   Corporate P/HRM
Director   Functional Director

Plant/Branch   or   Corporate P/HRM
P/HRM   Specialist

P/HRM Manager-   or   Employment
middle-sized plant   Communications
                                              Etc.

P/HRM Manager-   or   Employment   Labor relations
small plant   Communications   Training and development
                                      Salary administration   Safety

Employment   or   Compensation   or   Communications   or   Employee   or   Labor
Supervisor   Administration   Supervisor   Training   Relations
                            Assistant   Manager   Supervisor

Employment   or   Benefits   or   Communications   or   Training
Assistant   Planning   Assistant   Specialist
                              Analyst

hierarchy. Or the specialist at a large organization can move to a smaller organization as the chief P/HRM executive. Typically, a person with a college degree and P/HRM training can move up the career ladder without much difficulty if he or she is willing to work hard.

Career Development for the P/HRM Professional

The P/HRM specialist can advance his or her knowledge of the field by reading specialized journals. Appendix B provides information on trade, professional, and scholarly journals and literature that can provide relevant P/HRM information, data, and statistics.

Accreditation One move to increase the professionalism of P/HRM executives is the American Society of Personnel Administrators Accreditation Program. ASPA has set up the ASPA Accreditation Institute (AAI) to offer P/HRM executives the opportunity to be accredited as specialists (in a functional area such as employment, placement and P/HRM planning, training and development, compensation and benefits, health, safety and security, employee and labor relations, and personnel research), or generalists (multiple specialties). Specialists can qualify as accredited P/HRM specialists (accredited personnel specialist—APS) or the more advanced accredited P/HRM diplomates (accredited personnel diplomate—APD). Accreditation requires passing three-hour examinations developed by the Psychological Corporation of New York. Tests are given by ASPA in these P/HRM activity areas:

- Employment, placement, and personnel planning.
- Training and development.
- Compensation and benefits.
- Health and safety.
- Employee and labor relations.
- Personnel research.

The American Society for Training and Development is comprised of over 22,000 members who are concerned with the training and development of human resources.[32] The ASTD professional development committee is working to identify the competencies needed to master training and development activities.

The International Association for Personnel Women (IAPW) was founded in 1950. Its purpose is to expand and improve the professionalism of women in P/HRM. Its approximately 2,000 members are generalists and specialists working in various industries.[33]

---

[32] Ibid.

[33] Ibid.

A RETURN TO THE P/HRM · IN · ACTION

Don Brokop

Don Brokop is ready to make an important career decision. He now understands the role that personnel/human resource management plays at Melody. He can see that P/HRM is important not only to his firm but also to society. The people business is the job of all managers in all organizations. Don has decided to accept the assistant director position and to really become involved on a full-time basis with P/HRM activities.

The activities that Don will learn about first-hand are what this book is about. As you learn more about P/HRM think about Don Brokop and how he stepped from the operating level of management into the P/HRM role in the Melody plant. His on-the-job training will be invaluable in his personal growth and development. However, Don will also have to supplement this first-hand experience with reading and self-learning. Your job now is to dig into the type of reading and self-learning that Don will use to make himself a more successful P/HRM practitioner.

Questions for Review and Discussion

1. Why is the P/HRM department today playing a more significant role in organizational strategic planning processes than it did 20 years ago?
2. Why is it correct to conclude that all managers are involved in the personnel/human resource management (P/HRM) function?
3. What type of P/HRM jobs are available at the entry level for college graduates?
4. Why has the P/HRM function increased in stature and influence in many organizations?
5. Do accreditation procedures make the P/HRM field professional? That is, are lawyers, doctors, and P/HRM managers professional?
6. In your opinion, what type of educational background is needed to become an executive in the P/HRM field?

7. Peter Drucker seems to be incorrect when he states that work in P/HRM is nothing more than the work of a file clerk. What has happened in the world of work to make this statement wrong?
8. How would a hospital use a P/HRM unit or department?
9. Why should even very small firms (with 10 to 100 employees) be concerned about P/HRM?
10. What is the chief or primary P/HRM effectiveness measure?

GLOSSARY

Personnel/Human Resource Management (P/HRM). A function performed in organizations which facilitates the most effective use of people (employees) to achieve organizational and individual goals. Terms used interchangeably with P/HRM include *personnel, human resource management,* and *employee development.*

P/HRM Objectives. Objectives are the ends a department such as P/HRM is attempting to accomplish. Some of the specific P/HRM objectives are: (1) to provide the organization with well-trained and well-motivated employees; (2) to communicate P/HRM policies to all employees; and (3) to employ the skills and abilities of the work force efficiently.

P/HRM Policy. A general guide to decision making in important decision areas.

P/HRM Procedure. A specific direction to action. It tells a person how to do a particular activity.

APPLICATION CASE 1–1

The Personnel/Human Resource Manager and Time Management*

At 7:30 A.M. on Monday, Sam Lennox, personnel manager of the Lakeview plant of Supreme Textile Corporation, pulled out of the driveway of his suburban home and headed for work. It was a beautiful day; the sun was shining in a bright blue sky, and a cool breeze was blowing. The plant was about nine miles away, and the 15-minute ride gave Sam an opportunity to think about business problems without interruption.

Supreme Textile Corporation owned and operated five plants: one yarn-spinning operation, two knitting plants, and two apparel-making operations. Supreme enjoyed a national reputation for quality products, specializing in men's sports shirts. Corporate headquarters was located in Twin-Cities adjacent to two of the plant operations. The Hillsville, Eastern, and Lakeview Plants were 100–200 miles distant. Each employed 70–100 people. About 250 employees were located in Twin-Cities.

Sam had started with Supreme's Eastern plant after college. He progressed rapidly through several staff positions. He then served two years as a night foreman. He became known for his ability to organize a "smooth team," never having a grievance procedure brought against him. While his productivity figures were not outstanding, he was given credit by many people in the company for being the person who prevented the union from successfully organizing the Eastern plant. As a result he was promoted to assistant personnel manager.

Sam's progress was noted by Glen Johnson, corporate vice president of personnel. Glen transferred Sam to the Lakeview plant, which was having some personnel problems, as a special staff assistant. Six months later he was made personnel manager when the incumbent suddenly resigned. Sam had been able to work out most of the problems and was beginning to think about how to put together a first-rate personnel program.

Sam was in fine spirits as his car picked up speed, and the hum of the tires on the newly paved highway faded into the backgound. He said to himself, "This is the day I'm really going to get things done."

He began to run through the day's work, first one project, then another, tyring to establish priorities. After a few minutes, he decided that the Management by Objectives (MBO) program was probably the most important. He frowned for a moment as he recalled that, on Friday, Glen Johnson had asked him if he had given the project any further thought. He had been meaning to

---

* This case was prepared by Jack D. Ferner, Lecturer in Management, Babcock Graduate School of Management, Wake Forest University, Winston-Salem, N.C.

get to work on this idea for over three months, but something else always seemed to crop up. "I haven't had much time to sit down and really work it out," he said to himself. "I'd better hit this one today for sure." With that, he began to break down the objectives, procedures, and installation steps. "It's about time," he told himself. "This idea should have been followed up long ago." Sam remembered that he and Johnson had discussed it over a year ago when they had both attended a seminar on MBO. They had agreed it was a good idea, and when Sam moved to the Lakeview plant it was decided to try to install it here. They both realized it would be met with resistance by some of the plant managers.

A blast from a passing horn startled him, but his thoughts quickly returned to other projects he was determined to get underway. He started to think about ideas he had for supervisory training programs. He also needed to simplify the employee record system. The present system not only was awkward, but key information was often lacking. There were also a number of carryover and nagging employee grievance problems. Some of this involved weak supervisors, some poor working conditions, and some just poor communication and morale. There were a few other projects he couldn't recall offhand, but he could tend to them after lunch, if not before. "Yes, sir," he said to himself, "this is the day to really get rolling."

Sam's thoughts were interrupted as he pulled into the parking lot. He knew something was wrong as Al Noren, the stockroom foreman, met him by the loading dock. "A great morning, Al," Sam greeted him cheerfully.

"Not so good, Sam; my new man isn't in this morning," Al growled.

"Have you heard from him?" asked Sam.

"No, I haven't," replied Al.

Sam frowned as he commented, "These stock handlers assume you take it for granted that if they're not here, they're not here, and they don't have to call in and verify it. Better call him."

Al hesitated for a moment before replying. "Okay, Sam, but can you find me a man? I have two cars to unload today."

As Sam turned to leave, he called, "I'll call you in half an hour, Al," and headed for his office.

When he walked into the personnel office there were several plant employees huddled around his secretary, Terry. They were complaining that there was an error in their paychecks. After checking their files and calling payroll twice he found an automatic pay increase had not been picked up properly. He finally got everyone settled down.

He sat down at his desk, which was opposite Terry's and two other clerks. One of the clerks brought him a big pile of mail. He asked her to get him some office supplies and started to open the mail. The phone rang; it was the plant manager asking him about find a new secretary. As Sam hung on the phone listening to all the problems the "old man" had with secretaries, he thought, "Fussbudget." He started to call a couple of foremen to see if they had someone to fill in for Al in the stockroom when he was interrupted by one of his clerks asking him to check over several termination reports. He was trying to decide whether any of these represented trouble spots when the phone rang again.

Glen Johnson was on the other end. With an obvious edge in his voice, he asked, "I've heard rumblings about some of the grievances we can't seem to solve. What about it?" Sam responded that he hadn't had time, but would. There followed a series of questions. The conversation ended with, "Sam, you really need to get after those problems." Sam sighed. Terry was at his desk asking him to approve a couple of rate changes.

Several job applicants came into the office as a result of want ads the company had run over the weekend. There was a buzz as the applications and interviews progressed. Sam started to help out. Sam was talking with one applicant when Cecil Hardy came in. Cecil was the plant engineer, who liked to stop by to chat and have a cup of coffee. He was approaching retirement and today wanted to talk about the company's pension benefits. He also described in detail a round of golf he had played Sunday afternoon. Sam had played a lot when he was in school and enjoyed an occasional game with Cecil.

It was suddenly 10:45 and time to go to a staff meeting. They were going to discuss something about quality control and Sam wasn't awfully interested, but the plant manager wanted all the department heads at staff meetings. "They always drag on so long and we get off on things that don't seem real important to all of us," Sam reflected as he headed toward the conference room.

Sam went to lunch with a friend who owned a plastics fabrication business. He called an hour ahead to say he wanted to discuss a major medical package which had been proposed by an insurance company. They drove across town to a new restaurant.

When Sam returned at about 2 P.M. the office was busy again with job applicants. He suddenly remembered the replacement stock clerk. "Too late now," he mused. He sat down and began to assemble the files relating to the grievances. The production superintendent called to discuss his need for several production people. He wanted experienced people and wasn't happy with some of the prospects Sam's department had sent him. Sam took a break to get a soft drink from the storage room. He noticed some of the confidential employee files had been pulled out and not returned. As he straightened them out he thought, "I wonder who did this?"

Sam returned to his desk to find a Boy Scout troop selling advertisements in a program for a rally they were putting on. This was one of the odd tasks Sam had been assigned by the plant manager. As the afternoon wore on, Sam became increasingly irritated at not being able to make much progress with the grievances. "Trouble is, I'm not sure what should be done about the Sally Foster and Curt Davis cases."

At 4:45 the personnel manager at the Eastern plant called to ask about some employee matters Sam had handled when he was there. When he finished, it was 5:30 and he was the only one left in the office. Sam was tired. He put on his coat and headed toward the parking lot. He also ran into Al Noren who was also heading for his car. "Thanks for the stock clerk," Al grumbled as he drove off.

With both eyes on the traffic, Sam reviewed the day he had just completed. "Busy?" he asked himself. "Too much so—but did I accomplish anything?" His mind raced over the day's activities. "Yes and no" seemed to be the answer.

"There was the usual routine, the same as any other day. The personnel function kept going, and we must have hired several new people. Any creative or special project work done?" Sam grimaced as he reluctantly answered, "No."

With a feeling of guilt, he probed further. "Am I a manager? I'm paid like one, respected like one, and have a responsible assignment with the necessary authority to carry it out. Yet, one of the greatest values a company derives from a manager is his creative thinking and accomplishments. You need some time for thinking. Today was like most other days; I did little, if any, creative work. The projects that I so enthusiastically planned to work on this morning are exactly as they were last week. What's more, I have no guarantee that tomorrow will bring me any closer to their completion. There must be an answer."

Sam continued, "Night work? Yes, occasionally. This is understood. But I've been doing too much of this lately. I owe my wife and family some of my time. When you come down to it, they are the people for whom I'm really working. If I am forced to spend much more time away from them, I'm not meeting my own personal objectives. What about church work? Should I eliminate that? I spend a lot of time on it, but I feel I owe God some time, too. Besides, I believe I'm making a worthwhile contribution. Perhaps I can squeeze a little time from my fraternal activities. But where does recreation fit in?"

Sam groped for the solution. By this time, he had turned off the highway onto the side street leading to his home—the problem still uppermost in his mind. "I guess I really don't know the answer," he told himself as he pulled into his driveway. "This morning, everything seemed so simple, but now. . . ." His son ran toward the car, calling out, "Mommy, Daddy's home."

Questions

1. Personnel/human resource management consists of numerous activities. What areas were illustrated by Sam's schedule on this particular day?
2. List the areas of ineffective management and time robbers that are affecting Sam.
3. Discuss Sam's career progress. Is he now promotable?

A DIAGNOSTIC APPROACH TO PERSONNEL/HUMAN RESOURCE MANAGEMENT

LEARNING OBJECTIVES

After studying this chapter, you should be able to:

- **Describe** how a diagnostic P/HRM model can be used to examine people problems.
- **Explain** the difference between external and internal environmental forces that affect P/HRM problems.
- **Discuss** the role that P/HRM can play in accomplishing the organization's strategic plan.
- **Identify** how P/HRM activities contribute to a firm's productivity.

KEY TERMS

External P/HRM Influences
Internal P/HRM Influences
Motivation
Personality
Productivity
Strategy
Work Group

CHAPTER OUTLINE

P/HRM · IN · ACTION

Martha   Lenny   Harry

Martha Winston is the newly appointed manager of the National Pancake House in Ft. Lauderdale, Florida, which is known for its beach area. Officially, the restaurant is known as unit 827. National is a large chain. Martha believes that if she does a good job of managing 827, she has an excellent chance to be promoted at National. She is also thinking about opening her own restaurant someday.

Martha entered National's management training program after completing college at a small liberal arts school that is well known in her part of the country. The focus of the training program was technical. Martha learned all about the equipment a typical National restaurant has. She also learned about National's finance and accounting system, theft control, and advertising. She was taught a great deal about National's goals for the firm and for unit 827. The topics included sales goals, financial return goals, cleanliness goals, customer service goals, and so on.

She has been at 827 three weeks now and is adjusting pretty well. She is not reaching all the goals National set up for her yet, but she feels she will do so in time. She often wishes the training program had taught her more about the people part of the success equation. Her college courses were not much help to her on this, either.

This problem was on her mind as she sat in her office one morning staring at her paperwork over a cup of coffee. She was thinking of the two cooks on duty, Lenny and Harry. Lenny Melvina is about 24. He's been with National as a cook for almost six years. He finished high school locally. It's the only job he's ever had. He arrives on time, works hard, and leaves on time. He's never absent except for perhaps one day a year for illness. This is what his personnel file shows.

Everyone likes Lenny: the other help, his managers, the customers. It's easy to see why. He does his job well and in a friendly manner. For example, today Martha watched Lenny deal with a customer. National has a policy that second helpings are free. A girl, about 13, came up to Lenny and asked for seconds. He asked her in a friendly manner how many more pancakes she wanted. She said: "Oh, I don't know, one or two."

Instead of having her wait at the serving line, he suggested that she be seated and he'd bring her the pan-

(continued)

cakes. He delivered a plate with three pancakes on it that looked like this:

The customer and her family were very pleased with his effort to please her and give them a little joke too. They told Martha they'd come back again.

The other cook is Harry Bennis. Harry is about 19. He didn't finish high school. He's worked at National for two years. Harry is tolerated rather than liked. Most of his co-workers tend to ignore him. He rarely says anything beyond the minimum to co-workers, bosses, and customers. He is often late or absent. In about 1 case in 10, his food is sent back. He's not surly, but not too pleasant either. He's not bad enough to fire, but not good enough to be pleased with.

Martha wonders why there are these differences in Lenny and Harry. And what, if anything, she can do about it. It affects her now because she must hire a cook. Business at 827 has been growing faster than usual, even for this busy season. So the staff needs to be expanded to include at least one

new cook. Martha wondered how she can be sure to choose a person like Lenny, not another Harry.

It's also raise time. She doesn't have enough money to give everyone a raise. And to hire the new cook she may have to pay close to what she pays Lenny, because few cooks are out of work at present. Yet company policy says she must pay senior people like Lenny more. And if things weren't complicated enough, the pay must be above the government minimum wage.

Many of the employees at 827 told Martha they wanted more pay because the job wasn't too pleasant: the stove was hot, and they had to deal with the public. What should she do?

To help her make an intelligent, effective decision she went to visit a friend, Amy Adams, who had majored in personnel/human resource management at the university. Amy spent an afternoon with Martha explaining how to deal with the three personnel problems Martha faced (employee satisfaction, performance, selection, and pay) by understanding how three sets of factors affects P/HRM and organizational effectiveness.

These are:

- People.
- The internal and external environment of the organization.
- The organization, task, work group, and leadership.

Think about how Martha must diagnose the present situation and work with people at the restaurant.

A DIAGNOSTIC P/HRM MODEL

When you're experiencing pain and must see a physician, you are typically asked a number of questions. Where do you hurt? When did the pain start? What does the pain feel like—is it sharp or dull and aching? The doctor examines you and may also run a number of tests. What the doctor is doing is diagnosing the problem. He or she is performing a diagnosis by examination and observation.

The problem faced by Martha at National Pancake House could also be examined through a systematic diagnosis. A personnel/human resource management *diagnostic model* might be of help to her. A diagnostic model in P/HRM is a framework that can be used to help managers focus on a set of relevant factors. The model is a map that aids a person in seeing the whole picture or parts of the picture. The three factors that Martha was concerned about (people, the internal and external environment, and the organization itself) would be included as parts of any P/HRM diagnostic model.

Exhibit 2-1 presents the diagnostic model that will be used throughout the book. The model emphasizes some of the major external and internal environmental influences that directly and/or indirectly affect the match between P/HRM activities and people.

By studying the diagnostic model you should see that in order to work with people effectively a number of P/HRM activities must be efficiently practiced. For example, to encourage individuals to use their abilities, it may not be sufficient to have only a properly analyzed job. A sound performance evaluation, equitable benefits and services, and an attractive work schedule may also be needed. P/HRM activities are all related to each other and have a combined effect on people. It is because of this effect on people and, ultimately, on effectiveness criteria that the P/HRM function is now recognized as an important part of organizational management. The objectives of the P/HRM functions must be accomplished in order for an organization to remain competitive and to survive in the environment.

Each area of the diagnostic model is important in achieving the eight P/HRM objectives presented in Chapter 1. Again, it should be pointed out that a significant reason for the eventual success of any P/HRM activity is that the organization's employees are the best qualified and are performing jobs that suit their needs, skills, and abilities. The matching of people and activities to accomplish desirable goals is made easier by use of a diagnostic map. Of course, the map shown in Exhibit 2-1 can't include every important environmental influence, P/HRM activity, or effectiveness criterion. Instead, it is designed to provide an orderly and manageable picture of how P/HRM diagnosis should proceed.

EXTERNAL ENVIRONMENTAL FORCES

Exhibit 2-1 is intended to show that a P/HRM program in an organization does not operate in a vacuum. It is influenced by and has influence on the external

EXHIBIT 2–1 A Diagnostic Model for Personnel/Human Resource Management

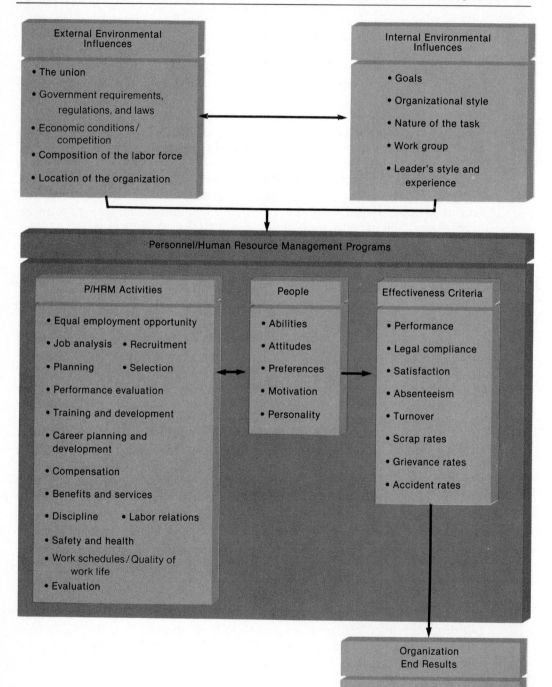

External Environmental Influences

- The union
- Government requirements, regulations, and laws
- Economic conditions/competition
- Composition of the labor force
- Location of the organization

Internal Environmental Influences

- Goals
- Organizational style
- Nature of the task
- Work group
- Leader's style and experience

Personnel/Human Resource Management Programs

P/HRM Activities

- Equal employment opportunity
- Job analysis • Recruitment
- Planning • Selection
- Performance evaluation
- Training and development
- Career planning and development
- Compensation
- Benefits and services
- Discipline • Labor relations
- Safety and health
- Work schedules/Quality of work life
- Evaluation

People

- Abilities
- Attitudes
- Preferences
- Motivation
- Personality

Effectiveness Criteria

- Performance
- Legal compliance
- Satisfaction
- Absenteeism
- Turnover
- Scrap rates
- Grievance rates
- Accident rates

Organization End Results

- Competitive product(s)
- Competitive service(s)

(outside the organization) and the internal (inside the organization) environments. On the one hand, factors external to the organization—such as government laws and regulations, union procedures and requirements, economic conditions and the labor force—have a significant impact on P/HRM programs. On the other hand, the P/HRM program of a firm must operate within guidelines, limits of available resources, and competencies produced by the organization. P/HRM is one important function among other internal functions, including finance, accounting, research and development, marketing, and production. The interaction of these internal programs sets the tone of the entire organizational system.

At the National Pancake House, Martha's P/HRM problems are aggravated by external environmental factors. Remember that Martha is faced with a tight labor market and government wage legislation. Let's look at some external environmental factors.

The Union

The presence of a union directly affects most aspects of P/HRM—recruiting, selection, performance evaluation, promotion, compensation, and benefits, among others. These effects will be discussed later in the book. Chapters 16 and 17 focus directly on relations with labor unions.

Unions differ just as people differ. There are cooperative unions and combative unions, just as there are sensitive organizations and socially irresponsible organizations. Those familiar with union history are aware of the kind of toughness a James Hoffa or a John L. Lewis can bring to the employment scene. The union leadership of the Air Line Pilots Association; State, Local, and Municipal Workers; Baseball Players Association; and others is not so well known, because they have different bargaining styles and philosophies.

At one time unions were concentrated in a few sectors of the economy, such as mining and manufacturing, and were influential in only a few sections of the United States, primarily the highly industrialized areas. But the fastest growing sectors for unions in the United States are in the public and third sectors. It is no longer useful to think of the unionized employee as a blue-collar factory worker. Engineers, nurses, teachers, secretaries, salespersons, college professors, professional football players, and even physicians belong to unions. In sum, unions often play a significant role in P/HRM programs.[1]

Government Requirements and Regulations

Another powerful, external environmental influence is government law and regulations, which affect many organizations directly. Many federal regulations limit the flexibility of city and state jurisdictions.

---

[1] E. Herman, Alfred Kuhn, and Ronald L. Seeber, *Collective Bargaining and Labor Relations* (Englewood Cliffs, N.J.: Prentice-Hall, 1987), pp. 1–27.

The government regulates and influences some aspects of personnel more directly than others. The major areas of legislation and regulation include:

Equal employment opportunity and human rights legislation, which indirectly affects recruiting, selection, evaluation, and promotion directly, and employment planning, orientation, career planning, training and development.

Employment of illegal aliens.

Sex and age discrimination.

Compensation regulation, which affects pay, hours of work, unemployment, and similar conditions.

Benefits regulation, which affects pension and retirement.

Workers' compensation and safety laws, which affect health and safety.

Labor relations laws and regulations, which affect the conduct of collective bargaining.

Privacy laws.

Government regulation is increasing substantially. In 1940 the U.S. Department of Labor administered 18 regulatory programs; in 1988 it administered over 140.[2] And that's just *one* government agency affecting managers and the activities of the P/HRM department.

John Dunlop lists a number of the problems government regulation imposes on management.[3] All of these make the operating and P/HRM managers' job more difficult:

■ Regulation encourages simplistic thinking on complicated issues. Small enterprises are treated like large ones. Different industries are regulated the same.

■ Designing and administering regulations is an incredibly complex task, leading to very slow decision making.

■ Regulation does not encourage mutual accommodation but rather leads to complicated legal manuevering.

■ Many regulations are out of date and serve little social purpose, yet they are not eliminated.

■ There is increasing evidence of regulatory overlap and contradictions between different regulatory agencies.

To cope with increasing governmental control, management has tried to influence the passage of relevant legislation and the way it is administered. Managements have sued to determine the constitutionality of many of the laws. When such efforts fail to influence the process as management prefers, it has learned to adapt its P/HRM policies.

In sum, there are almost no P/HRM decisions that remain unaffected by

---

[2] U.S. Department of Labor Office of Information and Public Affairs, Telephone Communication, February 1988.

[3] John Dunlop, "The Limits of Legal Compulsion," *Labor Law Journal,* February 1976, pp. 69–70.

FRANK AND ERNEST

© 1978 by NEA, Inc. Reprinted by permission of NEA.

government. In what ways and to what degree government affects the P/HRM function will be discussed in each chapter, beginning with Chapter 3.

Economic Conditions

Three aspects of economic conditions affect P/HRM programs: productivity, the nature of competition, and the nature of the labor market.

Productivity There is growing evidence that the productivity of employees is an important part of a nation's general economic condition. Managers are becoming more concerned with productivity because they feel it is a representative indicator of the overall efficiency of an organization. Productivity is defined as:

> Output of goods and services per unit of input of resources used in a production process.[4]

Inputs, as applied in productivity measurement, are expressions of the physical amount or the dollar amount of several elements used in producing a good or a service, including labor, capital, materials, fuel, and energy.

Before productivity can be effectively managed and improved, it must be measured. This can be done by isolating the outputs—division by division, department by department, work team by work team, individual by individual, or even product line by product line. Next, the costs that went into producing the output must be determined, including labor costs (salaries, bonuses, fringes), heating, lighting, and capital costs.[5] Then, using last year as

---

[4] Arthur S. Herman, "Productivity Gains Continued In Many Industries During 1985," *Monthly Labor Review,* April 1987, p. 48.

[5] Michael B. Packer, "Measuring the Intangible in Productivity," *Technology Review,* March 1983, pp. 48–57.

a baseline period, the manager must compare this year's figures with last year's. Some period of comparison is needed to make necessary adjustments. While productivity improvement is a worthy goal, managers should, before they rush into changes, lay the groundwork for measuring and monitoring productivity.

The industrial world's productivity growth passed through three major cycles during the past century.[6]

1. A slow cycle for eight decades (1870–1950), averaging about 1.7 percent a year.
2. Unprecedented growth during the two post–World War II decades, with such rates as Japan's 7.9 percent a year.
3. Although the productivity rate in the United States was virtually zero (no growth) from 1978 through 1982, there are today some signs of hope.[7] The annual rate for the 1985–91 period is headed for a rate of 3 percent a year. The improvement in U.S. productivity does not appear to be a flash in the pan. It is being fueled by technological advances, a more experienced labor force, and a new era of some improvement in labor-management cooperation. Despite the recent new optimism about productivity in the United States, the setbacks in the 1970s have had a lasting effect. Managers now realize that if productivity is to continue growing, they will have to play an active and efficient role in performing their jobs. Just sitting back will not make productivity growth happen.

The increasing disparity of productivity gains in Western economies can be traced in part to:

- The rebuilding of war-torn industry in Japan and Western Europe with modern technology, aided by massive U.S. economic aid and the transfer of technical and managerial knowledge.
- The defense umbrella that the United States provided to Japan, Korea, and West Germany. This required a large expenditure for the defense effort.
- Lower investment in industrial renovation and restoration, as well as for research and development.
- Legislative controls for reducing pollution and improving occupational safety and health.

These and other factors have contributed to the 1970s productivity crises in the United States and in much of the industrialized world.[8] Hopefully, U.S.

---

[6] "The Reward of Productivity," *Business Week,* February 13, 1984, pp. 92–96; and Elliott S. Grossman, "Total Factor Productivity Dynamics," in *Productivity Perspectives* (Houston: American Productivity Center, 1980), pp. 2–10.

[7] Arthur S. Herman, "Productivity Declined in 1982 in a Majority of Industries Measured," *Monthly Labor Review,* January 1984, pp. 80–83.

[8] Ralph E. Winter, "Productivity Debate Is Clouded by Problem of Measuring Its Lag," *The Wall Street Journal,* October 13, 1980, pp. 1 and 19.

managers, through the efficient utilization of P/HRM activities, can sustain the present improvement in productivity into the 1990s.

Some suggested solutions for enhancing productivity growth include the reduction of government controls, more favorable income tax incentives to invest in new plans and equipment, and the reindustrialization of the entire business/industrial complex (such as plants and equipment). These suggested solutions have both proponents and opponents.[9] For example, there are many citizens who believe that reducing or eliminating legislative controls will have an adverse effect on the quality of life and society for decades to come. Toxic wastes, radiation, air pollution, and other forms of destruction must be carefully controlled. In reality, the P/HRM executive or specialist has little control over the environmental pollution problem. Certainly, he or she is concerned, but has little power to initiate policies or programs in this area.

On the other hand, the P/HRM staff can influence productivity through the utilization of the sound application of P/HRM programs. There are specific activities and practices that can improve individual performance and, consequently, organizational productivity. For example, recruitment and selection techniques can be used to attract and hire the best performers. Motivational and compensation techniques can be used to retain employees and improve job performance. Training and development can be used to improve skill and competency deficiencies which, in turn, increase performance.

A study conducted by McKersie and Klein showed how the productivity problem is linked to a firm's P/HRM policies and programs.[10] Corporate staff personnel and operating employees were asked to identify restraints to increase productivity. Interviews and questionnaires were used to collect the data. Operating employees identified as major productivity restraints such factors as worker resistance to change, poor motivation, government regulations, and ineffective work rules. The productivity improvement programs most widely mentioned and used were training programs, employee involvement (e.g., quality circles and labor-management committees) and relating pay directly to performance.

A number of procedures to overcome restraints to productivity improvement were suggested by Charles Kepner of Kepner-Tregoe, Inc., and they included: commitment to improve productivity, teaching employees at all levels how to be effective problem solvers, leaders who encourage followers to use their problem-solving skills, and rewards for successful problem solving.[11]

Productivity problems will not be solved without concern for the P/HRM

---

[9] Burton G. Malkiel, "Productivity—The Problem Behind the Headlines," *Harvard Business Review,* May–June 1979, pp. 81–91. Also see Joel Ross, *Productivity, People, and Profits* (Reston, Va.: Reston Publishing, 1981).

[10] Robert B. McKersie and Janice A. Klein, "Productivity: The Industrial Relations Connection," *National Productivity Review,* Winter 1983–84, pp. 26–35.

[11] "Productivity," *Personnel Management Policies and Practices* (Englewood Cliffs, N.J.: Prentice-Hall, 1983), pp. 23, 71–72.

function and the activities it performs. Every P/HRM activity covered in the diagnostic model (Exhibit 2–1) can affect productivity. Thus, productivity pressure from the external environment directly and indirectly affects an organization's P/HRM program and vice versa.

The Nature of Competition The nature of competition is mainly measured by the degree of competition. In industry, competition is considered high when there are many producers competing for the customer's business. The result is usually price pressures. A similar condition can exist in nonprofit or governmental institutions. For example, if there are more dormitory rooms than there are students at universities, competitive pressures operate on tuition charges, extra services offered, and so on. This can happen in hospitals as well. In the public sector, competition for budget increases for an agency can be fierce when the total budget (in real dollars) is stable or declining.

The greater the competitive pressure, the less able the organization is to offer additional inducements, such as higher pay or benefits, to its employees. Effective organizations under economic pressure can compete for good employees by offering nonmonetary rewards: they can provide greater job satisfaction through better reward systems or through job placement, thus facilitating personal fulfillment or self-actualization.

If there is less competitive pressure, the organization has greater flexibility in the variety of P/HRM programs it can offer. For example, the onetime director of the M.B.A. program at Michigan State University interviewed two engineers who wanted to enter the program. They were both employed by a defense contractor in Detroit, 90 miles away. When it was pointed out there was no night program, they said they could come during the day. This was astonishing. Further questioning revealed that they had done nothing for the company for two years except to bring in coffee and do odds and ends. The company was on a cost-plus contract; thus it could "stockpile" them *in case* they were needed and could still recoup their salaries *plus* their built-in profit percentage. Obviously there was no economic or competitive pressure in this situation. The company could afford to be very generous in pay, benefits, and so on. Contrast this with the competitive food industry, in which an additional 20 cents on a $15 case of vegetables could lose the order. Firms that have to watch their pennies are concerned with the costs of large wage increases and excessive fringe benefits.

The Nature of the Labor Market The labor market also directly affects P/HRM programs. When there are more workers than jobs, employers find recruiting costs minimal. Employees apply readily, and selection is less difficult; the employer may be able to choose from five or more qualified applicants for each position. Work attitudes tend to be work-ethic oriented. Martha Winston, in the opening P/HRM In Action, has significant staffing problems at the National Pancake House because this is not the case. When the work ethic predominates in employee attitudes, output increases and performance evaluation can be a motivating experience. A surplus of labor can also reduce employee pressures for compensation and benefit increases. Disciplinary problems, absenteeism, and turnover are likely to decrease, and equal employment opportunity goals may be easier to fill.

The employer must be aware of several labor markets. The primary concern is the local labor market, from which most blue- and white-collar employees are drawn. Managerial, professional, and technical employees may be recruited from a regional, or even a national, market.

It is possible that the local labor market is different from the regional or national markets. For example, in January 1988, there was about 5.8 percent unemployment nationwide, but in Laredo, Texas, 20 percent of the workers were unemployed.[12] Recruiting blue-collar workers in Laredo is three or four times easier than in Austin, Texas.

Even though the national land and local labor markets differ significantly, there will still be some exchange between them. Thus, if Laredo's unemployment rate stays consistently high, those among the unemployed who are younger, have knowledge of jobs elsewhere, and have the money and motivation to move will do so. This movement tends to increase the labor supply in areas with shortages. There also are international labor markets. Illegal aliens who come to the United States to seek work change the labor market balance. It was estimated that there were over 6 million illegal aliens working in the United States in 1988.[13]

In addition to labor markets defined by geographic boundaries are markets determined by skill and age considerations. If you are seeking an accountant, a general labor market surplus is not much help if accountants remain scarce. The supply of labor with a particular skill is related to many factors: the number of persons of work age; the attractiveness of the job in pay, benefits, and psychological rewards; the availability of training institutes; and so on. With regard to age, the U.S. Department of Labor predicted in 1983 that by 1995 workers aged 25–54 will rise by 24 million, while the number of teenagers available to the labor market will decline by almost 3 million.[14]

In sum, the P/HRM function is affected fundamentally by the state of the labor market not only in the organization's location in the region, but in the nation and the world as well. Also, the specific markets for the kinds of employees the enterprise seeks will affect that function.

The Work Sector of the Organization The diagnostic model presented in Exhibit 2–1 does not take into consideration the work sector in which the organization is located. This was done so that the model could remain relatively uncluttered.

About 60 percent of professional P/HRM specialists work in the *private sector,* consisting of businesses owned by individuals, families, and stock-

---

[12] "Reagonomics: The Good, the Bad, and the Ugly," *Business Week,* February 1, 1988, pp. 59–62 and "USA Employment," *USA Today,* January 11, 1988, p. 6B.

[13] "Fast Times on Avenida Madison," *Business Week,* June 6, 1988, p. 62.

[14] Howard N. Fullerton, Jr., and John Tschetter, "The 1995 Labor Force: A Second Look," *Monthly Labor Review,* November 1983, pp. 3–10.

holders, while 30 percent of all P/HRM employees in the United States work in the *public sector,* which is that part of the economy owned and operated by the government. Many economists define other institutions in society that are neither government nor profit oriented as the *third sector.* Examples of these institutions are museums, symphony orchestras, private schools and colleges, not-for-profit hospitals and nursing homes, and voluntary organizations such as churches and social clubs. About 10 percent of P/HRM specialists and employees work in the third sector.

In general, private- and third-sector P/HRM work is structured similarly. Hospitals have different internal organization problems than most businesses, though. For example, the presence of three hierarchies—physicians, administrators, and the board of trustees (representing the public)—can lead to conflicts. Pressures from third-party payees such as Blue Cross or Medicare can lead to other conflicts. Hospitals employ professional groups that zealously guard their "rights," which also leads to conflict. Structurally, P/HRM work in the private and third sectors is similar, but because of organizational differences jobs in the P/HRM function vary.

P/HRM in the public sector is *fundamentally different* from the other two sectors because it varies *structurally.* And the public manager faces a different world. In fact, a manager who moves from the private or third sector to the public sector will find the P/HRM role much more complicated. P/HRM in the public sector generally is much more laden with direct outside pressures. Politicians, the general public, pressure groups, and reporters influence the P/HRM manager much more than in a private business or in the third sector.

For example, most public managers must deal with a central personnel bureau such as the Civil Service Commission. A special problem faced by these managers has always been political appointments. Formerly, politicians always saw to it that their party workers were rewarded with government jobs between elections; this is usually called the "spoils systems." In an attempt to ensure that public jobs are assigned on the basis of merit rather than political pull, the Civil Service Commission and equivalent central personnel bureaus were established to set personnel policies governing public employment. Civil service standardized examinations are now required as part of the selection process of many public-sector jobs. This system was intended to establish merit as the criterion for public employment, but it also increases the system's rigidity and entrenches bureaucracy.

The differences among public-, private-, and third-sector P/HRM activities are largely in the structure of the P/HRM function and the environment of the public manager's job. The P/HRM function does vary by sector, and these differences will be discussed where they are significant.

Composition of the Labor Force

In 1988, the U.S. population was approximately 245 million and the labor force comprised about 115 million persons. By 1990, about 120 million persons will be in the labor force. In the current labor force, about 62 percent of the males 16 years and older are employed: about 47 percent are aged 16–17 and 25 percent are over 65 years old. The largest percentage of employed males is about 96 percent of all males 25–44 years of age. Female employment participation is now 50 percent and growing. About 34 percent of females ages 16–17 are employed. The highest employee proportion is about 54 percent of women 45–54, and only 9 percent of women over 65. From 1947 to 1975, the female population increased 52 percent, but the percentage of women working increased 123 percent.[15]

The U.S. labor force is now composed of more single and fewer married persons. One third of all workers are single, and 90 percent of the recent growth in the labor force has been in unmarried workers.

More participation in the labor force has become possible as the life span of the population has lengthened. In the United States, men live about 72 years, and women live about 78 years.

The percentage of the labor force employed by manufacturing, construction, mining, and agriculture has stabilized or declined. It is estimated that by 1990 two times as many persons will be employed in service industries, such as transportation, utilities, trade, financial, general services, and government, as in the stabilized industries. As far as type of workers is concerned, by 1990 it is predicted that farm workers will represent about 2 to 3 percent; service workers, about 16 percent; blue-collar workers (skilled, semiskilled, and unskilled operating level employees—assembly line worker, steelworker), 31 percent; and the rest—over 50 percent—will be white-collar workers (professional and technical, clerical, sales, and managers). Blue-collar workers, especially unskilled workers, are declining in relative importance. One of the fastest growing segments of employment is state and local government workers. From 1950 to 1986, total employment was up 70 percent, while state and local government employment increased by over 200 percent.

Women In 1988, about 50 percent of the full-time U.S. work force consisted of women. The number of married women in the labor force has increased 230 percent since 1947, at the same time that the number of male married employees has increased by 30 percent. In the mid-70s, 52 percent of married women with children aged 6–17 held full-time jobs, and 35 percent of married women with children aged 6 or under worked. Fifty-one percent of black children and 37 percent of white children 18 and under had mothers in the labor force.

Although women are supposed to have equal job opportunities, it is difficult to argue with the facts of discrimination against women in the workplace. Women today typically hold the lower status, low-pay jobs. For example, one study of 163 companies found that 31 percent had 50 percent or more women employees, and 82 percent employed at least 19 percent women. If discrimination were not practiced, at least half of the companies with 50 percent women

[15] U.S. Department of Labor, "Tomorrow's Jobs," in *Occupational Outlook Handbook, 1982–1983* (Washington, D.C.: U.S. Government Printing Office, 1983), pp. 1–24; John W. Wright, *The American Almanac of Facts, 1982* (Maplewood, N.J.: Hammond Almanac, 1982).

workers should have a majority of women in higher status, higher paying jobs. This study found, however, that less than 10 percent of the high-pay, high-status jobs were held by women. Similar conditions exist also in the public and third sectors.[16]

Minorities The situation for racial and ethnic minorities in the United States is similar to that of women. Large numbers of minority peoples, such as Hispanics, blacks, and American Indians, are employed in low-skill, low-pay jobs, and few are in high-status, high-pay jobs.

Historically, the most recent immigrant groups took the lowest level jobs offered. This was true of the Irish, Polish, Yugoslavs, and Jews. One difference between the immigrant groups and other minorities like blacks, Hispanics, and Indians is that the minority groups were living in the United States long before the immigrants arrived. The Indians have been in the United States since the time of discovery, as were many of the Hispanics in the Southwest, and the blacks since the mid-1700s. They have not advanced to the degree that the immigrants have, however. The Indians were kept on reservations, and the Hispanics remained in the areas that once belonged to the Mexican Republic (except for the Cuban and Puerto Rican immigrants, who came much later). Most blacks worked in southern agriculture until relatively recently. These minorities represent about 13 percent of the U.S. population. They have been less educated than the majority, although recent programs have attempted to improve this situation. In 1986, 13 percent of adult black workers and 10 percent of Hispanics were college graduates, compared with 26 percent of whites. Movement to jobs with better pay and higher status has been a problem for racial and ethnic minorities, as it has for women. For example, data indicate that of all "officials and managers" only 4.3 percent were black, including 1.6 percent black females.[17] However, college-educated blacks have been closing the gap with whites; they now earn 82 percent, as much as a similarly educated white, up from 78 percent in 1970.[18]

The Older Employee The age discrimination legislation defines an older employee as one between the ages of 40 and 70. About 21 percent of the labor force currently is in this category. This portion of the labor force is protected by law because some employers hold negative stereotypes about older workers.[19]

Probably one of the most difficult employment problems today is the older employee who loses a job through no personal fault. In some cases, employers assume that because a person is older, he or she is less qualified to work and less able to adapt to changes. Also, benefit plans (which may amount to one

---

[16] Louis F. Fitzgerald and Sandra L. Shullman, "The Myths and Realities of Women in Organization," *Training and Development Journal,* April 1984, pp. 65–73.

[17] Edmond W. Jones, Jr., "Black Managers: The Dream Deferred," *Harvard Business Review,* May–June 1986, p. 84.

[18] Michael Brody, "The 1990's," *Fortune,* February 2, 1987, p. 22.

[19] Eric G. Flamholtz, Yvonne Randle, and Sonja Sackmann, "Personnel Management: The Terror of Today," *Personnel Journal,* July 1987, pp. 60–70.

third of base compensation) are set up in such a way that it costs more to employ older people (the cost of insurance premiums is higher for older people).

One thing to remember is that each person ages at a different rate. As we grow older, we lose some of our faculties. But this process is ongoing: Rarely is a swimmer better than in his or her midteens, for example. The key, then, is to match employees with jobs. Older workers may be less efficient on some jobs requiring quick physical response rates. But speed of response is more important for a race driver or airline pilot than a stock analyst or social worker.

Most studies indicate that even for jobs requiring physical work, employees over 45 have no more accidents than do younger employees. Older employees also have the same or lower rates of absenteeism—at least until age 55. The worst accident rate observed in one study was for employees under 35 years old.[20] When total performance is considered (including factors such as speed, accuracy, judgment, loyalty), the older employee has been found to be at least as effective as the younger one. Yet our society tends to assume that the older employee is less effective.

Handicapped Workers According to census data, approximately 21 million Americans are handicapped.[21] Of the 21 million handicapped in our society, more than 6.5 million are members of the work force. Studies of employed handicapped persons indicate that they are of all age groups, of both sexes, and in many occupations. About 56 percent have been disabled by disease, 30 percent by accident, and 14 percent congenitally. In the latter category, the largest group of people have lost the use of limbs or have back problems. The next largest number are amputees and blind (or partially blind) employees.[22]

The Federal Rehabilitation Act of 1973 defines a handicapped person as anyone who:

1. Has a physical or mental impairment that substantially limits one or more major life activities.
2. Has a record of such an impairment.
3. Is regarded as having such an impairment.

Major life activities include communication, ambulation, self-care, socialization, education, transportation, and employment.

Many handicapped persons have had difficulty finding employment of any kind because employers and fellow workers believe that they could not do the job or would cause an excessive number of accidents. However, few people use all their faculties on a job, and there are many jobs for those who do not have all their faculties. When the handicapped are properly matched to jobs, studies

---

[20] Sydney P. Freedberg, "Forced Exits? Companies Confront Wave of Age Discrimination Suits," *The Wall Street Journal*, October 13, 1987, p. 33, and H. Kahne et al., "Don't Take the Older Workers for Granted," *Harvard Business Review*, January 1957, pp. 90–94.

[21] Sara M. Freedman and Robert T. Keller, "The Handicapped in the Workforce," *Academy of Management Review*, July 1981, pp. 449–58.

[22] Bernard De Lury, "Equal Job Opportunity for the Handicapped Means Positive Thinking and Positive Action," *Labor Law Journal*, November 1975, pp. 679–85.

show that two thirds of the physically handicapped produce at the same rate as nonhandicapped workers, 24 percent perform at higher levels, and only 10 percent perform at a lower rate. Absenteeism and turnover are normally lower for the handicapped for two reasons—the handicapped have had their abilities matched to their jobs better, and most handicapped workers seem better adjusted to working and have more favorable attitudes toward work. Thus, they are better motivated to do a good job. Most studies indicate that handicapped persons have fewer accidents than nonhandicapped persons.[23]

Of course, some handicapped people are physically or psychologically unable to work. Some who are marginally employable can work in training jobs at sheltered organizations such as Goodwill Industries. But for those handicapped able to work, it is most important to be treated as normally as other workers. They will respond better to fair treatment than to paternalism. They want a chance.

Veterans Veterans are former servicemen and women released from active duty by the military. They are not easily recognized as special employees by employers, but they do have a readjustment to make to civilian life. The government has attempted to ease reentry to civilian life of Vietnam veterans for whom there are several programs.

About one fourth of all returning veterans have resumed their interrupted educational careers. But the great majority have entered the civilian labor market, many seeking their first full-time jobs. As of January 1, 1981, there were 545,000 Vietnam veterans aged 20–34 unemployed in this country. The overall unemployment rate for veterans was 8.9 percent while the average unemployment rate was 7.7 percent. In the 20–24 age bracket, the veterans' unemployment rate was 18 percent.[24]

Congress has provided specific reentry adjustments for veterans, usually referred to as *reemployment rights*. In addition to reemployment, Congress has enacted laws making it easier for veterans to enter the federal career service. These include a preference system of points added to test scores for veterans, the Veterans Readjustment Appointment, waivers of physical requirements, the restriction of certain jobs to veterans, preference for retention in case of reduction of force, and similar procedures. The Veterans' Administration also assists veterans who are seeking employment through job marts and apprenticeship training programs. Priority for referral to appropriate training programs and job openings is given to eligible veterans, with first consideration to the disabled veteran. Other federal benefits have also become available to veterans operating their own businesses from the Small Business Administration. Similarly, unemployment compensation for veterans provides a weekly income for a limited period of time, varying with state laws.[25]

---

[23] R. B. Nathanson, "The Disabled Employee: Separating Myth from Fact," *Harvard Business Review,* May–June 1977, pp. 6–8.

[24] Bureau of National Affairs, *Fair Employment Practices—Summary of Latest Developments,* May 21, 1981 (Washington, D.C., 1981).

[25] Ibid.

Geographic Location
of the Organization

The location of the organization influences the kinds of people it hires and the P/HRM activities it conducts. A hospital, plant, university, or government bureau located in a rural area confronts different conditions than one located in an urban area. For example, the work force in a rural area might be more willing to accept a bureaucratic organization style. Recruiting and selection in rural areas will be different in that there may be fewer applicants. Yet the organization may find a larger proportion of hirable workers ingrained with the work ethic. It also may be harder to schedule overtime if workers are supplementing farm incomes with an eight-hour shift at a factory. There may be fewer minority "problems," but it also may be difficult to recruit professional/technical personnel, who have shown a preference to work near continuing education and cultural opportunities. While pay may be lower in rural areas, so are costs of living.

An urban location might be advantageous for recruiting and holding professional workers. Urban locations provide a bigger labor force but generally call for higher wages. The late shifts may be a problem here, too, but for different reasons. Workers may not feel safe late at night in the parking lots or going home.

Geographic location, therefore, influences the kinds of workers available to staff the organization. The location or setting is extremely significant for companies operating in other countries. The employees may speak a different language, abide by the Napoleonic legal code, practice different religions, have different work attitudes, and so on. Let's consider some of the major differences between home-based and multinational organizations.

Educational Factors Examples include the number of skilled employees available, attitudes toward education, and literacy level. Educational deficiencies in some countries can lead to a scarcity of qualified employees, as well as a lack of educational facilities to upgrade potential employees.

Behavioral Factors Societies differ in factors such as attitudes toward wealth, the desirability of profits, managerial role, and authority.

Legal-Political Factors Laws and political structures differ and can encourage or discourage private enterprise. Nations also differ in degree of political stability. Some countries are very nationalistic (even xenophobic). Such countries can require local ownership of organizations or, if they are so inclined, expropriate foreign concerns.

Economic Factors Economies differ in basic structure, inflation rate, ownership constraints, and the like. The nations of the world can be divided into three economic categories: fully developed, developing, and less developed. The fully developed nations include the United States and Canada, Australia, Israel, Japan, South Africa, and most European countries (the United Kingdom, West Germany, France, the USSR, Belgium, Luxembourg, the Netherlands, Switzerland, Italy, Sweden, Denmark, Norway, Finland). In these countries, American and Canadian managers will find fewer differences in educational, behavioral, economic, and legal-political factors than they are likely to encounter in developing or less developed countries.

The developing nations are those that are well along in economic development but cannot yet be said to be fully developed. Examples include Brazil, Mexico, Argentina, Venezuela, Spain, Nigeria, Saudi Arabia, India, and Eastern Europe. These countries provide more constraints in all four factors than developed countries do.

Third-world nations—the less developed countries—are the most difficult to work in because of significant constraints in all four factors. The remaining 90 or so countries in the world are in this group. A sample list would include Ethiopia, Bolivia, and Pakistan.

To be successful abroad, P/HRM managers must learn all they can about the countries in which they will be working. There are many sources of this kind of information. Knowledge of differences among nations in educational, behavioral, legal-political, and economic factors is essential for managerial success abroad. It is equally important (and more difficult) for the enterprise to obtain managers with proper attitudes toward other countries and their cultures. A manager with the wrong set of attitudes may try to transfer North American ways of doing things directly to the host country, without considering the constraints in these four factors. The more significant the differences, the more likely they are to cause problems for the unperceptive manager.

Effective managers who work abroad must adapt their P/HRM practices to conditions in the host country and learn to understand the new culture. A whole new field is developing for human resource planning in multinational organizations. There are significant challenges in such P/HRM activities. Just as the tools of management science do not work on very unstable problems, leadership styles and P/HRM activities that work for educated, achievement-oriented employees may not do so for uneducated nonachievers.

In sum, the physical location of the organization (rural or urban, at home or abroad) can have a significant impact on how P/HRM programs are used and which activities are conducted. The manager using a diagnostic orientation will be better able to closely examine, consider, and understand the complexities involved with physical location differences.

INTERNAL ENVIRONMENTAL INFLUENCES

The internal environmental influences listed in Exhibit 2–1—goals, organization style, nature of the task, work group, and leader's style and experience—involve characteristics and factors that are found within the organization. Let's examine how each of these influences affects the P/HRM program.

Goals

The goals of organizations differ within and between departments. All departments probably have goals that include employee satisfaction, survival, and adaptability to change. The differences arise in the *importance* the decision makers place on the different goals. In some organizations, profit is of such major importance that other goals such as increased employee satisfaction are not well developed. In these organizations where profits take precedent, P/HRM goals involving the human resources are paid only minimal attention. The result of such negligence is typically problems in the effectiveness area of the diagnostic model (e.g., high absenteeism, performance decrements, high grievance rates). In other organizations, P/HRM-related goals are highly regarded by decision makers. Thus, how much the P/HRM function is valued and how it is implemented are affected by these goals.

Organization Style

Modern organization theory provides many ways to organize. At one extreme is the *bureaucratic approach*. In this approach, the organization usually centralizes decision making, designs specialized jobs, departmentalizes by function, has standardized policies, uses small spans of control, has clearly defined objectives, and encourages communication through the chain of command.[26] The opposite extreme—the *participative approach*—uses decentralized decision making. It enlarges jobs, departmentalizes by product, uses few detailed policies, has large spans of control, and encourages free-flowing multidirectional communication. These two styles reflect fundamentally different managerial philosophies about the nature of people, the role of work in life, and the most effective ways to supervise. Basic beliefs about how employees are to be treated translate into ideas about the kinds of P/HRM programs that are made available to employees.

Obviously, there are many approaches to organization that fall *between* these two extremes, and most work organizations practice an intermediate, or mid-range, approach. Some organizations for example, are likely to prefer more formalized P/HRM policies, tighter controls on employees, more direct job-related training, compensation policies tied to actual performance, and so on. It seems reasonable to hypothesize that truly bureaucratic and truly participative organizations would have different P/HRM policies. Of course, most organizations are made up of some units that are bureaucratic and some that are participative in outlook, so P/HRM policies would also vary within these dimensions. In these ways, the organization's style influences the P/HRM program.

---

[26] James L. Gibson, John M. Ivancevich, and James H. Donnelly, *Organizations: Behavior, Structure, Processes,* 6th ed. (Plano, Tex.: Business Publications, Inc., 1988), p. 381.

Nature of the Task

Many experts believe that the task to be performed is one of the two most vital factors affecting P/HRM. They describe P/HRM as the effective matching of the nature of the task with the nature of the employee performing the task.[27]

There are perhaps unlimited similarities and differences among jobs that attract or repel workers and influence the meaning of work for them. Some of the most significant are:

Degree of Physical Exertion Required Contrast the job of ditch digger with that of a computer programmer. In general, most people prefer work involving minimal amounts of physical exertion. Some companies, like IBM, believe that working with the mind is better for curing productivity problems than working with the back. Exhibit 2–2 captures some of IBM's thinking on this matter.

Degree of Environmental Unpleasantness Contrast the environment of a coal miner with that of a bank teller. People generally prefer physically pleasant and safe conditions.

Physical Location of Work Some jobs require outside work; others, inside. Contrast the job of a telephone craftsperson during the winter in Minnesota with that of a disc jockey. Some jobs require the employee to stay in one place. Others permit moving about. Contrast the job of an employee on an assembly line with that of a traveling sales representative. There are individual differences in preference for physical location.

Time Dimension of Work Some jobs require short periods of intense effort, others long hours of less taxing work. In some jobs the work is continuous; in others, intermittent.

Human Interaction on the Job Some jobs require frequent interaction with others. Contrast the position of a radar operator in an isolated location who rarely sees anyone else with that of a receptionist in a busy city hall.

Degree of Variety in the Task The amount of freedom and responsibility a person has on the job determines the degree of *autonomy* provided for in the work. Contrast the autonomy of a college professor with that of an assembly-line worker.

Task Identity The degree of wholeness in a job—the feeling of completing a whole job as opposed to contributing to only a portion of a job—is its *task identity*. Contrast the job of an auto assembler with that of a tax accountant.

---

[27] "The New Industrial Relations," *U.S. News & World Report,* May 11, 1981, pp. 85–87, 89–90, 92, 94, 96, 98.

Task Differences and Job Design Because jobs are not created by nature, engineers and specialists can create jobs with varying attention to the characteristics described here. There are a number of approaches to those aspects of job design that affect variety, autonomy, task identity, and similar job factors. These approaches will be covered in Chapter 4.

How do these task factors affect P/HRM decisions? They obviously affect recruiting and selection, since employees will probably be more satisfied and productive if their preferences are met. As was mentioned, few jobs match all preferences exactly—there are too many of them. With jobs that are difficult, dirty, or in smoky or hot environments, the manager must provide additional incentives (more pay, shorter hours, or priority in vacations) because few people prefer such jobs. Or the manager may try to find employees who can handle the conditions better.

Work Group

Groups play a major role in the life of an individual. You probably belong to family, friendship, and student groups. Once a person joins an organization, his or her experiences are largely influenced by a work group.

> A **work group** consists of two or more people who consider themselves a group, who are interdependent with one another for the accomplishment of a purpose, and who communicate and interact with one another on a more or less continuous basis. In many cases (but not always), they work next to each other.

An effective group is one whose:

- Members function and act as a team.
- Members participate fully in group discussion.
- Group goals are clearly developed.
- Resources are adequate to accomplish group goals.
- Members furnish many useful suggestions leading to goal achievement.

Most effective work groups are small (research indicates that 7 to 14 members is a good range), and their members have eye contact and work closely together. Effective groups also generally have stability of membership, and their members have similar backgrounds. Their membership is composed of persons who depend on the group to satisfy their needs.[28] An effective work group will help achieve the goals of the organization. Thus, it is in the manager's interest to make the groups effective. It is also in the interest of employees, because effective groups serve their members' social needs.

Although the effective group supports management and the organization's

---

[28] Gibson et al., *Organizations*, p. 277.

goals, it can also work against them. This is usually the case when the group perceives the organization's goals as being in conflict with its own. If the work group is effective and works with management, the manager's job is easier, and objectives are more likely to be achieved. If the group is working against the manager, an effort must be made to change the group's norms and behavior by the use of the manager's leadership, discipline, and reward powers, or by the transfer of some group members.

Work groups are directly related to the success of P/HRM activities. If the work group opposes P/HRM programs, it can ruin them. Examples of programs that can be successes or failures depending on work-group support or resistance include incentive compensation, profit sharing, safety, and labor relations. Operational and P/HRM managers who desire success in such programs should at least consider permitting work-group participation in designing and implementing P/HRM.

Leader's Style and Experience

The experience and leadership style of the operating manager or leader directly affects P/HRM activities because many, if not most, programs must be implemented at the work-unit level. Thus the operating manager-leader is a crucial link in the P/HRM function.

Leaders must orchestrate the distinctive skills, experiences, personalities, and motives of individuals. Leaders also must facilitate the intragroup interactions that occur within work groups. In his or her role a leader provides direction, encouragement, and authority to evoke desired employee behaviors.[29] In addition, leaders reinforce desirable behavior so that it is sustained and enhanced. The leader is an important source of knowledge about the tasks, the organization, the P/HRM policies, programs, and goals. The experience and operating style of a leader will influence which P/HRM programs are communicated, implemented, and effective.

PEOPLE AND THE P/HRM DIAGNOSTIC MODEL

People—the human resource element—are the most important concern in the diagnostic model. Simply putting together P/HRM activities without paying attention to people characteristics would be ill advised. The most carefully designed and implemented P/HRM activity may backfire because adjustments for individual differences were not built into the program. In the P/HRM In Action earlier in the chapter, Martha is attempting to understand why Lenny and Harry behave differently on the job at the National Pancake House. She will discover that people differ in many characteristics. Lenny and Harry differ

---

[29] John W. Gardner, "The Tasks of Leadership," *New Management*, Spring 1987, pp. 9–14.

in their abilities, attitudes, and preferences. They also have different styles, intellectual capacities, and ways of doing the job.

Abilities of Employees

Some employee differences affecting P/HRM programs are due to differences in abilities. Abilities can be classified by mechanical, motor coordination, mental, or creative skills. According to many psychologists, some abilities are caused by genetic factors that are rarely subject to change through training. Examples of these differences are finger dexterity and response time. Other abilities, such as interpersonal skills and leadership, are much more easily subject to change. People learn abilities at home, at school, and at work; their present inventories of abilities are, at least partly, a consequence of this past learning.

Because people differ in abilities, the extent to which they can be trained in a specific skill varies. In most cases an aptitude can be developed into an ability by training and experience. But in other cases it's more sensible to place people with certain abilities in jobs requiring those abilities. Not everyone will have all the abilities necessary to do every job, and a manager does not always have the time or money needed to train people who do not have them.

The importance of a manager's understanding of employee ability differences is emphasized by the example of Harry at National Pancake. Does he lack the abilities to do the job? If it appears that Harry's problem is in fact ability, Martha would have at least two options. One is training, whereby Harry's aptitudes would be developed into the ability needed for the job. The other is placement, whereby Harry could be transferred to another job, such as busboy or cashier.

Do you think Harry's problem is an ability problem?

Employee Attitudes and Preferences

How an individual thinks, feels, and behaves toward work and the place of work in his or her life forms one important attitude.

> An attitude is a characteristic and usually long-lasting way of thinking, feeling, and behaving toward an object, idea, person, or group of persons. A preference is a type of attitude which evaluates an object, idea, or person in a positive or negative way.

People are motivated by powerful emotional forces, and work provides an opportunity for the expression of both aggressive and pleasure-seeking drives. Besides offering a way to channel energy, work also provides the person with income, a justification for existence, and the opportunity to achieve self-esteem and self-worth. The amount of energy directed toward work is related to the amount directed to family, interpersonal relations, and recreation.

What kinds of attitudes about work do Lenny and Harry have?

How can an awareness of work attitudes and preferences help managers understand workers and improve their effectiveness? Many P/HRM programs (job enlargement, compensation, leadership, and participation programs) are designed to create a more favorable individual attitude toward work. The assumption is that a positive attitude will result in higher-quality performance and increased production. Recall, however, that performance is also influenced by learning, perception, abilities, and motivation.

Motivation of Employees

Work motivation is concerned with those attitudes that channel a person's behavior toward work and away from recreation or other life activity areas. The motivation to work is likely to change as other life activities change.

> Motivation is that set of attitudes which predisposes a person to act in a specific goal-directed way. Motivation is thus an inner state that energizes, channels, and sustains human behavior to achieve goals.

A number of theories have attempted to explain work motivation. The theories differ in their assumptions about how rational persons are and to what degree the conscious and the unconscious mind directs behavior. All of these theories have received some research support, but none has been overwhelmingly substantiated. At the moment, attention is focused on the importance of individual motivation in achieving organizational and individual goals.

How will the knowledge of employee motivation help a person be a more effective manager of people? As with work attitudes, a manager who can determine what the work motivations of the employees are will make more effective P/HRM decisions. For employees who appear to be work oriented and motivated toward working hard, incentive compensation systems will likely lead to more production and higher-quality work. Those who are consciously motivated to do a better job benefit from performance evaluation techniques like management by objectives. Managers who can determine or predict which employees are motivated can create the work environment that will most optimally sustain the motivation. The determination of a person's state of motivation is undoubtedly very difficult. Remember, motivation is *within* a person, and a manager must infer the individual's motivational level by his or her behavior. The manager uses his or her understanding of individual motivation to select the best possible P/HRM program.

Personality of Employees

Each employee has a unique personality. Because of this, it is highly unlikely that a single set of P/HRM activities or leadership approaches will be equally successful for *all* employees.

> Personality is the characteristic way a person thinks and behaves in adjusting to his or her environment. It includes the person's traits, values, motives, genetic blueprint, attitudes, emotional reactivity, abilities, self-image, and intelligence. It also includes the person's visible behavior patterns.

Behavioral scientists have found that:

1. The employee, as a person, is both rational and intuitive-emotional in makeup and behavior. Therefore, his or her choices and behavior are a consequence of rational (conscious) and emotional (unconscious) influences. Choices are occasionally entirely influenced by one or the other, but most behavior is influenced by both.
2. A person acts in response to internal inclinations and choices and environmental influences.
3. Each person is unique, and acts and thinks in a certain way, because of

   ■ The personality the person develops.
   ■ The abilities the person has or learns.
   ■ The attitudes and preferences the person has or develops.
   ■ The motives the person has or develops.

This section has touched briefly on some relevant concepts from the behavioral sciences that will be developed further in later chapters. Theory and research indicate that the nature of the employee has a great influence on P/HRM decisions. The effective manager realizes that the employee's nature is a crucial variable in P/HRM activities and organizational effectiveness. The implications of this knowledge of human behavior for the various P/HRM activities will become more obvious as we move into the book.

STRATEGIC P/HRM: AN IMPORTANT KEY TO SUCCESS

There is now little disagreement with the position that the P/HRM function is a vital contributor to the organization's mission. Therefore, P/HRM managers are becoming more involved in the establishment of the strategy formulation and implementation in the organization. A **strategy** indicates what an organization's key executives hope to accomplish in the long run.[30] There is also an intermediate and a short-term strategy position in an organization. Exhibit 2–3 presents the three levels of strategy, strategic, managerial, and operational, as they apply to five specific P/HRM activities.

The efforts to formulate and implement sound P/HRM strategies at the three levels presented in Exhibit 2–3 are designed to achieve desirable end

---

[30] Lee Dyer, "Bringing Human Resources into the Strategy Formulation Process," *Human Resource Management,* Fall 1983, pp. 257–71.

EXHIBIT 2–3   Personnel and Human Resource Activities by Level

Level	Employee Selection/Placement	Rewards (Pay and Benefits)	Appraisal	Development	Career Planning
Strategic (long-term)	Specify the characteristics of people needed to run business over long term Alter internal and external systems to reflect future	Determine how work force will be rewarded over the long term based on potential world conditions Link to long-term business strategy	Determine what should be valued in long term Develop means to appraise future dimensions Make early identification of potential	Plan developmental experiences for people running future business Set up systems with flexibility necessary to adjust to change	Develop long-term system to manage individual and organizational needs for both flexibility and stability Link to business strategy
Managerial (medium-term)	Make longitudinal validation of selection criteria Develop recruitment marketing plan Develop new markets	Set up five-year compensation plans for individuals Set up cafeteria benefits packages	Set up validated systems that relate current conditions and future potential Set up assessment centers for development	Establish general management development program Provide for organizational development Foster self-development	Identify career paths Provide career development services Match individual with organization
Operational (short-term)	Make staffing plans Make recruitment plans Set up day-to-day monitoring systems	Administer wage and salary program Administer benefits packages	Set up annual or less frequent appraisal system Set up day-to-day control systems	Provide for specific job skill training Provide on-the-job training	Fit individuals to specific jobs Plan next career move

Source: From M. A. Devanna, C. Fombrun, and N. Tichy, "Human Resources Management: A Strategic Perspective." Reprinted by permission of the publisher from *Organizational Dynamics*, Winter 1981, p. 55. Copyright © 1981 by AMACOM, a division of American Management Associations. All rights reserved.

results such as competitive products and/or services. In other words, sound strategies are intended to result in productivity, profits, and survival. One study of corporations with publicly recognized accomplishments showed that these recognized productivity leaders act by emphasizing the importance of P/HRM in strategic decision making.[31] The study compared the practices of productivity leaders and comparison firms from *Fortune* 500 corporations. Five practices differentiated the leaders from the comparison firms.

- Leaders define the P/HRM role in terms of the function's participation in business decisions and in the implementation of business strategies.
- Leaders focus the current resources devoted to the P/HRM function on important problems before they add new programs or see additional resources.
- Leaders' P/HRM staffs initiate programs and communication with line managers.
- Leaders' line management share in the responsibility for P/HRM programs.
- Leaders' corporate staffs share responsibility for human resource policy formulation and program administration across organizational levels.

The study clearly showed that the P/HRM function is a major force in developing the strategic thrust in the successful firms. In contrast, in the comparison companies the P/HRM function was not in the mainstream of developing organizational strategies.

Strategic planning by an organization leads to informed, purposeful actions. By articulating a clear common vision of what the organization exists for, now and in the future, a strategic plan provides direction and a cornerstone for making important P/HRM decisions. The planning process when applied to P/HRM activities expands awareness of possibilities, identifies strengths and weaknesses, reveals opportunities, and points to the need to evaluate the probable impact of internal and external forces.

A well-designed organizational strategic plan permits the P/HRM department to be better prepared to cope and deal with changes in both the internal and external environments presented in Exhibit 2–1. The concept of using P/HRM activities and plans with the organization's strategic plan to cope with changes is not new. Each organization can adopt a specific form of strategy that best fits its goals, environments, resources, and people. Gerstein and Reisman have identified five corporate strategies and the employee characteristics that fit each strategy. Exhibit 2–4 presents some P/HRM activities that represent a "best fit" for each strategy. The matching of an organization's strategic plan, employee characteristics, and P/HRM activities is important for achieving desirable organizational end results—competitive products and competitive services.

---

[31] Kenneth F. Misa and Timothy Stein, "Strategic HRM and the Bottom Line," *Personnel Administrator,* October 1983, pp. 27–30.

EXHIBIT 2–4   P/HRM Practices and Organizational Strategy

Strategy Type	Needed Employee Characteristics	HRM Practice Choices
Entrepreneurial: Projects with high financial risk are undertaken, minimal policies and procedures are in place, resources are insufficient to satisfy all customer demands, and multiple priorities must be satisfied. The focus here is on the short run and getting the operation off the ground.	To varying degrees, employees need to be innovative, cooperative, longer-term oriented, risk taking, and willing to assume responsibility. It is critical that key employees remain.	a. Employee selection/placement—seek out risk takers; high need for achievement people. b. Rewards—competitive, external equity, and employee-preference-based when possible. c. Appraisal—results-based; not too rigid. d. Development—informal, mentor-oriented. e. Career planning—focus on interest of employees and matching jobs with personal interests.
Dynamic growth strategy: Risk taking on projects is more modest. The constant dilemma is between doing current work and building support for the future. Policies and procedures are starting to be written, as the need is for more control and structure for an ever-expanding operation.	Employees need to have high organizational identification, be flexible to change, have a high task orientation, and work in close cooperation with others.	a. Employee selection/placement—seek out flexible and loyal individuals. b. Rewards—internal and external equity, high recognition-based program. c. Criteria-based. d. Development—emphasis on quality of work life programs, participation. e. Career planning—present opportunities, multiple career paths.
Contract profit rationalization strategy: The focus is on maintaining existing profit levels. Modest cost-cutting efforts and employee terminations may be occurring. Control systems and structure are well developed along with an extensive set of policies and procedures.	The focus is on quantity and efficiency, the short term, and results with a relatively low level of risk and a minimal level of organizational identification.	a. Employee selection/placement—very selective, some outplacement. b. Rework—merit based, seniority, internal equity. c. Appraisal—specific, results oriented, carefully reviewed. d. Development—emphasis on task competence, developing experts in narrow area. e. Career planning—narrow, few opportunities and paths available.

EXHIBIT 2-4—(concluded)

Strategy Type	Needed Employee Characteristics	HRM Practice Choices
Liquidation/divestiture strategy: The focus involves selling off assets, cutting further losses, and reducing the work force as much as possible. Little or no thought is given to trying to save the operation, as declining profits are likely to continue.	Employees need a short-term, narrow orientation, low organizational commitment, a low need to remain, and a limited focus on high quantity.	a. Employee selection/placement—not likely because of cutbacks. b. Rewards—merit based, few perks, no incentives. c. Appraisal—rigid, formally conducted, based on management based criteria. d. Development—limited, task competence based. e. Career planning—those with required skills will have opportunities.
Turnaround strategy: The focus is to save the operation. Although cost-cutting efforts and employee reductions are made, they are short-term programs for long-run survival. Worker morale may be somewhat depressed.	Employees need to be flexible to change, have a high task orientation, have a longer-term task focus, and engage in some non-repetitive behavior.	a. Employee selection/placement—need multi-talented individuals. b. Rework—incentive systems, merit reviews, and employee participation. c. Appraisal—results-oriented, encourage participation. d. Development—increased opportunities, carefully select participants. e. Career planning—multiple career paths, encourage participation.

Source: R. S. Schuler, "Personnel and Human Resource Management Choices and Organizational Strategy," in *Readings in Personnel and Human Resource Management*, 3d ed., ed. R. S. Schuler, S. A. Youngblood, and V. Huber (St. Paul: West Publishing, 1987).

P/HRM Manager Close-Up

James O. Wilson
Cooper Hospital/
University Medical Center

Biography

James O. Wilson is vice president of Cooper Hospital/University Medical Center in charge of human resources and general services.

Mr. Wilson, raised in Philadelphia, is a graduate of LaSalle College and received his M.B.A. from Temple University in Philadelphia.

He worked for the *Philadelphia Inquirer* and *Daily News* for over 12 years in various capacities, including manager of employee relations.

For over two years he was vice president/human resources for National Railway Utilization Corporation; he has held his current position with Cooper Hospital for almost five years. His responsibilities include recruitment, compensation, benefits, employee relations, safety, and employee health with additional responsibilities outside of personnel such as security, housekeeping, dietary, and other support functions.

Personnel—A Proactive Function: Mr. Wilson's View

It was not too many years ago that the responsibility for personnel was frequently placed in the hands of an executive in the twilight of his career, to be managed in a caretaker fashion. Personnel was a department that kept records in good order and *responded* to demands as they arose.

It is no longer appropriate to think of the personnel function in that light.

Personnel *can* and *should* be a department where the action takes place. Truly the personnel function has the potential to be proactive and should serve as the catalyst for change and improvement. At Cooper Hospital/University Medical Center, the personnel department is involved at all levels of the organization whenever decisions are made and in fact, because of our proactive stance, is the initiator of much change.

The posture taken by the Depart-

(continued)

ment relative to employees could almost be labeled "forced communication." Historically, in almost every instance of interpersonal, interdepartmental or labor/management conflict, the root cause usually can be identified as poor or lacking communication with the employee population.

For that reason Cooper Hospital seizes every opportunity to meet with any or all our 2,000 employees, who are spread over three shifts and a seven-day work week.

Some of the devices used to encourage communication are:

1. Town meetings, which are meetings scheduled around the clock. Employees are invited to meet and discuss concerns with our president, chief operating officer, and other senior managers, and lively discussion usually ensues.
2. Monthly personnel rounds are conducted on the second Thursday of each month. Representatives from the personnel department visit each department on second and third shifts to handle problems relating to pay, policy interpetation, and so forth. Additionally, the personnel staff involved are attuned to listen for rumors and grievances, so that these items can surface and be handled.
3. Coffee klatches are held on a regular basis with groups not larger than 20 to generate conversation regarding problems, opportunities, perceptions, and so forth. Personally conducted by our chief operating officer, they are invaluable in developing a humanness to management that might otherwise be lacking.
4. Ad hoc department task forces are created whenever particular departments appear to be experiencing employee unrest. The purpose of the task force, made up of departmental employees and chaired by personnel, is to pinpoint problems and potential remedies for those problems. Follow-up action by the personnel department and the department involved always results.
5. Employee relations interviews are conducted on an ongoing basis by the personnel department. These interviews are scheduled with members of a department individually. The employee responds to a structured interview and frequently spins conversation into areas of concern not addressed by the firm. The individual responses are held in confidence by the personnel interviewer, but broad brush summaries are provided to the department manager to aid the manager in lessening tension or improving morale in the department.

It is through extensive communication that large organizations like Cooper can foster a personal feeling in the work environment. As long as people treat one another as people, I believe that significant and potentially disastrous labor relations problems will not materialize nor be insurmountable if they do develop.

It is the personnel department that can serve as the linking pin between employees and management. As a barometer of the workplace climate, it becomes personnel's responsibility to initiate appropriate responses. Truly, this function can be the primary catalyst for internal improvement in many organizations.

The days of viewing the personnel or P/HRM area as only a highly specialized and technical staff activity are over. Human resources are vitally important to the firm's success, and the P/HRM function must be involved in all aspects of an organization's operation. The end results of having competitive products and/or services means that employees must be performing at an optimal level so that the overall strategy and goals can be achieved. The P/HRM unit must make everyday contributions to the organization. Thus, the P/HRM programs must be comprehensive, adaptable with the organization's culture, and responsive to employee needs. This means that management creativity and action must be exerted to match an organization's overall strategy with its P/HRM programs, activities, and talents.

HOW TO USE THE P/HRM DIAGNOSTIC MODEL

You've now had a chance to learn something about the role that can be played by P/HRM in strategy development and implementation. You have also been introduced to the diagnostic model, this book's way of providing a map of the important factors affecting P/HRM. The model tells you that three sets of factors—external, internal, and people—influence the P/HRM activities used by an organization.

It is reasonable to conclude that managers who must make P/HRM decisions are more effective if they think about the three sets of factors influencing P/HRM activities and effectiveness before they make a decision. Chapters 3–20 tell you *how* each of these factors affects a specific P/HRM decision.

Managers concerned with the P/HRM function, activities, and role in strategy development and implementation need some kind of model to guide the way. First, they need to analyze the P/HRM problem—or the person with a problem—by looking at all the data at hand. Then they decide which causes are operating and how the problem can be solved. They do not give up if the most probable cause does not seem to be operating. Rather, they proceed down the list of causes until the underlying source of the problem is found.

Suppose, for example, that a manager notices from the weekly production reports that productivity in the department has been declining over the past few weeks. There could be a number of reasons for this decline. Perhaps the equipment in the department has become defective and is not working properly, or the materials and supplies have been of a comparatively lower quality. Or the cause might be the employees: Perhaps some of the more highly skilled employees have been promoted, transferred to other departments, or have quit, and their replacements lack the necessary skills and experience to perform the work effectively. Or, perhaps the problem is one of poor employee morale.

In investigating the problem, the manager using a diagnostic framework may find that turnover in the department has been quite high, that absenteeism has been increasing, and that there have been more complaints and grievances of late. All of these are symptoms of low employee satisfaction and detract from the organization's effectiveness. If the manager concludes that

A RETURN TO THE P/HRM ‣ IN ‣ ACTION

Martha   Harry

Martha picked up her cup of coffee and thought: Amy helped me a lot. But it is my job to figure out what to do. She wonders what factors could cause the differences between Lenny and Harry. It could be personality differences. Lenny is an outgoing person, and Harry tends to be introverted. There are some differences in abilities. Lenny is more agile. He uses his hands well. Harry seems a bit clumsier. And Lenny is more experienced—he's been on the job four more years than Harry.

Lenny and Harry have the same leader and work group. They do the same task at the same time. The environment is the same. These couldn't cause the differences.

This narrows the option down to motivation and attitude differences. Was there a good match of interests and abilities with the job? Martha decided to discuss the issues formally with Harry. Later that day, she invited Harry to have a chat with her.

Martha Harry, this is the first chance I've had to chat with you for very long. How do you like it at National by now?

Harry It's O.K. It's a job.

Martha Is there anything we can do to make it better than just a job for you?

Harry Not really. Jobs are jobs. They're all the same.

Martha All of them? Did you ever have a dream about what you wanted to do?

Harry Sure. I've always wanted to be a disc jockey, but I hated school. So I quit. Then I got married and I'm locked in. I can't go back to school and make it.

Martha I didn't know you wanted to go back to school. I'm sure you could go to night school.

Harry I might be ready for that now.

Martha If I can help by scheduling you differently, let me know. Everyone should get all the schooling they can. And who knows? You could go on to be assistant manager here—or even a disc jockey.

After talking with Martha, Harry did go back to school. His work improved, as did his willingness to be friendlier with co-workers and customers. Martha's chats became more frequent with all the employees, including Harry. Harry did graduate from high school and now is an assistant manager for National. He's very happy in his job.

(continued)

What about Lenny? He's chief cook at 827. He's had several opportunities to become assistant manager, but he loves his work and has refused to be transferred. As Lenny put it, "I've found my niche. I do my job, then go to the beach. No worries. And I get to talk to lots of nice people."

What about the new cook? The pay issue had to be settled first. Martha contacted the home office, emphasizing that business had been steadily increasing at 827. When she told them that she needed more money to hire an extra cook to handle the increased business, they gave her more, but not enough to completely satisfy everyone.

Instead of hiding this fact from the rest of her employees, Martha explained the situation and asked them for their suggestions. Their solution was to help her recruit a cook with some experience, but one who would not demand so high a salary that their raises would be eliminated. All of the employees asked their friends for leads to fill the vacancy. Martha called guidance counselors at schools and the state employment service.

Within a week, Martha had hired Dan, a friend of Harry's. Lenny, Harry, and all the other employees liked him very much, and he worked out well as the third cook. Besides that, employee satisfaction improved all around. Not only could Martha pay Dan what he expected as a beginning wage, but all the other employees got a slight increase in pay, too.

the most likely cause of poor production in the department is the low satisfaction of employees, a solution for this problem will be sought. The manager may consider such solutions as: providing better working conditions, increasing pay and other financial benefits, improving communication between supervisor and employees, redesigning the jobs to make them more interesting and challenging, or modifying the manager's own leadership style. If, after treating the morale problem, productivity is still low, the manager will turn to the next most probable cause of the problem and continue down the list of causes until the right one is found and corrected.

Now after learning about the diagnostic model, let's find out what happened at National Pancake House 827. A Return To The P/HRM In Action will show you how Martha worked on the problem and solved the mystery of Harry's behavior.

SUMMARY

The main objective of this chapter has been to introduce you to the diagnostic model of P/HRM. The model will serve as the framework for observing, analyzing, and solving P/HRM problems. The chapter also briefly reviews some concepts from the behavioral sciences to show you how they apply to P/HRM decisions. It further examines two other aspects of the environment of the

P/HRM function: the physical location of the organization in a labor market and the work sector in which it is located. This book has been written with the assumption that effective P/HRM programs are more likely to occur if the manager or specialist follows a diagnostic approach.

To summarize the major points covered in this chapter:

1. A sound P/HRM program can contribute to organizational effectiveness.
2. The diagnostic approach suggests that before you choose a P/HRM program you should examine the nature of the employees, the external and internal environmental influences on the organization, and organizational factors. These factors act as moderating variables in P/HRM decisions, and P/HRM activities are influenced by them.
3. Various factors in the external environment, such as unionization of employees, government regulations, and competitive pressure, also exert strong influences on the P/HRM function.
4. Understanding the characteristics and composition of the labor force is important when designing a P/HRM program.
5. The work sector in which the organization is operating—public, private, or third—determines the complexity and bureaucratic level of the P/HRM function.
6. Organization factors, including goals of organization style, the nature of the task, makeup of the work group, and leader's style and experience, must all be taken into account to maximize the effectiveness of the P/HRM function.
7. An attitude is a characteristic and usually is a long-lasting way of thinking, feeling, and behaving. A preference is a type of attitude that evaluates an object, idea, or person in a positive or negative way.

Questions for Review and Discussion

1. How are specialists involved in P/HRM programs performing work similar to physicians who must conduct a diagnosis before treating a patient?
2. What individual differences play a major role in P/HRM decision making?
3. Why is it important for a P/HRM department to be respected by other units when an organization is developing its strategic plan?
4. How can a P/HRM department make daily contributions to the goals of an organization?
5. Why must external environmental forces be considered when designing a P/HRM program?
6. What does the term *third sector* mean?
7. What effectiveness criteria are used to examine the success of a P/HRM program?
8. Why should even small firms engage in developing clearly stated strategic plans?
9. Someone stated that, "If unemployment in the national and local labor markets differs, there will be a natural movement of people between the markets." What did she mean by this statement?
10. What did you like about Martha's leadership style at National Pancake House 827?

GLOSSARY

External P/HRM Influences. The environmental forces outside the organization, such as unions, government, and economic conditions.

Internal P/HRM Influences. Those internal (inside the organization) environmental forces, such as goals, organizational style, tasks, work group, and the leader's style of influencing.

Motivation. The attitudes that predispose a person to act in a specific goal-directed way. It is an internal state that directs a person's behaviors.

Personality. The characteristic way a person thinks and behaves in adjusting to his or her environment. It includes the person's traits, values, motives, genetic blueprint, attitudes, abilities, and behavior patterns.

Productivity. The output of goods and services per unit of input of resources used in a production process.

Strategy. What an organization's key executives hope to accomplish in the long run.

Work Group. Two or more people who work together to accomplish a goal and who communicate and interact with each other.

EXERCISE 2–1   Dissecting the Diagnostic Model and Its Application

Objective   The objective of this exercise is to have students examine in detail the main diagnosic model used in this book (Exhibit 2–1).

SET UP THE EXERCISE

1. Each student is to individually examine the various parts of Exhibit 2–1. Note the three main parts of P/HRM programs—activities, people, and effectiveness criteria.
2. Set up groups of four students. Each student is to take a hypothetical organization type—a large manufacturing firm, a medium-sized community hospital (350 beds), a government agency such as the equal employment opportunity commission, and a small mom-and-pop department store that employs 10 full-time and 15 part-time employees.
3. Each student is to develop an analysis of the type of environmental influences, P/HRM activities, people characteristics, criteria, and results that pertain to their organization type. Thus, each group will have four separate analyses being prepared. The analyses should use Exhibit 2–1 as the diagnostic model for putting together the analyses.
4. Students will bring their analyses to a group meeting for discussion and to compare similarities and differences.
   a. What are the criteria used in the different organizations?
   b. What are the end result factors?
   c. What environmental forces are important for the various organizations?

A Learning Note

This exercise will require individual and group work. It should show that the diagnostic model (Exhibit 2–1) can be applied to large, medium, and small organizations.

3

THE LAW AND PERSONNEL/HUMAN RESOURCE MANAGEMENT

P/HRM · IN · ACTION

Hugo

Gregory

Osanna

Hugo Gerbold, the director of personnel/human resource management at Reliable Insurance, is sitting in his office, thinking. The problem is equal employment opportunity. Reliable is a middle-sized company in the Midwest which specializes in homeowners', auto, and, to a lesser extent, life and health insurance. As is typical of firms of this type, the top-management team members are all white, in their 60s, and have been with the firm all their careers. The work force is mainly composed of:

Salespersons—98 percent white males, the rest white females and black males.

Underwriters—98 percent white males, 2 percent white females.

Claims agents—90 percent white males, 8 percent white females, 2 percent black males.

Clerical staff—90 percent white females, 10 percent black females.

Other administrative personnel: Computer programmers, marketing staff, security, etc.—95 percent white males, 5 percent white females.

Reliable is located in an area where at least 35 percent of the labor force is black.

Hugo knows many firms just like Reliable have been fined back-pay differentials and ordered to set up affirmative action plans. At a recent conference, Reliable's lawyers devoted much time to discussing the laws and recent cases. This had prompted Hugo to visit the company president, Gregory Inness.

Gregory, 64 years old and a lawyer by training, did not give Hugo much hope that things were going to change at Reliable with regard to equal employment opportunities.

It is a few days after this meeting. Hugo has just received a call from a professor at one of the local universities. The professor had encouraged Osanna Kenley to apply at Reliable for a management trainee position which had been advertised. She had been discouraged by the P/HRM department because, they said, she was a liberal arts major. She'd also been told there were no positions. In fact, the company had just hired a white male for a trainee position. Somehow she'd found out about this.

The professor informed Hugo that Osanna is going to file a complaint against the firm with the Equal Em-

(continued)

ployment Opportunity Commission (EEOC). He suggests Hugo talk with her before she goes to the EEOC. In fact, she is on her way over to see Hugo right now.

Hugo and Osanna have a pleasant talk, but it is clear that she means to open up Reliable to all applicants, even if she personally does not get a job there. He arranges to see Gregory right after Osanna leaves.

Hugo: Gregory, remember how I was just talking about equal employment opportunities? Well, we may have a

case on our hands. And remember the insurance company that just paid out $15 million in back pay and had to hire their fair share of minorities as a result?

Gregory: Well, maybe we should hire this young woman. That ought to take care of the problem, won't it?

Hugo: No, it won't. We'd better get going on an EEO program now.

Hugo then explains the legal details of recent court cases on affirmative action.

INTRODUCTION

The impact of law on the P/HRM function is indicative of the development of laws governing all business and societal activities. Around 1970, people began to want to be legally protected from every problem. Patients sued doctors, consumers sued manufacturers of faulty products, children even began to sue parents for not being supportive and nurturing. In 1960 there were about 59,000 civil suits filed in U.S. district courts. By 1983, this figure had increased to over 200,000, an increase of over 200 percent, in a period when the population increased by only 25 percent.[1]

Although suits by consumers against manufacturers of defective products account for a large proportion of the increased litigation, suits by employees or job candidates against employers are increasing rapidly.[2] Therefore, it is in the best interest of the organization for the P/HRM function executives to develop policies and procedures that comply with the law. The best way to begin studying the relationship between P/HRM functions and the law is to devote time and attention to equal employment opportunity (EEO). No other regulatory area has so thoroughly affected P/HRM as EEO. EEO has implications for almost every activity in P/HRM: hiring, recruiting, training, terminating, compensating, evaluating, planning, disciplining, and collective bargaining.[3] **Equal employment opportunity (EEO) programs** are implemented by

---

[1] 1987 *Annual Report of Director of Administrative Office of U.S. Courts* (Washington, D.C.: U.S. Government Printing Office, 1987).

[2] Kenneth Sovereign, *Personnel Law* (Reston, Va.: Reston Publishing, 1984), p. 22.

[3] For an excellent discussion of federal regulations applied to P/HRM see James Ledvinka, *Federal Regulation of Personnel and Human Resource Management* (Boston: Kent, 1982), p. 21.

employers to prevent employment discrimination in the workplace or to take remedial action to offset past employment discrimination.

EEO cuts across every P/HRM activity, and this means that P/HRM officials and managers in every function of the organization are involved. Top managers must get involved in EEO issues and programs to make sure that the organization is in compliance with the law, to avoid fines, and to establish a discrimination-free workplace. Operating managers must help by changing their attitudes about protected-category employees and helping all employees to adjust to the changes EEO is bringing to the workplace.

Exhibit 3–1 highlights the key factors in the P/HRM diagnostic model that affect equal employment opportunities. Some of these were noted in the introduction union requirements, goals of the organization, and P/HRM activities involved. Others are discussed later in the chapter: societal values, preferences of workers as reflected in economic status of minorities and women, and government regulations. Knowledge of these factors can contribute to an understanding of why EEO developed and how it operates. To be effective, P/HRM managers must pay close attention to EEO in designing each P/HRM activity and program.

HOW DID EEO EMERGE?

The three main influences on the development of EEO were: (1) changes in societal values; (2) the economic status of women and minorities; and (3) the emerging role of government regulation. The first two are briefly discussed in this section; information on the third factor is discussed in detail in the next section.

Societal Values and EEO

Throughout history, Western society has accepted the principle that people should be rewarded according to the worth of their contributions. When the United States became a nation, that principle was embodied in the American dream: the idea that any individual, through hard work, could advance from the most humble origins to the highest station, according to the worth of her or his contributions. In America, success did not depend on being born into a privileged family; equal opportunity was everyone's birthright. To this day, the American dream, with its emphasis on merit rather than privilege, is widely accepted by the public.

Another value that has encouraged equal opportunity is the profit motive. Nondiscrimination makes good business sense. If a company limits opportunities to white males it cuts itself off from the vast reservoir of human talent comprised of women and minorities. Moreover, it adds to such societal problems as poverty, crime, high taxes, and civic disorder, which also hurt the business community.

Until the early 1960s it was not unusual for many people, while believing in the American dream of rewards based on merit, to also believe that blacks (and

EXHIBIT 3–1　Factors Affecting Equal Employment Opportunity Programs

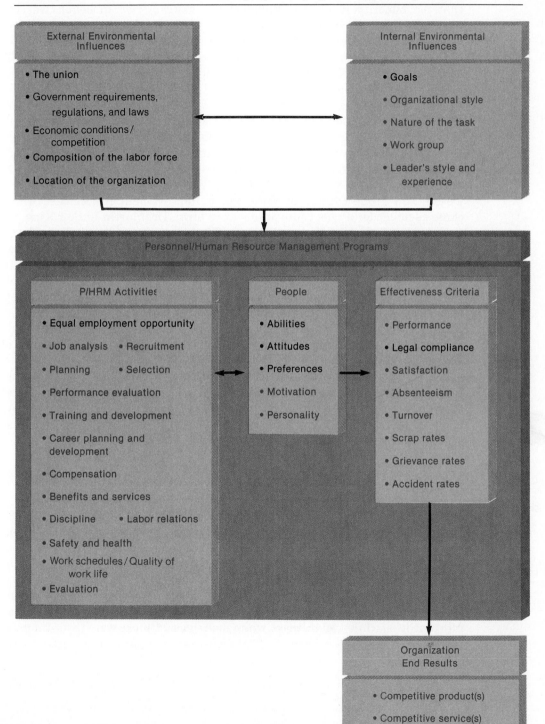

External Environmental Influences

- The union
- Government requirements, regulations, and laws
- Economic conditions/competition
- Composition of the labor force
- Location of the organization

Internal Environmental Influences

- Goals
- Organizational style
- Nature of the task
- Work group
- Leader's style and experience

Personnel/Human Resource Management Programs

P/HRM Activities

- Equal employment opportunity
- Job analysis　• Recruitment
- Planning　• Selection
- Performance evaluation
- Training and development
- Career planning and development
- Compensation
- Benefits and services
- Discipline　• Labor relations
- Safety and health
- Work schedules/Quality of work life
- Evaluation

People

- Abilities
- Attitudes
- Preferences
- Motivation
- Personality

Effectiveness Criteria

- Performance
- Legal compliance
- Satisfaction
- Absenteeism
- Turnover
- Scrap rates
- Grievance rates
- Accident rates

Organization End Results

- Competitive product(s)
- Competitive service(s)

other minorities) had their "place"—a place largely cut off from the rewards that the majority received. This apparent contradiction in beliefs was the American dilemma as observed even in the 1940s by the distinguished Swedish economist, Gunnar Myrdal, in his studies of American race relations for the Carnegie Corporation. Blacks were often excluded from schools, public accommodations, jobs, and voting; and economic realities for blacks belied the ideals of the American dream.[4]

The differences between American ideals and American realities lent special significance to the civil rights conflict of the 1960s. The conflict began in Montgomery, Alabama, on December 1, 1955, when Mrs. Rosa Parks, a black department store worker in her 50s, was arrested for refusing to give up her bus seat to a white man. Out of that single act of protest emerged a previously unthinkable act—a bus boycott by blacks. At the center of the boycott was a loosely knit group called the Montgomery Improvement Association, which chose as its leader a new young minister in town, Dr. Martin Luther King, Jr.

Then came years of demonstrations, marches, and confrontations with the police that captured headlines throughout most of the early 1960s. Television accounts included scenes of civil rights demonstrators being attacked with cattle prods, dogs, and fire hoses. These events shocked the public into recognition that civil rights was a serious social problem in the United States. Gradually, overt discrimination declined and recognition of the problems faced by minorities grew. The business community shared in this attitude change, voluntarily supporting such EEO-related efforts as the National Alliance of Businessmen.

As the U.S. Congress turned its attention to civil rights, laws were passed prohibiting discrimination in education, voting, public accommodations, and the administration of federal programs, as well as discrimination in employment. The civil rights movement was instrumental in raising congressional concern and stimulating the passage of this legislation.

Economic Status of Minorities: Before 1964

Undeniable economic inequality helped focus national attention on employment as a specific area of discrimination. Unemployment figures for blacks were twice as high as for whites, and higher still among nonwhite youth. While blacks accounted for only 10 percent of the labor force, they represented 20 percent of total unemployment and nearly 30 percent of *long-term* unemployment. Moreover, in 1961, only one half of black men worked steadily at full-time jobs, while two thirds of white men did so. Blacks were three times as

---

[4] Gunnar Myrdal, *An American Dilemma: The Negro Problem and American Democracy* (New York: Harper & Row, 1944).

likely as whites to work less than full time. Similar statistical differences existed for other minorities, such as Hispanics and Indians.[5]

When they did find work, minorities were relegated to lower-status jobs, and consequently their income was far below that of whites. Minorities such as blacks were over three times as likely as whites to be unskilled laborers. Whites were over three times as likely as blacks to be in professional or managerial positions. While only 9 percent of black men were skilled crafts-workers, 20 percent of white men were. In the tobacco, paper, and trucking industries, blacks were ordinarily segregated into less desirable lines of pro-gression or sections of the company. In the building trades, they were concen-trated in the lower paying "trowel trades," such as plastering and bricklaying. Some unions excluded blacks entirely, and others organized separate locals for them.

The inequalities are especially striking in the income comparisons between blacks and whites. In 1962, the average family income for blacks was $3,000, compared with nearly $6,000 for whites. More importantly, the relative posi-tion of blacks had been worsening during the preceding 10 years. While black family income was only 52 percent of white family income in 1962, it was 57 percent of white family income in 1952. These inequalities could not be at-tributed entirely to differences in educational level between blacks and whites. The average income of a black high school graduate was lower than the average income of a white elementary school graduate.[6]

The Government

There is no need to develop a detailed analysis to convince you that the government is playing an increasing role in all phases of life. According to some estimates, government expenditures on federal regulation have in-creased from $750 million in 1970 to over $4 billion in 1987.[7] But this is only a small fraction of the total cost of regulation. The public spends billions of dollars to comply with regulations.

In organizations, much of the compliance burden has been directed to the P/HRM department. The growth of equal employment opportunity has given employees specific rights in their relationship with their employers. Employee rights were not widely publicized or seen as front-page news prior to the early 1970s.

---

[5] Charles Silberman, *Crisis in Black and White* (New York: Random House, 1964).

[6] St. Clair Drake, "The Social and Economic Status of the Negro in the United States," in *The Negro American,* ed. Talcott Parsons and Kenneth B. Clark (Boston: Houghton Mifflin, 1966), pp. 3–46.

[7] The estimate was provided in discussions with EEOC representative, Houston, Texas office on June 30, 1987.

THE 1964 CIVIL RIGHTS ACT AND TITLE VII

Today, there are many laws and executive orders (issued by presidents which have the force and effect of laws enacted by congress) prohibiting employment discrimination. Since it would be impossible to discuss all of them in a single chapter, this chapter will primarily focus on **Title VII** of the **1964 Civil Rights Act** and a few of the presidential executive orders. Considerable understanding of the entire legal framework can be gained by examining how these regulations operate.

Title VII: A Major Part of Civil Rights Guarantees

Employers, unions, employment agencies, and joint labor-management committees controlling apprenticeship or training programs are prohibited from discriminating on the basis of race, color, religion, sex, or national origin by Title VII of the 1964 Civil Rights Act. Other laws protect the aged, the handicapped, and special classes of veterans.[8] Title VII prohibits discrimination with regard to any employment condition, including hiring, firing, promotion, transfer, compensation, and admission to training programs. The Equal Employment Opportunity Act of 1972 amended Title VII by strengthening its enforcement and expanding its coverage to include employees of state and local governments and of educational institutions, as well as private employment of more than 15 persons. However, Indian tribes and private membership clubs are not covered, and religious organizations are allowed to discriminate on the basis of religion in some cases. Federal government employees are also covered by Title VII, but enforcement is carried out by the Civil Service Commission with procedures that are unique to federal employees.

The EEO coverage of government employees is noteworthy. While discrimination has been illegal in government employment since the end of the spoils system and the advent of open competitive examinations in the public service, race and sex inequalities have persisted in public service. The "merit system" in government employment has had a mixed record. Some of its features have held back minorities over the years. With the 1972 amendments to Title VII, public administrators found themselves subject to the same sorts of EEO burdens that managers in private enterprise had shouldered since the passage of Title VII in 1964.

One clause of Title VII permits employers to discriminate based on sex, religion, or national origin if these attributes are a "bona fide occupational qualification" (BFOQ). This seems like a loophole, but it is a small one indeed. For instance, courts have said that the clause does not allow an employer to

---

[8] For an excellent discussion and presentation of the federal laws regarding discrimination, see Lee Modjeska, *Handling Employment Discrimination Cases* (Rochester, N.Y.: Lawyers Cooperative, 1980).

From The Wall Street Journal, *with permission of Cartoon Features Syndicate.*

"Can't those Equal Opportunity people leave well enough alone?"

discriminate against women simply because they feel that the work is "inappropriate" for them or because customers might object. The best example of this reasoning was the decision in *Diaz* v. *Pan American Airways* that an airline could not limit its employment of flight attendants to women. Pan American Airways was challenged in court by a male applicant. The airline pointed to section 703(e) of Title VII and claimed that sex was a "bona fide occupational qualification" for the position of flight attendant. As evidence, the airline offered the following:

- Passenger preference: Surveys showed that passengers preferred women to men as flight attendants.
- Psychological needs: A clinical psychologist testified that women, simply because they were women, could provide comfort and reassurance to passengers better than men could.

▪ Feasibility: An industrial psychologist testifed that sex was the best practical screening device to use in determining whom to hire for the position.

At the time, the idea of a male flight attendant was unusual, but that was not a legal justification for Pan American's refusal to hire Diaz in that position.[9]

When *is* sex a bona fide occupational qualification? One obvious but unusual situation is when one sex is by definition unequipped to do the work—as in the case of a wet nurse. Another is when the position demands one sex for believability—as in the case of a fashion model. A third instance is when one sex is required for a position in order to satisfy basic social mores about modesty—as in the case of a locker room attendant.

Executive Order 11246 was issued by President Lyndon B. Johnson in 1965, superseding President John F. Kennedy's Executive Order 10925. Employment discrimination by federal government contractors, subcontractors, and federally assisted construction contracts is prohibited. While Executive Order 11246 prohibits the same actions as Title VII does, it carries the additional requirement that contractors must develop a written plan of affirmative action and establish numerical integration goals and timetables to achieve equal opportunity. The affirmative action planning requirement is discussed in greater detail later in this chapter.

Virtually every state also has some form of equal employment law. In 41 states, plus the District of Columbia and Puerto Rico, there are comprehensive state "fair employment" laws similar in operation to Title VII. In fact, some of these state laws antedate Title VII. If a state's law is strong enough, charges of discrimination brought under Title VII are turned over by the federal government to the state fair employment practices agency, which has the first chance at investigating it.

Discrimination: A Legal Definition

All the laws discussed above are designed to eliminate discrimination. Would you believe the laws never defined it? It's true; the courts have had to do this when they have interpreted the laws. The courts arrive at definitions by looking at the history behind a statute, examining the *Congressional Record* to gain insight into the social problems Congress hoped it would solve. Then they define terms like *discrimination* in a way to help solve these problems. For Title VII, the history of the civil rights conflict clearly identifies the problems: economic inequality and the denial of employment opportunities to blacks and other minorities.

The courts have defined discrimination in three different ways since the first days of federal involvement in employment practices.[10] Initially, during World War II, discrimination was defined as *prejudiced treatment:* harmful

---

[9] *Diaz* v. *Pan American Airways,* 442 F. 2d 385.

[10] Alfred Blumrosen, "Strangers in Paradise: *Griggs* v. *Duke Power Co.* and The Concept of Employment Discrimination," *Michigan Law Review,* November 1972, pp. 59–110.

actions motivated by personal animosity toward the group of which the target person was a member. However, that definition was ineffective as a means of solving the problem of economic inequality, because it is difficult to prove harmful motives, and that made it difficult to take action against many employment practices that perpetuated inequality.

Then the courts redefined discrimination to mean *unequal treatment*. Under this definition, a practice was unlawful if it applied different standards or different treatment to different groups of employees or applicants. This definition outlawed the practice of keeping minorities in less desirable departments (different treatment), and it also outlawed the practice of rejecting women applicants with preschool-aged children (different standards). The employer was allowed to impose any requirements, so long as they were imposed *on all groups alike*.

To enable Title VII to solve the social problems that congress wanted it to, the U.S. Supreme Court arrived at the third definition of employment discrimination: *unequal impact*. In the case of *Griggs* v. *Duke Power Co.,* the Court struck down employment tests and educational requirements that screened out a greater proportion of blacks than whites.[11] These practices were prohibited because they had the *consequence* of excluding blacks disproportionately, *and* because they were not *related* to the jobs in question. The practices were apparently not motivated by prejudice against blacks. And they certainly were applied equally: both whites and blacks had to pass the requirements. But they did have an adverse impact on blacks. Today both unequal treatment and unequal impact are considered discrimination.

By way of a summary, the determination for EEO and affirmative action compliance or noncompliance can theoretically be reduced to two criteria. In question format the criteria are:

1. Does an employment practice have unequal or adverse impact on the groups covered by the law? (Race, color, sex, religious, or national origin groups.)
2. Is that practice job related or otherwise necessary to the organization?

A practice is prohibited *only* if the answers to *both* questions are unfavorable. Even practices that are unnecessary and irrelevant to the job are legal if they have equal impact on the groups covered by the law. This means that employers do not have to validate tests or follow the employee selection regulations if their tests do not exclude one group disproportionately.

This two-question approach does have some exceptions, and getting a straight answer to the second question is especially difficult because of the stringent guidelines that employers must follow. Nevertheless, the two questions are a good place to begin in understanding EEO and affirmative action. It is important to remember that new cases are constantly being decided, and guidelines are undergoing important changes. Therefore, EEO programs are in a period of total uncertainty. Nevertheless, these two basic questions remain as underlying principles through all the changes.

---

[11] *Ibid.*

The Discrimination Case Process In a discrimination case a person alleges that he or she is being, or has been, discriminated against due to an unlawful employment practice. The person filing the suit is called the *plaintiff*. The person or organization against whom the charge of discrimination is made is called the *defendant*. The plaintiff must demonstrate that a prima facie (evidence exists) violation has occurred by gathering evidence showing that the employment practice has had an adverse impact.[12] The **adverse impact** criterion refers to the total employment process that results in a significantly higher percentage of a protected group in the available population being rejected for employment, placement, or promotion.

This means that the minority applicant for a job would have to show that the P/HRM activity (e.g., testing, promotion, selection) had an adverse impact on his or her minority group. For example, a plaintiff might demonstrate that out of 50 black and 50 white applicants for a job who completed a test, no blacks were hired, but 15 whites were placed on the job. This would be evidence of adverse impact, and a prima facie violation of Title VII would be established.

Those in P/HRM use what is called the **4/5ths rule** for judging adverse impact. This rule notes that discrimination typically occurs if the selection rate for a protected group is less than 80 percent of the selection rate for a majority group. Thus, if 20 out of 100 white applicants are selected (20 percent), at least 16 percent (4/5ths or 80 percent of 20) of minority applicants (e.g., black or Hispanic) should be selected to avoid being accused of adverse impact. It should be pointed out that adverse impact need not be considered for groups that constitute less than 2 percent of the relevant labor force.

Once adverse impact has been demonstrated the burden of proof shifts to the defendant. The defendant must demonstrate that the testing or selection activity at issue is job related or has some business necessity. If the defendant cannot demonstrate the job-relatedness of the testing activity, the judgment will probably be awarded to the plaintiff.

The "shifting burden of proof" model is applied in most suits in which there is a claim of employment discrimination. Exhibit 3–2 presents the model graphically. This model and adverse impact and job-relatedness criteria are important in understanding most court judgments.

Other Federal Laws

There are a number of federal laws that are related to EEO and Title VII. These include the Age Discrimination Act of 1967, as amended in 1978, the Equal Pay Act of 1963, the Rehabilitation Act of 1973, and the Vietnam Era Veteran's Readjustment Assistance Act of 1974. Exhibit 3–3 briefly presents important sections of the Civil Rights Act of 1964, as amended by the Equal Employment Opportunity Act of 1972 and these other EEO relevant laws.

---

[12] Richard D. Arvey, *Fairness in Selecting Employees* (Reading, Mass.: Addison-Wesley Publishing, 1979), pp. 50–52.

EXHIBIT 3–2   Shifting Burden of Proof Model

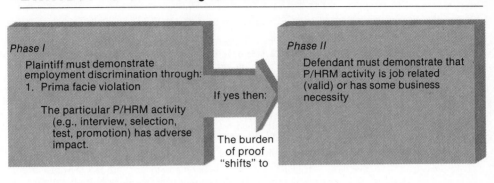

Phase I

Plaintiff must demonstrate employment discrimination through:
1. Prima facie violation

   The particular P/HRM activity (e.g., interview, selection, test, promotion) has adverse impact.

If yes then:

The burden of proof "shifts" to

Phase II

Defendant must demonstrate that P/HRM activity is job related (valid) or has some business necessity

The total impact of the type of laws and regulations presented in Exhibit 3–3 are made clear by the following example. Notice in the example in Exhibit 3–4 that a plaintiff could lose her claim in 11 different forums, yet still end up winning a judgment from the employer in the 12th.[13]

AFFIRMATIVE ACTION

In 1967 Executive Order 11246 was amended to conform with Title VII by including sex. The basic theory of all executive orders is that it is a privilege to do business with the federal government and therefore to continue doing such business, certain conditions must be followed. The condition imposed by order 11246 is that a contractor or subcontractor cannot discriminate in employment because of race, sex, creed, color, or national origin.

Many employers took Executive Order 11246 more seriously than Title VII, probably because under Title VII, a charge had to be filed and a long period of contestation resulted, while under 11246 the firm complied or lost its contracts with the government request.[14] One response to equal opportunity laws and executive orders such as 11246 is the development of affirmative action plans (AAP).

Affirmative action has different meanings to different people. Various meanings that have emerged over the years are:

1. Recruitment of underrepresented groups.
2. Attempting to eliminate conscious and unconscious prejudices that some managers have toward underrepresented groups.
3. Removing discriminatory obstacles that work to the disadvantage of underrepresented groups.

---

[13] Kenneth J. McCulloch, *Selecting Employees Safely under the Law* (Englewood Cliffs, N.J.: Prentice-Hall, 1981), pp. 7–8.

[14] Sovereign, *Personal Law*, p. 80.

EXHIBIT 3–3   Major Equal Employment Opportunity Laws and Regulations

Civil Rights Act of 1964, as amended by the Equal Employment Opportunity Act of 1972

Sec. 703(a)   It shall be an unlawful employment practice for an employer (1) to fail or refuse to hire or to discharge any individual, or otherwise to discriminate against any individual with respect to his compensation, terms, conditions, or privileges of employment, because of such individual's race, color, religion, sex, or national origin; or (2) to limit, segregate, or classify his employees or applicants for employment in any way which would deprive or tend to deprive any individual of employment opportunities or otherwise adversely affect his status as an employee, because of such individual's race, color, religion, sex, or national origin.

Age Discrimination in Employment Act of 1967, as amended in 1978

Sec. 4(a)   It shall be unlawful for an employer (1) to fail or refuse to hire or to discharge any individual or otherwise discriminate against any individual with respect to his compensation, terms, conditions, or privileges of employment, because of such an individual's age.

Sec. 12(a)   The prohibitions in this Act shall be limited to individuals who are at least 40 years of age but less than 70 years of age.

Equal Pay Act of 1963

Sec. 3(d)(1)   No employer having employees subject to any provisions of this section shall discriminate, within any establishment in which such employees are employed, between employees on the basis of sex by paying wages to employees in such establishment at a rate less than the rate at which he pays wages to employees of the opposite sex in such establishment for equal work on jobs the performance of which requires equal skill, effort, and responsibility, and which are performed under similar working conditions, except where such payment is made pursuant to (i) a seniority system; (ii) a merit system; (iii) a system which measures earnings by quantity or quality of production; or (iv) a differential based on any other factor other than sex . . .

Rehabilitation Act of 1973

Sec. 503(a)   Any contract in excess of $2,500 entered into by any federal department or agency for the procurement of personal property and non-personal services (including construction) for the United States shall contain a provision requiring that, in employing persons to carry out such contract the party contracting with the United States shall take affirmative action to employ and advance in employment qualified handicapped individuals . . .

Vietnam Era Veterans' Readjustment Assistance Act of 1974

Sec. 2012(a)   Any contract in the amount of $10,000 or more entered into by any department or agency for the procurement of personal property and non-personal services (including construction) for the United States, shall contain a provision requiring that the party contracting with the United States shall take affirmative action to employ and advance in employment qualified special disabled veterans and veterans of the Vietnam era.

Executive Order 11246 (1965), as amended by Executive Order 11375 (1967) and Executive Order 12086 (1978)

Sec. 202(1)   The contractor will not discriminate against any employee or applicant for employment because of race, color, religion, sex, or national origin.

EXHIBIT 3–4 The Wide Reach of the Law

A minority female with a heart murmur who is over 40 and working in New York City for an employer who is a government contractor can precipitate legal or administrative action, or both, against that employer in 12 different forums because of alleged discrimination. Theoretically, she could lose in 11 forums, yet still receive relief from the employer in the 12th.

She could accuse the employer of discrimination on the basis of race or sex under Title VII.,[4] thereby precipitating "enforcement" either by EEOC or herself. In any event, she would precipitate an investigation by such a charge.

She could accuse the employer of discrimination on the basis of age, under the Age Discrimination in Employment Act of 1967,[5] and thereby precipitate court enforcement action by EEOC or herself. At a minimum, this would cause an attempted conciliation by EEOC.

She could file a lawsuit in federal court on the basis of race discrimination under the Civil Rights Act of 1866, 42 U.S.C. *1981.

She could file a claim of discrimination under the Equal Pay Act of 1963,[6] and thereby precipitate court enforcement action by either EEOC or herself. At a minimum, this charge would trigger an investigation.

She could file a claim of discrimination based upon her status as "handicapped"[7] and precipitate court enforcement action by the U.S. Department of Justice or herself[8] under the Rehabilitation Act of 1973. The same charge could also precipitate sanctions against the employer under the Rehabilitation Act of 1973, and the rules and regulations issued pursuant to that law.[9] Thus, this charge would trigger an investigation that could lead to an administrative hearing and, alternatively, federal court proceeding[10]—as two possible forums.

By filing a charge of discrimination with OFCCP claiming race or sex discrimination in violation of Executive Order 11246,[11] she could precipitate sanctions against the employer because the employer is a government contractor. At a minimum, this charge would trigger an investigation, and it could precipitate an administrative hearing or a federal court action by the federal government[12]—again, two possible forums.

She could file a charge of discrimination on the basis of race, sex, disability, or age with the New York State Division of Human Rights and thereby precipitate an investigation.[13] She can either go to court directly herself, or await the administrative proceedings and then appeal an adverse determination to court. The New York statute offers her two distinct forums.[14]

She can file a charge of discrimination based on age, sex, race, or disability with the New York City Commission on Human Rights and thereby precipitate an investigation and an administrative determination, with court review.[15]

She can file a charge of discrimination based on age, sex, race, or disability under the Mayor's Executive Order, thereby precipitating sanctions against the employer because the employer is a city contractor. At a minimum, this charge would lead to another investigation.

If the woman were a disabled veteran, she could file a charge of discrimination with OFCCP on that basis, thereby precipitating possible sanctions against the employer because it is a government contractor and, possibly, court action initiated by either the Department of Justice or herself, or an administrative hearing.[16]

If the woman were covered by a collective bargaining agreement, she could precipitate an arbitration if there were a nondiscrimination clause in the agreement, or a lawsuit, under the Labor-Management Relations Act, against the union and the employer.[17]

If the employer were a New York State defense contractor, a charge of discrimination on the basis of race could lead to investigation and criminal conviction of a misdemeanor.[18]

---

[4] 42 U.S.C. **2000e *et seq.*

[5] 29 U.S.C. **621 *et seq.* (now enforced by EEOC).

[6] 29 U.S.C. *206(d) (Now enforced by EEOC).

[7] U.S.C. *701.

[8] In *Carmi* v. *St. Louis Sewer District,* 20 FEP Cases 162 (E.D.Mo.1979), the court recognized the individual's right of action, but ruled against the plaintiff on the merits. *Carmi* discusses the cases which have split on the issue of whether there is an independent right of action available to a private party under the Rehabilitation Act.

[9] 41 C.F.R. *60–741.

[10] See *Davis* v. *Bucher,* 451 F.Supp.791 (E.D.Pa.1978).

[11] 3 C.F.R. *339.

[12] See *United States* v. *New Orleans Public Services, Inc.,* 553 F.2d 459 (5th Cir.1977), vacated and remanded, 436 U.S. 942 (1978).

[13] N.Y. Exec. Law **290–301 (McKinney 1972); 3 Empl. Prac. Guide (CCH) **26000 *et seq.*

EXHIBIT 3–4   *(concluded)*

[14] Under Section 291 of the New York State Human Rights Law, the opportunity to obtain employment without discrimination because of age, race, creed, color, national origin, sex, or marital status was recognized and declared to be a civil right. As such, it is enforceable by direct court action. Additionally, a complainant may follow the procedures outlined in Section 297, which leads to administrative action and possible court review.

[15] The New York City Commission on Human Rights and its powers are described in the Administrative Code of the City of New York, **B1–1.0 *et seq.* Commissions such as the new York City Commission are allowed to exist pursuant to the General Municipal Law, Article 12-D, **239 *et seq.* That law, apparently, did not grant to cities full hearing and court enforcement powers. See General Municipal Law, *239-R. However, in interpreting the law, the New York Court of Appeals has ruled that the New York City Commission on Human Rights does have jurisdiction to decide a controversy raised by a discrimination claim. See *Maloff* v. *City Commission on Human Rights,* 38 N.Y.2d.563, 379 N.Y.S.2d 788 (1975).

[16] The possibility of a court enforcement proceeding by the Department of Justice is indicated by 41 C.F.R. *60-250.28(b). The possibility of an administrative hearing is indicated by 41 C.F.R. *60–250–29 and 41 C.F.R. *60–250.26(g) (3). The possibility of an independent right of action for an individual claiming to be aggrieved by a violation of the Vietnam Era Readjustment Act of 1974 is enhanced by the Supreme Court's decision in *University of California Board of Regents* v. *Bakke,* 438 U.S. 265 (1978), 17 EPD (CCH) #8402 (June 28, 1978).

[17] 29 U.S.C. **141 *et seq.*

[18] See N.Y. Civ. Rights Law **44, 44a (McKinney 1976); 3 Empl. Prac. Guide (CCH) #26,105.

Source: Kenneth J. McCulloch, *Selecting Employees Safely Under the Law,* © 1981, pp. 7–8. Reprinted by permission of Prentice-Hall, Inc., Englewood Cliffs, New Jersey.

4. Hiring and staffing preferentially for underrepresented groups.[15]

The most controversial interpretation and definition is the fourth. It suggests that affirmative action gives preferential treatment in hiring, recruitment, promotion, termination, and development to groups that have been discriminated against.

The legality of preferential treatment depends in part on whether the affirmative action is involuntary (court ordered) or voluntary (not court ordered). When an employer violates the law an affirmative action plan (AAP) may be required. Any employer having a contract with the federal government of at least $50,000 and employing at least 50 people must put their AAP in writing. Although not all employers are required to have AAP, some have elected to develop them as an indication of being a socially responsible business. By having AAP the organization is suggesting to the public and the courts that it is attempting to deal with discrimination.

Affirmative Action Guidelines

The regulation that suggests the format and parts of AAPs is Revised Order No. 4, issued by the Office of Federal Contract Compliance Programs, a subdivision of the U.S. Department of Labor. Three main planning steps are presented in Revised Order No. 4.

1. *Perform a utilization analysis*—This analysis compares employment of women and minorities in the employer's work force with the availability of women and minorities in the labor market. The analysis will show the percentage of the employer's work force that belongs to the group in question (e.g., Hispanic) and the percentage of the available labor supply that belongs to that group (e.g., Hispanic). If there is a smaller percentage in the

[15] Ledvinka, *Federal Regulation,* pp. 118–19.

work force than in the labor supply, then the group is said to be "under-utilized."

2. *Goals and Timetables*—This step specifies the percentage of a job group (one or a group of jobs having similar content wage rates and opportunities) to be filled by women or minorities and the date by which that percentage is to be attained. Goals and timetables are required for all job groups in which underutilization is found.

3. *Action Steps*—These are steps that can be taken by employers to reduce underutilization and achieve their goals. Steps mentioned include publicizing the firm's AAP, both inside and outside the firm, communicating top management's support for the program, removing any barriers to employment, validating job specification and selection methods, and auditing the entire affirmative action program.

Affirmative action does not demand that underutilization be correct, but that a good faith effort be made by the organization to increase the number of women and minorities in certain job groups. It appears that in order for AAPs to have a chance to succeed they must be written down, and they must be vigorously supported and communicated by top management. Without top-management support, it is difficult to show that there is a good faith effort being exerted to deal with discrimination.

Despite lingering controversy, AAPs are now found in many organizations. It is likely, no matter which way the courts rule, that affirmative action will remain a part of P/HRM programs. Almost on a daily basis, there is a critic, supporter, or legal analyst making statements about affirmative action. For example, in June 1984, the Supreme Court ruled that seniority is more important than affirmative action goals when layoffs take place. Only employees who can prove that they are victims of discrimination can benefit from affirmative action in layoff cases.[16] The last-hired, first-fired ruling is considered by some people to mean that there will be less pressure on firms to push affirmative action. Others feel that this Supreme Court ruling will have no noticeable effect on affirmative action. They feel that AAPs are an ingrained part of overall policies and P/HRM programs. Stephen Byrd, vice president for human resources of Schering-Plough Corporation, stated "We've had these programs in place for 10 years and we're not turning our backs on them now."

AT&T's Affirmative Action Program for Women Outside-Crafts

Of all employers in the United States, probably none has received more attention for its affirmative action program than the American Telephone and Telegraph Company.[17] AT&T was involved in the largest back-pay settlement in the history of equal employment. As part of that settlement, the company

---

[16] "Affirmative Action Ruling Pleases Firms, Angers Minorities, Women," *The Wall Street Journal,* June 14, 1984, p. 31.

[17] "AT&T: In the Throes of Equal Employment," *Fortune,* January 15, 1979, pp. 44–57.

was required to make significant strides in increasing employment opportunities for women and minorities. The program that resulted from the settlement exemplifies some of the more advanced EEO efforts in American industry.

The scope of AT&T's affirmative action program is so vast that it is impractical to focus on more than a small segment here. One particularly interesting segment of AT&T's program is its provisions for increasing the employment of women in outside-crafts positions: the various lineworkers, telephone installers, and repair workers whose work is mostly done outdoors. These components are an integral part of affirmative action for any job at any company.

Step 1: Analyzing Underrepresentation and Availability AT&T found a problem simply by examining the sex composition of their job classes: There were almost no women in outside-crafts positions. But how great was the extent of underrepresentation? Many organizations find the answer to this question in the statistics compiled for affirmative action plans by state labor departments in every state, which show the number of women and minorities in each of 10 or 20 broad occupational groups. Others use the overall population figures compiled by the U.S. Census. Both sets of data are readily available from the appropriate government agencies. In addition, some larger firms are investing in sophisticated labor market studies to arrive at a more accurate estimate of availability. Of course any set of statistics is open to criticism. Many employers strive to collect statistics that put them in the best light. While some may argue that such a strategy is manipulative, it often does succeed in reducing enforcement pressures. Employers are likely to continue using it until such time as there emerges a generally accepted statistical definition of availability.

Step 2: Goal Setting Once the statistics are agreed upon, the organization sets goals to help achieve greater minority representation in the job in question. The EEO goals have to be realistic, and they have to be attainable without discriminating against those in the majority. Nevertheless, while good availability statistics help make goals realistic, there is no way to be sure that goals will not discriminate in reverse, unless the means by which the company seeks to attain them are carefully planned.

Step 3: Specifying How Goals Are to Be Attained If the means to goal attainment are to be nondiscriminatory against white males, management should find out the causes of underrepresentation of women and minorities in the company's work force. Otherwise, it will not know what discriminatory employment practices must be changed in order to increase representation without preferential treatment of women and minorities. For example, the underrepresentation of women in a certain job class may be caused by a company's reputation for being rough on women or by a policy that unnecessarily schedules work shifts so that women workers cannot meet family responsibilities. If management knows the cause, it can attempt to increase the representation of women by working on its public image and by exploring the possibility of retiming the shifts. But if management doesn't know it, it may attempt to increase the representation of women by lowering the requirements for women applying from the outside, or by granting transfers to women employees while refusing to grant them to more qualified men employees. This would not only increase the risk of discrimination charges from white males, it would also contribute to morale problems and foster resentment against women in the company.

At AT&T 24 reverse discrimination cases eventually went to court. In one case the union claimed that reverse discrimination resulted because of promotion policies favoring qualified women and minorities. The district court and appeals court ruled against the union and supported preferential treatment and quotas. The court reasoned that such treatment was justified to correct the abuses of past discrimination.

The AT&T case illustrates that even a large company (at the time of the initial court case AT&T employed 980,000 employees) can take specific action to alleviate discrimination. AT&T took these steps:

- It tried to change the image of outside-crafts employees from male to neutral by advertising, public relations, and relationships with guidance counselors.
- It redesigned the jobs so that women could perform them more easily.

From The Wall Street Journal, *with permission of Cartoon Features Syndicate*

"Are you sure you won't quit after a year or two to get married?"

- It provided detailed information to the Department of Labor on the status of the AAP. The information provided exceeds what is ordinarily required by federal rules.[18]

IMPORTANT COURT DECISIONS

Knowledge about the law and affirmative action is important to the P/HRM manager. However, the court's interpretation of the laws and regulations must also be followed. Numerous court cases involving employment discrimination laws have become public record.[19] There are, however, a few cases that have been widely publicized and used as important precedent-setting cases involving the law and P/HRM.

Griggs v. Duke Power (1971)

Willie Griggs was an applicant for a job as a coal handler at the Duke Power Company.[20] Duke required coal handlers to be high school graduates and receive a satisfactory score on two aptitude tests. Griggs claimed that these requirements were unfairly discriminatory in that they were not related to job success. Thus, they resulted in a disproportionate number of blacks being disqualified.

Duke Power Company lost this suit. Supreme Court Chief Justice Burger ruled that (1) discrimination need not be overt; (2) the employment practice must be shown to be job-related; and (3) the burden of proof is on the employer to show that the hiring standard is job related.

Perhaps the most important aspect of the *Griggs* decision was the emphasis on the consequences of an employment practice in addition to the examination of the intent involved. It opened the door for giving serious consideration to what the actual consequence of a practice was. The use of statistical methods in reviewing consequences became accepted.

Albermarle Paper Company v. J. Moody (1975)

The *Albermarle* case is important because the courts provided details on how an employer should go about validating a test; that is, how an employer must prove that the test predicts on-the-job performance.

Albermarle had required applicants for employment to pass various tests. The court found that the Albermarle tests were not validated for all jobs for

---

[18] "AT&T Signs Accord to Review Hiring of Women, Minorities," *The Wall Street Journal*, November 26, 1982, p. 3.

[19] For an up-to-date summary of cases, awards, and remedies see *Employment Practices*, published twice monthly by Commerce Clearing House, Inc., 4025 W. Petersen Avenue, Chicago, Ill. 60646.

[20] *Griggs* v. *Duke Power Co.*, 401 U.S. 424, 1971.

which people were recruited.[21] This court decision indicated that tests or other screening tools that had the effect of screening out a disproportionate number of minorities or women (that is, those tests that had an adverse impact) had to be validated properly. The test had to validly predict performance.

Washington v. Davis (1976)

The *Washington* v. *Davis* case involved a metropolitan police department (Washington, D.C.), which had been using a test for the selection of police recruits. Between 1968 and 1971, 57 percent of the blacks failed the exam compared to 13 percent of whites. The police department demonstrated that the test score was related to examinations given during the police recruits' 17-week training course.[22]

The Supreme Court ruled that the city of Washington, D.C., did not discriminate unfairly against minority police recruits because the test was job-related. The decision was a departure from previous court decisions. The implication was that a job-related test is not illegal simply because a large percentage of minorities do not successfully pass it. This decision provided test users with hope that testing could still be used as a screening device.[23]

Bakke v. University of California (1978)

The central issue of the now famous *reverse discrimination* case involving Allan Bakke (a white male) was the legality of the admission policy of the University of California at Davis Medical School. The Davis system set aside 16 of 100 places in its entering classes for "disadvantaged" applicants who were members of racial minority groups. Competitors for these places were evaluated in terms of lower than normal standards. Thus, Bakke sued the university under the "equal protection" clause of the 14th Amendment. The suit claimed that Bakke could compete for only 84 of the 100 places, while minorities could compete for all 100. All individuals were therefore not treated equally.

Justice Lewis Powell, writing the key opinion, concluded that the Davis racial quota system was not acceptable because it disregarded Bakke's right to equal protection of the law. However, the Court also stated that AAPs in general are permissible, as long as they consider applicants on an individual basis and do not set aside a rigid number of places.[24]

The *Bakke* case indicated that P/HRM selection decisions must be made on an individual, case-by-case basis. Certainly race can be a key factor in an

---

[21] James Ledvinka and Lyle Schoenfeldt, "Legal Developments in Employment Testing: Albermarle and Beyond," *Personnel Psychology*, Spring 1978, pp. 1–13.

[22] *Washington* v. *Davis*, 12 FEP 1473 (1976).

[23] Arvey, *Fairness in Selecting Employees*, p. 76.

[24] "The Bakke Ruling," *The Wall Street Journal*, June 29, 1978, pp. 1, 17, and 18.

applicant's favor, but the final decision must be made on the basis of a combination of factors.

Weber v. Kaiser (1979)

Brian Weber, a laboratory analyst at a Kaiser Aluminum plant in Louisiana, brought suit under Title VII of the 1964 Civil Rights Act. He had been bypassed for a crafts-retraining program in which the company and the union jointly agreed to reserve 50 percent of the available training places for blacks.[25]

The company and the union were faced with a dilemma. To eliminate the affirmative action-training plan would risk suits by minority employees. However, to retain the plan would run the risk of reverse discrimination charges by white employees. As discussed earlier affirmative action goes beyond equal employment opportunity. It is a systematic plan that specifies goals, timetables, and audit procedures for an employer to make an extra effort to hire, promote, and train those in a protected minority. Kaiser's affirmative action plan focused on giving preference to blacks in the crafts-retraining program.

On June 27, 1979, the U.S. Supreme Court ruled that employers can give preference to minorities and women in hiring and promoting for "traditionally segregated job categories." Thus, where there has been a societal history of purposeful exclusion of blacks from the job category, resulting in a disparity between the proportion of blacks in the labor force and the proportion of blacks who hold jobs in the category, preference can be given. The Court also noted that the Kaiser plan was a "temporary measure" to eliminate a racial imbalance in a job category.[26] This decision definitely put pressure on employers to establish AAPs.

Fire Fighters Local Union 1784 v. Stotts (1984)

The Weber decision did not guarantee that all affirmative action programs would be approved. The Supreme Court ruled in *Fire Fighters Local Union 1784* v. *Stotts* that a bona fide seniority system cannot be overriden in a layoff situation to protect an affirmative action program.[27] The City of Memphis, Tennessee, had a budget deficit and decided to lay off some employees. The city believed that the most equitable procedure would be to use a last-hired, first-fired seniority system. The union and the city went to court on behalf of nonminority employees. Stotts appealed the layoff sequence asking for an

---

[25] Michael J. Phillips, "Paradoxes of Equal Employment Opportunity: Voluntary Racial Preferences and the Weber Case," *Business Horizons,* August 1980, pp. 41–47.

[26] Ibid.

[27] *Memphis Fire Department* v. *Stotts*, 82–206, 1984, U.S. Supreme Court.

EXHIBIT 3–5   Six Precedent Setting Supreme Court Decisions

Case	Outstanding Feature(s) of Court's Ruling
Griggs v. *Duke Power* (1971)	If adverse impact is established defendant must demonstrate that selection practice is valid.
Albermarle v. *Moody* (1975)	Validation is not proven unless test can predict job success.
Washington v. *Davis* (1976)	If a test is job related it is not illegal simply because a greater percentage of minorities do not successfully pass it.
Bakke v. *University of California* (1978)	Reverse discrimination is not allowed; race can be used as a factor in selection decisions.
Weber v. *Kaiser* (1979)	Employers can give preference to minorities and women in hiring and promoting for "traditionally segregated job categories."
Fire Fighters Local Union 1784 v. *Stotts* (1984)	A bona fide seniority system cannot be overridden in a layoff situation to protect minority employees with less seniority.

order forbidding the layoff of any black employee. The union and city last-hired, first-fired plan ultimately prevailed. Both the District Court and the Appeals Court ruled in favor of Stotts, but the Supreme Court overturned the ruling. In ruling for the minority, Justice White stated that, "Title VII does not permit the ordering of racial quotas in business or unions."[28]

These six cases are landmarks in discrimination law. They have provided prospective plaintiffs and defendants with insight on the Supreme Court's view of discriminatory practices. Exhibit 3–5 provides a concise summary of these six landmark cases and the outstanding feature(s) of the Supreme Court's decision.

ENFORCING THE LAWS

Most employment discrimination laws provide for enforcement agencies that issue the regulations that affect P/HRM administrators most directly. Exhibit 3–6 provides an overview of the complex agency scene, showing some of the principal laws, the agencies that enforce them, and the guidelines issued by these agencies. The units of government *most* responsible for enforcing the regulations considered here are the **U.S. Equal Employment Opportunity Commission (EEOC)** and the federal courts, which enforce Title VII; and the Office of Federal Contract Compliance Programs (OFCCP), which enforces Executive Order 11246.

---

[28] Louis P. Britt, III., "Affirmative Action: Is There Life after Stotts," *Personnel Administrator*, September 1984.

Equal Employment Opportunity Commission

Title VII originally gave EEOC the rather limited powers of resolving charges of discrimination and interpreting the meaning of Title VII. Later, in 1972, Congress gave EEOC the power to bring lawsuits against employers in the federal courts, but the agency still does not have the power to issue directly enforceable orders, as many other federal agencies have. Thus EEOC cannot order an employer to discontinue a discriminatory practice, nor can it direct an employer to give back pay to victims of discrimination. However, the EEOC has won these issues in out-of-court settlements, and it has made effective use of the limited powers it does have.

EEOC has the power to:

Require employers to report employment statistics. Typically, they do so by completing a form called EEO— each year (see Exhibit 3–7).

Process charges of discrimination, as follows:

- The preinvestigation division interviews the complainants.

- The investigation division collects facts from all parties concerned.
- If there seems to be substance to the charge, the EEOC tries to work out an out-of-court settlement through conciliation.
- If conciliation fails, the EEOC can sue the employer.

Is the EEOC Effective? In 1985 the EEOC had approximately 500 lawsuits.[29] Job bias charges received by the EEOC during 1986 totaled over 70,000 complaints.[30] When the EEOC sought to clear away some of the backlog, its employee union complained this was a speedup and forced employees to violate the law in processing the cases and charges too hastily. Each year, the agency tries to deal with the backlog by requesting sharp increases in its budget. As a result of the backlog, charges can take years to be investigated. During that time, records get lost and memories fade, making it hard for investigators to determine how justifiable the original charge was. Besides that problem, critics claim that investigations are often not conducted competently enough to uncover all the information that is available, which leads to selective enforcement of the law.

The result of these problems is that only a very small percentage of charges

---

[29] Estimate provided by EEOC administrator in Washington, D.C., June 16, 1988.

[30] "New Focus For EEOC," BNAC Communicator 7, no. 1 (Spring 1987), pp. 1–3 and George T. Milkovich and John W. Boudreau, *Personnel/Human Resource Management: A Diagnostic Approach* (Plano, Tx.: Business Publications, Inc., 1988), pp. 87–88.

EXHIBIT 3-6 **Partial Summary of Major Employment Discrimination Laws and Orders, Enforcement Agencies, and Regulations**

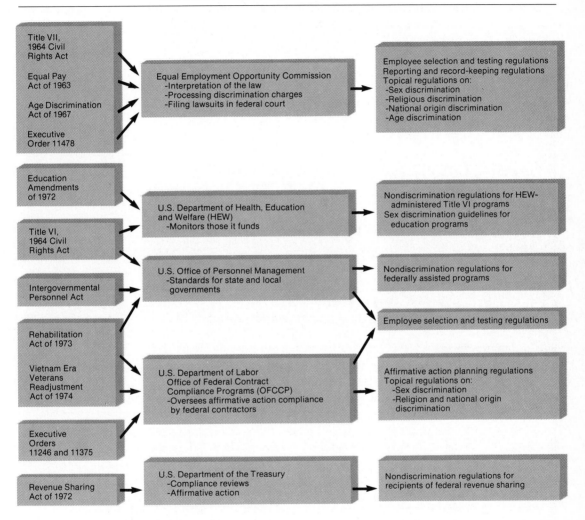

ever get resolved by the EEOC or the courts. Consequently civil rights advocates are not happy with the agency, and of course, many employers are less than enthusiastic about it (or any regulatory agency, for that matter).[31] In spite of this, the EEOC has made legal history. It provides individuals and groups with a government contact point to voice their complaints.

---

[31] Tony Marino, "How the EEOC Is Reaching Out to Employees," *Nation's Business*, August 1984, pp. 25–26.

EXHIBIT 3–7   EEO–1 Form

Standard Form 100
(Rev 12 76)
Approved GAO B-180541 (R0077)
Expires 12 31 78

EQUAL EMPLOYMENT OPPORTUNITY
EMPLOYER INFORMATION REPORT EEO-1

Joint Reporting Committee

- Equal Employment Opportunity Commission
- Office of Federal Contract Compliance Programs

Section A — TYPE OF REPORT
Refer to instructions for number and types of reports to be filed.

1. Indicate by marking in the appropriate box the type of reporting unit for which this copy of the form is submitted (MARK ONLY ONE BOX)

(1) ☐ Single-establishment Employer Report

Multi-establishment Employer

(2) ☐ Consolidated Report

(3) ☐ Headquarters Unit Report

(4) ☐ Individual Establishment Report (submit one for each establishment with 25 or more employees)

(5) ☐ Special Report

2. Total number of reports being filed by this Company (Answer on Consolidated Report only) _____

Section B — COMPANY IDENTIFICATION *(To be answered by all employers)*

OFFICE USE ONLY

1. Parent Company

    a. Name of parent company (owns or controls establishment in item 2) omit if same as label

a

Name of receiving office | Address (Number and street)

b

City or town | County | State | ZIP code | b Employer Identification No

2. Establishment for which this report is filed (Omit if same as label)

    a. Name of establishment

c

Address (Number and street) | City or town | County | State | ZIP code

d

    b Employer Identification No | (If same as label skip)

3. Parent company affiliation

(Multi-establishment Employers
Answer on Consolidated Report only)

    a. Name of parent—affiliated company | b Employer Identification No

Address (Number and street) | City or town | County | State | ZIP code

Section C — EMPLOYERS WHO ARE REQUIRED TO FILE   *(To be answered by all employers)*

☐ Yes ☐ No **1** Does the entire company have at least 100 employees in the payroll period for which you are reporting?

☐ Yes ☐ No **2** Is your company affiliated through common ownership and/or centralized management with other entities in an enterprise with a total employment of 100 or more?

☐ Yes ☐ No **3** Does the company or any of its establishments (a) have 50 or more employees **AND** (b) is not exempt as provided by 41 CFR 60-1.5, **AND** either (1) is a prime government contractor or first-tier subcontractor. and has a contract, subcontract, or purchase order amounting to $50,000 or more or (2) serves as a depository of Government funds in any amount or is a financial institution which is an issuing and paying agent for U S Savings Bonds and Savings Notes?

NOTE If the answer is yes to ANY of these questions. complete the entire form, otherwise skip to Section G

EXHIBIT 3-7 *(concluded)*

Section D — EMPLOYMENT DATA

Employment at this establishment--Report all permanent, temporary, or part-time employees including apprentices and on-the-job trainees unless specifically excluded as set forth in the instructions. Enter the appropriate figures on all lines and in all columns. Blank spaces will be considered as zeroes.

JOB CATEGORIES	OVERALL TOTALS (SUM OF COL. B THRU K) A	MALE					FEMALE				
		WHITE (NOT OF HISPANIC ORIGIN) B	BLACK (NOT OF HISPANIC ORIGIN) C	HISPANIC D	ASIAN OR PACIFIC ISLANDER E	AMERICAN INDIAN OR ALASKAN NATIVE F	WHITE (NOT OF HISPANIC ORIGIN) G	BLACK (NOT OF HISPANIC ORIGIN) H	HISPANIC I	ASIAN OR PACIFIC ISLANDER J	AMERICAN INDIAN OR ALASKAN NATIVE K
Officials and Managers											
Professionals											
Technicians											
Sales Workers											
Office and Clerical											
Craft Workers (Skilled)											
Operatives (Semi-Skilled)											
Laborers (Unskilled)											
Service Workers											
TOTAL											
Total employment reported in previous EEO-1 report											

(The trainees below should also be included in the figures for the appropriate occupational categories above)

Formal On-the-Job trainees	White collar										
	Production										

1. NOTE On consolidated report, skip questions 2-5 and Section E.
2. How was information as to race or ethnic group in Section D obtained?
   1 ☐ Visual Survey
   2 ☐ Employment Record
   3 ☐ Other — Specify ....
   ....
3. Dates of payroll period used –

4. Pay period of last report submitted for this establishment
   _____
5. Does this establishment employ apprentices?
   This year? 1 ☐ Yes 2 ☐ No
   Last year? 1 ☐ Yes 2 ☐ No

Section E — ESTABLISHMENT INFORMATION

1. Is the location of the establishment the same as that reported last year?
   1 ☐ Yes 2 ☐ No 3 ☐ Did not report last year 4 ☐ Reported on combined basis

2. Is the major business activity at this establishment the same as that reported last year?
   1 ☐ Yes 2 ☐ No 3 ☐ No report last year 4 ☐ Reported on combined basis

OFFICE USE ONLY

3. What is the major activity of this establishment? (Be specific, i.e. manufacturing steel castings, retail grocer, wholesale plumbing supplies, title insurance, etc. Include the specific type of product or type of service provided, as well as the principal business or industrial activity.)

e.

Section F — REMARKS

Use this item to give any identification data appearing on last report which differs from that given above, explain major changes in composition or reporting units, and other pertinent information.

Section G — CERTIFICATION (See Instructions G)

Check one
1. ☐ All reports are accurate and were prepared in accordance with the instructions (check on consolidated only)
2. ☐ This report is accurate and was prepared in accordance with the instructions.

Name of Certifying Official	Title	Signature		Date
Name of person to contact regarding this report (Type or print)	Address (Number and street)			
Title	City and State	ZIP code	Telephone Area Code	Number	Extension

Office of Federal Contract Compliance Programs (OFCCP)

This office was originally established to enforce Executive Order 11246. Now it also enforces laws covering employment of veterans and the handicapped. OFCCP has the power to remove a federal contractor's privileges of doing business with the government, but it seldom exercises that power.

Is the OFCCP Effective? Some data have indicated few positive effects on employment gains for black males; fewer gains for white males; zero or negative effect for other minorities and women; and zero effects on wage and occupational gains for all minority groups. Some experts doubt that the OFCCP can alter employment distributions of minorities.[32]

One reason for the limited success of the OFCCP is the need to delegate its compliance review authority to 13 other agencies. It is no surprise, then, that contractors complain of conflicting agency regulations. Moreover, the 13 agen-

---

[32] "Increase In Affirmative Action Enforcement," *Personnel Journal*, February 1988, p. 34.

cies are principally in business for some reason other than equal employment. For instance, the Department of Defense had an EEO operation housed in the bureau that was principally responsible for making sure that defense contracting was carried out well, with the right goods and services delivered at the right time. Undue concern with EEO, however, could be seen as impeding contract fulfillment. Thus, EEO was not an overriding concern in some of these agencies. President Carter in 1978 consolidated these compliance functions, as shown in Exhibit 3–6.

The Courts

Besides federal and state agencies, the courts are constantly interpreting the laws, and rulings can conflict. Appellate courts then reconcile any conflicts. All the employment discrimination laws provide for court enforcement, often as a last resort if agency enforcement fails. With regard to Title VII, the federal courts are frequently involved in two ways: settling disputes between the EEOC and employers over such things as access to company records, and deciding the merits of discrimination charges when out-of-court conciliation efforts fail. The possible legal routes for complaints against an employer's P/HRM activities are presented in Exhibit 3–8.

Legal maneuvering often makes the court enforcement picture confusing, largely because every step of the process can be appealed. And with three parties involved—the EEOC, the plaintiff, and the defendant—appeals are commonplace. All these possibilities for trial, appeal, retrial, and even appeal of the retrial can cause several years' delay before an issue is settled. When that delay is added to the EEOC's charge-processing delay, the result is discouraging to the parties involved.

Once a final court decision is reached in a Title VII case, it can provide drastic remedies: back pay, hiring quotas, reinstatement of employees, immediate promotion of employees, abolition of testing programs, creation of special recruitment or training programs. In a class action suit against Georgia Power Company that sought back pay and jobs for black employees and applicants, the court ordered the company to set aside $1.75 million for back pay, and another $388,925 for other purposes. Moreover, the court imposed numerical goals and timetables for black employment in various job classes. If Georgia Power failed to meet the goals, then the court order provided for mandatory hiring ratios: One black was to be hired for each white until the goal percentages were reached. Other courts have ordered companies to give employees seniority credit for the time they have been discriminatorily denied employment.[33]

Many court orders are not so drastic, however. Much depends, of course, on

---

[33] U.S. Supreme Court, *Teamsters Union*, U.S. 14 EPD (1977), 7579.

EXHIBIT 3–8   Legal Courses for Complaints against an Employer's P/HRM Policies

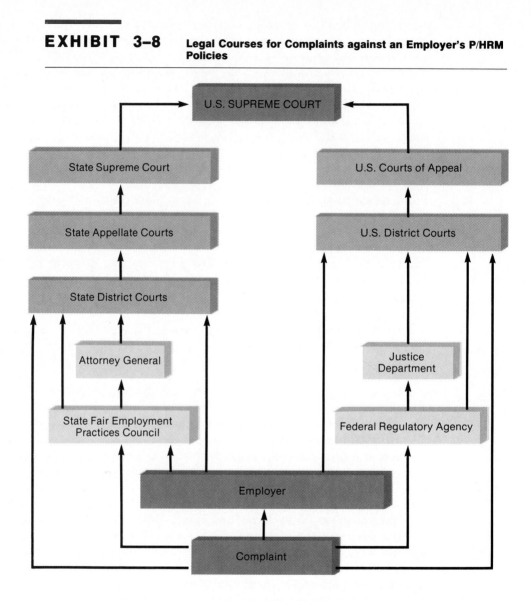

the facts surrounding the case. One important factor is whether the employer is making any voluntary efforts to comply with employment discrimination laws. If the company shows evidence of successfully pursuing an AAP, the court may decide to impose less stringent measures. This situation is discussed further in the section on costs and benefits of AAPs later in this chapter.

OFCCP has the power to order an employer to:

Survey the labor market and determine the availability of minorities.

Prepare an affirmative action plan to show the jobs minorities are under-represented in.

Set goals and timetables for making the work force representative of the labor market.

Audit the affirmative action plan to see if the goals are being met.

If the investigator decides that the contractor is not in compliance with Executive Order 11246, he may have a "show cause" order issued against the contractor. This order triggers a lengthy sequence of administrative decisions and appeals, which can culminate in the contractor being debarred from government contract work.

VARIOUS GROUPS AND EEO

As already mentioned, EEO permeates most P/HRM activities. It can require changes in employment planning, recruiting, selecting, evaluating, career planning, training, and other activities. Rather than discuss each P/HRM activity, this section focuses on some special features of EEO programs for various groups. In future chapters the law as it pertains to a specific P/HRM activity will be discussed.

Women

In many companies, EEO for women is more a matter of career design than job design. Women often find themselves locked into their positions with no career path upward; this situation is especially true for clerical positions. Typists and secretaries usually have little likelihood of promotion to supervisory or managerial positions.

Sometimes the solution to that problem involves training or job rotation for clerical workers. Management training can give them the specific skills they need to assume higher-level positions, and job rotation can give them the breadth of experience they need to become effective managers. In other cases, the problem is that the employees of the organization, women included, are unaware of the promotion and transfer opportunities it offers. Larger companies often establish very thorough and elaborate systems to inform employees of job openings in the company. Among other things, these systems may include individual career counseling for employees, which helps identify promising talent at the same time it keeps employees informed.

A second problem area for women involves insurance and leaves for pregnancy. Prior to the **Pregnancy Discrimination Act of 1978**, women could be forced to resign or take a leave of absence because of pregnancy. Furthermore, employers did not have to provide disability or medical coverage, even when coverage was provided for other disabilities and medical problems. The Pregnancy Discrimination amendment to the 1964 Civil Rights Act now prevents this form of discrimination against women. The act makes it an unfair employment practice to discriminate on the basis of pregnancy, childbirth, or related medical conditions in hiring, promotion, suspension, discharge, or in any other term of employment. The act prohibits an employer from failing to pay medical and hospital costs for childbirth to the same extent that it pays for medical and hospital costs for other conditions.[34]

An interesting court ruling was issued in 1984 involving women returning to work after maternity leave. The U.S. District Court in Los Angeles ruled that a 1978 California law guaranteeing a job following childbirth is unconstitutional. It was judged to discriminate against men and, therefore, was a violation of Title VII.[35] Lillian Garland was a receptionist at California Federal Savings and Loan Association when she took maternity leave. After eight weeks, she returned and found that her position had been filled.[36] No other jobs were available at that time, she was advised. Under the California law, firms were told they must offer the same or equivalent jobs to women returning from maternity leave, regardless of what was being offered other workers. If a man was out of work for an operation and a company refused to rehire him, that was allowed under the state law. However, every woman was owed a job-secure leave of up to four months if disabled by childbirth.

The judge in the case ruled that the California law was in direct conflict with Title VII. Pregnancy had to be treated like any other disability. Receiving special treatment meant that females had different rights than males, which is illegal according to the federal law. A study of maternity and paternity leave policies among the 1,500 largest industrial, financial, and service companies showed that only 38 percent of the companies guaranteed women their same jobs back after a disability leave for childbirth. Another 43 percent provided a comparable job, and 6 percent more gave returning mothers some job. Thirteen percent made no promise of any job.[37]

A third problem area involves sexual harassment on the job. **Sexual harassment** is unwelcome sexual attention that causes the recipient distress and results in an inability on the part of the recipient to effectively perform job requirements.[38] One research study of 9,000 women revealed that 90 percent of the respondents had experienced unwanted sexual attention at work, ranging from leers and remarks to overt requests for sexual favors.[39] This and

---

[34] Richard Trotler, Susan Rawson Zacur, and Wallace Gatewood, "The Pregnancy Disability Amendment: What the Law Provides: Part 1," *Personnel Administrator*, February 1982, pp. 47–54.

[35] "Guaranteed Job Law," *Resource*, May 19, 1984, pp. 1–2.

[36] "Maternity Leave Case Gives Birth to Bitter Debate," *Chicago Tribune*, July 30, 1984, p. 2.

[37] Ibid.

[38] "Sexual Harassment—Already a Major Concern May Become Even a Higher Priority," *Human Resources Management Ideas and Trends*, January 14, 1986, pp. 9–12.

[39] Robert W. Schupp, Joyce Windham and Scott Draugh, "Sexual Harassment under Title VII: The Legal Status," *Labor Law Journal*, April 1981, p. 230; and Catherine A. MacKinnon, *Sexual Harassment of Working Women* (New Haven, Conn.: Yale University Press, 1979). See also Donald J. Peterson and Douglass Massengill, "Sexual Harassment: A Growing Problem in the Workplace," *Personnel Administrator*, October 1982, pp. 79–89.

other studies suggest that sexual harassment is a serious problem. Women facing sexual harassment are often subjected to mental anxiety, humiliation, reprimand, or loss of job or promotion.

In order for a woman to recover on a claim of sexual harassment under Title VII of the Civil Rights Act, she must allege and establish that submission to the sexual suggestion constituted a term or condition of employment. A course of action cannot arise from an isolated incident or a mere flirtation.

An analysis of court decisions provides insight into the various types of sexual harassment cases being argued. One type of sexual harassment is sexual favors being exchanged for employment opportunities. In order for this type of activity to be considered sexual harassment under Title VII, it must be shown that job opportunities would be denied if sexual favors were refused.

Another type of sexual harassment is referred to as *environmental sexual harassment.* This is where no job opportunities are involved, just unwanted attraction of one sex to another. The comments or innuendos of a sexual nature, physical contact, or other overt acts that convey a message that going further would be desirable fall in this category. This type of harassment is considered a violation by some courts because the employees contend that it interferes with work performance or makes work unpleasant.

The existence of sexual harassment is often difficult to determine because consent is not known until after the act is committed.[40] Any degree of consent would make the conduct a normal consequence of one sex being attracted to another.

The court also looks at the employer's knowledge of the conduct. In a leading case in the area of employer knowledge, a worker subjected a female co-worker to verbal sexual advances, made sexually derogatory remarks, and on one occasion physically grabbed her while she was bending over. The female complained to her supervisors, who did nothing to stop the harassment. The company was found liable under the Minnesota discrimination law because an employee complained and it took no action.[41]

In another leading sexual harassment case, *Bundy* v. *Jackson,* Title VII was used as the basis for a discrimination claim. Sandra Bundy, a vocational rehabilitation specialist, in 1972 received and rejected sexual propositions by a fellow employee. The accused employee eventually became director of the agency that employed Bundy. After being passed over for promotion for alleged inadequacy of work performance, Bundy filed an informal complaint with the EEO officer and a formal complaint with the department. The director failed to investigate the complaints. However, two and a half years later, Bundy received a promotion. She filed a complaint in the district court. The court concluded that Bundy was not entitled to relief because sexual harassment did not constitute discrimination within the meaning of Title VII. The District of Columbia Circuit Court of Appeals in 1981 reversed the earlier ruling.[42]

---

[40] Sovereign, *Personal Law*, p. 146.

[41] *Continental Can Co.* v. *State of Minnesota*, 297 N.W. 241 (Minn. Sup. Ct. 1980).

[42] *Bundy* v. *Jackson*, 641 F. 2d 934 (D.C. Cir. 1981).

Pepper . . . and Salt

THE WALL STREET JOURNAL

From The Wall Street Journal, *reprinted with permission of Cartoon Features Syndicate*

"He asked if he can carry my books home from school, Miss Thompson. Is that sexual harassment?"

In a precedent-setting decision, the EEOC in 1984 found a restaurant owner responsible for the sexual harassment of an employee by a customer, since the owner had it within his power to take corrective action, but failed to do so.[43] A waitress had complained to the owner about four male customers—friends of the owner—but the owner ignored her complaints. The customers made loud jokes and comments of a sexual nature about the waitress. When she tried to take their order one man made grabbing gestures toward her and then grabbed and pinched her. The owner claimed he had spoken to the men, but no apology was forthcoming. The waitress refused to serve the men again, and the owner said he might not be able to continue her employment.

[43] "EEOC Finds Employer Liable for Harassing Act of Restaurant Customers," *Resource*, April 1984, p. 3.

After the waitress said an attorney had advised her to have a witness present if her job was to be discussed, she was fired. The EEOC found that "evidence corroborates the plaintiff's allegation that she was harassed." No previous EEOC decision had addressed the issue of an employer's responsibility for the sexual harassment of an employee by a nonemployee.

Sexual harassment suits need not result in liability for an employer.[44] What the employer needs to do is to establish a policy and communicate it to all employees. Second, there is a need to establish an easy-to-use grievance procedure. Alleged victims must feel free to use such a system without fear of retribution (such as being given more difficult job assignments, laid off, or unfairly bypassed for promotion). Third, violators of sexual harassment guidelines need to be promptly and fairly disciplined for their conduct. Finally, managers and other employees must be educated on what constitutes sexual harassment. Company newspapers, harassment notices placed on bulletin boards, and training programs may all prove beneficial in improving employee's awareness of what constitutes sexual harassment.[45]

In June 1986, the United States Supreme Court issued a significant decision in *Meritor Savings Bank, FSB* v. *Vinson* (1986).[46] The case firmly established the principle of employer liability for sexual harassment of employees under Title VII of the Civil Rights Act of 1964, while simultaneously limiting the extent of that liability. In the case, the plaintiff, a female assistant bank manager, claimed that her supervisor, a male vice president made repeated sexual advances, resulting in sexual intercourse "some 40 or so times" over several years. The vice president and the bank denied the plaintiff's allegations. The court ruled in favor of the plaintiff because of the hostile environment she worked in and also suggested that the existence of an effective grievance procedure could insulate an employer from liability for sexual harassment.[47]

This case implies that employers must perform specific corrective actions that halt sexual harassment once they have learned of a violation. At a minimum, if an employer's investigation reveals that sexual harassment did occur, immediate imposition of counseling or progressive discipline should be initiated. It is important not only to have a specific program, but also that the program function efficiently.

[44] Elizabeth C. Wesman, "Shortage of Research Abets Sexual Harassment Confusion," *Personnel Administrator*, November 1983, pp. 60–65.

[45] *Heelan* v. *Johns-Manville Corporation*, 451 Federal Supplement (DC Colo., 1978), 16 EPD No. 8330; and Donna C. Ledgerwood and Sue Johnson-Dietz, "Sexual Harassment: Implications for Employer Liability," *Monthly Labor Review*, April 1981, pp. 45–47.

[46] *Meritor Savings Bank* v. *Vinson*, 91, L. Ed. 2d 49 (June 9, 1986).

[47] Jonathon S. Mount and Angel Gomez, "Sexual Harassment: The Impact of *Meritor Savings Bank* v. *Vinson* on Grievances and Arbitration Decisions," *The Arbitrator Journal*, December 1986, pp. 24–29.

Older Employees

Age discrimination has been called the "third wave" and a "sleeper" in equal employment opportunity.[48] There has been a dramatic increase in the number of employment-related age discrimination complaints filed with state and federal agencies. For example, in 1979 over 5,000 complaints were filed. In 1980, there were over 11,000 complaints filed. During 1981, over 15,000 complaints were filed; in 1982 the number filed was up to 19,187. The yearly increase is likely to continue into the future. As complaints increase, so has the number of age-related lawsuits filed by the EEOC. From 16 in 1979, the number rose to 89 in 1981.[49] In cases in which the EEOC became involved, the employer won only 21.6 percent of the time (versus 50 percent overall). Apparently, the EEOC picks cases and brings its resources into action when it has a high likelihood of winning.[50]

The Age Discrimination Employment Act of 1967 and the amendments of 1978 and 1986 protect workers between the ages of 40 and 70 from job discrimination. In the past, the enforcement agencies did not press too hard on discrimination against older persons, but recent actions suggest this will no longer be true. The law prevents employers from replacing their staffs with younger workers, whether the purpose is to give the company a more youthful image or to save money in the pension program. The October 7, 1986, amendment eliminates a 70-year-old age cap for most private-sector employees. While age requirements are illegal in most jobs, the law does not cover all of them. For example, Greyhound was allowed to refuse bus driver jobs to applicants over age 40 with the justification that aging brings on slow reaction times, which can adversely affect safety.[51] Greyhound claimed that physical changes that begin around age 35 have an adverse effect on driving skills. Chronological age was used as an indicator of the physical changes.

A number of barriers face older workers in many organizations. Some are a matter of company economics, others a matter of management attitudes.[52] The economic reasons include the added expense of funding pensions for older workers and the increased premiums necessary for health and life insurance benefit plans. The attitude problems are more difficult to pin down. Perhaps

---

[48] Nicholas J. Beutrell, "Managing the Older Worker," *Personnel Administrator*, August 1983, p. 31.

[49] Robert H. Roley, Lawrence S. Kleiman, and Mark L. Lengnick- Hall, "Age Discrimination and Personnel Psychology: A Review and Synthesis of the Legal Literature with Implications for Future Research," *Personnel Psychology*, Summer 1984, pp. 327–50.

[50] Nicholas J. Mathys, Helen LaVan, and Frederick Schwerdtner, "Learning the Lessons of Age Discrimination Cases," *Personnel Journal*, June 1984, pp. 30–31.

[51] *Brennen* v. *Greyhound Lines, Inc.*, 9 FED Cases 58 (1975).

[52] Jerome M. Rosow and Robert Zagar, "Work in America Institute's Recommendations Grapple with the Future of the Older Workers," *Personnel Administrator*, October 1981, pp. 47–54, 80.

P/HRM Manager Close-Up

Herbert J. Ayers
J. A. Jones Construction
Services Company

Biography

Herbert J. Ayers is equal employment opportunity officer for J. A. Jones Construction Services Company. Mr. Ayers, originally from New York City, holds a masters degree in Applied Behavioral Science from Whitworth College, and a B.A. degree from Gonzaga University, both in Spokane, Washington.

He joined J. A. Jones after a 13-year career with the American Red Cross. He has served as a caseworker, community programs director, public relations director, and manager of a regional blood service.

Mr. Ayers, in addition to his EEO responsibilities, works as the company's employee assistance counselor and internal management consultant.

He serves on the board of the local chapter of the American Society for Personnel Administration and is a member of the national planning committee of the American Association for Affirmative Action.

Mr. Ayers is a writer and performs private research in family systems communication and its relation to work.

How to Avoid Sexual Harassment: The J. A. Jones Construction Services Company Approach

The burly construction worker wearing his hard hat and flirting with every woman who walks by; the "all-male" craft work force whose members intimidate, taunt, and connive to keep women "in their place" and out of construction activities are stereotypical images of construction companies. In reality, this is hardly the case today. Making money, maintaining a good reputation, and working within the law are well-established principles for most construction companies.

For example, J. A. Jones Construction Services Company, Richland, Washington, employs hundreds of craft

(continued)

workers and professional people each year. Upon joining the company, each person quickly learns the policies that prohibit sexual harassment, intimidation, and coercion. They learn that such behavior will not be tolerated in the workplace, and they learn how to identify behaviors that constitute sexual harassment. Before a new employee even begins work, he or she knows the consequences of such behavior.

Should an allegation be brought to the attention of a personnel officer or member of management, the company Equal Employment Opportunity officer immediately initiates a fact-finding investigation. Counseling also begins at the time with the alleged victim and with the alleged perpetrator. The employees concerned are interviewed separately. If there are witnesses, they too are interviewed. An effort is then made to resolve the problem to everyone's satisfaction. Sometimes a third-party consultation is held with the victim and the perpetrator, while at other times, work may proceed with the two separately. The seriousness of the charge (the alleged actions and effects on the victim and the degree of policy violation) is also considered, and a determination is made about how to resolve the problem. Actions by an employee that are deemed serious may result in a written warning or even in termination of employment. In less serious instances, work is done with the two parties to help them resolve the problem and form a new relationship. All interviews and actions taken by the company are thoroughly documented.

Should an employee be terminated

for sexual harassment, it is J. A. Jones's policy that no other Jones's affiliates, subsidiaries, or projects rehire that person.

It is believed by management that half-hearted attempts to control sexual harassment work against the company and hinder employee morale and productivity. Therefore, the company president periodically meets with his department managers and tells them that such behavior will not be tolerated. The chief executive makes it clear to them that they must explain to him personally why an incident could not have been avoided should one occur in their department. All managers are rated on their EEO effectiveness during their annual performance appraisal.

Managers inform their supervisors of the company president's concern that all forms of sexual harassment be avoided and the managers provide them with ongoing training. All current and newly hired employees view a slide series depicting those behaviors that are prohibited. It also explains how to obtain help when faced with a problem. All newly hired female craft workers also meet with the EEO officer or company women's coordinator and the message is reinforced.

J. A. Jones Construction Services Company suffers few problems stemming from sexual harassment. Employees are well informed on the subject; the company faces the issue from the top down and acts quickly when problems arise. Because of this attitude and practice, mutual respect is enhanced, and everyone cooperates in avoiding such problems.

From The Wall Street Journal, *with permission of Cartoon Features Syndicate*

"Edwards, it's a marvelous face lift but I'm afraid retirement at sixty-five is mandatory."

some managers feel that older workers lose their faculties, making them less effective on the job. Yet there is evidence that the intelligence levels of many older employees increase as they near retirement age. Besides, there are other advantages to hiring older workers: lower turnover, greater consciousness of safety matters, and longer work experience.[53]

Racial and Ethnic Minorities

The laws prohibit discrimination against a person because of race, color, and national origin. The specifically protected minorities are blacks, Hispanics, American Indians, Asian-Pacific Islanders, and Alaskan natives. These groups historically have had higher unemployment and underemployment and have held the lowest level jobs.

While every ethnic and racial minority is unique, one problem facing them all is adverse P/HRM policies. Examples of such practices are numerous. Height and weight requirements, which have an adverse impact on Asian

---

[53] "Aging and the IQ: The Myth of the Twilight Years," *Psychology Today*, March 1974, pp. 35–40.

Americans and Hispanic Americans, were, until recently, commonplace among police departments in the United States. Seniority and experience requirements based on time in a department tend to lock in blacks who move out of segregated departments. They find themselves at the bottom of the seniority lists in their new departments, even though they have had many years with the company. Vague, subjective performance evaluations by supervisors are so subject to bias that many minority group members find they cannot attain high enough ratings to get promotions or merit pay increases. All these practices, along with others, are prime targets for change in the EEO program.

Some barriers are more difficult to change, even though they have an adverse impact on minorities. College degree requirements are common for some jobs, although one study found that 65 percent of the jobs reserved for college graduates could be performed by workers with no more than a high school education.[54] Employers should examine their own job specifications to see if educational requirements can be reduced without sacrificing job performance. Where the requirements cannot be reduced, the organization might consider redesigning or breaking down the job so that people with less education could perform satisfactorily. While job redesign is usually a big step, the resulting increase in opportunities for minorities may make it worthwhile for the organization.

Religious Minorities

The EEO-type laws prohibit discrimination in employment based on religious preference, but there have been few cases thus far charging that employers have discriminated against religious groups in employment and promotion. This is surprising, given the reality that certain employers have had a policy of limited or no hiring of persons who are Jewish, Orthodox Christian, or Roman Catholic, at least for the managerial class. Roman Catholics, for example, are seriously underrepresented in managerial and professional groups in the United States.[55]

The focus of religious discrimination cases has been on hours of work and working conditions. The cases largely concern employers telling employees to work on days or at times that conflict with their religious beliefs—at regular times or on overtime. For example, employees who are Orthodox Jews, Seventh-Day Adventists, or Worldwide Church of God members cannot work from sunset Friday through sundown Saturday.

One important religious discrimination case involved Trans World Airlines and an employee, Larry G. Hardison. Mr. Hardison was a member of the

---

[54] Virginia Herwegh, "Compliance in the Real World of Business," presentation at the Equal Employment Opportunity Seminar of the American Society for Personnel Administration, June 29, 1976.

[55] EEOC, "Guidelines on Religious Discrimination," 1977.

Worldwide Church of God.[56] His seniority enabled him to avoid Saturday work; however, when he asked to be transferred to another department, his low seniority in the new unit required him to work on Saturday. The employer permitted the union to seek a work-scheduling change for Hardison, but the union refused to change seniority provisions to accommodate Mr. Hardison's religious requirements.

The Supreme Court upheld the employer's discharge of Hardison for refusing to work on Saturdays. The Court reasoned that the employer would have to incur overtime costs to replace Hardison on Saturday, which constituted an undue hardship. Although this court ruling may appear to be unsympathetic to religious minorities, some observers believe that the First Amendment of the Constitution supersedes discrimination laws from mandating an employer's accommodation to a person's religion.

In another interesting case, a Jewish employee requested time off to observe Rosh Hashanah and Yom Kippur. She met with no resistance from her employer, a city housing authority. The employer gave her the time off.[57] However, the employer's policy stated that, "Excused absence for (religious observance) may be charged against personal leave, vacation leave, or compensatory leave." That is, the employee had to charge the time off to one of the leave categories, or she could take the days off without pay.

The employee filed suit. The New York State court that heard the case ruled that the employer did make accommodations by giving the employee time off. Thus, the employee could be forced to charge the days she took off to leave if she wanted to be paid for them.[58]

Physically and Mentally Handicapped Workers

As of 1988 about half of the 21 million disabled citizens of the United States fit to work could not find jobs. Tales of crippled, blind, or deaf Americans who send out waves of résumés without success are still quite common.[59] The **Rehabilitation Act of 1973** has slowed down but not stopped discrimination in hiring and promoting the disabled. Section 503 of the Vocational Rehabilitation Act of 1973, which is enforced by OFCCP, requires that all employers with government contracts of $2,500 or more must set up affirmative action programs for the handicapped. At present these programs require no numerical goals. They do call for special efforts in recruiting handicapped persons, such as outreach programs; communication of the obligation to hire and promote

---

[56] *Trans World Airlines, Inc.* v. *Hardison*, 432 U.S. 63 (1977).

[57] *State Division of Human Rights* v. *Rochester Housing Authority*, NY-Sct, 446 NYS 2d 736.

[58] "Time Off for Religious Observance: At Whose Expense?" *Fair Employment Practices*, October 1983, p. 6.

[59] "For Disabled, Jobs Few—But Many Make It," *U.S. News & World Report*, September 8, 1980, p. 45.

the handicapped; the development of procedures to seek out and promote handicapped persons presently on the payroll; and making physical changes that allow the handicapped to be employed (e.g., ramps). Employers who are dedicated to improving the handicappeds' chances also will set up training programs and partially redesign jobs so the handicapped can perform them effectively.[60]

Two court rulings, *Dean* v. *Metro* (1985)[61] and *Clarke* v. *Shoreline School District* (1986),[62] provide guidelines as to how far employers are required to go to accommodate handicapped employees. In Dean, the court ruled that a municipal insurance company was obligated to help an employee, whose failing eyesight prevented him from continuing to drive a bus, find other work with the company for which he was qualified. The state of Washington court implied, however, that the employer was not required to retrain the worker or create a job for the employee. In the Clarke case the court indicated again that the employer has no duty to create a job for the handicapped worker, nor hire him in preference to a more qualified employee.[63]

The biggest hurdle that handicapped persons must face is not their physical (or mental) handicap, but myths and negative attitudes about their ability to do the job. It has been demonstrated that the handicapped can perform successfully. Affirmative action may help give them the chance to use their abilities.

Research has pointed out the contributions that the handicapped make to organizations. DuPont studied over 1,400 employees with various types of handicaps. They found that few disabled workers required special work arrangements and that the handicapped workers had on the average good job performance, excellent safety records, and good job attendance.[64]

There are wonderful stories of disabled people making it to the top. There are blind judges like Criss Cole of Houston, paraplegic mayors like W. Mitchel of Crested Butte, Colorado, and deaf actresses like Phyllis Frelich, who won the Tony Award as the best Broadway actress and Marlee Matlin who won an Academy Award. Max Cleland, who lost his legs and one arm in Vietnam, headed the Veterans Administration in the Carter administration (1976–80) and is a visible symbol of hope for 2.2 million disabled veterans.[65]

Veterans

The Vietnam Era Veterans Readjustment Act of 1974 requires federal contractors to take affirmative action for the employment of disabled veterans and

---

[60] Gopal C. Pati, "Countdown on Hiring the Handicapped," *Personnel Journal*, March 1978, pp. 144–53.

[61] *Dean* v. *Metro*, 104, Wn. 2d 627 (1985).

[62] *Clarke* v. *Shoreline School District*, 106 Wn. 2d 102 (1986).

[63] Clemens H. Barnes, "Court Rulings Define Scope of Employer's Duty to Accommodate Handicapped Workers," *Personnel Law Update*, October 1986, p. 5.

[64] Robert B. Nathanson, "The Disabled Employee: Separating Myth from Fact," *Harvard Business Review*, May–June 1977, pp. 6–8.

[65] "For Disabled, Jobs Few," p. 45.

veterans of the Vietnam conflict. This act imposes fewer obligations than the other employment discrimination laws. No numerical goals are required, but the organization must show it makes special efforts to recruit them. In determining a veteran's qualifications, the employer cannot consider any part of the military record that is not directly relevant to the specific qualifications of the job in question.

White Males

If you are a white male, you are by now probably thinking: Women and minorities are getting a better chance for employment and promotion than they used to. But what does this do for me? Will I get a job? Will I get promoted to a better job? Or is reverse discrimination likely in my future? This concern is natural. The *Bakke* v. *University of California* and the *Weber* v. *Kaiser* cases show the concern of white males about reverse discrimination. These cases will have a significant impact on future EEO programs. Title VII prohibits discrimination based on race and sex, and that includes discrimination against white males. The laws that were originally passed to give better opportunities to women and minorities are now being interpreted as protecting the rights of the majority as well.

The obligations of the organization to white males are the same as its obligations to other groups: It must not discriminate for or against any race, sex, religion, or minority group. This presents a problem to employers with numerical affirmative action goals. How are goals to be attained without favoring the disadvantaged groups? The answer is to seek *other* means for satisfying goals that do not in turn discriminate against the advantaged groups. For example, employers could undertake more intensive recruiting efforts for women and minorities, as well as eliminating those employment practices that inhibit their hiring and promotion.

Employers should *never* set numerical goals so high that they can be attained *only* through reverse discrimination. If the goals are already too high, action should be taken to lower them. The courts are increasingly saying that employers cannot use their numerical affirmative action goals as an excuse to discriminate against white males.

At present there appear to be problems in interpreting these rules. For example, the New York Bell Division of AT&T promoted a woman rather than a white male who had greater seniority and better performance evaluation ratings. The judge ruled that the company should have promoted the woman to meet its EEO goals, but the male was discriminated against. The judge ordered the promotion to go through but also ordered the company to pay the white male $100,000 in damages.[66]

The courts themselves may still impose goals that discriminate against

---

[66] Equal Opportunity Agreement, U.S. Department of Labor, January 18, 1973, Commerce Clearing House *Labor Law Reports*, No. 373, 1973.

white males. But federal agencies may not impose such goals on employers, and employers may not impose them on themselves.

The conclusion that emerges is that employment discrimination laws were passed for the benefit of those groups that have historically been the victims of discrimination; nevertheless, these laws do not allow the employer to bestow such benefits voluntarily by depriving white males of their rights.

COST/BENEFIT ANALYSIS OF EEO PROGRAMS

The cost of an equal employment opportunity plan can be calculated for an employer. It includes the added expense of recruitment, special training programs, test validation, job-posting systems, equipment redesign, and whatever other programs the organization includes in its plan. The calculation also must include an added cost for the preparation of reports. The P/HRM manager or specialist may have to compute these costs and justify the expense of such a plan to higher management by citing the benefits to be derived.

Unfortunately, the benefits are difficult to compute. Even if they can be computed, they may not outweigh the costs in the short run. Consequently, some top managers may tend to view EEO as a necessary evil, something that must be done because the government requires it, not because of any benefits to be derived by the organization. This consequence can do much to destroy the P/HRM manager's position as the person responsible for the plan, because top-management attitudes are contagious. If higher management does not provide the necessary support and resources, then lower levels of management may be reluctant to cooperate.

Therefore, it is important for managers to be aware of the benefits of EEO programs, even if they are long-range ones that are difficult to quantify. One immediate benefit is that EEO increases the likelihood that the company will stay eligible for government contracts. Another benefit is an increase in the pool of eligible employees that results from providing opportunities to women and minorities. Then there is the obvious benefit of better public relations and increased goodwill among employees that comes from a properly administered EEO program.

One benefit that EEO does not provide is insulation from liability in discrimination court cases. While a good EEO plan may make employees more satisfied and less likely to file charges of discrimination, it provides no presumption of innocence if an employee does take a charge to court. For instance, one General Motors plant had a good record of hiring minorities, but that did not keep a court from finding that it was guilty of discrimination in promoting them.[67] Still, EEO programs can help an employer in court. Some courts have been less stringent when companies seem to be making progress with their AAPs. This alone may make the costs of EEO worth it.

---

[67] *Rowe* v. *General Motors Corp.*, 457 F. 2d 348, 5th Cir., 1972.

A RETURN TO THE P/HRM · IN · ACTION

Hugo Gerbold has just returned from his discussion with Gregory Inness, company president. Gregory seemed impressed with Hugo's presentation. But he is still doubtful that more women and minorities would "fit in" at Reliable. Hugo had pointed out that the EEOC and the courts wouldn't think much of this reasoning. He wondered if Gregory would take the next step in instituting an EEO plan at Reliable Insurance.

Hugo decided to be ready, just in case. He prepared an EEO program designed to focus on the areas where he felt Reliable was in the worst shape. He prepared a list of current employees, primarily in the clerical ranks, who could be promoted to underwriters and claims agents. These promotions could increase female representation in better jobs fairly quickly. They would require training, but it could be done.

To get minorities represented fairly in all categories would require special recruiting efforts. Hugo prepared a plan to increase Reliable's recruiting efforts in all categories of employment. The plan was drawn up to protect the position of current white male employees and applicants. In no case would a person be hired with fewer qualifications than white male applicants.

Luckily, Reliable was growing and was hiring more people as it expanded. Attrition would also open positions in most lower managerial, professional, and sales positions.

After spending quite a bit of time on development of the plan, Hugo waited. When he didn't hear from Gregory, he made an appointment to see the president.

Hugo: Gregory, you recall we discussed the EEO issue. We hired Osanna, but that's as far as our effort went. I've prepared an EEO. . . .

Gregory: Hugo, after we discussed it, I checked with the rest of the management. We feel we're OK as is. We don't want to upset our loyal work force with an EEO plan. Now, about the pay plan for next year. . . .

And that was that. Hugo took his EEO plan and placed it in a folder in his desk drawer.

Six months later, another female employee, Dot Greene, filed a complaint. The EEOC came to investigate, and the investigation indicates that Reliable has not taken the necessary steps to eliminate job discrimination. The company is instructed to develop an EEO plan to correct the problem.

SUMMARY

This chapter focused on EEO programs designed to eliminate bias in P/HRM programs. The role of EEO and the law as a significant force in shaping P/HRM policies and programs is now an accepted fact in society. The law, executive orders, and the courts' interpretations will continue to have an influence on every phase of P/HRM programs and activities. This influence will become clearer as specific P/HRM activities are discussed in Chapters 4–20. This chapter provides only the general theme of the importance of the law in P/HRM. The remaining chapters will at times spell out specifically how the law impacts P/HRM.

To summarize the major points covered in this chapter:

1. Equal employment opportunity is one of the most significant activities in the P/HRM function today.
2. The three main influences on the development of EEO were:
   a. Changes in societal values.
   b. The economic status of women and minorities.
   c. The emerging role of government regulation.
3. Laws prohibiting employment discrimination that were discussed in this chapter are:
   a. Title VII of the 1964 Civil Rights Act.
   b. Executive Order 11246.
   c. The Vocational Rehabilitation Act.
   d. The Age Discrimination Act.
   e. Pregnancy Discrimination Act.
4. Three different definitions of discrimination have been arrived at by the courts over the years:
   a. Prejudiced treatment.
   b. Unequal treatment.
   c. Unequal impact.
5. The criterion for EEO and affirmative action compliance can theoretically be reduced to two questions:
   a. Does an employment practice have unequal or adverse impact on the groups covered by the law (race, color, sex, religious, or national origin groups)?
   b. Is that practice job related or otherwise necessary to the organization?
6. The government units *most* responsible for enforcing EEO regulations are:
   a. U.S. Equal Employment Opportunity Commission (EEOC)—Title VII.
   b. Office of Federal Contract Compliance Programs (OFCCP)—Executive Order 11246.
7. Courts are constantly interpreting the laws governing EEO. Due to numerous appeals, an EEO complaint can be years in reaching ultimate settlement.
8. EEO planning can be used as a preventive action to reduce the likelihood of employment discrimination charges and ensure equal employment opportunities for applicants and employees.
9. There are special aspects of EEO planning for each of these groups:
   a. Women.
   b. Older employees.
   c. Racial and ethnic minorities.
   d. Physically and mentally handicapped workers.
   e. Veterans.
   f. White males.

EXHIBIT 3–9 EEO Programs for Model Organizations

Type of Organization	Who is responsible for organization's EEO program?			How are women and minorities recruited in EEO program?			Other activities engaged in by organization to encourage EEO		
	Separate Department	Separate Program Director	Part of Manager's Job	State Employment Service	Liaison with Community Groups	Separate Offices, etc.	Longer Training Periods	Transportation to Work	Financial Counseling
1. Large size, low complexity, high stability	X		X	X	X	X	X	X	X
2. Medium size, low complexity, high stability		X	X	X	X	X	X		X
3. Small size, low complexity, high stability			X	X	X		X		
4. Medium size, moderate complexity, moderate stability		X	X	X	X		X		X
5. Large size, high complexity, low stability	X		X	X	X	X	X	X	X
6. Medium size, high complexity, low stability		X	X	X	X		X		X
7. Small size, high complexity, low stability			X	X			X		

Exhibit 3–9 lists some recommendations for effective EEO programs using the model organization presented in Chapter 1 (Exhibit 1–8).

Questions for Review and Discussion

1. The EEOC suggests that every organization should have an affirmative action policy. Is this a good suggestion? Why?
2. What is the meaning of the term *adverse impact?*
3. What can employers do to minimize their chance of litigation and being found negligent in sexual harassment matters?
4. How is goal setting used in an organization's affirmative action program?
5. Why is the *Griggs* v. *Duke Power Company* court decision considered a landmark case?
6. How did the Equal Employment Opportunity Act of 1972 affect Title VII of the 1964 Civil Rights Act?
7. Why are the *Bakke* v. *University of California* and *Weber* v. *Kaiser* rulings considered significant for the P/HRM area of an organization?
8. What is meant by the term *bona fide occupational qualification* (BFOQ)?
9. What can an employer do to make it easier for handicapped people to be active and contributing employees of an organization?
10. What does unequal treatment mean in terms of discrimination?

GLOSSARY

Adverse Impact. A situation in which a significantly higher percentage of members of a protected group (women, blacks, Hispanics) in the available population are being rejected for employment, placement, or promotion.

Affirmative Action. Gives preferential treatment in hiring, recruitment, promotion, and development to groups that have been discriminated against.

Age Discrimination Act of 1967 (Amended 1978). Protects workers between the ages of 40 and 70 against job discrimination.

Civil Rights Act, Title VII 1964. An important law that prohibits employers, unions, employment agencies, and joint labor-management committees controlling apprenticeship or training programs from discriminating on the basis of race, color, religion, sex, or national origin.

Equal Employment Opportunity Commission (EEOC). The Civil Rights Act, Title VII, 1964 gave the EEOC limited powers of resolving charges of discrimination and interpreting the meaning of Title VII. Later in 1972, Congress gave EEOC the power to bring lawsuits against employers in the federal courts.

Equal Employment Opportunity Programs (EEO). Programs implemented by employers to prevent employment discrimination in the workplace or to take remedial action to offset past employment discrimination.

Pregnancy Discrimination Act of 1978. This law makes it unlawful to discriminate on the basis of pregnancy, childbirth, or related medical conditions in employment-type decisions.

Rehabilitation Act of 1973. An act that is enforced by the Office of Federal Contract Compliance Programs (OFCCP), requires that all employers with government contracts of $2,500 or more must set up affirmative action programs for the handicapped.

Sexual Harassment. Unwelcome sexual attention that causes the recipient distress and results in an inability on the part of the recipient to effectively perform the job requirements.

The 4/5ths Rule. Discrimination is likely to occur if the selection rate for a protected group is less than 4/5ths of the selection rate for a majority group.

APPLICATION CASE 3–1   Meeting the Challenge of Sexual Harassment*

At a Goldman, Sachs & Co. office in Boston, some male employees allegedly pasted photos of bare-breasted women on company newsletters, next to biographies of new female employees (suggesting that the photos were pictures of the new staff members). Copies of the newsletters were circulated around the office. So allegedly was sexist literature such as "The Smart Man's Creed or Why Beer is Better than Women" ("After you've had a beer, the bottle is still worth a dime.") Kristine Utley, a former Goldman sales associate has made these allegations in a suit charging that the environment at Goldman, Sachs & Co. constitutes sexual harassment. Fired for refusing a transfer to a New York office, she is suing to gain reinstatement and damages and to eliminate the harassment.

Joanne Barbetta has filed a similar suit seeking damages for harassment caused by an environment that she asserted "was poisoning my system." Ms. Barbetta reports that during her tenure as a clerk at Chemlawn, male employees circulated pornographic magazines and pinup posters. She viewed a slide presentation that included suggestive pictures (e.g., a nude woman) put there, said management, "to keep the guys awake," according to Barbetta. After these experiences and continual breast-grabbing shenanigans by a male employee, Ms. Barbetta quit.

Marie Regab, formerly an 18-year employee of Air France, has filed similar charges concerning the Washington office where she worked as a salesperson. She alleges that several characteristics of the office environment combined to create harassment including propositions by one of her bosses, circulation of *Playboy* and *Penthouse* magazines in the office, and open discussion of sexual activity by male employees. "It was sickening and an insult to women in the office," she claims. Ms. Regab was fired; she is suing to gain reinstatement, for $1.5 million in damages, and to eliminate the harassment in the office.

These three situations are examples of a growing number of suits being filed in courts by women who are charging that a sexist environment in the workplace constitutes sexual harassment and that their employers are therefore liable. Plaintiff actions in this area have been fueled by the U.S. Supreme Court's ruling that sexist behavior which creates an "intimidating, hostile, or offensive working environment" is sexual harassment and violates Title VII of the 1964 Civil Rights Act.

* Written by Kim Stewart and adapted from Joseph Pereira, "Women Allege Sexist Atmosphere in Offices Constitutes Harassment," *The Wall Street Journal,* February 10, 1988, p. 19; Cathy Trost, "With Problem More Visible, Firms Crack Down on Sexual Harassment," *The Wall Street Journal,* August 28, 1986, p. 19; Walter Kiechel III, "The High Cost of Sexual Harassment," *Fortune,* September 14, 1987, p. 147ff; and Marisa Manley, "Dealing with Sexual Harassment," *Inc.,* May 1987, p. 145ff.

The Court's ruling has spurred an increasing number of companies to act to prevent sexual harassment in the work place and to deal with it effectively when the problem occurs. Other factors have triggered company action. Employers are realizing that the costs of harassment can be high in terms of lowered productivity, absenteeism, and turnover. One study of female employees in the federal government concluded that the government loses about $200 million each year to the effects of sexual harassment. Costs can also be high if an employee sues. Even if the plaintiff opts for an out-of-court settlement, the costs of these settlements are often in the six figures, and it's the company who pays. Companies are also realizing that sexual harassment is a very real issue in today's and tomorrow's workplace; from 20 to over 50 percent of working women have experienced sexual harassment (and so have at least 15 percent of male employees).

Thus, companies are tackling the issue; the more effective strategies developed so far contain four primary features:

1. *Training programs that educate employees concerning the meaning of sexual harassment and the behaviors that comprise a hostile and harassing workplace:* Training is especially important simply because men and women often differ in their perception of what behaviors are and aren't harassment. Most training is in the form of seminars and workshops often with films and videos. Philip Morris USA conducts a mandatory training program for its field managers that includes viewing a video called "Shades of Gray." General Motors conducts an awareness seminar for employees and offers this benchmark for judging the appropriateness of office conduct: "Would you be embarrassed to see your remarks or behavior in the newspaper or described to your own family?"

   Du Pont has developed one of the most comprehensive anti-harassment programs in business (begun in 1981). Recently, the corporation added a $500,000-funded course on personal safety, rape, and harassment prevention primarily for its female employees (many of whom are moving into traditionally male jobs at Du Pont such as agricultural products sales). The course offers no-nonsense advice on how to handle a harasser. For example, if a male customer fondles a woman's knee, Du Pont advises that she "firmly remove his hand . . . and then say, 'Let's pretend this didn't happen.'" If she receives a verbal proposition, Du Pont advises that she say, "No, I wouldn't want our business relationship to be jeopardized in any way." About 1,600 employees have completed the course.

   Like General Motors, Du Pont offers its employees a guideline for evaluating their behavior. Said a Du Pont spokesman, "We tell people: It's harassment when something starts bothering somebody."

   Some other companies provide advice concerning how to handle harassment. One popular piece of advice: document the incident as soon as possible by describing on paper what happened in full detail and talking to someone informally about the incident. A relatively mild case of harassment can be handled by talking to the harasser, explaining what he or she did, how it made you feel, and telling the harasser to stop. In a more serious situation, communicating these points via a certified letter sent to the harasser with the victim keeping a copy is often recommended (and reportedly proven to be quite effective).

2. *An internal complaint procedure:* Ideally, the procedure provides for fast action and confidentiality and ensures that the employee can report the problem to a manager who is not involved in the harassment. Some companies encourage employees to report a problem to their immediate supervisor but also designate an individual (often a woman) in the P/HRM department as someone employees can speak with in cases where the immediate supervisor is involved in the problem. To ensure speedy action, some companies require that an investigation begin within 24 hours after the harassment complaint has been reported. The procedure also ideally stipulates how investigations will be conducted.

3. *Speedy, corrective action that solves the problem:* If the investigation supports the employee's claims, corrective action is quickly taken. Such action can range from simply talking to the harasser to discharge, depending on the severity of the offense. One federal agency requires offending employees to publicly apologize to the individuals they've harassed. Staffing changes also sometimes occur. One New York bank faced a problem of a highly talented male executive who generated much profit for the bank—and also several costly EEOC complaints from his secretaries. The bank solved the problem by assigning the executive an all-male secretarial staff. Corrective action is particularly important because it communicates to both potential offenders and victims that harassment will not be tolerated.

4. *A written and communicated antiharassment policy:* The written policy is documented and distributed to all employees. The policy contains a definition of harassment, the company's position prohibiting harassment, the grievance procedure, and penalties.

While a growing number of companies are implementing antiharassment policies the courts have yet to establish a consistent record concerning the "hostile environment" as illegal harassment issue. For example, a federal district court in Michigan dismissed a claim by Vivienne Rabidue that sexual posters and obscene language in her office at Osceola Refining Co. constituted illegal sexual harassment.

However, Joanne Barbetta has won the first round of her court battle with Chemlawn. The judge hearing her complaint rejected ChemLawn's motion to dismiss the suit; he has ordered Ms. Barbetta's case to trial. Chemlawn is expected to present a vigorous defense, asserting that the men involved in the newsletter incident have been disciplined and that the situations Ms. Barbetta cites occurring "over the course of two years fall far short" of creating a hostile, harassing environment.

Questions for Thought

1. Assume that you are an P/HRM executive for a company that manufactures and sells agricultural products (for example, fertilizers and grain feeds).

The company's workforce of 1,200 employees is 70 percent male and 30 percent female. Drawing from this case and the chapter content, develop an antiharassment policy/program. What are the major challenges you see in implementing the policy?

2. Many experts assert that reported cases of sexual harassment comprise a small percentage of the total number of incidents that actually occur in the workplace. If their assertions are true, why do many cases go unreported? How would your P/HRM policy on harassment address this situation?

3. As research indicates, people widely differ in their perceptions of sexual harassment. What is a harmless remark to one individual can be an annoying, even infuriating insult to another. In your view, what separates harmless conduct from harassing behavior? In the same vein, when does a sexist environment become a "hostile," harassing one?

ANALYSIS, PLANNING, AND STAFFING

Part Two consists of four chapters. Chapter 4, Job Analysis and Design, defines the techniques of job analysis and design, then reviews and critiques them. Chapter 5, Human Resource Planning (HRP), looks at HRP in organizations and emphasizes the important role of planning. In Chapter 6, recruitment strategies are discussed. Different approaches to recruitment are presented and evaluated. In Chapter 7, Selection, the various steps in the selection process are presented and analyzed.

JOB ANALYSIS AND DESIGN

After studying this chapter, you should be able to:

- **Define** what is meant by the terms *job analysis, job description,* and *job specification.*
- **Illustrate** the uses that job analysis information can serve in an organization's P/HRM program.
- **Describe** four methods used to collect job analysis information.
- **Interpret** what kind of job code and information is found in the *Dictionary of Occupational Titles.*
- **List** the five core job dimensions used in job enrichment programs.

Autonomy
Feedback
Functional Job Analysis (FJA)
Job

Job Analysis
Job Analysis Information Format
Job Characteristics Model
Job Description
Job Enrichment
Job Family
Job Specification
Management Position Description Questionnaire (MPDQ)
Position
Position Analysis Questionnaire (PAQ)
Process Chart
Skill Variety
Task
Task Identity
Task Significance

P/HRM · IN · ACTION

Tim Huggins

Tim Huggins is the new director of human resources of Sprowl Manufacturing, a division of the MBTI corporation. Tim wanted to start a job analysis program immediately. Six weeks after he took over, job analysis questionnaires (six pages each) were given to employees. The results were puzzling. Responses from the operating employees (machinists, lift operators, technicians, draftspeople, and mechanics) were quite different from responses from their supervisors about these jobs.

The fact that supervisors viewed the jobs differently from those doing the work fueled Tim's desire to do a job analysis. He wanted to study and specifically define the jobs so that misunderstandings, arguments, and false expectations could be kept to a minimum.

The supervisors listed job duties as simple and routine. The operating employees disagreed and claimed that their jobs were complicated; constrained by limited resources. They complained that work areas were hot, stuffy, and uncomfortable. These disagreements soon became the basis for some open hostility between supervisors and workers. Finally, Nick Mannis, a machinist, confronted supervisor Rog Wilkes and threatened to punch him out over the "lies" Rog and other supervisors had concocted in the job analysis.

Tim was worried that the job analysis program was getting totally out of hand. He had to do something about it. Everyone was getting up in arms over a program Tim felt was necessary.

Should a manager like Tim, who knows a lot about P/HRM, but who was not trained in the specifics of job analysis, undertake this kind of program?

INTRODUCTION

Organizations have evolved because the overall mission and objectives of most institutions are too large for any single person to accomplish. The cornerstone of the organization is the set of jobs performed by employees. The set of jobs is what provides the input needed to accomplish the mission and objectives.

These jobs must fit together, coordinate, and link directly to the mission if the organization is to be successful.[1] Thus, studying and understanding jobs is a vital part of any P/HRM program. **Job analysis** involves the formal study of jobs.

Job analysis provides answers to questions such as:

How much time is taken to complete important jobs tasks?

Which tasks are grouped together and are considered a job?

How can a job be designed or structured so that employee performance can be enhanced?

What kinds of behaviors are needed to perform the job?

What kind of person (traits and experience) is best suited for the job?

How can the information acquired with a job analysis be used in the development of P/HRM programs?

In this chapter the contributions made by job analysis to an organization's P/HRM program and specific activities will become clearer. Furthermore, the careful planning needed and various general and specific techniques of a job analysis program will also be highlighted. Finally, the importance of job analysis in the design of jobs will be discussed. The chapter will show that job analysis is a necessary part of P/HRM. It is this necessity that is pushing Tim in his drive to institute job analysis at Sprowl Manufacturing.

Job Analysis Vocabulary

The language of job analysis must be learned before the specific process and the techniques are understood. To establish the vocabulary some key terms must be clarified. The following definitions are consistent with those provided by the U.S. Employment Service and the U.S. Office of Personnel Management.[2]

> *Job analysis.* The process of defining a job in terms of tasks or behaviors and specifying the education, training, and responsibilities needed to perform the job successfully.
>
> *Job description.* The job analysis provides information about the job that results in a description of what the job entails.
>
> *Job specification.* The job analysis also results in the specification of what kind of traits and experiences are needed to perform the job.
>
> *Task.* A coordinated and aggregated series of work elements used to produce an output (e.g., units of production of service to a client).
>
> *Position.* Consists of responsibilities and duties performed by an individual. There are as many positions as there are employees.

---

[1] E.T. Cornelius, "Practical Findings from Job Analysis Research," in *Handbook of Job Analysis,* ed. S. Gall (New York: John Wiley & Sons, 1987).

[2] Bureau of Intergovernmental Personnel Programs, "Job Analysis: Developing and Documenting Data" (Washington, D.C.: U.S. Government Printing Office, 1973).

Job. A group of positions that are similar in their duties, such as a computer programmer or compensation specialist.

Job family. A group of two or more jobs that have similar job duties.

These terms illustrate that, in order to prevent confusion and improper usage the specific meaning of words must be understood. Terms such as *job* and *task* are often used interchangeably. This, however, is technically incorrect (as you can see from the definitions just listed). Since precision is required by federal and state legislation, it is important for the P/HRM manager to use these terms accurately.

THE STEPS IN JOB ANALYSIS

A number of steps are performed in the job analysis process.[3] Exhibit 4–1 depicts these steps. The process outlined in Exhibit 4–1 assumes that the job analysis process is occurring in an ongoing organization; in other words, an organization that is already in operation as opposed to a new venture. Step 1 is important, since it provides an overall view of the organization. The fit of each job in the total fabric of the organization is what is being considered. Organization charts and process charts (which will be discussed later) are used to complete Step 1. Step 2 encourages those involved to determine how the job analysis and job design information will be used. This step will be further explained in the next section. Since it is usually too costly and time consuming to analyze every job, a representative sample of jobs needs to be selected. In Step 3, attention is called to the selection of jobs that are to be analyzed.

Step 4 involves the use of acceptable job analysis techniques. The techniques are used to collect data on the characteristics of the job, the required behaviors, and the employee characteristics needed to perform the job. The information collected in Step 4 is then used in Step 5 to develop a job description. Next, in Step 6, a job specification is prepared.

Tim failed to explain these steps at Sprowl. He simply handed out questionnaires. Naturally, this resulted in concern among supervisors and operating employees. The people whose jobs were being analyzed and their supervisors simply were not informed of what Tim had in mind. Tim knew what job analysis was, but he was never actually trained in the "how to" specifics. Unfortunately, other people at Sprowl were not sure what job analysis was, because Tim failed to communicate what he had in mind.

The knowledge and data collected in Steps 1–6 are then used to engage in Step 7, job design. A job's *design* is how the elements, duties, and tasks are put together to achieve optimal employee performance and satisfaction. The suc-

---

[3] Jai Ghorpade and Thomas J. Atchison, "The Concept of Job Analysis: A Review and Some Suggestions," *Public Personnel Management Journal,* Summer 1980, pp. 134–44; Ronald A. Ash and Edward L. Levine, "A Framework for Evaluating Job Analysis Methods," *Personnel,* November–December 1980, pp. 53–59.

EXHIBIT 4–1   **Steps in the Job Analysis Process (1–6) and Job Design (7–8)**

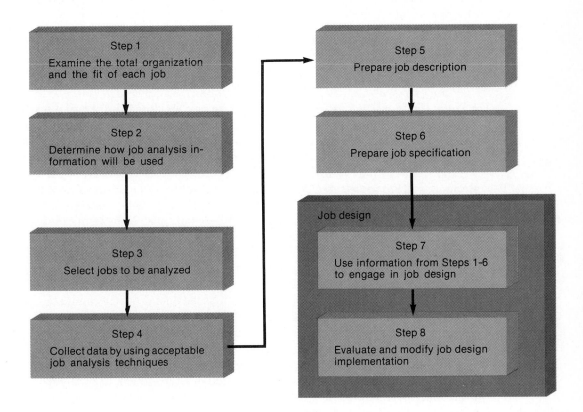

cess or failure of any job design attempt should be evaluated and will probably have to be modified. These actions are spelled out in Step 8. Steps 7 and 8 focus on job design as an output of the job analysis process.

THE USES OF JOB ANALYSIS

P/HRM managers, specialists, and managers in general know that job analysis has many uses. Some believe that there is no longer a choice about whether job analysis should be conducted. The administrative guidelines accompanying the civil rights/EEO laws now require that organizations conduct a formal job analysis to defend their P/HRM activities.[4] For example, the EEOC's Uniform Guidelines on Employee Selection states that:

---

[4] M. G. Miner and J. B. Miner, *Uniform Guidelines on Employee Selection Procedures* (Washington, D.C.: The Bureau of National Affairs, 1979).

> There should be a job analysis which includes an analysis of the important work behaviors required for successful performance. . . . Any job analysis should focus on work behavior(s) and the tasks associated with them.[5]

Job analysis is specifically linked to various laws.[6] Therefore, if for no other reason than to comply with the law, a valid and reliable job analysis technique should become a part of the P/HRM activities in all organizations.[7] For example, job analysis is linked to the following legislation:

- *Equal Pay Act (1963)*—In order for work to be considered the same, the jobs must involve equal skill, equal effort, and equal responsibility and be performed under similar working conditions in the same establishment. A job analysis can be used to show similarities or differences in skill, effort, responsibility, and working conditions to warrant compensation payments.

- *Fair Labor Standards Act (1938)*—Exempt employees do not have to be paid overtime pay, generally after 40 hours per week. Typically, managers, technical workers, and professionals are considered exempt. Nonexempt employees are required to receive overtime pay for working in excess of 40 hours per week. Generally, blue-collar, clerical, and semiskilled workers are classified as nonexempt. The job analysis clarifies into which category, exempt or nonexempt, employees are placed.

- *Civil Rights Act (1964)*—A job description based on a properly conducted job analysis can provide support for preparing a defense against unfair discrimination charges. Not having job analysis data weakens the defense against discrimination charges. For example, stating that certain physical requirements (e.g., strength of stamina) are needed to perform a job without having determined their necessity through job analysis can subject the employer to discrimination charges.

- *Test Validation*—Landmark cases discussed in Chapter 3 such as *Griggs* v. *Duke Power Co.* (1971) and *Albermarle Paper Company* v. *J. Moody* (1975) established the legal need for job analysis in the validation of employee selection procedures. For example, the court held that Albermarle's test validation effort was inadequate because there had been "no analysis of the attributes of, or the particular skills needed in, the structured job group."[8]

In addition to legal compliance requirements, in order to defend P/HRM activities, job analysis is intricately tied to P/HRM programs and activities. It is used in these areas:

---

[5] Section 14.C.2 of the EEOC's *Uniform Guidelines on Employee Selection Procedures,* 1978.

[6] James W. Hunt, *The Law of the Workplace* (Washington, D.C.: Bureau of National Affairs, 1984).

[7] Donald W. Myers, "The Impact of a Selected Provision in the Federal Guidelines on Job Analysis and Training," *Personnel Administrator,* July 1981, pp. 41–45.

[8] Duane E. Thompson and Toni A. Thompson, "Court Standards for Job Analysis in Test Validation," *Personnel Psychology,* Winter 1982, pp. 865–74.

1. Preparation of *job descriptions*. A complete description contains a job summary, the job duties and responsibilities, and some indication of the working conditions.
2. Writing *job specifications*. The job specification describes the individual traits and characteristics required to perform the job well.
3. *Job Design*. Job analysis information is used to structure and modify the elements, duties, and tasks of specific jobs.
4. *Recruitment*. Job analysis information is useful when searching for the right person to fill the job. It helps recruiters to seek and find the type of people that will contribute to and be comfortable with the organization.
5. *Selection*. The final selection of the most qualified people requires information on what job duties and responsibilities need to be performed. This type of information is provided in the job description.
6. *Performance evaluation*. The evaluation of performance involves comparison of actual versus planned output. Job analysis is used to acquire an idea of acceptable levels of performance for a job.
7. *Training and development*. Job analysis information is used to design and implement training and development programs. The job description provides information on what skills and competencies are required to perform the job. Training and development work is then conducted to satisfy these skill and competency requirements.
8. *Career planning and development*. The movement of individuals into and out of positions, jobs, and occupations is a common procedure in organizations. Job analysis provides clear and detailed information to those considering such a career movement.
9. *Compensation*. The total job is the basis for estimating its worth. Compensation is usually tied to a job's required skill, competencies, working conditions, safety hazards, and so on. Job analysis is used to compare and properly compensate jobs.
10. *Safety*. The safety on a job depends on proper layout, standards, equipment, and other physical conditions. What a job entails and the type of people needed also contribute information to establish safe procedures. Of course, this information is provided by job analysis.

Taken together, these uses of job analysis information are comprehensive. They cover the entire domain of P/HRM activities. Exhibit 4–2 provides a sample of the list of activities that benefit from job analysis information. Job analysis is such an important source of information that it transcends P/HRM programs and activities. Managers involved in planning, organizing, controlling, and directing functions also can and do benefit from job analysis information.

WHO DOES THE JOB ANALYSIS?

Conducting a reliable and valid job analysis is a job for a trained professional. However, some firms use a job analyst, others use the supervisor, the

---

EXHIBIT 4-2   How Job Analysis Information Is Used

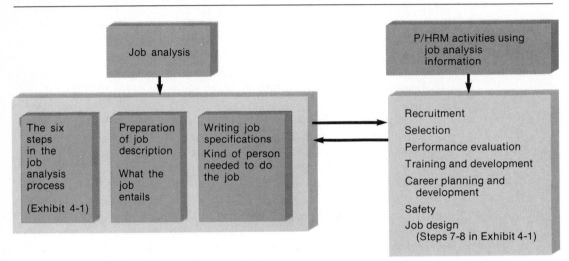

jobholder, or some combination of these to collect job analysis information. The steps spelled out in Exhibit 4–1 indicate that care and planning are important features of any job analysis effort. As the opening P/HRM In Action illustrates, Tim really didn't take the care and planning that he should have to start the job analysis program—he started the program too abruptly. Regardless of who collects the data, some training in job analysis procedures is required.

There are some managers who do not respect the work of the job analyst. This statement presents an interesting message about job analysis:

> Although job analysis is an essential feature of almost every activity engaged in by industrial-organization psychologists, the subject is treated in textbooks in a manner which suggests that any fool can do it, and thus it is a task which can be delegated to the lowest level technician. This is quite contradictory to the position taken by Otis (1953 . . . , and is clearly at variance with the statements in the EEOC Selection Guidelines. . . . Job analysis for these purposes is not accomplished by rummaging around in an organization; it is accomplished by applying highly systematic and precise methods.[9]

The individuals conducting a job analysis should understand people, jobs, and the total organizational system. These individuals should also understand how work flows within the organization. An understanding of how P/HRM fits into the overall structure of the organization is also important.

The job analyst could be located in a P/HRM or industrial engineering

---

[9] E. P. Prien, "The Functions of Job Analysis in Content Validation," *Personnel Psychology,* Summer 1977, pp. 167–74. The "Otis (1953)" reference in the quote is in J. L. Otis, "Whose Criterion?" Presidential address to Division 14 of the American Psychological Association, 1953.

department or in a unit that is solely responsible for job analysis. Some firms, because of only an occasional need for job analysis information or due to cost constraints, may hire a temporary job analyst from outside the organization. Whatever the organizational arrangement, the job analyst is not an amateur. He or she is a trained specialist who plays a vital role in P/HRM.

SELECTING METHODS AND PROCEDURES: THE USE OF CHARTS

The job analyst has to select the best methods and procedures available to conduct the job analysis. However, even before this selection is made, an overview of the organization and jobs is required. An overview provides the job analyst with an informed picture of the total arrangement of departments, units, and jobs.

The Organization Chart

An organization chart presents the relationship among departments and units of the firm. The line functions (the individuals performing work duties) and staff functions (the advisers) are spelled out.

A typical organization chart for a manufacturing firm is presented in Exhibit 4–3. This chart shows the vertical levels in the organization and the various departments. It provides the job analyst with a general picture of what departments exist and the hierarchy and formal communication networks in the organization. Emphasis is placed on the word *general*. A chart shows the way the organization is *supposed* to be arranged. The actual arrangement of the organization and the flow of communication is often different from the plan on the chart. However, even a partial view aids in forming a broad-based conception of the organization.

Process Chart

A **process chart** is more specific than an organization chart.[10] It displays how jobs are connected to each other. Exhibit 4–4 is a process chart showing how four jobs are related to each other. Specific attention is paid to the technician job. The job analyst would be interested in the flow of work to and from the technician job. The process chart in Exhibit 4–4 shows the flow of activities necessary to prepare the specs for the construction of an engineering prototype (model).

Organization charts provide a broad overview; process charts provide a more detailed analysis of specific jobs. These and other similar sources should be consulted before actual job analysis collection methods are used.

---

[10] Richard I. Henderson, *Compensation Management* (Reston, Va.: Reston Publishing, 1987), p. 195.

EXHIBIT 4–3 **Organization Chart (Sample)**

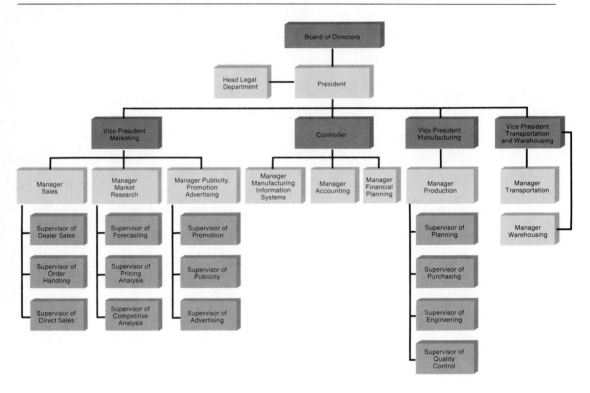

EXHIBIT 4–4 **Process Chart of Job Relationships**

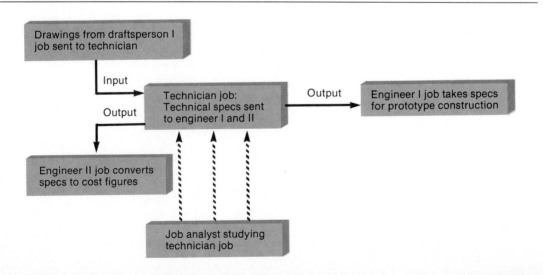

JOB ANALYSIS: METHODS
OF DATA COLLECTION

There are four methods used separately or in combination to collect job analysis data—observation, interview, questionnaires, and job incumbent diary/logs. In each of these methods, the information about the job is collected and then the job studied in terms of tasks completed by the job incumbent (person presently working on the job). This type of job analysis is referred to as *job oriented*. On the other hand, a job can be analyzed in terms of behaviors or what the job incumbent does to perform the job (such as computing, coordinating, negotiating). This is referred to as *work-oriented* job analysis.[11] Both of these orientations are acceptable under the 1978 Uniform Guidelines on Employee Selection procedures as long as they identify job duties and behaviors that are critical to performing the job.

Thus, the four methods—or any combination of them—must collect what is called critical information. Since time and cost are considerations, managers need to collect comparable, valid data. Consequently, some form of core information is needed no matter what data collection method is used.[12] A professional job analyst typically conducts extensive interviews with incumbents and supervisors, collects records about the job, and if feasible directly observes job incumbents performing the job.[13]

A questionnaire called the **Job Analysis Information Format (JAIF)** can provide the basic core information for use of any job analysis method—observation, interview, questionnaire, or job incumbent diary/log. It permits the job analyst to collect job information that provides a thorough picture of the job, job duties, and requirements.

Job incumbents are asked to complete the JAIF. These answers (of course, some questions may not be answered or can't be answered because of a lack of job incumbent knowledge about the question) are then used to specifically structure the data collection technique that will eventually be implemented. Exhibit 4–5 presents a copy of one type of JAIF.

Observation

Direct observation is used for jobs that require manual, standardized, and short-job cycle activities. Jobs performed by an automobile assembly-line worker, an insurance company filing clerk, or an inventory stockroom employee are examples of these. The job analyst must observe a representative

---

[11] E. J. McCormick, *Job Analysis: Uses and Application* (New York: AMACOM, 1979), and E. J. McCormick, ed., "Job and Task Analysis," in *Handbook of Industrial and Organizational Psychology,* ed. M. D. Dunnette (Chicago: Rand McNally, 1976), pp. 652–53.

[12] Henderson, pp. 146–152.

[13] Lee Friedman and Robert J. Harvey, "Can Recruiters with Reduced Job Description Information Provide Accurate Position Analysis Questionnaire (PAQ) Ratings?" *Personal Psychology,* Winter 1986, p. 774.

EXHIBIT 4–5

JOB ANALYSIS INFORMATION FORMAT

Your Job Title _____ Code _____ Date _____

Class Title _____ Department _____

Your Name _____ Facility _____

Supervisor's Title _____ Prepared by _____

Superior's Name _____ Hours Worked ____ AM/PM ____ to ____ AM/PM

1. What is the general purpose of your job?

2. What was your last job? If it was in another organization, please name it.

3. To what job would you normally expect to be promoted?

4. If you regularly supervise others, list them by name and job title.

5. If you supervise others, please check those activities that are part of your supervisory duties

   — Hiring   — Coaching   — Promoting

   — Orienting   — Counseling   — Compensating

   — Training   — Budgeting   — Disciplining

   — Scheduling   — Directing   — Terminating

   — Developing   — Measuring performance   — Other _____

6. How would you describe the successful completion and results of your work?

7. *Job Duties*—Please briefly describe *what* you do and, if possible, *how* you do it. Indicate those duties you consider to be most important and/or most difficult.

   a. *Daily duties*—

   b. *Periodic duties*—(Please indicate whether weekly, monthly, quarterly, etc.)—

   c. *Duties performed at irregular intervals*—

   d. How long have you been performing these duties?

   e. Are you now performing unnecessary duties? If yes, please describe.

EXHIBIT 4–5 *(continued)*

---

    f. Should you be performing duties not now included in your job? If yes, please describe.

8. *Education.* Please check the blank that indicates the educational *requirements* for the job, not your *own* educational background.

    a. _____ No formal education required.

    b. _____ Less than high school diploma.

    c. _____ High school diploma or equivalent.

    d. _____ 2-year college certificate or equivalent.

    e. _____ 4-year college degree.

    f. _____ Education beyond under-graduate degree and/or professional license.

List advanced degrees or specific professional license or certificate required.

Please indicate the education you had when you were placed on this job.

9. *Experience.* Please check the amount needed to perform your job.

    a. __ None.

    b. __ Less than one month.

    c. __ One month to less than six months.

    d. __ Six months to one year.

    e. __ One to three years.

    f. __ Three to five years.

    g. __ Five to 10 years.

    h. __ Over 10 years.

Please indicate the experience you had when you were placed on this job.

10. *Skill.* Please list any skills required in the performance of your job. (For example, amount of accuracy, alertness, precision in working with described tools, methods, systems, etc.)

Please list skills you possessed when you were placed on this job.

11. *Equipment.* Does your work require the use of any equipment? Yes __ No __. If Yes, please list the equipment and check whether you use it rarely, occasionally, or frequently.

	Equipment	Rarely	Occasionally	Frequently
a.	_____	_____	_____	_____
b.	_____	_____	_____	_____
c.	_____	_____	_____	_____
d.	_____	_____	_____	_____

12. *Physical Demands.* Please check all undesirable physical demands required on your job and how often you are required to do them: Rarely, occasionally, or frequently.

EXHIBIT 4–5 *(continued)*

		Rarely	Occasionally	Frequently
a.	_____ Handling heavy material	_____	_____	_____
b.	_____ Awkward or cramped positions	_____	_____	_____
c.	_____ Excessive working speeds	_____	_____	_____
d.	_____ Excessive sensory requirements (seeing, hearing, touching, smelling, speaking)	_____	_____	_____
e.	_____ Vibrating equipment	_____	_____	_____
f.	_____ Others: _____	_____	_____	_____

13. *Emotional Demands.* Please check all undesirable emotional demands placed on you by your job and whether they occur rarely, occasionally, or frequently.

		Rarely	Occasionally	Frequently
a.	_____ Contacts with general public	_____	_____	_____
b.	_____ Customer contact	_____	_____	_____
c.	_____ Close supervision	_____	_____	_____
d.	_____ Deadlines under pressure	_____	_____	_____
e.	_____ Irregular activity schedules	_____	_____	_____
f.	_____ Working alone	_____	_____	_____
g.	_____ Excessive traveling	_____	_____	_____
h.	_____ Others:	_____	_____	_____

14. *Workplace Location.* Check type of location of your job and if you consider it to be unsatisfactory or satisfactory.

		Unsatisfactory	*Satisfactory*
a.	_____ Outdoor	_____	_____
b.	_____ Indoor	_____	_____
c.	_____ Underground	_____	_____
d.	_____ Pit	_____	_____
e.	_____ Scaffold	_____	_____

15. *Physical Surroundings.* Please check whether you consider the following physical conditions of your job to be poor, good, or excellent.

		Poor	Good	Excellent
a.	_____ Lighting	_____	_____	_____
b.	_____ Ventilation	_____	_____	_____
c.	_____ Sudden temperature change	_____	_____	_____
d.	_____ Vibration	_____	_____	_____
d.	_____ Comfort of furnishings	_____	_____	_____

EXHIBIT 4–5   *(concluded)*

16. *Environmental Conditions.* Please check the objectionable conditions under which you must perform your job and check whether the condition exists rarely, occasionally, or frequently.

		Rarely	Occasionally	Frequently
a.	_____ Dust	_____	_____	_____
b.	_____ Dirt	_____	_____	_____
c.	_____ Heat	_____	_____	_____
d.	_____ Cold	_____	_____	_____
e.	_____ Fumes	_____	_____	_____
f.	_____ Odors	_____	_____	_____
g.	_____ Noise	_____	_____	_____
h.	_____ Wetness	_____	_____	_____
i.	_____ Humidity	_____	_____	_____
j.	_____ Others:	_____	_____	_____

17. *Health and Safety.* Please check all undesirable health and safety factors under which you must perform your job and how often they occur: rarely, occasionally, or frequently.

		Rarely	Occasionally	Frequently
a.	_____ Height of elevated workplace	_____	_____	_____
b.	_____ Radiation	_____	_____	_____
c.	_____ Mechanical hazards	_____	_____	_____
d.	_____ Moving objects	_____	_____	_____
e.	_____ Explosives	_____	_____	_____
f.	_____ Electrical hazards	_____	_____	_____
g.	_____ Fire	_____	_____	_____
h.	_____ Others: _____	_____	_____	_____

Signature _____ *Date* _____

Supervisory review

Do the incumbent's responses to the questionnaire accurately describe the work requirements and the work performed in meeting the responsibilities of the job? _____ Yes _____ No. If No, please explain and list any significant omissions or additions.

_____   _____   _____
Date   Title   Signature

sample of individuals performing these jobs. Observation is usually not appropriate where the job involves significant amounts of mental activity, such as the work of a research scientist, a lawyer, or a mathematician.

The use of the observation technique requires that the job analyst be trained to observe *relevant* job behaviors. In conducting an observation, the job analyst must remain as unobtrusive as possible. He or she must stay out of the way so that the work can be performed.

Interview

Interviewing job incumbents is often done in combination with observation. Interviews are probably the most widely used job analysis data collection technique. They permit the job analyst to talk face to face with job incumbents. The job incumbent can ask questions of the job analyst, and this interview serves as an opportunity for the analyst to explain how the job analysis knowledge and information will be used.

Interviews can be conducted with a single job incumbent, a group of individuals, or with a supervisor who is knowledgeable about the job. Usually a structured set of questions will be used in interviews so that answers from individuals or groups can be compared.

One major problem with interviewing is that inaccurate information may be collected. For example, if a job incumbent believes that the job analysis interview will be used to set the job's compensation amount, he or she may provide inaccurate information. Therefore, interviewing more than one person (job incumbents and supervisors), careful planning, good questions, and establishing rapport between the job analyst and interviewees are extremely important guidelines. Using the guidelines is time consuming, but their use improves the quality of information collected. Interview information can be further refined by use of observation and/or questionnaires.

Questionnaires

The use of questionnaires is usually the least costly method for collecting information. It is an effective way to collect a large amount of information in a short period of time. The JAIF presented in Exhibit 4–5 is a structured questionnaire. It includes specific questions about the job, job requirements, working conditions, and equipment. A less structured, more open-ended approach would be to ask job incumbents to "describe their job in their own terms." This open-ended format would permit job incumbents to use their own terms and ideas to describe the job.

The format and degree of structure that a questionnaire should have are debatable issues. Job analysts have their own personal preferences on this matter. There really is no best format for a questionnaire. However, here are a few hints that will make the questionnaire easier to use:

- Keep it as *short as possible*—people do not generally like to complete forms.

- *Explain* what the questionnaire is being used for—people want to know why it must be completed. Tim Huggins (in the P/HRM In Action in this chapter) failed to explain his job analysis questionnaire. Employees wanted to know why the questions were being asked and how their responses would be used.
- Keep it *simple*—do not try to impress people with technical language. Use the simplest language to make a point or ask a question.
- *Test* the questionnaire before using it—in order to improve the questionnaire ask some job incumbents to complete it and to comment on its features. This pretest will permit the analyst to modify the format before using the questionnaire in final form.

Job Incumbent Diary/Log

The diary/log is a recording by job incumbents of job duties, frequency of the duties, and when the duties were accomplished. This technique requires the job incumbent to keep a diary/log on a daily basis. Unfortunately, most individuals are not disciplined enough to keep such a diary/log.

If a diary/log is kept up to date, it can provide good information about the job. Comparisons on a daily, weekly, or monthly basis can be made. This permits an examination of the routineness or nonroutineness of job duties. The diary/log is useful when attempting to analyze jobs that are difficult to observe, such as those performed by engineers, scientists, and senior executives.

Any of these four methods can be used in combination. In fact, all four can be used to acquire a comprehensive picture of a job. Of course, using all four would take time and be rather costly. The analyst decides which method or combination is needed to do a thorough job analysis. Job analysts often use a more specific, widely used technique that incorporates various features of these four general techniques and provides a quantitative score.

JOB ANALYSIS: SPECIFIC QUANTITATIVE TECHNIQUES

The four job analysis methods of data collection just described are presented in general terms. They form the basis for construction of specific techniques that have gained popularity across many types of organizations. These specific techniques provide systematic and quantitative procedures that yield information about what job duties are being accomplished and what skills, ability, and knowledge are needed to perform the job. Currently, there is no ideal job analysis technique available that fits all jobs and meets reliability and validity standards.[14] There simply is no general agreement on what format provides

---

[14] Edward L. Levine, Ronald A. Ash, Hardy Hall, and Frank Sistrunk, "Evaluation of Job Analysis Methods by Experienced Job Analysts," *Academy of Management Journal,* June 1983, pp. 339–48.

the best information. Three popular quantitative-based techniques are: **functional job analysis (FJA);** the **position analysis questionnaire (PAQ);** and the **management position description questionnaire (MPDQ).**

Functional Job Analysis

The U.S. Training and Employment Service (USTES) has developed what is called *functional job analysis (FJA)*.[15] FJA is used to describe the nature of jobs, to prepare job descriptions, and to provide details on employee job specifications. The result of FJA is a description of a job in terms of data, people, and things.

FJA assumes that:

- Jobs are concerned with data, people, and things.
- It is important to make a distinction between what gets done and what job incumbents do to get things done.
- Mental resources are used to describe data; interpersonal resources are used with people; physical resources are applied to people.
- Each function performed on a job draws on a range of worker talents and skills to perform job duties.

The job incumbents' activities associated with data, people, and things are listed in Exhibit 4–6. These activities are used to describe more than 20,000 jobs in the *Dictionary of Occupational Titles (DOT)*.[16]

The DOT classifies jobs on the basis of a nine-digit code. If someone is interested in a general description of a job, the DOT could be used. Exhibit 4–7 provides DOT descriptions of five jobs. The first three digits of any listing (e.g., Disc Jockey—159) specify the occupational code, title, and industry. The next three digits (147) designate the degree to which a job incumbent typically has responsibility and judgment over data, people, things. The lower the numbers' value, the greater the responsibility and judgment. The final three digits (014) are used to classify the alphabetical order of the job titles within the occupational group having the same degree of responsibility and judgment.[17]

The DOT descriptions offer a starting point for learning about a job. The FJA can then be used to clarify and elaborate on the standard DOT listing.

The FJA form of analyzing the job of a dough mixer appears in Exhibit 4–8. The dough mixer's activities in terms of data, people, and things are quan-

---

[15] Sidney A. Fine and Wretha W. Wiley, *An Introduction to Functional Job Analysis: A Scaling of Selected Tasks from the Social Welfare Field* (Methods for Manpower Analysis no. 4.) (Kalamazoo, Mich.: W. E. Upjohn Institute for Employee Research, 1973).

[16] U.S. Department of Labor, *Dictionary of Occupational Titles,* 4th ed. (Washington, D.C.: U.S. Government Printing Office, 1977).

[17] Pamela S. Cain and Donald J. Treiman, "*The Dictionary of Occupational Titles* as a source of Occupational Data," *American Sociological Review,* June 1981, pp. 353–78.

EXHIBIT 4–6   Activities to Be Rated: Data, People, and Things

Data	People	Things
0 Synthesizing	0 Mentoring	0 Setting up
1 Coordinating	1 Negotiating	1 Precision working
2 Analyzing	2 Instructing	2 Operating/controlling
3 Compiling	3 Supervising	3 Driving/operating
4 Computing	4 Diverting	4 Manipulating
5 Copying	5 Persuading	5 Tending
6 Comparing	6 Speaking/signaling	6 Feeding/offbearing
	7 Serving	7 Handling
	8 Taking instructions/helping	

Source: Adapted from U.S. Department of Labor, Employment Service, Training and Development Administration, *Handbook for Analyzing Jobs* (Washington, D.C.: U.S. Government Printing Office, 1972), p. 73.

titatively rated a 5, 6, and 2 in item 5. These ratings are based on the analyst's judgment concerning the activities presented in Exhibit 4–6. That is, a dough mixer must be able to copy data (5), speak effectively (6), and control (2) his or her work.

If the job analyst were examining the job of an executive secretary, the quantitative score might be 5, 6, 5 (copying, speaking-signaling, tending). On the other hand, a research scientist in a laboratory might be rated a 2, 0, 1.

The advantage of the FJA is that each job has a quantitative score. Thus, jobs can then be arranged for compensation or other P/HRM purposes. For example, all jobs with 5, 6, 2, or 2, 0, 1 scores could be grouped together.[18]

Position Analysis Questionnaire (PAQ)

A structured questionnaire for quantitatively assessing jobs was developed by Purdue University researchers and is called the *Position Analysis Question-naire (PAQ)*.[19] Typically a job analyst completes the PAQ. The PAQ contains 194 items (11 of these are shown in Exhibit 4–9). The job analyst decides whether the item is important in performing the job. For example, measuring

---

[18] Sidney A. Fine, *Functional Job Analysis Scales: A Desk Aid, Methods for Manpower Analysis No. 7* (Kalamazoo, Mich.: W. E. Upjohn Institute for Employment Research, 1973).

[19] E. J. McCormick, O. R. Jeanneret, and R. C. Mecham, "A Study of Job Characteristics and Job Dimensions as Based on the Position Analysis Questionnaire (PAQ)," *Journal of Applied Psychology,* August 1972, pp. 347–68, and E. J. McCormick, P. R. Jeanneret, and R. C. Mecham, *User's Manual for the Position Analysis Questionnaire System II* (West Lafayette, Ind.: Purdue University Press, 1978).

EXHIBIT 4-7 DOT Descriptions of Jobs

159.147-014 DISC JOCKEY (radio & tv broad.)
   Announces radio program of musical selections: Selects phonograph or tape recording to be
played based on program specialty and knowledge of audience taste. Comments on music and
other matters of interest to audience, such as weather, time, or traffic conditions. May
interview music personalities. May specialize in one type of music, such as classical, pop, rock,
or country and western. May be designated COMBINATION OPERATOR (radio & tv broad.)
when operating transmitter or control console.

159.167-018 MANAGER, STAGE (amuse. & rec.)
   Coordinates production plans and directs activities of stage crew and performances during
rehearsals and performance: Confers with DIRECTOR, STAGE (amuse. & rec.) concerning
production plans. Arranges conference times for cast, crew, and DIRECTOR, STAGE (amuse. &
rec.), and disseminates general information about production. Reads script during each
performance and gives cues for curtain, lights, and sound effects, and prompting performers.
Interprets stage-set diagrams to determine stage layout. Supervises stage crew engaged in
placing scenery and properties. Devises emergency substitutes for stage equipment or
properties. Keeps records to advise PRODUCER (amuse. & rec.) on matters of time, attendance,
and welfare benefits. Compiles cue words and phrases to form prompt book. Directs activities of
one or more assistants. May instruct understudy, replacement, or extra. May call performers at
specified interval before curtain time.

313.381-014 BAKER, PIZZA (hotel & rest.)
   Prepares and bakes pizza pies: Measures ingredients, such as flour, water, and yeast,
using measuring cup, spoon, and scale. Dumps specified ingredients into pan or bowl of mixing
machine preparatory to mixing. Starts machine and observes operation until ingredients are
mixed to desired consistency. Stops machine and dumps dough into proof box to allow dough to
rise. Kneads fermented dough. Cut out and weighs amount of dough required to produce pizza
pies of desired thickness. Shapes dough sections into balls or mounds and sprinkles each
section with flour to prevent crust forming until used. Greases pan. Stretches or spreads dough
mixture to size of pan. Places dough in pan, adds olive oil and tomato puree, tomato sauce,
mozarella cheese, meat, or other garnish on surface of dough, according to kind of pizza
ordered. Sets thermostatic controls and inserts pizza into heated oven to bake for specified
time. Removes product from oven and observes color to determine when pizza is done.

187.167-094 MANAGER, DUDE RANCH (amuse. & rec.)
   Directs operation of dude ranch: Formulates policy on advertising, publicity, guest rates,
and credit. Plans recreational and entertainment activities, such as camping, fishing, hunting,
horseback riding, and dancing. Directs activities of DUDE WRANGLERS (amuse. & rec.).
Directs preparation and maintenance of financial records. Directs other activities, such as
breeding, raising, and showing horses, mules, and livestock.

732.684-106 SHAPER, BASEBALL GLOVE (sports equip.) steamer and shaper.
   Forms pocket, opens fingers, and smooths seams to shape baseball gloves, using heated
forms, mallets, and hammers: Pulls glove over heated hand-shaped form to open and stretch
finger linings. Pounds fingers and palm of glove with rubber mallet and ball-shaped hammer to
smooth seams and bulges, and form glove pocket. Removes glove from form, inserts hand into
glove, and strikes glove pocket with fist while examining glove visually and tactually to ensure
comfortable fit.

devices (item 6) play a very substantial role 5 for the job being analyzed in
Exhibit 4–9.
   The PAQ's 194 items are placed in six major sections:

1. *Information input.* Where and how does job incumbent get job information?
2. *Mental processes.* What reasoning, decision-making, and planning processes
   are used to perform the job?

EXHIBIT 4–8   **Sample of Result of Job Analysis**

U.S. Department of Labor
Manpower Administration
(USTES)

JOB ANALYSIS SCHEDULE

1. Established Job Title _____ DOUGH MIXER _____

2. Ind. Assign _____ (bake prod.) _____

3. SIC Code(s) and Titles(s) _____ 12051 Bread and other bakery products _____

_____

4. JOB SUMMARY:

Operates mixing machine to mix ingredients for straight and
sponge (yeast) doughs according to established formulas, directs
other workers in fermentation of dough, and cuts dough into pieces
with hand cutter.

5. WORK PERFORMED RATINGS:

	D	P	(T)
Worker Functions	Data	People	Things
	5	6	2

Work Field _____ Cooking, Food Preparing _____

6. WORKER TRAITS RATINGS: (To be filled in by analyst)
   Training time required
   Aptitudes
   Temperaments
   Interests
   Physical Demands
   Environment Conditions

3. *Work output.* What physical activities and tools are used to perform the job?
4. *Relationship with other people.* What relationships with others are required to perform the job?
5. *Job contacts.* In what physical and social context is the job performed?
6. *Other job characteristics.* What activities, conditions, or characteristics other than those described in Section 1–5 are relevant?

Computerized programs are available for scoring jobs on the basis of seven dimensions—decision making, communication, social responsibilities, per-

EXHIBIT 4–9 **Portions of a Completed Page from the Position Analysis Questionnaire**

INFORMATION INPUT

1 INFORMATION INPUT

   1.1 Sources of Job Information

Rate each of the following items in terms of the extent to which it is used by the worker as a source of information in performing his job.

	Extent of Use (U)
NA	Does not apply
1	Nominal/very infrequent
2	Occasional
3	Moderate
4	Considerable
5	Very substantial

1.1.1 Visual Sources of Job Information

1 | 4 Written materials (books, reports, office notes, articles, job instructions, signs, etc.)

2 | 2 Quantitative materials (materials which deal with quantities or amounts, such as graphs, accounts, specifications, tables of numbers, etc.)

3 | 1 Pictorial materials (pictures or picturelike materials used as *sources* of information, for example, drawings, blueprints, diagrams, maps, tracings, photographic films, x-ray films, TV pictures, etc.)

4 | 1 Patterns/related devices (templates, stencils, patterns, etc., used as *sources* of information when *observed* during use; do *not* include here materials described in item 3 above)

5 | 2 Visual displays (dials, gauges, signal lights, radarscopes, speedometers, clocks, etc.)

6 | 5 Measuring devices (rulers, calipers, tire pressure gauges, scales, thickness gauges, pipettes, thermometers, protractors, etc., used to obtain visual information about physical measurements; do *not* include here devices described in item 5 above)

7 | 4 Mechanical devices (tools, equipment, machinery, and other mechanical devices which are *sources* of information when *observed* during use or operation)

8 | 3 Materials in process (parts, materials, objects, etc., which are *sources* of information when being modified, worked on, or otherwise processed, such as bread dough being mixed, workpiece being turned in a lathe, fabric being cut, shoe being resoled, etc.)

9 | 4 Materials *not* in process (parts, materials, objects, etc., not in the process of being changed or modified, which are *sources* of information when being inspected, handled, packaged, distributed, or selected, etc., such as items or materials in inventory, storage, or distribution channels, items being inspected, etc.)

10 | 3 Features of nature (landscapes, fields, geological samples, vegetation, cloud formations, and other features of nature which are observed or inspected to provide information)

11 | 2 Man-made features of environment (structures, buildings, dams, highways, bridges, docks, railroads, and other "man-made" or altered aspects of the indoor or outdoor environment which are *observed* or *inspected* to provide job information, do not consider equipment, machines, etc., that an individual uses in his work, as covered by item 7)

Note: This exhibits 11 of the "information input" questions or elements. Other PAQ pages contain questions regarding mental processes, work output, relationships with others, job context, and other job characteristics.

Source: From *Position Analysis Questionnaire*, Occupational Research Center, Department of Psychological Sciences, Purdue University. Position Analysis Questionnaire, copyright 1979 by Purdue Research Foundation, West Lafayette, Indiana 47807. Reprinted by permission.

forming skilled activities, being physically active, operating vehicles and/or equipment, and processing information. These scores permit the development of profiles for jobs analyzed and the comparison of jobs.

Like every job analysis technique the PAQ has some advantages and disadvantages. One advantage is that the PAQ has been widely used and researched. The available evidence indicated that it can be and is an effective technique.[20] It is a reliable technique in that there is little variance among job analysts' rating the same jobs. Furthermore, it also seems to be valid in that jobs rated higher with the PAQ prove to be those paying higher compensation rates.

A major problem with the PAQ is its length. It requires time and patience to complete. In addition, since no specific work activities are described, behavioral activities performed in jobs may distort actual task differences in the jobs. For example, a police officer's profile is similar to a homemaker. They both are involved in troubleshooting and crisis-handling situations.[21] There is also research available that suggests that the PAQ is capable of measuring only job stereotypes. The implication of this is that the PAQ may only be providing common knowledge about a job.[22]

Management Positions Description Questionnaire (MPDQ)

Conducting a job analysis for managerial jobs offers a significant challenge to the analyst because of the disparity across positions, levels in the hierarchy, and type of industry (e.g., industrial, medical, government). An attempt to systematically analyze managerial jobs was conducted at Control Data Corporation. The result of this work is the *Management Position Description Questionnaire (MPDQ).*[23]

The MPDQ is a checklist of 208 items related to the concerns and responsibilities of managers. The latest version of the MPDQ is classified into 10 parts.[24]

---

[20] E. J. McCormick, A. S. De Nisi, and J. B. Shaw, "Use of the Position Analysis Questionnaire for Establishing the Job Component Validity of Tests," *Journal of Applied Psychology,* February 1979, pp. 51–56.

[21] Wayne F. Cascio and Elias M. Awad, *Human Resource Management* (Reston, Va.: Reston Publishing, 1981), pp. 157–58.

[22] Angelo S. De Nisi, Edwin T. Cornelius, III, and Allyn G. Blencoe "Further Investigation of Common Knowledge Effects on Job Analysis Ratings," *Journal of Applied Psychology,* May 1987, pp. 262–268 and R. J. Harvey and T. L. Hayes, "Monte Carlo Baselines for Interrater Reliability Correlations Using the Position Analysis Questionnaire, *Personnel Psychology,* Spring 1986, pp. 345–57.

[23] Walter W. Tornow and Patrick R. Pinto, "The Development of a Managerial Job Taxonomy: A System for Describing, Classifying, and Evaluating Executive Positions," *Journal of Applied Psychology,* August 1976, pp. 410–18.

[24] Cascio and Awad, *Human Resource Management,* pp. 158–59.

1. General information.
2. Decision making.
3. Planning and organizing.
4. Supervising and controlling.
5. Consulting and innovating.
6. Contacts.
7. Monitoring business indicators.
8. Overall ratings.
9. Know-how.
10. Organization chart.

Part 6 of the MPDQ is presented in Exhibit 4–10. The job incumbent (manager) responds to the type of questions shown in Exhibit 4–10. These responses are then used to update job descriptions, identify career ladders and facilitate career planning, validate managerial performance appraisal scales, and explore new job evaluation methods.

There are many other specific job analysis techniques available. For the most part the FJA and the MPDQ are job focused and the PAQ is individual or behavior focused. The FJA and MPDQ focus on job activities, while the PAQ is designed to describe jobs in terms of standard behaviors and activities. When a specific job analysis technique provides a reliable and valid quantitative score, jobs can be classified for such purposes as compensation, training, and career development. The quantification feature is an important reason why the FJA and PAQ techniques are so popular.

Instead of using one of the four job analysis methods, Tim Huggins decided to develop a tailor-made, six-page questionnaire for Sprowl. Whether this job analysis will yield reliable or valid data is an issue he should have considered. The opening P/HRM In Action suggests that he didn't think enough about this issue before he started the job analysis program at Sprowl. What do you think?

JOB DESCRIPTIONS AND JOB SPECIFICATIONS

As previously mentioned, the job description (see Exhibit 4–2) is one of the outputs provided by a systematic job analysis. It provides a description of what the job entails. While there is no standard format for a job description, it usually includes:[25]

Job title. A title of the job. The *Dictionary of Occupational Titles* contains over 20,000 titles.

Job summary. A brief one- or two-sentence statement of what the job entails.

Job activities. A description of the tasks performed, material used, and extent of supervision given or received.

---

[25] Mark A. Jones, "Job Descriptions Made Easy," *Personnel Journal,* May 1984, pp. 31–34.

Working conditions and physical environment. Heat, lighting, noise level, and hazardous conditions are described.

Social environment. Information on size of work group and interpersonal interaction required to perform the job.

Exhibit 4–11 presents a job description for a personnel/human resource manager.

The job specification shown in Exhibit 4–12 evolves from the job description. It addresses the question "What personal traits and experience are needed to perform the job effectively?" The job specification offers guidelines for recruitment and selection. For example, suppose that you were looking for a trained and experienced machinist. The job specification would probably indicate the need for formal training and previous work experience. If certain traits and experience are stated as requirements to perform a job they must be shown to be needed to do the work.

Federal and state legislation has placed new emphasis on job descriptions and job specifications. For example, the Equal Pay Act requires equal pay for all employees performing equal work (in terms of equal effort, skill, ability, and working conditions).[26] Therefore, the job description and job specification are consulted to determine compliance with the law. To the extent that job specifications (e.g., height, weight, educational requirements, etc.) are not essential for effective job performance, they may violate Title VII of the 1964 Civil Rights Act.

JOB DESIGN

The information provided by job analysis, job descriptions, and job specifications can be very useful in designing jobs; that is, structuring job elements, duties, and tasks in a manner to achieve optimal performance and satisfaction. There is no one best way to design any job. Different situations call for different arrangements of job characteristics. Two of the many available approaches to job design are the rational approach and job enrichment.

The Rational Approach

Job design was central to the view of scientific management by F. W. Taylor. In 1911, he stated:

> Perhaps the most prominent single element in modern scientific management is the task idea. The work of every workman is fully planned out by the management at least one day in advance, and each man receives in

---

[26] Philip C. Grant, "What Use Is A Job Description?" *Personnel Journal,* February 1988, pp. 44–53 and James Brennan, "Job Descriptions and Pay: The Inevitable Link," *Personnel Journal,* July 1984, p. 18.

EXHIBIT 4–10   Contacts

To achieve organizational goals, managers and consultants may be required to communicate with employees at many levels within the corporation and with influential people outside the corporation.

The purposes of these contacts may include such functions as:

- Informing
- Receiving information
- Influencing
- Promoting
- Selling
- Directing
- Coordinating
- Integrating
- Negotiating

DIRECTIONS:

Describe the nature of your contacts by completing the charts on the opposite page as follows:

STEP 1

Mark an "X" in the box to the left of the kinds of individuals that represent your major contacts internal and external to Control Data Corporation.

STEP 2

For each contact checked, print a number between 0 and 4 in *each* column to indicate how significant a part of your position that PURPOSE is. (Remember to consider both its *importance* in light of all other position activities and its *frequency* of occurrence.)

0-***Definitely not*** a part of the position.
1-A ***minor*** part of the position.
2-A ***moderate*** part of the position.
3-A ***substantial*** part of the position.
4-A ***crucial*** and ***most significant*** part of the position.

STEP 3

If you have any other contacts please elaborate on their nature and purpose below.

226 _____
_____
_____
_____
_____
_____
_____
_____
_____
_____

EXHIBIT 4–10 *(concluded)*

STEP 1   **STEP 2**

CONTACTS	PURPOSE		

INTERNAL	Share information regarding past, present or anticipated activities or decisions	Influence others to act or decide in a manner consistent with my objectives	Direct and/or integrate the plans, activities, or decisions of others
Executive or senior vice president and above 159	167	175	183
Vice president 160	168	176	184
General/regional manager, 161 director, or executive consultant	169	177	185
Department/district manager, or senior consultant 162	170	178	186
Section/branch manager or consultant 163	171	179	187
Unit manager 164	172	180	188
Exempt employees 165	173	181	189
Nonexempt employees 166	174	182	190

EXTERNAL	Provide, obtain or exchange information or advice.	Promote the organization or its products/ services.	Sell products/ services.	Negotiate contracts, settlements, etc.
Customers at a level equivalent to or above a Control Data general/ regional manager 191	198	205	212	219
Customers at a level lower than a Control Data general/ regional manager 192	199	206	213	220
Representatives of major suppliers, for example, joint ventures, subcontractors for major contracts 193	200	207	214	221
Employees of suppliers who provide Control Data with parts or services 194	201	208	215	222
Representatives of influential community organizations 195	202	209	216	223
Individuals such as applicants, stockholders 196	203	210	217	224
Representatives of federal or state governments such as defense contract auditors, government inspectors, etc. 197	204	211	218	225

EXHIBIT 4–11   **Job Description of a Manager**

JOB TITLE: PERSONNEL/HUMAN   Department: P/HRM
           RESOURCE MANAGER   Date: Jan. 1, 1989

General Description of the Job

Performs responsible administrative work managing personnel activities of a large state
agency or institution. Work involves responsibility for the planning and administration of a
P/HRM program that includes recruitment, examination, selection, evaluation, appointment,
promotion, transfer, and recommended change of status of agency employees, and a system of
communication for disseminating necessary information to workers. Works under general
supervision, exercising initiative and independent judgment in the performance of assigned
tasks.

Job Activities

Participates in overall planning and policymaking to provide effective and uniform personnel
    services.
Communicates policy through organization levels by bulletin, meetings, and personal contact.
Interviews applicants, evaluates qualifications, classifies applications.
Recruits and screens applicants to fill vacancies and reviews applications of qualified persons.
Confers with supervisors on personnel matters, including placement problems, retention or
    release of probationary employees, transfers, demotions, and dismissals of permanent
    employees.
Supervises administration of tests.
Initiates personnel training activities and coordinates these activities with work of officials and
    supervisors.
Establishes effective service rating system, trains unit supervisors in making employee
    evaluations.
Maintains employee personnel files.
Supervises a group of employees directly and through subordinates.
Performs related work as assigned.

> most cases complete written instructions, describing in detail the task
> which he is to accomplish. . . . This task specifies not only what is to be
> done but how it is to be done and the exact time allowed for doing it.[27]

The principles offered today by scientific management to job design remain
today as follows:

- Work should be scientifically studied (note: this is what job analysis attempts to do).
- Work should be arranged so that workers can be efficient.
- Employees selected for work should be matched to the demands of the job
  (note: job description and job specification used in recruitment and selection
  should achieve this).
- Employees should be trained to perform the job.
- Monetary compensation should be used to reward successful performance of
  the job.

---

[27] F. W. Taylor, *The Principles of Scientific Management* (New York: Harper & Row, 1911), p.
21.

EXHIBIT 4-12 Job Specification for Personnel/Human Resource Manager

General Qualification Requirements

Experience and Training
  Should have considerable experience in area of P/HRM administration. Six-year minimum.

Education
  Graduation from a four-year college or university, with major work in personnel, business administration, or industrial psychology.

Knowledge, Skills, and Abilities
  Considerable knowledge of principles and practices of P/HRM selection and assignment of personnel; job evaluation.

Responsibility
  Supervises a department of three P/HRM professionals, one clerk, and one secretary.

Although these scientific management principles were introduced around the early 1900s, they are still significant today. The work of Taylor and scientific management principles initiated interest in research and studying jobs. For example, large research efforts have been devoted to analyzing jobs so that information is available for making rational recruitment, selection, training, compensation, and career development decisions.

Many managers find scientific management principles to job design appealing because they point toward increased organizational performance. Jobs designed according to the principles tend to be specialized (the job incumbent performs only a few duties) and routine (the same duties are repeated again and again). It is assumed that specialization and routineness result in job incumbents' becoming experts rather quickly. This then leads to high levels of output and only minimum training to master the job.

Despite the assumed gains in efficiency, behavioral scientists have found that some job incumbents dislike specialized and routine jobs.[28] These workers are not challenged enough to satisfy their need for growth, recognition, and responsibility. When jobs are viewed in this way, workers often attempt to compensate by being absent, resorting to horseplay while on the job, and even quitting.

Although scientific management has introduced important rational guidelines, the bottom line is that the principles do not work for all individuals. Likewise a program of job enrichment is suited for some employees but may be detrimental to other employees.

A Behavioral Approach: Job Enrichment

In the past two decades, much work has been directed to changing jobs so that job incumbents can satisfy their needs for growth, recognition, and responsibility. Herzberg's research popularized the notion of enhancing need satisfaction

---

[28] David A. Nadler, J. Richard Hackman, and Edward E. Lawler, III, *Managing Organizational Behavior* (Boston: Little, Brown, 1979), p. 79.

EXHIBIT 4–13 Key Job Core Dimensions

Skill variety	The degree to which the job requires a variety of different activities in carrying out the work, which involves the use of a number of an individual's skills and talents.
Task identity	The degree to which the job requires completion of a "whole" and identifiable piece of work—that is, doing a job from beginning to end with a visible outcome.
Task significance	The degree to which the job has a substantial impact on the lives or work of other people—whether in the immediate organization or in the external environment.
Autonomy	The degree to which the job provides substantial freedom, independence, and discretion to the individual in scheduling the work and in determining the procedures to be used in carrying it out.
Feedback	The degree to which carrying out the work activities required by the job results in the individual's obtaining direct and clear information about the effectiveness of his or her performance.

through what is called *job enrichment*.[29] There are many different approaches to job enrichment, yet all of them attempt to help the job incumbent satisfy personal needs while performing the job.

One widely publicized approach to job enrichment uses what is referred to as the **job characteristics model**.[30] The model is based on the view that three key psychological states of a job incumbent affect motivation and satisfaction on the job. The three states are:

1. *Experienced meaningfulness*. The degree to which the job incumbent experiences work as important, valuable, and worthwhile.
2. *Experienced responsibility*. The extent to which the job incumbent feels personally responsible and accountable for the results of the work performed.
3. *Knowledge of results*. The understanding that a job incumbent receives about how effectively he or she is performing the job.

The more these three states are experienced, the more the job incumbent will feel internal work motivation. To the extent that these three states are important for the job incumbent, he or she will be motivated to perform well.

Research has indicated a number of core job dimensions that lead to these psychological states.[31] Exhibit 4–13 presents the five core job dimensions, while Exhibit 4–14 illustrates the job characteristics model.

---

[29] F. Herzberg, B. Mausner, and B. Snyderman, *The Motivation to Work* (New York: John Wiley & Sons, 1959).

[30] Richard Hackman, "Work Design," in J. Richard Hackman and J. L. Suttle, *Improving Life at Work* (Santa Monica, Calif.: Goodyear Publishing, 1976), pp. 96–162.

[31] Richard Hackman and R. G. Oldham, "Motivation through the Design of Work: Test of a Theory," *Organizational Behavior and Human Performance*, August 1976, pp. 250–79, and J. Richard Hackman, G. Oldham, R. Janson, and K. Purdy, "A New Strategy for Job Enrichment," *California Management Review*, Summer 1975, pp. 57–71.

EXHIBIT 4-14   The Job Characteristics Mode of Work Motivation

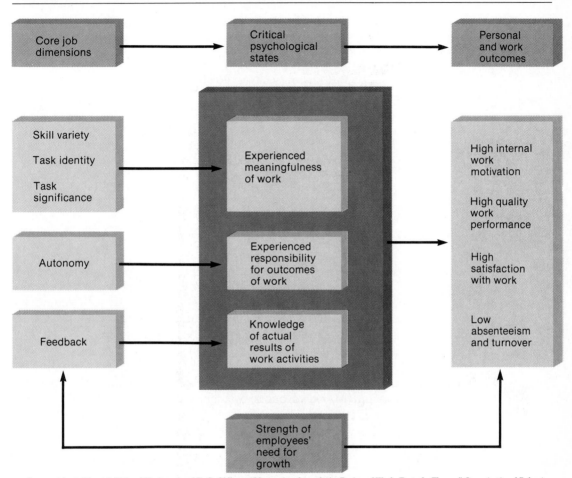

Source: Adapted from J. Richard Hackman and R. G. Oldham, "Motivation through the Design of Work: Test of a Theory," *Organizational Behavior and Human Performance*, August 1976, p. 256.

As presented in Exhibit 4-13, three job dimensions—**skill variety, task identity,** and **task significance** all contribute to a sense of meaningfulness. **Autonomy** is directly related to feelings of responsibility. The more control job incumbents have over the job, the more they feel responsible. **Feedback** is related to knowledge of results.

The job characteristics model presents four sets of factors—core job dimensions, psychological states, personal and work outcomes, and need strength. Since different people have different capabilities and needs, it is important to be aware of individual differences that can moderate the linkages shown in Exhibit 4-14. If a person does not have a need for growth, job enrichment in any or all of the job core dimensions will probably have little impact.

Work behavior and individual job incumbent feelings appear to be more

---

EXHIBIT 4–15   Degree of Individual of Job Match

Degree of Job Enrichment	Intensity of Desire for Job Enrichment	
	High	**Low**
Enriched	"Match" 1. Performance quality is high. 2. Satisfaction is high. 3. Absenteeism and turnover are low.	"Mismatch" 1. Employee is overwhelmed and possibly confused. 2. Performance is poor. 3. Absenteeism and turnover are high.
Simple	"Mismatch" 1. Employees feel underutilized. 2. Job satisfaction is low. 3. Absenteeism and turnover are high.	"Match" 1. Employees can be motivated by pay incentives in the absence of intrinsic motivation. 2. Performance is high.

---

positive where there is a fit between the job and the person. Exhibit 4–15 depicts the results of a match and mismatch between individuals and the job.[32] The managerial implication of Exhibit 4–15 is that not all jobs should be designed to be high on the core job dimensions, and that the personal traits and characteristics of the persons holding the job must be considered.

The job analysis, job description, and job specification can be extremely valuable in determining whether or not a job can be enriched on any of the five core job dimensions. Thus, before job enrichment is even attempted two actions seem to be needed. First, the job has to be thoroughly understood. Job analysis can provide this needed information. Second, individual preferences about job enrichment need to be considered. Does the employee want job enrichment? Can he or she tolerate an enriched job?

Prudential Life Insurances' Job Enrichment Program The chief executive officer of Prudential decided that all jobs at Prudential should be made as interesting as possible. Each unit was charged with redesigning its own jobs with special attention to be paid to enrichment. The workers redesigned their jobs. The results were impressive:

- 57 percent of the units reported improvements in employee attitudes; only 4 percent indicated a deterioration.
- 31 percent of the units reported a decrease in turnover; only 5 percent reported an increase.
- 93 percent of the units indicated that the abilities of workers were being more fully utilized.

---

[32] John P. Wanous, "Who Wants Job Enrichment?" *S.A.M. Advanced Management Journal,* Summer 1976, pp. 15–22.

[33] James O'Toole, *Making America Work* (New York: Continuum, 1981), pp. 67–68.

General Food's Topeka Plant Job Enrichment Program General Foods constructed a new plant to manufacture pet foods. Management worked at designing a plant that contained enriched jobs—maximum variety, autonomy, and feedback.[34] The early results in the new plant were outstanding:

- Quality control improved.
- Turnover was down.
- Job attitudes were better than at other plants.
- Cost savings amounted to about $2 million per year.

These successes, however, began to fade about five or six years after the plant was built. One former employee noted:

> Creating a system is different from maintaining it. There were pressures almost from the inception, and not because the system didn't work. The basic reason was power. We flexed in the face of corporate policy. People like stable states. This system has to be changing or it will die.

In fact, 70 workers ran the entire Topeka operation. The need for middle managers in the plant was eliminated. The result of the new plant arrangement was a power struggle of managers versus workers. Lyman Ketchum (the manager who had thought up the redesign experiment) was fired.

The Prudential experiment was a success, while the Topeka plant experiment with job enrichment resulted in mixed findings—some successes and some failures. These two cases illustrate that job enrichment, or any redesign strategy, is not always successful. Some of the common problems with job enrichment reported in the management and P/HRM literature include:

1. Technological constraints—the job simply can't be enriched because of machine constraints.
2. Costs—the costs of starting and sustaining job enrichment for tools, training, and consultants are often high.
3. Failure to recognize job incumbent preferences—not everyone wants an enriched job.
4. Mickey Mouse changes—minor, insignificant changes in core dimensions are called job enrichment; they are so minor that they have no impact.
5. Managerial and union resistance—managers are sometimes threatened by increased subordinate autonomy. The union also may feel threatened because it sees its power base shrinking.[35]

Job design is a process that influences the behavior and attitude of a job incumbent. The job is so important that it needs to be clearly understood, as

---

[34] Richard E. Walton, "Teaching an Old Dog New Tricks," *Wharton Magazine,* Winter 1978, pp. 38–48.

[35] M. Fein, "Job Enrichment: A Revolution," *Sloan Management Review,* Winter 1974, pp. 69–88; and E. A. Locke, D. Sirota, and A. D. Wolfson, "An Experimental Case Study of the Successes and Failures of Job Enrichment in a Government Agency," *Journal of Applied Psychology,* December 1976, pp. 701–11.

A RETURN TO THE P/HRM ‣ IN ‣ ACTION

Tim Huggins

What do you now think about Tim Huggins' job analysis process? Do you now see why some type of training in job analysis is required? Tim really lacked sufficient training, and this lack was clearly revealed as the process got out of hand. Using questionnaires requires preparation and careful initial steps. A trained job analyst knows that distribution of questionnaires without an explanation is bound to set off negative feelings. Tim failed to plan thoroughly what he wanted to do. He was a new boss, and this alone is threatening to many people. A new person has to establish rapport with the employees before changing things. In the case of Sprowl manufacturing, Tim's haste and poor preparation has now reached the boiling point. He needs to backtrack and slow down. Perhaps the distribution of memos, open discussions with informal leaders, and using the expertise of trained job analysts can improve the atmosphere at Sprowl.

What would you advise him to do about job analysis at this point?

well as modified in many situations. Jobs are not something that exist in a vacuum. They are dynamic and changing. Consequently, job analysis is an important technique that can capture and change the nature of jobs so that the best job design decisions can be made and implemented. P/HRM managers are involved in both job analysis decisions and decisions that reflect on job design. Exhibit 4–16 provides recommendations for use of job analysis and job design in terms of model organizations.

EXHIBIT 4–16 Recommendations for Job Analysis and Job Design for Model Organizations

Type of Organization	Has a Permanent Job Analysis Unit	Use of JAIF-Type Instrument	Formal Job Analysis Program	Observation Method Used	Interview Method Used	Questionnaire Method Used	Diary/Log Method Used
1. Large size, low complexity, high stability		X	X		X	X	
2. Medium size, low complexity, high stability		X	X		X	X	
3. Small size, low complexity, high stability		X	X		X	X	X
4. Medium size, moderate complexity, moderate stability	X	X	X	X	X	X	
5. Large size, high complexity, low stability	X	X	X	X	X	X	
6. Medium size, high complexity, low stability	X	X	X	X	X	X	
7. Small size, high complexity, low stability		X	X	X	X	X	X

SUMMARY

This chapter has emphasized the major role that job analysis plays in P/HRM activities and programs. Each part of the diagnostic P/HRM model is in some way affected by job analysis. The job is the major building block of an organization. Therefore, it is essential that each characteristic of the job's presence in an organization is clearly understood.

To summarize the major points covered in this chapter:

1. There are six sequential steps in job analysis, starting with examining the total organization and fit of jobs and concluding with the preparation of a job specification (see Exhibit 4–1).
2. The uses of job analysis information seem endless. Recruitment, selection, training, compensation, and job design actions all benefit immensely from job analysis information.
3. Job analysis is not for amateurs to conduct. Training is required.
4. Before conducting a job analysis, organization and process charts should be consulted to acquire an overview of the organization.
5. Four general job analysis techniques can be used separately or in some combination. They are observation, interviews, questionnaires, and job incumbent diary/logs.
6. Functional job analysis (FJA) is used to describe the nature of jobs, prepare job descriptions, and provide details on employee job specifications. The job is described in terms of data, people, and things.
7. The *Dictionary of Occupational Titles* is a listing of over 20,000 jobs on the basis of occupational code, title, industry.
8. The Position Analysis Questionnaire (PAQ) is a 194-item structured instrument used to quantitatively assess jobs on the basis of decision making, communication/social responsibilities, performing skilled activities, being physically active, operating vehicles and/or equipment, and processing information.
9. The Management Position Questionnaire (MPDQ) is a checklist of 208 items that assesses the concerns and responsibilities of managers.
10. Job design involves structuring job elements, duties, and tasks to achieve optimal performance and satisfaction.
11. Job design was a concern of F. W. Taylor, the famous industrial engineer and father of what is called scientific management.
12. Job enrichment involves designing jobs so that job incumbent needs for growth, recognition, and responsibility are satisfied.

EXERCISE 4–1   Conducting A Job Analysis

Objective: This exercise is designed to permit students to become familiar with the U.S. Department of Labor method and form for conducting a functional job analysis.

SET UP THE EXERCISE

1. Reread the discussion of functional job analysis (FJA) in the chapter.
2. Secure a copy of the *Handbook For Analyzing Jobs* (U.S. Government: Department of Labor). Your school or local library will have a copy of the Handbook.
3. Set up groups of four or five students. After reading the *Handbook* on job analysis your instructor will assign the following jobs—one to each group.

   A. Police officer   F. Prison warden
   B. Lathe operator   G. Military officer
   C. Computer programmer   H. Radio disc jockey
   D. Movie stunt artist   I. Tennis coach
   E. Airplane pilot   J. Operating room nurse
4. Complete the job analysis form for the assigned job. Meet with your group to discuss similarities and differences in the job analysis.

A Learning Note

This exercise will illustrate the difficulty in conducting a job analysis and in reaching a consensus among analysts.

1. ESTABLISH JOB TITLE _____

2. JOB SUMMARY:

3. WORK PERFORMED RATINGS

Worker functions	D Data	P People	T Things

   Work Field _____

4. WORKER TRAITS RATINGS

GED	1 2 3 4 5 6 __ __ __ __ __ __ __ __ __
SVP	1 2 3 4 5 6 7 8 9
Aptitudes	G __ V __ N __ S __ P __ Q __ K __ F __ M __ E __ C __
Temperaments	D F I J M P R S T V
Interests	1a 1b 2a 2b 3a 3b 4a 4b 5a 5b
Phys. demands	S L M H V 2 3 4 5 6
Environ. cond.	1) B 2 3 4 5 6 7

5. GENERAL EDUCATION
   a. Elementary _____ High school _____ Courses _____
   b. College _____ Courses _____

6. VOCATIONAL PREPARATION
    a. College _____ Courses _____
    _____
    b. Vocational education _____ Courses _____
    _____
    c. Apprenticeship _____
    _____
    d. Inplant training _____
    _____
    e. On-the-job training _____
    f. Performance on other jobs _____

7. EXPERIENCE _____

8. ORIENTATION _____

9. LICENSES, etc. _____

10. RELATION TO OTHER JOBS AND WORKERS
    Promotion: From _____ To _____
    Transfers: From _____ To _____
    Supervision received _____
    Supervision given _____

11. MACHINES, TOOLS, EQUIPMENT, AND WORK AIDS

12. MATERIALS AND PRODUCTS

13. DESCRIPTION OF TASKS

14. DEFINITION OF TERMS

15. GENERAL COMMENTS

Questions for Review and Discussion

1. What role could job analysis play in the recruitment and selection of employees?
2. Are job descriptions the same as job specifications?
3. What role can a properly coordinated and valid job analysis play in a legal case concerning performance appraisal or promotion?
4. What are the six major steps in the job analysis process?
5. Why would a manager be interested in using a combination of job analysis methods to collect information?
6. What is the problem with the claim that, "All jobs should be enriched"?
7. What is the job characteristics model?
8. It is claimed that "Job analysis is the cornerstone to all P/HRM activities." Do you agree? Explain.
9. Why is the PAQ considered a behavior focused and quantitative job analysis technique?
10. Should managerial jobs be subjected to job analysis? Why?

GLOSSARY

Autonomy. The degree to which the job provides substantial freedom, independence, and discretion to the individual in scheduling the work and in determining the procedures to be used in carrying it out.

Feedback. The degree to which carrying out the work activities required by the job results in the individual's obtaining direct and clear information about the effectiveness of his or her performance.

Functional Job Analysis (FJA). A job analysis method that attempts to identify what a worker does in performing a job in terms of data, people, and things.

Job. A group of positions that are similar in their duties, such as a computer programmer or compensation specialist.

Job Analysis. The process of defining a job in terms of tasks or behaviors and specifying the education, training, and responsibilities needed to perform the job successfully.

Job Analysis Information Format. A questionnaire that provides the core information about a job, job duties, and job requirements.

Job Characteristics Model. A mode of job design that is based on the view that three psychological states toward a job affect a person's motivation and satisfaction level. These states are experienced meaningfulness, experienced responsibility, and knowledge of results. A job's skill variety, identity, and task significance contribute to meaningfulness; autonomy is related to responsibility; and feedback is related to knowledge of results.

Job Description. The job analysis provides information about the job that results in a description of what the job entails.

Job Enrichment. A method of designing a job so that employees can satisfy needs while performing the job. The job characteristics model is used in establishing a job enrichment strategy.

Job Family. A group of two or more jobs that have similar job duties.

Job Specification. The job analysis also results in the specification of what kind of traits and experience are needed to perform the job.

Management Position Description Questionnaire (MPDQ). A checklist of 208 items related to concerns and responsibilities of managers.

Position. The responsibilities and duties performed by an individual. There are as many positions as there are employees.

Position Analysis Questionnaire (PAQ). A structured questionnaire of 194 items used to quantitatively assess jobs. It assesses information input, mental processes, work output, relationships, job contacts, and various other characteristics.

Process Chart. A chart that displays how jobs are linked or related to each other.

Skill Variety. The degree to which the job requires a variety of different activities in carrying out the work, which involves the use of a number of an individual's skills and talents.

Task. A coordinated and aggregated series of work elements used to produce an output (units of production or service to a client).

Task Identity. The degree to which the job requires completion of a "whole" and identifiable piece of work—that is, doing a job from beginning to end with a visible outcome.

Task Significance. The degree to which the job has a substantial impact on the lives or work of other people—whether in the immediate organization or the external environment.

HUMAN RESOURCE PLANNING

LEARNING OBJECTIVES

After studying this chapter, you should be able to:

- **Discuss** the importance of human resource planning in organizations of any size.
- **Describe** how the managers forecast demand for and analyze the supply of employees in the organization.
- **List** four forecasting techniques that are used in personnel and employment planning.
- **Define** what is meant by the terms *skills inventory* and *replacement chart*.
- **Identify** reasons why a computerized human resource planning system could be useful to an organization.

KEY TERMS

Handicapped Person
Human Resource Information System
Human Resource Planning
Replacement Chart
Skills Inventory

CHAPTER OUTLINE

P/HRM · IN · ACTION

Ted Sloane and Anne Wilson

"What do you mean we're going to lose the government contract?" asked the company president, Ted Sloane.

"We're going to lose it," said the personnel/human resource management vice president, Anne Wilson. "We don't have trained personnel to meet the contract specifications. We have to furnish records to show that we have an adequate number of employees with the right technical qualifications who meet the government's equal employ- ment opportunity goals. I don't have those kinds of records available at a moment's notice. You know I asked you to let me set up a human resource information system (HRIS). "Why didn't we get around to it?"

Ted didn't know what Anne had in mind. Everything he ever heard about computer systems suggested that they were expensive and complex. He wanted to learn more about HRIS.

Experiences like Ted's are common and suggest that many managers fail to plan for human resource needs. They never know what their needs are because they neglect human resource planning.

> Human resource planning is the process that helps to provide adequate human resources to achieve future organizational objectives. It includes forecasting future needs for employees of various types, comparing these needs with the present work force, and determining the numbers and types of employees to be recruited or phased out of the organization's employment group.

People are asking: "How do I get promoted? When will I be promoted? Will I have to relocate to be promoted? What is my future going to be?[1] Human

---

[1] See Charles F. Russ, Jr., "Manpower Planning Systems: Part I," *Personnel Journal,* January 1982, pp. 40–45; and Charles F. Russ, Jr., "Manpower Planning Systems: Part II," *Personnel Journal,* February 1982, pp. 119–24.

resource planning is a process that provides answers to these questions. Employees should know about the opportunities, plans, and development programs that exist for them.[2]

INTRODUCTION TO HUMAN RESOURCE PLANNING

Exhibit 5–1 models the human resource planning process. As the model indicates, top management examines the environment, analyzes the strategic advantages of the organization, and sets objectives for the coming period. Then the manager makes strategic and operating decisions to achieve the objectives of the organization. The P/HRM capabilities of the organization are among the factors analyzed in the strategic management process. An example of a strategic decision is General Electric's decision to sell its computer business. This meant that General Electric's supply of employees was cut when the business was sold to another company.

Once the strategy is set, the P/HRM unit does its part to ensure the strategy's success and to achieve the organization's objectives. It does this by comparing the present supply of human resources with projected demand for them. This comparison leads to action decisions: add employees, cut employees, or reallocate employees internally.

Reasons for Human Resource Planning

All organizations perform human resource planning, formally or informally. The formal employment techniques are described in this chapter because informal methods are typically unsatisfactory for organizations requiring skilled human resources in a fast-changing labor market. It is important to point out that most organizations do more talking about formal employment planning than actual performance.[3] Therefore, personnel and employment planning as a P/HRM activity is in Stage II of development, or early development (see Exhibit 1–7).

The major reasons for formal employment planning are to achieve:

- More effective and efficient use of human resources.
- More satisfied and better developed employees.
- More effective equal employment opportunity planning.

---

[2] L. James Harvey, "Effective Planning for Human Resource Development," *Personnel Administrator,* October 1983, pp. 45–52, 112.

[3] W. S. Wikstrom, "Manpower Planning: Evolving Systems," Report no. 521 (New York: Conference Board, 1971).

EXHIBIT 5-1 **The Human Resource Planning Process**

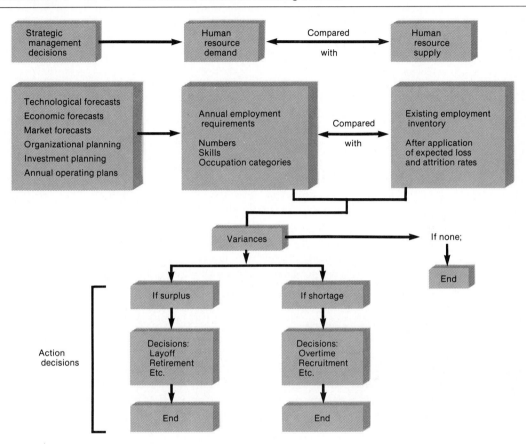

More Effective and Efficient Use of People at Work

Human resource planning should precede all other P/HRM activities. For example, how could you schedule recruiting if you did not know how many people you needed? How could you select effectively if you did not know the kinds of persons needed for job openings? Careful analysis of all P/HRM activities shows that their effectiveness and efficiency, which result in increased productivity, depend on human resource planning.

More Satisfied and Better Developed Employees

Employees who work for organizations that use good human resource planning systems have a better chance to participate in planning their own careers and to share in training and development experiences. Thus, they are likely to feel their talents are important to the employer, and they have a better chance to utilize those talents. This situation often leads to greater employee satisfaction and its consequences: lower absenteeism, lower turnover, fewer accidents, and higher quality of work.

More Effective EEO Planning

As pointed out frequently in this book, government has increased its demands for equal employment opportunities. Information systems that focus on personnel and employment planning to help organizations formally plan employment distribution.[4] Therefore, it is easier to complete the required government reports and respond satisfactorily to EEO demands using human resource planning.

In sum, effective human resource planning ensures that P/HRM activities and programs will be built on a foundation of good planning. Proper planning should cut down on the number of surprises that occur involving human resource availability, placement, and orientation. Not having the right person in the right place at a particular moment is a surprise and usually a problem. These kinds of surprises can be reduced through effective personnel and employment planning.

Who Performs the Planning?

Effectiveness in P/HRM activities requires the efforts and cooperation of P/HRM managers and operating managers. The activities described in this chapter are outlined in Exhibit 5-2, which shows the kind of planning activities that are performed by operating and P/HRM managers.

A DIAGNOSTIC APPROACH TO HUMAN RESOURCE PLANNING

Exhibit 5-3 highlights the factors in the diagnostic model that are most important to planning. One of the most significant factors affecting planning involves the goals of the controlling interests in the organization. If planning and effective utilization of human resources are not a significant goal for the organization, employment planning will not be performed formally, or it will be done in a slipshod manner. If the goals of top management include stable growth, employment planning will be less important than if the goals include

---

[4] A. Charnes, W. W. Cooper, K. A. Lewis, and R. J. Niehaus, "Equal Employment Opportunity Planning and Staffing Models," *Human Resource Planning,* Spring 1978, pp. 103–12.

EXHIBIT 5–2   **Human Resource Activities Performed by P/HRM and Operating Managers**

Human Resource Planning Activities	Operating Manager (OM)	P/HRM Manager
Strategic management decisions	Performed by OM with inputs from P/HRM	Provides information inputs for OM
Forecasting demands		Performed by P/HRM based on strategic management decisions
Job analysis	Provides information inputs for P/HRM	Performed by P/HRM with information inputs from OM
Analysis of supply of employees	Provides information inputs for P/HRM	Performed by P/HRM with information inputs from OM
Work scheduling decisions	Joint responsibility	Joint responsibility
Action decision: Analyzing the composition of the work force		Performed by P/HRM
Action decision: Shortage of employees	Provides information inputs for P/HRM	Performed by P/HRM with information inputs from OM
Action decision: Surplus of employees	Policy decisions by OM with inputs from P/HRM	Implementation decisions by P/HRM

rapid expansion, diversification, or other factors with a significant impact on future employment needs.

Government policies are another important factor in planning. Requirements for equal employment opportunity and promotion call for more personnel planning for women and other employees in minority groups and special categories. Other examples are the government's raising the age of mandatory retirement and the encouragement of hiring handicapped employees and veterans (see Chapter 3).

The conditions in the labor market also have a significant impact on the amount and type of employment planning done in an enterprise. For example, when there is 20 percent unemployment in, for instance, Laredo, Texas, an employer in that city could be more selective than another employer in Dallas, Texas where there is a 5 percent rate of unemployment.

To a lesser extent than the government, unions may restrict the ability to hire and promote employees, so they, too, are a factor in planning. In discussing the planning activity it is more realistic to take into consideration the important role played by the segments highlighted in Exhibit 5–3.

The types of people employed and the tasks they do also determine the kind of planning necessary. Need for unskilled employees does not have to be planned two years ahead; but computer salespersons, for example, need years of training before coming on track. Planning for highly skilled employees usually requires more care and forecasting.

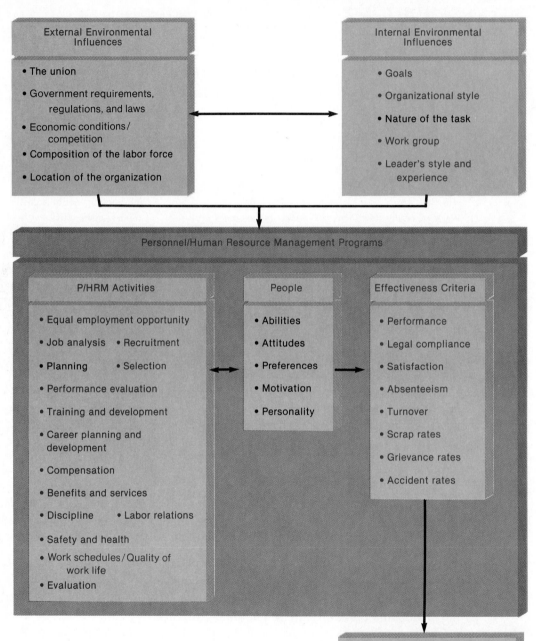

FORECASTING FUTURE DEMAND FOR EMPLOYEES

Forecasting human resource needs is a major concern in the human resource planning process. Forecasting yields the advance estimates or calculations of staffing required to accomplish the organization's objectives. It depends heavily on human judgment, yet since the future is so uncertain, forecasting is sometimes rather imprecise, and is always a considerable challenge. There is no generally recognized forecasting procedure that fits all circumstances and guarantees accurate results.[5] Rather, P/HRM experts and line managers must develop a process that will enable them to have the right numbers and kinds of people in the right place, at the right time, to perform the job.

The techniques of forecasting human resource needs range from the highly subjective to the mathematically complex. In some instances, managerial estimates or guesses of needs are adequate. However, in other circumstances, such as when government law is involved or where competition for individuals with certain skill levels is intense, more advanced and sophisticated techniques are almost required.

Employment Forecasting Techniques

Essentially, there are three organizational approaches to human resource forecasting. The headquarters can forecast the total demand (top-down approach); the units can forecast their own demand (bottom-up approach); or there can be a combination of the two.[6]

Four forecasting techniques will be described here: three top-down techniques—expert estimate, trend projection, and modeling—and the bottom-up unit forecasting technique.

The Expert-Estimate Technique The least sophisticated approach to employment planning—yet the one most frequently used—is for an "expert" to forecast the employment needs based on her or his own experience, intuition, and guess. The P/HRM manager may do this by thinking about past employment levels and questioning future needs. This method is an informal system. The expert-estimate technique can be more effective if the experts use the Delphi technique.

The Delphi technique is a set of procedures originally developed by the Rand Corporation in the late 1940s.[7] Its purpose is to obtain the most reliable consensus of opinion of a group of experts. Basically, the Delphi technique consists of intensive questioning of each expert, through a series of question-

---

[5] Walker, *Human Resource Planning,* p. 100.

[6] D. J. Bartholomew, ed., *Manpower Planning* (Harmansworth, England: Penguin Books, 1976). Also see Kendrith M. Rowland and Scott L. Summers, "Human Resource Planning: A Second Look," *Personnel Administrator,* December 1981, pp. 73–80.

[7] N. Dalkey, *The Delphi Method: An Experimental Study of Group Opinion* (Santa Monica, Calif.: Rand, 1969).

naires, to obtain data that can be used to make "educated" forecasts. The procedures are designed to avoid direct meetings between the experts in order to maximize independent thinking.

A person who serves as intermediary in the questioning sends the questionnaires to the experts and asks them to give, for example, their best estimates of employment needs for the coming year. The intermediary prepares a summary of the results, calculating the average response and the most extreme answers. Then the experts are asked to estimate the number again. Usually the questionnaires and responses tend to narrow down over these rounds. The average number is then used as the forecast.

A forecast by a single expert is the most frequently used approach to forecasting employment. It works well in small- and middle-sized enterprises that are in stable environments. However, the Delphi technique improves these estimates in larger and more volatile organizations.

The Trend Projection Technique The second technique is to develop a forecast based on a past relationship between a factor related to employment and employment itself. For example, in many businesses, sales levels are related to employment needs. The planner can develop a table or graph showing past relationships between sales and employment. Exhibit 5–4 gives an example of a trend projection forecast for a hypothetical company, Rugby Sporting Goods Company. Note that as Rugby's sales increased, so did the firm's employment needs. But the increases were not linear. Suppose that in late 1985 Rugby instituted a productivity plan that led to 3 percent increased productivity per year. As Rugby forecasted employee needs, it adjusted them for expected productivity gains for 1989 and 1990.

Trend projection is a frequently used technique, though not as widely used as expert-estimate or unit demand. Trend projections are an inexpensive way to forecast employment needs.

EXHIBIT 5–4   Sample Trend Protection Employment Forecast for Rugby Sporting Goods Company

Year Actual Data	Sales	Employee Census	Employee Forecast Adjusted for Annual Productivity Rate Increase of 3 Percent
1985	$100,000,000	5,000	5,000
1986	120,000,000	6,000	5,825
1987	140,000,000	7,000	6,598
1988	160,000,000	8,000	7,321
Forecast	**Sales Forecast**	**Employee Forecast**	
1989	$180,000,000	9,000	7,996
1990	200,000,000	10,000	8,626

EXHIBIT 5–5   Movement of Nurses Changes during 1988

Hospital	1988 Level of Nurses	Gain	Loss	1989 Level of Nurses
I	200	60	40	220
II	500	40	50	490
III	300	35	45	290

Modeling and Multiple-Predictive Techniques The third top-down approach to prediction of demand uses the most sophisticated forecasting and modeling techniques. Trend projections are based on relating a single factor (such as sales) to employment. The more advanced approaches relate many factors to employment, such as sales, gross national product, and discretionary income. Or they mathematically model the organization and use simulations, utilizing such methods as Markov models and analytical formulations such as regression analysis. These are the most costly approaches to employment forecasting because of the cost of computer time and salaries of highly paid experts to design the models.

The use of the Markov chain analysis involves developing a matrix. This matrix shows the probability of an employee moving from one position to another or leaving the organization. A full treatment of P/HRM applications of Markov analysis is found in management science or operations management literature.[8]

Markov analysis begins with an analysis of staffing levels in various levels from one period to another time period. Suppose that professional nursing employees have shifted from hospital I, II, and III in the Houston Medical Center complex. That is, they quit working in one hospital and went to work for another in the Medical Center (i.e., a complex of 11 hospitals in Houston that employs approximately 30,000 people). A P/HRM specialist in hospital I is interested in analyzing the human resource shifts that are occurring between her hospital and hospitals II and III. Exhibit 5–5 illustrates the movement of nurses.

The P/HRM specialists could next calculate transition probabilities for all three hospitals. That is, the probability that a hospital will retain its nurses can be calculated. Exhibit 5–6 illustrates the transition probabilities for the retention of professional nurses.

The data in Exhibit 5–6 indicate that hospital I has a probability of .80 of retaining its nurses. On the other hand, hospital II has a probability of .90 of retaining its nurses, and hospital III has a probability of .85 of retaining its nurses. Both hospitals II and III have a higher probability of retaining their nursing staff. Therefore, the P/HRM specialist in hospital I needs to study

---

[8] Richard I. Levin and Charles A. Kirkpatrick, *Quantitative Approaches to Management* (New York: McGraw-Hill, 1980).

EXHIBIT 5-6   Nurse Transition Probabilities

Hospital	1988	Nurses Lost	Nurses Retained	Probability of Retention
I	200	40	160	160/200 = .80
II	500	50	450	450/500 = .90
III	300	45	255	255/300 = .85

further the issue of why her hospital has a lower probability of retention. Is it because of some particular P/HRM program? Markov analysis can help identify the lower retention probability, but it does not suggest any particular solution to the potential problem.

Regression analysis is a mathematical procedure in which predictions of the dependent variable are made through knowledge of factors known as *independent variables*.[9] When only one dependent and one independent variable are studied, the process is known as *simple linear regression*. When there is more than one independent variable being considered, the technique used is referred to as *multiple regression*.

Most uses of multiple regression emphasize prediction from two or more independent variables, X_i, to a dependent variable, Y. For example, suppose a P/HRM manager wants to predict how many manufacturing workers are needed. Assume that the manager is attempting to predict the number of workers (the dependent variable) by using sales, efficiency of the work force, and productivity per worker as the independent variables.

A simplified example of an application of regression analysis is presented in Exhibit 5-7. The number of lathe operators (the dependent variable) is predicted by the level of production. Data compiled by the organization for the years 1977 to 1988 are used to forecast the number of lathe operators needed in 1989. In the example, management assumes that 40,000 units will be produced in 1989.

The discussion of the specific statistical notations and procedures presented in Exhibit 5-7 are beyond the scope of coverage of this book. More details on regression analysis can be found in most applied statistics books.[10]

The Unit Demand Forecasting Technique The unit (which can be an entire department, a project team, or some other group of employees) forecast is a bottom-up approach to forecasting demand. Headquarters sums these unit forecasts, and the result becomes the employment forecast. The unit manager

---

[9] A concise and clear discussion of regression analysis can be found in R. Dennis Middlemist, Michael A. Hitt, and Charles R. Green, *Personnel Management* (Englewood Cliffs, N.J.: Prentice-Hall, 1983), pp. 112–15.

[10] Dennis E. Hinkle, William Wiersma, and Steven G. Jurs, *Applied Statistics for the Behavoral Sciences* (Skokie, Ill.: Rand McNally, 1979); and Fred N. Kerlinger and Elazar J. Pedhazur, *Multiple Regression in Behavioral Research* (New York: Holt, Rinehart & Winston, 1973).

EXHIBIT 5–7 Regression Analysis Demand Forecast

Year (I)	Units of Production (000)(x)	Number of Lathe Operators (y)	$(x_i - \bar{x})$	$(x_i - \bar{x})^2$	$(y_i - \bar{y})$	$(x_i - \bar{x})(y_i - \bar{y})$
1977	11	21	−8	64	−8	64
1978	13	22	−6	36	−7	42
1979	14	23	−5	25	−6	30
1980	14	25	−5	25	−4	20
1981	17	28	−2	4	−1	2
1982	16	30	−3	9	1	−3
1983	19	32	0	0	3	0
1984	21	31	2	4	2	4
1985	20	32	1	1	3	3
1986	24	34	5	25	5	25
1987	28	34	9	81	5	45
1988	31	36	12	144	7	84

$\Sigma x_i = 228$
$\Sigma y_i = 348$
$\Sigma(x_i - \bar{x})^2 = 418$
$\Sigma(x_i - \bar{x})(y_i - \bar{y}) = 316$

$N = 12 \quad \bar{x} = \dfrac{\Sigma x_i}{N} = 19 \quad \bar{y} = \dfrac{\Sigma y_i}{N} = 29$

Simple regression formula:

$y = \alpha + Bx + \epsilon$

where

$B = \dfrac{\Sigma[(x - \bar{x})(y - \bar{y})]}{\Sigma(x - \bar{x})^2} = \dfrac{316}{418} = .76$

$\alpha = \bar{y} - B\bar{x} = 29 - (.76)(19) = 14.56$

ϵ is assumed equal to zero.

Forecast for the 1989 production goal of 40,000 units is:

$Y = 14.56 + (.76)(40) = 44.96 = 45$ lathe operators

Source: Formula adapted from R. S. Pindyck and D. L. Rubenfeld, *Economic Models of Economic Forecasts* (New York: McGraw-Hill, 1976), pp. 11–16.

analyzes the person-by-person, job-by-job needs in the present as well as the future. By analyzing present and future requirements of the job and the skills of the incumbents, this method focuses on quality of workers.

Usually the manager will start with a list of the jobs in the unit by name. This list will also record the number of jobholders for each job. The manager evaluates both the numbers and skills of the present personnel. Consideration is given to the effects of expected losses through retirement, promotion, or other reasons. Whether the losses will require replacement and what the projected growth needs will be are questions the manager must answer and project into his or her calculations in determining net employment needs.

A manager's evaluation that is based on the present number of employees has two assumptions built into it: (1) that the best use has been made of the available personnel, and (2) that demand for the product or service of the unit will be the same for next year as for this. With regard to the first assumption, the manager can examine the job design and workload of each employee. The manager may also attempt to judge the productivity of the employees in the unit by comparing the cost per product or service produced with those of similar units in the organization and others. Past productivity rates can be compared with present ones, after adjusting for changes in the job; or subjective evaluations can be made of the productivity of certain employees compared to others. In addition, it may be necessary to base employment needs on work force analysis, with adjustments for current data on absenteeism and turnover.

The unit analyzes its product or service demand by projecting trends. Using methods similar to the trend technique for the organization, the unit determines if it may need more employees because of a change in product or service demand. Finally, the unit manager prepares an estimate of total employment needs and plans for how the unit can fulfill these needs.

In larger organizations, a P/HRM executive at headquarters who is responsible for the employment demand forecast will improve the estimates by checking with the P/HRM and operating managers in the field. If the units forecast their own needs, the P/HRM executive would sum their estimates, then this becomes the forecast. What happens if both the bottom-up and top-down approaches are used, and the forecasts conflict? In all probability, the manager reconciles the two totals by averaging them or examining more closely the major variances between the two. The Delphi technique could be used to do this. One or several forecast techniques can be used to produce a single employment forecast.

In the employment-demand forecasting aspect of human resource planning, the bottom-up or unit-forecasting method calls for each unit to determine the number of people needed to accomplish the unit's objectives. The basic building blocks of this forecast is the number of jobs to be filled. The number of jobs in a unit can be reduced by more efficient job design, as discussed in Chapter 4. Recall that closely related to job design are job information procedures. Information about jobs is derived from job analysis, job descriptions, and job specifications.

Typically, these four forecasting methods, which use statistics-based techniques and computers, are resisted by some managers.[11] They are resisted because:

- They are made difficult to understand by the forecasters and users of the data and information.
- They are assumed to require an understanding of advanced statistics.
- They are often irrelevant in terms of the overall corporate strategic plan.

---

[11] John D. Gridley, "Who Will Be Where When? Forecast the Easy Way," *Personnel Journal*, May 1986, pp. 50–58.

As the simplified four forecasting examples show, however, these points of resistance can be minimized. Any forecasting method that is to prove itself useful must be understood by the forecasters and users, as accurate and reliable as possible, and linked to the overall corporate strategic plan. Furthermore, the use of advanced statistics, if it is reliable, should be left to experts who have a responsibility to break them down and explain them to nonexperts. Most users of forecasting data and information do not have advanced statistics expertise.

ANALYSIS OF THE SUPPLY OF PRESENT EMPLOYEES

After a manager has projected the employment needs of the organization, the next step in planning is to determine the availability of those presently at work in it—the supply of employees. On the basis of strategic management decisions, the P/HRM manager compares the demand for people needed to achieve the organization's objectives with the present supply of people to determine the need to hire, lay off, promote, or train. These are the *action decisions*.[12] The major tool of analysis used to compute the employment supply is the *skills inventory*. In some organizations, a separate skills inventory, called a *management inventory,* is developed just for the managerial employees.

Good skills inventories enable organizations to determine quickly and expediently what kinds of people with specific skills are presently available, whenever they decide to expand to accept new contracts or change their strategies. Skills inventories are also useful in planning for training, management development, promotion, transfer, and related personnel activities.

> A skills inventory in its simplest form is a list of names, certain characteristics, and skills of the people working for the organization. It provides a way to acquire these data and makes them available where needed in an efficient manner.

For a small organization, it is relatively easy to know how many employees there are, what they do, and what they can do. A mom-and-pop grocery store may employ only the owners and have two part-time helpers to "plan" for. When they see that one part-time employee is going to graduate in June, they know they need to replace him. Sources of supply could include their own children, converting their other part-time helper into a full-time assistant, or the school's employment office.

---

[12] George T. Milkovich and Thomas A. Mahoney, "Human Resource Planning Models: A Perspective," *Human Resource Planning,* Spring 1978, pp. 19–30.

It is quite a different situation with a school system employing hundreds at numerous locations, or such mammoth organizations as Procter & Gamble and IBM. These kinds of organizations must know how many full-time and peripheral employees they have working for them, and where. They must know what skills prospective employees would need to replace people who have quit, retired, or have been fired, or to relocate employees for new functions or more work.

The methods for assessing the labor market range from simple records on 3-by-5-inch index cards to sophisticated statistical and mathematical techniques such as simulation and Markov chain analysis.[13] But the basic tool for assessing the supply of people and talents available within the organization is the skills inventory. Skills inventory tools can range from simple pieces of paper or forms to sophisticated computer information systems.[14] The degree of sophistication necessary is related to the size, complexity, and volatility of the organization.

In smaller manual systems of skills inventories, the data are entered on cards, the more advanced cards having notches or loops that can be "pulled" by the use of long metal bars (Cardex). Thus, if an organization wants to know which employees speak French fluently, it pulls all the cards notched at a particular place or with look 15, for example, on the card. If there are multiple criteria, this subset is then checked for the next characteristic. This can also be done with summary overlays: all those with certain characteristics are punched onto cards; several of these summary cards are laid atop one another, and only those still visible on the last overlay fit the criteria for selection.

At the other extreme are very complex and sophisticated systems.[15] Organizations such as IBM, RCA, and the U.S. Civil Service Commission have computerized inventories that allow them to plan employees' career, monitor career progress, and match the right person with the best job for his or her skills.[16] These systems are referred to as human resource information systems (HRIS).

The HRIS at firms such as General Electric, Bank America, Citicorp, Hitachi, FMC, American Cyanamid, and Southern California Gas, and also at smaller firms, are organized in such a way that they provide information in a timely manner to help make human resource decisions.[17] A HRIS is defined as

---

[13] H. G. Heneman III and M. G. Sandver, "Markov Analysis in Human Resource Administration," *Academy of Management Review,* October 1977, pp. 535–42.

[14] Donald L. Miller, "Computers: A Boon for HRM," *Personnel Administrator,* May 1987, pp. 82–89.

[15] Albert L. Lederer, "Information Technology: I. Planning and Developing a Human Resources Information System," *Personnel,* May-June 1984, pp. 14–27.

[16] George Milkovich, Lee Dyer, and Thomas Mahoney, "HRM Planning" in *Human Resources in the 1980's,* eds. Stephen J. Carroll and Randall S. Schuler (Washington, D.C.: Bureau of National Affairs, 1983), pp. 21–29.

[17] Sidney Simon, "HRIS Uses In Small Companies: An Explanation of Tables," *Personnel Journal,* June 1986, pp. 107–111.

the method used by an organization to collect, store, analyze, report, and evaluate information and data on people, jobs, and costs. Computer technology and HRIS have enabled P/HRM units to play a more active role in strategic planning, integrate personnel information in a simple database and to efficiently and regularly compare costs and benefits of programs, so that assessments of effectiveness can be conducted.

In the organization that maintains records and qualifications for thousands of employees, a manual system is not efficient or even feasible.[18] Thus, to deal with the need to plan for human resource needs, companies such as IBM have computerized their employment planning systems. The IBM system is called IRIS (IBM Recruiting Information System). Employees complete a booklet periodically called a data-pak. They answer questions about age, experience, education, skills, and qualifications. When there is a need to fill a vacancy, a manager describes the position and what he or she is looking for in terms of individual qualifications. The manager's requirements are entered into the computer. The IRIS system is used to match available candidates for the position described by the manager. The manager then receives a computer listing of possible candidates.[19]

Another computerized system is called MicroHRIS. It is a stand-alone human resource information system offered by Personnel Consulting Services, Inc.[20] The database of MicroHRIS provides information regarding employees' personal statistics, EEOC classifications, employees' compensation and performance evaluation, and the firm's benefit structure (life insurance amounts, health insurance coverage, etc.).

Although computers are becoming more prominent in the P/HRM function, little is known about the desire to automate specific P/HRM activities.[21] A study of P/HRM administrators was conducted to determine the future use of computers in the P/HRM area.[22] Exhibit 5–8 indicates the size of the 706 organizations in the final sample and the computer use in various P/HRM activities within the firms. The percentages in the computer application section indicate the proportion of respondents in each group that ranked the particular area in the top five. For example, of the 231 organizations with 500 to 2,000 full-time employees, 111 of them (48.1 percent) ranked recruitment-tracking as one of the five areas they would like to computerize. The findings suggest that organizations of all sizes desire computerized support and help in conducting various P/HRM activities.

---

[18] For an excellent discussion, see "Automating the Human Resource Function," *Employee Relations and Human Resources Bulletin,* Special Report, July 21, 1984, pp. 1–24.

[19] Gary Dessler, *Personnel Management* (Reston, Va.: Reston Publishing, 1984), p. 120.

[20] The 1985 database for organizations is available by contacting Personnel Consulting Services, Inc., 901 State Street, Suite 318, Erie, Pennsylvania 16501.

[21] David S. Zurakowski and William G. Harris, "Software Applications in Human Resource Management," *Personnel Administrator,* August 1984, pp. 77–84.

[22] David Mahal, "Microcomputers, Software Buyers Guide," *Personnel Journal,* April 1987, pp. 73–88.

EXHIBIT 5–8   Organization Size and Software Ranked in Top Five

	Organization Size	
Group	Full-Time Employees	Percent of Organizations (N = 706)
1	Fewer than 500	38.0% (268)
2	500–2,000	32.7 (231)
3	2,000 or more	29.3 (207)

**Software Ranked in Top Five
Size Groups (Full-Time Employees)**

Computer Application for the Future	Group 1*		Group 2†		Group 3‡	
	N	Percent	N	Percent	N	Percent
Job analysis	69	25.8	72	31.2	69	33.3
Automated applications	22	8.2	29	12.6	25	12.1
Work samples	10	3.7	2	0.9	5	2.4
Ability/aptitude tests	26	9.7	21	9.1	17	8.2
Vocational tests	8	3.0	11	4.8	5	2.4
Personality tests	10	3.7	6	2.6	6	2.9
EEO/AA records	128	47.8	122	52.8	98	47.3
Recruitment/tracking	103	38.4	111	48.1	90	43.5
Job previews	11	4.1	9	3.9	9	4.3
Person-job matching	45	16.8	35	15.2	50	24.2
Adaptive testing	10	3.7	7	3.0	10	4.8
Performance appraisal	91	34.0	83	35.9	67	32.4
In-basket techniques	4	1.5	4	1.7	5	2.4
Assessment centers	11	4.1	14	6.1	12	5.8
Training needs	43	16.0	35	15.2	38	18.4
Stress management	9	3.4	7	3.0	2	1.0
Career pathing	33	12.3	38	16.5	68	32.9
Outplacement counseling	5	1.9	5	2.2	7	3.4
Attitude questionnaires	39	14.6	42	18.2	29	14.0
Suggestion systems	10	3.7	7	3.0	5	2.4
Management information systems	159	59.3	151	65.4	125	60.4
Personnel inventories	162	60.4	141	61.0	113	54.6

* Fewer than 500 full-time employees; N = 268.
† 500 to 2,000 full-time employees; N = 231.
‡ 2,000 or more full-time employees; N = 207.
   Source: David S. Zurakowski and William G. Harris, "Software Applications in Human Resource Management," *Personnel Administrator*, August 1984, p. 80.

Exhibit 5–9 presents a summary of the current use and satisfaction among users who participated in the study. Computers are used most in EEO/affirmative action record keeping, development of HRIS systems, and development of personnel inventories.

EXHIBIT 5–9   Computer Use and Satisfaction (N = 706)

	Current Use		Overall Satisfaction Percent
Application	**N**	**Percent**	
Employee selection			
Job analysis	57	8.1	79.0
Automated applications	14	2.0	50.0
Work samples	2	0.3	50.0
Ability/aptitude tests	27	3.8	81.5
Vocational tests	10	1.4	80.0
Personality tests	8	1.1	87.5
EEO/AA records	450	63.7	68.0
Recruitment/tracking	142	20.1	73.2
Job previews	5	0.7	20.0
Person-job matching	35	5.0	65.7
Adaptive testing	7	1.0	57.2
Employee evaluation			
Performance appraisal	90	12.7	74.4
In-basket techniques	3	0.4	66.7
Assessment centers	9	1.3	66.7
Employee development			
Training needs	30	4.3	66.7
Stress management	5	0.7	20.0
Career pathing	36	5.1	50.0
Outplacement counseling	6	0.9	50.0
General personnel			
Attitude questionnaires	44	6.2	79.5
Suggestion systems	5	0.7	80.0
Management information systems	395	56.0	61.5
Personnel inventories	311	44.1	60.1

Source: David S. Zurakowski and William G. Harris, "Software Applications in Human Resource Management," *Personnel Administrator*, August 1984, p. 82.

The computer has tremendous ability to store and digest data.[23] However, many individuals are concerned that computers can violate their privacy. Federal employees are protected by the Privacy Act of 1974. The act requires federal agencies to permit employees to examine, copy, correct, or amend employee information. If there is a dispute about the accuracy of computer-stored information or what information is to be stored, an appeal procedure is available.[24] The act prohibits, with certain exceptions, the disclosure of information to outsiders without written consent of the employee.

Eight states currently have laws allowing private employees to exercise

[23] Robert J. Mitsch, "Ensuring Privacy and Accuracy of Computerized Employee Record Systems," *Personnel Administrator*, September 1983, pp. 37–41.

[24] Suzanne H. Cook, "Privacy Rights: Whose Life Is It Anyway?", *Personnel Administrator*, April 1987, pp. 58–65.

their right to privacy in finding out, with few exceptions, the content of their personnel files. P/HRM managers using an IRIS-type system certainly need to keep the legal issues of data privacy in mind. If they do not, the alternative may be more and more laws that restrict the use of computer-based information.

Another device that is less sophisticated than an IRIS-type system is the **replacement chart.** The replacement chart is used primarily with technical, professional, and managerial employees. It is a display of summary data about individuals currently in the organization. The replacement chart is a concise map that can be readily reviewed to pinpoint potential problem areas in terms of human resource planning.

Exhibit 5–10 presents a replacement chart that can be reviewed easily by Wiley Department Store managers. This chart provides information about

EXHIBIT 5–10   Replacement Chart: Wiley Department Stores

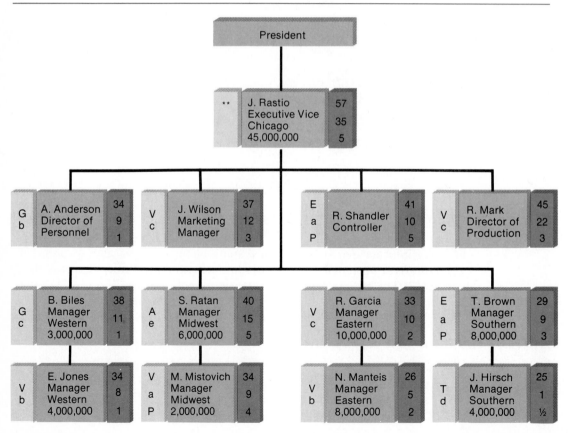

EXHIBIT 5–10 *(concluded)*

| 5. Performance and Potential Codes | 1. Name
2. Title
3. Store Name and Classification
4. Volume | 6. Age
7. Length of Service
8. Time in Job |

1. Name—first name/middle initial/last name.
2. Title—example: Mgr.
3. Store name and classification.
4. Total sales volume in region.
5. Performance and potential codes (see below).
6. Age in years.
7. Length of service—number of years of unbroken service with company.
8. Time in job—number of years in current position.

PERFORMANCE CODE		POTENTIAL CODE
E—Excellent	—Represents the top 10% of all executives in all categories.	*a.* Promotable now. One of two subdesignations must be made:
V—Very good	—Represents upper 25% in performance and generally indicates a high level of achievement of objectives.	P—"up"—will indicate readiness for promotion to a higher level. L—"lateral"—will indicate readiness for lateral promotion or transfer.
G—Good	—Represents the level of performance expected from most of our experienced executives and indicates upper-middle level of performance.	
A—Adequate	—Represents the minimum level of performance that is acceptable under usual circumstances.	*b.* Promotable within two years or less. *c.* Potentially promotable—time uncertain. *d.* Potential good, but at present level only. *e.* Potential and future is questionable.
U—Unsatisfactory	—Represents an unsatisfactory level of performance and indicates that failure to improve will result in termination or change of position.	
T—Too new to rate		

individuals in the organization in terms of age, performance, and tenure. This type of information can be combined with more extensive background data on each of the individuals shown on the chart to make planning decisions.

More on Skills Inventory Systems

Suppose that a manager decides that because of costs, a skills inventory system will be used. The challenge facing the manager is what data the system should contain. An organization can only retrieve what is designed into the system.

EXHIBIT 5-11   **Skill Inventory Components**

I. Data summarizing the employee's past.
  A. Titles and brief job description highlights from positions held in the last two to five years.
    1. This organization.
    2. Previous organization(s).
  B. Critical skills needed or developed while in these positions.
    1. Manual.
    2. Cognitive.
    3. Creative.
  C. Educational achievements.
    1. High school: job-relevant classes.
    2. College.
      a. Major.
      b. Minor.
      c. Job-relevant courses.
  D. Significant special projects accomplished during the last three years.
    1. This organization.
    2. Previous organization(s).
II. Data summarizing present skills' status.
  A. Skill-related highlights: last three performance appraisals.

  B. Employee's perception of what is done well on present job, i.e., skill competencies, perceptions of how skills could be improved or augmented.
  C. Same data as II.B, from the employee's superior.
III. Data that focuses on the future.
  A. Personal career goals.
    1. One year.
    2. Three years.
    3. Identify specific positions and aspirations. Avoid global generalities, i.e., "higher up."
  B. The views of the individual's present superior(s) as to what he or she could be prepared to become. List specific positions.
  C. Specific training and development efforts the individual is motivated to undertake.
    1. On-the-job.
    2. Off-the-job.
    3. Classrooms.
    4. Experiential.

Source: By permission of *Personnel Journal,* March 1987, p. 130.

The list of data coded into skills inventories is almost endless, and it must be tailored to the needs of each organization. Some of the more common items include: name, employee number, present location, date of birth, date of employment, job classification or code, prior experience, history of work experience in the organization, specific skills and knowledge, education, field of education (formal education and courses taken since leaving school), knowledge of a foreign language, health, professional qualifications, publications, licenses, patents, hobbies, a supervisory evaluation of the employee's capabilities, and salary range. Items often omitted, but becoming increasingly important, are the employee's own stated career goals and objectives, including geographical preferences and intended retirement date.

The elements in a skills inventory are shown in Exhibit 5-11.[25] Note the main category headings: I. Data summarizing the employee's past; II. Data summarizing present skills status; and III. Data that focuses on the future.

The data collected by a skills inventory are used to identify employees for

[25] John Lawrie, "Skills Inventories: Pack For The Future," *Personnel Journal,* March 1987, pp. 127-30.

specific job roles and assignments that will fulfill the organization's objectives, as well as individual career and job objectives.

Maintaining the Skills Inventory

While designing the system is the most difficult part of developing a skills inventory, planning for the gathering, maintaining, handling, and updating of data is also important. The two principal methods for gathering data are the interview and the questionnaire. Each method has unique costs and benefits. The questionnaire is faster and less expensive when many employees are involved, but inaccuracies often prevail. People often do not spend enough time on a questionnaire. There are those who contend, therefore, that the trained interviewer can complete the reports more quickly and accurately, a procedure which in the long run more than offsets the costs of the interviewer.

A procedure for keeping the files updated also must be planned. The procedure depends on the frequency of change and the uses of the data. For some organizations, an annual update is adequate. In others, where changes are made often and use is frequent, shorter update periods may be necessary. Some organizations make provisions for monthly updating of changeable data and annual checks for less changeable data. One method is to include updating forms in payroll envelopes.

Finally, a decision whether to store the data manually or on the computer must be made. This decision is based on cost of the computer and frequency of use of the data. The computer also provides the possibility of using comparative analyses of employment over a period of time.

Skills inventories are useful only if management uses the data in making significant decisions. Top management support is necessary here. Before a manager uses the skills inventory as an aid in selection decisions, he or she must be trained to avoid system abuse. Examples of this are:

- Making requests simply on the basis that "it would be nice to know."
- Making requests for searches that are not backed up by bona fide requisitions that have been budgeted.
- Specifying too many characteristics for a desired employee so that no one fits all the characteristics.

As an example of the third type of abuse, consider the following request of a skills inventory system:

> Wanted—A person with the following qualifications: B.S. in business, experience in finance and marketing, with at least two years with the company and willing to relocate overseas.

Assume that the organization has 1,000 employees. The chance of finding a person with all these characteristics is the product of the percent of probability in each category. Thus, if 20 percent of the 1,000 have a B.A. in business, 10 percent have experience in finance, 10 percent have experience in marketing, 70 percent have two years or more seniority, and 40 percent are willing to relocate overseas, the chance of finding such a person is $0.20 \times 0.10 \times 0.70 \times 0.40$, or 0.0056, or less than 1 chance in 1,000. Those who set requirements must recognize that being overly specific reduces the chance of finding any suitable employee.

ACTION DECISIONS IN HUMAN RESOURCE PLANNING

There are several managerial decisions to be made once the demand for people has been forecast and compared to the supply. Another action decision that is increasingly important today involves analyzing the work force to comply with government equal employment opportunity programs. This problem is discussed first.

Analyzing the Composition of the Work Force

The extent to which the work force of an organization approximates the composition of the total work force for the area is an essential consideration in EEO programs. As stated in Chapter 3, government agencies enforce the EEO laws. The makeup of the present labor force in the United States and some discrepancies between the ideal of equal employment opportunity and the reality of these opportunities for certain groups was described in Chapter 2.

The organization must keep records of the distribution of employees by categories, levels (top management, professional, operative, and so on), and pay groups. If the statistics show that the organization's employment patterns are substantially different from the overall population in its geographic areas and by employment category, the employer is vulnerable to EEO legal action, which might involve back-pay liability, mandatory hiring goals for women and minorities, and the like. Many socially responsible employers have voluntarily tried to improve the employment opportunities of these groups.

Antidiscriminatory programs enforced by government or promoted by popular opinion make it essential for the employer to examine the distribution of employees in protected categories (race, sex, and so on) at all levels to see if the organization has *in fact* discriminated against any group in its hiring and promotion practices. The organization cannot discriminate against any group solely on the basis of their personal characteristics. The purpose of this analysis is to ensure that all potential employees of equal ability have an equal chance at hiring and promotion and other rewards. The specific programs used for analysis of these items will be discussed throughout the book.

Action Decisions with No Variance in Supply and Demand

It is possible for the organization, after matching demand for employees with the supply at hand, to find that previous planning has been so excellent that the demand is matched exactly with the supply. In this case, employment planning has served its purpose well in helping the organization to meet its objectives.

An exact match is rare. More frequently the total supply is correct, but there are variances in subgroups. These data become inputs to facilitate decisions about training, promotion, demotion, and similar decisions. Exhibit 5–12 presents a personnel supply and demand report for 1989–1992. For two years, there is no need to find and identify a new district manager. However, suppose that in 1991 the present district manager will retire. The firm has Bob Ratky available to fill the district manager vacancy. Thus, the variance would be zero for 1991. However, for the director of unit maintenance job, there is a different situation. In 1989 there is a need for a director and no one available inside the firm to fill the position. Also in 1991 there is a vacancy and no one available. Thus, the firm would need to look outside the organization or train someone inside to fill these vacancies. The personnel supply and demand chart will clearly illustrate to the P/HRM specialist variance, shortage, and surplus circumstances.

Action Decisions with a Shortage of Employees

When employment specialists comparing demand to supply find the supply of workers is less than the demand, several possibilities are open to the organization. If the shortage is small and employees are willing to work overtime, it can be filled with present employees. If there is a shortage of highly skilled employees, training and promotions of present employees, together with the recruitment of lower-skilled employees, are a possibility. This decision can also include recalling previously laid-off employees. Outside the organization, additional part-time or full-time employees can be hired, or some of the work can be contracted out to other organizations.

Action Decisions in Surplus Conditions

When comparison of employee demand and supply indicates a surplus, the alternative solutions include attrition, early retirements, demotions, layoffs, and terminations. Surplus employee decisions are some of the most difficult decisions managers must make, because the employees who are considered surplus are seldom responsible for the conditions leading to the surplus. A shortage of a raw material such as fuel, or a poorly designed or marketed product can cause an organization to have a surplus of employees.

As a first approach to deal with a surplus, most organizations avoid layoffs by such means as attrition, early retirement, and work creation. Many organizations can reduce their work force simply by not replacing those who retire or quit (attrition). Sometimes this approach is accelerated by encouraging employees close to retirement to leave early, but this approach can amount to layoffs of older employees if the organization is not careful.

EXHIBIT 5–12   Personnel Supply and Demand Report

Manpower Report

	1989 Needs	Variance	1990 Needs	Variance	1991 Needs	Variance	1992 Needs	Variance
District manager	0	0	0	0	1 Ratky, Bob	0	0	0
Manufacturing superintendent	0	0	0	0	1 Tracey, Mark	0	0	0
Mechanic shop manager	0	0	1	1	0	0	0	0
Director of unit maintenance	1	1	0	0	1	1	0 Maria, Donna	1
Floor manager	0	0	1 Semoski, John	0	0	0	0	0
Safety engineer	0	0	1 Wittsell, Mark	0	0	0	0	0
Quality control supervisor	0	0	0	0	0	0	1	1

© Adapted from Charles F. Russ, Jr., "Manpower Planning Systems: Part II," *Personnel Journal*, 1982, p. 122.

P/HRM Manager Close-Up

Paul S. Bernius

Biography

Paul S. Bernius is the director of compensation and industrial relations at Hilti, Inc., in Tulsa, Oklahoma. Previously he held several positions with Sea Land Service, Inc., a subsidiary of R. J. Reynolds Industries, including director of personnel administration and employee relations, manager of training and development, and manager of personnel services (European Division). He also did extensive personnel administration and employee relations work with Standard Oil Company of California.

Bernius received a bachelors degree in sociology and psychology from St. Francis College in 1965. He later received a masters degree in human resource development from the New School for Social Research in 1975.

Manpower Planning Problem at Hilti

Hilti was faced with a manpower planning problem. The firm had a need to:

1. Determine which high-level managerial positions were backed up by an available internal candidate.
2. Determine which high-level managers represented a risk to the company in terms of potential turnover, poor performance, and so on.
3. Determine if managerial talent was available to operate in the near future.
4. Provide development for the managerial staff.

Although succession planning systems had been around for some time, Hilti wanted to develop a fresh approach that not only responded to the first two needs above, but also responded to the third and fourth, in that specific developmental actions were identified and implemented for the key managerial personnel.

The P/HRM response was to create a management development committee, consisting of the company's six top executives, which was chartered to meet four times a year. The committee approach gave Hilti three things:

(continued)

1. Representation for all personnel across division and functional lines.
2. A vehicle for reaching agreement on specific manpower actions.
3. A method of gaining an evaluation of each key manager based on several managers' experience, rather than relying totally on the present supervisor's individual appraisal.

The committee takes the lists of key positions and key personnel and answers the following questions in sequence that are implied first by a Succession/Management Development Planning Form and then a Development Plan Form.

1. Does the incumbent represent a risk?
2. Is there a backup for this position?
3. What are the strengths and weaknesses of the incumbent versus managerial dimensions?
4. For what specific positions is the incumbent a candidate?
5. What are the employee's career interests?
6. What are the specific developmental actions needed?

The system is nonbureaucratic, action-plan oriented, and has identified more internal (lateral, promotional, etc.) and external (seminar, workshop) activities than have been identified in the past.

With this approach, the manpower needs of the company are balanced with the career interests of employees and management development activities aimed at assisting the company meet its ambitious objectives.

Another variation of this approach is work sharing, which will be discussed in detail in Chapter 19. Instead of attempting to decide whom to lay off the organization asks all employees to work fewer hours than normal and thus share the work. Many unions favor this approach. During recessions, many firms give the employees a say in how to deal with surplus conditions, and some groups of employees decide for work sharing.

If there is a surplus of employees at higher levels in the organization, demotion can be used to reduce the work force. After World War II, as the U.S. Army reduced its size, it had too many higher-level officers to staff the number of positions left. As a result, many officers were demoted to the "permanent" rank, not the one they held in 1945. The numerous ways demotion can be handled include: lowering job status with the same salary or lowered salary; the same status with lower compensation; bypassing in seniority for promotion; changing to a less desirable job; the same formal status, but with decreased span of control; exclusion from a general salary increase; insertion of positions above the person in the hierarchy; or moving to a staff position. Demotions are very difficult for employees to accept, and valued employees may leave because of them.[26]

---

26 Bill Saporito, "Cutting Costs Without Cutting People," *Fortune*, May 25, 1987, pp. 26–32.

A RETURN TO THE P/HRM ⋅ IN ⋅ ACTION

Ted Sloane   Anne Wilson

After reading this chapter, talking to friends from other firms, and examining some literature, Ted Sloane was not at all confused about HRIS. He called his vice president of personnel/human resource management, Anne Wilson, and said, "Anne, I want to thank you for calling my attention to how we could use and benefit from a HRIS. Without good forward planning, we are going to be in trouble with the law. Let's move ahead and set up a HRIS. By the way, are you familiar with the IBM IRIS system? It's a dandy."

Organizations such as Kaiser Cement, UNIROYAL, Inc., and TWA have asked employees to make concessions on pay, benefits, and work roles. A few of the giveback concessions are presented in Exhibit 5–13.[27] The givebacks or concessions can hurt, but the alternative—layoff—can be even more painful.[28] Managers, however, are advised to negotiate concessions in as conciliatory manner as possible. In a situation where there is a surplus of employees, management can afford to ask for concessions.

In managing a surplus through layoffs, employers take the surplus employees off the payroll temporarily to reduce the surplus. Some employers may feel more willing to accept this method because unemployment compensation plans are now available (see Chapter 11). If the layoff is likely to be semipermanent or permanent, it is in effect a termination and results usually in the payment of severance pay, as well as unemployment compensation.

From 1984 through 1987, Allegis, Firestone, GM, B.F. Goodrich, and Owen-Illinois laid off employees in the hope of becoming more profitable. However, other firms such as Hallmark, Pacific Northwest Bell, Digital Equipment, and

---

[27] David Kirkpatrick, "What Givebacks Can Get You," *Fortune,* November 24, 1986, pp. 60–72.

[28] Carrie R. Leana and John M. Ivancevich, "Involuntary Job Loss: Institutional Interventions and a Research Agenda," *Academy of Management Journal,* April 1987, pp. 301–12.

EXHIBIT 5–13   **Examples of Givebacks In Different Industries**

Industry	Company	Givebacks
Steel	Wheeling-Pittsburgh	Eliminated cost-of-living adjustment (COLA), six paid holidays, one week of vacation.
	Bethlehem	Cut pay 8%; reduced premium for Sunday work.
	LTV	Cut pay $1.14 per hour; reduced premium for second and third shift.
Meat-packing	John Morrell	Eliminated profit sharing and implemented lower pay for new hires.
	Wilson Foods	Tied pay increases solely to company's profitability.
Airline	TWA	Reduced job classifications and medical benefits.
	American	Instituted longer probation and eliminated medical coverage for first-year machinists and ground workers.
	Eastern	Cut pay for pilots and flight attendants 20% and won two-tier pay scale for pilots.
Mining	Phelps Dodge	New workers hired during strike decertified union.
	Kennecott	Reduced average wage $3.22 per hour; eliminated 12 pay levels and COLA.
	Pinto Valley	Cut pay 20%.
Trucking	Some 110 trucking companies	Lowered starting salary 30% for new hires; cut pay 8% for supplementary workers.
Grocery store	P&C Food Markets	Eliminated COLA and reduced premium pay.
	Eagle Food Stores	Reduced premium pay and number of paid personal days.
	Kroger, National, and Schnuck Markets	Cut top pay rates, premium pay, and number of paid personal and sick days.

Source: *Fortune,* November 24, 1986, p. 64.

Micro Devices approached the surplus of employee problem differently. At Hallmark production schedules were removed, work was transferred to other factories, employees were transferred to other jobs, and cross-training was performed so that employees were not laid off.[29]

Pacific Northwest Bell is using a computerized job skills bank to help keep all employees working. The company and its union, the Communications Workers of America worked out a cost reduction for employment security agreement. Therefore, after the AT&T breakup the firm was committed to keeping employees on the job. The computerized job skills bank provides a weekly listing of job openings and job candidates. When a match-up occurs the employee is notified. Each employee who wants to pursue the in-house opening is then provided career counseling.

[29] Sapouto, pp. 26–32.

Digital Equipment Corporation found that they had 5,000 employees who could be considered surplus. They conducted an analysis of the skills needed for the firm's new manufacturing system and the skills of the employees. Where shortages existed a retraining program was installed. Pacific Northwest Bell and Digital Equipment Corporation have been able to cut costs without laying off employees.

How does a manager decide whom to lay off? Two criteria have been used: merit and seniority. In the past, the most senior employee was laid off last. A second approach now is to lay off those with lower merit ratings. Merit means that those who do the job the best are kept; those who perform poorly are laid off. If merit ratings are not precise, unions may fight their exclusive use as a reason for laying off particular employees.

Using seniority as the only criterion may mean that recently hired minorities and women are laid off first. The last-hired, first-laid-off policy pits minority rights against seniority rights, and courts have been hard pressed to resolve the conflict. In a significant ruling, the United States Supreme Court in June 1984 stated that seniority, not race or sex, must dictate policy for employee layoffs.[30] This ruling triggered off a number of lawsuits. In Boston, where 265 police officers and 157 fire fighters were laid off under affirmative action rules, union leaders are considering lawsuits for back pay and damages for workers involved. It is still too early to interpret the full impact of the Supreme Court's last-hired, first-laid-off ruling. However, there is likely to be confusion, disappointment, and a rash of lawsuits filed because of the ruling.

Terminating or firing an employee is generally used only as a last resort.[31] Anyone who has watched Willy Lohman in *Death of a Salesman* or the star of Neil Simon's *Prisoner of Second Avenue* knows why. Termination is usually very painful to both the employer and employee. EEO requirements apply to terminations as well as layoffs. When terminations take place, many employers engage in *outplacement,* which is a serious attempt by the organization to help terminated employees find suitable jobs.

SUMMARY

This chapter has pointed out the significant factors in the diagnostic model that affect human resource planning. It began by emphasizing that this P/HRM activity is an integral aspect of strategic planning by top management. This P/HRM function ensures organizational success in maintaining its P/HRM capacities by comparing the present supply of human resources with the projected demand for them.

To summarize the major points covered in this chapter:

---

[30] M. J. Zuckerman, "Seniority Ruling Stirs Up Controversy," *USA Today,* June 15, 1984, p. 12.

[31] Beth Brophy, "You're Fired," *U.S, News & World Report,* March 23, 1987, pp. 50–54.

1. The major reasons for formal employment planning are intended to achieve:
   a. More effective and efficient use of human resources.
   b. More satisfied and better developed employees.
   c. More effective equal employment opportunity planning.
2. The human resource planning process is a joint responsibility of P/HRM and operating managers, with each performing specific functions in the process.
3. Four forecasting techniques used to determine work force needs described in the chapter are: expert-estimate, trend projection, modeling, and unit-forecasting techniques.
4. An important step in the planning process is to determine the availability of those presently employed by the organization who can fill projected vacancies. The skills inventory can serve this purpose.
5. Action decisions in an employee shortage situation depend on the magnitude of the shortage: overtime, retraining of lower skilled employees, hiring additional employees, and subcontracting some of the work.
6. A growing number of firms are now using computerized inventories of their employees' skills, job experience, and personal work history. MicroHRIS is a computerized system that has been used with some success.
7. Action decisions in surplus conditions include attrition, early retirement, demotions, layoffs, and terminations.
8. Organizations need to analyze the supply-demand match of employees in advance so they can take necessary steps to reschedule, recruit, or lay off employces. The organization should analyze work force composition to determine that it meets legal constraints.

Human resource planning can be an integral part of the P/HRM program. It is most directly related to recruitment, selection, training, and promotion. By matching employment supply and demand, the organization can know how many persons of what type it needs to fill positions from within (by promotion or training) and how many it must acquire from outside (by recruitment and selection). (See Exhibit 5-14)

Chapters 6 and 7 are devoted to recruitment and selection, in which employment needs are filled from outside the organization when personnel and employment planning decisions show this need.

Questions for Review and Discussion

1. What is human resource planning? How does it relate to other personnel activities?
2. What have been the results of using computer technology and a HRIS?
3. Describe how you would choose a forecasting technique for several kinds of organizations, such as a small manufacturer of ashtrays, a large steel company, or a moderate-sized general hospital.
4. How could a replacement chart and a computerized system like IRIS be used to make better employment planning decisions?

EXHIBIT 5–14   **Recommendations on Personnel and Employment Planning for Model Organizations**

Type of Organization	Analysis of Supply (Skills Inventory)		Method of Demand Analysis				Level Where Planning Is Analyzed		
	Manual	Computerized	Expert	Trend	Model/ Multiple	Unit	HQ	Unit	Both
1. Large size, low complexity, high stability		X			X	X	X		
2. Medium size, low complexity, high stability	X	X			X	X	X		
3. Small size, low complexity, high stability	X	X		X			X		
4. Medium size, moderate complexity, moderate stability	X			X		X		X	
5. Large size, high complexity, low stability		X		X		X			X
6. Medium size, high complexity, low stability	X	X		X		X		X	
7. Small size, high complexity, low stability	X	X	X					X	

5. What benefits could result in a firm that makes every attempt to not lay off employees?
6. What is a skills inventory? Discuss how to design an effective skills inventory.
7. Why should an organization analyze the composition of its work force? How?
8. What action decisions can be made when there is a worker shortage? Which is best?
9. What action decisions can be made when there is a worker surplus? Which is best?
10. Why have forecasting methods been resisted or not used by managers?

GLOSSARY

Handicapped Person. Any person who has a physical or mental impairment that may limit his/her work or job activities.

Human Resource Information System (HRIS). The method used by an organization to collect, store, analyze, report, and evaluate information and data on people, jobs and costs.

Human Resource Planning. The process that helps to provide adequate human resources to achieve future organizational objectives. It includes forecasting future needs for employees of various types, comparing these needs with the present work force, and determining the numbers or types of employees to be recruited or phased out of the organization's employment group.

Replacement Chart. A display or chart usually of technical, professional, and managerial employees. It includes name, title, age, length of service, and other relevant information on present employees.

Skills Inventory. A list of the names, personal characteristics, and skills of the people working for the organization. It provides a way to acquire these data and makes them available where needed in an efficient manner.

APPLICATION CASE

Computers and Human Resource Planning*

Computers are becoming a widely used tool for human resource planning. Southland Corporation, which owns and operates the 7-Eleven convenience food stores, is one company that has computerized aspects of its planning function. The company inputs results from the twice-yearly personnel evaluations of its management into a computer system. Southland regularly obtains computer analyses on the promotability of each manager and the impact of future promotions on job openings and staffing requirements. Southland also uses computers in establishing career development programs for its employees. The computer software identifies skills gaps for each employee and even suggests remedies (a special assignment, training, college coursework.)

Tenneco Inc., a Houston-based international conglomerate, uses a $15,000 program called Executive Track to track its 800 executives. Each year the company uses the program to conduct an annual resource review, analyzing promotions, transfers, and performance of its executive corp and evaluating the probability and location of future executive openings. When an opening occurs in one of Tenneco's 11 divisions, Executive Track provides a written preliminary screening analysis that provides a list and summary of all employees who meet the stated qualifications for the position. Tenneco's P/HRM department uses the analysis to prepare a written report for division management. The computer's preliminary analysis is provided in minutes; before computerization the task required hours to complete.

Executive Track also performs a "position blockage" analysis that identifies high performers who have not been promoted for at least two years because the jobs above them are filled.

P/HRM departments that have computerized elements of their succession planning assert that computerization affords at least three advantages. Computerization makes succession planning more objective because the system evaluates all potential candidates for promotion using the same, specified criteria (a particular performance rating, number of years of experience, etc.). Politics or the old boy's network aren't a factor.

Second, computerization opens up succession planning in the organization because it can more easily evaluate a larger number of people as potential candidates to fill open positions. Consider that in companies the size of Tenneco, for example (100,000 employees), a computer can evaluate in a matter of

* Written by Kim Stewart and adapted from: William M. Bulkeley, "The Fast Track: Computers Help Firms Decide Whom to Promote," *The Wall Street Journal,* September 18, 1985, p. 33; "Tenneco Tracks Its Executives," *Computer Decisions,* July 15, 1985, p. 98; and Richard B. Frantzreb, "Microcomputer Software for Human Resources: A Directory," *Personnel Administrator,* July 1986.

seconds scores of employees (some of whom otherwise wouldn't be considered simply because of the hours required for the task).

Third, computerization provides sophisticated analysis for human resource planning. Many P/HRM departments have used programs to conduct "if-then" scenarios concerning possible turnover in key positions. One executive asserts that computerization is very useful in contingency planning for what he calls "the truck problem—what you do if a guy is hit by a truck." Computer analysis can calculate and layout the "domino effect" that vacancies in the upper levels of an organization can have on positions on lower levels when filled internally. Computer analysis can also uncover potential snags in human resource planning. For instance, one employee may emerge as clearly the most qualified candidate for one job; however, he or she could be the only qualified person for a critical position that will probably open a few months down the road. Well-designed computer programs catch potential pitfalls that are difficult to spot when manually reviewing stacks of personnel files.

However, computerized human resource planning has its critics. Some cite that computers tend to impersonalize planning and that relying too much on computer-provided analysis may produce poor decisions. However, one executive notes, "The computer doesn't make the decisions. People make the decisions. It's just a catcher of information."

Questions for Thought

1. The case and chapter describes some uses of computers in human resource planning. In what other ways can computers be used in performing human resource planning tasks?
2. Some consultants assert that many CEOs aren't enthusiastic about using computers in succession planning. Why? As a P/HRM manager, how could you deal with this problem?
3. Besides the issue of privacy and critics' concerns stated in this case, are there other shortcomings in computerizing elements of human resource planning? Explain.

RECRUITMENT

LEARNING OBJECTIVES

After studying this chapter you should be able to:

- **Discuss** how to develop an effective recruiting program for an organization.
- **Describe** the recruiting process; who does it, how they do it, and where they find recruits.
- **Define** what is meant by a realistic job preview.
- **Identify** typical flaws that college students find in recruiters.
- **List** sources of candidates for blue-collar, gray-collar, white-collar, and managerial, technical, and professional positions.

KEY TERMS

Employee Leasing
Immigration Reform and Control Act
  of 1986
Job Posting
Job Search
Realistic Job Preview
Recruiting

CHAPTER OUTLINE

P/HRM · IN · ACTION

Clark   Lewis   Ed

Clark Kirby is just entering the office of the vice president of personnel/ human resource management, Lewis Yates. Clark has worked for Gunther Manufacturing for 10 years, in Los Angeles. After a short management training program, Clark spent almost two years as operating supervisor in a plant. After that, a position opened up in the P/HRM department. Clark had majored in personnel at California State University at Los Angeles and wanted to try personnel work.

He moved up in the department headquarters in Chicago during the next seven years.

Gunther is a growing firm. For a middle-sized operation, it has one of the fastest growth records in the industry. Now, Gunther is opening up a new plant in the quickly expanding Tampa market.

Lewis has selected Clark to be the Tampa plant personnel/human resource manager. This was what Clark had been waiting for: a chance to be on his own and to show what he can do for Lewis, who has been very supportive of his career, and for Gunther. He was very excited as he entered Lewis' office.

Lewis greeted him with, "Well,

Clark, I hope you realize how much we are counting on you in Tampa. Shortly you'll be meeting your new plant manager, Ed Humphrey. You'll be working for him, but responsible to me to see that Gunther's P/HRM policies are carried out.

"The plant will be staffed initially with the following employees. These are, in effect, your recruiting quotas:

Managers	38
Professional/technical	10
Clerical	44
Skilled employees	104
Semiskilled employees	400

Also note that you will receive a budget for maximum initial pay for this group shortly.

"You and Ed should work out the details. You are eligible to recruit some employees from the home office and other plants. But excessive raiding is not allowed. Remember, too, that Gunther has an equal employment opportunity problem. Wherever possible, try to hire qualified minorities and women to help us meet our goal.

"Your own P/HRM office consists of yourself, one P/HRM specialist to help you run the employment office, and one clerical employee. Good Luck!"

Clark quickly arranged for a meet-

(continued)

ing with Ed, his new boss. Ed is about 50 years old. He is a high school graduate who started with Gunther as a blue-collar employee when he was 18 years old. After 10 years in various blue-collar positions, Ed became a foreman. Eight years later he was selected as an assistant to the plant manager. After several years in this position, he was made one of the three assistant plant managers at one of Gunther's plants in Chicago. He held that position until being given the position of plant manager at the new Houston plant.

After introductions, Clark and Ed talked.

Clark: Here are the figures for employees that Lewis gave me. He also said we could recruit some people from Gunther, but not to raid beyond company policy. Also, Lewis said we needed to do an exceptional job recruiting minorities and women because we have an EEO problem.

Ed: Let's get something straight right off. You work for me now, not Lewis. Here's a list of 20 managers I want to take with me. It's your job to convince them to come to Tampa with me. In cases where my help might persuade some to come along, call on me. But I'm very harassed now trying to get machinery ordered, the plant laid out, financing arranged, and so on. Call on me only when you must, you *understand?*

Oh, one more thing. That EEO * # /OX, you can forget that. The Tampa plant is going to be the most efficient in the company, or else! And if that means hiring the best workers and they all turn out to be white men, that's tough, you get me? Keep me

posted on what's happening. Good to have you on board.

After some thought, Clark decided to use job posting as a method of attracting professional/technical and managerial employees at the Los Angeles office to the new plant in Tampa. He also made the personal contacts Ed asked for in recruiting managerial employees, and the skills inventory was used to come up with more applicants. Clark contacted these also. He did not use job posting or the skills inventory for clerical, skilled, or semiskilled employees. He knew that for Gunther, as with most organizations, these categories of employees rarely wish to move to another location. Most companies don't want to pay relocation costs for these categories of employment, either.

Clark went to Tampa and set up the employment office at the new location. He ran an ad in Tampa's afternoon paper and placed a job listing with a private employment agency for the P/HRM specialist and clerk-typist for his office. Then he hired these two employees and set up the office to receive walk-ins. He provided application blanks and policy guidelines on when selection would proceed.

Clark listed the available positions with the U.S. Employment Service. He also contacted private agencies. He selected the private agencies after calling a number of P/HRM managers in the Tampa area in similar businesses and who were also ASPA members. The P/HRM specialist notified the high schools, vocational-technical schools, and colleges of the positions. The schools selected included all the vocational-technical schools, the junior colleges, and the colleges in the Tampa

(continued)

area. Also, all high school guidance counseling departments were notified. Now Clark wonders what other media he ought to use to publicize the positions.

Clark found out quickly, as you will find in this chapter, recruitment is a little more complicated than he originally thought.

Before an organization can make a job offer, it must find people who want the job. This chapter describes effective ways to recruit the people needed to offset shortages in human resources that become apparent as a result of the human resource planning process.

> Recruiting is that set of activities an organization uses to attract job candidates who have the abilities and attitudes needed to help the organization achieve its objectives.

Job search is the set of activities a person undertakes to seek and find a position that will provide him or her with sustenance and other rewards. Recruiting is related directly to a number of P/HRM activities, as shown in Exhibit 6–1.

The average cost to recruit and relocate a new professional or managerial employee in most medium or large companies is in the $30,000 to $40,000 range. Though most of the cost comes from a company's relocation policy provisions, a substantial portion comes from the recruitment budget. The estimated recruitment charge for a manager is between 30 and 40 percent of the expected salary. Thus, to recruit a $40,000 per year manager, a company

EXHIBIT 6–1　　**Recruiting and Other Personnel Activities**

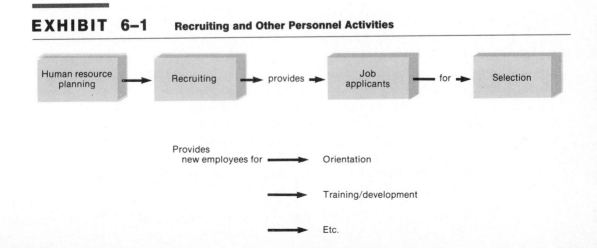

can expect recruitment expenses of between $12,000 and $16,000. The expenses include advertising costs, recruiter and candidate travel, agency search firms fees, relocation costs, and recruiter's salary and benefits.[1] Although recruitment is an expensive activity, it is not a well-developed P/HRM function.

A DIAGNOSTIC APPROACH TO RECRUITMENT

Exhibit 6–2 examines how the recruiting process is affected by various factors in the environment. The recruiting process begins with an attempt to find employees with the abilities and attitudes desired by the organization and to match them with the tasks to be performed. Whether potential employees will respond to the recruiting effort depends on the attitudes they have developed toward those tasks and the organization on the basis of their past social and working experiences. Their perception of the task will also be affected by the work climate in the organization.

How difficult the recruiting job is depends on a number of factors: external influences such as government and union restrictions and the labor market, plus the employer's requirements and candidates' preferences. External factors are discussed in this section, and the important interaction of the organization as a recruiter and the employee as a recruit is examined in the next section.

Since Clark Kirby has just moved to Tampa, he will have to learn about the external influences in the new location. Each area of the country has its own unique culture, problems, and situations that a P/HRM manager must study and understand. Clark will be doing a lot of studying of his new location.

External Influences

Government and Union Restrictions Government regulations prohibiting discrimination in hiring and employment have a direct impact on recruiting practices. As described in detail in Chapter 3 government agencies can and do review the following information about recruiting to see if an organization has violated the law:

- The list of recruitment sources (such as employment agencies, civic organizations, schools) for each job category.
- Recruiting advertising.
- Estimates of the firm's employment needs for the coming year.
- Statistics on the number of applicants processed by category (sex, race, and so on) and by job category or level.
- Checklist to show what evidence was used to verify the legal right to work.

---

[1] Margaret Magnus, "Is Your Recruitment All It Can Be?" *Personnel Journal*, February 1987, pp. 55–63.

EXHIBIT 6–2 Factors Affecting Recruitment of Employees

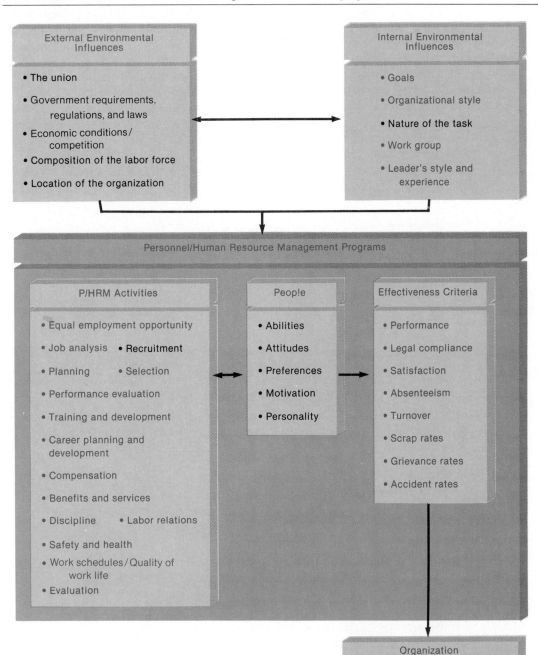

External Environmental Influences

- The union
- Government requirements, regulations, and laws
- Economic conditions / competition
- Composition of the labor force
- Location of the organization

Internal Environmental Influences

- Goals
- Organizational style
- Nature of the task
- Work group
- Leader's style and experience

Personnel/Human Resource Management Programs

P/HRM Activities

- Equal employment opportunity
- Job analysis • Recruitment
- Planning • Selection
- Performance evaluation
- Training and development
- Career planning and development
- Compensation
- Benefits and services
- Discipline • Labor relations
- Safety and health
- Work schedules / Quality of work life
- Evaluation

People

- Abilities
- Attitudes
- Preferences
- Motivation
- Personality

Effectiveness Criteria

- Performance
- Legal compliance
- Satisfaction
- Absenteeism
- Turnover
- Scrap rates
- Grievance rates
- Accident rates

Organization End Results

- Competitive product(s)
- Competitive service(s)

The government may require an organization to use EEO programs to recruit qualified employees who are not well represented in the present work force. For example, a firm with no female managers may be required to recruit at women's colleges offering degrees likely to lead to management positions with the organization.

Exhibit 6–3 provides a guide to what recruiters can and cannot legally do or ask in recruiting interviews. Other personal characteristics recruiters need to be wary of, because they may discriminate or do not relate directly to performance, are birthplace; use of second names or aliases; religious affiliation; citizenship; membership in clubs, societies, and lodges; and social security numbers. In some states, it is illegal to ask about the type of military discharge and past police records. Many public organizations must be careful to follow state or local statutes on recruiting.

EXHIBIT 6–3   Do's and Don'ts in Recruiting Interviews: The Law

Subject	Can Do or Ask	Cannot Do or Ask
Sex	Notice appearance.	Make comments or notes unless sex is a bona fide occupational qualification.
Race	General distinguishing characteristics such as scars, etc., to be used for identification purposes.	Color of applicant's skin, eyes, hair, etc., or other direct or indirect questions indicating race or color.
Handicap	Are you able to carry out necessary job assignments and perform them well and in a safe manner?	What is the nature and/or severity of any handicaps you have?
Marital status	Ask status *after* hiring, for insurance purposes.	Are you married? Single? Divorced? Engaged? Are you living with anyone? Do you see your ex-spouse?
Children	Ask numbers and ages of children *after* hiring, for insurance purposes.	Do you have children at home? How old? Who cares for them? Do you plan to have more children?
Physical data	Explain manual labor, lifting, other requirements of the job. Show how it is performed. Require physical exam.	How tall are you? How heavy?
References	By whom were you referred for a position here?	Requiring the submission of a religious reference.
Criminal record	If security clearance is necessary, can be done prior to employment.	Have you ever been arrested, convicted, or spent time in jail?
Military status	Are you a veteran? Why not? Any job-related experience?	Why type of discharge do you have? What branch did you serve in?
Age	Age *after* hiring. Are you over 18?	How old are you? Estimate age.
Housing	If you have no phone, how can we reach you?	Do you own your home? Do you rent? Do you live in an apartment or a house?

Source: Clifford M. Doen, Jr., "The Pre-Employment Inquiry Guide," *Personnel Journal*, October 1980, p. 825–29. Reprinted with permission of *Personnel Journal*, Costa Mesa, Calif., all rights reserved; and *Business Week*, May 26, 1975, p. 77. Also see Stephen Sahlein, *The Affirmative Action Handbook* (New York: Executive Enterprises Publishing).

Obviously, these government restrictions affect who can be recruited, how, and where. In addition, some union contracts restrict recruiting to union hiring halls (as will be discussed in Chapter 7). This restriction does not apply for many employers; but where it does, the recruiting function is turned over to the union, at least for those employees who are unionized.

The Immigration Reform and Control Act (IRCA) of 1986 has placed a major responsibility on employers in stopping the flow of illegal immigration to the United States. The employer—not the government—is the chief enforcer of the prohibition against the unauthorized recruitment and employment of foreign-born individuals.[2] Under the law's "employer sanctions" arrangement, all employers are required to screen every applicant's eligibility for lawful employment and maintain records demonstrating employment authorization.

The IRCA is a complex piece of legislation, but its basic features fit into four broad categories:

1. The employer's duty not to recruit, hire, or continue to employ "unauthorized aliens".
2. The employer's duty to verify the identity and work authorization of every new employee.
3. The employer's duty not to discriminate on the basis of citizenship or natural origin.
4. The amnesty rights of certain illegal aliens who are eligible to achieve temporary or permanent resident status in the country.

The IRCA went into effect in May 1988, 18 months after the bill became law, to ensure a period of education among employers.[3] Initial penalties for employers who violate the IRCA entail a cease and desist order along with a fine from $250 to $2,000 for each unauthorized alien. Second violations result in a fine of between $2,000 and $5,000 per unauthorized alien. Third offenses lead to fines of $3,000 to $10,000 per unauthorized alien. A person or firm may be charged criminally for having a pattern of violations, with a maximum sentence of six months imprisonment and/or a $3,000 fine per violation.[4]

The IRCA and existing civil rights laws indicate that employers must avoid hiring illegal immigrants while not discriminating against prospective employees just because they look or sound foreign. This type of enforcement and nondiscrimination role is extremely difficult to perform effectively.[5] Every employee—white, black, Hispanic, Asian—recruited and hired must provide acceptable documentation of their status: a valid U.S. passport, unexpired Immigration Authorization Service, unexpired work permit, birth certificate,

---

[2] Bruce D. May, "Law Puts Immigration Control in Employer's Hands," *Personnel Journal,* March 1987, pp. 106–11.

[3] David P. Berry and Jeff T. Appleman, "Policing The Hiring of Foreign Workers: Employers Get the Job," *Personnel,* March 1987, pp. 48–51.

[4] Philip R. Voluck, "Recruiting, Interviewing, and Hiring: Staying within the Boundaries," *Personnel Administrator,* May 1987, pp. 45–52.

[5] David S. Bradshaw, "Immigration Reform: This One's for You," *Personnel Administrator,* April 1987, pp. 37–40.

driver's license, social security card. In the first two months of the law's existence, 64 complaints were reported in New York alone and 350 complaints have been filed with California, Illinois, and Texas offices of the Mexican American Legal Defense and Education Fund.[6]

Even with the complexities and ambiguities of the IRCA, most major employers appear to be committed to abiding by the law. The IRCA created another formal step in the recruitment and selection process that puts a part of immigration control in the hands of employers.[7]

Labor Market Conditions Another external environmental factor affecting recruiting is labor market conditions (these were described in some detail in Chapter 2). The labor market affects recruiting in this way: If there is a surplus of labor at recruiting time, even informal attempts at recruiting will probably attract more than enough applicants. But when full employment is nearly reached in a area, skillful and prolonged recruiting may be necessary to attract any applicants that fulfill the expectations of the organization.

The employer can find out about the current employment picture in several ways. The federal Department of Labor issues employment reports, and state divisions of employment security and labor usually can provide information on local employment conditions. There are also sources of information about specific types of employees. Craft unions and professional associations keep track of employment conditions as they affect their members. Current college recruiting efforts are analyzed by the Conference Board, A. C. Nielsen, and the Endicott Report, which appears in *The Journal of College Placement.* Various personnel journals, the *Monthly Labor Review,* and *The Wall Street Journal* also regularly report on employment conditions.

Other sources provide summary data such as indexes of employment. One of the most interesting indexes is that of the Conference Board, which keeps track of help-wanted advertising in 52 major newspapers across the nation, using 1967 as a base year of 100. Local conditions are more important than national conditions, unless the employer is recruiting nationwide.

Composition of Labor Force and Location of Organization The influence of P/HRM law on activities was noted in Chapter 3. As the number of legal requirements has increased, it has become important for an organization to analyze the composition of its work force. Such an analysis is done to determine whether the firm's employment practices are discriminatory.

The location of the organization and the relevant labor market will play a major role in the composition of the work force. That is, the number of black, Hispanic, Asian or Pacific Islander, American Indian, or Alaskan native em-

---

[6] Dianna Soles, "Double Bind: Employers Who Share Illegals Risk Discrimination Charges," *"The Wall Street Journal,* June 5, 1987, p. 8.

[7] Dianna Soles, John R. Enshiviller, and Alfredo Corchado, New Immigration Law Brings Much Anxiety to U.S. Workplaces," *The Wall Street Journal,* June 5, 1987, pp. 1 and 8; and Dianna Soles, "Immigration Cops: New Law Puts Task of Enforcement on Employers," *The Wall Street Journal,* May 7, 1987, pp. 28–29.

ployees in the work force depends largely on the availability of these minority employees in the relevant labor market.

Therefore, government and union restrictions, labor market conditions, the makeup of the work force, and the location of the organization are external forces that affect each other. None of these forces is necessarily more important than any other force. Each of them must be considered in developing a sound recruitment plan that results in an effectively functioning organization.

INTERACTIONS OF THE RECRUIT AND THE ORGANIZATION

After considering how external factors such as government, unions, labor market conditions, composition of the work force, and location of the organization restrict the options of an organization to recruit (an applicant to be recruited), the next step in understanding the recruiting process is to consider the interaction of the applicants and the organization in recruiting.

In Exhibit 6-2 (the diagnostic model for recruitment), the nature of the organization and the goals of the managers are highlighted, as is the nature of the task. The techniques used and sources of recruits vary with the job. As far as the applicants are concerned, their abilities, attitudes, and past work experience affect how they go about seeking a job.

The recruiting process consists of the matching of the employer's desired qualifications with the applicant's qualifications.[8] The employer offers a job with associated rewards; the organization is looking for certain characteristics in a potential employee. The recruit has abilities and attitudes to offer and is looking for a kind of job that meets his or her minimum expectations. A match is made when sufficient overlap exists between these two sets of expectations. The recruiting process usually requires some modifications and compromises on both sides.

The Organization's View of Recruiting

Several aspects affect recruiting from the organization's viewpoint: the recruiting requirements set, organization policies and procedures, and the organizational image.

Requirements for Recruits Organizations specify the requirements they consider ideal in applicants for positions. The employer easily can have unrealistic expectations of potential employees: An employer might expect applicants who stand first in their class, are president of all extracurricular activities, have worked their way through school, have Johnny Carson's ability to charm, are good-looking, have 10 years' experience (at age 21), and are

---

[8] Ann Coil, "Job Matching Brings Out the Best in Employees," *Personnel Journal*, January 1984, pp. 54–61.

willing to work long hours for almost no money. Or, to meet federal requirements, they might specify a black woman, but one who is in the top 2 percent of her graduating class and has an undergraduate degree in engineering and an M.B.A.

As contrasted with this unrealistic approach, the effective organization examines the specifications that are absolutely necessary for the job. Then it uses these as its beginning expectations for recruits (see the section on job analysis, job description, and job specifications in Chapter 4).

Organization Policies and Practices In some organizations P/HRM policies and practices affect recruiting and who is recruited. One of the most important of these is promotion from within. For all practical purposes, this policy means that many organizations only recruit from outside the organization at the initial hiring level. They feel this is fair to present loyal employees and assures them a secure future and a fair chance at promotion, and most employees favor this approach. Some employers also feel this practice helps protect trade secrets. The techniques used for internal recruiting will be discussed later in this chapter.

Is promotion from within a good policy? Not always. An organization may grow so stable that it is set in its ways. The business does not compete effectively, or the government bureau will not adjust to legislative requirements. In such cases, promotion from within may be detrimental, and new employees from outside might be helpful.

Other policies can also affect recruiting. Certain organizations have always hired more than their fair share of the handicapped, or veterans, or ex-convicts, for example, and they may look to these sources first. Others may be involved in nepotism to favor relatives. All these policies affect who is recruited.

Organizational Image The image of the employer generally held by the public also affects recruitment. There are differences in attracting engineers, systems analysts, tool and die makers, marketing researchers, cost accountants, and employment specialists for such diverse organizations and situations as:

NASA at the height of the space program, when men were walking on the moon.

Chrysler hiring engineers during the current upswing in the company's history.

A small soap company, competing with Procter & Gamble in trying to hire salespersons.

IBM trying to recruit research scientists for its lab.

As you can imagine, the good or bad, well-known or unknown images of these organizations will affect how they are viewed by the public and job recruits. The organization's image is complex, but it is probably based on what the organization does and whether or not it is perceived as providing a good place to work. The larger the organization, the more likely it is to have a well-developed image. A firm that produces a product or service the potential employee knows about or uses is also more likely to have an image for the applicant. The probability is that a potential employee will have a clearer image of a chewing gum company than a manufacturer of subassemblies for a cyclotron.

The organization's image is also affected by its industry. These images change. In the past, petroleum had a positive image. The ecology movement has changed this universally good image. Petroleum organizations, such as Exxon, Shell, and Gulf, now actively advertise their positive contributions to society and try to improve their public images.

How does this image affect recruiting? Job applicants seldom can have interviews with all the organizations that have job openings of interest to them. Because there are time and energy limits to the job search, they do some preliminary screening. One of these screens is the image the applicants have of the organization, which can attract or repel them.

In sum, the ideal job specifications preferred by an organization may have to be adjusted to meet the realities of the labor market, government or union restrictions, the limitations of its policies and practices, and its image. If an inadequate number of quality people apply, the organization may have to adjust the job to fit the best applicant or increase its recruiting efforts.

The Potential Employee's View of Recruiting

Exhibit 6–2 highlighted several factors relevant to how a recruit looks for a job. The applicant has abilities, attitudes, and preferences based on past work experiences and influences by parents, teachers, and others. These factors affect recruits two ways: how they set their job preferences, and how they go about seeking a job. Understanding these is vital to effective recruiting organizations.

Preferences of Recruits for Organizations and Jobs Just as organizations have ideal specifications for recruits, so do recruits have a set of preferences for a job. A student leaving college may want a job in San Diego because of its quality of life, paying $30,000 a year, and with little or no responsibility or supervision. This recruit is unlikely to get *all* his expectations fulfilled. The recruit also faces the limits of the labor market (whether there are a lot of job openings or very few), government and union restrictions, and the limits of organizational policies and practices. The recruit must anticipate compromises just as the organization does.

From the individual's point of view, organization choice is a two-step process. First, the individual makes an occupational choice—probably in high school or just after. Then she or he makes a choice of the organization to work for within the occupation chosen.

What factors affect the organization-choice decision? A number of re-

Pepper ... and Salt

THE WALL STREET JOURNAL

From The Wall Street Journal, *reprinted with permission from Cartoon Features Syndicate*

"You have an honest face."

searchers have found that more educated persons know the labor market better, have higher expectations of work, and find organizations that pay more and provide more stable employment. Although much of the research suggests that this decision is fairly rational, the more careful studies indicate that the decision is also influenced by unconscious processes, chance, and luck.

Some studies have indicated that the organizational choice tends to be correlated with single factors. One study found blue-collar workers went after the highest paying jobs;[9] another found workers trying to match multiple needs with multiple job characteristics, such as high pay and preferred job type;[10] and a third found the approach varied by personality differences.[11]

---

[9] Dale Yoder, *Job Seeking Behavior of Workers* (New York: Organization for Economic Cooperative Development, 1965).

[10] Joseph Champagne, "Job Recruitment of the Unskilled," *Personnel Journal,* April 1969, pp. 259–68.

[11] John Morse, "Person-Job Consequence and Individual Adjustment and Development," *Human Relations,* December 1970, pp. 841–61.

Job Search and Finding a Job:
The Recruit

Exhibit 6–4 outlines the pattern followed by effective job searchers. Examine Step 1: Realize that the first job choice is part of a career plan. Is this job the first in a chain of jobs with this company? Or, is this just a job to get experience before starting your own business?

Step 2 is fulfilled by reading newspapers and professional publications in the area where the recruit wants to live. If a person is interested in working in the Chicago area, he or she would read the publications circulated in that area. College placement offices have job information, as do professional associations, employment agencies, and search firms. Personal contacts also are a good source of information.

The data from Step 2 allow you to complete Step 3 with regard to industry. To decide the company type and job function, you need to analyze the answers to certain kinds of questions about potential employers.

At this point, you may have determined, for example, that what you really want is a job near home in the toy industry, in a small firm that you can buy

EXHIBIT 6–4   Career Decision Strategy

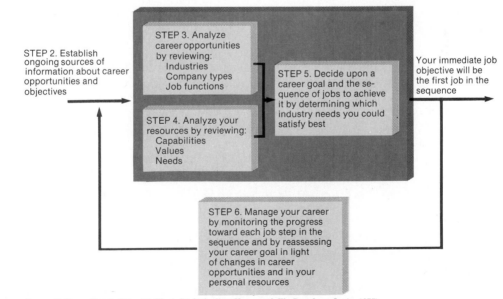

STEP 1. Realize that you're looking for a career objective and the sequence of jobs you'll use to achieve it

STEP 2. Establish ongoing sources of information about career opportunities and objectives

STEP 3. Analyze career opportunities by reviewing:
Industries
Company types
Job functions

STEP 4. Analyze your resources by reviewing:
Capabilities
Values
Needs

STEP 5. Decide upon a career goal and the sequence of jobs to achieve it by determining which industry needs you could satisfy best

Your immediate job objective will be the first job in the sequence

STEP 6. Manage your career by monitoring the progress toward each job step in the sequence and by reassessing your career goal in light of changes in career opportunities and in your personal resources

Source: B. Greco, *How to Get a Job That's Right for You* (Homewood, Ill.: Dow Jones-Irwin, 1975).

out some day. Answers to these questions will help you narrow the list of potential employers to a reasonable size.

With Step 4, there are several questions you need to answer about your values and needs. Questions of this type are almost unlimited. What you must do first is rank them in importance so you know the trade-offs between them. You *will not* find a job with *all* the characteristics you choose.

Then you need to analyze what you have to offer that comprises your comparative advantages. These resources can include education (for example, grades, kinds of courses, skills developed), interpersonal skills, personality traits, and personal contacts.

After completing Steps 3 and 4, you are ready to look for a job. Use all the sources available to you: employment agencies, personal contacts, professional associations, and so on. If you use mail to send résumés, the letters should be personalized, and telephone follow-up is necessary. Personal contacts should be used wherever possible.

Questions about Employers:

1. Do I have a size preference: small, medium, or large, or no certain size?
2. Do I have a sector preference (private, not for profit, public sector)?
3. What kinds of industries interest me? This question is usually based on interests in company products or services. Do I prefer mechanical objects or counseling people? This is a crucial question.
4. Have I checked to make sure that the sector or product or service has a good future and will lead to growth and opportunity?

Questions about Me:

1. How hard do I like to work?
2. Do I like to be my own boss, or would I rather work for someone else?
3. Do I like to work alone, with a few others, or with large groups?
4. Do I like work at an even pace or in bursts of energy?
5. Does location matter? Do I want to work near home? In warmer climates? In ski country? Am I willing to relocate?
6. How much money do I want? Am I willing to work for less money but in a more interesting job?
7. Do I like to work in one place or many? Indoors or outdoors?
8. How much variety do I want in work?

One study of over 200 personnel managers who normally screen applicants for positions found that it is essential for cover letters accompanying résumés to be personally typed, no longer than one page, and truthful.[12] They should include these items, in order of importance.

---

[12] Hubert Feild and William Holley, "Resume Preparation: An Empirical Study of Personnel Managers' Perceptions," *Vocational Guidance Journal*, March 1976, pp. 229–37.

Pepper . . . and Salt

THE WALL STREET JOURNAL

"Tell me about yourself, Kugelman—your hopes, dreams, career path, and what that damn earring means."

Position you are seeking.
Specific job objectives.
Your career objectives.
Reason you are seeking employment.
An indication that you know something about the organization.

The same study found that preferred résumés were personally typed, no more than two pages in length, on high-quality paper, and so on. The most important items the managers surveyed in this study were looking for on a résumé were, in order: current address; past work experience; college major; job objectives and goals; date of availability for the job; career objectives; permanent address; tenure on previous jobs; colleges and universities attended; specific physical limitations; and job location requirements. Other items they preferred were, in order: overall health status; salary requirements; travel limitations; minor in college; grades in college major; military experience; years in which degrees were awarded; overall grade point average; membership in organizations; and awards and scholarships. A sample of a résumé is presented in Exhibit 1, in Appendix C.

Video résumés are now being used by job seekers. Individuals are paying up to $300 to put themselves and their qualifications on a video tape. Some consider such approaches a costly gimmick. However, some employers prefer video résumés mainly to screen from a large pool of recruits.[13]

---

[13] John Knowlton, "Smile for the Camera: Job Seekers Make More Use of Video Resumes," *The Wall Street Journal,* June 22, 1987, p. 25.

Successful job seekers prepare for job interviews. Some suggestions for doing this are given in Chapter 7. As with other skills, practice makes perfect. If one is available, record a practice interview on a videotape with a friend playing the interviewer role. You can learn from each other.

Once you have had job interviews, be sure to follow up those that interest you by sending a letter or calling the interviewer. This requires you to write down and remember the interviewer's name and some details of the job being offered.

WHO DOES THE RECRUITING?

Clark Kirby's situation at Gunther illustrates that he is responsible for recruiting employees. This is an extremely important responsibility that will in the long run determine whether Gunther will be successful in the Houston area. The roles of operating and P/HRM managers in recruiting are shown in Exhibit 6–5.

Human resource planning gives operating managers the data needed to set recruiting quotas. Sometimes this process is formalized by authorizations. That is, a budget is prepared showing the maximum number of people to be recruited and the maximum salary that can be paid. Lewis gave these items to Clark at Gunther Corporation.

Who does the recruiting? In larger organizations, the P/HRM department does it. The branch of the department with this responsibility is called the employment office or department. It is staffed by recruiters, interviewers, and clerical employees. This group also does the preliminary selection, as will be described in Chapter 7. Employment offices are specialized units that provide a place to which applicants can apply. They conduct the recruiting, both at the work site and away from it.

EXHIBIT 6–5   **The Roles of Operating and P/HRM Managers in Recruitment**

Recruiting Function	Operating Manager (OM)	Personnel/Human Resource Manager (P/HRM)
Set recruiting goals	Set by OM with advice of P/HRM	Advises OM on state of labor market
Decide on sources of recruits and recruiting policies	Policy decision, outside versus inside, set by OM with advice of P/HRM	Advises OM on status of possible inside recruits
Decide on methods of recruiting	OM advises P/HRM on methods of recruiting	P/HRM decides on recruiting methods with advice of OM
College recruiting	OM occasionally recruits at colleges	P/HRM normally recruits at colleges
Cost/benefit studies of recruiting	OM evaluates results of cost/benefit studies and decides accuracy	P/HRM performs cost/benefit studies

Drawing by Lorenz; © 1973 *The New Yorker* Magazine, Inc.

"We'll be happy to put you on file, Mr. Bannister, but we don't have anything for an underling at the moment."

When applicants appear in person at the work site, the employment office serves a similar purpose. This initial meeting might be called the reception phase of employment. The applicant is greeted, supplied with an application blank, and perhaps given some information on present hiring conditions and the organization as a place of work. If the applicant is treated indifferently or rudely at this phase, he or she can form a lasting poor impression of the workplace.[14] The reception phase is a great deal like the initial contact a salesperson makes with a prospective customer. What kind of impression did the prospective employee in the cartoon get?

All applicants are potential employees, as well as clients for the organization's services or products. Therefore, it is vital that those who greet and process applicants (in person or by phone) be well-trained in communication techniques and interpersonal skills. They should enjoy meeting the public and helping people in stressful conditions, for job seeking can be a difficult experience for many applicants.

In smaller organizations, multipurpose P/HRM people do the recruiting, along with their other duties, or operating managers may take time to recruit

---

[14] Donn L. Dennis, "Are Recruitment Efforts Designed to Fail?" *Personnel Journal,* September 1984, pp. 60–67.

and interview applicants.[15] Sometimes the organization puts together a recruiting committee of operating and P/HRM managers.

The role of recruiter is very important. The recruiter is usually the first person from the organization that an applicant meets. Applicants' impressions about the organization are based to a large degree on their encounter with the recruiter. Effective recruiter behavior is described later in this chapter as an aspect of college training.

SOURCES OF RECRUITS

Once the organization has decided it needs additional employees, it is faced with two recruiting decisions: where to search (sources), and how to notify applicants of the positions (methods). Two sources of applicants could be used: internal (present employees), and external (those not presently affiliated with the organization). Exhibit 6–6 lists many of the sources of recruits and the perceived effectiveness of each source. Effectiveness was judged by a representative of the P/HRM function who participated in the Bureau of National Affairs survey.

The data portrayed in Exhibit 6–6 suggest that many different sources are used to recruit personnel. There appear to be some interesting effectiveness patterns. For example, newspaper advertising is about equally effective for recruiting office/clerical, professional/technical, and management recruits. Private employment agencies are most effective for sales, professional/technical, and management personnel. Walk-ins are most effective in the recruitment of office/clerical and plant service recruits. The patterns presented by the data in Exhibit 6–6 suggest that each recruiting source should be examined in terms of costs, advantages, and disadvantages before a decision is made on how recruits will be attracted.

Internal Sources

An organization's own policies and procedures can affect the recruitment effort. A sound human resource planning system can provide internal alternatives in sufficient numbers. Job vacancies filled by present employees provide opportunities for advancement. When present employees witness promotions from within they become aware of opportunities.

Organizations need to use both internal and external sources of recruitment. Some of the advantages and disadvantages of each are presented in Exhibit 6–7.

Job Posting and Bidding If the employee shortage is for higher-level employees, and if the organization approves of promoting from within, it will use the skills inventories to search for candidates (see Chapter 4). But P/HRM man-

---

[15] Barry M. Farrell, "The Art and Science of Employment Interviews," *Personnel Journal,* May 1986, pp. 91–94.

EXHIBIT 6–6 Sources Used for Recruitment by Employee Occupations and Their Perceived Effectiveness

Source	Employee Group				
	Office/ Clerical N-184	Plant/ Service N-155	Sales N-96	Professional/ Technical N-182	Management N-181
Employee referrals	92% (20)	94% (5)	74% (17)	68% (67)	65% (7)
Walk-ins	87 (24)	92 (37)	46 (5)	46 (7)	40 (2)
Newspaper advertising	68 (39)	88 (30)	75 (30)	89 (38)	82 (35)
Local high schools or trade schools	66 (2)	61 (2)	6 (0)	27 (0)	7 (0)
U.S. Employment Service	63 (5)	72 (6)	34 (0)	41 (1)	27 (1)
Community agencies	55 (1)	57 (3)	22 (0)	34 (1)	28 (2)
Private employment agencies	44 (10)	11 (2)	63 (23)	71 (25)	75 (27)
Career conferences/job fairs	19 (0)	16 (1)	19 (2)	37 (2)	17 (1)
Colleges/universities	17 (1)	9 (1)	48 (8)	74 (15)	50 (2)
Advertising in special publications	12 (0)	6 (0)	43 (3)	75 (5)	57 (8)
Professional societies	5 (0)	19 (1)	17 (1)	52 (0)	36 (2)
Radio and TV advertising	5 (0)	8 (1)	2 (0)	7 (0)	4 (1)
Search firms	1 (0)	2 (0)	2 (2)	31 (5)	54 (17)
Unions	1 (0)	12 (2)	0 (0)	3 (0)	0 (0)

Note: *N* refers to number of companies. Percentages are based on number of companies providing data for each employee group. Columns may add to more than 100 percent because of multiple responses or less than 100 percent because of nonresponses.
First number in each entry indicates percent of respondents who use source.
Figure in parentheses indicates percent who consider source effective.

Source: Adapted by permission from Mary Green Miner, *Personnel Policies Forum No. 126: Recruiting Policies and Practices*, July 1979, pp. 2, 5, copyright 1979 by The Bureau of National Affairs, Inc., Washington, D.C.

agers may not be aware of all employees who want to be considered for promotion, so they use an approach called *job posting* and *bidding*. In the **job posting system,** the organization notifies its present employees of openings, using bulletin boards, company publications, and so on. About 25 percent of white-collar firms in one survey conducted by Dahl and Pinto used the system,

EXHIBIT 6-7

Source	Advantages	Disadvantages
Internal	Example of opportunities are made realistic and help morale	Political infighting can create hostile atmosphere
	More accurate assessment of on the job behavior	Inbreeding may stifle creativity and new ideas
	Company is aware of strengths and weaknesses	Poor attitude among those employees not selected
	Limited cost for recruiting	
External	Larger group of people to select from	Longer adjustment period
	Infusion of competitors, ideas, secrets	Morale problem among internal employees
	A new beginning with no political intrigue	On the job behavior is not precisely known

as did most large Minnesota firms.[16] Most firms found the system useful; for example, the Bank of Virginia filled 18 percent of its openings as a result of job posting.

Dahl and Pinto provide a useful set of guidelines for effective job-posting systems.

- Post all permanent promotion and transfer opportunities.
- Post the jobs for about one week prior to recruiting outside the enterprise.
- Clarify eligibility rules. For example, minimum service in the present position might be specified as six months. Seniority may be the decision rule used to choose between several equally qualified applicants.
- List job specifications. Application forms should be available.
- Inform all applicants what happens in the choice.

Inside Moonlighting and Employees' Friends

If there is a labor shortage and it is short term, or if a great amount of additional work is not necessary, the organization can use inside moonlighting. It could offer to pay bonuses of various types to people not on a time payroll. Overtime procedures are already developed for those on time payrolls.

Before going outside to recruit, many organizations ask present employees to encourage friends or relatives to apply. In his study of the job-search behavior of 1,500 men, Ornstein found that 23 percent of white and 29 percent of black men found their jobs through friends, and 31 percent of both whites and blacks found their first jobs through help of the family.[17] These are *first* jobs; there presently are no data on what percentage of applicants for later jobs use these sources. These data indicate how powerful this source of recruits could be for organizations, should they use it wisely. Some equal employment

---

[16] Dave Dahl and Patrick Pinto, "Job Posting: An Industry Survey," *Personnel Journal,* January 1977, pp. 40–42.

[17] Michael Ornstein, *Entry into the American Labor Force* (New York: Academic Press, 1976).

P/HRM Manager Close-Up

William M. Read
Atlantic Richfield Company

Biography

William M. Read is senior vice president of Atlantic Richfield Company in charge of employee relations.

Mr. Read, a native of Philadelphia, Pennsylvania, is a graduate of Washington and Lee University, Lexington, Virginia. He attended the University of Pennsylvania Graduate School.

He joined the Atlantic Refining Company in 1943 as a personnel clerk at the Philadelphia Refinery. He has served as training assistant, manager of training, and manager of personnel administration before being elected a vice president in 1972 and a senior vice president in 1978.

Views of William M. Read— Atlantic Richfield

At Atlantic Richfield our employee relations professionals see their mission as one of helping managers achieve excellence in the management of their human resources. In carrying out this mission, the professional has four roles: (1) service, (2) consulting, (3) advocacy, and (4) catalytic.

The decade ahead offers a number of interesting human resource challenges:

1. National demographics indicate that there will be a shortage of persons with critical skills resulting from the zero population growth in the 50s and 60s. We in the Employee Relations profession must work with our management to intensify the training and development of minorities and females to fill this void and intensify efforts to retain older workers; that is, those who might be expected to retire.

2. We also face a middle-management crunch caused by the same demographics. Persons 35 to 45 who might anticipate rapid promotional movement will, in many companies in the second half of the decade, become blocked and frustrated by comparatively young managers filling the top-management jobs. This will require some creative re-thinking of how to retain the interest and enthusiasm of this important segment of the employee population.

opportunity programs prohibit using friends as a major recruiting source, however.

Employee referrals have to be carefully used by organizations. In a case involving *EEOC* v. *Detroit Edison* (1975), the U.S. Court of Appeals, Sixth Circuit found a history of racial discrimination that was related to recruitment.[18] The court stated:

> The practice of relying on referrals by a predominately white work force rather than seeking new employees in the marketplace for jobs was found to be discriminating.

This case suggests some caution about employee referrals. Unless the work force is racially and culturally heterogeneous to begin with, the referrals of friends tend to be the same in background, race, and attitude.

External Sources

Exhibit 6–6 also indicates a number of external sources of recruits and which sources supply applicants for various types of jobs. When an organization has exhausted internal sources, these sources are used. Studies indicating when each external source is used are not extensive.

The most fruitful of the outside sources is walk-ins. Ornstein found that one third of his sample got their first jobs that way.[19] Private employment agencies place some white-collar employees and serve as a source of recruits for many employers. Counselors in schools and teachers can also help, usually for managerial, professional, technical, and white-collar employees. The state employment security offices, partially using federal funds, have tried to serve more applicants and organization needs, but these agencies still provide primarily blue-collar and gray-collar applicants. They try to tie into school counseling services, too. Still, most studies are very critical of the costs and benefits of the public agencies. They do not help employees or applicants as much as they should. Thus, even though there appear to be many sources from which employees can be recruited, employers use only a few to recruit each type of employee.

Alternatives to Recruitment

An organization's human resource plan may suggest that additional or replacement employees are needed. However, because of the cost and permanency of recruiting individuals an alternative to recruitment may be used.

Overtime When a firm faces pressures to meet a production goal, it may mean that employees need to work overtime. By having employees work overtime,

---

[18] *EEOC* v. *Detroit Edison Company,* U.S. Court of Appeals, Sixth Circuit (Cincinnati), 515 F. 2d. 301 (1975).

[19] Michael Ornstein, *Entry into the American Labor Force* (New York: Academic Press, 1976).

organizations avoid the costs of recruiting and having additional employees. Overtime can provide employees with additional income. However, there are potential problems with fatigue, increased accidents, and increased absenteeism.

On a limited and short-term basis working some employees overtime may be an alternative to recruitment. However, continuous overtime has often resulted in higher labor costs and reduced productivity.

Temporary Employment There are temporary help agencies such as Kelly Services and M. David Lowe that fill needs of organizations. The temporary employee that possesses skills needed for the job can handle excess or special work assignments. An advantage of using temporary personnel is that the organization does not have to provide fringe benefits, training, or a compensation and career plan. The temporary can move in and out of the firm when the workload requires such movement. A disadvantage of hiring temporary help is that these individuals do not know the culture or workflow of the firm. This unfamiliarity distracts from the temporary's commitment to organizational and department goals.

Employee Leasing Employee leasing involves the payment of a fee to a leasing company which performs all the P/HRM recruiting, hiring, training, compensating, and evaluating.[20] The employee leasing firm is paid to provide a ready-made labor pool. Small- and medium-size firms find advantages in the employee leasing arrangement because they do not have to become involved in P/HRM and other administrative activities. Employee leasing is similar to the temporary help arrangement, but under leasing the employees are not temporary.

Many leasing firms have employment areas they specialize in. One company, for example, specializes in supplying labor to the transportation industry—truck drivers, dock workers, maintenance personnel.[21]

METHODS OF RECRUITING

A number of methods may be used to recruit external applicants: advertising, personal recruiting, computerized matching services, special-event recruiting, and summer internships are discussed here. There is also a separate section on college recruitment of potential managers and professionals.

To decide which methods to use, the organization should know which are most likely to attract potential employees. Relatively few studies of the jobseeking procedures used by applicants have been made, but Exhibit 6–8 suggests the most likely media for various categories of employees.

---

[20] Paul C. Driskell, "A Manager's Checklist for Labor Leasing," *Personnel Journal,* October 1986, pp. 108–12.

[21] Marion R. Selter, "On the Plus Side of Employee Leasing," *Personnel Journal,* April 1986, pp. 87–91.

EXHIBIT 6–8 Methods of Recruiting for Various Types of Employees

Method	Blue Collar	Gray Collar	White Collar	Managerial, Professional, Technical
Media advertisements				
Newspaper want ads	X	X	X	X
Professional journals and other media	X	X	X	X
Recruiters				X
Computer matching services				X
Special-event recruiting				X
Summer internships				X
Co-op programs	Select highly skilled	Select highly skilled	Select highly skilled	

Media Advertisements

Organizations advertise to acquire recruits. Various media are used, the most common of which are the daily newspaper help-wanted ads. Organizations also advertise for people in trade and professional publications. Other media used are billboards, subway and bus cards, radio, telephone, and television. Some job seekers do a reverse twist; they advertise for a situation wanted and reward anyone who tips them off about a job.

In developing a recruitment advertisement, a good place to begin is with the corporate image. General Mills used its Trix cereal logo to create instant recognition among MBA graduates: The ad featured the Trix rabbit with the headlines: "It's Not Kid Stuff Anymore". The copy continued: "Now you're an MBA who's looking for a dynamic growth-directed career environment . . . look to General Mills. Because it's not kid stuff anymore. It's your future."[22]

An innovative way to attract nurses was used in an ad campaign for Children's Hospital Medical Center in Cincinnati. The ad appealed to nurses' sense of pride in themselves and their profession. The ad ran in the *Cincinnati Engineer* newspaper. The headlines, "Nurses are smart and they know how to make you feel better," "Nurses are there to make sure you don't get real scared," "Nurses are kind and they don't laugh when you cry," are written in a child's handwriting and combined with hand-drawn pictures of nurses and children.

Another innovative way to attract prospective employees with particular skills is the use of recorded want ads. Want ad recordings were used by 40 companies recruiting engineers and scientists at a New York City convention. At a special recruiting center, job hunters were able to pick up a telephone and

---

[22] Margaret Magnus, "Recruitment Ad Vantages," *Personnel Journal*, August 1986, pp. 58–79.

hear a three-minute taped recruiting message that included a job description and company contact details.

Help-wanted ads must be carefully prepared. Media must be chosen, coded for media study, and impact analyzed afterwards. If the organization's name is not used and a box number is substituted, the impact may not be as great, but if the name is used, too many applicants may appear, and screening procedures for too many people can be costly. This is a difficult decision to make in preparing recruitment advertisements.

In addition, the ad must not violate EEO requirements by indicating preferences for a particular racial, religious, national origin, or sex group. The advertisement shown in Exhibit 6–9 is the type that will create trouble for a firm. Look at the questions that could be raised by this ad.

Use of Recruiters

Some organizations use recruiters or scouts who search the schools (as baseball scouts search the ball diamonds) for new talent. Recruiters can be ineffective as screeners of good applicants if they use stereotypes in screening or are more influenced by recent interviews than earlier ones. This problem will be addressed in the discussion of college recruiters in this chapter and the problems of interviewing in Chapter 7.

Computer Matching Services

Systems similar to the computer dating services that flourished a few years ago have been developed to match people desiring jobs and organizations needing people. These amount to extraorganizational skills inventories, and they are a natural use of the computer. The U.S. Employment Service's Job

---

EXHIBIT 6–9   A Questionable Want Ad

You can get into trouble very easily when you're hiring people these days. Look at this ad, and try to learn from its mistakes.

Is sex a bona fide occupational qualification for this job? Probably not under federal laws. You're in trouble.

Can you prove the age requirement is a business necessity? If you can't show that someone over age 40 can't do the job, you might be subject to a bias suit.

HELP WANTED

Telephone Sales

Women, age 25-40, needed for telephone sales. Must have high school diploma and good credit rating. Call Mr. Smith at Acme Manufacturing Co. Inc., 555-3333.

Is this necessary for the successful performance of the job? Another strike against you.

Will your business suffer without this condition? Is a person's credit rating important when you're talking about his or her ability to sell by phone? Think again.

Bank is attempting to fill the need for a nationwide job-matching network to reduce unemployment. In addition to this government service, there are private-sector systems.

A number of firms now provide for a fee computerized listings of jobs or job candidates. Connexions of Cambridge, Massachusetts, charges high-technology companies $600 for an eight-paragraph want ad.[23] Job seekers are charged $15 to look at a computerized listing of advertisements for two hours. If a job seeker sees a job that is appealing, Connexions helps the person apply immediately from his or her own terminal.

One of Connexions' advertisers is Digital Equipment Corporation, a computer manufacturer based in Maynard, Massachusetts. William Baker, Digital's human resources manager, believes computerized recruiting "will evolve to be a major factor in the next two or three years."

Some companies make job seekers pay to put their résumés in the computer. Plenum Publishing Corporation's Career Placement Registry, Inc., in Alexandria, Virginia, says it has 11,000 résumés on file after a year of operation. "Employees can punch in the qualifications they want and have the résumé come on-line," says Robert A. Goldberg, Marketing Manager. Job seekers pay $15 to $40, depending on salary expectations. Career Systems, Inc., in West Palm Beach, Florida, charges $49.50 each to list résumés. It has listed 7,000, 40 percent of them from people who are unemployed.

Special-Event Recruiting

When the supply of employees available is not large or when the organization is new or not well-known, some organizations have successfully used special events to attract potential employees. They may stage open houses, schedule headquarters, visits, provide literature, and advertise these events in appropriate media. To attract professionals, organizations may have hospitality suites at professional meetings. Executives also make speeches at association meetings or schools to get the organization's image across. Ford Motor Company conducted symposia on college campuses and sponsored cultural events to attract attention to its qualifications as a good employer.

One of the most interesting approaches is to provide job fairs and native daughter and son days. A group of firms sponsors a meeting or exhibition at which each has a booth to publicize jobs available. Some experts claim recruiting costs have been cut 80 percent using these methods. They may be scheduled on holidays to reach college students home at that time or to give the presently employed a chance to look around. This technique is especially useful for smaller, less well-known employers. It appeals to job seekers who wish to locate in a particular area and those wanting to minimize travel and interview time.

---

[23] William M. Bulkeley, *The Wall Street Journal*, February 8, 1983, p. 35.

Summer Internships

Another approach to recruiting and getting specialized work done that has been tried by some organizations is to hire students during the summer as interns. This approach has been used by businesses (Sherwin-Williams Company, Chase Manhattan Bank, Standard Oil Company of Ohio, Kaiser Aluminum, First National City Bank), government agencies (City of New York), and hospitals. Students in accredited graduate hospital programs, for example, serve a summer period called a *preceptorship*.

There are a number of purposes for these programs. They allow organizations to get specific projects done, expose them to talented potential employees who may become their "recruiters" at school, and provide trial-run employment to determine if they want to hire particular people full time. Interns also typically bring high levels of creative energy and new, fresh, and unbiased ideas to a job.[24]

From the student's point of view, the summer internship means a job with pay; some experience in the world of work; a possible future job; a chance to use one's talents in a realistic environment; and in some cases, earning course credit hours. In a way, it is a short form of some co-op college work and study programs.

The organization usually provides supervision and a choice of projects to be done. Some of the projects the City of New York's college interns worked on during one summer were snow emergency planning, complaint handling, attitude survey of lower-level employees, and information dissemination.

There are costs to these programs, of course. Sometimes the interns take up a lot of supervisory time, and the work done is not always the best. But the major problem some organizations have encountered concerns the expectations of students. Some students expect everything to be perfect at work. When it is not, they get negative impressions about the organization they have worked for, assuming that it is less well-organized than others in the field. Such disillusioned students become *reverse recruiters*. This effect has caused some organizations to drop the programs. Others have done so when they found they were not able to recruit many interns.

COLLEGE RECRUITING

The college recruiting process is similar in some ways to other recruiting. However, in college recruiting the organization sends an employee, usually called a recruiter, to a campus to interview candidates and describe the organization to them. Coinciding with the visit, brochures and other literature

---

[24] Robert E. Hite, "How to Hire Using College Internship Programs," *Personnel Journal*, February 1986, pp. 110–112.

about the organization are often distributed. The organization may also run ads to attract students or conduct seminars at which company executives talk about various facets of the organization.

In the typical procedure, those seeking employment register at the college placement service. This placement service is a labor market exchange providing opportunities for students and employers to meet and discuss potential hiring. During the recruiting season (from about mid-October to mid-March), candidates are advised of scheduled visits through student newspapers, mailings, bulletin boards, and so forth. At the placement service, they reserve preliminary interviews with employers they want to see and are given brochures and other literature about the firms. After the preliminary interviews and before leaving the campus, each recruiter invites the chosen candidates to make a site visit at a later date. Those lower on the list are told they are being considered and are called upon if students chosen first decide not to accept employment with the firm.

Students who are invited to the site are given more job information and meet appropriate potential supervisors and other executives. They are entertained and may be given a series of tests as well. The organization bears all expenses. If the organization desires to hire an individual, he or she is given an offer prior to leaving the site or shortly thereafter by mail or phone.[25] Some bargaining may take place on salary and benefits, depending on the current labor market. The candidate then decides whether to accept or reject the offer. The college recruiting process is modeled in Exhibit 6-10. As you can see, effective recruiting requires the attention of both personnel and operating executives.

Various persons influence the applicant in job choice: peers, family, wife/ husband or companion, and professors. The main influence appears to be the recruiter. You can learn a lot about the job situation by knowing what happens on the recruiter's side of the desk. Mary Kale, a recruiter for Bethlehem Steel, often has a recruiting day like the one described in the P/HRM Manager Close-Up later in this chapter.

The Effective College Recruiter

In college recruiting, generally three elements are involved: the organization, the applicant, and the intervening variable—the recruiter. The recruiter is the filter and the matcher, the one who is actually seen by the applicants and is studied as a representative of the company. The recruiter is not just an employee but is viewed as an example of the kind of person the organization employs and wants in the future.

Students prefer recruiters who have work experience in their specialties and have some personal knowledge of the university they are visiting. Stu-

---

[25] Thomas J. Bergman and M. Susan Taylor, "College Recruitment: What Attracts Students to Organizations," *Personnel,* May-June 1984, pp. 34–36.

EXHIBIT 6–10   The College Recruiting Process

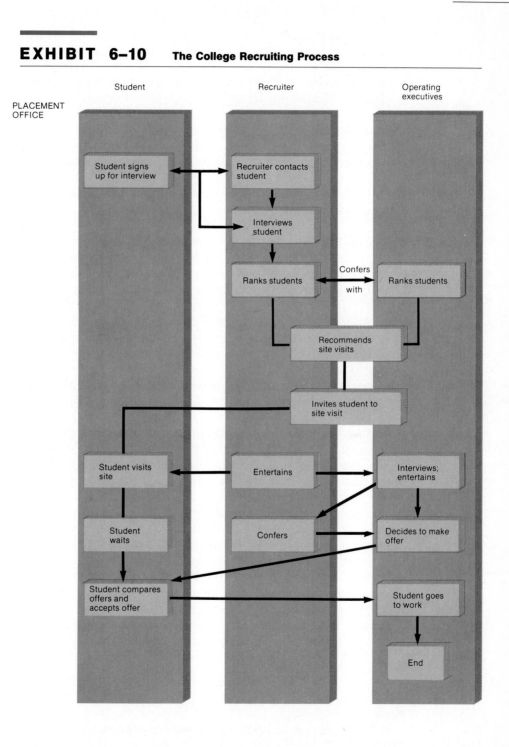

dents also have preferences for specific behavior during the recruiting interview. Characteristics in the recruiter they want most are: friendliness, knowledge, personal interest in the applicant, and truthfulness. Second, some applicants prefer enthusiastic and knowledgeable communicators.[26]

Major flaws students have found in typical recruiters are:

Lack of Interest in the Applicant Students infer indifference if the recruiter's presentation is mechanical—bureaucratic—programmed. One student reported, "The company might just as well have sent a tape recorder."

Lack of Enthusiasm If the recruiter seems bored, students infer that he or she represents a dull and uninteresting company.

Stress or Too-Personal Interviews Students resent too many personal questions about their social class, their parents, and so forth. They want to be evaluated for their own accomplishments. They, like most people, also unanimously reject stressful or sarcastic interviewing styles.

Time Allocation by Recruiters The final criticism of recruiters has to do with how much time they talk and how much they let applicants talk or ask questions. From the point of view of the applicant, much of the recruiter's time is wasted with a long canned history of the company, number of employees, branches, products, assets, pension plans, and so forth. Many of the questions the recruiter asks applicants are answered on the application blank, anyway.

Realistic Job Preview It is also important for recruiters to provide realistic expectations of the job. When they do so, there is significantly lower turnover of new employees, and the same number of people apply. Researchers have found that most recruiters give general, glowing descriptions of the company rather than a balanced or truthful presentation.

Research suggests that recruitment can be made more effective through the use of **realistic job previews (RJPs).**[27] A realistic job preview provides the prospective employee with pertinent information about the job without distortion or exaggeration. In traditional job previews, the job is presented as attractive, interesting, and stimulating. Some jobs are all of these things. However, most jobs have some unattractive features.[28] The RJP presents the full picture, warts and all, as suggested in Exhibit 6–11.

Exhibit 6–11 presents the typical consequences of traditional previews versus job previews. Studies conducted at Southern New England Telephone,

[26] John Boudreau and Sara Rynes, "Giving It the Old College Try," *Personnel Administrator,* March 1987, pp. 78–85.

[27] John P. Wanous, "A Job Preview Makes Recruiting More Effective," *Harvard Business Review,* 1975, pp. 121–25.

[28] Larry Reibstein, "Crushed Hopes: When a New Job Proves to Be Something Different," *The Wall Street Journal,* June 10, 1987, p. 25.

EXHIBIT 6–11   Typical Consequences of Job Preview Procedures

Traditional Preview	Realistic Preview
Set initial job expectations too high ↓	Set job expectations realistically ↓
Job is typically viewed as attractive, stimulating and challenging ↓	Job may or may not be attractive, depending on individual's needs ↓
High rate of job offer acceptance ↓	Some accept, some reject job offer ↓
Work experience disconfirms expectations ↓	Work experience confirms expectations ↓
Dissatisfaction and realization that job not matched to needs ↓	Satisfaction; needs matched to job ↓
Low job survival, dissatisfaction, frequent thoughts of quitting	High job survival, satisfaction, infrequent thoughts of quitting

Source: Adapted from John P. Wanous, "Tell It Like It Is at Realistic Job Preview," *Personnel*, July-August 1975, p. 54.

Prudential Insurance Co., Texas Instruments, and the U.S. Military Academy have used and reported on the RJP.[29] The results indicate that:

> Newly hired employees who received RJPs have a higher rate of job arrival than those hired using traditional previews.
> Employees hired after RJPs indicate higher satisfaction.
> An RJP can "set" the job expectations of new employees at realistic levels.
> RJPs do not reduce the flow of highly capable applicants.

An analysis of 15 realistic job preview experiments that involved over 5,000 subjects revealed that RJPs can be expected to result in at least a 9% reduction, on average, in job turnovers.[30] The analysis, however, suggested that the reduction was moderated by job complexity. In jobs lower in complexity there was a smaller reduction in turnover than in jobs higher in complexity.

These findings suggest that RJPs can be used as an innoculation against disappointment with the realities of a job. At this stage of development, however, there is not conclusive evidence supporting the effectiveness of realistic job previews.[31] Although it seems clear that RJPs can have beneficial

---

[29] Paula Popovich and John P. Wanous, "The Realistic Job Preview as a Persuasive Communication," *Academy of Management Review*, October 1982, pp. 570–78, and John P. Wanous, *Organizational Entry* (Reading, Mass.: Addison-Wesley, 1980), pp. 51–61. Also see J. Weitz, "Job Expectancy and Survival," *Journal of Applied Psychology*, August 1956, pp. 245–47; and R. M. Macedonia, *Expectations—Press and Survival* (Unpublished doctoral dissertation, New York University, 1969).

[30] G. M. McEvoy and W. F. Cascio, "Strategies for Reducing Employee Turnover: A Meta-Analysis," *Journal of Applied Psychology*, May 1985, pp. 342–353.

[31] S. L. Premack and J. P. Wanous, "A Meta-Analysis of Realistic Job Preview Experiments," *Journal of Applied Psychology*, December 1985, pp. 706–19, and James A. Breaugh, "Realistic Job Previews: A Critical Appraisal and Future Research Directions," *Academy of Management Review*, October 1983, pp. 612–19.

P/HRM Manager Close-Up

Mary E. Kale
Bethlehem Steel Corporation

Mary Kale works for Bethlehem Steel Corporation. She was a metallurgist for two years and has been a recruiter for five. Recently, she recruited 26 of the 106 persons Bethlehem hired and has a high acceptance rate among her recruits. She is one of the 3,500 full-time recruiters in the United States today.

Two recent weeks are typical of her work life. One week she interviewed for five days at Cornell; she had to drive three hours through a snow squall to get there. The next week, she flew and drove on Sunday to Grove City to interview there Monday. She drove to Youngstown, Ohio, and interviewed there Tuesday, then drove back to Pittsburgh. Wednesday and Thursday she interviewed at Carnegie Mellon and other Pittsburgh schools. Friday was spent in a hotel interviewing.

What's her day like? She eats an early breakfast and begins interviewing at 9 A.M. She interviews candidates for 30 minutes each, takes a 30-minute walk instead of lunch, and resumes interviews until 5:30 P.M. In brief open periods she tries to line up other candidates, but typically she interviews 54 people a week. After a quick supper, she spends the evening in her hotel room writing reports on the day's recruits, calling recruit prospects for later interviews, and reading the résumés of the next day's prospects.

In each interview, she begins by putting the recruit at ease, then asks the recruit about himself or herself. Next she discusses the job requirements and what the company has to offer, and asks for questions. She sees herself as much as a job counselor as recruiter. She wants to help recruits find a direction for their lives, and also to acquire the best employees for Bethlehem.

Biography

Mary E. Kale, senior college relations representative for Bethlehem Steel Company, earned a B.S. in chemistry at Chatham College, Pittsburgh. Before her present position with Bethlehem Steel, Mary was a manage-

(continued)

ment trainee, metallurgical engineer, assistant college relations representative, and college relations representative. She travels extensively throughout the United States, meeting with industrial and government leaders as well as college placement officers and students. Mary has done videotaped news releases in connection with Bethlehem's communication effort and has served on specially appointed task forces and committees.

Job Description

At Bethlehem Steel Corporation, a recruiter's job consists primarily of visiting college and university campuses to interview graduating seniors for employment with the corporation. During the interview, the recruiter's objective is to learn as much as possible about the candidate's academic qualifications, motivation, experience, and goals, in order to evaluate her or his overall suitability for the jobs available. This task requires an in-depth knowledge of the corporation and the types of jobs to be filled. Once the recruiter evaluates the students, he or she must complete a written record of the interview, obtain a completed application form, and refer the file to the appropriate corporate department for further consideration and interview if desired.

In addition to interviewing, representatives visit key faculty and administration personnel on every campus at which the corporation conducts recruiting. Administrative tasks involved in college relations work include handling all correspondence with placement and faculty people concerning the campus visit, the completion of specification sheets describing the types of positions available and the degree required, and coordination of special events on campus, such as career fairs.

effects, at present there is still uncertainty as to why RJPs have the effects they do, and in what contexts they are likely to be the most effective.

Companies that wish to influence applicants should also review their recruiting literature to make sure it appeals to the most successful students. This literature, plus advertisements and articles in trade publications, are major factors in the students' organization-choice decision.

COST/BENEFIT ANALYSIS OF RECRUITING

Many aspects of recruitment, such as the effectiveness of recruiters, can be evaluated. Organizations assign goals to recruiting by types of employees. For example, a goal for a recruiter might be to hire 350 unskilled and semiskilled employees, or 100 technicians, or 100 machinists, or 100 managerial employees per year. Then the organization can decide who are the best recruiters. They may be those who meet or exceed quotas and those whose recruits stay with the organization and are evaluated well by their superiors.

EXHIBIT 6-12   Yields of Recruiting Methods by Various Calculations

Source of Recruit	Yield	Total Yield (percent)	Ratio of Acceptance to Receipt of Résumé	Ratio of Acceptance to Offer
Write-ins	2,127	34.77%	6.40	58.37
Advertising	1,979	32.35	1.16	39.98
Agencies	856	14.00	1.99	32.07
Direct college placement	465	7.60	1.50	13.21
Internal company	447	7.30	10.07	65.22
Walk-ins	134	2.19	5.97	57.14
Employee referrals	109	1.78	8.26	81.82

Sources of recruits can also be evaluated. In college recruiting, the organization can divide the number of job acceptances by the number of campus interviews to compute the cost per hire at each college. Then it drops from the list campuses that are not productive.

The methods of recruiting can be evaluated by various means. Exhibit 6-12 compares the results of a number of these methods. The organization can calculate the cost of each method (such as advertising) and divide it by the benefits it yields (acceptances of offers). After the interviews, the organization can also examine how much accurate job information was provided during the recruitment process.

Another aspect of recruiting that can be evaluated is what is referred to as the *quality of hire*. This measure can provide management with an assessment of the quality of new employees being recruited and hired.[32] The quality of hire measure is calculated as follows:

$$QH = PR + HP + HR/N$$

where

QH = quality of recruits hired
PR = average job performance ratings (20 items on scale) of new hirees (e.g., 4 on a 5-point scale or 20 items × 4)
HP = percent of new hirees promoted within one year (such as 35 percent)
HR = percent of hirees retained after one year (e.g., 85 percent)
N = number of indicators used

---

[32] This measure was developed by Jac Fitz-enz in *How to Measure Human Resources Management* (New York: McGraw-Hill, 1984), pp. 86–87.

A RETURN TO THE P/HRM · IN · ACTION

Clark Kirby got prices of ads from all the Houston papers, including suburban papers and ethnic papers. He also discussed the impact and readership of the papers with the personnel/human resource managers he'd befriended. On this basis, he chose the major Houston afternoon paper, the leading black newspaper, the leading Hispanic paper, and a suburban paper in an area near the plant.

He also investigated the leading radio stations and selected the one that had the highest rating of the top three and the lowest commercial cost. He chose commuter times to run the radio ads. The advertising approach was innovative.

The pay and working conditions offered at the Houston plant were competitive. After Clark's recruiting campaign, he had the following numbers of applicants:

Managerial positions	68
Professional/technical	10
Clerical	78
Skilled employees	110
Semiskilled employees	720

Clark notified Ed of the results. The job now was to select the best of the applicants. Clark knows that is no easy job. Effective selection/hiring is the subject of Chapter 7.

Therefore,

$$QH = 80 + 35 + 85/3$$
$$= \$200/3$$
$$= 66.6\%$$

The 66 percent quality of hire rate is a relative value. It will be up to management whether this represents an excellent, good, fair, or poor level.

Some caution must be exercised with the quality of hire measure when evaluating the recruitment strategy. Performance ratings and promotion rates are all beyond the control of a recruiter. A good new employee can be driven away by few promotion opportunities, inequitable performance ratings, or job market conditions that have nothing to do with the effectiveness of the recruiter. Nevertheless, the quality of hire measure can provide some insight into the recruiter's ability to attract employees.

SUMMARY

This chapter has demonstrated the process whereby organizations recruit additional employees, suggested the importance of recruiting, and shown who recruits, where, and how.

To summarize the major points covered in this chapter:

1. Recruiting is the set of activities an organization uses to attract job candidates who have the abilities and attitudes needed to help the organization achieve its objectives.

2. External factors that affect the recruiting process include influences such as government and union restrictions, the state of the labor market, composition of the labor force, and the location of the organization. The passage of the Immigration Reform and Control Act of 1986 has placed a major responsibility on employers in stopping the flow of illegal immigration to the United States.

3. Three aspects affect recruiting from the organization's viewpoint: the recruiting requirements set, organization policies and procedures, and the organizational image.

4. Applicants' abilities, attitudes, and preferences, based on past work experiences and influences by parents, teachers, and others, affect them in two ways: how they set job preferences, and how they go about seeking a job.

5. In larger organizations the P/HRM department does the recruiting; in smaller organizations, multipurpose P/HRM people or operating managers recruit and interview applicants.

6. Two sources of recruits could be used to fill needs for additional employees: present employees (internal) or those not presently affiliated with the organization (external).
    a. Internal sources can be tapped through the use of job posting and bidding; moonlighting by present employees; and seeking recommendations from present employees regarding friends who might fill these vacancies.
    b. External sources include walk-ins, referrals from schools, and state employment offices.

7. Alternatives to recruiting personnel when work must be completed include overtime, temporary employees, and employee leasing.

8. Advertising, personal recruiting, computerized matching services, special-event recruiting, and summer internships are methods that can be used to recruit external applicants.

9. The criteria that characterize a successful college recruiter include:
    a. Showing a genuine interest in the applicant.
    b. Being enthusiastic.
    c. Employing a style that is neither too personal nor too stressful.
    d. Allotting enough time for applicants' comments and questions.

10. A better job of recruiting and matching employees to job will mean lower employee turnover and greater employee satisfaction and organizational effectiveness.

11. In larger organizations, recruiting functions are more extensively planned and elevated.

Likely approaches used on the seven-model organizations specified in Exhibit 1–9 (Chapter 1) are summarized in Exhibit 6–13. It should be noted that several of the model organizations employ different categories of employees.

Type of Organization	Employment Conditions Affect Recruiting		Importance of Image		Methods of Recruiting							
	Greatly	Little	Crucial	Not too Important	Employment Agencies	Newspaper Ads	Radio Commercials	Present Employees	Computer Matching	Special Events	College Recruiting	Summer Internships
1. Large size, low complexity, high stability	X			X	X	X	X		X		X	X
2. Medium size, low complexity, high stability		X		X	X	X		X	X		X	
3. Small size, low complexity, high stability	X		X		X	X	X	X		X		
4. Medium size, moderate complexity, moderate stability	X		X		X	X	X	X	X	X	X	
5. Large size, high complexity, low stability		X		X	X	X	X		X		X	X
6. Medium size, high complexity, low stability		X	X		X	X	X	X		X	X	
7. Small size, high complexity, low stability	X		X		X	X	X	X		X		X

For example, a small, volatile hospital and a small, volatile toy company employ different kinds of employees, and the sources of recruits used would vary in such organizations. Only a few of the aspects of recruitment have been summarized in this table.

Questions for Review and Discussion

1. Why is the Immigration Reform and Control Act of 1986 a complex piece of legislature?
2. Of what value would a realistic job preview be in attempting to reduce turnover?
3. Give some do's and don'ts in recruiting interviews in terms of questions it is legal to ask.
4. Describe a model of the recruiting/attraction process. How do organization requirements, organizational policies, and organizational pay affect the process?
5. How do career planning and job preferences relate to effective job finding? Outline an approach to specify the job characteristics you want prior to job search.
6. Why would a firm use employee leasing as a method of completing work?
7. What are the major disadvantages of recruitment from within?
8. What sources of recruits do organizations use for blue-collar, gray-collar, white-collar, and managerial recruits?
9. Compare and contrast the effectiveness of the methods of recruiting, such as advertising, special events, internships, and others.
10. How do organizations recruit college students for jobs? What are effective and ineffective recruiters like?

GLOSSARY

Employee Leasing. Paying a leasing firm to provide the organization with a ready-made pool of human resources.

Immigration Reform and Control Act of 1986. All employers are required to screen every job applicants' eligibility for lawful employment. Thus, the employer has a major responsibility for not permitting illegal immigrants to be or remain employed.

Job Posting. A listing of job openings that includes job specifications, appearing on a bulletin board or in company publications.

Job Search. The set of activities a person (job candidate) initiates to seek and find a position that will be comfortable and rewarding.

Realistic Job Preview. A briefing that provides a job candidate with accurate and clear information about the attractive and unattractive features of a job. Being realistic so that expectations are accurate is the objective of a realistic job preview.

Recruitment. The set of activities an organization uses to attract job candidates who have the abilities and attitudes needed to help the organization achieve its objectives.

APPLICATION CASE 6–1

So Long to the Sunday Classifieds*

In a time when many companies are cutting costs across their operations, a growing number of P/HRM departments are changing the ways they recruit. Their goal: to boost recruiting efficiency (reducing recruiting costs per hire). Their means: innovative recruiting approaches that bring imagination and aggressiveness to a company's overall recruiting function. Innovations are occurring in several elements of the recruiting process. Here is a look at innovations in five areas.

Recruitment Advertising

An increasing number of companies are supplementing and even replacing the traditional classified ad approach to advertising with creative, clever, and eye-catching ads. These ads are essentially a company's resume and cover letter, designed to send a unique and memorable message about the company to sought-after prospective applicants. Recently, *Personnel Journal* reviewed several hundred ads submitted by subscribers and reported some trends in this type of advertising. They include:

1. Use of Employees in Ads Instead of the traditional testimonials, more company ads are spotlighting employees, talking about their skills, jobs, and accomplishments. For example, General Dynamics has run a series of ads which, by comparison to great inventors, compliments profiled employees and their colleagues. For example, one ad headline in the series proclaims, "We're looking for another Newton. . . . And another Newman" (Howard Newman, one of General Dynamic's senior project engineers). The ad's text showcases Mr. Newman's accomplishments and long tenure with the company and then urges those interested and qualified to "join Howard in the pursuit of technology excellence and discovery, apply for a position with us. . . . Who knows? You might become the next Newman." In some other ads in the series, General Dynamics has declared, "We're looking for another Edison. . . . And another Hardison" (electrical engineer Corrine Hardison), and another Da Vinci. Like

---

* Written by Kim Stewart and adapted from: Bob Martin, "Recruitment Ad Ventures," *Personnel Journal*, August 1987, pp. 46–54; J. Scott Lord, "Contract Recruiting Comes of Age," *Personnel Administrator*, November 1987, pp. 49–53; Maury Hanigan, "Campus Recruiters Upgrade Their Pitch," *Personnel Administrator*, November 1987, pp. 55–58; and Margaret Magnus, "Is Your Recruitment All It Can Be?" *Personnel Journal*, February 1987, pp. 54–63.

many employee-spotlight ads developed by other companies, this series portrays the corporation as a place where very talented and dedicated people work and reach their potential.

2. Promotion of Intangible Benefits In cases where a job is highly attractive and thus doesn't need promoting, employers have turned to emphasizing certain intangible benefits of the company such as advancement opportunities, employment security, creative freedom, and entrepreneurial opportunities. Lockheed Missile & Space Company has run a series of sports-related ads that promote company benefits. One such ad is entitled "Net Gain." Featuring a tennis racket and tennis balls in a partly closed briefcase, the text offers, "Along with a diverse and challenging project list, Lockheed Missile & Space Company makes a point of providing employees with truly comprehensive recreational programs and facilities." The St. Paul Medical Center has developed a series of one-word headline ads that promote certain themes such as "Commitment" (describing the center's commitment to patient care and employee career development) and "Balance" ("between caring professionals . . . between tradition and technology . . . between performance and opportunity"). Washington University in St. Louis uses creative advertising to promote its flexible work schedules, and in one ad entitled "Even you-know-who rested on the seventh day," the company published its nursing salaries.

3. Point-of-Purchase Recruitment A growing number of service companies with high turnover in low-skilled jobs are recruiting using point-of-purchase ads. For example, Pizza Hut places recruiting coupons on their carry-out boxes. Featuring a drawing of a large lead pencil, the ad suggests, "If you want a good job, get the lead out." The coupon provides a mini resume form for prospective applicants who don't have resumes. The Quik Wok chinese food takeout chain uses bag-stuffers that picture a broken fortune cookie and proclaim "Not everyone will have the good fortune to work at Quik Wok." The stuffer describes job opportunities. The success of point-of-purchase ads has eliminated Quik Wok's use of classified ads. Other users have found the strategy to be a low-cost, highly efficient and flexible form of recruiting; when a new position needs to be filled, they simply distribute the bag stuffers.

Contract Recruiting

Companies in fast-growing industries are seeking the expertise of a relatively new type of external specialist: the contract recruiter. This specialist is contracted on a temporary basis to perform recruiting functions for different job openings. The recruiter screens résumés, conducts telephone and in-person interviews, coordinates campus recruiting, prepares and executes formal offers, and performs any number of contractual recruiting responsibilities. He or she is not affiliated with an employment agency and does not receive a commission or a percentage of the hiree's salary. Rather, the recruiter is self-employed and is paid at an hourly rate negotiated with the client company.

These self-employed specialists are becoming popular because they can provide several benefits to client companies. When a company is undergoing exceptionally fast growth with immediate hiring needs, a recruiter can be quickly brought in to handle the suddenly burdensome task. The recruiting is performed without hiring permanent (and later unnecessary) staff. For example, when GTE in Needham, Massachusetts suddenly found itself with a Department of Defense contract requiring 1,200 professional employees to be hired in 16 months, GTE turned to 12 contract recruiters who become an instant employment department. They set up the system, completed the task, and then trained their replacements before departing 16 months later. Cosmetics manufacturer Helene Curtis Inc., regularly calls on contract recruiters to help the company handle its 15- to-20 percent yearly growth. The company cites suffering flexibility that contract recruiters provide as a major benefit. Recruiters can also serve as an external, objective advisor to the company's personnel function.

Some contract recruiters develop expertise in certain employment fields (such as electrical engineering or computer software design). Companies with hiring needs in these areas benefit from the specialists' contacts and highly focused capabilities. Some companies hire the same recruiters time and again, finding that the subsequent knowledge of the company's recruiting needs and functions that the recruiter acquires helps to further reduce per-hire costs.

Campus Recruiting

With declining college enrollments and growing demand for recruits with college degrees, companies are finding that recruiting on college campuses has become very competitive. As a result, many are launching strategies to both boost their offer-acceptance rates and lower recruiting costs.

Rather than select recruits from the Placement Office's résumé file, some companies are identifying a number of students in their junior year and focusing efforts on these select recruits. More firms are establishing programs that educate professors more fully on the company's career opportunities for graduates. For example, Macy's brings professors to a showcase store where the educators spend a day observing trainees and meeting with managers. Other companies such as Citibank hires professors to lecture in the company's training programs. Organizations such as Texas Instruments also provide executives as guest lecturers at several universities. These actions are designed to enhance the professors' knowledge of the company which hopefully is communicated to students and to develop executives' relationships with certain schools.

Some companies are also refining their recruitment brochures. Rather than providing the traditional, very general brochure on the company, firms are now developing smaller, more individualized publications that provide information on particular jobs and departments, and information on the respective community where a prospective applicant would work (for instance, information on cost of living, community recreation facilities). Invitation letters to a campus interview are being personalized, often explaining why the company is interested in that particular student. More companies are producing recruiting videos for show on campus. Companies are also paying more attention to the quality of their on-campus interviewers, providing their recruiters with communications skill training. And many firms are replacing the form rejection letter with one that is more tactful and considerate. Firms are mindfully aware of the impact that a word-of-mouth reputation created by an inconsiderate, disinterested recruiter can have on a company's campus recruiting efforts.

Computer Databases

Computer databases are being developed as job and résumé data banks. One example: Job Stores Inc., has developed a franchise chain of "stop and shop" employment centers located in high-traffic shopping malls. At any center, a job hunter can tap the Job Stores Network computer database by obtaining a computer printout on job openings in the local area and nationwide. The fee: $75 for 90 days' access to the network. Any company can list its job openings on the network at no charge. In seeking participation from businesses, Job Stores' franchisees focus on jobs in the $11,000–$22,000 pay range, job openings which companies usually don't fill via employment agencies.

JobNet, another computer database network, allows job hunters to place their résumés in the network at no charge. Companies pay a fee for access to the database which has over one million résumés of technical professionals on line. A company can search the database by specifying any of a number of criteria, such as the résumé's recency. Career Technologies runs the network and obtains résumés via job fairs, advertising, and exclusive contracts with over 20 professional associations and societies.

Some college placement centers are also establishing computer databases to link students with prospective jobs. For example, the Career Connection Company, of State College, Pennsylvania, has established Job Search, a computer database of job information. The network provides job listings (up to 20 lines each provided by companies) and is available for all students.

Employee Referrals

Lastly, companies are adding pizzazz to the widely used employee referral/ bounty system. A growing number of companies are aggressively promoting referral campaigns with special themes and prizes. Referral bonuses run the gamut from money and trips to time off and credit used to "buy" items from a special catalog. Many referral programs are periodically given a boost with new bonuses and new themes.

Questions for Thought

1. Assess the effectiveness of a recruitment advertising strategy that relies on imaginative, highly visual and eye-catching ads. What are the potential strengths and drawbacks of this approach to recruitment advertising?
2. What type of company (in what kind of industry) would most benefit from contract recruiters? What type would least benefit?
3. Suppose you are faced with the task of developing a college recruiting strategy for obtaining talented business school graduates with degrees in management information systems (developing and managing a company computer information network). Demand for these individuals is currently very high; supply is limited. Develop a recruiting strategy that addresses innovations discussed in the case and includes your own ideas.

7

SELECTION

LEARNING OBJECTIVES

After completing this chapter, you should be able to:

- **Define** the steps in the selection process.
- **List** what selection criteria are available and how they can be used to make selection more effective.
- **Describe** how to use selection tools such as interviews and biodata more effectively.
- **Compare** the different types of validity—content, construct, and criterion-related.
- **Illustrate** the methods used to observe and evaluate the performance of individuals in an assessment center.

KEY TERMS

Assessment Center
Content Validity
Construct Validity
Criterion-Related Validity
Genetic Screening
Reliability
Selection
Structured Employment Interview
Weighted Application Blank

CHAPTER OUTLINE

P/HRM · IN · ACTION

(Continued from Chapter 6)

Clark Kirby is satisfied. He and his assistants have recruited 986 applicants for the 596 positions Gunther will have at its Tampa plant. But before getting too satisfied, he realized that there is a big job ahead of him. Which 596 of the 986 should be hired? And who should do the hiring?

The P/HRM specialist has done some preliminary screening. Most of the applicants have completed an application blank. But where does he go from here?

Clark called Ed Humphrey, the plant manager, and asked if he wants to be involved in the hiring. Ed said that he only had time to choose his top management team. The rest is up to Clark. Ed reminded Clark that the company didn't want them to raid other plants. Raiding other plants for employees was simply against company policy. Clark said he knew that and would abide by company policy.

Clark is now faced with making 596 selection decisions. As this chapter will show, selection involves making many decisions. Selection is a vital and continuous process in an organization. Employee selection is important because the goals of the organization can only be accomplished if the right match is made between the person and the job.

> Selection is the process by which an organization chooses from a list of applicants the person or persons who best meet the selection criteria for the position available, considering current environmental conditions.

This definition emphasizes the effectiveness aspect of selection, but selection decisions must also be efficient. The second purpose of selection is to improve the proportion of successful employees chosen from the applicant list at the least cost. Selection costs can be high. In 1987, it was estimated that it cost an organization approximately $32,000 to select a top-level executive, $8,000 to select a middle manager, $6,000 for a supervisor, $8,000 for an engineer, $10,000 for an accountant, and $2,800 for a secretary.[1]

The basic objective of selection is to obtain the employees most likely to meet the organization's standards of performance. The employees' satisfaction and complete development of their abilities are included in this objective.

---

[1] Based on conversations with directors of P/HRM functions in large organizations in urban areas such as Chicago, Houston, Dallas, and San Diego.

A DIAGNOSTIC APPROACH
TO THE SELECTION PROCESS

As Clark Kirby sets out to hire 596 employees, he will follow a selection process influenced by many factors. These factors are highlighted in the diagnostic model in Exhibit 7-1. We'll begin by examining the factors in the external and internal environment.

Environmental Circumstances
Influencing Selection

The Internal Environment The nature of the organization doing the selecting affects the process it uses. The private and third sectors use similar methods, but the public sector is different. Traditionally, selection in the public sector has been made on the basis of either political patronage or merit. The patronage system gives jobs to those who have worked to elect public officials. This was the only method used in the public sector until the civil service reforms of the late 1800s. In the private and third sectors, friendship with managers or employees can become a factor in the choice, but this is not the same thing as patronage. Pure "merit" selection (choice based on the employee's excellence in abilities and experience) is an idea that systematic personnel selection tries to achieve but seldom does.

Other aspects of the organization that affect selection are the organization's size, complexity, and technological volatility. Systematic, reliable, and valid P/HRM selection techniques are sometimes costly to develop and use. When this is so, typically only large organizations can afford to use them. To justify the development of these techniques, there must be a sufficient number of jobs to fill and a pool of candidates to fill them. If the organization is complex and has a large number of jobs with only a few occupants, sophisticated selection techniques are not cost-effective. The extent to which size dictates the number of employees in each work group also affects the usefulness of the techniques. In sum, the size, complexity, technological volatility, and nature of the organization will determine which selection techniques are cost-effective for the organization.

Nature of the Labor Market The second circumstance affecting the selection process is the labor market within which the organization functions. If there are many applicants, the selection decision can be complicated. When there are few applicants, it is relatively easy. The labor market for the organization is affected by the labor market in the country as a whole, the region, or the city in which the organization is located. It is further affected by the working conditions the organization offers, the job itself, and the organization's image. (These were discussed earlier in the book and will be covered in Chapters 9–11.) For example, hospital dieticians trying to hire dishwashers or food preparation helpers do not have much of a selection decision to worry about.

EXHIBIT 7–1 Factors Affecting Selecting of Human Resources and Effectiveness

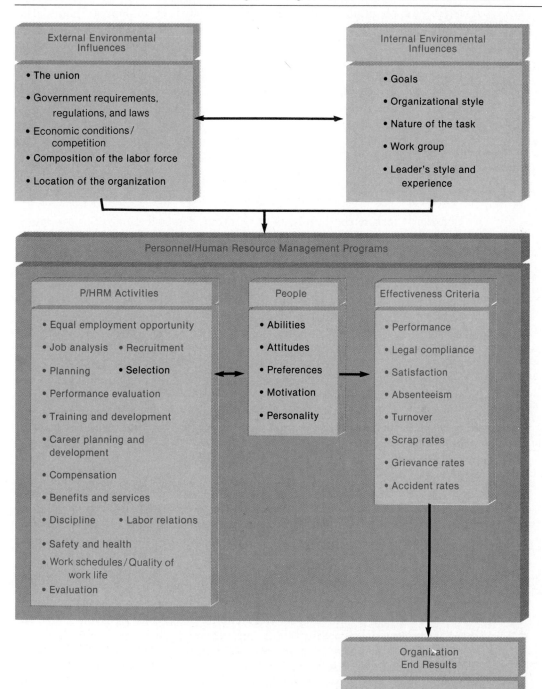

External Environmental Influences

- The union
- Government requirements, regulations, and laws
- Economic conditions/competition
- Composition of the labor force
- Location of the organization

Internal Environmental Influences

- Goals
- Organizational style
- Nature of the task
- Work group
- Leader's style and experience

Personnel/Human Resource Management Programs

P/HRM Activities

- Equal employment opportunity
- Job analysis
- Recruitment
- Planning
- Selection
- Performance evaluation
- Training and development
- Career planning and development
- Compensation
- Benefits and services
- Discipline
- Labor relations
- Safety and health
- Work schedules/Quality of work life
- Evaluation

People

- Abilities
- Attitudes
- Preferences
- Motivation
- Personality

Effectiveness Criteria

- Performance
- Legal compliance
- Satisfaction
- Absenteeism
- Turnover
- Scrap rates
- Grievance rates
- Accident rates

Organization End Results

- Competitive product(s)
- Competitive service(s)

The job can be unpleasant, and it is performed at unpopular hours (the breakfast crew might have to arrive at 5:30 A.M.). The workday can be long, the pay is not good, and frequently there are no possibilities for promotion. For such jobs, an applicant who walks in the door and is found to be free of a communicable disease will usually be hired. Rarely are there enough applicants. A civil service administrator who must choose from hundreds of applicants for foreign service postings to European embassies has a much more difficult selection decision to make.

Those who work in personnel/human resource management analyze this labor market factor by use of the selection ratio:

$$\text{Selection ratio} = \frac{\text{Number of applicants selected}}{\text{Number of applicants available for selection}}$$

Consider Clark Kirby's problem at Gunther. The selection ratios are: managers 38/68, or about 1:2; professional/technical, 10/10, or 1:1; clerical, 44/78, or about 1:2; skilled, 104/110, or about 1:1; semiskilled, 400/720, or almost 1:2. When the selection ratio is 1:1, the selection process is short and unsophisticated. It also means there are few applicants from which to select. With a selection ratio of 1:2, the process can be quite detailed. The larger ratio also means the organization can be quite selective in its choice. It is more likely that employees who fit the organization's criteria for success will be hired when the ratio is 1:2 than when it is 1:1.

Union Requirements If the organization is wholly or partly unionized, union membership prior to or shortly after hiring is a factor in the selection decision. Sometimes the union contract requires that seniority (experience at the job with the company) be the only criterion—or at least a major one—in selection. If the union has a hiring hall, the union makes the selection decision for the organization. In many ways, openly and subtly, a union can affect an organization's selection process.

Government Requirements The fourth circumstance affecting selection is government. In the United States, governments have passed laws designed to guarantee equal employment opportunity and human rights. Some of the requirements were described in detail in Chapter 3 on selection decisions.

Composition of the Labor Force Organizations often attempt to hire a labor force that reflects the makeup of their clients or customers. Even if government requirements regarding equal employment opportunity did not exist, it would be advisable for an organization to examine the composition of the labor force to help meet the needs of clients or customers. For example, in predominantly Spanish-speaking sections in Denver, the police department attempted to hire some Spanish-speaking police officers. To do so, the Denver police department attempted to recruit and select police officers who could speak Spanish fluently. Unfortunately, the police department found a shortage of police recruits who could speak fluent Spanish.

Location of the Organization The location of the organization also affects the selection process. Many high-technology firms have located their facilities in the Silicon Valley of California; Austin, Texas; and Boston, because of the abundant supply of job applicants. These regions of the country have attracted many skilled individuals who are properly trained to work for high-technology firms.

The Immediate Environment and Selection

You will note that in Exhibit 7–1 the people factor is emphasized. The basic objective, selection—to obtain high-performing employees—may be modified by the operating managers or controlling interests. It is management's responsibility to set selection objectives, such as:

- Employees who have high-quality standards.
- Employees who will stay with the company many years.
- Employees who have low accident rates.
- Employees who get along with their co-workers.
- Employees who get along with the customers.

These characteristics can influence the kind of employees selected. They do not, however, always correlate exactly with the optimal level of performance.

Selection seeks to identify the abilities and attitudes of the applicant so that these can be matched up with job requirements. Chapter 2 discussed how human beings differ on every possible characteristic: physical, mental, and psychological. All of these characteristics are important considerations in making a selection decision.

Selection also seeks to identify the nature of the task. From a job analysis (described in Chapter 4), up-to-date job specifications related to behavior are developed. The job specifications are used to define the characteristics (criteria) needed for a person to perform a certain task effectively. The essence of selection is to match the right applicant, one who has the right abilities and attitudes, with the right job and its specifications.

One more factor, which is not shown in Exhibit 7–1, influences the selection decision. This is the amount of time available to make the selection decision. If there is adequate time the organization may be able to use all the selection tools it normally uses. If there is an emergency, the selection decision may be shortened by dropping one or several of the steps in the selection process.

The selection activity is in Stage IV of development or maturity (see Exhibit 1–7, Chapter 1). It is well-developed, and many studies have been conducted that analyze the use of the various selection methods.

WHO MAKES SELECTION DECISIONS?

In smaller organizations with no P/HRM unit, the operating manager makes selection decisions. In medium-sized and larger organizations, both operating

EXHIBIT 7-2   The Role of Operating and Personnel Managers in Selection

Selection Function	Operating Manager (OM)	Personnel/Human Resource Manager (P/HRM)
Choice of selection criteria	Selected by OM	Recommends and implements the selection criteria based on job specifications
Validation of criteria		Performed by P/HRM
Screening interview		Normally performed by P/HRM
Supervision of application/ biodata form		Normally by P/HRM representative
Employment interview	OM and P/HRM	OM and P/HRM
Testing		Performed by P/HRM
Background/reference chart		Normally performed by P/HRM
Physical exam		Normally performed by P/HRM
Selection/decision	OM decides after considering P/HRM recommendation	Recommendation by P/HRM to OM

and P/HRM managers are involved in selection decisions, as Exhibit 7-2 indicates.

In larger organizations, the P/HRM manager in charge of selection is usually called the employment manager. An example is Audrey Johnson, employee relations manager of the Gillette Company (see the P/HRM Manager Close-Up in this chapter).

Some organizations also give employees a voice in the selection choice. Applicants are interviewed by employees, who are then asked to express their preferences. This procedure is used in university departments where the faculty expresses its preferences on applicants, and at the Lincoln Electric Company in Cleveland, where the work group recruits and selects replacements or additions.

Generally, more effective selection decisions are made when many people are involved in the decision and when adequate information is furnished to those selecting the candidates. The operating manager and the work group should have more to say about the selection decision than the P/HRM specialist.

SELECTION CRITERIA

If a selection program is to be successful, the employee characteristics believed necessary for effective performance on the job should be stated explicitly in the job specification. The criteria usually can be summarized in several categories: education, experience, physical characteristics, and personal characteristics. Basically, the selection criteria should list the characteristics of present em-

From The Wall Street Journal *with permission of Cartoon Features Syndicate*

"What we're really looking for is a not-too-bright young man with no ambition and who is content to stay on the bottom and not louse things up."

ployees who have performed well in the position to be filled.[2] As in human resource planning, however, if the list of characteristics desired is too long, it may be impossible to select anyone. And with no list of criteria, the wrong prospects are likely to be selected. Sometimes, because of limits on what the organization can offer or management's objectives, one gets criteria like those in the above cartoon.

Formal Education

An employer selecting from a pool of job applicants wants to find the person who has the right abilities and attitudes to be successful. These cognitive, motor, physical, and interpersonal attributes are present because of genetic predisposition and because they were learned in the home, at school, on the job, and so on. Most employers attempt to screen for abilities by specifying educational accomplishments.

Employers tend to specify as a criterion a specific amount (in years) of formal education and types of education. For the job of accountant, the em-

---

[2] Scott T. Rickard, "Effective Staff Selection," *Personnel Journal*, June 1981, pp. 475–78.

P/HRM Manager Close-Up

Audrey Johnson
The Gillette Company

Biography

Audrey Johnson, a graduate of the
University of Minnesota with an
M.B.A. in industrial relations, holds
the title of employee relations manager
for the Gillette Company, St. Paul,
Minnesota. She holds a B.A. from St.
Olaf College and is a graduate of the
Harvard-Radcliffe Program in Business
Administration. Johnson has had broad
personnel experience. Before joining
Gillette she worked as a personnel rep-
resentative at the University of
Minnesota. In her current position she
has:

Developed and instituted a comprehensive affirmative action plan that
   successfully stood a federal audit.
Streamlined and systematized employment practices and procedures to
   ensure their legality and efficiency.
Instituted compensation program with
   guidelines and controls to ensure
   uniform and equitable treatment for
   all employees.

Managed significant benefits changes,
   including installing a new dental insurance program and offering an
   HMO (Health Maintenance Organization) option.
Assessed training and development
   needs for all exempt employees.

Job Description

The position of employee relations
manager for all P/HRM administrative
functions in the manufacturing center
of the Gillette Company, one of the nation's largest personal care
manufacturers, involves responsibility
for employment, affirmative action,
compensation, work force, development
and training, benefits, and employee
services, along with a complete budget
responsibility of $300,000. The em-
ployee relations manager also
supervises a full-time staff of seven
subordinates.

ployer may list as an educational criterion a bachelor's degree in accounting. The employer may even prefer that the degree be from certain institutions, that the grade point average be higher than some minimum, and that certain honors have been achieved. To be legal, such criteria must relate to past performance of successful accountants at the firm.

Formal education can indicate ability or skills present, and level of accomplishment may indicate the degree of work motivation and intelligence of the applicant. In general, other things being equal, employers tend to prefer more to less education and higher to lower grades. But these characteristics must be correlated with job success if the criterion is to be an effective predictor.

The educational criteria must be validated against job performance. The employer must examine the amount and type of education that correlates with job effectiveness at the organization and use it as the selection criterion. This procedure is more effective than relying on preferences, and is the legal, ethical way to set an educational criterion.

Experience

Another useful criterion for selection is experience. Employers often equate experience with ability, as well as with attitude, reasoning that a prospect who has performed the job before and is applying for a similar job likes the work and will do it well. Since loyalty to the job and the organization is important, most employers prefer to hire from within, as discussed in Chapter 6.

One way to measure experience within the organization is to provide each employee with a seniority rating, which indicates the length of time he or she has been employed in the organization. In the military, the date of rank is an equivalent seniority measure. Seniority is measured in various ways: as total time worked for the firm, or time worked for the firm on a particular job or in a certain unit. Because some organizations in the past did not allow various groups to hold certain jobs, the courts and the EEOC are assigning retroactive and compensatory seniority to some employees.[3]

Physical Characteristics

In the past, many employers consciously or unconsciously used physical characteristics (including how an applicant looked) as a selection criterion. Many times this practice discriminated against ethnic groups and females. The practice is now illegal unless it can be shown that a physical characteristic is directly related to work effectiveness. Studies show that employers were more likely to hire and pay more to taller men, airlines chose flight attendants on the basis of beauty (or their definition of it), and receptionists were often chosen on the same basis.

---

[3] Alfred J. Walker, "Management Selection Systems That Meet the Challenges of the 80s," *Personnel Journal*, October 1981, pp. 775–80.

There are some tasks that require certain physical characteristics, usually stamina and strength, which can be tested. Candidates cannot legally be screened out by arbitrary height, weight, and similar requirements. The organization should determine the physical characteristics of present successful employees and use an attribute as a criterion *only* when all or most of them have it.

Personal Characteristics and Personality Type

The final criterion category is a catch-all called *personal characteristics* and *personality types*. One personal characteristic is marital status. Some employers have preferred "stable" married employees, assuming this characteristic would lead to lower turnover and higher performance. Other firms prefer divorced or single persons because they are more willing to be transferred or to work weekends. Discrimination in selection based on marital status is illegal in some places; and unless an organization has data to support the relation of this criterion to performance, it makes little sense.

A second personal characteristic is age. It is illegal to discriminate against persons over 40 years old in the United States. It is not illegal to discriminate against young people, although protecting this group also has been proposed. Any age criterion should be examined by seeing how it relates to present successful employees.

Employers may prefer certain "personality" types for jobs. To use Carl Jung's classification, they may prefer extroverts to introverts.[4] An outgoing personality can be an important characteristic for employees who deal with the public, such as receptionists, salespersons, and caseworkers; it may not be useful for other jobs, such as actuaries, lab technicians, or keypunch operators. The personality type specified should be based on past experience or be weighted lower than other, more directly relevant criteria.

RELIABILITY AND VALIDITY OF SELECTION CRITERIA

Before the organization can specify the characteristics to be sought in selection, the success criteria must be defined. Job analysis can indicate that the employee who meets minimum standards for a particular position processes 10 claims per hour, for example. This employee also receives an error rating of less than 5 percent and is absent fewer than six days per year.[5]

The next step is to determine ways of predicting which of the applicants can

[4] H. Read, M. Fordham, G. Adler, eds., C. G. Jung, *Collected Works* (Princeton, N.J.: Princeton University Press, 1953).

[5] L. R. Aiken, *Psychological Educational Testing* (Boston: Allyn & Bacon, 1971).

reach these levels of expectation. Sometimes direct success indicators (such as 10 claims per hour) are available. At other times proxies, such as levels of intelligence, the presence of specified abilities, or certain amounts and types of experience are used.

Reliability

The main purpose of selection is to make decisions about individuals. One attempt to predict which candidates will be successful is to give applicants tests or simulations (more will be said about these later). If these selection tools are to be useful they must be dependable or *reliable*. Thus, if Dan scores a 70 on an employment test on Monday, a 40 on a similar version of the test on Wednesday, and a 95 on Friday, it would not be possible to determine which score is the best measure of Dan's ability. The test is too unrealiable to use (assuming that Dan was not sick or tired on test days). The *reliability* of any selection technique refers to its freedom from systematic errors of measurement, or its consistency under different conditions.

Unless interviewers judge the potential of a job applicant to be the same one day as they did yesterday or a few days ago, their judgments are unreliable. Likewise, Dan's test scores are unreliable. In practice, one way to assess reliabilities is to correlate the scores of applicants given the same or similar tests or interviews on two different occasions. This correlation indicates the *stability* of scores over time. Reliability can also be determined by correlating scores from two alternate forms of a selection device (for example, test or interview). If the scores are the same or similar, the test is said to yield reliable scores.[6]

Interrater reliability is another estimate of reliability. It is calculated by having scores independently assessed by two or more raters (for example, performance evaluation, personality test). When nonobjective measures are used (e.g., performance evaluation), interrater reliability is important.

Validity

In addition to having reliable selection decision information, it is important, legally and organizationally, to have valid information. *Validity* refers to the extent to which a score or measure is an accurate predictor of success. It should be noted that validity refers to the inferences made from the use of a procedure, not to the procedure (test) itself. Siegel contrasts reliability and validity in this way: He points out that the yardstick is a reliable measure of space; no matter how many times you measure a person's height, the result will be the same.[7]

---

[6] Rober M. Guion, *Personnel Testing* (New York: McGraw-Hill, 1965), pp. 29–31.

[7] L. Siegel, *Industrial Psychology* (Homewood, Ill.: Richard D. Irwin, 1969). For a thorough discussion of validity, see *Principles for the Validation and Use of Personnel Selection Procedures* (Berkeley, Calif.: Division of Industrial Organizational Psychology, American Psychological Association, 1980).

But a yardstick has no validity as a measure of muscular coordination. The message is: A selection technique can be reliable without being valid. That is, if it is not valid, it is not measuring what it is suppose to measure.

It should be noted that reliability is *internally referenced:* It measures how well scores correlate with themselves, regardless of what they measure. On the other hand, validity is *externally referenced:* It measures how well scores relate to some other measure of behavior, such as job performance.

There are various types of validity that the P/HRM specialist should be familiar with: (1) content, (2) construct, and (3) criterion-related.[8] Knowledge of these forms of validity are needed to comply with EEO regulations involving P/HRM activities, such as selection, performance evaluation, and job analysis.

Content Validity The degree to which a test, interview, or performance evaluation measures the skill, knowledge, or ability to perform the job is called *content validity*. For example, employment tests used in the plumbing, bricklaying, and electrical construction trades are considered content valid when test content and job content correspond closely. Test and job content are directly observable, meaning that content validity is an appropriate type of validity.

An example of a content-valid test is a typing test for a secretarial position. Such a test can roughly replicate conditions on the job. The applicant can be given a typical sample of typing work under working conditions, and his or her performance on the sample can be evaluated. Assuming that the sample of typing work constitutes a random sample of typical work, the test is content valid. The typing test score is used to predict how successful a person will be in performing a job involving typing.[9] It is important to select a sample of work that closely resembles the type of work that will be done on the job.[10]

Content validity is not appropriate for more abstract job behaviors, such as leadership potential, leadership style, or work ethic. When selection procedures involve the use of tests to measure leadership characteristics and/or personality, construct validity rather than content validity is appropriate.

Construct Validity A construct is a trait; a test is construct valid when it measures a trait that is important for a job.

Construct validity is defined as:

> a demonstrated relationship between underlying traits or "hypothetical constructs" inferred from behavior and a set of test measures related to

---

[8] American Psychology Association, American Educational Research Association, and National Council on Measurement in Education Joint Committee. *Standards For Educational and Psychological Testing* (Washington, D.C.: American Psychological Association, 1985).

[9] R. H. Foley and E. Surdstrom, "Content Representatives: An Empirical Method of Evaluation," *Journal of Applied Psychology,* 1985, pp. 567–71.

[10] Robert M. Guion, "Scoring of Content Domain Samples: The Problem of Fairness," *Journal of Applied Psychology,* August 1978, pp. 449–506.

those constructs. Construct validity is not established with a simple study but only with the understanding that comes from a large body of empirical evidence.[11]

To use an example, if leadership is important for performing the work of a project manager, a test that measures leadership is said to have *construct validity*. To prove construct validity, an employer has to prove that the test actually does measure the trait (leadership), and that the trait actually is necessary for the job. It is extremely difficult to prove construct validity.[12]

The Uniform Guidelines on Employee Selection Procedures regulation, which provides the standards used by federal EEO agencies, has established three stringent requirements to show construct validity.[13]

- A job analysis must systematically define both the work behaviors involved in the job and the constructs that are believed to be important to job performance.
- The test must measure one of those constructs. In the example of the project manager, there must be evidence that the test validly measures leadership. For example, scores on the test might have correlated with leadership ratings given to other employees in other organizations upon previous administration of the test.
- The construct must be related to the performance of critical work behavior. For example, it must be shown that leadership ability is correlated with job performance for the position of project manager. That is, it is necessary that a criterion validity study between leadership and job performance be conducted, or that such data collected by another test user be used to support the claim of construct validity.

Criterion Validity The extent to which a selection technique is predictive of or correlated with important elements of job behavior is called *criterion-related validity*. Performance on a test or in some simulated exercise is checked against actual on-the-job performance. The job performance is called the *criterion*. A criterion can be units of output, a supervisor's rating, an end-of-training program test, sales results, or whatever outcome is appropriate.[14]

Two types of criterion-related validity popularly used are predictive and concurrent. *Predictive validity* can be determined by following a sequence of steps. For example, suppose that a battery of tests are given to a number of

---

[11] American Psychological Association, Division of Industrial and Organizational Psychology, *Principles for the Validation and Use of Personnel Selection Procedure*, 1986.

[12] James W. L. Cole, *Statistical Proof of Discrimination* (New York: McGraw-Hill, 1980).

[13] T. G. Abram, "Overview of Uniform Selection Guidelines: Pitfalls for the Unwary Employer," *Labor Law Journal*, August 1979, pp. 495–502.

[14] Robert H. Foley, "The Implications of Professional and Legal Guidelines for Court Decisions Involving Criterion Related Validity: A Review and Analysis," *Personnel Psychology*, Winter 1985, pp. 803–33.

applicants for an insurance agent position. Multiple tests are given so that there is a better chance of obtaining at least one valid test. Once the tests are administered, the results are kept confidential, and hiring decisions are made. The hiring decision is made without consulting the applicant's test scores. The test scores are kept on file until the applicants hired become proficient on the job. The test scores are kept secret because knowledge of them could bias the performance ratings.

Assume that the insurance agent became proficient after 15 months. At this time a performance evaluation rating is made. The ratings would then be correlated with the previously obtained and filed test scores. Those tests that are correlated significantly with the performance ratings would then be used in the future to help make selection decisions. The predictively valid tests would then be administered to new insurance agent applicants, and the test scores would be a valuable input in making hiring decisions.

In conducting a predictive validity test, the procedure is as follows:

1. Measure individuals for the job.
2. Select individuals using the results of the measurement.
3. Collect measurements of criterion performance over a period of time.
4. Assess the strength of the predictor-criterion relationship.

Predictive validity is an important form of criterion validity, but it does have a major drawback—namely, the employer must wait for a period of time to use the tests in selection decisions. The waiting period problem is reduced by using concurrent validity instead.

Concurrent validity is determined by using data obtained from the present work force. In concurrent validation, the first step is to administer tests to present employees performing the job. Next, performance ratings for these employees are collected. The test scores are then correlated with the performance ratings. If a test is significantly related to the ratings, it would be a candidate for future use in the selection process.

A difference in concurrent and predictive validity is that to establish concurrent validity, both test scores and performance measures are collected at the same time.

There are some problems with the use of current employees in validating a test. First, this method involves the use of experienced employees. If job experience is important in job performance, the results of such validation will be biased in favor of having experience. Second, present employees often balk at completing tests. They are puzzled by the requests to take a battery of tests, and often they will not provide honest or best answers. Therefore, the test scores may not be a true indicator of their skills and abilities. Third, there is a self-selection bias that can restrict the range of test scores. Among present employees, there is likely to be a restriction because the least skilled and able workers have been termininated, demoted, or transferred, and the most skilled and able have been placed in more responsible jobs. The restriction of range in test scores causes the correlation between test scores and performance ratings to be understated.

THE SELECTION PROCESS

All organizations make selection decisions, and most make them at least in part informally. The smaller the organization, the more likely it is to take an informal approach to selection decisions. Formal or systematic selection decisions were developed during World Wars I and II, when employee shortages brought tremendous placement problems, and the military had to select and place large numbers of workers in many different jobs very quickly and efficiently.

In the past, selection was often thought to be an easy decision. The boss interviewed applicants, sized them up, and let his or her gut reaction guide the choice. Decisions were based on the subjective "likes" or "dislikes" of the boss. Selection tools were designed to aid this gut reaction. For most selection decisions, that is all the tools were intended to do; they were designed to increase the proportion of successful employees selected. Today, selection is viewed as more than simply relying on intuition.

The selection decision is usually perceived as a series of steps through which applicants pass. At each step, a few more applicants are screened out by the organization, or more applicants accept other job offers and drop from the applicant list. Exhibit 7–3 illustrates a typical series of steps for the selection process.

This series is not universally used; for example, government employers test at Step 3 instead of Step 4, as do some private- and third- sector employers. It is important to note that few organizations use all steps, for they can be time consuming and expensive; and several steps, such as 4, 5, and 6, may be performed concurrently or at about the same time. Generally speaking, the more important the job, the more each step is likely to be used formally. Most organizations use the screening interview, application blank, and interview. Tests are used by a relatively small number of employers. Background and reference checks and physical exams are used for some jobs and not others. Exhibit 7–4 presents results of a study of 437 firms and the procedures used to make selection (hiring and promotion) decisions.

Step 1: Preliminary Screening
Interview

Different organizations can handle Step 1 in various ways—ineffectively or effectively. For some types of jobs, applicants are likely to walk into the employment office or job location. In these cases, a P/HRM specialist or line manager usually spends a few moments with applicants in what is called the *preliminary screening*. The organization develops some rough guidelines to be applied in order to reduce the time and expense of actual selection. These guidelines could specify, for example, minimum education or the number of words typed per minute. Only those who meet these criteria are deemed potential employees and are interviewed.

If general appearance and personal characteristics are deemed important,

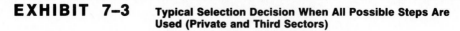

EXHIBIT 7–3 Typical Selection Decision When All Possible Steps Are Used (Private and Third Sectors)

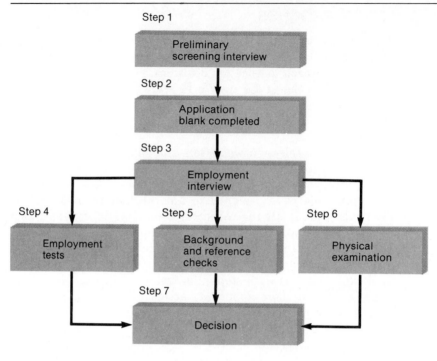

Step 1 — Preliminary screening interview

Step 2 — Application blank completed

Step 3 — Employment interview

Step 4 — Employment tests

Step 5 — Background and reference checks

Step 6 — Physical examination

Step 7 — Decision

EXHIBIT 7–4 Selection Procedures Used in Hiring and Promoting

	Percent of Companies (*n* = 437)	
	Procedures for Outside Applicants	Procedures for Candidates for Promotion
Reference/record check	97% (426)	67% (292)
Unstructured interview	81 (355)	70 (305)
Skill performance test/work sample	75 (329)	40 (176)
Medical examination	52 (229)	8 (34)
Structured interview	47 (206)	32 (142)
Investigation by outside agency	26 (112)	3 (14)
Job knowledge test	22 (94)	15 (64)
Mental ability test	20 (89)	10 (44)
Weighted application blank	11 (49)	7 (30)
Personality test	9 (39)	4 (18)
Assessment center	6 (28)	7 (30)
Physical abilities test	6 (27)	4 (16)
Polygraph test/written honesty test	6 (27)	1 (4)
Other	3 (13)	2 (9)

Source: Bureau of National Affairs, "Employee Selection Procedures," *Bulletin to Management,* ASPA-BNA Survey No. 45, May 5, 1983, p. 2. Reprinted by permission.

preliminary screening is often done through a brief personal interview in which the personnel/human resource specialist or manager determines key information and forms a general impression of the applicant. On this basis, the successful applicant then moves to the next step in selection, perhaps with the knowledge that the lack of an essential characteristic has lessened the chances of being seriously considered for the job. In smaller organizations, if the applicant appears to be a likely candidate for the position, the preliminary screening can proceed as an employment interview (Step 3).

The employer must be sure that the criteria used in this first step do not violate government antidiscrimination requirements. The EEOC has a publication, *Affirmative Action and Equal Employment: A Guidebook for Employers,* which provides help on this issue (vol. 1, pp. 40–44). Copies can be found in any office U.S. Government Printing Bookstore.

Step 1 is part of the reception portion of recruiting (see Chapter 6). The organization has the opportunity to make a good or bad impression on the applicant in this step.

Step 2: Completion of Application Blank/Biodata Form

Applicants who come to an employment office are asked to complete an application blank after a screening interview. Recruiters often follow a similar procedure.

One of the oldest instruments in P/HRM selection is the application blank.[15] Surveys show that all but the smallest organizations have applicants complete an application form or other biodata instrument (such as a biographical data form, biographical information blank, and individual background survey, or an interview guide). Biodata forms are useful in selection, career planning and counseling, and performance evaluation. They are most likely to avoid the EEOC's criticisms of other selection techniques.

Of course, application blanks and biodata forms could be illegal if they include items not relevant to job content. Items on the application blank should be kept to a minimum and should ask primarily for data that the enterprise's biodata studies indicate best predict effective performance. Exhibit 7–5 is an example of an application blank for Dr Pepper Company.

Essentially, those advocating the biodata approach argue that past behavior patterns are the best predictor of future behavior patterns. Thus, data should be gathered on a person's demographic, and attitudinal characteristics and previous work experience in a form that lends itself to psychometric evaluation and interpretation. In constructing the biodata form, a variety of approaches can be used. According to experts, the form should be brief; the items should be stated in neutral or pleasant terms; the items should offer all possible answers or categories plus an "escape clause"; and numbered items should add to a

---

[15] Wayne F. Cascio, "Accuracy of Verifiable Biographical Information Blank Responses," *Journal of Applied Psychology,* December 1975, pp. 767–70.

EXHIBIT 7-5

DR PEPPER COMPANY
APPLICATION FOR EMPLOYMENT

INTERVIEWER _____

INTERVIEWER _____

POSITION APPLIED FOR

PERSONAL DATA

FIRST NAME	MIDDLE NAME	LAST NAME	DATE

STREET ADDRESS	CITY AND STATE	ZIP CODE	SOCIAL SECURITY NUMBER

DATE OF BIRTH*	ARE YOU A U.S. CITIZEN? YES ☐ NO ☐	IF NO, RESIDENT CARD NUMBER	AREA CODE - TELEPHONE NUMBER

CAN YOU WORK IRREGULAR HOURS? YES ☐ NO ☐	CAN YOU WORK OVERTIME? YES ☐ NO ☐	DO YOU HAVE TRANSPORTATION TO YOUR JOB? NO ☐ YES ☐

DO YOU HAVE ANY FRIENDS OR RELATIVES WORKING HERE? IF YES, NAME AND LOCATION;   NO ☐   YES ☐

HAVE YOU EVER BEEN CONVICTED OF A CRIME OR REFUSED SURETY BOND? IF YES, GIVE DATE, PLACE AND REASON: NO ☐   YES ☐

NAME AND ADDRESS OF PERSON TO BE NOTIFIED IN CASE OF EMERGENCY:	NAME	STREET ADDRESS	CITY AND STATE	TELEPHONE

PHYSICAL RECORD

PRESENT STATE OF HEALTH	*PHYSICAL HANDICAPS OR LIMITATIONS: IF YES DESCRIBE: NO ☐ YES ☐

DO YOU HAVE OR HAVE YOU HAD ANY ALLERGIES (INCLUDING ASTHMA)? NO ☐ YES ☐	DO YOU HAVE HISTORY OF NERVOUS CONDITION? IF YES, EXPLAIN: NO ☐ YES ☐
HAVE YOU HAD ANY OPERATION OR MAJOR ILLNESS IN LAST 5 YEARS? IF YES, EXPLAIN: NO ☐ YES ☐	HAVE YOU EVER HAD BACK TROUBLE OR INJURY? IF YES, EXPLAIN: NO ☐ YES ☐

HAVE YOU EVER RECEIVED WORKMAN'S COMPENSATION FOR ANY ACCIDENT OR DISABILITY? IF YES, EXPLAIN:
NO ☐   YES ☐

EDUCATION

CIRCLE HIGHEST GRADE COMPLETED:	GRAMMAR SCHOOL 1 2 3 4 5 6 7 8	HIGH SCHOOL 9 10 11 12	COLLEGE 1 2 3 4

HIGH SCHOOL	NAME(S)	LOCATION(S)	DATES FROM	TO	GRADE AVERAGE	GRADUATE? YES ☐ NO ☐

COLLEGE	NAME	LOCATION	FROM	TO	DEGREE/MAJOR	GRADUATE? YES ☐ NO ☐

OTHER SCHOOLING

U. S. MILITARY SERVICE

ARE YOU IN THE MILITARY RESERVE? NO ☐ YES ☐ STATUS: ACTIVE ☐ INACTIVE ☐	WERE YOU EVER IN THE SERVICE? NO ☐ YES ☐	DATE ENTERED	DATE DISCHARGED	RANK AT DISCHARGE

DO YOU RECEIVE A V.A. PENSION CAUSED BY DISABILITY INCURRED DURING U.S. MILITARY SERVICE? NO ☐ YES ☐	IF YES, STATE PERCENT OF BENEFIT, IF ANY:

SKILLS / SCHOOLS DURING SERVICE

OFFICE SKILLS   INDICATE THOSE SKILLS YOU HAVE

TYPEWRITER? NO ☐ YES ☐ SPEED	DICTAPHONE? NO ☐ YES ☐	ADDING MACHINE? NO ☐ YES ☐	CALCULATOR? NO ☐ YES ☐ WHAT TYPE?
DO YOU TAKE SHORTHAND? NO ☐ YES ☐ SPEED	BOOKKEEPING MACHINE? NO ☐ YES ☐ WHAT TYPE?		DATA PROCESSING? NO ☐ YES ☐ WHAT TYPE?

*ALL LEGAL REQUIREMENTS PERTAINING TO FAIR EMPLOYMENT PRACTICES ARE COMPLIED WITH BY DR PEPPER CO. HENCE ITEMS COVERING INFORMATION WHICH IN YOUR STATE MAY NOT BE LEGALLY REQUIRED (INCLUDING ITEMS WITH ASTERISKS) SHOULD NOT BE COMPLETED. DR PEPPER IS AN EQUAL OPPORTUNITY EMPLOYER.

EXHIBIT 7–5 *(concluded)*

EMPLOYMENT RECORD — BEGIN WITH MOST RECENT POSITION AND WORK BACK, BEING SURE TO ACCOUNT FOR ANY TIME LAPSE. INCLUDE SUMMER AND PART TIME JOBS

DATES		NAME OF FIRM			JOB TITLE	REASON FOR LEAVING
FROM	TO					
		ADDRESS		TELEPHONE	SUPERVISORS NAME	
		CITY	STATE	ZIP CODE	FULL TIME ☐ SALARY PART TIME ☐	
		GENERAL DUTIES				
FROM	TO	NAME OF FIRM			JOB TITLE	REASON FOR LEAVING
		ADDRESS		TELEPHONE	SUPERVISORS NAME	
		CITY	STATE	ZIP CODE	FULL TIME ☐ SALARY PART TIME ☐	
		GENERAL DUTIES				
FROM	TO	NAME OF FIRM			JOB TITLE	REASON FOR LEAVING
		ADDRESS		TELEPHONE	SUPERVISORS NAME	
		CITY	STATE	ZIP CODE	FULL TIME ☐ SALARY PART TIME ☐	
		GENERAL DUTIES				
FROM	TO	NAME OF FIRM			JOB TITLE	REASON FOR LEAVING
		ADDRESS		TELEPHONE	SUPERVISORS NAME	
		CITY	STATE	ZIP CODE	FULL TIME ☐ SALARY PART TIME ☐	
		GENERAL DUTIES				
FROM	TO	NAME OF FIRM			JOB TITLE	REASON FOR LEAVING
		ADDRESS		TELEPHONE	SUPERVISORS NAME	
		CITY	STATE	ZIP CODE	FULL TIME ☐ SALARY PART TIME ☐	
		GENERAL DUTIES				

ACCEPTABLE STARTING WAGE _____

DRIVING RECORD

DRIVER'S LICENSE NO. TYPE AND STATE ISSUED:	YEARS OF DRIVING EXPERIENCE:	INDICATE NUMBER OF VEHICLE ACCIDENTS INVOLVED IN LAST:
ARE THERE ANY RESTRICTIONS ON YOUR DRIVER'S LICENSE? NO ☐ YES ☐ COMMENT:		12 MONTHS _____ 5 YEARS _____ EXPLAIN:
HAVE YOU EVER HAD YOUR DRIVER'S LICENSE SUSPENDED OR REVOKED? NO ☐ YES ☐ COMMENT:		MOVING TRAFFIC VIOLATIONS IN LAST: 12 MONTHS _____ 5 YEARS _____COMMENT:

I CERTIFY THAT ALL OF THE FOREGOING STATEMENTS ARE TRUE AND CORRECT TO THE BEST OF MY ABILITY. I UNDERSTAND THAT MISREPRESENTATION OR OMISSION OF FACTS IS CAUSE FOR DISMISSAL.
I AM WILLING TO TAKE PHYSICAL OR OTHER EXAMINATIONS WHEN REQUIRED. I UNDERSTAND THAT AN INVESTIGATIVE REPORT MAY BE MADE WHEREBY INFORMATION IS OBTAINED FROM THIRD PARTIES. THIS INQUIRY INCLUDES INFORMATION AS TO YOUR CHARACTER, GENERAL REPUTATION, PERSONAL CHARACTERISTICS, MODE OF LIVING, ETC. AND RELEASE OF SCHOOL AND OR COLLEGE TRANSCRIPTS. YOU HAVE THE RIGHT TO MAKE A WRITTEN REQUEST WITHIN A REASONABLE PERIOD OF TIME FOR A COMPLETE DISCLOSURE OF ADDITIONAL INFORMATION CONCERNING THE NATURE AND SCOPE OF THE INVESTIGATION.

_____
SIGNATURE OF APPLICANT

DO NOT WRITE BELOW THIS LINE — FOR COMPANY USE ONLY

INTERVIEWER'S COMMENTS:

MVR_____ DATE ORDERED_____ REF CHECK_____ PHYSICAL_____ DATE SENT_____ DATE & TIME OF RETURN_____

START DATE_____ LOCATION _____ DEPARTMENT_____ POSITION _____ WAGE_____

ITEM #CP-026 W/10-1-80 Qty.

scale.[16] It is argued that sequenced items are preferable to nonsequenced items, and select-one option items are better than multiple-choice items.

An important biodata substitute or supplement for the application blank is the *biographical information blank (BIB)*. The BIB usually has more items than an application blank and includes different kinds of items relating to such things as attitudes, health, and early life experiences. It uses the multiple-choice answer system. Instead of asking just about education, it might ask:

How old were you when you graduated from the 6th grade?

1. Younger than 10
2. 10–12
3. 13–14
4. 15–16

It also asks opinion questions, such as:

How do you feel about being transferred from this city by this company?

1. Would thoroughly enjoy a transfer.
2. Would like to experience a transfer.
3. Would accept a transfer.
4. Would reject a transfer.

To use the BIB as a selection tool, the P/HRM specialist correlates each item on the form with the selection criteria for job success. Those criteria that predict the best for a position are used to help select applicants for that position.

Another variety of biodata form is the **weighted application blank,** an application form designed to be scored as a systematic selection device. Weighted application blanks have been used for predicting success and turnover for office, manufacturing, hospital, and banking jobs.[17] The purpose of a weighted application blank is to relate the characteristics of applicants to success on the job. It has been estimated that to develop a weighted blank for a job takes about 100 hours.

The typical approach is to divide present jobholders into two or three categories (in half, high or low; or in thirds, high, middle, or low), based on some success criterion such as performance as measured by production records, supervisor's evaluation, or high versus low turnover. Then the characteristics of high and low performers are examined. For many characteristics for a particular organization and job, there may be no difference by age or education level, but there may be differences for where applicants live and years of experience, for example. A weight is assigned to the degree of differences: for no difference, 0; for some difference, ± 1; for a big difference, ± 2. Then these weights are totaled for all applicants, and the one with the highest positive

[16] W. Owens, "Background Data," in *Handbook of Industrial and Organizational Psychology,* ed. M. Dunnette (Skokie, Ill.: Rand McNally, 1976), pp. 609–44.

[17] D. G. Lawrence, B. L. Salsburg, J. G. Dawson and Z. D. Fasman, "Design and Use of Weighted Application Blanks," *Personnel Administrator,* March 1982, pp. 47–53.

score is hired, assuming that the score meets the minimum that past and currently successful employees have attained.

These predictive characteristics vary by job and occupation. For example, sometimes the age of the applicant is a good predictor; other times it is not. They may also change over time. Weights need to be recomputed every several years or so, and the weighted application blank must be validated for each job and organization.

Most researchers have found that biodata approaches are reliable. They also find that biodata approaches have very high validity. Studies indicate, however, that although most organizations use application blanks, fewer than a third of the *larger* organizations have utilized weighted application blanks or other biodata approaches. Given the problems with tests, references, and other selection techniques, the percentage of organizations using biodata approaches is likely to increase.[18]

Step 3: Employment Interview

Employment interviews are part of almost all selection procedures. Studies indicate that over 90 percent of selection decisions involve interviews.[19] And a number of them indicate that the interview is the *most important aspect* of the selection decision. Clark Kirby in P/HRM In Action is going to learn a lot about interviewing especially if he gets involved in interviewing applicants for the 596 positions at Gunther.

Types of Interviews There are a number of general types of employment interviews. Some organizations use more than one type to help them make a selection decision:

- Structured.
- Semistructured.
- Unstructured.

While all employment interviews are alike in certain respects, each type is also unique in some way. All three include interaction between two or more parties, an applicant and one or more representatives (people serving on an interview panel hold what is called a *group interview*) of the potential employer, for a predetermined purpose. This purpose is consideration of an applicant for employment. Information is exchanged, usually through questions and answers. The main differences in employment interviews lie in the interviewer's approach to the process, and the type used depends both on the kind of information desired and the nature of the situation.

In the *structured employment interview,* the interviewer prepares a list of

---

18 Bureau of National Affairs, *Employee Selection Procedures,* Washington, D.C.: AJPA-BNA Survey No. 45, May 5, 1983.

19 William L. Donoghy, *The Interview: Skills and Applications* (Glenview, Ill.: Scott, Foresman, 1984).

questions in advance and does not deviate from it. In many organizations a standard form is used on which the interviewer notes the applicant's responses to the predetermined questions. Many of the questions asked in a structured interview are forced-choice in nature, and the interviewer need only indicate the applicant's response with a check mark on the form.

If the approach is highly structured, the interviewer may also follow a prearranged sequence of questions. In such an interview the interviewer is often little more than a recorder of the interviewee's responses, and little training is required to conduct it. The structured approach is very restrictive, however. The information elicited is narrow, and there is little opportunity to adapt to the individual applicant. This approach is equally constraining to the applicant who is unable to qualify or elaborate on answers to the questions. The Bureau of National Affairs survey found that 19 percent of the companies used a written interview form, while 26 percent employed a standard format for employment interviews.[20] Exhibit 7–6 is an example of a form used for a structured employment interview.

In the *semistructured interview* only the major questions to be asked are prepared in advance, though the interviewer may also prepare some probing questions in areas of inquiry. While this approach calls for greater interviewer preparation, it also allows for more flexibility than the structured approach. The interviewer is free to probe into those areas that seem to merit further investigation. With less structure, however, it is more difficult to replicate these interviews. This approach combines enough structure to facilitate the exchange of factual information with adequate freedom to develop insights.

The *unstructured interview* involves little preparation. The interviewer prepares a list of possible topics to be covered and sometimes does not even do that. The overriding advantage of the unstructured type is the freedom it allows the interviewer to adapt to the situation and to the changing stream of applicants. Spontaneity characterizes this approach, but under the control of an untrained interviewer, digressions, discontinuity, and eventual frustration for both parties may result.

While the unstructured approach lends itself to the counseling of individuals with problems, it is not limited to guidance. Students frequently encounter P/HRM recruiters whose sole contribution, other than the opening and closing pleasantries, is "Tell me about yourself." When used by a highly skilled interviewer, the unstructured interview can lead to significant insights that might enable the interviewer to make fine distinctions among applicants. As used by most employment interviewers, however, that is not the case, and it is seldom appropriate for an employment interviewer to relinquish control to such an extent.

Some interviewers try to induce stress into the employment interview process. For example, the interviewer may ask questions in a hostile tone or deliberately interrupt the interviewee. It is assumed that stressful situations

---

[20] Bureau of National Affairs, *Personnel Policies Forum*, Survey 114, September 1976.

EXHIBIT 7-6 Patterned Interview Form—Executive Position

Date _____ 19 ___

SUMMARY

Rating [1] [2] [3] [4]   Comments: _____
In making final rating, be sure to consider not only what the applicant can do but also his/her stability, industry, perseverance, loyalty, ability to get along with others, self-reliance, leadership, maturity, motivation, and domestic situation and health.

_____

_____

_____

Interviewer: _____ Job considered for: _____

Name _____ Date of birth _____ ; Phone No. _____
The age discrimination in the employment act and relevant FEP Acts prohibit discrimination with respect to individuals who are at least 40 but less than 65 years of age.

Present address _____ City _____ State _____ How long there? _____

Were you in the Armed Forces of the U.S.? Yes, branch _____ Dates _____ 19 __to _____ 19 _____
(Not to be asked in New Jersey)   _____ 19 __ to _____ 19 _____

If not, why not? _____

Where you hospitalized in the service? _____

Are you drawing compensation?   Yes ___ No ___

Are you employed now?   Yes ☐ No ☐. (If yes) How soon available? _____
What are relationships with present employer?

Why are you applying for this position? _____
Is his/her underlying reason a desire for prestige, security, or earnings?

WORK EXPERIENCE. Cover all positions. This information is very important. Interviewer should record last position first. Every month since leaving school should be accounted for. Experience in Armed Forces should be covered as a job (in New Jersey exclude military questions).

LAST OR PRESENT POSITION

Company _____ City _____ From _____ 19 __ to _____ 19 __

How was job obtained? _____ Whom did you know there? _____
Has applicant shown self-reliance in getting jobs?

Nature of work at start _____ Starting salary _____
Will applicant's previous experience be helpful on this job?

In what way did the job change? _____
Has applicant made good work progress?

Nature of work at leaving _____ Salary at leaving _____
How much responsibility has applicant had?   Any indication of ambition?

Superior _____ Title _____ What is he/she like? _____
Did applicant get along with superior?

How closely does (or did) he/she supervise you? _____ What authority do (or did) you have? _____

Number of people you supervised _____ What did they do? _____
Is applicant a leader?

Responsibility for policy formulation _____
Has applicant had management responsibility?

To what extent could you use initiative and judgment? _____
Did applicant actively seek responsibility?

will show how a person really reacts under pressure. Generally speaking, creating stress in the interview is dysfunctional to the selection process. However, introducing stress is still used when interviewing individuals for high-pressure jobs, such as police work, emergency care centers, and fire fighting.[21]

Interviewing Errors Whether an interview accomplishes its purpose depends largely on how it is conducted. There are a number of interviewing errors that detract from the interview's usefulness. First, there is a tendency for interviewers to make up their minds based on the first impression of the applicant. Based on the first observation of the applicant and the first few minutes of discussion, a judgment of the applicant is made. Second, interviewers often use nonverbal behavior patterns as a basis of reaching a decision. That is, how the person looks, sits in the chair, and maintains eye contact may be the major factors considered in rating the applicant.[22]

In one research study, 52 P/HRM specialists observed videotaped job interviews in which the verbal content expressed by the applicants was identical. However, the videotaped applicants' nonverbal behavior differed significantly. The applicants in one group displayed little eye contact, a low energy level, and low voice modulation. The applicants in a second group demonstrated the opposite behavior. Of the 26 P/HRM specialists who saw the high eye contact-high energy applicant, 23 would have invited the candidate back for a second interview. On the other hand, all 26 of the P/HRM specialists who saw the little eye contact-low energy applicant would not have recommended that person for a second interview.[23] One implication of this error is that an interviewer must closely examine verbal and nonverbal behaviors. Paying too much attention to nonverbal behaviors can result in bypassing competent applicants.

A third interview problem involves the applicant's attractiveness and sex. One study found that whether attractiveness was a help or a hindrance to applicants depended on the sex of the applicant and the nature of the job being filled. Attractiveness was a major advantage for male applicants seeking managerial jobs.[24] However, attractiveness tended to work against a woman interviewing for a managerial job.

Another interview problem involves the interviewer's lack of knowledge about the job. An interviewer that is not clear about a job's responsibilities often has difficulty providing a good impression to the applicant about the

21 Richard A. Fear, *The Evaluation Interview* (New York: McGraw-Hill, 1984).

22 Richard Arvey and James Campion, "The Employment Interview: A Summary and Review of Recent Research," *Personnel Psychology*, Summer 1982, pp. 281–322.

23 T. V. McGovern and H. E. Tinsley, "Interviewer Evaluations of Interviewees' Non-Verbal Behavior," *Journal of Vocational Behavior*, October 1978, pp. 163–71.

24 Madeline Heilmann and Lewis Sariwatari, "When Beauty Is Beastly: The Effects of Appearance and Sex on Evaluations of Job Applicants for Managerial and Nonmanagerial Jobs," *Organizational Behavior and Human Performance*, June 1979, pp. 360–72.

organization. This impression by an applicant can play a role in his or her final decision about accepting a position.

There is also the potential problem of making contrast errors. These errors occur when an interviewer is overly influenced, for or against, by the interviews of previous applicants. For example, if a qualified applicant follows an exceptional applicant, his or her qualifications tend to pale in comparison. This situation is unfortunate, since the qualified candidate may be rejected because of the contrast error.

These and other interview errors must be understood so that they can be avoided. Interviewers often make errors in interviewing because they do not understand the errors and they are not formally trained to conduct interviews. A trained interviewer is likely to make fewer errors because he or she understands potential errors, has learned how to ask questions effectively, is able to establish a positive relationship with applicants, and has systematically organized the interview. These are characteristics of effective interviewing that would be stressed in interview training programs.

Following is a concise summary of some key points to follow when conducting an interview:

1. Work at listening to what and how the applicant communicates to you. Unlike hearing, listening is an active process and requires concentration. Many interviewers plan their next question when they should be listening to the applicant's present response.

2. Be aware of the applicant's nonverbal cues as well as the verbal message. In attempting to get as complete a picture of the applicant as possible, you must not ignore what some consider the most meaningful type of communication, body language.

3. Remain aware of the job requirements throughout the interview. No one is immune to the halo effect, which gives undue weight to one characteristic. You must constantly keep the requirements of the job in mind. Sometimes an applicant possesses some personal mannerism or trait that so attracts or repels the interviewer that the decision is made mostly on the strength of that characteristic, which may be completely irrelevant to the requirements of the job in question.

4. Maintain a balance between open and overly-structured questions. Too many of the former, and the interview becomes a meandering conversation; while too many of the later turn the interview into an interrogation.

5. Wait until you have all of the necessary information before making a decision. Some interviewees start more slowly than others, and what may appear to be disinterest may later prove to have been an initial reserve that dissipates after a few minutes. *Don't evaluate on the basis of a first impression.*

6. Do not ask questions that violate equal employment opportunity laws and regulations (see list in Chapter 3). Focus the interview on the variables identified as crucial criteria for selection.

A number of studies have examined whether employment interviews are reliable sources of data.[25] Generally speaking, the more structured the interview and the more training the interviewer has, the more reliable the interview.

Interviewing is a skill that can be learned. The following section describes the purposes and phases of effective interviews.

Purposes of Selection Interviews Many employment interviewers perceive their only task as that of screening and selecting those individuals best suited for employment. While this is unquestionably the *main* function of the employment interview, it is not the only one. A second purpose is public relations, that is, to impress the interviewees with the value of the interviewer's employer.

In addition to the selection and public relations roles, the employment interviewer also must function as an educator. It is the interviewer's responsibility to "educate" the applicants concerning details of the job in question that are not immediately apparent. The interviewer must be able to answer the applicant's questions with honesty and candor. To be effective, the interviewer must remain aware of all three of these functions while conducting the employment interview.

Step 4: Employment Tests

A technique some organizations use to aid their selection decisions is the employment test. An employment test is a mechanism (either a paper-and-pencil test or a simulation exercise) that attempts to measure certain characteristics of individuals, such as manual dexterity. Psychologists or P/HRM specialists develop these tests with a procedure that is similar to that described for the weighted application blank. First, those most knowledgeable about the job are asked to rank (in order of importance) the abilities and attitudes essential for effective performance in a job. Thus for a secretarial position, the rank might be (A) ability to type, (B) ability to take shorthand, and (C) positive work attitudes. The psychologist prepares items or simulations that are thought to measure these required characteristics. The items are tried to see if they can, in fact, separate the qualified from less qualified (on A and B), and easygoing from less easygoing (on C). For such items, psychologists prefer those that about half the applicants will answer with "right" answers, and half answer incorrectly.

The terms or simulations that distinguish the best from the worst are combined into tests. A measure of effectiveness (a criterion) is developed, such as typing 75 words per minute with a 1-percent error rate. All new applicants are given the test. After about two years, those items that prove to have been

---

25 W. F. Cascio and R. A. Ramos, "Development and Application of a New Method for Assessing Job Performance in Behavioral/Economic Terms," *Journal of Applied Psychology,* February 1986, pp. 20–28.

FRANK AND ERNEST

© 1976 by Nea, Inc. Reprinted by permission of NEA.

the best predictors of high performance are kept in the test used for selection, and those found not to be predictive are dropped. This is the validation process.

It is not easy or cheap to validate a test. In a study of 2,500 American Society of Personnel Administrators (ASPA) members, it was found that, on average, a validation study costs $5,000 per job, and some studies cost as much as $20,000.[26] This same study found the use of tests is declining, and that tests are used most frequently for clerical jobs. About half of the surveyed employers use tests in selection. Middle-sized firms are most likely to use them, followed by larger firms. The smaller firms are least likely to use them. Some industries (transportation, communications, office, and insurance) are more likely to use tests than manufacturers, hospitals, and retailers.

Of the 2,500 personnel managers consulted in this survey, 37.9 percent considered tests "about the same in importance," and 36.5 percent considered them less important than other selection techniques such as the interview and biodata. Less than 20 percent said they disqualified applicants on the basis of test scores alone.

Because of criticisms of the courts and P/HRM practitioners that tests discriminate against minority employees, separate validity studies may be required for minorities. Because it is expensive, many employers have abandoned the use of tests for minority employees. This criticism applies more to paper-and-pencil tests than performance tests.

Few organizations have the personnel, time, or money to develop their own tests. Instead, they often purchase and use tests developed elsewhere. The test organization provides a key (or notation) that lists the enterprises that have

[26] "The Personnel Executive's Job," *Personnel Management: Policies and Practices* (Englewood Cliffs, N.J.: Prentice-Hall, 1976).

used the test in the past and the typical performance of good and bad employees. This is not enough, however; the test must be validated in each organization and for minority and nonminority employee groups before it can be useful.

There are various kinds of tests. Work sample performance tests, simulations of performance, paper-and-pencil tests, personality and temperament inventories, and others will be discussed later in this chapter.

Job Sample Performance Tests A job sample performance test is an experience that involves actually doing a sample of the work the job involves in a controlled situation.[27] Examples of performance tests include:

1. A programming test for computer operators.
2. Employees running a miniature punchpress.
3. A standard driving course as performance test for forklift operators.
4. The auditions used by symphony orchestras for hiring purposes. For example, when symphony orchestras select new musicians, the selection panel listens to them play the same piece of music with the same instrument. The applicants are hidden behind a screen at the time.
5. A tool dexterity test for machine operators.
6. Standardized typing tests. The applicants are asked to type some work. The speed and accuracy are then computed.

Variations of these performance tests exist in many organizations. The applicants are asked to run the machines they would run if they got the job, and quality and quantity of output are recorded.

Job sample tests tend to have the highest validities and reliabilities of all tests because they systematically measure behavior directly related to the job. This is not surprising. Imagine that you are an artist who is applying for graduate work in art. You typically must take the Graduate Record Exam, a paper-and-pencil test designed to measure verbal and mathematical "ability." You also must present 12 paintings, drawings, and watercolors (a portfolio) to the art department. Which of these selection devices appears likely to be the more reliable and valid measure of your painting ability? Or recall that when you applied for your driver's license, you took two tests: a paper-and-pencil test, and, when you drove the car, a performance test. Which better tested your driving ability: the paper-and-pencil test, or that tension-filled drive with the observer who rated your driving ability? A similar principle applies to job selection. Which would be a better predictor of the forklift operator's job performance: the standardized test, in which the applicant drives the truck down and around piles of goods, or a paper-and-pencil test of driving knowledge, intelligence, or whatever?

Reliability and validity figures for all the standardized tests discussed here are available from the test developers. Many are reviewed in regular summaries, such as the *Annual Review of Psychology*.

---

[27] James J. Asher and James A. Sciarrino, "Realistic Work Sample Tests: A Review," *Personnel Psychology*, Winter 1974, pp. 519–33.

Performance Simulations A performance simulation is a non-paper-and-pencil experience designed to determine abilities related to job performance. For example, suppose job analysis indicates that successful job occupants of a specific job require highly developed mechanical or clerical abilities. A number of simulations are available to measure these abilities. The simulation is not the actual performance of part of the job, but it comes close to that through simulation. You may have learned to drive by performing first on simulation machines; it was not the same as on-the-street driving, but it was closer than reading about it or observing other drivers.

There are many of these simulation tests. Here are some:

Revised Minnesota Paper Form Board Test Exhibit 7–7 is an excerpt from the MPFB, which is a test of space visualization. It is used for various jobs. For example, to be a draftsperson requires the ability to see things in their relation to space. The applicant must select the item (A–E) that best represents what a group of shapes will look like when assembled.

Psychomotor Ability Simulations There are a number of tests that measure such psychomotor abilities as choice reaction time, speed of limb movement, and finger dexterity. One of these is the O'Connor Finger and Tweezer Dexterity Test (see Exhibit 7–8). The person being tested picks up pins with the tweezer and row by row inserts them in the holes across the board, or inserts the pins with the hand normally used. These tests are used for positions with

EXHIBIT 7–7   **Excerpt from Revised Minnesota Paper Form Board Test**

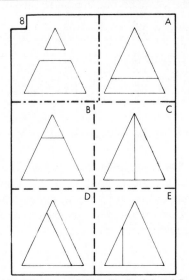

EXHIBIT 7–8   O'Connor Finger and Tweezer Dexterity Test Equipment

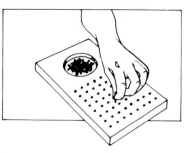

high manual requirements for success, such as assemblers of radio or TV components and watches.

Clerical Abilities Exhibit 7–9 is the first page of the Minnesota Clerical Test. It is a typical test for clerical abilities. This simulation requires the applicants to check numbers and names, skills frequently used in clerical tasks.

Paper-and-Pencil Tests In the third group of tests are paper-and-pencil tests, designed to measure general intelligence and aptitudes.[28] Many employers assume that mental abilities are an important component of performance for many jobs. Intelligence and mental ability tests attempt to sample intellectual mental development or skills.

Some examples of paper-and-pencil tests are:

Otis Quick Scoring Mental Ability Test This test samples several intellectual functions, including vocabulary, arithmetic skills, reasoning, and perception, totaling them to one score. It includes items such as the following:

(a) Which one of the five things below is soft?
(1) glass (2) stone (3) cotton (4) iron (5) ice
(b) A robin is a kind of:
(6) plant (7) bird (8) worm (9) fish (10) flower
(c) Which one of the five numbers below is larger than 55?
(11) 53 (12) 48 (13) 29 (14) 57 (15) 16

Wechsler Adult Intelligence Scale The Wechsler is a comprehensive paper-and-pencil test of 14 sections grouped into two scores. The verbal score includes general information, arithmetic, similarities, vocabulary, and other items. The performance score includes picture completion, picture arrangement, object assembly, and similar items.

---

[28] Anne Anastasi, *Psychological Testing* (New York: MacMillan, 1982).

EXHIBIT 7-9

MINNESOTA CLERICAL TEST
(formerly the Minnesota Vocational Test for Clerical Workers)
by Dorothy M. Andrew, Donald G. Patterson, and Howard P. Longstaff

Name _____   Date _____

TEST 1—Number Comparison   TEST 2—Name Comparison

Number Right _____   Number Right _____
Number Wrong _____   Number Wrong _____
Score = R − W _____   Score = R − W _____
Percentile Rating _____   Percentile Rating _____
Norms Used _____   Norms Used _____

INSTRUCTIONS

On the inside pages there are two tests. One of the tests consists of pairs of names and the other of pairs of numbers. If the two names or the two numbers of a pair are exactly the same make a check mark (√) on the line between them: if they are different, make no mark on that line. When the examiner says "Stop!" draw a line under the last pair at which you have looked.

SAMPLES done correctly of pairs of NUMBERS
79542____79524
1234567 √ 1234567

SAMPLES done correctly of pairs of NAMES
John C. Linder____John C. Lender
Investors Syndicate √ Investors Syndicate

This is a test for speed and accuracy. Work as fast as you can without making mistakes. Do not turn this page until you are told to begin.

Wonderlic Personnel Test The Wonderlic is a shortened form of the Otis test using a variety of perceptual, verbal, and arithmetical items which provide a total score. Other well-known tests include the Differential Aptitude Test, the SRA Primary Mental Abilities Test, and multiple aptitude tests.

The above three tests are administered to individuals and are paper-and-pencil tests similar to those taken in school. There are also tests of mental ability designed to be administered to groups, including the following example.

California Test of Mental Maturity (adult level) This test is administered to groups and scored by machine. Scores are developed from a series of short tests on spatial relationships, verbal concepts, logic and reasoning, numerical reasoning, memory, and others. The scores are converted to IQ equivalents, and profiles are developed for analyzing performance.

The reliability and validity of paper-and-pencil tests have been studied extensively. In general, they are not as reliable as performance tests or other selection devices, such as biodata forms or structured interviews.

Personality Inventories and Temperament Tests The least reliable of the employment tests are those instruments that attempt to measure a person's personality or temperament. The most frequently used inventory is the Minnesota Multiphasic Personality Inventory. Other paper-and-pencil inventories

EXHIBIT 7–10   An Inkblot of the Type Employed in the Rorschach Technique

are the California Psychological Inventory, the Minnesota Counseling Inventory, the Manifest Anxiety Scale, and the Edwards Personal Preference Schedule.

A different approach, not as direct as the self-reporting inventory, utilizes projective techniques to present vague stimuli, the reactions to which provide data on which psychologists base their assessment and interpretation of a personality. The stimuli are purposely vague in order to reach the unconscious aspects of the personality. Many techniques are used. The most common are the Rorschach Inkblot Test and the Thematic Apperception Test.

The Rorschach Inkblot Test was first described in 1921. The test involves 10 cards, on each of which is printed a bilateral symmetrical inkblot similar to that illustrated in Exhibit 7–10.[29] The person responding is asked to tell what he or she sees in the inkblot. The examiner keeps a verbatim record of the responses, the time taken to make the responses, emotional expressions, and other incidental behavior. Then a trained interpreter analyzes the data set and reaches conclusions about the personality patterns of the person being examined.

The Polygraph and Honesty Tests Another method currently used by some employers to test employees is the polygraph, sometimes erroneously called a lie detector. The polygraph is an instrument that records changes in breathing, blood pressure, pulse, and skin response associated with sweating of palms, and then plots these reactions on paper. The person being questioned with a polygraph attached is asked a series of questions. Some are neutral, to achieve a normal response, others stressful, to indicate a response made under pressure. Thus the applicant may be asked: "Is your name Smith?" Then, "Have you ever stolen from an employer?"

---

[29] H. Rorschach, *Psychodiagnostics: A Diagnostic Test Based on Perception* (Berne, Switz.: Huber, 1942).

Drawing by D. Fradon; © 1974 The New Yorker *Magazine, Inc.*

Why does a fireman wear red suspenders?

A. □ The red goes well with the blue uniform.
B. □ They can be used to repair a leaky hose.
C. □ To hold up his pants.

    Although originally developed for police work, the great majority of polygraph tests today are used to check data during selection. Approximately one fifth of American businesses use the polygraph today.[30] It is understandable why organizations need to determine certain facts about potential employees. On-the-job crime has increased tremendously, and it is estimated that dishonest employees cost employers about $5 billion per year. A good reference check may cost $100; a polygraph test only $25. Some employers offer applicants a choice: Take a polygraph test now, making it possible to make an immediate selection decision, or await the results of a reference check and run the risk of losing the job. Local, state, and federal agencies have begun to use the polygraph, especially for security, police, fire, and health positions.
    There are many objections to the use of the polygraph in personnel selection.

---

[30] Thomas L. Bright and Charles J. Hollen, "State Regulation of Polygraph Tests at the Workplace," *Personnel,* February 1985, pp. 50–56.

One is that use of this device is an invasion of the applicant's privacy and thus a violation of the Fourth Admendment to the Constitution. Second, it is believed that its use could lead to self-incrimination, a violation of the Fifth Amendment. A third objection is that it insults the dignity of the applicant.

As severe as these objections are, *the most serious question is whether the polygraph is reliable and can get the truth.* The fact is that the polygraph records *physiological* changes in response to stress, not lying or even the conditions necessarily accompanying lying. Many cases have come to light in which persons who lie easily have beaten the polygraph, and it has been shown that the polygraph brands as liars people who respond emotionally to questions. There is evidence that polygraphs are neither reliable nor valid. This conclusion was reached following studies by a congressional committee and the Pentagon, which made a thorough analysis of all the available data. Compounding this deficiency, one expert has estimated that 80 percent of 1,500 polygraph practitioners are not sufficiently trained to interpret the results of the tests, even if they were reliable and valid.[31]

An increasing number of organizations are asking job applicants to complete a paper-and-pencil honesty test. As many as 2 million job applicants annually for jobs ranging from bank teller to pharmaceutical sales person are asked to answer carefully crafted questions.[32] The Stanton Inventory is an honesty test that uses 96 questions to detect dissatisfaction, hostility, and overall work attitude. Questions are general ("How would you rate this company as a desirable place to work?") and also very open ("How does (would) your nearest loved one feel about you working here?").

Research indicates that 18% of high-risk job applicants actively admit that they would steal from a company. White-collar crime alone is estimated to cost business over $67 billion a year.[33] Thus, honesty tests are being used as one piece of evidence to screen out those job applicants who do not score favorably with preferred norms or group profiles.[34]

The test results from a reliable honesty test are only one aspect of information gathered about the job applicant.[35] Other performance tests, previous work experience, reference checks, and previous employer recommendations should also be carefully screened. Because of the problems and costs of employee theft, espionage, and dissatisfaction it is likely that honesty tests will continue to be used as part of the selection process in the future.

Such criticisms have lead to the banning of the polygraph for employee selection in many jurisdictions. Arbitrators have held against forcing employ-

[31] John E. Reid and Fred E. Inbau, *Truth and Deception: The Polygraph Technique* (Baltimore: Williams & Wilkins, 1966).

[32] Labor Letter, *The Wall Street Journal,* April 16, 1985, p. 1.

[33] S. L. Jacobs, "Owners Who Ignore Security Make Worker Dishonesty Easy," *The Wall Street Journal,* March 11, 1985.

[34] Ed Bean, "More Firms Use Attitude Tests to Keep Thieves off the Payroll," *The Wall Street Journal,* February 27, 1987, p. 35.

[35] P. R. Sackett and M. M. Harris, "Honesty Testing for Personnel Selection: A Review and Critique," *Personnel Psychology,* 1984, pp. 221–45.

ees to take such tests, and polygraph evidence is not admissible in court unless both sides agree. As a result of congressional hearings, the federal government has severely reduced the use of polygraphs. In spite of these criticisms, however, it appears that the use of the polygraph in job selection will continue.

Employment Testing and the Law Perhaps the first event signaling the involvement of the courts in employment testing was the *Myart* v. *Motorola* (1964) case.[36] In 1963, Leon Myart, a black, was refused a job as a "television phaser and analyzer" at one of Motorola's plants because his score on a five-minute intelligence test was not high enough, although he had previous job-related experience. Myart filed a complaint charging that he had been racially discriminated against in his denial of the job. At the hearing, an examiner for the Illinois Commission ruled that: (1) Myart should be offered a job; (2) the test should no longer be used; and (3) every new test developed in its place should take into account environmental factors contributing to cultural deprivation. Although this ruling was eventually overturned for lack of evidence by the Illinois State Supreme Court, it set the precedent to hear employment testing complaints in the courts.

The National Research Council's 19-member Committee on Ability Testing prepared two books that examine employment testing and the law.[37] Among the conclusions reached by the committee were these:

- No alternative to a standardized test has been found that is equally informative, equally adequate technically, and also economically and politically viable.
- Validation of tests is important, but it should be recognized that it is an expensive and time-consuming process.
- Standardized tests do not necessarily discriminate against minorities, but employers should not rely on them solely to make selection decisions.
- Tests have been used to bring about increased government involvement in the selection process of organizations.

These conclusions and the content of the books suggest that valid and reliable tests do not alone ensure EEO compliance, but remain accurate predictors of job performance and a force against discrimination in employment. However, no test is infallible or immune from legal repudiation.[38]

Testing will undoubtedly remain a part of many organizational selection programs. However, it is advisable for an organization to choose selection tests carefully, to examine the reliablity and validity of the tests used, and to validate the tests used, since it is likely that they will be challenged by some individuals. Furthermore, P/HRM specialists involved in testing should be

---

[36] *Myart* v. *Motorola*, 110 Congressional Record 5662–64 (1964).

[37] *Ability Testing: Uses, Consequences, and Controversies. Parts I and II* (Washington, D.C.: National Academy Press, 1982).

[38] Dale Yoder and Paul D. Staudohar, "Testing and EEO: Getting Down to Cases," *Personnel Administrator*, February 1984, pp. 67–76.

familiar with the enforcement activities of the EEOC, OFCCP, and the Uniform Guidelines on Employee Selection Procedures.

Step 5: Reference Checks and Recommendations

If you have ever applied for a job, at some point you were asked to provide a list of references of past supervisors and others. In general, you picked people who could evaluate you effectively and fairly for your new employer—people who know and express your good and bad points equally.

For years, as part of the selection process, applicants have been required to submit references or recommendation letters.[39] These indicate past behavior and how well the applicant did at her or his job. Studies indicate that this has been a common practice for white-collar jobs.

For a letter of recommendation to be useful, it must meet certain conditions:

The writer must know the applicant's performance level and be competent to assess it.

The writer must communicate the evaluation effectively to the potential employer.

The writer must be truthful.

If the applicant chooses the references, the first two conditions may not be met. With regard to the third, many people are reluctant to put in writing what they really think of the applicant, since he or she may see it. As a result, the person writing the reference either glosses over shortcomings or over-emphasizes the applicant's good points. Because of these and other shortcomings, studies of the validity of written references have not been comforting to those using them in selection.

Kessler and Gibbs propose a method for potentially improving the validity of letters of reference as a selection tool.[40] In their approach, letters of reference are required only for jobs that have had job analysis performed to develop job specifications (see Chapter 4). A panel of judges (three to six persons) familiar with the job ranks the specifications for relative importance. Then a reference letter is drafted, asking the respondent to rate the applicant on the job specifications, which are listed randomly. A sample of such a reference letter is shown in Exhibit 7–11. The references must be familiar with the applicant's past employment. The rankings of the panel and the references are correlated, and the greater the correlation, the more likely is the applicant to be hired.

---

[39] Carole Sewell, "Pre-Employment Investigations: The Key to Security in Hiring," *Personnel Journal,* May 1981, pp. 376–79.

[40] Clemm C. Kessler III, and Georgia J. Gibbs, "Getting the Most from Application Blanks and References," *Personnel,* January-February 1975, pp. 53–62.

EXHIBIT 7–11   **Sample Reference Letter for Applicant for Employment Interviewer Positions**

Dear _____

_____ is applying for a position with our company and has supplied your name as a reference. We would appreciate it if you would take a few moments to give us your opinions about him.

Listed below is a series of items that may describe skills, abilities, knowledge, or personal characteristics of the applicant to a greater or lesser degree. Will you please look at this list and rank them from most to least like the applicant by placing the appropriate letter in the space below. If you do not have an opinion about a specific item, skip it and rank what you can, beginning with Space 1.

A. Has the ability to develop scheduled and nonscheduled interview formats for various jobs.
B. Can conduct an interview using the nondirective approach.
C. Has a neat appearance (clothes clean, in good condition).
D. Makes checks to see if people understand his meaning when he speaks to them.
E. Checks to see if he understands people when they speak to him.

1. _____ (Most characteristic of the applicant)
2. _____
3. _____
4. _____
5. _____ (Least characteristic of the applicant)

Now, on the rating scale below, please indicate with a check in the appropriate space the degree to which the applicant possesses the last ranked skill, ability knowledge or personal characteristic. If he is very high in the characteristic, give a rating of 5; if he is very low, give him a rating of 1. Place your check in between the two extremes if you consider that a more appropriate rating.

Very low ⌐ | | | | ⌐ Very high
         1   2   3   4   5

Comments about the applicant:

Congress has passed the Privacy Act of 1974 and the Buckley Amendment.[41] These allow applicants to view letters of reference in their files. The laws apply to public-sector employees and students. But private- and third-sector employers are afraid that the laws will soon apply to them, so many of them will now give out only minimal data: dates of employment, job title, and so on. If this becomes a common practice, reference letters may not be very useful.

_____

[41] J. D. Rice, "Privacy Legislation: Its Effect on Pre-Employment Reference Checking," *Personnel Administrator*, February 1978, pp. 46–51.

When there is a need to verify biodata, a more acceptable alternative for a letter might be a phone call to the applicant's previous supervisors to cross-check opinions or to probe further on doubtful points. Most studies indicate that few employers feel written references alone are a reliable source of data. A majority of organizations combine telephone checks, written letters of reference, and data obtained from the employment interview. Items checked most frequently are previous employment and educational background (in that order).

Although little data on phone references are available, phone calls appear to be very useful to find out how the applicant performed on previous jobs. This can be the most relevant information for predicting future work behavior. Reference checks should be conducted for the most crucial jobs at any time. Costs of these checks vary from a few cents for a few quick telephone calls to several hundred dollars for a thorough field investigation.

Step 6: Physical Examinations

Some organizations require that those most likely to be selected for a position complete a medical questionnaire or take a physical examination. The reasons for such a requirement include:

- In case of later workers' compensation claims, physical condition at the time of hiring should be known.
- It is important to prevent the hiring of those with serious communicable diseases. This is especially so in hospitals, but it applies to other organizations as well.
- It may be necessary to determine whether the applicant is physically capable of performing the job in question.

These purposes can be served by the completion of a medical questionnaire, a physical examination, or a work physiology analysis. Chase has discussed the latter technique, which is neither a physical examination nor a psychomotor test.[42] Commonly used for selection of manual workers who will be doing hard labor, it attempts to determine, by physiological indexes (heart rate and oxygen consumption), the true fatigue engendered by the work. Fatigue is analyzed through simulated job performance. First, the analyst measures applicants and obtains baseline information on these indexes while they are seated. Then data are gathered while they are working. The data are analyzed and the workers are ranked; those with the lowest heart rate and oxygen consumption should be hired (all other factors being equal).

Genetic screening, a type of physical examination that uses blood and urine samples, is now being used in some organizations to determine whether a job applicant carries genetic traits that could predispose him or her to adverse health effects when exposed to certain chemicals.[43] For example, an applicant having a specific genetic condition that makes him or her more susceptible to occupational diseases or to toxins could be screened out of "unhealthy" jobs.

A study of 366 companies indicated that 6 were using genetic testing, 17 had used it in the past 12 years, and 59 were considering using genetic testing in the next five years. Apparently a growing number of firms plan to implement genetic screening as part of the selection and placement process.[44] To date, however, genetic screening devices have not proven to be accurate and reliable predictors of hypersusceptibility.

Genetic screening, as it becomes more widely implemented, is likely to raise a number of legal implications. The use of genetic screening may trigger discrimination suits under Title VII of the Civil Rights Act, because there is some evidence suggesting that genetic impairments differ as a function of ethnicity.[45] Suits under workers' compensation law may also increase. It is difficult to establish cause and effect relationships between toxins and subsequent disease, largely because of the latency period between exposure and disease onset. Genetic screening would help an employer determine employees' predisposition to a disease. The genetic data could be used to support the

---

[42] Richard Chase, "Working Physiology," *Personnel Administrator,* November 1969, pp. 47–53.

[43] Judy D. Olian and Tom C. Snyder, "The Implications of Genetic Testing," *Personnel Administrator,* January 1984, pp. 19–27.

[44] Office of Technology and Assessment, *The Role of Genetic Testing in the Prevention of Occupational Disease* (Washington, D.C.: Government Printing Office, 1983).

[45] Ibid.

employer's placement of present employees who file workers' compensation claims or lawsuits.[46]

Physical examinations have *not* been shown to be very reliable as a predictor of future medical problems.[47] This is at least partially so because of the state of the art of medicine. Different physicians emphasize different factors in the exam, based on their training and specialties. There is some evidence that correlating the presence of certain past medical problems (as learned from the completion of a medical questionnaire) can be as reliable as a physical exam performed by a physician and is probably less costly.

Preemployment and present employee drug testing as a part of a physical examination is growing in popularity in more and more organizations. It is estimated that approximately one third of all Fortune 500 companies are conducting some form of drug testing. This trend toward drug testing has been hampered, but not halted by an increasing number of lawsuits.

Employees have been bombarded with a growing number of drug abuse statistics that have motivated them to take preemployment steps to screen out drug abusers before they become employees. Some of the statistics are that:

- 6 million Americans regularly use cocaine (900 died from cocaine abuse in 1986).
- 22 million Americans use marijuana at least once a month.
- Approximately 5 million adults are dependent on drug use as a way of life.[48]

These statistics, employer concerns about productivity and safety, and government initiated publicity has encouraged a growing number of firms to require all job applicants to pass a urinalysis test for cocaine and marijuana. In general, approximately 15 percent of those tested are eliminated from the selection process because of testing results.[49]

The legality and reliability of urinalysis is being severely questioned. Drug testing legal cases involve a cluttered web of technical problems, relating to such issues as forensic toxicology and psychopharmacology, in addition to contractual and due process questions.

In the case of present employees being asked to submit to a drug test, the issue of violating the Fourth Amendment stricture against unreasonable searches and seizures is broached. There is also the issue of whether drug testing violates the privacy rights clause written into some state constitutions, collective bargaining agreements, or the Federal Rehabilitation Act of 1973. However, in the case of job applicants, there have been few lawsuits filed by those who are not hired, because urinalysis is often conducted as part of a physical examination required for employment. Job applicants may never know that they have been tested for drug use.

---

[46] R. L. Jennings, "Medical Removal Protection and the Sensitive Worker," *Annals of the American Conference on Government Industrial Hygienists,* 1982, pp. 147–50.

[47] Mitchell S. Novitt, "Physical Examinations and Company Liability: A Legal Update," *Personnel Journal,* January 1982, pp. 47–53.

[48] Jack Gordon, "Drug Testing: As a Productivity Booster?" *Training,* March 1987, pp. 22–34.

[49] Tia Schneider on *Denenberg and Richard* v. *Denenberg,* "Employee Drug Testing and The Arbitrator: What Are the Issues?" *The Arbitrator Journal,* June 1987, pp. 19–31.

When employers conduct urinalysis tests for job applicants they should be aware of the questionable reliability of urine tests—that is, their propensity for delivering false positives as often as one third of the time.[50] Reports indicate that false positives occur mistaking Advil for marijuana, Contac for amphetamines, and tonic water for heroin. The National Institute of Drug Abuse issued some words of caution about drug testing reliability. They stated that until there is a widely accepted accreditation system or routine proficiency evaluation, the booming "diagnostics industry" will remain highly competitive. The race to be the swiftest with results may not necessarily mean that the results will be the most reliable.[51]

Chemists from the Centers for Disease Control mailed a number of urine samples which either had been spiked with known chemical substance such as cocaine and barbiturates or were blank to 13 drug testing laboratories. The results were dramatic. The laboratory results contained a large proportion of false negatives and false positives in 66 percent of the reports.[52] Thus, quality control is important in any drug testing program for job applicants or present employees.

To avoid legal entanglements, morale problems, and public image difficulties, employers need to:

1. Inform all job applicants of the organization's drug testing screening program.
2. Establish a high-quality control testing procedure with a reliable testing laboratory.
3. Perform any drug tests in a professional, non-threatening manner.
4. Keep all drug test results confidential.

These four common sense approaches should be used for preemployment screening.[53] At present there are no general legal limitations on preemployment drug testing. At a minimum, however, an organization needs to consider the dignity, privacy, and personal well-being of job applicants.

SELECTION OF MANAGERS

The process of selecting managers and the tools used vary with the type of employee being hired. The preceding section focused on blue-, gray-, and white-collar employees, but the general process is similar for the managerial employee.

Before a manager is hired, the job is studied. Then the criteria for hiring are selected, based on the characteristics of effective managers in the organization

---

[50] Joan W. Hoffman and Ken Jennings, "Will Drug Testing in Sports Play for Industry?" *Personnel Journal*, May 1987, pp. 52–59.

[51] Anne Marie O'Keefe, "The Case against Drug Testing," *Psychology Today*, June 1987, pp. 34–38.

[52] National Report on Substance Abuse, Bureau of National Affairs, February 4, 1987, pp. 1–2.

[53] Victoria Corcoran, "Surviving the Pre-Employment Legal Minefield," *Management Review*, October 1986, pp. 36–38.

at present and likely future needs. *Each* organization must do this, since the managerial task differs by level, function, industry, and in other ways. Studies of successful managers across these groups have concluded that many (not all) successful executives have intelligence, drive, good judgment, and managerial skills. Most studies avoid real-world problems like these: Candidate A scores high on intelligence and motivation, low on verbal skills, and moderate on hard work. Candidate B scores moderate on intelligence, high on motivation, moderate on verbal skills, and high on hard work. Both have good success records. Which one would you choose? The trade-offs must be assessed for particular jobs and particular organizations.

One recruiter stated:

> I've read the studies about high intelligence, test scores, and so on in managerial selection. But I've found I've got to look at the job. For example, our most successful *sales managers* are those who grew up on a farm where they learned to work hard on their own. They went to the nearest state college (all they could afford) and majored in business. They got good to better-than-average grades. They might have done better gradewise if they hadn't had to work their way through school. Our best *accounting managers,* however, did not have that background.

The message is that these studies can indicate the likely predictors of success *in general,* but executive success must be analyzed in each organization. Each of the factors mentioned must be correlated with success measured several ways to see which works for the organization. However, the focus of selection must be on *behavior,* not just on scores on tests or general impressions.

Once the criteria of managerial success are known, the selection tools to be used are chosen. In general, tests are not frequently used in managerial selection. Reference checks have been a major source of data on managerial applicants, but the legal problems with this tool also apply for executives. Biodata analysis is a major tool used for managerial selection. It is stated that, "Very often, a carefully developed typical behavior inventory based on biographical information has proved to be the single best predictor of future job behavior. . . . biographic information has proved particularly useful for assessing managerial effectiveness."[54]

The most frequently used selection tool for managers is the interview. More often than not, it is used in conjunction with the other methods. But if only one method is used by an organization, it is likely to be the personal interview.

Studies indicate that more successful managers are hired using judgments derived in employment interviews than decisions based on test scores. This is no doubt so, because these judgments can be based on factorially complex behavior, and typical executive performance is behaviorally complex. The interview is likely to continue to be the most used selection method because

[54] John P. Campbell, Marvin Dunnette, Edward E. Lawler III, and Karl E. Weick, Jr., *Managerial Behavior, Performance and Effectiveness* (New York: McGraw-Hill, 1970), p. 146.

organizations want to hire managers they feel they can trust and feel comfortable with.

Assessment Centers

An assessment center is not a building or a place. Assessment centers are designed to provide a view of individuals performing critical work behaviors.[55] The assessees are asked to complete a series of evaluative tests, exercises, and feedback sessions. The popularity of the assessment center can be attributed to its capacity for increasing an organization's ability to select employees who will perform successfully in management positions. The assessment center was first used by the German military in World War II. The Office of Strategic Services (OSS) in the United States began to use it in the mid-1940s. American Telephone and Telegraph Company (AT&T) in the 1950s introduced assessment centers to the business world. Since 1956, AT&T has used assessment centers to evaluate more than 200,000 employees.[56]

The core of an assessment center is the use of simulations, tests, interviews, and observations to obtain information about candidates (assessees). Exhibit 7–12 presents briefly a typical 2½-day assessment-center schedule. Finkle states that "assessment center . . . refers to a group-oriented, standardized series of activities that provides a basis for judgments or predictions of human behaviors believed or known to be relevant to work performed in an organization setting.[57]

Most assessment centers are similar in a number of areas.

1. Groups of 12 individuals are evaluated. Individual and group activities are observed and evaluated.
2. Multiple methods of assessment are used—interviewing, objective testing, projective testing, games, role plays, and other methods.
3. Assessors doing the evaluation are usually a panel of line managers from the organization. They can, however, be consultants or outsiders trained to conduct assessments.
4. Assessment centers are relevant to the job and have higher appeal because of this relevance.

As a result of participating in the group and as individuals, completing exercises, interviews, and tests, the assessors have a large volume of data on each individual. Individuals are evaluated on a number of dimensions, such as organization and planning ability, decision-making decisiveness, flexibility, resistance to stress, poise, and personal styles.

The rater judgments are consolidated and developed into a final report. Each assessee's performance in the center can be described if the organization

---

[55] Paul R. Sackett, "Assessment Centers and Content Validity: Some Neglected Issues," *Personnel Psychology,* Spring 1987, pp. 13–25.

[56] "Assessment Centers," *Small Business Report,* June 1987, pp. 22–24.

[57] R. B. Finkle, "Managerial Assessment Centers" in *Handbook of Industrial and Organizational Psychology,* ed. M. Dunnette (Chicago: Rand McNally, 1976), pp. 861–88.

EXHIBIT 7–12   Assessment Center Schedule (2½ Days)

Day 1

A. Orientation of approximately 12 ratees.

B. Breakup into groups of four or six to play management simulated game. (*Raters* observe: planning ability, problem-solving skill, interaction skills, communication ability.)

C. Psychological testing—Measure verbal and numerical skills.

D. Interview with raters. (*Raters* discuss goals, motivation, and career plans.)

E. Small group discussion of case incidents. (*Raters* observe confidence, persuasiveness, decision-making flexibility.)

Day 2

A. Individual decision-making exercise—Ratees are asked to make a decision about some problem that must be solved. (*Raters* observe fact-finding skill, understanding of problem-solving procedures, and risk-taking propensity.)

B. In-basket exercise. (*Raters* observe decision making under stress, organizing ability, memory, and ability to delegate.)

C. Role play of performance evaluation interview. (*Raters* observe empathy, ability to react, counseling skills, and how information is used.)

D. Group problem solving. (*Raters* observe leadership ability and ability to work in a group.)

Day 3

A. Individual case analysis and presentation. (*Raters* observe problem-solving ability, method of preparation, ability to handle questions, and communication skills.)

B. Evaluation of other ratees. (Peer evaluations.)

---

wants this type of report. Portions of the individual reports are fed back to each assessee, usually by one or more members of the assessment team.

The assessment center exercises, tests, and interviews; the final reports permit the organization to make a number of decisions, such as:

1. The qualifications of individuals for particular positions.
2. The promotability of individuals.
3. How individuals function in a group.
4. The type of training and development needed to improve behaviors of individuals.
5. How good assessors are in observing, evaluating, and reporting on the performance of others (assessees).

The results of research on assessment centers have been encouraging. The initial work at AT&T indicated that assessment centers can predict future success with some accuracy. Assessor ratings were kept secret for eight years after one assessment center was conducted. In a sample of 55 candidates who achieved the middle-management level, the center correctly predicted 80 percent of them. Of 73 people who did not move beyond the first level of management, 95 percent were correctly predicted by the assessors.[58] Other research

---

[58] Douglas W. Bray and Donald L. Grant, "The Assessment Center in the Measurement of Potential for Business Management," *Psychological Monographs* 80, no. 625 (1966), p. 25.

also indicates that the assessment center can be, if implemented correctly, an unbiased selection technique.[59]

In spite of some supportive research findings, assessment centers are not without some disadvantages. Dunnette and Borman caution about the fact that "the rapid growth of assessment centers may be accompanied by sloppy or improper application of assessment procedures."[60] Everyone's jumping on the bandwagon often leads to exaggerated claims and improper use. Another disadvantage is cost. Assessors' time, assessees' time, materials, exercises, and other center expenses cost money. Costs can be as high as $4,000 to $5,000 per assessee.

Why hasn't more work been devoted to costing out assessment center activities? In concise terms, it is not an easy task. In fact, it requires quantifying many intangible characteristics. The work to quantify may certainly be worth the effort. A survey of 64 organizations reported on the cost and benefits from their assessment centers. Total yearly costs including staff personnel, facilities, and initial setup consultant fees averaged about $88,000, while yearly assessment center savings were estimated to be $364,000.[61]

COST/BENEFIT ANALYSIS
FOR THE SELECTION DECISION

One way to evaluate which selection techniques should be used is to consider the probabilities that particular methods will select successful candidates and the costs of these methods. The seven steps in the selection procedure and their probable costs are:

Method	Cost
1. Preliminary screening interview	Negligible
2. Application blank/biodata	Negligible
3. Employment interview	Time used × cost per hour
4. Employment tests	$5–$1,000
5. Background and reference checks	$100
6. Physical examination	$100
7. Decision	

Each of these steps can be regarded as a hurdle that will cull out the least qualified candidates. Steps 1, 2, and 3 probably will be used in most cases. The

59 W. C. Byham Assessment Centers: More Than Just Predicting Management Potential, Monograph VII (Pittsburg Pa.: Development Dimensions International, 1986); Linda L. Kolb, "Use of Assessment Center Methodology for Appraising Performance," *Personnel Administrator,* October 1984, pp. 68–72, 130; and Larry Alexander, "An Exploratory Study of the Utilization of Assessment Center Results," *Academy of Management Journal,* March 1979, pp. 152–57.

60 M. D. Dunnette and W. Borman, "Personnel Selection and Classification Systems," in *Annual Review of Psychology,* ed. M. Rosenzweig and L. Porter (1979), pp. 477–526.

61 Stephen L. Cohen, "Validity and Assessment Center Technology: One and the Same?" *Human Resource Management,* Winter 1980, pp. 2–11.

A RETURN TO THE P/HRM · IN · ACTION

What did Clark Kirby do? He didn't have the resources or time to hire all 596. Besides, he believed that operating managers should participate in decisions. So his strategy was to hire the managers first. Then he had the managers help screen and hire the clerical and semiskilled employees.

As far as selection objectives were concerned, Clark accepted the home office's objectives. These were to hire those employees who were most likely to be effective and satisfied. He accepted the job specifications for the most similar positions he could find in the Chicago plant. These specifications listed minimum requirements in education and experience for managers and professional/technical employees. For clerical employees, the emphasis was on minimum experience, plus performance simulation test scores. For skilled employees, the job specifications included minimum experience and test scores on performance simulation tests. The same criteria were used for semiskilled employees.

Clark decided that because of time pressures and the nature of the job differences, he would use the following selection process.

Managers: screening interview, application blank, interview, reference check.
Professional/technical: screening interview, application blank, interview, reference check.
Clerical: screening interview, application blank, interview, tests.
Skilled: screening interview, application blank, tests and interviews for marginal applicants.
Semiskilled: screening interview, application blank, tests and interviews for marginal applicants.

Clark and Ed hired the managers. Clark himself hired the professionals. While these groups were being hired, the personnel specialist administered the tests to the clerical employees and supervised the reference checking process on the managers and professionals. The P/HRM specialist hired the clerical employees. But the managers and professionals were involved in hiring the clerical personnel to be under their direct supervision.

Then Clark and the P/HRM specialist administered the tests to skilled and semiskilled employees. Clark hired the clearly well-qualified semiskilled employees, except in marginal cases. Candidates received a review and were interviewed by the managers to whom they would report. A similar process was used to hire the semiskilled employees. Since there were few choices among professional/technical and skilled employees, it was more efficient not to involve the new managers, too.

Several problems developed. Clark and Ed had no trouble agreeing on 20 managerial candidates. But in 18 additional cases, Clark felt he had found better candidates. Ed wanted more Chicago people he knew. Lewis, reflecting the position of Chicago managers, objected. Clark found many more qualified minority and female managerial candidates than Ed wanted to accept. They compromised. Ed gave up

(continued)

half his choices to Clark, and Clark did likewise.

There were also problems in the skilled professional categories. These people generally wanted more pay than the budget called for. And the last 20 percent hired were somewhat below minimum specifications. Clark appealed for more budget, given these conditions. The home office gave him half of what he needed. He had to generate the other half by paying less for the bottom 20 percent of the semiskilled and clerical employees. Clark alerted Ed to the probable competence problem. He promised Ed that he'd be-

gin developing a list of qualified applicants in these categories in case they were needed.

In sum, Clark hired the people needed within the adjusted budget, on time, and generally with the required specifications. He was able to make a contribution to equal employment opportunity objectives by hiring somewhat more minorities and women than the total population, less than he could have and less than Lewis wanted, but more than Ed wanted. All were qualified. No reverse discrimination took place.

questionable ones are 4, 5, and 6 for many persons, and Step 6 may not be appropriate. As for Step 5, the checks need not be used for many jobs that do not involve much responsibility. Each selection technique can be evaluated in terms of costs and benefits.

Costs of training and selecting personnel may have trade-off features that can be calculated. One final comment about the selection decision: The greater the number of sources of data used in the decision, the more probable it is that the final decision will be a good decision. Tests alone will not suffice. Interviews supplemented by background checks and some test results are better.

SUMMARY

This chapter was designed to help you understand what is involved in making effective selection decisions. The basic objective of selection is to obtain the employees who are most likely to meet the organization's standards of performance and who will be satisfied and developed on the job.

To summarize the major points covered in this chapter:

1. Selection is influenced by environmental characteristics: whether the organization is public or private, labor market conditions and the selection ratio, union requirements, and legal restrictions on selection.
2. Reasonable criteria for the choice must be set prior to selection.
3. The selection process can include up to six steps:
   a. Preliminary screening interview.
   b. Completion of application blank/biodata form.
   c. Employment interview.
   d. Employment tests.

    e. Reference checks and recommendation letters.

    f. Physical examinations.

4. For more important positions (measured by higher pay and responsibility), the selection decision is more likely to be formalized and to use more selection techniques.

5. The effective organization prefers to select persons already in the organization over outside candidates.

6. More effective selection decisions are made if both P/HRM managers and the future supervisors of potential employees are involved in the selection decision.

7. Using a greater number of accepted methods to gather data for selection decisions increases the number of successful candidates selected.

8. Larger organizations are more likely to use sophisticated selection techniques.

9. For more measurable jobs, tests can be used in the selection decision more effectively.

10. For lower jobs in the hierarchy, tests can be used more effectively in the selection decisions.

11. Even if the most able applicant is chosen, there is no guarantee to successful performance on the job.

Exhibit 7–13 summarizes the recommendations for use of the various selection methods in the model organizations (see Exhibit 1–8). While selection appears to be a universally used personnel activity, the techniques adopted are likely to be based on the types of personnel selected rather than the types of organization doing the selection.

Questions for Review and Discussion

1. What is personnel selection? Who makes these decisions? What factors influence personnel selection? How?

2. What are some of the disadvantages associated with using an assessment center?

3. What is a selection ratio? How does it apply to P/HRM selection?

4. What is the difference between content and construct validity?

5. Describe the typical selection process you would see for a manual laborer; top executive; typist.

6. How are biodata forms used in selection? How effective are they? Are they reliable and valid? How frequently are they used?

7. What is an employment interview? How often is it used? What are three types of interview styles? Which are the most reliable?

8. What is a performance test? A simulation? A paper-and-pencil test? An honesty test?

9. When would you use reference checks? For which jobs? How would you do the checks?

10. Why are more and more organizations interested in using drug testing as a selection technique at preemployment?

EXHIBIT 7–13   Recommendations on Selection Methods for Model Organizations

Type of Organization	Screening Interview	Appli-cation Blank, Biodata	Employ-ment Interview	Perfor-mance and Ability Tests*	Telephoned Background Reference Check†	Physical Exam
1. Large size, low complexity, high stability	X	X	X	X	X	Hospital
2. Medium size, low complexity, high stability	X	X	X	X	X	
3. Small size, low complexity, high stability	X	X				
4. Medium size, moderate complexity, moderate stability	X	X	X	X	X	
5. Large size, high complexity, low stability	X	X	X	X	X	Hospital
6. Medium size, high complexity, low stability	X	X	X			
7. Small size, high complexity, low stability	X	X	X			Hospital

* Usually for blue- and white-collar positions.
† Usually for white-collar and managerial positions.

GLOSSARY

Assessment Center. A selection technique that uses simulations, tests, interviews, and observations to obtain information about candidates.

Content Validity. The degree to which a test, interview, or performance evaluation measures skill, knowledge, or ability to perform.

Construct Validity. A demonstrated relationship between underlying traits inferred from behavior and a set of test measures related to those traits.

Criterion-Related Validity. The extent to which a selection technique is predictive of or correlated with important elements of job behavior.

Genetic Screening. The use of blood and urine samples to determine whether a job applicant carries genetic traits that could predispose him or her to adverse health effects when exposed to certain chemicals or job-related toxins.

Reliability. Refers to a selection technique's freedom from systematic errors of measurement or its consistency under different conditions.

Selection. The process by which an organization chooses from a list of applicants the person or persons who best meet the selection criteria for the position available, considering current environmental conditions.

Structured Interview. Interview that follows a prepared pattern of questions that were structured before the interview was conducted.

Weighted Application Blank. An application form designed to be scored and used in making selection decisions.

APPLICATION CASE 7–1

Bechtel Power Corporation's Use of Objective Welding Tests*

Charles Ligons, a black, was a welder at the Iowa Electric Light and Power, Duane Arnold Energy Center Construction site at Palo, Iowa. He worked at the site for Bechtel Power Corporation. Bechtel required that its welders be qualified in accordance with standards of the American Society of Mechanical Engineers Code. That code prescribes objective criteria for testing welders on various types of welding work and for placing them in two categories: (1) A-LH, under which a welder qualifies to perform general welding jobs, and (2) AT-LH, involving more difficult welding procedures.

Prior to his arrival to the Palo site, Ligons passed a test that qualified him under AT-LH to perform heliarc welding. During his first week of employment, however, Ligons was required to report to the test shop for training and testing as a result of observations made by a welding engineer of a weld which Ligons had improperly prepared. Following a one-week training period, Ligons passed a simple plate welding test, but failed the same heliarc welding test he had passed before coming to Palo. Ligons spent several weeks on at least three separate occasions training for upgrading testing to improve his competence in heliarc welding.

On February 9, approximately 18 months after coming to the Palo site, Ligons was laid off with 58 other welders, all of whom were white. Ligons was informed that he was eligible for rehire when more welders were needed. The layoff was a result of a general reduction of the Palo work force.

Ligons was rehired in September. He required further training and testing for recertification. After about one month of training, he passed only the test qualifying him for the least difficult type of welding. About four months after being rehired he was again laid off with five other welders.

Ligons believed that race was a motivating factor in the decision to lay him off. Bechtel claimed, however, that its testing procedures for upgrading a welder's qualifications had a relationship to the jobs for which they were used. They stated that the welding tests were based on objective welding standards set by the American Society of Mechanical Engineers. Bechtel was contractually bound to ensure that its welders were qualified and, that all welding performed on the job complied with the American Society of Mechanical Engineers Code.

* Based on *Ligons* v. *Bechtel Power Corporation*, 23EPD 9 16, 233.

Questions for Thought

1. Do you believe that welding tests are necessary for the type of job Charles Ligons worked on?
2. Was the first layoff of Ligons legitimate?
3. Did the company make an attempt to help Ligons maintain and upgrade his welding competence?

EXERCISE 7–1   Practicing the Selection Interview

Objective: The exercise is designed to have students participate in structured and unstructured interviews involving selection decisions.

SET UP THE EXERCISE

1. The class or group is to be divided into equal numbers of 6, 8, 10, 12, or 14 people. The best number to work with is 10.
2. Suppose that 10 people are in the group (make adjustments based on size of group). Two individuals will play the role of the job applicant Nick Thomas. The autobiography of Nick should be read.
3. Two other group members are to play the role of interviewers using the unstructured format. They should review the unstructured interview material in Chapter 7, the job description for the position, and Nick's job application.
4. Two other group members should conduct interviews with a structured format. Consult Chapter 7 on the structured format. Also read the job description for the position, and Nick's job application (see page 316).
5. The remaining four members are to act as a panel of observers that will evaluate the structured versus unstructured format. Read all materials—Chapter 7 on interviews, job description, autobiography, and application.
6. First, the unstructured interview should be conducted (take no more than six or seven minutes.)
7. Second, conduct the structured interview (take no more than six or seven minutes).
8. Observers should rate the interviewers using these criteria:
   a. Which format yielded the most valuable information?
   b. Which format was easiest to conduct?
   c. Which format was able to probe the applicant's attitudes and feelings?

A Learning Note

This exercise will illustrate that interviewing is a rather intricate task. One must be fully prepared to conduct any interview.

The Situation

Dante Foods is a chain of food stores operating in 20 locations in the Chicago area. The night manager of the Palmer Park store suddenly resigned, leaving a vacancy. The Palmer Park store has 40 full- and part-time employees. A brief job description of the night manager position was developed. Dante has a number of applicants and wants to fill the position as soon as possible. Nick Thomas seems a likely candidate for the vacancy.

Brief Job Description of Dante Night Manager

1. Reports directly to store manager.
2. Makes decisions concerning store tasks when on duty; usually from 6 P.M. to 12 midnight.
3. Supervises all night shift employees—full- and part-time.
4. Handles all emergencies and problems when on duty (e.g. customers, deliveries, special food orders).
5. Closes books at end of shift and prepares morning orders for stockouts— canned goods, produce, and bakery products.

Nick Thomas Autobiography

I have lived in Chicago for the past 12 years. I was born in Washington, D.C., and lived for 11 years in Arlington, Virginia. I enjoy school and really like to work with people.

My work experience ranges from delivering papers as a youngster to my present position of produce manger. I plan to become an executive in the food business working for a chain or even starting my own business.

My strongest trait is a dogged determination to do the job well. In anything I do I work hard and always give my best effort. My weakest trait is that I sometimes become impatient with those people who do not do their best.

I enjoy fishing, listening to music, and staying in shape. Every year for the past three I have spent at least two weeks fishing on Lake Baribou in Wisconsin. I actively work out with Nautilus equipment and weights at least four times a week.

I would like to finish my degree at the University of Illinois at Chicago within the next four or five years. I have to keep working to put myself through school. This is the only way that I can receive a college education.

Job Application—Dante Foods

Name: ___Nick Thomas___

Address: ___1711 Western Avenue, Chicago, Ill. 60615___

How Long at Present Address: ___3 years___

Date of Birth: ___March 18, 1960___

Marital Status: ___Single___

Number of Children: _____

U.S. Citizen: ___Yes___

Do you have any physical defects? ___No___ If Yes, describe _____

Have you had any major illness in the past two years? ___No___

If yes, describe _____

Please List Former Employers

Year	Name and address	Position	Reason for leaving
From 1976 to 1978 (Summers)	Gassmans 3514 E. 92 Street Chicago, Illinois	Clerk	College
From 1978 to Present	Safeway 10136 Commercial Chicago, Illinois	checker, assistant produce manager, and produce manager	—
From to			
From to			

Hobbies: _____ Fishing, Listening to Music, Exercise _____

Civic Organizations: _____
Professional Organizations: _____
_____

Education	Date of Graduation	Major	Rank in Class and Grade Point Average
High School			
Bower	1978		65/275
College			3.1/4.0
University of		Business	65 credits
Illinois at Chicago			completed

When could you begin to work for Dante?
Next Week 7/20

PERFORMANCE EVALUATION AND COMPENSATION

Part Three discusses an extremely important part of a firm's overall P/HRM program: performance evaluation and compensation.

Chapter 8, Performance Evaluation, introduces the job of evaluating the performance of employees. This is an extremely difficult job that requires care in the development of measures to assess performance.

The subject of compensation and pay is introduced in Chapter 9, Compensation: An Overview. It discusses the potential impact of pay on employees and discusses pay level, pay structure, and individual pay determination. Chapter 10, Compensation: Methods and Policies, completes this discussion by focusing on incentives and pay programs, managerial compensation, and several significant policy issues regarding compensation.

Chapter 11, Employee Benefits and Services, covers benefits, services, and pensions. The potential impact of benefits and services is considered, and the major benefits that employers provide for employees are discussed.

PERFORMANCE EVALUATION

LEARNING OBJECTIVES

After studying this chapter, you should be able to:

- **Define** what is meant by the term *performance evaluation.*
- **Discuss** various types of rating errors that raters can make in performance evaluation programs.
- **Compare** the advantages of various performance evaluation techniques.
- **Explain** the role of a manager and his or her subordinate in a management by objectives program.
- **Describe** the process of and skill required for a feedback interview.

KEY TERMS

Behaviorally Anchored Rating Scale (BARS)
Behavioral Observation Scale (BOS)
Central Tendency Error
Critical Incident
Halo Error
Harshness Rating Error
Leniency Rating Error
Performance Evaluation
Personal Bias Rating Error
Recency of Events Rating Error

CHAPTER OUTLINE

P/HRM · IN · ACTION

Hector

Ed Smart went to work in the maintenance department of Partridge Enterprise, a middle-sized firm, about a year ago. He enjoys working in maintenance, since he has always liked to work with his hands. His supervisor, Hector Garcia is a good maintenance man who helps Ed when he doesn't understand a problem. But Ed has often wished he knew what Hector thinks of him on the job. Hector never tells Ed how he is doing. It seems that Hector chews him out about once a month. Ed wonders: Doesn't he think I am trying to do a good job? Doesn't he think I am a good maintenance man?

Knowing answers to these questions is important to Ed, because someday he'd like to move up. He hears that Joe is going to retire next year. Joe's job is better and pays more. Ed wonders if he has a chance to get the job. He also has heard that business is not good right now at some branches. People have been laid off. If the crunch hits the New York branch where Ed works, he might get laid off. He knows seniority is a factor in layoffs. But so is performance. He wishes he knew how he was doing so that he could improve himself, move up, and avoid getting laid off. Ed wants some kind of feedback from his boss.

This chapter focuses on *performance evaluation*—the P/HRM activity designed to satisfy Ed's needs for performance feedback.

> Performance evaluation is the P/HRM activity that is used to determine the extent to which an employee is performing the job effectively.

Other terms for performance evaluation include *performance review, personnel rating, merit rating, performance appraisal, employee appraisal, or employee evaluation.*

In many organizations, two evaluation systems exist side by side: the formal and the informal. Supervisors often think about how well employees are doing; this is the informal system. It is influenced by political and interpersonal processes so that employees who are liked better than others have an edge. On the other hand,

> A formal performance evaluation is a system set up by the organization to *regularly* and *systematically* evaluate employee performance.

This chapter focuses only on formal performance evaluation systems.

A DIAGNOSTIC APPROACH TO PERFORMANCE EVALUATION

Exhibit 8–1 highlights the relevant factors from the diagnostic model that have significance for performance evaluation. One factor is the task. A white-collar or supervisory task is more likely to be formally evaluated than a blue-collar task. In addition, the performance evaluation technique used will differ with the task being evaluated. Other factors affecting performance evaluation are government requirements, regulations, and laws. Since the passage of antidiscrimination legislation, the government has investigated to determine if organizations discriminate against protected categories of employees in promotions, pay raises, and other rewards. Performance evaluation is the personnel method for allocating these rewards. By inducing organizations to keep better records to support their decisions, government action has indirectly encouraged better performance evaluation systems.

Other factors influencing performance evaluation are the attitudes and preferences of employees. For people such as Ed, whose values fit the work ethic, evaluations can be very important. But if this process is badly handled, turnover increases, morale declines, and productivity can drop. For employees with instrumental attitudes toward work, performance evaluation is just another process at work. Since work is not too important to them, neither are evaluations. They want a job to earn money, and that is it.

An important factor that can affect performance evaluation is the leader's (supervisor's) style. Supervisors can use the formal system in a number of ways: fairly or unfairly, in a supportive manner or punitively, positively or negatively. If the supervisor is punitive and negative with an employee who responds to positive reinforcement, performance evaluation can lead to the opposite of the results expected by the enterprise.

Finally, if there is a union present in the organization, performance evaluations might be affected. Different unions take different positions in support of or in opposition to formal performance evaluations. Most oppose the use of nonmeasurable, nonproduction-related factors in performance evaluation. They have good reason to doubt unclear factors such as "initiative" or "potential."

EXHIBIT 8–1   Factors Affecting Performance Evaluation

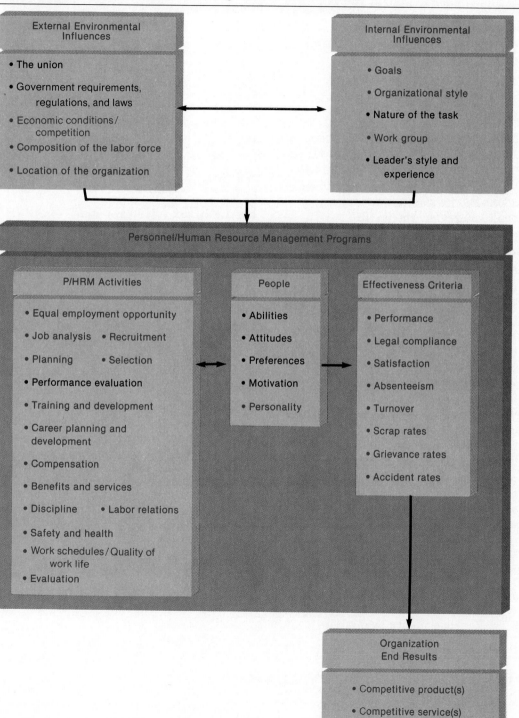

P/HRM · IN · ACTION

The setting: Office of the executive vice president of Partridge Enterprises. Present are the executive vice president and the vice presidents of the corporation.

Tom Smith (executive vice president): As you know, we're here to make a recommendation to John (the president) on what if anything to do about Mary's suggestion. Mary, why don't you review the issue?

Mary Hartford (vice president, personnel/human resource management): You all received a copy of my memo to J.B. As you know, when I came here three years ago I felt one of our top priorities in P/HRM would be to get an evaluation system really running on-line. I want this because performance evaluation is an outstanding motivation technique. After much thought and planning, the results are in my memo. I recommend we institute management by objectives-type evaluation systems for vice presidents through section heads, and a graphic rating scale for below that. The MBO would be done quarterly, the rating scale semiannually, and we'd tie rewards such as raises and promotions to the results of the evaluation.

The details are in the memos. We're too big and geographically dispersed now to continue using our informal system.

Tom: Sounds good to me.

Dave Artem (vice president marketing): Me too.

Will Roxer (vice president, finance): Looks fine, Mary.

Fred Fairfax (vice president, manufacturing): Well, it doesn't to me. We had one of these papermill forms systems here 10 years ago, and it was a waste of time. It just meant more paper work for us down on the firing line. You staff people sit up here dreaming up more for us to do. We're overburdened now. Besides, I called a few buddies in big firms who have P.E. They say it involves a lot of training of evaluators, and it makes half the employees mad when they don't get 100 percent scores on the "grade report." It gets down to a lot of politics when it's all said and done.

If you recommend this, I'll send J.B. a counterproposal.

These are the major factors affecting the performance evaluation process. The next section will briefly examine the case for and against the use of formal performance evaluation.

TO EVALUATE OR NOT TO EVALUATE

Why hasn't Ed ever been evaluated by his supervisor? In order to answer that question, consider the above situation in P/HRM in Action.

In Favor of Evaluation

This meeting illustrates many of the arguments, pro and con, on formal performance evaluation. Let's sum them up. Those who favor formal performance evaluation contend that it serves several purposes:

Developmental purposes. It can determine which employees need more training and helps evaluate the results of training programs. It helps the subordinate-supervisor counseling relationship, and it encourages supervisors to observe subordinate behavior to help employees.

Reward purposes. It helps the organization decide who should receive pay raises and promotions. It can determine who will be laid off. It reinforces the employee's motivation to perform more effectively.

Motivational purposes. The presence of an evaluation program has a motivational effect: it encourages initiative, develops a sense of responsibility, and stimulates effort to perform better.

Legal compliance. It serves as a legally defensible reason for making promotion, transfer, reward, and discharge decisions.

Personnel and employment planning purposes. It serves as a valuable input to skills inventories and personnel planning.

Compensation. It provides information that can be used to determine what to pay and what will serve as an equitable monetary package.

Communications purposes. Evaluation is a basis for an ongoing discussion between superior and subordinate about job-related matters. Through interaction, the parties get to know each other better.

P/HRM research purposes. It can be used to validate selection tools, such as a test program.

These and other purposes served by a formal performance evaluation system indicate how important this P/HRM activity is to the organization. They also show how performance evaluation is job-related and linked to other P/HRM activities—planning, selection, training and development, research evaluation, and equal employment opportunity. Of all of the relationships between performance evaluation and other P/HRM activities, the one between evaluation and equal employment opportunity has become extremely crucial.

Performance Evaluation and the Law

As mentioned in Chapter 3, the Equal Employment Opportunity Commission (EEOC) is responsible for administering and enforcing the Civil Rights Act of 1964. The EEOC issued the Uniform Guidelines on Employment Selection Procedures in 1978. These guidelines definitely have an impact on performance evaluation because evaluations are viewed as a selection procedure.[1] The guidelines state that a procedure such as a performance evaluation must not adversely impact any group protected by the Civil Rights Act.

Most performance evaluation procedures rely on paper-and-pencil methods

---

[1] Richard Henderson, *Performance Appraisal* (Reston, Va.: Reston Publishing, 1984), p. 337.

to identify specific work behavior. Once ratings are made, they are used as input in making promotion, pay, transfer, and other human resource decisions. In making these decisions, there is the potential for bias and poor judgment in many parts of the evaluation process.[2] For example, managers who are serving as raters could use criteria that are not important in performing a job or place too little weight on significant job performance criteria.

A number of court rulings have identified the responsibilities of management in developing and using a performance evaluation system.

> *Griggs* v. *Duke Power Company* (1971). Recall from Chapter 3 that the central issue in this case was that an educational restriction on an employment decision is useless unless it can be proved that there exists a bona fide occupational qualification (BFOQ) between the test and actual job performance. The burden of proof is on the employer to show nondiscrimination in any employment decision related to discrimination.
>
> *Brito* v. *Zia Company* (1973). The Zia Company was found in violation of the law when a disproportionate number of protected group members were laid off on the basis of low performance evaluation scores. The court ruled that the company had not shown that its performance evaluation instrument was valid in the sense that it was related to important elements of work behavior in the jobs for which the employees were being evaluated. For example, some raters had little daily contact with the ratees.
>
> *Moody* v. *Albermarle Paper Company* (1975). The court ruled that in the process of validating their tests, the company had not conducted a job analysis to identify the critical requirements of jobs.
>
> *Mistretta* v. *Sandia Corp.* (1977). The courts ruled that an employer must be able to justify the need for any layoff. Sandia Corporation claimed that the plaintiff's performance declined with age. The Court ruled that the appraisal decision, which resulted in the early retirement of Mistretta, was not based on definite, identifiable criteria that were supported by the record. The appraisal system used was ruled to be age-biased.[3]

Since employers have been winning only about 5 percent of the race, sex, and age discrimintion cases, understanding the law would seem to be a major concern. Previous court rulings such as the four just cited provide managers with guidelines on the issues of criteria, validity, and reliability. These three concepts are extremely important if a case reaches the federal courts. An audit is necessary to ensure that an organization's performance evaluation system is able to withstand review by the courts and the EEOC. Exhibit 8–2 summarizes some of the suggested steps for developing and implementing an evaluation system that can be defended by the employer in a court.

---

[2] See footnotes in Chapter 3 and Wayne F. Cascio and H. John Bernardin, "Implications of Performance Appraisal Litigation for Personnel Decisions," *Personnel Psychology,* Summer 1981, pp. 211–26.

[3] *Mistretta* v. *Sandia Corp.,* 15 FEP Cases 1680 (1977); 24 FEB Cases 316 (1980).

EXHIBIT 8–2   **Suggestions to Follow for Developing and Implementing Legally Defensible Appraisal Systems**

1. Procedures for personnel decisions must not differ as a function of the race, sex, national origin, religion, or age of those affected by such decisions.
2. Objective-type, nonrated, and uncontaminated data should be used whenever available.
3. A formal system of review or appeal should be available for appraisal disagreements.
4. More than one independent evaluator of performance should be used.
5. A formal, standardized system for the personnel decision should be used.
6. Evaluators should have ample opportunity to observe ratee performance (if ratings must be made).
7. Ratings on traits such as dependability, drive, aptitude, or attitude should be avoided.
8. Performance appraisal data should be empirically validated.
9. Specific performance standards should be communicated to employees.
10. Raters should be provided with written instructions on how to complete the performance evaluations.
11. Employees should be evaluated on specific work dimensions rather than a single overall or global measure.
12. Behavioral documentation should be required for extreme ratings (e.g., critical incidents).
13. The content of the appraisal form should be based on a job analysis.
14. Employees should be provided with an opportunity to review their appraisals.
15. Personnel decision makers should be trained on laws regarding discrimination.

Source: J. Bernardin and W. Cascio, "Performance Appraisal and the Law," in R. S. Schuler, S. A. Youngblood, and V. Huber, eds. *Readings in Personnel and Human Resource Management,* 3d ed. (St. Paul, Minn., West Publishing, 1987).

POTENTIAL PERFORMANCE EVALUATION PROBLEMS

Opposition to Evaluation

Most employees are wary of performance evaluation. Perhaps the most common fear is that of rater subjectivity. Introducing subjective bias and favoritism are real problems that create opposition to most performance evaluation systems. These fears are hidden, and other, more general arguments are provided. For example, those who oppose the use of formal performance evaluation systems argue that:

- They increase paperwork and bureaucracy without benefiting employees much. Operating managers do not use them in reward decisions (systems problems).
- Managers and employees dislike the evaluation process. Raters especially have problems with reaching decisions about the performance levels of employees.
- Employees who are not evaluated in the top performance category experience a reverse motivation effect: They slow down (employee problems).

System Design and Operating Problems

Performance evaluation systems break down because they are poorly designed. The design can be blamed if the criteria for evaluation are poor, the technique used is cumbersome, or the system is more form than substance. If the criteria used focus solely on activities rather than output results, or on personality traits rather than performance, the evaluation may not be well-received. Some evaluation techniques take a long time to do or require extensive written analysis, both of which many managers resist. If this is the problem, another technique can be chosen. Finally, some systems are not on line and running. Some supervisors use the system, but others just haphazardly fill out the paperwork. Top management's support for performance evaluation can remedy this problem of ritualism.

Too often a typical manager is like Hector. He knows there is a formal performance evaluation system, but he disregards it. Performance evaluation systems have to be so good that they can't be disregarded.

Rater Problems

Even if the system is well designed, problems can arise if the raters (usually supervisors) are not cooperative and well trained. Supervisors may not be comfortable with the process of evaluation, or what Douglas McGregor called "playing God."[4] This is often because they have not been adequately trained or have not participated in the design of the program. Inadequate training of raters can lead to a series of problems in completing performance evaluations including:

- Standards of evaluation.
- Halo effect.
- Leniency or harshness.
- Central tendency.
- Recency of events.
- Personal bias (same as me or different from me).

Standards of Evaluation Problems with evaluation standards arise because of perceptual differences in the meaning of the words used to evaluate employees. Thus *good, adequate, satisfactory,* and *excellent* may mean different things to different evaluators. Some teachers are "easy As," while others almost never give an A. *They* differ in their interpretation of *excellent.* If only one rater is used, the evaluation can be distorted. This difficulty arises most often in graphic rating scales but may also appear with essays, critical incidents, and checklists.

For example, Exhibit 8–3 presents a rating scale with unclear standards for four difficult-to-rate performance dimensions. What does "good" performance for quality of work mean? How does it differ from a "fair" rating? How would you interpret the quality or quantity of performance? This rating scale is ambiguous as it now stands. Perhaps defining the meaning of each dimension

---

[4] Douglas McGregor, "An Uneasy Look at Performance Appraisal," *Harvard Business Review,* May 1957.

EXHIBIT 8–3   A Graphic Rating Scale for Laboratory Scientists

Performance Dimension	Scale: Place an X for Rating of _____				
	Outstanding	Good	Fair	Below Accepted	Poor
Quality of technical reports					
Quantity of technical reports					
Creativeness					
Social interaction ability					

and training raters to apply the five ratings consistently could reduce the potential rating problem.

The Halo Effect Halo error in ratings is one of the major problems in most performance evaluation systems. It occurs when a rater assigns ratings on the basis of an overall impression (positive or negative) of the person being rated (ratee).[5] Suppose that a retail store floor manager (rater) sees and overhears an argument between a clerk and a customer. If the rater assumed that because of this argument the clerk was not good at servicing customers, processing complaints, and ordering inventory, he or she would be making a halo error. The one negative aspect of the clerk's behavior caused the rater to see the ratee in a negative light on other dimensions.

Eliminating halo rating errors are difficult.[6] One procedure to reduce this type of error is to have the rater evaluate all subordinates on one dimension before proceeding to another dimension. The theory of this practice is that thinking in terms of one dimension at a time forces the rater to think in specific instead of overall terms when evaluating subordinates.

Leniency or Harshness Error Performance evaluations require the rater to objectively reach a conclusion about criteria of performance. Being objective is difficult for everyone. Raters have their own rose-colored glasses with which they "objectively" view subordinates. What some raters see is everything

---

[5] Steve W. J. Kozlowski and Michael P. Kirsch, "The Systematic Distortion Hypothesis, Halo, and Accuracy: An Individual Level Analysis," *Journal of Applied Psychology,* May 1987, pp. 252–61.

[6] E. Pulakos, N. Schmidt, and C. Ostroff, "A Warning about the Use of a Standard Deviation across Dimension within Rates to Measure Halo," *Journal of Applied Psychology,* February 1986, pp. 29–32.

P/HRM · IN · ACTION

Hector and Bob Woods

Let's get back to Ed and his supervisor, Hector. Now that the vice presidents have had their meeting about performance evaluation, the tentative decision to start up Mary's plan has been passed on to the department heads.

Bob Woods (department head): I'm just reviewing your suggested pay and promotion recommendations for your unit, Hector. You know I try to delegate as much as I can. But I know some of the people you have set here for big raises and promotions, and I notice some surprising omissions. Since I'm responsible for the whole department, I'd like to review this with you. Understand, I'm not trying to undercut you, Hector.

Hector Garcia (supervisor): Oh, I understand, Bob. No problem! Where do you want to start?

Bob: Let me just highspot. I note that Mo Gibbs, who's always been in our high reward group, isn't here, nor is Ed Smart, a good worker. And you do have Joe Berlioz in your high reward group. In the past, he never appeared there. How did you make these recommendations?

Hector: I looked my people over and used my best judgment.

Bob: Well Hector, what facts did you use—did you look at the quarterly output printout, their personnel files, or what? How about performance evaluations? Partridge is thinking about a formal system to evaluate employees and help decide who should be promoted and get raises.

Hector: I believe I know my people best. I don't need to go through a lot of paperwork and files to come up with my recommendations.

good—these are lenient raters. Other raters see everything bad—these are harsh raters.

Exhibit 8–4 shows the distributions of lenient and harsh raters on a dimension called quality of work performance.[7] Suppose that Jack is an employee

[7] Wayne Cascio, *Applied Psychology in Personnel Management* (Reston, Va.: Reston Publishing, 1987) p. 83

EXHIBIT 8–4   **Distributions of Lenient and Harsh Raters**

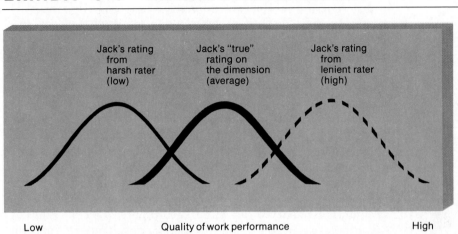

Jack's rating from harsh rater (low)   Jack's "true" rating on the dimension (average)   Jack's rating from lenient rater (high)

Low   Quality of work performance   High

working for this particular rater. His ratings would be low if rated by the harsh rater and high if rated by the lenient rater.

Raters can assess their own harsh and lenient rating tendencies by examining ratings. This self-assessment is sometimes startling. Another method used to reduce harsh and lenient rating tendencies is to ask raters to distribute ratings—forcing a normal distribution (e.g., 10 percent of the subordinates will be rated excellent, 20 percent rated good, 40 percent rated fair, 20 percent rated below fair, and 10 percent rated poor).

Central Tendency Error Many raters avoid using high or low ratings. They resort to a philosophy that everyone is about average and rate subordinates around a 4 on a 1 to 7 scale or a 3 on a 1 to 5 scale. This type of "average" rating is almost useless. It fails to discriminate between subordinates. Thus, it offers little information for making P/HRM decisions regarding compensation, promotion, training needs, or what should be fed back to ratees. Raters must be made aware of the importance of discriminating across ratees and the use of evaluations. This sometimes stimulates raters to use less central (or average) ratings.

Recency of Events Error One difficulty with many of the evaluation systems is the time frame of the behavior being evaluated. Raters forget more about past behavior than current behavior. Thus many persons are evaluated more on the results of the past several weeks than on six months' average behavior. This is called a *recency of events rating error.*

Some employees are well aware of this difficulty. If they know the dates of the evaluation, they make it their business to be visible and noticed in many positive ways for several weeks in advance. Many evaluation systems suffer from this difficulty. It can be mitigated by using a technique such as critical incident or management by objectives (MBO) or by irregularly scheduled evaluations.

Personal Bias Error Various studies have indicated that raters' biases can influence their evaluation of employees.[8] If raters like certain employees better than others, this can influence the ratings they give. This problem is related to the effects of prejudices against groups of people. There is also personal bias error when a rater gives a higher rating because the ratee has qualities or characteristics similar to him or her. Likewise giving a ratee a rating lower than he or she deserved because the person has qualities or characteristics dissimilar to the rater is a form of personal bias error.[9] Pressures from governmental agencies and managerial rules of fairness should lead to equal opportunity and fair performance evaluation. The result should be equitably distributed merit pay increases and promotions, and more positive career experiences for all employees of both sexes and all races, religions, and nationalities. Some evaluation techniques (e.g., forced choice, field review, performance test, and MBO) tend to reduce this problem.

Bias has been pointed out in a number of studies. One study found a systematic tendency to evaluate subordinates over 60 years of age lower on "performance capacity" and "potential for development" than younger subordinates.[10] In other research, high-performing females were often rated significantly higher than high-performing males.[11]

Some of the evaluation difficulties and errors made in rating can perhaps be reduced through the use of better performance evaluation instruments (forms or scales used). By clearly defining the dimensions being rated and the scale value or descriptors (what is meant by the term *excellent, good, fair*), raters could become more confident about their ratings. Unfortunately, research to date indicates that improved instruments have little positive influence on reducing leniency and halo errors.[12] However, more research is needed before concluding that a clear, unambiguous, and meaningful rating scale is not more effective than an unclear, ambiguous, and meaningless rating scale.

Another approach used in reducing rater problems involves training. Training can be of many types: how to rate effectively, present rater tendencies and ways to become more accurate, how to feed back evaluation information, and how to get subordinates more involved in evaluation.[13] Several research stud-

---

[8] Walter C. Borman, "Format and Training Effect on Rating Accuracy and Rater Errors," *Journal of Applied Psychology,* August 1979, pp. 410–21.

[9] Lawrence H. Peters et al., "Sex Bias and Managerial Evaluations: Replication and Extension," *Journal of Applied Psychology,* May 1984, pp. 349–52.

[10] B. Rosen and T. H. Jerdee, "The Nature of Job Related Age Stereotypes," *Journal of Applied Psychology,* April 1976, pp. 180–83.

[11] William J. Bigoness, "Effect of Applicant's Sex, Race, and Performance on Employer's Performance Ratings: Some Additional Findings," *Journal of Applied Psychology,* February 1976, pp. 80–84.

[12] Donald P. Schwab, Herbert G. Heneman III, and Thomas A. DeCotiis, "Behaviorally Anchored Rating Scales: A Review of the Literature," *Personnel Psychology,* Winter 1975, pp. 549–62.

[13] S. Zedeck and W. F. Cascio, "Performance Appraisal Decisions as a Function of Rating Training and Purpose of the Appraisal," *Journal of Applied Psychology,* December 1982, pp. 752–58.

ies indicate that even brief training programs can reduce some of the rating errors so prevalent in performance evaluation programs.[14]

Employee Problems with Performance Evaluation

For the evaluation system to work well, the employees must understand it, feel it is fair, and be work-oriented enough to care about the results. One way to foster understanding is for the employees to participate in system design and be trained to some extent in the process of performance evaluation. Another is the use of a self-evaluation system. With regard to fairness, performance evaluation is in some ways like grading systems in schools. If you have received grades that you thought were unfair and inequitable, that were incorrectly computed or based on the "wrong things" (always agreeing with the instructor), you know what your reactions were! Students will say "I got an A" for a course in which they worked hard and were fairly rewarded. They will say *"He* (or she) gave me a D" if they feel it was unfair. Their reactions sometimes are to give up or to get angry. Similar response can come from employees as well. If performance evaluation raters are incompetent or unfair, the employees may resist, sabotage or ignore them.

Performance evaluation may also be less effective than desired if the employee is not work-oriented and sees work only as a means to an end sought off the job. It might be seen only as paperwork, unless the evaluation is so negative that the employee fears termination.

Some critics believe that employees who are rated poorly will not improve their performance but will give up. This problem is compounded if the technique used is viewed as a zero-sum game—that is, some win and some lose as a result of it. With a system such as forced distribution, 90 percent of the employees must be told they are not highly regarded, whether they are or not. One study found that 77 percent of General Electric's personnel ranked themselves high.[15] In a forced choice system only 10 percent would be rated high, so 67 to 77 percent of them would find such an evaluation a deflating experience. Some of the performance evaluation tools (forced distribution, ranking, paired comparisons) do not include an explanation of why employees received their rank. It might be argued that everyone cannot be tops, so the best are rewarded, and the worst will leave. Sometimes just the opposite happens. Of those who were evaluated poorly at GE, 60 percent lost heart but stayed because they figured they had nowhere else to go.

But this analysis is too simple. In one summary of the research in how a person's expectations in the evaluation affected his or her reactions to evalua-

---

[14] John M. Ivancevich, "Longitudinal Study of the Effect of Rater Training on Psychometric Errors in Rating," *Journal of Applied Psychology,* October 1979, pp. 502–8.

[15] Paul H. Thompson and Gene W. Dalton, "Performance Appraisal: Managers Beware," *Harvard Business Review,* January-February 1970, pp. 149–57.

tion and behavior afterward, it was found that reaction to positive and negative feedback varied depending on a series of variables: (1) the importance of the task and the motivation to perform it; (2) how high the employee rates the rater; (3) the extent to which the employee has a positive self-image; and (4) the expectations the employee had prior to the evaluation—for example, did the employee expect a good evaluation or a bad one?

FORMAL EVALUATION

To provide information that can serve the organization's goals and that complies with the law, a performance evaluation system must provide accurate and reliable data. The ability to generate accurate and reliable data is enhanced if a systematic process is followed. These six steps can provide the basis for such a systematic process:

1. Establish performance standards for each position and the criteria for evaluation.
2. Establish peformance evaluation policies on when to rate, how often to rate, and who should rate.
3. Have raters gather data on employee performance.
4. Have raters (and employees in some systems) evaluate employees' performance.
5. Discuss the evaluation with the employee.
6. Make decisions and file the evaluation.

Step 1 was performed when job analysis and work measurement took place (see Chapter 4). But the key issue is: What is and should be evaluated?

The factors on which an employee is evaluated are called the criteria of the evaluation. Examples include quality of work, quantity of work, and cost of work. One of the major problems is that some systems make *person evaluations* rather than *performance evaluations*.

The criteria used are critical in effective performance evaluation systems. They must be established to keep EEO agencies satisfied, too. After a thorough review of the literature, Smith listed four characteristics of effective criteria.[16]

Relevant—Reliable and valid measures of the characteristics being evaluated, and as closely related to job output as possible.
Unbiased—Based on the characteristic, not the person.
Significant—Directly related to enterprise goals.
Practical—Measurable and efficient for the enterprise in question.

The evidence is clear that single performance measures are ineffective because success is multifaceted. Most studies indicate that multiple criteria are necessary to measure performance completely. The multiple criteria are

---

[16] Patricia Smith, "Behaviors, Results, and Organizational Effectiveness," in *Handbook of Industrial and Organizational Psychology,* ed. M. D. Dunnette (Skokie, Ill.: Rand McNally, 1976), pp. 745–75.

Drawing by Frascino; © 1973 The New Yorker Magazine, Inc.

"Your work is fine, Perkins. It's your aftershave I can't stand."

added together statistically or combined into a single multifaceted measure. The criteria choice is not an easy process. One must be careful to evaluate both activities (for example, number of calls a salesperson makes) and results (for example, dollars of sales). A variation is to evaluate both results and how they were accomplished.

Probably a combination of results and activities is desirable for criteria. How do you weigh the importance of multiple criteria? For example, if a salesperson is being evaluated on both number of calls and sales dollars and is high on one and low on the other, what is the person's overall rating? Management must weigh these criteria.

Keeley studied the evaluation of research scientists whose job duties were not clear.[17] When the tasks are not clear and performance standards are hard to specify, he found the organization responds by asking third persons (such as employee peers and other supervisors) for their opinions of the employee's performance.

---

[17] Michael Keeley, "Subjective Performance Evaluation and Person-Role Conflict under Conditions of Uncertainty," *Academy of Management Journal*, June 1977, pp. 301–14.

The criteria selected depend on the purpose of the evaluation. If the purpose is to improve performance on the job, they should be performance-related. If social skills or personality are vital on this or future jobs, these should be stressed.

A BNA study found that for white-collar workers, performance factors such as the following were used by these percentages of organizations surveyed: quality of work (93 percent), quantity of work (90 percent), job knowledge (85 percent), and attendance (79 percent).[18] Personality factors used were initiative (87 percent), cooperation (87 percent), dependability (86 percent), and need for supervision (67 percent). The data for blue-collar workers were parallel: performance factors included quality of work (used by 91 percent), quantity of work (91 percent), attendance (86 percent), and job knowledge (85 percent). Personality factors surveyed were dependability (86 percent), initiative (83 percent), cooperation (83 percent), and need for supervision (77 percent).

This study found that hard-to-measure personality traits are widely used. The key issue, however, is weighing the factors. The personality factors may be evaluated, but not weighed equally with performance.

Whether the evaluation should be based on actual or potential performance depends on the major purpose of the evaluation for the P/HRM function. In this respect there are three principal purposes of performance evaluation:

- Improvement of performance.
- Promotion consideration.
- Salary and wage adjustments.

If the main purposes are improved performance or wage adjustment, the evaluation should be based on actual performance. If the main purpose is possible promotion, a different evaluation is needed, one that will assess potential performance on a new job. This situation is similar to the selection decisions, in which past performance on one job must be projected to possible performance on a different one: it is easier to do if the employee has had experience that is relevant to the new job. But here the emphasis is different, and assessment of future potential on a different job is more difficult than actual assessment of past performance. Exhibit 8–5 presents a promotability form used at Armstrong.

Set Policies on When, How Often, and Who Evaluates

When Should Evaluation Be Done? There are two basic decisions to be made regarding the timing of performance appraisal: one is when to do it, and the other is how often. In many organizations, performance evaluations are scheduled for arbitrary dates, such as the date the person was hired (anniversary date). Or every employee may be evaluated on or near a single calendar date.

---

[18] Bureau of National Affairs, "Employee Performance: Evaluation and Control," *Personnel Policies Forum,* Survey 108 (Washington, D.C., February 1975).

EXHIBIT 8-5

Armstrong

CONFIDENTIAL BUSINESS INFORMATION

PERSONNEL PROMOTABILITY

Name _____ Employee No. _____

Following the Personnel Performance and Development Review with the individual, complete as appropriate:

A. PROMOTABILITY WITHIN UNIT. It appears that this individual has the potential to advance beyond the present position in this organizational unit, as follows:

	Ready Now	Ready By (Date)
(Title)		
(Title)		

B. PROMOTABILITY INTO OTHER UNITS. This individual should be considered for opportunities outside this organizational unit. It is suggested that these recommendations be reviewed with appropriate unit (s) management, where practical.

_____

_____

_____

C. INDIVIDUAL IS NOT PROMOTABLE. It appears this individual is not promotable beyond the present position. (Mark (X) for appropriate reasons.)

☐ Own desire, unwilling to change work locations, or similar personal reasons.

☐ Capabilities are now fully utilized.

☐ Other factors. (Specify) _____

_____

_____

_____

Evaluated by _____

Date evaluated _____

Reviewed by (Rater's Supervisor): _____

Please enclose the white copy of this form with Form 43289 and return to Director, Employee Relations, Lancaster. Retain buff copy.

Although the single-day approach is convenient administratively, it probably is not a good idea. It requires raters to spend a lot of time conducting evaluation interviews and completing forms at one time, which may lead them to want to "get it over with" quickly. This probably encourages halo effect ratings, for example. In addition, it may not be related to the normal task cycle of the employee; this factor can make it difficult for the manager to evaluate performance effectively.

It makes more sense to schedule the evaluation at the completion of a task cycle. For example, tax accountants see the year as April 16 to April 15. Professors consider that the year starts at the beginning of the fall term and terminates after the spring term. For others without a clear task cycle based on dates, one way to set the date is by use of the MBO technique, whereby the manager and employee agree upon a task cycle, terminating in evaluation at a specific time. Another approach is to schedule an evaluation when there is a significant change (positive or negative) in an employee's performance.

How Often Should Evaluation Be Done? The second question concerns how often evaluation should be done. A BNA study found that 74 percent of white-collar and 58 percent of blue-collar employees were evaluated annually, and 25 percent of white-collar and 30 percent of blue-collar employees were evaluated semiannually. About 10 percent were evaluated more often than semiannually.[19]

Organizations use two basic timing periods for most employees. They are referred to as the anniversary date (date the person entered the current job or a common review date). Under a common review date system all employees are evaluated and compared so that such decisions as promotions and merit pay increases have a common period of time being covered for all employees.

Researchers have found that feedback on performance should be given frequently, and the closer the feedback to the action, the more effective it is. For example, it is more effective for a professor to correct an error on a computer program the first time the error appears and show the student how to change it than to wait and flunk the student at the end of the term.[20]

Why, then, do so few firms evaluate frequently? Generally speaking, it is because managers and employees have lots of other things to do. One way to reconcile the ideal with the reality in this respect is for the manager to give frequent feedback to employees informally, and then formally summarize performance at evaluation time. This, of course, is based on the assumption that employees value evaluation and feedback.

Another reason that some managers resist frequent subordinate evaluations is that they produce stress, especially if a rater has to use a system in which he or she has little faith or confidence. There is also the stress associated with having to inform another person that he or she is not performing at

---

[19] Ibid.

[20] D. R. Ilgen and J. M. Feldman, "Performance Appraisal: A Process Focus," in *Research in Organizational Behavior,* ed. B. M. Staw and L. L. Cummings (Greenwich, Conn.: JAI Press, 1983).

EXHIBIT 8–6   **Involvement of Personnel and Operating Managers in Performance Evaluation**

Performance Evaluation Function	Operating Manager (OM)	Personnel Manager P/HRM
Establish performance standards	Approves the standards	Calculated by P/HRM and engineers
Set policy on when performance evaluation takes place	Approves the policy	Recommends the policy
Set policy on who evaluates	Approves the policy	Recommends the policy
Set policy on criteria of evaluation	Approves the policy	Recommends the policy
Choose the evaluation system	Approves the system	Recommends the system
Train the raters		Done by P/HRM
Review employee performance	Done by OM	
Discuss the evaluation with the employee	Done by OM	
File the performance evaluation		Done by P/HRM

acceptable levels.[21] Researchers have found that raters under stress tend to notice and recall negative information about those being evaluated. This recall, of course, is likely to result in the giving of less favorable evaluations.

As Exhibit 8–6 shows, performance evaluation is another P/HRM activity that involves both line managers and P/HRM specialists. For performance evaluation to be more than a yearly paperwork exercise, top management must encourage its use and use it to make reward decisions.

Who Should Evaluate the Employee? Exhibit 8–6 indicates that the operating manager (the supervisor) does so. This is true in the vast majority of cases. Other possibilities include:

Rating by a Committee of Several Superiors The supervisors chosen are those most likely to come in contact with the employee. This approach has the advantages of offsetting bias on the part of one superior alone and adding additional information to the evaluation, especially if it follows a group meeting format.

Rating by the Employee's Peers (Co-workers) In the peer evaluation system, the co-workers must know the level of performance of the employee being evaluated. For this system to work, it is preferable for the evaluating peers to

---

[21] Shanthi Srinivas and Stephen J. Motowidlo, "Effects of Raters' Stress on the Dispersion and Favorability of Performance Ratings," *Journal of Applied Psychology,* May 1987, pp. 247–51.

trust one another and not be competitive for raises and promotions. This approach may be useful when the tasks of the work unit require frequent working contact among peers.

Rating by the Employee's Subordinates Exxon has used this system, and it is used in some universities (students evaluate faculty). It is used more for the developmental aspects of performance evaluation than are some of the other methods.

Rating by Someone outside the Immediate Work Situation Known as the field review technique, this method uses a specialized appraiser from outside the job setting, such as a personnel specialist, to rate the employee. This approach is often costly, so it is generally used only for exceptionally important jobs. It might be used for the entire work force if accusations of prejudice must be countered. A crucial consideration is that the outside evaluator is not likely to have as much data as evaluators in any of the other four approaches, and the data developed are from an atypical situation.

Self-Evaluation In this case the employee evaluates herself or himself with the techniques used by other evaluators. This approach seems to be used more often for the developmental (as opposed to evaluative) aspects of performance evaluation. It is also used to evaluate an employee who works in physical isolation.

Finally, a combination of these approaches can be used. The supervisor's evaluation can be supplemented by a self-evaluation; when evaluation is done jointly, it can be an MBO exercise. The supervisor's results could be supplemented by subordinates' or peers' evaluations.

An example of the use of a combination program is the one at Glendale Federal Savings and Loan Association, Glendale, California.[22] The program has three critical elements:

1. Independent manager and employee completion of an evaluation instrument (see Exhibit 8–7 for employee's section, which is similar to manager's section).
2. Two-way (rater-ratee) communication of job performance, career goals, and additional job responsibilities.
3. High-level managerial review of the completed appraisal.

The multiple-approach program involving a number of managerial levels has been well received. Managers complete their evaluations on time, and key training and development data are extracted from the forms.

Unlike the combination Glendale Federal program, evaluation by superiors only is the most frequently used method, as has been noted. Self- evaluation is used in about 5 percent of evaluations. Peer evaluation is sometimes used by the military and universities but is rarely used elsewhere.

It is probable that evaluation by superiors will continue to be the principal approach used. If the primary purpose of the evaluation is developmental, the

---

22 William J. Birch, "Performance Appraisal: One Company's Experience," *Personnel Journal,* June 1981, pp. 456–60.

EXHIBIT 8–7

SECTION I: EMPLOYEE'S COMMENTS
(To be completed by Employee)

MAJOR ACCOMPLISHMENTS: Briefly describe the major accomplishments you achieved in your position during the past appraisal period.

SUPPORT NEEDED: What type of assistance, guidance or support do you need from your supervisor or Glendale Federal Savings to improve your job related performance in the future?

MAJOR AREA(S) OF RESPONSIBILITY: Indicate 1 or 2 major areas of responsibility in your job that you would like to focus on during the next appraisal period.

DEVELOPMENTAL ACTIVITIES: Describe any developmental activities you are presently engaged in or have completed this appraisal period—i.e., courses, workshops, work assignments.

PERFORMANCE FACTORS: In each category below indicate ONE area you would describe as one of your major strengths by checking the appropriate circle. If strength is not evident, leave category blank. NOTE: Select only those factors which are appropriate for this job.

COMMUNICATING
- Writes clearly & concisely
- Speaks clearly & concisely
- Works well with peers
- Works well with subordinates
- Works well with superiors
- Courteous & helpful to customers
- Presents ideas persuasively
- _____

JOB SKILLS/KNOWLEDGE
- Completes work assignments
- Knows major aspects of job
- Needs little supervision
- Makes few errors
- Meets schedules
- Keeps up to date on current developments in field
- _____

PLANNING
- Sets realistic goals
- Analyzes needs accurately
- Gets results
- Develops a variety of solutions
- Effectively identifies & solves problems
- _____

ORGANIZING
- Keeps files & resources up to date
- Delegates tasks appropriately
- Checks effectiveness of actions
- Establishes work priorities
- Uses time efficiently
- _____

SUPERVISING
- Accurately judges subordinates' performance
- Trains & prepares subordinates
- Demonstrates effective leadership
- Motivates subordinates
- _____

CONTROLLING
- Adheres to policies & procedures
- Maintains acceptable quality standards
- Keeps within expense limits
- _____

OTHER
- Knows where to find information
- Develops creative ideas
- Works well under pressure
- Adjusts to changes
- Makes good decisions
- _____

Indicate specific area(s) from the lists above you would like to improve upon. NOTE: Indicate only areas that are job related.

1. _____ 2. _____ 3. _____

CAREER INTEREST: If appropriate, indicate other areas of career interest or long-range career goals.

EMPLOYEE'S SIGNATURE _____ **DATE** _____

When you have completed SECTION I give this form to your supervisor.

Source: "Performance Appraisal: One Company's Experience," By William J. Birch, copyright June 1981, p. 457. Reprinted with the permission of *Personnel Journal*, Costa Mesa, Calif.; all rights reserved.

P/HRM Manager Close-Up

John C. Midler
Archer Daniels Midland Co.

Biography

John "Jack" C. Midler is director of personnel and labor relations at Archer Daniels Midland Co. Mr. Midler, a native of Minnesota, graduated from Macalester College in Minneapolis after serving in the United States Air Force. He joined ADM as a wage and salary analyst and became director of personnel and labor relations in 1971.

Mr. Midler's assets include his patience; listening skills; and broad experience in labor, including negotiations, arbitrations and mediations, personnel policy and procedure, and wage and salary administration.

The Importance of Listening Skills: An Important Part of Performance Evaluation

At Archer Daniels Midland Company, the name Jack Midler conjures up the image of an organized, can-do manager. A sharper focus reveals an even more responsive, determined manage-ment style laced with no-nonsense and grit.

Unafraid of hard work and challenges, Midler effectively directs the areas of Personnel and Labor Relations. Whatever he does, Midler acts out of conviction, using his excellent listening skills and wonderful sense of humor. "Don't talk until you have to; you don't usually lose anything by waiting" was his response when asked about his listening philosophy.

"I've never consciously thought about how I was going to deal with people." His expectations are basic. "Your word is your bond," and "Everyone is allowed one mistake." Thinking some and with a deeper grin, he states, "Every dog is allowed one bite before it's classified as a biter."

One of Midler's working philosophies is the multivalued approach, where he is consistently seen as being open-minded and flexible. When addressed with a problem, instead of singling out one specific cause and declaring it

(continued)

responsible, he likes to see the larger picture and firmly supports the belief that every problem can and usually does have more than one cause or cure. He firmly announces, "If you have a problem and you bring it to me, you'd better have several alternative answers that you'll be willing to consider."

As responsive as Midler is, it is hard to imagine how one can stay on top of everything. Asked how he juggles everything with such enthusiasm and energy, he replies, "All you can do is all you can do."

organization might consider supplementing it with subordinate evaluations or self-evaluation. If the purpose of the process is reward, then the organization might consider adding peer evaluation to superior's ratings. The field review approach would be used only in special cases. The key to successful performance evaluation appears to be well-trained, carefully selected raters who are knowledgeable about the performance of those being evaluated.

Gathering Data on Employees

With regard to gathering data on employees, the raters collect information by observation, analysis of data and records, and discussion with the employees. The data they gather are influenced by the criteria used to evaluate, the primary purpose of the evaluation, and the technique used to do the evaluation.

SELECTED EVALUATION TECHNIQUES

A number of techniques for evaluation will be described here. There are several ways to classify these tools. The three categories used here are: individual evaluation methods, multiple-person evaluation methods, and other methods.

Individual Evaluation Methods

There are a number of ways to evaluate employees individually.[23] In these systems, employees are evaluated one at a time without *directly* comparing them to other employees.

Graphic Rating Scale The most widely used performance evaluation technique is a graphic rating scale.[24] It is also one of the oldest techniques in use.

---

[23] Henderson, *Performance Appraisal,* pp. 155–98.

[24] Robert L. Taylor and Robert A. Zawacki, "Trends in Performance Appraisal: Guidelines for Managers," *Personnel Administrator,* March 1984, pp. 71–80.

EXHIBIT 8-8   Typical Graphic Rating Scale

Name _____ Dept. _____ Date _____

	Out-standing	Good	Satis-factory	Fair	Unsatis-factory
Quantity of work Volume of acceptable work under normal conditions Comments:	☐	☐	☐	☐	☐
Quality of work Thoroughness, neatness and accuracy of work Comments:	☐	☐	☐	☐	☐
Knowledge of job Clear understanding of the facts or factors pertinent to the job Comments:	☐	☐	☐	☐	☐
Personal qualities Personality, appearance, sociability, leadership, integrity Comments:	☐	☐	☐	☐	☐
Cooperation Ability and willingness to work with associates, supervisors, and subordinates toward common goals Comments:	☐	☐	☐	☐	☐
Dependability Conscientious, thorough, accurate, reliable with respect to attendance, lunch periods, reliefs, etc. Comments:	☐	☐	☐	☐	☐
Initiative Earnestness in seeking increased responsibilities. Self-starting, unafraid to proceed alone? Comments:	☐	☐	☐	☐	☐

Using this technique, the rater is presented with a set of traits such as those shown in Exhibit 8–8 and asked to rate employees on each of the characteristics listed. The number of characteristics rated varies from a few to several dozen.

The ratings can be in a series of boxes as in the exhibit, or they can be on a continuous scale (0–9, or so). In the latter case, the rater places a check above

EXHIBIT 8–9   **Standards of Performance: Excerpts from Graphic Rating Scale**

Far below standard rating:

1. Has serious gaps in technical-professional knowledge
   Knows only most rudimentary phases of job
   Lack of knowledge affects productivity
   Requires abnormal amount of checking

2. Reluctant to make decisions on his own
   Decisions are usually not reliable
   Declines to accept responsibility for decisions

3. Fails to plan ahead
   Disorganized and usually unprepared
   Objectives are not met on time

4. Wastes or misuses resources
   No system established for accounting of material
   Causes delay for others by mis-management

descriptive words ranging from *none* to *maximum*. Typically, these ratings are then assigned points. For example, in Exhibit 8–8, *outstanding* may be assigned a score of 4 and *unsatisfactory* a score of 0. Total scores are then computed. In some plans, greater weights may be assigned to more important traits. Raters are often asked to explain each rating with a sentence or two.

Two modifications of the scale have been designed to make it more effective. One is the Mixed Standard Scale.[25] Instead of just rating a trait such as *initiative,* the rater is given three statements to describe the trait, such as:

> She is a real self-starter. She always takes the initiative, and her superior never has to stimulate her. (Best description.)
> While generally she shows initiative, occasionally her superior has to prod her to get her work done.
> She has a tendency to sit around and wait for directions. (Poorest description.)

After each description the rater places a check mark (the employee fits the description), a plus sign (the employee is better than the statement), or a minus sign (the employee is poorer than the statement). The resulting seven-point scale, the authors contend, is better than the graphic rating scale.

The second modification is to add operational and benchmark statements to describe different levels of performance. For example, if the employee is evaluated on job knowledge, the form gives a specific example: "What has the employee done to actually demonstrate depth, currency or breadth of job knowledge in the performance of duties? Consider both quality and quantity of work." The performance description statement to guide the rater gives these examples of persons deserving that rating (see Exhibit 8–9).

Forced Choice The forced-choice method of evaluation was developed because other methods used at the time led to too many high ratings. In forced choice

---

[25] Fritz Blanz and Edwin Ghiselli, "The Mixed Standard Scale: A New Rating System," *Personnel Psychology,* Summer 1972, pp. 185–99.

EXHIBIT 8–10   **Forced-Choice Items**

Instructions: Rank from 1 to 4 the following sets of statements according to how they
describe the manner in which _____ performs
(name of employee)
the job. A rank of *1* should be used for the most descriptive statement, and a
rank of *4* should be given for the least descriptive. No ties are allowed.

1. _____   Does not anticipate difficulties
   _____   Grasps explanations quickly
   _____   Rarely wastes time
   _____   Easy to talk to
2. _____   A leader in group activities
   _____   Wastes time on unimportant things
   _____   Cool and calm at all times
   _____   Hard Worker

the rater must choose from a set of descriptive statements about the employee.
Typical sets of these statements are given in Exhibit 8–10. Typically, P/HRM
specialists prepare the items for the form, and supervisors or others rate the
items for applicability. That is, they determine which statements describe
effective and ineffective behavior. The supervisor then evaluates the employee. The P/HRM department adds up the number of statements in each
category (for example, effective behavior), and they are summed into an
effectiveness index. Forced choice can be used by superiors, peers, subordinates, or a combination of these in evaluating employees.

Essay Evaluation In the essay technique of evaluation, the rater is asked to
describe the strong and weak aspects of the employee's behavior. In some
organizations, the essay technique is the only one used; in others, the essay is
combined with another form, such as a graphic rating scale. In this case, the
essay summarizes the scale, elaborates on some of the ratings, or discusses
added dimensions not on the scale. In both of these approaches, the essay can
be open-ended, but in most cases there are guidelines on the topics to be
covered, the purpose of the essay, and so on. The essay method can be used by
raters who are superiors, peers, or subordinates of the employee to be evaluated.

Management by Objectives In most of the traditional performance evaluation systems, the rater makes judgments of past performance behavior. Any
person making judgments is in a difficult and somewhat antagonistic role.
McGregor believed that instead of creating antagonisms because of judgments,
the superior should work with subordinates to set goals. This would enable
subordinates to exercise self-control and management over their job performance behaviors. From the early beliefs of McGregor, Drucker, and Odiorne has
emerged the management by objectives (MBO) approach.[26]

---

[26] Douglas M. McGregor, *The Human Side of Enterprise* (New York: McGraw-Hill, 1960);
Peter F. Drucker, *The Practice of Management* (New York: Harper & Row, 1954); and George S.
Odiorne, *Management by Objectives* (New York: Pitman Publishing, 1965).

MBO is more than just an evaluation program and process. It is viewed as a philosophy of managerial practice, a method by which managers and subordinates plan, organize, control, communicate, and debate. By setting objectives through participation or by assignment from a superior, the subordinate is provided with a course to follow and a target to shoot for while performing the job. Usually an MBO program follows a systematic process such as the following:

1. The superior and subordinate conduct meetings to define key tasks of the subordinate and to set a limited number of objectives (goals).
2. The participants set objectives that are realistic, challenging, clear, and comprehensive.
3. The superior, after consulting with the subordinate, establishes the accomplishment of the objectives.
4. Intermediate progress review dates.
5. The superior and subordinate make any required modifications in original objectives.
6. A final evaluation by the superior is made and a meeting is held with the subordinate in a counseling, encouragement session.
7. Objectives for the next cycle are set by the subordinate after consulting with the superior, keeping in mind the previous cycle and future expectations.

MBO-type programs have been used in organizations throughout the world.[27] Approximately 200 of *Fortune*'s 500 largest industrial firms report use of MBO-type programs. Various types of objectives have been set in these programs. A sample of some objectives taken from actual MBO evaluation forms is presented in Exhibit 8–11. Most of these objectives are stated in the language of the job or occupation. Some of them are routine, others are innovative, and some are personal, such as the accountant's objectives.

Research indicates that a well-stated objective is clear, specific, challenging, and timely.[28] The criteria are easier to attain if the objectives are stated in quantitative terms and also specify a target date. A challenging objective leads to higher levels of performance if the objective is accepted by the subordinate. Thus, many firms have used participative goal setting to encourage subordinate acceptance of superior-subordinate established objectives.

An important feature of any MBO program is that discussions about performance evaluation center on results. The results hopefully are objective in nature and associated with certain work behaviors. The superior and subordinate dissect the objectives achieved and not achieved, and analysis serves to help subordinates improve in the next cycle of objective setting.

---

[27] Steve Kaufman, "Going for the Goods," *Success*, January-February 1988, pp. 38–41; and Gary P. Latham and Gary A. Yukl, "A Review of Research on the Application of Goal Setting in Organizations," *Academy of Management Journal*, December 1975, pp. 824–43; and Gary P. Latham and Edwin A. Locke, "Goal Setting: A Motivational Technique That Works," *Organizational Dynamics*, Autumn 1979, pp. 68–80.

[28] George Labovitz and Lloyd S. Baird, "MBO As an Approach to Performance Appraisal," in *The Performance Appraisal Sourcebook*, ed. Lloyd S. Baird, Richard W. Beatty, and Craig Eric Schneier (Amherst, Mass.: Human Resource Development Press, 1982), pp. 51–56.

EXHIBIT 8–11   **Examples of MBO Evaluation Form Objectives**

Occupation in Organization	Type Organization	Objective Statement
Sales representative	Medium: Petrochemical firm	To contact six new clients in West AVA region and to sell at least two of these new clients within the next semiannual cycle.
Product manager	Large: Food processing plant	To increase market share of creamy peanut butter by at least 3.5 percent before next objective meeting (nine months from today) without increasing costs by more than 2 percent.
Skilled machinist	Small: Job shop	To reduce flange rejects by 8 percent by August 15.
Accountant	Small: CPA firm	To attend two auditing seminars to improve and update audit knowledge by the end of summer (September 15).
Plant manager	Medium: Assembly line plant	Decrease absenteeism of operating employees from 18.9 percent to under 10 percent by January 1.
Engineer	Large: Construction company	To complete power plant tower project within 30 days of government specified target date of November 10.

After three decades of interest there is still cautious support for MBO among many practicing managers. First, MBO appeals to people because it doesn't require a superior to sit as judge. Second, MBO seems simple to implement. Nothing can be further from the truth. In fact, MBO requires patience, objective writing skill, interview skills, and overall trust between superiors and subordinates. These attributes are complex and difficult to maintain in MBO programs. Third, the literature cites example after example of MBO success stories. Unfortunately, many of these success stories are based on anecdotal statements of consultants who are in the business of selling MBO to clients. As reviews of the literature indicate there are few rigorously designed field studies of MBO that find that it has a positive, long-lasting effect on performance.[29]

A number of pitfalls and problems with MBOs have been identified. Some of these include:

- Too much paperwork.
- Too many objectives are set, and confusion occurs. (It appears to be more efficient to work with four, five, or six objectives.)
- MBO is forced into jobs where establishing objectives is extremely difficult.

---

[29] Jeffrey S. Kane and Kimberly A. Freeman, "MBO Performance Appraisal: A Mixture That's Not a Solution," *Personnel*, December 1986, pp. 26–36.

- Failure to tie in MBO results with rewards. "Why are we doing this?" is an often-asked question.
- Too much emphasis on the short term.
- Failure to train superiors in the MBO process and the mechanics involved.
- Never modifying originally-set objectives.
- Using MBO as a rigid control device that intimidates rather than motivates.

These and other problems need to be minimized or overcome if MBO is to have any chance for success.[30] MBO in some situations is very effective; in other cases, it is costly and disruptive. Just like the other evaluation techniques available, managers need to examine the purposes, costs, and benefits, and their preferences before selecting or discarding an MBO program.

Critical Incident Technique In this technique, P/HRM specialists and operating managers prepare lists of statements of very effective and ineffective behaviors for an employee. These are the *critical incidents*. The specialists combine these statements into categories, which vary with the job. For example, Kircher and Dunnette described 13 categories they used for evaluating salespersons at the 3M Company.[31] Two of the categories are calling on all accounts and initiating new sales approaches. Another set of categories for evaluating managers generally includes, for example, control of quality, control of people, and organizing activities.

Once the categories are developed and statements of effective and ineffective behavior are provided, the rater prepares a log for each employee. During the evaluation period, the evaluator records examples of critical (outstanding good or bad) behaviors in each of the categories, and the log is used to evaluate the employee at the end of the period. An example of a *good* critical incident of a sales clerk is the following:

> May 1—Dan listened patiently to the customer's complaint, answered the woman's questions, and then took back the merchandise, giving the customer full credit for the returned product. He was polite, prompt, and interested in her problem.

On the other hand, a *bad* critical incident might read as follows:

> August 12—Dan stayed eight minutes over on his break during the busiest part of the day. He failed to answer three store manager's calls on the intercom to report to cash register 4 immediately.

The use of critical incidents is valuable during the evaluation interview, since it avoids recency bias, and the rater can be specific in making positive and negative comments. The critical incident technique is more likely to be used by superiors than in peer or subordinate evaluations.

---

[30] J. N. Kondrasuk, "Studies in MBO Effectiveness," *Academy of Management Review,* 1981, pp. 419–30.

[31] W. E. Kircher and M. D. Dunnette, "Using Critical Incidents to Measure Job Proficiency Factors," *Personnel,* September-October 1957, pp. 54–59.

Checklists and Weighted Checklists Another type of individual evaluation method is the checklist. In its simplest form, the *checklist* is a set of objectives or descriptive statements. If the rater believes that the employee possesses a trait listed, the rater checks the item; if not, the rater leaves it blank. A rating score from the checklist equals the number of checks.

A variation of the checklist is the *weighted checklist*. Supervisors of P/HRM specialists familiar with the jobs to be evaluated prepare a large list of descriptive statements about effective and ineffective behavior on jobs, similar to the critical incident process. Judges who have observed behavior on the job sort the statements into piles describing behavior that is scaled from excellent to poor. When there is reasonable agreement on an item (for example, when the standard deviation is small), it is included in the weighted checklist. The weight is the average score of the raters prior to use of the checklist.

The supervisors or other raters receive the checklist without the scores and check the items that apply, as with an unweighted checklist. The employee's evaluation is the sum of the scores (weights) on the items checked. Checklists and weighted checklists can be used by evaluators who are superiors, peers, or subordinates, or by a combination.

Behaviorally Anchored Rating Scales Smith and Kendall developed what is referred to as the *behaviorally anchored rating scale (BARS)* or the *behavioral expectation scale (BES)*.[32] The BARS approach relies on the use of critical incidents to serve as anchor statements on a scale. A BARS rating form usually contains 6 to 10 specifically defined performance dimensions, each with 5 or 6 critical incident anchors. Exhibit 8–12 presents one performance dimension for engineering competence. The anchor statement for a rating of 9 is: "This engineer applies a full range of technical skills and can be expected to perform all assignments in an excellent manner." The rater would read the anchors and place an X at some point on the scale for the ratee.

A BARS scale usually contains the following features:

1. Six to 10 performance dimensions are identified and defined by raters and ratees (a group is selected to construct the form).
2. The dimensions are anchored with positive and negative critical incidents.
3. Each ratee is then rated on the dimensions.
4. Ratings are fed back using the terms displayed on the form.

The exact construction of a BARS scale is too complex for presentation here.[33] However, it should be noted that usually two to four days are needed to

---

[32] P. C. Smith and L. M. Kendall, "Retranslation of Expectations: An Approach to the Construction of Unambiguous Anchors for Rating Scales," *Journal of Applied Psychology,* April 1963, pp. 149–55.

[33] Gary P. Latham and Kenneth N. Wexley, *Increasing Productivity through Performance Appraisal* (Reading, Mass.: Addison-Wesley Publishing, 1981), pp. 51–64; and R. S. Atkin and E. J. Conlon, "Behaviorally Anchored Rating Scales: Some Theoretical Issues," *Academy of Management Review,* January 1978, pp. 119–28. Also see Frank J. Landy and James L. Fair, "Performance Rating," *Psychological Bulletin,* February 1980, pp. 72–107.

EXHIBIT 8–12 Sample BARS Dimension

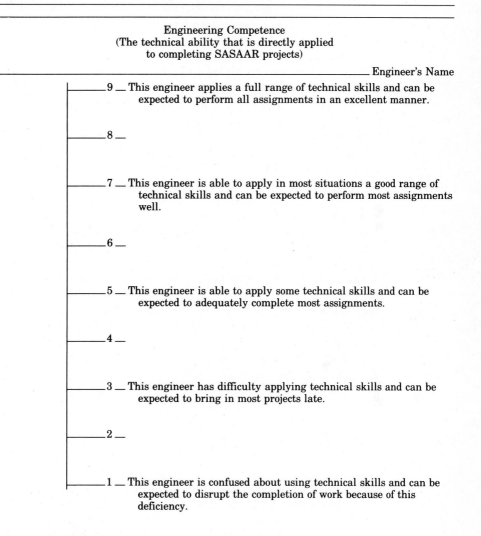

Engineering Competence
(The technical ability that is directly applied
to completing SASAAR projects)

_____ Engineer's Name

9 — This engineer applies a full range of technical skills and can be expected to perform all assignments in an excellent manner.

8 —

7 — This engineer is able to apply in most situations a good range of technical skills and can be expected to perform most assignments well.

6 —

5 — This engineer is able to apply some technical skills and can be expected to adequately complete most assignments.

4 —

3 — This engineer has difficulty applying technical skills and can be expected to bring in most projects late.

2 —

1 — This engineer is confused about using technical skills and can be expected to disrupt the completion of work because of this deficiency.

develop a BARS. The result of the developmental work is a job-related, jargon-free, superior-subordinate scale.

In terms of rating errors and problems, research fails to show the superiority of BARS over other techniques. Raters using BARS still make halo, harsh, and lenient rating errors.[34] However, there appear to be some impor-

---

[34] Walter C. Borman and M. D. Dunnette, "Behavior-Based v. Trait-Oriented Performance Ratings: An Empirical Study," *Journal of Applied Psychology,* October 1975, pp. 561–65; and Paul O. Kingstrom and Alan R. Bass, "A Critical Analysis of Studies Comparing Behaviorally Anchored Rating Scales (BARS) and Other Rating Formats," *Personnel Psychology,* Summer 1981, pp. 263–89.

tant spin-offs from using a BARS program. It appears that subordinates involved with a BARS program are more committed, less tense, and more satisfied than counterparts using other programs.[35] Another possible benefit is that managers have feedback in the form of critical incident statements that are meaningful to subordinates. Thus, although the BARS system is costly, time-consuming, and complex, it may make performance evaluation easier to accept for subordinates. After all, they are usually involved in the development of the rating instrument.

In the decision of evaluation approaches and techniques, we have implied that each person is evaluated independent of others, unless the employee is one of the few being evaluated with a multiperson evaluation technique. However, this may not be strictly true: the evaluation of one employee can be affected by the evaluations of the others in the work group.

Laboratory research has indicated that when a work group included one employee with poor work attitudes who refused to obey orders, the supervisor evaluated other employees higher. In one study, 59 supervisors of 473 clerical employees were asked to evaluate their employees.[36] The researchers examined how the supervisors evaluated and rewarded the employees who were poor in ability and work attitudes (and the proportion of the work group they comprised) affected how the supervisors evaluated *all* the employees. Specifically, when there is one or a small percentage of noncompliant employees, the supervisor gave a *much lower* evaluation of the noncompliant employees and a slightly higher evaluation to the compliant employees. As the percentage of noncompliant employees increased, the supervisors raised the evaluations of the compliant employees *much higher*.

Case study research also indicates that some supervisors may perceive pressure not to evaluate all employees at the top of the range. They modify the ratings so that all employees do not seem "excellent." Therefore, at least some of the time evaluators are likely to be influenced in their evaluations of one employee by their evaluations of others in the work group, even when individual evaluation techniques are used.

Behavioral Observation Scales Latham and associates developed the behavioral observation scale (BOS) performance evaluation approach.[37] Like BARS, the BOS uses the critical incident technique to identify a series of behaviors that cover the domain of the job. A major difference between BARS and BOS is that, instead of identifying those behaviors exhibited by the ratee during a rating period, the rater indicates on a scale how often the ratee was actually observed engaging in the specific behaviors identified in the BOS.

---

[35] John M. Ivancevich, "A Longitudinal Study of Behavioral Expectations Scales: Attitudes and Performance," *Journal of Applied Psychology,* April 1980, pp. 139–46.

[36] Ronald Grey and David Kipnis, "Untangling the Performance Appraisal Dilemma: The Influence of Perceived Organizational Context on Evaluative Processes," *Journal of Applied Psychology,* June 1976, pp. 329–35.

[37] Gary Latham, Charles H. Fay, and Lise M. Saari, "The Development of Behavioral Observation Scales for Appraising the Performance of Foremen," *Personnel Psychology,* Summer 1979, pp. 290–311.

EXHIBIT 8–13 Sample BOS Items for Supervisor

Is accurate in preparing cost reports for Johnson project crew.

Almost Never	1	2	3	4	5	Almost Always

Practices sound energy conservation in supervising project crews.

Almost Never	1	2	3	4	5	Almost Always

Is available for technical consultation when needed.

Almost Never	1	2	3	4	5	Almost Always

Develops fair and equitable work schedule.

Almost Never	1	2	3	4	5	Almost Always

Exhibit 8–13 presents four behavior items that are used to appraise the performance of a first line supervisor in a manufacturing plant. In this BOS appraisal form 25 behavioral items are identified. The maximum score is 125 (25×5), and the minimum score is 25. Those supervisors with scores above 115 are considered excellent performers, while a score in the 25 to 34 range is considered extremely poor. Each firm using a BOS must determine the meaning and importance of the total score for their ratees.

A limitation of the BOS is the time and cost needed to develop it for actual use in ratings. There is also the issue of measurement. The BOS method uses a five-point frequency scale. The five rating intervals have constant definitions for all the behavioral descriptions rated (such as 1 = 0–64 percent, 2 = 65–74 percent, 3 = 75–84 percent, 4 = 85–94 percent, 5 = 95–100 percent). This method ignores the possibility that a given frequency interval (e.g., 65–74 percent) may indicate a higher level of satisfaction for some behaviors, especially those that are difficult to accomplish, than for others.[38]

Multiple-Person Evaluation Methods

The techniques that have been described are used to evaluate employees one at a time. Three techniques that have been used to evaluate an employee in comparison with other employees being evaluated are discussed in this section.

Ranking In using the ranking method, the evaluator is asked to rate employees from highest to lowest on some overall criterion. This is very difficult to do

---

[38] See the series of debates on the limitations in H. John Bernardin and Jeffrey S. Kane, "A Second Look at Behavioral Observation Scales," *Personnel Psychology,* Winter 1980, pp. 809–14; Gary P. Latham, Lise M. Saari, and Charles Fay, "BOS, BES, and Baloney: Raising Kane with Bernardin," *Personnel Psychology,* Winter 1980, pp. 815–21; and K. R. Murphy, C. Martin, and M. Garcia, "Do Behavioral Observation Scales Measure Observation?" *Journal of Applied Psychology,* October 1982, pp. 562–67.

if the group of employees being compared numbers over 20. It is also easier to rank the best and worst employees than it is to evaluate the average ones. Simple ranking can be improved by alternative ranking. In this approach, the evaluators pick the top and bottom employee first, then select the next highest and next lowest, and move toward the middle.

Paired Comparison This approach makes the ranking method easier and more reliable. First, the names of the persons to be evaluated are placed on separate sheets (or cards) in a predetermined order, so that each person is compared to all others to be evaluated. The evaluator then checks the person he/she feels is the better of the two on a criterion for each comparison. Typically, the criterion is overall ability to do the present job. The number of times a person is preferred is tallied and results are indexed based on the number of preferences compared to the number being evaluated.

These scores can be converted into standard scores by comparing the scores to the standard deviation and the average of all scores. This method can be used by superiors, peers, subordinates, or some combination of these groups.

Forced Distribution The forced-distribution system is similar to grading on a curve. The rater is asked to rate employees in some fixed distribution of categories, such as 10 percent in low, 20 percent in low average, 40 percent in average, 20 percent in high average, and 10 percent in high. One way to do this is to type each employee's name on a card and ask the evaluators to sort the cards into five piles corresponding to the ratings. This should be done twice for the two key criteria of job performance and promotability.

Exhibit 8–14 shows the results of forced-distribution evaluation of 20 employees. One reason forced distribution was developed was to try to alleviate such problems as inflated ratings and central tendency in the graphic rating scale.

A variation of forced distribution is the point allocation technique (PAT). In PAT, each rater is given a number of points per employee in the group to be

---

EXHIBIT 8–14 **Forced-Distribution Evaluation of Employees in a Marketing Research Unit**

High 10 Percent	Next 20 Percent	Middle 40 Percent	Next 20 Percent	Low 10 Percent
Leslie Moore	Cinde Lanyon	Max Coggins	Art Willis	Wayne Allison
Tina Little	Sharon Feltman	Tina Holmes	Debbie Salter	Sherry Gruber
	Eddie Dorsey	Julis Jimenex	Tom Booth	
	Johnny Dyer	Lis Amendale	Lance Smith	
		Vince Gaillard		
		Missy Harrington		
		Bill King		
		Shelly Sweat		

evaluated, and the total points for all employees evaluated cannot exceed the number of points per employee times the number of employees evaluated. The points are allocated on a criterion basis. The forced distribution and PAT are most likely to be used by superiors, but could be used by peers or subordinates.

Which Technique to Use

Perhaps you now feel overwhelmed by the large number of evaluation techniques. You should know that not all of them are used very often. It is generally recognized that the graphic rating scale is the most widely used technique. Studies indicate that the essay method is also widely used, usually as part of a graphic rating scale form. And, checklists are also widely used. Studies show that other methods, such as forced choice, critical incident, BARS, BOS, performance tests, field review, and MBO, *combined* equal only about 5 percent. Ranking and paired comparison are used by 10 to 13 percent of employers. MBO is most likely to be used for managerial, professional, and technical employees, not production and office personnel.[39]

Which technique should be used in a specific instance? The literature on the shortcomings, strengths, reliabilities, and validities of each of these techniques is vast. In essence, there are studies showing that each of the techniques is sometimes good, sometimes poor. The major problems are not with the techniques themselves, but *how they are used* and *by whom*. Untrained raters or those that have little talent or motivation to evaluate well can destroy or hamper *any* evaluation technique. The rater is more critical than the technique in developing effective evaluation systems.

Evaluation techniques can be judged on a series of criteria, such as costs and purposes. As noted in the discussion of the approaches to evaluation above, at least two major purposes are served by evaluation: Counseling and personal development and evaluation for rewards, such as an aid in promotion and decision. Some evaluation techniques serve one purpose better than others. Some systems cost more to develop and operate than others. Exhibit 8–15 scales the techniques on these criteria to help in the choice.

If the primary purpose of the evaluation is development, for example, the knowledgeable organization will use BARS, BOS, essay, critical incident, MBO, and field review tools. If the primary purpose of the evaluation is rewards, the organization might use graphic rating scales, field review, performance tests, forced distribution, MBO, critical incident, BARS, or BOS. If the primary purpose of the evaluation is developmental, and costs are not a concern currently, then field review, MBO, or critical incident methods should be chosen. And if the primary purpose is development and costs are a consideration, the BARS or essay methods might be chosen.

---

[39] Bureau of National Affairs, "Employee Performance: Evaluation and Control."

EXHIBIT 8–15 Selected Criteria for Choice of Performance Evaluation Techniques

Evaluative Base	Graphic Rating Scale	Forced Choice	MBO	Essay	Critical Incident	Weighted Checklist	BARS	BOS	Ranking	Paired Comparison	Forced Distribution	Performance Test	Field Review
Developmental cost	Moderate	High	Moderate	Low	Moderate	Moderate	High	High	Low	Low	Low	High	Moderate
Usage costs	Low	Low	High	High supervisory costs	High	Low	Low	Low	Low	Low	Low	High	High
Ease of use by rater	Easy	Moderately difficult	Moderate	Difficult	Difficult	Easy	Easy	Easy	Easy	Easy	Easy	Moderately difficult	Easy
Ease of understanding by those evaluated	Easy	Difficult	Moderate	Easy	Easy	Easy	Moderate	Moderate	Easy	Easy	Easy	Easy	Easy
Useful in promotion decisions	Yes	Yes	Yes	Not easily	Yes	Moderate	Yes	Yes	Yes	Yes	Yes	Yes	Yes
Useful in compensation and reward decisions	Yes	Moderate	Yes	Not easily	Yes	Moderate	Yes	Yes	Not easily	Not easily	Yes	Yes	Yes
Useful in counseling and development of employees	Moderate	Moderate	Yes	Yes	Yes	Moderate	Yes	Yes	No	No	No	Moderate	Yes

THE FEEDBACK INTERVIEW

After the rater has completed the evaluation, it should be discussed with the employee. Some organizations use split evaluations to accomplish the dual purposes of evaluations. In evaluation for developmental purposes, the ratings are communicated and appropriate counseling takes place. And in evaluation to determine pay, promotion, and other rewards, the ratings sometimes are not given to the employee. In the usual evaluation, however, the employee acknowledges the evaluation in some way, often by signing a receipt form.

In 97 percent of organizations with formal performance evaluation systems, the employee receives feedback, normally in the form of an evaluation interview.[40] The rater and ratee get together for an interview, which allows the evaluator to communicate the employee's ratings and to comment on them.

Norman Maier describes three generally used approaches to these interview situations: tell and sell, tell and listen, and problem solving.[41] These are shown in Exhibit 8–16. Research on when each should be used indicates that the tell-and-sell approach is best for new and inexperienced employees, and that the problem-solving approach, which encourages employee participation, is useful for more experienced employees, especially those with strong work ethic attitudes.

The suggestions for conducting an effective evaluation interview are designed to reduce the arbitrariness and improve the clarity of the superior-subordinate interaction. Regardless of how or when the performance evaluation occurs, there should be a formal evaluation interview. The closer the suggestions are followed, the more effective the interview. It is the superior's responsibility to be a clear communicator, a good listener; he or she should set a respectful tone and cover not only past performances but also future expectations and objectives.

The interviewing skills that are needed by a rater are an ability to talk clearly, listen carefully, gather and analyze information thoroughly, and negotiate the availability and use of resources. A poor feedback interview occurs because of poor preparation, error and miscalculation about the purpose of the session, and failure to achieve some accuracy in understanding each other in the perceptions of the rater and the ratee. A rater should always realize that a ratee's perception is reality to him or her.[42]

A well-planned and -conducted feedback interview will facilitate the sharing of information and perceptions between rater and ratee.[43] This doesn't mean that a rater should not criticize poor performance, or that some ratees will not become defensive. In fact, some ratees react to criticism in the form of

[40] Bureau of National Affairs, "Employee Performance: Evaluation and Control," also see Randall Brett and Alan J. Fredian, "Performance Appraisal: The System Is Not the Solution: *Personnel Administrator,* December 1981, pp. 61–68.

[41] Norman Maier, *The Appraisal Interview: Three Basic Approaches* (La Jolla, Calif.: University Associates, 1976).

[42] Henderson, *Performance Appraisal,* p. 267.

[43] Brian L. Davis and Michael K. Mount, "Design and Use of a Performance Appraisal Feedback System," *Personnel Administrator*, March 1984, pp. 91–97.

EXHIBIT 8-16 Three Types of Evaluation Interviews

Method	Tell and Sell	Tell and Listen	Problem Solving
Role of interviewer	Judge	Judge	Helper
Objective	To communicate evaluation To persuade employee to improve	To communicate evaluation To release defensive feelings	To stimulate growth and development in employee
Assumptions	Employee desires to correct weaknesses if he knows them Any person can improve who so chooses A superior is qualified to evaluate a subordinate	People will change if defensive feelings are removed	Growth can occur without correcting faults Discussing job problems leads to improved performance
Reactions	Defensive behavior suppressed Attempts to cover hostility	Defensive behavior expressed Employee feels accepted	Problem-solving behavior
Skills	Salesmanship Patience	Listening and reflecting feelings Summarizing	Listening and reflecting feelings Reflecting ideas Using exploratory questions Summarizing
Attitude	People profit from criticism and appreciate help	One can respect the feelings of others if one understands them	Discussion develops new ideas and mutual interests
Motivation	Use of positive or negative incentives or both (Extrinsic in that motivation is added to the job itself)	Resistance to change reduced Positive incentive (Extrinsic and some intrinsic motivation)	Increased freedom Increased responsibility (Intrinsic motivation in that interest is inherent in the task)
Gains	Success most probable when employee respects interviewer	Develops favorable attitude to superior which increases probability of success	Almost assured of improvement in some respect
Risks	Loss of loyalty Inhibition of independent judgment Face-saving problems created	Need for change may not be developed	Employee may lack ideas Change may be other than what superior had in mind
Values	Perpetuates existing practices and values	Permits interviewer to change his or her views in the light of employee's responses Some upward communication	Both learn, since experience and views are pooled Change is facilitated

Source: Reproduced from Norman R. F. Maier, *The Appraisal Interview; Three Basic Approaches* (La Jolla, Calif.: University Associates, 1976). Used with permission.

Suggestions for Effective Evaluation Interviews
Steps and Skills

1. Raters and ratees should prepare for the meeting and be ready to discuss the employee's past performance against the objectives for the period.
2. The rater should put the employee at ease and stress that the interview is not a disciplinary session, but a time to review past work in order to improve the employee's future performance, satisfaction, and personal development.
3. The rater should budget the time so that the employee has approximately half the time to discuss the evaluation and his or her future behavior.
4. The rater should use facts, not opinions. Evidence must be available to document the claims and counterclaims.
5. The rater should structure the interview as follows:

   First, open with *specific positive remarks*. For example, if the employee's quantity of work is good, the superior might say, "John, your work output is excellent. You processed 10 percent more claims than was budgeted."

   Second, sandwich performance shortcomings between two positive result discussions. Be specific, and orient the discussion to *performance* comments, *not personal criticisms*. Stress that the purpose of bringing the specific issues up is to alleviate the problems in the *future,* not to criticize the past. Probably no more than one or two important negative points should be brought up at one evaluation. It is difficult for many people to work toward improving more than two points. The handling of negative comments is critical. They should be phrased specifically and be related to *performance,* and it should be apparent to the employee that their purpose is not to criticize but to improve future performance. Many people become very defensive when criticized. Of course, the interviews should be private, between the employee and the evaluator.

   Third, conclude with *positive* comments and overall evaluation results.
6. The rater should guard against overwhelming the ratee with information. Too much information can be confusing, while too little information can be frustrating. The rater must balance the amount of information that is provided.
7. The rater should encourage ratee involvement and self-review and evaluation. Ask the ratee to do his or her own evaluation on a periodic basis.
8. The final aspect of the interview should focus on *future* objectives and how the superior can help the employee achieve enterprise and personal goals. Properly done, the interviews contribute importantly to the purposes of performance evaluation.

feedback by becoming angry or sullen. However, taking the steps outlined above and practicing the skills mentioned should diminish the probability of an angry, nonproductive feedback interview session. By focusing on job-related problems, involving the ratee in setting realistic performance goals, and providing useful information in a nonthreatening manner, a rater can effec-

A RETURN TO THE P/HRM · IN · ACTION

Hector and Ed Smart

Hector Garcia was not very happy about having to take time out from his supervisory duties to attend a training session about the new evaluation system. But he'd had some problems with his boss, Bob Woods, over pay and promotions. So even though it sounded like more paperwork and time, he decided to see what the trainers had to say.

The session began with some short lectures. But most of the session involved practice on how to complete the rating forms for several kind of employees. The supervisors were encouraged to review their employees' files and to jot down notes about employees' good and bad performances. They also practiced the evaluation interviews on each other. Given the ratings, they completed interviews on a very good, average, and a poor employee. Other policies were also covered. They learned about the new MBO system and how it was going to work. Still, Hector was a bit skeptical.

Hector thought he'd better start the evaluations, since Bob had asked him how they were going. Hector decided to do Ed first. He still was a little worried about how it would go. Ed had been trained in what to expect. "Hope they haven't built him up too high." Hector thought. In reviewing the files, his notes, and his observations, Hector realized he had overlooked how well Ed had come along. He had done an excellent job, and so Hector rated him high.

Hector called Ed in for the interview. Hector referred to his notes and started and ended the interview on a positive note. He talked just a little about the shortcoming he'd noticed and offered to help Ed improve. At the beginning of the interview, Ed had been nervous. But he beamed at the end.

Hector finished the interview by saying he was recommending Ed for a good raise at the earliest change. Over the next few days, Ed seemed to be especially happy. Maybe it was Hector's imagination, but he seemed to be working a bit harder, too, although he was already a good worker.
The training, formal system, and well-prepared feedback interview seemed to pay off. (As shown in this chapter, there are specific requirements and skills associated with a well-designed performance appraisal system.)

tively use the interview. The feedback interview is designed to accomplish goals such as: (1) recognizing and encouraging superior performance so that it will continue; (2) sustaining acceptable behaviors; or (3) changing the behavior of ratees whose performance is not meeting organizational standards of acceptance.

MAKE DECISIONS AND FILE THE EVALUATION

Once the employees and their supervisor have discussed the evaluation, the superior reviews the evaluation. BNA found that 80 percent of office employees and 76 percent of production employees surveyed had their evaluations reviewed in this manner. Next, the P/HRM department reviews the evaluation and places it on file.[44]

If the employee is unhappy with the evaluation, BNA found that 68 percent of the production employees and 56 percent of the office employees surveyed could appeal it through the union (if they are unionized) or to the rater's superior. This is less common in nonbusiness organizations than businesses. For more data on evaluation in P/HRM, see Chapter 20.

These reviews are designed to prevent situations such as Ed Smart's confusion and Hector Garcia's failure to give him positive feedback. If the evaluation has been properly done, the employee knows where he or she stands and has received positive feedback on accomplishments and help on shortcomings. This is the developmental aspect of performance evaluation. The reward aspect can include pay raises (see Chapters 9 and 10).

SUMMARY

Formal performance evaluation of employees is the P/HRM process by which the organization determines how effectively the employee is performing the job. It takes place primarily for white-collar, professional/technical, and managerial employees. It rarely is done for part-time employees, and only about half of all blue-collar employees experience it. Although the data are not entirely clear, it appears that, properly done, performance evaluations and feedback can be useful for most organizations and most employees.

To summarize the major points covered in this chapter:

1. Factors in the diagnostic model that have significance for performance evaluation are:
   a. The task performed.
   b. The government.
   c. The attitudes and preferences of the employee.

---

[44] Bureau of National Affairs, "Employee Performance: Evaluation and Control."

  d. The leader's or supervisor's style.

  e. The union (if the employees are unionized).

2. The purposes that formal performance evaluation can serve include:

  a. Developmental.

  b. Reward.

  c. Personnel planning.

  d. Compensation.

  e. Validation.

3. For formal performance evaluation to be effective, five steps must be taken:

  a. Establish performance standards for each position.

  b. Establish performance evaluation policies on when and how often to evaluate, who should evaluate, the criteria for evaluation, and the evaluation tools to be used.

  c. Have raters gather data on employee performance.

  d. Discuss the evaluation with the employee.

  e. Make decisions and file the evaluation.

4. Performance evaluation systems have problems because of:

  a. Systems design and operating difficulties.

  b. Problems with the rater:

   (1) Standards of evaluation.

   (2) The halo effect.

   (3) Leniency or harshness.

   (4) Recency of events.

   (5) Personal biases.

  c. Employee problems with performance evaluation:

   (1) Employees don't understand the system or its purpose.

   (2) Employees are not work oriented.

   (3) Evaluation may be below the employee's expectations.

5. Performance appraisal interviews that involve feeding back evaluation information are dreaded because of the arbitrariness of many evaluation programs. Selecting the best program for the employees and supervisors to use is an important P/HRM decision.

6. Properly performed, performance evaluation can contribute to organizational objectives and employee development and satisfaction.

  Exhibit 8–17 provides recommendations for the usage of evaluation tools in terms of the ability of the model organizations to use them. You can see from this exhibit that some tools are more universally applicable (essay, critical incident, graphic rating scale, MBO, ranking, forced distribution). Others have fewer applications (performance test, field review, forced choice), and still others are in the middle (assessment centers, BARS, BOS, weighted checklist).

Questions for Review and Discussion

1. What advantages would a combination performance evaluation system (for example, the use of more than one technique) provide to managers responsible for evaluating subordinates?

2. Why would training in conducting performance evaluations be an important issue for organizations to consider?

EXHIBIT 8–17 Recommendations on Evaluation Techniques for Model Organizations

Type of organization	Graphic Rating Scale	Forced Choice	MBO	Essay	Critical Incident	Weighted Checklist	BARS	BOS	Ranking	Paired Comparison	Forced Distribution	Performance Test	Field Review
1. Large size, low complexity, high stability	X	X	X		X	X	X	X	X	X	X	X	X
2. Medium size, low complexity, high stability	X		X	X	X	X	X	X	X	X	X		
3. Small size, low complexity, high stability	X		X	X	X				X	X	X		
4. Medium size, moderate complexity, moderate stability	X		X	X	X	X			X	X	X		
5. Large size, high complexity, low complexity	X	X	X	X	X				X	X	X		X
6. Medium size, high complexity, low stability	X		X	X	X				X	X	X		
7. Small size, high complexity, low stability	X		X	X	X				X	X	X		

3. Describe the major problems that can arise for the system, the rater, and the ratee in performance evaluation.
4. How often should performance evaluation take place? Informal ones? How often do they take place?
5. Who usually evaluates employees in organizations? Who should do so? Under what circumstances? What criteria should be used to evaluate employees? Which ones are used?
6. Compare and contrast performance evaluation techniques. If you were to choose one to be used to evaluate you, which one would it be? Why?
7. Describe how to conduct an effective feedback interview with a new, inexperienced employee. With an experienced employee.
8. What role would job analysis (Chapter 4) play in the development of an equitable and valid performance evaluation system?
9. What did McGregor mean when he said that managers, when they are involved in making judgments, are placed in an antagonistic role?

GLOSSARY

Behaviorally Anchored Rating Scale (BARS). A rating scale that uses critical incidents as anchor statements placed along a scale. Typically 6 to 10 performance dimensions, each with 5 to 6 critical incident anchors, are rated per employee.

Behavioral Observation Scale (BOS). A method similar to the BARS that uses the critical incident technique to identify a series of behaviors that describe the job. A 1 (Almost Never) to 5 (Almost Always) format is used to rate the behaviors.

Central Tendency Error. A rating tendency to give ratees an average rating on each criteria. That is, on a 1 to 7 scale, circling all 4s, or on a 1 to 5 scale, selecting all 3s.

Critical Incident Rating. The system of selecting very effective and ineffective examples of job behavior and rating whether an employee displays the type of behaviors specified in the critical incidents.

Halo Error. A rating error that occurs when a rater assigns ratings on the basis of an overall impression (positive or negative) of the person being rated.

Harshness Rating Error. The tendency to rate everyone low on the criteria being evaluated.

Leniency Rating Error. The tendency to rate everyone on every criteria high or excellent.

Performance Evaluation. The P/HRM activity that is used to determine the extent to which an employee is performing the job effectively.

Personal Bias Rating Error. The bias that a rater has about individual characteristics, attitudes, backgrounds, and so on influence a rating more than performance.

Recency of Event Rating Error. A rating tendency to use the most recent events to evaluate a ratee's performance instead of using a longer, more complete time frame.

APPLICATION CASE 8–1

Performance Evaluation of Store Managers at Firestone Tire & Rubber

The Firestone Tire & Rubber Co. is the second largest tire company in the United States with about 18 percent of the market. Firestone manufactures and sells tires and related products for cars, trucks, buses, tractors, and airplanes. The tires are sold to automakers and consumers through 2,100 Firestone stores and many independent dealers, including Montgomery Ward. The stores are the vital link with the ultimate consumer.

A vital person in the link with consumers is the store manager. It is the store managers who are the key human resource in determining whether sales and profits will be sufficient. The following list is a description of the store managers' duties and a portion of the performance evaluation form used to appraise store managers. Each store manager is evaluated annually by his or her immediate supervisor.

Description of Store Manager Responsibilities
Summary of Duties

Has responsibility for securing maximum sales volume and maximum net profits. Supervises all phases of store operation—selling, merchandise display, service, pricing, inventories, credits and collections, operation, and maintenance. Responsible for the control of all store assets and prevention of merchandise shortages.

Interviews, selects, trains, and supervises all employees, following their progress and development. Conducts employee meetings and follows closely for satisfactory productivity.

Sets sales quotas for employees and follows for accomplishment. Works with salespeople and personally calls on commercial and dealer accounts.

Interprets and explains store operating policies and procedures to subordinates and follows for adherence. Investigates complaints and makes adjustments. Maintains store cleanliness.

A. *Personnel administration*—30 percent
   1. Directly supervises pivotal employees and, through them, the other employees, directing activites, scheduling duties and hours of work, following for productivity and sales results. Instructs or directs the instruction of new and present employees in work procedure, results expected, sales quota program, product and price information, etc., and follows for adherence to instructions. (Daily)
   2. Interviews applicants, obtains formal applications, determines qualifications (using employment questionnaires), and makes se-

lection of best persons for open jobs or files applications for future consideration. (Weekly)

3. Determines number of employees needed for profitable store operations, considering individual sales productivity, salary expense, anticipated personnel requirements, etc. (Monthly)

4. Prepares plans for and conducts employee meetings, instructing concerning new products and policies, developing sales enthusiasm, explaining incentive programs, holding sales demonstrations, etc. (Semimonthly)

5. Trains and directs the training of new employees, following established training programs for effective utilization, conducting on-the-job training, and supervising training activities for own employees and those being trained for other assignments. (Weekly)

B. *Selling and sales promotion*—30 percent

1. Breaks down stores sales into individual daily amounts for each employee, follows progress of employees in meeting quotas, determines and takes action necessary to help them reach the objective. (Daily)

2. Works with salesperson in setting up sales objectives and reviewing accomplishments, using call and sales record sheets, and following to secure maximum sales effort effective use of time. Makes calls with salespeople to determine effectiveness of contacts, reasons for lack of progress, etc., giving help in closing sales, and securing additional business. (Daily)

3. Contacts personally and by telephone, inactive accounts and prospective customers, promoting and soliciting and sale of merchandise and services, and following to close the sales. Reviews prospect cards, assigns them to employees, and follows to secure sales from each. (Daily)

4. Contacts selected commercial and dealer accounts for special sales promotion and solicitation, determining sales possibilities and requirements, selling merchandise and services, etc. (Daily)

5. Prepares advertising copy, following merchandising program suggestions, and arranges for insertion of advertisements in local newspaper. Makes certain employees are alerted and store has merchandise to back up advertising. (Weekly)

6. Maintains a firm retail, commercial, and wholesale pricing program according to established policies.

C. *Inventory sales and expense control*—15 percent

1. Reviews stock turnover records for overstock conditions, determines steps necessary to correct, and takes the appropriate action. Establishes stock levels and orders accordingly based on sales results as recorded in the stock ledgers for new tires and retreads. (Also major appliances.)

2. Prepares sales and expense budget covering projected sales and expenses for the period. (Monthly)

EXHIBIT I   Setting Standards and Recording Results

Instructions: This worksheet is to be used during the year for the purpose of providing supporting information for the annual employee assessment. First list the six most important job duties of the employee in decreasing order of importance. Establish standards for each major job duty. Record the employee's performance against the standard established (1, 2, 3, or 4). Refer to the employee's work results in the performance feedback or post-assessment interview.

Major Job Duties (Taken From Job Description)	Standard of Performance (Measure Or Criterion Of Success)	Employee's Performance (Percentage Of Time Standard is Met)			
		Less Than 50%	50% to 75%	76% to 89%	90% or More
1.					
2.					
3.					
4.					
5.					
6.					

3. Reviews expense control sheet, comparing actual expenses with budget figures, determines and takes action necessary to keep within the approved budget. (Daily)
4. Is responsible for the completeness and accuracy of all inventories, accounting inventories, markup, markdown inventories, etc.

D. *Checking*—10 percent
1. Checks stock, automotive equipment, service floor, etc., continually observing store activities, and determining that equipment is maintained in good operating condition. Makes inspection trips through all parts of the store, checking observance of safety and fire precautions, protection of company assets, etc. Checks credit information secured for commercial and dealer accounts, and works with office and credit manager in setting up credit limits. (Weekly)
2. Is responsible for and investigates all cash shortages, open tickets, and missing tickets.

EXHIBIT II   **Work Review Comments**

Instructions: Review the employee's performance against the standards established. Analyze the employee's performance in terms of quality (how good), quantity (how much), and work methods (how the employee went about getting work results). What job duties are being handled particularly well by the employee? What job standards are not being met? Complete this section before conducting the interview with the employee.

PERFORMANCE STRENGTHS ABOVE JOB STANDARDS: _____

PERFORMANCE AREAS BELOW JOB STANDARDS: _____

III. INTERVIEW RESULTS AND DEVELOPMENT PLAN

Instructions: The work counseling interview is an important part of any work results program. Section III should be completed after holding the interview. Comment on the employee's reaction to performance feedback and the plan you and the employee have developed for improving work results. Be specific in your description of the results of the interview and the developmental steps you and the employee have agreed upon.

EMPLOYEE REACTION TO PERFORMANCE FEEDBACK: _____

PLAN FOR IMPROVING WORK RESULTS: _____

Employee's Signature

RATER TO PROCEED TO SECTION IV

    3. Investigates customer complaints, making adjustments or taking appropriate action for customer satisfaction. (Daily)

E. *Miscellaneous functions*—15 percent

    1. Reads and signs Store Operating Policy and Office Procedure Letters, analyzes and puts into operation new policies and procedures as received. (Weekly)

    2. Prepares letter to district manager covering progress of the store, store plans, results secured, market and special conditions, etc. (Monthly)

    3. Inspects tires and other merchandise in for adjustment, determines appropriate settlement, prepares claim forms, and issues credit, replaces, etc. (Makes all policy adjustments.) (Daily)

4. Attends district sales and civic organization meetings, and takes part in civic affairs, community drives, etc. (Weekly).

Questions for Thought

1. Do you consider the description of the Firestone store managers' responsibilities as important information that the raters of managers need to be knowledgeable about?
2. Does the portion of the performance evaluation form used at Firestone require any subjective judgments or considerations on the part of the rater?
3. Suppose that a Firestone manager received an outstanding performance evaluation. Does this mean that he or she is promotable? Why?

APPLICATION CASE 8–2

The Politics of Performance Appraisal*

Every Friday, Max Steadman, Jim Cobun, Lynne Sims, and Tom Hamilton meet at Charley's Food Place after work for refreshments. The four friends work as managers at Eckel Industries, a manufactureer of arc welding equipment in Minneapolis. The one-plant company employs about 2,000 people. The four managers work in the manufacturing division. Max, 35, manages the company's 25 quality control inspectors. Lynne, 33, works as a supervisor in inventory management. James, 34, is a first-line supervisor in the metal coating department. Tom, 28, supervises a team of assemblers. The four managers' tenures at Eckel Industries range from one year (Tom) to 12 years (Max).

The group is close-knit; Lynne, Jim, and Max's friendship stems from their years as undergraduate business students at the University of Minnesota. Tom, the newcomer, joined the group after meeting the three at an Eckel management seminar last year. Weekly get-togethers at Charley's has become a comfortable habit for the group and provides an opportunity to relax, exchange the latest gossip heard around the plant, and give and receive advice about problems encountered on the job.

This week's topic of discussion: performance appraisal, specifically the company's annual review process which the plant's management conducted in the last week. Each of the four managers completed evaluation forms (graphic rating scale format) on each of his or her subordinates and met with each subordinate to discuss the appraisal.

Tom: This was the first time I've appraised my people, and I dreaded it. For me it's been the worst week of the year. Evaluating is difficult; it's highly subjective and inexact. Your emotions creep into the process. I got angry at one of my assembly workers last week, and I still felt the anger when I was filling out the evaluation forms. Don't tell me that my frustration with the guy didn't overly bias my appraisal. I think it did. And I think the technique is flawed. Tell me— what's the difference between a five and a six on "cooperation"?

Jim: The scales are a problem. So is memory. Remember our course in personnel/human resource management in college? Philips said that according to research, when we sit down to evaluate someone's performance in the past year, we will only be able to actively recall and use 15 percent of the performance we observed.

---

* Written by Kim Stewart. Several of the perspectives presented here were drawn from an insightful study reported in Clinton O. Longenecker, Henry P. Sims, Jr., and Dennis A. Gioia, "Behind The Mask: The Politics of Employee Appraisal," *The Academy of Management Executive*, August 1987, pp. 183–91.

Lynne: I think political considerations are always a part of the process. I know I consider many other factors besides a person's actual performance when I appraise him.

Tom: Like what?

Lynne: Like the appraisal will become part of his permanent written record that affects his career. Like the person I evaluate today, I have to work with tomorrow. Given that, the difference between a five and a six on cooperation isn't that relevant, because frankly, if a five makes him mad, and he's happy with a six . . .

Max: Then you give him the six. Accuracy is important, but I'll admit it— accuracy isn't my primary objective when I evaluate my workers. My objective is to motivate and reward them so they'll perform better. I use the review process to do what's best for my people and my department. If that means fine tuning the evaluations to do that, I will.

Tom: What's an example of fine tuning?

Max: Jim, do you remember three years ago when the company lowered the ceiling on merit raises? The top merit increase that any employee could get was 4 percent. I boosted the ratings of my folks to get the best merit increases for them. The year before that, the ceiling was 8 percent. The best they could get was less than what most of them received the year before. I felt they deserved the 4 percent, so I gave the marks that got them what I felt they deserved.

Lynne: I've inflated ratings to encourage someone who is having personal problems but is normally a good employee. A couple of years ago, one of my better people was going through a painful divorce, and it was showing in her work. I don't think it's fair to kick someone when they're down, even if their work is poor. I felt a good rating would speed her recovery.

Tom: Or make her complacent.

Lynne: No, I don't think so. I felt she realized her work was suffering. I wanted to give her encouragement; it was my way of telling her she had some support and that she wasn't in danger of losing her job.

Jim: There's another situation where I think fine tuning is merited—when someone's work has been mediocre or even poor for most of the year, but it improves substantially in the last two, three months or so. If I think the guy is really trying and is doing much better, I'd give him a rating that's higher than his work over the whole year deserves. It encourages him to keep improving. If I give him a mediocre rating, what does that tell him?

Tom: What if he's really working hard, but not doing so great?

Jim: If I think he has what it takes, I'd boost the rating to motivate him to keep trying until he gets there.

Max: I know of one or two managers who've inflated ratings to get rid of a pain-in-the-neck, some young guy who's transferred in and thinks he'll be there a short time. He's not good, but thinks he is, and creates all sorts of problems. Or his performance is okay, but he just doesn't fit in with the rest of the department. A year or two of good ratings is a sure trick for getting rid of him.

Tom: Yes, but you're passing the problem on to someone else.

Max: True, but it's no longer my problem.

Tom: All the examples you've talked about involve inflating evaluations. What about deflating them, giving someone less than you really think he deserves? Is that justified?

Lynne: I'd hesitate to do that because it can create problems. It can backfire.

Max: But it does happen. You can lower a guy's ratings to shock him, to jolt him into performing better. Sometimes, you can work with someone, coach them, try to help them improve, and it just doesn't work. A basement-level rating can tell him you mean business. You can say that isn't fair, and for the time being, it isn't. But what if you feel that if the guy doesn't shape up, he faces being fired in a year or two, and putting him in the cellar, ratings-wise, will solve his problem? It's fair in the long run if the effect is that he improves his work and keeps his job.

Jim: Sometimes, you get someone who's a real rebel, who always questions you, sometimes even oversteps his bounds. I think deflating his evaluation is merited just to remind him who's the boss.

Lynne: I'd consider lowering someone's true rating if they've had a long record of rather questionable performance, and I think the best alternative for the person is to consider another job with another company. A low appraisal sends him a message to consider quitting and start looking for another job.

Max: What if you believe the situation is hopeless, and you've made up your mind that you're going to fire the guy as soon as you've found a suitable replacement. The courts have chipped away at management's right to fire. Today, when you fire someone, you must have a strong case. I think once a manager decides to fire, appraisals become very negative. Anything good that you say about the subordinate can be used later against you. Deflating the ratings protects yourself from being sued and sometimes speeds up the termination process.

Tom: I understand your points, but I still believe that accuracy is the top priority in performance appraisal. Let me play devil's advocate for a minute. First, Jim, you complained about our memory limitations introducing a bias into appraisal. Doesn't introducing politics into the process further distort the truth by introducing yet another bias? Even more important, most would agree that one key to motivating people is providing true feedback—the facts about how they're doing so they know where they stand. Then you talk with them about how to improve their performance. When you distort an evaluation—however slightly—are you providing this kind of feedback?

Max: I think you're overstating the degree of fine tuning.

Tom: Distortion, you mean.

Max: No, fine tuning. I'm not talking about giving a guy a seven when he deserves a two or vice versa. It's not that extreme. I'm talking about making slight changes in the ratings when you think that the change can make a big difference in terms of achieving what you think is best for the person and for your department.

Tom: But when you fine tune, you're manipulating your people. Why not give them the most accurate evaluation, and let the chips fall where they may? Give them the facts, and let them decide.

Max: Because most of good managing is psychology. Understanding people, their strengths and shortcomings. Knowing how to motivate, reward, and act to do what's in their and your department's best interest. And sometimes total accuracy is not the best path.

Jim: All this discussion raises a question. What's the difference between fine tuning and significant distortion? Where do you draw the line?

Lynne: That's about as easy a question as what's the difference between a five and six. On the form, I mean.

Questions for Thought

1. In your opinion, and from a P/HRM perspective, what are the objectives of employee performance evaluation?
2. Based on these objectives, evaluate the perspectives about performance appraisal presented by the managers.
3. Assume you are the vice president of P/HRM at Eckel Industries and that you are aware that fine tuning evaluations is a prevalent practice among Eckel managers. If you disagree with this perspective, what steps would you take to reduce the practice?

EXERCISE 8–1   The Selection and Appraisal of Administrative Assistants at Row Engineering*

Objective: The exercise is designed to have the student use knowledge about selection and performance appraisal to design an appraisal system.

Introduction

Row Engineering (name disguised) is a major engineering contractor, supplying aerospace firms, NASA, and the military with sophisticated equipment designs. Because of their rapidly expanding business, Row executives decided that a formal management information system (MIS) was needed. The MIS could be used to monitor progress on projects, limit employee access to classified information, reduce unnecessary duplication across similar projects, and generally increase efficiency by insuring that the proper managers or engineers received timely and relevant information for decision making.

---

* This exercise was developed by Dr. William H. Ross, Jr., University of Wisconsin, La Crosse.

◥ ROW ENGINEERING	**HOURLY JOB DESCRIPTION**

Job Title: Administrative Assistant   4-11-1193

I.   Function:

　　 To provide administrative support to a company organization.

II. Controls:

　　 Works under the direct supervision of a higher level administrator or
　　 technical manager but must exercise considerable judgement in the
　　 performance of assignments.

III. Major Duties:

　　 A.   Utilizes a thorough knowledge of functions, activities, personnel,
　　 and organizations to perform various administrative duties
　　 incidental to the efficient operation of a company element.

　　 B.   Prepares charts and reports to reflect performance and overall
　　 efficiency of operations. Prepares, analyzes and evaluates data
　　 pertaining to cost and maintains systems for effective cost control.

　　 C.   Confers with operating managers to determine requirements for
　　 space, equipment, supplies, and other facilities. Provides co-
　　 ordination with Purchasing, Plant Services, and other company
　　 service organizations in meeting these requirements.

　　 D.   Conducts introductory non-technical interviews with job applicants,
　　 briefing them on general functions of the company element and
　　 obtaining pertinent information for use in subsequent technical
　　 interviews. Keeps management informed of interviews, schedules,
　　 job offers extended, rejections, acceptances, and anticipated
　　 starting dates.

　　 E.   Coordinates the induction and indoctrination of new employees to
　　 the company element. Compiles materials for use in indoctrination
　　 lectures, welcomes new employees and arranges for tours of
　　 facilities. Ensures that all required paperwork is completed.

IV. Requirements:

　　 Requires a high school education, with college level courses highly
　　 desirable, and approximately five (5) years administrative experience or
　　 a B.S. degree in Business Administration.

ROW FORM NO. 06206 ORIG.

Row has four major design facilities scattered throughout the southern and eastern United States in areas where approximately 50 percent of all high school graduates are Blacks. Engineers at the different facilities typically work on different projects. Thus, Row executives decided that one MIS department should be established for *each* of the four facilities. While these would be linked by computer, each MIS department would have a great deal of autonomy.

Each MIS department will be comprised of one administrator, seven administrative assistants, numerous technical personnel (for example, computer programmers) and clerical staff (for example, data entry personnel). The 28 administrative assistant positions will be key entry-level managerial positions. The administrative assistants will be responsible for securing and maintaining information for their assigned MIS area. Also, some may eventually be promoted to middle-level management positions in the future.

Typical administrative assistant duties will include:

A. Determining appropriate information needs from various projects for the MIS database. To do so requires cooperation with project engineers and mangers as well as personnel from other departments.

B. Working with other MIS administrative assistants to develop standardized information reporting procedures. Such procedures facilitate the aggregation and comparison of specific types of information from different projects.

C. Creating and distributing user-instruction manuals outlining correct information reporting and information acquisition procedures for various departments. Sometimes administrative assistants would provide orientation sessions for company personnel.

D. Insuring that necessary and timely information is supplied by each project or department using standardized reporting procedures.

E. Supervising technical and clerical staff who are responsible for data input and retrieval.

F. Supervising technical staff who develop and purchase information-based software.

G. Maintaining project security. Illustrative duties include: documenting computer analyses, insuring that only authorized personnel receive relevant information, supervising clerical staff, and preventing unauthorized photocopying of specific types of information.

H. Supplying information, as requested, to project managers, specific departments, and contract monitors.

I. Documenting and supplying information to the fiscal services department regarding monthly time and computer-use expenditures for various projects. Fiscal services uses this information when comparing actual and estimated (budgeted) expenditures for various projects and departments.

J. Determining the MIS department's own budget needs.

About one year ago, the personnel department conducted a formal job analysis of all existing administrative assistant positions throughout the corporation. From this analysis, a common job description was derived. This job description is reproduced below:

Designing the Performance Appraisal System

Currently, all Row Engineering employees, including administrative assistants, are evaluated using a one-item, 10-point global rating scale. Ratings of either Unsatisfactory (1) or Superior (10) must be accompanied with written documentation. In addition to the rating supervisor, the department head and the evaluated employee must sign the form, indicating that they have read the evaluation.

Recently, the personnel director has become concerned about the use of this type of rating scale. He has hired your personnel consulting firm to design a

◤ ROW ENGINEERING				EMPLOYEE REVIEW
EMPLOYEE NAME		EMPLOYEE NO.	COST CENTER	DATE
RATING SUPERVISOR – APPROVAL	DEPARTMENT HEAD – APPROVAL		EMPLOYEE	
CIRCLE APPROPRIATE RATING				
UNSATISFACTORY 2 3 4 5 6 7 8 9 SUPERIOR				
(WRITTEN DOCUMENTATION REQUIRED FOR RATINGS OF SUPERIOR OR UNSATISFACTORY AND FOR CLASSIFICATION CHANGES)				

better performance appraisal system for the administrative assistant position with all the MIS departments.

Assignment: Write a three- to six-page report to this company describing and explaining your selection system. Your report should incorporate the following points:

A. A tactful explanation of the limitations of the present performance appraisal system.
B. An identification of the relevant dimensions (criteria) that should be measured in the new performance appraisal system. That is, how will the company distinguish the superior administrative assistants from those whose performance is merely adequate (or even inadequate)? Assume that the provided job description is correct.
C. How will *each* dimension be measured?
D. If you use some type of overall measure of performance, tell how you will measure it on a 100-point scale (100 = best). If you have several performance measures tell how they will be combined into a composite criterion score. This composite score should be measured on a 100-point scale.
E. What weaknesses (if any) exist in your system? How will these be overcome?

A Learning Note

This exercise encourages the student to consider the uses, strengths, and weaknesses of a performance appraisal system.

9

COMPENSATION: AN OVERVIEW

LEARNING OBJECTIVES

After studying this chapter, you should be able to:

- **Define** what is meant by the job evaluation process.
- **Describe** four widely used methods of job evaluation.
- **Discuss** how pay surveys help managers compare their pay systems to other organizations.
- **Explain** how external factors influence pay levels and policies.
- **Illustrate** a pay-class graph and pay trend line.

KEY TERMS

Classification or Grading System
Comparable Worth
Exempt Employee
Factor Comparision Method
Job Evaluation
Minimum Wage
Nonexempt Employee
Pay Class
Pay Surveys
Point System
Ranking of Jobs
Red Circle Rates

CHAPTER OUTLINE

P/HRM · IN · ACTION

Joe and Guido

Cardeson National Bank is a small firm that was founded in suburban Pittsburgh 14 years ago. For the first year and a half, it operated out of a prefabricated building on a small lot across from a shopping center. Then it built a nice building on the site. Later it added two branch offices in adjoining suburbs. CNB now employs about 150 persons.

The founder of the bank and still president is Joseph Paderewski, an entrepreneur who made his first career in construction and building. Joe is 55 years old. He has spent most of his energies building the bank by raising money from the original stockholders, developing a marketing plan to get enough depositors to use CNB, and finding good locations at which to build banks.

Joe does almost all the hiring. He also establishes the pay rates for each employee, based on experience, potential, and how much the employee needs to help support self and family. Recently, Guido Panelli, his executive vice president, started bringing Joe some problems he didn't have time for. Guido has mentioned something about salaries, but Joe hasn't given it much thought.

Joe has always had an open-door policy. Yesterday a teller, Arte Jamison, came in to see him.

Arte Jamison: Joe, you hired me five years ago. I came in to tell you that I'm quitting. I had to tell Mr. Panelli about this problem a couple of times and nothing happened. So I'm gone. I'm going to work for Pittsburgh National Bank for more money.

Joe: Arte, don't quit for money. What do you need? I'll take care of it.

Arte: That's not the point. You keep hiring in people with less experience than me at more pay. There's no future here with a situation like that. I quit.

Joe: Sure sorry to see you go, Arte.

Poppa Joe sat in his office. He'd always liked Arte. What was happening? He called in Guido.

Joe: Guido, what's happening around here? Arte Jamison just quit. He's a good man.

Guido: Boss, I've tried to bring the subject up lots of times, and you're always too busy. We've got a poor pay system around here.

Joe: What do you mean? I've always been fair.

Guido: You think you've been fair. But you're too busy to do all you've been doing. You hire some people at one pay level and others doing the same job at another. Some get behind and never get a raise. It's a mess.

I've asked one of our vice presidents, Mary Renfro, to take a course at the University of Pittsburgh's night MBA program on P/HRM, and to look es-

pecially at compensation. She's done it. Now: Should I ask her to study the problem and talk to us about it?

Joe: O.K., let her do a study. But I'm not convinced we've got such a big problem because a few people quit.

Guido: Please boss, let's keep an open mind about this. Pay has an awfully important impact on employees.

INTRODUCTION

Compensation is a part of a transaction between an employee and an employer that results in an employment contract. From the employee's point of view, pay is a necessity in life. The compensation received from work is one of the chief reasons people seek employment. Pay is the means by which they provide for their own and their family's needs. For people with instrumental attitudes toward work (as discussed in Chapter 2), compensation may be the only (or certainly a major) reason why they work. Others find compensation a contributing factor to their efforts. Pay can do more than provide for the physiological needs of employees, however. What a person is paid indicates his or her worth to an organization.

Compensation is one of the most important P/HRM functions for the employer, too. Compensation often equals 50 percent of the cash flow of an organization, and for some service organizations, it is an even larger percentage. It may be the major method used to attract employees as well as a way to try to motivate employees' more effective performance. Compensation is also significant to the economy. For the past 30 years, salaries and wages have equaled about 60 percent of the gross national product of the United States and Canada.

Objectives of Compensation

The objective of a compensation system is to create a system of rewards that is equitable to the employer and employee alike, so that the employee is attracted to the work and *motivated* to do a good job for the employer. Patton suggests that in compensation policy there are seven criteria for effectiveness.[1] The compensation should be:

---

[1] Thomas Patton, *Pay* (New York: Free Press, 1977).

- *Adequate*—Minimum governmental, union, and managerial levels should be met.
- *Equitable*—Each person should be paid fairly, in line with his or her effort, abilities, and training.
- *Balanced*—Pay, benefits, and other rewards should provide a reasonable total reward package.
- *Cost effective*—Pay is not excessive, considering what the organization can afford to pay.
- *Secure*—Pay should be enough to help an employee feel secure and aid him or her in satisfying basic needs.
- *Incentive-providing*—Pay should motivate effective and productive work.
- *Acceptable to the employee*—The employee should understand the pay system and feel it is a reasonable system for the enterprise and himself or herself.

Do you think Cardeson National Bank's pay plan is achieving these objectives?

Compensation Decision Makers

A number of persons are involved in making compensation decisions. Top management makes the decisions that determine the total amount of the budget that goes to pay, the pay form to be used (time pay versus incentive pay), and pay policies. Top management also set the pay strategy, which is discussed later in the chapter. Usually the P/HRM department advises them of all these issues. As always, the operating managers at the supervisory and middle-management level also have an impact on P/HRM decisions, including pay. The relationships between P/HRM and operating managers in pay matters are given in Exhibit 9–1.

The exhibit describes the roles performed by the compensation manager for P/HRM. This person normally is a department head in a P/HRM department.

Compensation is a Stage IV P/HRM function. It is mature in that all work organizations compensate employees, and there is a good deal of empirical data with which to analyze the relative effectiveness of various compensation methods.

Compensation Decisions

Perhaps you believe that pay can be determined by a manager and employee sitting down and talking it over, or that the government or unions determine pay. In fact, pay is influenced by a series of internal and external factors. The diagnostic approach can be used to help you understand these factors better.

Pay can be determined absolutely or relatively. Some people have argued that a pay system set by a single criterion for a whole nation or the world, the absolute control of pay, is the best procedure. Since absolute pay systems are not used, the pay for each individual is set *relative* to the pay of others.

EXHIBIT 9–1 The Roles of Operating and P/HRM Managers in Making Pay Decisions

Pay Decision Factor	Operating Manager (OM)	P/HRM Manager (P/HRM)
Compensation budgets	OM approves or adjusts P/HRM preliminary budget	P/HRM prepares preliminary budget
Pay-level decisions: Pay survey design and interpretation		P/HRM designs, implements, and makes decisions
Pay-structure decisions: Job evaluation design and interpretation		P/HRM designs, implements, and makes decisions
Pay classes, rate ranges, and classification design and interpretation		P/HRM designs, implements, and makes decisions
Individual pay determination	Joint decision with P/HRM	Joint decision with OM
Pay policy decisions: method of payment	OM decides after advice of P/HRM	P/HRM advises OM
Pay secrecy	OM decides after advice of P/HRM	P/HRM advises OM
Pay security	OM decides after advice of P/HRM	P/HRM advises OM

Nash and Carroll point out that pay for a particular position is set relative to three groups.[2] These are:

- Employees working on similar jobs in other organizations (Group A).
- Employees working on different jobs within the organization (Group B).
- Employees working on the same job within the organization (Group C).

The decision to examine pay relative to Group A is called *the pay-level decision*. The objective of the pay-level decision is to keep the organization competitive in the labor market. The major tool used in this decision is the pay survey, which will be discussed later in this chapter. The pay decision relative to Group B is called *the pay-structure decision*. This uses an approach called job evaluation. The decision involving pay relative to Group C is called *individual pay determination*.

Consider Pete Johnson, custodian at Cardeson National Bank. Pete's pay is affected first by the pay-level policy of the bank—whether CNB is a pacesetter or a going-wage employer. Next, his pay is affected by how highly ranked *his* job is relative to other jobs within the bank, such as teller. Finally, his pay depends on how good a custodian he is, how long he has been with the enterprise, and other individual factors (individual pay determination).

---

[2] Allen Nash and Stephen J. Carroll, Jr., *The Management of Compensation* (Monterey, Calif.: Brooks/Cole Publishing, 1975).

P/HRM Manager Close-Up

Henry Oliver
University Computing Company

Biography

Henry Oliver is manager of compensation and benefits for University Computing Company. Prior to his present assignment, he served the company as administrator of compensation of benefits and as a staff recruiter. He has been with UCC since 1976. Before his association with UCC, he was regional director of personnel for the Massachusetts Indemnity and Life Insurance Company and a national accounts officer with the First City National Bank of Houston. He was born in Houston, Texas, and holds a B.A. degree in economics from the University of the South at Sewanee, Tennessee.

Job description

Henry Oliver is responsible for ensuring that UCC's employees are compensated at an equitable level relative to each other and to people who hold similar positions outside the company. He is also charged with the responsibility of maintaining benefits at levels that remain competitive and which provide real assistance to an employee at a time of death, disability, or retirement. Additionally, Oliver also recruits professionals for the company's corporate staff and provides personnel-related assistance for a remote subsidiary.

A DIAGNOSTIC APPROACH TO COMPENSATION

Exhibit 9–2 highlights the diagnostic factors most important to compensation as a P/HRM activity. The nature of the task affects compensation primarily in

EXHIBIT   9–2   Factors Affecting Compensation and Results

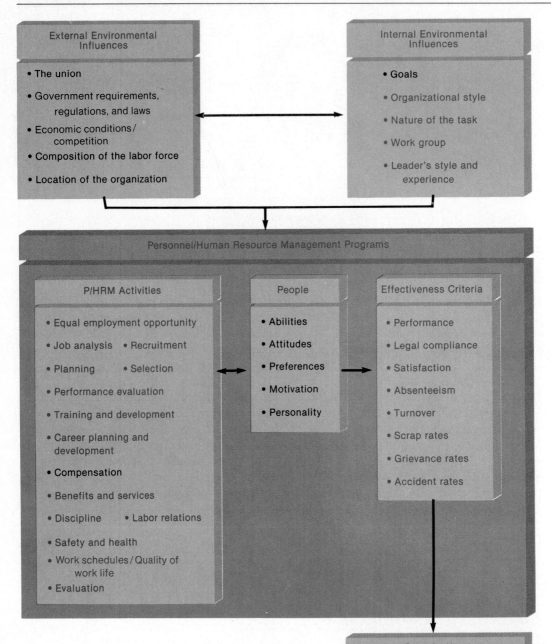

External Environmental Influences

- The union
- Government requirements, regulations, and laws
- Economic conditions/competition
- Composition of the labor force
- Location of the organization

Internal Environmental Influences

- Goals
- Organizational style
- Nature of the task
- Work group
- Leader's style and experience

Personnel/Human Resource Management Programs

P/HRM Activities

- Equal employment opportunity
- Job analysis   • Recruitment
- Planning   • Selection
- Performance evaluation
- Training and development
- Career planning and development
- Compensation
- Benefits and services
- Discipline   • Labor relations
- Safety and health
- Work schedules/Quality of work life
- Evaluation

People

- Abilities
- Attitudes
- Preferences
- Motivation
- Personality

Effectiveness Criteria

- Performance
- Legal compliance
- Satisfaction
- Absenteeism
- Turnover
- Scrap rates
- Grievance rates
- Accident rates

Organization End Results

- Competitive product(s)
- Competitive service(s)

the method of payment for the job, such as payment for time worked or incentive compensation. Incentives and executive compensation, which differ in many ways from other types, are discussed in Chapter 10.

One of the most significant factors in compensation is the nature of the employee. How employee attitudes and preferences directly affect performance is discussed in the section. Employee attitudes and preferences also affect the pay structure.

There are other factors affecting compensation. Factors external to the organization—the government, unions, economic conditions, and labor market conditions—all have an effect in pay or wage surveys. Organizational factors are managerial goals and pay structures, labor budgets, and the size and age of the organization. Discussion of these factors in the sections that follow illustrates why employees and managers are paid the amounts they receive and which methods are used to pay people.

COMPENSATION AND EMPLOYEE SATISFACTION

Does a well-designed pay system motivate employees to greater performance, higher-quality performance, or greater employee satisfaction? The answer to this question has varied from the yes of scientific management in the early 1900s to the no of human relations theorists in the 1930s. The controversy still rages. It is not possible to settle this age-old dispute here, but the various positions will be presented briefly.

All would agree that effective compensation administration is desirable in efforts to increase employee satisfaction. And satisfaction with pay is important because, as many researchers have found, if pay satisfaction is low, job satisfaction is low.[3] As a consequence, absenteeism and turnover will be higher and more costly.

A summary of research on pay satisfaction indicates a number of important points.[4]

Salary level. The higher the pay, the higher the pay satisfaction within an occupational group at each job level. (For example, higher paid presidents are more satisfied than lower paid presidents.)

Community cost of living. The lower the cost of living in a community, the higher the pay satisfaction.

Education. The lower the educational level, the higher the pay satisfaction.

Future expectations. The more optimistic the employee is about future job conditions, the higher the pay satisfaction.

Other personal characteristics. The more intelligent, self-assured, and decisive a person is, the lower the pay satisfaction.

Pay basis. The more pay is perceived to be based on merit or performance, the greater the pay satisfaction.

---

[3] Graef S. Crystal, "Pay for Performance—Even if It's Just Luck," *The Wall Street Journal*, March 2, 1981, p. 16.

[4] J. D. Dunn and Frank Rachel, *Wage and Salary Administration* (New York: McGraw-Hill, 1971).

From The Wall Street Journal, *with permission of Cartoon Features Syndiate*

"Oh, I've found inner peace. Now I'm seeking financial peace."

In sum, most people believe it is desirable to have a pay system that leads to pay satisfaction. However, research indicates a relatively weak relationship between pay and pay satisfaction.[5] One reason that the relationship is not stronger is that people have different ideas about what their pay should be. Another reason for the weak relationship is that how pay is determined is not clearly understood by employees. That is, nonjob factors such as being agreeable with the boss, having a pleasant personality, or making donations to the supervisor's favorite charity, may be factors in the pay decision. Whether they are or not is sometimes not known to the employees.

COMPENSATION AND EMPLOYEE PERFORMANCE

High performance requires much more than employee motivation. Employee ability, adequate equipment, good physical working conditions, effective leadership and management, employee health, and other conditions all help raise employee performance levels. But employee motivation to work harder and better is obviously an important factor. And most compensation experts believe that pay affects the motivation of employees. A number of studies indicate that if pay is tied to performance, the employee produces a higher quality and quantity of work.[6]

Not everyone agrees with this—some researchers argue that if you tie pay to performance, you will destroy the intrinsic rewards a person gets from doing

---

[5] George Milkovich and Jerry M. Newman, *Compensation* (Plano, Texas: Business Publications, Inc., 1987), pp. 293–94.

[6] Edward J. Lawler III, *Pay and Organizational Effectiveness* (New York: McGraw-Hill, 1971).

the job well.[7] These are powerful motivators too. But the research behind these concerns has been limited to only a few studies. The importance of money to employees varies among individuals. And if the organization claims to have an incentive pay system and in fact pays for seniority, the motivation effects of pay will be lost.

In sum, theorists disagree over whether pay is a useful mechanism to motivate and satisfy employees. Because of individual differences in employees and jobs, it seems more fruitful to redirect this research to examine (1) the range of behaviors that pay can affect positively or negatively; (2) the amount of change pay can influence; (3) the kind of employees that pay influences positively and negatively; and (4) the environmental conditions that are present when pay leads to positive and negative results.

The point is that, although compensation in the form of pay for performance has intuitive appeal, it is extremely difficult to perfectly fit a pay for performance system together. Developing a system that employees consider as showing that pay is tied to performance requires a number of managerial skills. First, managers must be able to allocate pay on the basis of merit. Any merit pay increase must be meaningful, not a token, if it is to be motivational. Second, managers must be willing to specifically discriminate among subordinates, in terms of rating and rewarding performance. Third, the pay system must be communicated at the time of employment in terms of initial pay, expected long-term progression, and adjustments.[8] This information should be communicated by the manager, who informs the employee as well what performance levels are required to obtain the pay increases, Finally, managers must have the ability to discuss the pay for performance linkage with subordinates.

One reason that organizations have failed to tie the pay and performance for their employees is that it requires quite a bit of work, effort, and commitment by management.[9] A more simplified strategy is to conduct business as usual or to not work on creating a pay for performance perception among subordinates. The first step in the direction of creating a pay for performance work culture is to develop performance evaluation systems that are considered equitable, meaningful, and comprehensive by managers and employees.

Chapter 8 pointed out the difficulty of measuring performance. When pay rewards cannot be linked to measurable performance, management has a problem. This is, if performance measures are poorly developed, employees will have difficulty perceiving the connection between pay and performance. Thus, if compensation is to have any influence on motivation, it is extremely important to develop accurate measures of performance.

---

[7] Herbert Meyer, "The Pay for Performance Dilemma," *Organizational Dynamics*, Winter 1975, pp. 39–50; and Edward Deci, *Intrinsic Motivation* (New York: Plenum Publishing, 1975).

[8] Ibid., pp. 42–46.

[9] See debate on this subject in Richard E. Kopelman, "Linking Pay to Performance Is a Proven Management Tool," and William L. Mihal, "More Research Is Needed; Goals May Motivate Better," *Personnel Administrator*, October 1983, pp. 60–68.

EXTERNAL INFLUENCES
ON PAY LEVELS

Besides being concerned about pay satisfaction and the pay for performance linkage, managers have to consider other influences when designing a compensation program. Among the factors that influence pay and compensation policies are those outside the organization: the government, unions, the economy, and the labor market.

Government Influences

The government directly affects compensation through wage controls and guidelines, which prohibit an increase in compensation for certain workers at certain times, and laws directed at the establishment of minimum wage rates, wage and hour regulations, and the prevention of discrimination directed at certain groups.

Wage Controls and Guidelines Several times in the past quarter century or so the United States has established wage freezes and guidelines. President Harry Truman imposed a wage and price freeze from January 1951 to 1953, and President Richard Nixon imposed freezes from 1971 to 1974, which came to be called Phases I–IV. Wage freezes are government orders which permit no wage increases. Wage controls limit the size of wage increases. Wage guidelines are similar to wage controls, but they are voluntary rather than legally required restrictions.

Economists and compensation specialists differ on the usefulness of wage and price freezes. Critics argue that controls are an administrative nightmare, which seriously disrupt the effective resource allocation market process and lead to frustration, strikes, and so on. Even the critics admit, however, that during times of perceived national emergencies and for relatively brief periods, the controls might help slow (but not indefinitely postpone) inflation. Those favoring them believe that controls reduce inflation. The important point is that employers must adjust their compensation policies to any governmental wage guidelines and controls. Considerable data gathering is necessary when such programs are in effect, and the employer must be prepared to justify any proposed wage increases. Even when the controls have been lifted, there are frequently wage and price advisory groups—government or quasi-government groups that some politicians use to try to "jawbone" executives into keeping price increases lower. These bodies at times might influence prices, which in turn could limit the profits needed to give wage increases. One proposed solution is *TIP (tax-based income policy)*. Under a TIP, when employers give employees bigger raises than government standards, the employer receives a tax increase; when the raise is below standards, he receives a tax reduction.

Wage and Hour Regulations The Fair Labor Standards Act of 1938 is the basic pay act in the United States. It has been amended many times, contains minimum wage, overtime pay, equal pay, and child labor provisions. Government agencies such as the Department of Labor's Wage and Hour Division enforce the wage and hour law. It has the right to examine employers' records and issue orders for back pay, get an injuction to prohibit future violations and prosecute violators and send them to prison. For example, the department estimates that in 1984, U.S. employers underpaid employees by $125 million, in violation of minimum wage and overtime regulations. The department forced employers to pay $60 million to 385,000 employees for minimum wage violations, and 300,000 workers recovered $52 million from employers violating overtime regulations. In 1984 over 60 million American workers were covered by the Fair Labor Standards Act. The law includes the following provisions.

Minimum Wages All employers covered by the law (all but some small firms and some specific exemptions) must pay an employee at least a minimum wage per hour. Exempt are small businesses whose gross sales did not exceed $325,000 in 1980, or $362,000 in 1981. In 1938, the minimum wage was 25 cents per hour. In 1984, the minimum was $3.35 per hour. A brief history of minimum wage rates is shown in Exhibit 9–3. A number of economists question the desirability of minimum wages, arguing that this law may price the marginal worker out of a job. The minimum wage law does not apply to all employees. For example, full-time students only have to be paid at 83 percent of the wage. Thus, a full-time student could be paid only $2.78 per hour for a period of up to one year. There are also other exceptions granted for apprentices, handicapped workers, and learners.

Overtime Pay An employee covered by the law who works more than 40 hours per week must be paid one-and-one-half times the base wage. If bonuses are also paid on a monthly or quarterly basis, the overtime pay equals one-and-one-half times the base pay and bonuses. Overtime pay tends to reduce the scheduling of longer hours of work.

The Fair Labor Standards Act provisions regarding minimum wages and overtime pay applies to employees classified as nonexempt, but does not apply

EXHIBIT 9–3   **Historical Progression of Minimum Wage Rate**

Year	Rate per Hour
1938	$0.25
1939	0.30
1945	0.40
1956	1.00
1968	1.60
1974	2.00
1979	2.90
1981	3.35

to exempt employees.[10] An *exempt employee* is classified to mean an executive, administrative, professional, or outside salesperson. *An executive employee* would be a manager who has authority over subordinates. An *administrative employee* would be a staff employee such as the president's assistant public relations coordinator. *A professional* is a person who has special knowledge acquired through education such as a company physician or lawyer. An *outside salesperson* sells goods or services to customers away from the organization.[11]

Nonexempt employees do not fit any of the above categories. Most noticeably nonexempt employees are blue-collar workers, such as skilled and semiskilled manufacturing workers, truck drivers, and assembly line workers. Nonexempt employees are covered by the minimum wage and overtime provisions of the law.

Child Labor Prohibition The law prohibits employing persons between the ages of 16 and 18 in hazardous jobs such as meatpacking and logging. Persons under age 16 cannot be employed in jobs in interstate commerce except for nonhazardous work for a parent or guardian, and this requires a temporary permit.

The Equal Pay Act (1963) amendment to the Fair Labor Standards Act is the first antidiscrimination law relating directly to females. The act applies to all employers and employees covered by the Fair Labor Standards Act, including executives, managers, and professionals. The Equal Pay Act requires equal pay for equal work for men and women and defines equal work as work requiring equal skills, effort, and responsibility under similar working conditions.[12]

Under the Equal Pay Act, an employer can establish different wage rates on the basis of (1) seniority, (2) merit, (3) performance differences—quantity and quality, and (4) any factor other than sex. Shift work differentials are also permissible. All these exemptions, however, must apply equally to men and women.

The doctrine of comparable worth (sometimes called *pay equity*), is not a position that provides that women and men be paid equally for performing equal work. It is a concept that attempts to prove and remedy the allegation that employers systematically discriminate by paying women employees less than their work is intrinsically worth, relative to what they pay male employees who work in other comparable professions.[13]

Advocates of comparable worth depend primarily upon two sets of statistics to demonstrate that women employees are discriminated against by employers. First, they point to statistics that show that women earn from 59 percent

[10] Description of exemption is found in the U.S. Department of Labor, *Executive Administration, Professional and Outside Salesmen Exemption* (Washington, D.C.: U.S. Government Printing Office, 1973).

[11] Robert M. Pattison, "Fine Tuning Wage and Hour Practices," *Personnel Journal*, September 1987, pp. 166–69.

[12] Based on Richard I. Henderson, *Compensation Management* (Reston, Va.: Reston Publishing, 1985), pp. 71–74.

[13] Anne Armstrong, *Comparable Worth*, Austin, Texas, Texas Womens Alliance Report, 1986.

to 72 percent less than men employees overall and tend to be concentrated in lower paying predominately female jobs (for instance, 99.2 percent of secretaries are female; 94.6 percent of registered nurses are female; 77.7 percent of cashiers are female).[14] They are relying on statistics gathered by job evaluators, whose function is to compare the amount of education, skill, effort, responsibility, and working conditions involved in different occupations.

Comparable worth has become a hotly debated political issue. The majority of political debate is being contested in state courts. Fourteen states have adopted the equal pay for comparable work standard as amendments to their equal pay acts.[15]

Comparable Worth Today, American women working full time earn only about 60 percent of what men earn.[16] In an effort to close this earnings gap, there has been a growing movement in the last few years to have the widely accepted concept of equal pay for equal jobs expanded to include equal pay for comparable jobs. The issue of comparable worth has been ruled on by the Supreme Court. In a five to four decision on June 9, 1984, the Supreme Court ruled that a sex discrimination suit can be brought under the 1964 Civil Rights Act on a basis other than discrimination based on "equal or substantially equal work."[17] The suit involved Washington County, Oregon, prison matrons claiming sex discrimination because male prison guards, whose jobs were somewhat different, received substantially higher pay. The county had evaluated the male's jobs as having 5 percent more job content than the female jobs, and paid the males 35 percent more. On July 1, 1984, the state of Washington began wage adjustment payments to approximately 15,000 employees. For example, women in female-dominated jobs receive $4.17 more per week. This is the first of several adjustments aimed at eliminating state pay disparities between male and female jobs by 1993.[18]

Until the *Gunther* v. *Washington* prison matron's case, the courts were split on the issue of comparable worth.[19] The ruling, although not mentioning the comparable worth concept, now permits women to bring suit on the grounds that they are paid less than men holding jobs of comparable, or less than comparable worth—based on job content evaluation.

In another case involving the State of Washington, the *AFSCME* (American Federation of State, County, and Municipal Employees) v. *State of Wash-*

---

[14] "Pay Gap Narrows But Women Still Earn Less Than Men," *Houston Chronicle*, September 4, 1987, p. 13.

[15] "Pay Equity and Comparable Worth, BNA Special Report (Washington, D.C.: Bureau of National Affairs, 1984).

[16] Geoffrey, Cowley, "Comparable Worth," *Across the Board*, May 1984, p. 45.

[17] Michael F. Carte, "Comparable Worth: An Idea Whose Time Has Come?" *Personnel Journal*, October 1981, pp. 792–94.

[18] Robert Buchele and Mark Aldrich, "How Much Difference Would Comparable Worth Make?" *Industrial Relations*, Summer 1985, pp. 222–33.

[19] James T. Brinks, "The Comparable Worth Issue: A Salary Administration Bombshell," *Personnel Administrator*, November 1981, pp. 37–40; and Richard J. Schonberger and Harry W. Hennessey, Jr., "Is Equal Pay for Comparable Work Fair?" *Personnel Journal*, December 1981, pp. 964–68.

ington, the court found that the state was guilty of direct, overt, and institutionalized pay discrimination. The court found that jobs held predominantly by women had lower pay rates than jobs dominated by men, even when jobs were rated the same in job evaluation studies. The court contended that the female job pay rates were incorrectly tied to market forces and not to job content. After all appeals are heard, it is possible that Washington state employees could be awarded as much as $500 million in salary adjustments and three years of back pay.[20]

In another important comparable worth case in San Jose, California, in 1981, several hundred women employees of the city walked off their jobs over the comparable worth issue. One eye-opening example in this situation was that senior librarians, typically female, earned 27 percent less than senior chemists, typically male, although the two jobs were rated comparably.

The union and city reached a settlement on July 14, 1981, with the city agreeing to pay $1.45 million in raises for several hundred female employees to make their pay more equitable with men. A few other pay equity cases have involved:[21]

1. Nurses working for the city of Denver, Colorado, starting at $1,000 per year less than painters, tree trimmers, and tire servicemen.
2. Jobs held primarily by females in a Westinghouse plant in Trenton, New Jersey, in general paying less than male jobs that were rated comparably by the company's job evaluation system.
3. Women handling health and beauty aids for a division of Super Valu Stores, Inc., in western Pennsylvania, eastern Ohio, and northern West Virginia, being paid $3,500 less annually than men handling perishable food.

In each of these cases and almost every instance of a case reaching the court, the claim revolved around the job evaluation system (job evaluation will be discussed later in this chapter).

Although there are various methods used in job evaluation to make comparisons, one of the most common involves assigning a numerical score to each separate component of a job and constructing a rating scale. The assigned points serve as a basis for comparing the intrinsic value of one job with another. Comparable worth proponents find employer discrimination by comparing predominately female jobs with predominately male jobs. This type of inequity is brought out in Exhibit 9–4.

This sample of jobs suggests that women are not paid equitably. For example, the job of senior legal secretary received 226 job evaluation points, the same as the job of senior carpenter. However, the female secretary is paid $375 less per month than the male carpenter. The female librarian, although her job

[20] E. James Brennan, "Why Laws Have Failed to End Pay Discrimination," *Personnel Journal*, August 1984, p. 20.

[21] Benson Rosen, Sara Rynes, and Thomas A. Mahoney, "Compensation, Jobs, and Gender," *Harvard Business Review*, July–August 1983; p. 170, and Carter, "Comparable Worth," p. 793.

EXHIBIT 9–4 Inequalities in Point-to-Dollar Relationships

A. Inequality of pay in relation to job evaluation points

City or State	Job Title	Monthly Salary	Difference	Number of Points
Minnesota	Registered nurse (F)	$1,723	$537	275
	Vocational education teacher (M)	2,260		275
San Jose, California	Senior legal secretary (F)	665	$375	226
	Senior carpenter (M)	1,040		226
	Senior librarian (F)	898	$221	493
	Senior chemist (M)	1,119		493
Washington State	Administrative services manager A (F)	1,211	$500	506
	Systems analyst III (M)	1,711		426
	Dental assistant I (F)	608	$208	120
	Stockroom attendant II (M)	816		120
	Food service worker (F)	637	$332	93
	Truck driver (M)	969		94

B. Inequality of job evaluation points in relation to pay

City or State	Job Title	Monthly Salary	Point Difference	Number of Points
Minnesota	Health program representative (F)	$1,590	82	238
	Steam boiler attendant (M)	1,611		156
	Data processing coordinator (F)	1,423	65	199
	General repair work (M)	1,564		134
San Jose, California	Librarian I (F)	750	140	228
	Street sweeper operator (M)	758		124

Note: F = Female; M = Male.

Source: Ronnie J. Steinberg, "Identifying Wage Discrimination and Implementing Pay Equity Adjustments," in *Comparable Worth: Issue for the 80's*, Vol. 1 (Washington, D.C.: U.S. Commission on Civil Rights, 1985).

is rated 104 points higher than that of the male street sweeper, receives $8 less monthly in pay.

P/HRM specialists must be extremely careful about how job evaluation data are used in determining pay. They also must work at developing job evaluation systems that are valid and reliable. Comparable worth is an issue that requires a number of P/HRM responses such as:

- A sound job evaluation system.
- Comparing pay across jobs on a regular basis. Are low-paying jobs being occupied by females and minorities? If so, look at this closely.
- Documentation of the pay system.
- Clarifying and documenting the role that performance appraisal plays in pay.

There is some opposition to the notion of comparable worth. Job evaluation plays a major role in determining if two dissimilar jobs are comparable in worth.[22] The question raised is whether job evaluation can provide accurate

---

[22] Daniel Seligman, "Pay Equity Is a Bad Idea," *Fortune*, May 14, 1984, pp. 133–40.

results. It's not clear that it can, since every job evaluation system (some will be discussed later) involves subjectivity. Thus, job evaluation experts differ among themselves about what job factors to measure and what weights to assign to the factors.

A second problem is that job evaluation scores don't reveal anything about the labor market. Even if jobs are rated as comparable, shouldn't the ease or difficulty of filling the job be considered? For example, although the San Jose, California, Personnel Department determined that librarians (female-dominated) and electricians (male-dominated) are comparable, should they receive the same pay? First-rate librarian applicants are in abundance, while qualified electricians are difficult to locate in Silicon Valley.

The notion of value is extremely important when examining pay differentials. Most people would agree that water is more valuable than diamonds, but diamonds are much more expensive than water. This differential arises because the supply of water is abundant relative to demand. When secretaries, librarians, registered nurses, and cashiers are in short supply what employers will have to pay is likely to rise.

Comparable worth will continue to be a controversial issue as more court rulings are issued. It appears that P/HRM departments will become more embroiled in the controversy. Special equity adjustments ruled by the courts in comparable worth cases are going to have to be paid by someone. Both men and women are finding that comparable worth has been and will remain a costly problem.

Other Pay Legislation The Civil Rights Act of 1964, and the Age Discrimination Act of 1967 are designed to assure that all persons of similar ability, seniority, and background receive the same pay for the same work. The Equal Employment Opportunity Commission enforces the Civil Rights Act, while the Wage and Hour Division enforces the Equal Pay Act and the Age Discrimination Act.

The Walsh-Healy Act of 1936 requires firms doing business with the federal government to pay wages at least equal to the industry minimum rather than the market area minimum. It parallels the Fair Labor Standards Act on child labor and requires time-and-a-half pay for any work performed after eight hours a day. It also exempts some industries. The Davis-Bacon Act of 1931 requires the payment of minimum prevailing wages of the locality to workers engaged in federally sponsored public works. The McNamara-O'Hara Service Contract Act requires employers who have contracts with the federal government of $2,500 per year or more, or who provide services to federal agencies as contractors or subcontractors, to pay prevailing wages and fringe benefits to their employees.

In addition to federal laws, 47 states have minimum-wage laws covering intrastate employees and those not covered by federal laws. Some of these minimums are higher than the federal minimum. In such cases, the state minimums apply.

The government directly affects the amount of pay the employee takes home by requiring employers to deduct funds from employees' wages. Deductions include federal income taxes (withholding taxes), social security taxes, and possibly state and local income taxes.

The federal government also has other laws governing pay deductions. The Copeland Act (1934) and Anti-Kickback Law (1948) are designed to protect the employee from unlawful or unauthorized deductions. The Federal Wage Garnishment Act (1970) is designed to limit the amount deducted from a person's pay to reduce debts. It also prohibits the employer from firing an employee if the employee goes in debt only once and has his pay garnisheed. The employer may deduct as much from the paycheck as required by court orders for alimony or child support, debts due for taxes, or bankruptcy court requirements.

Other Government Influences In addition to the laws and regulations just discussed, the government influences compensation in many other ways. If the government is the employer, it can legislate pay levels by setting statutory rates. For example, the pay scale for teachers can be set by law or by edict of the school board, and pay depends on revenues from the current tax base. If taxes decline relative to organizations' revenue streams, no matter how much the organization may wish to pay higher wages, it cannot.

The government affects compensation through its employment-level policy too. One of the goals of the government is full employment of all citizens seeking work. The government may even create jobs for certain categories of workers, thus reducing the supply of workers available and affecting pay rates.

Union Influences on Compensation

Another important external influence on an employer's compensation program is labor unionization. Unions have an effect whether or not the organization's employees are unionized, if the organization is an area where unionized enterprises exist. Unions have tended to be pacesetters in demands for pay, benefits, and working conditions. There is reasonable evidence that unions tend to increase pay levels, although this is more likely where an industry has been organized by strong unions. If the organization elects to stay in an area where unions are strong, its compensation policies will be affected.

During hard economic times, union and nonunion employees have made concessions in the form of wage cuts, wage freezes of previously negotiated increases, benefit reductions, work rules changes, and other forms of givebacks. Uniroyal, Inc.'s 16,000 employees gave up $27 million in compensation in 1980 and 1981. This savings was essential for Uniroyal to survive. Public Service Electric and Gas Co. extended the workweek for 3,000 employees at its Newark, New Jersey, headquarters to 40 hours from 35 hours. This increase in hours occurred without any pay increase and meant that the firm gets more work for the same payroll dollar.[23] At American Motors and Quality Aluminum Company, employees have given back millions of dollars. However,

---

[23] Ralph E. Winter, "More Employees Accept Cuts in Pay to Help Their Companies Survive," *The Wall Street Journal*, October 22, 1980, p. 23.

the union and management in these two firms reached agreement that all wage concessions are to be paid back under a plan based on improved company performance.[24]

A series of legal cases has required employers to share compensation information with the unions if employees are unionized. For example, in *Shell Development* v. *Association of Industrial Scientists—Professional Employees,* Shell was requried to provide the union with a written explanation of salary curves and the merit system, as well as copies of current salary curve guides, merit ratings, and so on. In *Time Incorporated* v. *Newspaper Guild*, Time was required to provide the union with a list of salaries of employees. In *General Electric* v. *International Union of Electrical Workers*, GE was required to provide the union with the pay survey information it had gathered to form compensation decisions. Thus employers would do well to communicate with and try to influence the union on compensation policy and levels.

Unions do try to bargain for higher pay and benefits, of course. The union is more likely to increase the compensation of its members when the organization is financially and competitively strong; when the union is financially strong enough to support a strike; when the union has the support of other unions; and when general economic and labor market conditions are such that unemployment is low and the economy is strong.[25]

Unions also bargain over working conditions and other policies that affect compensation. There is a tendency for unions to prefer fixed pay for each job category, or rate ranges that are administered primarily to reflect seniority rather than merit increases. This is true in the private and other sectors. Unions press for time pay rather than merit pay when the amount of performance expected is tied to technology (such as the assembly line).

Economic Conditions and Compensation

Also affecting compensation as an external factor are the economic conditions of the industry, especially the degree of competitiveness, which affects the organization's ability to pay high wages. The more competitive the situation, the less able is the organization to pay higher wages. Ability to pay is also a consequence of the relative productivity of the organization or industry or sector. If a firm is very productive, it can pay higher wages. Productivity can be increased by advanced technology, more efficient operating methods, a harder working and more talented work force, or a combination of these factors.

One productivity index used by many organizations as a criterion in the determination of a general level of wages is the Bureau of Labor Statistics' "Output per Man-Hour in Manufacturing." This productivity index is published in each issue of the *Monthly Labor Review*. For about 70 years, produc-

---

[24] Peter Cappeli, "What Do Unions Get in Return for Concessions?" *Monthly Labor Review*, May 1984, pp. 40–41.

[25] William T. Dickens and Kevin Lang, Labor Market Segmentation and the Union Wage Premium (Cambridge, Mass.: NBER Working Paper 1883), April 1986.

tivity increased at an average annual rate of approximately 3 percent. The percentage increase in average weekly earnings in the United States is very closely related to the percentage change in productivity, plus the percentage change in the consumer price index. Unfortunately, in the 1970–1987 period, productivity improvement in the United States had been less than 2 percent annually.

The degree of profitability and productivity is a significant factor in determining the ability of firms in the private and third sector to pay wages. In the public sector, the limitations of the budget determine the ability to pay. If tax rates are low or the tax base is low or declining, the public-sector employer may be unable to give pay increases even if they are deserved.

Nature of the Labor Market and Compensation

The final external factor affecting compensation to be discussed is the state of the labor market. Although many feel that human labor should not be regulated by forces such as supply and demand, it does in fact happen. In times of full employment, wages and salaries may have to be higher to attract and retain enough qualified employees; in depressions, the reverse is true. Pay may be higher if few skilled employees are available in the job market. This situation may occur because unions or accrediting associations limit the numbers certified to do the job. In certain locations, due to higher birthrates or a recent loss of a major employer, more persons may be seeking work. These factors lead to what is called *differential pay levels*. At any one time in a particular locale, unskilled labor rates seek a single level, and minimally skilled clerical work rates seek another. Research evidence from the labor economics field provides adequate support for the impact of labor market conditions on compensation.

Besides differences in pay levels by occupations in a locale, there are also differentials between government and private employees and exempt and nonexempt employees, as well as international differences. For example, there are differences in pay levels between the United States and Canada.

Increases in productivity are typically passed on to employees in the form of higher pay. In general, employers do not exploit employees when market conditions do not favor the employees. Employers use compensation surveys and general studies of the labor market in the area to serve as inputs to their pay-level compensation decision. The pay survey is the major pay-level decision tool.

ORGANIZATIONAL INFLUENCES ON PAY LEVELS

In addition to the external influences on compensation already discussed, several internal factors affect pay levels: the size and age of the organization, the labor budget, and the goals of its controlling interests.

EXHIBIT 9–5   **Allocation Decisions on Labor Budget**

Position	Responsibility
Employees' immediate supervisor	Appraises performance; makes pay recommendation to supervisor.
Department head	Reviews each recommendation and initiates action based on budgeted amounts.
P/HRM: Compensation specialists	Review department head recommendations and consider equity, budget, objectives, and future plans. Consult with department heads on specialist's recommendations.
Senior or top-level management	Makes final decision on pay recommendations. Decision is based on labor budget and departmental allocations plus recommendations passed through various levels (supervisor, head, specialist).

We don't know a great deal about size and pay. Generally speaking, it appears that larger organizations tend to have higher pay levels. Little is known about age of the organizations and pay, but some theorists contend that newer enterprises tend to pay more than old ones.

The Labor Budget

The labor budget of an organization normally identifies the amount of money available for annual employee compensation. Every unit of the organization is influenced by the size of the budget.[26] A firm's budget normally does not state the exact amount of money to be allocated to each employee, but it does state how much is available to the unit. The discretion in allocating pay is then left to department heads and supervisors. These allocations form the basis of a manager's strategy.

The department heads and supervisors are in the best position to allocate the unit's labor budget dollars, assuming that they have the closest contact and best view of the employees. Theoretically, the contract and performance evaluation should permit a proper allocation of dollars. Thus, the department heads and supervisors take the budget amounts and, based on observation and evaluation, recommend who should get what amount of compensation. Exhibit 9–5 briefly describes some of the pay allocation decisions. Each of these decisions is significantly influenced and constrained by what amount is budgeted to a particular unit.

Goals of Controlling Interests and Managerial Pay Strategies

Another organizational influence deals with the goals of controlling interests and the specific pay strategy that managers select. The final authority in pay

---

[26] Henderson, *Compensation Management*, p. 415.

P/HRM · IN · ACTION

Mary   Guido

Guido Panelli went to Mary Renfro as he had promised Joe. He told her to go ahead and prepare a report that would point out the problems in P/HRM, especially in compensation, that CNB was facing. Mary remembered worrying about the situation at Cardeson National Bank after learning about the effect of pay on performance and satisfaction. At the bank some employees seemed to be paid for seniority, others for family need. People doing the same job at about the same performance levels received different paychecks, and they knew it. This seemed to be a bomb about to go off.

She knew the bank was following the legal requirements of compensation with regard to minimum wage and overtime. But equal-pay requirements were another situation. Often single people were paid less than married people, and married people with several children were paid more than those who were childless or had only one child. Single females were paid the least.

At present the bank was not unionized; few banks were. The labor market was good for the bank right now. There always were more applicants than needed. This factor had helped CNB with its problem of high turnover, for there were many eager replacements. But what would happen if the labor market should change or if the inequities in the pay rates were not corrected?

decisions as shown in Exhibit 9–5 is top-level or senior management. The views of managers and supervisors about pay differ as much as the employees' view.3. For example, some believe their employees should be compensated at high pay levels because they deserve it. They also accept or reject the idea that high pay or merit pay leads to greater performance or employee satisfaction. These attitudes are reflected in the pay-level strategy chosen by the managers of the organization. This is a major strategic choice top managers must make. Essentially, three pay-level strategies—high, low, or comparable—can be chosen by supervisors and managers (the term *manager* will henceforth be used to reflect these two levels of compensation decision makers).

FRANK AND ERNEST

© 1975 by NEA, Inc. Reprinted by permission of NEA.

The High Pay-Level Strategy In this strategy, the managers choose to pay higher than average pay levels. The assumption behind this strategy is that you get what you pay for. These managers believe that paying higher wages and salaries will attract and hold the best employees, and this is the most effective long-range policy. Organizations that use this strategy are sometimes called *pacesetters*. The strategy may be influenced by pay criteria such as paying a living wage or paying on the basis of productivity.

The Low Pay-Level Strategy At the opposite extreme is the low-pay strategy. In this case, the manager may choose to pay at the minimum level needed to hire enough employees. This strategy may be used because this is all the organization can pay—the ability to pay is restricted by other internal or external factors such as a limited labor budget or a forecasted decline in sales and profits.

The Comparable Pay-Level Strategy The most frequently used strategy is to set the pay level at the going wage level. The wage criteria are comparable wages, perhaps modified by cost of living or purchasing power adjustments. For example, the Federal Pay Comparability Act of 1970 limits federal government compensation to the comparable pay paid in the private sector at the time. This going wage is determined from pay surveys. Thus the policy of a manager of this type is to pay the current market rate in the community or industry, ±5 percent or so.

These three strategies are usually set for the total organization, although the strategy might have to be modified for a few hard-to-fill jobs from time to time. The choice of strategy in part reflects the motivation and attitudes held by the manager. If the manager has a high need for recognition, the high-pay strategy might be chosen; otherwise, the low-pay strategy might be chosen. Another factor is the ethical and moral attitude of the manager. If the manager is ethically oriented, then a low-pay strategy is not likely to be chosen willingly.

PAY SURVEYS AND COMPARABLE PAY LEVELS

Pay Surveys (also called *wage surveys*) are surveys of the compensation paid to employees by all employers in a geographic area, an industry, or an occupational group. Surveys must be carefully designed because their results are quoted and used in making pay decisions. They are the principal tool used in the pay-level decision.

Who Conducts Wage Surveys?

Pay surveys are made by large employers, professional and consulting enterprises, trade associations, and the government. Some examples are described here.

Professional and Trade Association Surveys *American Management Association.* AMA conducts surveys of professional and managerial compensation and provides about 12 reports on U.S. executives' salaries and 16 reports on foreign executives' salaries. The *Top Management Report* shows the salaries of 31,000 top executives in 75 top positions in 3,000 firms in 53 industries. The *Middle Management Report* covers 73 key exempt jobs between supervisor and top executives. The sample includes 460 firms with 15,000 middle-level executives. The *Administrative and Technical Report* covers jobs below the middle management level. The sample is 568 firms. The *Supervisory Management Report* provides national and regional data on salaries of 55 categories of foremen and staff supervisors in 700 companies.

Administrative Management Society This group compiles records on the compensation of clerical and data processing employees. AMS surveys 7,132 firms with 621,000 clerical and data processing employees in 132 cities throughout the United States, Canada, and the West Indies. The data are gathered for 20 positions. A directory published every other year by cities and regions reports interquarterly ranges of salaries.

American Society for Personnel Administration ASPA conducts salary surveys for personnel executives and others every other year.

Surveys by Other Organizations Other organizations that do pay surveys include Pay Data Service (Chicago); Management Compensation Services; Bureau of National Affairs; Hay Associates; Abbott, Langer and Associates; and American Society of Corporate Securities. Many journals report on compensation, including: *Compensation Review, Business Week, Dun's, Forbes, Fortune, Hospital Administration, Nation's Business, and Monthly Labor Review.*

Government Surveys U.S. government pay surveys include those by Federal Reserve banks, which survey private industry pay to set their employees' pay, and the Bureau of Labor Statistics (BLS). The BLS publishes three different surveys:

Area Wage Surveys Annually, BLS surveys about 200 areas (usually the Standard Metropolitan Statistical Areas) on the pay and benefits for white-collar, skilled blue-collar, and indirect manufacturing labor jobs (in alternate years).

Industry Wage Surveys The BLS surveys 50 manufacturing industries, 20 service industries, and public employees. Blue- and white-collar employees are covered. The surveys are done on one-, three- and five-year cycles. Some industries are surveyed nationally (utilities, mining, manufacturing), and others by metropolitan area (finance, service, and trade).

Professional, Administrative, Technical, and Clerical (PATC) Surveys BLS also annually surveys 80 occupational work-level positions on a nation-wide basis. Occupations covered by the PATC (Professional, Administrative, Technical, and Clerical) survey include accountancy, legal services, engineering, drafting, clerical, and chemistry. Although the BLS studies tend to follow the most sophisticated survey methods, they often do not relate to the area in which a firm is doing business.

How Pay Surveys Are Conducted and Used

How are these surveys done? One method is the personal interview, which develops the most accurate responses but is also expensive. Mailed questionnaires are probably the most frequently used method, and one of the cheapest. The jobs being surveyed by mail must be clearly defined, or the data may not be reliable. Telephone inquiries are used to follow up the mail questionnaires to gather data. This procedure is quick, but it is also difficult to get a great deal of detailed data over the phone.

There are a number of critical issues determining the usefulness of the surveys: the jobs to be covered, the employers to be contacted, and the method to be used in gathering the data. Other employers cannot be expected to complete endless data requests for all the organization's jobs, so the jobs that are surveyed should be the 2 to 20 most crucial ones. If the point method of job evaluation is used (described later in the chapter), the key jobs might be selected for surveying, since they cover all ranges. The jobs that most employees hold should also be on the list (clerk-typists, underwriters, and keypunch operators for an insurance company, for example).

The second issue concerns who will be surveyed. Most organizations tend to compare themselves with similar competitors in their industry. American Airlines might compare its pay rates to those of United Airlines, for example. It has been shown that employees might not compare their pay to that offered by competitors at all. Their basis of comparison might be friends' employers, or employers that they worked for previously. If the survey is to be useful, employees should be involved in choosing the organizations to be surveyed. The employers to be surveyed should include the most dominant ones in the area and a small sample of those suggested by employees.[27]

27 D. W. Belcher, N. Bruce Ferris, and John O'Neill, "How Wage Surveys Are Being Used," *Compensation and Benefits Review*, September–October 1985, pp. 34–51.

Government agencies use pay surveys of comparable private-sector jobs to set their pay levels. The evidence suggests that private-sector organizations use their own pay surveys rather than those provided by the government or other services, primarily as general guidelines or as one of several factors considered in pay-level decisions. In fact, there is some evidence that organizations weigh job evaluation and individual pay determination more heavily than external pay comparisons. This makes sense, because pay surveys are not taken often (perhaps yearly) and are sometimes hard to interpret meaningfully.

Much care and thought must go into how the pay survey is conducted, and many factors, such as the source of data, must be considered.[28] An employer might not know if there is a pay differential between the job the firm offers and others. The difference might be due to differences in the job, fringe benefits provided, the time of the survey, or the pay level of the two areas. Remember too that there are many surveys an employer can use and many organizations and locales it can survey. This can give the employer a great deal of maneuvering room to handle problems such as relative ability or inability to pay certain wages or to deal with cost-of-living problems, and similar pay bargaining issues.

THE PAY-LEVEL DECISION

The pay-level decision is made by managers, who compare the pay of persons working inside the organization with those outside it. This decision is affected by multiple factors in interaction with one another, as shown in Exhibit 9–6, which affect pay levels laterally, upward, or downward. When factors such as managerial attitudes, the labor market, and competition change, the pressures on pay level shift.[29]

But remember: The many external factors affecting the process, such as government and unions, are compounded by employees' job preferences, which include pay and nonpay aspects. And many employees do not have a sophisticated or comprehensive knowledge of all these factors. So you can see that the organization has a great deal of maneuvering room in the pay-level decision.

PAY STRUCTURES

In addition to relating pay to pay levels paid for comparable jobs in other organizations, the enterprise must also determine pay structures for its employees having different jobs *within* the organization. Factors similar to those affecting pay levels affect these pay structures, too.

Managers can cope with the attempt to provide equal pay for positions of

---

[28] Gary D. Fisher, "Salary Surveys—An Antitrust Perspective," *Personnel Administrator*, April 1985, pp. 87–97, 154.

[29] Robert J. Greene, "Thoughts on Compensation Management in the 80s and 90s," *Personnel Administrator*, May 1980, pp. 27–28.

EXHIBIT 9–6 Factors Affecting the Pay-Level Decision

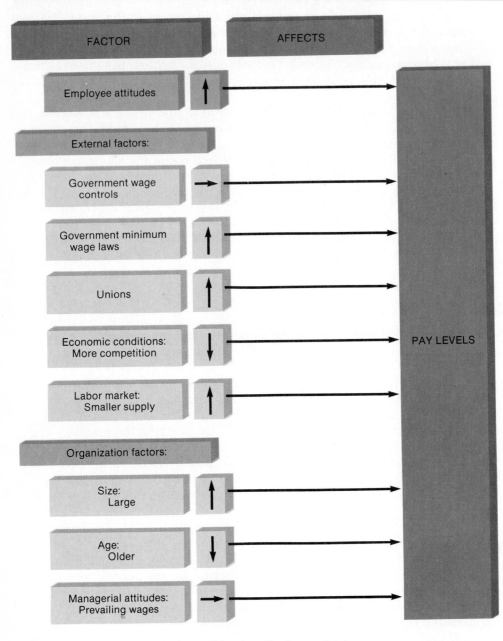

FACTOR

AFFECTS

Employee attitudes

External factors:

Government wage controls

Government minimum wage laws

Unions

Economic conditions: More competition

Labor market: Smaller supply

Organization factors:

Size: Large

Age: Older

Managerial attitudes: Prevailing wages

PAY LEVELS

Direction affecting pay level

approximately equal worth by arbitrary management decisions, collective bargaining, or job evaluation. If managers try to make these decisions without help from tools such as job evaluation, unsystematic decision making is likely to lead to perceived inequities. Bargaining alone can lead to decisions based solely on relative power. Therefore, most management experts suggest that managerial decisions should be influenced both by the results of collective bargaining and job evaluation.

Job Evaluation

Job evaluation is intended to determine the relative worth of a job. A systematic comparison of the worth of one job to another eventually results in the creation of a wage or salary hierarchy.

> Job evaluation is the formal process by which the relative worth of various jobs in the organization is determined for pay purposes. Essentially, it attempts to relate the amount of the employee's pay to the extent that her or his job contributes to organizational effectiveness.

It is not always easy to evaluate the worth of all jobs in an organization. The fact is that job evaluation involves making judgments that are subject to errors on the part of job evaluators.[30] It may be obvious that the effective physician will contribute more to the goals of patient care in the hospital than the nurse's aide. The point at issue is *how much* the differential is worth which means that a judgment must be made.

Since computing exactly how much a particular job contributes to organizational effectiveness is difficult, proxies for effectiveness are used. These proxies include skills required to do the job, amount and significance of responsibility involved, effort required, and working conditions. Compensation must vary with the differing demands of various jobs if employees are to be satisfied and if the organization is to be able to attract the personnel it wants.

Job evaluation is widely used. At least two thirds of all jobs have been evaluated. The following are among the reasons often cited for using a job evaluation program:[31]

- To establish a systematic and formal structure of jobs based on their worth to the organization.
- To justify an existing pay structure or to develop one that provides for internal equity.
- To provide a basis for negotiating pay rates when a firm bargains collectively with a union.

---

[30] Henderson, *Compensation Management*, p. 235.

[31] Michael K. Mount and Rebecca A. Ellis, "Investigation of In-Job Evaluation Ratings of Comparable Worth Study Participants," *Personnel Psychology*, Spring 1987, pp. 85–96.

- To identify to employees a hierarchy of pay progression.
- To comply with equal pay legislation.
- To develop a basis for a merit or pay for performance program.

Once an organization decides to use job evaluation, a series of decisions must be made to ensure its effectiveness. Part of the decision to use job evaluation, or the first step in using it effectively, is for management to involve employees (and, where appropriate, the union) in the system and its implementation. Most experts emphasize that job evaluation is a difficult task that is more likely to be successful if the employees whose jobs are being evaluated are involved in the process. Employees should be allowed to express their perceptions of the relative merits of their jobs compared to others. This participation affords an opportunity to explain the fairly complicated process of job evaluation to those most directly affected by it, and it will usually lead to better communication and improved employee understanding.

After the program is off to a cooperative start, usually a committee of about five members evaluates the jobs. Ideally, the committee includes employees, managers, and P/HRM specialists. All members should be familiar with the jobs to be evaluated.

Job evaluation is usually performed by analyzing job descriptions and occasionally job specifications. Early in the process, it is imperative that job evaluators check the availability and accuracy of the job descriptions and specifications (see Chapter 4). It is usually suggested that job descriptions be split into several series, such as managerial, professional/technical, clerical, and operative. It makes sense in writing job descriptions to use words that are keyed to the job evaluation factors.

Another essential step in effective job evaluation is to select and weigh the criteria (compensable factors) used to evaluate the job. Although there is not a lot of research in this area, it appears that the results are the same whether all factors or just a few factors are considered, especially if the job evaluation is carefully designed and scaled. Typical of the most frequently used factors for job evaluation are education, experience, amount of responsibility, job knowledge, work hazards and working conditions. It is important that the factors used be accepted as valid for the job by those being evaluated.

Once the method of evaluating the job (to be discussed) is chosen, the evaluators make the job evaluations. Basically, those familiar with the jobs tend to rate them higher, especially if they supervise the jobs. It seems useful for each committee member to evaluate each job individually. Then the evaluators should discuss each job on which the ratings differ significantly, factor by factor, until agreement is reached.

Job Evaluation Methods The four most frequently used job evaluation methods are:

Job ranking.
Factor comparison.

EXHIBIT 9–7 Comparison Job Evaluation Systems

Comparison Basis	Nonquantitative Comparison (Job as Whole)	Quantitative Comparison (Parts of Factors of Jobs)
Job versus job	Job ranking	Factor comparison
Job versus scale	Job grading or classification	Point system

Classification.

The point system.[32]

Job evaluation systems can be classified as shown in Exhibit 9–7.

Ranking of Jobs The system used primarily in smaller, simpler organizations, is job ranking. Instead of analyzing the full complexity of jobs by evaluating parts of jobs, the job-ranking method has the evaluator rank order *whole* jobs, from the simplest to the challenging.

Sometimes this is done by providing the evaluator with the information on cards. The evaluator sorts the jobs into ranks, allowing for the possibility of ties. If the list of jobs is large, the paired-comparison method, whereby each job is compared to every other job being evaluated, can be used. The evaluator counts the number of times a particular job is ranked above another, and the one with the largest number of highest rankings is the highest ranked. There is no assurance that the ranking thus provided is composed of equal-interval ranks. The differential between the highest job and next highest may not be exactly the same as that between the lowest and next lowest. If the system is used in an organization with many jobs to be rated, it is clumsy to use, and the reliability of the ratings is not good. Because of these problems, ranking is probably the least frequently used method of job evaluation.

Classification or Grading System The *classification* or *grading system* groups a set of jobs together into a grade or classification. Then these sets of jobs are ranked in levels of difficulty or sophistication.

The most publicized example of a classification system is the United States Office of Personnel Management General Schedule (GS). It has 18 grades with 10 pay steps within the pay grades. This classification system is used for making compensation decisions for over 2.5 million employees. Exhibit 9–8 presents the federal government general schedule and pay steps.

Each grade has a general definition that differentiates it from other grades on the basis of skill, responsibility, effort, and working conditions. For example, a Grade GS–10 includes those jobs that have duties to:

---

[32] John D. McMillan and Cynthia G. Brondi, "Job Evaluation: Generate the Numbers," *Personnel Journal,* November 1986, pp. 56–63.

EXHIBIT 9-8   General Schedule Pay Systems

	1	2	3	4	5	6	7	8	9	10
GS-1	$ 8,342	$ 8,620	$ 8,898	$ 9,175	$ 9,453	$ 9,615	$ 9,890	$10,165	$10,178	$10,439
2	9,381	9,603	9,913	10,178	10,292	10,595	10,898	11,201	11,504	11,807
3	10,235	10,576	10,917	11,258	11,599	11,940	12,281	12,622	12,963	13,304
4	11,490	11,873	12,256	12,639	13,022	13,405	13,788	14,171	14,554	14,937
5	12,354	13,282	13,710	14,138	14,566	14,994	15,422	15,850	16,279	16,706
6	14,328	14,806	15,284	15,762	16,240	16,718	17,196	17,674	18,152	18,630
7	15,922	16,453	16,984	17,515	18,046	18,577	19,108	19,639	20,170	20,701
8	17,634	18,222	18,810	19,398	19,986	20,574	21,162	21,750	22,338	22,926
9	19,477	20,126	20,775	21,424	22,073	22,722	23,371	24,020	24,669	25,318
10	21,449	22,164	22,879	23,594	24,309	25,024	25,739	26,454	27,169	27,884
11	23,566	24,352	25,138	25,924	26,710	27,496	28,282	29,068	29,854	30,640
12	28,245	29,187	30,129	31,071	32,013	32,955	33,897	34,839	35,731	36,723
13	33,586	34,706	35,326	36,946	38,066	39,186	40,306	41,426	42,546	43,666
14	39,689	41,012	42,335	43,658	44,981	46,004	47,627	48,950	50,273	51,696
15	46,485	48,241	49,797	51,353	52,909	54,465	56,021	57,577	59,133	60,689
16	54,765	56,580	58,405	60,230	62,055	63,390	65,705	67,530	69,055	
17	64,142	66,280	68,418	70,656	72,694					
18	75,177									

Source: *Federal Register* 46, no. 200, Friday, October 16, 1981, pp. 50,922.

A. Perform, under general supervision, highly difficult and responsible work along special technical, supervisory, or administrative lines in offices, business, or fiscal administration requiring:
   1. Somewhat extended specialized, supervisory, or administrative training and experience so that employee has demonstrated capacity for sound independent work.
   2. Thorough and fundamental knowledge of a specialized and complex subject matter, or of the profession, art, or science involved.
   3. Considerable latitude for the exercise of independent judgment.
B. To perform other work of equal importance, difficulty, and responsibility, and requiring comparable qualifications.

Examples of various jobs and their GS classification are janitor (light work, GS-1), sewing machine operator (GS-6), welder and machinist (GS-10), assistant department manager (GS-13), and instrument maker (GS-15).[33]

A welder or machinist who is classified as a GS-10 could be paid annually

---

[33] William H. Holley and Kenneth M. Jennings, *Personnel Management* (Hinsdale, Ill.: Dryden Press, 1983), p. 316.

between $21,449 and $27,884. The amount of specific pay for a GS–10 would be determined on the basis of when the person was hired, the seniority a person has in the grade, and the merit increases that have been earned for good performance.

The Point System The greatest number of job evaluation plans use the point system. It is the most frequently used because it is more sophisticated than ranking and classification systems, but it is relatively easy to use.

Essentially, the point system requires evaluators to quantify the value of the elements of a job. On the basis of the job description or interviews with job occupants, points are assigned to the degree of various compensable factors required to do the job. For example, skill required, physical and mental effort needed, degree of dangerous or unpleasant working conditions involved, and amount of responsibility involved in the job. When these are summed, the job has been evaluated.

Many point systems evaluate as many as 10 aspects or subaspects of each job. The aspects chosen should not overlap, should distinguish real differences between jobs, should be as objectively defined as possible, and should be understood and acceptable to both management and employees. Because all aspects are not of equal importance in all jobs, different weights reflecting the differential importance of these aspects to a job must be set. These weights are assigned by summing the judgments of several independent but knowledge-able evaluators. Thus, a clerical job might result in the following weightings: education required, 50 percent; experience required, 25 percent; complexity of job, 12 percent; responsibility for relationships with others, 8 percent; working conditions and physical requirements, 5 percent.

Once the weights are agreed upon, reference to a point manual is appropriate. Experience required by jobs varies, as does education. A point manual carefully defines degrees of points from first (lowest) to fifth, for example. Experience might be defined in this way:

First degree, up to and including three months	25 points
Second degree, more than three months but less than six	50 points
Third degree, more than six months to one year	75 points
Fourth degree, more than one year and up to three years	100 points
Fifth degree, more than three years	125 points

These definitions must be clearly defined and measurable to ensure consistency in ratings of requirements from the job description to the job evaluation. The preliminary point manuals must be pretested prior to widespread use.

As displayed in Exhibit 9–9, factor 1, education, has five degrees, as do factors 2 and 3. On the other hand factor 4 has three degrees, while factor 5 has four degrees. The maximum number of points is calculated by multiplying the points in the system by the assigned weights. For education, the maximum points would be 250 (50 percent weight multiplied by 500 maximum points).

An advantage of the point system is that it can be easily interpreted and

EXHIBIT 9–9   **Evaluation Points for Insurance Clerical Job**

Factor	Weight	Degree Points (500 point system)				
		1st	2nd	3rd	4th	5th
1. Education	50	50	100	150	200	250
2. Experience	25	25	50	70	100	125
3. Complexity of job	12	12	24	36	48	60
4. Relationships with others	8	8	24	40		
5. Working conditions	5	10	15	20	25	

explained to employees. On the other hand, it is a time-consuming process to develop a point system.

Factor Comparison The *factor comparison method* was originated by Eugene Benge. Like the point system, it permits the job evaluation process to be done on a factor-by-factor basis. It differs from the point method in that jobs are evaluated or compared against a "benchmark" of key points. A factor comparison scale, instead of a point scale, is used. Five universal job factors used to compare jobs are:

- *Responsibilities*—The money, human resource, records, and supervisor responsibilities of the job.
- *Skill*—The facility in muscular coordination and training in the interpretation of sensory requirements.
- *Physical effort*—The sitting, standing, walking, lifting, moving, and so on.
- *Mental effort*—The intelligence, problems solving, reasoning, and imagination.
- *Working conditions*—The environmental factors such as noise, ventilation, hours, heat, hazards, fumes, and cleanliness.

The evaluation committee follows six formal steps in examining jobs. First, the comparison factors are selected and defined. The five universal job factors will be used in working through an example. Factors, of course, could differ across executive supervisory, and operating employee jobs. Second, the benchmark or key jobs are selected. These are common jobs found in the firm's labor market. Often a committee is used to select from 10 to 20 benchmark jobs. Third, the evaluators rank the key jobs on each of the compensation factors. The ranking is based on job descriptions and job specifications. Four benchmark jobs for the Moser Manufacturing Company of Tulsa, Oklahoma, are presented in Exhibit 9–10.

Fourth, job evaluators allocate a part of each key job's wage rate to each job factor as shown in Exhibit 9–11. The proportion of each wage assigned to the different critical factors depends on the importance of the factor. Each evaluator first makes an independent decision. Then the committee or group of

EXHIBIT 9-10   Ranking Four Benchmark Jobs by Factors

	Factors				
Jobs	Responsibility	Skill	Physical Effort	Mental Effort	Working Conditions
Tool and die maker	2*	1	2	2	3
Shipping clerk	4	2	1	4	4
Systems analyst	1	4	4	1	2
Secretary	3	3	3	3	1

* 1 is high, 4 is low. For working conditions, the higher the rating the poorer the conditions.

evaluators meets to arrive at an apportionment consensus about assigning money values to the factors.

Fifth, the two sets of ratings (the ranking and assigned money), are compared to determine the evaluator's consistency. Exhibit 9-12 displays this consistency of rating comparisons at Moser.

Sixth, a job comparison chart displays the benchmark jobs, and the money values for each factor is constructed. The chart is used to rate other jobs as compared to the benchmark jobs. These jobs would be placed in an appropriate position in the chart. Exhibit 9-13 illustrates the Moser job comparison chart.

The factor comparison method has some advantages and disadvantages. One advantage is that it is a step-by-step formal method of evaluation. Furthermore, it permits you to see how the differences in factor rankings translate into dollars and cents. Probably the most negative aspect of the factor comparison method is its complexity. Although the method is easy to explain to subordinates, it is difficult to show them how such a system is developed. There is also the issue of subjectivity. Despite the systematic nature of the factor comparison method, it still relies on a committee or a group of evaluators' subjective judgment. Of course, subjectivity is also a problem with each of the other job evaluation methods.

EXHIBIT 9-11   Apportionment of Wages to Benchmark Jobs

		Factors				
Jobs	Hourly Wage =	Responsibility +	Skill +	Physical Effort +	Mental Effort +	Working Conditions
Tool and die maker	$8.40	2.00 (2)	2.50 (1)	1.60 (2)	1.50 (2)	.80 (3)
Shipping clerk	5.80	.60 (4)	1.90 (2)	1.80 (1)	.60 (4)	.90 (4)
Systems analyst	7.10	2.30 (1)	1.10 (4)	1.20 (4)	1.90 (1)	.60 (2)
Secretary	5.00	1.00 (3)	1.50 (3)	1.30 (3)	1.00 (3)	.20 (1)

EXHIBIT 9–12 **Rank versus Money Comparisons**

Jobs	Responsibility R† $‡		Skill R $		Physical Effort R $		Mental Effort R $		Working Condition* R $	
Tool and die maker	2	2	1	1	2	2	2	2	3	3
Shipping clerk	4	4	2	2	1	1	4	4	4	4
Systems analyst	1	1	4	4	4	4	1	1	2	2
Secretary	3	3	3	3	3	3	3	3	1	1

* Note that working condition is reversed—poorer conditions receive more money.
† Rankings.
‡ Money amounts.

Pay Classes, Rate Ranges, and Classifications

After completion of the job evaluation, the pay-structure process is completed by establishing pay classes, rate ranges, and job classifications.[34] A *pay class* (also called a *pay grade*) is a grouping of a variety of jobs that are similar in terms of work difficulty and responsibility. If an organization uses the factor comparison or point system of job evaluation, this is accomplished by use of

---

EXHIBIT 9–13 **Moser Job Comparison Chart**

Money Amounts	Responsibility	Skill	Physical Effort	Mental Effort	Working Conditions
$2.50		Tool and die maker			
	Systems analyst				
2.00	Tool and die maker	Shipping clerk		Systems analyst	
			Shipping Tool and die maker		
1.50		Secretary	Tool and die maker	Tool and die maker	
			Secretary Systems analyst		
1.00	Secretary	Systems analyst		Secretary	
					Shipping clerk Tool and die maker
0.50	Shipping clerk			Shipping clerk	Systems analyst
					Secretary

---

[34] Nash and Carroll, *Management of Compensation.*

EXHIBIT 9–14   **Pay Classes and Pay Curve**

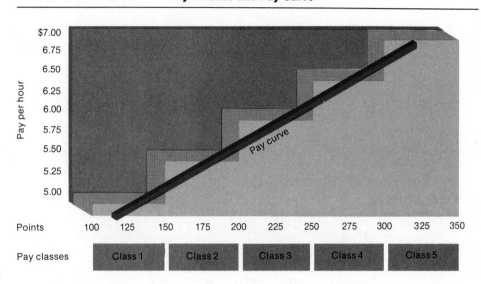

pay-class graphs or point conversion tables. An example of a pay-class graph used by Dexter electronics is given in Exhibit 9–14.

At intervals of say 50 points, a new pay class is marked off. The pay curve illustrated in Exhibit 9–14 is based on information obtained from wage and salary surveys and modified as necessary to reflect Dexter's policy to pay at, above, or below prevailing rates. This exhibit shows a single-rate pay system rather than a rate-range system in that all jobs within a given labor class will receive the same rate of pay. In this example, pay classes are determined by the point value determined through a point system method of job evaluation used by Dexter.

Exhibit 9–15, another pay-class graph, demonstrates how wage and salary survey data are combined with job evaluation information to determine the pay structure for an organization. A compensation trend line is derived by first establishing the general pay pattern, plotting the surveyed rates of key jobs against the point value of these jobs. The trend line can then be determined by a variety of methods, ranging from a simple eyeball estimate of the pay trend to a formalized statistical formulation of a regression line based on the sum of the least squares method. The appropriate pay rate for any job can then be ascertained by calculating the point value of the job and observing the pay level for that value as shown by the trend line. By taking a set percentage (e.g., 15 percent) above and below the trend line, minimum and maximum; limit lines can be established. These limit lines can be used to help set the minimum and maximum rates if a pay range is used instead of a single rate for each job. The limit lines can also be used in place of the trend line for those organiza-

EXHIBIT 9–15   Pay-Class Graph with Range of Pay

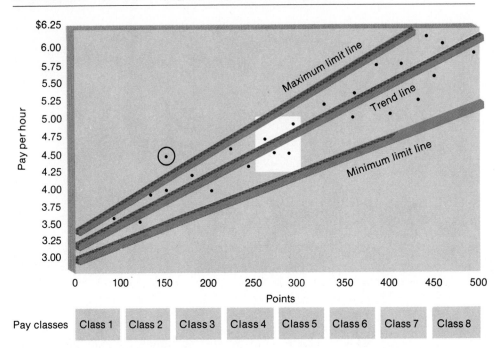

tions that wish to establish pay levels above market—the pay leaders—or those that want to pay slightly under the prevailing rates.

Although it is possible for a pay class to have a single pay rate (as in Exhibit 9-14), the more likely condition is a range of pays. These ranges can have the same spread, or the spread can be increased as the pay rate increases. An example of a pay structure with increasing rate ranges is given in Exhibit 9-15. The ranges are usually divided into a series of steps. Thus, within Class 4 (250–300 points), there might be four steps:

	Pay Range
Step 1	$4.20–4.40
Step 2	4.40–4.60
Step 3	4.60–4.85
Step 4	4.85–5.10

These steps in effect are money raises within a pay range to help take care of the needs of individual pay determination (to be discussed shortly). Similar ranges would ordinarily be determined for all other classes to illustrate the pay structure for all jobs in the pay plan. Within-grade increases are typically based upon seniority, merit, or a combination of both, as described in the next section.

The entire pay structure should be evaluated periodically and adjusted to reflect changes in labor market conditions, level of inflation, and other factors

P/HRM · IN · ACTION

Mary

Mary sat at her desk a few days later. She thought over the problems the bank was facing again. She had spent weeks learning about pay surveys, job evaluation, pay classifications, rate ranges—all the aspects of pay-level and pay-structure decisions. CNB had done nothing about any of these issues. How could they keep employees without much attention to pay practices?

As Mary wondered about these issues, she had the report she'd prepared for her P/HRM class before her. It compared the turnover and absenteeism rates at CNB to those of other banks like it in the Pittsburgh area. CNB was clearly in the worst shape.

She had interviewed supervisors and others who had talked with employees leaving CNB. A large number gave better pay as the reason for leaving. And even more often, fairness in treatment of pay was the reason given. She'd passed her report on to Guido. But would anything happen other than receiving a grade in class for her report?

affecting pay. Although the typical structure is shown as linear, generally a more fair structure is curvilinear, with rates increasing exponentially as pay increases.

In Exhibit 9–15 the pay rate for a set of class 2 jobs is well above the maximum limit line. These jobs are paid too much relative to other jobs in the firm. These types of jobs are called *red circle* or overrated. They were presented in the exhibit as ⊙.[35] Management has several methods that can be used with overpaid red circle jobs. One is to freeze the pay to individuals with the red circle rates until pay increases in the other jobs bring them in line. Second, transferring or promoting employees in red circle jobs so that their rate of pay can be justified may be possible.[36] Third, the rate may have to be cut back to the maximum level for the job class. The pay-class graph can illustrate red

---

[35] Jobs can also be underrated and underpaid. They would be red circled or, as found in the Dexter Company, they are green circled, which indicates an underrated level.

[36] Paul R. Reed and Mark J. Kroll, "Red-Circle Employees: A Wage Scale Dilemma," *Personnel Journal*, February 1987, pp. 92–95.

circle jobs, but solving the problems associated with them is a challenging task for managers and compensation experts.

SUMMARY

Chapter 9 has begun the discussion of compensation that will be concluded in Chapter 10. The objectives of compensation have been stated, and premises dealing with the multiple meanings of pay at work, pay level, external and internal factors influencing pay level, and pay structures and their determination have been covered.

To summarize the major points covered in this chapter:

1. Pay is the monetary reward paid by an organization for the work done by an employee.
2. To promote employee satisfaction, compensation should be adequate, equitable, balanced, cost effective, secure, incentive providing, and acceptable to the employee.
3. Compensation decisions are the joint responsibility of operating executives, supervisors, and P/HRM specialists.
4. Because of individual employee preferences and jobs, research on motivation and compensation should be directed to examine:
   a. The range of behaviors that pay may affect positively or negatively.
   b. The amount of change pay can influence.
5. Determining the worth of a job is difficult, because it involves measurement and subjectively based decisions. Using systematic job evaluation procedures is recommended for determing a job's worth.
6. The four most widely used methods of job evaluation are job ranking, classification, the point method, and factor comparisons.
7. Most managers group similar jobs into what are called pay classes or rate ranges.
8. The wage curve (or line) illustrates the average target wage for each pay class.

Questions for Review and Discussion

1. What is compensation? How does it fit into the total reward system of an organization?
2. Why is comparable worth considered to be a political issue?
3. Does compensation affect employee satisfaction? Performance?
4. What problems would a P/HRM have explaining or correcting jobs that are overrated (red circle jobs)?
5. Discuss the major laws affecting compensation. How do they affect the organization's pay level?

A RETURN TO THE P/HRM · IN · ACTION

Guido

Guido called Mary the next day to go over her findings. She decided to use her term report to illustrate possible solutions for CNB's dilemma.

Guido: I've read your paper. I like the way it deals with the problems here at CNB. It was a good idea to calculate how much turnover costs the bank. This may have an impact on Joe. You've also prepared recommendations for changes in our pay program, as I asked you to do. Let me see if I understand your plan. Basically, you propose setting up a point system of job evaluation and establishing standardized pay classes and ranges that would allow for pay variations based on individual pay factors. You also recommend that we set up a pay policy according to going wages. In view of our profit picture, that seems reasonable. I'll present this plan to Poppa Joe tomorrow, with my endorsement.

Mary: I'll be interested to see if it has any impact.

The next day Guido gave the report to Joe to read and comment on.

(This case will be continued in Chapter 10.)

6. What is a pay survey? What is the best way to conduct a survey?
7. What are the organization factors affecting pay level?
8. How does management's pay strategy affect pay level? Give an example of the most typical pay strategy. Which strategy would you pursue?
9. What are the external factors affecting pay level decisions? How do they affect the organization's pay level?
10. Why is the reliability of ranking jobs a problem in this type of job evaluation technique?
11. What is job evaluation? What are the techniques for performing it?
12. Distinguish and describe the interrelationships among pay classes, rate changes, and pay classifications.

GLOSSARY

Classification or Grading System. A job evaluation method that groups jobs together into a grade or classification.

Comparable Worth. An issue that has been raised by women and the courts in recent years. It means that the concept of equal pay for equal jobs should be expanded to the notion of equal pay for comparable jobs. If a job is comparable to other jobs as determined by job content analysis, that job should be comparable.

Exempt Employee. A person working in a job that is not subject to the provisions of the Fair Labor Standards Act (1938) with respect to minimum wage and overtime pay. Most professional, executives, administrators, and outside salespersons are classified as exempt.

Factor Comparison Method. A job evaluation method that uses a factor-by-factor comparison. A factor comparison scale, instead of a point scale, is used. Five universal job factors used to compare jobs are; responsibilities, skills, physical effort, mental effort, and working conditions.

Job Evaluation. The formal process by which the relative worth of various jobs in the organization is determined for pay purposes.

Minimum Wage. The Fair Labor Standards Act of 1938, as amended, states that all employers covered by the law must pay an employee at least a minimum wage. In 1984 the minimum was $3.35 per hour.

Nonexempt Employee. A person working in a job that is subject to the minimum wage and overtime pay provisions of the Fair Labor Standards Act. Blue-collar and clerical workers are two major groups of nonexempt employees.

Pay Class. A convenient grouping of a variety of jobs that are similar in their work difficulty and responsibility requirements.

Pay Surveys. Surveys of the compensation paid to employees by all employers in a geographic area, an industry, or an occupational group.

Point System. The most widely used job evaluation method. It requires evaluators to quantify the value of the elements of a job. On the basis of the job description or interviews with job occupants, points are assigned to the degree of various factors required to do the job.

Ranking of Jobs. A job evaluation method often used in smaller organizations, in which the evaluator ranks jobs from the simplest to the most challenging—for example, clerk to research scientist.

Red Circle Rates. A pay rate above a wage or salary level that is considered maximum for the job class. This means that the job is overpaid and overrated.

APPLICATION CASE   9–1

The Comparable Worth Debate*

Twin Oaks Hospital is a privately owned facility that serves Lexington, Colorado (population approximately 250,000). The 100-bed hospital has a staff of 350 employees, including over 200 nurses and 40 clerical and secretarial employees (an almost exclusively female group). In the last month, discontent concerning pay levels has been mounting among the hospital's nurses and secretarial/clerical employees. Discontent was spurred by recent developments at the Lexington Memorial Hospital, a public facility. There, the hospital administration agreed to demands by nurses and secretarial/clerical workers for a 5 percent pay increase. The administration further agreed to launch a job evaluation program that would evaluate the nursing and secretarial/clerical jobs on the basis of comparable worth. The administrators pledged that the study's findings would be used as the basis for any further pay adjustments.

The administration's moves came after demonstrations by nurses and clerical/secretarial workers and by a clear threat of unionization by the Union of American Nurses and the United Office Workers. Union organizers had held discussions with the nurses and office employees, and circulated the results of one comparable-worth study to illustrate the extent of pay inequities (shown in Exhibit 1).

David Hardy, director of personnel at Twin Oaks, was acutely aware of the troubles brewing at his hospital. He knew that union organizers were meeting with employees and distributing the study flier. Overall, Twin Oak's pay levels for its nurses and office staff were very similar to the levels at Lexington Memorial before the 5 percent increase. However, the levels were not competitive with compensation available in Denver which is located about 100 miles north of Lexington. In the last week, Hardy had met with representatives of the two employee groups at their request. There, the spokeswomen made three requests: An immediate 5 percent pay increase, the establishment of a job evaluation program based on the concept of comparable worth, and a pledge to make wage adjustments based on study findings.

Hardy informed James Bledsoe, the hospital director, of the employees' requests; Bledsoe asked for a recommendation for action within three days. Before developing an action plan, Hardy met with his two top aides (Janet Sawyer and Charles Cooper) for an initial, informal discussion of the situation. In Hardy's view, the key question focused on whether to evaluate the jobs based on comparable worth.

---

* Written by Kim Stewart. The situation, names and characters are fictitious. Facts and some perspectives are drawn from: Peter B. Olney, Jr., "Meeting the Challenge of Comparable Worth: Part I," *Compensation and Benefits Review,* March-April 1987, pp. 34–44; Barbara R. Bergmann, "Pay Equity—Surprising Answers to Hard Questions," *Challenge,* May-June 1987, pp. 45–51; and Daniel Seligman, "Pay Equity is a Bad Idea," *Fortune,* May 14, 1984, p. 133ff.

EXHIBIT 1   Findings from One Comparable Worth Study

	Head Nurse	Electrician	Clerk/Typist	Truck Driver
Knowledge and Skills	**244** RN license; good judgment; people skills	**122** Apprenticeship; technical know-how	**106** High-school diploma; type 60 wpm	**61** Chauffeur's license
Mental Demands	**106** Life-and-death decisions; administer doctor's orders; emotional stability	**30** Troubleshooting; public safety	**26** Always told what to do; pressure to get work done; monotony	**10** Heavy traffic; speed limits
Responsibility	**122** Supervise patient care; manage ward staff	**30** Order supplies; safe wiring	**35** Neat documents; manage small tasks	**13** Truck maintenance; on-time deliveries
Working Conditions	**11** Always on feet; constant demands; rotating shifts	**15** Cramped quarters; strenuous assignments; fairly dangerous	**0** Padded seat; constant interruptions; regular hours	**13** Crazy schedule; tight space, long hours
Total Points	**483**	**197**	**167**	**97**
Monthly Salary	**$2,390**	**$2,047**	**$1,264**	**$1,670**

"I favor launching the job evaluation program," said Janet Sawyer. "Nationwide, there is a disturbingly large gap between the pay levels of predominantly male and female jobs. Consider that there's no difference in the median education levels of men and women—about 12.6 years. Yet with the same median amount of education, women earn 40.8 percent of a man's median pay. If we take a close look at our compensation levels across jobs from the perspective of comparable worth, we'd likely find some pretty disturbing gaps of our own.

"There's a growing precedent for comparable worth-based pay adjustments," she continued. "Over 30 states have comparable worth bills pending or commissions that are studying the issue. Minnesota has had comparable worth-based pay policies for its employees since 1983, and several city governments have implemented the concept."

"That's precedent in the public sector, not private industry," said Charles Cooper. "I would favor a pay increase, perhaps 5 percent, to keep us competitive with Lexington Memorial. However, agreeing to a job evaluation based on comparable worth is opening the door to a very questionable and costly concept.

"I'm troubled by the concept of comparable worth for three reasons," he continued. "First, if you implement comparable worth, you destroy our free market system. The market does discriminate but on the basis of supply and demand which accurately reflects a job's worth. The market is blind to gender."

"I'm not so sure about its visual shortcomings in that regard," Janet said.

"I agree with Janet that a sizable wage gap does exist," Charles continued. "But according to some studies, much of that gap is not due to gender. For example, I've just reviewed a study by the U.S. Labor Department that found that over 50 percent of the gap between men's and women's pay is due to vocational training, the industries that women choose, and geographical location. The remaining gap could be due to sex discrimination, but frankly I'm not willing to destroy the free market system to find out.

"Second, there's the issue of implementation," Charles continued. "Here, comparable worth floats in a sea of subjectivity. If we conduct the evaluation, we must evaluate all jobs in the hospital, not just the nurses, secretaries, and clerical workers. Doing so requires one evaluation system with one set of job factors. Which factors do we use? How do we weigh the factors in calculating a job's worth? Few objective guidelines exist for us to use.

"And suppose we did implement comparable worth," he continued. "We might create internal pay equity across our jobs but it would not address our need to be externally competitive. For example, suppose we determine that two jobs are very similar in worth, almost identical. Using comparable worth as a basis, we provide the same pay for both jobs. However, marketwise we're paying far too much for one job and far too little for another. How do we attract people for the underpaid position? We end up with too many applicants for jobs already filled and not enough for jobs that go unfilled.

"Third, there's our primary concern—costs. We won't know how much comparable worth will cost us until we're into the evaluation program. However, given adjustments made in clerical and secretarial pay by government offices that have implemented comparable worth, the cost should be hefty. Look at the estimated price tag for implementing comparable worth nationwide—over $150 billion. Business and society would pay the bill via higher inflation and lowered productivity."

"We could conduct an effective job evaluation program—other companies have," Janet countered. "General Electric has overhauled its job evaluation methods to reflect comparable worth concerns. BankAmerica has also made some changes; it's incorporated job factors into predominately female jobs that weren't there before such as physical demands for computer VDT operators and bank tellers. We could also talk with Lexington Memorial about how they plan to conduct their job evaluation program.

"I'd suggest that we develop a job evaluation plan that's tailor-made for our hospital," Janet continued. "We could form a committee composed of 6 to 10 members with representatives from all functional areas. The committee would be charged with identifying the elements that should be considered in evaluating all jobs in the hospital. It would also determine the weights for all factors. For some factors such as knowledge and experience, accountability and judgment would be more difficult. But we could do it; others have."

"What about costs?" David Hardy asked.

"Charles is right," Janet replied. "We won't really know until the evaluation task is complete. But as a very rough estimate, I'd say we would be raising the nursing and office workers' pay by at least 10 percent, probably more. However, we can phase in the increase over a number of years, a bit at a time."

"What happens if the evaluation determines that some male-dominated jobs are overpaid?" asked Charles. "Do we reduce their pay while boosting the women's? Threat of unionization is a factor in regard to the nurses and clerical staff. What about the possibility of male employees unionizing because of pay cuts?"

"We'd have to address that question," Janet replied. "But given that most of our staff are women, overall our employees would be benefitting from comparable worth."

"You know, I've heard a lot about women benefitting from comparable worth," said David Hardy. "But over the long term, I'm not so sure. It seems to me that if the concept is implemented nationwide, companies will have a higher wage bill with no increase in productivity. So they may pay the bill by reducing the number of jobs with the highest wage increases—jobs that women hold. Many women may find themselves out of work."

"That might be," Janet said. "However, that hasn't happened in countries like Australia and Great Britain that have actively closed much of the gender-based wage gap in recent years."

"Any other thoughts?" asked David.

"We should take a good look at a pay increase and perhaps even more than the 5 percent requested," Charles said. "But stay away from comparable worth. For private business, it is unchartered and dangerous territory."

"This whole situation has raised questions in my mind about the fairness and validity of our pay structure," Janet said. "We may have problems. Let's look at it; and let's consider comparable worth. We may not be able to go the full 90 yards. How about a first few steps?"

Questions for Thought

1. In your view, is comparable worth a legitimate strategy for determining job compensation?

2. As the director of Twin Oaks' P/HRM department, what recommendations would you make to James Bledsoe?

3. From a P/HRM perspective, what are the challenges of implementing comparable worth?

COMPENSATION: METHODS AND POLICIES

P/HRM · IN · ACTION

(Continued from Chapter 9)

Joe Paderewski sat in his big office in the rear of the Cardeson National Bank. Guido Panelli, his executive vice president, came in to drop off Mary Renfro's report on compensation, and to discuss other problems CNB was having with people and pay.

"For one thing, Joe, our executive turnover has been increasing. Mary is wondering if the executive compensation package is contributing to the problem. The employees who have quit have indicated a lack of adequate compensation, but we all know this is the most acceptable reason to give an employer for leaving. In any case, it's a problem, and we have to face it."

"CNB pays the going rate for salaries," Joe declared. "And there's our bonus system—when profits allow it."

"But some of those leaving said their new employers would have performance-share programs," Guido said.

Joe wondered what that meant, and he thought, "Maybe I should hire a consultant to advise us on the executive compensation program."

Meanwhile, over at Branch 1, Tom Nichols, the manager of the branch, was having a meeting with the tellers' supervisors to discuss pay. He hadn't wanted to attend the meeting; he didn't like meetings, and he knew this one would be bad. The tellers were never satisfied with their pay. Back in school, Tom had learned that pay was one thing that was never easily settled; people were always griping about it.

The meeting went like this:

Chet: Tom, we're here because the troops are unhappy.

Tom: The troops are always unhappy.

Chet: Sure, but this time it's serious. My people are tired of punching time clocks and getting paid by the hour. Everyone else here at the bank gets salaries—52 weeks a year. Why don't my tellers?

Tom: Well, you know, it's always been done that way. Besides . . .

Chet: Don't give me that "it's-always-been-done-that-way" stuff. You can do something about it. Talk to Joe. My people want the security of a regular paycheck and the dignity of no time clock. You know the union's been around. What are we going to do about it?

The other supervisors shook their heads, and Tom didn't know what to say.

Branch 2 was having its own problems. One day there was an incident involving two tellers and a supervisor. It all started when the following dialogue took place:

Martha: Did you hear that Joanne makes $1.50 more an hour than me? I've been here longer than she has.

Sandra: Why not go to June about it? She's the boss.

Martha: (to June) How come Joanne makes $1.50 more than me? I've been here longer.

June: How do you know that's true? We don't reveal salaries around here, and it's against company policy to discuss other people's pay.

Martha: Never mind how I found out. And let's cut the company policy stuff.

(continued)

Why is Joanne paid more than I am?

It is now raise time again, and Joe is getting flak from all sides. He believes he can afford about 10 percent for raises. But who should get them?

After Guido left his office, Joe went over the situation in his mind. "Some deserve no raise, really," he thought. "Others deserve something; a few deserve a lot. But how should I divide the money? Should I really give no raise at all to some? With inflation what it is, that's like getting a pay cut, and they don't deserve *that*. And how much should the *average* employee get? The cost of living has gone up 7 percent. If I give them much more than that, there won't be enough to give big raises to the people who really deserve them, like Mary and Guido. And that says nothing about the people who deserve raises because, as Mary keeps saying, their base pay is too low, and what about the people who are being promoted? How am I going to allocate this raise money?"

After thinking it over, Joe decided to talk to Mary about the problems and her report. He asked her to come in and give him a brief summary of some of the major points about compensation she learned in the college course she had taken.

Joe: Mary, I'm having problems with pay again, as you know. Will you give me a rundown on some of the highlights of that course you took? I don't have a lot of time, though. That's why I'd rather have you tell me than read your report.

Mary: I know you don't have much time. Let's cover some basics that we haven't discussed already.

With that, Mary briefed Joe on pay methods, executive compensation, and some key compensation issues raised in the incidents she and Guido had told him about.

Let's pick up where we ended in Chapter 9 and complete the discussion of the seven criteria for effective compensation introduced there. A compensation system that meets all these criteria will accomplish the objective of providing a system of rewards equitable to employer and employee alike, so that the employee's satisfaction and production are both heightened. As was discussed, an effective compensation system should be:

Adequate. Chapter 9 gave the legal definition of adequacy as set forth in minimum wage and other legislation. The managerial definition of adequacy, or pay-level policies designed to pay the going wage, was also described.

Equitable. Chapter 9 discussed job evaluation as one technique to be used to attain equity. The present chapter will touch upon the related policy issue of whether all employees should be paid salaries.

Incentive providing. Chapter 9 discussed the theory behind the merit or incentive pay system. This chapter will discuss how incentive pay systems are designed and how raises are used as a form of incentive.

The other four criteria, which will be discussed primarily in this chapter, state that the compensation plan should be:

Secure. The extent to which the employee's pay seems secure to him or her.

Balanced. The extent to which pay is a reasonable part of the total reward package, which includes benefits, promotions, and so on. Chapter 11 discusses benefits.

Cost-effective. The extent to which the pay system is cost-effective for the organization.

Acceptable to the employee. Whether employees think the pay system makes sense. Three aspects of this will be discussed: whether pay should be secret; compensation communication to achieve acceptability; and employee participation in pay decision making.

METHODS OF PAYMENT

Employees can be paid for the time they work, the output they produce, or a combination of these two factors.

Payment for Time Worked

The majority of employees are paid for time worked in the form of wages or salaries. Paying for time worked and establishing compensation systems based on time were the compensation methods discussed in Chapter 9. Pay surveys are used to establish competitive pay for the industry, and job evaluation is the principal method for setting time-pay schedules.[1] Then, pay ranges, pay classifications, and similar tools are developed for individual pay determination, the final step in a time-based pay system.

Salaries for Everyone? An increasing number of employees are paid salaries. Exceptions are blue-collar and some clerical employees, who are paid hourly wages. One issue in the time-pay system is whether everyone should be paid a salary. (Tom Nichols' dilemma in dealing with hourly paid employees is an example.) Would you rather be paid strictly by the hour and not know your income week to week, month to month, or be paid a salary so you could plan your budget? In general, most blue-collar employees are given hourly pay, but there has been a movement to place all employees on salaries and give them the same benefits and working conditions others have. Firms such as IBM, Texas Instruments, Polaroid, and Avon have experimented with this plan.

One advantage claimed for this move is that blue-collar workers become more integrated into the organization, thus improving the climate of employee relations. No study claims that it improves productivity, and the reports of its

---

[1] Ellen Wojahn, "How to Value Your Employee," *Inc.*, August 1983, pp. 93–96.

effects on absenteeism are mixed.[2] Some studies claim absenteeism decreases. Others have found that it increases, but management controls and peer pressure later bring it down to acceptable levels.[3]

Some individuals propose that if all employees are paid salaries, it is possible that the long-run security of positions will be diminished. With hourly workers, if business is down it is relatively easy for an organization to reduce the hours worked daily or weekly, save the labor costs, and adjust to the realities of the marketplace. On the other hand, if everyone is on salary, management tends to look toward full layoffs or reduction in the labor force by attrition or terminations. *Providing salaries for everyone changes labor costs from variable to fixed with serious employment security implications.*

The success of a total-salaries program requires stable, mature, responsible employees, a cooperative union, willing supervisors, and a work load that allows continuous employment. Caution is urged in adopting this approach until the full range of possible consequences is carefully evaluated.[4]

The methods for paying employees on the basis of output are usually referred to as incentive forms of compensation. Incentives can be paid individually, to the work group, or on an enterprisewide basis. Incentive compensation assumes it is possible and useful to tie performance directly to pay, an issue discussed in detail in Chapter 9.

Merit Incentives

The wages and salaries of employees are typically adjusted at some point during the year. Historically, the adjustments have resulted in pay increases; at various times employees at Ford, Uniroyal, Continental Airlines, and U.S. Steel have given back some of their pay raises. When pay is adjusted upward it is usually based on four types of increases: *(a)* a general, across-the-board increase for all employees; *(b)* merit increases paid to employees based on some indicator of job performance; *(c)* a cost-of-living adjustment (COLA) based on the consumer price index (CPI); and *(d)* seniority.

Typically hourly employees in unionized firms are likely to receive general increases, whereas exempt salaried employees are more likely to receive merit pay increases.[5]

Exhibit 10–1 shows how a merit pay raise is related to performance ratings in Rialto Manufacturing Co., a medium-size firm located in Florida. The merit increase is also based on the individual's position in the salary classification. Typically, the lower the position in the range (first third), the larger the percentage of the merit increase.

---

[2] Edward E. Lawler III, *Pay and Organizational Effectiveness: A Psychological View* (New York: McGraw-Hill, 1971).

[3] Ibid.

[4] W. J. Keaney, "Pay for Performance? Not Always," *MSU Business Topics.* Spring 1979, p. 6.

[5] Charles A. Peck, *Compensating Salaried Employees During Inflation: General vs. Merit Increases* (New York: Conference Board, 1981), p. 9.

EXHIBIT 10–1 Rialto Manufacturing Co., Position in Salary Classification (1989)

Employee's Performance	Bottom Third	Middle Third	Top Third
Outstanding	12–15%	9–11%	5–8%
Good	8–11	6–8	4–5
Average	4–7	4–5	2–3
Marginally satisfactory	1–3	3	1
Unsatisfactory	No increase	No increase	No increase

Merit pay advocates propose that it is the most valid type of pay increase, since it is tied directly to performance.[6] Rewarding performers, instead of marginal or nonperformers, is claimed to be a powerful motivator. On the other hand, some individuals suggest that the validity of a merit pay system serving as an incentive rests on the quality of the performance evaluation system.[7] If the performance evaluation is biased, unreliable, or not well received by employees, the merit pay increase will be tainted. There is also the problem of receiving no increase or a small increase relative to others. This has a long-lasting effect and can demoralize the average or below-average performer. If a person is regularly performing below average, he or she must show improvement, be transferred, or be fired.[8] However, some individuals may have a bad year, and receiving no increase or a small increase may affect them for many years.[9]

Individual Incentives

Perhaps the oldest form of compensation is the individual incentive plan, in which the employee is paid for units produced. Today the individual incentive plan takes several forms: piecework, production bonus, and commissions.[10] These methods seek to achieve the incentive goal of compensation.

Straight piecework usually works like this. An employee is guaranteed an hourly rate (probably the minimum wage) for performing an expected minimum output (the standard). For production over the standard, the employer pays so much per piece produced. This is probably the most frequently used incentive pay plan. The standard is set through work measurement studies, as

---

[6] Bruce R. Ellig, "What's Ahead in Compensation and Benefits," *Management Review,* August 1983, pp. 56–61.

[7] E. James Brennan, "Compensation and Benefits," *Personnel Journal,* February 1984, p. 16

[8] Edward Mandt, "Who Is Superior and Who's Merely Very Good," *Across the Board,* April 1984, pp. 16–23.

[9] Philip Kienast, Douglas MacLachlan, Leigh McAlister, and David Sampson, "The Modern Way to Redesign Compensation Packages," *Personnel Administrator,* June 1983, pp. 127–33.

[10] Richard I. Henderson, *Compensation Management* (Reston, Va.: Reston Publishing, 1985, pp. 487–526).

modified by collective bargaining. The amount of the base rate and piece rates may emerge from data collected by pay surveys.

A variation of the straight piece rate is the differential piece rate. In this plan, the employer pays a smaller piece rate up to standard and then a higher piece rate above the standard. Research indicates that the differential piece rate is more effective than the straight piece rate, although it is *much less* frequently used.[11]

Production bonus systems pay an employee an hourly rate. Then a bonus is paid when the employee exceeds standard, typically 50 percent of labor savings. This system is not widely used.

Commissions are paid to sales employees. Straight commission is the equivalent of straight piecework and is typically a percentage of the price of the item. A variation of the production bonus system for sales is to pay the salesperson a small salary and commission or bonus when she or he exceeds standards (the budgeted sales goal).

Individual incentives are used more frequently in some industries (clothing, steel, textiles) than others (lumber, beverage, bakery), and more in some jobs (sales, production) than others (maintenance, clerical).

Are individual incentives effective? The research results are mixed.[12] Most studies indicate they do increase output. Although production increases, other performance criteria may suffer. For example, in sales, straight commission can lead to less attention being paid to servicing accounts. Working on hard-to-sell customers may be neglected because the salesperson will elect to sell to easy customers. There is also evidence that there are individual differences in the effect of incentives on performance.[13] Some employees are more inclined to perform better than others. This should not surprise you, since we know that people have varying motivations to work.

Incentive systems may be designed to affect outputs other than performance. For example, employers may use them to try to lower absenteeism and turnover. At least for some employees, incentive pay may lower satisfaction, however. Employees may be dissatisfied if they have to work harder or if they feel manipulated by the system.

For incentive plans to work, they must be well designed and administered. It appears that an individual incentive plan is likely to be more effective under certain circumstances.[14] These are when:

- The task is liked.
- The task is not boring.

---

[11] Edwin Locke et al., "Goods and Intentions as Mediators of the Effects of Monetary Incentive on Behavior," *Journal of Applied Psychology,* April 1968, pp. 104–21.

[12] George T. Milkovich and Jerry M. Newman, *Compensation* (Plano, Tex.: Business Publications, Inc., 1987), pp. 303–307.

[13] Mitchell Fein, "Let's Return to Now for Incentives," *Industrial Engineering,* January 1979, pp. 34–37.

[14] Allan Nash and Stephen Carroll, *The Management of Compensation* (Monterey, Calif.: Brooks/Cole Publishing, 1975), Chapter 7.

Reprinted by permission of George Dole

"Our incentive plan is quite simple. Make one mistake and your through!"

- The supervisor reinforces and supports the system.
- The plan is acceptable to employees and managers and probably includes them in the plan's design.
- The incentive is financially sufficient to induce increased output.
- Quality of work is not especially important.
- Most delays in work are under the employees' control.

Group Incentives

Piecework, production bonuses, commissions, and other individual incentives can also be paid to groups of individuals. This might be done when it is difficult to measure individual output, when cooperation is needed to complete a task or project, and when management feels this is a more appropriate measure on which to base incentives. Group incentive plans also reduce administrative costs.

Group incentive plans are used less frequently than individual incentive plans. Less research has been done on group incentives, though some studies suggest that group incentives are less effective than other incentive plans but more effective than straight-time wages or salaries.[15] A problem is that the

---

[15] Manual London and Greg Oldham, "A Comparison of Group and Individual Incentive Plans," *Academy of Management Journal*, March 1977, pp. 34–41.

group may not work well together, or less motivated members might decide to coast along on the work of others.

There are a number of logical reasons why a group incentive plan is used. In some situations, jobs and work output are so interrelated that it is impossible to specifically pinpoint individual performance. In this situation a group incentive could be used. The Japanese have used group incentives to help foster group cohesiveness and reduce jealousy. They assume that rewarding only one individual or a few workers will discourage a sense of teamwork.[16]

Although the Japanese assumptions about teamwork may have some merit, there are disadvantages with group incentive plans. When an individual does not perceive a connection between individual effort and reward there may be a dampening of motivation. In the United States, there is an individual spirit and self-confidence that is not always fully supported by a teamwork or group approach. Thus, there may be a clash between group incentive pay plans and societal norms.

Organization Incentive Plans

In an attempt to minimize the problems of interindividual and intergroup competition, some organizations have elected to use organization-level incentive plans. Competition can result in withholding information or resources, political gamesmanship, not helping others, and even sabotaging the work of others. These behaviors can certainly be costly to an organization that uses this type of plan.

In an interesting use of an organization incentive plan, Robert Collings, president of Data Terminal Systems (DTS) used a vacation reward program.[17] DTS was experiencing some growing problems with too much interdepartmental conflict and jealousy. Collings gave employees an offer that was difficult to refuse: If the firm doubled sales and earnings he would treat everyone to a week's vacation in Disney World or London. Sales didn't quite make that goal, but earnings more than doubled. Collings closed the doors for one week and off the employees went (310 employees, 326 dealers, and about 300 husbands, wives, and friends [they paid their own way]). The vacation incentive cost DTS about $200,000.

The next year, Collings offered a trip to Rome. Again the goals were met and off the company went. Each employee received full pay, most expenses, $100 spending money, and cost rates for their families. The Rome travels and leisure cost DTS about $500,000. But DTS remained committed to organizationwide incentives because the entire employee team was able to pull together to accomplish a common or superordinate goal.

Four approaches to incentive plans are used at the organizational level: suggestion systems, company group incentive plans, profit sharing, and stock ownership plans.

---

[16] John P. Alston, "Awarding Bonuses the Japanese Way," *Business Horizons,* September–October, 1982, pp. 6–8.

[17] S. Solomon, "How a Whole Company Earned Itself a Roman Holiday," *Fortune,* January 15, 1979, pp. 80–83.

Drawing by Herbert Goldberg: © 1974 The New Yorker Magazine, Inc.

"Dear Sir: Here are 2,000 suggestions for the betterment and efficiency of the corporation. One . . ."

Suggestion Systems Many large- and medium-sized organizations have suggestion systems designed to encourage employee input for improvements in organization effectiveness. Typically, the employee submits the suggestion in writing, perhaps placing it in a suggestion box. If, after being screened by a committee, the idea is tried and proved useful, the employee receives a financial reward. If the savings due to the idea are hard to compute, the employee is given a standard reward, such as $25 or $100. If they are measurable, the employee receives a percentage of the first year's savings, typically 10 to 20 percent.

Effective administration of the suggestion program is essential to its success. General Electric has disbursed over $3 million to its employees in one year for more than 69,000 suggestions.[18] The reasons for rejecting a suggestion must be carefully explained to the submitter. If a group idea is successful, it is useful to reward the whole group rather than an individual. In general, suggestion systems seem to be useful incentive plans. But this is not always true. Some of the reasons for failure are:

1. Management lacks interest and fails to support the system.

2. There has been insufficient time to review and analyze the suggestions.

3. Those developing suggestions fear the impact of changes brought about by the suggestions on co-workers (e.g., improving technology, equipment, and work flow may result in layoffs or cutbacks in overtime pay).

---

[18] Henderson, *Compensation Management*, p. 519.

4. Supervisors consider suggestions to be a personal threat.[19]

Company Group Incentive Plans Several companies have developed elaborate group incentive and participation schemes that generally have been quite successful. Productivity, or sharing plans, which are now referred to as gainsharing plans, are specifically designed for sharing the benefits of improved productivity, cost reductions, or quality improvement.[20] The most successful group incentive or productivity sharing plan at a single company is the Lincoln Electric Plan.[21] The benefits of the plan are impressive: stable prices for customers, good employee-management relations, and large financial rewards to employees. Individual workers have received huge bonuses year in and out, into the thousands of dollars, in addition to competitive wages. From 1933 to 1951, the bonuses per worker averaged $40,000! For 1987, the year-end bonus averaged $18,773 per employee. The employee's share in the bonus is based on a merit rating three times a year.[22]

Lincoln Electric, with $370 million yearly in sales of welding and similar equipment, has multiple incentives for its workers tied to a participation scheme. An advisory board of several executives and about 30 employees reviews and makes suggestions for company improvements. The suggestion system pays 50 percent of savings in the first year. The base rate of wages is a piece rate. The firm also has a stock purchase plan in which about two thirds of the employees participate; they now own about one third of the total stock. The stock is privately traded and not sold on any exchange.

Lincoln Electric has been extraordinarily successful in mobilizing employee energies. Employees hire the replacements for vacancies in their work group. The company basically subcontracts the work to the work group, using its past performance and time studies as standards. When these standards are beaten, the employees share generously. This bonus is not used as a substitute for adequate wages and benefits, either. Needless to say, some individuals bid to go to work for Lincoln Electric.

Scanlon Plan The Scanlon Plan is a combination group incentive, suggestion, and employee participation scheme that has been adopted by primarily small- and medium-sized manufacturing firms.[23] It is named after Joseph Scanlon, its designer. The Scanlon Plan avoids many of the problems of the other group incentive schemes. Here is how it works. Each department of the firm has a production committee composed of the foreman and employee representatives elected by the members or appointed by the union. The committee screens the suggestions for improvements made by employees and management. The number of suggestions that come from workers in these plans is about double

---

[19] Ibid., pp. 379–80.

[20] Christopher S. Miller and Michael H. Schuster, "Gainsharing Plans: A Comparative Analysis," *Organizational Dynamics*, Summer 1987, pp. 44–67.

[21] Bruce G. Posner, "Right From The Start," *Inc.*, August 1988, pp. 95–96; and James Lincoln, *Incentive Management* (Cleveland, Oh.: Lincoln Electric Co., 1986, pp. 10–12).

[22] Harvey Shore, "Mr. Lincoln and His System," *Business Quarterly*, Summer 1986, pp. 10–12.

[23] R. J. Bullock and Edward E. Lawler III, "Gainsharing: A Few Questions and Fewer Answers," *Human Resource Management*, Spring 1984, pp. 18–20.

the normal suggestion-plan rate, and about 80 perent of them are usable. If accepted, the cost of savings is paid to the work group, not just to the person suggesting it.

The plan also involves a wage formula. Gains from increased productivity are paid in bonus form to all employees: operative workers, supervisors, indirect workers such as typists, and salespersons. They receive bonuses in proportional shares. Management receives its share of productivity gains in increased profits.

Exhibit 10–2 shows how a company uses the Scanlon Plan. A database year (1986 in this case) is used to calculate the Scanlon ratio of 30 percent. In 1988, sales increased to $1.2 million; according to the Scanlon ratio, the payroll costs should be $360,000. However, because of worker suggestions, improved efficiency, and better work methods, the actual 1988 payroll costs were only $310,000. Thus, a savings of $50,000 was achieved. Workers typically would share in 75 percent of the savings or $37,500. The remaining $12,500 would be given to the company. The $37,500 was distributed to employees based on their wage levels.

Advocates of the Scanlon Plan contend that there are positive results for everyone. These include increased participation by employees, better acceptance of change on everyone's part, greater efficiency for the company, and improved union-management relations. Despite their promise, a number of Scanlon Plans have failed. The plans have had more success when there are fewer than 1,000 participants and when employees fully understand the features of the plan.

The Scanlon Plan is a promising incentive system. The ultimate success of the plan requires management involvement and commitment. All employees must provide their fair share of suggestions and work. The union must develop a new degree of cooperation. It is likely to be more successful in small- and medium-sized organizations. It also has worked well in troubled companies, providing there are the necessary conditions of participation, communication, and identification.

Improshare Mitchell Fein developed an industrial-engineering-based produc-

---

EXHIBIT 10–2   A Company Scanlon Plan for 1988

1986 Database Year

Average sales value of production for 1987	= $1,000,000
Average payroll costs for 1987	= 300,000
Scanlon ratio = $\frac{\$300,000}{\$1,000,000}$	= 30%

1988

Average sales value of production	= $1,200,000
Allowable payroll cost	= .30 ($1,200,000)
	= 360,000
Actual payroll cost	= 310,000
Savings available for bonus distribution	= $50,000

tivity measurement and sharing plan in the mid-1970s, which he calls *Improshare*. This plan uses past production records to establish base performance standards. Typically, employees (hourly and salaried) and the organization share equally in all productivity gains.

The first step is to identify those participants in the plan. Next, a base period, the base period product cost, and the base productivity factor (BPF) are determined.[24] The *base period product costs* are those costs used by management during the base period that represent the direct labor hours to produce a product by major operations and by total products being produced. The BPF represents the relationship in the base period between the actual hours worked by all employees in the plan and the value of work in standard worker hours produced by these employees, as determined by the product costs used by management for the base period.

Next, management calculates current performance in hours worked and output. A comparison can then be made between current output and hours worked against base period standards, which provides an hours-saved figure, called the *Improshare earned hours*. Management then uses the Improshare hours gained to calculate the employees' share of the improvements.

There are three controls established in the Improshare plan: (1) a ceiling on productivity improvements is set at 160 percent; (2) a cash buy-back of measurement standards is established; and (3) an 80/20 share of capital equipment improvements is set.[25]

Employees receive the productivity monthly gain as a percent increase in their regular pay. If particular gains are over 160 percent, management has the cash buy-back right. Suppose that gains are at 180 percent and that employees receive 50 percent of the difference (180 − 160) or .50 × 20 = 10 percent in a one-time-around bonus. Assume the employee's hourly rate of pay was $8 and work hours totaled 2,000 a year. The buy-back hours for the employee would be calculated as:

(20% buy-back) × 50% (division of gain) × $8 (per hour)
    × (2,000 (hours worked) = $1,600 (buy-back bonus paid to worker).

Management would then change the base period standard for future calculations:

$$1.8/1.6 = 2.25.$$

There is still significant interest in the concept of gainsharing such as that emphasized in the Scanlon and Improshare plans.[26] Gainsharing plans are usually introduced for a number of reasons: To make labor costs reflect the economic conditions surrounding the business; to improve manager-employee trust, respect, and communications; and to improve productivity. However, the

---

[24] Mitchell Fein, *An Alternative to Traditional Managing* (Hillsdale, N.J.: Mitchell Fein, 1980), pp. 28–41.

[25] Henderson, *Compensation Management*, pp. 504–505.

[26] Michael Schuster, "Gainsharing: Do It Right The First Time," *Sloan Management Review*, Winter 1987, pp. 17–25.

effectiveness of any gainsharing plan appears to depend upon such factors as: Initially defining the plan's strategic objectives; devoting the required resources to feasibility assessment and plan design; a genuine top-management public commitment to the program; and careful, well-planned implementation. Above all else, it is recommended that a firm avoid using a canned or textbook-recommended program, and instead design one specifically suited for the firm, its employees, and the strategic goals being sought.[27]

Profit-Sharing Plans Profit sharing is still a widely used form of group incentive. *Profit sharing* is defined as any procedure under which an employer pays or makes available to regular employees, subject to reasonable eligibility rules, in addition to the normal rate of pay, special current or deferred sums based on the firm's profitability.[28] There are essentially three types of profit-sharing plans:

- *Cash or current payment*—Profits are immediately distributed quarterly or annually.
- *Deferred plan*—A portion of current profits is credited to employee accounts, with payment made at the time of retirement, disability, or severance. This is the most popular profit-sharing plan because of tax advantages of deferring income.
- *Combined plan*—A profit-sharing plan that incorporates features of the current payment and deferred plans.

The enactment of Employee Retirement Income Security Act (ERISA) and various Internal Revenue Service rulings have placed a number of administrative and financial responsibilities on firms using profit-sharing plans. The laws have actually resulted in many firms changing their profit-sharing programs to provide for an annual payment.

Advocates of profit sharing contend that the plans successfully motivate greater performance by employees. Many firms also see profit sharing as a way to increase employee satisfaction and quality and to reduce absenteeism and turnover. Essentially, they contend that employees who have profit-sharing plans identify more closely with the company and its profit goals, and thus they reduce waste and increase productivity.[29]

However, there are some potential problems with profit sharing.[30] First, an organization cannot share what it does not have. And in bad years, there are no profits to share. The employees may have cut costs and worked hard, but perhaps a recession slowed sales and thus profits, or management chose an expensive but ineffective marketing program. After several bad years the employee no longer links his or her extra efforts to increased financial rewards. Often, even in good years, it is difficult for the employee to see the

---

[27] Carl G. Thor, "Employee Involvement and Productivity Gainsharing," *Industrial Management*, July–August 1987, pp. 21–25.

[28] Henderson, *Compensation Management*, p. 366.

[29] "Employee Wrath Hits Profit-Sharing Plans," *Business Week*, July 18, 1977, pp. 25, 28.

[30] Randy G. Swad, "Stock Ownership Plans: A New Employee Benefit," *Personnel Journal*, June 1981, pp. 453–55.

significance of extra work to profit sharing a year away, or worse, at retirement 40 years later.

Profit sharing has had limited success because of the difficulty of tying individual rewards to effort and the problems raised when there are no profits to share. The plans probably are more succesful in smaller firms, because the employees can identify more closely with a smaller organization and can see the relation between their productivity and company profits more easily. Plans restricted to executives have been more successful, as will be discussed later in the chapter.

Stock Ownership Plans Many companies encourage employee purchase of company stock (often at advantageous prices), to increase employees' incentive to work, satisfaction, and work quality, and to reduce absenteeism and turnover. Purchase plans often allow for payroll deductions or company financing of the stock. Sometimes the company will agree to buy the stock back at a guaranteed rate if it appears that the employee would take a significant loss. Companies use these plans for the same reasons as they do profit-sharing plans: When employees become partners in the business, they work harder.

Some of these plans (such as Procter & Gamble's) are very successful. In general, stock purchase plans have most of the disadvantages of profit sharing. It is hard for the truck driver to identify his or her working harder with an increase in the value of his stock. It is more difficult when the stock drops in price. Many stock ownership plans were terminated in the 1930s because of big drops in stock prices.

A major change in U.S. laws may have increased the usage of stock ownership plans.

Congress authorized an establishment of an employee stock ownership plan (ESOP) through the mechanism of an employee stock ownership trust (ESOT). Firms have a number of incentives for setting up an ESOT. ERISA views an ESOT as an employee benefit plan. The Tax Reduction Act of 1975 allows firms with an ESOT to take an extra 1 percent investment tax credit in addition to the 10 percent investment tax credit.

Leveraged ESOP The whole ESOP phenomenon grew out of the ideas of Louis Kelso, a San Francisco-based lawyer.[31] In basic form, the leveraged ESOP is as follows:

- The ESOP trust obtains a loan to buy company stock.
- The company makes annual, tax-deductible contributions sufficient to repay the loan.
- The ESOP buys newly issued stock from the company, and the company uses the money to finance new capital.
- Each year, the ESOP uses the company's tax-deductible contributions to repay the loan.

The term *leveraged ESOP* is used because the trust borrows money to buy capital stock.

---

[31] John J. Miller, "ESOPS, TRASOPS, and PAYSOPS: A Guide for the Perplexed," *Management Review*, September 1983, pp. 40–43.

The number of employee-owned (or partially owned) companies is approximately 8,100 with over 8 million employees owning stock.[32] Employee-owners make steel beams at Weirton Steel, stock shelves at Publix Supermarkets, publish the *Milwaukee Journal* newspaper, and do research and development work on new high-technology products at W. L. Gore Associates.

The tax incentives have proven so attractive to companies that ESOPs are expected to increase. The 1986 Tax Reform Act has made ESOPs attractive. Businesses can still deduct contributions to ESOPs from corporate income taxes. If an ESOP brings stock in a closely held firm, the owner can defer taxation on the sale. Other laws allow an ESOP to borrow money and use the loan to purchase company stock; the company can make tax-deductible contributions to the ESOP to pay off the loan. The 1986 Tax Reform Act permits workers to continue to deduct 50 percent of the interest income they receive from the ESOP debt.

A number of studies suggest that the performance of ESOP companies is good. Unfortunately, most of these studies only examined ESOP companies after the plans had been set up. However, a well-designed, pre-post longitudinal study reported by Rosen and Quarrey shows promising results.[33] They studied 45 ESOP companies, looking at data for each during the five years before it instituted the plan and the five years after. A total of at least five comparison companies (in the same industry) for every ESOP company was used in the data sample. Data were collected from ESOP and non-ESOP firms on sales and employment growth. The ESOP firms grew faster in terms of sales and employment.

Regardless of company size or the size of employee contributions or even the percentage of the company owned by the ESOP, the most significant correlation was between corporate performance and workers' perceptions of their managers' attitudes toward worker participation. ESOP companies that instituted participation plans grew at a rate three times faster than ESOP firms that did not.

The Rosen and Quarrey research cited the example of the Cost Cutter grocery chain, based in Bellingham, Washington. The establishment of the ESOP seemed to increase employee expectations about their role in the firm. After group meetings between management and employees, managers began interviewing employees one-on-one asking for opinions about how to improve productivity. Since these meetings, productivity has skyrocketed.

The results of the ESOP at Weirton Steel have also been outstanding. In 1984, Weirton's 7,000 employees bought the firm to keep it from closing.[34] They set up training programs to teach employees how to run teams of employees; the firm installed television monitors throughout the plant to keep employees informed; and it shared detailed financial and production data—good

---

[32] Michael Quarry, Joseph Blasi, and Corey Rosen, *Taking Stock: Employee Ownership at Work* (Cambridge, Mass.: Ballinger, 1986).

[33] Corey Rosen and Michael Quarry, "How Well Is Employee Ownership Working?," *Harvard Business Review*, September–October 1987, pp. 126–28 and 132.

[34] William E. Fruham, Jr., "Management Labor and The Golden Goose," *Harvard Business Review*, September–October 1985, p. 131.

and bad—with the employee-owners. Weirton now employs 8,500 people and has made a profit for 14 straight quarters, a record unmatched among integrated steelmakers.

An example of the esprit generated through ESOP is captured in what James Lucas, a cabinetmaker for Maximum Building Corporation of Williamson, West Virginia, has to say: "Every time I put a hammer to a nail, I tell myself, do it right, now. Be sure of what you're doing, because everything you do comes back to you. What I do matters, because I own this company. We all own it." Lucas is part of Maximum's ESOP.[35]

Not everyone has a positive opinion about ESOPs. Some critics feel it is a loophole in ERISA and can endanger employee pension funds. The problem with profit-sharing plans (if stocks decline in value, so will retirement funds) could be worse for ESOPs if all the funds are invested in the company stock. ESOPs also have the effect of diluting earnings per share and thus stockholder equity.[36]

TRASOP into PAYSOP Tax-credit ESOPS, created by the Tax Reduction Act of 1975, became known as TRASOP (Tax Reduction Act Stock Ownership Plans). The Economic Recovery Act of 1981 has changed tax-credit ESOPs from a capital investment basis to a payroll basis. As of January 1, 1983, available tax credits were based on the payroll of participants—hence the term *PAYSOPS*. Approximately 3 million employees participated in the PAYSOP plan. However, the PAYSOP plan was eliminated with the 1986 Tax Reform Act.

EXECUTIVE COMPENSATION

Executives in the public and third sectors are normally compensated by salaries. In the private sector, business executives receive salaries too, but many of them also receive incentive compensation, such as bonuses. In addition, executives in all sectors receive benefits and special treatment that are usually called *perquisites (perks)*.

A fundamental question in executive compensation is why business executives should be paid incentives as well as salaries. A number of answers can be given. First, it is argued that these incentives improve performance, and that is good for stockholders and employees. A second reason is that incentive compensation is a way of retaining talented executives. Many have alternative employment opportunities with other corporations or as entrepreneurs. The third reason is that business executives are more likely to control their own compensation in the private sector than in the public sector, where legislative bodies determine it, or in the third sector, where boards, normally from outside the enterprise, have a great deal of control. For these and other reasons, the

---

[35] Ellen Wojahn, "Getting the Most out of an ESOP," *Inc.*, July 1983, pp. 91–92.

[36] Based on William G. Flanagan, "More Sweets to the Suite," *Forbes*, June 8, 1981, pp. 107–44.

EXHIBIT 10-3   The Ten Highest Paid Executives: 1986 (in thousands)

		1986 Salary and Bonus	Long-Term Compensation	Total Pay
1. Lee A. Iacocca, Chairman	Chrysler	$10,984	$9,558	$20,542
2. Paul Fireman, Chairman	Reebok Intl.	13,063	–	13,063
3. Victor Posner, Chairman	DWG	8,400	–	8,400
4. John J. Nevin, Chairman	Firestone	785	5,570	6,355
5. Charles E. Exley, Jr., Chairman	NCR	938	5,357	6,295
6. Sidney J. Sheinberg, President	MCA	559	5,520	6,079
7. Maurice R. Greenberg, President	American Intl. Group	823	3,780	4,603
8. Donald E. Petersen, Chairman	Ford	1,961	2,375	4,336
9. Rand V. Araskog, Chairman	ITT	1,665	2,590	4,255
10. Alan C. Greenberg, Chairman	Bear Stearns	4,078	–	4,078*

* Compensation for six months only; data for full year unavailable.

Source: Standard & Poor's Compustat Services, Inc.

compensation of business executives tends to be lucrative and innovative enough to sidestep the everchanging tax laws.

Executive Salaries

Salaries of executives in the public sector are generally known to the public. Salaries of executives in the third sector have not been widely studied. In general, the highest salaries are paid in the private sector.[37] There are many studies of this form of compensation.

To give you some idea of the salaries and bonuses of some top executives in organizations you probably have done business with, look at some 1986 data shown in Exhibit 10-3. Remember, these figures are just for the salary and bonus portions of compensation. The exhibit provides a look at 10 executives in companies that are in the news.

Some studies have been done on the relationship of the size and kind of business to salary amount. With regard to size, in general, as the firm increases in size, the top executive's salary increases. Several studies have examined the relative salaries of executives in different industries. For example, one study found that in companies with sales larger than $10 billion, motor vehicle companies paid the highest, followed (in order) by conglomerates and firms in office machines and oil.[38] In the $5 billion category, the order was: Motor vehicles, office machines, conglomerates, and oil. In the $2.5 billion

---

[37] John A. Byrne, "Executive Pay: Who Got What in '86," *Business Week*, May 4, 1987, pp. 50–58.

[38] Arch Patton, *Men, Money and Motivation* (New York: McGraw-Hill, 1961).

P/HRM · IN · ACTION

Mary and Joe's conversation on compensation continues:

Mary: In summary, Joe, one of our problems is that we pay some people salaries, and pay others by the hour. That was the problem Chet brought to Tom Nichols at Branch 1. Of course, lots of banks do this, but we could change it.

We also have not tried incentive pay here. Most banks don't offer it, but we might consider it. At least we probably ought to have a suggestion system. We might even consider a Scanlon Plan or profit sharing.

Joe: I don't know. What about our executive compensation problem?

Mary: I'm going to get to that next.

sales category, the order was: Pharmaceuticals, packaged goods, forest products, chemicals, and food processors. In the $500 million sales category, the order was: Packaged goods, pharmaceuticals, chemicals, office machines, and forest products.

Various experts have tried to explain industry differences in executive compensation. Patton suggested that industries that pay higher salaries are dynamic, decentralized, and results-oriented. Industries that pay poorly tend to be static, centralized, seniority-oriented, and monopolies with a great deal of regulation. In a later study he added that high-paying companies tend to have stock that is widely held.[39]

Most studies also find that the salaries below the CEO level fit a percentage pattern by industry grouping. For example, the second highest ranked executive is usually paid about 71 percent of the CEO's salary in all industries except retail trade, where it is 84 percent. The third highest ranked executive tends to be paid 55–60 percent of the CEO's salary.

If top managers believe that pay is a motivator to higher performance, it follows that they will pay themselves in a way that rewards performance. and if performance is defined as more profits, pay should be correlated with profits. Some studies indicate that this is done. Other studies show that top executive pay is correlated with sales, a proxy for size.[40]

More sophisticated studies point out that simple correlations such as these are not likely to explain very much. The factors that influence executive pay are ownership and market concentration. One study found that in closely held firms, executive pay was correlated with profitability. Other studies agree

---

[39] Robert Sibson, "Executive Pay: The Long Term Is Where the Action Is," *Nation's Business*, November 1971, pp. 29–33.

[40] Marc Wallace, "Type of Control, Industrial Concentration and Executive Pay," *Proceedings* (National Academy of Management, 1976).

with this, and it makes sense.[41] In firms where the owners can put on pressure, executives are likely to encourage higher profitability. In firms with no strong ownership interest, executives can set their salaries similar to those of executives in equal-size firms, regardless of profitability.

Louis Brindisi of Booz, Allen, & Hamilton, Inc. argues that corporations should be tying executive pay more closely to shareholder gains in stock value and dividends. This is one method of measuring worth of contribution.[42]

Borden, Inc. is gradually phasing in a return on equity pay plan for its top 300 to 400 managers.[43] And at Libbey-Owens-Ford Company they are using monthly management reports that pinpoint the contribution to the creation of shareholder value each division makes. These companies along with Sears, Emhart, and Combustion Engineering are doing more than talking about tying pay to performance. They are phasing in specific pay for performance plans that are intended to motivate participants.

Labor unions are certainly one group that complains about the amount of salaries and bonus received by top executives. They believe that the total compensation paid to Lee Iacocca and others is obscene and unfair.[44] Compared to top executives, the pay of union leaders (usually in the $100,000 to $150,000 range) is pretty skimpy. Of course, the question one must ask is whether the pay differentials between top business managers and top union leaders are warranted. Do you think that business leaders are overpaid or that union leaders are underpaid?

Bonuses

A *bonus* is a compensation payment that supplements salary and can be paid in the present or in the future. In the latter case, it is called a *deferred bonus*. A majority of large and some small firms pay bonuses in the belief that doing so leads to better profitability and other advantages for organizations. Bonuses involve large expenditures of funds. They vary from 80 percent of top executives' salaries to 20 percent of the salaries of lowest level participants. In spite of wide usage and high costs, there is little research support for their effectiveness. Unless more research does support the payment of bonuses, many may conclude they are an example of management's power to pay itself whatever it wants. This is an issue that can have an impact on the image the public holds about the ethics of corporate executives.

Bonus practices in large firms are typically based on percentage of net profits after deducting a reasonable earnings per share for the stockholders. In

---

[41] Daniel Seligman, "Believe It or Not, Top-Executive Pay Makes Sense," *Fortune*, June 11, 1984, pp. 57–62.

[42] "Executive Pay: The Top Earners," *Business Week*, May 7, 1984, pp. 88–116.

[43] "Rewarding Executives for Taking the Long View," *Business Week*, April 2, 1984, pp. 99–100.

[44] "Growing Furor over Pay of Top Executives," *U.S. News & World Report*, May 21, 1984.

smaller firms, bonuses are based on attaining sales goals, as a percentage of sales, as a percentage of net profits, or are totally discretionary. In fact, one study of small growing firms indicated that 81 percent of the firms used bonus compensation and that 51 percent of them based the bonus payment on a discretionary basis. Although some of the firms used fixed and annual formulas most of them had no set formula or procedure.[45] This finding does lend support to the public image of chief executives paying themselves what they feel is fair.

Stock Options, Performance Shares, and Book-Value Devices

Another form of executive compensation used in the private sector is a set of devices tied to the firm's stock. The oldest form is the *stock option*, which gives executives the right to purchase company stock at a fixed price for a certain period of time. The option's price usually is close to the market price of the stock at the time the option is issued. The executive gains if the price rises above the option price during the option period enough to cover the capital gains tax on the stock should it be purchased.

The popularity of stock options has risen and fallen with the tax laws (especially the 1976, 1981, and 1986 laws), the level of interest rates, the state of the stock market, and the feelings of stockholders about them. At present, because of tax law changes and these other factors, the use of stock options as incentive compensation is decreasing.

Is this a great loss? Probably not. There was little research to indicate that stock options led to better performance; what evidence there was tended to indicate that they did not. But one implication of the research is that as management's income from ownership-related sources (dividends and capital gain) increases, these instruments can serve to improve performance.

Innovative tax lawyers and tax accountants have worked up some new compensation forms to replace the stock option and still provide ownership and incentive compensation. Several variations are primarily incentive compensation-oriented, others ownership-oriented, and still others a mix of the two. The ownership-oriented devices are:

Market-Value Purchases The company lends the executive funds at low interest rates to buy company stock at current market value. The executive repays the loan by direct payment or receives credits on the loan payments for staying with the company and/or achieving a certain performance level.

Book-Value Purchases The executive is offered a chance to buy the company stock at book value (or some similar nonmarket value measure) but can resell it to the company later, using the same formula price.

---

[45] Ellen Wojahn, "The Take at the Top," *Inc.*, September 1984, pp. 44–56.

Exercise Bonuses Payment to an executive when he or she exercises a stock option that is equal to or proportionate to the option gain is called an exercise bonus. This helps the executive keep the stock rather than sell it to pay the taxes on the gain.

One device appears to be primarily a form of compensation that is linked to stocks. This is *performance shares and performance units*, used by such companies as General Motors, Gulf, Texaco, Pepsico, and International Nickel. Performance shares grant stock units due the executive in the future (such as five years later) if performance targets are met. These units appreciate or depreciate as the stock does. Performance units are performance shares paid in cash instead of stock. The units are compensation unless they are to be used to buy stock. Both are viewed as compensation by the IRS.

Another device, *stock appreciation rights*, can be either compensation or ownership oriented. This device, attached to a stock option, allows the executive to accept appreciation in value in either stock or cash.

Most of these devices are fairly new and are still rarely used. All could have performance implications for the organization, but there is inadequate research at this stage to determine under what conditions they do so. The key to their success is the definition and identification of what constitutes performance.

Executive Perquisites

All over the world and in all sectors of the economy, executives receive perks. These tend to be larger in Europe than in the United States. The European executive can receive free housing and other niceties in lieu of or in addition to higher salaries. The differences can be easily explained. Some perks are taxed elsewhere.

The American Management Association studied perks in 742 companies: 34 perks were examined, but only 7 were regularly available in more than half of the companies studied. These include better office decor, choice office location, a company car, reserved parking, a car for personal use, and first-class airline tickets.[46]

A list of executive perks is presented in Exhibit 10–4. Some of these perks are also called benefits (as noted in the exhibit, these are discussed in Chapter 11). Research indicates that executives prefer the following perks the most: insurance, company car, club memberships, financial counseling, travel, loans, company airplane, and annual physical examinations.[47]

A recent survey by the Japan Economic Institute found that while American companies try to base an executive's compensation package (salary, bon-

---

[46] Robert Sbarra, "The New Language of Executive compensation," *Personnal*, November–December 1975, pp. 10–18.

[47] Ibid., p. 55; and Edward Meadows, "New Targeting for Executive Pay," *Fortune*, May 4, 1981, pp. 176–77, 180, 184.

EXHIBIT 10–4   Executive Perquisites: A Selected List

Company-provided car. The employee is able to use the car for both business and personal use. (According to IRS, the employee must pay a flat monthly maintenance charge or a mileage charge for personal use.)

Parking. Special no-cost, readily accessible to work site parking services.

Chauffeured limousine. Normally provided only to the CEO or key officials. The chauffeur may also act as bodyguard.

Kidnap and ransom protection. A service of recent vintage aimed at protecting key officials who may be victims of such action.

Counseling service. Includes financial and legal services. Tax-related expenses are tax-deductible; cost of nonbusiness-related services is considered taxable income.

Attending professional meetings and conferences. Opportunity to enhance professional knowledge and enjoy activities at selected sites.

Spouse travel. The company pays for expenses incurred in taking a spouse to a convention or on a business trip.

Use of company plane and yacht. Opportunity to mix use of company plane and yacht for personal enjoyment and business purposes.

Home entertainment allowance. Executives who do considerable entertaining are frequently provided with a domestic staff or given a home servants allowance. The allowance may include cost of food and beverages and payment of utility bills.

Special living accommodations. Executives required to perform business activities at odd hours or at a considerable distance from home are provided with an apartment or permanent hotel accommodations.

Special dining rooms. The business provides special dining facilities for key officials and their business guests.

Special relocation allowance. A variety of relocation allowances is provided only to key officials. This includes low interest loans to purchase a new home and complete coverage of all relocation expenses.

Use of company credit card. No waiting period for reimbursement of company-related charges and use of card for personal service and delay in repayment to the company.

Medical expense reimbursement. Coverage for all medical care.

College tuition reimbursement for children. Special programs that provide for college tuition.

Source: Richard I. Henderson, *Compensation Management* (Reston, Va.: Reston Publishing, 1985), pp. 655–56. Used with permission.

---

sus, perks) on his or her ability to produce profit or earn money for shareholders, most Japanese firms say that the differential in compensation between managers and nonmanagers is critical.[48] The Japanese work at not having too wide a gap in pay between managers and nonmanagers.

The Japanese manager works for firms that take into account a person's needs in relation to age, seniority, and job position. The perks received by Japanese managers are very attractive. Companies pay up to 50 percent of interest charges on mortgages. As an executive moves up the hierarchy, the

---

[48] Lisa Miller Mesday, "Are You Underpaid?" *Fortune*, March 19, 1984, pp. 20–25.

company provides a car, chauffeur, large expense account, and memberships in exclusive golf clubs and social clubs. The Japanese example of rewarding heavily with perks suggests that, when making simple salary comparisons between Japanese, American, and other nations' managers one must include the perks received as well as the currency exchange rates and taxes. For example, in Japan an executive who earns over $335,000 would pay a national tax of 75 percent and municipal taxes of 14 percent. The American counterpart would be faced with the maximum tax rate of 28 percent under the 1986 Tax Reform Act.

Executive Compensation Policy

How does an organization choose the compensation package for its executives? Effective executive compensation must meet the needs of both the organization and the individual executive. For the organization, the total compensation must be competitive with that of similar enterprises. Thus it makes no sense to look at total compensation of executives, or averages. The effective firm determines the compensation of executives in similar-sized organizations in the same industry group with the same degree of competitiveness. Executive compensation must also be directly tied to the organization's strategy and objectives, so executive rewards will promote achievement of the organization's goals.

One way organizations try to satisfy the needs and desires of their executives is to adjust compensation methods to changing tax laws. This often leads to the use of more deferred compensation methods. Another way is to study the preferences and attitudes of executives toward the various compensation approaches. However, since each executive is different and has differing needs for compensation, studies of pay preferences are only partly indicative of what an enterprise should do. In one study of the pay preferences of 300 executives in seven large companies, it was found that executives' compensation preferences vary widely.[49] One consistency was a preference for 75 percent of total compensation in cash and 25 percent in benefits and deferred items, which would mean a shift from the present 85/15 percent division to include more benefits.

A way to deal with these differences is to set up a *cafeteria compensation system*. The cafeteria approach permits executives to determine the range of their compensation between present pay, deferred compensation, and benefits and services. This approach is described in more detail Chapter 11, where the cafeteria approach to benefits is considered for all employees. It does not change the total compensation (that could lead to perceived inequities), but the mix of how the compensation is received. Although there are administrative hurdles to be overcome, this approach fits compensation theories and makes sense.

At present the cafeteria system is not feasible in the public sector because of

---

[49] Wilbur Lewellen and Howard Lanser, "Executive Pay Preferences," *Harvard Business Review*, September–October 1973, pp. 115–22.

the usual rigid pay classifications and the system of a single salary plus fixed benefits. But it is feasible and is being used in the private and third sectors.[50] Cafeteria-style compensation was first introduced in 1974. TRM Systems and Energy Group and the Educational Testing Service were the first companies to implement such a system.[51] However, there are still only approximately 200 firms currently using cafeteria-style plans.[52]

COMPENSATION ADMINISTRATION ISSUES

Managers must make policy decisions on four issues in compensation administration for employees and executives. These issues involve the extent to which (1) compensation will be secret, (2) compensation will be secure, (3) pay is compressed, and (4) compensation is two-tiered.

Pay Secrecy or Openness

The first compensation issue to be discussed is the extent to which the pay of employees is known by others in the enterprise. (This is the issue Martha raised in the beginning of the chapter.) How would you feel if your co-workers could find out what you make? Would you care? As in other issues, employees differ on this.

There are degrees of secretiveness and openness on pay information. In many institutions and organizations, pay ranges and even an individual's pay

---

[50] R. B. Cockrum, "Has the Time Come for Employee Cafeteria Plans?" *Personnel Administrator*, July 1982, pp. 66–72.

[51] Paul A. Tanker, "Why Flexible Benefits Are So Appealing," *Management World*, March 1987, p. 18.

[52] Dale Gifford, "The Status of Flexible Compensation," *Personnel Administrator*, May 1984, pp. 19–25.

P/HRM · IN · ACTION

Mary: So you see, boss, we've really only scratched the surface on compensation at CNB. Our executive compensation system consists of salaries (and not high ones at that), and a few perks, like free club memberships. We haven't tried bonuses or stock options, performance shares, or anything else. Our executive turnover is probably related to our executive compensation system.

Joe: Yeah, but high turnover also could be happening because we've hired a great group of executives. Now we're a likely target for others to pirate executives from.

Mary: I doubt it, boss.

Joe: OK. What's left?

Mary: What's left are some key compensation administration issues.

are open to the public and fellow employees. Examples are public-sector salaries (federal, state, and local governments), some universities, and unionized wage employees. This is called the *open system*.

The opposite is the *secret system*, in which pay is regarded as privileged information known only to the employee, her or his superior, and such staff employees as P/HRM and payroll. In the most secrecy-oriented organizations, employees are told they cannot discuss pay matters and, specifically, their own pay. The National Labor Relations Board has ruled that this is not a legitimate policy.

A survey of 183 firms by the Bureau of National Affairs revealed that in only 45 did mangers have a general knowledge of the salaries of other managers at their own or higher levels of management. In this survey 112 of the firms made available salary ranges, but not individual salaries.[53]

Should this be changed? Research is mixed. Some findings favor the open system, others the secret system. Before an open system is tried, the individual's performance must be objectively measurable, and the measurable aspects of the jobs to be rewarded must be the significant ones. There should be little need for cooperation among jobs, and employees in the system should have a direct causal relationship on performance. The employees must also prefer the open system.

There is increasing recognition that some employees want a more open pay system. The opening up of a system and providing more information to employees certainly has its costs and benefits. However, if an organization wishes to reduce the manipulative aura surrounding pay, actual or perceived, it is going to have to share additional pay information with employees. As more firms

[53] Staff of Bureau of National Affairs, Wage and Salary Administration (Washington, D.C.: Bureau of National Affairs, 1981), p. 23.

post job openings to make employees aware of opportunities, information on pay becomes a critical decision point.

As a step in deciding how much secrecy or how much openness is needed, managers first must clearly determine through observation (listening, talking, discussions in groups) what their employees want to know about pay. Then managers must decide if providing pay information will harm or benefit the firm. Finally, the condition cited above concerning the objective measuring of performance, degree of interdependence, and causal relationships on performance must be carefully weighed.

Pay Security

Current compensation can be a motivator of performance. But the belief that there will be future security in compensation may also affect it. Various plans for providing this security have been developed: the guaranteed annual wage, supplementary unemployment benefits, severance pay, seniority rules, and the employment contract.

A few companies provide a guaranteed annual wage to employees who meet certain characteristics. For this type of plan to work, general employee-management relations must be good. And the demand for the product or service must to be steady. The best known such plans are those of Procter & Gamble, Hormel Meats, and the Nunn-Bush Shoe company. In one plan, the employer guarantees the employee a certain number of weeks of work at a certain wage after the worker has passed a probation period (say, two years). Morton Salt Company guarantees 80 percent of full-time work to all employees after one year of standard employment. Procter & Gamble has invoked its emergency clause only once since 1923—in 1933 for a brief period at three plants. In the Hormel and Spiegel plans and others, a minimum income is guaranteed.[54]

In the supplementary unemployment benefits approach, the employer adds to unemployment compensation payments to help the employee achieve income security, if not job security (as in the GAW). The auto, steel, rubber, garment, and glass industries, among others, contribute to a fund from which laid-off employees are paid. During the 1973–74 recession, many of these funds in the auto industry went bankrupt. They provided less income security than was thought. Studies on plans in which unemployment was less severe than in autos show the system has helped in employment security.

In many organizations, the employer provides some income bridge from employment to unemployment and back to employment. This is *severance pay*. Typically, it amounts to one week's pay for each year of service. About 25 percent of union contracts require such severance pay. It doesn't guarantee a job, but it helps the employee when a job is lost.

In times of layoff, the basic security for most employees is their seniority. If an organization is unionized, the contract normally specifies how seniority is to be computed. Seniority guarantees the jobs (and thus the compensation) to

---

[54] Robert Zager, "Managing Guaranteed Employment," *Harvard Business Review*, May–June 1978, pp. 103–15.

P/HRM Manager Close-Up

Betty Bessler
Mary Kay Cosmetics, Inc.

Biography

Betty Bessler, vice president of human resources, joined Mary Kay Cosmetics, Inc. in 1975 to establish a personnel function in a subsidiary of Mary Kay. Prior to joining Mary Kay she was personnel manager of Liquid Paper Corporation, where she established the corporate personnel function.

Ms. Bessler earned a bachelor's degree from the University of Dallas, and has done graduate work in business at the University of Dallas and Southern Methodist University. She also attended Harvard University's executive development program in human resource management. Ms. Bessler has served as an officer in the Dallas Personnel Association and is a member of ASPA. She was the recipient of ASPA's 1985 Yoder-Heneman Personnel Creative Application Award and was one of 50 women selected for the 1983 Leadership Texas program.

Job Description

In 1986 Ms. Bessler was promoted to her present position which includes responsibility for employment, employee relations, compensation, benefits, management and organizational development, and security. She has a staff of 45 employees and serves on the Mary Kay Executive Committee and the Mary Kay Profit Sharing Committee.

Views

The present corporate environment of mergers, acquisitions, buyouts and the all-too-frequent downsizing which results, presents opportunities for human resource professionals to significantly impact corporate strategy. Our company has experienced an LBO (leveraged buy-out) and a RIF (reduction in force) which have changed us

(continued)

significantly. We are a new company with new ownership, new customers, new products, and a new strategy. We have had to learn how to communicate in a new way, too.

During change, communication, which is always important, becomes critical. A true partnership between the company and its employees is critical to survival in the changing business environment today. There must be two-way communications, and employees must understand that job security today only is assured when every employee becomes a team member contributing to the profitability of the company. And companies must become more adept at "incenting" and rewarding those employees who join the team. This is an arena in which human resource professionals who choose to be proactive can excel. And it is in this arena that those in our profession can participate in developing and implementing corporate strategy.

A Compensation Task Force Structure

When commitment from implementers is necessary to the success of the project, it is important to involve those people in the decision-making process. Even when there may be strong disagreement, it is probably best to allow the difference to be aired. While personnel professionals are usually strong advocates of participatory problem solving, they are sometimes guilty of establishing policies and procedures for others to implement without soliciting their input. Two situations Betty has

recently been involved in are good examples.

In 1984, Mary Kay decided to form a task force to evaluate the implementation of a PAYSOP, 401K deferred compensation plan, and a flexible benefits plan. The company treasurer, a member of the legal department, the head of the compensation department, and Betty worked with a consulting group and decided to implement the proposed programs within the following nine months.

It became evident that the members of the personnel staff who would be charged with communicating the new plans were concerned that the company was making too many changes at one time, and that the proposed changes in the health care plan would have a negative effect on employee morale. The task force realized that the lack of commitment probably stemmed from the lack of involvement in the plan design. The task force agreed that the communicators would have to be enthusiastic about the changes if the changes were to be accepted by Mary Kay's employees. The decision was made to have the consultant give a presentation of the program to the 10 staff members, and that the task force would go ahead with the implementation only if the 10 voted to move ahead after an opportunity to air disagreements and challenge the changes. With more comprehensive knowledge of the changes and knowing that they as a group would decide if the changes would be made, they were unanimous in their support, and the new plans were in place at the beginning of 1985.

the employees with the longest continuous employment in the organization or work unit. Even in nonunionized situations, a strong seniority norm prevails, which gives some security to senior employees.

The United Auto Workers (UAW) and General Motors entered a job security agreement in 1984. It was decided that if jobs were eliminated by technological advances or because General Motors decided to buy more parts from cheaper sources rather than make them itself, those workers would be given other jobs within the company at the same pay—and retrained if necessary. Eligibility is determined by seniority; it is assumed that lifetime jobs are guaranteed for about 60 to 70 percent of the workers. This is roughly the same percentage of workers in major Japanese auto companies who have such pay and job security.

General Motors, under the job security agreement, is allowed to eliminate as many as 100,000 jobs as it continues to install more robots on its assembly line and to farm out more parts orders to nonunion and foreign firms. How General Motors will absorb workers as they technologically move forward is still a problematic issue.[55]

Exhibit 10–5 traces some landmarks in pay, concessions, and pay-job-security issues involving management and labor. From 1948 with the annual cost-of-living adjustment (COLA) to the 1984 agreement on job security and pay the auto workers and management have set precedents for other industries. One study reports that COLA plans are used in over 50 percent of the firms surveyed.[56]

Pay Compression

The Fair Labor Standards Act (FLSA) sets a legal minimum wage that must be paid employees. However, union power and labor market conditions often push for higher minimum rates of pay. These pressures often result in setting higher levels of pay. This further results in what is called *pay compression*.

Pay compression exists when jobs requiring advanced levels of education and experience, more skills, and higher degrees of responsibility receive smaller increases in compensation opportunities. Those performing jobs requiring more knowledge, greater skills, and increased responsibilities find that rewards are inadequate for these added contributions.

To illustrate pay compression, suppose that the job of a mechanic in a food processing plant of General Mills is difficult to fill. Furthermore, pay for mechanics has increased by 12 percent, partly because of the shortage of

---

[55] "Detroit Breaks New Ground," *Newsweek*, September 24, 1984, pp. 48–49. Also see Dale D. Buss, "Lifetime Job Guarantees in Auto Contracts Arouse Second Thoughts among Workers," *The Wall Street Journal*, April 18, 1983, p. 27.

[56] In a COLA plan the Bureau of Labor Statistics cost-of-living index is used to make wage and salary adjustments. The consumer price index (CPI) is used as a cost-of-living index. It is a measure of changes over time of a hypothetical basket of goods and services. The adjustment is not based on performance. See Milkovich, pp. 442–48; C. R. Deitsch and D. A. Dilts, "The COLA Clause: An Employee's Bargaining Weapon?" *Personnel Journal*, March 1982, pp. 220–23; and "Inflation's COLA Cure," *Time*, July 29, 1980, p. 57.

EXHIBIT 10–5   **From Paid Vacations to Quality Control Programs**

1940

Establishment of 40 hours of annual paid vacation for employees with at least one year on the job.

1948

An annual cost-of-living allowance (COLA) is written into Big Three contracts for the first time.

1949

The Ford Motor Co. agrees to fund the auto industry's first blue-collar pension plan.

1955

UAW president Walter Reuther vows to win a guaranteed annual wage—but settles for a supplemental unemployment benefit (SUB) fund.

1961

The first profit-sharing plan is negotiated at tiny American Motors Corp.—but AMC did not make enough money that year to pay off.

1970

Pension plans are redrawn to allow retirement after 30 years' service.

1980

UAW president Douglas Fraser is elected to the Chrysler Corp. board of directors.

1982

Trapped in their worst peacetime sales slump since the 1930s, the Big Three wring an an estimated $3.5 billion in wage concessions from the UAW.

1984

UAW and General Motors agree to job and pay security plan for between 60 and 70% of firm's union members.

1987

A moratorium on plant closings and union involvement in quality control.

Source: Adapted from "Detroit Breaks New Ground," *Newsweek*, September 24, 1984, p. 49; Donald F. Ephlin, "Evolution By Revolution: The Changing Relationship Between GM and the UAW," *Academy of Management Executive*, February 1988, pp. 63–66; John Hillkirk, "Ford, UAW Reach Accord on Contract," *USA Today*, September 18, 1987, p. 1B.

---

qualified candidates. There is, however, an abundant supply of mechanic supervisors, so that their pay increases this year averaged about 6.5 percent. The pay differential between the operative mechanic and the mechanic supervisor has become smaller—it has been compressed. To overcome pay compression problems, some firms state that there must be at least a 15 percent differential between the pay received by the highest level nonmanagerial personnel and that of their immediate supervisors.[57]

---

[57] John M. Ivancevich, "Management and Compensation," in *Making Organizations Humane and Productive*, ed. H. Meltzer and Walter R. Nord (New York: John Wiley & Sons, 1981), p. 82.

P/HRM · IN · ACTION

Joe and Mary

In summing up what she had told Joe about compensation, Mary Renfro said, "Joe, that's it. We've discussed a lot of personnel/human resource management problems." Then she summarized the situation at Cardeson National Bank for him, as follows:

- You are making all the pay decisions. You hire people and pay them what you think they are worth, based on their experience (as you see it), their potential (as you see it), and their needs (as you see them). This has caused us a lot of inequity problems. Remember Arte Jamison? He was really underpaid and we lost him. You don't use pay surveys. You don't use job evaluation. You don't have pay classifications—nothing. It's all in your head, and it varies with your feelings at the moment. You have ignored the equal pay laws.
- You give raises similarly and throw in some factor for seniority—how, we don't know.
- Our turnover and absenteeism are high. I think that's largely because of pay problems. Turnover and absenteeism are complex factors, like profit. But you have been hearing a lot of complaints about pay lately, haven't you? Where there's smoke. . . . I've shown you the cost figures on turnover and absenteeism. It's a real cost. And that doesn't count morale problems directly—surly tellers, and so on.
- Executive turnover is high, too. It appears low pay and few incentives are one cause.
- There is pressure to put everyone on salary—as Tom Nichols knows.
- In spite of our pay secrecy policy, word about the differential pay situation is getting out. Remember Martha?
- We don't have a raise policy. We don't have a pay strategy.
- Should we continue time pay only, or go to an incentive plan, like a suggestion system or profit sharing?

While Joe is pondering these points, Guido stops by the office to help Mary make her points.

Guido: Boss, Mary has some specific suggestions for you. They're all in her report that I've given you. I've discussed them with some of the other VPs and they generally agree. . . .

Joe: Oh, they do, do they? I'll bet it'll all cost a lot of money. How can you

(continued)

build a bank like I'm trying to do and give away all the profits? I've been fair with everybody. And what do I get—complaints!

Well, Mary, show me where your specific suggestions for our personnel needs are in your report and I'll read them. I'll let you know.

Mary's report contained the following recommendations:

1. That one of the vice presidents be delegated to handle day-to-day P/HRM matters. Joe would deal only with policy decisions.
2. That a job evaluation point system be set up to determine proper pay. No person would have his or her pay lowered. But some people being paid below the suggested pay level should be raised as soon as possible.

Those overpaid should be held at the same level until they are in the right category.

3. That area wage surveys be consulted in making pay decisions.
4. That a pay structure be set up.
5. That a pay strategy of paying going wages be approved.
6. That a systematic raise policy be established as soon as possible, fixing timing amount, and criteria for raises.
7. That the pay secrecy policy be continued.
8. That current use of hourly pay and salaries be continued.
9. That the possibility of incentive pay for executives and other employees be investigated.

Some firms are also paying supervisory personnel for overtime work. Supervisory personnel typically are exempt under the FLSA from overtime pay. However, overtime pay is one way to attract more qualified employees into the managerial field and provide fair compensation. Overtime pay may not start until the exempt employee has worked 45 hours, there may be a cap placed on overtime hours worked, or a limit set by base pay (e.g., employees with a base pay of greater than $40,000 are not eligible for overtime pay).[58] Each firm has to review its compensation plan and be aware of possible pay-compression problems. With changes in market conditions, technological changes requiring more specialists, and reorganizations occurring, it is likely that pay compression will continue to be an issue that P/HRM managers must continue to address creatively.

Two-Tiered Compensation Plans

Two-tiered compensation plans for nonmanagers date back to the 1930s. Today, however, they are growing in use in a number of industries.[59] Basically, the idea is to protect the wages of workers hired before a certain date, but new

---

[58] Henderson, *Compensation Management*, pp. 296, 424–25.

[59] Steven Flax, "Pay Cuts before the Job Starts," *Fortune*, January 9, 1984, pp. 75–77.

A RETURN TO THE P/HRM · IN · ACTION

Guido   Mary

A week later, Mary and Guido caught Joe in his office. He'd spent much of the time since their last meeting at the branch offices—very unusual behavior for him.

Guido: Boss, are you free?

Joe: I'm very busy. But come in for a moment.

Guido: Mary and I have been wondering if you've had a chance to decide on those pay policy issues.

Joe: Yes, I have. I believe we are a small bank. We don't need a lot of paperwork and bureaucracy. So I decided to chuck the whole report in the wastebasket.

Then I thought it over and decided I ought to compromise. So I accept suggestions 5, 7, and 8. I've already appointed John Bolts to investigate who is letting out the salary information around here. Now, I'm very busy. So please excuse me.

Six months later, Mary Renfro left the bank. Executive and employee turnover had continued to increase. Guido Panelli took a position with another company about six months after Mary left. The bank still has two branches and about the same number of employees. Profitability has declined some, but the bank is still profitable.

workers start at a lower pay rate. Thus, older (in terms of company tenure, not necessarily age) and new workers, although working side by side, would be paid differently. Management has supported two-tiered plans in order to lower labor costs.

Examples of the new worker differentials covered by labor contract agreements in various firms are presented in Exhibit 10–6. Under some two-tiered plans, new employees eventually attain the level of wages or salaries earned by older employees. Other plans are structured so that new workers will never attain the pay level of older workers. For example, newly hired employees at Kohler Company are frozen into a plan that pays them about 15 percent less than older employees.

There is some risk associated with two-tiered plans. The new workers may eventually question the equity of such a plan. There is also the possibility of

EXHIBIT 10–6   **Two-Tiered Wage Pay Plan**

Company	Workers Covered	Rate of Pay: Older Workers	Rate of Pay: New Workers	Difference
Boeing	26,000	$11.38/hour	$6.70/hour	$4.68
Giant Food	12,000	$5.96/hour	$5.00/hour	$1.95
American Airlines (pilots)	4,000	$36,000/year	$18,000/year	$18,000
Briggs & Stratton	8,000	$8.00/hour	$5.50/hour	$2.50
Dow Chemical	2,600	$7.08/hour	$6.90/hour	$0.18

Source: Adapted from Steven Flax, "Pay Cuts Before the Job Even Starts," *Fortune,* January 9, 1984, pp. 75–77.

legal liability. A union that agrees to such a plan may be liable for not representing all members equally under the duty of fair representation. However, when pay scales reach such levels that the costs are exorbitant or are noncompetitive, there may be few alternatives to job loss except a two-tiered pay system.[60]

Most reports of the two-tiered plan have been based on anecdotal comments. However, one study of 1,935 employees in retail stores assessed commitment to the union and employer, perceived pay equity, and other similar relationships.[61] Low-tier employees perceived significantly lower pay equity and lower ability of their union in helping members obtain fair pay. This type of field research needs to be replicated in other settings to understand more fully the impact of two-tiered pay plans on employee attitudes and behaviors.

SUMMARY

Chapter 10 has continued the discussion of compensation by adding some very important concepts: methods of payment, executive compensation, and compensation administration issues.

To summarize the major points covered in this chapter:

1. Methods of payment are:
    a. (1) Hourly wage.
        (2) Salary.
    b. Incentive plans.
        (1) Individual incentives.
        (2) Group incentives.
        (3) Organization incentives.

---

[60] "Two-Tier Wage Plans Can Help Control Wage Costs if Administered Properly," *Management Review,* September 1984, p. 4.

[61] James E. Martin and Melanie M. Peterson, "Two-Tier Wage Structures: Implications for Equity, Theory," *Academy of Management Journal,* June 1987, pp. 297–315.

2. Most employees are paid salaries; exceptions are blue-collar and some clerical employees.
3. Individual incentive plans are the most effective methods to tie pay to performance; group incentive plans are the next most effective; organizationwide plans, the least effective.
4. Group and organization incentive plans provide more nonpay rewards (such as social acceptance, esteem) than individual incentive plans.
5. The least effective plans for tying pay to performance are across-the-board raises and seniority increases.
6. Executives are the most likely to think that pay should be tied to performance.
7. The more executive compensation is tied directly to performance for executives, the greater the impact on performance.
8. Pay secrecy is still practiced by a majority of firms. Knowing salary ranges instead of the salaries of other employees is the preferred practice in the majority of organizations.
9. Pay compression can have a demoralizing effect on employees. Some type of formal policy to maintain an equitable pay differential between managerial and nonmanagerial employees is recommended by P/HRM experts.

Questions for Review and Discussion

1. What is the most typical payment method: time-based or output-based? Why?
2. Are individual incentive pay plans effective? Which of the individual incentive pay plans are used most frequently?
3. What factors or ingredients are needed to help gainsharing plans be successful?
4. Compare and contrast the positive and negative aspects of suggestion plans, company group incentive plans, profit sharing plans, the Scanlon Plan, Improshare, and the stock ownership plan.
5. What do you feel is a fair pay for a top level executive in a large firm in a competitive industry? Explain.
6. Are executive salaries effective in increasing performance? Are perks? Bonuses? Stock options and performance shares?
7. Should compensation be kept secret? Why or why not?
8. What type of formalization in policy is needed to prevent disruptive pay compression?
9. When should raises be given? Should raises be given for cost-of-living changes?
10. What type of research is needed to examine the impact of two-tiered pay plans?

GLOSSARY

Bonus. A compensation payment that supplements salary and can be paid in the present or in the future.

COLA Plans. The adjustment of pay by automatic cost-of-living adjustment (COLA). In COLA plans, when the Bureau of Labor Statistic's Cost of Living Index increases by a rounded percentage, the wages and salaries are automatically increased by that percentage.

ESOP. An employee stock ownership plan under which employees, through stock purchases, become owners of a firm.

Gainsharing Plans. An organizational-based plan such as the Scanlon Plan designed to permit employer-employee sharing in the benefits resulting from improved productivity, cost reductions, or quality improvements.

Improshare Plan. An industrial engineering-based productivity measurement and sharing plan developed in the mid-1970s by Mitchell Fein. In this plan there is an equal sharing among participating employees in all productivity gains.

Incentive Compensation. Paying employees on the basis of output.

Pay Compression. A pay situation in which jobs requiring advanced levels of education and experience, more skills, and higher degrees of responsibility receive smaller increases in compensation opportunities.

Profit-Sharing Plan. A compensation plan in which payment of a regular share of company profits to employees is made as a supplement to their normal compensation.

Scanlon Plan. A combination group incentive, suggestion, and employee participation plan developed by Joseph Scanlon. Gains from increased productivity are paid in bonus form to all employees.

Stock Option. Provides employees with the right to purchase company stock at a fixed price for a certain period of time.

Two-Tiered Pay Plans. A pay structure in which the top pay for new employees is substantially lower than that for old (tenured) employees.

APPLICATION CASE 10–1

The "Money Motivates" Strategy At Nucor Manufacturing*

Nucor Manufacturing Company is a shining exception in the American steel industry where most companies contend with low profits and poor productivity. As the country's largest builder/operator of steel "mini-mills," Nucor is very profitable. The *Fortune 500* company sells over $800 million in steel products each year and has grown at a compound rate of over 23 percent in each of the last 10 years. Nucor is also very productive; its production employees in the company's 18 plants produce on average 950 tons per worker each year. This productivity is over twice the level achieved by the top five American steel companies (averaging 347 tons per worker year) and even by the Japanese steel competitors (480 tons).

Productivity produces profits at Nucor, and in many observers' views, the company's performance-based incentive compensation system produces the productivity. The company operates five types of incentive compensation plans:

Production incentive compensation: This plan applies to all employees whose work is directly tied to production (about 2,600 of the company's 4,000 employees). Each production employee works in a "bonus" group of 25 to 35 members which performs a complete task such as coating steel. Overall, nine bonus groups exist in each steel plant. A production standard is set by management; the group receives a bonus for production above standard. For example, in the coating group, 12 tons of good billets per hour is the standard; once the group exceeds the standard, members receive a bonus of 4 percent (of their base pay) for each additional ton per hour produced. Each employee receives the bonus in a separate check at the end of the week along with the base pay check. Bonuses are paid weekly instead of yearly to clearly communicate the link between performance and reward. There is no maximum limit for bonuses, and for almost all employees, the bonus check exceeds their base pay. However, the bonus system is demanding. Employees are allotted only four "forgiveness" days for absenteeism each year. Those who take more days (except for military or jury duty) lose their bonus for the respective week. If an employee is late five minutes to work, the bonus for the day is forfeited; if 30 minutes late, the bonus for the week is lost. Annual pay averages over $30,000 for production employees who are unskilled/semiskilled when first hired.

Department manager incentive compensation: Nucor employs about five or six department managers in each plant, and their bonus compensation is based

---

* Written by Kim Stewart and adapted from: George Gendron, "Steel Man Ken Iverson," *Inc.*, April 1986, pp. 40–44; and John Ortman, "Nucor's Ken Iverson on Productivity and Pay," *Personnel Administrator*, October 1986, pp. 46–48ff.

solely on their department's return on assets utilized. The maximum bonus is set at about 74 percent of base salary.

Nonproduction employee incentive compensation: This plan applies to employees who are not in a production function or are not at the department manager level. The bonus they receive is based on either the plant's return on assets or the corporation's return on assets. Every month each plant receives a report showing, on a year-to-year basis, its return on assets. This chart is posted in the employee cafeteria or break area, together with the chart showing the bonus payout.

Executive incentive compensation: Executives (general manager/vice president) receive a base salary that is about 75 percent of the average for the steel industry. Their bonus is based solely on the company's return on equity, which often averages 20 percent each year. If the company surpasses a 9 percent return (about the industry average), 5 percent of the company's net earnings for the year are placed in an executive bonus pool. Bonuses are allocated based on salary and are received in cash and in stock. Bonuses top out at a 24 percent return on equity, which provides an executive with about 300 percent of his/her base salary.

Profit sharing: Nucor does not have a pension or retirement plan; instead, all employees except top executives participate in a profit sharing plan where 10 percent of the company's pretax earnings each year are set aside for employees. Most of the employee's share is placed in a deferred trust; 20 percent is paid to the employee in cash in March of the following year. Vesting in the profit sharing trust is much like that of a retirement plan. An employee is 20-percent vested after a year in profit sharing, with an additional 10-percent vesting each year thereafter.

Another example of incentive at Nucor is the service awards program. Instead of handing out pen and pencil sets or gift certificates for seniority, Nucor issues company stock. After five years of service, an employee receives five shares of Nucor stock. After another five years of service, he or she receives another five shares, and so on. In 1987, the market price for Nucor stock ranged from about $30 to $50 a share.

Interestingly, because of the system's design, managers take a deeper pay cut than the plant's employees when times are bad (reduced product demand, sales, and production). In such times, employees' work week is cut to four or three-and-a-half days rather than a layoff (no layoff has occurred in the last 15 years). Thus, workers' pay is reduced by about 20 to 25 percent. However, with the lower earnings and use of assets, the department manager's pay is cut about 35 to 40 percent. Given that return on equity is even more substantially affected by production cutbacks, top executives find their pay reduced by 60 to 80 percent. This effect is what Nucor CEO Ken Iverson terms the "Share the Pain" program which he believes is equitable. He says, "Management should take the biggest drop in pay (in bad times) because they have the most responsibility . . . for making the decisions that make the company successful or not. . . ." Under his system, Iverson was the lowest paid CEO in the *Fortune 500* during 1983.

The compensation system also attracts particular types of individuals: managers with the confidence to make their divisions a success and employees who are highly goal-and money-oriented. Because production bonuses are based on group performance, group expectations of members are high, and the pressure on lower-performing employees can be intense. Recalls Iverson, "It gets pretty tough sometimes. We had a situation once in a joist plant—the group there is a whole production line—where the group chased a guy around the plant with a piece of angle iron. They were going to put him out of commission because he wasn't making his contribution." The work groups provide many productivity improvement ideas which ultimately boost their own bonus pay.

Because of the hard work and required commitment, turnover often runs as high as 200 percent during the first year of a new plant's operation. Many people just don't want to work that hard. However, once workforce adjustments are made, turnover becomes virtually nonexistent, often annually averaging 4 to 10 people (excluding retirements) in a plant of 500 employees.

Besides the unique compensation system, other factors contribute to Nucor's exceptional success. Iverson places the company's lean management structure near the top of the list. With a workforce of 4,000 employees, Nucor has a corporate staff of only 16 individuals and four management levels (chairman and president, plant manager/vice president, department head, and foreman). In Iverson's view, keeping the structure lean produces quick, clear decision making and better communication with employees.

Management-employee relations are also enhanced by the absence of any class distinctions between managers and employees. Everyone receives the same vacation and benefits, wears the same color hard hat (green), and eats in the same company cafeteria. There are no executive parking spaces, washrooms, or perks that the nonsupervisory employees don't receive.

To further enhance communication with employees, Iverson requires that all production supervisors receive company training in communication skills and conducts a survey of about half the company's workforce every two years. Company policy also requires that every plant general manager have dinner with plant employees (in groups of less than 50) at least once a year. After dinner and brief comments from the manager, the rest of the evening is for the employees to talk about their concerns involving their work and the company.

Overall, Nucor's system works, but Iverson admits that the company's way of work and compensation is not for everyone. Besides high initial turnover, the company has had problems with employees who've worked years in the steel industry for other companies. The compensation system is also applicable only in cases where small groups of people work on an identifiable task and the output is objectively measurable.

Questions for Thought

1. Evaluate Nucor's production incentive compensation program (including profit sharing) using the eight criteria for an effective compensation system presented in the chapter. Which criteria does the plan most (and least) effectively fulfill?
2. What is your opinion of Nucor's executive incentive plan? Would most executives like to work under such a plan? Why?
3. In your view, why has Nucor had problems with employees who've worked or managed years with another steel company?

EXERCISE 10–1   Paying People for Work

Objective: The exercise encourages students to think about job conditions and occupations in terms of the most appropriate, if
any, method of payment.

SET UP THE EXERCISE

1. Listed below are several job conditions. Decide whether payment should be
made on the basis of time worked (hour, week, month), or on the basis of
number of units produced or output (for instance, generators, cars painted,
vouchers filed).

Job Condition	Time Payment	Output Payment
1. Quality is very important.	_____	_____
2. Quantity is difficult to measure.	_____	_____
3. Workers perceive little relationship between effort/performance and rewards.	_____	_____
4. Equipment is unreliable; thus there are large chunks of down-time.	_____	_____
5. Management wants to create more competition between workers.	_____	_____
6. Incentive systems have been very successful.	_____	_____

Now examine the jobs listed here. Decide whether payment should be made
on the basis of time or output.

Job	Time Payment	Output Payment
Police officer	_____	_____
Auto worker	_____	_____
Coal miner	_____	_____
College professor	_____	_____
Trucker	_____	_____
Neurosurgeon	_____	_____
Professional baseball player	_____	_____
Air traffic controller	_____	_____
Homemaker	_____	_____
Accountant	_____	_____
Judge (lawyer)	_____	_____
Carpenter	_____	_____
Nurse	_____	_____
Cashier at checkout	_____	_____

2. The instructor will form groups to discuss the individual ratings.
3. What did each group find? Were there a lot of similarities or differences in opinions? Have a group spokesperson discuss the findings.

A Learning Note

This exercise encourages you to think about how payment for work decisions is made difficult by the characteristics of the job. It also raises issues concerning how individuals in various occupations are paid.

EXERCISE 10–2   Developing a Positive Reinforcement Sales Program

Objective: The exercise is designed to have students apply principles of motivation in designing a positive reinforcement program for sales personnel.

SET UP THE EXERCISE

1. Please read the facts individually.

Palmay Cosmetics is a small firm with 15 salespeople in the New York City area. The salespeople put on demonstrations to sell a full line of women's cosmetics in the homes of customers. Each demonstration will have between 10 to 15 neighborhood women in attendance. The Palmay salesperson has a specific New York area territory. Usually the territories are the areas in which the salesperson lives. The salespeople receive commissions at the rate of 12 percent on gross sales. Bonuses are paid if sales exceed a previously set sales goal established jointly by the sales director and each salesperson. Pension and insurance benefits are paid by the company.

Two years ago Palmay had four salespersons. Currently the company has 15 salespersons and plans to add 15 more in two years because of the growth in sales. Unfortunately, there has been some turnover (five women have left and been replaced) in the past nine months.

The president of Palmay, Sonja Kimslow, believes that applying behavior modification can improve performance, reduce turnover, and increase the morale of the sales force. She would like a skeleton plan that outlines what the company can do in terms of a positive reinforcement program to accomplish these objectives.

2. The class or group is to be divided into groups—six, seven, or eight persons are ideal.
3. Each group is to develop a positive reinforcement program for Sonja's review. Think about the following points in developing the plans:

   a. What reinforcers should be used? How were they determined to be what was needed?
   b. How and when should the reinforcers be used?
   c. How should the consequences be assessed?
   d. Should punishment be included in any plan to improve performance at Palmay?
   e. What assumptions did the group make in putting their plan together?
4. A spokesperson for each group should present the group's plan to the class.

A Learning Note

This exercise should illustrate that there are some problems and difficulties associated with implementing a positive reinforcement program. The evaluation of such programs is one of these difficulties.

EMPLOYEE BENEFITS AND SERVICES

P/HRM · IN · ACTION

Carl Reems and Pete Lakich

Carl Reems was the president of Coy Manufacturing of Whiting, Indiana. It was Carl's intention to keep his work force as satisfied and productive as possible. A number of problems concerning the Coy employee benefits and services package have come to a head over the past few months. Carl listened to a presentation that Pete Lakich, Coy's director of personnel/human resources, made to the firm's executive committee. In the presentation, Pete used some figures that seemed wrong to Carl. Pete claimed that in manufacturing firms in the Whiting area (located just southeast of Chicago), the average fringe benefit and services costs per worker totaled $6,240. In fact, Pete gave a specific item-by-item breakdown of these costs to the committee.

After the meeting Carl had this talk with Pete:

Carl: Pete, where did you get those fringe benefit figures? They seem wrong.

Pete: Carl, these are facts based on my program of monitoring costs and benefits of fringes.

Carl: We must be paying the highest fringe benefits in the entire area!

Pete: As a matter of fact, we are a little on the low end of the scale. Among similar firms in our area we are in the bottom one third in fringe benefit costs.

Carl: Do you think this is one of the reasons we are not able to recruit and hold skilled employees?

Pete: I'm not certain, but there is probably some connection. You know how employees exchange and compare wage, fringe, and service information.

Carl: Let's look at the entire range of our fringe benefits and services and see what is needed to become more competitive. We would probably even improve production and morale by improving benefits and services.

Pete: We do need to take a look, but we can't be so certain that more and better fringes and services can make productivity and morale jump up.

Carl: Pete, you're just too conservative about the power of money. The carrot and the stick can always do the job, even in Whiting, Indiana.

Pete: Don't jump to conclusions.

Do you agree with Carl or Pete about the motivational power of benefits and services?

INTRODUCTION

Unlike pay for performance programs and incentive plans, benefits and services are made available to employees as long as they are employed by an organization.

> Employee benefits and services are a part of the rewards of employment that reinforce loyal service to the employer. Major benefits and services programs include pay for time not worked, insurance, pensions, and services.

This definition of benefits and services is applied to hundreds of programs. Programs that are sometimes called benefits or services (for example, stock purchase plans) have already been discussed. This chapter will show that Pete's opinions about the impact of benefits and services is a valid position in most situations.

Why do Employers Offer Benefits and Services?

The programs offered in work organizations today are the product of efforts in this area for the past 40 years. Before World War II, employers offered a few pensions and services because they had the employees' welfare at heart, or they wanted to keep out the union. But most benefit programs began in earnest during the war, when wages were strictly regulated.

The unions pushed for nonwage compensation increases, and they got them. Court cases in the late 1940s confirmed the right of unions to bargain for benefits: *Inland Steel* v. *National Labor Relations Board* (1948) over pensions, and *W. W. Cross* v. *National Labor Relations Board* over insurance. The growth of these programs indicates the extent to which unions have used this right. In 1929, benefits cost the employer 3 percent of total wages and salaries; by 1949, the cost was up to 16 percent; and in the 1970s, it was nearly 30 percent. By 1990, costs of benefits and services are expected to total about 50 percent.[1]

Some employers provide these programs for labor market reasons; that is, to keep the organization competitive in recruiting and retaining employees in relation to other employers. Or they may provide them to keep a union out or because the unions have won them during contract negotiations.

Another reason often given for providing benefits and services is that they increase employee performance. Is this reason valid? In a study of benefits, it was found that none of these reasons explained the degree to which benefits and services were provided.[2] The researchers found that only the *size* of the

---

[1] Kenneth H. Loeffler, "Benefits," *Personnel Journal*, June 1983, pp. 106–12.

[2] Robert Ashall and John Child, "Employee Services: People, Profits, or Parkinson?" *Personnel Management*, Fall 1972, pp. 10–22.

organization explained this factor. Thus, as organizations grow in size, they offer more benefits. According to these researchers, the move to provide employee benefits and services is just another manifestation of the bureaucracy.

Who Is Involved in Benefit Decisions?

P/HRM executives often seek professional advice from specialists such as a member of the Society of Professional Benefit Administrator. These persons are independent consultants or are employed by benefit carriers like insurance companies. In very large organizations, the compensation department may have a specialist in benefits, usually called a manager or director of employee benefits, such as Ernest Griffes of Levi Strauss & Co. Exhibit 11–1 shows who is involved in benefit decisions within an organization. How the benefits and services decision is made is discussed later in the chapter.

Benefits are still primarily a Stage I function. Many authorities argue that all organizations should have benefits and services, but there is little concrete evidence that they affect employee productivity or satisfaction.

A DIAGNOSTIC APPROACH TO BENEFITS AND SERVICES

Exhibit 11–2 highlights the most important factors in the diagnostic model of the P/HRM function that affect the administration of employee benefits and services. Unions have had a great impact on benefits. In the 1940s and 1950s, a major thrust of their bargaining was for increased or innovative benefits. Union pressure for additional holidays is being followed by demands for such benefits as group auto insurance, dental care, and prepaid legal fees. Union leaders have varied the strategy and tactics they use to get "more." The long-

---

EXHIBIT 11–1   The Role of Operating and P/HRM Managers in Benefits and Services

Benefits and Services Function	Operating Manager (OM)	P/HRM Manager (P/HRM)
Benefits and services budget	Preliminary budget approved or adjusted by top management	Preliminary budget developed by P/HRM
Voluntary benefits and services	Programs approved by OM (top management)	Programs recommended by P/HRM
Communication of benefits and services	OM cooperates with P/HRM	Primary duty of P/HRM
Evaluation of benefits and services		Done by P/HRM
Administration of benefits and services programs		Done by P/HRM

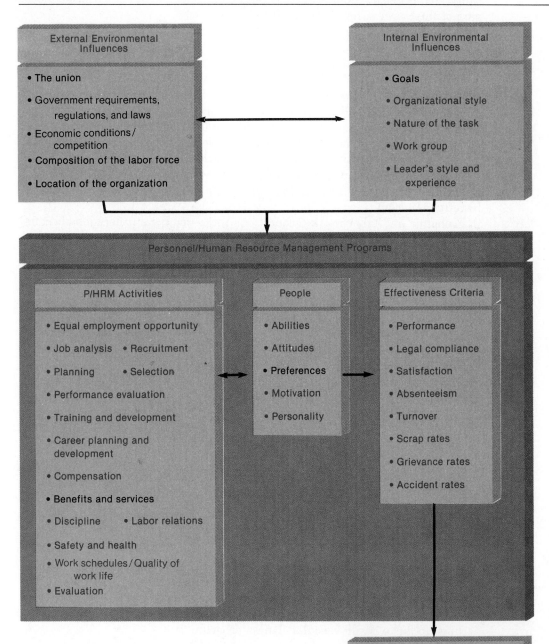

External Environmental Influences

- The union
- Government requirements, regulations, and laws
- Economic conditions/competition
- Composition of the labor force
- Location of the organization

Internal Environmental Influences

- Goals
- Organizational style
- Nature of the task
- Work group
- Leader's style and experience

Personnel/Human Resource Management Programs

P/HRM Activities

- Equal employment opportunity
- Job analysis • Recruitment
- Planning • Selection
- Performance evaluation
- Training and development
- Career planning and development
- Compensation
- Benefits and services
- Discipline • Labor relations
- Safety and health
- Work schedules/Quality of work life
- Evaluation

People

- Abilities
- Attitudes
- Preferences
- Motivation
- Personality

Effectiveness Criteria

- Performance
- Legal compliance
- Satisfaction
- Absenteeism
- Turnover
- Scrap rates
- Grievance rates
- Accident rates

Organization End Results

- Competitive product(s)
- Competitive service(s)

range goal is getting employers to perceive benefits not as compensation but as part of their own social responsibility.

Government requirements have affected the benefits area significantly. Three major benefits are legally required: workers' compensation, unemployment compensation, and social security. Progressive income taxes and the policy of the Internal Revenue Service to allow deductions of benefits costs as expenses have encouraged their development. In 1971 the federal government mandated four long holiday weekends. Passage of the Welfare Fund Disclosure Act requires descriptions and reports of benefits plans. The National Labor Relations Board and the courts have stringent rules on eligibility for benefits and the employer's ability to change an established benefits plan. Finally, the government's tax policy influences benefits. At present, benefits are tax free, though some agencies (in Canada, for example) appear interested in taxing benefits as income.

Economic and labor market conditions influence benefit decisions because in tight labor markets, organizations seeking the best employees compete by offering better benefits and services pakcages, which are nontaxable income.

The goals of managers and controlling interests affect the benefits-services package offered. Managers or owners may aim at employee satisfaction or may oppose unions. Other goals also can influence whether a benefits program is set up and how generous it is.

Competition can induce an organization to add to or adjust its benefits-services plan. Certain companies are pacesetters in benefits; they introduce the newer benefits first. Examples of pacesetters in benefits are American Telephone & Telegraph Company, IBM, Texas Instruments, Apple Computer, and Time, Inc.[3]

Let us look closely at the benefits offered by a sample company. Few companies can match the benefits that Time, Inc. employees receive. For example:

- If an employee works past 8 P.M. in New York, he or she not only receives $20 toward dinner, but also the right to take a cab all the way home (even if home is in New Jersey or Connecticut).
- The entire premium for medical and dental insurance for the whole family is paid by Time, Inc.
- The profit-sharing plan deposits into an employee's account 10 percent of his or her annual compensation, plus bonuses.
- The pension plan is completely paid into by the company.
- Education is paid if it's job-related, up to 100 percent of tuition.
- The company pays 50 percent of membership in an athletic club, provided the club has a cardiovascular fitness program.

Other leading employers follow the practices of pacesetters like Time, Inc. The benefits managers of the pacesetting companies regularly discuss benefit trends and read surveys of what the competition is offering.

---

[3] Robert Levering, Milton Moskowitz, and Michael Katz, *The 100 Best Companies to Work for in America* (Reading, Mass.: Addison-Wesley Publishing, 1984), p. 369.

In addition to observing and following pacesetters, many firms examine the preferences and attitudes of their employees toward them. For benefits to have an effect on employee satisfaction:

- Employees must know about their benefits.
- Employees must prefer the organization's benefits to those offered by other organizations.
- Employees must perceive the organization's benefits as satisfying more of their needs than competing employers' benefits would.

Presumably, if employees are satisfied with their benefits package, they will be absent less, be reluctant to quit, produce higher-quality products, and have fewer accidents. For benefits to have an affect on employee performance:

Employees must see them as a strongly preferred end.

Employees must perceive that by performing better they can increase their benefits.

MANDATED BENEFIT PROGRAMS

There are three benefit programs that the private- and third-sector employers have no choice but to offer to employees. An employer who wishes to change these programs or to stop offering them must get involved in the political process and change the laws. These three programs are unemployment insurance, social security, and workers' compensation (see Chapter 18 for further discussion).

Unemployment Insurance

In the 1930s, when unemployment was very high, the government was pressured to create programs to take care of people who were out of work through no fault of their own. Unemployment insurance (UI) was set up in the United States as part of the Social Security Act of 1935.

Unemployment insurance is designed to provide a subsistence payment to employees between jobs. The employer contributes to the UI fund (in Alabama, Alaska, and New Jersey, so do employees). The base payment is increased if there is more than an average number of employees from an enterprise drawing from the fund (this is called the *experience rating*). Unemployment insurance and allied systems for railroad, federal government, and military employees covers about 65 million employees. Major groups excluded from UI are self-employed workers, employees of small firms with less than four employees, domestics, farm employees, state and local government employees, and nonprofit employers such as hospitals.

To be eligible for compensation, the employee must have worked a minimum number of weeks, be without a job, and be willing to accept a suitable position offered through a state Unemployment Compensation Commission. A Supreme Court decision granted unemployment insurance benefits to strikers after an eight-week strike period. The Court ruled that neither the Social Security Act nor the National Labor Relations Act specifically forbids making

P/HRM Manager Close-Up

Ernest J. E. Griffes
Levi Strauss & Company

Biography

Ernest J. E. Griffes is director of employee benefits with Levi Strauss & Co. in San Francisco. A graduate of Grand Valley State College, Allendale, Michigan, with a bachelors degree in economics, Griffes has previously held positions as a bank operations manager, an office manager-personnel officer, a consultant (employee benefit plans), and a personnel and financial officer. Over the past several years, he has achieved a highly respected national reputation through his frequently published articles, his participation in seminars and workshops, and his lectures on the subjects of pension planning and legislation. He serves as chairman of the American Society for Personnel Administration (ASPA) National Committee on Retirement Income Systems. Griffes prepared

ASPA's position paper to the U.S. Congress on the subject, "Providing Adequate Retirement Income for the American People," in which he outlined ASPA's position on pension legislation.

Job Description

The primary responsibility of this position is dynamic, results-oriented management of employee benefit plans to maximize the cost effectiveness of benefit expenditures for both company an employee. The incumbent develops and installs new or modified plans, administers existing plans, ensures compliance with all laws, determines whether "to make or buy" group insurance, and also develops and implements corporate benefit policies, alerting management to trends.

benefits payments to strikers. Each state decides on whether to permit or prohibit such payments.[4]

The employee receives compensation for a limited period. Typically, the maximum is 26 weeks, although a few states extend the term beyond this in emergency situations, such as when the number of insured unemployed reaches 6 percent.[5] The payment is intended to be about 50 percent of a typical wage and varies from a few dollars to over $200 a week in some states. Unemployment compensation averages about $109 a week nationally.

The unemployment insurance program is jointly run by the federal and state governments and is administered by the states. Federal guidelines indicate that presently the tax is 6.2 percent on the first $7,000 earned by each employee. Each state has its own set of interpretations and payments. Payments by employers and to employees vary with benefits paid, the experience ratings of organizations, and the efficiency of different states in administering the program.

Hard economic times seem to tempt more Americans to cheat on unemployment. Some individuals keep collecting and cashing unemployment checks after they find work. It is estimated that approximately $3 billion a year may be wasted through unemployment insurance fraud.[6] In 1982 the government initiated a program to cut unemployment insurance fraud. The government is now using computers and extensive interviews to block costly fraudulent claims.

What can the employer do about UI cost increases? Responsible employers want to pay their fair share, but do not want to support abusers. They also do not want their experience ratings to increase costs. Much expert advice has been offered on how to cut costs to the program by stabilizing employment, keeping good records, challenging fraudulent claims, and issuing effective claim control procedures. Careful hiring and separation procedures, and claims verification and control can also cut cost. Effective managers try to control the costs of unemployment insurance just as much as inventory, advertising, or other costs.

Social Security

In 1935 the pension portion of the social security system was established under the Old-Age, Survivors and Disability Insurance (OASDI) program. (See Chapter 18 for disability and other provisions.) The goal of the pension portion was to provide *some* income to retired persons to *supplement* savings, private

---

[4] *New York Telephone Co. et al.* v *New York State Department of Labor et al.*, U.S. Supreme Court, No. 77–961, March 21, 1979.

[5] C. Arthur Williams, John S. Turnbull, and Earl F. Cheit, *Economic and Social Security* (New York: John Wiley & Sons, 1982).

[6] Joann S. Lublin, "Government Starts Cracking Down on Unemployment Insurance Fraud," *The Wall Street Journal*, February 9, 1982, p. 27.

pensions, and part-time work. It was created at a time when the wealthy continued to live alone, the average person moved in with relatives, and the poor with no one to help them were put in a "poor house," or government-supported retirement home.

The program has a worthwhile objective. No one wants older people to live out their last years in crushing poverty and with little or no dignity. Anyone whose grandparents had to live with their children because they could not survive any other way knows how hard this can be on everyone involved.

The basic concept was that the employee and employer were to pay taxes that would cover the retirement payments each employee would later receive in a self-funding insurance program. Initially, two goals were sought: adequate payments for all, and individual equity, which means that each employee was to receive what he or she and the employer had put into the fund. In the past 15 years, however, individual equity has lost out.

Social security taxes are paid by *both* employers and employees. Both pay a percentage of the employee's pay to the government. Respectively, the percentage will rise to 7.65 percent for employee and employer in 1990. The maximum tax increased to $3,046 in 1987 for an employee earning $42,600 or 7.15 percent. How much is paid by employee and employer is calculated on the average monthly wage (weighted toward the later years).

Those receiving social security pensions can work part time, up to a maximum amount that is increased each year to reflect inflation. The maximum a person aged 65 to 70 can earn before loss of social security benefits is $6,600 in 1983 and thereafter. Just about all employees except civilian federal government employees are eligible for social security coverage. Self-employed persons can join the system. They will pay 10.75 percent in 1990, a tax of $4,579 for a person earning $42,600.

Employees become eligible to receive full benefits at age 65 or reduced benefits at age 62. If an employee dies, a family with children under 18 receives survivor benefits, regardless of the employee's age. An employee who is totally disabled before age 65 becomes eligible to receive insurance benefits. Under Medicare provisions of the social security system, eligible individuals aged 65 and older receive payments for doctor and hospital bills, as well as other related benefits and services. Exhibit 11–3 provides a payment schedule for retired employees or dependents. A person who retires at age 65 and whose pay averages $10,000 annually would receive a monthly check of $534.70. If this person retires at age 62, the monthly check would be $427.80.

Presidents Reagan and Carter called attention to some of the problems with the social security system. Specifically, they pointed out that the trust fund set up to pay the pensions was being rapidly depleted. This was happening for a number of reasons:

- Unrealistic inflation rate assumptions by the system's actuaries.
- Inaccurate assumptions of the birthrate.
- Unrealistic assumptions of the productivity increases by employees.
- Addition by Congress of beneficiaries who did not pay into the system fully.
- Withdrawal of many government employees from the system.

EXHIBIT 11–3 Monthly Retirement Benefits for Workers and Dependents

| Average Yearly Earnings | Amount Workers Receive Monthly | | | | Monthly Amount for Dependents* or Spouse | | | | Family† Benefits |
	At 65	At 64	At 63	At 62	At 65 or Child	At 64	At 63	At 62	
$ 1,200	$156.70	$146.30	$135.90	$125.40	$ 78.40	$ 71.90	$ 65.40	$ 58.80	$235.10
2,600	230.10	214.80	199.50	184.10	115.10	105.50	95.90	86.40	345.20
3,000	251.80	235.10	218.30	201.50	125.90	115.40	104.90	94.50	384.90
3,400	270.00	252.00	234.00	216.00	135.00	123.80	112.50	101.30	434.90
4,000	296.20	276.50	256.80	237.00	148.10	135.70	123.40	111.10	506.20
4,400	317.30	296.20	275.00	253.90	158.70	145.40	132.20	119.10	562.50
4,800	336.00	313.60	291.20	268.80	168.00	153.90	140.00	126.00	612.70
5,200	353.20	329.70	306.20	282.60	176.60	161.80	147.20	132.50	662.70
5,600	370.60	345.90	321.20	296.50	185.30	169.80	154.40	139.00	687.10
6,000	388.20	362.40	336.50	310.60	194.10	177.80	161.70	145.60	712.10
6,400	405.60	378.60	351.60	324.50	202.80	185.80	169.00	152.10	737.10
6,800	424.10	395.90	367.60	339.30	212.10	194.30	176.70	159.10	762.30
7,200	446.00	416.30	386.60	356.80	223.00	204.30	185.80	167.30	788.90
7,600	465.60	434.50	403.60	372.50	232.80	213.30	194.00	174.60	814.70
8,000	482.60	450.50	418.30	386.10	241.30	221.10	201.10	181.00	844.50
8,400	492.90	460.10	427.20	394.40	246.50	225.80	205.40	184.90	862.60
8,800	505.10	471.50	437.80	404.10	252.60	231.40	210.50	189.50	883.80
9,200	516.00	481.60	447.20	412.80	258.00	236.40	215.00	193.50	903.00
9,400	520.40	485.80	451.10	416.40	260.20	238.40	216.80	195.20	910.40
9,600	524.60	489.70	454.70	419.70	262.30	240.30	218.50	196.80	918.00
9,800	530.40	495.10	459.70	424.40	265.20	234.00	221.00	198.90	928.00
10,000	534.70	499.10	463.50	427.80	267.40	245.00	222.80	200.60	935.70

* If a person is eligible for both a worker's benefit and a spouse's benefit, the check actually payable is limited to the larger of the two.
† The maximum amount payable to a family is generally reached when a worker and two family members are eligible.

Source: U.S. Department of Health and Human Services, Social Security Administration, SSA Publication No. 05–10088, June 1982.

Another area of concern for the social security system is that many people continue to believe that social security is not just a supplement but should provide full support in retirement, at almost the same standard of living they had when they were working. Unfortunately, some voters reward congresspersons and senators who vote their way on a single issue. Social security is such an emotionally charged issue that voters listen very carefully to how a politician regards this benefit. The goal of providing full retirement support through social security benefits simply cannot be reached without a dramatic increase in taxes.

Probably the best way to save social security is to create a significant *communication* program to tell people the facts about retirement and social security. Everyone must understand these facts and comprehend how the facts apply to their own situations.

BENEFIT AND RETIREMENT PLANS

In addition to the benefits required by the law, many employers also provide other kinds of benefits: compensation for time not worked, insurance protection, and retirement plans. There are many differences in employers' practices regarding these benefits.

Compensation for Time Off

Can you imagine a life in which you went to work six days a week, 12 hours a day, 52 weeks a year for life? That's what life used to be like, although it has been shown that employees did not always work hard all that time. The concept of a paid holiday or vacation with pay did not exist. Now most employers compensate for time that employees have not worked: break time, get-ready time, washup time, clothes changed time, paid lunch and rest periods, coffee breaks, and so on. Employers also pay employees when they are not actually at work—holidays, vacations, sick leave, funeral leave, jury duty, and other personal leaves, such as to fulfill military obligations.

Studies of employees' preference indicate that work breaks are not strongly preferred; they are just expected.[7] Vacations are generally a highly preferred benefit. Preferences for holidays vary, and lower-paid and women employees have stronger preferences for sick leave. Unions have negotiated hard for added time off to give their members more leisure and to create jobs.

Let us take a closer look at some of the time off offered by employers.

Paid Holidays Probably the most frequently offered of these times-off-with-pay are paid holidays. At one time, every employee was paid only for actual holidays off with pay. The typical number of paid holidays has been increasing. Currently, 10 or more paid holidays are provided to full-time employees. The most typical holidays are: New Year's Day, Memorial Day, July 4, Labor Day, Thanksgiving Day, and Christmas. The new minivacation dates created by Congress through the federal Monday-holiday law allow for three-day weekends in February for President's Day, in May for Memorial Day, in October Columbus Day, and in November for Veterans' Day.

Paid Vacations Another example of voluntary compensation offered for time not worked is paid vacations. This is the most expensive benefit for American employers. Most organizations offer vacations with pay after a certain minimum period of service. The theory behind vacations is that they provide an opportunity for employees to rest and refresh themselves; when they return, hopefully, they will be more effective employees. Employees have pressed for more leisure to enjoy the fruit of their labors.

Government and military employees traditionally have been given 30 days

---

[7] Robert C. Wender and Ronald L. Sladky, "Flexible Benefit Opportunities for the Small Employer," *Personnel Administrator*, December 1984, pp. 111–18.

Jack Markou, from True Magazine.

"Let me see that vacation schedule again, Hawkins."

vacation. The typical vacation is one week of paid vacation for an employee of less than a year's service, and two weeks for 1–10 years service. Three-week vacations are offered annually to veterans of 10–20 years, and four weeks to the over-20-year tenured. Over one fourth of the companies studied by the Personnel Survey now offer five-and six-week vacations, usually for 25-year employees.[8] The trend in paid vacations for unionized employees is upward. As you can see from the cartoon above, vacations need to be well planned to allow the firm to continue to operate effectively.

In some organizations, if employees don't take their vacation by the end of the year or a specified date, they forfeit the vacation days. Also in some firms, if an employee is sick during a vacation, rescheduling the vacation is permitted. In a personnel survey of 137 firms, it was determined that some employ-

---

[8] "1984 Vacation Policies," *Personnel Management Policies and Practices* (Englewood Cliffs, N.J.: Prentice-Hall, May 7 1984), pp. 223–29.

ers, about 34, permitted employees to get double pay instead of time off for vacations. The firms that permitted this practice did so primarily because of particularly heavy workloads.[9]

Personal Time Off Many employers pay employees for time off for funerals, medical/dental appointments, sickness in the family, religious observances, marriage, personal-choice holidays, and birthdays as holidays. If an organization uses flexitime scheduling (see Chapter 19), the need for time off is minimized. A BNA survey found that 9 out of 10 firms provide paid jury duty; 9 out of 10 provide paid leave for funerals of close relatives; and 7 out of 10 provide paid leave for military duty time. Typically, the pay is the difference between normal pay and military pay. Many policies apply to leaves for personal reasons, such as sickness in the family or marriage. A typical policy is to allow no more than five days per year personal time.[10]

Sick Leave

Illness has a significant effect on the productivity of an organization. In most situations, organizations allow and pay for one sick day per month, or 12 per year. The attitudes, expectations, and interests in society toward improved health has certainly found its way into organizations. There is now a trend toward emphasizing wellness instead of sick pay among employees. People are now placing a higher value and are more interested in maintaining good health. Consequently, there is now a growing interest in rewarding good health through organizational programs.

At Scherer Brothers, a lumber company in Minnesota, a wellness program has been implemented.[11] The firm has removed candy machines, cigarette machines, caffeinated coffee, and high-fat foods from the noontime meals served free to employees. In addition, recreation facilities are available for use by employees and their families, including a gym, exercise equipment, and a sauna. Coupled with this is well pay—two hours' extra pay for employees who have been neither tardy nor absent during the previous month. The result is that absenteeism is now 0.3 percent, compared to an industry rate of between 3 and 4 percent.

A review of organization sick-leave programs shows some common characteristics:[12]

- Sick pay accrues over time (usually every pay period).

---

[9] Ibid., p. 227.

[10] Bureau of National Affairs, *Paid Leave and Leave of Absence Policies*, Personnel Policies Forum, Survey III Washington, D.C., November 1975.

[11] Miriam Rothman, "Can Alternatives to Sick Pay Reduce Absenteeism?" *Personnel Journal*, October 1981, pp. 788–90.

[12] Barron H. Harvey, Judy A. Schultz, and Jerome F. Rogers, "Rewarding Employees for Not Using Sick Leave," *Personnel Adminstrator*, May 1983, pp. 55–59.

- Upon termination of employment, no compensation is given for accrued sick leave.
- Sick pay is granted when a worker is absent from work due to a short-term illness.

The central objective of such leave is to provide short-term insurance to workers against loss of wages due to short-term illness.

Some firms are using what are called sick-leave banks to cut down on sick leave. Employees deposit a set portion of their earned sick leave days into a company pool. Should an employee use all of his or her compensated sick leave, an application for withdrawal from the sick-leave bank can be made. However, these requests are carefully screened by a committee. The sick-leave bank has psychological benefits. Members become conservative in using banked days, using only what they need so that co-workers will have what they need in case of long-term illnesses or accidents.

Employer-Purchased Insurance

The many risks encountered throughout life—illness, accident, and early death, among others—can be offset by buying insurance. Many employers can buy insurance cheaper than their employees can, and insurance is frequently offered as a benefit. The employer may provide it free to the employee or pay part of it, and the employee "participates" by paying a share. Four major forms of insurance are involved: health, life, disability-accident, and maternity leave.

Health Insurance Medical costs are almost out of control in the United States. In 1985, over $400 billion was spent on health care costs in the United States. To put this in perspective, if that money were a gross national product, it would represent the eight largest nations in the world. One of the most costly kinds of insurance, health or medical insurance, is financed at least partially by employers as a benefit for employees. Health insurance can be purchased from Blue Cross (hospital expenses), Blue Shield (physician expenses), life insurance firms, or from a health maintenance organization (HMO). Studies indicate that employees prefer health insurance over most other benefits. Health insurance includes hospitalization (room and board and hospital service charges), surgical fees (actual surgical fees or maximum limits), and major medical fees (maximum benefits, typically $5,000–$10,000 beyond hospitalization and surgical payments). In the 1980s, increased coverage has been provided in major medical and comprehensive health insurance plans. Surveys report that almost all organizations have hospitalization plans, almost all nonblue-collar workers are provided with surgical and major medical plans, and about three fourths of blue-collar employees have major medical insurance. The rising cost of hospital care, as shown in Exhibit 11–4, point out how important health insurance is to employees.

Typically, all employees get basic coverage. Beyond this, plans differ. Plans

EXHIBIT 11–4 **Cost of Hospital Care**

	1987 Cost	1995 Estimate
Semiprivate room rate (per day)	$ 180.00	$ 240.00
Laboratory test (P)	12.00	20.00
X ray (P)	20.00	30.00
Nursing (P)	75.00	85.00
Bandages, supplies (P)	16.00	26.00
Medicines (P)	18.00	25.00
Food (P)	12.00	20.00
Ambulance	45.00	75.00
Emergency room	70.00	120.00
Operating room	310,00	550.00
Recovery room	50.00	100.00
Anesthesiologist	70.00	125.00
Appendectomy	500.00	700.00
Tonsils and adenoids	350.00	600.00
Hemorrhoidectomy	600.00	800.00
Heart bypass	13,500.00	17,000.00
Pacemaker	2,500.00	3,000.00
Vasectomy	250.00	500.00
Cesarean birth	600.00	1,000.00
Hysterectomy	1,000.00	2,000.00

for salaried employees typically are of the major medical variety and provide "last-dollar coverage." This means that the employee must pay the first $200 of the cost or a similar deductible. The benefits may be based on either a specific cash allowance for various procedures or a service benefit that pays the full amount of all reasonable charges.[13]

Negotiated plans for time-pay workers generally have expanded coverage that provides specific benefits rather than comprehensive major medical coverage. This approach is preferred by union leaders because they feel individual benefits that can be clearly labeled will impress union members; and these benefits can be obtained with no deductible payments by employees. Also, until recently, coverage of some desired services was not available under major medical plans. Some of the more rapidly expanding benefits of the negotiated plans are prescription drugs, vision care, mental health services, and dental care. For example, typical dental care ranges from $1,000 to $2,000 yearly. About one employer in four provides this insurance now.[14]

The Health Maintenance Organization (HMO) Act of 1973 was intended to stimulate a prepaid health care system. An *HMO* is a medical organization

---

[13] "A Report Card on Health Cost Strategies," *Employee Benefits News*, March 1987, pp. 15–19.

[14] "Free Program on Dental Reimbursement," *Employee Benefits News*, September 1987, p. 27.

consisting of medical and health specialists (surgeons, internists, psychiatrists, nurses). HMOs offer outpatient services as well as hospital coverage for a fixed, monthly, prepaid fee. Care is available 24 hours a day, seven days a week. The emphasis of an HMO is on preventive medicine so that problems are caught in their early stages. Typically, the number of hospital days per 1,000 HMO members is about half the national average.[15]

Section 162(k) of the Consolidated Omnibus Budget Reconciliation Act of 1985 (COBRA) stipulates that employers with more than 20 employees are required to offer continuation of health care coverage for 18 to 36 months after an employee termination.[16] Thus, employees who are fired, quit, or laid off are given the option to continue health care coverage for themselves and their families. If an employer fails to comply with COBRA regulations, the employer will not be allowed to deduct contributions made to that or any other group health plan. Employers complain that the legal details of COBRA will become a recordkeeping nightmare. What triggers COBRA coverage is a qualifying event—death of a covered employee, divorce, legal separation, employee strikes, layoffs, when a child ceases to be a dependent. Keeping track of qualifying events is causing anxiety and concern for P/HRM managers who must comply with COBRA.[17]

Life Insurance Group life insurance is one of the oldest and most widely available employee benefits. The employer purchases life insurance for each employee to benefit the employee's family. Group life insurance plans provide coverage to all employees without physical examinations with premiums based on the characteristics of the group as a whole.

Employee preference for group life insurance is not high. Surveys indicate that almost all employers offer group life insurance. In a typical program for a large company, the amount of insurance provided by the plan increases as salary increases, the typical amount being twice the salary in life insurance. But about a third of the companies surveyed have different plans for blue-collar employees, who usually get a flat amount (usually $5,000–$10,000). Initially, the organization pays part of the premium, the employee the rest (contributory plan). The trend is moving toward noncontributory plans in which the company pays it all. But 34 percent of blue-collar, 38 percent of white-collar, and 40 percent of managerial plans are still contributory. In view of employee preferences, it probably should stay that way. Continued life insurance coverage after retirement, usually one third the coverage while working, is provided by 72 percent of large American companies.[18]

---

[15] David Albertson, "HMO—Only Move Gaining Popularity," *Employee Benefits News*, April 1987, pp. 3, 31.

[16] Anita Bruzzese, "COBRA Regs Hit Benefits Arena," *Employee Benefits News*, July/August 1987, pp. 1, 36, 38.

[17] Anita Bruzzese, "Employers Examine COBRA," *Employee Benefits News*, September 1987, p. 1, 31–33.

[18] Berkeley Rice, "Why Am I in This Job?" *Psychology Today*, January 1985, pp. 54–59.

Long-Term Sickness and Accident Disability Insurance What happens to employees who have accidents at work that leave them unable to work, temporarily or permanently? Workers' compensation pays a very small part of these costs, since it was designed primarily to take care of short-term disability problems (see Chapter 18). Employer-funded, long-term disability insurance is designed to cover these cases, with payments supplementing benefits from workers' compensation, social security, and other agencies.

Some disability payments are very large. A roofer in Georgia who fell off a roof received over $5 million. About 75 percent of larger firms have this kind of insurance. Usually blue-collar workers are covered by flat-amount coverage (usually $5,000–$10,000). For other employees coverage is tied to salary level. Usually there is noncontributory coverage for all employees. The goal is to provide employees with at least half pay until pension time, but the primary recipients have been nonblue-collar employees.

The majority of long-term sickness and accident disability insurance plans provide benefits for up to 26 weeks. But about 20 percent provide these benefits for a year. About 75 percent of organizations provide such sickness and accident coverage.[19]

Maternity Leave Benefits

The Pregnancy Discrimination Act is technically an amendment to Title VII of the Civil Rights Act. The Pregnancy Discrimination Act became law in 1978. It requires that pregnancy be treated just like any other temporary disability. Before the act, temporary disability benefits for pregnancies were paid in the form of either sick leave or disability insurance, if at all. It was common organizational practice to limit pregnancy benefits to about six weeks.

A recent U.S. Supreme Court decision upheld a California law granting women up to four months of unpaid disability leave for maternity care. This decision may prod more employers to adopt formal policies on pregnancy leave.[20] A study by Columbia University found that no more than 40 percent of all working women get any salary protection when returning from pregnancy leave. The newly upheld California law requires employers to grant up to four months of unpaid disability leave and to guarantee women a return to their job positions.

Currently five states—California, New York, New Jersey, Rhode Island, and Hawaii—require employers to provide at least 10 weeks maternity leave at half to two-thirds pay. Pregnancy claims in California and New York have not climbed significantly as had been feared by opponents of the paid leave policies.[21]

---

[19] Jerry S. Rosenbloom and Victor G. Hallman, *Employee Benefit Planning* (Englewood Cliffs, N.J.: Prentice-Hall, 1981).

[20] James D. Snyder, "Pregnancy Issue Grows in Courts and Congress," *Employee Benefits News*, April 1987, p. 5 and 36.

[21] "Fertility Unaffected by Maternity Leave," *Employee Benefits News*, May/June 1987, p. 26.

Catalyst, a New York city-based career resource and research center, surveyed the Fortune 1500 largest firms and found the following:[22]

1. Three types of leave policies are used: (*a*) Disability is paid to natural mothers treating pregnancy as a short-term physical disability exactly like any other; (*b*) paid leave may be offered to fathers as well as to mothers. Like disability, it guarantees that employees will have jobs to come back to; and (*c*) unpaid leave also guarantees jobs and is increasingly offered to both parents as "child care" or "personal" leave.
2. Only 30 percent of the surveyed firms guarantee women the same job after being absent for childbirth.
3. Few women get a fully paid leave (only 7.4 of the firms offer paid leave, while 51.7 percent offer unpaid leave).
4. Managers and nonmanagers are subject to the same leave policy.

In addition to maternity leaves, a few organizations (about 10 percent included in the Forbes Market Value 500) provide paternity leaves. A *paternity leave* is given to fathers who, when a child is born, is assumed by some to share in the child care activities.[23] For example, Bell Telephone gives fathers and mothers the option to take a six-month leave without pay but without the loss of benefits (e.g., insurance) when a child is born. The fathers and mothers who take maternity or paternity leave are guaranteed the same job, or a similar one, at the same pay when they return to work. Few men have ever taken paternity leaves in the United States.

An interesting program was initiated by American Telephone & Telegraph Co. (AT&T). AT&T established a program under which new fathers can take up to six months of unpaid leave to help care for a newborn and still return to their jobs. Workers of either sex adopting infants are also eligible for the unpaid six-month leave. Pregnant employees at AT&T can take paid leave as long as they have been certified by a physician as unable to work. As long as the employee is certified as disabled, she can receive 52 weeks of half-pay maternity benefits (with six months of service) or 52 weeks of full pay (with 25 years of service). Certainly the program is innovative, but one must ask about the 52 weeks of full-pay provision. How many women with 25 or more years of service are having babies? Probably not very many, even in a firm as large as AT&T.

INCOME IN RETIREMENT

Retired employees can receive income from a number of sources: (1) savings and investments, (2) individual retirement accounts, (3) government pensions, and (4) employer pension plans. The first two are discussed in this section, and the government and employer pension plan are discussed in separate sections.

---

[22] Judy Linscott, "What Companies Really Do about Maternity Leaves," *Savvy*, October 1984, p. 40; and Snyder, p. 5.

[23] Nancy Norman and James T. Tidechi, "Paternity Leave: The Unpopular Benefit Option," *Personnel Administrator*, February 1984, pp. 39–43.

Retirement Income from Savings and Work

An important source of retirement income is from savings. Studies find that persons save more (percentage-wise and absolutely) the higher their income, and those with private pensions are more likely to save money for retirement than those without them.[24]

Until the mid-1970s, little change in savings took place after social security started. As people were forced to pay social security taxes, their private savings for retirement tended to decline. But social security does not allow much work after retirement, and thanks to medical science and improved life style, people are living longer. So employees have seen the need to save more during their working years and have begun to do so. More persons will have to work to supplement social security payments in view of inflation, but if social security benefits increase substantially, people will save less during their work years.

IRAs and the 1986 Tax Reform Act

Under the 1981 law, any employee could make annual tax-excludable contributions of up to $2,000 to an individual retirement account (IRA) even if he or she was already enrolled in a company pension plan. If the employee contributed to a separate IRA for a nonworking spouse, they could make an overall annual contribution of $2,250. However, under the 1986 Tax Reform Act no deductible IRA contributions can be made by active participants in an employer-sponsored retirement program, either for themselves or for their spouses, if their income is above the cutoff point of $50,000 of adjusted gross income on joint returns, or $35,000 on single. The term *active participant* is defined as one who participated, whether vested or not, in a private or public employer-sponsored retirement plan for any part of the plan year ending within the individual's taxable year.[25] Qualified voluntary employee contributions (QVECs), which allow an employee to contribute to a retirement plan and receive a tax benefit, are not permitted under the 1986 law.

Reducing deductibility for IRAs will discourage some individuals from saving for their retirement, which is not a desirable consequence. The final verdict on the impact of the 1986 law on retirement savings and conditions will not be apparent for a number of years.

An employee can have both a qualified voluntary employee contribution (QVEC) plan and an IRA.[26] A *qualified voluntary employee contribution* means that the employee pays, but the employer does not. The money is deposited

---

[24] Alicia Munnell, *The Effect of Social Security on Personal Savings* (Cambridge, Mass.: Ballinger, 1974).

[25] William M. Mercer-Meidinger, "How Will Reform Tax Your Benefits," *Personnel Journal*, December 1986, pp. 49–63.

[26] Philip M. Alden, Jr., "New Tax Law's Voluntary Employee Contributions Forcing Management to Make Hard, Long-Term Choices," *Management Review*, December 1981, pp. 21–23.

with a qualified pension, profit sharing, or similar plan. An employee who contributes, say, $1,000 to a QVEC can deposit only $1,000 in an IRA.

The employer has a number of alternatives under the 1981 law. The employer can add a QVEC provision to one or more of its existing plans or adopt a new plan offering employees a QVEC opportunity. Also the employer can ignore QVECs altogether. Employees under the law will probably turn to the many IRAs offered by banks, insurance companies, and other financial institutions if they wish to accumulate tax-deductible contributions.[27] Some employers have decided to sponsor an IRA by arranging for withholding of employee pay and the transmittal of contributions to the employee-designated IRA agency. What management chooses, and how it affects its choice, is likely to have long-term implications for a company's benefit program and for its P/HRM policies overall.[28]

The 401(k) Plan

Internal Revenue Code Section 401(k) allows employees to save on a tax-favored basis by entering into salary deferral agreements with their employer. Since the Internal Revenue Service issued the 401(k) regulations, most large companies have adopted the savings plan. The 1981 law permitted maximum salary deferral of $30,000 annually. The 1986 Tax Reform Act, however, reduced the salary deferral to $7,000 subject to slight increases as the cost of living increases. Deferrals to a 401(k) plan must be coordinated with other salary deferrals if the individual participates in other plans.[29]

The 401(k) used to be a tool for employees interested in saving for their retirements. For example, Wargo & Co. set up one in 1983. In the first four years of the program Wargo's 30 employees contributed their own money to the 401(k) plan.[30] The company matched annual employee contributions by an amount as high as 10 percent of a person's base salary and allowed participants to borrow against their accounts. The 1986 Tax Reform Act thus placed a cap of $7,000 on personal contributions, which makes capital accumulation much tougher. In addition, lower personal income tax rates may make any kind of salary deferral less attractive than it used to be.

PRIVATE PENSIONS

As we shall see shortly, the Employee Retirement Income Security Act of 1974 (ERISA) requires that all persons participating in pensions must be notified about them in writing and in language *they can understand.* The U.S. Depart-

---

[27] G. Christian Heil, "Fierce Competition for IRA Cash Breaks Out in the Financial Industry," *The Wall Street Journal,* January 18, 1982, p. 23.

[28] Frederick W. Rumack and David H. Gravitz, "New Opportunities in Compensation and Benefits under the 1981 Tax Act," *Management Review,* November 1981, pp. 8–12.

[29] William M. Mercer-Merdinger, *Tax Reform Commentary,* Louisville, Ky. 40202, 1987.

[30] Bruce G. Posner, "The Brave New World," *Inc.,* September 1987, p. 67.

ment of Labor set out a six-page notification form in "laymen's language" that employers could use to notify retirees about their pensions. One firm sent this report, littered with pension terms such as *vested benefits* and *fiduciary,* to its retirees. "The reaction of retired employees who received the letters was near hysteria," according to Mr. Donnelly, personnel director at Vulcan, and the company's pension-plan administrator. "Nearly half of them called the company, desperate to learn whether the gobbledygook meant their pensions were going to be raised or cut."[31] Let's examine some of the so-called pension terms.

Vesting—This is the right to participate in a pension plan. Pension plans state how long an employee must be employed before he or she has a right to a pension or a portion of it should the employee quit. When the employee has completed the minimum time after which he or she has a right to a pension, he or she is said to be vested in the pension.

Portability—This is the right to transfer pension credits accrued from one employer to another. It becomes possible when several employers pool their pensions through reciprocal agreements.

Contributory or Noncontributory—Some pension plans require employees to pay some of the costs of the pensions during employment (contributory). Other employers pay all the pension costs (noncontributory).

Funded or Nonfunded—Some pension plans finance future payments by setting money aside in special funds. These are called funded pension plans. Nonfunded or pay-as-you-go plans make pension payments out of current funds.

Insured or Uninsured—Funded plans can be administered by insurance companies. Under the insured method, the payments made for each employee buy that worker an annuity for the retirement years. An uninsured or trustee plan is usually administered by a bank or trust company. In these cases, the administrators invest the pension funds in securities, real estate, and so on, from which pension payments are generated.

Pension Payments—Pensions can be paid in one of two ways: a flat or defined dollar payment, or an annuity. The defined benefit approach uses a benefit formula, as described in the next section. In an annuity, the payments vary according to the value of the investment trust used to pay the pensions. If the value increases, the payment increases, and *the reverse* is also true. In the stock market decline of the early 1980s, some pensioners learned that valuable annuities vary downwards as well as upward.

Fiduciary—Fiduciaries are persons responsible for pension trust funds, such as pension trustees, officers, or directors of the company, controlling shareholders, and attorneys.

Benefit Formula—A benefit formula is used to calculate the size of a pension payment. It expresses the relationship between wages and salaries earned while employed and the pension paid.

---

[31] David Ignatius, "Paper Weight," *The Wall Street Journal,* July 16, 1987, p. 12.

The first step in determining the formula is to indicate which earnings figure should be used as a base in this computation.[32] Some experts have noted a trend toward using the average of the final several years of employment as the base earnings figure. An earlier approach was to average career earnings, but this is not fair in an inflationary period.

Once average earnings are determined, by whichever formula approach is used, the actual pension benefit is determined by multiplying the average earnings times the number of years of service times the stipulated percentage, generally between 1 and 3 percent. Some firms offset this figure to some degree by social security benefits. This approach is generally designed to yield a monthly benefit, including social security; that is, approximately 50 percent of the individual's projected salary during the final year of employment.

Criticisms of Private Pensions

Most elderly Americans believe that security in the later years rests on a three-legged stool consisting of social security, savings, and private pensions. An average retired couple has an income of about $14,700 per year, of which 33 percent comes from social security, 13 percent from private pensions, and 17.5 percent from savings, stocks, or other assets. At this time, that stool is very shaky. Personal savings are no longer considered a secure nest egg. Inflation has wiped out some of the puchasing power of money in the bank.[33]

Since two of the stool legs are shaky, people are looking more closely at their private pensions programs. There are now about 500,000 private employer pensions plans that cover more than 75 percent of America's nonfarm workers over age 25. Exhibit 11–5 shows the percentage of people receiving income from specific sources and what each source contributes to a family's income.

There is loud criticism of the private pension system. The criticisms center on mismanagement, misrepresentation of funds, and failure to keep up with inflation. For example, some people who thought they were covered were not because of complicated rules, insufficient funding, irresponsible financial management, and employer bankruptcies. Some pension funds, including both employer-managed and union-managed funds, have been accused of mismanagement, and others have required what the critics considered unusually long vesting periods. Over the years, therefore, pension regulation laws have been regularly debated. ERISA was passed in 1974 to respond to some of the criticisms.

Status of Private Pensions

Like many other benefits, private pensions are relatively new; the private pension plans in existence prior to 1950 covered less than one sixth of the

---

[32] Allen Stiteler, "Finally Pension Plans Defined," *Personnel Journal,* February 1987, pp. 44–53.

[33] "Facing the Pension Dilemma," *Time,* October 19, 1981, pp. 76–77.

EXHIBIT 11–5   Sources of Income: Retirement

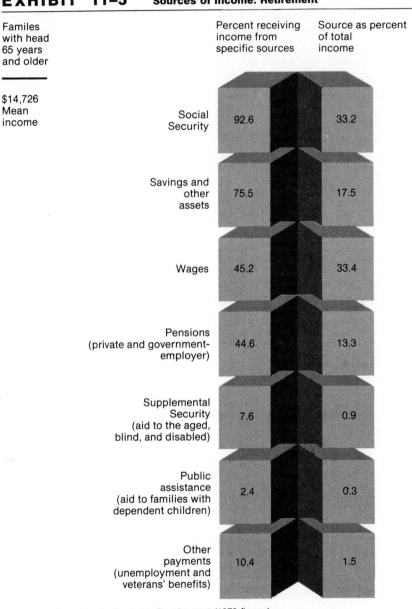

Families with head 65 years and older	Percent receiving income from specific sources	Source as percent of total income
$14,726 Mean income		
Social Security	92.6	33.2
Savings and other assets	75.5	17.5
Wages	45.2	33.4
Pensions (private and government-employer)	44.6	13.3
Supplemental Security (aid to the aged, blind, and disabled)	7.6	0.9
Public assistance (aid to families with dependent children)	2.4	0.3
Other payments (unemployment and veterans' benefits)	10.4	1.5

Source: Committee for Economic Development (1979 figures).

nonagricultural work force. In the 1950s many new plans were introduced and coverage doubled, so that by 1960 about 15 million workers were covered. Coverage during the 1960s remained rather stable, and the percentage participating had also stabilized. Studies have found that the kinds of employees covered vary greatly. Certain industries (mining; manufacturing, especially nondurable goods; construction; transportation; communication; and public utilities) tend to provide pensions more than others (retailing and services). Larger firms are more likely than smaller firms to have pensions. The higher the employee's income, the more probable it is that a pension exists. Unionized employees are more apt to be covered than nonunion employees. And everyone working for employers with pension plans is not covered by them; the Treasury Department estimates that 35 to 45 percent of employees of companies with pension plans are not covered. Part-time employees, for example, are rarely included in pension plans.

Inflation Protection More and more companies are beginning to design pension plan options that provide at least some inflation protection. H. J. Heinz Co. has introduced an indexing option. A worker can choose to take a lower initial retirement benefit, and pension checks will be increased each year by a fixed percentage based on the increase in the consumer price index. The pension benefit is tied (indexed) to the consumer price index.

Other organizations have voluntarily increased the pensions of their retirees because of inflation. For example, Exxon boosted the annual benefits for 21,000 former employees. Similar steps were taken by RCA, the Continental Group, and New York's Chemical Bank.[34]

GOVERNMENT REGULATION OF PRIVATE PENSIONS

The law regulating private pensions is the Employee Retirement Income Security Act (ERISA) of 1974. As noted above, ERISA was designed to cover practically all employee benefit plans of private employers, including multi-employer plans. Basically, the legislation was developed to ensure that employees covered under pension plans would receive the benefits promised.

Existing regulations were tightened in ERISA, but the major impact of the law is in the minimum standards established, which all plans are required to meet. ERISA *does not require an employer to have a private pension plan*. Indeed, many existing private pension plans were terminated rather than meet ERISA's requirements. The major provisions of the law are as follows:

Eligibility Requirements

Organizations were prohibited from establishing requirements of more than one year of service, or an age greater than 25, whichever is later. An employee hired before the age of 22 who continues unbroken service must at age 25 be given at least three years' service credit for vesting purposes. An exception is

---

[34] George T. Milkovich and Jerry M. Newman, *Compensation* (Plano, Tex.: Business Publications, Inc., 1987), p. 408.

allowed employers who provide immediate 100 percent vesting in that they may require a three-year eligibility period.

Vesting Practices

The employer may choose from three vesting alternatives: (1) the 10-year service rule, whereby the employee receives 100 percent vesting after 10 years of service; (2) the graded 15-year service rule, whereby the employee receives 25 percent vesting after 5 years of service, graded up to 100 percent after 15 years; and (3) the rule of 45, which provides 50 percent vesting when age and service equal 45 (if the employee has at least five years of service), graded up to 100 percent vesting five years later.

The new vesting standards appear to provide a major advantage to employees. Previously, those who changed employment after 10 or 15 years of service did not receive benefits; now they will. Although small, the benefits received will increase the total income at retirement.

The vesting schedule used by a firm is often dictated by the demographic makeup of the workers.[35] An employer with a high-turnover situation may want to use the 100 percent vesting, 10-year scheduling. This means that any employee with fewer than 10 years service at the time he or she quits or is terminated receives no vested pension benefits.

Portability Practices

From the employee's point of view, it is desirable for pensions to be transferable or portable. Employers, however, find portability an expensive provision. Under ERISA, portability becomes a voluntary option of the employee and his or her employer. If the employer agrees, a vested employee leaving a company is permitted to transfer (tax free) the assets attributable to his or her vested pension benefits or vested profit-sharing or savings plan funds to an individual retirement account (IRA). The benefit to employees is in the opportunity to defer the payment of taxes on the funds.

Fiduciary Responsibility

Because of the need to provide more effective safeguards for pension funds, the law has imposed new standards for fiduciaries and parties-in-interest such as trustees, officers or directors of the company, controlling shareholders, or attorneys. The "prudent man" rule is established as the standard for handling and investing pension plan funds.

A fiduciary is prohibited from engaging in certain activities. He may not: (1) deal with the fund for his own account; (2) receive personal consideration from any party dealing with the fund in connection with a transaction involving the fund; (3) make loans between the fund and a party-in-interest; and (4) invest

---

[35] Ibid.

more than 10 percent of the assets of the pension plan in securities of the employer. These prohibitions have caused a great deal of concern, and it is expected that Congress will amend the standards.

Other Provisions

ERISA provides for plan termination insurance to ensure vested pension benefits (similar to FDIC provisions at banks). The Pension Benefit Guaranty Corporation was set up to pay pensions to employees of firms whose pension plans become bankrupt.

Reporting and disclosure provisions of the law require the employer to provide employees with a comprehensive booklet describing major plan provisions, and to report detailed information concerning the operation and financing of the plan annually to the Secretary of Labor. The act also imposes limits on contributions and benefits and changes the tax rules related to lump-sum distributions to employees.

What about those who have no employer-sponsored pension plan or who are self-employed? Persons having an employer but without a pension plan can set aside 15 percent of their compensation or $1,500, whichever is less, and pay no taxes on this income until they are 70.5 years old. IRAs are managed by banks and other financial institutuons. ERISA limits the investment of these funds to specific choices: savings accounts, certificates of deposit, retirement annuities, endowment or retirement income policies, mutual funds, trust accounts, individual retirement bonds, and others. The money cannot be withdrawn before age 59.5 without tax penalty. Firms without pension plans can set up IRAs for their employees. Self-employed persons can set up IRAs or Keogh plans. Legislation allows a self-employed person to set aside up to $7,000 in tax-deferred trusts.

PUBLIC PENSIONS

Employees in the public sector also receive pensions. The Tax Foundation estimates pensions are not almost universally available at the state and local levels. Federal employees are covered by civilian or military pensions plans, and about two thirds of state and local government employees are also covered by social security. Typically, public pensions are contributory. The bulk of the cost is paid by the government and investment income. The employee usually contributes about 7 percent of wages or salary.

One study comparing private with public pensions found that the benefit levels of the latter are approximately *twice* the level of those in private industry.[36] Even adjusting for the portion paid for by the employees themselves, public pensions are still one third larger than industry's. The plans are

---

[36] Robert Tilove, *Public Employee Pension Funds,* Twentieth-Century Fund Report (New York: Columbia University Press, 1976).

not coordinated with social security. Since public pension and social security payments have been rising dramatically, a number of public servants now retire at greater net income than they had when working. Needless to say, this is a strong inducement to retire and has helped lead to a crisis in public pensions. The crisis is this: As public pensions rose (often because politicians gave public employees greater pensions than wage increases and left the bill for their successors to pay), funding did not. All the studies show a consistent pattern: a rising spread between funds and payouts.

There are only two ways to take care of this: raise taxes *dramatically,* or lower pension checks. A third answer, to place the public plans under ERISA, is not helpful. A better solution is to reform the public pensions so that benefit payouts are coordinated with social security and total no more than private industry's payout of about 55 percent of final salary. The length of service required to receive full pensions should be more like that in private industry, too. Taxes must rise or benefits must fall, or the total government budget could be going to pensions.

PRERETIREMENT AND RETIREMENT

Retirement has mixed meaning for people: some look forward to it, others dread it. Various policies affect the way people will live in retirement. These include compulsory or flexible retirement policies, early retirement policies, and employer preretirement programs.

Compulsory or Flexible Retirement

A major issue regarding retirement has been whether it should be compulsory or flexible. There are advantages to both of these policies. Flexible retirement policies take account of individual differences, but can cause difficulty in administration, especially in regard to favoritism. Compulsory retirement assures a predictable turnover of older employees, opening up positions for younger ones, and equality of treatment for all employees. When new job openings come up, EEO requirements can be fulfilled more easily. However, those closest to retirement age favor flexible retirement policies, not compulsory ones.

Nevertheless, legislation that became effective January 1, 1979, stipulated that the private and third sectors cannot have mandatory retirement policies that specify less than 70 years of age. The only exception is that firms may retire top executives and policymakers who at age 65 have employer-financed pension or retirement benefits of at least $27,000 per year (exclusive of social security). Prior to this new legislation, federal employees could be forced to retire at age 70. There now is no maximum age limit for federal employment.

Early Retirement

The opposite of the movement to keep older employees working is early retirement. Some employees prefer not to work up until normal retirement

HOW ABOUT ONE MORE COMMANDMENT, ABOUT A MANDATORY RETIREMENT AGE?

FRANK & ERNEST

THAVES 6-2

© 1978 by NEA, Inc. Reprinted by permission of NEA.

age. In recent years, more than 90 percent of pension plans studied have made provision for early retirement.

Typically, the minimum age for early retirement is 55; others call for a minimum age of 60. Most early retirement plans require a minimum number of years of work (typically 10 or 15 years) before the employee is eligible for early retirement. As far as benefits are concerned, all plans will pay the actuarial equivalent of the normal retirement benefits, but 30 percent of the plans pay more than that. One study found that in a typical year an average of 10 percent of those eligible retire early, but this is related to the benefits paid. Only 5 percent of those with nonliberalized payments retire early; whereas 30 percent of those eligible for early retirement with liberalized benefits do so.[37] The U.S. Census Bureau found that more men than women retire early.

Several studies have examined which employees take early retirement. They have found that black men have a lower propensity to retire early than white men.[38] One study also found that the employee is more likely to retire early the higher the pension benefits, the smaller the number of dependents, the higher the assets, and the poorer the health. Blue-collar workers are more likely to retire early than white-collar workers. Executives are especially averse to early retirement. Government workers retire early more frequently than private-sector employees. But in general, people are reluctant to retire early in times of inflation.

Employers' Preretirement Programs

Today there are about 30 million retirees and 60 million people are over 50 years old. What have American employers done to smooth the way for these potential retirees? Until recently, very little.

---

[37] Meyer and Fox, "Profile of Employee Benefits."

[38] "Hanging in There after 65," *Business Week*, January 17, 1977, pp. 22–21.

In more recent years, many organizations have begun providing preretirement counseling. A recommended comprehensive preretirement program includes these topics:

First meeting: Developing a healthy attitude for a happy retirement. This session emphasizes the positive steps society has taken to ease the financial burdens on senior citizens by reducing the costs of recreation, housing, and taxes. The potential retirees are encouraged to keep mentally and physically active, and programs designed to help, such as adult education, are discussed.

Second meeting: Leisure time converted to happiness. Potential retirees are acquainted with the variety of leisure time activities, and they are encouraged to choose specific goals and to take steps to develop plans that will bring them to fruition.

Third meeting: Is working in retirement for me? Retirees are given lectures on service projects and part-time job experiences that may provide variety in the retirement periods.

Fourth meeting: Money matters. This session discusses the sources of funds available to retirees: social security, pensions, and supplementary jobs. Personal budgets can be developed for each retiree to help him or her adjust to the new income level more smoothly.

Fifth meeting. Relocation in retirement. The advantages and disadvantages of living in retirement communities, staying in present quarters (if possible), or moving in with children are discussed.

Sixth meeting: Other subjects. Rights under Medicare are discussed. Retirement publications such as *Harvest Years* and *Modern Maturity* are analyzed. The preparation of wills is encouraged. Social and marital adjustment problems during retirement are covered.

At present, the great majority of firms do the counseling when employees are 64 or 65 years old. About a third counsel employees between the ages of 60 to 65. Very few do so prior to age 60. Preretirement counseling is an inexpensive benefit that can help the employee a great deal.

EMPLOYEE SERVICES

"Employee services" is something of a catch-all category of voluntary benefits. It includes all other benefits or services provided by employers. These are such varied programs as cafeterias; saunas and gyms; free parking lots; commuter vans; infirmaries; ability to purchase company products at a discount; and death, personal, and financial counseling. Several of the more frequently provided services will be discussed here.

Education Programs

Many organizations provide off-the-job general educational support for their employees. This varies from teaching basic skills such as reading to illiterate workers, to tuition-refund programs for managers, to scholarship and loan plans for employees' children.

When employers provide for tuition refunds for courses, they usually place some restrictions on them. The courses must be relevant to the work being done and a minimum grade level must be achieved. One study of some 620 U.S. and Canadian firms found some form of educational assistance at 96 percent of the companies.[39] A large majority required the course of study to be either directly or indirectly related to the employee's present job in order to qualify for reimbursement. Approximately half of the companies paid 100 percent of the tuition costs. A few firms based the degree of remuneration on the grade attained in the course. More than 75 percent of the firms made refunds only upon completion of the course.

Child Care Facilities

The Census Bureau reports that working mothers pay about $11.1 billion per year for child care while they work. The Labor Department predicts that by 1995, more than 80 percent of the women between the ages of 25 and 44 are expected to be working outside the home. This fact suggests that corporate-sponsored child care will become a necessity. Studies indicate that company child care programs improve recruitment, retain valuable employees, increase morale, and reduce absenteeism.[40]

Despite these benefits, employers are not working aggressively on plans or programs that include corporate-sponsored child care.[41] Currently, there are still only about 3,000 companies providing child care assistance. Such assistance ranges from resource-referral programs to on-site centers.[42] Another 1,000 companies reportedly give funds to support local child care programs, and 1,000 run seminars for working parents.

Work/Family Directors, a Boston company, organized the information-referral network being used by some 220,000 IBM employees in more than 300 locations. The program, which costs IBM approximately $2 million annually, has been a major force in creating 300 new child care centers. In addition, local agencies have recruited and trained more than 240 people to provide in-house care for IBM employees.

On-site centers have proved to be a beneficial recruitment tool for some firms. A Florida bank reports that after opening its on-site center, it received over 2,000 applications from women, many who stated that they hadn't applied before because high-quality child care was not available.

Although on-site child care has not caught on, many employers are working

---

[39] Meyer and Fox, "Profile of Employee Benefits."

[40] Lynn E. Densford, "Make Room For Baby: The Employer's Role in Solving the Day Care Dilemma," *Employee Benefits News,* May/June 1987, pp. 19–37.

[41] Stuart A. Youngblood and Kimberly Chambers-Cook, "Child Care Assistance Can Improve Employee Attitudes and Behavior," *Personnel Administrator,* February 1984, pp. 45–46, 93–95.

[42] Cathy Trost, "Child Care Center at Virginia Firm Boosts Worker Morale and Loyalty," *Wall Street Journal,* February 12, 1987, p. 25.

on other options so that the benefits associated with child care support can become a reality. Some of the options include:

1. Developing programs that reduce the need for child care by minimizing the amount of time parents are away from the children. Examples would be flexitime work schedules, job sharing, and work at home (all covered in Chapter 19).
2. Hiring a part- or full-time child care coordinator to establish an information and referral center in the firm.
3. Subsidizing the costs of child care by making it a part of the benefit package.

As more and more organizations investigate the benefits, there is likely to be more probing by employers of the attitudes of employees about child care. Exhibit 11–6 is a questionnaire that can be used to investigate employee attitudes and feelings about child care. Information provided by such a survey could be used to help management decide what course to take in the child care area.

Financial Services

Some organizations give their employees help and encouragement to save funds through employee savings plans, credit unions, and thrift plans. Essentially, savings plans encourage employee thrift by matching all or part of an employee's contribution, up to, say 5 percent of the wage or salary. Credit unions help employees by providing loans at reasonable and market competitive rates of interest.

In the thrift plans, most funds are often invested for distribution at retirement. When companies have thrift plans, about 85 percent of employees participate. As with many services, it is difficult to tie performance or even employee satisfaction to such plans. However, they may contribute to the perception of the organization as a good place to work and thus attract better employees.[43]

Relocation Services

A domestic relocation costs, on average, more than $40,000. This means that American organizations spend over $14 billion annually to relocate employees.[44] A survey of 608 of *Fortune* magazine's top 1,000 industrial firms found that:

- On average, companies relocated 132 employees per year. At a cost of about $40,000 per employee, these firms spent, on average, about $5.28 million.

---

[43] "Hanging in There," p. 21.

[44] Arlene A. Johnson, "Relocation: Getting More for the Dollars You Spend," *Personnel Administrator*, April 1984, pp. 29–35, 136.

EXHIBIT 11–6   Child Care Planning and Attitude Survey

Those planning a child care program may want to survey employees and/or non-employees who live within recruiting range. The new edition of Employers and Child Care suggests these frequently asked questions.

QUESTIONNAIRE

1. Would you be willing to give some time and your expertise to help organize (identify the program being proposed)?
   Many people, including some with no children, might volunteer to help organize or manage a program that is parent controlled.

2. Do you have dependent children under six years old living at home? If so, how are they cared for while you work?

3. How much do you pay for child care services for each child using services?
   $ _____ for _____ hours per week for child _____ years old.
   The amount an employee presently pays may indicate what parents are willing to pay.

4. Would you be interested in enrolling a dependent child in a child care center located close to where you work?
   The answer to this question, of course, does not constitute a commitment to enroll a child, but asking the question may avoid surprise that so many (or so few) are interested.

5. What is the age of the child (children) that you would be interested in enrolling in the child care center?
   List ages, using age brackets, that determine teacher-child ratios for state licensing laws. Some centers have reported more demand for infant care (seldom available in the community) rather than preschool care.

6. What hours and days would you need child care?

7. Do any of the children that you're interested in enrolling have a handicap? If so, what is the child's condition?
   Planners may or may not be able to accommodate handicapped children, depending on the kind of handicap and the number of children affected.

8. What would you be willing to pay for care for one child in a child care center near work?
   List alternative ranges of fees. Answers may be lower than parents are willing to pay once the center has opened. A better indicator of what employees will pay may be a comparison of family income with fees currently being paid at other centers.

9. What is your total gross family income?
   A rule of thumb often used is that a family can spend 10 percent of its gross income for child care. If planners are considering a sliding scale that will charge high-income families more, will there be enough high-income interest to balance enrollment by low-income families?

10. If all the following forms of child care service were available to you, which would be your first choice?

11. Do you believe a service at the company (or nonprofit organization) that supplied you with names of child care providers in your community would help you in making your own child care arrangements?

continued

EXHIBIT 11-6 *(concluded)*

---

12. How would you describe your present child care arrangements.
    ■ Cost of care
    _____ too expensive
    _____ moderate
    _____ inexpensive
    ■ Location of care
    _____ close to home
    _____ close to work
    _____ inconvenient distance to travel
    _____ other: _____
    ■ Hours of care
    _____ available during times needed
    _____ not available as early as needed
    _____ not available as late as needed
    Other items could include evaluation of activities for children in present program, adequacy of staff, etc.

13. Have you missed work during the past six months because (give number of days)
    _____ child was ill
    _____ sitter was ill
    _____ needed to find new care arrangements
    _____ other

14. Were you late for work during the past six months because of child care problems?
    _____ No
    _____ Yes
    How many times? Describe problems: _____

15. Have you left work early during past six months because of child care problems?
    _____ No
    _____ Yes
    How many times? Describe problems: _____

16. Do you ever waste time or make mistakes because you are worried about your child care problems?
    _____ No
    _____ Some
    _____ A lot
    What problems bother you most? _____

Source: Commerce Clearing House, Ideas and Trends, December 30, 1982, p. 229.

■ Nearly all companies provided relocated employees with assistance in selling their current homes.
■ Cost-of-living allowances were given by 18 percent of the companies as an incentive to employees transferring to high-cost areas.
■ About 26 percent of the companies offered some type of job-seeking assistance for the spouse.[45]

---

[45] "1983 Survey of Employer Relocation Policies," *Personnel Administrator*, April 1984, p. 91.

The 1986 Tax Reform Act has had an effect on how moving expense deductions are made. Thus, income tax preparation counseling and support is needed. For example, before 1987, employees deducted moving expenses from their gross income.[46] Beginning in 1987, transferred employees had to itemize deductions on their returns to include moving expenses that result from relocation. The changes in what is deductible, how reimbursed moving expenses are added to income, and other tax-related issues need to be addressed by individuals with income tax knowledge.

In addition to paying for moving expenses, granting cost-of-living allowances, providing assistance in selling homes, and dealing with taxes, organizations are now showing more concern about the spouse, family, and psychological aspects of relocation.[47] A family that relocates experiences stress in spite of any financial benefits package. Relocation is stressful to some because it involves change and uprooting. Any time relocation occurs, there is anticipation, anxiety, and adjustment. Therefore, more and more firms, such as Baxter Travenol Laboratories, are providing personal and family counseling and assistance, in addition to financial benefits, to minimize the disruption, stress, and adjustment that inevitably is a part of relocation.[48]

Social and Recreational Programs

Today more than 50,000 organizations provide recreation facilities for employees, on or off the job. Some experts foresee a growing trend to release employees from work time to participate in company-sponsored sports activities, which are intended to keep employees physically fit and tie them to employers. In one survey, three fourths of companies responding said they sponsored recreation programs, and half of them sponsored athletic teams.[49] The median expenditure is $6 per employee per year.

There are no available studies of the value, if any, of such benefits to the employer. These plans could be extensions of the paternalistic antiunion activities of some employers in the 1920s and later. Studies of the preferences of employees indicate that recreational services are the *least preferred* of all benefits and services offered by organizations.

MANAGING AN EFFECTIVE BENEFIT PROGRAM

When top managers make benefit and services decisions, such as the cost decision discussed above, they must consider the following facts:

[46] Runzheimer International, "Relocation," *Personnel Journal,* September 1987, pp. 153–64.

[47] Linda Cecere, "The Loneliness of the Long-Distance Manager," *Working Woman,* October 1983, p. 137.

[48] "Relocation," *Personnel Journal,* September 1984, pp. 89–90.

[49] Meyer and Fox, "Profile of Employee Benefits." Also see Karen Debats, "Industrial Recreation Programs: A New Look at an Old Benefit," *Personnel Journal,* August 1981, pp. 620–27.

- At present, there is little evidence that benefits and services really motivate performance. Nor do they necessarily increase satisfaction.
- The costs of benefits and services are escalating dramatically.
- Regarding mandated programs, managers have no choice but to offer them.
- With regard to voluntary programs, unions, competitors, and industry trends put pressures on managers to provide or increase benefits.

To manage the benefit program effectively, certain steps are necessary. Four of these are discussed in this section.

Step 1: Set Objectives and Strategy for Benefits

There are three strategies for benefits:

1. *Pacesetter strategy*. Be first with the newest benefits employees desire.
2. *Comparable benefit strategy*. Match the benefit programs similar organizations offer.
3. *Minimum benefits strategy*. Offer the mandatory benefits and those which are most desired and least costly to offer.

The decision about which strategy to use is made on the basis of management's goals, as discussed early in the chapter. The third strategy may be chosen because of inability to pay more benefits, or because management believes the employees want more pay and fewer benefits. Before these costly benefits and services are offered, management must set objectives that fit its benefit strategy.

Step 2: Involve Participants and Unions in Benefit Decisions

Whatever strategy is chosen, it makes sense to find out what those involved desire in benefits and services. Yet in most organizations, top managers *alone* judge which benefits the employees prefer. Without getting some employee-preference input, it is impossible to make these decisions intelligently. It is similar to a marketing manager trying to decide on consumer preferences with no market research input.

Therefore, it is wise to permit (and encourage) employee participation in decision making on benefits and services. When employees share in benefit decisions, they show more interest in them. One way for employees to participate in the decisions is to poll them with attitude surveys. Another is to set up employee benefits advisory commitees.

Will these devices work? Many believe so, but others think employees are not well enough informed to be of much help. Others oppose asking employees about benefits because to do so might raise their expectations so that they expect more. Instead, supervisors and union leaders might be asked about workers' preferences; most research shows they are good predictors of employee preferences.

A more direct way of allowing employee participation in benefit decisions and dealing with the problem of major preference differences is called the cafeteria approach to benefits. Each employee is told how much money the employer has set aside for benefits plans, after provision for mandated programs and minimal health insurance. Then the employee can choose to receive the funds in cash in lieu of benefits, or decide which benefits are wanted. This approach lets employees know how much the employer is spending on the programs. Because they pick the benefits they want for themselves, the employees' performance and satisfaction are more likely to be affected favorably.

When the organization is unionized, it is vital that the union leadership be involved. Many times the leadership knows what employees want in benefits. Sometimes, the leadership tries to maximize benefits without having determined what employees want. It is useful to involve the union leadership in preference studies so that all parties are seeking benefits desired by the employees.

Step 3: Communicate Benefits Effectively

Another method for improving the effectiveness of benefits and service is to develop an effective communication program. How can benefits and services affect the satisfaction and performance of employees if they do not know about the benefits or understand them? Yet most studies of employees and executives indicate they are unaware of the benefits or significantly undervalue their cost and usefulness.

It has always been desirable to improve benefit communications for this reason. But now there is another reason. For pensions ERISA requires employers to communicate with employees by sending them an annual report on the pension plan and basic information on their pensions in language they can understand.

Many communication media can be used: employee handbooks; company newspaper, magazines, or newsletters; booklets; bulletin boards; annual reports; payroll stuffers; and employee reports. Other communication methods include filmstrips, cassettes, open houses and meetings with supervisors and employees. A typical employee report is Exhibit 11–7 which spells out the value of the benefits to each employee. How much employees would need to save to provide this coverage themselves should be stressed. Another direct means of communication is to send employees copies of bills paid by the company for medical expense on their behalf.

The problem of communication is retention of the message and learning it in its entirety. Most organizations handle these problems by using multiple media and sending the message many times. For example, when the First National Bank of Chicago changed its benefits package, it told about the plan with a range of communications. These included, from first to last, the following:

EXHIBIT 11–7   **Summary Page from a 1988 Benefit-Audit Statement**

YOUR TOTAL PAY PACKAGE

	Your Yearly Contributions	Estimated Cost if You Bought It All
Basic and major medical	$315	$ 1,575
Salary continuation and disability insurance	none	2,750
Life and accident insurance	none	1,314
Pension plan	none	6,875
Social security	600	2,492
Total	$915	$12,006
Net value of benefits	$11,091	
Annual salary	41,000	
Total pay package value	$52,091	

This report tells you what your company-provided benefits can mean to you and your family at retirement or in case of illness, disability, or death. There is no way of knowing how many dollars you will actually receive. This table, however, shows your yearly contributions and the estimated cost in annual individual insurance and benefit policy premiums if you were to buy this protection and income yourself. The company pays the full cost of your basic and major medical insurance, salary continuation, long-term coverage, and your pension. You and the company together share the cost of social security and the medical insurance program.

A letter from the president sent to each employee's home to explain the purpose and general nature of the changes. This letter was tested out on 15 "typical" employees for readability prior to sending it.

The company newsletter carried several articles per week for weeks after.

Employee handouts were distributed to explain the plan.

Meetings of 40 employees each were held.

Every employee was exposed to easy-to-read loose-leaf binders explaining the benefits.

Finally, employees received their individual annual benefits reports explaining what the benefits meant to them.

In sum, organizations are spending billions on benefits and very little on benefit communications. To make these billions pay off, they need to increase the quantity and improve the quality of their communications about the benefits they provide.

Step 4: Monitor the Costs Closely

In addition to considering costs in choice of benefits, it is vital that managers make sure the programs are administered correctly. Expecially important is the review of insurance claims. Miller has shown how Rockwell International and Goodyear Tire and Rubber have lowered insurance costs by studying claims to make sure they are reasonable and covered by the policy.[50] Large savings have resulted. More efficient administration procedures using computerized methods also can lead to greater savings and more satisfied employees.

Together, these four steps will make any benefit program more effective.

COST/BENEFIT ANALYSIS OF BENEFITS

Conrad Fiorello tells the story about a gunman who suddenly appeared at the paymaster's window at a large plant and demanded: "Never mind the payroll, Bud. Just hand over the welfare and pension funds, the group insurance premiums, and the withholding taxes." As indicated earlier, costs of benefits are going up twice as fast as pay.

When benefit costs increase the price of products and services, they are less competitive with other products, especially those from countries where the government pays for benefits. Higher benefits can reduce permanent employment, also, since it is cheaper to pay overtime or to hire part-time employees than to pay full-time wages and benefits. It may also reduce employee mobility, but most evidence thus far shows that it does not affect turnover at all.

It is rational for employees to want additional benefits since they are tax-free income. For example, in 1986, the typical employee in the petroleum industry received over $11,755 in fringe benefits—tax free. The costs of such benefits, however, have been rising substantially, and many organizations cannot afford to offer benefits and high wages as well. Just what does it cost employers to provide these benefits for their employee?

Various groups, including the Department of Labor and the U.S. Chamber of Commerce, report on the costs of benefits. Exhibits 11–8 and 11–9 present some of the latest Chamber figures, by industry and per employee. These studies indicate that benefits (not including services) cost 14–60 percent of payroll, although they vary by size of employer and industry. The most typical figures are 20–30 percent. For example, retailers and textile firms offer low benefits. Petroleum, chemical, and public utility firms offer a high level of benefits. The most costly benefits are time off with pay (holidays, rest periods, vacations), insurance (especially health insurance), and pensions. In sum, benefits are very costly and getting more so.

In addition to the direct costs of benefits, there are added burdens, or indirect costs. One is the administration of these plans. They can become complicated, and paperwork proliferates. Because administrative costs at smaller organizations are especially high, some smaller organizations get together in joint benefit plans for their employees.

Financing benefits can also be complicated. Some companies have found

---

[50] Allan Miller, "How Companies Can Train Employee Health Benefit Claims," *Harvard Business Review,* January–February 1978, p. 608.

EXHIBIT 11-8

Individual Benefits Costs, 1986

	Per Employee, Per Year
Old-age, survivors, disability and health insurance	$1,588
Unemployment compensation	258
Workers' compensation	277
State sickness benefits insurance	211
Retirement and savings plans contributions	1,762
Life insurance and death benefits	127
Medical insurance (current employees)	1,604
Medical insurance (retirees)	157
Short-term disability insurance	139
Long-term or salary-continuation insurance	50
Dental insurance	148
Other medically related payments	86
Paid rest periods (coffee and lunch breaks, etc.)	879
Paid vacations, holidays and sick leave	2,608
Maternity and parental leave	48
Discounts on goods and services	63
Meals furnished	26
Education expenditures	41
Child care	159
Miscellaneous	53
Total Benefits Costs	**10,283**

Source: Albert G. Holzinger, "The Real Costs of Benefits," *Nation's Business*, February 1988, p. 32.

that they can save money by creating tax-exempt trusts for benefit funds as disability pay: Examples include Westvaco, General Electric, TRW, and FMC Corporation.

An organization can compare its costs to those of other firms with the aid of data from an industry or professional group or published sources such as the United States Chamber of Commerce. Some other examples of such sources are the Conference Board, *Employee Benefit News*, Bureau of Labor Statistics, *Nation's Business*, and *Business Week*.

1. Total cost of benefits annually for all employees.
2. Cost per employee per year—basis 1 divided by number of employee hours worked.
3. Percentage of payroll—basis 1 divided by annual payroll.
4. Cost per employee per hour—basis 2 divided by employee hours worked.

Cost of benefits can be calculated fairly easily. The benefits side of the equation is another issue, however. There has been little significant empirical research on the effects of benefits on productivity.

EXHIBIT 11–9

Average Benefits Costs, 1986

	Per Employee, Per Year
All Industries	**$10,283**
Manufacturing Industries	**12,035**
Food, beverages and tobacco	7,580
Textile products and apparel	4,743
Pulp, paper, lumber and furniture	9,922
Printing and publishing	6,919
Chemicals and allied products	11,287
Petroleum	11,755
Rubber, leather and plastic	13,450
Stone, clay and glass	7,748
Primary metals	13,402
Fabricated metals (excluding machinery and transportation equipment)	8,497
Machinery (excluding electrical)	10,461
Electrical machinery, equipment and supplies	9,380
Instruments and miscellaneous manufacturing	10,403
Nonmanufacturing Industries	**8,917**
Public utilities	12,712
Department stores	5,102
Trade (wholesale and retail other than department stores)	6,107
Banks, finance companies and trust companies	7,153
Insurance companies	8,315
Hospitals	7,172
Miscellaneous nonmanufacturing	9,494

Source: Albert G. Holzinger, "The Real Costs of Benefits," *Nation's Business*, February 1988, p. 30.

SUMMARY

Chapter 11 has described benefits and services as part of the rewards that reinforce loyal service to the employer. The Chapter described mandated and voluntary employee benefits and some critical benefit decisions such as communication, administration, retirement benefits, and employee participation.

To summarize the major points covered in this chapter:

1. Mandated benefit programs in the private and third sectors include:
   a. Unemployment insurance.
   b. Social security.
   c. Workers' compensation (Chapter 18).

A RETURN TO THE P/HRM · IN · ACTION

Carl Reems

After talking to other presidents and reading some literature that Pete gave him, Carl better understood Pete's conservatism about benefits and services. Carl reviewed what researchers have found and became convinced that pouring money into benefits and services doesn't mean that absenteeism will decrease, production will increase, and loyalty toward Coy Manufacturing will improve. "Employees have simply come to expect employers to provide competitive benefits and services," Carl thought, "I'm sure glad Pete brought this to my attention."

2. To be eligible for unemployment insurance, an employee must have worked a minimum number of weeks, be without a job, and be willing to accept a position offered through a state Unemployment Compensation Commission.
3. Three kinds of benefits many employers provide voluntarily are:
    a. Compensation for time not worked (break time, coffee breaks, clothes change time, holidays, sick leave, vacations, and so on).
    b. Insurance protection (health, disability-accident, and life).
    c. Employee services (various benefits that can include cafeterias, gyms, free parking lots, discounts, and so forth).
4. Retirement income is received from three principal sources:
    a. Savings, investments and part-time work.
    b. Private pension plans.
    c. Government program—social security.
5. The employee Retirement Income Security Act of 1974 is the law regulating private pensions.
6. To manage the benefit program effectively, follow these steps:
    a. Develop objectives and a benefit strategy.
    b. Involve participants and unions in the benefit program.
    c. Communicate the benefits effectively.
    d. Monitor the costs closely.

7. To avoid administrative nightmares, employers should concentrate on fewer benefit plans and if possible implement those preferred by most employees.

The benefit plans recommended for the model organizations are given in Exhibit 11–10.

Remember, for the benefits and services program to be effective, the operating manager and P/HRM manager must work together. The operating man-

EXHIBIT 11–10   Recommendations on Benefit and Service Programs for Model Organizations

Type of Organization	Benefits and Services							
	Legally Required Benefits	Vacation Plans	Paid Holidays	Group Life Insurance	Hospital-Medical Insurance	Accident-Disability Insurance	Employee Pension Program	Services
1. Large size, low complexity, high stability	X	*	*	*	X	X	X	*
2. Medium size, low complexity, high stability	X	*	*	*	X	X	X	*
3. Small size, low complexity, high stability	X	*	*	*	X	X	X	*
4. Medium size, moderate complexity, moderate stability	X	*	*	*	X	X	X	*
5. Large size, high complexity, low stability	X	*	*	*	X	X	X	*
6. Medium size, high complexity, low stability	X	*	*	*	X	X	X	*
7. Small size, high complexity, low stability	X	*	*	*	X	X		*

* Minimized.

ager helps the P/HRM manager know what the employees prefer in benefits and asks for help in explaining the benefits and getting administrative problems cleared up. The P/HRM manager helps the operating manager communicate the benefits to employees and administer the program.

Questions for Review and Discussion

1. What type of monitoring and auditing problems are employers faced with in administering COBRA?
2. Why do employers have benefit and service programs?
3. Which benefit and services do employees prefer? Which do you prefer? Why are these preferences significant.
4. Describe government-mandated benefits and services. Should these programs exist? How can they be improved?
5. Why would an employee have to be careful about making investments under a 401(k) plan?
6. Are early retirement programs a good idea? Have they been successful?
7. What are the major provisions of ERISA regarding vesting and portability?
8. What effects did the 1986 Tax Reform Act have on benefits?
9. Do you feel that an organization should provide child care benefits for employees? Why?
10. Should employers be required by law to provide paid pregnancy leave for three months? Why?

GLOSSARY

Individual Retirement Account. A plan in which a person is able to save or invest for retirement up to $2,000 which is not subject to taxes. A person can also contribute to an IRA for a nonworking spouse at a rate of $2,250 for both of them.

Portability. The right of an employee to transfer pension credits accrued from one employer to another.

Unemployment Insurance. Established by the Social Security Act of 1935 to provide a subsistence payment to employees when they are between jobs. The employer and employee contribute to a fund which then pays when the employee is out of work.

Vesting. The right of employees to participate in a pension plan.

COBRA. The Consolidated Omnibus Budget Reconciliation Act of 1985 requires that employers with more than 20 employees must offer continuation of health care coverage for 18 to 36 months after an employee is fired, quits, or is laid off.

APPLICATION CASE 11–1   The Maternity/Paternity Leave Debate*

Since the early 1980s, an ongoing debate has emerged among businesses, government, and women concerning maternity leave for pregnant employees. The debate has centered on three issues: (1) the form and degree of maternity leave benefits provided by companies (especially whether the employee recives pay while on leave and is guaranteed her previous or comparable job upon return): (2) whether leave should be granted to fathers; and (3) whether leave benefits should be mandated by law or provided by companies on a voluntary basis.

Two factors have intensified interest in the issue. First, pregnant employees are increasingly common in the workplace because women are comprising a growing proportion of the workforce. About 44 percent of the nation's employees are women, and women will comprise over two thirds of the new entrants into the workforce from now through the early 1990s. Over 70 percent of these women will become pregnant sometime during their working years. In a workforce increasingly characterized by expectant workers, the issue of maternity leave is of obvious interest.

Second, many assert that maternity leave is inadequate for most working women. The Pregnancy Discrimination Act mandates paid short-term maternity leave for employees of companies that provide disability insurance (usually six to eight weeks of paid leave), and five states (California, New York, New Jersey, Rhode Island, and Hawaii) require paid short-term maternity leave benefits by all companies. These state-mandated benefits usually amount to 50 to 66 percent of a woman's base pay for about 10 weeks. However, many small companies outside these five states aren't affected because they do not offer disability coverage. Thus, about 60 percent of America's working women don't receive any type of paid or job-protected maternity leave. According to a two-year study of 384 large companies by the Catalyst organization, too often a job-protected employee returning after taking leave, "may lose out by having to return to a different job and essentially work her way back up."

Maternity leave advocates thus assert that most women are unjustly penalized financially and professionally for having children. Society also pays a price; because of financial need, many women return to work within a few weeks after delivery. Many pediatricians and psychologists assert that this

---

* Written by Kim Stewart and adapted from: Dana E. Friedman, "Liberty, Equality, and Maternity!" *Across The Board*, March 1987, pp. 10–17; Rosa Harris-Adler, "Who Pays for Pregnancy?" *Report on Business*, March 1987, pp. 60–63; Melissa A. Berman, "What Do Women Get," *Across The Board*, March 1987, pp. 18–20; Dana E. Friedman, "Work vs Family: War of the Worlds," *Personnel Administrator*, August 1987, pp. 36–38; Sheila B. Kamerman and Alfred J. Kahn, "Company Maternity-Leave Policies: The Big Picture"; Lesly Berger, "The Corporate Scene," *Working Woman*, February 1984, pp. 79–82; and Karen Krett, "Maternity, Paternity, and Child Care Policies," *Personnel Administrator*, June 1985, pp. 125–36.

early separation between mother and child threatens the child's cognitive and emotional growth because the separation hinders the development of a secure mother-child relationship which is the foundation of a child's psychological growth. Many experts advise that a solid bonding requires four months of full-time parental attention. Said one advocate, "If society wants women to make economic contributions as well as nurture the next generation, some accommodations seem to be necessary. It is impossible for women to accomplish both work and family tasks without some support."

Congress is responding to these concerns with the Family and Medical Leave Bill. If passed, the law would require companies with 15 or more employees to provide up to 18 weeks of leave with job guarantees for the birth, adoption, or illness of a dependent. Both fathers and mothers would be eligible for leaves with protected seniority and pension credits and health benefits and could resume work on a gradual schedule. The leave is unpaid; however, the bill would also establish a commission to study the feasibility of a paid leave policy. The bill's supporters are quick to assert that the United States is the world's only industrialized nation without a national parental leave policy. Companies in Western Europe provide an average of six months paid maternity leave. The European Economic Community has proposed a plan where all member countries require a parental leave of at least three months per employee per child to be used before the child is two years old.

Though endorsed by over 80 organizations, the Family and Medical Leave Bill is highly controversial and opposed by formidable critics. They include the U.S. Chamber of Commerce and CARE (Concerned Alliance of Responsible Employers), a 150-organization-strong lobby which is working hard to defeat the bill. Critics present five reasons for opposing the bill:

1. *Economic impact*: The bill would cost the private sector $2.6 billion a year due to the costs of temporarily losing employees, hiring and training temporary employees, and the lowered productivity of newly trained employees.
2. *Small-business impact*: The financial burden of carrying nonworking employees and temporary substitutes and lowered productivity would bankrupt many small businesses. (Interestingly, the National Association of Women Business Owners opposes the bill due to concern about negative impact on small business.)
3. *Discrimination against Women*: Because women employees would be viewed as more expensive, businesses would be less inclined to hire them.
4. *Voluntary benefits*: Parental leave benefits should be provided by companies voluntarily, with each company providing benefits geared to the company's and its employees' specific needs.
5. *Imbalance between the pregnant employees' rights and responsibilities*: If the law mandates maternity leave rights for employees, it should also mandate employee responsibilities. Employees should provide companies with more advance notice before taking leave. They should also provide several weeks notice if, once on leave, they intend to quit. Failing to give adequate notice creates major problems in personnel planning and for employees temporarily hired or promoted to fill the gap. The bill does not mandate employee responsibilities.

Regardless of whether the Family and Medical Leave Bill becomes law, support for mandated maternity leave is gaining momentum in many states. In 1987, 28 states introduced legislation to provide some sort of maternity, paternity, and child care leave, and more states are expected to consider parental leave bills. Although not required by law, a growing number of companies are implementing more generous parental leave policies. These companies are primarily large with pools of employees who can more easily assume the workload of a temporarily absent worker. For example, a 1984 survey of America's 1,500 largest companies found that 95 percent of the responding firms, provide about five to eight weeks maternity leave and most leaves are paid. About half of the companies provide job-protected leaves.

Many high-tech companies with highly skilled (and difficult-to-replace) employees and companies with many women in the management ranks (e.g., companies in the banking, real estate, and insurance industries) also tend to have more progressive parental leave policies. For example:

1. Levi Strauss & Co provides up to 120 days of paid maternity leave with the employee's length of tenure determining the number of days paid at full salary. Employees with one or more years of service receive four weeks at full salary and the remaining weeks at 70 percent pay; those employed 11 years or more receive full pay for the full period. Employees can add sick days, vacation days at full pay, or an unpaid child care leave to their disability period.
2. Johnson & Johnson Baby Products provides expecting employees full pay for up to 26 weeks after delivery and 90 days of unpaid leave for parents of natural or adopted children. J&J's "Baby Power" program also enables former J&J employees who left to raise families to fill jobs temporarily vacated by employees on leave.
3. Ameritrust Bank provides expectant mothers with up to two weeks of paid leave before delivery, six weeks of paid leave after delivery, and six months of unpaid leave with job protection. The employee's length of tenure determines the specific amount of leave provided. The company also maintains the "Perfectly Pregnant" program which holds a meeting each month with pregnant employees to discuss company parental benefits and provide instruction in exercise and nutrition during pregnancy.

Although many companies are developing progressive policies for expecting mothers, few companies are offering leave for expectant fathers (14 percent according to a 1985 survey). Reports indicate that few fathers are taking paternity leave because they believe that their employer, while offering the leave, would not approve. According to the Catalyst study of 384 large companeis, these employees' perceptions may be accurate. According to the study, over 40 percent of the companies providing paternity leave responded that they didn't view any paternity time off as reasonable. Catalyst researcher Phyllis Silverman concluded that many companies provide paternity leave only to protect themselves from possible discrimination suits.

Questions for Thought

1. Assume that you are the P/HRM director for a manufacturing company that employs approximately 500 individuals (35 percent are women) and that the Family and Medical Leave Bill is not law. Outline the provisions for a parental leave policy for the company. Be specific.
2. What are the key challenges facing management in implementing the policy?
3. Do you support a federally-mandated, paid parental leave policy? Explain your position.

TRAINING AND DEVELOPMENT FOR BETTER PERFORMANCE

Part Four covers the training and development of employees. Chapter 12, Orientation and Training, discusses the orientation and training of employees. It focuses on improving the abilities and skills of employees. Chapter 13, Management and Organization Development, discusses the development of human resources with specific attention paid to managers. Chapter 14, Career Planning and Development, looks at career planning, an area of growing importance in organizations. In Chapter 15, Discipline and the Difficult employee, positive discipline, as well as punishment, are examined in terms of where, when, and why each may be appropriate.

12

ORIENTATION AND TRAINING

P/HRM · IN · ACTION

Harold   Gwen

Harold Matthews was unhappy. He'd just had an unpleasant visit with his boss, William Custer. Harold is vice president of operations of Young Enterprises, a firm employing about 1,600 persons in the Los Angeles area. The firm manufactures parts for a large aircraft firm nearby.

Since Young Enterprises serves primarily one customer, costs are a major factor in their negotiations. Bill Custer told Harold that the new contract was not as good as the last one. Costs needed to be cut. Since labor costs are a high percentage of the total, Harold must begin to work on these. At the same time, Purchasing was working on reducing materials costs and Finance was trying to find ways to reduce the cost of capital.

Harold has decided to consult two groups of persons about the cost cutting: P/HRM and his supervisors. First he called a meeting of the department heads and key supervisors and prepared his figures. The facts are:

- Young Enterprises' labor costs are rising faster than their competitors' are, and faster than the cost of living.

- These costs are higher any way you measure them: number of employees per unit of output, cost per unit of output, and so on. What's more, the trend is worsening.

At the meeting, Harold explained the facts. Then he asked the supervisors for suggestions. He gave them strong "encouragement" to supervise each employee closely and to make sure that the firm gets a fair day's work for a fair day's pay. Harold took notes of the comments his supervisors made. Some of the better ones were:

Sally Feldman (supervisor): One of my problems is that the people P/HRM sends me are not producing at the output standards of the people I've lost through quits and retirement.

Art Jones (department head): Let's face it, when you look at the records, our recent output isn't up to what we expected when we installed the new machines.

Sam Jacobs (supervisor): The problem is our current crop of employees. They ain't what they used to be!

Harold wondered if they were just passing the buck—or it there was some truth to the complaints. He invited

(continued)

Gwen Meridith, the personnel/human resource management vice president, in for help.

Harold: Gwen, production costs are up and labor efficiency is down. The supervisors are blaming it on the employees. We put new machinery in to get production up. It's up, but not to what it should be, given our investment. What do you think is going on?

Gwen: I suspect that part of what they say has some truth to it. Lately, the job market is tight. Last week, I had 20 jobs to fill and only 20 applicants. About half really were somewhat mar-

ginal. And let's face it, we put the new machinery in with little preparation of the employees.

Harold: What can we do? We have a serious cost problem.

Gwen: The job market is still tight. I don't see any improvement in the quality of labor in the near future. Sounds like we ought to gear up that training program I've been talking about.

Harold: You prepare something for Bill. Then you and I will go to see him about it.

Orientation and training are processes that attempt to provide an employee with information, skills, and an understanding of the organization and its goals. Orientation involves starting the employee in the right direction and training is designed to keep or to help a person continue to make positive contributions in the form of good performance.

Sam Lavalle reported to P/HRM as the notice of employment said to do. After about six of the new employees were there, orientation began. Miss Wentworth welcomed them to the company and then the "paper blitz" took place. In the next 30 minutes, she gave them a lot of paper—work rules, benefits booklets, pay forms to fill out, and so on. Sam's head was swimming. Then he got a slip telling him to report to his new supervisor, Andrew Villanueva, in Room 810. Andrew took Sam around the facility for three minutes, pointed out Sam's new workbench, and wished him good luck. Sam's case is an example of what most employees encounter: a formal orientation program that is brief and leaves a lot of questions unanswered.

> Orientation is the P/HRM activity that introduces new employees to the organization and to the employee's new tasks, managers, and work groups.

Walking into a new job is often a lonely and confusing event. The newcomer doesn't usually know what to say or whom to say it to, or even where he or she is supposed to be. Getting started is difficult for any new employee simply because the newness means not knowing what to expect, having to cope with a major life change (the job), and being unsure of the future. These ingredients suggest that newness anxiety will naturally be significant. It takes time to learn the ropes, and a good orientation program can help make this time be a positive experience. The first few days on the job are crucial in helping the employee get started in the right direction with a positive attitude and feeling.[1]

Orientation has not been studied a great deal.[2] Little scientific research has been done on whether orientation programs are adequate. Some experts view orientation as a kind of training.

THE PURPOSES OF ORIENTATION

Effectively done, orientation serves a number of purposes. In general, the orientation process is similar to what sociologists call socialization. Socialization occurs when a new employee learns the norms, values, work procedures, and patterns of behavior and dress that are expected in the organization. The principal purposes of orientation are:

To Reduce the Start-Up Costs for a New Employee

The new employee does not know the job, how the organization works, or whom to see to get the job done. This means that for a while the new employee is less efficient than the experienced employee, and additional costs are involved in getting the new employee started. These start-up costs have been estimated for various positions as follows: top manager, $2,000; middle manager, $1,000; supervisor, $1,000; senior engineer, $900; accountant, $750; and secretary, $400.[3] Effective orientation reduces these start-up costs and enables the new employee to reach performance standards sooner.

To Reduce the Amount of Anxiety and Hazing a New Employee Experiences

Anxiety in this case means fear of failure on the job. It is a normal fear of the unknown focused on the ability to do the job. This anxiety can be made worse when old employees haze the new employee.

Hazing takes place when experienced employees "kid" the new employee. For example, experienced employees may ask the new worker, "How many

---

[1] Michael C. Gallegher, "The Economics of Training Food Service Employees," *The Cornell H.R.A. Quarterly,* May 1977, pp. 54–56.

[2] David F. Jones, "Developing a New Employee Orientation Program," *Personnel Journal,* March 1984, pp. 86–87.

[3] Robert Sibson, "The High Cost of Hiring," *Nation's Business,* February 1975, pp. 85–86.

toys are you producing per hour?" When she answers, she is told, "You'll never last. The last one who did that few wasn't here after two days."

Such hazing serves several purposes. It lets the recruit know he or she has a lot to learn and thus is dependent on the others for his or her job, and it is "fun" for the old-timers. But it can cause great anxiety for the recruit. Effective orientation alerts the new person to hazing and reduces anxiety.

To Reduce Employee Turnover

If employees perceive themselves to be ineffective, unwanted, or unneeded they may react to these feelings by quitting. Turnover is high during the break-in period, and effective orientation can reduce this costly reaction.

To Save Time for Supervisor and Co-Workers

Improperly oriented employees must still get the job done, and to do so they need help. The most likely people to provide this help are the co-workers and supervisors, who will have to spend time breaking in new employees. Good orientation programs save everyone time.

To Develop Realistic Job Expectations, Positive Attitudes toward the Employer, and Job Satisfaction

In what sociologists call the older professions (law, medicine) or total institutions (the church, prison, the army), job expectations are clear because they have been developed over long years of training and education. Society has built up a set of attitudes and behaviors that are considered proper for these jobs. For most of the world of work, however, this does not hold true. New employees must learn realistically what the organization expects of them, and their own expectations of the job must be neither too low nor too high.[4] Each worker must incorporate the job and its work values into his or her self-image.

Orientation helps this process. One way to illustrate how orientation serves these purposes is with the story in Exhibit 12–1 of how Texas Instruments developed its new orientation program.

WHO ORIENTS NEW EMPLOYEES?

Exhibit 12–2 describes how operating and P/HRM managers run the orientation program in middle-sized and large organizations. In smaller organ-

---

4 Walter D. St. John, "The Complete Employee Orientation Program," *Personnel Journal*, May 1980, pp. 373–78.

EXHIBIT 12–1   **Orientation at Texas Instruments**

Texas Instruments knew that anxieties existing in the early period of work reduced competence and led to dissatisfaction and turnover. The anxiety resulted from awareness on the part of the female assemblers that they must reach the competence level they observed in the experienced employees around them. Many times they did not understand their supervisors' instructions but were afraid to ask further questions and appear stupid. Sometimes this anxiety was compounded by hazing.

Anxiety turned out to be a very important factor in the study at Texas Instruments, which investigated whether an orientation program designed to reduce anxiety would increase competence, heighten satisfaction, and lower turnover. The control group of new recruits were given the traditional orientation program: a typical two-hour briefing on the first day by the personnel department. This included the topics normally covered in orientation and the usual description of the minimum level of performance desired. Then they were introduced to the supervisor, who gave them a short job introduction, and they were off.

The experimental group was given the two-hour orientation the control group received and then six hours of social orientation. Four factors were stressed in the social orientation:

1. They were told that their opportunity to succeed was good. Those being oriented were given facts showing that over 99 percent of the employees achieved company standards. They were shown learning curves of how long it took to achieve various levels of competence. Five or six times during the day it was stressed that all in the group would be successful.
2. They were told to disregard "hall talk." New employees were tipped off about typical hazing. It was suggested that they take it in good humor, but ignore it.
3. They were told to take the initiative in communication. It was explained that supervisors were busy and not likely to ask the new worker if she "needed help." Supervisors would be glad to help, but the worker must ask for it, and she would not appear stupid if she did so.
4. They were told to get to know their supervisor. The supervisor was described in important details—what she liked as hobbies, whether she was strict or not, quiet or boisterous, and so forth.

This social orientation had dramatic results. The experimental group had 50 percent less tardiness and absenteeism, and waste was reduced by 80 percent, product costs were cut 15 to 30 percent, training time was cut 50 percent, and training costs cut about 66 percent.

---

izations, the operating manager does all the orienting. In some unionized organizations, union officials are involved. P/HRM also helps train the operating manager for more effective orientation behavior.

A new and progressive idea about who should orient employees is being used at Hewlett Packard (H-P) in San Diego, California. At this H-P plant and also one in Waltham, Massachusetts, retired employees perform the orientation training. The response, according to Joe Costi, employee relations man-

---

EXHIBIT 12–2   **Relationship of Operating and P/HRM Managers in Orientation**

Orientation Function	Operating Manager (OM)	P/HRM Manager (P/HRM)
Design the orientation program		P/HRM is consultant with OM
Introduce the new employee to the organization and its history, personnel policies, working conditions, and rules. Complete paperwork.		P/HRM performs this
Explain the task and job expectations to employee	OM performs this	
Introduce employee to work group and new surroundings.		
Encourage employees to help new employee	OM performs this	

ager at the San Diego facility, has been fantastic. "Many newcomers comment this must be a good place to work, if retirees come back."[5]

HOW ORIENTATION PROGRAMS WORK

Orientation programs vary from quite informal, primarily verbal efforts, to formal schedules that supplement verbal presentations with written handouts. Formal orientations often include a tour of the facilities, or slides, charts, and pictures of them. Usually, they are used when a large number of employees must be oriented.

An example of areas that are covered in comprehensive orientation programs is presented in Exhibit 12–3.

After an employee has received a general orientation of the organization it is recommended that a more job-specific orientation be given. Exhibit 12–4 presents the areas that can be covered in a job-specific orientation program.

THE ORIENTATION INFORMATION OVERLOAD

As Exhibits 12–3 and 12–4 indicate, a new employee during orientation is provided with a great amount of information. The intent of providing the

---

[5] "Companies Calling Retirees Back to the Workplace," *Management Review,* February 1982, p. 29.

EXHIBIT 12–3   Areas Covered in a Comprehensive Orientation Program

---

1. **Overview of the company**
   - ☐ Welcoming speech
   - ☐ Founding, growth, trends, goals, priorities, and problems
   - ☐ Traditions, customs, norms, and standards
   - ☐ Current specific functions of the organization
   - ☐ Products/services and customers served
   - ☐ Steps in getting product/service to customers
   - ☐ Scope of diversity of activities
   - ☐ Organization, structure, and relationship of company and its branches
   - ☐ Facts on key managerial staff
   - ☐ Community relations, expectations, and activities

2. **Key policies and procedures review**

3. **Compensation**
   - ☐ Pay rates and ranges
   - ☐ Overtime
   - ☐ Holiday pay
   - ☐ Shift differential
   - ☐ How pay is received
   - ☐ Deductions; required and optional, with specific amounts
   - ☐ Option to buy damaged products and costs thereof
   - ☐ Discounts
   - ☐ Advances on pay
   - ☐ Loans from credit union
   - ☐ Reimbursement for job expenses
   - ☐ Tax shelter options

4. **Fringe benefits**
   - ☐ Insurance
   - ☐ Medical-dental
   - ☐ Life
   - ☐ Disability
   - ☐ Workers' compensation
   - ☐ Holidays and vacations (patriotic, religious, birthday)
   - ☐ Leave: personal illness, family illness, bereavement, maternity, military, jury duty, emergency, extended absence
   - ☐ Retirement plans and options
   - ☐ On-the-job training opportunities
   - ☐ Counseling services
   - ☐ Cafeteria
   - ☐ Recreation and social activities
   - ☐ Other company services to employees

5. **Safety and accident prevention**
   - ☐ Completion of emergency data card (if not done as part of employment process)

- ☐ Health and first aid clinics
- ☐ Exercise and recreation centers
- ☐ Safety precautions
- ☐ Reporting of hazards
- ☐ Fire prevention and control
- ☐ Accident procedures and reporting
- ☐ OSHA requirements (review of key sections)
- ☐ Physical exam requirements
- ☐ Use of alcohol and drugs on the job

6. **Employee and union relations**
   - ☐ Terms and conditions of employment review
   - ☐ Assignment, reassignment, and promotion
   - ☐ Probationary period and expected on-the-job conduct
   - ☐ Reporting of sickness and lateness to work
   - ☐ Employee rights and responsibilities
   - ☐ Manager and supervisor rights
   - ☐ Relations with supervisors and shop stewards
   - ☐ Employee organizations and options
   - ☐ Union contract provisions and/or company policy
   - ☐ Supervision and evaluation of performance
   - ☐ Discipline and reprimands
   - ☐ Grievance procedures
   - ☐ Termination of employment (resignation, layoff, discharge, retirement)
   - ☐ Content and examination of personnel record
   - ☐ Communications: channels of communication—upward and downward—suggestion system, posting materials on bulletin board, sharing new ideas
   - ☐ Sanitation and cleanliness
   - ☐ Wearing of safety equipment, badges, and uniforms
   - ☐ Bringing things on and removing things from company grounds
   - ☐ On-site political activity
   - ☐ Gambling
   - ☐ Handling of rumors

7. **Physical facilities**
   - ☐ Tour of facilities
   - ☐ Food services and cafeteria
   - ☐ Restricted areas for eating
   - ☐ Employee entrances
   - ☐ Restricted areas (e.g., cars)
   - ☐ Parking
   - ☐ First aid
   - ☐ Rest rooms
   - ☐ Supplies and equipment

(continued)

EXHIBIT 12-3 *(concluded)*

8. Economic factors
- ☐ Costs of damage by select items with required sales to balance
- ☐ Costs of theft with required sales to compensate
- ☐ Profit margins
- ☐ Labor costs
- ☐ Cost of equipment
- ☐ Costs of absenteeism, lateness, and accidents

EXHIBIT 12-4   **Areas Covered in Job-Specific Orientation Program**

1. Department functions
- ☐ Goals and current priorities
- ☐ Organization and structure
- ☐ Operational activities
- ☐ Relationship of functions to other departments
- ☐ Relationships of jobs within the department

2. Job duties and responsibilities
- ☐ Detailed explanation of job based on current job description and expected results
- ☐ Explanation of why the job is important, how the specific job relates to others in the department and company
- ☐ Discussion of common problems and how to avoid and overcome them
- ☐ Performance standards and basis of performance evaluation
- ☐ Number of daily work hours and times
- ☐ Overtime needs and requirements
- ☐ Extra duty assignments (such as changing duties to cover for an absent worker)
- ☐ Required records and reports
- ☐ Checkout on equipment to be used
- ☐ Explanation of where and how to get tools, have equipment maintained and repaired
- ☐ Types of assistance available; when and how to ask for help
- ☐ Relations with state and federal inspectors

3. Policies, procedures, rules, and regulations
- ☐ Rules unique to the job and/or department
- ☐ Handling emergencies
- ☐ Safety precautions and accident prevention
- ☐ Reporting of hazards and accidents
- ☐ Cleanliness standards and sanitation (such as cleanup)
- ☐ Security, theft problems and costs
- ☐ Relations with outside people (e.g., drivers)
- ☐ Eating, smoking, and chewing gum, etc., in department area
- ☐ Removal of things from department
- ☐ Damage control (e.g., smoking restrictions)
- ☐ Time clock and time sheets
- ☐ Breaks/rest periods
- ☐ Lunch duration and time
- ☐ Making and receiving personal telephone calls
- ☐ Requisitioning supplies and equipment
- ☐ Monitoring and evaluating of employee performance
- ☐ Job bidding and requesting reassignment
- ☐ Going to cars during work hours

4. Tour of department
- ☐ Rest rooms and showers
- ☐ Fire-alarm box and fire extinguisher stations
- ☐ Time clocks
- ☐ Lockers
- ☐ Approved entrances and exits
- ☐ Water fountains and eye wash systems
- ☐ Supervisors' quarters
- ☐ Supply room and maintenance department
- ☐ Sanitation and security offices
- ☐ Smoking areas
- ☐ Locations of services to employees related to department
- ☐ First aid kit

5. Introduction to department employees

information is to present an understanding of how the organization and department operates. However, it is virtually impossible for any person to digest and learn the volume of orientation information that can be provided. Thus the orientation should provide for the employee's receiving the information over more than a one-day or one-week period.

Developing an orientation program that takes place over a one-month period seems to be well suited for absorbing the volume of information needed by new employees. Unfortunately, too many organizations overload new employees with orientation information. They usually provide the information in a standard operating procedures manual and ask the employee to take a day or two to examine the material. Once this brief period is over, the employee is asked if there are any questions. When any questions are answered, the new employee begins to work.

Instead of a quick and information overloaded orientation program, a more systematic and guided procedure is appropriate. A few guidelines for such a program are these:

1. Orientation should begin with the most relevant and immediate kinds of information and then proceed to more general policies of the organization. It should occur at a pace that the new employee is comfortable with.
2. The most significant part of orientation is the human side, giving new employees knowledge of what supervisors and co-workers are like, telling them how long it should take to reach standards of effective work, and encouraging them to seek help and advice when needed.
3. New employees should be "sponsored" or directed in the immediate environment by an experienced worker or supervisor who can respond to questions and keep in close touch during the early induction period.
4. New employees should be gradually introduced to the people with whom they will work, rather than given a superficial introduction to all of them on the first day. The object should be to help them to know their co-workers and supervisors.
5. New employees should be allowed sufficient time to get their feet on the ground before job demands on them are increased.

ASSIGNMENT, PLACEMENT, AND ORIENTATION FOLLOW-UP

The final phase of a well-designed and systematic orientation program is the assignment of the new employee to the job. At this point, the supervisor is supposed to take over and continue the orientation program. But as the Texas Instruments study demonstrated, supervisors are busy people, and they can overlook some of the facts needed by the new employee to do a good job.

One way to ensure adequate orientation is to design a feedback system to control the program, or use the management by objectives technique. A form could be used to communicate this feedback from the trainee. The new employee could be instructed to: "Complete this checklist as well as you can. Then take it to your supervisor, who will go over it with you and give you any additional information you may need." The job information form is signed by employee and supervisor. An appointment set up with the orientation group in the first month on the job provides a follow-up opportunity to determine how well the employee is adjusting and permits evaluation of the orientation program. The form is designed not to test knowledge but to help improve the process of orientation.

INTRODUCTION TO TRAINING

Training is extremely important for new or present employees. Training is, in short, an attempt to improve current or future employee performance. The following specific points are important to know about training:

- *Training* is the systematic process of altering the behavior of employees in a direction to increase organization goals.
- A *formal training program* is an effort by the employer to provide opportunities for the employee to acquire job-related skills, attitudes, and knowledge.
- *Learning* is the act by which the individual acquires skills, knowledge, and abilities that result in a relatively permanent change in his or her behavior.
- Any behavior that has been learned is a skill. Therefore, skills improvement is what training will accomplish. Motor skills, cognitive skills, and interpersonal skills are targets of training programs.

One way to display the meaning and comprehensiveness of training and development is to present a graphic model. Exhibit 12–5 illustrates such a model. The needs assessment phase serves as the formulation for decisions that must be made at later phases. It is important for the needs assessment to be complete, timely, and accurate. After the needs assessment is completed, instructional objectives are needed. These objectives lead to the selection and design of instructional programs. If assessment and the selection and design of programs are done carefully, the evaluation of the training and development can be accomplished. As Exhibit 12–5 indicates, evaluation can provide information about when various training goals have been accomplished. Some important goals are:

- *Training validity*—Did the trainees learn skills, or acquire knowledge or abilities during the training?
- *Transfer validity*—Did the knowledge, skills, or abilities learned in training lead to improved performance on the job?
- *Intraorganizational validity*—Is the job performance of a new group of trainees in the same organization that developed the program comparable with the job performance of the original training group(s)?
- *Interorganizational validity*—Can a training program that has been validated in one organization be used successfully in another firm?

EXHIBIT 12-5 **A General Systems Model of Training and Development**

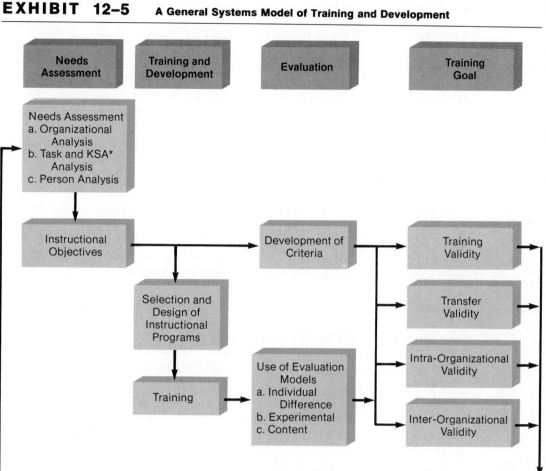

* KSA = Knowledge, Skills, Abilities

Source: From I. L. Goldstein, *Training in Organizations: Needs Assessment, Development, and Evaluation*, 2nd ed (Monterey, Calif.: Brooks/Cole, 1986) p. 16. Reprinted by permission of the publisher.

These questions (goals) result in different evaluation procedures being employed to examine what, if anything, training and development has accomplished.[6]

Since training is a form of education, some of the findings regarding learning theory logically might be applicable to training. These principles can be important in the design of both formal and informal training programs. The

---

[6] I. L. Goldstein, *Training in Organizations: Needs Assessment Development and Evaluation* (Monterey, Calif.: Brooks/Cole, 1986).

following is a brief summary of the way learning principles can be applied to job training.[7]

The Trainee Must Be Motivated To Learn In order to learn, a person must want to learn. In the context of training, motivation influences a person's enthusiasm for training, keeps attention focused on the training activities, and reinforces what is learned. Motivation is influenced by the belief and perceptions of the trainee as displayed in Exhibit 12–6.

Four important factors including the work environment and three beliefs are portrayed in Exhibit 12–6. To the extent that these factors are present, the motivation to learn is likely to be high. If these motivational factors are missing, a trainer may leave a training program with nothing at all accomplished.

The Learning Must Be Reinforced Behavioral psychologists have demonstrated that learners learn best with fairly immediate reinforcement of appropriate behavior. The learner must be rewarded for new behavior in ways that satisfy needs, such as pay, recognition, and promotion. Standards of performance should be set for the learner. Benchmarks for learning will provide goals and give a feeling of accomplishment when reached. These standards provide a measure for meaningful feedback.

The Training Must Provide for Practice of the Material Learning requires time to assimilate what has been learned, to accept it, to internalize it, and to build confidence in what has been learned. This requires practice and repetition of the material.

The Material Presented Must Be Meaningful Appropriate materials for sequential learning (cases, problems, discussion outlines, reading lists) must be provided. The trainer acts as an aid in an efficient learning process.

The learning methods used should be as varied as possible. It is boredom that destroys learning, not fatigue. Any method—whether old-fashioned lecture or programmed learning or the jazziest computer game—will begin to bore some learners if overused.

The Material Presented Must Be Communicated Effectively Communication must be done in a unified way, and over enough time to allow it to be absorbed.

The Material Taught Must Transfer to the Job Situation The trainer must do her or his best to make the training as close to the reality of the job as possible. Thus, when the trainee returns to the job, the training can be applied immediately.[8]

---

[7] E. R. Hilgard and G. H. Bower, *Theories of Learning* (New York: Appleton-Century-Crofts, 1966).

[8] Elaine I. Berke, "Keeping Newly Trained Supervisors from Going Back to Old Ways," *Management Review*, February 1984, pp. 14–16.

EXHIBIT 12–6   **Factors That Affect Motivation In Training Program**

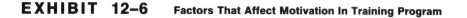

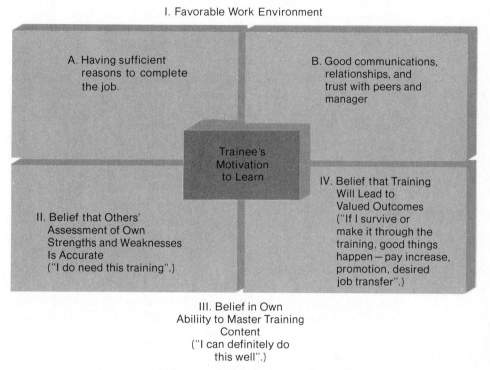

I. Favorable Work Environment

A. Having sufficient reasons to complete the job.

B. Good communications, relationships, and trust with peers and manager

Trainee's Motivation to Learn

IV. Belief that Training Will Lead to Valued Outcomes ("If I survive or make it through the training, good things happen—pay increase, promotion, desired job transfer".)

II. Belief that Others' Assessment of Own Strengths and Weaknesses Is Accurate ("I do need this training".)

III. Belief in Own Abiliity to Master Training Content ("I can definitely do this well".)

Source: Adapted from Wayne F. Cascio, *Applied Psychology In Personnel Management* (Englewood Cliffs, N.J.: Prentice Hall, 1987), p. 367.

As each aspect of training program design and implementation is discussed, you will see how these learning theory principles are applied. Training and management development are closely related to many P/HRM activities. For example, performance evaluation provides the data needed for training. Employment planning decisions may also dictate the need for added training.

Employee training is moderately well developed—a Stage III or possibly Stage IV function in P/HRM. But management development is a Stage II P/HRM function. Most people do it, but scientific evaluation of its results is rare.

A DIAGNOSTIC VIEW OF TRAINING

The most important determinants of training are the task to be done and the employees' abilities and attitudes. If the current employees have work ethic attitudes and the skills needed to do the jobs, training may not be too important for the organization. More often, because of conditions in the labor market, the organization is losing some employees to other enterprises that provide better rewards.

It is also unlikely that the task demands are stable. More frequently, because of volatile technology and market conditions, the jobs are changing, requiring more training so that employees can meet current effectiveness standards. For example, when computers are introduced or new production or operating techniques are instituted, employees must be retrained.[9]

The U.S. government also is becoming a vital influence on training. This has been happening in two ways. One is the pressure for equal employment opportunities and human rights. If in an organization minorities and women work only at the lowest paid, least skilled positions, pressure will be applied to upgrade the skills of those who have the potential for upward mobility thus increasing the demand for training or retraining.

The second way government influences training is that it provides many training programs. These programs frequently have public policy purposes, such as reducing unemployment, upgrading the incomes of minority groups, or increasing the competitiveness of underdeveloped regions of the country.

In the United States, the federal government, through the Comprehensive Employment and Training Act (1974) and other work force legislation, has allocated large sums of money for the training of potential workers for jobs.[10] The government reimburses training organizations (schools, business, unions) or trains the workers itself.

The California Employment Training Panel is a unique, state-sponsored program. The panel has provided $20 million in funds diverting unemployment insurance money for finance training that will reduce the states' jobless rolls.[11] The money helps companies hire and train unemployed workers, or retrain workers threatened with losing their jobs unless they learn new skills. The California program permits employers to pick their own trainees and choose whether they want to train in-house or use local colleges. It pays only for workers who complete the training course and succeed in holding jobs.

Some unions are also involved in employee training, especially in industries such as construction, in which the union is larger than the employer. In these cases, the union often does most or all of the training. A large proportion of this type of training occurs in apprenticeship programs.

Finally, the goals of management also affect training and development. For example, organization development programs are likely to be chosen by managers who feel that full development of employees is an appropriate enterprise goal.

The implications are that employee training is a major undertaking for employers. Almost all large organizations and most medium-sized ones run their own training programs. They employ 50,000 full-time trainers and spend approximately $100 billion per year on their programs.[12] As P/HRM personnel

---

[9] Bradley R. Schiller, "Training Keeps the Job Machine Running," *The Wall Street Journal,* June 24, 1987, p. 24.

[10] William Mirengoff and Lester Rindler, "The Comprehensive Employment and Training Act: Impact on People, Places, and Programs (Washington, D.C.: National Accademy of Sciences, 1976).

[11] Michael Brody, "Helping Workers to Work Smarter," *Fortune,* June 8, 1987, pp. 86–88.

[12] John Naisbitt, "Retraining Managers," *Management Review,* April 1985, pp. 33–35.

EXHIBIT 12–7   **Average Costs of Training a Salesperson***

Type of Firm	1986
Industrial products (an engineering salesperson)	$27,525
Consumer products (a person selling food products to a grocery store)	19,320
Services†	20,460

* Includes salary, instructional materials, transportation, and living expenses incurred for training, instructional staff, outside seminars, and management time when it is part of training budget.
† Includes insurance, financial, utilities, transportation, and sales personnel.
Reprinted with permission from *Sales & Marketing Management* magazine. Copyright February 16, 1987, p. 62.

know, training can be a costly endeavor. Exhibit 12–7 illustrates how an industrial firm could easily spend $50,000–$100,000 or more training just three or four salespeople. Whether an organization has management or professional development programs depends a great deal on its size. Smaller enterprises rarely run their own formal development program; the programs are informal at best. Larger organizations have elaborate formal programs combining on-the-job with off-the-job development.[13] Others, such as General Motors, the U.S. Military, Exxon, and AT&T, have established large complex training and development centers for their managers. McDonald's runs Hamburger University in Oak Brook, Illinois, while Arthur Andersen trains accountants on an old college campus west of Chicago.[14] The Federal Executive Institute at Charlottesville, Virginia, is set up to develop federal government executives, as is the Executive Seminar Center in Berkeley, California, and the U.S. Post Office Center in Norman, Oklahoma. Aetna Insurance Institute was built at a cost of $42 million to handle over 31,000 Aetna Corporation students per year.[15] There has been tremendous growth in this area in the past 20 years, and the trend is expected to continue.

The corporate classroom is now a growing business. Engineers can take classes that could lead to a masters degree. It is estimated that close to 100 companies—Eastman Kodak, Westinghouse Electric Co., and NCR among them—offer in-house course work that can lead to academically-accredited degrees. National Technology University (NTU) based in Fort Collins, Colorado, is unique among corporate colleges with its electronic satellite network.[16] The university combines the resources of 22 member universities and several corporate sponsors to transmit advanced degree courses across the country. NTU students attend classes at their worksite, watch satellite trans-

---

[13] Constance Mitchell, "Corporate Classes: Firms Broaden Scope of Their Education Programs," *The Wall Street Journal*, September 28, 1987, p. 27.

[14] Mary William Walsh, "Company Built Retreats Reflect Firms' Culture and Personalities," *The Wall Street Journal*, August 26, 1984, p. 25.

[15] Ibid.

[16] A. Vice Short, "Are We Getting Our Money's Worth?" *New Management*, Winter 1987, pp. 23–26.

EXHIBIT 12–8 The Role of Operating and P/HRM Managers in Training

Training Activites	Operating Manager (OM)	P/HRM Manager (P/HRM)
Determining training needs and objectives	Approved by OM	Done by P/HRM
Developing training criteria	Approved by OM	Done by P/HRM
Choosing trainer	Jointly chosen: nominated by OM	Jointly chosen: approved by P/HRM
Developing training materials	Approved by OM	Done by P/HRM
Planning and implementing the program		Done by P/HRM
Doing the training	Occasionally done by OM	Normally done by P/HRM
Evaluating the training	OM reviews the results	Done by P/HRM

missions, and talk with professors via telephones or electronic mail. After about 3½ years of study, they can earn various degrees.

WHO IS INVOLVED IN TRAINING?

For training to be effective, top management must support it in an open manner. Employees must see that top management is supporting training personally and financially. As with other P/HRM activities, both operating and P/HRM managers are involved in training. Exhibit 12–8 indicates how. Occasionally, more than these two groups are involved. For example, at General Telephone of Florida, the training, labor relations, and public affairs departments combined forces to prepare video training programs to train managers to handle grievances and arbitration. Community theater actors performed the roles to show participants how to perform while on the job.

In larger organizations, the P/HRM manager most involved in the work described in Chapters 12 and 13 is called the training director or training and development manager. A manager involved in training is Naomi Garner. She works for First National Bank of Hot Springs, Arkansas, and a few of her thoughts are presented here.

MANAGING THE TRAINING PROGRAM

Determining Training Needs and Objectives

The first step in managing training is to determine training needs and set objectives for these needs. In effect, the trainers are preparing a training forecast (this is the assessment phase in Exhibit 12–5).

P/HRM Manager Close-Up

Naomi Garner
First National Bank
of Hot Springs

Biography

Naomi Garner is vice president and director of human resources of First National Bank of Hot Springs, responsible for personnel administration, training, and recruitment.

Ms. Garner is a graduate of Louisiana State University, Graduate School of Banking of the South, class of 1983.

She joined First National Bank of Hot Springs in October 1973 as executive secretary to the president and chief executive officer. She assumed the additional responsibility of payroll clerk and was then promoted to director of human resources. Her next promotion was to her present position of vice president.

A Training Program at First National Bank

Under the direction of Naomi Garner, director of human resources, and assisted by the then facilitator, Phyllis Rogers, a study was conducted of available productivity and quality circle material. The program was written to meet the needs of employees and then introduced at a staff meeting of all employees. Enthusiasm was high, and the program was kicked off with the bank's nine branches as a pilot group.

Following the introduction, breakfast meetings in one-hour time frames were conducted for eight weeks. The high-performance units (HPUs) were trained by Ms. Garner in a variety of skills necessary to ensure success of the program. The quality circle concept was explained in detail, and such topics as brainstorming, creative thinking, group and team dynamics, and presentation skills were covered.

After the training was completed, each branch manager (named as the "Leadership Rep") then designated a "Pacesetter Rep" from his or her unit, the pacesetter being the spokesperson for the unit and who passed productivity ideas from the group to the leadership representative.

The leadership representative has the responsibility for judging the merit of productivity ideas. If the represen-

(continued)

tative thinks the suggestion has merit, he or she and the branch administration division manager have the authority to approve it.

If the idea involves another area of the bank, it goes to the advisory committee for a decision. This six-member management committee, which meets monthly, must rule on the validity of the idea within 48 hours after its presentation. This committee consists of division managers from the controller, marketing, human resource, branch administration, and operations areas.

Members of high-performance units were told during initial training that their ideas could involve housekeeping, communication, customer service, work methods, or suggestions for cutting costs or saving time. Ms. Garner said the first ideas from the units involved housekeeping and included such things as inadequate lighting and poor arrangement of work areas.

"The group found that doing something as simple as moving a desk a few feet could account for a productivity gain," Ms. Garner stated. "From these meager beginnings, our high-performance units are now branching out and looking at the bigger picture; they are coming up with ideas that touch on the other productivity categories and producing real benefits for the bank."

Some of the "creative ideas" that the bank's management team feels has improved not only the image of the bank but customer service include: interdepartmental cross-training, smiling as they answer the telephone, "check-only system" for utility payments, call-up deposit procedure, creating a commercial account window at the branches,

and a "Hold File" to keep accounts current.

G. Michael Sigman, president and chief executive officer of First National, has called this program "one of the best programs we have ever implemented." "Too often," Mr. Sigman stated, "we get involved in trying to manage from the top down when the really successful organizations have proven time and again that the most effective way is to start with the individual doing the actual day-to-day work."

After two years, 26 units are functioning, and each employee is involved in a high-performance unit. Every employee is more aware of the real costs associated with "running a bank" and the need to be constantly aware of customer needs. With the units now participating, First National Bank has seen a substantial drop in absenteeism, a decrease in turnover, and supply costs cut in some divisions by 35 percent. In addition, a change in one procedure has resulted in a significant reduction of unnecessary telephone calls between tellers and the bookkeeping department.

Through continued training updates and small group "brainstorming" sessions, the employees have gotten involved in their jobs like never before. They realize that their job responsibilities involve more than just "putting in their eight hours." They know that they are accountable for constant improved customer service and realize their importance when they can personally curb diminished customer service.

P/HRM · IN · ACTION

Bob

Young Enterprises did not have a separate training department. So Gwen, with the assistance of Bob McGarrah, the director of training and development, began to think about a training program to help Harold Matthews reach his goal. The program might not have been needed if the job market weren't so tight. But since applicants are so scarce, the training program was very important at this point.

Gwen: Bob, what we need to determine is what training programs we should have right now. What do you suggest we do?

Bob: The typical approach is to use organizational analysis, operational analysis, and person analysis. Besides, we need to do some sort of feasibility of cost/benefits analysis to see if the training is worth the effort. This will give us a set of training objectives for a program or set of programs. Then we design the program content and methods around these. After the program is run, we evaluate it.

Gwen: At this point, let's set the objectives and design the program. Then we'll go back to Harold to see if he has any additional suggestions.

There are four ways to determine the training needs:[17]

1. Observe employees.
2. Listen to employees.
3. Ask supervisors about employees' training needs.
4. Examine the problems employees have.

In essence, any gaps between expected and actual results suggest training needs.[18] Active solicitation of suggestions from employees, supervisors, managers, and training committees can also provide training needs ideas.

---

[17] Donald Kirkpatrick, "Determining Training Needs," *Training and Development Journal,* February 1977, pp. 22–25.

[18] Vicki S. Kaman and John P. Mohr, "Training Needs Assessment in the Eighties: Five Guideposts," *Personnel Administrator,* October 1984, pp. 47–53.

Performance Analysis By observation, asking, and listening, a manager or P/HRM specialist is actually conducting a performance analysis.[19] There are a number of specific steps that are taken in using a performance analysis to determine training needs. Exhibit 12–9 outlines the steps that are used in conducting a performance analysis.

Step 1: Behavioral Discrepancy The first step is to appraise employees' performance. How are the employees doing now and how should they be doing? If a secretary is using a Wang word processor to prepare budgets and takes an average of 7.5 hours to complete the work, this record of performance can be used to assess her performance. This performance may be 2.0 hours over what is expected. Thus, there is a behavioral discrepancy—a difference between actual and expected.

Step 2: Cost/Value analysis Next the manager must determine the cost and value of correcting the identified behavioral discrepancy. Is it worth the cost, time, and expense to have the secretary prepare the budgets in less than 7.5 hours?

Step 3: Is It a Can't or Won't Do Situation It is important to determine if the employee could do the expected job if she wanted to. Three questions need to be answered: *(a)* Does the person know what to do in terms of performance? *(b)* Could the person do the job if she wanted to? and *(c)* Does she want to do the job? Answering these questions requires observation, listening, and asking skills on the part of the person conducting the performance analysis.

Step 4: Set Standards If a secretary doesn't know what the standard is, she may underperform. Establishing a standard and clearly communicating it can improve performance.

Step 5: Remove Obstacles Not being able to complete budgets on time may be caused by frequent breakdowns of the equipment (the Wang system) or not receiving a job on time. Time, equipment, and people can be obstacles that result in behavior discrepancies.

Step 6: Practice Practice, practice, practice may be one avenue to performing a job better. Does the manager permit the employee the needed practice time?

Step 7: Training If the performance analysis indicates that behaviors need to be altered, training becomes a viable consideration before any training approaches can be weighed and considered as being best suited to correct the behavior discrepancy.

Step 8: Change the Job Redesigning the job through job enrichment, job simplification, or job enlargement may be the best solution.

Step 9: Transfer or Terminate If all else has failed, the employee may have to be transferred or terminated.

Step 10: Create a Motivational Climate In some cases a skilled and able employee may not want to perform the job as required, posing a motivational problem. A manager may then have to use a motivational approach that converts this undermotivated person into a motivated high performer. Re-

---

[19] Donald Michalak and Edwin Yager, *Making the Training Process Work* (New York: Harper & Row, 1979).

EXHIBIT 12–9   **Performance Analysis: Analyzing Training Needs**

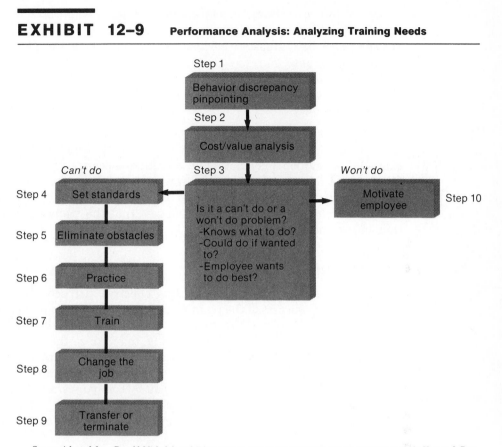

Source: Adapted from Donald Michalak and Edwin Yager, *Making the Training Process Work* (New York: Harper & Row, 1979).

wards, punishment, discipline, or some combination may be needed to create a positive climate that results in the employee utilizing his or her skills optimally.

A performance analysis is a sound procedure that can provide insight into training needs and objectives. Such an analysis may illustrate that training is not the best solution to the behavior discrepancies identified. If this is the case other solutions will surface as the performance analysis is conducted.[20]

If, however, the performance analysis identifies a training problem, then it is necessary to establish specific, measurable training objectives. Training objectives should be expressed in behavioral terms, if at all possible. The behavioral training objectives of a Bandell Manufacturing supervisory training program are:

---

[20] Carol Haig, "A Line Manager's Guide to Training," *Personnel Journal,* October 1984, pp. 42–45.

- To improve supervisory understanding of laws pertaining to the use of the performance appraisal system.
- To improve listening and feedback skills for use in the performance appraisal program.
- To reduce by 20 percent for the year's program, the formal supervisor complaints that are filed with the P/HRM unit about the performance appraisal system.

By using behaviorally-based objectives, the intent of the training program is identified. In some cases it is difficult to specify behavioral objectives. For example, a new job may not have objectives because the manager is still attempting to clarify what behaviors are required. However, if behaviors can't be identified, one might be inclined to ask what the reason for the training is. A vague, ambiguous answer might suggest that the training purpose is not that important.

Choosing Trainers and Trainees

Great care must be exercised in choosing effective instructors or trainers. To some extent, the success of the training program depends on proper selection of the person who performs the training task.[21] Personal characteristics (the ability to speak well, to write convincingly, to organize the work of others, to be inventive, and to inspire others to greater achievements) are important factors in the selection of trainers. The process of needs analysis and training program development can be accomplished by company trainers. P/HRM specialists or hired outside consultants who report to the P/HRM manager or other top managers are used to perform a needs analysis and to conduct the training.[22]

Although much formal training is performed by professional trainers, often operating supervisors may be the best trainers technically, especially if the training manager helps them prepare the material. Using operating managers as trainers overcomes the frequent criticism that "Training is OK in the classroom, but it won't work on the shop floor or back on the job." The presence of *trained* trainers is a major factor in whether the training program is successful. It will help if these principles of learning are followed:

- Provide time for practice of the material.
- Require practice and repetition of the material.
- Communicate the material effectively.

Another planning factor is the selection of trainees who will participate in the programs. In some cases this is obvious; the program may have been designed to train particular new employees in certain skills. In some cases, the

---

[21] Lary E. Greiner, "Confessions of an Executive Educator," *New Management,* Winter 1987, pp. 35–38.

[22] Stephen B. Wehrenberg, "Inside or Outside Resources: Which Are Best for Training?", *Personnel Journal,* July 1984, pp. 23–24.

training program is designed to help with EEO goals; in others it is to help employees find better jobs elsewhere when layoffs are necessary or to retrain older employees. Techniques similar to selection procedures may be used to select trainees, especially when those who attend the program may be promoted or receive higher wages or salaries as a result.

The selection of trainees is not always limited to promising future leaders or newcomers who need to learn specific job-related skills. More and more companies now offer training programs for employees nearing retirement.[23] Some examples of such programs follow:

- Chrysler has a seven-week training program relating to retirement issues, problems, and adjustments co-sponsored by the company and the United Auto Workers.
- AT&T sponsors a retiree group called the Telephone Pioneers of America. Preretirement and postretirement activities occur in meetings, discussions, and with personal counselors.
- Citicorp holds seminars with guest speakers and consultants who discuss health, aging, financial planning, and insurance.

The way a company treats its retirees is seen by all employees. The intent of pre- and postretirement training and educational programs is to provide accurate information and an open exchange of ideas about the experience of retiring.

TRAINING AND DEVELOPMENT PHASE

After needs and objectives have been determined and trainees and trainers have been selected, the program is run. This is the second phase shown in Exhibit 12–5. This phase includes selection of content and methods to be used and the actual training.

Selection of Training Content

From the analysis of the training needs and translating them into behavioral objectives, the training director derives the content of the training. Since there are well over 20,000 jobs listed in the *Dictionary of Occupational Titles,* the number of skills to be developed can be quite large. For example, communication, leadership, and budgeting skills are frequent subjects of training programs. But all kinds of skills can be taught.[24] The ones *to be* taught are derived from the training needs analysis. They can vary from typing skills improvement to learning a new computer language to effective use of a new machine.

---

[23] Stephen B. Wehrenberg, "Preparing to Retire: Educational Programs that Help Employees," *Personnel Journal,* September 1984, p. 41–42.

[24] William J. Rothwell, "Curriculum Design in Training: An Overview," *Personnel Administrator,* November 1983, pp. 53–57.

Training Approaches for Employees

Both training for the unskilled and retraining for an employee follow one of four approaches, which combine elements of the *where* and *what* of training. The four principal types of training are apprenticeship, vestibule, on-the-job training, and off-the-job training.

Apprentice Training Apprentice training is a combination of on-the-job and off-the-job training. It requires the cooperation of the employer, trainers at the workplace and in schools (such as vocational schools), government agencies, and the skilled-trades unions.

Governments regulate apprentice training. In the United States, the major law is the Apprenticeship Act of 1937. Typically, the government also subsidizes these programs. The U.S. Department of Labor funds apprenticeship programs in the building trades, mining, auto repair, oil, and other fields. The department also issues standards and regulations governing these programs. About 30,000 persons are trained yearly by this method.

The apprentice commits to a period of training and learning that involves both formal classroom learning and practical on-the-job experience. These periods can vary from 2 years or so (barber, ironworker, foundry worker, baker, meat cutter, engraver) through 4 or 5 years (electrician, photoengraver, tool and die maker, plumber, job press worker), up to 10 years (steelplate engraver). During this period, the pay is less than that for the master workers. A weakness of apprenticeship training is that the amount of time a person serves as an apprentice is predetermined by members of the trade. The trade fails to take into consideration individual differences in learning time.

Research evaluating construction workers trained by the apprenticeship method versus on-the-job training indicates that apprentices are better trained, get promoted sooner, and experience less unemployment later.[25]

Vestibule Training In vestibule training, the trainee learns the job in an environment that simulates the real working environment as closely as possible. An example would be the simulated cockpit of a Boeing 767 used to train airline pilots in operating that specific aircraft.[26] United Airlines had 16 jet simulators in use in 1982. A machine operator trainee might run a machine under the supervision of a trainer until he or she learns how to use it properly. Only then is the trainee sent to the shop floor. This procedure can be quite expensive if the number of trainees supervised is not large, but it can be effective under certain circumstances. Some employees trained in the ves-

---

[25] William Franklin, "A Comparison of Formally and Informally Trained Journeymen in Construction," *Industrial and Labor Relations Review,* July 1973, pp. 1086–94.

[26] Shelby Hodge, "Flights of Fancy Qualify Pilots on the Ground," *Houston Chronicle,* August 9, 1981, p. 3AA.

[27] Carol Harg, "Clinics Fill the Training Niche," *Personnel Journal,* September 1987, pp. 134–39.

tibule method have adjustment problems when they begin full-time work, since the vestibule area is safer and less hectic.

A form of vestibule training is now called "clinic training" at firms such as Wells Fargo Bank. For example, a Wells Fargo Bank branch manager may need to train tellers who can work the branches' busiest hours.[27] In a "clinic," trainees work in peer groups to learn and practice new skills. They attend a short, instructional session presented during a staff meeting or at a central location.

They are taught, coached and evaluated by a line employee, usually the manager. The typical Wells Fargo clinic is between 75 minutes and three hours long. In the clinic, the tellers are coached and observed as they practice the needed skills. The clinic requires few resources and delivery of training costs stay low because travel, classroom, and instructor expenses are minimal.

On-the-Job Training Probably the most widely used method of training (formal and informal) is on-the-job training. It is estimated that more than 60 percent of training occurs on the job. The employee is placed into the real work situation and shown the job and the tricks of the trade by an experienced employee or the supervisor. Although this program is apparently simple and relatively less costly, if it is not handled properly the costs can be high in damaged machinery, unsatisfied customers, misfiled forms, and poorly taught workers. To prevent these problems, trainers must be carefully selected and trained. The trainee should be placed with a trainer who is similar in background and personality. The trainer should be motivated by training and rewarded for doing it well. The trainer should use effective training techniques in instructing the trainee.

One approach to systematic on-the-job training is the job instruction training (JIT) system developed during World War II.[28] In this system, the trainers first train the supervisors, who in turn train the employees. Exhibit 12–10 describes the steps of JIT training as given in the War Manpower Commission's bulletin, "Training within Industry Series in 1945." These are the instructions given to supervisors on how to train new or present employees.

The Bay Area Rapid Transit District (BART) is a mass transit system in the San Francisco–Oakland Bay area. It was built for $1.6 billion and opened for its first paying customers on September 11, 1972.[29] BART became a classic joke because of its problems. Late to work, for whatever reason? "I took BART" was the main joke for years. BART today has turned around and boasts a 55.5 million ridership and an "on-schedule and on-time" rate of 95 percent. Training has played a major role in the turnaround.

Vehicle electricians, computer specialists, train-control technicians, line supervisors, and other technical/line specialists have been involved in formal

---

[28] Fred Wickert, "The Famous JIT Card: A Basic Way to Improve It," *Training and Development Journal,* February 1974, pp. 6–9.

[29] Chris Lee, "Is This Any Way to Train a Railroad?", *Training,* June 1984, pp. 20–26.

EXHIBIT 12–10   Job Instruction Training (JIT) Methods

First, Here's what you *must do* to *get ready* to teach a job:
1. Decide what the learner must be taught in order to do the job efficiently, safely, economically, and intelligently.
2. Have the right tools, equipment, supplies, and material ready.
3. Have the workplace properly arranged, just as the worker will be expected to keep it.

Then, you should *instruct* the learner by the following *four basic steps:*

Step I—*Preparation* (of the learner)
1. Put the learner at *ease.*
2. Find out what he or she already knows about the job.
3. Get the learners interested and desirous of learning the job.

Step II—*Presentation* (of the operations and knowledge)
1. *Tell, show, illustrate* and *question* in order to put over the new knowledge and operations.
2. Instruct slowly, clearly, completely, and patiently, one point at a time.
3. Check, question, and repeat.
4. Make sure the learner really knows.

Step III—*Performance tryout*
1. Test learner by having him or her perform the job.
2. Ask questions beginning with *why, how, when* or *where.*
3. Observe performance, correct errors, and repeat instructions if necessary.
4. Continue until *you know learner knows.*

Step IV—*Follow-up*
1. Put the employee "on his own."
2. Check frequently to be sure learner follows instructions.
3. Taper off extra supervision and close follow-up until person is qualified to work with normal supervision.

Remember—if the learner hasn't learned, the teacher hasn't taught.

on-the-job training programs. New technicians, for example, find themselves in the classroom and on the job receiving training for approximately one year. Training must be successfully completed before a technician goes out on the job without an experienced worker.

Electricians and other technical specialists at BART must pass an initial certification when they are hired or promoted and must be recertified every two or three years. To maintain their certification, employees attend training programs that require written and performance exams, in addition to on-the-job competency testing. At BART the training experience means that the training programs must show results to be continued. A former white elephant, BART has become a success story, and training has played a major role.

IBM manufactures typewriters in Lexington, Kentucky. Until recently the typewriters were produced by hand. However, technological changes required a new set of employee skills. Consequently, IBM developed a two-tiered combined training system of on-the-job *and* classroom instruction to retain automated assembly line workers.[30] The retraining opportunity means that employees apply for a position in the program. The candidate's experience, performance, and education are used to decide who will be given the retraining opportunity. So far, IBM has about 10 candidates for each retraining slot. On-the-job retraining is important to a company like IBM, since having the best skill mix available to meet future changes and challenges is so vital for sustaining success in a rapidly changing field.

On-the-Job Training Experiences for Managers There are four approaches to on-the-job training. These programs are not mutually exclusive; often they are run simultaneously. On-the-job management training is the preferred type from many points of view, especially because of its relevance and immediate transferability to the job.

Coaching and Counseling One of the best and most frequently used methods of training new managers is for effective managers to teach them.[31] The coach-superior sets a good example of what a manager does. He or she also answers questions and explains why things are done the way they are. It is the coach-superior's obligation to see to it that the manager-trainee makes the proper contacts so that the job can be learned easily and performed in an adequate way. In some ways, the coach-superior-manager-trainee relationship resembles the buddy system in employee training.

One technique the superior may use is to have decision-making meetings with the trainee. During these meetings procedures are agreed upon. If the trainee is to learn, the superior must give him or her enough authority to make decisions and perhaps even make mistakes. This approach not only provides opportunities to learn, it requires effective delegation, which develops a feeling of mutual confidence. Appropriately chosen committee assignments can be used as a form of coaching and counseling.

Although most organizations use coaching and counseling as either a formal or an informal management development technique, it is not without its problems. Coaching and counseling fail when inadequate time is set aside for them, when the subordinate is allowed to make no mistakes, if rivalry develops, or the dependency needs of the subordinate are not recognized or accepted by the superior.

In sum, many experts contend that coaching and counseling, when coupled with planned rotation through jobs and functions, are effective techniques. It can fit the manager's background and utilize the principle of learning by doing that has proven effective. Finally, the method involves the supervisors, which is essential to successful management development.

Transitory, Anticipatory Experiences Another approach to management training is to provide transitory experiences. Once it has been determined that

---

[30] Hastings H. Huggins, Jr., "IBM's Retraining Success Based on Long-Term Manpower Planning," *Management Review,* August 1983, pp. 29–30.

[31] Walter Mahler and William Wrightnour, *Executive Continuity* (Homewood, Ill.: Richard D. Irwin, 1973), chapters 6 and 7.

a person will be promoted to a specific job, provision is made for a short period before the promotion in which she or he learns the new job, performing some new duties while still performing most of the old ones. This intermediate position is labeled differently in various organizations as assistant-to, understudy, multiple management, or management apprenticeship.

The main characteristic of this type of program is that it gives partial prior experience to a person likely to hold a position in the future.[32] In some approaches, the trainee performs a part of the actual job; thus, an assistant-to does some parts of the job for the incumbent. In multiple management, several decision-making bodies make decisions about the same problem and compare them—a junior board or group's decisions are compared to those of senior management groups. Another variation is to provide trainees with a series of assignments that are part of the new job in order to train them and broaden their experiences.

To the extent that transitory experiences simulate the future job and are challenging, they seem to provide an eminently reasonable approach to management development. Little systematic study has been made of the effectiveness of this approach, however, and it appears to be used less often than coaching or counseling.

Transfers and Rotation In another on-the-job approach, trainees are rotated through a series of jobs to broaden their managerial experience. Organizations often have developed programmed career plans that include a mix of functional and geographic transfers.

Advocates of rotation and transfer contend that this approach broadens the manager's background, accelerates the promotion of highly competent individuals, introduces more new ideas into the organization, and increases the effectiveness of the organization. But some research evidence questions these conclusions.[33] Individual differences affect whether or not the results will be positive, and generalists may not be the most effective managers in many specialized positions.

Geographic transfers are desirable when fundamentally different job situations exist at various places. They allow new ideas to be tried instead of meeting each situation with the comment, "We always do it that way here." As in many other types of development, trained supervisors can make this technique more effective.

In general, because of the perceived relevance of on-the-job experience, it should be provided in management development programs. Because of individual differences in development and rewards by organizations, however, off-the-job development programs should supplement them where expertise is not readily available inside the organization. Exclusively on-the-job programs lead to a narrow perspective and the inhibition of new ideas coming into the organization.

---

[32] Roger O'Meara, "Off the Job Assignments for Key Employees," in *Manpower Planning and Programming*, ed. Elmer Burack and James Walker (Boston: Allyn & Bacon, 1972), pp. 339–46.

[33] Robert Pitts, "Unshackle Your 'Comers'," *Harvard Business Review*, May 1977, pp. 127–36.

EXHIBIT 12–11   Training Directors' Ratings of Effectiveness of Alternative Training Methods for Specific Training Objectives

Training Method	Knowledge Acquisition Mean Rank	Changing Attitudes Mean Rank	Problem Solving Skills Mean Rank	Interpersonal Skills Mean Rank	Participant Acceptance Mean Rank	Knowledge Retention Mean Rank
Case study	2	4	1	4	2	2
Conference (discussion) method	3	3	4	3	1	5
Lecture (with questions)	9	8	9	8	8	8
Business games	6	5	2	5	3	6
Movie films	4	6	7	6	5	7
Programmed instruction	1	7	6	7	7	1
Role playing	7	2	3	2	4	4
Sensitivity training (T-group)	8	1	5	1	6	3
Television lecture	5	9	8	9	9	9

Note: 1 = highest rank.
   Source: Adapted from Stephen J. Carroll, Frank T. Paine, and John M. Ivancevich, "The Relative Effectiveness of Training Methods—Expert Opinion and Research," *Personnel Psychology* 33 (1972), pp. 495–509.

Off-the-Job Training Other than apprenticeship, vestibule training, and on-the-job training, all other training is off-the-job training, whether it is done in organization classrooms, vocational schools, or elsewhere. Organizations with the biggest training programs often use off-the-job training. The majority of the 50,000 trainers in the United States and the $100 billion spent on training is in off-the-job training. A survey of training directors in *Fortune 500* companies examined their views of which off-the-job training techniques were the most effective for specific objectives. The training directors indicated that if knowledge acquisition were the objective, it would be best to use programmed instruction. On the other hand, if the training was intended to improve the problem-solving skills of participants, then it would be better to use the case method of training (i.e., having participants analyze job-related cases). Exhibit 12–11 summarizes the major results of the study. The most frequently used methods for off-the-job training are the conference/discussion, programmed instruction, computer-assisted, and simulation approaches.[34]

Conference/Discussion Approach The most frequently used training method is for a trainer to give a lecture and involve the trainee in a discussion of the material to be learned. The effective classroom presentation supplements the verbal part with audiovisual aids such as blackboards, slides, and mockups. Frequently these lectures are videotaped or audiotaped. The method allows the trainer's message to be given in many locations and to be repeated as often as needed for the benefit of the trainees. Videotape recording also

---

[34] Goldstein, *Training*.

allows for self-confrontation, which is especially useful in such programs as sales training and interpersonal relations.[35] The trainee's presentation can be taped and played back for analysis.

Programmed Instruction and Computer-Assisted Instruction A popular method used in organizational training is programmed instruction.[36] Material can be presented on teaching machines or in text form, and behaviorist learning principles are followed closely. Programmed instruction is a useful method for self-instruction when the development cost of the materials has been paid by another organization and the materials are available. It might also be a useful method if there are enough trainees to amortize the development cost, if the trainees are likely to be motivated enough to move ahead with this approach, and if the material presented is suitable to the method. Programmed instruction has been described as follows:

> Programmed instruction is a technique for instructing without the presence or intervention of a human instructor. It is a learner-centered method of instruction, which presents subject-matter to the trainee in small steps or increments, requiring frequent responses from him and immediately informing him of the correctness of his responses. The trainee's responses may be written, oral, or manipulative. A response may be constructed, as in the completion type; it may be selected from among several alternatives, as in the multiple-choice type; or it may assume one or more of a variety of other styles.[37]

Features of programmed instruction are:

> Instruction is provided without the presence or intervention of a human instructor. The learner learns at his own rate (conventional group instuction, films, television, and other media and methods that do not allow learner control do not satisfy this criterion).
>
> Instruction is presented in small incremental steps requiring frequent responses by the learner; step size is a function of the subject matter and the characteristics of the learner population.
>
> There is a participative overt interaction, or two-way communication, between the learner and the instructional program.
>
> The learner receives immediate feedback informing him of his progress.
>
> Reinforcement is used to strengthen learning.
>
> The sequence of lessons is carefully controlled and consistent.
>
> The instructional program shapes and controls behavior.

---

[35] Willard Thomas, "Shoot the Works with Videobased Training," *Training and Development Journal,* December 1980, pp. 83–87.

[36] A. N. Nash, Jan P. Muczyk, and F. L. Vettori, "The Role and Practical Effectiveness of Programmed Instruction," *Personnel Psychology,* Autumn 1971, pp. 397–418.

[37] Leonard Silvern, "Training: Man-Man and Man-Machine Communications," in *Systems Psychology,* ed. K. yon De Greene (New York: McGraw-Hill, 1970), pp. 383–405.

Programmed instruction can have wide application in organizational training programs, especially for programs whose characteristics fit those discussed above. It can also be developed in computer-assisted forms.

Many firms are now using *computer-assisted instruction (CAI)* to train employees. CAI permits self-paced learning and immediate feedback. A CAI system works as follows: A trainee sits at a terminal with a monitor. The computer is programmed with the training materials. The trainee communicates by programming or using the keyboard to input commands or requests. In one company managers are able to learn how to use the inventory control system with CAI. They can make requests and assess how changes in their requests will influence their end-of-month budget statements.

Control Data Corporation has developed a computer program called Plato. With Plato, an airline pilot uses the CAI and is able to reduce the vestibule training time spent in the jet simulator. The CAI provides a computer view of the instrument panel that is found in the simulator and the actual airplane.[38] However, instead of training in the simulator or the airplane, the pilot can become familiar with the instrument panel by using the computer. This form of corporation training results in more personal instruction and reduced training time.

Steelworkers are now being retrained in a state-funded program at the Pittsburgh Control Data Institutes, one of 26 Plato-equipped institutes in major cities. The eight-month course in computer technology is being attended by unemployed steelworkers. Because of industry's need for CAI, Plato is starting to have competitors. Digital Equipment Corporation now has a Plato-like system. Dozens of software houses are starting to emulate Plato programs, or training "courseware."[39]

Other examples of CAI can be found in such companies as Motorola, Detroit Edison, and the National Association of Security Dealers.[40] At Motorola, technicians and engineers are trained with courseware in basic electronics, microprocessors, and BASIC programming. Detroit Edison uses computers to train maintenance operators in uniform procedures to isolate and mark all equipment scheduled for maintenance with various colored tapes and tags. The National Association of Security Dealers uses computers to test more than 100,000 brokers annually.

The potential for computer-based training is limited only by the number of training needs. It is generally agreed that because of such advantages as self-pacing, privacy, immediate feedback, convenience, and adaptability CAI will become one of the most popular training approaches available.

---

[38] Gary Dessler, *Personnel Management* (Reston, Va.: Reston Publishing, 1984), p. 247.

[39] "Computerized Training May Finally Be About to Take Off," *Business Week,* March 28, 1983, p. 88.

[40] William A. Hultyen, "An Introduction to Computerized Training," *Personnel Journal,* October 1984, pp. 22–23.

A RETURN TO THE P/HRM ▸ IN ▸ ACTION

After Bob and Gwen performed the training needs analysis, they isolated the skills training necessary. The supervisors and employees told him the key need was improved training in the use of the new equipment. He also identified other work-related skills that appeared to decrease employee efficiency.

Then Bob prepared a proposed training program. The training needs analysis had identified the employees who needed the training the most. For trainers, he decided to propose that the manufacturer of the new equipment should provide a trainer. This person would train Bob and several supervisors who appeared to have the greatest potential to run employee training programs. He also proposed that the manufacturer provide a mockup of the machines to use in the training (if available). Lacking that, slides would be used. Then the firm would use several machines for training alone—a semivestibule approach. The cost would be minimal. The manufacturer would provide the training free.

Harold approved the plan, and the training sessions were conducted. Two months after the training was completed, however, there was little change in results. Gwen realized that they had not done as good a job in cost feasibility study as they should have.

No formal evaluation of the training had been planned or done.

Gwen and Bob went back to the supervisors to interview them on what had happened. Some of the comments were:

Sandy Feldman (supervisor): I told you people the problem was who you hired. Training bimbos like I got won't help.

Sam Jacobs (supervisor): I thought that training would help. It did a little, for a while. But my problem has become discipline. They know how to do the job—they just don't seem to want to do it.

Harry Samson (supervisor): Maybe the problem was *how* the training was done—I don't know. I see few real results so far.

Bob and Gwen decided to do a formal evaluation of training on the next program. As for what to do now, performance evaluation time was coming up. Maybe the use of rewards for better employees would help. Maybe more and better training would have results. And maybe the labor market had opened up and some terminations and rehirings would be the answer. They'd just have to keep working on it until they could really help Harold and the company. (There will be more about this case in Chapter 13.)

No matter which training approach is used, it must be evaluated. This is the third phase of the model shown in Exhibit 12–5. Evaluation of training and development will be discussed in Chapter 13.

SUMMARY

To summarize the major points covered in this chapter:

1. The principal purposes of orientation include:
   a. To reduce start-up costs for a new employee.
   b. To reduce fear and anxiety of the new employee and hazing from other employees.
   c. To reduce turnover.
   d. To save time for supervisors and co-workers.
   e. To develop realistic job expectations, positive attitudes toward the employer, and job satisfaction.
2. In small enterprises the operating manager does all the orienting; in middle-sized or larger enterprises the operating and P/HRM managers share this task.
3. Training is a form of education to which the following learning principles can be applied:
   a. The trainee must be motivated to learn.
   b. The learning must be reinforced.
   c. The training must provide for practice of the material.
   d. The material presented must be meaningful.
   e. The material taught must transfer to the job situation.
4. Purposes of training and development include:
   a. To improve the quantity of output.
   b. To improve the quality of output.
   c. To lower the costs of waste and equipment maintenance.
   d. To lower the number and costs of accidents.
   e. To lower turnover and absenteeism and increase employee job satisfaction.
   f. To prevent employee obsolescence.
5. When employee turnover is great, it is more important for the organization to provide formal technical training for employees.
6. Effective organizations design their training programs only after assessing the organization's and individual's training needs and setting training objectives.
7. Effective training programs select trainees on the basis of the trainees' needs as well as organizational objectives.
8. Effective training programs carefully select and develop trainers for the programs.
9. Training approaches for employees are:
   a. Apprenticeship.
   b. Vestibule.
   c. On-the-job training (coaching and counseling; transitory experiences; self-improvement programs; transfers and rotation).
   d. Off-the-job training (conference/discussion; programmed instruction; computer assisted; simulation approaches).

EXHIBIT 12–12   Recommendations on Management Training and Development Programs for Model Organizations

Type of Organization	Formal Program	Informal Program	On-the-Job Programs	Off-the-Job Programs
1. Large size, low complexity, high stability	X		X	X
2. Medium size, low complexity, high stability		X	X	
3. Small size, low complexity, high stability		X	X	
4. Medium size, moderate complexity, moderate stability		X	X	X
5. Large size, high complexity, low stability	X		X	X
6. Medium size, high complexity, low stability		X	X	
7. Small size, high complexity, low stability		X	X	

The recommendations on management training and development programs for model organizations are presented in Exhibit 12–12.

Questions for Review and Discussion

1. What are the main purposes of orientation programs? What aspects of orientation seem to be the most neglected?
2. Describe the study of Texas Instruments' orientation program. What does it indicate to you about how to operate an orientation program?
3. Describe a typical orientation program. Which parts of it would you describe as important, very important, or less important? To the employee? To the employer?
4. Describe why a performance analysis may indicate that training is not what is needed to solve a particular problem.
5. What role, if any, does a trainee's motivation play in his or her ability to learn?
6. What principles of learning affect training? How?
7. Why would employees prefer to use corporate classrooms to earn various college-type degrees?
8. Who is involved in the planning and operating of formal training in organizations?
9. How do training managers determine training needs and objectives? Why do they do so (or should they)?
10. In the future is training less or more likely to grow in importance in the strategic plans of an organization? Explain.

GLOSSARY

Apprentice Training A combination of on-the-job and off-the-job training. The apprentice, while learning the job, is paid less than the master worker. Some of the jobs in which one serves as an apprentice include electrician, barber, tool and die maker, and plumber.

Learning. The act by which a person acquires skills, knowledge, and abilities that result in a relatively permanent change in his or her behavior.

Management Development. The process by which managers gain the experience, skills, and attitudes to become or remain successful leaders in their organizations.

Orientation. The P/HRM activity that introduces new employees to the organization and the employee's new tasks, superiors, and work groups.

Performance Analysis. A systematic procedure that is used to determine if training is needed to correct behavior deficiencies.

Training. The systematic process of altering the behavior of employees in a direction to increase organizational goals.

Vestibule Training. A trainee learns a job in an environment that closely resembles the actual work environment. For example, pilots at United Airlines train (vestibule) in a jet simulation cockpit.

APPLICATION CASE 12–1

Dunkin' Donuts and Domino's Pizza: Training for Quality and Hustle*

Dunkin' Donuts and Domino's Pizza share the same requirement for business success: Provide a high-quality product at impressive speed. Domino's guarantees a hot, tasty pizza delivered to your doorstep within 30 minutes (a considerable challenge given that 80 percent of a day's orders at a Domino's franchise are typically received during three hours of a 12- hour day). Dunkin' Donuts promises fresh donuts every four hours and fresh coffee every 18 minutes.

To meet this requirement, both fast-food companies face the same training challenge: Train a very young (typically aged 18–21) and inexperienced workforce to meet rigorous performance standards. Both companies must train in an industry where turnover averages 300–400 percent yearly and where company locations are widely dispersed. Domino's operates 3,800 stores throughout the United States and seven foreign countries; Dunkin' Donut's 1,400 shops span the United States and 12 foreign countries.

The two companies approach this training challenge with a highly decentralized training function. At Domino's Pizza, 85 percent of a nonsupervisory employee's training occurs on the job and is provided by the store manager or franchise owner. Each employee is usually trained to fill most of the shop's five hourly jobs (order taker, pizza maker, oven tender, router, driver) which helps during rush hours when a crew member doesn't appear for work. Performance standards are demanding; the order taker must answer a call within three rings and take the order within 45 seconds. The pizza maker must make the pizza and place it in the oven within one minute. The oven tender must take one pizza out while putting another one in within five seconds and cut and box the pizza by the count of 15. Domino's encourages dedication to speed by keeping tabs on the fastest service and delivery times reported by its stores and publishing them as "box scores" in *The Pepperoni Press*, the company newspaper.

Although the bulk of training is on the job far away from corporate headquarters, Domino's corporate training staff maintains some control over training by providing a variety of training aids. The staff makes available to shop management 14 video tapes (with instructors' manuals) on such tasks as delivery, dough management, image, and pizza making. Each shop is equipped with a VCR. The videos are upbeat, fast-moving and musical (MTV-styled)

---

* Written by Kim Stewart and adapted from: Dale Feuer, "Training for Fast Times," *Training*, July 1987, pp. 25–30; and Dale Feuer, "Training at Dunkin' Donuts: Taking It to the Stores," *Training*, July 1985, pp. 55, 59–61.

with a heavy dose of comedy geared to its high school and college-aged audience. Young Domino's employees play the roles in the videos.

Each shop also displays corporate-produced training posters on job hints/reminders throughout the work area. Above the production line, for example, are large color pictures of how a pizza should look at each step of the production process. Two popular posters: a glossy color picture of "The Perfect Pepperoni" pizza, and a picture of a pizza cursed with the 10 common flaws (scorched vegetables, air bubbles). The training materials communicate many key points with Domino's-styled lingo, "Dominese." For example, getting "blown away" means missing the "TMS" which stands for Domino's infamous 30-minute delivery guarantee. How to avoid this costly mistake? Sharp "PRP," prerush preparation.

Store managers (aged 21–25) are trained by means of a six- course, typically six-month MIT program that includes coursework in pizza dough management, people management, cost management, and in how to conduct on-the-job training of hourly employees. Manager trainees progress through five levels of training with higher performance requirements and more responsibilities added at each level. On-the-job training is an important part of the training program.

Many franchise owners (and all company-owned stores) send management trainees to the regional training center for classes taught by corporate trainers; however, management training often is decentralized with franchise owners conducting the MIT courses themselves. Franchise owners must be certified to conduct the formal courses for their manager trainees. The certification process requires that the owner complete the "Training Dynamics" course on how to teach manager trainees, observe certified teachers training the MIT series of courses, and then co-teach the series with a regional trainer who must approve the franchisee's performance. The quality of training provided by franchise owners is enhanced by the owners' substantial in-store management experience. Only Domino's store managers may apply for franchise ownership.

Domino's corporate training staff is also involved in developing franchise owners by means of a rigorous training program for all prospective owners. The training includes a series of courses on contracts, site selection, store construction, and marketing, with an early, heavy emphasis on the nitty-gritty aspects of ownership to discourage those who are less than totally committed.

Like Domino's Pizza, Dunkin' Donuts' corporate training staff conducts a demanding training program for its franchise owners. Prospective franchisees undergo six weeks of training at the Dunkin' Donuts University in Braintree, Mass. There, they spend four weeks in production training, learning how to make donuts, coffee, soup, and other products, and how to operate and maintain the production equipment. Performance standards are rigorous; the final production test requires that a trainee make 140 donuts within eight hours (enough to fill a shop's donut case). Each batch of donuts is weighed and measured for length and height. If a batch of six cake donuts is one ounce too light or heavy, for example, the batch fails the test.

Franchisees spend the last two weeks focusing on financial aspects of the business and on developing employee management skills (for example, supervising, performance appraisal, interpersonal communication). The 12-member training staff conducting the program are all former store managers or district sales managers with about 10 years of experience with the company.

Training of hourly employees is totally decentralized. Franchise owners serve as trainers and receive how-to instruction for this task. Like Domino's Pizza, Dunkin' Donuts' corporate training staff also provides training video cassettes for owners to use. Quarterly clinics on quality control are also conducted by the company's district managers and technical advisers.

Dunkin' Donuts uses a different and decentralized approach to training its store managers who are not franchise owners. Rather than have franchise owners conduct the training, the company selects experienced store managers and trains them as store manager trainers. There trainers train new managers using a program and materials developed by the corporate staff. This decentralized approach is relatively new for Dunkin' Donuts and was adopted after the company dropped its 12-week training program conducted totally at corporate headquarters. With the centralized approach, new manager turnover was 50 percent during training. Under the new decentralized, on-site approach, turnover during training is about .5 percent, and annual training costs have decreased from $418,000 to $172,000.

People-related management skills are emphasized in training both franchise owners and store managers. Dunkin' Donuts credits this emphasis as a major reason why its annual turnover rate for hourly workers (80 percent) is considerably less than the industry average.

Questions for Thought

1. What are the strengths and shortcomings of a decentralized approach to training managers and hourly employees? Discuss.
2. Develop a plan for determining the training needs of the hourly paid staff of a Domino's Pizza franchise.
3. In your opinion, why was the turnover rate among management trainees in Dunkin' Donuts centralized program so high?

MANAGEMENT AND ORGANIZATION DEVELOPMENT

P/HRM · IN · ACTION

Gwen

(Continued from Chapter 12)

Later the same year, Gwen Meridith, Young Enterprise's P/HRM vice president was faced with another problem. She received the results of Young's third annual attitude survey from the firm's consultant. (An attitude survey is an instrument to measure employee's feelings about their employer.)

Bob McGarrah, the director of training and development, was called in to discuss them.

Gwen: Bob, look at the results of the items on training and development. Even though we have not had the desired results on our new training program, Item 17 indicates that the blue-and white-collar employees are very satisfied with our technical training program. So are the managers. Now look at the questions on development. There seems to be serious dissatisfaction there on the part of the employees and managers. With regard to the employee dissatisfaction, this may be related to Item 27. There is a fair amount of dissatisfaction with their supervisors' management styles.

Maybe that is why our training program has not given us the desired results! What do you think?

Bob: Well, Gwen, we haven't done much on nontechnical training here at Young. We have not tried to run off-the-job development programs. We don't do career development. Nor have we ever considered organizational development programs. How do you feel about them?

Gwen: As you know, Bob, my background is labor relations. I have kept up in other areas such as EEO, OSHA, and compensation. But I'm asking for your help on this. I'm not too familiar with these programs. Why don't you get together a report to tell me what's happening in development these days.

Bob prepared a summary of the current trends and happenings in development for managers and employees. The next section covers many of the points Gwen wanted to know about development programs.

INTRODUCTION TO MANAGEMENT DEVELOPMENT

This chapter completes the two-chapter unit on training and development of human resources employees. Chapter 12 focused primarily on the training of employees to improve their abilities. In addition, an organization must be concerned about the development of the management team—supervisors, middle-level managers, and top-level executives. Management development focuses on developing in a systematic manner the knowledge base, attitudes basic skills, interpersonal skills, and technical skills of the managerial cadre.[1]

Since managers are such a vital cog in the success of any organization, an entire chapter is devoted specifically to the development of managers. Technical or operating employees must also be trained and developed, but it is very important to have a managerial cadre that possesses knowledge, skills, and motivation.

APPROACHES FOR DEVELOPING MANAGERS

There are numerous management development approaches available. Brochures, testimonials, books, and articles extol the virtues of the management development approach. The programs offer a number of advantages as expressed by consultants, managers, or others familiar with the particular approach. Unfortunately, few of the approaches have been scientifically evaluated, and there is relatively little known about where to use a particular approach and what kind of managers (personality type, experience, education) is able to derive the most benefit from a particular approach.[2]

A safe assumption is that different levels of management have different development needs. A survey indicates that at the executive level managing time and team building are crucial needs, while at the supervisory level instituting motivation programs and appraising subordinates are important needs.[3] Exhibit 13–1 summarizes the results of a survey that determined the 15 most important development needs at three levels of management—executive, middle, and supervisory.

The earliest programs designed to affect managerial attitudes, called *human relations programs*, were oriented toward individual development. Human relations programs were an outgrowth of the human relations movement, which fostered consideration of the individual in the operation of industry in the 1930s to the 1950s. The rationale of the movement from the organization's point of view was that an employee-centered, liberal super-

---

[1] Jay Lorsch, ed., *Handbook of Organizational Behavior* (Englewood Cliffs, N.J.: Prentice-Hall, 1987) and Alan Mumford, ed., *Handbook of Management Development* (Brookfield, Vt.: Gower, 1986).

[2] Robert Townsend, *Further Up the Organization* (New York: Alfred A. Knopf, 1984).

[3] Lester Digman, "Management Development: Needs and Practices," *Personnel*, July–August 1980, pp. 45–57.

EXHIBIT 13-1 Most Frequent Development Needs: A Survey of Managers by Level

Executive Level	Middle Level	Supervisory Level
1. Managing time Team building	1. Evaluating and appraising employees	1. Motivating others
3. Organizing and planning Evaluating and appraising employees	2. Motivating others	2. Evaluating and appraising others
	3. Setting objectives and priorities	3. Leadership
	4. Oral communication	4. Oral communication
5. Coping with stress Understanding human behavior	5. Organizing and planning	5. Understanding human behavior
7. Self-analysis Motivating others	6. Understanding human behavior	6. Developing and training subordinates Role of the manager
9. Financial management Budgeting	7. Written communica- tion Managing time	7. Setting objectives and priorities Written communication
11. Setting objectives and priorities Holding effective meetings	9. Team building Leadership Decision making	10. Discipline Organizing and plan- ning
13. Oral communication	10. Holding effective meetings Delegation Developing and train- ing subordinates	11. Managing time Counseling and coaching
14. Labor/management relations		14. Selecting employees
15. Decision making Developing strategies and policies	15. Selecting employees	15. Decision making

Source: Lester Digman, "Management Development: Needs and Practices," *Personnel*, July–August 1980, p. 56.

visory style would lead to more satisfied employees. This, in turn, would reduce absenteeism, employee turnover, and strikes. Sometimes the style also increased performance. But, as was discussed in Chapter 2, effective performance has multiple causes, and supervisory attitudes and behavior are only one factor influencing it.

The effectiveness of these general human relations programs was measured by direct improvement in objectively measured results, such as a reduction in turnover. The programs were also called effective if they changed the attitudes of the managers in the direction desired or if the managers participating said the programs were worthwhile. In reviewing the evidence on the effectiveness of human relations programs, it has been determined that 80 percent of the programs evaluated had significant positive results, as measured by attitudes and opinions about these programs.[4]

Such positive results have encouraged organizations to continue to conduct interpersonal skills and attitude-change programs. A number of the in-class training techniques are used in interpersonal skills and attitude-change devel-

[4] John P. Campbell, Marvin D. Dunnette, Edward E. Lawler III, and Karl E. Weick, Jr., *Managerial Behavior, Performance and Effectiveness* (New York: McGraw-Hill, 1970).

opment programs. Those most frequently used are the case, role playing, in-basket, and management games techniques.[5]

The Case Method

One widely used technique is the case method. A case is a written description of a real decision-making situation in the organization or a situation that occurred in another organization. Managers are asked to study the case to determine the problems, analyze the problems for their significance, proposed solutions, choose the best solution, and implement it. More learning takes place if there is interaction between the managers and instructor. The instructor's role is that of a catalyst and facilitator. A good instructor is able to get everyone involved in solving the problem.

The case method lends itself more to some kinds of material (business policy analysis) than to well-structured material. It is easier to listen to a lecture and be given a formula than to tease the formula out of a case, for example. With good instructors and good cases, the case method is a very effective device for improving and clarifying rational decision making.[6]

The instructor using the case method must guard against (a) dominating the discussion, (b) permitting a few people to dominate the discussion, or (c) leading the discussion toward his or her preferred solution. As a catalyst the instructor should encourage divergent viewpoints, initiate discussion on points the managers are missing, and be thoroughly prepared.[7]

Variations on the Case Method One variation of the case method is the incident method. In the incident method, just the bare outlines of a problem are given initially, and the students are assigned a role in which to view the incident. Additional data are available if the students ask the right questions. Each student "solves" the case, and groups based on similarity of solutions are formed. Each group then formulates a strong statement of position, and the groups debate or role play their solutions. The instructor may describe what actually happened in the case and the consequences, and then everyone compares their solutions with the results. The final step is for participants to try to apply this knowledge to their own job situations.

Role Playing

Role playing is a cross between the case method and an attitude development program. Each person is assigned a role in a situation (such as a case) and

---

[5] John P. Campbell, "Personnel Training and Development" in *Annual Review of Psychology* (Palo Alto, Calif.: Annual Reviews, 1971); and B. M. Bass and J. A. Vaughan, *Training in Industry* (Belmont, Calif.: Wadsworth Publishing, 1966).

[6] Kenneth N. Wexley and Gary P. Latham, *Developing and Training Human Resources in Organizations* (Glenview, Ill.: Scott, Foresman, 1981), p. 193.

[7] Chris Argyris, "Some Limitations of the Case Method: Experiences in a Management Development Program," *Academy of Management Review*, April 1980, pp. 291–98.

asked to play the role and to react to other players' role playing. The player is asked to pretend to be a focal person in the situation and to react to the stimuli as that person would. The players are provided with background information on the situation and the players. There is usually a brief script provided to the participant. Sometimes the role plays are videotaped and reanalyzed as part of the development situation. Often role playing is done in small groups of a dozen or so persons. The success of this method depends on the ability of the players to play the assigned roles believably. If done well, role playing can help a manager become more aware of and sensitive to the feelings of others.

Although role playing is a cross between the two, comparison of the general forms of role playing and the case method suggest a few differences between the two:[8]

Case Study	Role Playing
1. Presents a problem for analysis and discussion.	1. Places the problem in a real-life situation.
2. Uses problems that have already occurred in the company or elsewhere.	2. Uses problems that are now current or are happening on the job.
3. Deals with problems involving others.	3. Deals with problems in which participants themselves are involved.
4. Deals with emotional and attitudinal aspects in an intellectual frame of reference.	4. Deals with emotional and attitudinal aspects in an experiential frame of reference.
5. Emphasis is on using facts and making assumptions.	5. Emphasis is on feelings.
6. Trains in the exercise of judgments.	6. Trains in emotional control.
7. Furnishes practice in analysis of problems.	7. Provides practice in interpersonal skills.

The In-Basket Technique

Another method used to develop managerial decision-making abilities is the in-basket technique. The participant is given materials (typically memos or descriptions of things to do) which include typical items from a specific manager's mail and a telephone list. Important and pressing matters, such as out-of-stock positions, customer complaints, or the demand for a report from a superior, are mixed in with routine business matters, such as a request to speak at a dinner or a decision on the date of the company picnic four weeks hence. The trainee is analyzed and critiqued on the number of decisions made in the time period allotted, the quality of decisions, and the priorities chosen for making them. In order to generate interest the in-basket, materials must be realistic, job-related, and not impossible to make decisions on.

---

[8] A. R. Solem, "Human Relations Training: Comparison of Case Study and Role Playing," *Personnel Administrator*, September–October 1960, pp. 27–37.

Management Games

Essentially, management games describe the operating characteristics of a company, industry, or enterprise. These descriptions take the form of equations that are manipulated after decisions have been made.

In a typical computerized management game procedure, teams of players are asked to make a series of operating (or top-managment) decisions. In one game, for example, the players are asked to decide on such matters as the price of the product, purchase of materials, production scheduling, funds borrowing, marketing, and R&D expenditures. When each player on the team has made a decision, the interactions of these decisions are computed (manually or by computer) in accordance with the model. For example, if price is linearly related to volume, a decrease in price of X percent will affect the volume, subject to general price levels. Players on the team first reconcile their individual decisions with those of the other team members prior to making a final decision. Then each team's decision is compared with those of the other teams. The result of that team's profit, market share, and so forth is compared, and a winner or best team performance is determined.

Looking Glass is a management game that is used to permit individuals to operate or participate as managers in the simulation of a hypothetical glass manufacturing company with 4,000 employees and $200 million in annual sales.[9] Executives from IBM, AT&T, Monsanto, and Union Carbide have used Looking Glass to provide a picture to participants of their management style. Looking Glass was developed at the Center for Creative Leadership, a nonprofit think tank in Greensboro, North Carolina.

Another management game used to develop managers is Simmons Simulator, Inc., a make-believe high-technology multinational firm with $3 billion in annual sales. It is used to train top managers at IBM in the company's corporate planning process. Financial Services Industry is a game that simulates a business day in which managers grapple with planning decisions that are influenced by technological change and government deregulation of the financial industry. Management games emphasize problem-solving skill development.

Hard evaluation evidence is scarce on whether Looking Glass, Simmons Simulator, or Financial Services accomplish the desired outcomes. A major concern is to rigorously assess whether participation in management games means that the manager is a better performer back on the job.

Advantages of games include the integration of several interacting decisions, the ability to experiment with decisions, the provision of feedback experiences on decisions, and the requirement that decisions be made with inadequate data, which usually simulates reality. The main criticisms of most games concern their limitation of novelty or reactivity in decision making, the cost of development and administration, the unreality of some of the models, and the disturbing tendency of many participants to look for the key to win the

---

[9] Peter Petre, "Games That Teach You to Manage," *Fortune*, October 29, 1984, pp. 65–72.

EXHIBIT 13–2 Model of Behavior Modeling Training Program

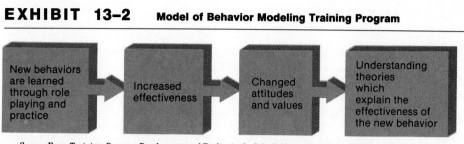

Source: From *Training: Program Development and Evaluation* by I. L. Goldstein. Copyright © 1974 by Wadsworth Publishing Company, Inc. Reprinted by permission of the publisher, Brooks/Cole Publishing Company, Monterey, California.

game instead of concentrating on making good decisions. Many participants seem to feel the games are rigged, so that a few factors or even a single factor may be the key to winning.

Behavior Modeling

A development approach for improving interpersonal skills is *behavior modeling*, which is also called *interaction management or imitating models*.[10] The key to behavior modeling is learning through observation or imagination. Thus, modeling is a "vicarious process" that emphasizes observation. The development model as formed by Goldstein and Sorcher is shown in Exhibit 13–2.[11]

One behavior modeling approach begins by identifying 19 interpersonal problems that employees, especially managers, face. Typical problems are: gaining acceptance as a new supervisor, handling discrimination complaints, delegating responsibility, improving attendance, effective discipline, overcoming resistance to change, setting performance goals, motivating average performance, handling emotional situations, reducing tardiness, and taking corrective action.[12]

There are four steps in the process:

1. Modeling of effective behavior—often by use of films.
2. Role playing.
3. Social reinforcement—trainees and trainers praise effective role plays.
4. Transfer of training to the job.

[10] See Allen Kraut, "Developing Managerial Skills via Modeling Techniques: Some Positive Research Findings—A Symposium" (other articles in this series cover modeling), *Personnel Psychology*, Autumn 1976, pp. 325–61; and Gary Latham and Lise Saari, "Application of Social Learning Theory of Training Supervisors through Behavior Modeling," *Journal of Applied Psychology*, June 1979, pp. 239–46.

[11] A. P. Goldstein and M. Sorcher, *Changing Supervisory Behavior* (Elmsford, N.Y.: Pergamon Press, 1974).

[12] D. Johnson and M. Socher, "Behavior Modeling Training: Why, How, and What Results," *Journal of European Training*, 76 no. 2, pp. 62–72.

EXHIBIT 13–3   Behavior Modeling

Administrator announces the interaction skill being considered and
  the supervisors read an overview of the interaction skill . . . .   5 minutes
Administrator describes critical steps in handling the interaction. . . . .   5 minutes
Administrator shows a film or video tape of a supervisor effectively
  handling the interaction with an employee. . . . .   10 minutes
Administrator and supervisors discuss how the supervisor depicted
  handled the critical steps . . . .   5 minutes
Three supervisors take turns in skill practice exercises by handling
  similar situations with employees. Background information is
  provided the "supervisor" and "employee" in each skill practice
  exercise. The handling of the situations is observed by the other
  supervisors and the administrator using specially prepared Observer
  Guides. The use of positive reinforcement by the observers helps to
  build confidence and skill in skill-practicing supervisors . . . .   60 minutes
Supervisors write their own interaction situations based on job-related
  problems, using forms provided in workbooks . . . .   10 minutes
Supervisors take turns in skill practice sessions by becoming the
  "employee" in the participant-written situations, while other
  supervisors use the interaction skills to handle these situations.
  These skills practice exercises are also observed and discussed. . . . . .   60 minutes
Supervisors read a summary of the skill module. Using specially
  designed forms, they plan on-the-job applications of the interaction
  skills. The administrator hands out a Critical Steps card for
  supervisors to utilize on the job . . . .   10 minutes

Source: William Byham and James Robinson, "Interaction Management: Supervisory Training That Changes Performance," *The Personnel Administrator*, February 1976.

A typical behavior modeling module is shown in Exhibit 13–3. Modeling applies the principles of learning described in Chapter 12 to the development situation. Exhibit 13–4 shows how.

Behavior modeling has been introduced into a number of organizations including AT&T, General Electric, IBM, RCA, Boise Cascade, Kaiser Corporation, Olin, and B. F. Goodrich. So far, the research evidence is generally positive. In a series of studies, the groups trained in behavior modeling have outperformed those who received no training or traditional management development training.[13]

One interesting program using behavior modeling was reported in a study conducted in the manufacturing operation of a major forest products com-

---

[13] Charles C. Manz and Henry P. Sims, Jr., "Vicarious Learning: The Influence of Modeling on Organizational Behavior," *Academy of Management Review*, January 1981, pp. 105–14; and B. L. Rosenbaum, "New Uses of Behavior Modeling," *Personnel Administrator*, July 1978, pp. 27–28.

EXHIBIT 13–4   **Learning Theory Principles Applied to Behavior Modeling**

	Behavior Modeling
Learning Principles	**Method**
Principles whereby learner:	
Is motivated to improve	
Understands desired skills	Modeling
Actively participates	⎫
Gets needed practice	⎬ Role playing
Gets feedback on performance	⎫
Is reinforced for appropriate skills	⎭ Social reinforcement
Experiences well-organized training	Transfer of training
Simple to complex	
Easy to hard	
Undergoes training performance	
akin to job	

Source: Allen Kraut, "Developing Managerial Skills via Modeling Techniques," *Personnel Psychology* 29 (1976), pp. 325–28.

pany.[14] The program was divided into seven weekly workshop sessions, each lasting about six hours. The sessions focused on a particular problem-solving situation, such as dealing with a performance problem or motivating a subordinate.

The specific parts to the behavior modeling approaches used were:

1. A conceptual lecture.
2. A videotape demonstration of the skills being taught.
3. A rehearsal period for practicing the behaviors.
4. A feedback and reinforcement period for refining the behaviors.
5. Participants entered into contracts and committed themselves to the newly acquired skills on the job.
6. A follow-up discussion on how things were going on the job.

These six phases were built into each workshop session. Each session covered critical incidents selected from a survey of all first-line supervisors in the company. The supervisors had been asked to identify the most difficult problems they faced in managing their subordinates.

The second phase of each session involved a modeled demonstration. The supervisors in the training program observed a videotape that depicted a company supervisor successfully employing skills to solve the problem. The videotaped model performed each step in solving the problem. As participants watched, they were asked to identify the steps being taken and make com-

---

[14] Jerry I. Porras and Brad Anderson, "Improving Managerial Effectiveness through Modeling-Based Training," *Organizational Dynamics,* Spring 1981, pp. 60–77.

ments in their notebooks for future reference. After observing the models, the participants rehearsed the skill in the classroom.[15]

Improved supervisory behavior in dealing with 10 difficult problems led to improved performance on the job. Average daily production of trained supervisors versus controls increased. Furthermore, grievance rates decreased and absenteeism steadily declined. This behavior modeling program, then, has the kind of positive impact organizations desire.

Behavior modeling offers a number of promising possibilities in organizations.[16] One especially important need in organizations is to develop effective leaders. Modeling appears to offer some promise for leadership skills development, if used in conjunction with videotape methods.[17] The participants can view their style, behaviors, strengths, and weaknesses and learn from this personal, first-hand view. A person who sees herself or himself in action has a vivid reminder that she or he can benefit from practice.

Which Development Approach Should Be Used?

Deciding on the development approach or combination of approaches must be done on the basis of weighing various criteria. The choice can be made on the basis of the number of managers to be developed, each program, the relative costs per manager for each method, the availability of development materials in various forms (including the instructor's capabilities), and the employees' relative efficiency in learning. In general, it is true that the more active the manager, the greater the motivation to learn. The probability of success is higher in that instance. If there are only a few instructors, individualized programmed instruction may be considered. If none of the managers is capable of giving certain instructions, outside instructors may be contacted, or movies or videotapes might be used. Finally, the method used should reflect the degree of active participation desired for the program, as illustrated in Exhibit 13–5.

Inevitably, the question as to the effectiveness of each form of development or training must be answered. There are studies to support the effectiveness of all methods; if a method is appropriate for the particular program in question, it should be used.

Studies show that the following development methods are used by larger companies with advanced P/HRM practices: 53 percent used the lecture method; 29 percent, the conference method; and 20 percent, programmed instruction.[18] One survey found that almost all organizations used lectures

---

[15] P. J. Decker and B. R. Nathan, *Behavior Modeling Training Principles and Applications,* (New York: Praeger Publishers 1985).

[16] James C. Robinson, *Developing Managers through Behavior Modeling* (San Diego: University Associates, 1982), Chapter 2.

[17] Henry P. Sims, Jr., and Charles C. Manz, "Modeling Influences on Employee Behavior," *Personnel Journal,* January 1982, pp. 58–65.

[18] NICB, *Office Personnel Practices,* no. 197; *Personnel Practices in Factory and Office* (New York: The Conference Board, 1965).

EXHIBIT 13–5 Roles of Participants Affected by Different Approaches

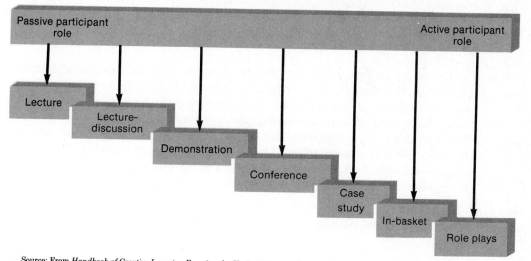

and conferences. Other techniques, such as simulation, role playing, and programmed instruction, were used by about 15 percent of the companies.[19]

Each of the techniques just mentioned—the case method, role playing, the in-basket technique, and management games—are classroom practices used in both skills training and development programs. In addition to these popular methods behavior modeling has become widely used.

ORGANIZATION DEVELOPMENT: AN OVERVIEW

Organizations and their environments are dynamic and constantly changing. New technologies are developed, competitors enter and leave markets, inflation increases, and productivity fluctuates. These are the kind of changes that managers in general and specifically P/HRM Managers face. Organizational development (OD) is a process of change that involves the continuing development of human resources. It is a newly emerging area of study directed toward using behavioral science knowledge to deal with problems of change.[20] There

---

[19] S. B. Utgaard and R. V. Davis, "The Most Frequently Used Training Techniques," *Training and Development Journal*, April 1970, pp. 40–43.

[20] Robert L. Smith, "OD Can Be a Discipline," *Training and Development Journal*, January 1984, pp. 102–4.

is still no definition of organization development that is universally accepted. Perhaps the most quoted definition of OD is that it is:

> an effort (a) planned, (b) organizationwide, (c) managed from the top, to (d) increase organization effectiveness, and health through (e) planned intervention in the organization's "processes" using behavioral science knowledge.[21]

According to this definition, OD is planned, since it requires systematic diagnosis, development of a program, and the mobilization of resources (trainers, participants, teaching aids). It involves either the entire system or an entire unit. It must have top-management commitment if it is to be a success. The definition also suggests that OD is not a specific technique such as behavior modeling, transactional analysis, or sensitivity training. These techniques and others often are part of an OD effort, but they are used only after their relevance and utility is demonstrated by a careful diagnosis.

The Importance of Diagnosis: OD's Base

An important characteristic of any OD intervention is that it should follow diagnosis.[22] A manager's perception of a problem is not a sufficient reason to implement a technique such as behavior modeling. Only after data are collected in a scientific way through interviews, observations, questionnaires, and/or checks of records should a planned OD intervention be considered and selected. Exhibit 13–6 presents the diagnosis phase of OD in a schematic diagram.

The collection of diagnostic data is considered to be a part of the action research orientation of OD.[23] Action research involves seven main steps:

1. Problem identification.
2. Consultation among experts. This could involve hired consultants, P/HRM specialists, and senior executives.
3. Data collection and diagnosis.
4. Feedback of findings to key people.
5. Group discussion of the diagnostic data and findings.
6. Action. The adoption of techniques such as sensitivity training, transactional analysis, and team building.
7. Evaluation of the action steps taken in Step 6.

The P/HRM department of specialists may be involved in any or all of these seven action research steps. For the purposes of this book, the action step is

---

[21] This definition was originally developed by R. Beckhard, *Organization Development: Strategies and Models* (Reading, Mass.: Addison-Wesley Publishing, 1969), p. 16.

[22] David Nadler, *Feedback and Organization Development: Using Data-Based Methods* (Reading, Mass.: Addison-Wesley Publishing, 1977), pp. 34–40.

[23] Peter A. Clark, *Action Research and Organizational Change* (New York: Harper & Row, 1972).

EXHIBIT 13–6   **Diagnosis Steps in OD Programs**

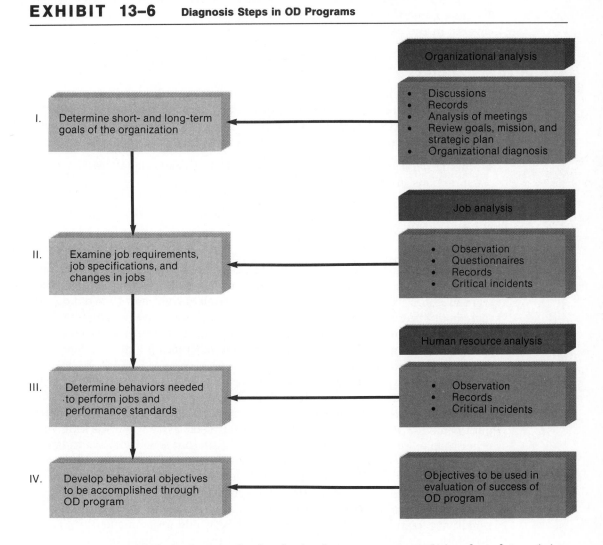

extremely important for developing human resources; it involves determining which planned interventions or techniques are available for use as part of OD programs.

OD: INDIVIDUAL AND INTERPERSONAL TECHNIQUES

One way to classify OD techniques is on the basis of the target area they are intended to affect. There are four target areas: Individual, interpersonal, group, and organizational. Sensitivity training or T-group training is designed to improve the awareness of individuals. Transactional analysis is supposed to help people understand the principles of transactions with others so that more meaningful interpersonal interactions occur. Team building, which focuses on the group, and the grid, which addresses the organization as a target, will be covered in the next sections.

Sensitivity Training

The first sensitivity training course was held in 1946 in New Britain, Connecticut. Since this beginning it has been used by psychotherapists, counselors, trainers, and P/HRM specialists.[24] Overall sensitivity training (also referred to as T-Group, process group, and encounter group) focuses on:

■ Making participants aware of and sensitive to the emotional reactions and expressions in themselves and others.

■ Increasing the ability of participants to perceive, and to learn from, the consequences of their actions through increased attention to their own and other's feelings.

The Group The sensitivity group process varies from trainer to trainer. However, a typical meeting involves a group of 10 to 12 people, meeting away from the job.[25] The emphasis is on: "How do you feel right now?" "What do you feel about others in the group?" "What will it take to make you feel better?" There is little structure imposed by the trainer on the group. Each group member is encouraged to say what he or she is thinking and how each sees others in the group.

Because of its nature, the sensitivity training group is a controversial OD technique. Some believe that it is unethical, impractical, and dangerous.[26] However, some research suggests that sensitivity training can change participant behavior. Participants can increase their sensitivity when working with other people. Furthermore, a few studies indicate that sensitivity training can improve organizational performance. It has, however, been shown that sensitivity training can increase the anxiety levels of some participants.[27]

A survey of personnel directors of large firms found that about twice as many of the respondents indicated a negative response toward the use of sensitivity training as those who said they would recommend it.[28] These directors may be listening more closely to the critics than to some of the supportive research results. Two things are certain about sensitivity training; only qualified trainers should be used, and only employees who volunteer to participate should attend this type of training program.

[24] Leland Bradford, Jack R. Gibbs, and Kenneth Bene, eds., *T-Group Theory and Laboratory Method* (New York: John Wiley & Sons, 1964).

[25] K. Back, *Beyond Words: The Story of Sensitivity Training and the Encounter Movement* (New York: Russell Sage Foundation, 1972).

[26] George Odiorne, "The Trouble with Sensitivity Training," *Training Directors Journal,* October 1963, pp. 19–37.

[27] Robert J. House, "T-Group Training: Good or Bad? *Busines Horizons,* December 1969, pp. 69–77.

[28] William J. Kearney and Desmond D. Martin, "Sensitivity Training: An Established Management Development Tool?" *Academy of Management Journal,* December 1974, pp. 755–60.

P/HRM Manager Close-Up

J. William Streidl
Tenneco Inc.

Biography

J. William Streidl is director of management education and development for Tenneco Inc. in Houston, Texas. After receiving his B.S. degree from the School of Natural Resources at the University of Michigan, Streidl worked for a short time as an industrial engineer for the Hamilton Manufacturing Company. He served as an army officer in Korea and returned to the University of Michigan where he received his M.B.A. degree majoring in personnel and industrial management.

Streidl joined the Filer City, Michigan Paper Mill of Packaging Corporation of America (a Tenneco company) as an employment supervisor in 1955. He moved through various personnel, labor relations, training and organization, planning and development assignments until becoming director of manpower planning and development for Packaging Corporation in 1967. He was promoted and transferred to the corporate staff of Tenneco Inc. in 1975.

Job Description

As director of management education and development for Tenneco Inc., Steidl directs the activities of the professional staff that carries out formal management education and development programs for all Tenneco companies on an international basis. In addition, he ensures the effective use of university-level executive development programs and ensures that enrollments in such programs are related to corporate executive resource plans.

Views about Personnel Development—J. William Streidl

The human assets of any organization can appreciate rather than depreciate over a period of time if the organization provides the environment and resources for such appreciation to occur.

This "personal growth environment" depends upon:

(continued)

- The individual employee, who must be personally concerned with self-development.

- The employee's immediate supervisor, who must ensure that the job environment sustains and reinforces the employee's self-development efforts.

- The resources provided by the organization as a whole. These resources in larger organizations are typically assigned to the education and development staff.

Tenneco's management education and development staff provides formal programs designed to accelerate the acquisition of participants' management

concepts and skills so they can perform more effectively on their current or future jobs. Our management course participants come from almost all of the United States and many countries of the free world. They represent many different industries, organizational levels, and national cultures because of the diversity of Tenneco's companies and their operations. It is a challenge to provide meaningful and helpful programs that provide the opportunity for continual personal development for those who participate.

Tenneco's management firmly believes that it will be successful as long as it provides such opportunities for human resource development on a continuing basis.

A form of sensitivity training is practiced in Japanese management training camps. Kanrisha Training camp offers a 13-day experience in self-analysis and development. A typical day at the camp begins at 5 A.M. and ends at 9 P.M.[29] It starts with similarly dressed (white exercise clothes) managers doing a round of calisthenics. The exercises are timed by observant instructors. The managers wear on their clothes ribbons of shame that indicate their personal shortcomings—speech, relating to people, writing ability.

The camp instructors push each manager every day in calisthenics, classroom teachings, skill development exercises, personal self-assessment exercises, group discussion meetings, and speech making. Most of the participants have been hand-picked because they are considered to be highly promotable by their firms. The camp is intended to put pressure on the participants so that they must use every skill, amount of energy, and knowledge that they possess to survive. Survival means that the self must overcome the pressures; the screaming instructors; and the long, tiring days. The Japanese have begun to refer to the experience as "Hell Camps."

Transactional Analysis

Transactional analysis (TA) is not really accepted by most OD experts as a full-fledged technique to use in developing human resources. Instead, TA is consid-

---

[29] Richard Phalon, "Hell Camp," *Forbes*, June 18, 1984, pp. 56–58.

ered a useful tool or technique to help people better understand themselves. Organizations such as Polaroid, Texas Instruments, American Airlines, and Bank of America use TA.

Eric Berne is usually credited with starting the interest in TA with his book, *Games People Play*.[30] TA remains popular because it is based on the psychoanalytic theories of Freud.[31] Three important ego states are used in TA: child, adult, and parent.

Child State This is the state where a person acts as an impulsive child. Immature behavior is displayed. An example would be an employee who, when reprimanded by a boss after doing a job, throws a temper tantrum and shouts, cusses, and screams about the unfairness of the system.

Adult State In this state the person acts like a mature adult. The adult state person is fair, objective, and careful in what he or she does. An example would be a manager who in reviewing the production record of a subordinate states, "Well, output is down a little, but we can look at it together and see what went wrong—was it equipment, not enough help, or poor quality parts?"

Parent State In this state people act like domineering, nagging parents. They are critical and all-knowing in their interactions, often talking down to others. A manager who states, "You shouldn't horse around because we are paying you to put in a fair day's work, not to play and hold down performance."

Generally people exhibit all three ego states, but one often dominates the other two. The emphasis in TA development training seminars is on encouraging participants to engage in *adult state behaviors*. It is this state that leads to effective interpersonal relations. A TA training program emphasizes the analysis of the transactions between people. It is these interactions of ego states that can significantly influence behavior.

Exhibit 13–7 shows effective interaction between a P/HRM manager and a subordinate. The two ego states involved are adult to adult. The two parties are communicating at the same ego state.

A different kind of interaction is displayed in Exhibit 13–8. The P/HRM manager speaks as an adult, but the specialist replies as a child, thus weakening the communication between the two.

In Exhibit 13–9 there is a breakdown in interaction. The adult P/HRM manager speaks to the adult in the specialist. However, the child in the specialist replies to the parent in the P/HRM manager.

Two other concepts in TA are strokes and games. *Strokes* mean that people need cuddling, affection, recognition, and praise. Strokes can be viewed as reinforcers. A "Good morning," a "Hello," or a "How are you doing?" from a boss may be a positive stroke which helps interactions.[32]

---

[30] Eric Berne, *Games People Play* (New York: Ballantine Books, 1964).

[31] Sigmund Freud, "Psychopathology of Everyday Life," *The Standard Edition of the Complete Psychology Works of Sigmund Freud*, ed. J. Strackey (London: Hogarth Press, 1960).

[32] Dorothy Jonerward and Philip Seyen, *Choosing Success* (New York: John Wiley & Sons, 1978).

EXHIBIT 13–7   **Effective Interaction**

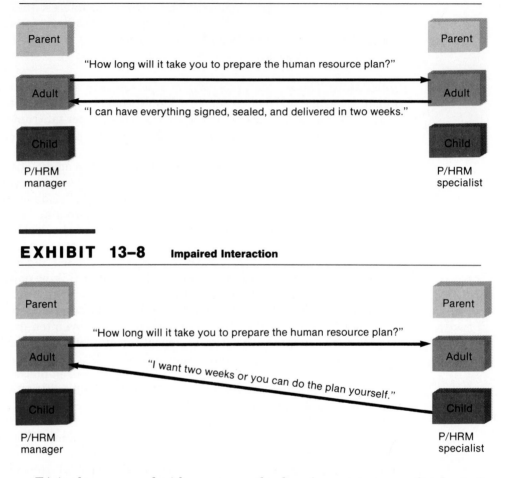

EXHIBIT 13–8   **Impaired Interaction**

TA is also concerned with games people play. A game is a superficial set of transactions. The outcome of games is that one person wins and another loses. Some of the frequently played games are presented in Exhibit 13–10.

When used as an OD technique, TA is designed to develop more adult states in people so that effective interactions occur. To date few studies have been reported on the scientific analysis of TA interventions.[33] Instead, testimony of TA consultants dominates the literature supporting this approach.[34] Until more rigorous research is conducted on the effectiveness of TA as an OD tool, P/HRM managers and specialists must cautiously consider its relative value for their situation or problem.

---

[33] Donald D. Bowen and Rayhu Nath, "Transactional Analysis in OD: Applications within the NTL Model," *Academy of Management Review,* January 1978, pp. 86–87.

[34] Wexley and Latham, *Developing and Training Human Resources,* p. 188.

EXHIBIT 13–9   A Breakdown in Interaction

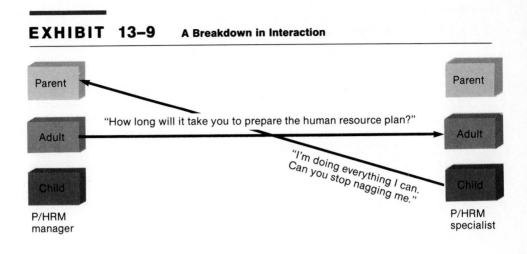

OD: A GROUP TECHNIQUE

There are numerous OD techniques that focus on improving the effectiveness of groups (the target), such as process consultation, survey feedback, and team building. In order to understand more fully these types of techniques, team building is presented.

Team Building

Team building is a development process that helps or prepares organizational members to work more efficiently or effectively in groups. It is designed to enhance the problem-solving, communication, and sensitivity-to-others skills of individual team members.[35]

Any organization depends on the cooperation of a number of people if it is to be successful. Consequently, teams of people have to work on a temporary or permanent basis in harmony.[36] Task forces, committees, project teams, or interdepartmental groups are the kinds of teams that are frequently brought together.

In one organization, team building followed this pattern.[37]

1. A *teams skills workshop.* Production teams in the firm went through a 2½ day workshop working on various experiential exercises.

---

[35] Malcolm Shaw, "Work Team Development Training," in *Human Resources Management and Development Handbook,* ed. William R. Tracey (New York: AMACOM, 1985), pp. 1113–24.

[36] W. G. Dyer, *Team Building: Issues and Alternatives* (Reading, Mass.: Addison-Wesley Publishing, 1977).

[37] Warren R. Nielsen and John R. Kimberly, "The Impact of Organizational Development on the Quality of Organizational Output," *Academy of Management Proceedings,* 1973, pp. 528–29.

EXHIBIT 13–10   Games People Play in Organizations

Name of Game	Brief Description of Game
1. Now I've Got You You S.O.B. (N.I.G.Y.Y.S.O.B.)	One employee gets back at another by luring her into what appears to be a natural work relationship. Actually the situation is rigged so that the other will fail. When the inevitable mistake is made, the game player pounces on the associate and publicly embarrasses her.
2. Poor Me	The employee depicts himself to the boss as helpless. Criticisms for inadequate performance are avoided because the boss truly feels sorry for the individual, who may actually begin to feel sorry for himself.
3. Blemish	The boss appears to be objectively evaluating an employee's total performance. In reality, the boss is looking for some minor error. When the error is found, the employee is berated for the poor performance, the inference being that the whole project/task/report is inadequate.
4. Hero	The boss consistently sets up situations in which employees fail. At some point, the boss steps in to save the day miraculously.
5. King of the Hill	The boss sets up situations in which employees end up in direct competition with her. At the end, she steps in and demonstrates her competence and superiority while publicly embarrassing her employees.
6. Cops and Robbers	An employee continuously walks a fine line between acceptable and unacceptable behavior. The boss wastes unnecessary time desperately trying to catch the employee, while the employee stays one step ahead and laughs to himself through the day.
7. Prosecutor	The employee carefully carries around a copy of the union contract or organization regulations and investigates management practices. This employee dares the boss to act in an arbitrary manner. Once he does, the employee files a grievance and attempts to embarrass the boss.
8. If It Weren't for You . . .	The employee discusses her problems openly but carefully works the conversation around so that she can rationalize her failure by blaming the boss for everything that goes wrong.
9. Yes, But . . .	In this game the boss responds with "yes, but . . ." to every good answer or idea that the subordinate may have. By doing this the boss can maintain a superior position and keep subordinates in their place. It represents a form of pseudo-participation; that is, the boss asks for participation but answers every suggestion with "yes, but . . ."

Source: Adapted from Fred Luthans and Mark J. Martinko, *The Practice of Supervision and Management.* Copyright © 1979 McGraw-Hill, pp. 386–87, which in turn is adapted from the literature on transactional analysis. Used with the permission of McGraw-Hill Book Company.

2. *Data collected.* Attitude and job data were collected from all teams (individual members).
3. *Data confrontation.* Consultants presented data to teams. It was discussed and problem areas sorted out. Priorities were also established by each team.
4. *Action planning.* Teams developed their own tentative plans to solve problems.
5. *Team building.* The teams finalized plans to solve all the problems identified in Step 4 and to consider barriers to overcome.
6. *Intergroup team building.* The groups that were interdependent met for two days to establish a mutually acceptable plan.

When team building is successful participation is encouraged and sustained. There also can be improved communication and problem solving within and between teams. Team building has proven to be most successful when the technique is tailored to fit the needs and problems of the groups involved.[38]

OD: AN ORGANIZATIONWIDE TECHNIQUE

By "organizationwide," OD experts mean the total system is involved or that a clearly identifiable unit, department, or plant is the target. The independence of the identifiable system or subsystem is extremely important when using an organizationwide technique.

Grid OD

One of the most publicized programs in OD was first introduced and researched by Blake and Mouton and is called the Managerial Grid®.[39] It consists of six phases directed toward enhancing organizational performance. The completion of the six-phase Grid program would cover a period of three to five years.

The Grid OD program is built upon a framework for understanding leadership styles of managers, as presented in Exhibit 13–11. The Grid depicts five different patterns of leadership, although 81 cells represent the two leadership concerns, production and people. Each person completes a questionnaire resulting in a determination of their leadership style. Blake and Mouton propose that the best way to lead is to be a 9, 9—which typifies high concern for both production and people.

The specific objectives of a Grid OD program are to:

- Study the organization as an interacting system and apply techniques of analysis in diagnosing problems.

---

[38] Robert R. Blake, Jane Srygley Mouton, and Robert L. Allen, *Spectacular Teamwork* (New York: John Wiley & Sons, 1987).

[39] Robert R. Blake, Jane S. Mouton, *The New Management Grid* (Houston: Gulf Publishing, 1978).

EXHIBIT 13–11   **Managerial Grid®**

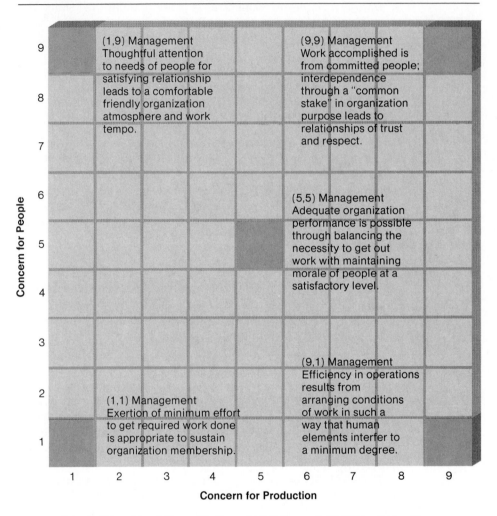

Source: Robert R. Blake and Jane S. Mouton, *The Managerial Grid* (Houston: Gulf Publishing, 1964), p. 10.

- Understand the rationale of systematic change.
- Gain insight into the strategies of Grid OD for increasing performance.
- Examine the documents and forms used in different phases and simulate their application to the participant's own situation.
- Evaluate the styles of leadership and techniques of participation most likely to produce high-quality results.
- Assess the effort and expense required and risks involved relative to the potential of increased profit and human effectiveness.[40]

---

[40] Brochure from Scientific Methods, Inc. Austin, Texas.

These objectives are accomplished, according to Blake and Mouton, by following the six-phase program.[41]

Phase I: *Study of the Grid.* Concepts about the various leadership styles are taught. The participants' styles are evaluated and reviewed. 50 hours of problem-solving tasks and exercises are completed.

Phase II: *Team Development.* Participants spend time analyzing their leadership styles and group skills. The key objective in the first two phases is to build trust and respect within the teams.

Phase III: *Intergroup Development.* Emphasis is on intergroup relationships. Joint problem solving is used in simulated situations.

Phase IV: *Developing an Organization Model.* The emphasis is on the importance of strategic planning and bringing together top- and lower-management groups. Linking the top and lower levels by establishing a framework is one result of this phase.

Phase V: *Implementing the Model.* Groups are given tasks to implement the Phase IV-developed model. Structural, process, and personnel plans are established to use the model.

Phase VI: *Evaluation.* The evaluation of the overall Grid is part of this phase. Modifications are made and a critique of the program is also part of this final phase. A standardized 100-item questionnaire is part of the evaluation in order to examine such areas as individual behavior, teamwork, intergroup relations, problem solving, and corporate strategy.

The Grid has been adopted totally, or in part, by thousands of organizations and hundreds of individuals. A large amount of the support for Grid OD comes from its founders, Blake and Mouton.[42] However, a comprehensive review of OD does give some support to Blake and Mouton's claims.[43] It has been found to have a positive impact on intergroup relationship and teamwork, as well as on performance and satisfaction. But, as is true with most training and development techniques, Grid OD needs to be researched more. P/HRM managers considering the use of Grid OD must cautiously weigh the potential costs and benefits of this extremely popular technique.

EVALUATION OF TRAINING AND DEVELOPMENT

In Chapter 12, the problem Gwen Meridith and Harold Matthews faced was deciding whether the training offered was effective. They had not designed a formal evaluation of the training program. This section focuses on the evaluation.

---

[41] A summary is provided in Robert R. Blake and Jane S. Mouton, "An Overview of the Grid," *Training and Development Journal,* May 1975, pp. 29–37.

[42] Fred Luthans, *Organizational Behavior* (New York: McGraw-Hill, 1981), p. 618.

[43] Jerry Porras and P. O. Berg, "The Impact of Organizational Development," *Academy of Management Review,* April 1978, pp. 259–60.

The evaluation step is the final phase of the training and development program. Cost/benefit analysis generally is more feasible for training and development than for many other P/HRM functions. Costs are relatively easy to compute: They equal direct costs of training (trainer cost, materials costs, and lost productivity, if training is done on company time) and indirect costs (a fair share of administrative overhead of the P/HRM department).[44]

Essentially, the evaluation should be made by comparing the results (the benefits) with the objectives of the training and development program that were set in the assessment phase. It is easier to evaluate the results of some programs (e.g., typing) than others (e.g., decision making and leadership).[45] The criteria used to evaluate training and development depend on the objectives of the program and who sets the criteria: management, the trainers, or the trainees. For example, one study found that trainees who were asked to develop their own evaluative criteria chose standards that varied from knowledge of the subject to the amount of socializing allowed during training sessions.[46]

Criteria for Evaluation

There are three types of criteria for evaluating training: internal, external, and participant reaction. *Internal criteria* are directly associated with the content of the program—for example, whether the employee learned the facts or guidelines covered in the program. *External criteria* are related more to the ultimate purpose of the program—for example, improving the effectiveness of the employee. Possible external criteria include job performance rating, the degree of learning transferred from training and development sessions to on-the-job situations and increases in sales volume, or decreases in turnover. *Participant reaction,* or how the subjects feel about the benefits of a specific training or development experience, is commonly used as an internal criterion.

Most experts argue that it is more effective to use multiple criteria to evaluate training.[47] Others contend that a single criterion, such as the extent of transfer of training to on-the-job performance or other aspects of performance, is a satisfactory evaluation approach.

One view of a multiple-criterion evaluation system was developed by Kirkpatrick.[48] He suggests measuring the following:

---

[44] Robert O. Brinkerhoff, *Achieving Results From Training* (San Francisco: Jossey-Bass, 1987).

[45] Harold E. Fisher, "Make Training Accountable: Assess Its Impact," *Personnel Journal,* January 1988, pp. 73–75.

[46] R. A. Guzzo, R. D. Jette, and R. A. Katzell, "The Effects of Psychologically Based Intervention Programs On Work Productivity: A Meta-Analysis," *Personnel Psychology,* Spring 1985, pp. 275–292.

[47] Darlene F. Russ-Eft and John H. Zenger, "Common Mistakes In Evaluating Training Effectiveness," *Personnel Administrator,* April 1985, pp. 57–62.

[48] Donald L. Kirkpatrick, ed., *Evaluating Training Programs* (Madison, Wis.: American Society for Training and Development.

Participant Reaction. Whether subjects like or dislike the program. The participant indicates his or her satisfaction with the program.

Learning. The extent to which the subjects have assimilated the knowledge offered and skills practiced in the training program. Does the participant score higher on skill demonstration tests after the training or development than before?

Behavior. An external measure of changes or lack of changes in job behavior. The ratings a participant received on the performance appraisal (comparison of before and after appraisal ratings).

Results. The effect of the program on organizational dimensions such as employee turnover, productivity, volume of sales, or error-free letters typed.

At present, many firms assess reaction, but very few measure behavioral results. The reaction measure is relatively easy to collect, while results are somewhat difficult to assess.[49]

A number of evaluation instruments and methods can be used to measure results of training and development (see the highlighted listing of evaluation methods). Data that can be used for evaluation include information on the trainee in the program; the trainee's immediate superiors and superiors above immediate supervisors; the trainee's subordinates (where applicable); nonparticipants from the work setting, including the subject's peers, company records, and nonparticipants from outside the work setting who might be affected by the program (e.g., clients).

Evaluation Methods for Training and Development Programs:

Company Records. Either exiting records or those devised for the evaluation of training or development, used to measure production turnover, grievances, absenteeism, and so on.

Observational Techniques. Interviewing, field observation, and other methods to evaluate skills, ability, communication, and productivity.

Critical Incidents. Using crucial incidents that occur on the job.

Ratings. Judgments of ability, performance, or ratings of satisfaction with various factors.

Questionnaires. A variety of types to measure decision making, problem solving, attitudes, values, personality, perceptions, and so on.

Tests. Written examinations or performance tests to measure changes in ability or knowledge.

---

[49] Jack Phillips, *Handbook of Training Evaluation and Measurement Methods* (Houston: Gulf Publishing, 1983).

A Matrix Guide

One useful device to address the evaluation issue is to work with a systematic evaluation matrix. A matrix, because of its organization, can help those involved with training and development programs to systematically review relevant issues or questions. Exhibit 13–12 presents such a matrix that could be used as a guideline for evaluating any of the programs and techniques covered in Chapters 12 and 13.

The relevant issues, skill improvement, training and development materials, costs, and long-term effects are crucial questions that can be answered by use of evaluation. It is important to understand that the issues and questions provide only the direction that evaluation can take. The actual design and data collection of the evaluation phase of training and development requires following the scientific method as used by behavioral scientists. Simply asking participants if they liked the program after attending a sensitivity group or a behavioral modeling session is not very scientific. What would you expect to be the answer? Certainly, most of us like new experiences, new ideas. However, this does not mean that a program is good or beneficial for improving perform-

EXHIBIT   13–12   An Evaluation Matrix: Issues to Consider

The Relevant Issues to Cover and Evaluate	Examples of What to Measure	What to Examine for Answers	How to Collect Data to Answer Issue Questions
1. Are the participants learning, changing attitudes, and/or improving skills?	Participants' attitudes and/or skills before and after (even during training or development sessions)	Comments Method of participation Co-workers Superiors	Interview Questionnaires Records Observation
2. Are the training or development materials used on the job?	Participants on-the-job performance, behavior, and style	Subordinate performance, attitudes, and style	Records Interview Questionnaires Critical incidents Observation
3. What are the costs of training and development programs and techniques?	The fixed and variable costs of conducting the training or development	Cost of trainers Participant time Travel expenses Consultant fees Training aids Rent Utilities	Budget records
4. How long does the training or development have an effect on participants?	Participants' on-the-job performance, behavior, and style over an extended period of time.	Subordinate performance, attitudes, and style	Records Interview Questionnaires Critical incidents Observation (collected a number of times)

EXHIBIT 13–13   One Group: Baseline/After Design

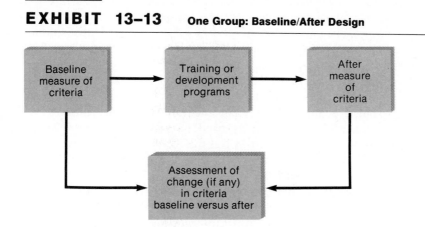

ance or increasing interpersonal skills on the job. Perhaps the most pressing question is whether what is learned in training transfers to the job. Another crucial issue is what strategies can management use to facilitate positive training to job transfer of learning.[50]

Someone in authority (usually someone above the P/HRM specialist involved in the training or development, such as a director of human resources or vice president of operations) must hold those who train and develop employees accountable. The efficient use of people, dollars, and facilities must be clearly shown. This can only be done if the evaluation phase is completed and sound reseach designs are used. Evaluation is certainly not easy, but it is a necessary and often glossed over part of training and development.[51]

In sum, formal training and development has been shown to be more effective than informal or no training and development. However, the results tend to be assumed rather than evaluated for most training and development programs.

Research Designs

There are numerous research designs that can be used to assess the effectiveness of training and development effectiveness. The more rigorous the design, the more confidence that can be placed on the principle that changes learning, behavior, or results are due to the program.[52]

A simple design is shown in Exhibit 13–13. One group of participants in the

[50] Kenneth N. Wexley and Timothy T. Baldwin, "Posttraining Strategies For Facilitating Positive Transfer: An Empirical Exploration," *Academy of Management Journal,* September 1986, pp. 503–520.

[51] For an interesting view of one of the pioneers of OD, see "A Dialogue with Warren Bennis," *Training and Development Journal,* April 1981, pp. 19–26.

[52] Donald L. Kirkpatrick, "Four Steps to Measuring Training Effectiveness," *Personnel Administrator,* November 1983, pp. 19–25.

program is assessed before and after the experience. The differences in the measures, baseline versus after design, may be due to the training or development or there may be a "Hawthorne Effect"—that is, the employees conclude that they are being studied, so they work harder than usual. There is also the probability that over time employees gain experience and acquire ways to do the job better. Self-development may have nothing to do with the training or development program. The baseline/after one-group design doesn't address the Hawthorne or natural job experience improvement issues.

A research design that is used to address the Hawthorne and the job experience issues is shown in Exhibit 13–14. This is a two-group design. One group receives the training or development program, while the other group receives no training.

This design is an improvement over the one-group design, but we don't know if the groups were comparable to begin with. Perhaps the no-training or development group were initially significantly better performers. Since no baseline measures were taken, the conclusions drawn are somewhat debatable.

Exhibit 13–15 shows a two-group design that uses baseline measures. This is a better design than the one-group or the no-baseline, two-group design. It permits the researcher to conclude with some confidence that differences in the criteria (learning, behavior, results) may be attributable to the training or development program.

Other much more sophisticated research designs are available. The manager must decide which design will be used. It is recommended that some type

EXHIBIT 13–14   **Two Groups: After Design**

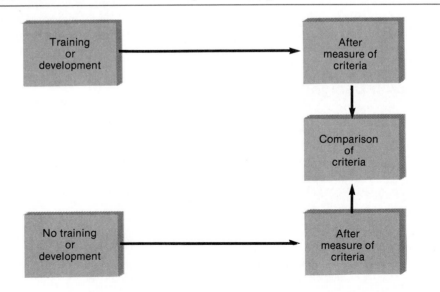

EXHIBIT 13–15   Two Groups: Baseline/After Design

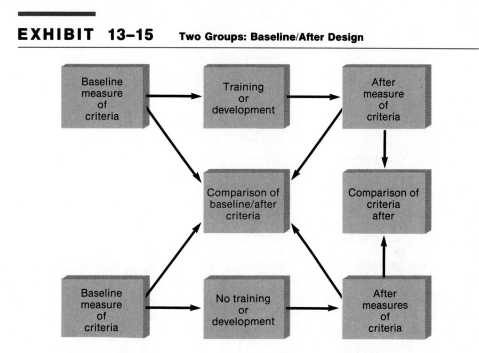

of design be used to evaluate training or development programs to determine their value, if any, to the organization.[53] For too long, managers have accepted opinions, personal testimonials, and publicity as the reason why they do or do not incorporate a training or development approach.

SUMMARY

This chapter has introduced the important areas of the development of human resources and the evaluation of training and development programs.

To summarize the major points covered in this chapter:

1. Management development is the process by which managers gain the experience, skills, and attitudes to become or remain successful leaders in their organization.
2. Management and professional development is designed to reduce obsolescence and to increase employee satisfaction and productivity.

---

[53] William D. Hicks and Richard J. Klimoski, "Entry into Training Programs and Its Effects on Training Outcomes: A Field Experiment, *Academy of Management Journal*, September 1987, pp. 532–42.

Gwen

After absorbing the material Bob has brought her, Gwen approaches Lester Young, Young Enterprise's president, on an informal basis.

Gwen: You know, Les, our last attitude survey indicated major dissatisfaction with our development program at Young. We've been doing some research in our shop about development programs. I'm sure I couldn't work it into this year's budget. But we're only six weeks away from the new budget time. I feel the program is very important at this time. As you know, we were not completely satisfied with the training program on the new machinery. In addition, one or two of our supervisors have come in to complain about the lack of any organization development program for them. How would you like us to proceed?

Lester: I have heard some talk about OD at a recent American Manufacturers Association meeting. I hear it's quite costly. We may have some problems in this area, but we're in no position to make a major investment in development at the present time in view of our earnings situation. Why not work up a modest program for presentation to the budget and goals

meeting six weeks from now—no more than 5 percent of your current budget as an increment.

Gwen: Will do, Les.

Gwen and Bob put together a proposal that they viewed as Phase 1. They proposed a supervisory development program with some help from the P/HRM department for one half of 1 percent of current budget.

After investigating the potential costs of an OD consultant, they felt they should begin to move in the development area. They proposed some beginning funds for planning an OD program, the first phase of which would involve initial diagnosis and small sample data collection. They proposed to set up an experiment using a behavior-modeling program in one unit for supervisory style, with a control group. Evaluation procedures were to be formal. They specified desired outputs: better readings from the attitude survey, some improvements in turnover and absenteeism, and some results in the productivity problem.

Lester and the budget and goals committee accepted the proposal. Phase 1 began, and it was successful. Little by little, the company accepted a development program.

3. Methods used to modify employee and managerial attitudes and interpersonal skills include behavior modeling, sensitivity training, transactional analysis, and team building.
4. A popular organizationwide OD program is the Managerial Grid, which was first introduced by Blake and Mouton.
5. Organization development programs, such as the Grid, overlap the other methods. The Grid seeks to change attitudes, values, organization structure, and managerial practices to improve performance.
6. The final phase of any training and development program is evaluation. It is unfortunately often bypassed by organizations.

Exhibit 13–16 provides some recommendations for the use of various OD programs and techniques for the model organization.

EXHIBIT 13–16 Recommendations for Use of OD in Model Organizations

	Types of OD				
Type of Organization	Behavior Modeling	Sensitivity Training	Transactional Analysis	Team Building	Grid OD
1. Large size, low complexity, high stability		X	X		
2. Medium size, low complexity, high stability		X	X		
3. Small size, low complexity, high stability			X		
4. Medium size, moderate complexity, moderate stability	X	X	X	X	X
5. Large size, high complexity, low stability	X	X	X	X	X
6. Medium size, high complexity, low stability	X	X	X	X	X
7. Small size, high complexity, low stability	X		X	X	

Questions for Review and Discussion

1. How can you describe the characteristics of a few OD programs designed to improve interpersonal skills and attitudes?
2. What would be some of the possible consequences of not being involved in state-of-the-art management development programs for employees?
3. How could a person's expectations about training influence what they learn in a formal training program?

4. Why do you think many organizations fail to evaluate their training and development programs?
5. Why do you think TA is such a popular technique?
6. What type of organization would implement a full-fledged Grid OD program?
7. Present a research design that could be used to evaluate the effectiveness of a team-building development program.
8. Should management be concerned about what amount of training transfers to the actual job? Why?
9. Why would an organization enter into attitude-change and interpersonal skills training programs?
10. The predecessor current development programs was called human relations programs. What was the major emphasis of these programs, and how effective were they?

GLOSSARY

Behavior Modeling. Participants learn by observing a role model behavior. The fundamental characteristic of modeling is that learning takes place by observation or imagination of another individual's experience.

Case Method. A training technique in which a description (a case) of a real situation is analyzed by participants. The interaction of the participants and trainer is valuable in improving the degree of learning that occurs.

Grid OD. A program that involves six phases designed to improve organizational performance. The phases include determining the participants' leadership styles, team building, intergroup development, and evaluation.

Role Playing. The acting out of a role by participants. Participants play act a role that others in the training session observe.

Participants play an active part in role plays.

Sensitivity Training. A training technique that was first used in 1946. In it small groups of participants focus on emotions and how they feel about themselves and the group. Usually little structure is imposed by the trainer. The group members are encouraged to say or do what they feel.

Team Building. A development method that attempts to improve the cooperation between teams.

Transactional Analysis. A training technique designed to help the people participating better understand their own ego states and those of others; to understand the principles behind transactions; and to interact with others in a more comfortable way.

APPLICATION CASE 13–1

General Food's Method of Needs Assessment*

The history of training development at General Foods Corporation is a long one; training and development continues to be supported throughout the company. General Foods relies on it to achieve optimum performance levels. Some of General Food's (GF) philosophy is captured in statements made by executives of the firm:

- GF believes people want and should be given the opportunity for individual growth and development and should be encouraged to increase their knowledge and improve their skills.
- Training and development is the responsibility of each employee and his/her manager.
- The results of training and development must be evaluated.

At the hub of the training and development process is the determination of needs. All of the aspects of training and development revolve around "needs." Thus, the first important step of training and development is the identification of needs. The exhibit on p. 595 presents the needs model used at GF's plants. Note that the needs assessment is a cooperative effort of employees, supervisors, management, and P/HRM staff. The purpose of this first crucial training and development step is to collect qualitative and quantitative data.

The needs assessment at GF is conducted at the organizational and individual levels—separately or concurrently. This is considered an important requirement for acquiring a total picture of needs. GF placed significant emphasis on the role of the line manager in assessing needs. Since managers are concerned about performance, they must be responsible for closing the gap between actual and expected performance.

It is, however, the responsibility of the P/HRM department to act as consultants once the line managers assess their needs. Thus, a dual responsibility for training and development at GF rests in line managers and the P/HRM department.

Training and development needs-identification determines plant objectives and activities necessary for an efficient operation to accomplish those objectives.

Based on		As Discovered by		To Determine
1. Analysis of organizational problems and conditions and 2. Analysis of employees' performance, problems, and potential	1. Asking—	Employees Supervisors Top management Staff offices	Questionnaire Interview Surveys	1. What is the problem or situation that makes us want to do something? 2. What causes this problem or situation? 3. Exactly what do we really want? 4. What do we have now? 5. What do we need? 6. Which of these needs have greatest priority? 7. What can we do about them? 8. How shall we go about doing it?
	2. Observing—	Employees Their work Work flow Relationships		
	3. Studying—	Records and reports Public reaction to service Jobs (job analysis) Organization structure Program plans Organization policies		

A cooperative effort of employees, supervisors, management, and P/HRM staff

* Adapted from J. I. Lazer, A. W. Olkewicz, and J. W. Bevans, "Training in Plants: A Realistic Approach," *Training and Development Journal*, October 1980, pp. 91–96.

Questions for Thought

1. Would the General Foods needs model be of any value to the General Foods line manager?
2. Why does General Foods collect qualitative and quantitative data in the needs assessment step?
3. Since there is a dual responsibility between line managers and the P/HRM department at General Foods, do you think they will cooperate with each other? Explain.

EXERCISE 13–1   Making Responses

Objective: The exercise is designed to have students apply the three ego states of transactional analysis—child, adult, parent.

SET UP THE EXERCISE

1. Divide the class into groups of four or five.
2. Individually complete the transactional analysis response form.
3. Discuss in the group the individual responses. Consult Chapter 13 to review the child, adult, parent states.

Transactional Analysis Response Form

Make a child, adult, and parent response to each of the following statements:

A. Is the P/HRM an important function in organizations?
Child:

Adult:

Parent:

B. Eating nutritional food is good for your health.
Child:

Adult:

Parent:

C. Are you a good driver?
Child:

Adult:

Parent:

D. Do you litter the highways?
Child:

Adult:

Parent:

E. Jim (Anne) is a good student in this course (program).
Child:

Adult:

Parent:

F. You always force your views on other people.

Child:

Adult:

Parent:

4. Which of these states is the dominant one for you?

A Learning Note

This exercise will illustrate clearly the differences in the three ego states. It will also illustrate that the adult state is much more relevant and effective when answering any kind of question or issue.

CAREER PLANNING AND DEVELOPMENT

LEARNING OBJECTIVES

After studying this chapter, you should be able to:

- **Define** the term *career*.
- **Describe** why mentoring is an important part of career development
- **Explain** why organizations need to be concerned about dual careers.
- **Discuss** how career pathing can be used within an organization.
- **State** how career planning is done in organizations.

KEY TERMS

Career
Career Path
Career Stages
Dual Careers
Job Layoff
Job Loss
Mentoring Relationships
Midcareer Plateau
Outplacement

CHAPTER OUTLINE

P/HRM · IN · ACTION

Jim Lucio and Norbert Wislinski

Jim Lucio was a 50-year-old executive with Neal Engineering Construction Company in Mesa, Arizona, a suburb of Phoenix. Despite his professional engineering training, and his good position with the company, Jim had an identity problem. This conversation between Jim and Norbert Wislinksi, his boss, indicates a midcareer concern.

Norb: Jim, you're really moving on the Salt River Project. Costs are under control and you've been able to control Tony (the chief engineer).

Jim: To be honest, Norb, I'm sick of the project, Tony, and everything about the job. I can't sleep, eat, or relax.

Norb: I'm sorry to hear that. Do you need some time off?

Jim: No. I need to rethink my whole career. I've just lost my intensity. It hasn't been sudden. It's been growing over the last year.

Norb: You know I'll do anything I can to help you. You're what made this company a success.

Jim: Thanks. But I have to really do some soul-searching. I've always wanted to own my own business, be my own boss. I just haven't been brave enough to take the plunge.

Norb: Jim, you know I'm selfish. I need you here at Neal, but if you make the break, I'll help you any way I can

Jim: Thanks again, Norb. I have to think more about this. It is a whole career change. Serious business for a 50-year-old engineer.

Jim Lucio has changed and now he is trying to cope with his thoughts and feelings. This is a difficult time in Jim's life. He seems to have it all, but something is missing. He is not satisfied. Norb is an understanding manager who also seems to realize that Jim Lucio is at a midcareer point in life and wants to make a change.

Because of organizational change and growth, managers must pay attention to developing people and placing them in key positions. Organizational growth through expansion, mergers, and acquisitions creates new management positions and changes the responsibilities of existing positions. Capable people must be available to fill the new and bigger jobs. Moreover, the contemporary concern for developing the full potential of all employees through job opportunities that provide responsibility, advancement, and challenging work reinforces such efforts. Even organizations facing a stable or a contracting future recognize that a key to performance is the development of human resources.

As organizations change, so do their employees. For example, a recently hired P/HRM manager has different needs and aspirations than does the midcareer or the preretirement P/HRM manager. All of us move through a fairly uniform pattern of phases during our careers. The different phases produce different opportunities and stresses that affect job performance. Effective managers comprehend these implications and facilitate the efforts of employees who wish to confront and deal with their career and life needs.

Finally, it should be noted that managers should be concerned with their own career development. By their nature, managers are likely to be concerned with their career goals and with the paths that are most likely to lead to those goals. Yet managers often lack the ability and the information needed to develop their career plans in systematic and explicit ways. But we see more and more evidence of growing interest in providing individuals with information that will help them to identify their goals and to understand what they should do to reach them.

In this chapter we will review a number of programs that organizations and managers can use to plan and develop careers. Some of these programs have been used in management for many years to identify and select promising managerial talent. For example, assessment centers and performance appraisal programs have long been used to develop managers, though the traditional emphasis of these programs has been placed on the satisfaction of organizational needs. More recently, the programs have been revised to include the consideration of employee needs as well.

A DIAGNOSTIC APPROACH
TO CAREER PLANNING
AND DEVELOPMENT

Exhibit 14–1 highlights the diagnostic factors most important to career planning and development as a P/HRM activity. People have always had careers, but only recently has serious P/HRM attention been directed to the way careers develop and the type of planning that is needed to achieve career satisfaction. The key to the diagnostic factors influencing careers is not in the person, external environmental influences, or the internal influences themselves, but rather the ways in which these major factors interact.

Certainly, careers do not just happen in isolation from environmental and personal factors. Every person's career goes through a series of stages. Each of these stages may or may not be influenced by attitudes, motivation, the nature of the task, economic conditions, and so forth. The P/HRM employee must be sensitive to the "career cycle" and the role that different influences such as those shown in Exhibit 14–1 can play at different points.

An adequate matching of individual needs, abilities, preferences, moti-

EXHIBIT 14-1

Factors Affecting Career Planning and Development

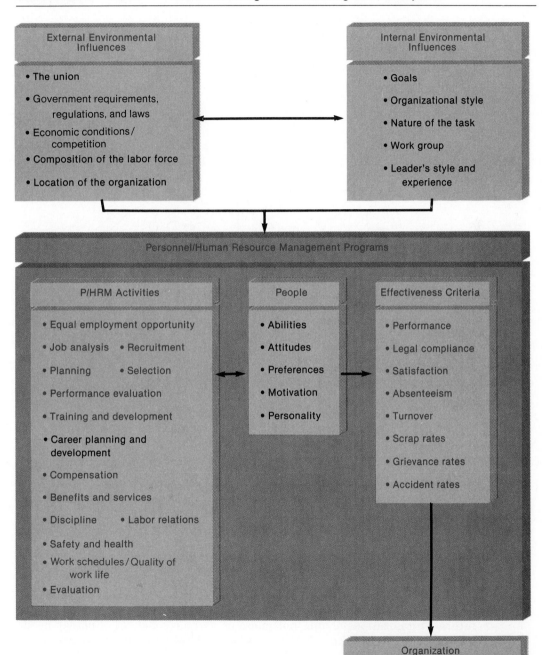

External Environmental Influences

- The union
- Government requirements, regulations, and laws
- Economic conditions/ competition
- Composition of the labor force
- Location of the organization

Internal Environmental Influences

- Goals
- Organizational style
- Nature of the task
- Work group
- Leader's style and experience

Personnel/Human Resource Management Programs

P/HRM Activities

- Equal employment opportunity
- Job analysis • Recruitment
- Planning • Selection
- Performance evaluation
- Training and development
- Career planning and development
- Compensation
- Benefits and services
- Discipline • Labor relations
- Safety and health
- Work schedules/Quality of work life
- Evaluation

People

- Abilities
- Attitudes
- Preferences
- Motivation
- Personality

Effectiveness Criteria

- Performance
- Legal compliance
- Satisfaction
- Absenteeism
- Turnover
- Scrap rates
- Grievance rates
- Accident rates

Organization End Results

- Competitive product(s)
- Competitive service(s)

From *The Wall Street Journal*, with permission of Cartoon Features Syndicate

"I find this work truly fulfilling in many ways—there's the exercise, the sense of accomplishment, and, most important, the opportunity to make lots of noise."

vation, and organizational opportunities will not just happen. Individuals, organizations, and experts in areas such as P/HRM all must take responsibility for things they can control. For example, organizations and P/HRM employees must realize the needs of employees. On the other hand, employees must have a clear picture of the opportunities available now and anticipated in the future. Organizations should not guess or assume some set of career needs. Likewise, employees should not have to guess how career development occurs in "the organization." A sharing of information, and understanding of the "career stage" and concern about the kind of forces highlighted in Exhibit 14–1 must be established as part of an ongoing career planning and development effort. Anything less will probably result in the inefficient use of human resources.

THE CONCEPT OF CAREER

The concept of career has many meanings. The popular meaning is probably reflected in the idea of moving upward in one's chosen line of work—making more money; having more responsibility; and acquiring more status, prestige, and power. Although typically restricted to lines of work that involve gainful employment, the concept of career can apply to other life pursuits. For example, we can think of homemakers, mothers, and volunteer workers as having careers. For they too advance in the sense that their talents and abilities to handle larger responsibilities grow with time and experience. A mother of teenagers plays a far different role than she did when the children were preschoolers.

Here our discussion will center on the careers of those in occupations and professions. A concise definition of career that emphasizes important factors is the following:

> A career is the individually perceived sequence of attitudes and behaviors associated with work-related experiences and activities over the span of the person's work life.[1]

This definition emphasizes that the term *career* does not imply success or failure except in the judgment of the individual, that a career consists of both attitudes and behaviors, and that it is an ongoing sequence of work-related activities. Yet, even though the concept of career is clearly work-related, it must be understood that a person's nonwork life and roles play a significant part in a career. For example, the attitudes of a 50-year-old midcareer manager (*midcareer* means at about the midpoint of a person's working tenure) about a job advancement involving greater responsibilities can be quite different from those of a manager nearing retirement. A single person's reaction to a promotion involving relocation is likely to be different from that of a father or a mother of school-age children.

Now that you have started to think about the notion of careers, it would be useful for you to consider your own career aspirations. The exercise that follows will enable you to think about a career and its meaning. Although you can do the exercise without input from others, it would be helpful to share and compare the results. The exercise is presented in a step-by-step format, and it can be completed on a separate sheet of paper.

1. Draw a horizontal line that depicts the past, present, and future of your *career*. On that line, mark an *X* to show where you are now.
2. To the left of the *X*, that part of the line which represents your *past*, identify the events in your life which gave you genuine feelings of fulfillment and satisfaction.

---

[1] Douglas T. Hall, *Careers in Organizations* (Santa Monica, Calif.: Goodyear Publishers, 1976), p. 4.

3. Examine these historical milestones, and determine the specific factors that seem to have caused those feelings. Does a pattern emerge? Did the events occur when you were alone or when you were with other people? Did you accomplish some objective alone or with other people? Write down as much as you can about the events and your reactions to them.

4. That part of the line to the right of the *X*, represents your *future*. Identify the career-related events from which you expect to realize genuine fulfillment and satisfaction. You should describe these events as explicitly as possible. If you are only able to write such statements as "Get my first job" or "get my first raise," you probably have ill-defined career expectations.

5. After you have identified these future career-related events, rank them from high to low in terms of how much fulfillment and satisfaction you expect to derive from them.

6. Now go back to Step 3 and rank the historical events from high to low in terms of the actual fulfillment and satisfaction you derived from them. Compare your two sets of ranked events. Are they consistent? Are you expecting the future to be the same as or different from the past? If you expect the future to be considerably different from the past, are you being realistic about the fulfillment and satisfaction that you think the future events will provide?

7. Discuss your results with your classmates and your instructor. How do you compare with your classmates in terms of your self-understanding and your understanding of the role of a career in providing personal fulfillment and satisfaction?

Career Stages

The idea that individuals go through distinct, but interrelated, stages in their careers is widely recognized. The simplest version includes four stages: (1) the prework stage (attending school), (2) the initial work stage (moving from job to job), (3) the stable work stage (maintaining one job), and (4) the retirement stage (leaving active employment). Most working people prepare for their occupation by undergoing some form of organized education in high school, trade school, vocational school, or college. They then take a first job, but the chances are that they will move to other jobs in the same organization or in other organizations. Eventually over the course of the career, they settle into a position in which they remain until retirement. The duration of each stage varies among individuals, but most working people go through all of these stages.

Studies of career stages have found that needs and expectations change as the individual moves through the stages.[2] Managers in American Telephone and Telegraph (AT&T) expressed considerable concern for safety needs during the initial years on their jobs. This phase, termed the *establishment* phase,

---

[2] Douglas T. Hall and Khalil Nougaim, "An Examination of Maslow's Need Hierarchy in an Organizational Setting," *Organizational Performance and Human Behavior*, 1968, pp. 12–35.

ordinarily lasted during the first five years of employment. Following the establishment phase in the *advancement* phase, which lasts approximately from age 30 to age 45. During this period the AT&T managers expressed considerably less concern for the satisfaction of safety needs and more concern for achievement, esteem, and autonomy.

The *maintenance* phase follows the advancement phase. This period is marked by efforts to stabilize the gains of the past. Although no new gains are made, the maintenance phase can be a period of creativity, since the individual has satisfied many of the psychological and financial needs associated with earlier phases. Although each individual and each career will be different, it is reasonable to assume that esteem and self-actualization would be the most important needs in the maintenance phase. But as we will see, many people experience what is termed the *midcareer* crisis during the maintenance phase. Such people are not achieving satisfaction from their work, and consequently they may experience physiological and psychological discomfort.

The maintenance phase is followed by the *retirement* phase. The individual has, in effect, completed one career, and he or she may move on to another one. During this phase the individual may have opportunities to experience self-actualization through activities that it was impossible to pursue while working. Painting, gardening, volunteer service, and quiet reflection are some of the many positive avenues that have been followed by retirees. But the individual's financial and health status may make it necessary to spend the retirement years in satisfying safety and physiological needs. Exhibit 14–2 summarizes the relationship between career stages and needs.

The fact that individuals pass through different stages during their careers is evident. It is also understandable that individual needs and motives are different from one stage to the next. But managing the careers of others requires a more complete description of what happens to individuals during these stages. One group of individuals whose careers are of special significance to the performance of modern organizations are the *professionals*. Knowledge workers—such as professional accountants, scientists, and engineers—are one of the fastest growing segments of the work force. This segment constitutes 32

EXHIBIT 14–2   **Career Stages and Important Needs**

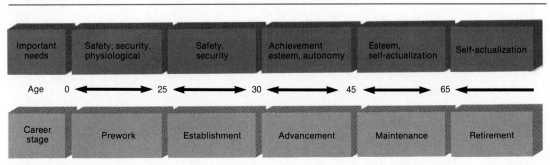

Important needs	Safety, security, physiological	Safety, security	Achievement esteem, autonomy	Esteem, self-actualization	Self-actualization
Age	0 ← → 25	← → 30	← → 45	← → 65	←
Career stage	Prework	Establishment	Advancement	Maintenance	Retirement

percent of the work force at present (blue-collar workers make up 33 percent).[3] Many professionals spend their careers in large, complex organizations after having spent several years in obtaining advanced training and degrees. The organizations which employ them expect them to provide the innovativeness and creativity for organizational survival in dynamic and competitive environments. Obviously, the performance levels of professional employees must be of the upmost concern for the organizations' leaders.

The effective management of professionals begins with understanding the crucial characteristics of the four stages of professional careers. Professional employees could avoid some disappointments and anxieties if they also understood more about their own career stages.

Stage 1 Young professionals enter an organization with technical knowledge, but often without an understanding of the organization's demands and expectations. Consequently, they must work fairly closely with more experienced persons. The relationship that develops between the young professionals and their supervisors is an *apprenticeship*. The central activities in which apprentices are expected to show competence include *learning* and *following directions*. To move successfully and effectively through Stage I, one must be able to accept the *psychological state of dependence*. And some professionals cannot cope with being placed in a situation similar to that which they experienced while in school. They find that they are still being directed by an authority figure, just as they were in school, whereas they had anticipated that their first job would provide considerably more freedom.

Stage II Once through the dependent relationship characteristic of Stage I, the professional employee moves into Stage II, which calls for working independently. Passage to this stage depends on the employee having demonstrated competence in some specific technical area. The technical expertise may be in a content area, such as taxation, product testing, or quality assurance, or it may be in a skill area, such as computer applications. The professional's primary activity in Stage II is to be an *independent contributor* of ideas in the chosen area. The professional is expected to rely much less on direction from others. The *psychological state of independence* may pose some problems because it is in such stark contrast to the state of dependence required in Stage I. Stage II is extremely important for the professional's future career growth. However, those who fail at this stage do so because they do not have the necessary self-confidence to do so.

In the case at the beginning of this chapter, there is an indication that Jim Lucio is at Stage II in his career development. As the opening P/HRM in Action stated, Jim really values his independence. He wants to be his own boss, run his own business. Independence is a high priority for him as it is for most professionals at Stage II.

---

[3] Phillip R. Harris, "Future Work," *Personnel Journal*, June 1985, pp. 52–58.

Stage III Professionals who enter Stage III are expected to become the mentors of those in Stage I. They also tend to broaden their interests and to deal more and more with people outside the organization. Thus, the central activities of professionals at this stage are *training* and *interaction* with others. Stage III professionals assume *responsibility for the work of others*, and this characteristic of the stage can cause considerable psychological stress. In previous stages the professional was responsible only for his or her own work. But now it is the work of others that is of primary concern. Individuals who cannot cope with this new requirement may decide to shift back to Stage II. Individuals who derive satisfaction from seeing other people move on to bigger and better jobs will be content to remain in Stage III until retirement.

In the *Change Masters*, Kanter argued that all companies that want to achieve excellence should encourage managers to become mentors to their employees.[4] Kotter agreed that mentors, sponsors, coaches, and role models can be especially important in helping others in their careers. He stated, "Virtually all of the successful and effective executives I have known have had two or more of these kinds of relationships early in their careers.[5]

As defined by Kram, a *mentoring relationship* is a relationship between a junior and senior colleague that is viewed by the junior as contributing positively to his or her development.[6] The junior person is developed by a range of career advancement activities (coaching, exposure and visibility, and protection) that the senior person facilitates. Also the mentoring relationship provides the junior person with support that helps him or her acquire a sense of personal identity. The person in Stage III serving as a mentor can derive tremendous satisfaction from the growth, development, and advancement of a protégé.[7] In some organizations such as J. C. Penney, Sears, and IBM, Stage III professionals will not be promoted until they can demonstrate an ability to prepare junior subordinates for promotion and more job responsibilities.[8]

Mentoring relationships have been hard to form for women and minority workers.[9] Researchers have suggested that some men hesitate to act as mentors for female protégés because of the sexual innuendoes that often accompany such relationships. Some firms are attempting to overcome barriers of race and sex by assigning mentors to promising young executives. At Bank American Corporation, a senior manager may be asked to serve as a coach and mentor to three or four juniors for a year at a time.

---

[4] Rosabeth Kanter, *The Change Masters* (New York: Simon and Schuster, 1984).

[5] John Kotter, *Power and Influence* (New York: Free Press, 1985).

[6] K. E. Kram, *Mentoring at Work* (Glenview, Ill.: Scott, Foresman, 1984).

[7] Robert D. Bretz, Jr. and George F. Dreher, "Sponsored verus Contest Mobility: The Role of Mentoring In Managerial Careers," in R. S. Schuler, S. A. Youngblood, and V. L. Herbert, eds., *Readings in Personnel and Human Resource Management* (St. Paul: West Publishing, 1987) pp. 311–19.

[8] Charles D. Orth, Harry E. Wilkinson, and Robert C. Benfari, "The Manager's Role As Coach and Mentor," *Organizational Dynamics,* Spring 1987, pp. 66–74.

[9] Sebywyn Fernstein, "Women and Minority Workers in Business Find a Mentor Can Be a Rare Commodity," *The Wall Street Journal,* November 10, 1987, p. 31.

Stage IV Some professional employees remain in Stage III; for these professionals, Stage III is the career maintenance phase. Other professionals progress to yet another stage. This stage is not experienced by all professionals, because its fundamental characteristic involves *shaping the direction of the organization itself.* Although we usually think of such activity as being undertaken by only one individual in an organization—its chief executive—in fact it may be undertaken by many others. For example, key personnel in product development, process manufacturing, or technological research may be Stage IV types. As a consequence of their performance in Stage III of the careers, Stage IV professionals direct their attention to long-range strategic planning. In doing so, they play the roles of manager, entrepreneur, and idea generator. Their primary job relationships are to *identify* and *sponsor* the careers of their successors and to interact with key people outside the organization. The most significant shift for a person in Stage IV is to accept the decisions of subordinates without second-guessing them. Stage IV professionals must learn to influence; that is, practice leadership through such indirect means as idea planting, personnel selection, and organizational design. These shifts can be difficult for an individual who has relied on direct supervision in the past.

The concept of career stages is fundamental for understanding and managing career development. It is necessary to comprehend *life stages* as well. Individuals go through career stages as they go through life stages, but the interaction between career stages and life stages is not easy to understand.

Life Stages

Our understanding of the stages of life for children and youth is relatively well developed as compared to our understanding of adult life stages. Psychology has provided much insight into the problems of early childhood, but far less insight into the problems of adulthood. More and more, however, we are finding that adulthood is defined by rather distinct phases. The demands, problems, and opportunities presented in these phases must be taken into account by managers who are concerned with developing the careers of their subordinates.

One view of the life stages emphasizes developmental aspects. That is, each life stage is marked by the need to work through a particular developmental task before the individual can move successfully into the next stage.[10] In this regard, moving through the stages of life is analogous to Maslow's need hierarchy. The stages and their developmental tasks are as follows.

Adolescence For most people, this stage occurs from age 15 to 25. Prior to this stage is *childhood,* but since our primary concern is the life stages as related to the career stages, childhood is relatively unimportant for our purposes. Essential for normal progression through adolescence is the achieving of

---

[10] Erik H. Erikson, *(Childhood and Society,* 2nd ed. (New York: W. W. Norton, 1963), as presented in Hall, *Careers in Organizations,* pp. 48–52.

ego identity. Adolescents are much concerned with settling on a particular career or occupational choice. They can become confused by the apparent gaps between what they think they can do and what they think they must do to succeed in a career. The latter years of the adolescent stage usually coincide with initial employment; and if ego identity has not been achieved, one can expect difficulties during this first employment opportunity.

Young Adulthood The years between 25 and 35 ordinarily involve the development of *intimacy and involvement with others*. During this life stage, individuals learn to become involved not only with other persons but also with groups and organizations. The extent to which individuals pass through this phase successfully depends on how successful they were in establishing their ego identities as adolescents. In terms of career stages, young adulthood corresponds with the *establishment* of a career and the initial stages of *advancement*. Conflicts may develop between life stage demands and career stage demands if, for example, the demands of the career stage include behaviors that are inconsistent with the development of relationships with others.

Adulthood The 30 years between 35 and 65 are devoted to *generativity,* a term that implies concern for actions and achievements which will benefit *future generations*. Individuals experiencing this life stage emphasize the productive and creative use of their talents and abilities. In the context of work experience, adulthood involves building organizations, devising new and lasting products, coaching younger people, and teaching others. This life stage coincides with the later years of the advancement career stage and the full duration of the maintenance stage. Successful development of the adulthood stage depends on having achieved ego identity and commitment to others, the developmental tasks of the preceding two stages.

Maturity The last life stage is maturity, and people pass through this stage successfully if they achieve *ego integrity;* that is, they do not despair of their lives and of the choices they have made. In a sense, this stage represents the culmination of a productive and creative life served in the interests of others to the satisfaction of self. This life stage coincides with the retirement career stage.

The relationships between life stages and career stages are shown in Exhibit 14–3. Successful careers are often a result, in part, of achieving certain career stages at certain ages. For example, a study of scientists in two research and development companies attempted to determine the relationship between performance and career stage for those over 40. The results are shown in Exhibit 14–4. In these two companies it is apparent that individuals whose career stages were not in step with their life stages were relatively low performers. Notice that 100 percent of the employees over 40 who were classified at Stage I of their careers were considered to be below-average performers. For whatever reasons, these employees were unable to establish themselves as independent contributors of ideas and thus to move on to Stage II. Perhaps this was because they had been unable to achieve ego identity during the early

EXHIBIT 14–3 The Relationships between Career Stages and Life Stages

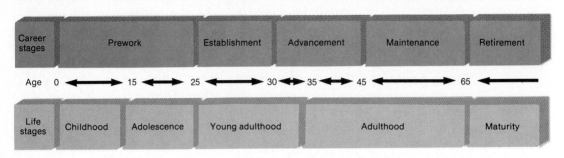

EXHIBIT 14–4 Relationship between Age, Career Stage, and Performance (40 Years or Older)

	Stage I	Stage II	Stage III	Stage IV
Above-average performance	0%	18%	79%	100%
Below-average performance	100	82	21	0

Source: Based on Gene W. Dalton, Paul H. Thompson, and Raymond L. Price, "The Four Stages of Professional Careers—A New Look at Performance by Professionals," *Organizational Dynamics*, Summer 1977, p. 36.

stages of their lives. Managers must recognize the interaction between career stages and life stages in designing effective career development programs.

CAREER CHOICES

Perhaps the most important decision a person makes is what career he or she should pursue. At some point, you will likely make a career decision and ask yourself career questions such as: What do I want to be when I grow up? What are my strengths and weaknesses? Why can't I sell more products?

John L. Holland, a career counseling expert, has proposed and researched a theory of career (vocational) choice.[11] Holland suggests that the choice of a career is an expression of personality and not a random event, though chance can play a role. He also believes that what a person accomplishes and derives from a career depends on the congruence between his or her personality and the job environment.[12]

---

[11] John L. Holland, *Holland's Vocational Preference Inventory* (Palo Alto, Calif.: Consulting Psychologists Press, 1983).

[12] John L. Holland, *Making Vocational Choices: A Theory of Careers* (Englewood Cliffs, N.J.: Prentice-Hall, 1973).

Holland contends that each individual to some extent resembles one of six personality types:

- *Realistic*—This individual prefers activities involving the manipulation of machinery or tools—a machinist.
- *Investigative*—This individual prefers to be analytical, curious, methodical, and precise—a research scientist.
- *Artistic*—This person is expressive, nonconforming, original, and introperspective—an interior decorator.
- *Social*—This person enjoys working with and helping others and purposefully avoids systematic activities involving tools and machinery—a school counselor.
- *Enterprising*—This person enjoys activities that permit him or her to influence others to accomplish goals—a lawyer.
- *Conventional*—This individual enjoys the systematic manipulation of data, filing records, or reproducing materials—an accountant.

The more one resembles any given type, the more likely one is to display some of the behaviors and traits associated with that type.

Holland suggests that, whereas one personality type predominates, individuals use a wide range of strategies for coping with their environment and that many strategies fall within the boundaries of two or more types.[13] Holland has presented a hexagon to illustrate the closeness and distance between the six personality types. Exhibit 14–5 illustrates Holland's hexagon analysis. He has determined by research that the closer two orientations are in the hexagon arrangement, the more similar are the personality types. Therefore, he claims that the adjacent types realistic-investigative, social-enterprising are similar, while realistic-social and artistic-conventional are dissimilar.[14] Using Holland's analysis and logic one would conclude that if a person's predominant and secondary orientations are similar he or she will have a relatively easy time selecting a career. On the other hand, dissimilar orientations (predominant and secondary) may result in difficulty choosing a career.

Various quantitative instruments have been used to assess a person's resemblance to the six personality types.[15] The Vocational Preference Inventory asks a person to indicate the vocations that appeal to him or her from a list of 84 occupational titles (14 titles for each of the six scales). The person's responses are scored and profiled. The higher a person's score on a scale, the greater the resemblance to the type that scale represents.

The Strong Vocational Interest Blank has been used to assess a person's resemblance to each personality type by selecting six Strong scales to represent each type. The Vocational Exploration and Insight Kit (VEIK) is used to

---

[13] John L. Holland, D. C. Darger, and P. G. Power, *My Vocational Situation* (Palo Alto, Calif.: Consulting Psychologists Press, 1980).

[14] Gary Dessler, *Personnel Management* (Reston, Va.: Reston Publishing, 1984), p. 500.

[15] Stephen G. Weinrach, "Determinants of Vocational Choice: Holland's Theory," in *Career Choice and Development,* eds. Ursula Delworth and Gary R. Hanson (San Francisco: Jossey-Bass, 1984), pp. 61–93.

EXHIBIT 14–5   **Choosing an Occupational Orientation**

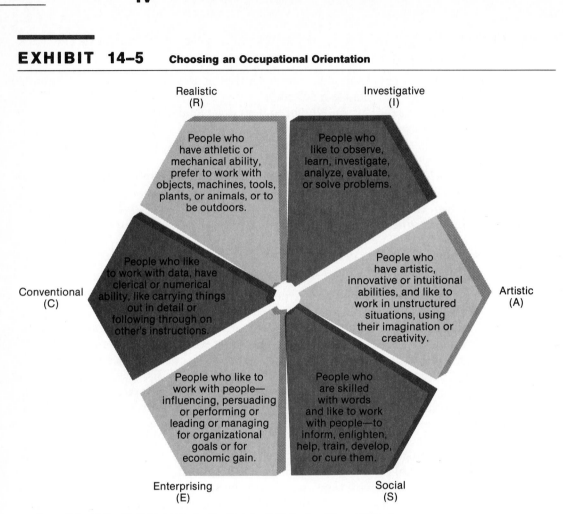

Source: Richard Bolles: *The Quick Job Hunting Map* (Berkeley, Calif.: Ten Speed Press, 1979), p. 5.

help individuals who are concerned about their career future. The VEIK requires each person to sort 84 cards to generate a measure of the interest the individual has in an occupation. The individual is then asked a series of questions about how he or she sorted (ranked) the occupations. The person is also asked to indicate what skills he or she possesses. An action plan for seeking additional information about preferred occupations is worked out.

Examining Your Skills

Determining what skills one has is extremely important in making career choices. Holland's work on career choice suggests that simply preferring one career or occupation over another is not enough. A person must have or be able to develop the skills required to perform the job. A person may have an investigative orientation, but whether he or she has the skills to be a research

EXHIBIT 14–6   The Three Basic Skill Categories

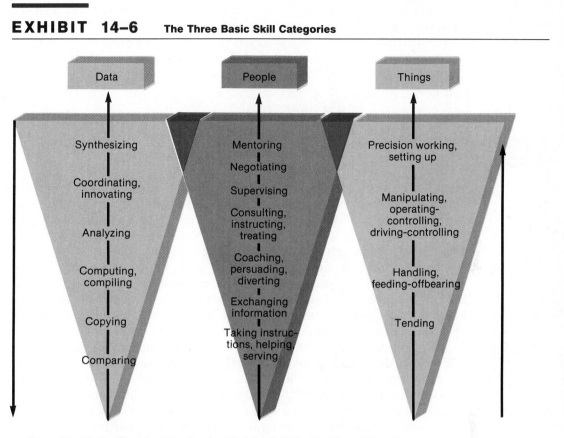

Data	People	Things
Synthesizing	Mentoring	Precision working, setting up
Coordinating, innovating	Negotiating	
	Supervising	Manipulating, operating-controlling, driving-controlling
Analyzing	Consulting, instructing, treating	
Computing, compiling	Coaching, persuading, diverting	Handling, feeding-offbearing
Copying	Exchanging information	Tending
Comparing	Taking instructions, helping, serving	

Source: Richard Bolles, *What Color is Your Parachute?* (Berkeley, Calif.: Ten Speed Press, 1976), p. 73.

scientist, physician, or biologist will play a significant part in which specific occupation is selected.[16]

The *Dictionary of Occupational Titles (DOT),* published by the U.S. Government Printing Office, provides information on the skills required for over 20,000 jobs. As discussed in Chapter 4, the DOT illustrates skills in three areas—data, people, and things. Exhibit 14–6 presents the three basic skill categories in a hierarchical form. For example, under people skills, taking instruction, helping, and serving is a low-key skill, while mentoring is the highest skill level.

Using the skill categories shown in Exhibit 14–6, identify which skills you enjoy and can use effectively. This self-assessment will initiate some consideration of the skills you possess or think can be developed. Now go back to the Holland hexagon in Exhibit 14–5 and determine where your preferred style is. This is not a scientific assessment, since Holland's Vocational Preference Inventory or VEIK would provide a more precise view.

---

[16] Donald E. Super, "Assessment in Career Guidance: Toward Truly Developmental Counseling," *Personnel and Guidance Journal,* May 1983, pp. 555–62.

By weighing your skills and your personality orientation, you are creating a better understanding of career choices and career compatibility. However, this is often not enough to ensure a successful career and more and more organizations are playing a significant role in helping employees reach their potential. As a result, more P/HRM resources are being devoted to career development programs.

CAREER DEVELOPMENT: A COMMITMENT

When an organization understands the importance of career development, it typically offers numerous opportunities to employees.[17] These opportunities can involve simply a tuition reimbursement program or a detailed counseling service for developing individual career path plans. An example of the type of career development programs available in various organizations and industries is presented in Exhibit 14–7.

The programs presented in Exhibit 14–7 are most valuable when they are: (1) regularly offered; (2) open for all employees; (3) modified when evaluation indicates that change is necessary. The overall objective of these programs is to match employee needs and goals with current or future career opportunities in the organization. Thus, a well-designed career development effort will assist employees in determining their own career needs, develop and publicize available career opportunities in the organization, and match employee needs and goals with the organization. This commitment to career development can delay the obsolescence of human resources that is so costly to an organization.

At Owens-Illinois, Inc., for example, a formal career opportunity program is used. It is the firm's policy to promote persons from within the company whenever possible. The career opportunity program provides several services to employees:

1. It makes available a broad range of information about available jobs and the qualifications needed to fill them.
2. It provides a system through which qualified employees may apply for these positions.
3. It helps employees establish career goals.
4. It encourages a meaningful dialogue between employees and supervisors about the employees' career goals.

Exhibit 14–8 presents one of the career opportunity response forms that is completed by employees and managerial personnel. The supervisor who makes the hiring decision explains why he or she made the decision that was reached. No matter who is selected for the job, the form is returned to the employee who submitted it for consideration.

Dow Jones & Company, Inc. publishes *The Wall Street Journal* and *Bar-*

---

[17] Manuel London and Stephen A. Stumpf, *Managing Careers* (Reading, Mass.: Addison-Wesley Publishing, 1982), p. 4.

EXHIBIT 14–7   Career Development Programs

Career counseling:
  Career counseling during the employment interview
  Career counseling during the performance appraisal session
  Psychological assessment and career alternative planning
  Career counseling as part of the day-to-day supervisor/subordinate relationship
  Special career counseling for high-potential employees
  Counseling for downward transfers

Career pathing:
  Planned job progression for new employees
  Career pathing to help managers acquire the necessary experience for future jobs
  Committee performs an annual review of management personnel's strengths and
    weaknesses and then develops a five-year career plan for each
  Plan job moves for high-potential employees to place them in a particular target job
  Rotate first-level supervisors through various departments to prepare them for upper
    management positions

Human resources:
  Computerized inventory of backgrounds and skills to help identify replacements
  Succession planning or replacement charts at all levels of management

Career information systems:
  Job posting for all nonofficer positions; individual can bid to be considered
  Job posting for hourly employees and career counseling for salaried employees

Management or supervisory development:
  Special program for those moving from hourly employment to management
  Responsibility of the department head to develop managers
  Management development committee to look after the career development of man-
    agement groups
  In-house advanced management program

Training:
  In-house supervisory training
  Technical skills training for lower levels
  Outside management seminars
  Formalized job rotation programs
  Intern programs
  Responsibility of manager for on-the-job training
  Tuition reimbursement program

Special groups:
  Outplacement programs
  Minority indoctrination training program
  Career management seminar for women
  Preretirement counseling
  Career counseling and job rotation for women and minorities
  Refresher courses for midcareer managers
  Presupervisory training program for women and minorities

EXHIBIT 14–8   Career Opportunity Response Form—Owens-Illinois

Form 5287-R6

Owens-Illinois Career Opportunity Program Response Form

Section 1

Name		Soc. Sec. No.		Home Phone	O-I Ext.	O-I Mail Location
Present Job Title		Div.	Department			☐ Hourly ☐ Salary
Present Supervisor			Supervisor's Signature *			
Is your supervisor aware that you have responded to this Career Opportunity Program? ☐ Yes ☐ No					Number of months on current position	

Job You Are Responding to

Job Title	Div.	Department	Rate Group/Points	Location
Divisional Personnel Coordinator	Posting Dates	HRS Requisition No.	Date Form Completed	

To Apply

1. Compare your experience, education, and skills against the selection criteria stated on the posting.

2. Complete Sections 1 and 2 of this form and the Career Summary Form and forward to
Career Opportunity Program – 2, OIB, Human Resource Systems.

3. Please do not keep any pages of this form. A copy of this form will be returned to you by the Divisional Personnel Coordinator.

* Supervisor Approval

4. Your supervisor must approve your responding to a job under the following policies:

- Non-exempt and hourly —
  if you have been on the job less than 12 months.

- Exempt through 129 points —
  if you have been on the job less than 18 months.

- Greater than 130 points —
  if you have been on the job less than 24 months.

- All personnel responding —
  before you may receive an interview.

Human Resource Use Only

Date Received

(**White** and **Canary** copies – Return to Employee, **Pink** copy – Retained by Division)

EXHIBIT 14–8 *(concluded)*

Form 5287-R6

Owens-Illinois Career Opportunity Program Response Form

Section 1

Name	Soc. Sec. No.		Home Phone	O-I Ext.	O-I Mail Location
Present Job Title	Div.	Department			☐ Hourly ☐ Salary
Present Supervisor		Supervisor's Signature			
Is your supervisor aware that you have responded to this Career Opportunity Program? ☐ Yes ☐ No				Number of months on current position	

Job You Are Responding to

Job Title	Div.	Department	Rate Group/Points	Location
Divisional Personnel Coordinator	Posting Dates	HRS Requisition No.	Date Form Completed	

Section 2

Candidate
State how your qualifications meet posted criteria

Section 3

Divisional Personnel Coordinator
1. Review all responses.   2. Turn down, interview or forward files to Selecting Supervisor.
3. If turned down, state reason why candidate is **not** being considered further and return Response Form and Career Summary Form to candidate.

Section 4

Selecting Supervisor
1. Review all responses.
2. If no further consideration is given, indicate reason why and return Response Form and Career Summary Form to Division Personnel Coordinator.
3. If you wish to interview, schedule interviews through your Division Personnel Coordinator.
4. If candidate is not offered position after the interview, state reason and return Response and Career Summary Forms to Div. Personnel Coordinator.

Date	Signed

Section 5

Divisional Personnel Coordinator
1. Complete Referral Summary Form indicating status of candidates and return form to HR Systems.
2. Return Response and Career Summary Forms to candidate.

Date	Signed

(White and **Canary** copies – Return to Employee, **Pink** copy – Retained by Division)

ron's. Until the past few years the company had no formal career development program for its approximately 4,500 employees. Now Dow Jones has a formal career development program that employees like Kevin Letz appreciate.[18] Kevin was a nighttime delivery driver for *The Wall Street Journal* in Naperville, Illinois. He worked in that capacity for five years while earning college credits during the day. He finally received an M.B.A. and a C.P.A. certificate. He informed his boss that he wanted to enter the firm's new "Druthers" program. It is called this since it suggests that the person would "druther" be working elsewhere in the firm.

Kevin was able to present his educational records and skills as indicators of his interest to move from the position of driver to accountant. He was chosen to fill an accountant position in the firm's South Brunswick, New Jersey office.

The Druther's program requires that employees show the initiative needed to make a job change. Qualified candidates for openings are interviewed. These current managers are asked questions about performance, attendance, and potential. In the past few years, 411 interdepartmental druthers requests have been submitted. The company has placed 131 employees in new positions, and another 61 employees are under consideration for appropriate vacancies as they arise.

Three points in the careers of individuals are particularly crucial for career development. The *recent hiree* begins his or her career with a particular job and position. Experiences on this first job can have considerable positive and negative effects on future performance. The *midcareer* person is subject to pressures and responsibilities different from those of the recent hiree, but he or she is also at a critical point. The *preretirement* person is uncertain and anxious about the future. The following sections describe some career development problems of recent hirees, midcareer managers, and preretirement employees.

CAREER DEVELOPMENT FOR RECENT HIREES

Recently hired employees face many anxious moments. They have selected their positions on the basis of expectations regarding the demands that the organization will make of them and what they will receive in exchange for meeting those demands.[19] Young managers, particularly those with college training, expect opportunities to utilize their training in ways that lead to recognition and advancement. In too many instances, recently hired managers are soon disappointed with their initial career decisions. Although the specific causes of early career disappointments vary from person to person, some general causes have been identified.

---

[18] Richard K. Broszeit, "If I Had My Druthers . . . A Career Development Program," *Personnel Journal,* October 1986, pp. 84–90.

[19] Arnon E. Reichers, "An Interactionist Perspective on Newcomer Socialization Rates," *Academy of Management Review,* April 1987, pp. 278–89.

Causes of Early Career Difficulties

Studies of the early career problems of young managers typically find that those who experience frustration are victims of "reality shock." These young managers perceive a mismatch between what they thought the organization was and what it actually is. Several factors contribute to reality shock, and it is important for young managers and their managers to be aware of them.

The Initial Job Challenge The first jobs of young managers often demand far less of them than they are capable of delivering. Consequently, young managers believe that they are unable to demonstrate their full capabilities and that in a sense they are being stifled. This particular cause is especially damaging if the recruiter has been overly enthusiastic in "selling" the organization to the managers when they were recruited.

Some young managers are able to *create* challenging jobs even when their assignments are fairly routine. They do this by thinking of ways to do their jobs differently and better. They may also be able to persuade their managers to give them more leeway and more to do. Unfortunately, many young managers are unable to create challenge. Their previous experiences in school were typically experiences in which challenge has been given to them by their teachers. The challenge has been created for them, not by them.

Initial Job Satisfaction Recently hired managers with college training often believe they can perform at levels beyond those of their initial assignments. After all, they have been exposed to the latest managerial theories and techniques, and in their minds at least, they are ready to run the company. Disappointment and dissatisfaction are the sure outcomes, however, when they discover that their self-evaluations are not shared by others in the organization. The consequences of unrealistic aspirations and routine initial assignments are low job satisfaction, in particular, and low satisfaction of growth and self-actualization needs, in general.

Initial Job Performance Evaluation Feedback on performance is an important managerial responsibility. Yet many managers are inadequately trained to meet this responsibility. They simply do not know how to evaluate the performance of their subordinates. This management deficiency is especially damaging to new managers. They have not been in the organization long enough to be socialized by their peers and other employees. They are not yet sure of what they are expected to believe, what values to hold, or what behaviors are expected of them. They naturally look to their own managers to guide them through this early phase. But when their managers fail to evaluate their performance accurately, they remain ignorant and confused as to whether they are achieving what the organization expects of them.

Not all young managers experience problems associated with their initial assignments. But those who do and who leave the organization as a consequence of their frustrations represent a waste of talent and money. One estimate placed the cost of replacing a manager (including recruiting costs, training expenses, and subpar performance during the early phases) at

$50,000 in the first year alone.[20] Thus, the cost of losing capable young managers outweighs the cost of efforts and programs designed to counteract initial job problems.

Programs and Practices to Counteract Early Career Problems

Managers who wish to improve the retention and development of young management talent have several alternatives.

Realistic Job Previews One way to counteract the unrealistic expectations of new recruits is to provide realistic information during the recruiting process. As was discussed in Chapter 6, this practice is based on the idea that a recruit should know both the bad and the good things to expect from a job and the organization. Through *realistic job previews* (RJPs), recruits are given opportunities to learn not only the benefits that they may expect, but also the drawbacks. Studies have shown that the recruitment rate is the same for those who receive RJPs as for those who do not.[21] More importantly, those who receive RJPs are more likely to remain on the job and to be satisfied with it than are those who have been selected without using realistic job previews. The practice of "telling it like it is" is used by a number of organizations, including the Prudential Insurance Company, Texas Instruments, and the U.S. Military Academy.

A Challenging Initial Assignment Managers of newly hired people should be encouraged to slot them into the most demanding of the available jobs. Successful implementation of this policy requires managers to take some risks, because managers are accountable for the performance of their subordinates. If the assignments are too far beyond the ability of the subordinates, both the managers and the subordinates share the cost of failure. Thus, most managers prefer to bring their subordinates along slowly by giving them progressively more difficult and challenging jobs, but only *after the subordinates have demonstrated their ability*. Newly hired managers have *potential for performance,* but have not *demonstrated performance*. Thus, it is risky to assign an individual to a task for which there is a high probability of failure. But studies have indicated that managers who experienced initial job challenge were more effective in their later years.[22]

An Enriched Initial Assignment Job enrichment is an established practice for motivating employees with strong growth and achievement needs. If the

---

[20] What Does It Cost to Train New People?" *Training/HRD,* March 1981, p. 16.

[21] John P. Wanous, *Organizational Entry* (Reading, Mass.: Addison-Wesley Publishing, 1980), pp. 51–79.

[22] Hall, *Careers in Organizations,* p. 67.

nature of the job to be assigned is not intrinsically challenging, the newly hired manager's manager can enrich the assignment. The usual ways to enrich a job include giving the new manager more authority and responsibility, permitting the new manager to interact directly with customers and clients, and enabling the new manager to implement his or her own ideas (rather than merely recommending them to the boss).

Demanding Bosses A practice that seems to have considerable promise for increasing the retention rate of young managers is to assign them initially to demanding supervisors. In this context, "demanding" should not be interpreted as "autocratic." Rather, the type of boss most likely to get new hirees off in the right direction is one who has high but achievable expectations for their performance. Such a boss instills in the young managers the understanding that high performance is expected and rewarded and, equally important, that the boss is always ready to assist them through coaching and counseling.

The programs and practices that are intended to retain and develop young managers—particularly recent hirees with college training—can be used separately or in combination. In all cases, a manager should seek to establish policies that would retain those recent hirees who have the highest potential to perform effectively. Although such practices are not perfect, they are helpful not only in retaining young managers, but also in avoiding the problems that can arise during the middle phase of a manager's career.

CAREER DEVELOPMENT FOR MIDCAREER MANAGERS

Managers in the midstages of their careers are ordinarily "key people" in their organizations. They have established a place for themselves in society, as well as at work. They occupy important positions in the community, often engage in civic affairs, and are looked upon as model achievers in our achievement-oriented culture. Yet popular and scholarly articles and books appear yearly that discuss the "midcareer crisis" and the "middle-aged dropout" and "midlife transition." These kinds of pressures cause executives to disappear from their jobs, drink heavily, or, at worst, to drop out totally. A person at midcareer is attempting to deal with the job, bodily decline, the realization of mortality, and aging. Such lost talent is expensive to replace, and more and more organizations are initiating practices to deal with the problems of the midcareer manager.

The Midcareer Plateau

Managers face the midcareer plateau during the adult stage of life and the maintenance phase of careers. At this point the likelihood of additional upward promotion is usually quite low. Two reasons account for the plateau. First, there are simply fewer jobs at the top of the organization, and even though the manager has the ability to perform at that level, no opening exists. Second, openings may exist, but the manager may lack either the *ability* or the *desire* to fill them.[23]

Managers who find themselves stifled in their present jobs tend to cope with the problems in fairly consistent ways. They suffer from depression, poor health, and fear and hostility toward their subordinates. Eventually they "retire" on the job or leave the organization physically and permanently. Any one of these ways of coping results in lowered job performance and, of course, lowered organizational performance.[24]

The midcareer, middle-aged crisis has been depicted in novels, movies, dramas, and psychological studies. Although each individual's story is different and unique, the scenario has many common features. Each story and research indicates that the midcareer crisis is real and has psychological and often physical effects that can become dangerous if not properly handled. Jim Lucio, for example, has insomnia, loss of appetite, and is on edge because of his midcareer crisis.

Of course, not all managers respond to their situations in the same ways. Some, perhaps most, cope constructively. A few examples of some individuals who coped effectively are the following:

- John W. Culligan, 70, currently chairperson of the executive committee at American Home Products, was 64 and had been a fixture in the company for 42 years, when he was promoted.
- Thomas S. Derek retired from a 30-year career as a life insurance agent and decided to start the Ugly Duckling Rent-A-Car agency in Tucson. Today he is 74 and owns a business that has 600 outlets and gross annual rentals of $84.5 million.
- Joyce Fox got her first job at 41 and is now a senior vice president in charge of international loans at American Express Bank.

There are many other stories of individuals who just play along and seem to be plateaued or never recognized.[25] However, some event or person triggers a series of changes and opportunities. John Culligan waited patiently after reaching a plateau; Thomas Derek changed careers; Joyce Fox decided that her age was not a detriment and entered the labor force exuding confidence, wisdom, and maturity. Each of these individuals used their own tailor-made career plateau coping strategy.

Programs and Practices to Counteract Midcareer Problems

Counteracting the problems that managers face at midcareer involves providing *counseling* and *alternatives*.

---

[23] Thomas P. Ference, James A. F. Stoner, and E. Kirby Warren, "Managing the Career Plateau," *Academy of Management Review,* October 1977, p. 604.

[24] C. V. Entrekin and J. G. Everett, "Age and Midcareer Crisis: An Empirical Study of Academics," *Journal of Vocational Behavior,* August 1981, pp. 84–97.

[25] Faye Rice "Lessons from Late Bloomers," *Fortune,* August 31, 1987, pp. 87–91.

Midcareer Counseling Organizations such as DuPont, Alcoa, and Western Electric employ full-time staff psychiatrists to assist employees in dealing with career, health, and family problems.[26] In the context of such counseling, midcareer managers are provided with professional help in dealing with the depression and stress they may experience. Since midcareer managers are usually well-educated and articulate, they often only need someone to talk to, someone skilled in the art of listening. The process of verbalizing their problems to an objective listener is often enough to enable midcareer managers to recognize their problems and to cope with them constructively.

Midcareer Alternatives Effective resolution of the problems of midcareer crises requires the existence of acceptable alternatives. The organization cannot be expected to go beyond counseling on personal and family problems. But when the crisis is precipitated primarily by career-related factors, the organization can be an important source of alternatives. In many instances, the organization simply needs to accept career moves that are usually viewed as unacceptable. Three career moves that have potential for counteracting the problems of midcareer managers are lateral transfers, downward transfers, and fallback positions.[27]

Lateral transfers involve moves at the same organizational level from one department to another. A manager who has plateaued in production could be transferred to a similar level in sales, engineering, or some other area. The move would require the manager to learn quickly the technical demands of the new position, and there would be a period of reduced performance as this learning occurred. But, once qualified, the manager would bring the perspectives of both areas to bear on decisions.

Downward transfers are associated in our society with failure; an effective manager simply does not consider a move downward to be a respectable alternative. Yet downward transfers are, in many instances, not only respectable alternatives, but entirely acceptable alternatives, particularly when one or more of the following conditions exist:

The manager values the quality of life afforded by a specific geographic area and may desire a downward transfer if required in order to stay in or move to that area.

The manager views the downward transfer as a way to establish a base for future promotions.

The manager is faced with the alternatives of dismissal or a downward move.

The manager desires to pursue autonomy and self-actualization in nonjob related activities—such as religious, civic, or political activities—and for that reason may welcome the reduced responsibility (and demands) of a lower-level position.

---

[26] Manfred F. R. Kets de Vries, "The Midcareer Conundrum," *Organizational Dynamics*, Autumn 1978, p. 58.

[27] Douglas T. Hall and Francine S. Hall, "What's New in Career Management," *Organization Dynamics*, Summer 1976, pp. 21–27.

The use of *fallback positions* is a relatively new way to reduce the risk of lateral and downward transfers. The practice involves identifying in advance a position to which the transferred manager can return if the new position does not work out. By identifying the fallback position in advance, the organization informs everyone who is affected that some risk is involved but that the organization is willing to accept some of the responsibility for it and that returning to the fallback job will not be viewed as "failure." Companies such as Heublein, Procter & Gamble, Continental Can, and Lehman Brothers have used fallback positions to remove some of the risk of lateral and upward moves. The practice appears to have considerable promise for protecting the careers of highly specialized technicians and professionals who make their first move into general management positions.

The suggestion that organizations initiate practices and programs to assist managers through midcareer crises does not excuse managers from taking responsibility for themselves. Individuals who deal honestly and construc- tively with their lives and careers will early on take steps to minimize the risk of becoming *obsolete* or redundant. At the outset of their management careers, they can begin to formulate their *career plans and paths*. Often they will be assisted in this process by the organization which employs them.

CAREER DEVELOPMENT FOR PRERETIREMENT

The extension of mandatory retirement to age 70 was signed into U.S. law in April 1978. It has given rise to the reference of the "graying of America." The impact of this legislation on career planning and development can be signifi- cant. Will people still want to retire at an earlier age than 70? What is the organization's responsibility in preparing employees for retirement? Will dis- satisfied workers and those with good pension plans retire early?

Too many organizations are ill-prepared to deal with the effects of the legislation, have few programs that cope with the preretirement employee, and are unable to answer the questions raised above.[28] Management needs to consider in much more depth the following issues:

- When do employees plan to retire?
- Who is attracted to early retirement?
- What do employees plan to do during retirement? Can the organization help them prepare for these activities?
- Do retirees plan a second career? Can the organization assist in this prepara- tion?
- Which retirees can still be consulted by the organization to help new employ- ees?

---

[28] Sydney P. Freedberg, "Forced Exits? Companies Confront Wave of Age-Discrimination Suits," *The Wall Street Journal*, Oct. 13, 1987.

Programs and Practices to Minimize
Retirement Adjustment Problems

These and other similar questions can be addressed through counseling and education programs for preretirees. Retirement is feared by some and anticipated by others. Counseling and education programs can make the transition from being employed to retirement much smoother.

In most cases the retired person must learn to accept a reduced role, to manage a less-structured life, and to make new accommodations to family and community. Educational workshops and seminars and counseling sessions are invaluable for the preretirement person to make the transition from work to retirement. These activities can be initiated by P/HRM departments.

IBM is one organization that has attempted to aid in this transition by offering tuition rebates for courses on any topic within three years of retirement. Many IBM preretirees have taken advantage of this program to prepare for second careers (learning new skills, professions, and small business management).[29]

Those P/HRM departments that are truly dedicated to the development of human resources will become more involved with the preretiree's problems, fears, and uncertainties in the 1990s. Perhaps a new measure of concern for human resources will be the degree of organizational commitment in the form of preretirement preparation for those who have devoted their careers.

CAREER PLANNING AND PATHING

Many of us sit and think about where we will be in 10 years careerwise. We also wonder how we are going to get there. This is a form of career thinking that can be brought into sharper focus by career planning.[30] Individuals and organizations are beginning to learn how important career planning is from a motivational perspective.

The practice of organizational *career planning* involves matching an individual's career aspirations with the opportunities available in an organization. *Career pathing* is the sequencing of the specific jobs that are associated with those opportunities. The two processes are intertwined. Planning a career involves the identification of the means for achieving desired ends; and in the context of career plans, career paths are the means for achieving goals. Although career planning is not entirely new—as early as 1920, General Electric and Western Electric had such programs—many organizations are just now beginning to use it as a way to proact rather than react to the problems associated with early career and midcareer crises.[31]

---

[29] Jeffrey Sonnenfeld, "Dealing with the Aging Work Force," *Harvard Business Review*, November/December 1978, pp. 81–92.

[30] Walter Kiechel III, "The Neglected Art of Career Planning," *Fortune*, June 27, 1983, pp. 153–55.

[31] Linda Brooks, "Career Planning Programs in the Workplace," in *Career Choice and Development*, ed. Ursula Delworth and Gary Hanson (San Francisco: Jossey-Bass, 1984), pp. 388–405.

EXHIBIT 14–9   **A Career Planning Process**

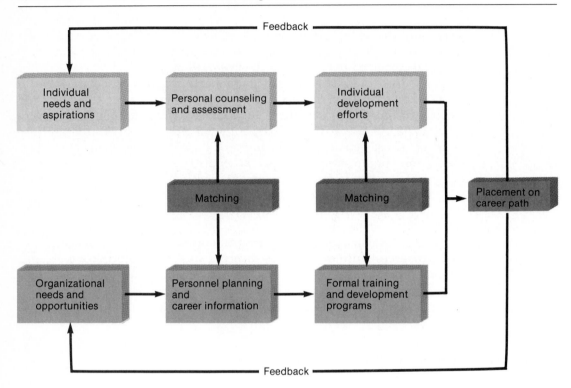

Source: Based on John C. Alpin and Darlene K. Gerster, "Career Development: An Integration of Individual and Organizational Needs," *Personnel*, March–April 1978, p. 25.

The career planning and career pathing process is depicted in Exhibit 14–9. Its successful employment places equal responsibility on the individual and the organization. The individual must identify his or her aspirations and abilities and, through counseling, recognize what training and development are required for a particular career path. The organization must identify its needs and opportunities and, through work force planning, provide the necessary career information and training to its employees. Such companies as Weyerhaeuser, Nabisco, Gulf Oil, Exxon, and Eaton use career development programs to identify a broad pool of talent available for promotion and transfer opportunities. Companies often restrict career counseling to managerial and professional staff, but IBM, GE, and TRW provide career counseling for both blue-collar and managerial personnel.

Career Planning

Individual and organizational needs and opportunities can be matched in a variety of ways. According to a recent American Management Association

(AMA) survey, the most widely used approaches are (1) informal counseling by the personnel staff and (2) career counseling by supervisors. These approaches are often quite informal. Somewhat more formal and less-widely, although increasingly, used practices involve workshops, seminars, and self-assessment centers.

Informal Counseling The P/HRM staffs of organizations often include counseling services for employees who wish to assess their abilities and interests. The counseling process can also move into personal concerns; and this is proper, since, as we have already seen, life concerns are important factors in determining career aspirations. In this context, career counseling is viewed by the organization as a service to its employees, but not as a primary service.

Career counseling by supervisors is usually included in performance evaluations. The question of where the employee is going in the organization arises quite naturally in this setting. In fact, the inclusion of career information in performance appraisal has created the current interest in career planning. A characteristic of effective performance evaluation is to let the employee know not only how well he or she has done, but also what the future holds. Thus, supervisors must be able to counsel the employee in terms of organizational needs and opportunities not only within the specific department, but throughout the organization. Since supervisors usually have limited information about the total organization, it is often necessary to adopt more formal and systematic counseling approaches.

Formal Counseling Workshops, assessment centers, and career development centers are being used increasingly in organizations. Typically, such formal practices are designed to serve specific employee groups. Management trainees and "high-potential" or "fast-track" management candidates have received most of the attention to date. However, women employees and minority employees have been given increased attention. Career development programs for women and minority employees are viewed as indications of an organization's commitment to affirmative action.

One example of a formal organizational career planning system is Syntex Corporation's Career Development Center. The center was the result of the realization that the managers in Syntex were unable to counsel their subordinates because they (the managers) were too caught up in their own jobs. The center's staff first identifies the individual's strengths and weaknesses in eight skill areas that Syntex believes to be related to effective management. These eight areas are: (1) problem analysis; (2) communication; (3) goal setting; (4) decision making and conflict handling; (5) selecting, training, and motivating employees; (6) controlling employees; (7) interpersonal competence; and (8) the use of time. On the basis of scores in the eight areas, each manager sets career and personal goals. The center's staff assists the manager to set realistic goals that reflect his or her strengths and weaknesses in the eight areas.

The highlight of each manager's career planning effort is attendance at a weeklong seminar. Usually attended by 24 managers at a time, the seminar places each participant into simulated management situations that require applications of the eight skill areas. Subsequently, each candidate reviews his or her own career plan, a plan that includes career goals, timetables, and required personal development. The purpose of the seminar is to encourage realistic self-appraisal. Following the seminar, participants meet with their immediate supervisors to set up their career development plans.

Organizations can use a variety of practices to facilitate their employees' career plans. One of the oldest and most widely used practices is some form of *tuition aid program*. Employees can take advantage of educational and training opportunities available at nearby schools, and the organization pays some or all of the tuition. J. I. Case, a Tenneco company with corporate offices in Racine, Wisconsin, is but one of many organizations that provide in-house courses and seminars as well as tuition reimbursement for courses related to the individual's job.

Another practice is *job posting*; that is, the organization publicizes job openings as they occur. The employees are thus made aware of the opportunities. Effective job posting requires more than simply placing a notice on the company bulletin board. At a minimum, job posting should meet the following conditions:

1. It should include promotions and transfers, as well as permanent vacancies.
2. The available jobs should be posted at least three to six weeks prior to external recruiting.
3. The eligibility rules should be explicit and straightforward.
4. The standards for selection and the bidding instructions should be stated clearly.
5. Vacationing employees should be given the opportunity to apply ahead of time.
6. Employees who apply but are rejected should be notified of the reason in writing, and a record of the reason should be placed in their personnel files.[32]

Whatever approach is used, the crucial measure of its success will be the extent to which *individual and organizational* needs are satisfied.

Career Pathing

The result of career planning is the placement of an individual into a job that is the first of a sequential series of jobs. From the perspective of the organization, career paths are important inputs into work force planning. An organization's future work force depends on the projected passage of individuals through the ranks. From the perspective of the individual a career path is the sequence of jobs that he or she desires to undertake in order to achieve personal and career

---

[32] David R. Dahl and Patrick R. Pinto, "Job Posting: An Industry Survey," *Personnel Journal,* January 1977, pp. 40–42.

goals. Although it is virtually impossible to completely integrate the organizational and individual needs in the design of career paths, systematic career planning has the potential for closing the gap between the needs of the individual and the needs of the organization.[33]

Traditional career paths have emphasized upward mobility in a single occupation or functional area. When recruiting personnel, the organization's representative will speak of engineers', accountants', or salespersons' career paths. In these contexts, the recruiter will describe the different jobs that typical individuals will hold as they work progressively upward in an organization. Each job, or "rung," is reached when the individual has accumulated the necessary experience and ability and has demonstrated that he or she is "ready" for promotion. Implicit in such career paths is the attitude that failure has occurred whenever an individual does not move on up after a certain amount of time has elapsed. Such attitudes make it difficult to use lateral and downward transfers as alternatives for managers who no longer wish to pay the price of upward promotion.

An alternative to traditional career pathing is to base career paths on real-world experiences and individualized preferences. Paths of this kind would have several characteristics:

1. They would include lateral and downward possibilities, as well as upward possibilities, and they would not be tied to "normal" rates of progress.
2. They would be tentative and responsive to changes in organizational needs.
3. They would be flexible enough to take into account the qualities of individuals.
4. Each job along the paths would be specified in terms of *acquirable* skills, knowledge, and other specific attributes, not merely in terms of educational credentials, age, or work experience.[34]

Realistic career paths, rather than traditional ones, are necessary for effective employee counseling. In the absence of such information, the employee can only guess at what is available.

An example of a career path for general management in a telephone company is depicted in Exhibit 14–10. According to the path, the average duration of a manager's assignment in first-level management is 4 years—$2\frac{1}{2}$ years as a staff assistant in the home office and $1\frac{1}{2}$ years as the manager of a district office in a small city. By the 14th year, the average manager should have reached the fourth level of management. The assignment at this level might be that of division manager of Commercial Sales and Operations Division. Obviously not all managers reach the fifth level, much less the seventh (president). As one nears the top of the organization, the number of openings declines and the number of candidates increases.

---

[33] John D. Gridley, "Who Will Be Where When?", *Personnel Journal*, May 1986, pp. 50–58.

[34] James W. Walker, "Let's Get Realistic about Career Paths," *Human Resource Management*, Fall 1976, pp. 2–7.

EXHIBIT 14–10   **Career Path, General Management in a Telephone Company**

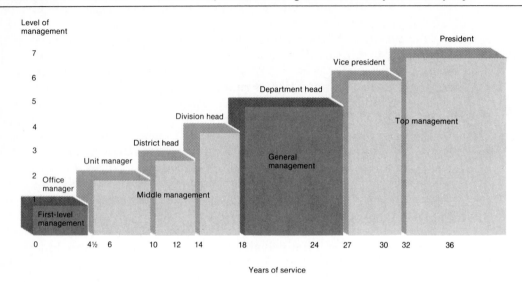

Years of service

CAREER DEVELOPMENT PROBLEMS AND ISSUES

Organizations that undertake career development programs are certain to encounter some difficult issues along the way.[35] The following problems are based on the actual experiences of some organizations.

Integrating Career Development and Work Force Planning

The relationship between career development and work force planning is obvious. Career development provides a *supply* of talents and abilities; work force planning projects the *demand* for talents and abilities. It would seem that organizations that undertake one of these activities would undertake the other. Surely it makes little sense to develop people and then have no place to put them; or to project needs for people, but have no program to supply them. In fact, some organizations do have one or the other but not both.

Even companies that make use of both career development programs and work force planning have difficulty in integrating the efforts of the two. One reason is that each is done by different specialists. Career development is often done by psychologists, and work force planning is the job of economists and systems analysts. Practitioners of these two disciplines have difficulty in

---

[35] This section is based on Hall and Hall, "What's New in Career Management," pp. 27–30.

communicating with each other. Their training and backgrounds create promotional barriers to effective communication.

A second reason for failure to integrate the efforts of career development and work force planning is related to the *organization structure*. Career development is usually the function of *personnel departments*. Work force planning is the function of *planning staffs*. The two activities are carried out in two organizationally distinct units. The manager who is responsible for both units may be the chief executive officer or a group executive.

Managing Dual Careers

As more and more women enter the working world and pursue careers, managers will increasingly confront the problems of *dual careers*. The problem arises because the careers of husbands and wives may lead them in different directions. There may be problems because each person works different shifts, one at night and one during the day.[36] There are a growing number of dual-career couples working on the same job as police officers, firefighters, machinists, and even managers.[37]

A more obvious problem can arise when the organization offers the husband or wife a transfer (involving a promotion) but is rejected because the required relocation is incompatible with the spouse's career plans. One study reports that one in three executives cannot, or will not, relocate because this would interfere with the career of the spouse.[38] Thus, organizations *and* individuals lose flexibility as a consequence of dual careers.

The incidence of dual careers will probably rise as more women enter the labor force. At present, more than 53 million employed men and women are two-career couples. There is no reason to believe that the number will decrease with time; in fact, the reasonable assumption to make is that both the number and the proportion of dual-career couples will increase.[39] The problems associated with this phenomenon are relatively new, but those who have studied these problems offer the following advice:

1. An organization should conduct an employee survey that gathers statistics and information regarding the incidence of dual careers in its *present* and *projected* work force. The survey should determine (*a*) how many employees are at present part of a two-career situation, (*b*) how many people interviewed for positions are part of a dual-career situation, (*c*) where and at what level in the organization the dual-career employees are, (*d*) what conflicts these employees now have, and (*e*) whether dual-career employees perceive company policy and practices to be helpful to their careers and careers of their spouses.

---

[36] Joanne S. Lublin, "Couples Working Different Shifts Take on New Duties and Pressures," *The Wall Street Journal,* March 8, 1984, p. 27.

[37] Glenn Slay, "Spouses in Blue," *Houston Chronicle,* November 15, 1987, pp. 1 and 13.

[38] Francine S. Hall and Douglas T. Hall, "Dual Careers—How Do Couples and Companies Cope with the Problem?" *Organizational Dynamics,* Spring 1978, p. 58.

[39] "A Job for the Trading Spouse; Too," *Business Week,* November 16, 1987, p. 239.

P/HRM Manager Close-Up

Adrianne H. Geiger
Owens-Illinois, Inc.

Biography

Adrianne H. Geiger is manager, human resource systems (HRS), for Owens-Illinois, Inc., Toledo, Ohio. She was graduated from Ohio State University with a B.A. in premedicine. While rearing a family of four and working part-time as a professional musician, she returned for graduate work. She holds an M.B.A. and a Ph.D. in organization development from the University of Southern California's School of Public Administration.

Dr. Geiger held faculty positions at several universities and was a private consultant in organizational effectiveness in California before going into industry in 1979. She joined Owens-Illinois as an organization development specialist, working in the manufacturing plants for several divisions of the company. She was also involved in the writing of programs for training middle management and supervisory skills training.

Job Description

As manager, HRS, Adrianne Geiger is responsible for management progression and succession planning systems, including forecasting, work force planning and career pathing. Additional responsibilities include improvement of career opportunity programs such as job posting and search activities and the performance appraisal systems. She also administers a wide variety of management development programs for high-level managers.

Views about the Changing Role of Personnel in the 1980s—Adrianne H. Geiger

The technical skills required to be a personnel professional have changed drastically over the past decade. The standard industrial relations specialist who traditionally negotiated the labor contracts and, therefore, rose to become head of the personnel department, has

(continued)

been replaced by the human resource specialist. A good grounding in psychology, human motivation, group dynamics, and organization development are essential to the personnel professional of the 1980s.

The next technical requirement will be mastery of computerized personnel information systems that enhance the ability of personnel professionals to better manage a company's people resources. The demographics of the 1980s and people's changing work values contribute to make employee demands ever present. They wish to know (1) how they're doing against standards of the job, (2) what their next career step will be, and (3) what their chances are of getting there. Employees want to be a part of the decision making—on the job, about the job, and for choices around the next job. All of this is difficult to do in large, complex organizations unless the computer keeps track of job performance, growth potential and career interests for you, the personnel professional. Human resource planning will be a necessity for all well-managed companies into the next century. It will affect bottom-line profits and productivity. The personnel professional will find the challenge an exciting one, but also one that mandates constant learning and updating of skills.

2. Recruiters should devise methods that present realistic previews of what the company offers dual-career couples. Orientation sessions conducted by P/HRM departments should include information that helps such couples identify potential problems.
3. Career development and transfer policies must be revised. Since the usual policies are based on the traditional one-career family, they are inapplicable to dual-career situations. The key is to provide more flexibility.
4. The company should consider providing career couples with special assistance in career management. Couples are typically ill prepared to cope with the problems posed by two careers. When wives earn more than their husbands, marriages often face strain and the need for adjustments.[40]
5. The organization can establish cooperative arrangements with other organizations. When one organization desires to relocate one dual-career partner, cooperative organizations can be sources of employment for the other partner.[41]
6. The most important immediate step is to establish flexible working hours. Allowing couples the privilege of arranging their work schedules so that these will be compatible with family demands is an effective way to meet some of the problems of managing dual-career couples.[42]

---

[40] Laurie Hays, "Pay Problems: How Couples React When Wives Out-Earn Husbands," *The Wall Street Journal*, June 15, 1987, p. 19.

[41] Gail Benson and Jane Holston, *Smart Moves* (Houston, Tex.: River Forest Publishing, 1987).

[42] E. J. Smith, "The Working Mother: A Critique of the Research," *Journal of Vocational Behavior*, October 1981, pp. 191–211.

It would be a mistake to believe that dual-career problems exist only for managerial and professional personnel. Nonmanagerial personnel are also members of dual-career families. Managers will confront problems in scheduling overtime for these people and in transferring them to different shifts.

One company that has responded to the needs of its dual-career employees is the Morgan Adhesives Company in Stow, Ohio. Tom and Vickie Barker are employed by the company. Vickie finally won her request to run a machine that applies an adhesive coating to films, foils, foams, and papers. She is responsible for monitoring and controlling the machine's output and for directing the work of two helpers. One of her helpers is her husband, Tom. After Vickie became a machine operator, Tom asked to be her helper so that they could be on the same shift. The company had no difficulty with the arrangement. As Bill Wyers, Morgan Adhesives' personnel manager said, "Our only policy is performance, and the Barkers are delivering."[43]

General Electric has set up a network with other firms to share information about job opportunities for dual-career couples. At Economics Laboratory, Inc., in St. Paul, companies in the area are advised of the availability of the spouses of relocated employees.[44]

Middle-Aged Women Looking for a Career

After 20 years of raising children, being a good wife, and doing her bit for the community, 43-year-old Ruth Sugerman, of Lawrenceville, New Jersey, wanted a job. But those 20 years had left a big gap in her résumé. To help fill the void, she became an intern. The intern program is run by Creative Alternatives for Women.[45]

The program Ruth joined offers women a chance to develop confidence in their abilities to succeed in business by involving them in courses, workshops, and seminars designed to help women identify their work interests.

After completing the classroom work, the women receive the internships. They are salaried and usually work three to six months. The jobs include market research, public relations, data processing, and banking.

Ruth Sugerman interned with Educational Testing Service, Inc. as a researcher. Now she is a full-time senior research assistant on the same project. The career reentry program restored Ruth's confidence and permitted her to retool while being paid. This, however, is a point of contention. Some P/HRM experts believe that interns shouldn't be paid since they are hired as unknown quantities. What do you think? Should interns, men or women, be paid?

---

[43] "At Home on the Coating Line," *Management Review*, September 1978, p. 46.

[44] Maria H. Sekas, "Dual-Career Couples—A Corporate Challenge," *Personnel Administrator*, April 1984.

[45] Erik Larson, "Firms Providing Business Internships Lure Middle-Aged Women Looking for Work," *The Wall Street Journal*, September 2, 1981, p. 21.

From *The Wall Street Journal*, with permission of Cartoon Features Syndicate

Dealing with EEO Problems

The initial thrust of affirmative action programs is to recruit and place women and minority employees into managerial and professional positions. Many organizations have been successful in that effort, but their success has created additional problems. For example, the career development needs of women and minority employees require nontraditional methods. A potentially-explosive additional problem is coping with the reactions of white male employees.

There is a limited amount of information about minority participation in major corporations. In a 1985 survey of 1,362 senior executives in Fortune 1000 companies, there were four blacks, six Asians, three Hispanics, and 29 women. This survey data suggests that women and minorities hold few of the top-level, decision-making positions in America's largest companies.[46]

---

[46] Edward W. Jones, Jr., "Black Managers: The Dream Deferred," *Harvard Business Review*, May–June 1986, pp. 84–93.

The importance of addressing the career development needs of women and minority employees must be addressed by top managers. Equal opportunity can not be achieved by placing a black on the board of directors or a hispanic in charge of a new plant. What is needed is a focused program that integrates recruitment, placement, and development efforts. For example, Virginia National Bankshares, the holding company of Virginia National Bank (VNB), has 155 offices throughout Virginia. Despite the fact that 72 percent of its employees are women, only 25 percent of them are in management positions. To correct the imbalance, VNB started a program designed to move more women into management. VNB appointed an advisory board consisting of eight women from various specialities within the bank. The advisory board interviewed all present female managers to determine what women considered to be their problems. The board then surveyed 109 nonmanagerial women to find out how many actually aspired to be managers.

The advisory board discovered a large number of women who were willing to undergo whatever training was necessary to move into management. The board also identified three crucial problem areas that had to be resolved before these women could realize their aspirations: (1) misconceptions about and outdated attitudes toward women, (2) lack of lending experience among women, and (3) lack of management skills among women. The bank's management accepted the advisory board's recommendation that a rotational program be implemented. Women would be placed in all major credit areas throughout the bank. They would be trained in three lending skills: accounting, economics/finance, and financial statement analysis. They would spend one month in each credit area: branch management, credit review, marketing, branch lending, commercial loans, mortgage loans, and national accounts. In addition to the rotational program, the bank sponsors seminars prepared by the National Association of Bank Women and conducts life planning seminars to help women function effectively in their careers and in other areas of their lives.[47]

The VNB program is representative of career development designed to meet the specific needs of employees in a specific situation. Traditional programs were directed toward mainstream employees and were too general in focus and content to meet the needs of women and minority employees. Although the VNB program's target group was women, its principles could be equally applicable to minority employees.

In the midst of EEO and affirmative action concerns, the employees most likely to feel threatened are white males of average competence. Above-average white males will usually progress; below-average performers will always lag behind. The threat is most keenly felt when the economy slows down and what few promotions are available go to women and minority employees. White males are not much comforted to be told that such practices are temporary and are intended to correct past injustices. So what can managers do to help?

No company practice can guarantee that average-performing white male

---

[47] "Making Room at the Top," *Management Review,* April 1978, p. 45.

employees will go along with affirmative action programs. But some practices offer promise. First, the company should provide open and complete information about promotions. Instead of being secretive about promotions (in the hope that if white males aren't told they are being passed over for promotion, they won't notice it), the organization should provide information that permits white males to see precisely where they stand. If given such information, they will be less likely to overestimate their relative disadvantage and will be able to assess their position in the organization more accurately.

A second practice that seems promising is to make sure that white males receive as much career development assistance as other groups. White males may also need information about occupational opportunities *outside the company*. Since their upward mobility may be temporarily stifled by the company's affirmative action efforts, the average white male should be given the opportunity to seek career mobility elsewhere. In summary, the management that is sincerely pursuing affirmative action through career development must not expect all employees to go along with and support the effort. Vested interests are at stake when one group progresses at the expense of another.

Job Layoffs and Loss

Business and farm bankruptcies, layoffs in manufacturing and service industries, permanent closing of obsolete plants, and other similar events have altered the lives of millions of workers and their families.[48] As of early 1988, about 6.7 percent (8.5 million) of the United States' labor force (including only those actively seeking work) was unemployed. Just as disturbing is the fact that it is estimated that three times that number would be told some time during 1988 that they are out of a job.

Layoffs exist when three conditions occur: (1) there is no work available at the time and the employee is sent home; (2) management expects the no-work situation to be temporary; and (3) management intends to recall the employee. Job loss, on the other hand, means that the employee has permanently lost his or her job.[49] In layoff and job loss situations there is inevitably a halt to any career development and progression.[50] No company is immune to eliminating jobs. Some of the pillars of the business world such as AT&T, Monsanto, American Airlines Inc., Sears Roebuck & Co., and ITT have laid people off.[51]

Research has shown that job loss produces dangerous increases in personal stress. For instance, the work of sociologist Harvey Brenner provides convincing evidence on the effects of job loss. He shows that higher levels of job loss (unemployment) have been associated with higher levels of social disorders,

---

[48] Barbara Rhine, "Business Closings and Their Effects on Employees: The Need for New Remedies," *Labor Law Journal*, May 1984, pp. 268–80.

[49] Dessler, *Personnel Management*, p. 512.

[50] Terry F. Buss and F. Stevens Redburn, *Mass Unemployment* (Beverly Hills, Calif.: Sage Publications, 1983).

[51] "You're Fired," *U.S. News and World Report*, March 23, 1987, pp. 50–54.

mental hospital first admissions, and suicide.[52] Such associations raise a number of important questions. Who is most vulnerable to the stress caused by job loss, and why? Do short-term layoffs have different effects than permanent job loss? How important are such factors as support from family and friends in conditioning the impact of job loss?

Cobb and Kasl conducted a two-and-a-half-year study of the effects of job loss on 100 employees prior to job loss and after losing their jobs.[53] They found that:

- Job loss is stressful and requires several months for a person to adjust.
- Job loss is associated with depression, anomie, and suspicion.
- Self-reports of illness and drug use were high during the anticipation phase, dropped at termination, and rose again at six months.
- Those who were unemployed longer and had less social support experienced more stress.

Although the Cobb and Kasl study is well-designed, it has a number of limitations. The sample size was only 100. Also, the sample was predominantly composed of white, middle-aged males. The Cobb and Kasl research and other similar studies has resulted in a number of tentative conclusions:[54]

- Denial or disbelief is a typical initial response to rumors of job loss.
- As rumors circulate and as individuals lose their jobs, there is a high level of anxiety among job stayers.
- Several weeks after job loss there is a period of relaxation and relief, of optimism, and vigorous efforts to find a new job.
- Friends and family can play a major support role.
- Four or more months after job loss, those workers still unemployed go through a period of doubt—in which some people experience panic, rage, and erratic behavior.

The likelihood that a person will experience all of these stages depends on the duration of unemployment (how long his or her career is halted). Differences of personality and circumstances (such as age and degree of financial security) influence the timing and the intensity of job loss effects.

Managerial Responses to Career Halt Consistently strong performance is one effective approach to guard against the need to use job layoffs or job loss approaches.[55] An efficient performance appraisal system can help management pinpoint poor performance and initiate corrective steps. Even when

[52] M. H. Brenner, *Mental Illness and the Economy* (Cambridge, Mass.: Harvard University Press, 1973).

[53] S. Cobb and S. V. Kasl, *Termination: The Consequences of Job Loss* (Cincinnati: Department of Health, Education, and Welfare, 1977).

[54] R. Catalano and C. D. Dooley, "Health Effects of Economic Instability: A Test of Economic Stress Hypotheses," *Journal of Health and Social Behavior,* March 1983, pp. 46–60.

[55] Gene L. Morton, "Helping Managers and Employees Cope with Work-Force Cutbacks," *Training and Developmental Journal,* September 1983, pp. 50–54.

managers use performance appraisal systems there may be other uncontrollable events such as cutback in market demand, reduced resources availability, and competitive forces that require some form of labor force cutback.

The best time to prepare for job layoff and job loss is when business is good. Establishment of *layoff criteria* is an important step. Typically, seniority is the most used criterion in determining who will be laid off. However, if a valued and reliable performance appraisal system is in place it could be used to make decisions. Some firms use a panel of managers from outside the work unit being cut back to decide who will be laid off and who will stay.

The creation of an *outplacement services* unit within the P/HRM unit or hiring an outplacement consultant is another valuable step in preparing for possible job layoff and job loss.[56] Outplacement consists of a variety of job placement services that an organization offers to people who are being asked to leave.[57] These services may include resume writing, use of company telephones for calling potential employers, letters of introduction, reference letters, payment of placement fees, and career counseling. In some cases, a company may pay for retraining as a person learns the skills necessary to begin the career again elsewhere or to enter a new career.[58] Outplaced employees sometimes form support groups so that they can exchange information about job openings and feelings.

In addition to outplacement services, organizations can provide payments so that individuals have some financial resources to draw upon during the transition between jobs. The most common is *severance pay,* based on the age of the employee and his or her years of services.

In 1979–1980 the Brown and Williamson Tobacco Company shut down its Louisville, Kentucky, plant and reduced its Richmond, Virginia, facility.[59] By following a number of guidelines, the company worked hard to reduce the stress and trauma of job loss and job layoffs. First, it gave employees 18 months advance notice of the employee reduction plan. Second, it worked closely with the union in communicating the plan and counseling employees. Third, it purposefully designed a gradual work force reduction program instead of summarily and suddenly letting people go.

Since job layoffs and job loss are expected to be problems that will continue into the foreseeable future, management must continue to study the problems and experiment with solutions.[60] There are still many gaps in our understanding of what happens to people when their careers are halted temporarily or permanently. We need more information on:

---

[56] Loretta D. Foxman and Walter L. Polsky, "How to Select a Good Outplacement Firm" *Personnel Journal,* September 1984, pp. 94–97.

[57] William J. Morin and Lyle York, *Outplacement Techniques* (New York: AMACOM, 1982), pp. 101–31.

[58] Nadeem Shahzel, "Outplacement Services at Interfaith Medical Center," *Personnel Administrator,* June 1984, pp. 59–63.

[59] Jerome M. Roscow and Robert Zager, *Employment Security in a Free Economy* (New York: Pergamon Press, 1984).

[60] H. G. Kaufman, *Professionals in Search of Work* (New York: John Wiley & Sons, 1982).

A RETURN TO THE P/HRM · IN · ACTION

After thinking about his goals, present position, and the future he saw at Neal, Jim Lucio made the decision to leave the company. It wasn't easy, and he had some fears, but Jim really felt that a second career was best for him. He didn't make a hasty decision; he knew all about the idea of a midcareer crisis. Jim decided to go after the thing he always wanted, his own business.

He now is a partner in a database management system company in Hamilton, Ohio. He felt good, slept well, and jumped into his second career with enthusiasm. Norb and everyone at Neal wished him well. His co-workers even had a party for Jim to show him that they really cared and wanted him to be happy in his new career as a business owner in the computer field.

- Women and minority worker reactions to job layoffs and loss.
- The longer-range effects of job loss.
- How personality predisposes reactions to job loss.
- The effectiveness of outplacement services.

Much work and managerial action need to be done on the effects of career halt. As stated by Harry Maurer,

> Work, if the longing of the unemployed is any indication, remains a fundamental need—even in the crushing form it has increasingly assumed in the modern world. It provides not simply a livelihood, but an essential passage into the human community. It makes us less alone.[61]

SUMMARY

This chapter has been designed to discuss the importance of career planning and development.

To summarize the major points covered in this chapter:

1. A career is an ongoing sequence of work-related activities. It is not something that occurs in isolation, but is work-related.
2. Individuals go through four career stages—prework, initial work stage, the stable stage, and the retirement stage.
3. Mentoring can be extremely important to a junior employee in terms of personal development.
4. In selecting a career individuals are expressing a part of their personality.
5. Three points in careers are of particularly crucial importance for career

---

[61] "The Stress of Job Loss," *Occupational Health and Safety,* June 1982, p. 26.

development—when a person is just hired, at midcareer, and at preretirement.

6. Programs to combat problems of the new hiree include realistic job previews, challenging initial assignments, and demanding bosses.
7. Programs to combat midcareer problems include counseling to illustrate and develop midcareer alternatives (transfers, retraining).
8. Programs to combat preretirement problems include counseling, workshops and seminars on what to expect, alternative careers, and coping with change.
9. Career pathing can inform people about the sequence of job opportunities in the organization.
10. Career planning involves matching a person's aspirations with opportunities. Some commonly used practices involve counseling, seminars, and even self-assessment centers.
11. A growing issue of importance is the dual-career couple. Organizations need to become more active in finding ways to minimize problems of dual-career couples.
12. Career progress and development can halt because of a temporary cutback in the work force or a permanent reduction in the work force. The layoff or job loss situation can create psychological and behavioral problems for individuals and families that are affected.

Questions for Review and Discussion

1. What kind of person and skills are needed to be an effective mentor?
2. Why do recently retired persons need to be prepared for the differences between work and retirement?
3. Why would a job layoff or job loss affect a person?
4. What is the meaning of the term *career success* to an individual?
5. Why are some people satisfied with what is identified as a midcareer plateau?
6. Should organizations be concerned about dual-career issues such as career conflict, job relocation, and salary differences? Why?
7. What can an employee learn from examining a career path that is developed specifically for him or her?
8. Have you made a career choice? What is it and do you have the skills and personality for the particular career? How do you determine this?
9. Why are women and other minorities concerned about survey's like that of Fortune 1000?
10. How could a manager evaluate the effectiveness (or lack of) of the outplacement services used in her or his firm?

GLOSSARY

Career. Individually perceived sequences of attitudes and behaviors associated with work-related experiences and activities over the span of an individual's work life.

Career Path. A sequence of positions through which an organization moves an employee.

Career Stages. The distinct stages that individuals go through in their careers, typically: prework, initial work, stable work, and retirement.

Dual-Career Couples. A situation in which a husband and wife have careers.

Job Layoff. A condition that exists when no work is available and the employee is sent home, management views the no-work situation as temporary, and management intends to recall the employee.

Job Loss. A condition in which there is no work and the individual is sent home permanently.

Midcareer Plateau. A point reached during the adult stage of life where a person feels stifled and not progressing as he or she had planned or would like.

Mentoring Relationship. A relationship between a junior and senior colleague that is considered by the junior person to be helpful in his or her personal development.

Outplacement. Service provided by some firms to individuals who are permanently asked to leave. The services may include resume preparation help, counseling, and training.

APPLICATION CASE 14–1   The Dual-Career Couple*

Until recently, America's workforce was largely comprised of the heads of traditional families—the husbands who work as the employed breadwinner while the wives remain home to raise the children. However, today the "traditional family" comprises less than 10 percent of all households. Increasingly, both spouses are launching careers and earning incomes. These dual-career couples now account for 40 percent of the workforce (over 47 million employees) and their numbers will substantially increase.

The advent of the dual-career couple poses challenges for the working spouses and for business. According to one recent survey of over 800 dual-career couples by Catalyst, couples experience a myriad of problems, most notably difficulties with allocating time (the top-ranked complaint), finances, poor communication, and conflicts over housework. For couples with children, meeting the demands of career and family usually becomes the top concern. Recent studies indicate that dual-career families need: (1) benefit plans that enable couples to have children without jeopardizing careers; (2) more flexible work arrangements to help balance family-career demands; (3) freedom from anxieties about child care while at work; and (4) employer assistance in finding spouse employment when the employee relocates (a need of both parents and childless couples).

For businesses, the challenge lies in helping to ease the problems of dual-career couples, especially those with children. According to a 1987 study commissioned by *Fortune* magazine, organizations are losing productivity and employees due to the demands of family life. The study found that, among the 400 working parents surveyed, problems with child care were the most significant predictors of absenteeism and low productivity. For example, 41 percent of those surveyed took at least one day in the three months preceding the survey to handle family matters; 10 percent took from three to five days. (These figures on a national scale amount to hundreds of millions of dollars in lost productivity.) About 60 percent of the parents polled expressed concerns about time and attention given to their children, and these anxieties were linked to lower productivity. Overall, many experts advise that companies that ignore the problems of dual-career couples (and working parents per se) stand to lose output and even valued employees.

Companies are beginning to respond to these needs in a number of ways. A growing number of organizations are:

---

* Written by Kim Stewart and adapted from: Veronica J. Schmidt and Norman A. Scott, "Work and Family Life: A Delicate Balance," *Personnel Administrator,* August 1987, pp. 40–46; Fern Schumer Chapman, "Executive Guilt: Who's Taking Care of the Children?" *Fortune,* February 16, 1987, pp. 30–37; Anastasia Toufexis, "Dual Careers, Doleful Dilemmas," *Time,* November 16, 1987, p. 90; Irene Pave, "Move Me, Move My Spouse," *Business Week,* December 16, 1985, pp. 57, 60; Ronald F. Ribaric, "Mission Possible: Meeting Family Demands," *Personnel Administrator,* August 1987, pp. 70–79; and Lawrence Rout, "Pleasures and Problems Face Married Couples Hired by Same Firms, *The Wall Street Journal,* May 28, 1980, pp. 1, 28.

1. *Hiring spouses of employees or helping them find jobs:* Studies indicate that more employees are refusing relocation assignments if their working spouses cannot find acceptable jobs. It is estimated that by 1990, 75 percent of all corporate moves will involve dual-career couples. In response, many companies have recently begun to offer services for "trailing spouses." These services include arranging interviews with prospective employers, providing instruction in resume writing, interviewing and contract negotiation, and even paying plane fares for job hunting trips. Some companies (General Mills, 3M, American Express) use outside placement services to find jobs for trailing spouses. Over 150 northern New Jersey companies created and use a job bank that provides leads for job-hunting spouses.

A small and growing number of companies (Chase Manhattan Bank; O'Melveny & Myers, one of the nation's largest law firms) are breaking tradition and hiring two-career couples. Martin Marietta maintains an affirmative hire-a-couple policy and hires about 100 couples a year in its Denver division. Proponents assert that couples who work for the same company share the same goals, are often more committed to the company, and are more willing to work longer hours. Hiring couples helps attract and keep top employees, and relocations are also easier for the couple and the company.

However, many companies still shun the practice, asserting that problems outweigh advantages. Often-cited problems include the consequences of unequal performance—one spouse being promoted faster than the other resulting in jealousy, or difficulties in firing one spouse while retaining the other. Forced competition can also be problematic as, "You always . . . have a built-in tension with couples comparing job assignments, salary levels, and so forth," said one personnel manager of Price Waterhouse & Co which opposes the practice. "Pillow talk" (couples exchanging confidential information), and problems inherent in the marriage going sour are also potential liabilities. A number of companies with hiring couple policies forbid spouses supervising each other.

2. *Providing day care assistance:* Over 3,000 companies now provide day-care services and financial assistance or referral services for child care (a 50 percent increase in company participation since 1984). Many experts predict that child care will become the fringe benefit of the 1990s.

About 150 companies currently operate on-site, or near-site, day-care centers. For example, American Savings and Loan Association established the Little Mavericks School of Learning in 1983 for 150 children of employees on a site within walking distance of several of its satellite branch locations. Established as a for-profit subsidiary and with a staff of 35, the center's services include regular day care, holiday care, sick-child care, Boy and Girl Scout programs, a kindergarten program, and afterschool classes. Service fees range from $135 to $235 a month depending on the type of service, and parents pay via payroll deductions. Company officials report that the center has substantially reduced employee absenteeism and personal phone calls and has been a substantial boon to recruitment and retention. However, as many companies have found, limited openings prohibit serving all parent employees, and some employees get preferential treatment, sometimes those who can afford external day-care services.

Many companies contract outside day-care services run by professional groups thus relieving the company of the headaches of running a center. For example, IBM contracted the Work/Family Directions child care consulting group to establish 16,000 home-based family centers and to open 3,000 day-care centers for IBM employees and other families throughout the United States. About 80 companies have created programs to help parents of sick children. If a child of an employee of First Bank System (Minneapolis) becomes ill, the company will pay 75 percent of the bill for the child's stay at Chicken Soup, a sick-child day-care center. The policy enables parents to still work and saves the company money. A growing number of companies arrange to send trained nurses to the sick child's home.

Other companies are providing partial reimbursement for child care services per se. Zayre Corporation pays up to $20 a week for day-care services for employees who work at corporate headquarters. A growing number of cafeteria fringe benefit programs enable employees to allocate a portion of fringe benefits to pay for day-care services. Chemical Bank pays these benefits quarterly in pretax dollars.

3. Providing flexible time off: A number of companies are combining vacation and sick leave to increase the amount of time off for family life. At Hewlett Packard, for example, employees receive their regular vacation days and plus five additional days of unused sick leave. Employees can take the time off in any increments at any time. Employees can carry a number of unused days over to the next year (the number is determined by tenure) and employees who leave the company receive cash value for their unused days (at current salary level).

4. Providing job sharing: This program enables two people to share the same job on a part-time basis and is a major boon to spouses who want to continue their careers while raising children. The program was first established by Steelcase Inc., in Grand Rapids, Michigan where company officials assert the program has reduced turnover and absenteeism, boosted morale, and helped achieve the company's affirmative action objectives. However, job sharing can be difficult to implement as the program requires that a job be divided into two related but separate assignments, that job sharers are compatible, and that the supervisor can provide task continuity between the two job sharers.

Questions For Thought

1. What are the advantages and potential liabilities of hiring two-career couples beyond those noted in the case?
2. Many of the services for dual-career couples and parent employees are provided by large corporations that have far greater financial resources than smaller companies. Identify and discuss potential ways in which a small company's P/HRM function can alleviate the challenges facing parent employees and employees with working spouses.
3. Suppose a dual-career couple involves spouses who are each in a different career stage. Does this situation pose problems for the couple? For the organization(s) that employ(s) them? Discuss.

EXERCISE 14–1   Career: A Self-Assessment

Objective: This exercise is designed to encourage students to think about themselves in terms of a career. It also requires students to engage in the development of a personal career plan of action.

SET UP THE EXERCISE

1. Individually complete the self-assessment career exercise. Take your time, give each section serious thought, and after careful thought make any necessary changes.
2. The instructor will set up groups of four or five to discuss any aspect of the self-assessment that individuals want to talk about. Each individual should discuss at least *one* part or issue of his or her career assessment.
3. After the discussion each individual is to complete the action plan form.

Career Self-Assessment Form

A. *What is the ideal* career?
   Describe briefly what appears to you to be the ideal career. This is not necessarily the career you want or are in, but what you feel is ideal.
B. What skills do I have?
   List the three most obvious skills that you possess.
   1.

   2.

   3.

C. List the job experience that you have had.
D. Rate each of the outcomes you want from a job.

	Extremely Important						Not Really Important
1. Job security	7	6	5	4	3	2	1
2. Pay	7	6	5	4	3	2	1
3. Advancement opportunity	7	6	5	4	3	2	1
4. Social interaction	7	6	5	4	3	2	1
5. Challenge	7	6	5	4	3	2	1
6. Travel	7	6	5	4	3	2	1
7. Respect of colleagues	7	6	5	4	3	2	1
8. Feedback	7	6	5	4	3	2	1
9. Variety	7	6	5	4	3	2	1
10. Autonomy	7	6	5	4	3	2	1
11. Power	7	6	5	4	3	2	1
12. Recognition	7	6	5	4	3	2	1

E. Describe how often you think about your ideal career. What kind of things do you usually think about?

Career Action Plan

Now that you have thought about a career and have discussed it in a group, it is time to consider preparing your own career action plan. State the kind of actions that you really plan to do. Also seriously consider the potential obstacles in your path. Only work on *two* specific career planning goals.

A Learning Note

The difficulty of career progress evaluation will be highlighted. It will also help students compare an ideal career with their own career plans, experience, and preferred outcomes.

Action For Goal	When Will I Do It	Obstacles	How Obstacles Can Be Overcome
Action for Goal I Description:			
Action for Goal II Description:			

Now describe how you will determine whether your two action plans were successful. That is, how will you evaluate the progress being made?

	Evaluation Description
Action Plan I	
Action Plan II	

DISCIPLINE AND THE DIFFICULT EMPLOYEE

LEARNING OBJECTIVES

After studying this chapter, you should be able to:

- **List** four behavioral categories of difficult employees.
- **Describe** steps that can be taken to prevent employee theft.
- **Discuss** the elements of a disciplinary system.
- **Define** termination-at-will.
- **Explain** why discharge is more widely used in a nonunionized situation as opposed to a unionized situation.

KEY TERMS

Dehiring
Hot Stove Rule
Progressive Pattern of Discipline
Termination-at-Will

CHAPTER OUTLINE

P/HRM · IN · ACTION

| Al | Susan | Joyce | Tom |

Managers supervise a variety of types of employees as part of their work. Most employees perform effectively most of the time. But any management development session eventually comes around to a discussion of employees like Al, Susan, Joyce, or Tom. These four employees are employed by a small conglomerate in the Boston area, Judge Incorporated. Judge owns manufacturing and retailing units.

- Al is the salesperson who had the largest sales increases of any of the sales force just after he was hired. Later, his sales dropped off. When his supervisor checked, Al was found to be making just enough sales calls to reach his quota.
- Susan is often a good worker. Then there are days when all the forms she types have serious errors on them. These are the days Susan is drinking.
- Joyce seems to do good work. She is courteous to the customers. She puts the stock up quickly and marks the prices accurately. But Joyce takes more than her paycheck home every week.
- Tom is a pretty good employee. But John, his supervisor, is driven up the wall by him. Tom just can't seem to follow the company rules. And when John tries to talk to him about it, Tom gives him a hard time and may even seem to threaten him if he tries to do anything about the problem.

At present, Judge Incorporated has no well-organized discipline system.

These examples illustrate a time-consuming and worrisome aspect of the P/HRM job: dealing fairly with the difficult employee. The seriousness of the problem is reinforced by the fact that the largest number of cases going to arbitration involves disciplinary matters. Unionized organizations have ways of dealing with these incidents, but most employees do not work in a unionized situation.

This chapter is concerned with the characteristics of difficult employees and some of the reasons for their problems. It also considers systems of discipline and appropriate means for rehabilitating difficult employees. Too often, discipline has been oriented toward punishment for past misdeeds. This is required in Joyce's case, but more important for the others is behavioral change to improve employee productivity.

The emphasis of the chapter will be *on-the-job behavior*. Organizations such as the military have tried to control the total behavior of the employee; the military often will court-martial and punish soldiers for civilian offenses, such as speeding, whether or not civilian authorities prosecute. The work organization, however, should be concerned with off-the-job behavior only when it affects work behavior. Thus, if Susan drinks before work so that she cannot do her job, this is of concern to her employer. If she has a few drinks after work and this in no way affects her job, it is none of her employer's business, even if the boss happens to be a teetotaler.

Generally, the operating supervisor is the person primarily involved in disciplining employees. P/HRM specialists may be involved as advisers if they are asked to do so by the operating manager. Sometimes the P/HRM manager serves as a second step in investigation and appeal of a disciplinary case. Or, when the union is involved, the P/HRM manager may advise the operating manager on contract interpretation for a specific case.

Discipline is a Stage III P/HRM activity as defined in Exhibit 1–7 (Chapter 1). Some studies have been performed on the topic, but there is a wide divergence in the disciplinary practices applied in various organizations.

A DIAGNOSTIC APPROACH TO DISCIPLINE

Exhibit 15–1 highlights the factors affecting the discipline process in an organization. As we have seen, an employee's attitude toward work is a crucial factor in productivity or performance, and discipline may play an important part in this attitude. (The kind of discipline system used is normally related to the organization.) It will be more formal in larger organizations, especially those that are unionized. It is quite informal in smaller organizations.

How strict discipline is depends on the nature of the prevailing labor markets. In times of high unemployment, for example, it can be quite strict. It is also related to the supportiveness of the work group (if the work group "covers" for the employee and feels the issue is unimportant, management's ability to discipline will be limited), and to the nature of the leader or supervior (an autocratic leader's approach to discipline will be quite different from a participative leader's). The government and the legal system may provide support for employer or employee.

The effective operating or P/HRM manager will try to diagnose each of these factors in the discipline situation. For example, the supervisor may try to diagnose the difficult employee's motivation, with a view to improving performance. This is not always easy to do. If the manager does not know the employee well, it may be virtually impossible. Discipline is one of the most challenging areas in the P/HRM function. The diagnostic approach has many advantages over the "give him a fair trial before you hang him" approach in dealing with the difficult employee.

EXHIBIT 15–1 Factors Affecting the Discipline of Personnel

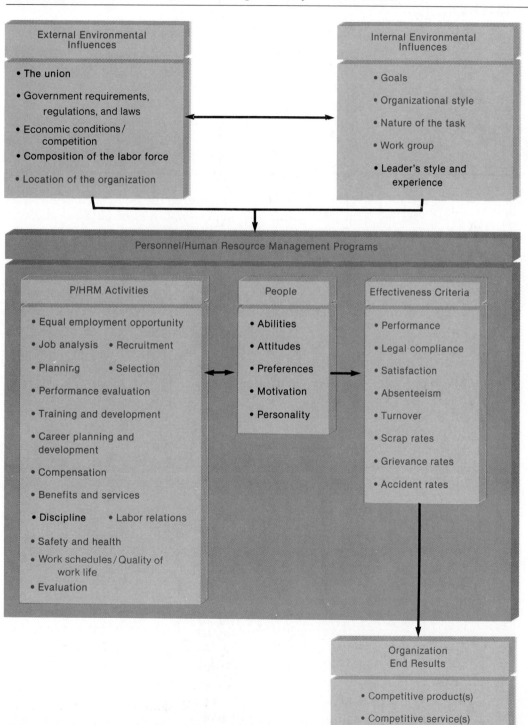

CATEGORIES OF DIFFICULT EMPLOYEES

Employees whose behavior can be described as difficult can be classified into one of four categories:

Categories of Difficult Employees:

Category 1.   Those whose quality or quantity of work is unsatisfactory due to lack of abilities, training, or job motivation. (Al is an example.)

Category 2.   Those whose personal problems off the job begin to affect job productivity. These problems can include alcoholism, drugs, or family relationships. (Susan is an example.)

Category 3.   Those who violate laws while on the job by such behavior as stealing from the organization or its employees or physical abuse of employees or property. (Joyce is an example.)

Category 4.   Those who consistently break company rules and do not respond to supervisory reactions. (Tom is an example.)

The difficulty of determining the causes of any human behavior pattern was noted in Chapter 2. It is especially difficult to assess the causes of undesired behavior, but Miner has devised a scheme for analyzing deficient behavior that provides a checklist of possible causes:[1]

A. Problems of intelligence and job knowledge.
B. Emotional problems.
C. Motivational problems.
D. Physical problems.
E. Family problems.
F. Problems caused by the work group.
G. Problems originating in company policies.
H. Problems stemming from society and its values.
I. Problems from the work context (e.g., economic forces) and the work itself.

Many of these causes can influence deficient behavior, which can result from behavior of the employee alone, behavior of the employer alone, or interaction of the employee and employer. Al's behavior (Category 1), which is directly related to the work situation, could be caused by emotional, motivational, or organizational problems. If Susan is drinking (Category 2) because of family problems or emotional problems, then the primary cause of her behavior is outside the control of the employer. Frequently, difficult behavior is caused by personal and employment conditions that feed one another. Joyce's behavior—theft and other illegal activites (Category 3)—is normally dealt with by security departments and usually results in termination and

---

[1] John Miner, *The Challenge of Managing* (Philadelphia: W. B. Saunders, 1975).

possibly prosecution of the employee. Tom's behavior (Category 4) is often caused by motivational, job, or emotional problems.

Category 1: The Ineffective Employee

Employees whose performance is due to factors directly related to work are theoretically the easiest to work with and to adjust. Chapter 12 introduced a systematic approach for investigating performance discrepancies. The approach is applicable not only for training but also for coping with ineffective, poor-performing employees. Recall that the approach indicates that there are some key issues that managers must consider. For example, the employee is not performing well; the manager thinks there is a training problem. There are three general follow-up questions a manager might use to analyze the problem:

1. *What is the performance discrepancy?* Why do I think there is a training problem? What is the difference between what is being done and what is supposed to be done? What is the event that causes me to say that things aren't right? Why am I dissatisfied?
2. *Is it important?* Why is the discrepancy important? What would happen if I left the discrepancy alone? Could doing something to resolve the discrepancy have any worthwhile result?
3. *Is it a skill deficiency?* Could he do it if he really had to? Could he do it if his life depended on it? Are his present skills adequate for the desired peformance?

If there is a skill deficiency, then it must be corrected. On the other hand, if the problem is not a skill deficiency, then the performance problem must be addressed in terms of removing obstacles, creating a more positive motivational climate, or by bringing about some type of job change.

In summary, ineffective performance may be the result of skill, job, or motivational climate factors. Each of these factors must be carefully weighed in considering Al's sales drop off described in the opening P/HRM In Action.

Category 2: Alcoholic and Drug Abusing Employees

The Alcoholic Employee Abusive alcohol consumption that affects an employee's job performance is a serious problem with effects on organizations everywhere throughout the world. More and more, alcoholism is being viewed by the courts and by therapists as an illness, a *treatable* illness.

Estimates of the number of alcoholics employed in America vary, but about 10 percent of the labor force are alcoholics and another 10 percent are borderline alcoholics.[2] The greatest incidence of alcoholism is in people aged 35–55 who have been employed at the same enterprise 14–20 years. The direct

---

[2] Herbert Peyser, "Stress and Alcohol," in *Handbook of Stress*, ed. Leo Goldberger and Shlomo Breznitz (New York: Free Press, 1982), pp. 585–98.

cost to industry alone is estimated at $8 billion a year in lost productivity and allied expenses. This estimate may be low because alcoholics often are sent home as "sick" rather than as drunk.

Of course, alcoholic consumption does not affect all employees the same at work, nor does it affect performance of tasks equally. Studies indicate that alcoholic intake tends to reduce some performance levels (for example cognitive and perceptual-sensory skills) more than others (psychomotor skills).[3] For many persons, it takes about an hour for the alcohol to affect performance negatively. Also compared to workers who are not alcoholic, problem drinkers take two-and-a-half times more absences of eight days or more, receive three times as much sick leave and accident benefits, and make five times as many workers' compensation claims.[4] About a third of America's largest employers have set up alcoholism control programs. Many medical plans now cover the costs of treatment for alcoholism. Many companies fire those employees who need help and do not take advantage of these programs.

Generally the successful program for alcoholics includes a conference between supervisor and employee. These points are covered:

- The supervisor documents the effects at work of the employee's alcoholism.
- The supervisor offers to help.
- The supervisor *requires* the employee to participate in a rehabilitation program such as Alcoholics Anonymous (which has been evaluated as by far the best program).
- The supervisor notifies the employee that the consequences of not participating in rehabilitation is loss of the job.

Many unions are now participating in joint employer-union programs designed to deal with alcoholism.

In larger organizations, the medical or occupational health department helps alcoholics. In medium-sized and smaller organizations, P/HRM refers them to consultants and to treatment programs. P/HRM and operating managers need such documentation to support their decisions in arbitration hearings if necessary.

The Drug Abusing Employee Employers also are finding more employees abusing drugs such as cocaine and heroin on the job. Drug abuse manifests itself in ways similar to alcoholism. Counselors at the Cocaine National Helpline polled callers of the 800-COCAINE hotline and found that 75 percent admitted to occasional cocaine use while at work and 69 percent said they regularly worked while under the influence of the drug. The problems may be less well-known to employers because of laws against possession and use of drugs, which causes employees to hide their abuse. However, it is estimated

---

[3] Jerrold Levine, Gloria G. Kramer, and Ellen N. Levine, "Effects of Alcohol on Human Performance: An Integration of Research Findings Based on an Abilities Classification," *Journal of Applied Psychology*, June 1975, pp. 285–93.

[4] Joseph F. Madonia, "Managerial Responses to Alcohol and Drug Abuse among Employees," *Personnel Administrator*, June 1984, pp. 134–39.

that drug use at the workplace costs American business over $50 billion per year.[5]

One Fortune 500 company released profiles of the typical drug abuser that indicate, compared to the norm for a working unit, the drug user:

- Functions at about 67 percent of his or her potential.
- Is 3.6 times more likely to be involved in an accident.
- Receives three times the average level of sick benefits.
- Is five times more likely to file a workers' compensation claim.
- Is repeatedly involved in grievance procedures.
- Misses 10, or more, times as many work days.[6]

In some industries, drug- and alcohol-influenced mistakes cost lives. Since 1975, approximately 50 train accidents have been attributed to workers under the influence of drugs or alcohol: 37 people were killed, 80 injured, and property valued at $34 million was destroyed.[7]

An increasing number of firms believe that some absenteeism, turnover, accidents, industrial espionage, and lower productivity are caused by drug addiction, and some thefts are caused by drug users trying to support their habit. What have they done about it? One survey of 108 companies on employees' use of drugs found that 81 percent tried to find out if the employee had used drugs prior to hiring, and 51 percent have company policies against drug use by employees.[8] Their responses to the problem include detection methods to determine the extent of the problem, more careful recruitment and selection, educational programs for supervisors, policy statements, and counseling programs that refer addicts to rehabilitation programs.

Companies follow similar control programs for drugs as they do for alcohol, although treatment methods vary more in the drug area. Drug usage is illegal, and public attitudes are much more negative on drugs than on alcohol. In industry, the company health department can try to rehabilitate drug users. Often, however, the ultimate decision is discharge and discipline, although this may lead to arbitration. A summary of arbitration rulings on the subject and a survey of members of the National Academy of Arbitrators by Levin and Denenberg found that because of the legal implications and the difficulty drug users would have in getting future jobs, arbitrators demand full and complete proof of drug usage.[9] This is sometimes difficult for employers to provide. Employers can help protect themselves by asking the employee to certify that he or she had no previous drug experiences. If it can be shown this record is

[5] Ian A. Miners, Nick N. Ykodyn, and Diane M. Samerdyke Traband, "Put Drug Detection to the Test," *Personnel Journal*, August 1987, pp. 90–97.

[6] J. Castro, "Battling the Enemy Within," *Time*, March 17, 1986, p. 53.

[7] Ibid.

[8] Carl D. Chambers and Richard Heckman, *Employee Drug Abuse* (Boston: Cahners Books, 1972). Also see William G. Wagner, "Assisting Employees with Personal Problems," *Personnel Administrator*, November 1982, pp. 59–64.

[9] Edward Levin and Tia Denenberg, "How Arbitrators View Drug Abuse," *The Arbitration Journal*, March 1976, pp. 97–108.

falsified, arbitrators view this as grounds for discharge or discipline. If company policy is to discipline or discharge employees who use drugs, company rules and employment controls should be explicit about this prohibition. Evidence must also be given that these prohibitions have been communicated clearly to all employees.

Kimberly-Clark has an employee assistance program (EAP) for chemical dependency and other special health problems affecting work performance.[10] The EAP screened over 250 employees and family members in 1980. About half of these had chemical dependency problems. The company's rehabilitation program was able to reduce chemical dependency and improve the job performance of about 65 percent of the participants. Absenteeism and accident data for employees in the EAP showed a 43 percent reduction in absenteeism and a 70 percent reduction in accidents for a one-year period following treatment (using a pre-and posttreatment design).

Arbitrators have discharged drug-using employees if their habit ruins a firm's reputation or causes it to lose business. They are more likely to uphold discharges for drug usage after conviction than after arrest alone, and they discipline drug pushers more severely than drug users. In general, arbitrators tend to urge employers to give drug-using employees a second chance if they agree to participate in rehabilitation programs.

Category 3: Participants in Theft, Crime, and Illegal Acts

Employers often have to deal with employees who engage in various illegal acts. Employees may steal (remember Joyce), misuse company facilities or property, disclose trade secrets, embezzle, or kidnap executives for terrorism purposes. They may sabotage products, or use company telephones and credit cards for personal use, or pirate company materials or labor to repair their own homes. One source estimates that 75 percent of stolen goods is taken by employees and suppliers. Yet some arbitrators have recently ruled that employee property (such as their cars in the parking lot) cannot be searched without a warrant. Organizations try to deal with employee theft, which is estimated to cost over $30 billion annually, and similar problems in a number of ways.[11] One is to try to screen out likely thieves. For example, a weighted application blank has been developed to help with this. Exhibit 15-2 lists other ways to prevent employee theft.

A method organizations can use to oversee theft and criminal prevention is to set up a security department or program. Often this responsibility is assigned to the P/HRM department. Typically, the protection program is called *industrial security* and includes security education, employment screening, physical security, theft and fraud control, and fire prevention.

---

[10] Robert E. Dedmon and Mary Katherine Kubiak, "The Medical Director's Role in Industry," *Personnel Administrator*, September 1981, pp. 59–64.

[11] Joshua Hyatt, "Easy Money," *Inc.*, February 1988, pp. 91–96 and Cliff Roberson, *Preventing Employee Misconduct*, Lexington, MA: Lexington Books, 1986, p. 1.

EXHIBIT 15–2   Ways to Prevent Employee Theft

1. The employee should be made to feel that the job is worth keeping, and it would not be easy to earn more elsewhere.
2. Normal good housekeeping practices—no piles of rubbish or rejects or boxes, no unused machines with tarpaulins on them, and no unlocked, empty drawers—will help ensure that there are no places where stolen goods can be hidden. The first act of the thief is to divert merchandise from the normal traffic flow.
3. Paperwork must be carefully examined and checked at all stages so invoices cannot be stolen or altered.
4. Employees' cars should not be parked close to their places of work. There should be no usable cover between the plant doors and the cars.
5. Do not allow employees to make sales to themselves, their friends, or their family members.
6. Whether the plant is open or closed at night, bright lights should blaze all around the perimeter, so no one can enter or leave without being seen.
7. There should be adequate measures to control issuance of keys. There have been cases where a manager or supervisor would come back at night for a tryst with a girlfriend and give her an armload of merchandise to take home with her. Key control is very important.
8. As far as possible, everyone entering or leaving should have an identification card.
9. Unused doors should be kept locked. If only two must be open to handle the normal flow of traffic, the rest should be bolted.
10. Everything of value that thieves could possibly remove, not just obvious items, must be safeguarded.

Most companies engage in at least minimal industrial security operations such as identification or "badge" systems, prior employment screening, special safeguards for or destruction of sensitive documents, and escort services for visitors. There is research available that suggests that the larger the organization, the greater the likelihood that theft prevention and security observation programs will be used.[12] Most organizations also attempt at least some industrial security planning in selecting sites and designs for remodeling or construction of facilities. Security vulnerabilities are assessed and structural barriers such as fences, lighting, and the building itself are designed to reduce security hazards.

Operating and P/HRM managers may both be involved in disciplinary matters involving Category 3 employees. Often firings and legal actions are considered. The organization must also be concerned with thefts and similar crimes by visitors and guests.

Category 4: The Rule Violators

Difficult employees of the fourth category consistently violate company rules, such as those prohibiting sleeping on the job, having weapons at work, fighting at work, coming in late, or abusing the supervisor. An especially difficult issue is verbal and physical abuse of supervisors. Recall Tom in the opening P/HRM In Action. It is useful (though not necessary) for the organization to have an established rule prohibiting verbal and physical abuse. Disputes charging

---

[12] Philip Puysiner, *Security and Loss Prevention*, (Boston: Butterworth, 1984).

abuse often go to arbitration. In general, arbitrators take the position that the decisions of supervisors deserve respect. Their rulings have been influenced by several facets of the cases:

The nature of the verbal abuse. If the shop talk is usually obscene, unless the employee personally applies the obscenities to the supervisor, arbitrators are not likely to uphold disciplinary measures for use of obscene words.

The nature of the threat. Discipline will be upheld if an employee *personally* threatens a supervisor, but not if the employee talks vaguely about threats.

The facts in physical abuse cases. If the employee directly attacks the supervisor personally or indirectly (e.g., abusive phone calls) *and if* the employee was not provoked, the disciplinary decision will be upheld by arbitrators.

One study found that in 54 percent of the cases studied, arbitrators have reduced disciplinary penalties given by supervisors.[13] They take into account mitigating circumstances like prior excellent work records and how fairly the management has treated the employee prior to and at the time of the incident. They also check to make sure that management has consistently disciplined other employees in similar cases.

Arbitrators have treated altercations between supervisors and union stewards differently from those between supervisors and other employees. They view the supervisor and steward as equal and feel the steward need not be as "respectful" as other employees.

It is more difficult to establish rules about other infractions. Many organizations prohibit gambling on company grounds to avoid lowering productivity and losing time from work because of fights over gambling losses. Yet few work very hard to prohibit nickel-dime poker at lunch.

Organizations usually have rules prohibiting employees from making decisions when there is a conflict of interest (such as a purchasing agent who has an interest in a supplier) or when the employee is indebted to others. Many organizations prohibit their employees from accepting gifts over some nominal value or from being guests at lavish parties. Conflict-of-interest dealings are usually specifically prohibited.

THE DISCIPLINE PROCESS

Exhibit 15–3 is a model of the discipline process. The employer establishes goals and rules and communicates them to employees. Employee behavior is then assessed, and modification may be found desirable. This process is an attempt to prevent difficulties and is positive in nature. It is designed to help employees succeed.

The first element in the process is the establishment of *work and behavior*

---

[13] Ken Jennings. "Verbal and Physical Abuse Toward Supervision," *Arbitration Journal*, December 1974, pp. 258–71.

EXHIBIT 15–3   Elements In a Disciplinary System

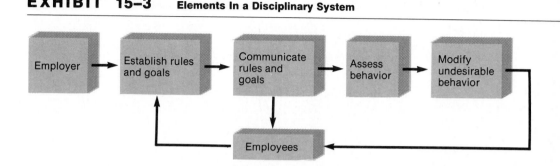

rules. Work goals and standards were discussed as part of performance evaluation (Chapter 8). Through whatever method is used (time and motion study, examination of past performance or performances by others, management by objectives), a set of minimally acceptable work goals is established. Behavior rules cover many facets of on-the-job behavior. They can be categorized as concerning behavior that is directly or indirectly related to work productivity. Both types are often negatively described as prohibited behavior. Exhibit 15–4 lists some examples of employee behavior rules.

The second important element in the disciplinary process is the *communication* of the rules to all employees. Unless employees are aware of the rules, they can hardly be expected to follow them. Closely related is a willingness to accept the rules and their enforceability. If employees or their representatives participate in the formation of the rules, their cooperation is more likely to be ensured. Employees must be convinced that the rule is *fair and related to job effectiveness.*

It is useful for management to seek employee advice on periodic revision of rules. The objective is to reduce the number of rules to the minimum and enforce those that are important. Customs and conditions change. Rules, like laws, need regular updating to achieve the respect and acceptance necessary for order in the workplace.

The third element of the disciplinary process is an *assessment mechanism.* In most organizations, performance evaluation is the mechanism for assessing work behavior deficiency. Rule-breaking behavior usually comes to the attention of management when it is observed or when difficulties arise and investigation reveals certain behavior as the cause.

Finally, the disciplinary process concludes with a system of *administering punishment or motivating change.* This varies from supervisory administration of discipline to formal systems somewhat like courts or grievance procedures.

APPROACHES TO DISCIPLINE

Discipline for each of the categories of employee behavior just discussed can be applied in various ways. A negative approach is to emphasize the punitive

---

EXHIBIT 15-4   **Examples of Employee Behavior Rules**

I. Rules Directly Related to Productivity
  A. Times rules
    1. Starting and late times.
    2. Quitting times.
    3. Maximum break and lunch times.
    4. Maximum absenteeism.
  B. Prohibited-behavior rules
    1. No sleeping on the job.
    2. No leaving workplace without permission.
    3. No drinking on the job.
    4. No drug-taking on the job.
    5. Limited nonemployer activities during work hours.
  C. Insubordination rules
    1. Penalties for refusal to obey supervisors.
    2. Rules against slowdowns and sit-downs.
  D. Rules emphasizing laws
    1. Theft rules
    2. Falsification rules.
  E. Safety rules
    1. No smoking rules.
    2. Safety regulations.
    3. Sanitation requirements.
    4. Rules prohibiting fighting.
    5. Rules prohibiting dangerous weapons.
II. Rules Indirectly Related to Productivity
  A. Prevention of moonlighting.
  B. Prohibition of gambling.
  C. Prohibition of selling or soliciting at work.
  D. Clothing and uniform regulations.
  E. Rules about fraternization with other employees at work or off the job.

---

effects on undesirable behavior. A more positive approach emphasizes what can be done to prevent the undesirable behavior from reoccurring.

Hot Stove Rule

One view of discipline is referred to as the *hot stove rule*. This approach to discipline is discussed in terms of what happens when a person touches a hot stove, the consequences are:

1. *A warning system.* A good manager has, before any behavior has occurred, communicated what are the consequences for the undesirable behavior.
2. *An immediate burn.* If discipline is required, it must occur immediately after the undesirable act is observed. The person must see the connection between the act and the discipline.
3. *Consistency.* There are no favorites—stoves burn everyone the same. Any employee who performs the same undesirable act will be disciplined similarly.
4. *Impersonality.* Disciplinary action is not pointed toward a person; it is meant to eliminate undesirable behaviors.

The hot stove rule assumes that the discipline being applied will be impersonal. However, a serious question arises on whether every employee is equal. Is a newly hired employee with only a few weeks on the job and unfamiliar with company rules and programs the same as an employee with 20 years of job tenure? People, situations, and the undesirable behaviors differ and the hot stove rule, if used to the letter, fails to recognize individual and situational differences.

Progressive Discipline

Progressive discipline is an approach in which a sequence of penalties is administered, each one slightly more severe than the previous one. The goal is to build a discipline program that progresses from less severe to more severe in terms of punishment. One example of a progressive discipline approach applied to unexcused absences is the program used at Hudson Manufacturing. The progressive steps are outlined in Exhibit 15–5.

Hudson's progressive approach becomes especially harsh after three unexcused absence violations. It is important in any disciplinary system to formally record what the policy is and what and when action was taken. The Hudson approach does this. The courts are especially sensitive to the quality of records kept by management in using a progressive discipline approach.

Positive Discipline

Hot stove rules and progressive discipline focus on past behavior. There is also the possibility that employees who are disciplined in a punitive way will rarely build time commitment into their jobs or feel better about the job or company

---

EXHIBIT 15–5 **Hudson Manufacturing Progressive Discipline For Unexcused Absences**

An unexcused absence is defined in the labor-management agreement Sec. 7, paragraph 12, p. 9–181 as any absence not approved by the immediate manager of the employee. Hudson permits absence for personal illness, jury duty, vacation, and death in the family according to Sec. 7, paragraph 15, p. 9–184 specifications. In each case the supervisor must be consulted. Other absences must be approved before they occur. Failure to comply with the unexcused absence guidelines will be subject to the following:

- First violation will result in an oral warning within 48 hours of return to work and a written record of the act being placed in the employee's file.
- Second violation will result in a written warning being placed in the employee's file within 48 hours of return to work.
- Third violation will result in a two-day layoff without pay and a statement of the layoff being placed in the employee's file.
- Fourth violation will result in a two-week layoff without pay and a statement of the layoff being placed in the employee's file.
- Fifth violation will result in the immediate and permanent dismissal of the employee.
- The record of unexcused absence will begin anew after three years. All unexcused absences on the record will be eliminated and a new file will begin every three years.

as a result. In contrast to punitive discipline approaches, positive discipline is another approach. The advocates of this approach view it as future-oriented, as working with employees to solve problems so that problems do not occur again.

General Electric (GE) Meter Business Department in Somersworth, New Hampshire, uses a positive discipline approach.[14] In General Electric's system, there are written reminders about behaviors and not warnings. There is provision for what is called a decision-making leave as the final disciplinary step instead of suspension or termination. If the employee, after the leave, fails to commit to the rules and policies of the firm, she or he is then discharged.

A cross section of supervisors and line managers implemented the GE positive discipline approach. The team developed a 12-phase communication program that included meetings, slide/tape presentations, brochures, and training to explain the program and its features to employees. In the first two years of the program there has been a significant reduction in the number of formal disciplinary steps taken compared to the previous period, when punitive discipline was used. In the second year of the program, 3,295 counseling sessions were conducted by supervisors to discuss a specific need for improvement and to gain the employee's agreement to make necessary corrections. The effectiveness of these meetings is demonstrated by the fact that only 65 oral reminders were issued. Seven employees were placed on decision-making leave; all seven returned without any need to discharge them.

Some of the employee comments on the GE positive discipline program are:

- "I think whenever a company will treat us like adults, as individuals, it's a good thing."
- "It certainly is an improvement. . . . Now when you do something wrong . . . they talk with you rather than talk down to you. You feel like an adult."
- "The decision-making leave with pay makes you feel guilty. I'd feel like a heel!"

The positive discipline approach is a program that recognizes that people make mistakes. It is a discipline program that deemphasizes punitive action by management. Yet, it is still a discipline program that uses the most punishing consequence of all, being discharged.

ADMINISTRATION OF DISCIPLINE

The hot stove rule, progressive discipline, and positive discipline approaches are each applied in a formal manner. Likewise, in unionized organizations, the employee has a formalized procedure that provides adequate protection: the grievance procedure discussed in Chapter 17. In nonunionized situations, the hierarchical system is the most prevalent. However, management today is no

---

[14] Allan W. Bryant, "Replacing Punitive Discipline with a Positive Approach," *Personnel Administrator*, February 1984, pp. 79–87.

longer free in any situation, union or nonunion, to administer discipline without concern for potential legal challenges.

Hierarchical Discipline Systems

Discipline is administered to most nonunion employees by the supervisor, who also evaluates the employee. If the employee is in need of discipline, the supervisor decides what is to be done. In this hierarchical system, the conditions allow a supervisor who might be arbitrary, wrong, or ineffective to be police officer, judge, and jury over the employee. In many of our courts, a person accused of a crime such as speeding can have counsel, the judge is not the arresting officer, and the penalty may be a $50 fine. In the employment situation, where the employee has none of these safeguards, the penalty for an infraction of work rules may be his or her job or salary. Even if convicted of speeding, the employee can appeal to a higher court. What can the employee do if he/she is unfairly fired by the supervisor? There is, of course, the *open-door policy:* The employee could appeal to the supervisor's superior. But this is usually no help at all. The whole value system of the hierarchy is based on support among supervisors to build a good management team. The informal open-door policy can lead to a quasilegal form of justice such as that developed by IBM, in which the employee's case is recorded and systematically reviewed at several levels. A strictly hierarchical justice system is more prevalent in businesses than in other work organizations.

A feeling of helplessness and lack of due process for employees can become a *powerful* force leading to the unionization of enterprises. To work at all, hierarchical systems must be considered fair by employees. There must be adequate proof of any deviance. Employees will support discipline only if they feel that the disciplined employee was treated fairly and consistently compared to other past offenders. Mitigating circumstances must be considered if disciplinary procedures are taken. The minimal safeguard to prevent serious injustice in the hierarchical system is the mandated right to job transfer in disputes with less than overwhelming evidence against the employee.

If hierarchical systems are to be effective and fair, operating and P/HRM managers must administer discipline equitably. There have been a few studies of the extent to which this is so. One study on the subject found that even in companies with a well-developed discipline system, discipline was unevenly administered.[15] Other studies have found that prejudice against minorities or union members had led to unequal discipline. The data on differences in degree of discipline provide reasons for having systems of appeal besides the open-door policy to supplement or supplant the hierarchical approach.[16]

If discipline is called for, the manager can apply a series of sanctions to improve future performance or behavior. These vary from a brief parental-type

---

[15] Edward L. Harrison, "Legal Restrictions on the Employer's Authority to Discipline," *Personnel Journal,* February 1982, pp. 136–41.

[16] Phillips Shaak and Milton S. Schwartz, "Uniformity of Policy Interpretation among Managers in American Industry," *Academy of Management Journal,* March 1973, pp. 77–83.

chat to discharging the employee. A typical discipline system follows a progressive pattern of steps. Each step in the progression proves more severe for the disciplined employee.

The first step in a progressive pattern involves what is called counseling or a verbal discussion or warning. This is the most frequent method of disciplinary action. The supervisor determines if, in fact, a violation took place, explains to the employee why the violation significantly affects productivity, and suggests that it should not happen again. Sometimes the supervisor pushes counseling to the "chewing out" stage.

If a second or more serious violation takes place, the supervisor again counsels the employee, this time noting that the incident will be entered in the employee's personnel file. This is actually called the written warning step in a progressive pattern of discipline. If the violation was sufficiently serious, the employee may also be given an oral or written warning of the consequences of a future reoccurrence. An example of an employee warning report from Dailey Oil Tools, Inc., is presented in Exhibit 15–6. This report is placed in the employee's file.

EXHIBIT 15–6　　**Employee Warning Report**

DAILEY OIL TOOLS, INC
L I Drilling Jars

EMPLOYEE WARNING REPORT

Employee's Name _____　Date of Warning _____ Dept. _____ Shift _____

Clock or
Payroll No. _____

Type of Violation		W A R N I N G	

Type of Violation

☐ Attendance　☐ Carelessness　☐ Disobedience
☐ Safety　　　☐ Tardiness　　☐ Work Quality
☐ Other _____

_____

_____

Violation Date _____

Violation Time _____ a.m. p.m.

Place Violation Occurred _____

Company Statement

Employee Statement

Check Proper Box

☐ I concur with the Company's statement.

☐ I disagree with the Company's statement for the following reasons:

I have entered my statement of the above matter.

Employee's Signature _____ Date _____

Warning Decision

Approved By _____

Name	Title	Date

List All Previous Warnings Below
When Warned And By Whom

I have read this "warning decision" and understand it.

Previous Warning:　　1st Warning
　　　　Date _____
　　　Verbal _____
　　　Written _____

Employee's Signature _____ Date

Previous Warning:　　2nd Warning
　　　　Date _____
　　　Verbal _____
　　　Written _____

Signature of person who prepared warning　Title　Date

Previous Warning:　　3rd Warning
　　　　Date _____
　　　Verbal _____
　　　Written _____

Supervisor's Signature　　　　　　　Date

Copy Distribution

☐ Employee　　　　☐ Supervisor　　　☐ Foreman
☐ Industrial Relations　☐　　　　　　☐ Union Rep.

DOT 704 (R 12/80)

If the incident concerns decreasing productivity, the employee may request transfer or be asked to transfer to another job. The employee may have been placed in the wrong job, there may be a personality conflict between the employee and the supervisor, or more training might help. In some rare cases, demotions or downward transfers are used.

If counseling and warnings do not result in changed behavior, and if a transfer is not appropriate, the next progressive step is normally a *disciplinary layoff.* If any damage resulted from the deviant behavior, the deductions can be made from employee's pay over a period of time. Most disciplinary action will not require such a severe step. The layoff is usually of short duration, perhaps a few days or up to a week.

The next most severe form of progressive discipline is what is referred to as *dehiring,* or what most people call getting an employee to quit.[17] Getting the unsatisfactory employee to quit has many advantages over termination, for both employee and employer. Both save face. The employee finds another job and then quits, telling the peer group how much better off he or she is at the new location. The employer is happy to have gotten rid of an ineffective employee without having to fire him or her. Dehiring is not a forthright approach to discipline. Many supervisors find it unethical. It should be used only if the supervisor prefers it to the next step: discharge.

The ultimate progressive discipline step is discharge or termination of employment. To many inexperienced managers, discharge is the solution to any problem with a difficult employee. Often discharge is not possible, because of seniority rules, union rules, too few replacements in the labor market, or a number of other reasons. Discharge has many costs, both direct and indirect. Directly, it leads to a loss of all the human resource investments already made, for recruiting, selection, evaluation, and training; many organizations also pay severance pay. Then these same investments must be made again for the replacement, and frequently there is a period during which the new employee is not as productive as the former employee. The indirect costs are the effect on other employees of firing one of their numbers. If it is a blatant case of severe inability or deviant behavior, there is not too much problem with peer group resentment. But too often, the facts are not clear, and other employees may feel the employer acted arbitrarily. Some employees may seek employment elsewhere to prevent an arbitrary action happening to them. Others may reduce productivity in protest.

Thus discharge is the *last alternative*—when all else fails or in very serious cases, such as discovery of fraud or massive theft. One subtle reason restrains many supervisors from suggesting discharges. If the supervisor has had the employee a long time, management may begin to ask: "If the employee is so bad, why wasn't he downgraded sooner? Why didn't the supervisor get rid of the employee sooner? Why did he hire him in the first place? Do you think he's a good judge of employees? Is he really supervisory timber?" Many discharges

---

[17] Lawrence Steinmetz, *Managing the Marginal and Unsatisfactory Performer* (Reading, Mass.: Addison-Wesley Publishing, 1969).

are reversed by arbitrators. For these reasons, actual discharges are rare and when they occur a record is made of the reasons. Exhibit 15–7 presents the documentation used at Dailey Oil Tools for terminated or discharged employees.

Termination-at-Will

Each year, American employers in the private sector fire about 3 million employees for noneconomic reasons.[18] Such terminations are called *discharge for cause*. Protection against unjust discharge is provided to a minority of all employees through collective bargaining, antidiscrimination laws, civil service, and teacher tenure laws.[19] All other employees are subject to the termination-at-will doctrine. As one court put it 100 years ago: "Employment relationships of an indefinite duration may be terminated at any time without notice for good cause, for no cause, or even for cause morally wrong."[20]

In recent years, however, an increasing number of state court decisions have found exceptions to the termination-at-will doctrine.[21] The three theories that have been advanced in support of wrongful discharge suits are based on claims of violation of public policy, the existence of an implied contract, and the covenant of good faith and fair dealing.[22]

From *The Wall Street Journal*, with permission of Cartoon Features Syndicate

"Basford, I want to put an end to this rumor that you're going to be fired. You're fired!"

---

[18] Jack Stieber, "Employment-At-Will: An Issue for the 1980s," in *Personnel and Human Resources Management,* eds. Randall S. Schuler, Stuart A. Youngblood, and Vandra L. Huber (St. Paul: West Publishing, 1987), pp. 379–86.

[19] David W. Ewing, *Do It My Way or You're Fired* (New York: John Wiley & Sons, 1983).

[20] *Payne v. Western Atlanta R.R.*, 81 Tenn. 507–20 (1884).

[21] Marco L. Colosi, "Who's Pulling the Strings on Employment at Will?" *Personnel Journal,* May 1984, pp. 56–68.

[22] *The Employment-At-Will Issue, a BNA Special Report* (Washington, D.C.: Bureau of National Affairs, 1982).

EXHIBIT   15–7   **Termination Report**

DAILEY OIL TOOLS, INC.
HOME OF THE
L. I. Drilling Jars
SPECIALTY SERVICE SINCE 1971

TERMINATION REPORT

PROFILE DATA (To Be Completed By Employee's Immediate Manager)

EMPLOYEE NAME	SOCIAL SECURITY NUMBER
ADDRESS	MANAGER/SUPERVISOR
POSITION	

☐ EXEMPT   ☐ NON-EXEMPT   ☐ FULL-TIME   ☐ PART-TIME   ☐ TEMPORARY

AGE	HIRE DATE	SALARY

LAST PERFORMANCE RATING

NOTICE GIVEN?   ☐ NO   ☐ YES, _____DAYS   ☐ VERBAL   ☐ WRITTEN

REASONS FOR TERMINATION (Check Appropriate Reason(s) and Explain Fully).

VOLUNTARY

____ Personal Reasons
____ Medical Reasons
____ Domestic Reasons
____ Another Position
____ Dissatisfied (Wgs., Hrs., Wk.)
____ Transportation Difficulties
____ Marriage
____ Leaving Area
____ Attend School
____ Military
____ Deceased
____ Retirement
____ Other (Specify)

INVOLUNTARY

____ Unadaptable or Unsatisfactory
____ Unsatisfactory Attendance
____ Attitude Unsatisfactory
____ Excessive Tardiness
____ Violation of Company Rules
____ Refused to do assigned work
____ Extensive Absence due to illness
____ Lack of Work
____ Other (Specify)

IMPACT ON COMPANY

Do the Circumstances of this Termination Qualify the Employee for Unemployment Benefits Taxable to the Company?
            ☐ YES   ☐ NO   ☐ QUESTIONABLE

EVALUATION (Check One and Explain Below)
☐ SIGNIFICANT LOSS (Key Employee)   ☐ LOSS   NO IMPACT   ☐ ADVANTAGE

WOULD YOU RECOMMEND REHIRE?   ☐ NO   ☐ YES   ☐ SIMILAR JOB   ☐ DIFFERENT JOB

INTERNAL CORRECTIVE ACTION INDICATED?   ☐ NO   ☐ YES

COMMENTS:

EVALUATION BY:	DATE

DOT-728 (R 4/81)

P/HRM Manager Close-Up

Kenneth W. Tynes
Cessna Aircraft Company

Biography

Kenneth W. Tynes is manager of professional employment for Cessna Aircraft Company.

Mr. Tynes, a native of Monroe, Louisiana, holds a masters degree from Webster University with a human resources management major and a bachelors degree in administrative management from Brigham Young University. He is also an Accredited Personnel Manager.

Mr. Tynes's experience has included personnel assignments in both the public and private sectors. He served as a personnel assistant, safety coordinator, and employee relations manager prior to joining Cessna in 1979. Previous assignments within the Cessna organization have included serving as wage and salary manager for the marketing divisions and as personnel and training manager for the finance subsidiaries.

A Performance Problem: How It Was Handled at Cessna

Human resource problems often provide the opportunity to affect people's lives while benefiting the company. One such example involved an older, minority employee with 30 years seniority in the company and a satisfactory performance record until recently. The employee (who is called John here) developed performance, attendance, tardiness, and attitude problems. Kenneth Tynes became involved when John's supervisor contacted him regarding possible disciplinary actions that could be taken against John.

This meeting yielded some interesting facts. John's performance was extremely poor, he was operating material-loading equipment in a hazardous manner, and he was no longer reliable. The supervisor wanted to terminate John's employment. How-

(continued)

ever, John had performed well for 30 years, with problems occurring only recently. Kenneth discussed with the supervisor the possibility that John's actions were symptoms of the problem rather than the problem itself. They agreed to investigate the matter before forming any conclusions.

The pattern created by John's behavior caused Kenneth to suspect a problem with alcohol. The supervisor and Kenneth met with John regarding his situation. They spoke candidly with him about the safety problems, the liability exposure, and the need for performance improvement. John expressed concern for his job. Once he felt comfortable with their motives, he opened up and really talked. Alcohol abuse was the main problem.

They explained the company's employee assistance program to John and made sure that he understood how the company could help if he desired to participate. John elected to enter the rehabilitation program at a local hospital. Six weeks later, John finished the program and returned to work.

The course pursued allowed John to regain his previous performance level in the company. In addition, John did not become another turnover statistic or worse—a discrimination claimant against the company. Cessna also demonstrated their commitment to their employees through this effort.

Public Policy Exception This view argues that an employer cannot fire an employee for reasons that violate public policy. Today 20 states have recognized this exception in cases in which an employee was fired for refusing to commit an unlawful act, for performing an important public obligation, or for exercising a statutory right or privilege. In general, cases involve refusing to give false testimony, reporting illegal conduct by an employer (called "whistle blowing"), or refusing to violate a professional code of ethics.[23]

In one of the earliest cases, the California Court of Appeals ruled in 1959 that it was against public policy for the Teamsters' Union to fire a business agent for refusing to give false testimony before a legislative committee.[24]

In an Illinois case, an employee alleged that he was fired for offering information to the police about possible criminal behavior on the job by another co-worker and for agreeing to help in the investigation.[25] The court held that there is a clear public policy favoring investigation and prosecution of criminal offenses.

Implied Contract Exception The implied contract exception as recognized in 13 states, has found an implied promise of job tenure for employees with satisfactory performance records, in employee handbooks, in personnel man-

---

[23] J. P. Near and M. P. Miceli, "Retaliation against Whistleblowers: Predictions and Effects," *Journal of Applied Psychology*, February 1986, pp. 137–45.

[24] Peterman v. International Brotherhood of Teamsters, Local 396, 174 C. A. 2d 184, 344, p. 2d 25, 1959.

[25] Palmeteer v. International Harvester Co., 85 Ill. 2d 124, 421 N.E.

uals, or in oral statements that an employee would not be discharged without just cause.

The California Court of Appeals found that evidence supported the claim that an implied promise was made to the employee based on the 32-year duration of his employment, his promotions and commendation, assurances he received, and the employer's personnel policies.[26] The employee claimed that he was discharged for refusing to participate in negotiations with a union because of a purported "sweetheart agreement" that enabled the company to pay women lower wages than male employees.

In a New York case an employee signed an application stating that employment would be subject to the company's handbook, which said that dismissal would occur only for just and sufficient cause.[27] He also received from the supervisor oral assurances of job security. The New York Court of Appeals held that there was sufficient evidence of a contract and a breach of contract to sustain a cause of action.

The Good Faith and Fair Dealing Exception In three states—California, Massachusetts, and Montana—it is held that no matter what an employer says or does to make it clear that termination is at-will and that an employee may be dismissed without cause, the employer must deal with the employee fairly and in good faith.

In Massachusetts, the Appellate Court ignored an explicit written contract that reserved to the employee the right to fire an employee for any reason.[28] The employee, a 61-year-old salesperson with 40 years of service, claimed that he was fired to avoid paying him sales commissions on a multimillion dollar order. The court held it was for a jury to decide, which the jury did, if the employer's motive in firing him was suspect.

In 1983, the Montana Supreme Court approved a jury award of $50,000 to a cashier who alleged that she was discharged without warning and was forced to sign a letter of resignation.[29] The employer claimed that she was fired for carelessness, incompetency, and insubordination. The court said that there was sufficient evidence for the jury to find fraud, oppression, or malice and held that an employer's breach of good faith and fair dealing is a reason for which damages may be recovered.

The principles and decision just presented may not appear surprising or unreasonable to nonlawyers. They merely support what is considered fair and decent employer behavior. However, in some jurisdictions the court's rulings are based on narrow interpretations of the law, public policy, implied contract, and good faith and fair dealing. For example, the District of Columbia Court of Appeals rejected a public policy exception claim when one employee stated that his employer had required that he testify in an administrative proceeding and then fired him in retaliation for testifying against the employer's inter-

---

[26] Pugh v. See Candies, Inc. 116 Cal. App. 3d 311, 171 Cal. reptr. 917, 1981.

[27] Weiner v. McGraw-Hill, 83 A.D. 2d 810, 442, N.Y.S. 2d 11 (1st Dept. 1981).

[28] Fortune v. National Cash Register, 373 Mass. 96, 364 N.E. 2d 1251, 1977.

[29] Gates v. Life of Montana Insurance Co., Mont. Sup. Ct. No. 83–468, August 5, 1983.

est.[30] Also, in New York a court ruled that a bank employee, who alleged that he had been discharged because he had uncovered evidence of illegal foreign currency manipulation, was terminated at will because he had no written employment contract.[31]

Even under the most liberal interpretation of the termination-at-will doctrine, the National Labor Relations Act, and Title VII of the Civil Rights Act, the recognized exceptions still only apply to a small percentage of the 3 million employees discharged each year. The overwhelming majority of discharged employees are fired for such acts as: excessive absenteeism, dishonesty, theft, insubordination, possession or use of intoxicants or illegal drugs, refusal to accept a job assignment, and falsifying company records or application forms.[32]

The Current State Current court interpretations, laws, and public sentiment indicate that an employee has a "right to a job" unless he or she fails to live up to rules, policies, and performance standards and gives just cause for termination, or the employer has a just cause (such as a business slow-down) to terminate the employee.[33] This right to a job is based on the contractual relationship (stated or implied) entered into by the employee and employer. It flows from the contract, its conditions, and the duty of fairness and good faith by both parties.[34]

A company might respond to the latest court interpretations of termination-at-will by stating that all employees, except those under written contract, are "at-will." In *Novosel* v. *Sears Roebuck & Co.* an employee-at-will alleged that Sears unfairly terminated him without just cause.[35] The Michigan court ruled against the employee saying that the application blank indicated termination-at-will. On the blank it stated:

> In consideration of my employment, I agree to conform to the rules and regulations of Sears, Roebuck & Company, and my employment and compensation can be terminated, with or without cause, and with or without notice, at any time, at the option of either the company or myself.

The court held that the obligations of both parties was stipulated on the application form.

Employers and employees need to carefully examine written policies and procedures as they relate to recruiting, hiring, compensation, appraisal, discipline, and termination. Is there any stated or implied promise of permanent

[30] Ivy v. Army Times Publishing Co., 428 A. 2d 831 (D.C. 1981).

[31] Edwards v. Citibank, 100 Misc. 2d 59, 418 N.Y.S. 269 (Supr. Ct. N.Y., 1979).

[32] F. Elkouri, *How Arbitration Works*, 3rd ed. (BNA, 1973), pp. 652–66.

[33] Pat Gray, "Employer's Right to Fire Is under Fire," *USA Today*, February 18, 1986, p. 33.

[34] Maria Leonard, "Challenges to the Termination-At-Will Doctrine," *Personnel Administrator*, February 1983, pp. 49–56.

[35] Court Action No. 69–73926 C.E.D. Mich. (SLIP OP 9/5/80).

employment? Is what you find what you prefer? It is the employer and the employee's responsibility to clearly understand what is meant by termination-at-will.[36] Instead of being frightened by court rulings for and against termination-at-will, it is recommended that everyone involved examine the law, court rulings, and company practices before making any changes in procedures, policies, and behavior.

Other Discipline and Appeal Systems

Although the progressive discipline and grievance system is *by far* the most used in industry, other employing organizations use different models more often. A few business organizations have also taken steps to design systems that may protect the employee from arbitrary supervisory action more effectively than the hierarchical model does. The alternatives to the hierarchical models are peer, quasi-judicial, and modified hierarchical approaches. In the *peer system,* a jury of peers evaluates and punishes. The *quasi-judicial approach* uses an independent arbitrator or ombudsman to resolve disputes. *Modified hierarchical systems* are regular appeals channels *inside* the organization, but including someone other than the supervisor's superior. One mechanism is to have all disputed dismissals or behavior modification plans submitted to specified management executive or executives far removed from the scene, who hear the facts, and judge whether proper action was taken.

Nonhierarchical systems are used by such varied organizations as unions like the United Auto Workers, the Civil Service Commission in the U.S. government, and the American military. The private sector almost never uses nonhierarchical systems.

It must be noted that there is little or no empirical evidence that providing nonhierarchical systems necessarily provides fairer treatment of employees. But a study of the history of justice under various systems in the public domain would indicate justice is much more likely under systems that provide for independent assessment of evidence and judgments than one in which the superior is prosecutor, judge, and jury.

THE DISCIPLINARY INTERVIEW: A CONSTRUCTIVE APPROACH

As previously mentioned, managers in some cases must tell an employee in clear terms that his or her behavior or job performance is below par. Suppose that this is accomplished through a discussion of poor performance, which is in essence a disciplinary interview.[37] There are several guidelines that can help

---

[36] Richard Greene, "Don't Panic," *Forbes,* August 29, 1983, p. 122.

[37] David N. Campbell, R. L. Fleming, and Richard C. Grote, "Discipline without Punishment—at Last," *Harvard Business Review,* July–August 1985, pp. 174–78; and Guvene G. Alpander, "Training First-Line Supervisors to Criticize Constructively," *Personnel Journal,* March 1980, pp. 218–21.

the manager accomplish a constructive discussion with the ineffective performer.

1. *Root out the Causes.* The manager needs to determine if personal problems are playing a role in the poor performance (e.g., fatigue, alcohol, insomnia). This can be done by listening to the employee, to his or her co-workers, and by observation of the employee on the job.
2. *Analyze Other Reasons for Poor Performance.* If personal problems are not the main cause of poor performance, examine such factors as:
    a. Lack of skill and training to do the job.
    b. Low effort.
    c. Situational circumstances beyond the employee's control.
3. *Prepare for the Disciplinary Interview.* After analyzing possible causes and reasons for poor performance, prepare for the interview. Check the employee's previous record and even talk to previous supervisors about the employee.
4. *Conduct the Interview with Care and Professionalism.*
    a. Keep it private—public criticism is too stark and often negative.
    b. Criticize selectively—emphasize job-related performance causes. Tell the employee what you think and try to avoid being aggressive. Stay calm and be polite at all times.
    c. Let the employee speak—be a good listener; don't rush the meeting. Allow the employee to give his or her side of the story. A good rule is to show that you are listening by asking questions that indicate you are receiving the message being delivered.
    d. Take one point at a time—don't confuse points. Focus on one problem at a time.
    e. Attack the problem and not the person—in focusing on each point, remember to attack the act and not the self-concept.
5. *Issuing the Discipline.* Don't make a joke of having to discipline the employee. There really is nothing funny about being disciplined for poor performance or inappropriate behavior. Prescribe the disciplinary steps to be taken in specific terms and with a specific timetable. Do not end the disciplinary interview until you are certain that the employee understands the discipline and what is expected. Also, assure the employee his or her future performance will be judged without considering past ineffective performance problems.
6. *Don't Expect to Win a Popularity Contest.* A person who administers discipline in an equitable and firm manner will not win popularity contests. However, this person will be respected, and a manager who is respected is invaluable to an organization. The disciplinary interview is a serious part of the management job that unfortunately must be conducted regularly.

These few guidelines are designed to correct a problem or modify ineffective behaviors and are not intended to embarrass or publicly ridicule an employee. A constructive disciplinary interview can play an instrumental role in converting an ineffective performer into a productive member of the organization.

A RETURN TO THE P/HRM · IN · ACTION

Jeremy Schultz, the P/HRM vice president at Judge Incorporated, is reflecting on the results of his interviews with four supervisors this week. These supervisors are responsible for Al, Susan, Joyce, and Tom.

Because of these four and many similar employees, Jeremy decides to set up a formal disciplinary system. In consultation with supervisors and selected employees, he sets up in written form the rules of working at Judge. The performance evaluation system is strengthened to make the goals clearer.

Jeremy runs some training sessions and communicates the new system to the employees. The new discipline system sets up a step-by-step process and a set of "costs":

1st violation or problem: Counseling by supervisor.

2nd violation or problem: Counseling by supervisor and recording in personnel file.

3rd violation or problem: Disciplinary layoff.

4th violation or problem: Discharge.

For alcohol or drug problems, mandatory counseling at counseling centers is required, or discharge will result.

Legal violations result in discharge and prosecution.

In all cases of disciplinary layoff, the employee will receive counseling from P/HRM. If there appear to be problems between supervisor and employee, Jeremy will serve as an ombudsman.

With regard to Al, Susan, Joyce, and Tom, Jeremy recommends the following actions:

Al: Transfer him to a new supervisor. There appeared to be a personality conflict between Al and his supervisor. (The transfer did not help. Eventually Al received a disciplinary layoff and was terminated, in spite of much counseling.)

Susan: Ask her to join Alcoholics Anonymous. (She did, and got her drinking problem under control.)

Joyce: Watch for evidence that she is stealing. (When the evidence was clear, she was terminated and prosecuted. The judge gave her a suspended sentence.)

Tom: Give him counseling about his behavior. (The supervisor reported later that Tom was a better employee.)

All in all, Jeremy felt the new disciplinary system was working rather well.

SUMMARY

Some of the most difficult human and personnel problems involve handling the difficult or ineffective employee. Guidelines for assessing the causes and how to deal with this situation follow:

1. Most deviant or difficult employees' problems probably have multiple causes. Some of these are listed below:
   a. Problems of intelligence and job knowledge.
   b. Emotional problems.
   c. Motivational problems.
   d. Physical problems.
   e. Family problems.
   f. Problems caused by the work group.
   g. Problems originating in company policies.
   h. Problems stemming from society and its values.
   i. Problems from the work context (e.g., economic forces) and the work itself.
2. Categories of employees that cause discipline problems include:
   a. The ineffective employee.
   b. Alcoholic and drug abusing employees.
   c. Participants in theft, crime, and illegal acts.
   d. The rule violators.
3. The discipline process involves:
   a. Employer establishes rules and goals.
   b. These rules and goals are communicated to the employees.
   c. Employee behavior is assessed.
   d. Undesirable behavior is modified, punished, and so on.
   e. Depending on the behavior, its severity, and the number of offenses, continued violation might result in termination.
4. Employers should concentrate on trying to modify the effects and advise rehabilitation and counseling for such problems as alcoholism and drug addiction.
5. For discipline systems to be effective, the disciplinary review must take place as soon after the action as possible. It must be applied consistently and impersonally.

Exhibit 15–8 gives recommendations for the use of different kinds of justice systems in the model organizations defined in Chapter 1.

It is important to remember that discipline is an area in which help is needed from many areas: supervisors, P/HRM, the work group, arbitrators, and top management. Each has a crucial role to play if the discipline system is to be effective.

Questions for Review and Dicussion

1. Why is the equity of a discipline program important for maintaining the respect of employees?
2. Should an employer have a right to terminate at will?
3. Would a union support a discipline program within an organization? Why?
4. What are limitations of applying the hot stove rule to all employees?
5. How serious a problem is the alcoholic employee at work? How should the alcoholic employee be handled?

EXHIBIT 15–8 Recommendations for Model Organizations on Difficult Employees and Discipline

Type of Organization	Hierarchical Justice Systems	Reinforce Hierarchical Justice Systems with:		
		Peer Committees	Ombudsmen	Outside Committees
1. Large size, low complexity, high stability	X		X	X
2. Medium size, low complexity, high stability	X		X	
3. Small size, low complexity, high stability	X	X		
4. Medium size, moderate complexity, moderate stability	X		X	
5. Large size, high complexity, low stability	X		X	X
6. Medium size, high complexity, low stablity				
7. Small size, high complexity, low stability	X	X		

6. What are the potential costs to the employer of drug abusers attempting to work on the job?
7. How serious is the problem of an employee who violates criminal laws? How should the employee be dealt with?
8. Describe the key elements in the discipline process.
9. Contrast the hot stove rule, progressive discipline, and positive discipline. Which one is most compatible with your views?
10. How would a union attempting to organize workers use termination-at-will in its organizing campaign?

GLOSSARY

Dehiring. Creating a work climate that encourages an employee to quit.

Hot Stove Rule. A discipline program that is described in terms of touching a hot stove. There is an immediate burn, a warning system, consistency, and impersonal application of discipline.

Progressive Pattern of Discipline. A discipline program that proceeds from less severe disciplinary actions (a discussion) to a very severe action (being discharged). Each step in the progression becomes more severe.

Termination-at-Will. A condition under which an employer is free to terminate the employment relationship, either for some specific reason, or even no reason at all. In a growing number of courts, the employer's right to terminate at will is being challenged.

APPLICATION CASE 15–1

The Case for and against Drug Testing*

In two short months, top management at Castulon Corporation realized that the company had an employee who might have a drug abuse problem. In October, an electronics engineer was found at his desk clearly stoned ("he literally fell off his chair," the engineer's supervisor said). In November, a security guard discovered two employees in the company parking lot during the lunch hour, snorting cocaine in a car. All three employees were fired. Bob McRary, CEO of Castulon Corp., was particularly disturbed by these incidents. Castulon manufactures electronic systems that monitor and control the levels of hazardous chemicals in industrial plants. Any mistakes made by drug-dependent employees in the design/production of a system could produce disastrous results for system users.

McRary assigned Michael O'Brien, vice president of personnel, the task of developing a written proposal for a drug testing program for Castulon's job applicants and 600 employees. The proposal would recommend procedures for establishing a program and propose the program's content. The proposal would also present a comprehensive coverage of the pros and cons of establishing drug testing at Castulon. Undecided, McRary wanted to review all sides of the question before making a decision.

Michael O'Brien sought the help of Norman Sterling, director of employee relations, and Beverly Shaver, director of employee recruitment and selection, in preparing the proposal. As he often did when handling difficult issues, O'Brien asked each director to assume one position—either for or against mandatory drug testing—and to prepare a 10-page position paper presenting their views based on research and a thorough consideration of the issues at hand. O'Brien would use the papers as input for the final proposal.

Today, Norman Sterling (who chose the advocate position) and Beverly Shaver (who selected the opponent's view) submitted their papers to O'Brien. Now in his office and at O'Brien's request, the two managers are discussing their positions.

"I accepted this assignment initially supporting a drug testing program, and after considering the issues, I'm more convinced we need one, for three primary reasons," Norman Sterling asserted.

"First, we have a responsibility for providing a safe workplace for our employees, and any drug use on the job compromises safety," he continued. "There's no question that drug use results in more accidents on the job. One

* Written by Kim Stewart. Facts and several perspectives were drawn from: Janice Castro, "Battling the Enemy Within," *Time,* March 17, 1986, pp. 52ff; Lewis L. Maltby, "Why Drug Testing Is a Bad Idea," *Inc.,* June 1987, pp. 152–53; Ian A. Miners, Nick Nykodym, and Diane M. Samerdyke-Traband, "Put Drug Detection to the Test," *Personnel Journal,* August 1987, pp. 90–97; and Anne Marie O'Keefe, "The Case against Drug Testing," *Psychology Today,* June 1987, pp. 34–36, 38.

study which compared employees who use drugs with nonusers found that an employee who uses drugs is almost four times more likely to be involved in a job-related accident.

"If you want more evidence, look at the transportation industry," Sterling continued, thumbing through his report to read a passage. "In the train industry alone, about 50 accidents since 1975 have been attributed to mistakes made by drug- or alcohol-impaired employees. Those accidents cost 37 lives, injured 80 others, and destroyed over $34 million in property. In our company, we should be very concerned because our manufacturing people work with heavy equipment. A drug user may not only hurt himself but injure other workers.

"Second, we have a responsibility to produce safe products for our customers. We manufacture electronic systems that monitor and control the levels of hazardous chemicals in plants. That's our business; we've installed thousands of systems worldwide. If a mistake is made in the design or manufacture of a system, toxic chemicals can overflow in a facility, and a tragedy the size of Bhopal, India could occur. Drug use increases the risk.

"Then there are the costs our company pays because of drug use," Sterling continued. "We have the costs of higher absenteeism. The study I mentioned also found that drug-using employees are absent 10 times or more as many days as nonusers. We bear the costs of higher insurance premiums given that drug-using employees receive three times the average level of sick benefits and are five times more likely to file a workers' compensation claim. There are the costs of lower productivity, impaired decision making, and employee theft from the company. Stories abound in the media of addicted employees stealing from their employers to support their drug habits. In one such reported case, a high-level advertising executive billed clients for work never performed and used the revenues to support a $2,000-a-week habit."

"I think you've raised some legitimate concerns, but I think we should first question whether we have a drug problem the size of which merits such a major action as mandatory drug testing," Beverly Shaver replied. "We've had two incidents, but only two. The high quality of our products and low accident and absenteeism record don't indicate widespread drug use among our employees.

"Since we're quoting studies, I found one that's very interesting," she continued. "Although the media paints a picture of a massive drug use problem nationwide, a recent study by the National Institute on Drug Abuse found that for all drugs except cocaine, current use levels are well below 1979, which was the peak year for drug use in the United States. Do we really have a problem?

"All it takes is one impaired employee who makes one design or manufacturing mistake and thousands of people could be killed," Sterling replied. "Also, we may not have a problem now, but we may very well have one soon. The figures are startling on young people now entering the workforce. One study says that about two-thirds of these new workers have taken illegal drugs and 44 percent have done so in the last year. Another survey among companies using preemployment drug test screening among applicants found that 20 to

50 per cent of applicants 18 to 25 years old tested positive. Some of these folks are our future employees."

Michael O'Brien interjected, "Let's assume for a moment that we have a drug problem. Is drug testing the way to solve it?"

"No. I think it creates more problems than it solves," Shaver asserted. "First is the inaccuracy problem. Suppose we tested using the EMIT test which is the most widely used procedure. It boasts a 97 percent accuracy rate under ideal conditions. But conditions are rarely if ever ideal. Samples are contaminated by employees or mishandled by labs or the test just fails. The figures are scary; the Centers for Disease Control re-analyzed urine samples from 13 labs chosen at random to test the accuracy rate. They found that the results of 66 percent of the lab tests were wrong—false positives. Other studies have found similar results."

"It's no wonder given that many over-the-counter drugs, and even foods test positive as illegal drugs," Shaver continued. "Cough syrups can test positive as cocaine. Datril, Advil, and Nuprine can test positive as marijuana, and even poppy seeds on hamburger buns can test positive as morphine. I wonder, given this high false positive rate, how many jobs have been unjustly lost and careers ruined?"

"We can solve the inaccuracy problem by performing second and even third tests when an initial positive finding is obtained," Sterling countered. "We could use a different and more thorough procedure and a different laboratory to reduce the chances of sample mishandling."

"We could, but costs are a big factor," Shaver replied. "The EMIT costs about $18 per test. We can expect a lot of false positives from what I've read. Given the high false positive rates, I wouldn't trust a second or even third followup EMIT test. We could use the most reliable test—the gas chromatography/mass spectroscopy test. It costs $60 per test. With 600 employees and a few hundred applicants each year, costs could get out of hand."

"What are the other issues?" O'Brien asked.

"There's the issue of individual rights," Shaver asserted. "Mandatory drug testing essentially involves searching the contents of an individual's most valued possession—his body, and searching without probable cause. Doesn't the 14th Amendment to the Constitution guarantee an individual's right to be secure against unreasonable searches without probable cause?"

"The 14th Amendment doesn't apply to most dealings between a private company and its employees, including drug testing," Sterling asserted. "We're on sure footing with a drug testing program as long as it is fairly and consistently administered and thoroughly documented, and as long as we don't reveal test results to a third party."

"Technically, the 14th Amendment doesn't apply, but the spirit of the amendment should," Shaver said. "Here's my most serious concern. When we implement mandatory drug testing, we are presuming that our employees are guilty, not innocent. That's what we're communicating to them. It's an act of distrust, and it violates the spirit of mutual trust we've maintained with our employees.

"We have the best employees in the industry," she continued. "They're highly committed to Castulon; they often go the extra mile on their own without being asked. I think that's the case because we've stayed out of their private lives but have been supportive. There's a deep, mutual trust here. Mandatory drug testing violates that trust, and I think it will undermine our relationship with employees."

"Yes, we could make our people feel like criminals if the program is badly handled," Sterling responded. "But it wouldn't be. No trust is violated if we explain the potential costs of drug use, and make employees feel as if they're cooperating to resolve a troublesome problem, not as if they're potential criminals."

"Norman, I'll quote Lewis Maltby, vice president of Drexel Engineering, who's written widely on why his company will not implement drug testing," Shaver said. "'When you say to an employee, 'You're doing a great job, just the same, I want you to pee in this jar and I'm sending someone to watch you,' you've undermined that trust.'"

"Folks, I feel like I'm moderating a debate," O'Brien said. "So, any closing remarks? Beverly?"

"Again, I'm disturbed about the effect that a drug testing program will have on our employees. And the issue of privacy. I wonder if we have the right to information that test results would give us—information about whether an employee is being treated for asthma, heart disease, diabetes, depression, or a host of other illnesses. But essentially, I feel that if we do have a drug problem, we can more effectively deal with it in other ways. As a preventive strategy, we can be very selective in our hiring by thoroughly evaluating job candidates, especially their past work record. We can train managers to identify employees who are possibly drug dependent. There are other strategies that don't have the potentially explosive results a testing program will have."

"If approached carefully, I don't think employees will be offended by the program," Sterling said. "As for more selective hiring, we are already very selective, and as far as drug use is concerned, our careful selection procedure has failed in at least three cases. We need a program that definitely works, and drug testing fits the bill."

Michael O'Brien rose from his desk. "Thank you both for your input," he said. "I'll send you a copy of the proposal once I submit it to Bob later this week. He says he'll make a decision soon after reviewing the proposal. I'll let you know."

Questions for Thought

1. Should Castulon Corporation establish a drug testing program? If so, recommend specific policy for the program that includes disciplinary procedures for dealing with employees who test positive for drug use.
2. What are the most difficult challenges facing an organization in establishing a drug testing program? Discuss.
3. Some observers assert that since alcohol abuse is more prevalent in the workplace and its effects just as costly, companies should also test for alcohol use. Do you agree? Explain.

EXERCISE 15–1   Making Difficult Decisions

Objective: To permit individuals to consider and decide whether the actions taken by management are fair, equitable, and legally defensible under the termination-at-will concept.

SET UP THE EXERCISE

1. Groups of four, six, or eight will form to discuss each of the following situations.
2. Prepare a brief group statement explaining the group decision.
3. Review in the total class each of the group decisions.

John Rogorski

John Rogorski was employed as a department manager in a retail store for three years. He maintained that during the initial job interview he was told that the firm expected to expand operations. The firm because of slow growth had to terminate John after three years of employment. The compnay maintained that John was given no guarantee of employment and was fired under the "at will" doctrine.

Was John's firing justified under the termination-at-will concept?

Peter Rybark

Peter Rybark was an untenured assistant professor at a private college in Oregon. He was sent a memo this past May stating that his annual academic year salary from September to May would be $31,000. He signed a statement about his salary and sent it to the college personnel director. In December, after the fall semester, Peter was informed that his services were no longer needed. He argued that he had an annual contract and was unfairly fired. The college informed him that it had the right to terminate an untenured professor whenever it chose to do so.

Was Peter's firing acceptable under the termination-at-will concept?

Dirk Mansfield

Dirk Mansfield was a technician in the machine shop of Millfield Corporation. He was meeting at lunchtime, during breaks, and after work with employees attempting to convince them to start and support a union. After six months of meetings Dirk was informed by his supervisor that he was fired. He was told that he had violated union organizing procedures and was using the company premises without permission to organize a union. Therefore, because of union organizing rules violations he was terminated.

Was Dirk's firing justifiable under the termination-at-will concept?

Learning Note

This exercise illustrates that in making termination decisions, consideration must be given to the law.

P A R T   V

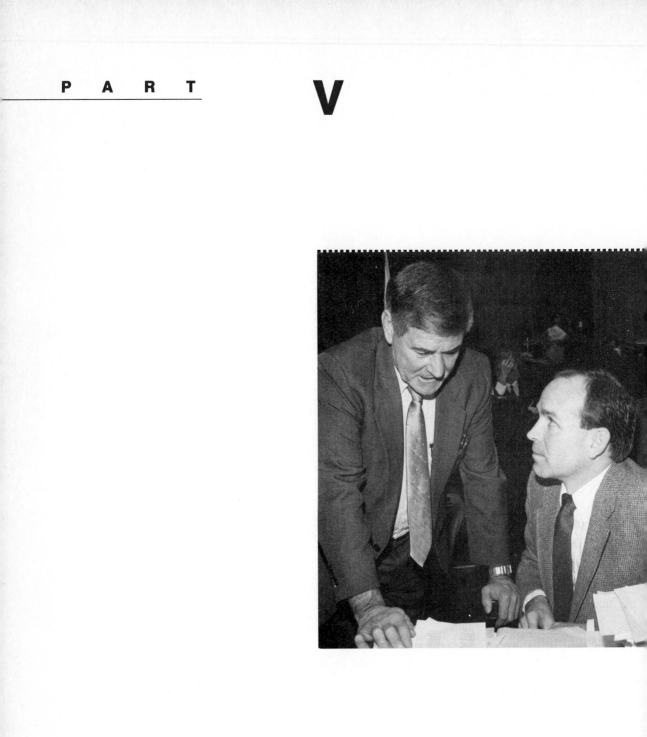

LABOR RELATIONS AND SAFETY AND HEALTH

Three chapters make up Part Five. Chapter 16, Labor Unions: History, Laws, and Issues, covers the history, laws, and some current issues facing labor unions, including unemployment, the quality of life, membership, and resistance to unions. Chapter 17, Organizing and Collective Bargaining, focuses on organizing campaign issues and strategies and collective bargaining. The rights of employees in nonunionized situations are also covered in this chapter. Chapter 18, Employee Safety and Health, covers such topics as the government involvement in safety and health, and new preventive health programs in firms such as Kimberly-Clark and Control Data are discussed and analyzed.

LABOR UNIONS: HISTORY, LAWS, AND ISSUES

LEARNING OBJECTIVES

After studying this chapter you should be able to:

- **Describe** the role that unions play in the lives of unionized employees.
- **Explain** why some employees are attracted to and others resist union membership.
- **Discuss** how labor legislation initially encouraged the growth of labor unions.
- **Define** the various types of union security.
- **Examine** and understand the role that the National Labor Relations Board plays in labor-management relations.

KEY TERMS

AFL-CIO
Agency Shop
American Federation of Labor (AFL)
Business Representative
Closed Shop
Congress of Industrial Organizations (CIO)
Craft Union
Guaranteed Annual Wages
Labor Relations
Landrum-Griffin Act

National Labor Relations Board
Open Shop
Preferential Shop
Restricted Shop
Right-to-Work Laws
Taft-Hartley Act
Union
Union Shop
Union Steward
Wagner Act
Yellow-Dog Contracts

CHAPTER OUTLINE

P/HRM · IN · ACTION

Tom Hardisty

Hardisty Manufacturing Company (HMC) is a fairly new firm that has grown substantially in its short history. Hardisty is located in the Boston area and manufactures consumer goods. It has a volatile technology and employs about 750 persons.

The president of the company is Tom Hardisty. He used to work for the largest firm in the industry, until he had a fight with his boss, quit, and went into competition with his former employer. Several of the key executives of Hardisty were recruited from the same firm.

The last year or two have seen increases in sales for HMC. But because of extreme competitive pressures, profits have been low or nonexistent. At times, HMC has had to lay off employees. And pay and benefit increases have not kept up with inflation. Tom has been too busy trying to keep sales up and financing available to notice the lack of positive change in his own paycheck. That isn't necessarily true for all the others at HMC. Stan Goebel, the P/HRM VP, has tried to bring this up with Tom from time to time. But Tom always seems to be too busy to talk about the problem.

Then one day, Stan came rushing into Tom's office.

Stan: Tom, there are union organizers on the parking lot trying to get our employees to sign authorization cards.

Tom: Authorization cards? What are they? We engineers don't know much about unions and don't like them much either.

Stan: An authorization card is the form the organizers use to get enough people to sign up to hold an election that can unionize us.

Tom: Stan, calm down. You're shaking! We have nothing to worry about. It's one happy family here. Our employees won't join a union.

Stan: Oh yeah? Then why are many of them signing the cards?

Tom: You saw some signing?

Stan: Yeah. Lots of them.

There was a pause while Tom thought for awhile.

Tom: What can we do?

Stan: Well, for one thing, we can't throw them off the parking lot. We allowed charities to solicit there. Remember, I warned you!

Tom: No. I meant, what should we do to keep the union out?

(continued)

Stan: The union must get 30 percent of the employees to sign the cards. . . .

Tom: They'll never get that many. The few malcontents will sign and the rest. . . .

Stan: I've talked to enough P/HRM people who've been through this. You can't assume that. You gotta do something.

Tom: Let's talk about unions and labor relations and decide what we should do. . . .

Stan then discussed some facts of life with Tom: About labor relations, unions, contracts, law, grievances, and similar issues affecting Hardisty Manufacturing Company.

This chapter is about a political and economic force in our society—the labor union. It discusses the union in the context of *labor relations*.

> Labor relations is a continuous relationship between a defined group of employees (represented by a union or association) and an employer. The relationship includes the negotiation of a written contract concerning pay, hours, and other conditions of employment and the interpretation and administration of this contract over its period of coverage.

Labor relations is a much-discussed P/HRM activity. Few employers or employees get as emotionally involved over recruiting methods or career development plans, for example, as they do over labor-management relations.[1] The reason is that collective bargaining goes to the heart of employee relations problems: power. Whoever has the power to fire an employee has power over whether that employee and his or her family can survive. Whoever has the power to discipline an employee because of poor performance has the power to affect significant human needs negatively, as noted in Chapter 2. Underlying the concept of leadership in management is the need for power.

Most employers and unions have used their power fairly. The majority of employers have hired employees, given them reasonable jobs, compensated them well, respected their dignity, and retired them after rewarding careers. However, some employers have not dealt with their employee as well. They have exploited them economically and wielded many a blow to their human dignity.

Likewise most unions and associations have represented the membership well. They have fought hard and fair for improved working conditions, better wages, human dignity, and a sharing of the fruits of labor. Some, however, have been corrupt, violent, and an embarrassment to the membership. In the United States, work conditions considered unfair or exploitative have led to the development of the collective bargaining process. Employees have joined

---

[1] John A. Fossum, *Labor and Relations* (Plano, Tex.: Business Publications, Inc., 1982).

together so that, as individuals, they do not have to stand alone against the power of a General Electric, a Department of Defense, a Yale University, or a Barnes Hospital.

In considering collective bargaining, one focus is the big picture: national and international unions all locked in major struggles with industry or in Congress. As interesting as this is, the focus of this chapter is primarily on the effects of labor relations activities on the P/HRM function of the employer. National contracts, and especially national contracts for a multiunit organization, are the business of a few top managers, a few top union officials, some staff lawyers and support persons, and a few government officials. Very few individuals are involved in these interactions. This chapter is concerned with how the collective bargaining process affects the *day-to-day operations* of an employer and its employees.

A DIAGNOSTIC APPROACH
TO LABOR RELATIONS

Exhibit 16–1 highlights the diagnostic factors that are important in labor relations. The attitudes of employees toward unions influence whether they will join or support a union in the workplace.[2] Managerial attitudes toward unions in general and the union officials they deal with in particular also affect labor relations.

The goals of the controlling interests influence managerial attitudes and behavior toward labor relations. If management is very antiunion, the negotiation and administrative process will not proceed smoothly. The union is the other focal organization in effective collective bargaining relationships. Union officials and management interact daily and at contract time. Union and managerial attitudes toward each other affect the degree of peace and effectiveness that can exist in labor-management relations.

In addition to union requirements, two other environmental factors influence the nature of collective bargaining. Labor market conditions influence both management and the unions in their relationships. If the labor market is tight and the demand for goods is soft and the labor market has a surplus, management has an advantage. It can sustain a strike, and perhaps even benefit economically from one. The other factor is government, which creates the legal environment within which labor relations take place. Government boards rule on legal differences in the system, and government mediators and conciliators often help settle disputes.

Labor relations vary by the sector in which the organization operates. As will be described shortly, unions relate to managers in the business world (private sector), in government settings (public sector), and in other settings such as health, education, and voluntary organizations (third sector). Differing labor relations among the sectors are due to institutional and legal differences.

---

[2] Arthur A. Sloane and Fred Witney, *Labor Relations* (Englewood Cliffs, N.J.: Prentice-Hall, 1988).

EXHIBIT 16–1　　**Factors Affecting Labor Relations**

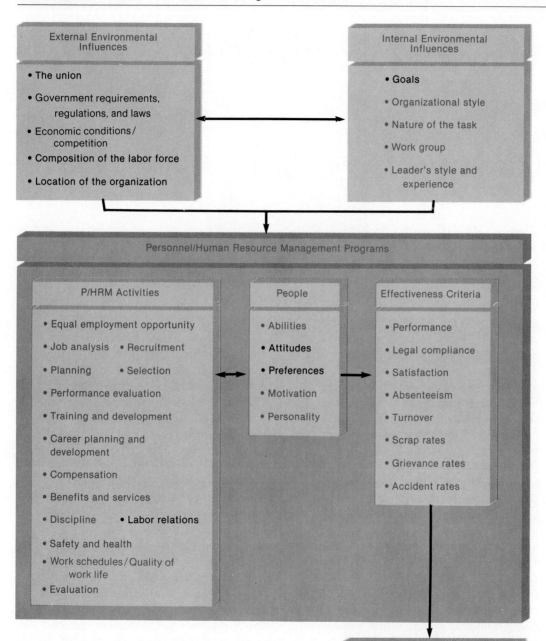

P/HRM Manager Close-Up

John L. Quigley, Jr.
Dr Pepper Company

Biography

With a degree in personnel management from Texas A&M, three years with Smith Protection Services as vice president of security operation for south Texas, and a position as assistant personnel director for Morton Foods, Inc., Division of General Mills, Inc., John Quigley had a strong personnel generalist background when he was recruited as director of personnel for the rapidly growing Dr Pepper Company in 1967. He participated in the management-leveraged buyout of the Dr Pepper Company in 1984, which took Dr Pepper Company private, and again when the Company was sold in 1986. He currently holds the dual position of vice president human resources for the Dr Pepper Company and The Seven-Up Co., a leveraged buyout being managed by the senior management of the Dr Pepper Company.

Job Description

As vice president for human resources, Mr. Quigley coordinates all human resource and personnel functions for the companies, including personnel policy development, employment and recruiting, benefit administration, EEO and affirmative action planning, labor relations, sales training, management development, compensation and security, facilities management, office services and corporate transportation, and flight operations. His responsibilities have grown from a centralized manual personnel system to managing a decentralized, highly responsive human resources and administrative system servicing the national company and several wholly owned domestic and international subsidiaries offering computerized support systems, personnel managers, professionals and specialists, and refined

(continued)

policies and programs designed to support the rapidly growing and expanding companies.

In addition to his work with Dr Pepper Company and The Seven-Up Co., Mr. Quigley has served in the American Society for Personnel Administration, as ASPA district director for north Texas, national vice chairman of the board of directors, and chairman of the board of directors. He is a past member of the board of the Personnel Accreditation Institution. His 18-year membership in ASPA has offered him service opportunities on behalf of growth of personnel professionalism across the continental United States as well as Hawaii, Alaska, and Mexico.

A BRIEF HISTORY OF AMERICAN LABOR UNIONS

Unions have a long history in the United States. Even before the Declaration of Independence, skilled artisans joined together to provide members' families with financial aid in the event of illness or death.[3] Today many blue- and white-collar employees have joined together in unions. Their philosophy is the same: In joining together, there is strength. In fact, a *union* is a group of employees who have joined together to achieve present and future goals that deal with employment conditions.

The power of employees joined together is evident at the bargaining table, where union and management meet to discuss numerous issues. Many of the P/HRM decisions discussed in this book were influenced by union-management bargaining agreements. Employers in unionized organizations must often consult with union officials before taking actions that affect union members. In addition, many nonunionized companies have a workers' committee or council that managers consult before taking action. Their P/HRM policies and practices may affect employees' interest in unionizing. Thus, managers should be concerned with unions; they may either negotiate with union representatives at the bargaining table or face employees who want to form a union. Union objectives, organization, leadership, and attitudes are important for managers to know about.

Unions have existed in the United States since the colonial era. They originally functioned as fraternal societies providing help for members. Today, most unions are part of national organizations, many affiliated with the AFL–CIO (American Federation of Labor–Congress of Industrial Organizations).

---

[3] U.S. Department of Labor, "Brief History of the American Labor Movement," *Bulletin 1000* (Washington, D.C.: U.S. Government Printing Office, 1976), pp. 1–104.

Early Unions

Employers successfully resisted the earliest efforts to organize unions. In 1806, a court ruling made it a "conspiracy in restraint of trade" for workers to combine or exert pressure on management. In effect, unions were illegal until 1842, when the Massachusetts Supreme Court, in *Commonwealth* v. *Hunt*, decided that criminal conspiracy did not apply if unions did not use illegal tactics to achieve goals.

Even then, employers still resisted by discharging employees who joined unions. It was also easy for employers to have employees sign *yellow-dog contracts*, which promised that a prospective employee (job applicant) would not form or join a union. Employers also obtained court injunctions against strikes.

Early unions promoted social reform and free public education. Some of the more militant groups—such as the secret society of anthracite miners called the Molly Maguires from the Pennsylvania coal mines—were considered socialist or anarchist. They were involved in a series of widely publicized murders, riots, and bloodshed initiated by both the employers in the coal regions of Pennsylvania and the Molly Maguires themselves.

LABOR LEGISLATION

The union-management pattern of interaction is governed by state and federal laws.[4] These laws have evolved through common law and through rulings by the National Labor Relations Board and the courts. Figuratively speaking, these laws swing back and forth like a pendulum, at times favoring management and at times favoring unions.

Early Labor Law

The first government legislation affecting unions and management was the Arbitration Act of 1888. This act encouraged the voluntary settlement of labor disputes in the railroad industry. In 1926 the Railway Labor Act was passed by Congress. It provided railroad employees with the right to organize and bargain collectively with management.

In the 1930s, the federal government became involved in labor disputes outside the railroad industry. The Norris-LaGuardia Act, also called the Anti-Injunction Act, was passed in 1932. The act limited the powers of federal courts to stop union picketing, boycotts, and strikes. *Injunctions*, court decrees to stop union activities, had provided employers with an easy way to hinder union activities. The Norris-LaGuardia Act also made the yellow-dog contracts unenforceable.

---

[4] See D. W. Twomey, *Labor Law and Legislation* (Cincinnati: South-Western Publishing, 1980).

The Wagner Act

The *National Labor Relations Act*, better known as the *Wagner Act*, was passed in 1935. The stated purpose of the act was to encourage the growth of trade unions and restrain management from interfering with this growth. This act made the government take an active role in union-management relationships by restricting the activities of management. Five unfair labor practices specified in the Wagner Act are summarized in Exhibit 16–2.

The power to implement the Wagner Act was given to a three-person National Labor Relations Board (NLRB) and a staff of lawyers and other personnel responsible to the board. The board sets up elections, on request, to determine if a given group of workers wishes to have a union as a bargaining representative. The board also investigates complaints of unfair labor practices. If an unfair labor charge is filed with the NLRB and investigation is initiated, the NLRB has an array of alternatives, as presented in Exhibit 16–3, that can be used to resolve the unfair labor practices claim.

The Taft-Hartley Act

The Wagner Act was considered prolabor. In order to swing the pendulum back toward management, Congress in 1947 passed the Taft-Hartley Act (also called the *Labor-Management Relations Act),* which amended and supplemented the Wagner Act. The Taft-Hartley Act guaranteed employee bargaining rights and specifically forbade the five unfair employer labor practices first established in the Wagner Act. But the act also specified unfair union labor practices. The union was restrained from such practices as those shown in Exhibit 16–4.

Union membership increased significantly after the Wagner Act was passed. Under aggressive union leadership, members were recruited, and the

---

EXHIBIT 16–2   Employer Unfair Labor Practices

- *To interfere with, restrain, or coerce employees in the exercise of their rights to organize* (threaten employees with loss of job if they vote for a union, grant wage increases deliberately timed to discourage employees from joining a union).
- *To dominate or interfere with the affairs of a union* (take an active part in the affairs of a union, such as a supervisor actively participating in a union, show favoritism to one union over another in an organization attempt).
- *To discriminate in regard to hiring, tenure, or any employment condition for the purpose of encouraging or discouraging membership in any union organization* (discharge an employee if he or she urges others to join a union, demote an employee for union activity).
- *To discriminate against or discharge an employee because he or she has filed charges or given testimony under the Wagner Act* (discriminate against, fire, or demote an employee because he or she gave testimony to NLRB officials or filed charges against the employer with the NLRB).
- *To refuse to bargain collectively with representatives of the employees; that is, bargain in good faith* (refuse to provide financial data, if requested by the union, when the organization pleads losses; refuse to bargain about a mandatory subject, such as hours and wages; refuse to meet with union representatives duly appointed by a certified bargaining unit).

EXHIBIT 16–3 **NLRB Alternatives for Handling Unfair Labor Practice Charges**

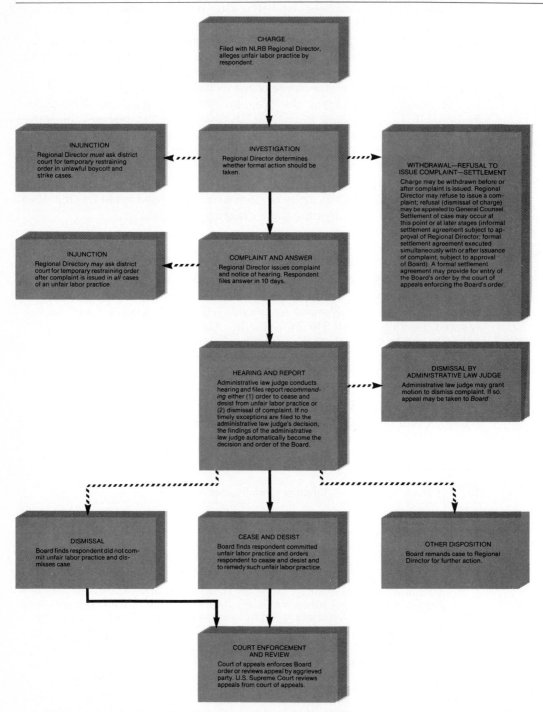

Source: Bruce Feldacker, *Labor Guide to Labor Law* (Reston, Va.: Reston Publishing, 1980), pp. 14–15.

EXHIBIT 16–4   Union Unfair Labor Practices

- *To restrain or coerce employees in the exercise of their right to join or not to join a union, except when an agreement is made by the employer and union that a condition of employment will be joining the union, called a union security clause authorizing a union shop* (picket as a mass and physically bar other employees from entering a company facility, act violently toward nonunion employees, threaten employees for not supporting union activities).
- *To cause an employer to discriminate against an employee other than for nonpayment of dues or initiation fees* (cause an employer to discriminate against an employee for antiunion activity, force the employer to hire only workers satisfactory to the union).
- *To refuse to bargain with an employer in good faith* (insist on negotiating illegal provisions such as the administration's prerogative to appoint (supervisors, refuse to meet with the employer's representative, terminate an existing contract or strike without the appropriate notice).
- *To engage, induce, encourage, threaten, or coerce any individual to engage in strikes, refusal to work, or boycott where the objective is to:*
  Force or require any employer or self-employed person to recognize or join any labor organization or employer organization.
  Force or require an employer or self-employed person to cease using the products of or doing business with another person, or force any other employer to recognize or bargain with the union unless it has been certified by the NLRB.
  Force an employer to apply pressure to another employer to recognize a union.
  Examples are: picketing a hospital so that it will apply pressure on a subcontractor (food service, maintenance, emergency department) to recognize a union; or forcing an employer to do only business with others, such as suppliers, who have a union, or picketing by another union for recognition when a different one is already certified.
- *To charge excessive or discriminatory membership fees* (charge a higher initiation fee to employees who did not join the union until after a union-security agreement is in force).
- *To cause an employer to give payment for services not performed (featherbedding)* (force an employer to add people to the payroll when they are not needed, force payment to employees who provide no services).

---

union cause became so popular that from 1935 to 1947 the membership rolls increased from 3 million to 15 million.

The other major effects of the Taft-Hartley Act include the following:

- It denied supervisors legal protection in organizing their own unions.
- It provided the president of the United States, through the attorney general, the right to seek an 80-day court injunction against strikes or lockouts that could affect the nation's health.
- The union was forbidden to deduct union dues from members' paychecks without prior written permission.
- Employers could express their views against unions as long as they made no attempt to threaten or bribe employees.

Soon after the Taft-Hartley Act was put into practice, a number of corrupt practices in the union movement were disclosed. Investigations uncovered union leaders who had misused and stolen union membership fees and funds. It was also determined that some union leaders were involved with organized crime. The AFL expelled the entire International Brotherhood of Teamsters when the leaders failed to correct a criminal act uncovered in Senate hearings.

In 1974 Congress extended the coverage of the Taft-Hartley Act to private nonprofit hospitals and nursing homes. The extension was a major matter. Approximately 2 million employees working in about 3,300 nonprofit hospitals were affected. Before 1974 the National Labor Relations Board (NLRB) as-

---

EXHIBIT 16–5   **Right-to-Work States**

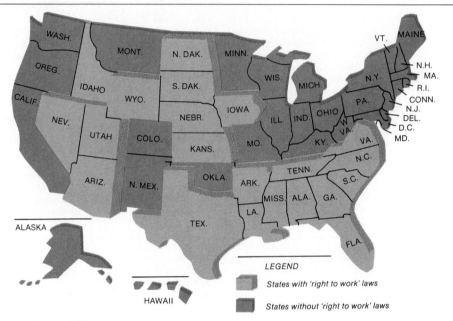

LEGEND

States with 'right to work' laws

States without 'right to work' laws

Data as of January 1988.

sumed jurisdiction over health care institutions. However, until the 1974 amendment, the NLRB was not authorized to handle cases in the nonprofit sector because the original law expressly excluded it from doing so.

Recognizing that hospitals supply a critical public service, the 1974 amendment established a special set of dispute-settling procedures. Unions representing hospital employees must give a 90 days' notice before terminating a labor agreement, 30 days more than Taft-Hartley requires in other industries. In addition, a hospital union cannot strike or picket unless it gives 10 days' notice. This notice requirement, not found in other industries, provides hospital management with the opportunity to make arrangements for the continuity of patient care.[5] There are other provisions of the 1974 amendment that apply to hospitals.

One of the most important elements of the Taft-Hartley Act is section 146, involving *right-to-work requirements*. Section 146 provided that, should any state wish to pass legislation more restrictive of union security than the union shop (i.e., to outlaw labor contracts that made union membership a condition of retaining employment), the state was free to do so. Exhibit 16–5 presents a map that shows the states (21) that have enacted right-to-work laws. These states ban any form of compulsory union membership.

---

[5] Sloane and Witney, *Labor Relations*, p. 84.

The Landrum-Griffin Act

In the 1950s, Congressional investigations uncovered a number of illegal practices on the part of unions. At this time, Congress assumed that the individual union members were still not protected enough by the labor laws in existence. In 1959 Congress passed the *Landrum-Griffin Act*, which is officially designated the *Labor-Management Reporting and Disclosure Act*. It was designed to regulate the internal affairs of unions.

This act, referred to as the *bill of rights of union members*, gave every union member the right to (1) nominate candidates for union office, (2) vote in union elections, and (3) attend union meetings. Union members also had the right to examine union accounts and records. In addition, the union was required to submit an annual financial report to the secretary of labor. Employers had to report any payments or loans made to unions, the officers, or members. This portion of the act was to eliminate what are called *sweetheart contracts*, under which the union leaders and management agree to terms that work to their mutual benefit, but maintain poor working conditions for other employees.

In general, labor unions were opposed to the passage of the Landrum-Griffin Act because it restricted union control over their organizations. The AFL–CIO believed it could handle any abuses through good internal management. However, the Senate Select Committee on Improper Activities in Labor and Management, headed by Senator McClellan, uncovered numerous abuses inside the union in the late 1950s. This Senate investigation weakened the prestige of unions and made it easier to pass the Landrum-Griffin Act.

As the shifts in labor legislation indicate, there have been noticeable shifts in public policy toward labor unions. It has moved in this century from encouragement and support to modified support with regulation, to specific regulations of union affairs. The American public is now, with television and other media, able to acquire an up-close look at union-management relationships and behavior. The future public policy toward these relationships and behaviors will depend largely upon what the American public sees and wants.

GOVERNMENT EMPLOYEE LEGISLATION

The second largest group of unionized employees is in the public sector. One half of the estimated 3.5 million unionized public employees work for the federal government. The rest are employed primarily by local government. There are also an estimated 3 million public employees who belong to professional and civil service associations that are not counted as belonging to labor unions. However, in many cases, they are very much like labor unions. For example, the National Education Association has 1.7 million members, many of whom are covered by collective bargaining agreements.[6]

---

[6] E. Edward Herman, Alfred Kuhn, and Ronald L. Seefer, *Collective Bargaining and Labor Relations* (Englewood Cliffs, N.J.: Prentice-Hall, 1987), pp. 405–415.

There are major differences between labor law and regulation in the private and public sectors.[7] In the private sector, the law tries to encourage management and labor to bargain as equals. In the public sector, the government defines itself as the superior through the use of the sovereignty doctrine, which has weakened in recent years. *The sovereignty doctrine* holds that the federal and state governments represent the sovereign power of the people. Consequently, only the government can delegate by legislation to various organizations or by voluntarily delegating authority to them in certain areas. In addition, responsibility for negotiating with employees is complicated by the separation of powers doctrine. Some managerial responsibility lies with the executive branch, some with the legislative.

Public sector collective bargaining is relatively new in the United States and has not been developed definitively. There is more clarity for federal employees than others. In the public sector, federal labor relations are regulated by executive orders issued by the president alone. Each new order rescinds previous orders on the same topic. In 1962, President John Kennedy issued Executive Order 10988, designed to parallel federal bargaining to private bargaining. It included a strong management-rights clause and banned strikes and the union shop. This was the first recognition ever on the part of the government that its employees could join unions and bargain collectively.

Executive Order 11491, issued by President Richard Nixon in 1969 to update 10988, was designed to bring public bargaining even closer to that in the private sector. Under this order, the secretary of labor has the authority to determine bargaining units, to supervise procedures for union recognition, and to examine standards for unfair labor practices and rule on them.

Executive Order 11491 also created the Federal Labor Relations Council (FLRC), which reviews decisions of the secretary of labor, chairman of the Civil Service Commission, and director of the Office of Management and Budget. The FLRC supervises the Federal Service Impasses Panel, comprised of seven neutral members appointed by the president from outside the federal service to settle labor disputes in that sector. Executive Order 11491 also required a simple majority of employees to choose an exclusive representative union and stipulated criteria for determining the bargaining unit.

Executive Order 11838, issued by President Gerald Ford in 1975, required federal agencies to bargain with their employees on all issues unless the agency could show *compelling need* not to negotiate. All P/HRM policies became subject to negotiation. The FLRC was appointed the final arbitrator on these issues and what constitutes compelling need. Subjects for grievances were also broadened. But this order still bans union-agency shops and has a strong management-rights clause.

Labor relations regulations for public employees at state and local levels are diverse and complicated. For example, 12 states have no applicable labor laws

---

[7] H. B. Frazier II, "Labor-Management Relations in the Federal Government," *Labor Law Journal*, March 1979, pp. 130–34.

at all for public employees. Another 20 states have such laws, and the other 18 have laws that cover certain aspects of labor relations for these employees.

For a time, it was thought the answer to this confusion might be a federal law applicable to state and local employees, but the Supreme Court and other federal courts have made it clear that the federal government cannot interfere with state and local employees. These rulings have also said that these government employees do not have to bargain with their employees. So the degree of public bargaining practiced and the methods used vary from state to state and city to city.

In January 1979, the executive orders were supplemented by what is called the *Federal Service Labor-Management Relations Statute*. The act applies to employees in federal agencies except the Postal Service (covered by the Taft-Hartley Act), the FBI, the General Accounting Office, the National Security Agency, the CIA, and agencies dealing with federal employee labor relations. Employees of the legislative and judicial branches were also excluded.

The Federal Labor Relations Authority is charged with overseeing the act in a manner similar to the National Labor Relations Board. Bargaining rights are limited under the statute. Federal employees may not bargain over wages and benefits, hiring or promotion, or classification of positions. The labor organization may not advocate a strike, and unauthorized strikes may lead to decertification (the union is no longer the representative of the employee) and discipline of individual members. These steps were taken by the government under this statute when the Professional Air Traffic Controllers (PATCO) union was decertified in 1981.

In addition to federal law, the states have passed labor laws affecting certain aspects of labor relations. Normally, these laws affect strikes, picketing, boycotts, and collective bargaining by public employees. These laws are varied across states and between employee groups within states.

THE STRUCTURE AND MANAGEMENT OF UNIONS

The turbulent 1870s and 1880s brought growing recognition of the labor union approach to social and economic problems. These experiences helped solidify the union movement and encouraged the development of a nationwide organization.[8]

The first union federation to achieve significant size and influence was the Knights of Labor, formed around 1869. This group attracted employees and local unions from all crafts and occupational areas. In general, there are two types of unions: industrial and craft. *Industrial union* members are all employees in a company or industry, regardless of occupation. *Craft union* members belong to one craft or to a closely related group of occupations. The strength of

---

[8] A. H. Raskin, "From Sitdowns to Solidarity: Passage in the Life of American Labor," *Across the Board,* December 1981, pp. 12–32.

the Knights was diluted because it failed to integrate the needs and interests of skilled and unskilled, industrial and craft members.

A group of national craft unions cut their relationships with the Knights of Labor around 1886 to form the *American Federation of Labor* (AFL). They elected Samuel Gompers of the Cigar Makers' Union president. At first the AFL restricted membership to skilled tradespeople, but it began to offer membership to unskilled employees when the Congress of Industrial Organizations began to organize industrial employees.

Growth in the union movement from 1886 to 1935 was slow. The government's attitude toward union organizing was neutral, indifferent, or negative. But with the passage of federal laws in the 1920s and 1930s protecting the union organizing process, union membership began to grow. (More will be said about organizing in Chapter 17.) Thus, formal laws helped unions grow during their formative years.

In 1935 the *Congress of Industrial Organizations* (CIO) was formed by John L. Lewis, president of the United Mine Workers, in cooperation with a number of presidents of unions expelled from the AFL. The CIO was formed to organize employees in industrial and mass-production jobs. The AFL organized craft employees, such as machinists, bricklayers, and carpenters; the CIO wanted to organize craft and unskilled employees within an industry, such as assembly-line workers, machinists, and assemblers.

Competition for new union members led to bitter conflicts between the AFL and CIO, but in 1955 they merged. The structure of the present AFL–CIO is shown in Exhibit 16–6.

The majority of national and international labor unions now belong to the AFL–CIO, although a number of unions, representing over 3 million members, are unaffiliated. However, in 1987, one of the most powerful unions, the Teamsters became reaffiliated with the AFL–CIO.

How does the AFL–CIO work? Its chief governing body is the biennial convention, which sets policy. Between conventions, the executive officers, assisted by the executive council and the general board, run the AFL–CIO. Executive officers are the *president,* who interprets the constitution between meetings of the executive council and heads the union staff, and the *secretary-treasurer,* who is responsible for financial affairs. The executive council also has 33 vice presidents. It meets three times a year and sets policy between conventions. The general board consists of the executive council and the head of each affiliated national union and department.

National headquarters provides many services to subsidiary union bodies: training for regional and local union leaders, organizing help, strike funds, and data to be used in negotiating contracts. Specialists available for consultation include lawyers, public relations specialists, and research personnel. Under the national union are regional groups of local unions which may provide office space and facilities for local unions.

Very large unions that are members of the AFL–CIO are those of the steelworkers, electrical workers, carpenters, machinists, and hotel and restaurant workers. The smallest national union—a unit in the printing trade—has 18 members.

EXHIBIT 16–6 **Structural Organization of the American Federation of Labor and Congress of Industrial Organization**

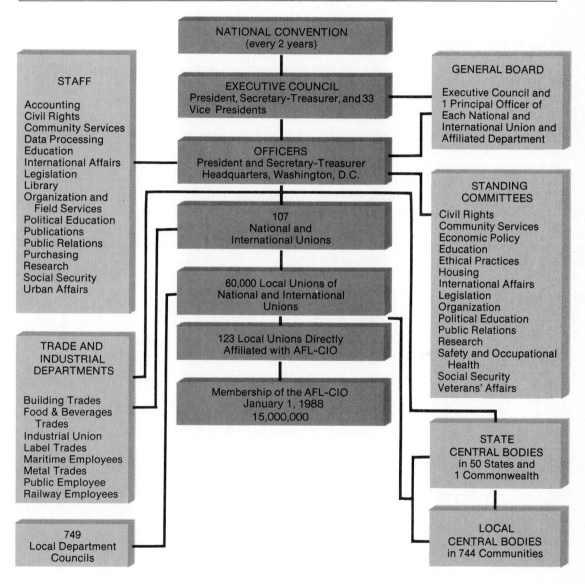

NATIONAL CONVENTION
(every 2 years)

EXECUTIVE COUNCIL
President, Secretary-Treasurer, and 33
Vice Presidents

OFFICERS
President and Secretary-Treasurer
Headquarters, Washington, D.C.

107
National and
International Unions

60,000 Local Unions of
National and International
Unions

123 Local Unions Directly
Affiliated with AFL-CIO

Membership of the AFL-CIO
January 1, 1988
15,000,000

STAFF

Accounting
Civil Rights
Community Services
Data Processing
Education
International Affairs
Legislation
Library
Organization and
  Field Services
Political Education
Publications
Public Relations
Purchasing
Research
Social Security
Urban Affairs

**TRADE AND
INDUSTRIAL
DEPARTMENTS**

Building Trades
Food & Beverages
  Trades
Industrial Union
Label Trades
Maritime Employees
Metal Trades
Public Employee
Railway Employees

749
Local Department
Councils

GENERAL BOARD

Executive Council and
1 Principal Officer of
Each National and
International Union and
Affiliated Department

**STANDING
COMMITTEES**

Civil Rights
Community Services
Economic Policy
Education
Ethical Practices
Housing
International Affairs
Legislation
Organization
Political Education
Public Relations
Research
Safety and Occupational
  Health
Social Security
Veterans' Affairs

**STATE
CENTRAL BODIES**
in 50 States and
1 Commonwealth

**LOCAL
CENTRAL BODIES**
in 744 Communities

The National Union

The constitution of the national union establishes the rules, policies, and procedures under which the local unions may be chartered and become members. Each national union exercises some control over the local unions. These controls usually deal with the collection of dues, the admission of new members by the local, and the use of union funds. The national union also provides the local unions with support for organizing campaigns, strikes, and the administration of contracts. There are approximately 100 national union organizations and about 50,000 local unions.

The Local Union

The labor movement has its foundation in the local craft union. The local has direct influence over the membership. Through the local, members exercise their complaints and pay the dues that support the national union.

The activities of locals are conducted by officials elected by the members. The elected officials include a president, vice president, secretary-treasurer, business representative, and committee chairperson. Elected officials of local unions often have full-time jobs in addition to their regular union duties.

In many local unions the *business representative* is the dominant person. The major responsibilities of the business representative are to negotiate and administer the labor agreement and to settle problems that may arise in connection with the contract. The business representative also collects dues, recruits new members, coordinates social activities, and arranges union meetings.

The *union steward* represents the interests of local union members in their relations with managers on the job. In the auto industry, the steward (called a *committee person*) devotes full time to solving disputes that arise in connection with the union-management labor contract.

The role of a district committeeman (union steward) named Charlie Bragg, who worked in a Ford Motor Company plant, was described as follows:

> He might be called, in fact, the fixer—the man to whom workers can turn in times of trouble. . . . Unofficially, Mr. Bragg is the union to his people and often the only representative they deal with. . . .
>
> The main function of a committeeman is to settle problems right on the floor. Mr. Bragg says, "I'm a mediator, a foot-soldier out here. Without the committeeman, Ford couldn't run this plant."
>
> It is Charlie Bragg and the men like him who are fighting disciplinary actions, getting supply racks fixed, arranging days off, getting bathrooms cleaned and drinking fountains unclogged. (On the average day, Mr. Bragg handles about 20 individual problems.)
>
> His prime goal, he says, is keeping his constituents happy. But, he also must remain on working terms with their supervisors, who, he feels must regard him as tough, but flexible.[9]

In United Steelworkers Union 1010 in East Chicago, Indiana the union steward is called a "griever." Alan Moseley is the busy, overworked, and highly stressed griever who is paid approximately $350 per month by the

---

[9] Walter S. Mossberg, "On the Line: A Union Man at Ford, Charlie Bragg, Deals in Problems, Gripes," *The Wall Street Journal,* July 26, 1973, p. 1.

union and who also is paid $16 per hour by Inland Steel for his regular work as a quality inspector.[10] Alan works a full job and is also the union steward. He blames the stress of handling hundreds of grievances and complaints a year for his 50-pound weight gain, sleepless nights, and little time off to be with his family.

Charlie Bragg and Alan Moseley are the union's direct link to management. They are the front-line representatives who must work for the workers they represent. They try hard to keep the lines of communication, trust, and respect open between union members and management.

Managing the Union

The job of managing a union at the national or local level is challenging and time-consuming. Union officials need to be dedicated, willing to work long hours, able to counsel members on personal problems, and skilled in influencing people. This combination of skills and abilities must also be obvious to members; tenure in office, especially at the local level, depends on projecting a favorable impression. Officers must run periodically for reelection. Some of the managerial problems facing union officials are member apathy, financial control, and recruitment of new members.

It is common knowledge that the majority of union members are apathetic about attending union meetings and voting on contracts or strike decisions. Thus, it is difficult for union officials to encourage members to take their union responsibilities more seriously.

Unions are financed through dues, fines, and initiation fees collected at the local level. However, union members resist high assessments. Union officials must convince members that, unless the union has a sound financial base, it won't have the power to secure favorable labor agreements.

The drive to organize more employees always faces union officials. Without new members, unions don't have the strength to carry out tactics to satisfy the needs, preferences, and interest of the membership. Developing effective organizing drives is the responsibility of local and national unions alike. Organizing will be discussed in more detail in Chapter 17.

WHY JOIN A UNION?

One important function of a union is to negotiate and administer the contract with the employer, which covers wages, hours, and the conditions of employment. The contract designates the formal terms of the union-management agreement in every specific language. It usually covers about two or three years. More details on contracts will be presented in Chapter 17. In addition to having a specific contract, there are many other attractive features of union

---

[10] Alex Kotlowitz, "Job of Shop Steward Has New Frustrations in Era of Payroll Cuts," *The Wall Street Journal,* April 1, 1987, pp. 1 and 19.

membership, and these appeal to different segments of the work force. There is no single answer to the question of why employees join a union. It is generally correct to state that employees join unions to satisfy needs that are important to them.[11] Certainly, needs and what is important differ among individuals.

First, many employees want some assurance that their jobs will exist in the future. They do not want to be fired or arbitrarily laid off because of a personality clash with a manager, an economic recession, or because of automation caused by the introduction of new technology. Unions, through collective bargaining, continually discuss and debate the issue of job security.

For 300 employees at the Bethlehem Steel plant in Johnstown, Pennsylvania, having a job for life is a reality. Since July, 1983, mechanical workers in the bar, rod, and wire divisions have been protected from any type of layoff.[12] It is estimated that only about 100 of the major employers in the United States have worked out plans to provide job security. IBM, a nonunion firm, is one firm that provides job security. IBM has had no layoffs in more than 40 years.

Second, people need to socialize and be part of a group. Unions meet these needs by bringing together people with similar interests and goals. Through meetings, social events, educational programs, and common projects, unions can build a strong bond of friendship and team spirit.

Third, a safe and healthy place to work is important to employees. Unions in the United States and Canada have pushed hard for good working conditions. This well-publicized emphasis on improved working conditions appeals to employees who are considering a union.

Perhaps one of the strongest motives for joining a union is that it provides employees with a communication link to management. This link enables them to express dissatisfactions and disagreements about the job, management, and other issues. One such link is the grievance procedure detailed in the union-management contract.

Finally, compensation is an important reason for working. Employees want to receive a fair day's pay for a fair day's work and good fringe benefits. They are very concerned with receiving pay and fringe benefits that are competitive in the community.

A national survey of workers in various organizations was conducted by the University of Michigan Survey Research Center. Its focus was on how workers perceived the goals of unions. Eighty-nine percent of the workers felt that unions have power to improve wages and working conditions, 87 percent believed unions improved job security, and 80 percent thought that unions can protect workers from unfair management action.[13]

A few unions have secured *guaranteed annual wages* (GAW) or guaranteed annual employment for members. The best known plans are found at Procter &

---

[11] Donna Sockell, "Toward a Theory of the Union's Role in an Enterprise," in *Advances in Industrial and Labor Relations,* ed. David B. Lipsky and Joel M. Douglas (Greenwich, Conn: JAI Press, 1983), pp. 221–32.

[12] "Unions' Latest Goal: A Job for Life," *U.S. News & World Report,* May 21, 1984, pp. 74–76.

[13] R. P. Quinn and G. L. Staines, *The 1977 Quality of Employment Survey* (Ann Arbor, Mich.: Institute for Social Research, Survey Research Center, University of Michigan, 1979).

Gamble, Hormel, and Nunn-Bush. These plans *guarantee* regular employees a certain amount of money or hours of work. The purpose of the GAW is economic security.[14] Most companies oppose this type of guarantee, because they are concerned about continuity to pay workers when sales are down. Another breakthrough in the area of income security was a plan developed between Ford and the United Auto Workers. This plan became known as the Supplemental Unemployment Benefits (SUB) program because it supplemented unemployment benefits instead of providing a guaranteed annual income. Some companies with SUB plans are American Can, Kaiser, Reynolds, and General Motors.[15]

In summary, a major reason why unions exist is that management has not satisfied the total set of employees' needs and wants. It seems impossible for any management to continually satisfy every need and want, but some companies, such as IBM, Delta Airlines, and Du Pont have not been unionized. IBM has worked at making wages, salaries, fringe benefits, and other programs very attractive to employees. This concerted effort has probably been one of the main reasons why IBM employees have not unionized.

UNION SECURITY

Labor unions have, since their beginning, stressed the importance of security for members. Labor legislation also addresses the issue of union security. Unions want to increase their security by requiring all employees to join the union once it is elected as the legitimate bargaining agent.

In some elections, the union is voted in by a slim margin. In such cases, some employees obviously don't want to join the union. Different types of union "shops" have developed as a result, and they represent various degrees of union security.

Restricted Shop

When management tries to keep a union out without violating any labor laws, a *restricted shop* exists. A restricted shop is an attitude rather than a formal arrangement. Management may try to provide wages and fringe benefits that make the union and what it can offer unattractive. This is a legal effort to make the union's organizing ineffective.[16]

It is illegal to create a restricted shop by dismissing employees who want to unionize; trying to influence employees who are thinking about starting a union; or promising rewards if the union is voted down. These activities could result in legal action against management.

---

[14] Norma Pope and Paul A. Brinker, "Recent Developments with the Guaranteed Annual Wage: The Ford Settlement," *Labor Law Journal,* September 1968, pp. 555–62.

[15] "Lifetime Security," *Business Week,* November 14, 1977, p. 56.

[16] Jeff Blyskal, "Beating the UAW—Three Times," *Forbes,* March 2, 1981, pp. 37–39.

Open Shop

An *open shop* is one in which there is neither a union present nor a management effort to keep the union out. The employees have total freedom to decide whether or not they want a union. This type of shop is a prime target for union organizing efforts.

Agency Shop

In the *agency shop,* all employees pay union dues whether or not they are members of the union. This means that no employee is a "free rider." Everyone pays dues for the services of an organized union even though some employees are not members.

Preferential Shop

In the *preferential shop,* the union is recognized, and union members are given preference in some areas. For example, when hiring new employees, union members are given preference over nonunion members. This type of preference may also be given in such areas as promotion and layoff. Many of these preferential decisions are in violation of the Taft-Hartley Act. If there is an excessive amount of preferential treatment, a closed shop may exist, which is also prohibited by the Taft-Hartley Act.

The Union Shop

The *union shop* requires the employee to join a union after being hired. An employer may hire any person, but within a period of time, that employee must join the union or lose the job. Under the Taft-Hartley Act, this period of time can be shorter than 30 days. But under the Landrum-Griffin Act, this period can be shortened to seven days in the construction industry only. Most union-management labor contracts provide for the union shop.

The Taft-Hartley Act allows states to forbid union shops by passing what are called *right-to-work laws.* Under these laws, two persons doing the same job must be paid the same wages, whether or not they belong to the union. The union believes this is unfair, because the nonunionized employees pay no dues but share in the benefits won by the union. Nineteen states, located primarily in the South, the Great Plains, and the Southwest have right-to-work laws. Some of the larger states with these laws are Texas, Florida, Georgia, and Arizona.

Closed Shop

The *closed shop* requires that a new employee be a union member when hired. The union itself provides labor to the organization. Although this type of shop is illegal, modified closed shops are found in the construction, printing, and maritime industries. For example, an ironworkers' union hall sends out union members to construction sites on request. A nonunion member has little chance to be sent from a union hall to a job, because the union's business agent makes the assignment. Union members elect the business agent, while the nonunion members have no vote.

LABOR-MANAGEMENT RELATIONS

The role of a labor relations manager is a very important one on the P/HRM team. Surveys indicate that labor relations is the most important issue to be faced in unionized forms. Both P/HRM and operating managers are involved in labor relations. P/HRM managers or specialists are, of necessity, technical experts on labor relations who train and advise operating managers on the contract provisions. They also bargain with the union on the contract and serve as a step in the grievance process. But operation managers are the persons who implement the contract. They advise P/HRM on problem areas in the contract so they can try to improve them during the next negotiations, and they face grievances first. An overall, vital influence in labor relations is exerted by top management. Top managers' attitudes toward unions strongly influence the attitudes of P/HRM and operating managers and help determine whether union-management relations will be amiable or combative. Top managers also strongly influence the negotiating process. The bargaining philosophy and strategy they assume at the time of negotiations will help determine whether and how soon a contract will be signed, or whether a strike, lockout, and arbitration or other processes will occur.

Labor-Management Stereotypes

There have been a number of studies of the attitudes of how labor and management view each other. In general, they show the unflattering, dysfunctional stereotypes they have developed of one another. These stereotypes can distort the data presented during discussions about working conditions, pay, and so on. One union stereotype of a labor relations manager is a "pretty boy," snobbish, country-club type, fawning over his boss, who could not find his way to the bathroom with a map and never worked a real day's work in his life. His job is only to cheat honest workers out of a few cents an hour to get a big bonus. Some labor relations managers, on the other hand, stereotype the union official as a loudmouth, uneducated goon who probably is stealing pension funds and no doubt beats up uncooperative workers. He will ruin the company because he does not understand the dog-eat-dog marketplace.

These differences in perceptions between the two groups are compounded by major differences in such factors as age, education, and social class background. Furthermore, the employer organizations are hierarchical: the labor relations manager has a boss to report to. The union is peer-oriented: the agreement must be approved by a vote of the members. The union leader has to be reelected to remain in office.

In sum, one of the challenges of labor relations is that on the union side of the table the representatives have more conflicts and less structure than those on the employer's side. There are conflicts within the management side, too, but usually there is an official, such as the president of the organization, who can settle these conflicts by a decision. This is not so on the union side.[17]

Government Officials and Others

The role players in labor relations are the employees, union officers, and labor relations executives. But others also do have an impact. The first are the government regulatory bodies that administer the labor laws. In the United States, the National Labor Relations Board (NLRB) administers the laws and regulations in the private and third sectors. Many states also have state boards to administer state labor laws.

Labor relations administrators have two major duties:

To supervise representation elections and certify unions as bargaining agents.

To hear appeals of alleged violations of the laws.

Most experts believe the boards do a satisfactory job with elections. Some contend they are too slow in processing violation appeals. However, they receive a large number of complaints, and it is not an easy job. For example, in a typical month over 4,000 new cases are filed with the NLRB.[18] Some who favor the union side contend that these delays benefit management, and management deliberately takes its time and regularly appeals violation decisions. For example, cases where management is charged with firing prounion employees might take two years (with appeals and delays) to decide. By then the fired employees have other jobs or are tired of the process. Management disputes this, and the NLRB and other boards have attempted to expedite these cases.

Others with a possible impact on labor relations include customers and the general public. Customers and clients of the organization may mobilize to move the negotiation process along faster. Customers who need goods or services may exert pressure on the employer directly to settle or lose the business. They also do this indirectly by buying elsewhere and letting the home office know it.

The general public tends to be neutral or uninterested in most labor-management incidents. Both sides try to mobilize public support through the media, however, because if the public is denied service, it can bring political or other pressure to bear on the settlement. This normally happens when the public is severely affected by the loss of the goods or services.

---

[17] John A. Fossum, "Labor Relations," *Human Resources in the 1980s,* ed. Stephen J. Carroll and Randall S. Schuler (Washington, D.C.: Bureau of National Affairs, 1983), pp. 7–12.

[18] Twomey, *Labor Law and Legislation.*

ISSUES FACING UNIONS

To attract and retain members, unions have concentrated their efforts on issues that employees are concerned about: public image, unemployment, social dilemmas, and recruiting members. These issues are an important part of the motivational forces influencing employees to unionize.

In February 1985, the AFL–CIO Committee on the Evolution of Work issued a landmark report entitled "The Changing Situation of Workers and Their Unions". The committee was composed of some two dozen American trade union leaders.[19] Among the committee's proposal were the following:

- Improve labor communications and the public image of unions.
- Establish new categories of membership. This would make it possible for former union members or those outvoted in an organizing drive, to have union-offered services and benefits.
- Establish organizing committees to organize workers in a particular industry, geographic area, or company.
- Increase members' participation in unions.
- Improve organizing techniques by renewing the emphasis on organizing and increasing the resources devoted to training organizers.
- Facilitate mergers which provide the best hope for many smaller unions to continue serving their workers.

Although labor considers the report a landmark, it remains to be seen whether the sharp decline in union membership can be stopped and reversed.[20] Perhaps the most important starting point should focus on the public's image of unions.

Labor Unions and the Public Image

Foreign competition from Japan, West Germany, and Australia is expanding a domestic market share and underselling many U.S. products abroad. Industry has been closing plants all across the country, but especially hard hit is the union heartland of the Northeast and Midwest. When new plants are built, preference goes to right-to-work states or foreign locations. The only labor segment in which unions are making some gains is the government. However, cutbacks in government spending could mean fewer new jobs and fewer workers to organize.

If any successful organizing gains are accomplished in the 1990s, they will be with new groups that are beginning to predominate the work force—engineers, programmers, and technical technicians. The union organizing

---

[19] James O'Toole, "Unions: The Good, the Bad, and the Necessary," *New Management,* Winter 1986, pp. 4–7

[20] Richard B. Freeman, "Unionization in Troubled Times," *New Management,* Winter 1986, pp. 8–10.

efforts in these areas will be different from the traditional ones. Instead of simply passing out handbills at a plant gate informing workers about the benefits of unionization, there will be a greater "Madison Avenue" touch. Television, newspaper, and carefully prepared pamphlets will be used by the unions. These campaigns will be resisted by equally as "slick" and professional management campaigns. Management will emphasize more of the individual spirit and skill theme that they claim will be dampened if a person joins a union that emphasizes collectivism and group solidarity.

In a Gallup Poll, it was determined that there is greater public disapproval of labor unions than at any time in the past 45 years.[21] At least part of Americans' disaffection with the union movement may be traced to their general disapproval of strikes or sick-outs by public employees such as air traffic controllers, police officers, and fire fighters.

If labor unions are to remain strong political and social forces, they must stem their recent decline and negative public image. Still, the majority of Americans believe that unions do more good than harm. Most people feel that strong unions provide the only way for many workers to get a fair piece of the economic pie. The union is also viewed as a legitimate representative for workers to voice complaints and grievances.

Perhaps some of the public's growing disapproval of labor unions is directed toward the behavior of labor union leaders rather than the union's objectives. Many people still believe that labor leaders are less likely than business leaders to act in the national interest. In fact, today the public shows a greater disdain for labor leaders than they do business leaders. It is evident that corrupt and autocratic labor leader behavior is given more media publicity than corrupt and autocratic business leader behavior.[22] However, as long as union leader corruption is publicized, the image of the union movement will remain more negative. Hopefully, union leaders who are aware of the problems poor image can cause will encourage and promote improved union leader behavior. Unless unions can improve their image, their efforts to remain a major force in society will fail.

Unemployment

Many organizations have searched for and found technological advances that resulted in increased productivity. American Telephone & Telegraph Company has cut some 120,000 jobs from its payroll because of automation. The U.S. Treasury Department has replaced workers by using computers. The steel industry (heavily unionized) has had to cut its work force from about 500,000 to slightly more than 200,000 because of technological changes. In many instances these advances were necessary in order for the organization to remain competitive. In some cases, the technology has displaced workers,

---

[21] "Approval of Labor Unions Remains at Low," *Gallup Report*, August 1981, pp. 6–8.

[22] "Union Corruption: Worse Than Ever," *U.S. News & World Report*, September 8, 1980, pp. 33–36.

many of whom belonged to unions. For years unions resisted technological changes that displaced labor. However, as it became apparent that improvements in productivity were the only way to increase compensation, many unions changed their attitude about technology. Some unions now support technological improvement and work with management representatives to minimize the displacement of workers. They bargain for compensation for displaced workers, retraining, and relocation assistance for laid-off employees.

In 1988, there were approximately 8 million unemployed Americans. Hardest hit by the recent jobless spiral were blue-collar workers, blacks, and teenagers. The heaviest concentration of unemployment in the late 1980s was in the auto, steel, and construction industries, clustered in factory towns in the Midwest and the industrial Northeast. These are union industries and geographic regions.[23] Five states alone—California, Illinois, New York, Ohio, and Pennsylvania—account for about half of all union members.

Even if the economy reverses, there are experts who believe that in some industries unemployment will never fully rebound. Industries seem to be searching for ways to expand the use of computers and robots to improve quality and reduce labor costs.[24] If this trend continues, the union will have fewer blue-collar workers to attract into the membership. Fewer members could mean less political power for the union.

Social Dilemmas

Labor unions support the principle of equal rights for all people regardless of race, sex, creed, or national origin. Furthermore, like employers, unions must comply with the provisions of the 1964 Civil Rights Act. In the West and Southwest, equal opportunity for Hispanic migratory workers has been a rallying point for union organizing efforts. One dilemma that unions face, along with management, is finding enough jobs for those who are capable and willing to work.

There is a growing pool of untrained workers who are ill-equipped for jobs in high-skill occupations. Thus, the union must push hard for improved skill training for these workers. However, unless the government and management are willing to support such training, there is little chance that high-skill occupations will be filled or that ill-equipped workers will find jobs.

Membership

Union membership significantly increased from 1933 to 1947. In 1933, there were only 3 million union members, accounting for about 7 percent of the total labor force; by 1947, there were 15 million union members.

The number of union members continued to increase until 1956, declined until 1963, and started to grow slowly until it reached 22 million workers in

---

[23] Bill Saporito, "The Smokestacks Won't Tumble," *Fortune*, February 2, 1987, pp. 30–32.

[24] Michael McFadden, "Protectionism Can't Protect Jobs," *Fortune*, May 11, 1987, pp. 121–128.

EXHIBIT 16–7   The 10 Largest Unions in the United States

Union	Affiliation	Members
Teamsters, Chauffeurs, Warehousemen and Helpers of America, International Brotherhood of	AFL–CIO	1,800,000
Automobile, Aerospace and Agricultural Implement Workers of America, International Union, United (UAW)	Independent	1,340,000
United Food and Commercial Workers	AFL–CIO	1,300,000*
Steelworkers of America, United	AFL–CIO	1,300,000
State, County and Municipal Employees, American Federation of	AFL–CIO	950,000
Electrical Workers, International Brotherhood of (IBEW)	AFL–CIO	900,000
Machinists and Aerospace Workers, International Association of	AFL–CIO	820,000
Carpenters and Joiners of America, United Brotherhood of	AFL–CIO	800,000
Laborers' International Union of North America	AFL–CIO	675,000
Service Employees' International Union	AFL–CIO	625,000

* Retail Clerks and Meatcutters merged in 1979 to form this union.
Source: U.S. Department of Labor, November 1987.

1980, or about 23 percent of the total labor force and 28 percent of non-agricultural employment.[25] However, since 1980 there has been a decline in union membership of about 3 million workers and today, January 1988, union members constitute about 18 percent of the labor force. Labor officials claim that corporate cost cutting, massive layoffs, deregulation, and plant closings will lead to more appeal among workers to join unions. The 1990s are predicted to be the turnaround and growth on membership decade by labor leaders.[26]

The 10 largest unions and their membership are presented in Exhibit 16–7. The three largest unions, with membership of more than 1 million each, are the Teamsters, UAW, and the United Food and Commercial Workers. Exhibit 16–8 shows the degree of union organization in selected industries. For example, at least 75 percent of the blue-collar employees in transportation are unionized, whereas less than 25 percent of local government employees are unionized.

The organizational and recruiting efforts of unions have varied according to changes in economic, social, and political conditions. New membership drives are taking place in the public sector, which includes military personnel, police, and fire fighters; among professionals, including teachers, medical personnel, athletes, and lawyers; among employees in service industries; and among agricultural workers.

Unions are very interested in attracting public employees. A 1962 executive order by President John F. Kennedy, which was strengthened by amendments in 1969 and 1971, set up a form of collective bargaining for federal government

---

[25] Sloane and Whitney, *Labor Relations*, p. 34.

[26] Alex Kotlowitz, "Unions May Be Poised to End Long Decline, Recover Some Clout," *The Wall Street Journal*, August 28, 1987, pp. 1 and 18.

EXHIBIT 16–8 The Degree of Union Organization in Selected Industries

---

75 Percent and Over

Transportation	Paper
Contract construction	Electrical machinery
Ordinance	Transportation equipment

50 Percent to less than 75 Percent

Primary metals	Manufacturing
Food and kindred products	Fabricated metals
Mining	Telephone and telegraph
Apparel	Stone, clay, and glass products
Tobacco manufacturers	Federal government
Petroleum	Rubber

25 Percent to Less than 50 Percent

Printing, publishing	Machinery
Leather	Chemicals
Furniture	Lumber
Electric, gas utilities	

Less than 25 Percent

Nonmanufacturing	State government
Textile mill products	Trade
Instruments	Agriculture and fishing
Service	Finance
Local government	

---

employees. As a result, public employee unions have become the fastest growing labor groups in the country.

In the past, professors, teachers, nurses, doctors, athletes, and other professionals have considered themselves above union goals, procedures, and tactics.[27] Yet these groups have recently begun to recognize union gains and adopt union strategies. For example, the American Federation of State, County and Municipal Employees won the right to represent 4,100 technical employees in the University of California hospital system after hiring a professional pollster to pinpoint workers' concerns, such as job safety.[28]

The union attempted and succeeded in organizing the 20,000 faculty members of California's 19-campus state university system. The California State (Cal State) system was a fertile ground for the union. Cal State evolved as a collection of teacher colleges in such cities as San Jose, Chico, and Fresno.[29] Money and legislative support have been a lingering problem at Cal State.

---

[27] Leon C. Megginson, *Personnel Management: A Human Resources Approach*, 4th ed. (Homewood, Ill.: Richard D. Irwin, 1981).

[28] Joanne S. Lublin, "Health Care Workers Are Target of Big Organizing Drive by Unions," *The Wall Street Journal*, February 24, 1984, p. 29.

[29] "California Says Yes to Unions," *Time*, February 15, 1982, p. 55.

Also, about 38 percent of the Cal State faculty were hired on a part-time or year-to-year basis. The result of these and other problems was a vote to unionize.

Another area that unions are attempting to unionize is agriculture. Organizing efforts are especially intense in the grape, lettuce, citrus, and cotton regions of California.

In addition to these new organizing efforts in industries and professions, unions are also attempting to attract white-collar, female, and black employees. In the past, white-collar employees identified more with management practices and antiunion ideals and philosophy. But now, because of boredom and frustration in many white-collar jobs, some employees have considered unionizing.

The proportion of working women who are members of labor unions is declining. However, the number of female union members is increasing to approximately 5.2 million. The Coalition of Labor Union Women, an alliance of blue-collar working women, was formed in 1974 to end sex discrimination in wages and hiring. It also is attempting to elect more women as union officials. With more women officials, other women might believe that unions welcome them and need their abilities and skills.

Black employees are another fast-growing segment and a target of union organizers. In 1988, there were approximately 2.8 million black trade unionists. However, blacks have not been represented in union management in proportion to their membership. Furthermore, several unions have been found guilty of discriminating against blacks. Both blacks and women are demanding more say in union decisions and will certainly acquire additional power as unions attempt to increase their membership.

Resistance to Unions

Despite well-planned and systematic organizing efforts, about 75 percent of the total labor force, or 90 million workers, still are not unionized. One reason is that many people distrust unions. Some people believe that unions stand against individualism and free enterprise. They feel that people should get ahead on their own skills and merits. They resent the union's position in favor of collectivism and the use of seniority in personnel decisions involving promotions, layoffs, and pay increases.

Many professionals resist unions because they view them as dominated by blue-collar employees. Doctors, lawyers, and professors assume that they should not be associated with blue-collar tactics and behavior. This attitude is somewhat contrary to some of the actions of such professional associations as the American Medical Association. (The major difference between an association and a union is that the association believes payment is a matter between the individual performing the service and the customer.)

Some employees resist unions because they choose to identify with management values and practices. Management typically does not support union tactics. These nonmanagers may consider their aspirations to be a part of management when they resist union organizing efforts.

A RETURN TO THE P/HRM · IN · ACTION

Stan Goebel and
Tom Hardisty

Tom Hardisty and Stan Goebel had lunch after their discussion about labor relations. After lunch, Stan said: "We could follow a strategy of fighting the union to keep it out. Or we could let nature take its course and live with it."

Tom replied, "That's what you think! I'm *not* running a unionized place. I'll sell out first! You need to figure out how to keep that #*&%$ union out of HMC!"

Stan then presented a communication program and proposed increases in pay and benefits as part of the "keep the union out" strategy. He costed out the proposed changes in pay and benefits and took these to Tom.

The reasons for resisting union organizing efforts may also be based on historical impressions and beliefs. Some well-known union leaders have been associated with illegal acts. One report found that about 450 union officers have been convicted of serious labor-related crimes from 1973 to 1980.[30] There has also been some union-incited violence during organizing campaigns, although such violence may have received more publicity than management-provoked violence. An accurate check of unbiased history books finds that company "thugs" were just as plentiful as union "thugs."[31]

SUMMARY

This chapter has introduced you to labor relations, a sometimes emotionally charged P/HRM activity. It has discussed the history of labor unions, why

---

[30] "Union Corruption: Worse Than Ever," *U.S. News & World Report*, September 8, 1980, p. 33.

[31] Raskin, "From Sitdowns to Solidarity," pp. 14–18.

unions appeal to some employees, some major issues facing unions, the structure and management of unions, and major labor legislation.

To summarize the major points covered in this chapter:

1. A union is a group of employees who have joined together to achieve present and future goals that deal with employee conditions.
2. Three major laws affecting labor-management relations in the United States are the Wagner Act (1935) as amended by the Taft-Hartley Act (1947), and the Landrum-Griffin Act of 1959.
3. The second largest group of unionized employees is 3 million employees in the public sector. In the public sector, federal labor relations are regulated by executive orders issued by the president of the United States and the Federal Service Labor-Management Relations Statute.
4. The National Labor Relations Board (NLRB) administers the laws and regulations in the private and third sector (health care and universities).
5. The contact point for the membership is the local union. Through the local, members exercise their complaints. The union steward or committeeperson or griever is the member with on-the-job contact. If a union member has a complaint that deals with the labor-management contract, the steward is contacted.
6. Unions appeal to some workers for various reasons. Some of the cited reasons are job security, strength in numbers, protection against unfair management action, and the communication link to management.
7. Some of the issues that unions must face today and in the future are declining membership, creating more positive public image, unemployment, equal rights for all people, attracting additional members, and some hard-core resistance to unions.

Questions for Review and Discussion

1. Why would merging two small unions into one be an important strategy for the AFL–CIO to promote and support?
2. Why do some individuals decide to join a union?
3. What will unions have to do to attract more blacks, women, and white-collar members?
4. Why has union membership significantly declined in the 1980s?
5. What kind of image do you now have of unions and the union movement?
6. Explain the impact of the Wagner Act on the growth of trade unions.
7. Under what conditions would a restricted shop be considered illegal?
8. The union steward is considered a key communication link between labor and management. Why?
9. Can federal employees unionize? Explain.
10. A person was heard to comment, "Unions do not have to exist. Look at IBM and Delta Airlines. They have been doing fine without them." What is your opinion of this comment?

GLOSSARY

AFL–CIO. A group of union members consisting of individuals that merged membership in 1955 from the American Federation of Labor and the Congress of Industrial Organizations.

Agency Shop. A situation in which all employees pay union dues whether or not they are union members.

American Federation of Labor (AFL). A union group devoted to improving economic and working conditions for craft employees.

Business Representative. The local union's representative who is responsible for negotiating and administering the labor agreement and for settling problems in connection with the contract.

Closed Shop. A situation in which a new employee must be a union member when hired. Popular in the construction, maritime, and printing industries.

Congress of Industrial Organizations (CIO). A union formed by John L. Lewis, president of the United Mine Workers. It was formed to organize industrial and mass-production workers and was devoted to improving economic and working conditions.

Craft Union. A group of individuals who belong to one craft or closely related group of occupations (e.g., carpenters, bricklayers).

Guaranteed Annual Wages. An agreement that guarantees regular employees a certain amount of money or hours of work. Its purpose is to provide some degree of economic security.

Labor Relations. The continuous relationship between a defined group of employees (e.g., a union or association) and an employer.

Landrum-Griffin Act. A labor law passed in 1959 that is referred to as the bill of rights of union members. It was designed to regulate and audit the internal affairs of unions.

Nation Labor Relations Board. A government regulatory body that administers labor laws and regulations in the private and third sectors.

Open Shop. A work situation in which neither a union is present nor is there a management effort to keep the union out.

Preferential Shop. The union is recognized and union members are given preference in some areas. These preferences are in violation of the Taft-Hartley Act.

Restricted Shop. A practice initiated by management to keep a union out without violating labor laws. A restricted shop is an attitude rather than a formal arrangement.

Right-to-Work Laws. A law that specifies that two persons doing the same job must be paid the same wages, whether or not they are union members. Nineteen states have right-to-work laws.

Taft-Hartley Act. A labor amendment of the Wagner Act, passed in 1947, that guaranteed employees bargaining rights and also specifed unfair labor union practices that would not be permitted.

Union. A group of employees who have joined together to achieve present and future goals that deal with employment conditions.

Union Shop. A situation in which an employee is required to join a union after being hired.

Union Steward. A union representative who works at the job site to solve disputes that arise in connection with the labor-management labor contract.

Wagner Act. A labor law passed in 1935 that was designed to encourage the growth of trade unions and restrain management from interfering with the growth.

Yellow-Dog Contracts. A contract (now illegal) that required that a person (such as a job applicant) would not join or form a union.

APPLICATION CASE 16–1   Modern Management, Inc.: Union Busters with Briefcases

In the old days they used billy clubs and brass knuckles. However, today's union busters go by the name "labor relations consultants"—but they're still out to stop unions from organizing employees. Union busters give private counseling on specific company policies, advising management how to circumvent union organizing efforts.

Herbert Melnick operates Modern Management, Inc., of Bannockburn, Illinois. His firm has 70 consultants engaged in helping firms avoid unionization. The consultants are paid over $700 plus expenses per day. The firm has had a 93 percent success rate. Today there are about 1,000 firms like Modern Management and another 1,500 independent practitioners in the union-busting business. Critics call their specialization psychological manipulation of the workers' attitudes in the workplace.

Nonunion companies want to prevent unionization. Management of a unionized shop wants to decertify the union. These goals are within the purview of Modern Management and other union busters. Are they successful? In the NLRB representation elections lost by unions, over 90 percent involve labor relations consultants.

House Subcommittee on Labor Management Relations issued a report on labor relations consultants. A key recommendation was that the Department of Labor should be more diligent in enforcing the reporting requirements for consultants under the Landrum-Griffin Act. "Virtually every union is required to and does report its activities under the provisions of the Act," the report says. "It is inequitable that the Department does not require consultants, even in instances when they are clearly running management's antiunion campaign, to disclose their involvement."

Some of the situations that led to the call for tighter controls involved PPG Industries, St. Francis Hospital (Milwaukee, Wis.), and Humana Corporation. Following are brief descriptions of these situations.

PPG Industries

The law firm representing PPG Industries' Lexington, N.C., plant reportedly trumped up an alienation of affection suit against Teamsters' organizer Pat Suporta filed in May 1979, seeking to discredit her. Suporta had helped win an election at the plant in July 1978. Even after the suit was withdrawn in June 1979, PPG attempted (but failed) to use it as new evidence to get the NLRB to overturn IBT certification. The company's law firm is Hogg, Allen, Ryce, Norton & Blue in Coral Gables, Fla. In a separate incident, PPG fired employee Terri Drake in March 1979, four days after she was identified as a union supporter. She and many others on the in-plant committee were blacklisted and couldn't get jobs in the Lexington area. The company also was found to have bugged an employees' cafeteria.

St Francis Hospital

In the first NLRB complaint directly against a labor consultant, the board charges that Modern Management, Inc., "independently violated the National Labor Relations Act by its having complete control and use of supervisory personnel at St. Francis Hospital in a systematic and antiunion campaign." The tactics included, the complaint says, "illegal interrogations, promises of benefits, promises of improved conditions of employment and threats of reprisal against employees for engaging in union activities." The St. Francis Federation of Nurses and Health Professionals, American Federation of Teachers, lost an October 1979 election by a vote of 100 to 95. NLRB set aside the election in July 1980.

Humana Corp.

Lloyd Laudermilch, a member of Operating Engineers Local 501 in Las Vegas, Nev., was coached by management at Sunrise Hospital, its parent company, Humana Corp., and its consultants, West Coast Industrial Relations, on how to initiate, gather support for, and file a decertification petition with NLRB. This is a clear violation of the law, which forbids an employer from discussing a decertification petition with employees. Laudermilch was asked—but refused—to sign an affidavit saying that he had never talked to any management people about filing the petition. For his efforts Laudermilch was promised a better job: busting unions at other hospitals owned by Humana. He kept the union informed of his activities, and the decertification effort failed.

Questions for Thought

1. Should union busters like Modern Management be permitted to stop union organizing efforts?
2. Why would union busting be a popular tactic among organizations?
3. Are union busters like Modern Management worth $700 a day plus expenses for each labor relations consultant? Why?

EXERCISE 16–1   Pro-, Neutral, and Antiunion?

Objective: To examine the reader's feelings, emotions, and attitudes about the union movement and joining a union.

SET UP THE EXERCISE

By the time you are enrolled in the present course you have developed an opinion about unions. Friends, parents, and the media have helped shape your opinion. Are your opinions logical or are they emotional? Would you ever become a spokesperson for the union? How do your opinions compare to others in the course?

Each person is asked to complete the following 15-item scale. There are no right or wrong answers. Circle the letter that best describes your opinion for each of the items. Your instructor will tell you how to score your responses and will ask you to discuss your score with others in the classroom. What does your score tell you about your attitudes toward unions, their goals, and their impact on society?

1. (a). Unions are needed to keep management interested in and responsive to rights.
   (b). Unions have served their purpose and are no longer needed.
2. (a). Unions are too concerned with job security.
   (b). Unions want their members to be highly productive members of an organization.
3. (a). Unions push hard for the autonomy of all members.
   (b). Unions are overly protective of the autonomy of too many nonproductive employees.
4. (a). Unions use their strike powers too frequently.
   (b). Unions only strike when they have to gain benefits for members.
5. (a). Unions are more democratically operated than management committees or councils.
   (b). Democracy and unionism are contradictory terms.
6. (a). Public employees should have every right to strike.
   (b). It is not in the best interest of society to permit public union members to strike.
7. (a). The union movement is the primary reason why Americans have a good standard of living.
   (b). Management has been the driving force behind technological advancement which has resulted in our high standard of living.
8. (a). Unions are too close to socialism for most Americans.
   (b). Unions in the United States are not political forces or a power like they are in European nations.

9. (a). Without unions more Americans would have become unemployed in the late 1980s.

   (b). The unions resistance to improvements, retraining, and change has resulted in a large number of plant closings and business failures.

10. (a). Union leaders are corrupt.

    (b). Union leaders are no more corrupt or unethical than managers.

11. (a). Unions advocate promotions based on merit.

    (b). Union politics dictates a posture that seniority is more important than merit in reward decisions.

12. (a). Union violence is a thing of the past.

    (b). Unions still beat and intimidate those opposed to their viewpoints.

13. (a). Managers would fire at will workers who opposed their orders.

    (b). Managers need the respect of workers and will only fire those who break cleanly stated rules.

14. (a). Unions are for the blue-collar, minimally educated person who can't stand up to management.

    (b). Unions can with their strength and prestige represent any employee—blue-collar or white-collar.

15. (a). Unions are responsible for the growth of the personnel/human resource management field.

    (b). Management supported, encouraged, and implemented the personnel/human resource management department to support their mission and goals.

ORGANIZING AND COLLECTIVE BARGAINING

LEARNING OBJECTIVES

After studying this chapter, you should be able to:

Describe what is meant by the term *organizing a bargaining unit.*

- **Discuss** the role of the National Labor Relations Board (NLRB) in an organizing campaign.
- **Define** the meaning of collective bargaining.
- **Explain** the steps taken before a grievance reaches the point of going to arbitration in a nonunion setting.
- **Cite** some examples of union-management cooperation on job-related issues.

KEY TERMS

Arbitration
Boycott
Collective Bargaining
Decertification Election
Grievance
Hot Cargo Agreement
Lockout
Mediation
Representation Election
Strike

CHAPTER OUTLINE

P/HRM · IN · ACTION

Stan Goebel and Tom Hardisty

Tom and Stan met to discuss the organizing situation and the communication program. Here is a part of the conversation.

Tom: The communication program looks good, Stan. We'll have personal visits with the employees to talk about the union problem. The supervisors will run some of the meetings. You and I will split up and attend as many as we can. You'll train the supervisors on why the employees shouldn't join the union. But we can't afford to add these pay and benefit increases at this time.

Stan: You know the union will exploit that. Our money situation, together with the lack of security because of layoffs, puts us at a big disadvantage.

Tom: I know it. But it's your job to keep the union out.

In the next days and weeks, Stan did his best. Lots of meetings were held. He also mailed letters to the employees' homes.

Who will represent or speak for whom in the collective bargaining process? *Collective bargaining* is a process by which the representatives of the organization (the employer) meet and attempt to work out a contract with representatives of the workers (the employee).[1] The employees' representative can be a union or a group of unions.

Organizing efforts at Hardisty Manufacturing (HMC) are what Tom and Stan are concerned about. The efforts at HMC are typical of thousands of others that involve a face-off between the union and management. More about the details of organizing will be presented in this chapter.

In the private, public, and third sectors of society, employees have the right to self-organization in order to collectively bargain through a *unit* of their choosing. A unit of employees is a group of two or more employees who share common employment interests and conditions and may reasonably be grouped

---

[1] John A. Fossum, *Labor Relations*, 4th ed. (Homewood, Ill.: BPI/Irwin, 1989), p. 6.

together.[2] In determining whether a proposed unit is appropriate, the following points are considered: (1) the history of collective bargaining in the organization, and (2) the desires of the employees in the proposed unit.

This chapter will first discuss how union organizing occurs in organizations and management's response to the organizing campaign. Next, the collective bargaining process and the administration of the labor-management contract will be discussed. Finally, the current public image of labor unions and what is being done about it will be discussed.

THE BARGAINING UNIT: THE WORKERS' CHOICE

A union can exist only if workers prefer to be unionized. Someone at Hardisty Manufacturing, or perhaps a group of employees, has called a union representative to come to the plant and "talk union" with the workers. The union considers the employees at Hardisty a viable unit that the union will attempt to win over. The employees who make up the bargaining unit can be decided upon jointly by labor and management, or by one or the other, but it is an important determination. Often union and management will disagree as to which employees or groups of employees are eligible for inclusion in a particular proposed unit. Obviously, both union and management want as much bargaining power as possible. Management may examine the make up of the proposed unit to determine if required exclusions (e.g., supervisors, security guards) have been made. If the union's proposed unit is not suitable, management may challenge the proposal and present its own proposed unit. In general, the union will seek as large a unit as possible, while management will attempt to restrict a unit's size.

The final determination by labor sector of the appropriate bargaining unit is in the hands of the following agencies and/or individual(s).

Private sector (e.g., General Motors, Xerox, USX)—The National Labor Relations Board (NLRB).

Railway and airline sector (e.g., Illinois Central, TWA)—The National Mediation Board.

Postal sector—The National Labor Relations Board (NLRB).

Federal sector (e.g., air traffic controllers)—Assistant Secretary of Labor for Labor-management Relations.

Public sector (e.g., California Highway Patrol, New York Sanitation Department)—Varies in accordance with state and local statutes.

Exhibit 17–1 represents a concise model that summarizes the union organizing and representation election process. The exhibit only applies to sectors in which the NLRB has jurisdiction. As shown, the organizing process leads to an

---

[2] Benjamin Taylor and Fred Witney, *Labor Relations Law* (Englewood Cliffs, N.J.: Prentice-Hall, 1987), p. 11.

EXHIBIT 17–1   **Sequence of Organizing Events**

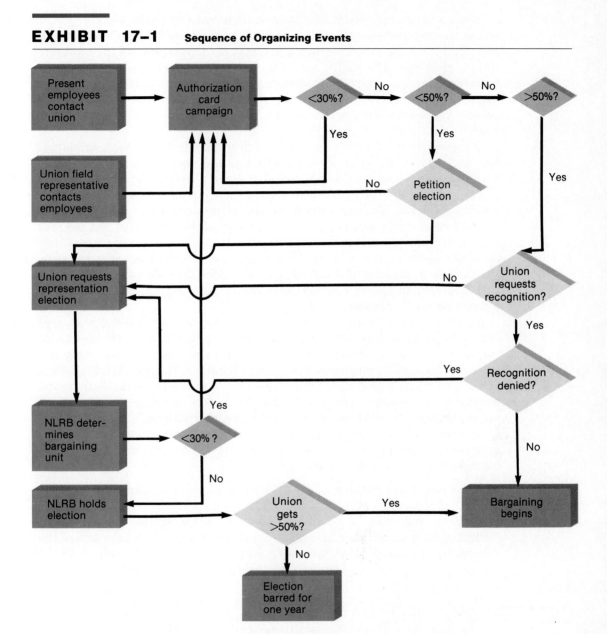

authorization card campaign. This is what Tom and Stan are suddenly confronted with. It is the union's way of finding out how many workers are for unionization. The card, when signed by an employee, authorizes the union to represent that employee during negotiations. At least 30 percent of the employees in the unit must sign before the NLRB will set up an actual election. If over 50 percent of the unit employees sign up, the union can directly demand to be recognized as the representative of the unit.

When a union believes that it represents a majority of the workers but is refused managerial recognition, it can petition the NLRB to hold a *representation election*.[3] If the union receives a majority of the votes cast in the representation election, the NLRB *certifies* it as the employees' bargaining representative and contract negotiations begin. If the union does not receive a majority (51 percent) of the votes cast, it cannot represent the employees, and no new representation election can be held for the unit for a period of one year.[4]

Occasionally the NLRB conducts *decertification elections*. Here, employees who are represented by a union vote to drop the union. If a majority of the bargaining unit votes against the union, it decertifies it as the representative.

For example, if employees have second thoughts about the desirability of retaining a union, they can—after one year of voting in a union—petition the NLRB for a decertification election.[5] A majority of the total votes cast rescinds the union. Employers cannot legally start the decertification process, but antiunion consultants can be used to encourage employees to start the process. Unions lose a majority of decertification elections. In 1986 over 1,000 decertification elections were conducted by the NLRB, and the union only won approximately 30 percent.[6]

Antiunion consultants or "union busters" as they are called, have had significant success in keeping unions out and helping management encourage employees to decertify unions. The AFL–CIO has identified 520 consulting and law firms that assist companies in warding off unions. The union feeling about these consultants is that they prevent employees from exercising their rights. Management, however, feels that they are important in helping organizations use legal means to remain nonunion or to decertify unions.[7]

Some examples of organizing campaigns illustrate the importance of efforts to organize workers (the unions) and resistance to organizing (the management and antiunion consultants):

- Grand Base is the only one of Alcan Aluminum Ltd.'s six Canadian smelters that has repeatedly voted against union efforts to organize.[8]
- Du Pont employees at 14 plants rejected representation by the United Steelworkers union after an eight-year drive by the union to organize the company. Six plants voted to retain their small independent locals while the others chose to remain nonunion. A total of about 11,500 workers are eligible

---

[3] Stephen I. Scholssberg and Frederick E. Sherman, *Organizing and the Law* (Washington, D.C.: Bureau of National Affairs, 1971).

[4] John E. Abodeely, *The NLRB and the Appropriate Bargaining Unit* (Philadelphia: Industrial Research Unit, Wharton School of Finance and Commerce, University of Pennsylvania, 1971).

[5] James P. Swann, Jr., "The Decertification of a Union," *Personnel Administrator*, January 1983, pp. 47–51.

[6] Arthur A. Sloane and Fred Witney, *Labor Relations* (Englewood Cliffs, N.J.: Prentice-Hall, 1988), p. 109; and Fifty-second Annual Report of The National Labor Relations Board for the fiscal year ended September 1986.

[7] Paul G. Engle, "Unionbusters or Morale Builders?" *Industry Week*, April 2, 1984, pp. 56–58.

[8] Alan Frieman, "In a Pro-Labor Area of Canada, Alean Plant Resists Repeated Attempts at Unionization," *The Wall Street Journal*, November 16, 1983, p. 33.

P/HRM · IN · ACTION

Stan sat in his office and went over his program. So far, the efforts of Hardisty's management to squelch the union through communication had not been as effective as Stan had hoped. He kept hearing more and more talk about the union—in fact, his communication program seemed to have backfired in some instances, having forced many employees to think seriously about unionization for the first time. Stan himself was beginning to feel that the union was inevitable.

He got out a pencil and paper and began to write down all the reasons he could think of for remaining non-unionized. (One reason he neglected to write down, of course, was the lecture he'd get from Tom if the union ever succeeded at Hardisty.)

to join the steelworkers union, and at least 93 percent turned out to vote in the representation election.[9]

- The Communication Workers recently won bargaining rights for 11,500 state-employed office workers in New Jersey.[10]
- The United Auto Workers have organized the Volkswagenwerk AG's Pennsylvania Rabbit factory.[11]
- J. P. Stevens & Co. denim plant workers in Rock Hill, South Carolina voted 433 to 299 not to be represented by the Amalgamated Clothing and Textile Workers Unions. This defeat occurred in the region that spawned the Hollywood movie about organizers, *Norma Rae*.[12]
- The American Federation of Teachers failed to organize 600 nurses at Fort Myers Memorial Hospital in Fort Myers, Florida, after the hospital hired consultants from Chicago; on the other hand, 200 nurses at Richmond Memorial Hospital in New York's Staten Island voted a union in.[13]

REPRESENTATION CAMPAIGNS:
THE UNIONS

The laws and executive orders covering labor relations require an employer to bargain with the representatives selected by the employees. The union's intention is to convince employees that being a member will lead to important

---

[9] "Steelworkers Effort to Organize Du Pont Is Turned Back by Employees at 14 Plants," *The Wall Street Journal*, December 14, 1981, p. 8.

[10] "Unions on the Run," *U.S. News & World Report*, September 14, 1981, p. 61.

[11] Robert L. Simison, "After Coaxing Japanese Car Makers to U.S., UAW Finds They Resist Union Organizing," *The Wall Street Journal*, August 26, 1980, p. 1.

[12] "Blue Jean Bombshell," *The Wall Street Journal*, September 1, 1981, p. 26.

[13] "Unions Move into the Office," *Business Week*, January 25, 1982, pp. 90–92.

EXHIBIT 17–2   Prevalent Union Campaign Issues

Issue	Percent of Campaigns
Union will prevent unfairness, set up grievance procedure/seniority system	82
Union will improve unsatisfactory wages	79
Union strength will provide employees with voice in wages, working conditions	79
Union, not outsider, bargains for what employees want	73
Union has obtained gains elsewhere	70
Union will improve unsatisfactory sick leave/insurance	64
Due/initiation fees are reasonable	64
Union will improve unsatisfactory vacations/holidays	61
Union will improve unsatisfactory pensions	61
Employer promises/good treatment may not continue without union	61
Employees choose union leaders	55
Employer will seek to persuade/frighten employees to vote against union	55
No strike without vote	55
Union will improve unsatisfactory working conditions	52
Employees have legal right to engage in union activity	52

Source: Adapted from Table 4–3 in *Union Representation Elections: Law and Reality*, by Julius G. Getman, Stephen B. Goldberg, and Jeanne B. Herman, © 1976 by Russell Sage Foundation, New York.

outcomes—better wages, fairer treatment from management, job security, and better working conditions. Unions attempt to stress issues that are meaningful, current, and obvious to employees.

Do unions stress important issues? This depends on the foresight and skill of the union determining the issues. A study of 33 representation elections found that 15 issues were raised by the union in at least half of these elections.[14] Exhibit 17–2 presents these issues and the number of elections in which each were stressed by the union. The union attempts to sell itself as a powerful force that can get the issues addressed in a way that is favorable to members. Which issues do you think the union will stress to the workers at the Hardisty plant?

REPRESENTATION CAMPAIGNS: MANAGEMENT

Most organizations prepare some type of campaign to oppose the union move to organize workers. It is important to know that the NLRB forbids management actions to suppress the union and intimidate employees considering unioniza-

---

[14] Julius Getman, Stephen Goldberg, and Jeanne B. Herman, *Union Representation Elections: Law and Reality* (New York: Russell Sage Foundation, 1976), pp. 80–81.

EXHIBIT 17-3 Prevalent Management Campaign Issues

Issues	Percent of Campaigns
Improvements not dependent on unionization	85
Wages good, equal to/better than under union contract	82
Financial costs of union dues outweigh gains	79
Union is outsider	79
Get facts before deciding; employer will provide facts and accept employee decision	76
If union wins, strike may follow	70
Loss of benefits may follow union win	67
Strikers will lose wages, lose more than gain	67
Unions not concerned with employee welfare	67
Strike may lead to loss of jobs	64
Employer has treated employees fairly/well	60
Employees should be certain to vote	54

Source: Adapted from Table 4–2 in *Union Representation Elections: Law and Reality*, by Julius G. Getman, Stephen B. Goldberg, and Jeanne B. Herman, © 1976 by Russell Sage Foundation, New York

tion. Neither management nor the union are permitted to engage in unfair labor practices.[15] For example, firing a union supporter or disciplining a worker that is involved in organizing efforts may be considered unfair management labor practices. If these actions are not supported with facts and are related to organizing efforts, management can become involved in lawsuits.

Normally, the P/HRM department is responsible for presenting management's side of the story. As previously discussed, outside consultants or anti-union experts trained in preventing organizing often are used. One popular management approach is to emphasize that a union is run by outsiders. The outsider is pictured as being uninformed, uninterested, and unqualified.[16] Management attempts to communicate clearly and forcefully to the employees about the advantages of remaining nonunionized. Speeches, question-and-answer sessions, bulletin board posters, personal letters to employees, and articles in the company newspaper are used to promote the nonunion advantages.

Exhibit 17–3 presents the issues covered by management in keeping employees nonunionized. The effectiveness of pointing to these kinds of issues depends to some extent on the thoroughness, clarity, and sincerity of management's efforts.

---

[15] Edward F. Murphy, *Management vs. the Union* (New York: Stein and Day, 1971), pp. 30–32.

[16] James F. Rand, "Preventive Maintenance Techniques for Staying Union-Free," *Personnel Journal*, June 1980, pp. 497–99.

THE ROLE OF THE NLRB:
WATCHING THE CAMPAIGN

The NLRB is responsible for conducting the election and certifying the results of organizing efforts in the private and public sectors. Often the NLRB is faced with preelection charges of one group against the other about unfair practices. The NLRB often has to decide whether a specific management or union tactic was fair under the guidelines of the law. The NLRB pays particular attention to the following areas:

Concerning the Employer

1. The NLRB makes sure that the questioning of employees about union membership is done in a fair and non-intimidating manner.
2. The NLRB checks to see if the union information provided to employees is truthful.
3. The NLRB does not allow any final presentations within 24 hours preceding the election.

Concerning the Union

1. The NLRB makes sure that no threats or intimidation are used to gain votes.
2. The NLRB guards the employees against the union's promises of special treatment for votes if the union wins.
3. No final presentations are allowed within 24 hours preceding the election.

The NLRB is a watchdog. Unfair labor practices charges can be filed by an employee, an employer, the union, or any person.[17] A formal charge requires the NLRB to officially review the claim. It is the NLRB in the private and postal sectors that guards against and prevents any interference in the lawful procedures to select the bargaining representative. If the interference is considered significant, an election can be set aside and rerun.

The NLRB has taken a significant stand concerning unfair employer practices. The board ruled that when an employer commits outrageous and pervasive unfair labor practices, the board will grant bargaining rights to the union even when the union is not able to persuade a majority of the employees to sign authorization cards during an organizing campaign. The board reasoned that employees would be afraid and intimidated to the point of not signing the cards. Although employers have been opposed to such involvement, the NLRB has actually ordered collective bargaining rights in about 1 percent of the cases. In all other cases, the status of the union is determined through the election process.[18]

---

[17] Louis Jackson and Robert Lewis, *Winning NLRB Elections* (New York: Practicing Law Institute, 1972).

[18] Conair Corp., 261 NLRB; No. 178 (1982).

If a union legally wins an organizing election, it is recognized as the bargaining representative of a unit. The NLRB requires that both the elected union and management must bargain in good faith. This requirement is spelled out in the Taft-Hartley Act as follows:

> For the purposes of this section, to bargain collectively is the performance of the mutual obligation of the employer and representative of the employees to meet at reasonable times and confer in good faith with respect to wages, hours, and other terms and conditions of employment, or the negotiation of an agreement, or any question arising thereunder, and the execution of a written contract incorporating any agreement reached if requested by either party, but such obligation does not compel either party to agree to a proposal or require the making of a concession.

If either party does not bargain in good faith, unfair labor practices can be charged. The costs, publicity, and hostility associated with not bargaining in good faith are usually too significant to disregard. Of course, good faith doesn't mean that the union or management must agree with each other about issues. This is the essence of collective bargaining—disagreement and negotiation. An absence of good faith would include:

1. An unwillingness to make counterproposals.
2. Constantly changing positions.
3. The use of delaying tactics.
4. Withdrawing concessions after they have been made.
5. Refusal to provide necessary data for negotiations.

COLLECTIVE BARGAINING

As stated at the beginning of the chapter, collective bargaining is a process by which the representatives of the organization meet and attempt to work out a contract with the employees' representative—the union. *Collective* means only that representatives are attempting to negotiate an agreement. *Bargaining* is the process of cajoling, debating, discussing, and threatening in order to bring about a favorable agreement for those being represented.

The collective bargaining process and the final agreement reached are influenced by many variables.[19] Exhibit 17–4 graphically identifies some of the variables influencing the union and management representatives. For example, the state of the economy affects collective bargaining. In a tight economy, a union push for higher wages is less likely to succeed, because it would be inflationary. The firm's representative must also consider whether the company can pay an increased wage based on current and expected eco-

---

[19] Reed Richardson, *Collective Bargaining by Objectives* (Englewood Cliffs, N.J.: Prentice-Hall, 1985).

nomic conditions. In the 1980s, American Airlines, United Airlines, TRW, Wilson Foods, and Ford have all asked for and received union agreement to give back some of the wages and fringe benefits won at the bargaining table.[20] The poor economy has been such a factor that plant after plant has been closed down because of high labor costs. For example, employees at Ford's Sheffield, Alabama, plant had to accept a 50 percent wage and benefit cut or face a closed plant.[21]

A concession bargaining situation exists when there is something of importance given back. Concessions can consist of wage cuts, wage freezes of previously negotiated increases, benefit reductions, work-rule changes that result in increased management flexibility, and other similar actions. An analysis by two labor relations researchers estimated that 30 to 50 percent of all unionized workers in major industries (e.g., machinery, air transportation, apparel, metal) had granted concessions.[22] However, some unions have fought back and have traded concessions for power and stock. For example, employees at Eastern Air Lines, Inc. traded concessions for stock and four board seats. In 1986 members of the United Steelworkers gained stock from LTV, Bethlehem Steel, Kaiser Aluminum, and Wheeling-Pittsburgh Steel.[23]

Each of the forces shown in Exhibit 17–4 involves a union and a management response. Each side of the collective bargaining table will be influenced by such factors as the economy and the environment. Unions and management are now painfully aware of how inflation, foreign competition, and the mood of a society can affect the issues being discussed at the bargaining table.

The actual process of collective bargaining involves a number of steps, such as: (1) prenegotiation; (2) selecting negotiators; (3) developing a bargaining strategy; (4) using the best tactics; and (5) reaching a formal contractual agreement.

Prenegotiation

In collective bargaining, both sides attempt to receive concessions that will help them achieve their objectives. As soon as a contract is signed by union and management, both parties begin preparing for the next collective bargaining session. Even with no union that is useful. Thus, the importance of careful prenegotiation preparation cannot be overemphasized.

---

[20] Leland B. Cross, Jr., "1982 and 1983: The Concession Bargaining Years," *Personnel Adminstrator*, November 1984, pp. 27–35; "Give-Backs Highlight Three Major Bargaining Agreements," *Personnel Administrator*, November 1983, pp. 33–35, 70–71; and Mark N. Doclosh, "Companies Increasingly Ask Labor to Give Back Past Contract Gains," *The Wall Street Journal*, November 27, 1981, p. 1.

[21] "A Dilemma in Sheffield," *Newsweek*, December 7, 1981, p. 77.

[22] Peter Capelli and Robert B. McKersie, "Labor and the Crisis in Collective Bargaining," in *Challenges and Choices Facing American Labor*, ed. Thomas A. Kocham (Cambridge, Mass.: MIT Press, 1985).

[23] Aaron Bernstein, "Move Over, Boone, Carl, and Ira—Here Comes Labor," *Business Week*, December 14, 1987, pp. 124–25.

EXHIBIT 17–4   The Forces Influencing the Bargaining Process

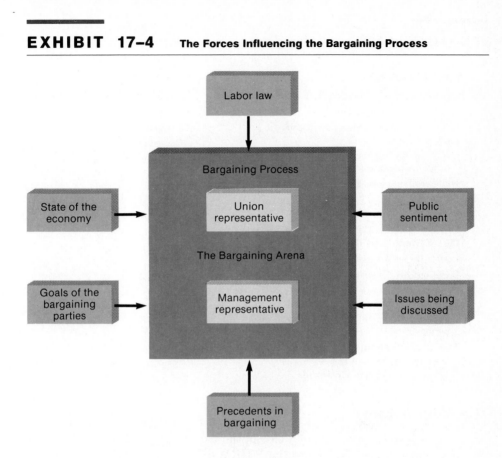

Data of all types are maintained by both unions and management. Exhibit 17–5 presents examples of data that is useful to both management and unions. In addition to the internal and external data it is also important to check the background of the union negotiators. This will allow management to interpret the style and personality of the negotiators.

The computer has now become a valuable tool for both the union and management in prenegotiation and actual negotiations.[24] The computer can store data, help negotiators prepare various economic scenarios, and interface with various database sources. One result of computer technology is that union and management negotiators have at their disposal in a short period detailed information that can be used or altered to fit their particular strategy. For example, a union negotiator requested information on the company's financial status and salaries paid to officers. Within 90 seconds this information was made available from a database.

---

[24] Deborah O. Cantrell, "Computers Come to the Bargaining Table," *Personnel Journal*, September 1984, pp. 27–30.

EXHIBIT 17–5   **Bargaining Data for Negotiators**

Internal to the Firm	**External to the Firm**
Number of workers in each job classification	Comparative industry wage rates
Compensation per worker	Comparative occupational wage rates
Minimum and maximum pay in each job classification	Comparative fringe benefits
	Consumer price index
Overtime pay per hour and number of annual overtime hours worked by job classification	Patterns of relevant bargaining settlements
Number of employees, by categories, who work on each shift	
Cost of shift differential premiums	
History of recent negotiations	
Cost of fringe benefits	
Cost-of-living increases	
Vacation costs by years of service of employees	
Demographic data on the bargaining unit members by sex, age, and seniority	
Cost and duration of lunch breaks and rest periods	
An outline of incentive, progresson, evaluation, training, safety, and promotion plans	
Grievance and arbitration awards	

The Negotiators

On the management side of the bargaining table may be any one of a number of people, including the P/HRM director, the executive vice president, or the company lawyer. Or management may field a team of negotiators, so that all forms of expertise are present. Typically, the team consists of a P/HRM expert, a lawyer, a manager or vice president with knowledge of the entire business organization, and an economist.

The union also uses a team approach. The union team generally consists of business agents, shop stewards, the local union president, and—when the negotiation is very important—representatives from national union head-quarters. When industrywide bargaining is taking place, as in the automobile industry, the chief negotiator is a representative from the national union.

The negotiating teams (union and management) meet independently before the actual bargaining sessions and plan the best strategy to use. This preparation identifies the chief spokesperson and the roles of each member of the team.

Mapping the Strategy

Because the labor agreement must be used for a long period of time, it is important to develop a winning strategy and tactics. The *strategy* is considered to be the plan and policies that will be pursued at the bargaining table. Tactics are the specific actions taken in the bargaining sessions. It is important to

P/HRM · IN · ACTION

Stan wanted to know more about the union. The vote had still not been taken, but he knew from talk around the plant that the union already had an edge. He called his researchers together to see if they could find out a little about the union's past history—particularly its success or failure at the bargaining table. Jim Rogers, Stan's assistant, came to Stan with the information.

Jim: It looks pretty grim for our side, Stan, if the union wins the election. They've got a very successful team of negotiators, starting with the local union president. They've won four out of six of their negotiations so far.

Stan: And with our money problems, we can't offer our people as much as the union can. What's this local president like?

Jim: He's a young guy, 35 years old; college man. His strategy in the past has been to let management do the talking first, then he comes up with points for the union's side. And he's

always armed with a lot of statistics and facts to back him up.

Stan: Well, we know his main argument will center around our refusal to increase pay and the threat of layoffs due to our financial situation.

Jim: He's got us there.

Two hours later, it was announced that Hardisty would be laying off 20 percent of its workers. Stan ran into Tom's office.

Stan: Tom, we can't lay these people off now, right in the middle of the union's campaign! We're practically handing ourselves over to the union if we do this!

Tom: Pipe down, Stan. It's your job to beat the union, but I've got to keep our heads above water, too.

Stan: I think this is the wrong move to make, Tom.

Tom: Too late now . . . it's done. Now what has your department found out about this union?

spell out the strategy and tactics because bargaining is a give-and-take process with the characteristics of a poker game, a political campaign, or a heated debate.[25]

An important issue in mapping out a strategy involves the maximum concessions that will be granted. By shifting a position during the bargaining, the other side may build up expectations that are difficult to change. By granting too much, one side may be viewed as weak. How far management or the union will go before it risks a work stoppage or lockout is considered before the sessions begin and are a part of the strategic plan.

Another part of management's strategic plan is to develop the total cost

[25] G. Edward Herman, Alfred Kuhn, and Ronald L. Seeber, *Collective Bargaining and Labor Relations* (Englewood Cliffs, N.J.: Prentice-Hall, 1987), pp. 243–47.

profile of the maximum concession package. This is, what will these concessions cost the company today and in the future? Will P/HRM policies or production procedures have to be changed if these concessions are granted? This form of future planning helps management determine how willing it is to take a strike. Planning for a strike is certainly difficult, but the issue should be included in strategy planning.

Tactics

Tactics are calculated actions used by both parties. Occasionally, tactics are used to mislead the other party. But they are also used to secure an agreement that is favorable to either management or the unions.

A number of popular tactics have been used by both the union and management to secure a favorable agreement.[26] These tactics are:

1. *Conflict Based*—Each party is uncompromising, takes a hard line, and resists any overtures for compromise or agreement. Typically, what happens is that what one party does the other party mirrors back.
2. *Armed Truce*—Each party views the other as an adversary. Although they are adversaries, it is recognized that an agreement must be worked out under the guidelines specified by the law. In fact, the law is literally followed to the letter to reach agreement.
3. *Power Bargaining*—Each party accepts the other party with the knowledge that a balance of power exists. It would be nonproductive to pursue a strategy of trying to eliminate the other party in the relationship.
4. *Accommodation*—Both parties adjust to each other. Compromise, flexibility, and tolerance in positive forms are used in favor of emotion and raw power. It is claimed that most managers and union leaders have engaged in accommodation for the bulk of union-management bargaining issues.
5. *Cooperation*—Each side accepts the other as a full partner. This means that management and the union work together not only on everyday matters but in such difficult areas as technological change, quality of work-life improvements, and business decision making.

These five tactics are only some of the many tactics that exist.

For example, General Electric used a tactic called *Boulwarism* (named after Lemuel Boulware, General Electric's vice president of public and employee relations who developed it). GE's management worked out an offer that was final and presented it to the union. No matter how heated or long negotiations became, the offer was final. The National Labor Relations Board ruled that the Boulware tactic was a failure to bargain in good faith.[27] GE appealed this decision and won in the lower courts. However, the Supreme Court informed GE that it could not give one best offer, but had to start lower in order to permit the union to obtain benefits and save face with the membership.

---

[26] Sloane and Whitney, *Labor Relations*, p. 223.

[27] Herbert R. Northrup, *Boulwarism* (Ann Arbor, Mich.: Bureau of Industrial Relations, University of Michigan, 1964).

By 1969, Boulwarism was starting to become an ineffective tactic. The long-competitive factions within the GE unions began to coordinate their bargaining efforts. There was also the attrition of GE managers who had worked with Boulwarism for years. A long and bitter strike in 1969, along with these other factors, resulted in adjustments in GE's negotiation procedures. Instead of making one—and only one—offer, there were modifications as negotiations occurred. Thus, Boulwarism as practiced in its heyday has become a historical reference point at GE.

The highly skilled and effective negotiator on either side must be in complete control of his or her emotions and be somewhat of an actor. There are times when a "performance" is given to make an effective point. In order to give these performances, the person must be in control of the situation. Threats, abusive language, and tirades are considered weak tactics by both parties. Logical presentations, good manners, and calmness seem to be more effective than threatening tactics.

The Contract

The union-management contract designates the formal terms of agreement. The average contract is designed to be in effect for two or three years, and it varies from a few typewritten pages to more than a hundred pages, depending on the issues covered, the size of the organization, and the union.

One of the continuing problems of union-management contracts is their readability. A study of 196 collective bargaining agreements from the Bureau of Labor Statistics analyzed contracts using readability indexes such as the Flesch, Farr-Jenkins-Patterson, and Gunning formulas.[28] The analyses indicated that contracts are difficult to read and that some sections are, in fact, incomprehensible. It is ironic that many of the contract sections that deal with seniority, discipline, and grievance procedures are not understandable to a rank-and-file employee who is most affected. Perhaps lawyers can understand what is presented, but stewards, union members, and other nonlawyers generally cannot make sense of the contract. Unfortunately, studies conducted over 30 years ago showed the same kind of results.[29]

The typical labor contract is divided into sections and appendixes. The standard sections that can be covered in some labor agreements are shown in Exhibit 17–6. The exhibit shows that a major part of the contract is concerned with such employment issues as wages, hours, fringe benefits, and overtime.

In general, the contract spells out the authority and responsibility of both union and management. Management rights appear in one of two forms. The first involves a statement that the control and operation of the business is the right of management except in cases specified in the contract. The second is a list of all management activities that are not subject to sharing with the union.

---

[28] James Suchan and Clyde Scott, "Readability Levels of Collective Bargaining Agreements," *Personnel Administrator*, November 1984, pp. 73–80.

[29] Jeanne Lauer and D. G. Patterson, "Readability of Union Contracts," *Personnel*, January 1951, pp. 36–40.

EXHIBIT 17–6 **Content of a Labor Agreement**

Purpose and intent of the parties	Vacations
Scope of the agreement	Seniority
Management	Safety and health
Responsibilities of the parties	Military service
Union membership and checkoff	Severance allowance
Adjustment of grievance	Savings and vacation plan
Arbitration	Supplemental unemployment benefits program
Suspension and discharge cases	S.U.B. and insurance grievances
Rates of pay	Prior agreements
Hour of work	Termination date
Overtime and holidays	Appendixes

Source: Adapted from USX Corporation and the United Steelworkers Union, "Labor Agreement."

Included are such topics as planning and scheduling production, purchasing equipment, and making final hiring decisions.

The union rights spelled out in the contract involve such issues as the role the union will play in laying off members or in such areas as promotion and transfer. The union stresses seniority as a means of reducing the tendency for discrimination and favoritism, in P/HRM decision making.

ADMINISTERING THE CONTRACT

Day-to-day compliance with contract provisions is an important responsibility of the first-line manager, who works closely with union members. As the representative of management, the first-line manager must discipline workers, handle grievances, and prepare for such actions as strikes.

Discipline

Most contracts agree that management in a unionized firm has a right to discipline workers, providing all discipline follows legal due process.[30] If an employee or union challenges a disciplinary action, the burden of proof rests on the company. Often management loses a case that is arbitrated (settled by an impartial third party) because improper disciplinary procedures have been followed.

Many union-management contracts specify the types of discipline and the offenses for which corrective action will be taken. Some of the infractions that are typically spelled out are:

- *Incompetence.* Failure to perform the assigned job.
- *Misconduct.* Insubordination, dishonesty, or violating a rule, such as smoking in a restricted area.

---

[30] "Understanding the Contract," *Personnel Journal*, August 1981, p. 612.

- *Violations of the contract.* Initiating a strike when there is no strike clause, for example.

The contract should list penalties for such infractions.[31] Inconsistent application of discipline is sometimes a problem as the discussion in Chapter 15 illustrated.

Grievances

A *grievance* is a complaint about a job that creates dissatisfaction or discomfort, whether it is valid or not. The complaint may be made by an individual or by the union.[32] It is important to note that, although the validity of the grievance may be questionable, it should be handled correctly. Even if an employee files an official grievance that seems absolutely without support, the manager should handle it according to formal contractual provisions.

Grievance procedures are usually followed in unionized companies, but they are also important channels of communication in nonunionized organizations. In the unionized organization, the contract contains a clause covering the steps to be followed and how the grievance will be handled. The number of steps varies from contract to contract. But a labor union is not essential for establishing a procedure.

Exhibit 17–7 illustrates a four-step grievance procedure used in a unionized company.[33]

1. The employee meets with the supervisor and the union steward and presents the grievance. Most grievances are settled at this point.
2. If the grievance is not settled at step 1, there is a conference between middle management and union officials (a business agent or union committee).
3. At this point, a top-management representative and top-union officials (for example, the union president) attempt to settle the grievance.
4. Both parties (union and management) turn the grievance over to an arbitrator who makes a decision. Arbitration is usually handled by a mutually agreed-upon single individual or a panel of an odd number.

Although most grievances are handled at step 1, there are a number of important principles for managers to follow. They should (1) take every grievance seriously; (2) work with the union representative; (3) gather all information available on the grievance; (4) after weighing all the facts, provide an answer to the employee voicing the grievance; and (5) after the grievance is settled, attempt to move on to other matters.

Even though the grievance procedure shown in Exhibit 17–7 is used typically in large unionized firms (e.g., AT&T, Proctor & Gamble, and Republic

---

[31] Richard Arvey and John M. Ivancevich, "Punishment in Organizations: A Review, Propositions, and Research Suggestions," *Academy of Management Review*, January 1980, pp. 123–32.

[32] Maurice S. Trotta, *Handling Grievances: A Guide for Labor and Management* (Washington, D.C.: Bureau of National Affairs, 1976), pp. 141–42.

[33] Thomas F. Gideon and Richard B. Peterson, "A Comparison of Alternate Grievance Procedures, *Employee Relations Law Journal*, Autumn 1979, pp. 222–33.

EXHIBIT 17–7   A Grievance Procedure: A Unionized Situation

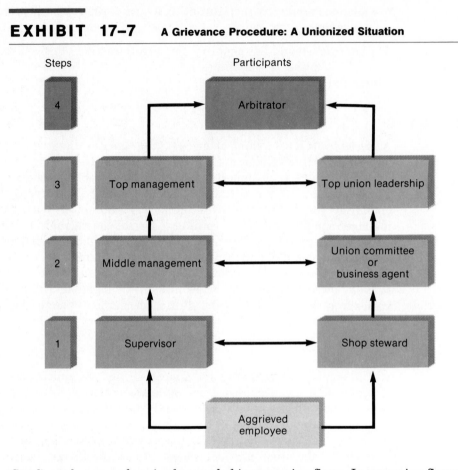

Steel), such a procedure is also needed in nonunion firms. In nonunion firms, a number of grievance approaches—open-door policy, ombudsman, juries of peers, hearing officers, and outside arbitration—have been used with some success.[34] The lack of any grievance procedure causes frustration, antagonism, and anxiety among many employees. These feelings and attitudes are not healthy for good employee-management relations. They also can spark an interest to organize a formal bargaining representative.

An example of a nonunionized employer with a formal grievance procedure is that of Duke University in Durham, North Carolina. Duke employs over 15,000 people of which two thirds work in the university's medical center.[35] In the current system as displayed in Exhibit 17–8, a grieving employee is allowed to choose an advocate (second-year M.B.A. students are selected as employee advocates) only from within the Duke community. The final step is a

---

[34] Alan Balfour, "Five Types of Non-Union Grievance Systems," *Personnel*, March–April 1984, pp. 69–76.

[35] Edmund M. Diaz, John W. Minton, and David M. Saunders, "A Fair Nonunion Grievance Procedure," *Personnel Journal*, April 1987, pp. 13–18.

EXHIBIT 17–8   **Duke University's Grievance Process for Nonunion Employees**

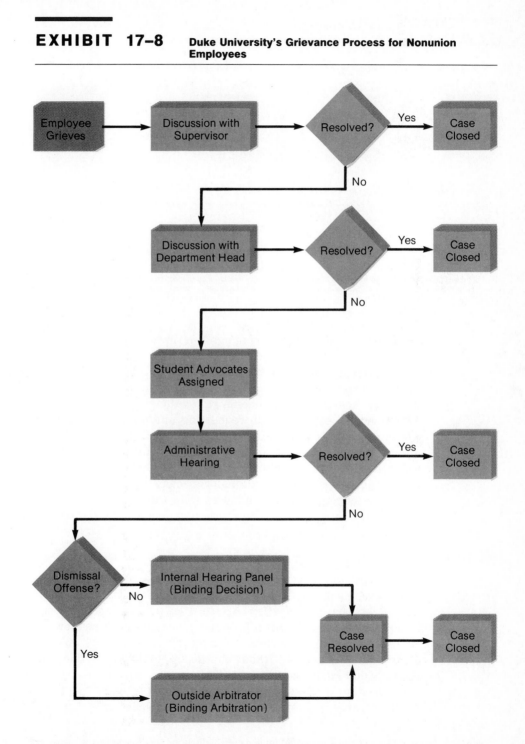

Source: Edmund M. Diaz, John W. Minton, and David M. Saunders, "A Fair Nonunion Grievance Procedure," *Personnel Journal*, April 1987, p. 14.

EXHIBIT 17–9   **The Grievance Procedure**

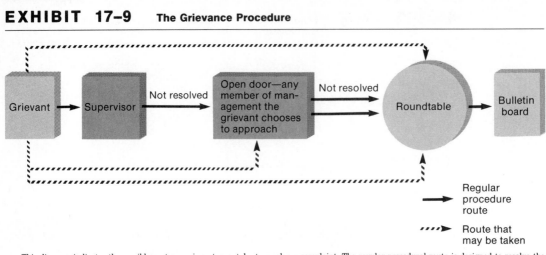

This diagram indicates the possible routes a grievant may take to resolve a complaint. The regular procedural route is designed to resolve the grievance at the lowest possible level—the supervisor. However, if the grievant feels uncomfortable approaching the supervisor, the grievance may be presented directly to any level of management via the open door policy or to the roundtable.

Source: *Personnel Adminstrator*, January 1983, p. 37.

jointly selected internal hearing panel or, in the case of termination, one of the panel of five professional arbitrators.

Interestingly, the main purpose of using M.B.A. student advocates to re-solve grievances was to avoid using legal counsel which usually led to long, drawn-out hearings. The students gain valuable "real world" experience from their hands-on experience in requesting and debating employee rights. The program has been successful for over three years. It is likely that a program similar to Duke's could work in other organizations if (1) there were an accepted grievance procedure in place, (2) a college or university interested in developing hands-on applications of grievance resolution were unavailable, and (3) management and employees were interested in grievance resolution instead of long, drawn-out, legal-oriented debates and political maneuvering.

Mediation

Mediation is the process in which a third party helps labor and management reach agreement. The Federal Mediation and Conciliation Service (FMCS) was created by the Taft-Hartley Act in 1947 as an independent agency. The Federal Service maintains offices in major cities such as New York, Chicago, St. Louis, and San Francisco. It employs approximately 300 mediators, who perform their services without charge to participants. The FMCS mediates about 20,000 labor disagreements a year.

The mediators make suggestions which may be accepted or rejected by both or either party.[36] A mediator's suggestion doesn't have the power of an ar-

---

[36] Steven Briggs, "Labor/Management Conflict and the Role of the Neutral," in *Personnel and Human Resource Management*, R. S. Schuler, S. A. Youngblood, and V. L. Huber (St. Paul: West Publishing, 1987), pp. 418–24.

bitrator's recommendation which must be accepted. A *mediator* is a reviewer of facts, a creative facilitator, and a professional listener. A mediator relies on the power of persuasion to get both parties to settle a dispute. If the mediator is going to be an effective persuader he or she must be neutral, fair, and decisive. These attributes are essential in order to have parties reconcile their differences.

Arbitration

The grievance procedure does not always result in an acceptable solution. When a deadlock occurs, most contracts (about 96 percent) call for arbitration. *Arbitration* is a quasijudicial process in which the parties agree to submit an unresolvable dispute to a neutral third party for binding settlement. Both parties submit their positions, and the arbitrator makes a decision.

The contract typically specifies how a dispute goes to arbitration. Normally, the case would have gone through the previous three steps in the grievance procedure (Exhibit 17–7). At the last step, for instance, if management denies the grievance or fails to modify its position sufficiently to satisfy the union, the union can request arbitration.

Procedures for selection of an arbitrator are usually written into the contract. The most typical arrangement is to use a single impartial arbitrator who hears the evidence and renders an award, or to have a tripartite board consisting of a management representative, a union representative, and an impartial chairperson.

The arbitrators generally come from three major sources. The first group consists of attorneys who are full-time arbitrators. The second group is made up of academics who are experts in labor law, personnel/human resources management, and labor economics. The third group includes respected members of the community, such as teachers and ministers.

The *award* is the decision reached by the arbitrator. It conveys the decision, a summary of the evidence, and the rationale for the decision. In preparing the award, the arbitrator must examine a number of issues:

1. Can the dispute be arbitrated?
2. Did the grievance allege an actual violation of the contract?
3. Were the grievance procedures followed in a timely manner?

If these criteria are met, the arbitrator then investigates the dispute.

The arbitrator works hard to ensure that the award draws from the framework and intent of the contract. Most contracts prohibit arbitrators from adding to or subtracting from the intent of the contract. The arbitrator must clearly show how the award fits the meaning of the contract.

Arbitration is criticized because of time delays and cost. An AFL–CIO publication reported that the average time for the filing of a grievance through the submission of an arbitration award was 223 days.[37] For 1981, the Federal

---

[37] John Zalusky, "Arbitration: Updating a Vital Process," *American Federationist* 83 (November 1976), p. 6.

EXHIBIT 17–10   **Arbitration Time Delays**

	Days
Grievance date to request for panel	68
Between request for panel and panel sent out	6
Panel sent out to appointment of arbitrator	45
Appointment of arbitrator to hearing date	61
Hearing date to arbitrator award	43
Total: Grievance date to award	223

Source: John Zalusky, "Arbitration: Updating a Vital Process," *AFL–CIO American Federationist* 83 (November 1976), p. 6.

Mediation and Conciliation Service (FMCS) reported that, on the average, 168 days elapsed from the time the parties requested a panel of arbitrators until an award was issued.[38] The time delays are presented in Exhibit 17–10.

The costs of arbitration may cause problems, especially for some unions. Although management and the union usually share equally the cost of arbitration, a financially poor union is sometimes reluctant to become involved in arbitration. This reluctance can detract from the members' respect and image of the union.

In order to expedite cases and maintain some cost control, grievants in the steel industry have the option of using a new procedure. Under this procedure, panels have been created from which arbitrators are designated to handle disputes on a rotating basis. Arbitration hearings must be held within 10 days of the appeal, and the award must be made within 48 hours after the hearing. The cases are presented by local management and union representatives rather than the "pros" or "big shots" from the union and management. Thus, instead of paying the arbitrator from $200 to $400 per day that he or she works on the case, the fee is $50 to $100 from each party and only for the hearing day.

Strikes

A *strike* is an effort to withhold employee services so that the employer will make greater concessions at the bargaining table. The strike, or a potential strike, is a major bargaining weapon used by the union. But before a union strikes, it needs to consider the legality of striking, the members' willingness to endure the hardships of a long strike, and the employer's ability to operate the organization without union members. The greater the employer's ability to operate the organization, the less chance the union will have of gaining the demands it makes.

There are a number of different types of strikes, including:

- *Economic strike.* Based on a demand for better wages or fringe benefits than the employer wants to provide.

[38] MVCS, 1981 *Annual Report*, p. 39.

- *Jurisdictional strike.* Exists when two unions argue over who has the right to perform a job. For example, bricklayers and ironworkers may both want to install steel rods in doorways. The rods are made a part of the brickwork and are needed to hold up heavy steel doors. If either group strikes to force the employer to grant the work to its members, a jurisdictional strike occurs. This type of strike is illegal under the Taft-Hartley Act.
- *Wildcat strike.* An unapproved strike that suddenly occurs because one union subgroup has not been satisfied by a grievance decision or by some managerial action. The union leaders do not sanction this type of strike.
- *Sitdown strike.* When employees strike but remain in the plant. Such strikes are illegal because they are an invasion of private property.

When any strike occurs, management must be able to function during the work stoppage, and the company property must be protected from strike sabotage.

Management generally views strikes with a mixture of fear and loathing. Even the threat of a strike can force concessions from management at the bargaining table, and any strike usually leaves an aftertaste that poisons labor relations for years. There appears to be a downward trend in the number of strikes being called in the United States. The total amount of working time lost has been low from 1974 to 1980. In 1980, 33,000 labor days (a workday) were lost to strikes, versus 48,000 labor days in 1974.[39] Strikes over non-economic issues have been drastically reduced. In 1976, there were 1,950 strikes during the course of contracts over working conditions and union jurisdiction. In 1984, there were just 389 strikes.

In what may be a first, a union voted to strike because the wage offer they received from management was too high.[40] Leaders and members of Local 32 of the International Association of Heat and Frost Insulators and Asbestos Workers in New Jersey decided to strike because they felt management was trying to inflate wages so more jobs would go to nonunion crews from other areas. Management offered $2.50 more an hour over two years, but the union struck until a final agreement of only 90 cents more per hour was reached.

The decline in strikes doesn't mean that the strike is not a powerful weapon available to unions. The strike will still be used even in rough economic times. However, because of economics, workers' desires, and increased technological changes, unions are less willing and able to mount strikes.[41] The government has also reduced the power of the strike weapon with the Omnibus Budget Reconciliation Act of 1981. Effective October 1, 1981, striking workers and their families were no longer eligible for food stamps.

The 1983 strike against AT&T was a prime example of the recent difficulties unions are having in using the strike weapon.[42] Most of AT&T's telephone

---

[39] Herbert E. Meyer, "The Decline of Strikes," *Fortune*, November 2, 1981, pp. 66–70.

[40] "Workers Strike for Smaller Pay Raise," *Houston Chronicle*, September 21, 1984, p. 11.

[41] "Hospital Staff Finds Strike Ineffective," *Dallas Morning News*, May 16, 1981, p. 21.

[42] Ben Burdetsky and Marvin S. Katzman, "Is the Strike Iron Still Hot?" *Personnel Journal*, July 1984, pp. 48–52.

activities are automated, and little disruption occurred when the union decided to strike. The company was able to use supervisory and management personnel, along with nonstrikers, to handle most of the operator-assisted calls. The union was not able to close down the system.

Strikes in the public sector or by government employees are troublesome for unions, management, and the government. Because of the essential nature of the work performed, the government is opposed to public employee strikes.[43] The issue of "government sovereignty" is raised to argue against such strikes. Of course, the public employee unions like the Professional Air Traffic Controllers (PATCO) argue against this claim of the government.[44] The union argues that taking away the strike weapon reduces public employee unions to a second-class type of power.

In the summer of 1981, 12,000 air traffic controllers went on strike. President Reagan cited that the strike violated the oath taken by the controllers not to strike. The typical and usually followed practice by which a strike by public employees is "glossed over" was replaced by the president's decision to fire every striking air traffic controller. The action by President Reagan to hold public employees to the no-strike provisions of the contract has served notice to other unionized employees in the U.S. Postal Service and in the state and local governments.[45] Most observers believe that PATCO leaders such as the president Robert Poli totally miscalculated public reaction. The strike by air traffic controllers, with average annual salaries of $35,000, didn't generate a groundswell of public support.[46] The PATCO strike was a setback for organized labor in government employment—which is the union's main target for growth.

If and when a union mounts a strike, it usually resorts to *picketing* procedures. The union hopes to shut down the company during a strike, so it places members at plant entrances to advertise the dispute and discourage persons from entering or leaving the buildings. Peaceful persuasion through the formation of a picket line is legal, but violence is not. Picketing may also take place, without a strike, to publicize union viewpoints about an employer.

Another type of union pressure is the *boycott*. In a primary boycott, union members do not patronize the boycotted firm. This type of boycott is legal. A secondary boycott occurs when a supplier of a boycotted firm is threatened with a union strike unless it stops doing business with the boycotted company. This type of boycott is generally illegal under the Taft-Hartley Act. A special type of boycott is the *hot cargo agreement*. Under this agreement, the employer permits union members to avoid working with materials that come from employers who have struck by a union. This type of boycott is illegal according

---

[43] Herbert R. Northrup, "The Rise and Demise of PATCO," *Industrial and Labor Relations Review*, January 1984, pp. 167–84.

[44] Peter Gall and John Hoerr, "How Labor Loses from the PATCO Strike," *Business Week*, August 24, 1981, p. 35.

[45] Ibid.

[46] Burdetsky and Katzman, "Is the Strike Iron Still Hot?" p. 51.

to the Labor-Management Disclosure Act except in the construction and clothing industries.

Management's response to these union pressures may be to continue operations with a skeleton crew of managerial personnel, to shut down the plant, or to lock the employees out. The *lockout* is an effort to force the union to stop harassing the employer or to accept the conditions set by management. Lockouts are also used to prevent union work slowdowns, damage to property, or violence related to a labor dispute. Many states allow locked-out employees to draw unemployment benefits, thereby weakening the lockout. In practice the lockout is more of a threat than a widely practiced weapon of management.

In 1987, the 28 owners of National Football League teams discovered that during the players' strike, the organizations were much more profitable.[47] The players' strike showed that a football team is a peculiar labor force. It is organized labor by definition, yet its members are both more and less cohesive than many workers. There is an enormous disparity in wages. There is also no strike fund to bolster players in time of need. Thus, the owners were able to take a strong stand for three weeks, and the players gave in and came back to play.

The team owners used players who crossed the picket lines and played for significantly less money than the regular players. The lower salary expenses per week ($854,000 regulars versus $230,000 replacement players) meant higher profits for management.[48] Therefore, although attendance decreased during the strike, the profits earned were higher. The owners, by locking out the regulars and using replacement players, could earn a profit. The 1987 National Football League strike is an example of what one party can do to the other when they have the resources, a united front, and a plan.

Some experts believe that too much attention is paid to money and benefits issues before, during, and after a strike. In fact, one study of unionized strike and unionized nonstrike companies suggests that workers vote for a strike only when they are frustrated because their needs, wants, and ideas go unheard or unanswered.[49] In such situations, management becomes the enemy, an adversary to be punished by a strike. Instead of waiting for a strike to happen, it has been suggested that management needs to be more aggressive in finding out about employee sentiments and needs.

There are some companies that are aggressively attempting to uncover employee needs and wants before they lead to a strike. At Sears, Roebuck, a program of regular managerial visits with employees, discussion sessions, and attitude surveys are used. Kraft, Inc. uses outside help to determine employee sentiment. A team of experts, headed up by the vice president of personnel, visits each production and retail facility to conduct interviews and to hold

---

[47] Robert Johnson, "Team Owners Discover the Strike Brings a Big Benefit: An Improved Bottom Line," *The Wall Street Journal*, October 14, 1987, p. 33.

[48] Bill Saporito, "The Life of a $725,000 Scab," *Fortune*, October 26, 1987, pp. 91–94.

[49] Woodruff Imberman, "Who Strikes—And Why," *Harvard Business Review*, November–December 1983, pp. 18–20, 24–28.

feedback sessions. Corrective action is taken as quickly as possible. Rockwell International uses a program headed by the vice president of personnel that involves holding regular discussion meetings with engineers. The meetings cover engineers' concerns about computer needs, materials, educational opportunities, and access to libraries. These meetings, according to the management of Rockwell, have led to a more stable and constructive relationship between employees and managers.

UNION-MANAGEMENT COOPERATION

American labor leaders have had little use for well-intentioned schemes to make them partners with management. Thomas R. Donahue, secretary-treasurer of the AFL–CIO, states that cooperative union-management efforts have been, "the worst kind of nonsense, perpetrated either by pied pipers who promised no supervisor and no assembly lines, or romantic academics espousing European-style codetermination." Either way, says Donahue, "they set everyone's teeth on edge."[50]

Another critic of union-management cooperation is Ed Sadlowski. He was the youngest district director of the United Steelworkers union. In 1976, at 37 years of age, he ran for the national union presidency and lost. Sadlowski made a lot of waves, even within the labor union movement, because he was aggressive, young, brash, and committed to an adversary stance against management.[51] A sample of Sadlowski's views are expressed as follows:

> There's economic blackmail today. When the Environmental Protection Agency gets on their butt about polluting the valleys and streams and air, the head of U.S. Steel says: We have to leave. Labor has been buffaloed on this score. Now they're gettin' wise. You can make steel and have clean air and still make a profit. . . . I don't expect the head of General Motors or U.S. Steel to sit down at the table and by virtue of my having supper with him give me anything I want. I'm going to demand it and take it. The sooner the laboring class—and it is a class question—realizes it, the better off they'll be.[52]

Despite the strong feelings of Donahue and Sadlowski, there is a groundswell movement in the United States toward more labor-management cooperation. Unions are becoming almost as interested as management in finding innovative efforts to give more say about how they work-programs like quality circles and quality of work-life systems that solicit ideas are becoming

[50] Charles G. Burck, "What's in It for the Unions?" *Fortune*, August 24, 1981, pp. 88–91. Also see David Lewin, "Collective Bargaining and the Quality of Work Life," *Organizational Dynamics*, Autumn 1981, pp. 37–53.

[51] "Ed Sadlowski," in Studs Terkel, *American Dreams Lost & Found* (New York: Ballatine Books, 1980), pp. 260–67.

[52] Ibid., pp. 264–65.

more popular.[53] Union leaders who once worried about being "management's lackeys" have been surprised to find that cooperating with management has raised their standing with members.

Union Action

The United Auto Workers, the United Steelworkers of America, the Communications Workers of America, the International Brotherhood of Electrical Workers, and the Telecommunications International Union—together representing about a fifth of the nation's organized workers—have signed national labor agreements committing themselves to plans for a better employee work life. Unions have convinced managers that many workers want to take their jobs seriously and want to be treated fairly.

Adverse economic times and foreign competition have helped the unions see that changes in relations with management were necessary. Unionized labor's share of the total work force has been declining, and many of its leaders believe that labor-management cooperation might be able to reverse the decline.

During the early 1970s, the major steel companies and the United Steelworkers agreed upon a bold plan to fight the growing threat of imported steel. Joint labor-management committees sat down together to analyze and offer solutions to the problem. Lloyd McBride, the now-deceased United Steelworker's president (he defeated Ed Sadlowski) said about the first of these meetings.

> The management guys came in and said, "Well, we want to talk about the productivity of this operation. Down in this department we could eliminate this job." The union sat there and then one representative said, "Well, that would create some problems for us. But the problems would not be so great if we could get rid of your brother-in-law down there who's not doing much. . . ."

Confrontation, war, and adversarial relations were hard to change, according to McBride. The early 1970s effort came to a halt because both parties were so locked in their previous styles of fighting against each other.[54]

At about the same time, the United Auto Workers were attempting to work with General Motors (GM) to solve productivity problems. GM had become more concerned about the lagging productivity per worker. The GM managers were aware that the traditional solutions from the top down were only somewhat successful when workers came in late or failed to report to work at all. Irving Bluestone, then director of the UAW's GM department, saw an opportunity to advance his belief that unions could cooperate with mnagement to advance the workers' responsibilities and stature. He pushed his idea hard and

---

[53] James W. Thacker, and Mitchell W. Fields, "Union Involvement in Quality-of-Worklife Efforts: A Longitudal Investigation," *Personnel Psychology*, Winter 1987, pp. 97–111.

[54] Irving H. Siegel and Edgar Weinberg, *Labor-Management Cooperation: The American Experience* (Kalamazoo, Mich.: W. E. Upjohn Institute, 1982).

in the 1973 contract negotiations, GM and the UAW signed the first national quality of work-life agreement in the United States.

The agreement has become the model of labor-management cooperation.[55] Nowhere in it did the word "productivity" appear. Management would seek its rewards from work improvements in higher product quality and lower absenteeism. All the quality of work-life programs would be strictly voluntary, and none would be used unilaterally to raise production rates or reduce human resource requirements. Labor-management work improvement committees that have been working at GM have given workers more job control and opened up communications between workers and supervisors.

Many union leaders initially feared that labor-management cooperation would undermine the collective bargaining process. After all, nothing could be further from the spirit of "us versus them" than mutually identifying and solving problems. Some unionists worried that management would use cooperative programs such as quality of work-life improvements to chip away at benefits won through bargaining.

In practice, the lines between cooperation and conflict have been relatively clear.[56] Few managers or labor leaders have tried to abuse the cooperation problem-solving activities. GM and Ford are pressing for UAW wage concessions, and the UAW is pushing them for more wages, more job security, and more benefits.

In 1987 United Auto Workers' contract with Ford and GM are considered to be important in labor's effort to gain secure employment.[57] Previously job-protection insurers applied only when the UAW could show that a laid-off worker was covered. The new agreement reverses the burden of proof. It guarantees the jobs of current workers under all circumstances except for falling sales. In return, the UAW agreed to set up joint labor-management committees at each plant. These cooperative committees will develop plans for boosting productivity and quality.[58]

Increased labor-management cooperation in autos and steel were unquestionably spurred by the crises those industries have faced. However, cooperation is also occurring in the communications industry. The Communications Workers of America and AT&T have worked out a quality of work-life improvement program. Union members were frustrated by job pressures.[59] AT&T was pushing job performance and looking at workers closely. AT&T managers even called absent workers at home to determine if they were sick, and they monitored (listened to) operators on the job to see if they were efficient. The new agreement has resulted in eliminating these and other

---

[55] Ibid.

[56] Robert E. Steiner, "The Labor Management Cooperation Act," *Personnel Journal*, May 1981, pp. 344–45.

[57] John Hillkirk, "UAW Reach Accord On Contract," *USA Today*, September 18, 1987, p. 1 (B).

[58] Aaron Bernstein, "A Demanding Year for Labor," *Business Week*, January 11, 1988; and Jacob M. Schlesinger, "GM, UAW Reach Tentative Pact: Officials Say It's Similar to Ford's," *The Wall Street Journal*, October 9, 1987, p. 2.

[59] Burck, "What's in It for the Unions?"

similar programs. The union is now a limited partner working on methods to improve productivity.

Opinions are still divided about whether labor-management cooperation is a threat or an aid to new organizing efforts. In some nonunion situations, management has used it to resolve problems that might have brought in a union. Yet some labor leaders believe that it is a plus for organizing efforts. Some people view the union as aggressive, hostile, and disruptive. The Telecommunications International Union has emphasized the desire to cooperate with management. The union has won 13 representative elections in Pacific Telephone Co. because workers consider it to be fair, professional, and concerned.[60]

Even in 1986, it was rare to find a union leader who would agree publicly to union-management cooperation committees and forums. However, given the current economic and competitive climate, unions, as well as managers, cannot afford to overlook the possibility of more labor-management cooperation. The long-run survival of many organizations and unions may depend somewhat on the degree of cooperation achieved.

Although union behavior in Canada is usually compared to that in the United States, it has become increasingly different over the past decade. The powerful and militant Canadian unions have pushed more for confrontation than for cooperation in collective bargaining.[61] For example, in late 1982 and early 1983 Canadian Chrysler workers went on a five-week strike. Historically, Chrysler negotiated with the United Auto Workers on both sides of the border simultaneously, and the final agreement was almost identical. However, in late 1982 when Chrysler attempted to settle without an initial wage increase, the Canadian workers refused to stay on the job with their American counterparts. The Canadian strike lasted until Chrysler agreed to a substantial wage increase.

In Canada, the Canadian Labour Congress (CLC) and most major Canadian unions are affiliated with and support the New Democratic Party (NDP), which contends for political power. The NDP has called for government ownership of major industrial sections. In contrast, U.S. unions show little interest in political movements and support private ownership in industry. This recognition of private ownership and the need to earn profits to survive explains the greater willingness of U.S. unions for more labor-management cooperation.

THE RIGHTS OF EMPLOYEES
IN NONUNIONIZED SITUATIONS

The rights of union members are spelled out in labor contracts. However, most employees—about 75 percent—do not belong to unions. Do these nonunionized

---

[60] Ibid.

[61] Donald J. Schneider, "Canadian and U.S. Brands of Unionism Have Distinctly Different Nationalities," *Management Review*, October 1983, pp. 31–32.

P/HRM Manager, Close-Up

Gregory Watts

Biography

Gregory M. Watts, APM, is a personnel director for Chicago Switch, Inc., a division of Illinois Tool Works, Inc.

Mr. Watts, a native of Chicago, is a graduate of Southern Illinois University in Carbondale, Illinois.

Mr. Watts is a member of the following professional groups: American Society for Personnel Administration, Midwest Industrial Management Association, and the Electronics Personnel Administration.

The Union Contract and Arbitration

Recently, management made a decision to discontinue the operation of a tool and die department due to a sales slump.

Twenty-four union employees lost their jobs, and two were kept on until operations were completely severed.

Under the firm's severance pay policy, each received a severance allowance under the following plan:

1–5 years of service	2 weeks
6–10 years of service	4 weeks
11–15 years of service	6 weeks
Over 15 years of service	8 weeks

Soon a vacancy developed among the two who were kept on, and the company hired someone from the outside to fill the job. One of the "severees" complained to the union, stating "the job should have been filled according to the seniority of those who got severance. After all, when there is layoff, workers are recalled according to their length of service."

The company did not see it that way and maintained that once a worker receives severance pay, he or she loses former rights.

The case eventually went to arbitration, and the company won. The arbitrator stated that "employees

(continued)

who accept severance pay are not entitled to claim any other benefits, because, by accepting severance pay, they have released any rights they may have had under the contract. Since seniority is a right under the contract, it cannot be used as a way to recall by those who received severance allowances."

members have working conditions, privacy, wage, and other rights?[62] There has been an emphasis among nonunionized members on the "rights of employment." Nonunion employees also want to have some say in their work destiny. The traditional view that "top management knows best" is being challenged more and more.

Privacy

The right to privacy is a part of constitutional law. However, nonunion organizations in most states give managers the right to monitor employees' conversation on company telephones without notifying the employees. Other invasions of privacy occur when an employer collects data about a worker—psychological tests, attitude surveys, and medical records. The privacy may be invaded again when the information collected is put to use. Management may use the information to make promotion decisions and answer inquiries from credit bureaus, insurance companies, and social agencies.

IBM, the most publicized nonunion organization in the United States, makes a major issue about employee rights and especially privacy.[63] At IBM:

1. Management can collect and keep in its personnel files only those facts about employees that are required by law or that are necessary to manage operations. IBM's job application forms no longer request previous addresses or information on whether the employee has relatives in the firm. Nor does it ask about prior mental problems, convictions dating back more than five years, or more recent criminal charges that have not resulted in conviction.
2. Performance evaluations more than three years old must be weeded from an employee's personnel file.
3. Employees are entitled to know how filed information about them is being used.
4. An employee is entitled to see most of the information on file about him or her. Management may withhold some information, such as a confidential discussion of an opportunity for promotion that was never given.

---

[62] David W. Ewing, "A Bill of Rights for Employees," *Across the Board*, March 1981, pp. 42–49.

[63] Interview with Frank Cary, "IBM's Guidelines to Employee Privacy," *Harvard Business Review*, September–October 1976, pp. 82–90.

5. Personality and general intelligence tests are not permissible information for employee records.

IBM believes that by being open and concerned about employee privacy, the workers are happier. It is proud of the employees' continuing eagerness to reject unions. IBM wants its employees to feel that unions are not necessary.

Firing Nonunion Workers

The right of employers in private industry to fire workers not protected by a union contract is coming under close scrutiny, as discussed earlier in Chapter 15. Court decisions in several states have awarded large settlements to employees who were judged to be fired capriciously.[64] This trend may eventually result in unprecedented job security for nonunion workers. It is estimated that between 1988 and 1990 400,000 mid and upper-level managers with three or more years of experience will be laid-off permanently.[65]

Courts in Washington and Michigan have upheld claims by nonunion workers that promises made in employee handbooks—and even orally—constitute a job contract that precludes dismissal except for "just cause." Workers in California have also won the right to seek punitive damages on top of lost wages in dismissal cases.[66]

Estimates indicate that companies in private industry discharge about 1 million permanent employees each year without a "fair hearing." The court actions have put employers on notice to proceed cautiously. Those involved in P/HRM activities will have to pay more attention to the dismissal of workers.

A major court test on dismissal occurred in 1974, when a worker named Olga Moore successfully sued Beebe Rubber Co. after she was fired for refusing to go on a date with her foreman. More recently, in 1980 a federal district court in New York ruled against a motion by Korvettes to dismiss a suit by Morton Savodnik, a 13-year employee who claimed the company dismissed him to avoid paying him a pension. The court cited the interest to protect an employee's rights.

A frequently cited case involved the Shriner's Hospital for Crippled Children, which fired registered nurse Juanita Vorhees. One evening she playfully tossed a few drops of water at a patient. The patient tossed some back; she repeated. Ms. Vorhees wiped up the water and everyone laughed, except the supervisor who reported the incident. She was fired for gross violation of her duties. She sued the hospital claiming that "just cause" for dismissal was not supported. The Superior Court of Seattle ruled that the hospital's manual implied a "just cause" dismissal policy. The court said that the hospital had failed to demonstrate this in dismissing Vorhees; her award—her job and back wages.

In another case, Wayne Pugh was fired by See Candy, Inc. of San Francisco.

---

[64] This section is based on "The Growing Cost of Firing Nonunion Workers," *Business Week*, April 6, 1981, pp. 95–98.

[65] Robert J. McCaffery, *Employee Benefit Programs* (Boston: PWS-Kent, 1988), p. 87.

[66] David W. Ewing, *Do It My Way or You're Fired* (New York: John Wiley & Sons, 1983), p. 104.

A RETURN TO THE P/HRM · IN · ACTION

The notes of the union versus management vote were counted at Hardisty Manufacturing Company. The union had gotten 30 percent of the employees to sign authorization cards. And the NLRB had stepped in to schedule the unionization election. Shortly after the NLRB examiner left, Tom called Stan into his office.

Tom: How could we lose this election? Why do I have a P/HRM manager if he can't beat the union?

Stan: It's not over yet. They still have to get a majority. But Tom, we've got to start thinking about a strategy . . . the tactics we'll use . . . this problem isn't going to just "go away" . . . we've got to face it. I've been in touch with some professional negotiators who've agreed to speak for us, in case the union wins.

Tom: Is that necessary?

Stan: I think it is. There's a lot going against us. We were really hurt by the pay item. You told me we had to lay people off to cut costs, but the layoffs came in the middle of the union's organizing campaign. A lot of people felt threatened. When people get threatened, they join unions.

Tom: I'm tired of excuses. Just do your job and shut out that union! Hire whoever you have to. And I promise you, we'll have no more layoffs. We just had to keep our heads above water, that's all, so we had to lay off some workers. But no more. I'll help you in any way I can. By the way, how's that communication program coming along?

Between then and the election, both sides campaigned, but Stan felt that the management's efforts weren't as organized or as effective as the union's. At the last minute, Tom called back the workers who had been laid off; the votes looked close. But when the representative votes were counted, the union had won. HMC challenged the votes of several persons, but in the end, the NLRB declared the union as the bargaining agent, and negotiation began.

One week later, Stan quit. Tom had refused to talk to him since the election. After the experience, both men felt hostile toward unions, but Stan blamed Tom more than anything. He felt that Hardisty's whole antiunion campaign had been mismanaged from the start.

Pugh, the vice president and director of See's, alleged that he was fired for objecting to an arrangement whereby the firm paid a lower wage than other candy makers to seasonal union employees. This interesting case is still in court, but it is being watched because it involves a management-level employee fighting the company for the right of operating-level employees.

Unfair discharge suits in nonunion firms will probably continue to increase in number in the future. There is a growing feeling among legal observers that a manager in a nonunion firm *or* union firm is not entitled to penalize an employee unfairly.

SUMMARY

This chapter has focused on union organizing campaigns and management resistance to them. In addition, the collective bargaining process is spelled out.

To summarize the major points covered in this chapter:

1. A union can exist only if workers prefer and vote to become unionized. If a union doesn't receive at least 51 percent of the votes cast in a representation election, it can't serve as the employees' bargaining unit.
2. Management and the union face off and campaign against each other. Each presents its view of the situation.
3. The union and management organizing campaigns in the private sector to win over the employees are watched very closely by the National Labor Relations Board.
4. Collective bargaining is a process by which the representatives of the organization meet and attempt to work out a contract with the employees' representative—the union.
5. The steps in the collective bargaining process include:
   a. Prenegotiation.
   b. Selecting negotiators.
   c. Developing a bargaining strategy.
   d. Using the best tactics.
   e. Reaching a formal contractual agreement.
6. The day-to-day compliance with union-management contract provisions is an important responsibility of the first-line supervisor. He or she can be involved in such contract-related issues as discipline procedures, grievance procedures, and strikes.
7. The grievance procedure does not always result in an acceptable solution. *Mediation* is the process in which a third party helps labor and management reach agreement. *Arbitration* is a quasi-judicial process in which the parties agree to submit an unresolvable dispute to a neutral third party for binding settlement.
8. The *strike* is the ultimate union weapon to encourage management to make greater concessions to the union. There appears to be a distinct trend toward fewer strikes by unions.
9. The traditional adversary union-management relationship has been giving way to less antagonism. Adverse economic times, foreign competition, and technological advancements have created more interest in both union and management to look for ways to cooperate.
10. The rights of employees in nonunion firms are being upheld by the courts. In the areas of privacy and dismissal, the courts are becoming more involved.

Questions for Review and Discussion

1. What is needed in a nonunionized situation before a grievance process such as that used at Duke University can have a fair chance of succeeding?

2. Do negotiators at a bargaining table have to possess some acting abilities? Explain.
3. Should employees have a right to privacy while on the job? Why?
4. Why would an agency like the NLRB be needed to supervise and oversee representation elections?
5. What skills would be important for a person to be a successful and respected mediator?
6. What are some of the typical delays in the grievance to arbitration process?
7. Should public employees, such as air traffic controllers, police officers, and postal workers, be permitted to strike? Why?
8. How would the economic situation in the country (United States or Canada) influence the type of labor-management cooperation that is pursued by both parties?
9. Why has concession bargaining become more popular in the 1980s?
10. Why would professionals such as nurses, engineers, and educators want to join unions, which historically have been associated with blue-collar workers?

GLOSSARY

Arbitration. A quasi-judicial process in which the parties agree to submit the unresolvable dispute to a neutral third party for binding settlement.

Boycott. A primary boycott finds union members not patronizing the boycotted firm. In a secondary boycott a supplier of a boycotted firm is threatened with a union strike unless it stops doing business with the firm. This type of boycott is illegal under the Taft-Hartley Act.

Collective Bargaining. The process by which the representatives of the organization meet and attempt to work out a contract with representatives of the union.

Decertification Election. An election in which employees who are represented by a union vote to drop the union.

Grievance. A complaint about a job that creates dissatisfaction or discomfort for the worker.

Hot Cargo Agreement. The employer permits union members to avoid working with materials that come from employers who have been struck by a union. This type of boycott is illegal.

Lockout. A management response to union pressures in which a skeleton crew of managerial personnel is used to maintain a workplace and the total plant is basically closed to employees.

Mediation. A process in which a neutral third party helps through persuasion to bring together labor and management. The dispute is settled because of the skills and suggestions of a mediator.

Representation Election. A vote to determine if a particular group will represent the workers in collective bargaining.

Strike. An effort by employees to withhold their services from an employer in order to get greater concessions at the collective bargaining table.

EXERCISE 17–1   Union-Management Contract Negotiations

Objective: To permit individuals to become involved in labor-management contract negotiations in a role-playing session.

SET UP THE EXERCISE

1. Groups (even number of groups) of four to eight people will form. Half of the groups will be union teams and the other half will be management teams.
2. Read the description of the Dana Lou Corporation of Hamilton, Ohio.
3. Review and discuss in groups the four bargaining issues and the data collected on competitors (15 minutes).
4. The instructor will provide the union team(s), the "union negotiators" instructions; and the management team(s), the "management negotiations" instructions.
5. Groups face off against each other (one management team versus one union team). The negotiator represents the team's position.
6. Individuals should answer the exercise questions after the negotiations— Step 2 of the negotiations.

Dana Lou Corporation

Dana Lou Corporation is a medium-sized company with about 1,100 employees in Hamilton, Ohio, a suburb of Cincinnati. It competes in the electronic repair parts industry and is slightly larger than most of its main competitors. The firm's success (profitability and growth) has been attributed to a dedicated work force that takes great pride in their work.

In 1964, the Communications Workers of America (CWA) organized the plant. Since then labor-management relations have been good, and there were only two days lost to a strike in 1972. Labor and management both feel that the cooperation between them is much better than that found in other firms of the same size in the area.

The current labor-management contract expires in three weeks. Representatives from the union and management have been negotiating a number of bargaining issues for the last three days, but there seems to be little agreement.

The Bargaining Issues

1. Republic National Medical and Dental Insurance Protection Present contract: Dana Lou pays 50 percent of premiums for all full-time employees.

 New contract issues: The CWA wants Dana Lou to pay the full premium; management wants to hold the line.

In terms of costs, the data look like this:

Percent of Premium Paid	Dana Lou Contribution	
0	–0–	
25	$ 55,000	
50	110,000	Present contribution
75	$165,000	
100	220,000	

2. Preventive health director, staff, and participation
   a. Present contract: Dana Lou has two part-time physicians and two full-time nurses (cost is $66,000 per year).
   b. New contract issues: The CWA wants a full-time fitness director, a full-time physician, counselors for alcohol and drug abuse problems, and partial payment for employee use of YMCA and YWCA exercise facilities (estimated increase over present arrangements, $108,000).
3. Vacation benefits
   a. Present contract: One-week full pay for the first year, two weeks for employees with 2 to 10 years of service, and three weeks for employees with over 10 years.
   b. New contract issues: CWA wants all employees with 15 or more years of service to have four weeks of full-paid vacation. Management wants no change in present program.
4. Wage increases for skilled quality inspectors
   a. Present contract: Inspectors rate is $5.95 per hour; inspector apprentices, $4.30.
   b. New contract issues: CWA wants an increase of $0.50 per hour for the plant's 95 inspectors and a $0.40 per hour increase for the plant's 25 inspector apprentices. Management wants to hold the line on salary increases because they believe that layoffs will have to occur.
   Union's proposal would cost Dana Lou $95 \times \$0.05 = \$47.50$ and $25 \times \$0.40 = \$10,00$ or 57.50 per hour.

Competitor Data (Hamilton, Ohio, Survey)

	Blue Fox Corp.	Wintex, Inc.	Lafley Mfg.
Company contribution to medical and dental insurance	100%	50%	50%
Preventive health director	No	No	No
Payment of physical fitness fees for employees	Yes	No	Yes
Vacation benefits	1 week in first year; 3 weeks all employees after 1 year	2 weeks all employees until 10 years of service and then 3 weeks	2 weeks all employees for first 5 years and then 3 weeks
Wage rates inspectors	$5.80	$5.97	$5.93
Inspector apprentices	$4.45	$4.50	$4.20

The Negotiations

1. One member from each of the two groups facing each other will negotiate the four issues. The rest of the group must remain *totally* quiet during the negotiations. The negotiators should role play for exactly 20 minutes. At the end of this time they should record the agreement points reached.

Final Agreements

Medical and dental protection _____

_____

Preventive health director/Staff and participation _____

_____

Vacation benefits _____

_____

Wage increases _____

_____

2. Each individual is to analyze the negotiations:
   How successful were the negotiators? _____
   Would you have negotiated differently? How? _____

   _____

   Were the negotiations prepared? _____

A Learning Note

This exercise will illustrate how difficult discussing issues can be when people have a fixed attitude or position.

EMPLOYEE SAFETY AND HEALTH

P/HRM · IN · ACTION

Clint

The ambulance had just pulled away from Lysander Manufacturing. It was headed for a Denver hospital, carrying Dale Silas. Dale had been badly hurt; there was already talk that he might be disabled for the rest of his life.

Clint Woodley, the plant manager, wondered if there was anything he could have done to prevent Dale's injury. It was not the first injury this year at Lysander. Clint decided to visit his friend, Bob Undine, who operated a similar plant in a nearby town. He called Bob and arranged to have lunch the next day.

At lunch, Clint explained how upset he was about Dale's injury. Dale had been with Lysander for 15 years— longer than Clint had been. He had a wife and five children to support. The word from the hospital was not very good.

Bob: Well, Clint, sometimes accidents happen. You know our business is dangerous. And sometimes the men are not following the safety rules. What is your safety record over the last few years?

Clint: I don't really know. We've only got records since OSHA (Occupational Safety and Health Act) came in. But the P/HRM guy, Otto Richmond, handles that paperwork. When our people are hired, we tell them to be careful. The supervisors are supposed to handle that.

Bob: You mean you don't have a safety unit?

Clint: No.

Bob: Then you probably don't do accident research, safety design and prevention, safety inspections, or safety training either, do you?

Clint: No. We do fill out the OSHA paperwork. Luckily, we've never been inspected by OSHA.

Bob: Well, then, maybe you ought to be upset about Dale. You aren't doing all you could to protect your employees. And if you don't do it, OSHA will make you.

Clint: I don't want that. Can I come back with you and see how you operate safety programs at your plant?

Bob: Sure.

This chapter covers some of the main points that Bob and his safety executive, Mary Lou Vaugh, explained to Clint.

> *Safety hazards* are those aspects of the work environment that have the potential of immediate and sometimes violent harm to an employee. Examples of injuries are loss of hearing, eyesight, or body parts; cuts, sprains, bruises, broken bones; burns and electric shock.
>
> *Health hazards* are those aspects of the work environment that slowly and cumulatively (and often irreversibly) lead to deterioration of an employee's health. Examples are cancer, poisoning, and respiratory diseases; as well as depression, loss of temper, and other psychological disorders. Typical causes include physical and biological hazards, toxic and cancer-causing dusts and chemicals, and stressful working conditions.

Safety violations have been the cause of some of the most tragic accidents that have taken lives.

In December 1984, the worst industrial accident in history occurred. Poisonous methyl isocyanate gas leaked from a storage tank at a Union Carbide plant in Bhopal, India killing 3,000 people and injuring another 300,000.[1] The accident was the result of operating errors, design flaws, maintenance failures, and training deficiencies.

Union Carbide was sued for billions of dollars; compensation settlements are still occurring and are likely to be over $1 billion. In many of the lawsuits, Union Carbide's own 1982 safety report on the plant has been used since it stated "a higher potential for a serious accident or more serious consequences if an accident should occur." Another comment stated:

> That report "strongly" recommended among other things, the installation of a larger system that would supplement or replace one of the plant's main safety devices, a water spray designed to contain a chemical leak. That change was never made, plant employees said, and [when the leak happened] that spray was not high enough to reach the escaping gas.[2]

In 1979, the Three Mile Island nuclear power plant had an accident leading to the near meltdown of the plant's reactor core. In the Kemery Commission Report (named after the President's commission chairman) it was stated that human error in terms of inadequate operator training was the main cause of

---

[1] Ian Mitroff, Paul Shrivastava, and Firdaus E. Udivactra, "Effective Crisis Management," November 1987, pp. 283–91.

[2] "Bhopal," *New York Times,* January 28, 1985, p. 24.

the accident. This error endangered the entire population of the Pennsylvania community in which the plant was located.[3]

In January 1986, America's space program was stopped cold by the loss of the shuttle Challenger and its seven-person astronaut flight crew. After 25 aborted countdowns of the flight, the routine monitoring with inboard computers of 2,000 vital functions, the critical rocket joints and O-ring tolerances were missed. Despite technological sophistication, there were cost constraints, tight schedules, and human errors that contributed to this tragic loss of lives.[4]

These three highly publicized accidents and their tragic losses indicate that safety and health issues need to be given a high priority in decision-making circles. Accidents are costly not only in terms of human lives, but also in terms of disabling injuries, the loss of public image, and insurance premiums.

How many safety and health hazards exist in workplaces today? On the average, 1 employee in 10 is killed or injured at work *each year*. But some occupations (such as dock workers) have many more injuries per year than others (such as file clerks), so the odds for some workers are worse than 1 in 10 each year. It is estimated that about one fourth of the 21.3 million disabled people in the United States are disabled because of job-related injuries.[5]

Statistics on safety and health hazards are debated. The official statistics indicate that about 400,000 persons per year contract an occupational disease, and deaths from this cause average 100,000 per year. But Ashford, who prepared a report for the Ford Foundation, cites data to indicate this figure is too low and argues that many occupationally contracted diseases are not reported as being caused by work.[6]

Reports indicate there are about 4,090 accidental deaths at work a year (nearly 21 a day, or 3 people every working hour) and about 4.75 million reported accidents.[7] All sources do not list the same death and accident figures. Note the use of the verb *reported*. A number of studies indicate that perhaps as few as half of all occupational accidents are reported.

The 4,090 fatalities in 1982, by industry, are shown in Exhibit 18–1. As indicated, there were 7.4 deaths per 100,000 full-time workers. The fatalities ranged form 44.3 per 100,000 full-time workers in mining industries to 2.5 in finance, insurance, and real estate industries.

Accidents and illnesses are not evenly distributed among occupations in the United States. Employees facing serious health and safety dangers include fire fighters, miners, construction and transportation workers, roofing and sheet metal workers, recreational vehicle manufacturers, lumber and woodworkers, and blue-collar and first-line supervisors in manufacturing and agriculture. A

---

[3] Steven Fink, *Crisis Management* (New York: AMACOM, 1986).

[4] Robert Marx, Charles Stubbart, Virginia Traub, and Michael Cavanaugh, "The NASA Space Shuttle Disaster: A Case Study," *Journal of Management Case Studies,* Winter 1987, pp. 300–318.

[5] James Lambrinos and William G. Johnson, "Robots to Reduce the High Cost of Illness and Injury," *Harvard Business Review,* May–June 1984, p. 24.

[6] Nicholas Ashford, *Crisis in the Workplace: Occupational Disease and Injury: A Report to the Ford Foundation* (Cambridge, Mass.: MIT Press, 1976), chapters 1 and 3.

[7] "BLS Reports Drop in Workplace Deaths and Injuries for 1982," *Resource,* January 1984, p. 3.

<hr>

EXHIBIT 18–1 Occupational Injury and Illness Fatalities and Fatality Incidence Rates for Employers with 11 Employees or More, by Industry Division, 1981–1982

	Fatalities				Fatality Incidence Rate*	
	1981		1982			
Industry Division	Number	Percent	Number	Percent	1981	1982
Agriculture, forestry, and fishing	130	3	180	4	21.2	28.4
Mining	500	11	440	11	46.6	44.3
Construction	800	18	720	18	29.2	28.7
Manufacturing	990	23	770	19	5.3	4.5
Transportation and public utilities	750	17	970	24	16.5	21.9
Wholesale and retail trade	730	17	490	12	5.6	3.8
Finance, insurance and real estate	120	3	100	2	3.1	2.5
Services	350	8	420	10	3.0	3.5
Total private sector	4,370	100	4,090	100	7.6	7.4

* The incidence rates represent the number of fatalities per 100,000 full-time workers and were calculated as $(NE/EH) \times 200,000,000$, where NE is the number of fatalities, EH is the total hours worked by all employees during calendar year, and 200,000,000 is the base for 100,000 full-time equivalent workers (working 40 hours per week, 50 weeks per year).
NOTE: Because of rounding, components may not add to totals.

Source: Janet Macon, "'BLS' 1982 Survey of Work-Related Deaths," *Monthly Law Review*, March 1984, p. 44.

few white-collar jobholders face relative danger: dentists and hospital operating room personnel, beauticians, and X-ray technicians.

All accidents and diseases are tragic to the employees involved, of course. There is pain at the time of the accident, and there can be psychological problems later. In addition to pain, suffering, and death, there are also direct measurable costs to both employee and employer. About 42 million workdays were lost in the United States because of health-related absenteeism in 1982—an average of 16 days per case, often resulting in direct costs of workers' compensation and indirect costs of lost productivity for the enterprise.[8] The average company's workers' compensation for disability payments is 1 percent of payroll, and the indirect costs are estimated to be five times greater. These indirect costs include cost of wages paid the injured employee, damage to plant and equipment, costs of replacement employees, and time costs for supervisors and personnel staff investigating and reporting the accident or illness. Both because of the humanitarian desire of management to reduce suffering and because of the huge direct and indirect costs of accidents, deaths, and illnesses, the effective enterprise tries hard to create safe and healthy conditions at work.

An unsafe or unhealthy work environment can also affect an employee's ability and motivation to work. As noted in Chapter 2, security/preservation is one of the most fundamental needs people have. Poor safety and health conditions are likely to endanger fulfillment of the security needs of employees.

Until recently, the typical response to concern about health and safety was

<hr>

[8] Lambrinos and Johnson, "Robots," p. 28.

to compensate the victims of job-related accidents with workers' compensation and similar insurance payments. This chapter will discuss various compensation approaches and organizational programs designed to *prevent* accidents, health hazards, and deaths at work.

A DIAGNOSTIC APPROACH
TO SAFETY AND HEALTH

The environmental factors important to health and safety are highlighted in Exhibit 18-2. Probably the most crucial factor is the nature of the task, especially as it is affected by the technology and working conditions of the organizational environment. For instance, health and safety problems are a lot more serious for coal miners—whose working conditions require them to breathe coal dust in the air—than for typists. An X-ray technician has a much greater chance of getting cancer as a result of working conditions than does an elementary school teacher. Some examples of potential job hazards are presented in Exhibit 18-3.

OSHA issued a "Hazard Communication" standard after years of study and debate.[9] The standard is designed to reduce the incident of chemically-related occupational illnesses and injuries among employees in the manufacturing sector. Basically, the regulations require chemical manufacturers and importers to label containers and provide material safety data sheets (MSDS), or fact sheets describing the dangers posed by each chemical to customers. In addition, manufacturing employers are required to provide such information to workers through container labels, material safety fact sheets and training procedures. This type of workplace hazard identification requires aggressive managerial action.

One group affected by the Hazards Communication standard is pregnant women. Since more pregnant women are working, they are potentially exposed to hazards that may adversely affect them, their pregnancy and/or their unborn child.[10] Some of the common environmental pollutants and industrial chemicals that pose a threat to the pregnant worker are:

- Lead—Increased stillbirths have been reported among female workers exposed to excessive concentrations.
- Mercury—Pregnancy problems with central nervous system damage, kidney damage, and mental retardation.
- Polychlorinated Biphenyls (PCBs)—Decreased birth weight and skin discoloration.
- Solvents—Studies report increased incidences of spontaneous abortions and birth defects among children born to mothers exposed to solvents during their pregnancy.

---

[9] John B. Dubeck and Peter A. Susser, "Hazard Communications: New Disclosure Burden on Management," *Personnel Administrator*, May 1984, pp. 79–83.

[10] Rebecca Anderson, "A Primer on Protecting the Pregnant Worker," *Personnel Administrator*, August 1983, pp. 61–64.

EXHIBIT 18–2   **Factors Affecting Safety and Health**

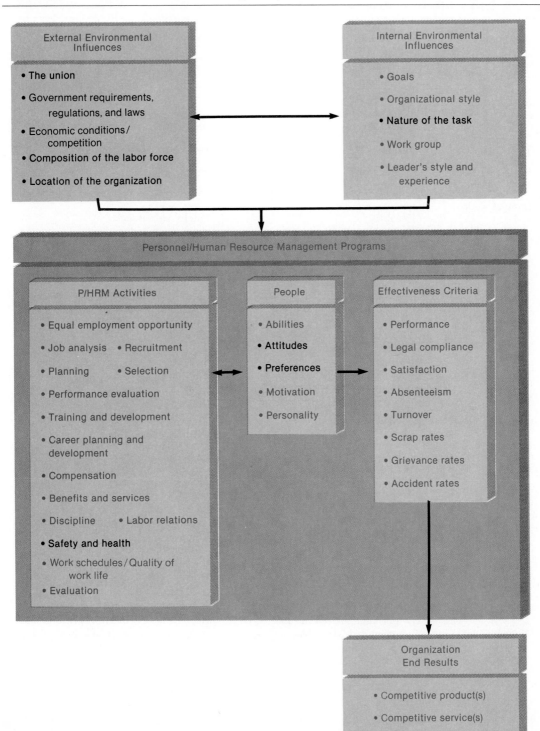

External Environmental Influences

- The union
- Government requirements, regulations, and laws
- Economic conditions/ competition
- Composition of the labor force
- Location of the organization

Internal Environmental Influences

- Goals
- Organizational style
- Nature of the task
- Work group
- Leader's style and experience

Personnel/Human Resource Management Programs

P/HRM Activities

- Equal employment opportunity
- Job analysis   • Recruitment
- Planning   • Selection
- Performance evaluation
- Training and development
- Career planning and development
- Compensation
- Benefits and services
- Discipline   • Labor relations
- Safety and health
- Work schedules/Quality of work life
- Evaluation

People

- Abilities
- Attitudes
- Preferences
- Motivation
- Personality

Effectiveness Criteria

- Performance
- Legal compliance
- Satisfaction
- Absenteeism
- Turnover
- Scrap rates
- Grievance rates
- Accident rates

Organization End Results

- Competitive product(s)
- Competitive service(s)

EXHIBIT 18–3   **Examples of Job and Safety Hazards**

Occupation	Potential Hazard	Possible Outcome
Textile workers	Cotton dust	Brown lung or byssinosis (a debilitating lung disease)
	Noise	Temporary or permanent hearing loss
	Chemical exposures	
	Aniline-based dyes	Bladder cancer and liver damage
	Formaldehyde	Dermatitis, allergic lung disease, possibly cancer
	Furfuraldehyde	Dermatitis, respiratory irritation, fatigue, headache, tremors, numbness of the tongue
	Moving machine parts without barriers	Loss of fingers or hands
Hospital workers	Infectious diseases	
	Hepatitis	Liver damage
	Herpes simplex virus	Painful skin lesions
	Chemical exposures	Spontaneous abortions
	Anesthetic gases	Poisoning of nervous system and kidneys
	Metallic mercury	
	Inorganic acids and alkalis	Irritation to respiratory tract and skin
	Physical hazards	Burns, birth defects, cancer
	Ionizing radiation	Sterility, harm to eyes, possible increased risk of cataracts
	Microwave radiation	
	UV light	Burning or sensitization of skin, skin cancer, cataracts
	Safety hazards	Back pain or permanent back injury
	Lifting or carrying	Infections
	Puncture wounds from syringes	
Welders	Infrared and visible light radiation	Burns, headache, fatigue, eye damage
	UV radiation	Burns, skin tumors, eye damage
	Chemical exposures	Cardiovascular disease
	Carbon monoxide	Asphyxiation, fire, explosion
	Acetylene	Contact dermatitis, eye irritation, respiratory irritation, metal fume fever (symptoms similar to the flu), possible kidney damage
	Metallic oxides	
	Phosphine	Lethal at even low doses: irritating to eyes, nose, skin; acts as anesthetic
Clerical workers	Improperly designed chairs and work stations; lack of movement	Backache, aggravation of hemorrhoids, varicose veins, and other blood-circulation conditions, eyestrain
	Noise	Hearing impairment, stress reactions
	Chemical exposures	
	Ozone from copy machines	Irritation of eyes, nose, throat; respiratory damage
	Benzene and toluene in rubber cement and "cleaners"	Benzene is associated with several blood diseases (including leukemia), and toluene may cause intoxication
	Methanol and ammonia in duplicating machine solvents	Irritation to eyes, nose, and throat

- Pesticides—Have been linked to abnormality of the offspring of exposed parents.

The short- and long-term effects of hazards such as pollutants and chemicals will be debated much more intensely in the future. The courts are likely to become even more involved than they are presently. Generally, the cost per case ranges from $156,000 to $305,000.[11] Currently, a number of asbestos hazard and dioxin hazard cases are being contested in many jurisdictions. It is estimated that there will be 350,000 deaths related to asbestos exposure that occurred between 1940 and 1980, with the peak mortality rate coming in 1995[12] Who should be held responsible? A group of 16 asbestos manufacturers have reached agreement to settle nearly 25,000 compensation claims pending in court for asbestos-related health claims.[13] Does this mean that the firms have finally accepted responsibility?

Charles Farley considered himself lucky to land a job at a Monsanto Co. plant in 1946.[14] Today, the ex-chemical worker is retired (at 55 years old) and is suffering from pain in his shoulders and legs. In 1982, he had a heart attack, and in February 1983 he underwent quadruple heart-bypass surgery. He attributes his premature health problems to long-term exposure to toxic chemicals. He is one of 172 former and current Monsanto workers and spouses suing the company. They are seeking more than $700 million in damages.

Monsanto has faced legal action before. The company was one of eight that settled for $180 million with Vietnam veterans charging contamination from Agent Orange, a defoliant used in the Vietnam War. In 1982, the company paid millions to settle suits by railroad workers after a railcar spilled chemicals made by the company.

A second vital factor is employee attitudes toward health and safety; they can vary from concern for safety and cooperation regarding safety programs, to apathy. If employees are apathetic, the best employer safety program and the most stringent safety inspection by the government or the safety specialists in the P/HRM department will not be successful in improving safety and health conditions.

A third factor affecting health and safety on the job is government. Federal and state governments have attempted to legislate conditions to improve safety and health for some years.[15] Some government programs currently in operation will be discussed later. However, perhaps the most publicity about government involvement has been the accident that closed down the Three

---

[11] Alan E. Dillingham, "Demographic and Economic Change and the Costs of Workers' Compensation," in *Safety and the Work Force*, ed. John D. Worrall (Ithaca, N.Y.: ILR Press, 1983).

[12] "Asbestos-Related Mortalities Expected to Reach 10,000 Annually by Year 2000," *Resource*, August 1984, p. 3.

[13] "Asbestos Manufacturers and Insurers Agree on Plan to Settle Claims," *Resource*, July 1984, p. 3.

[14] John Curley, "Monsanto and 172 Employees Go to Court over Allegations of Dioxin Contamination," *The Wall Street Journal*, June 20, 1984, pp. 31 and 45.

[15] Robert E. Harvey, "Industry Faces Costly Remedies for Occupational Illness," *Iron Age*, October 14, 1981, pp. 21–67.

Mile Island nuclear plant in 1979. This accident led to the discovery of dangers at other nuclear plants.[16] As a result, the Nuclear Regulatory Commission identified dozens of improvements—ranging from new equipment to better operator training—for the country's 72 operating nuclear reactors.

A fourth factor is the trade unions. Many unions have been very concerned about the safety and health of their employees and have pressured employers in collective bargaining for better programs. Some unions have taken extraordinary steps to protect their members' health and safety. For example, the Teamsters' Union hired a nationally known occupational health expert to investigate unexplained illnesses at the Robert Shaw Controls Company plant in Ohio. The United Rubber Workers' contract calls for a study of effects of benzene on employees. The Oil, Chemical and Atomic Workers Union has been subsidizing medical student interns and residents to study occupational health conditions in plants where their members work. Unions also have used their political power to get legislation passed to improve the safety and health of members.

A fifth factor is management's goals. Some socially responsible managers and owners had active safety programs long before the laws required them. They made safety and health an important strategic goal and implemented it with significant safety considerations designed into the enterprise's layout. The safety program included safety statistics, contests, and training sessions. Other managers, not so safety conscious, did little other than what was required by law. Thus managerial attitudes play a large part in the significance of the health and safety program of the enterprise.

The final factor affecting health and safety programs is economic conditions. We would accept the worst possible assumptions about human nature if we believed that any employer *knowingly* would choose to provide dangerous working conditions or would refuse to provide reasonable safeguards for employees. But there is a lack of knowledge about the consequences of some dangerous working conditions, and even when there is such knowledge, economic conditions can prevent employers from doing all they might wish. The risks of being a uranium miner are well known: 10 to 11 percent will die of cancer within 10 years. As long as there are no alternative methods and as long as there is a need for uranium, some employees will be risking shorter lives in these jobs. Engineers and scientists are constantly at work to determine the dangers and to prevent or mitigate the consequences. But the costs of some of the prevention programs are such that the enterprise may find them prohibitive and may consider the programs economically infeasible.

WHO IS INVOLVED WITH SAFETY AND HEALTH?

As with other P/HRM functions, the success of a safety and health program requires the support and cooperation of operating and P/HRM managers. But

---

[16] John R. Emshwiller, "Many Nuclear-Plant Perils Remain Three Years after Three Mile Island," *The Wall Street Journal*, February 26, 1982, p. 23.

P/HRM Manager Close-Up

William J. Danos
New Wales Chemicals, Inc.

Biography

William J. Danos, safety engineer of New Wales Chemicals, Inc., was graduated from Louisiana State University, Baton Rouge, with a degree in chemical engineering. He has had extensive training in the safety field, including the Industrial Hygiene Training Course (National Safety Council) and the Industrial Facilities Protection Program (Ft. Gordon, Georgia). Danos entered the safety field in 1959 as safety supervisor at Allied Chemical Corporation, Baton Rouge Works. Since that time he has held positions such as safety engineer for Boh Brothers Construction Company and safety supervisor for Uniroyal, Inc.

In addition, Danos was editor of *The Chemical Treat,* a magazine at Allied Chemical. He is a certified safety trainer and has served as national safety and health chairman for ASPA.

Job Description

As safety engineer at New Wales Chemicals, William J. Danos is responsible for total loss-control programs. This includes such areas as safety on the job, security, fire prevention, medical attention, and workers' compensation.

it is more complicated than that. In some organizations, safety is a separate-function of its own, though both operating managers and staff still have their parts to play to protect employees.

Top management must support safety and health with an adequate budget. Managers must give it their personal support by talking about safety and health with everyone in the firm. Acting on safety reports is another way top managers can be involved in these efforts. Without this support, the safety and health effort is hampered. Some organizations have responded to the environmental problems that can increase accidents, deaths, and disabilities by placing the responsibility for employee health and safety with the chief executive officer of the organization; the hospital administrator, the agency administrator, the company president. This is the approach taken by most smaller organizations that are concerned about health and safety.

Operating managers also are responsible, since accidents and injuries will take place and health hazards will exist in the work unit. They must be aware of health and safety considerations and cooperate with the specialists who can help them reduce accidents and occupational illness. In larger and some medium-sized organizations, there is a safety unit in the P/HRM department. This chapter will illustrate what a safety and health specialist does.

The success of the safety program rests primarily on how well employees and supervisors cooperate with safety rules and regulations. Often this relationship is formalized in the creation of a safety committee consisting of the safety specialist, representative employees, and managers.

Usually there are two levels of safety committees. At the policy level is the committee made up of major division heads; this committee sets safety policy and rules, investigates major hazards, and has budget responsibility. At the departmental level, both supervisors and managers are members. Safety committees are concerned with the organization's entire safety program: inspection, design, record-keeping, training, and motivation programs. The more people who can be involved through the committees, the more likely is the program to be successful. Finally, the government inspector plays a role in keeping the organization on its toes regarding the safety of the employees.

Employee health and safety is a mature P/HRM function—Stage IV, as described in Exhibit 1–7 (Chapter 1). Many studies have been made of it, especially by engineers and psychologists.

CAUSES OF WORK ACCIDENTS AND WORK-RELATED ILLNESSES

Work accidents and work-related illnesses have many causes. The major causes of occupational accidents are:

- The task to be done.
- The working conditions.
- The nature of the employees.

Some examples of causes in the task and working conditions area include poorly designed or inadequately repaired machines, lack of protective equipment, and the presence of dangerous chemicals or gases. Other working conditions that contribute to accidents include excessive work hours leading to employee fatigue, noise, lack of proper lighting, boredom, and horseplay and fighting at work. The National Institute for Occupational Safety and Health (NIOSH) is charged with finding out more about the causes of accidents and occupational health hazards.

There are data to indicate that some employees have more accidents than the average. Such a person is said to be an *accident repeater*. These studies indicate that employees who (1) are under 30 years of age, (2) lack psychomotor and perceptual skills, (3) are impulsive, and (4) are easily bored are more likely to have accidents than others.[17] Although some believe accident proneness can be measured by a set of attitude or motivational instruments, most experts who have examined the data carefully do not believe that attitudinal-motivational "causes" of accidents are a significant influence on accident rates. We need to know much more about accident proneness before such serious actions as attempting to screen out the "accident-prone" person are implemented.

ORGANIZATION RESPONSES TO SAFETY AND HEALTH

The safety department or unit and the safety committee can take three approaches to improving the safety of working conditions:

- Prevention and design.
- Inspection and research.
- Training and motivation.

Bob Undine's plant, mentioned at the beginning of this chapter, has taken all three approaches.

Safety Design and Preventive Approaches

Numerous preventive measures have been adopted by organizations in attempts to improve their safety records. One is to design more safety into the workplace through safety engineering. Engineers have helped through the study of human-factors engineering, which seeks to make jobs more comfortable, less confusing, and less fatiguing. This can keep employees more alert and less open to accidents.

Safety engineers design safety into the workplace with the analytical design approach. This total design approach analyzes all factors involved in the job. Included are such factors as speed of the assembly line, stresses in the work, and job design. On the basis of this analysis, steps are taken to improve safety precautions. Protective guards are designed for machinery and equipment. Color coding warns of dangerous areas. Standard safety colors, which should be taught in safety classes, include gray for machinery and red where the area presents danger of fire. Other dangers may be highlighted by bright orange paint.

Protective clothing and devices are also supplied for employees working in hazardous job situations. These can include:

---

[17] Bureau of Labor Statistics, *Injury Rates by Industry* (Washington, D.C.: U.S. Government Printing Office, 1978).

Head protection, principally with helmets.

Eye and face protection, with goggles, face shields, and spectacles.

Hearing protection, with muffs and inserts.

Respiratory protection, with air-purifying devices such as filter respirators and gas masks, and air-supplying devices.

Hand protection, with gloves.

Foot and leg protection, with safety shoes, boots, guards, and leggings.

Body protection, with garments such as suits, aprons, jackets, and coveralls.

Belts and lifelines to prevent those working in high places from falling.

The few studies on the effectiveness of these preventive design measures indicate that they do reduce accidents.[18]

Well-designed rest periods increase safety and productivity, as do clearly understood rules and regulations. These rules should be developed from analysis of equipment and conditions, such as flammability. No-smoking areas and hard hat areas where safety helmets are required for all employees and visitors are examples.

On April 27, 1984, the 85,000 employee Boeing Company in Seattle became the largest U.S. company to join a growing list of firms that have decided to ban smoking in the workplace.[19] Boeing's president, Malcolm Stammer, believes that "It is the responsibility of management in any company to provide the cleanest, safest, and most healthful environment possible for its employees." The Boyd Coffee Co. in Portland, Oregon, banned smoking on company property in 1973. Employees who wish to smoke may do so only in the employee parking lot and only during work breaks and lunch hour. Smoking is prohibited everywhere else—and the rule applies to everyone, even visitors and customers.

Approximately 36 percent of American companies have decided to control or prohibit employee smoking. There are currently 10 states and 260 communities that have laws that restrict smoking in public places.[20] Pacific Northwest Bell Telephone Co. put its 15,000 employees on notice one day that: In three months there would be no smoking allowed at work. What happened? Did anyone sue the firm? No. Nobody sued or resigned. Most of the company's 4,000 smokers cut down on their habit and within a year of the notice 350 had quit totally.

At the beginning of 1986, Blue Cross/Blue Shield of Maryland decided to create a smoke-free workplace. As of the end of 1986, the firm considered the program a success. The firm reviewed the medical histories of its 900 employees. The review indicated that 36 percent of the employees were smokers. It was estimated that costs due to illness, accidents and absenteeism of smokers averaged about $185,000. A three-phase program was installed:

---

[18] James Gardner, "Employee Safety," in *Handbook of Modern Personnel Administration*, ed. Joseph Famularo (New York: McGraw-Hill, 1978), chap. 48.

[19] William L. Weis, "No Smoking," *Personnel Administrator,* September 1984, pp. 52–58.

[20] Sherry C. Hammond, David A. DeCenzo, and Mollie H. Bowers, "How One Company Went Smokeless," *Harvard Business Review,* November–December 1987, pp. 44–45.

Phase I: All smoking was banned in meetings, conferences, and training sessions.

Phase II: Nine months after Phase I, all work areas were declared smoke-free. Smoking areas were established, but all cigarette vending machines were removed.

Phase III: Three months after Phase II, smoking was prohibited on all company premises. Employees who failed to comply faced the full range of disciplinary action: from warning to suspension and finally termination.

Now that the Blue Cross/Blue Shield no-smoking program is in place, employees do not smoke on company premises. Admittedly, one reason for such perfect compliance is that employees were warned about losing their jobs. The U.S. Surgeon General would like to see a "smoke-free" society by 2000.[21] The sales charts of the tobacco industry show that smoking in the United States is declining rapidly.[22] Today only about 30% of those over 18 smoke versus about half in the mid 50s. Perhaps the surgeon general and firms like Blue Cross/Blue Shield will be able to achieve the smoke-free society.

The no-smoking ban of firms like Boeing and Boyd Coffee has been attacked as being discriminatory.[23] Some claim that the high estimates cited for time lost per day for smoking (35 minutes a day) are biased, since they are obtained from interviews with employers who have instituted nonsmoking policies. These estimates do not show that time spent smoking is wasted in terms of lost productivity. Thus, a preventive approach such as establishing a no-smoking ban has triggered an interesting debate.

What is your opinion on a no-smoking ban?

Inspection, Reporting, and Accident Research

A second activity of safety departments or specialists is to inspect the workplace with the goal of reducing accidents and illnesses. The safety specialist is looking for a number of things, including answers to these questions:

Are safety rules being observed? How many near misses were there?
Are safety guards, protective equipment, and so on being used?
Are there potential hazards in the workplace that safety redesign could improve?
Are there potential occupational health hazards?

A related activity is to investigate accidents or "close calls" to determine the facts for insurance purposes. More important, such investigations also can

---

[21] Daniel Seligman, "Don't Bet against Cigarette Makers," *Fortune*, August 17, 1987, pp. 68–78.

[22] "No Smoking Sweeps America," *Business Week*, July 27, 1987, pp. 40–46.

[23] Lewis C. Solomon, "The Other Side of the Smoking Controversy," *Personnel Administrator*, March 1983, pp. 72–73, 101.

determine preventive measures that should be taken in the future. Following an accident requiring more than first aid treatment, the safety specialist, P/HRM specialist, or manager must *investigate* and report the facts to the government and insurance companies. These data are also used to analyze the causes of accidents, with a view to preventing possible recurrences.

Reporting of accidents and occupational illnesses is an important part of the safety specialist's job. Usually, the report is filled out by the injured employee's supervisor and checked by the safety specialist. The supervisor compiles the report because he or she usually is present when the accident occurs. And doing so requires the supervisor to think about safety in the unit and what can be done to prevent similar accidents.

At regular intervals during the work year, safety and personnel specialists carry out *accident research;* that is, systematic evaluation of the evidence concerning accidents and health hazards. Data for this research should be gathered from both external and internal sources. Safety and health journals point out recent findings which should stimulate the safety specialist to look for hazardous conditions at the workplace. Reports from the National Institute of Occupational Safety and Health, a research organization created by OSHA legislation, also provide important data inputs for research. Data developed at the workplace include accident reports, inspection reports by government and the organization's safety specialists, and recommendations of the safety committees.

Accident research often involves computation of organizational accident rates. These are compared to industry and national figures to determine the organization's relative safety performance. Several statistics are computed. Accident frequency rate is computed per million labor-hours of work, as follows:

$$\text{Frequency rate} = \frac{\text{Number of accidents} \times 1,000,000}{\text{Number of work hours in the period}}$$

The accidents used in this computation are those causing the worker to lose work time.

The second statistic is the accident severity rate. This is computed as follows:

$$\text{Accident severity rate} = \frac{\text{Number of workdays lost} \times 1,000,000}{\text{Number of work hours in the period}}$$

OSHA suggests reporting accidents as number of injuries per 100 full-time employees per year, as a simpler approach. The formula is:

$$\frac{\text{Number of illnesses and injuries}}{\text{Total hours worked by all employees for the year}} \times 200,000$$

The base equals the number of workers employed (100 full-time equivalent) working full time (for example, 40 hours per week and for 50 weeks if vacation is 2 weeks). OSHA visits workplaces in high-hazard industries and conducts inspections in firms with above-average lost-workday injury rates. The 1982 rate for manufacturing is 4.3 per 100 workers.

The organization's statistics should be compared with the industry's statistics and government statistics (from the Department of Labor and OSHA). Most studies find that although effective accident research should be very complex, in reality it is unsophisticated and unscientific.

Safety Training and Motivation Programs

The third approach organizations take to safety is training and motivation programs. Safety training usually is part of the orientation program. It also takes place during the employee's career. This training is usually voluntary, but some is required by government agencies. Studies of the effectiveness of such training are mixed. Some studies indicate that some methods, such as job instruction training (JIT) and accident simulations, are more effective than others. Others contend that the employees' perception that management really believes in safety training accounts for its success.[24] A few studies find that the programs make employees more *aware* of safety, but not necessarily safer in their behavior. Nevertheless, effectively developed safety training programs can help provide a safer environment for all employees.

Safety specialists have also tried to improve safety conditions and accident statistics by various motivation devices, such as contests and communication programs. These are intended to reinforce safety training. One device is to place posters around the workplace with slogans such as "A Safe Worker Is a Happy Worker." Posters are available from the National Safety Council or can be prepared for the enterprise. Communication programs also include items in company publications and safety booklets and billboards. The billboard in front of Bob Undine's plant, for example, reads:

Welcome to American Manufacturing Company

A Good Place to Work
A Safe Place to Work

We have had no accidents for
<u>182</u> days

Sometimes safety communications are tied into a safety contest. If lower accidents result over a period, an award is given. The little research that has

---

[24] Roger Dunbar, "Manager's Influence on Subordinate's Thinking about Safety," *Academy of Management Journal*, June 1975, pp. 364–69.

been done on safety communications and contests is mixed. Some believe they are useful. Others contend they have no effect or produce undesirable side effects, such as failure to report accidents or a large number of accidents once the contest is over or has been lost.[25]

In general, too little is known scientifically at this point to recommend use or reduction of safety motivation programs. One example of the needed research is a study that examined the conditions under which safety motivation and education programs were effective in a shelving manufacturing company. It found that:

- There are safety-conscious people and others who are unaware of safety. The safety-conscious people were influenced by safety posters.
- Safety booklets were influential to the safety-conscious employees when their work group was also safety-conscious.
- Five-minute safety talks by supervisors were effective when the work group was safety-conscious and when the supervisor was safety-conscious.
- Safety training was effective for the safety-conscious employee when the supervisor and top management were safety-conscious.
- Safety inspections were effective when the work group and supervisor were safety-conscious.

GOVERNMENT RESPONSES
TO SAFETY AND HEALTH PROBLEMS

Although many organizations (such as Bob Undine's) have done a good job of safeguarding the safety and health of their employees, with little or no supervision from government sources, others (as Clint Woodley's) have not. This has led governments to become involved in holding the organization responsible for prevention of accidents, disabilities, illnesses, and deaths related to the tasks workers perform and the conditions under which they work.

Prior to passage of the Occupational Safety and Health Act (OSHA) in 1970, the feeling was that private organizations had not done enough to assure safe and healthy working conditions. In 1936 alone, there were 35,000 workplace deaths reported. In 1970 the year in which OSHA became law, an estimated 14,200 workers died, 2.2 million suffered disabilities, and another 300,000 to 500,000 suffered from occupationally induced illnesses.[26] The federal law in effect, the Walsh-Healy Act, was thought to be too weak or inadequately enforced, and state programs were incomplete, diverse, and lacked authority. The basic requirements of OSHA are presented in Exhibit 18–4.

Lobbying by unions and employees led to the passage of several federal laws related to specific occupations, such as the Coal Mine Health and Safety Act of 1969 and the related Black Lung Benefits Act of 1972. The movement for

---

[25] Robert McKelvey et al., "Performance Efficiency and Injury Avoidance as a Function of Positive and Negative Incentives," *Journal of Safety Research,* June 1973, pp. 90–96.

[26] D. S. Thelam, D. Ledgerwood, and C. F. Walters, "Health and Safety in the Workplace: A New Challenge for Business Schools," *Personnel Administrator,* October 1985, pp. 37–38.

EXHIBIT 18–4 Job Safety and Health Protection Requirements per OSHA

The Occupational Safety and Health Act of 1970 provides job safety and health protection for workers through the promotion of safe and healthful working conditions throughout the nation. Requirements of the Act include the following:

Employers:
Each employer must furnish to each of his employees employment and a place of employment free from recognized hazards that are causing or are likely to cause death or serious harm to his employees; and shall comply with occupational safety and health standards issued under the Act.

Employees:
Each employee shall comply with all occupational safety and health standards, rules, regulations, and orders issued under the Act that apply to his own actions and conduct on the job. The Occupational Safety and Health Administration (OSHA) of the Department of Labor has the primary responsibility for administering the Act. OSHA issues occupational safety and health standards, and its Compliance Safety and Health Officers conduct jobsite inspections to ensure compliance with the Act.

Inspection:
The Act requires that a representative of the employer and a representative authorized by the employees be given an opportunity to accompany the OSHA inspector for the purpose of aiding the inspection. Where there is no authorized employee representative, the OSHA Compliance Officer must consult with a reasonable number of employees concerning safety and health conditions in the workplace.

Complaint:
Employees or their representatives have the right to file a complaint with the nearest OSHA office requesting an inspection if they believe unsafe or unhealthful conditions exist in their workplace. OSHA will withhold, on request, names of employees complaining. The Act provides that employees may not be discharged or discriminated against in any way for filing safety and health complaints or otherwise exercising their rights under the Act. An employee who believes he has been discriminated against may file a complaint with the nearest OSHA office within 30 days of the alleged discrimination.

Citation:
If upon inspection OSHA believes an employer has violated the Act, a citation alleging such violations will be issued to the employer. Each citation will specify a time period within which the alleged violation must be corrected. The OSHA citation must be prominently displayed at or near the place of alleged violation for three days, or until it is corrected, whichever is later, to warn employees of dangers that may exist there.

Proposed Penalty:
The Act provides for mandatory penalties against employers of up to $1,000 for each serious violation and for optional penalties of up to $1,000 for each nonserious violation. Penalties of up to $1,000 per day may be proposed for failure to correct violations within the proposed time period. Also, any employer who willfully or repeatedly violates the Act may be assessed penalties of up to $10,000 for each such violation. Criminal penalties are also provided in the Act. Any willful violation resulting in death of an employee, upon conviction, is punishable by a fine of more than $10,000, or by imprisonment for not more than six months, or by both. Conviction of an employer after a first conviction doubles these maximum penalties.

Voluntary Activity:
While providing penalties for violations, the Act also encourages efforts by labor and management, before an OSHA inspection, to reduce injuries and illnesses arising out of employment. The Department of Labor encourages employers and employees to reduce workplace hazards voluntarily and to develop and improve safety and health programs in all workplaces and industries. Such cooperative action would initially focus on the identification and elimination of hazards that could cause death, injury, or illness to employees and supervisors. There are many public and private organizations that can provide information and assistance in this effort, if requested.

Source: OSHA Bulletin.

federal supervision of health and safety programs culminated in passage of the Occupational Safety and Health Act administered by the Occupational Safety and Health Administration of the Department of Labor. To conduct research and develop safety and health standards, the act created the National Institute of Occupational Safety and Health (NIOSH).

OSHA, the product of three years of bitter legislative lobbying, was designed to remedy safety problems on the job. The compromise law that was enacted initially received wide support. Its purpose was to provide employment "free from recognized hazards" to employees. OSHA provisions originally applied to 4.1 million businesses and 57 million employees in almost every organization engaged in interstate commerce.[27]

OSHA has been enforced by federal inspectors or in partnership with state safety and health agencies. It encourages the states to assume responsibility for developing and administering occupational and health laws and carrying out their own statistical programs. Before being granted full authority for its programs, a state must go through three steps. First, the state plan must have the preliminary approval of OSHA. Second, the state promises to take "developmental steps" to do certain things at certain times, such as adjusting legislation, hiring inspectors, and providing for an industrial hygiene laboratory. OSHA monitors the state plan for three years, and if the state fulfills these obligations, the third step is a trial period at full-enforcement levels for at least a year. At the end of this intensive evaluation period, a final decision is made by OSHA on the qualifications of the state program.

If OSHA and the employer fail to provide safe working conditions, employees as individuals or their unions can seek injunctions against the employer to force it to do so or submit to an inspection of the workplace. The employer cannot discriminate against an employee who takes these actions. OSHA has many requirements, but the three that most directly affect most employers are:

Meeting safety standards set by OSHA.

Submitting to OSHA inspections.

Keeping records and reporting accidents and illnesses.

OSHA Safety Standards

OSHA has established safety standards, defined as those "practices, means, operations, or processes, reasonably necessary to provide safe . . . employment." The standards can affect any aspect of the workplace; new standards were established or proposed, for example, for such factors as lead, mercury, silica, benzene, talc dust, cotton dust, noise, and general health hazards. The standards may be industrywide or apply only to a specific enterprise.

The secretary of labor revises, modifies, or revokes existing standards or creates new ones on his own initiative or on the basis of petitions from interested parties (employees or unions). The National Institute of Occupa-

---

[27] "Will Reform Be the Death of OSHA?" *Nation's Business,* April 1980, pp. 55–58.

tional Safety and Health in the Department of Health and Human Services (HHS) is responsible for doing research from which standards are developed and for training those involved to implement them. Federal or national consensus standards (such as those of the National Fire Protection Association) have also become OSHA standards. And temporary emergency standards can be created for imminent danger. Employers may be granted temporary variances by showing inability to comply with a standard within the time allowed, if they have a plan to protect employees against the hazard.

The employer is responsible for knowing what these standards are and abiding by them. This is not easy. The *initial* standards were published in *The Federal Register* in 350 pages of small print, and interpretations of the standards are issued yearly *by volume*. One recent annual volume was 780 pages long! OSHA officers work with compliance operations manuals two inches thick. Even the *checklist* that summarizes the general industry standards is 11 pages long and lists 80 items. The responsible manager is subject to thousands of pages of such standards. If they are not met, an organization can be shut down, and the responsible manager can be fined or jailed for not meeting OSHA's standards.

OSHA Inspections

To make sure the law is obeyed, OSHA inspectors visit places of employment, on their own schedules or on invitation of an employer, union, or employee. An employee who requests an inspection need not be identified to the employer. If the employer is found guilty of a violation, the penalties include (1) willful or repeated violations, $10,000 per violation; (2) citation for serious violation, $1,000 each; (3) citation for less serious violation, up to $1,000 discretionary; (4) failure to correct cited violations, $1,000 per day; (5) willful violation causing death, up to $10,000 or up to six months in jail; (6) falsification of statements or records, up to $10,000 and/or six months in jail.

A Supreme Court decision ruled that employers can bar OSHA job safety inspectors from their workplaces if the inspectors don't have a search war-

© 1978 by NEA, Inc. Reprinted by permission of NEA.

rant.[28] But these warrants have been made easier to obtain. They can be issued by a court in advance without notifying the employer, so the surprise element of the inspection can be maintained.

OSHA inspectors examine the premises for compliance and the records for accuracy. They categorize a violation as imminent danger (in which case they can close the business), serious (which calls for a major fine), nonserious (fine up to $1,000) or de minimus (small—a notification is given, but no fine). Atlas Roofing (Georgia) and Frank Irey (Pennsylvania) argued that fining without court action violated the Seventh Amendment, but the Supreme Court supported OSHA unanimously.[29] The employer has the right to appeal fines or citations within OSHA (up to the level of the OSHA Review Commission) or in the courts.

OSHA Recordkeeping and Reporting

The third major OSHA requirement is that the employer keep standardized records of illnesses and injuries and calculate accident ratios. These are shown to OSHA compliance officers who ask to see them. The form used is illustrated in Exhibit 18–5. Accidents and illnesses that must be reported are those that result in deaths, disabilities that cause the employee to miss work, and medical care injuries that require treatment by a physician.

An OSHA guide to when to report and record an illness, injury, or death is shown in Exhibit 18–6. Injuries or illnesses that require only first aid and involve no loss of work time need not be reported. Employers go to great lengths to categorize incidents as "minor injuries," trying to treat them through first aid and keeping the employee on the job (even a make-work job), to avoid reporting them. To do so might lead to an OSHA inspection or raise their workers' compensation insurance rates. The employer must also report accident frequency and severity rates. The firm must also post OSHA Form 102 in a prominent place at work. It is a summary of the injuries and illnesses report.

Some Consequences of OSHA: Management's View

Most managers generally agree that OSHA has had a very rocky history.[30] They believe it has fallen far short of its promise. Let's examine some of the areas toward which managerial criticism is directed.

Safety Standards The general conclusion of most managers is that the agency's standards, more than 15 years after the law was passed, are still

---

[28] "Justices to Hear Test of Job Unit's Safety Checks," *The Wall Street Journal,* April 19, 1977, p. 14.

[29] "Justices Uphold Right of Job Safety Unit to Set Penalties Without Going to Court," *The Wall Street Journal,* March 24, 1977.

[30] Wade Swormstedt, "The New OSHA," *Screen Printing,* December 1981, pp. 58–63, 117–18.

EXHIBIT 18–5   OSHA Injury and Illness Reporting Form

VIII. Injury and Illness Summary (covering calendar year 1977)

Instructions:
- This section may be completed by copying data from OSHA Form No. 102 "Summary, Occupational Injuries and Illnesses," which you are required to complete and post in your establishment.
- Leave Section VIII blank if there were no recordable injuries or illnesses during 1977.
- Code 30 — Add all occupational illnesses (Code 21 + 22 + 23 + 24 + 25 + 26 + 29) and enter on this line for each column (3) through (8).
- Code 31 — Add occupational injuries (Code 10) and the sum of all occupational illnesses (Code 30) and enter on this line for each column (3) through (8).

Code (1)	Category (2)		Fatalities (deaths) (3)	Lost workday cases			Nonfatal cases without lost workdays*	
				Number of cases (4)	Number of cases involving permanent transfer to another job or termination of employment (5)	Number of lost workdays (6)	Number of cases (7)	Number of cases involving transfer to another job or termination of employment (8)
10	Occupational injuries							
21	Occupational illnesses	Occupational skin diseases or disorders						
22		Dust diseases of the lungs (pneumoconioses)						
23		Respiratory conditions due to toxic agents						
24		Poisoning (systemic effects of toxic materials)						
25		Disorders due to physical agents (other than toxic materials)						
26		Disorders due to repeated trauma						
29		All other occupational illnesses						
30		Sum of all occupational illnesses (Add Codes 21 through 29)						
31	Total of all occupational injuries and illnesses (Add Codes 10 + 30)							

*Nonfatal cases without lost workdays - Cases resulting in: Medical treatment beyond first aid, diagnosis of occupational illness, loss of consciousness, restriction of work or motion, or transfer to another job (without lost workdays).

Comments: _____

_____

IX.   Report prepared by: _____ Date: _____

Title: _____ Area code and phone: _____

unreadable, arbitrary, overly specific, too trivial, too costly to implement, and unworkable. An example of the trivia in the OSHA standards appears in a publication on ranch safety. It suggests to ranchers that "since dangerous

EXHIBIT 18–6   **Guide for Reporting and Recording Accidents, Illnesses, and Deaths**

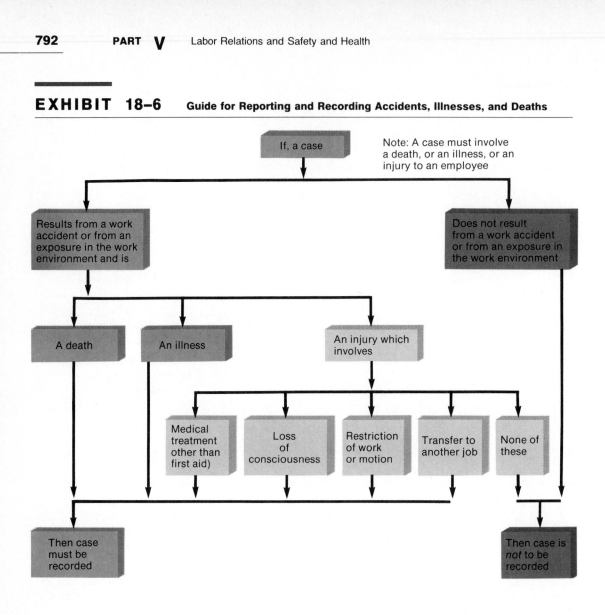

gases come from manure pits, you should be careful not to fall into manure pits." We don't suppose many ranchers willingly fall into them, with or without dangerous gases.

A more critical condition than the poor quality of the standards is the fact that many of them originally were not in written form. In the first five years, only three new sets of standards were written. Many others are still in the process. OSHA has difficulty writing standards for existing technology, but it *really* has problems with new technologies where no standards exist. It is very difficult to adjust old standards to new technologies. Managers believe that what is needed is a whole new strategy for standard setting and enforcement.[31]

In the same way, OSHA did not try to inspect all industries equally but created priorities based upon known hazardous occupations; however, managers feel all standards should not have equal emphasis. In the standards already set, the readability should be improved. More importantly, the agency should categorize the subparts of the standards into categories based on likelihood of accident or illness. These categories might be:

Most important. To be enforced at once and fully.
Of average importance. To be enforced later and in the spirit, not the letter, of the regulation.
Desirable. To be enforced when the most important standards and those of average importance are in full compliance.

If the standards were publicized to highlight these weights, employers could live with OSHA a bit more easily.

OSHA Inspections OSHA does not inspect each industry with equal frequency. Initially, they set up five target industries to be inspected often because of their high rates of accidents: roof and sheet metal work; meat packing; miscellaneous transportation (mobile homes), and lumber and wood products. Later, foundries and casting and metal-stamping industries were added to the target industries list. Target health hazard industries are those involving asbestos, carbon monoxide, cotton dust, lead, and silica.

Appealing Violations An employer who wishes to appeal a violation citation can do so within OSHA, through the Occupational Safety and Health Review Commission, or through the federal courts. Generally speaking neither management nor labor has been happy with the inspections, one side claiming too few, the other too many. The Supreme Court decision regarding the need for search warrants is a result. Because of a shortage of inspectors and this Court ruling and because OSHA recognizes that it cannot enforce the law without the employers' help, the agency has begun to emphasize voluntary compliance. This consists of educational programs and "dry run" inspections in which the employer is advised of hazards but is given a chance to correct them before a citation is issued. President Reagan used in his campaign in 1980 the rules of OSHA to point out the excesses of government involvement in business. Since he took office in January 1981, the number of OSHA inspectors have been cut to about 1,100.[32] Likewise, the inspections being carried out were cut by 15 percent.

Consequences of Recordkeeping and Reporting Few managers would quarrel with the need to keep adequate records on accidents and health and to calculate accident ratios. It seems reasonable for them to be recorded and reported in a standardized way, for ease in summarizing. But OSHA has been severely criticized by managers for the amount of paperwork required and the frequent changes in it.

---

[32] "A Deregulation Report Card," *Newsweek*, January 11, 1982, pp. 50–53.

Final Management Thoughts on OSHA

So far, there is only impressionistic managerial evidence on OSHA. Ashford, who had great hopes for OSHA, concluded his Ford Foundation report by saying "The OSHA Act has failed thus far to live up to its potential for reducing job injury and disease." General Motors pointed out that, although it was spending $15 per car to implement OSHA, and although in the first five years of OSHA the company has been inspected 614 times, received 258 citations, and spent $29 million to fulfill the requirements (and 11 million *worker-years* to get in compliance), "there was no correlation between meeting OSHA's regulations and reduction of accidents.[33]

Ultimately, whether OSHA succeeds or fails depends on a decrease in the number and severity of accidents and the incidence of occupational disease in the working population. OSHA's annual reports are phrased in bureaucratic "success" terms such as increases in numbers of inspections, pamphlets printed, and dollars of research spent. Until it can show that the *costs* of enforcement are exceeded by *benefits* in terms of reduced accidents and fewer disease victims, we shall have to wait and see whether the program should be called a success or a bureaucratic nightmare.

Management feels that an important factor is not presently covered in OSHA's approach: the worker's responsibility for his or her own health and safety. All the responsibility is placed on *management*. For example, if employees wish to skip medical tests to determine if they are developing an occupational disease, OSHA has ruled they can. If an employee refuses to cooperate in safety matters and an OSHA inspector finds a violation, the *company* is held responsible. For example, there are many instances of employees refusing to wear the safety equipment recommended by OSHA. If the inspector sees this, OSHA *fines the company*. All the company can do is discipline (or possibly fire) the employee.

What can the operating manager or P/HRM specialist do to help keep the enterprise in compliance with OSHA? The P/HRM specialist should know the standards that apply to the organization and check to see that they are being met. P/HRM is also responsible for keeping OSHA records up to date and filing them on time. The operating manager must know the standards that apply to her or his unit or department and see that the unit meets the standards.

As citizens, all managers should see to it that OSHA is effective at the organization. But, they can also write their congressional representatives to improve it so that:

Standards are understandable and focus on important items.
Advisory inspections are permitted.
Records and reports are minimized and efficient.

---

[33] Ashford, *Crises in the Workplace.*

Some Consequences of OSHA:
Union's Views

As would be expected, the union's view of OSHA is more favorable than management's. The union believes that the passage of OSHA and its history clearly demonstrate the need for a federal role in safety and health.[34] The identification of hazard is a task of such proportion that it can only be accomplished with the resources and authority of the federal government.

The union believes that OSHA has clearly made great strides despite managerial resistance. Fatalities have decreased 10 percent since OSHA, meaning that the lives of thousands of workers have been saved. Similarly, thousands of workers have been spared serious injuries, with a 15 percent overall decline in total injuries during OSHA's lifetime.

OSHA Regulations and Worker Involvement OSHA has provided workers access to the employer's records of illnesses and injuries. Consequently, many employers have encouraged the participation of workers in the enforcement process. Where effective, local union safety and health committees have been established to deal with problems at the plant level. Armed with training and education, and backed by their international unions, these local committees are having an impact on making the workplace safer and healthier. Health and safety is now the fastest growing among union programs. Each year, under OSHA's New Directions program, more than 20,000 workers are trained in recognition and control of hazards, more than half through union programs.

Justice Is Too Slow Every time a major standard to improve safety and health is proposed, management resists. They use every political and legal avenue to block standards. Management consultants are hired to argue against the standard's validity. Who suffers? The workers, say the unions. Their argument is that the courts take too long to make rulings.

The estimated time of standards development for changes in safety and health conditions is two and one half to three years. Judicial stays may add one or more years' delay. For example, the Coke Oven standard, subject of a United Steelworkers union petition for regulation in 1971, was still pending in 1982 before the U.S. Supreme Court.

OSHA Enforcement Differences The OSHA staff is still too small to do the job. A major purpose of the law was to achieve a nationwide, uniform, strong enforcement program. Despite the intent, enforcement is still somewhat unsystematic. There are differences in enforcement aggressiveness from area to area in the country. The union would like to see more aggressive enforcement

---

[34] Section is largely based on Lane Kirkland, "OSHA: A 10-Year Success Story," *AFL–CIO American Federationist*, July 1980, pp. 1–4.

across the country. Unfortunately, the cutbacks in staff and funding under the Reagan administration are considered to be reasons why enforcement variability will probably become even greater.

Union leaders like the United Auto Workers' Douglas Frazer have stated, "There seems to be a policy of weakening health standards to suit the interests of industry, rather than safeguarding workers' health and safety as a primary mission."[35] Frazer believes that the Reagan-initiated changes are a setback. Cuts in staff, budgets, and less interest in safety and health suggest that there will be less enforcement of OSHA. This, according to union leaders, means a return to more severe, more frequent, and more costly accidents and illnesses.

Some Jobs Are Still Adequately Covered There are still extremely dangerous jobs not covered by OSHA standards. Grain elevator and mill workers are not covered by a specific OSHA standard. Grain handlers face each day the threat of sudden death in an explosion or the development of an eventually incapacitating illness arising from their chronic exposures to grain dust and pesticides.[36]

The safety and health problems in grain elevators will not be significantly improved until OSHA standards are set. The problem, as mentioned above, is delay after delay. Setting standards and moving through the courts is a lengthy process. The union wants everyone to think about grain workers and others, who, even today, work in filthy, dangerous, and life-threatening jobs daily.

There were some Americans in the early 1900s who believed that leaving a light bulb burning in a room would cause deaths. Also, tomatoes had to be avoided because they were poisonous.[37] Today, the light bulb and the tomato have been replaced by the video display terminal (VDT), which is used with word processors, computers, and medical equipment. Rumors suggest that VDTs cause birth defects, cataracts, and stillbirths.[38]

Research and tests conducted in the United States and Canada have failed to find any radiation hazards from VDTs. There are, however some problems connected with their use, such as poor posture, eyestrain, skeletal-musculo aches, and general fatigue. Apparently, it is not the VDT but the workstation design, bad lighting, and poor job design that cause the problems.[39]

Maine and Connecticut have passed legislation on the study and eventual regulation of VDTs. No action has yet been taken by OSHA.[40] Maine's new law authorizes the state's Bureau of Labor Standards to collect statistics and medical information on the hazards of VDTs. The agency is also authorized to

---

[35] Swormstedt, "The New OSHA," p. 61.

[36] Robert F. Harbant, "A Dangerous Job with No Standards to Cover It," *AFL–CIO American Federationist,* July 1980, pp. 15–16.

[37] Vico Henriques and Charlotte LeGates, "A Look at VDTs and Their Impact on the Workplace . . . ." *Personnel Administrator,* September 1984, pp. 64–68.

[38] James W. Lahey, "Safety and the Future," *National Safety News,* October 1983, p. 63.

[39] "NIOSH Says VDT Use Not Harmful, But Undertakes a Three-Year Study to Prove It," *Resource,* July 1984, p. 3.

use the data collected to issue any rules which are needed to provide safe-guards for employees.

Another area not well covered by standards involves cases of robots injuring employees. Since more and more robots are being introduced into the work-place, there is likely to be a higher rate of people-robot accidents unless precautions are taken.[41] There have already been a few safety guidelines developed such as:

- Sharp edges and corners should be eliminated in the design of robots.
- Points of people-robot contact should be padded on the robot.
- Robots should be built with shear pins and breakaway sections to absorb the impact of collisions with people.[42]

Obviously, more safety rules, procedures, and laws will be introduced as the number of robots increases significantly in the next decade.

Final Union Thoughts on OSHA

The union believes that OSHA has resulted in better-informed employees, increased union involvement in safety and health, and better working condi-tions. These are all positive contributions. However, the union is still not satisfied that OSHA has achieved everything that it should. Workers are still needlessly being killed and subjected to work situations that are detrimental to their quality of life.

Unions now are fearful that the progress made under OSHA will be lost without support from President Reagan. His actions during 1981 indicated that OSHA would not be a top priority and that deregulation will be the rule rather than the exception.[43] However, the data indicate that in 1984, OSHA conducted 70,000 job safety inspections, the highest total since 1976. This indicates that OSHA is still a major force in helping bring about a safer and healthier workplace.[44]

HEALTH PROGRAMS

Health care costs Americans over $400 billion annually.[45] What is meant by the word *health?* While "the absence of disease" is one way of defining health, a

---

[40] Terminals Pose No Threat of Eye Damage," *Resource,* August 1983, pp. 1–2.

[41] Donald N. Smith and Richard C. Wilson, *Industrial Robots: A Delphi Forecast of Markets and Technology* (Dearborn, Mich.: Society of Manufacturers Engineers, 1982).

[42] Vincent M. Altamuro, "Working Safely with the Iron-Collar Worker," *National Safety News,* July 1983, pp. 33–37.

[43] "A Deregulation Report Card," p. 52.

[44] "Safety Inspections in Fiscal 1984 Expected to Be Highest in Nine Years," *Resource,* July 1984, p. 3.

[45] Stephen W. Hartman and Janet Cozzetto, "Wellness in the Workplace," *Personnel Admin-istator,* August 1984, pp. 108–17.

more informative definition is "a state of physical, mental, and social well-being.[46] This definition points to the relationships among body, mind, and social patterns. An employee's health can be harmed through disease, accident, or stress.[47] Managers now realize that they must be concerned about the general health of employees, and this includes psychological well-being. A competent manager or operator who is depressed and has low self-esteem is as nonproductive as a manager or operator who was injured and is hospitalized.

Today more than 750 organizations, such as Control Data, IBM, Prudential, Tenneco, and Kimberly-Clark, have initiated what are called *preventive health programs*.[48] The objectives of these programs are to achieve a higher level of employee "wellness" and to decrease health impairment costs by providing a program that is medically valid and responsive to workers' needs.

Preventive Health: Kimberly-Clark and Control Data Corporation

The Kimberly-Clark is highly publicized, is respected by its employees, and is being evaluated for its effects on cost, productivity, and well-being.[49] In 1977, Kimberly-Clark initiated its preventive health program, which consists of collecting information and samples from an employee to develop a medical history and health risk profile; medical tests of urine, blood, hearing, eyesight, extremity flexibility, and so on; exercise testing by treadmill or bicycle ergometer; health profile analysis by a physician; and recommendations to improve health. The company has constructed a 32,000-square-foot exercise facility that can be used to follow through on many health improvement recommendations.

The health screening at Kimberly-Clark has identified cases of hypertension, obesity, high cholesterol levels, cancer, ulcers, and high risk for heart attack. Cancer was detected in eight employees. Also, several employees required surgery for heart problems detected in the program.

Kimberly-Clark believes that they are investing in the long term with their preventive health program. Identifying health problems, improving wellness, and being concerned about employees are reasons why Kimberly-Clark is willing to invest so much in its preventive health program.

A program similar to Kimberly-Clark's is used by Control Data Corporation (CDC). The CDC Stay Well program was initiated in 1980.[50] It is offered as a

---

[46] Gloria C. Gordon and Mary Sue Henifin, "Health and Safety, Job Stress, and Shift Work," in *Making Organizations Human and Productive,* ed. H. Meltzer and Walter R. Nord (New York: John Wiley & Sons, 1981), p. 322.

[47] John M. Ivancevich and Michael T. Matteson, "Optimizing Human Resources: A Case for Preventive Health and Stress Management," *Organizational Dynamics,* Autumn 1980, pp. 4–25.

[48] John J. Hoffman, Jr., and Charles J. Hobson, "Physical Fitness and Employee Effectiveness," *Personnel Administrator,* April 1984, pp. 101–13, 126.

[49] Robert E. Dedmon and Mary Katherine Kubiak, "The Medical Director's Role in Industry," *Personnel Administrator,* September 1981, pp. 59–64.

[50] Murray P. Naditch, "Wellness Program Reaps Healthy Benefits for Sponsoring Employer," *Risk Management,* October 1981, pp. 21–24.

free corporate benefit to CDC's 57,000 U.S.-based employees and their spouses. There were 27,000 CDC employees in the program in 1981, and the company hoped to significantly increase that number each year.

For employees and their spouses, the CDC program consists of an orientation session, a health screening exam, a group interpretation session, and a series of courses that teach the skills necessary to change health-related behavior. CDC has a very strict confidentiality policy. No one at the company has access to any individual data except physicians who review the data. Individual participants decide whether they will share the information with their personal physicians. Each employee can decide what course of action to take after hearing and seeing the CDC physician's analysis of his or her health risk profile.

A four-year evaluation study of 15,000 Control Data employees showed workers with the worst life-style habits had the biggest medical bills. Health care costs for obese people were 11 percent higher than the average. People whose weekly exercise was equivalent to climbing less than five flights of stairs, or walking less than half mile, spent 114 percent more on health claims than those who climbed at least 15 flights of stairs or walked 1.5 miles weekly.

Kimberly-Clark, CDC, and hundreds of other organizations believe that preventive health programs made good sense. It is estimated that $18 billion–$25 billion is lost each year through nonmanagerial employee absenteeism, hospitalization, or death.[51] If these costs can be cut by as little as 5 percent through preventive health programs, they would be a significant bargain. Preventive health is an idea whose time has come for many corporations.

The preventive health move into organizations has brought with it some potential legal problems. Sentry Life Insurance has a $1.5 million fitness center at corporate headquarters in Stevens Point, Wisconsin.[52] Who is liable if an employee injures himself or herself in the center? This question was put to the test when an overweight man in his late 40s collapsed of a heart attack in the center. The man had reduced his weight from 270 to 180 pounds too fast and ignored the training regimen prescribed by the company. However, the firm continued to permit his use of the center. Fortunately for Sentry, a lawsuit based on a negligence claim was not filed.

To minimize legal risk, many corporations abide by guidelines established by the College of Sports Medicine. The guidelines recommend a series of tests to determine risks to program participants and prescribe training regimens. A health history and series of physical tests are used. Also, a stationary bike stress test to determine heart rate and blood pressure is administered. The test results help establish the safe parameters of a training program tailored to fit the person.

---

[51] This is a conservative estimate. Some experts estimate this figure actually to be closer to $100 billion. See John M. Ivancevich and Michael T. Matteson, *Stress and Work: A Managerial Perspective* (Glenview, Ill.: Scott, Foresman, 1980), pp. 18–19.

[52] Jonathan Miller, "Are You Liable to Be Liable?" *Corporate Fitness & Recreation*, December–January 1984, pp. 23–30.

From *The Wall Street Journal*, with permission of Cartoon Features Syndicate

"You need a good rest—can you just wheel without dealing for a while?"

Stress Management

Stress is a common experience that is a part of life. However, the concept of stress is a very difficult one to pin down in specific terms. There are experts who think of stress as the pressures in the world that produce emotional discomfort. Others feel that emotional discomfort is the stress that is caused by pressure or conditions that are called *stressors*. Still others view stress in terms of physiological or body reactions: blood pressure, heart rate, or hormone levels.[53] We will define *stress* as a person's physical, chemical, and mental reactions to stressors or stimuli in the environment. Stress occurs whenever environmental forces (stimuli) throw the bodily and mental functions of a person out of equilibrium.

Stress has typically been cast in terms of negative reactions. Of course, it can also be good for a person. Stress is what helps a person complete a report on

---

[53] For various interpretations of stress, see L. Kevin Hamberger and Jeffrey M. Lohr, *Stress and Stress Management* (New York: Springer Publishing Co., 1984); Tom Cox, *Stress* (Baltimore: University Park Press, 1978); Hans Selye, *The Stress of Life* (New York: McGraw-Hill, 1976); and K. Albrecht, *Stress and the Manager* (Englewood Cliffs, N.J.: Prentice-Hall, 1979).

time or generate a good, quick problem-solving procedure. This chapter acknowledges the positive aspects of stress—but our main attention will be on the negative aspects of stress.

Stress and Disease Job-related stress has been associated with a vast array of diseases such as coronary heart disease, hypertension, peptic ulcers, colitis, and various psychological problems such as anxiety and depression. Research has shown that stress affects the endocrine system, the cardiovascular system, the muscular system, and the emotions directly.[54] It also has a general arousal influence on the entire body.

Stress and disease linkage continues to be studied and is of interest to managers. A person who is emotionally troubled and depressed because of stress is often unable to function on the job and may even create problems for other workers if he or she attempts to work. In general, psychological job stress reactions are not severe psychoses. They are, however, frustrating; they do reduce a person's desire to work; they do cause feelings of fatigue. Thus, although many experts are concerned about the stress-coronary heart disease association there is also the possible stress-psychological reaction association.

The Person/Environment Fit Changes in the work and personal environment are inevitable. Too often, managers underestimate how changes can throw a person off kilter. A person who does not feel comfortable with his or her work environment is in what psychologists refer to as a state of disequilibrium. The person (skills, abilities, goals) does not fit with the work environment (boss, co-workers, compensation system). The costs of the lack of fit in person/environment can be many: subjective (feeling fatigued), behavioral (accident prone), cognitive (a mental block), physiological (elevated blood pressure), and/or organizational (higher absence rate).[55]

Research studies point out that these five levels of stress caused by disequilibrium or lack of fit are costly. The costs to an organization are found in premature deaths of employees, higher rates of accidents, performance inefficiencies, increased turnover, increased disability payments, and in many other areas.[56]

One way to attack the stress cost problem is to identify the stressors that contribute to it. Exhibit 18–7 is presented to show some of the major person and environmental stressors that lead to stress and dysfunctional consequences. This managerial model illustrates that stress is caused by the interaction of people with their environment. It is a person's perception of a work

---

[54] "For example, see J. G. Bruhn and S. Wolf, *The Roseto Story: An Anatomy of Health* (Norman, Okla.: University of Oklahoma Press, 1979); and K. R. Pelletier, *Mind as Healer, Mind as Slayer* (New York: Delacorte Press, 1977); and H. Weiner, *Psychobiology and Human Disease* (New York: Elsevier, North-Holland, 1977).

[55] Marilyn J. Davidson and Cary L. Cooper, "A Model of Occupational Stress," *Journal of Occupational Medicine*, August 1981, pp. 564–74.

[56] Cox, *Stress*.

EXHIBIT 18–7   A Managerial Model for Examining Job Stress

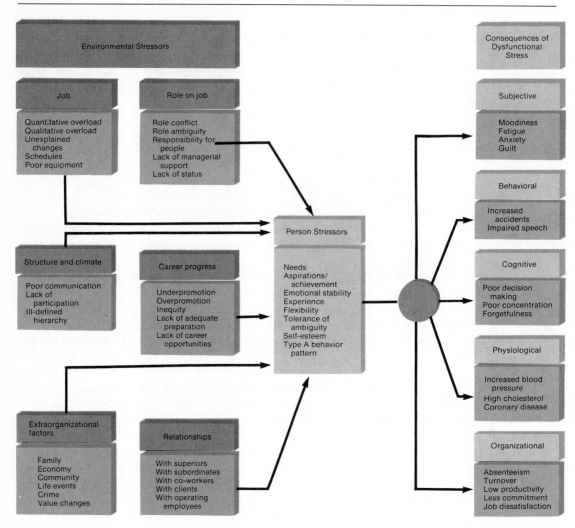

situation that can make a stressor stressful. This is what is portrayed in Exhibit 18–7. Covering each detail of Exhibit 18–7 is beyond the scope of this book. Consequently, only a few of the stressors will be examined.

Overload A person's workload can cause stress. Workload can relate to the quantity of the work (quantitative) or the quality (qualitative) of the activity to be completed (mental requirements). Underload can create problems as well as overload. Overload can cause a person to work long hours to stay even which can result in fatigue and more accidents. On the other hand, boredom can set in if a person is underloaded. A bored worker often avoids work by staying at home more frequently. The worker who is bored and stays at home often mopes around. The result—a lack of adequate exercise to maintain a healthy body.[57] It is a vicious circle.

Role Conflict How a person behaves in a given job depends on many factors. A combination of the expectations and demands an employee places upon him or herself and those of co-workers results in a set of forces called *role pressures*. When a situation arises in which two or more role pressures are in conflict with one another, role conflict exists. Role conflict exists whenever compliance with one set of pressures makes compliance with another set difficult, objectionable, or impossible.

Researchers have found that conflict is associated with job dissatisfaction and anxiety.[58] It has also been linked to heart disease, elevated blood pressure, and excessive eating. Role conflict seems to undermine a peaceful work state and leads to physiological and psychological changes.

Life Events Holmes and Rahe have studied how life events can contribute to a stressful life.[59] Based on their research they developed a numerical value for each life event, ranking the events in order of magnitude. After developing the scoring system, the medical histories and life events scores of patients were reviewed. It was found that patients who had a high score on what the researchers called the Social Readjustment Rating Scale (SRRS) were more likely to contract illness following the events. The SRRS is presented in Exhibit 18–8. People with scores of over 300 were very likely to contract some form of stress-related illness, such as ulcers, migraine headaches, colitis, and heart disease, in the near future.

The work of Holmes and Rahe with the SRRS points out the connection between life changes (stressors) and a lowered resistance to fight illness. This connection is illustrated by such information that 10 times as many widows and widowers die during the first year after the death of a spouse as non-widowed individuals in a similar age-group. Also, the illness rate for divorced persons during the first year after the divorce is 12 times higher than for married persons.

A Person Stressor: Type A Behavior Pattern In the 1950s two cardiologists, Friedman and Rosenman, began to look at the way a person's behavior pattern can be used to predict the incidence of coronary heart disease.[60] What they discovered was called the Type A behavior pattern. It is defined as:

---

[57] Michael J. Smith, "Recognition and Control of Psychosocial Job Stress," *Professional Safety,* August 1981, pp. 20–26.

[58] S. M. Sales and J. House, "Job Dissatisfaction as a Possible Risk Factor in Coronary Heart Disease," *Journal of Chronic Disease,* 1971, pp. 861–73.

[59] T. H. Holmes and R. H. Rahe, "The Social Readjustment Rating Scale," *Journal of Psychosomatic Medicine,* 1967, pp. 213–18.

[60] Meyer Friedman and Diane Ulmer, *Treating Type A Behavior and Your Heart* (New York: Alfred A. Knopf, 1984); and Meyer Friedman and R. Rosenman, *Type A Behavior and Your Heart* (New York: Alfred A. Knopf, 1974).

an action-emotion complex that can be observed in any person who is aggressively involved in a chronic, incessant struggle to achieve more and more in less and less time, and if required to do so, against the opposing efforts of other things or other persons.

The hard-core Type A person is hard-driving, competitive, has a sense of time urgency, and is chronically impatient with delays. (The opposite of the Type A is the Type B person.) Research has linked the Type A personality with coronary heart disease. Type A men have been found to experience 6½ times the incidence of heart disease than Type B men.[61] Also the Type A person has higher blood pressure than the Type B.

EXHIBIT 18–8   The Social Readjustment Rating Scale

Instructions: Check off each of these life events that has happened to you during the previous year. Total the associated points. A score of 150 or less means a relatively low amount of life change and a low susceptibility to stress-induced health breakdown. A score of 150 to 300 points implies about a 50 percent chance of a major health breakdown in the next two years. A score above 300 raises the odds to about 80 percent, according to the Holmes-Rahe statistical prediction model.

Life Events	Mean Value
1. Death of spouse	100
2. Divorce	73
3. Marital separation from mate	65
4. Detention in jail or other institution	63
5. Death of a close family member	63
6. Major personal injury or illness	53
7. Marriage	50
8. Being fired at work	47
9. Marital reconciliation with mate	45
10. Retirement from work	45
11. Major change in the health or behavior of a family member	44
12. Pregnancy	40
13. Sexual difficulties	39
14. Gaining a new family member (e.g., through birth, adoption, oldster moving in, etc.)	39
15. Major business readjustment (e.g., merger, reorganization, bankruptcy, etc.)	39
16. Major change in financial state (e.g., a lot worse off or a lot better off than usual)	38
17. Death of a close friend	37
18. Changing to a different line of work	36
19. Major change in the number of arguments with spouse (e.g., either a lot more or a lot less than usual regarding child rearing, personal habits, etc.)	35
20. Taking on a mortgage greater than $10,000 (e.g., purchasing a home, business, etc.)	31
21. Foreclosure on a mortgage or loan	30
22. Major change in responsibilities at work (e.g., promotion, demotion, lateral transfer)	29

---

[61] R. Rosenman, M. Friedman, R. Straus, C. Jenkins, S. Zyzanski, and M. Wurm, "Coronary Heart Disease in the Western Collaborative Group Study: A Follow-Up Experience of 4½ Years," *Journal of Chronic Disease,* 1970, pp. 173–90.

EXHIBIT 18–8 *(concluded)*

Life Events	Mean Value
23. Son or daughter leaving home (e.g., marriage, attending college, etc.)	29
24. In-law troubles	29
25. Outstanding personal achievement	28
26. Wife beginning or ceasing work outside the home	26
27. Beginning or ceasing formal schooling	26
28. Major change in living conditions (e.g., building a new home, remodeling, deterioration of home or neighborhood)	25
29. Revision of personal habits (dress, manners, associations, etc.)	24
30. Troubles with the boss	23
31. Major change in working hours or conditions	20
32. Change in residence	20
33. Changing to a new school	20
34. Major change in usual type and/or amount of recreation	19
35. Major change in church activities (e.g., a lot more or a lot less than usual)	19
36. Major change in social activities (e.g., clubs, dancing, movies, visiting, etc.)	18
37. Taking on a mortgage or loan less than $10,000 (e.g., purchasing a car, TV, freezer, etc.)	17
38. Major change in sleeping habits (a lot more or a lot less sleep, or change in part of day when asleep)	16
39. Major change in number of family get-togethers (e.g., a lot more or a lot less than usual)	15
40. Major change in eating habits (a lot more or a lot less food intake, or very different meal hours or surroundings)	15
41. Vacation	13
42. Christmas	12
43. Minor violations of the law (e.g., traffic tickets, jaywalking, disturbing the peace, etc.	11

NOTE: Today, items number 26 and 37 would have to be adjusted upward.

Source: Reprinted with permission from *Journal of Psychosomatic Research*, 11, no. 2, T. H. Holmes and R. H. Rahe, The Social Readjustment Rating Scale, pp. 213–18. Copyright 1967, Pergamon Press, Ltd.

There is little doubt that Type A behavior is associated in some ways to a number of diseases. The precise role it plays, however, is not clear. It is incorrect to definitely associate Type A with stress. Yet, there is likely to be more stress experienced by Type As. Type As tend to create stress for themselves by constantly exposing themselves to stressors that the Type B avoids, like work overload, handling too many projects, and always rushing to finish one job just to start a new job. The Type A person seems to be in a constant struggle with time and with other people. This behavior results in hyperaggressiveness that manifests itself as free-floating hostility.[62]

Pinpointing Worker Stress There are a number of methods available to managers for identifying stress within themselves and employees. The precise

---

[62] Matteson and Ivancevich, *Stress and Work*, p. 222.

identification of negative stress should be left to the professional. A well-trained behavioral scientist, physician, or counselor can use psychological tests, in-depth interviews, or medical history forms and medical tests to uncover stress problems.

The nonprofessional involved in pinpointing stress problems at work is the manager. He or she can also do some diagnosis. First, the manager should look for sudden, unexplained changes in mood, tensions, and loss of temper episodes. Second, when an efficient worker becomes sloppy or when a prompt worker becomes late, this signifies changes in behavior. This can be a signal that the person is experiencing stress.

Coping with Stress Stress in life is inevitable. However, when it hurts the person, co-workers, or the organization it must be addressed. There are two ways to cope with stress. The first is to eliminate the source of the stressor(s) that is causing the stress by changing policies, the structure, the work requirements, or whatever is necessary. The second approach is to deal with the stress individually or organizationally.

Individual stress coping programs include meditation, biofeedback, training, exercise, diet, and even prayer. These programs work for some people. They help the person feel better, relax, and regenerate energy. A few coping programs are briefly mentioned in Exhibit 18–9.

There are also organizational stress coping programs. In fact, some would call the Kimberly-Clark and Control Data Corporation approach a stress management program. Experts in organizations can use their knowledge about stress and employee health to develop and implement organizationally sponsored stress coping workshops and seminars.[63] In addition, these experts can recommend structural, job, and policy changes that can eventually improve the well-being of employees.

Levi Strauss & Co. has had an ongoing stress management program in which 1,500 employees have participated in an all-day seminar. Relaxation techniques and self-motivation procedures are taught, and the examination of life goals, identification of harmful personality traits, and behavior modification techniques are part of the program.[64]

At Employees Mutual Life Insurance Co. in Des Moines, Iowa, the stress coping program focuses on identifying individual stressors. Participants log a personal concerns inventory in which they rate the importance of 58 areas of concern for 21 days. It is assumed that just the identification of stressors is beneficial for helping individuals cope with stress.[65]

The P/HRM department has a role to play in stress coping programs. It can provide specialists, facilities, monitoring or evaluation, and other important resources. Organizations such as IBM, Tenneco, Control Data, Shell, and

---

[63] Michael T. Matteson and John M. Ivancevich, *Managing Job Stress and Health* (New York: Free Press. 1982).

[64] Susan Chase, "Putting the Stress on Control," *Corporate Fitness & Recreation,* August–September 1983, pp. 25–30.

[65] Ibid.

EXHIBIT 18–9   **Stress Coping Methods: A Few Samples**

Planning: Much stress in personal and work life can be managed by planning. Take some time to assess your personal and career goals. At work, set aside some time to plan tomorrows's activities. How do they relate to your goals or your company's goals?

Physical exercise: Regular exercise can contribute to the physical health of the individual, and it can also help the person overcome stress, both as an outlet and as physical conditioning. Of course, you should consult a physician before embarking on a strenuous exercise program.

Diet: Prolonged stress can deplete your body's supply of infection-fighting vitamins, leaving you susceptible to disease. Also, eating habits change under stress. The manager, up against a deadline, might well work through lunch or arrive late at dinner and unwind by downing a double scotch. During stressful periods, maintaining a good diet is essential.

Biofeedback: This therapeutic technique is used in the treatment of migraine headaches, high blood pressure, muscle tension, and other stress-related problems. It involves the monitoring of one or more body functions with electronic devices that signal the user with tones, clicks, or lights. For example, people can learn to control brain waves, pulse rate, blood pressure, and the temperature in their hands and feet.

Meditation or relaxation: Emerging from Far Eastern philosophies, these techniques include meditation, transcendental meditation, yoga, and Zen. The Americanization of meditation, which was popularized in Herbert Bensen's book *The Relaxation Response,* has a person sit in a comfortable chair in a quiet area with subdued lighting. The person closes his or her eyes, takes a deep breath, and exhales. Each time the person exhales, he or she repeats a single work or mantra. Repeating this single work helps to eliminate distracting throughts. This process takes approximately 20 minutes, although some individuals can achieve a refreshing relaxation in just a few moments.

Variations include tensing and relaxing muscles until relaxation of the entire body is reached. Others recommend thinking of a favorite vacation spot—a deserted beach or a calm lake—recalling all the sights and sounds.

Psychotherapy: A wide variety of interpersonal techniques are used that usually involve intensive one-to-one work with a professional therapist.

Psychoanalysis: This is a form of psychotherapy during which the therapist takes the patient into the depths of his or her personality to examine the root of abnormal behavior.

Prudential already have P/HRM employees performing such duties as setting up exercise classes, initiating fitness programs, and providing diet counseling. More and more organizations are expected to become concerned about and involved with stress management by the 1990s.

AIDS IN THE WORKPLACE

Since 1981 when the first known cases of Acquired Immune Deficiency Syndrome (AIDS) in the United States were reported, an estimated 1.5 million Americans have been infected with the virus. AIDS is an infectious disease in which the body's immune system is damaged in varying, often progressive degrees of severity. Evidence is mounting that the vast majority of people infected with the virus may eventually develop AIDS.

AIDS is clearly a devastating disease that is caused by a virus that breaks down part of the body's immune system, leaving a person defenseless against a variety of unusual, life-threatening illnesses. Each of the letters in AIDS stands for a word:

Acquired: The disease is passed from one person to another.

Immune: The body's defense system, which normally protects it from disease.

Deficiency: The defense system is not working.

Syndrome: A group of symptoms which, when they occur together, mean a person has a particular disease or condition.

Since AIDS was identified by the Centers for Disease Control (CDC), over 30,000 cases have been reported. Of these, 56 percent are deceased. Among adults, 66 percent of cases have occurred among homosexual and bisexual men; 17 percent among intravenous drug users; with an additional 8 percent among homosexual males who are also intravenous drug users; 1 percent among persons who are hemophiliacs or who have coagulation disorders, and the remaining 8 percent among persons who have contacted AIDS through heterosexual contact, transfusions, or who have no known risk factors.

AIDS has now been found in every state and in almost every foreign country. While ongoing research attempts to find both treatment and cure, no cure has yet been found—and the prognosis is that there may be no AIDS vaccine for 25 years or more. Today, a person with AIDS will incur between $40,000 and $140,000 in medical bills from diagnosis to death.[66]

By the year 1991, an estimated 324,000 will have contracted AIDS. Of these, 179,000 will have died. In addition, 10 million persons will be carriers. In 1991, an estimated 145,000 patients with AIDS will require health and support services that will cost between $8 and $20 billion.[67]

A poll conducted in 1987 of 600 senior personnel/human resource managers by Louis Harris and Associates, Inc., found that 89 percent of the respondents had no specific policy for dealing with employees who have AIDS. Eighty-five percent of those polled have no information program about AIDS for their employees, and 72 percent of those have no intention of implementing one.

Fear of AIDS At Work

A case of AIDS at work is a serious issue. Self-disclosure about AIDS raises the potential for retaliation from working peers, supervisors, and other employees in general.[68] At New England Telephone & Telegraph Company an employee named Paul told his supervisor that he had AIDS. The supervisor allegedly passed the information along to Paul's co-workers. Some of the co-workers began to threaten Paul. The AIDS victim sued his employers, charging handicap discrimination, breech of privacy, and other violations of Massachusetts state law. The case was settled out of court and Paul was reinstated. When Paul returned to work, his co-workers walked off the job. Medical experts were

---

[66] Michael Pollack, "Preparing for the Worst," *Nation's Business*, October 1987, pp. 28–30.

[67] Marilyn Chase, "In Lives and Dollars, the Epidemic's Toll Is Growing Inexorably," *The Wall Street Journal*, May 18, 1987, pp. 1 and 8.

[68] Mary P. Rowe, Malcom Russell-Einhorn, and Michael A. Baker, "The Fear of AIDS," *Harvard Business Review*, July–August 1986, pp. 28–36.

called in to discuss AIDS and how it is transmitted before the employees returned to work.

There are organizations that simply ignore AIDS since they do not want to be public about the disease. They fear tarnishing their image in the community. By not talking about AIDS, they hope that it will not become an issue. It is an issue and is likely to remain an issue for some time.

A firm that is attempting to alleviate fears about contracting AIDS is Levi Strauss & Co.[69] In 1982, Levi Strauss began bringing in medical experts on AIDS to speak to employees about the disease and answer questions during noontime sessions. The firm videotaped some of the sessions and made the tapes available to facilities in other parts of the country.

Today, the educational program at Levi Strauss is even more comprehensive. It features the package put together by the San Francisco AIDS Foundation which consists of a 23-minute video, informational brochures for employees, a manager's guide, and a guide for policy makers, medical specialists, and personnel/human resource management professionals. Small group sessions, usually lasting about 90 minutes, present the company's philosophy, health benefits, the disease and its transmission, as well as a medical update and a question-and-answer period. Levi Strauss employees fill the room up to get the best information they can about AIDS. Whether the Levi approach which works and is well received in San Francisco (a high AIDS incidence city) will work in other parts of the country is unfortunately questionable. Denying that AIDS is a workplace issue and concern is not going to reduce the fears of many people.

The Legal Battles About AIDS

AIDS is a debilitating disease with a potential for affecting job performance. Consequently, employers must consider the legal factors regarding AIDS victims as employees. There have been a growing number of lawsuits involving AIDS. In Chicago, a woman sued American Airlines because a ticket agent carrying the AIDS virus bit her in a scuffle over a boarding pass. American offered her $30,000 to settle the case, but the woman is seeking $10 million.[70]

When AIDS struck Vincent, the Orange County, California school system warned that the teacher might endanger his students lives. Its solution was to transfer him to office duties writing grant proposals. This transfer angered Vincent. He produced doctors' statements that he posed no health threat. A judge rejected Vincent's petition for a preliminary injunction to prevent his being moved from the classroom, but he is appealing the decision.[71]

John, a Raytheon employee, was placed on medical leave after he was diagnosed as having AIDS. His doctor said he posed no danger to co-workers.

---

[69] Dale Feuer, "AIDS at Work: Fighting the Fear," *Training*, June 1987, pp. 61–71.

[70] Roger Ricklefs, "AIDS Cases Prompt a Host of Lawsuits," *The Wall Street Journal*, October 7, 1987, p. 29.

[71] Ibid.

Raytheon claimed that the decision was based on the medical evidence available at the time and the uncertainty as to whether or not the health and safety of other employees would be threatened. The California Fair Employment and Housing Commission awarded lost pay and interest to John's estate. The commission stated that Raytheon's argument that AIDS might in the future be found to be casually transmissible was unsupported by any hard evidence. However, since Raytheon's misreading of the medical evidence was not malicious or oppressive, the Commission declined to award punitive damages.[72]

The American Federation of Government Employees sued the State Department to stop blood testing for AIDS employees and job applicants subject to overseas assignment. The State Department states that employees who might get sick should not be sent to areas with inadequate medical facilities. It says it will not hire applicants who test positive, but will retain current employees who do so. A federal judge in Washington denied the union's motion for a preliminary injunction against the testing program. He concluded that AIDS virus carriers are not suited for worldwide service.

The most important legislation affecting AIDS victims currently appears to be federal, state, and local laws dealing with handicap discrimination.[73] If AIDS is determined to be a handicap, then employers will be prohibited from discriminating against AIDS victims solely on the basis of the disease itself. At the federal level, Section 503 of the Vocational Rehabilitation Act of 1973 prohibits discrimination against the handicapped by employers receiving federal contracts, and Section 504 prohibits discrimination against the handicapped by employers receiving federal funds in their operations.

Most states have some form of handicap laws and some like Florida, Maine, Massachusetts, New Jersey, and New York have already acted to protect AIDS victims from discrimination based on their handicap statutes. California and Wisconsin have legislation protecting AIDS victims from employment discrimination.[74]

The courts interpretation of AIDS under various handicap statutes is an important decision. The trend points toward most courts considering AIDS victims to fall under the handicap category. In Florida, Todd was dismissed from his job because he was considered to pose a risk for co-workers who came into contact with him. The Florida Commission on Human Relations ruled that Todd was a victim of handicap discrimination. The commissioner also noted that employers could only discriminate based on handicap if the absence of the disability is a bona fide occupational qualification necessary to perform the job. This lawsuit was settled out of court, with the State of Florida agreeing to pay Todd $196,000 in back pay, medical bills, and attorney's fees, and to reinstate his health and life insurance.[75]

---

[72] Ibid.

[73] David L. Wing, "AIDS: The Legal Debate," *Personnel Journal,* August 1986, pp. 114–27.

[74] Robert H. Elliott and Thomas M. Wilson, "AIDS in the Workplace: Public Personnel Management and the Law," *Public Personnel Management,* Fall 1987, pp. 209–219.

[75] Ibid, p. 212.

The Center For Disease Control (CDC) claims that casual contact with persons with AIDS or who might be at risk for AIDS does not place an individual at risk for the illness. As of March 1988, no case of AIDS has been attributed to airborne infection or casual contact or touching. The CDC recommends that an employee with AIDS need not be restricted from work in any area including health care, food services, and dental care. For example, there is no evidence the AIDS virus is transmitted during the preparation or serving of food or beverages.

The CDC finds the greatest risk of transmission of the AIDS virus in the health care profession. To prevent transmission the CDC recommends health care workers wear gloves for direct contact with lesions, skin infections, and mucous membranes.[76] An employer's adherence to these precautionary recommendations has and will continue to be used in AIDS-related legal claims.

Developing and Implementing an AIDS Policy

As the Louis and Harris and Associate, Inc. survey of personnel/human resource managers shows there are few firms that have developed and implemented a workplace AIDS policy.[77] Employers and the courts are slowly beginning to face the realities of AIDS in the workplace. Before developing any policy there are a number of practical problems employers must be aware of regarding AIDS.

1. *Asking applicants if they have AIDS*. This is not an acceptable question. Asking whether a person is handicapped in such a way to inhibit him or her is acceptable. If the person volunteers that he or she has AIDS, an employer must determine if the disability will effect performance.
2. *Requiring job applicants to be tested for AIDS*. Some states prohibit employers from doing this test. Check the law and ask how the results will be used.
3. *If applicants' test positive for AIDS can they be denied a job?* They can be denied employment only if it is determined that the applicant can not perform the job.
4. *Can an employee with AIDS be disciplined, terminated, or placed on leave?* Again, as long as the job can be performed, he or she cannot be disciplined or terminated or placed on leave.
5. *Must an employer keep knowledge about an employee having AIDS or testing positive confidential?* Yes, there should be no medical information passed on to co-workers.
6. *Can an employer be held liable by employees who claim to have contracted AIDS on the job?* This is a difficult dilemma. The current state of medical knowledge indicates that AIDS cannot be transmitted through normal

---

[76] Thomas J. Coates, et al., "AIDS: A Psychosocial Research Agenda," *Annals of Behavioral Medicine,* Spring 1987, pp. 21–28.

[77] Phyllis S. Myers and Donald W. Myers, "AIDS: Tackling a Tough Problem through Policy," *Personnel Administrator,* April 1987, pp. 15, 97, 100, 102, 106–108, 143.

workplace interaction. Thus, it is questionable that the employer could be found guilty.

These practical guidelines should serve as the basis for developing an educational and support program on AIDS.[78] First, a policy statement that is medically accurate should be developed on AIDS. The AIDS virus, how the virus is spread, and the groups at greatest risk of contracting AIDS, should be spelled out in the policy documents. A statement regarding AIDS testing and the employer's position on such testing should be made clear. If the CDC guidelines are to be used the firm should state that they will not be conducting such tests for present employees. However, employers may establish pre-employment tests for all new potential employees.

If employees have AIDS or are expected to contract AIDS there is a need to state a position on continued employment. As long as performance standards are met employees should be assured of continued employment.

Information on physicians and counseling services and their confidentiality should be stated. There should also be information provided about insurance coverage. Knowledge and information in the form of a policy document can be useful in alleviating fear and correcting misinformation about AIDS.

The use of an in-house group such as those in the Employee Assistance Program (EAP) should be recommended. EAPs were originally designed as alcoholism-assistance programs. However, the services, support, and resources of such a group, if present in the firm, could be expanded to include AIDS victims.

The use of small group question and answer sessions such as those used by Levi Strauss could also be part of the AIDS program. Medical specialists, executives, and personnel/human resource specialists could serve as a panel to update and answer questions about AIDS in the workplace.

IBM has drafted an AIDS policy and also uses an AIDS brochure written by the Center for Disease Control. Every one of the 240,000 IBM domestic employees received the policies and brochures. IBMers affected by AIDS are encouraged to work as long as they are able, and they are assured of their privacy.[79] Until more firms like Levi Strauss and IBM develop and implement an AIDS policy and program there is little that can be said about how necessary and effective these programs are. Levi Strauss believes that their program is a success because of what has not happened. Approximately, 12 of 1,500 Levi Strauss, San Francisco employees have fallen victim to AIDS. There have been no lawsuits, employees refusing to work with AIDS victims, and demands for reassignments. Levi Strauss believes that their AIDS policy and program is working.

---

[78] William S. Waldo, "A Practical Guide for Dealing with AIDS at Work," *Personnel Journal,* August 1987, pp. 135–38.

[79] Marilyn Chase, "Corporations Urge Peers to Adopt Humane Policies for AIDS Victims," *The Wall Street Journal,* January 20, 1988, p. 25.

EMPLOYEE ASSISTANCE PROGRAMS (EAPs)

Instead of having separate preventive health, alcohol abuse, and drug abuse programs, some organizations have developed a total, all-encompassing approach that is called *employee assistance programs (EAPs)*. In 1972, General Motors began its own in-house EAP as a joint venture of labor and management. Specialists and interested individuals from labor management, and the company's medical department make up the EAP team.[80]

Some present-day EAPs retain a focus that is traced back to programs in the early 1940s that were designed wholly to address the problem of alcoholism.[81] However, other firms have EAPs to help employees with personal and work-related problems. AT&T has a program that deals with medical or behavioral problems. Counseling and help is provided by the EAP at AT&T for emotional problems, minor anxiety and depression, family, marital, or financial problems. The AT&T program is designed to help employees deal with their problems.[82]

EAPs are not therapy programs. They focus on minor problems as they occur or refer employees to an accredited professional if the problem is more pronounced. In most EAPs, like AT&T's, the cornerstone is voluntary participation. Posters, fliers, pay envelope inserts, and bulletin boards are used to inform employees how to use the EAP. A common theme is the confidential nature of the EAP.

A company's EAP can become a calming voice among overreactors to AIDS in the workplace. The EAP can serve as a resource in developing an AIDS policy. The professional personnel in an EAP can also help interpret and implement legislation dealing with AIDS.[83] Employees could enter an EAP that includes an AIDS support staff through self-referral or management referral. EAP directors teach managers to "constructively work with" employees who are AIDS victims.

Program directors have made claims that traditional EAPs have resulted in reduced absenteeism, lower medical care costs, and reduced replacement costs.[84] At AT&T, 59 participants in the EAP were judged to be in serious jeopardy of being terminated. Replacing them would have been costly. Unfortunately, most of the favorable comments about EAPs are based on opinion and not publicly documented research results. To date, there are no studies

---

[80] David Hall, "Employee Assistance Programs: The Helping Hand That's Good for All," *Corporate Fitness & Recreation*, October–November 1982, pp. 43–49.

[81] T. S. Denenberg and R. V. Denenberg, *Alcohol and Drugs: Issues in the Workplace* (Washington, D.C.: Bureau of Consumer Affairs, 1983).

[82] Lettieri, "Confronting Employee Drug Abuse," p. 35.

[83] *AIDS: The Workplace Issues,* New York: AMA Management Briefing, 1985.

[84] D. W. Meyers, "A Standard Measure of EAPs," *EAP Digest*, September–October 1984, pp. 15–20.

that evaluate how EAPs that deal with AIDS issues are doing in terms of effectiveness.

WORKERS' COMPENSATION AND DISABILITY PROGRAMS

Disability programs are designed to help workers who are ill or injured and cannot work (see Chapter 11). Employees show little preference for them. Although before his accident Dale Silas in the opening P/HRM In Action was probably not too interested in workers' compensation, he is now. He's also interested in Lysander's health insurance plan.

There are three programs in the United States for private- and third-sector employees. One is federal. The social security system is called OASDI, and the "DI" stands for disability insurance. A person who is totally disabled and unable to work can receive a small payment, perhaps $60 a week, from social security until age 65. As with other social security programs, this is financed by employer and employee payroll contributions.

The second program is the state-run workers' compensation, financed by employer payments. It pays for permanent partial, total partial, or total disability arising from employment. Requirements, payments, and procedures vary somewhat from state to state. Workers' compensation systems are compulsory in most states. For federal goverment employees, the Federal Employees Compensation Act of 1949 (last amended in 1974) provides for payments for accidents and injuries paralleling workers' compensation.

The compensation comes in two forms: monetary reimbursement and payment of medical expenses. The amount of compensation is based on fixed schedules of minimum and maximum payments. Disability payments are often based on formulas of the employees' earnings, modified by economic conditions and the number of dependents. There is usually a week's waiting period prior to the payment of the compensation and fixed compensation for permanent losses (such as, New Jersey's 1984 rate was $48,161 for the loss of an arm).

The employee receives workers' compensation no matter whose fault an accident is. Payment is made for physical impairments and for neuroses that may result from a physical loss. The employer must also pay compensation for diseases that result from occupations (such as black lung disease in mining) and for the results of undue stress laid on employees, such as hernias resulting from lifting heavy materials. Both workers' compensation laws and OSHA require the employer to keep detailed accident and death records.

The employer pays the entire cost of workers' compensation, usually by participating in private insurance plans or state-run systems or by self-insurance. The improvement of safety conditions at the work site can lead to lower insurance costs if accidents decline as a result.

The cost of workers' compensation varies by industry and type of work. For example, in a recent year, the average firm devoted less than 1 percent of its total compensation to workers' compensation. This varied from 1.5 percent for nonoffice, nonmanufacturing jobs to a low of 0.03 percent for office employees.

But workers' compensation claims went from $3.9 to over $20 billion from 1972 to 1981.[85]

In some states, if the employee will receive social security disability payments, workers' compensation is adjusted so that a joint maximum (for example, $80 per week) is not exceeded.

Criticism of workers' compensation programs centers on the fact that the systems were designed to prevent hardship but not to discourage return to work or rehabilitation of the injured worker. The National Commission on State Workers' Compensation was very critical of state workers' compensation plans. It found that the benefits are too low, and too many employers have inadequate accident prevention programs. The commission made 80 specific recommendations to the states that, if not actuated, should be legislated by Congress.

The third program under which employees receive workers' compensation is private disability insurance provided by employers. About two thirds of the companies surveyed provide accident and sickness insurance to their employees (usually for blue-collar workers). A variation for white-collar workers is sick pay-salary continuance insurance. About 85 percent of the companies surveyed have this. These plans pay wages or salaries to employees with short-term disabilities. Generally they supplement workers' compensation. Long-term disability pay or pensions for employees was also being offered by 74 percent of companies surveyed for managers, 62 percent for white-collar employees, and 28 percent for blue-collar workers. This insurance is designed to supplement government programs and bring total compensation up to a more livable level. Luckily for Dale Silas, Lysander does have disability coverage.

EVALUATION OF SAFETY AND HEALTH PROGRAMS

Health and (especially) safety programs have begun to receive more attention in recent years. The consequences of inadequate programs are measurable: increased workers' compensation payments, an increased number of lawsuits, larger insurance costs, fines from OSHA, and union pressures. A safety management program requires these steps:

1. Establishment of indicator systems (for example, accident statistics).
2. Development of effective reporting systems.
3. Development of rules and procedures.
4. Rewarding supervisors for effective management of the safety function.

Top-management support is needed, and proper design of jobs and worker-machine interactions is necessary, but probably the key is participation by employees.

A health and safety program can be evaluated fairly directly in a cost/

---

[85] Berkeley Rice, "Can Companies Kill?" *Psychology Today*, June 1981, pp. 80–85.

benefits sense. The costs of safety specialists, new safety devices, and other measures can be calculated. Reductions in accidents, lowered insurance costs, and lowered fines can be weighed against these costs. Studies evaluating safety and health programs show that safety is cost-effective.

In one study, 54 respondents were interviewed and another 86 respondents completed questionnaires in the chemical, paper, and wood-product industries in Texas.[86] It was determined that the most cost-effective safety programs were *not* the most expensive ones. They were programs that combined a number of safety approaches: safety rules, off-the-job safety, and safety training, safety orientation, safety meetings, medical facilities and staff, and strong top-management participation and support of the safety program. Engineering and nonengineeing approaches were used, but the emphasis was on the engineering aspects of safety. Cost/benefits studies for health and safety programs can be very helpful in analyzing and improving them.

SUMMARY

Effective safety and health programs can exist in all organizations. The nature of the safety program varies, of course, as the diagnostic approach emphasizes.

To summarize the major points covered in this chapter:

1. Safety hazards are those aspects of the work environment that have the potential of immediate and sometimes violent harm to an employee.
2. Health hazards are those aspects of the work environment that slowly and cumulatively lead to deterioration of an employee's health.
3. Some tragic safety and health problems have been highly publicized such as the Bhopal, India gas leak, the Three Mile Island accident, and the NASA Challenger loss.
4. Support from top management and unions for health and safety programs helps ensure their effectiveness.
5. The major causes of occupational accidents are the task to be done, the working conditions, and the employee.
6. Organizational responses to health and safety challenges include:
   a. Safety design and preventive approaches.
   b. Inspection, reporting, and accident research.
   c. Safety training and motivation programs.
   d. Auditing safety programs.
   e. Health programs for employees.
7. A growing number of firms are attempting to control or prohibit smoking at work.

---

[86] Foster Rinefort, "A New Look at Occupational Safety," *Personnel Administrator,* November 1977, pp. 29–36.

A RETURN TO THE P/HRM · IN · ACTION

After the visit to Bob's plant, Clint returned to his own. He did not feel good, thinking that maybe a safety unit could have prevented Dale's accident. That night, he drove to Denver to visit Dale in the hospital. There was good news: Dale would not be totally disabled. He would be handicapped, but he would be able to work about half the time after his recuperation.

Clint had taken the time to check with Otto Richmond of the P/HRM department about the company's disability plan and workers' compensation. He could tell Dale that, between the two plans, his compensation would be kept up at its normal level.

Clint: I feel very upset though, Dale. Maybe, just maybe, your accident needn't have happened. So I'm hiring a

safety specialist as soon as possible to try to avoid similar accidents in the future.

Dave: I'm glad you are. But it was my fault too. I've been at Lysander a long time. I know I shouldn't have done that with the machine. I just got sloppy.

Clint: The best news I've gotten in a long time is that you'll be back. Will you help me with the safety program?

Dale: I'm a living witness of what can happen if you're not safety-conscious. You can bet I'll be behind the safety program.

In the years that followed, Lysander's safety record improved. The improvement was at least partly due to the new safety program Clint installed.

8. The Occupational Safety and Health Act is the culmination of the movement for federal supervision of health safety programs. It has requirements such as:
   a. Meeting safety standards set by OSHA.
   b. Submitting to OSHA inspections.
   c. Keeping records and reporting accidents and illnesses.
9. Stress can play a major role in the health of employees. Thus, more firms are now concerned about understanding and managing stress. Individual- and organizational-based stress management programs are being used.
10. Today, more and more organizations have initiated preventive health programs. These are designed to improve the health and well-being of employees.
11. AIDS is a devastating disease that has become a problem that managers must address. Some firms are attempting to educate the workforce so that misconceptions and fear do not create a nonproductive work environment.
12. Employee assistance programs (EAPs) have been used to help employees deal with personal, family, and work problems. Present-day EAPs are

beginning to expand beyond focusing solely on alcoholism as they did in earlier programs in the 1940s. Developing an AIDS support program would seem to be an important expansion of EAP services.

13. Workers' compensation and disability programs are designed to help workers who are ill or injured and cannot work.

Exhibit 18–10 provides recommendations on health and safety for the model organizations described in Exhibit 1–7 (Chapter 1).

Questions for Review and Discussion

1. How do top managers, operating executives, employees, union officials, safety committees, and safety specialists interact to make the workplace healthy and safe?
2. Why would an EAP that is involved in AIDS education and support be needed in a highly productive and successful company?

EXHIBIT 18–10   Recommendations on Health and Safety for Model Organizations

Type of Organization	Formal Safety Department	Safety as Duty of P/HRM Specialist	Formal Health Department	Arrangement with Health Team	Preventive Health Programs	Stress Management Programs (Organizations)	AIDS Program
1. Large size, low complexity, high stability	X		X			X	X
2. Medium size, low complexity, high stability	X			X		X	X
3. Small size, low complexity, high stability		X		X			
4. Medium size, moderate complexity, moderate stability	X			X	X	X	X
5. Large size, high complexity, low stability	X		X		X	X	X
6. Medium size, high complexity, low stability	X			X	X	X	X
7. Small size, high complexity, low stability				X	X		

3. What is the meaning of the person/environment fit concept?
4. Why should organizations be concerned about the consequences of occupational stress?
5. Are smokers rights being violated by nonsmoking policies?
6. What are some major causes of accidents and work-related illnesses?
7. Describe some of the programs organizations used to prevent accidents and illnesses. Which are the most effective? Least effective?
8. Why is there some resistance in organizations regarding the development of an AIDS policy and program?
9. Why did the U.S. government legislate in the occupational safety and health area?
10. What legal requirements must an organization follow in the health and safety area?

GLOSSARY

Accident Research. The systematic evaluation of the evidence concerning accidents and health hazards.

AIDS. Acquired Immune Deficiency Syndrome is an infectious disease in which the body's immune system is damaged. Thus, AIDS victims are susceptive to many diseases.

Employee Assistance Programs. (EAP) A program designed to help employees with personal, family, and work problems. Although these programs are voluntary, managers are instructed on how to confront the problems when they occur.

Health. The state of physical, mental, and social well-being.

Health Hazards. Those aspects of the work environment which slowly and cumulatively (and often irreversibly) lead to deterioration of an employee's health.

Life Events. The changes in a person's life that can contribute to stress.

Occupational Safety and Health Act (1970). An act designed to protect the safety and health of employees. According to this act, employers are responsible for providing workplaces free from hazards to safety and health.

Occupational Safety and Health Administration (OSHA). The government agency responsible for carrying out and administering the Occupational Safety and Health Act.

Preventive Programs. A program instituted within an organization to achieve a high level of employee wellness and to decrease health impairment costs. Programs typically involve health screening exams, stress testing, and physician recommendations.

Safety Hazards. Those aspects of the work environment that have the potential of immediate and sometimes violent harm to an employee.

Stress. A person's physical, chemical, and mental reactions to stressors or stimuli in the environment—the boss, co-workers, P/HRM policies, and so on.

Type A Behavior Pattern. An action-emotion complex that can be observed in a person who is aggressive, in a struggle against time, competitive, and chronically impatient.

APPLICATION CASE 18–1   Du Pont: A Leader in Safety and Health*

At Du Pont, a company whose origins are in gunpowder, safety is very important. The Du Pont plant in Kinston, North Carolina, has a record of more than 66 million hours worked without a disabling injury. The hours started accumulating in 1964. The record went until 1977 when a worker slipped on an icy sidewalk outside the plant and sustained a head injury. If the Kinston plant had incurred injuries at the same rate as an average chemical plant of similar size, it would have experienced 366 injuries.

The story of Kinston is a classic one that shows that safety pays. Visitors to the plant are greeted by a large sign bragging about safety. This is the case throughout Du Pont plants. The founder of the corporation, Eleuthere Irene Du Pont, was a French immigrant who was an assistant to a chemist in France. At a time when most U.S. firms took few precautions to control accidents, fire, explosions, or employee injuries, Mr. Du Pont was ahead of his time. He designed his gunpowder mills to minimize the potential damage in the event of an explosion.

Each plant—located on the banks of the Brandywine Creek near Wilmington, Delaware—was built with three heavy stone walls. The fourth wall was made of light wood and faced the stream. In the event of an explosion, the risk was limited to one building; the force would vent itself by blowing the roof and wooden wall toward the water.

Today Du Pont, which has more than 130,000 employees at more than 140 manufacturing sites worldwide, produces more than 1,700 products. Du Pont is known as a safety leader and trend setter in 30 countries. In 1980, Du Pont's U.S. lost workday incidence rate was .039 injuries per 200,000 hours, representing a total of 40 injuries for a population of 106,000 employees. This means that the company's workers' compensation costs would be 68 times higher if its safety performance were no better than that of the rest of the U.S. industry. The motto at Du Pont is to use plant safety statistics to determine how well managers are performing.

The first step for new employees at the Kinston plant is to sign up at the payroll department. The second step is to pick up personal safety gear. Employees attend a 30-minute safety meeting once each month. Du Pont considers this so important that it pays its shift workers overtime for their attendance at these meetings.

The Kinston plant manager and his superintendents, about 10 in all, serve as the central safety committee; they meet each morning at the plant. Safety isn't the only topic the committee covers, but it is always first on the agenda.

* Adapted from John Teresko, "The Safest Plant in the World," *Industry Week*, October 5, 1981, pp. 45–47.

Each superintendent has a safety committee in his department. Production employees serve with supervisors on these committees.

As safety inspections are made so regularly, it is a safe assumption that, at almost any given time, an inspection is taking place somewhere in the plant. Each week the plant manager visits some area of the plant to make a safety inspection; each member of the central committee is also responsible for one inspection each week.

Bulletin boards throughout work areas have safety messages and posters. Videotaped safety presentations are shown to employees in the lunchroom. Off-the-job risks such as winter road hazards, home safety, firearms, and sports and fitness are also shown on videotapes.

Du Pont has a history of being safety and health leaders. In 1818, a Du Pont plant explosion killed 40 employees. Du Pont pensioned the widows and gave them houses to live in and undertook the education and medical care expenses of the children. In 1915, the company hired a full-time medical director. Records show that now Du Pont has approximately 73 full-time physicians, 58 part-time physicians, 150 physicians on a fee-for-service basis, and 202 full-time nurses. Also to safeguard the health of employees who work with Du Pont chemical products, the company in 1935 established the Haskell Laboratory for Toxicology & Industrial Medicine. In 1982 it had about 280 employees.

About the time OSHA came into existence, Du Pont began to market its in-house expertise in safety management. Du Pont's annual sales of "how to" expertise and equipment totals about $36 million. These sales have helped Du Pont's image as a safety and health leader and its balance sheet.

Behind Du Pont's internal safety performance and its success in merchandising its expertise is an appreciation of the high cost of work-related accidents. Du Pont estimates that the average cost to a company of a lost-time injury incident is between $10,000 and $11,000. Additional costs of workers' compensation, and lost-time injuries constitute a profit drain amounting to an estimated average of 4 percent of total profits.

Questions for Thought

1. What do you think about Du Pont's use of safety statistics in the appraisal of managers' performance?
2. Since Du Pont has such a successful history in safety and health management do you feel it is possible to attain a zero-risk accident and injury goal? Why?
3. Do you feel that Du Pont is a good model for other firms involved in manufacturing or working with dangerous products? Why?

VI

WORK SCHEDULING AND QUALITY OF WORK LIFE AND EVALUATION OF PERSONNEL/ HUMAN RESOURCE MANAGEMENT

A person's work schedule can have an impact on his or her work behavior and performance as well as affect activities outside of work. The importance of properly scheduling work and the quality of work life is emphasized in Chapter 19, Work Scheduling, Flexitime, part-time, job sharing, and compressed workweek schedules are analyzed in terms of employee reactions. Where, why, and how these types of schedules are used is covered. Quality circles and other worker participation programs are discussed in terms of benefits, costs, and limitations. In Chapter 20, evaluating the P/HRM Function, the methods required to examine the impact of the P/HRM function are examined. Measurement of the costs and benefits of the P/HRM function is an important practice occurring in an increasing number of organizations. This final chapter takes another look at P/HRM managers as they perform their important jobs in organizations of all sizes.

19

WORK SCHEDULING AND QUALITY OF WORK LIFE PROGRAMS

LEARNING OBJECTIVES

After studying this chapter, you should be able to:

- **Define** the traditional workweek, flexitime, permanent part-time employment, job sharing, and the compressed workweek.
- **Describe** why quality of work life programs are considered to be important for achieving organizational goals.
- Explain why fatigue may be an especially troublesome problem with the compressed workweek.
- **Discuss** some of the employee benefits derived from flexitime, part-time, and job-sharing schedules.
- **Distinguish** between quality of work life and productivity

KEY TERMS

Compressed Workweek (CWW)
Core Work Time
Flexitime Work Schedules
Flexible Work Time
Job Sharing
New Design Plants
Quality Circles
Quality of Work Life (QWL)

CHAPTER OUTLINE

P/HRM · IN · ACTION

Amanda Wilson

The turnover of registered nurses at La Grange Community Hospital in La Grange, Illinois, had become epidemic. The hospital, located in a suburb of Chicago, employed over 450 nurses. Amanda Wilson was hired about six months ago as the hospital administrator. She noticed that the turnover at La Grange Community was higher than any other hospital of similar size in the area. Amanda assigned Jack Quenton, an in-house (hospital-employed) P/HRM researcher, to examine the problem. Jack worked on the problem for about three months.

Last week Jack submitted a report to Amanda. The report was based on a review of the hospital's P/HRM programs, what other hospitals in the area were doing in terms of P/HRM programs, and exit interviews Jack had conducted with 30 nurses who had quit La Grange Community recently. As Amanda worked her way through the thorough report, she was especially astonished by the exit interview data. It showed that most of the "leavers"— the nurses who had quit—wanted a more flexible working schedule. They had objected to the standard eight-hour shifts.

The report recommended that La Grange Community immediately undertake a pilot experiment of instituting a flexitime working schedule in the medical-surgical wards. The experiment would run for one year and then decisions about schedules in other units such as maternity, emergency, operating room, and intensive care would be made.

Amanda asked Jack to provide her with more details on nontraditional work schedules like flexitime. She wanted to see what others had done and whether flexitime could be used in nursing. The details Jack presented to Amanda are similar to the material covered in this chapter.

Despite a growing number of experiments to change the length and arrangement of the five-day, 40-hour workweek it has remained a fixture in industry for over 40 years. Since 1940, the workweek has been relatively stable, despite a growing feeling that many people would derive more satisfaction from an increase in leisure time. The traditional work schedule remains: (1) five days,

40 hours; (2) from 9 A.M. to 5 P.M.; (3) Monday-Friday; and (4) with a standard lunch hour and a few coffee breaks daily.

From about 1970, however, industry, government, education, and health care institutions have become interested in new kinds of work schedules. This chapter will examine a few of the newer schedules, namely flexitime (in which employees vary their starting and stopping time), part-time, work sharing (in which two workers share the job; e.g., one works the morning, the other works the afternoon), and compressed workweeks (working less than five days, for instance, a four-day, 10-hour day schedule). P/HRM departments are naturally involved in the decision making that goes into work scheduling. Specifically, P/HRM specialists aid management in examining, implementing, and evaluating alternative work schedules. These P/HRM activities are extremely important in devising work schedules that contribute to improved morale, increased productivity, and enhanced leisure time gratification.

Breaking the traditional patterns of work scheduling for the sake of change is not the reason why newer work schedules are being considered by more and more organizations. They are being given serious consideration because in a number of experiments and settings they have been associated with improved end results—satisfaction, performance, and morale. This chapter will examine not only work scheduling, but also the kind of impact it is having on people and organizations. Ten years ago, the work schedules presented in this chapter were a German import—foreign, different, and of questionable value. There are about 9.5 million full-time workers in the United States using flexible work schedules and compressed workweeks, and an additional 11.8 million workers hold voluntary, permanent part-time jobs.[1] This constitutes about 20 percent of the entire labor force in the United States.

THE CHANGING WORK ENVIRONMENT

Changes and questioning about work schedules are occurring at an accelerated rate in organizations. In this chapter our focus is on work scheduling changes and questions that have been raised about scheduling practices. A few of these questions are:

- Most Americans work a 9-to-5 schedule, five days a week. Since 1940 this has been the predominant pattern. Is this what workers really want?
- The standard five-day, 40-hour-a-week work schedule offers organizations consistency, ease of administration, and predictability. What does it offer the worker?
- Many workers report dissatisfaction with their jobs. Is a major contributing cause the lockstep work schedules they have?
- Most workers pour into cities and towns to their jobs, lemminglike, at the same time every morning, and then leave together every evening. The result

---

[1] *New Work Schedules for a Changing Society* (Scarsdale, New York: Work in America Institute, 1981), p. 3.

is clogged roads, jammed public transportation, and frayed nerves. Is there any way this type of clogging and jamming can be reduced?[2]

These facts of everyday living pose interesting challenges to P/HRM specilists. The challenges and questions raised will be addressed by examining actual company use of new work schedules. Their answers will indicate that today's work environment is demanding changes in the traditional work schedules. The changes of expectations place a premium on improved management of organizational time and resources.

Workers' expectations about the job, the organization, and the family unit are different from those of a generation ago. Today, many workers are requesting jobs that have security, provide an acceptable level of earnings and fringe benefits, but also provide more autonomy, responsibility, and opportunity for self-development. The work ethic still exists, but there is now a request for increased self-dignity.

More and more workers claim that they would like to exchange some work time for more personal time. By personal time they mean time for leisure, family, household tasks, and education. Time to develop hobbies and to enjoy the fruits of hard work.[3]

Family structures have changed dramatically in the past 10 years. The "traditional family" of husband (breadwinner), wife (homemaker), and two children has all but vanished. Only 7 percent of all family units fit this model.[4] In many families, both husband and wife work; there are also more single-parent families, and a large number of single people. Many of these trends create the potential for conflict between work (the job) and home (the family, leisure time).

Productivity pressures, increased competition, and a concern about treating people more fairly have also encouraged many employers to examine new work schedules. The concept of viewing workers as assets in accounting terms is gaining acceptance in more organizations.

Another change is the employer's concern over energy and transportation problems. Despite increases in the fuel efficiency of smaller cars, the cost and time to commute by car from home to work and back is a continuing problem. Employers are responding to this problem by encouraging car pooling, offering van-pooling programs, and encouraging public transportation authorities to increase and improve their service.

Energy consumption and conservation are now regular agenda issues discussed by organizations. Ways to contain costs of heating, cooling, lighting, and operating offices and plants are constantly being examined. This examination includes paying attention to the impact of work schedules on energy costs.

---

[2] Stanley D. Nollen, "What Is Happening to Flexitime, Flexihour, Gliding Time, the Variable Day, and Permanent Part-Time Employment, and the Four-Day Week?" *Across the Board*, April 1980, p. 6.

[3] Paul Blyton, *Changes in Working Time: An International Review*, New York: St. Martins Press, 1985.

[4] *New Work Schedules for a Changing Society*, p. 20.

A DIAGNOSTIC APPROACH
TO WORK SCHEDULING

Exhibit 19–1 examines how work scheduling is affected by various factors in the environment. Work-scheduling decision makers must pay attention to external environment influences. The union in some cases has resisted changes in work scheduling. Unions have a disdain for tampering with overtime laws. It took the union time, patience, argument, and lobbying to gain the 8-hour day and the 40-hour week. Overtime work at a premium pay is something the union is fearful of losing with the move toward more part-time employment and compressed workweeks.

Government legislation affects work schedules. In fact, the Walsh-Healy Public Contracts Act of 1936 and the Fair Labor Standards Act of 1938 were passed to reduce hours of work and encourage the spreading of work among unemployed people.

Economic conditions also play a role in work scheduling. Downturns, stagflation, and other conditions have resulted in an increase in part-timers and a decrease in the number of hours worked by full-time employees.

The goals of management also play a major role in work scheduling. Management may feel that work schedules can affect morale, satisfaction, and productivity; and, if so, managers would be inclined to experiment with scheduling. On the other hand, management may want a schedule that is easy to administer; in that case, it is best to stay with the traditional one. However, other workers may not prefer a nontraditional work schedule. Determining these preferences, attitudes, and motivations about work schedules is the responsibility of line managers and P/HRM specialists. Implementing a changed work schedule without diagnosing what workers want and think is likely to be a costly, frustrating mistake.

LEGISLATION: THE GOVERNMENT

Unions have displayed positive interest in some of the new work schedules, but they are concerned about violations of the law. The union wants to protect its members from the exploitation that is possible through some of the new work schedules. Most collective bargaining agreements require premium pay (usually time and a half) after eight hours of work in a day. In fact, the Fair Labor Standards Act requires overtime pay after 40 hours a week for employees in interstate commerce and public administration.

Many compressed workweek schedules call for 9, 10, 11, or 12 hours of work a day. It would be uneconomical for employers to pay overtime rates for those extra hours. Flexitime with fixed workdays of eight hours or less are no problem with labor unions. But when the flexitime schedule permits variable length days (8½, 9, 10 hours), the union often raises the issue of exploitation and the law.

P/HRM specialists must consult and be knowledgeable about four federal statutes when considering changes in work schedules. The Fair Labor Standards Act of 1938 has already been presented. The Walsh-Healy Public Con-

EXHIBIT 19–1   **Factors Affecting the Work Scheduling Decisions**

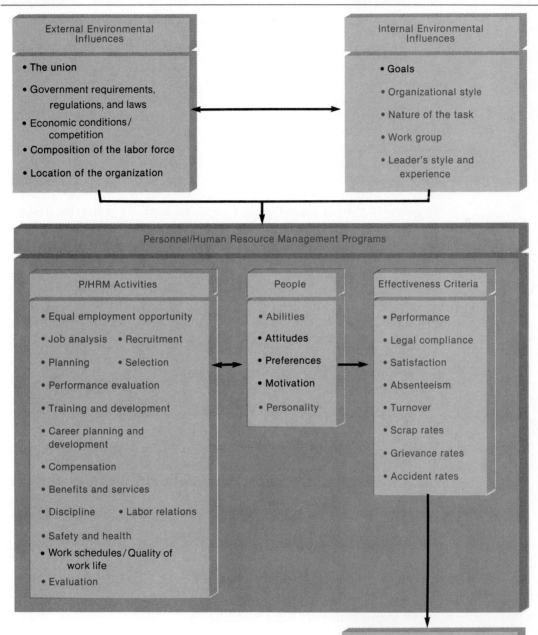

tracts Act requires overtime pay after eight hours a day for employees working on federal contracts of more than $10,000.[5] The Contract Work Hours and Safety Standards Act requires overtime pay after eight hours on federal construction contracts. The Federal Pay Act is applied to all nonexempt federal workers. It requires overtime pay after 8 hours a day or 40 hours a week. These laws exempt many supervisory and professional employees who have been able to be placed on new work schedules. Many blue-collar workers would like to have the same scheduling opportunities, but are hemmed in by the very laws that have protected them for years.

Several unions have been able to accept changes in traditional work schedules without giving up the protection of the law. Local 21 of the International Federation of Professional and Technical Employees, at the request of its members, negotiated flexitime agreements in California. About 1,000 union members, all white-collar employees, were covered. The agreement was that: (1) the contract contain explicit language about worker's protection and provide an appropriate grievance procedure for overtime disputes, and (2) the employees must be held accountable for meeting their time requirements. One contract with Almeda County set up an 80-hour pay period rather than a 40-hour week or 8-hour day.[6]

Of course, even in situations that are nonunion the laws must be followed regarding work scheduling. One challenge is to increase the flexibility of new work scheduling alternatives without violating the law. Building in such flexibility will require more cooperation and agreement between labor and management. Agreement can only occur if the details and specifics of each work scheduling alternative are clearly understood.

FLEXITIME

Flexible work hours (*flexitime* for short) means that employees are able to select their starting and quitting times within limits set by management.[7] A flexible schedule can differ in a number of ways: (1) daily versus periodic choice of starting and quitting time; (2) variable versus constant length of workday (crediting and debiting hours is allowed); and (3) core time—the management-imposed requirement of hours when all employees must be on the job. The different types of flexitime going from the least to the most flexible are:

> *Flexitour*. Requires employees to select specific starting and quitting time, and work on the schedule for a specific period like a week or month. The work period is usually eight hours.

---

[5] Richard I. Henderson, *Compensation Management* (Reston Publishing, 1985), p. 68.

[6] Stanley Nollen and Virginia Hider Martin, *Alternative Work Schedules* (New York: AMACOM, 1978).

[7] Many interesting examples of flexitime scheduling can be found in Stanley Nollen, *New Work Schedules in Practice: Managing Time in a Changing Society* (New York: Van Nostrand Reinhold, 1981).

EXHIBIT 19–2 Use of Flexitime in the United States by Occupation and Industry, 1980 (Full-Time Nonfarm Wage and Salary Workers)

Occupation and Industry	Number (000)	Percent
All occupations	7,638	11.9
Professional and technical workers	1,914	15.8
Managers and administrators	1,622	20.2
Sales workers	878	26.5
Clerical workers	1,296	9.8
Craft workers	753	7.4
Operatives, except transport equipment	387	4.4
Transport equipment operatives	388	14.3
Laborers	214	7.3
Service workers	569	8.7
Occupations excluding professional and technical workers, managers and administrators, and sales workers	3,608	8.1
All industries	7,922	11.9
Mining	83	10.6
Construction	439	10.1
Manufacturing	1,516	7.9
Transportation and public utilities	620	11.7
Wholesale and retail trade	1,633	4.7
Finance, insurance, and real estate	725	17.1
Professional services	1,555	11.4
Other services	696	16.9
Federal public administration, except postal	404	24.9
Postal service	47	7.6
State public administration	125	14.4
Local public administration	148	8.9

Source: U.S. Bureau of Labor Statistics, news release, February 24, 1981.

Gliding time. Variation in starting and quitting time is permitted, but workday total is usually eight hours.

Variable day. Credit and debit of work hours is permitted (such as working 10 hours one day and 6 hours on another day), as long as the total hours worked are even at the end of the week (40) or month (160).

Maniflex. Credit and debit hours are permitted, and a core time is not required on all days. The core may be 10 A.M. until 2 P.M. Monday and Friday only.

Flexiplace. An employee can change the location of work as well as the hours—working at home, at satellite locations, and so on, are examples.

As of 1980, the U.S. Bureau of Labor Statistics estimated that about 11.9 percent of all full-time nonfarm wage and salary workers use a form of flexitime.[8] There are also many professionals, sales personnel, professors, and managers who set their own work hours informally who are not counted in the flexitime statistics. Exhibit 19–2 presents a breakdown of flexitime by occupations and industries.

---

[8] U.S. Department of Labor, U.S. Bureau of Labor Statistics, "Ten Million Americans Work Flexible Schedules, 2 Million Work Full Time in Three to Four-and-a-Half Days," news release, (Washington, D.C.: Office of Information, February 24, 1981).

EXHIBIT 19–3   **Growth in Usage of Flexitime in the United States**

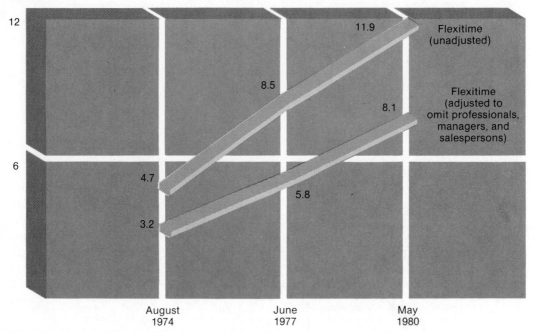

Note: Estimates are obtained from three different surveys whose methodology, coverage, and reliability differ.

Source: For flexitime data, for 1980: U. S. Bureau of Labor Statistics, news release, February 24, 1981; for 1977; Stanley D. Nollen and Virginia H. Martin *Alternative Work Schedules, Part 1: Flexitime* (New York: AMACOM, 1978); Work in America Institute; for 1974: calculated by Stanley D. Nollen from data by Virginia H. Martin.

The use of flexitime work scheduling has more than doubled from 1974 to 1980 from 3.2 percent to 8.1 percent (adjusted to omit professionals, managers, and sales personnel). Exhibit 19–3 shows the increase of flexitime work scheduling between August 1974 and May 1980.

Many types of jobs have converted to flexitime: they include bank tellers, accounting departments, engineers, keypunch operators, laboratory technicians, nurses, data processing, nonexempt production workers, and insurance clerks and claim examiners. A directory of the users of flexitime has even been published.[9]

Flexitime is difficult to implement in production units with assembly lines and multiple shifts. In such units it is impossible to have workers coming and going since work pace is largely machine controlled. Also, it is difficult to arrange flexitime for receptionists, retail sales clerks, bus drivers, or nurses

---

[9] *Alternative Work Schedule Directory* (Washington, D.C.: National Council on Alternative Work Patterns, 1978).

(e.g., operating room or intensive care units). In these cases, the job must be continuously covered thus limiting the type of work scheduling.

In flexitime systems, there are two major time periods—core time and flexible time. During the core time period, all employees in a unit or group must be at work. The flexible time period is the hours within which the employee is free to choose whether or not to be on the job. There is, of course, the requirement that during a day a required number of hours must be worked. A typical flexitime schedule is shown in Exhibit 19-4 for Verser Engineering and Construction Co., a medium-sized firm that has used this schedule since 1977.

Some Benefits of Flexitime

The reported success rates of flexitime programs is impresssive. Half or more of all user firms report dollar and cents improvements. Increased productivity lower unit labor costs, and improved morale have been attributed to flexitime.[10] There are also benefits in less paid absence and idle time, increased morale, and less overtime pay (because of less absence and higher productivity).[11]

One study of a flexitime schedule found that the most dramatic improvement was the increase of satisfaction with the work schedule. Satisfaction with interactions and friends also increased for those employees in a utility company, management and nonmanagement, who were on a flexitime schedule.[12]

One might ask, why are there productivity gains? Flexitime apparently

EXHIBIT 19-4 **Verser Engineering and Construction Company Flexitime Schedule** (Total for Workday Must Be Eight Hours)

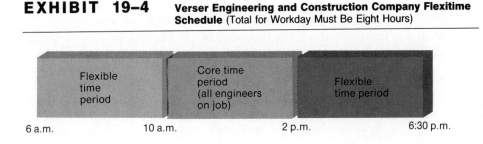

6 a.m.   10 a.m.   2 p.m.   6:30 p.m.

10 David A. Ralston, William P. Anthony, and David J. Gustafson, "Employees May Love Flexitime, But What Does It Do to the Organization's Productivity?" *Journal of Applied Psychology*, May 1985, pp. 272–79 and Stanley D. Nollen, "Does Flexitime Improve Productivity?" *Harvard Business Review*, September 1979, pp. 12, 16–18, 22.

11 C. W. Proehl, Jr., "A Survey of the Empirical Literature on Flexible Work Hours: Character and Consequences of a Major Innovation," *Academy of Management Review*, October 1978, pp. 837–53.

12 Randall B. Dunham and John L. Pierce, "The Design and Evaluation of Alternative Work Schedules," *Personnel Administrator*, April 1983, pp. 67–75.

increases the effective quantity of labor input. For example, if a car breaks down on the way to work the worker can stay later to make up the lost time. The firm gets more hours of work and, therefore, more productivity for the same cost. Also, because many workers like flexitime, an employer may have an easier time recruiting workers that prefer this type of work schedule. Again, because of the match between work schedule and worker preference, there is likely to be less absenteeism and turnover, reducing costs and increasing productivity.

There is another potential benefit of flexitime in that the schedule could be matched with the person's biological clock. Some of us are morning people—we are more productive in the A.M. Others are afternoon or early evening people. Flexitime permits employers in many cases to set up work schedules that optimize worker productivity and take advantage of the workers' biological clocks.

Some Problems of Flexitime

Productivity gains, morale improvements, cost containment—it sounds so attractive that we may wonder why every organization doesn't have flexitime work schedules. The reason is that flexitime can cause some major problems. Supervisors have to change their procedures and even work harder at the outset to implement flexitime schedules. Consequently, many supervisors drag their feet and resist flexitime.

There is also the increased cost in some organizations of heating and cooling buildings for longer workdays. The regular day is from 9 A.M. to 5 P.M. A flexitime schedule may require the building or plant to be open from 6:00 A.M. to 7:30 P.M. The result is more energy expenses.

There is also the problem of using flexitime in only some jobs. While some workers are on flexitime there are employees who are not able to have this kind of work schedule. What can happen is antagonism and jealousy across occupations between the "haves" and the "have nots."

The publicity given flexitime in the popular press and management literature has been overwhelmingly positive, yet some workers do not prefer flexitime. How can they say no when everyone around them is saying yes? This is a question that is not easy to answer. However, it points out that the assumption that everyone wants to go on a flexitime schedule may not be correct. What is a benefit to one worker may be a threat or inconvenience to another.

Managing Flexitime

There are a number of guidelines for successfully managing flexitime work schedules. Top-managment support is essential. Flexitime transfers some control over work from managers to workers. The top-management team must actively support this shifting of control. A climate of trust in the judgment of workers about their schedules is important. For example, if an honor system for checking in is used before flexitime is implemented, it would be a display of lack of trust if a formal sign-in, sign-out system is used after flexitime has been implemented. Top management has to encourage all levels of management to be supportive and trusting with flexitime schedules.

Another important guideline is to help the first-line supervisor. The job of this level supervisor gets more difficult with flexitime because he or she must: (1) still generate results, (2) balance the work schedules, (3) provide workers with some scheduling flexibility, and (4) plan further into the future. Thus, the first-line supervisor has fewer decisions to make about individual schedules, but still has responsibility to do the job. This responsibility is especially crucial in planning and coordinating activities.

A third management guideline is that supervisors should be trained to meet their new responsibilities and problems. The training should focus on what flexitime is, the supervisors' responsibilities, what research indicates about flexitime schedules, and some of the pitfalls to avoid. The supervisors need to understand a few important points that can be presented in training. They are:

- Work schedule choices, responsibility, and authority need to be clearly communicated to workers.
- The design of flexitime schedules must be understood—core hours (when everyone must be present), day length, timekeeping methods, disciplinary procedures.
- Jobs may have to be redesigned in order for flexitime to work. Training could cover job redesign approaches.

The fourth management guideline is that flexitime, like other work scheduling programs, should be evaluated. The schedule should be evaluated in terms of productivity, morale, energy costs, and the overall climate of the organization. A cost/benefit framework can be used to examine the effects of flexitime. It may also be worthwhile from a public goodwill standpoint to include in the evaluation an analysis of flexitime's impact on transportation efficiency. Cities such as Boston, Chicago, Seattle, and Ottawa, are examining the impact of flexitime work scheduling on commuting time, traffic congestion, and energy conservation.

In Ottawa, the number of federal employees who started work during the heavy 30-minute peak rush-hour period dropped from 78 to 40 percent after flexitime was implemented. In Toronto, after a year of citywide flexitime, almost half of the downtown employees on flexitime schedules elected to travel outside the peak rush hour in the morning.[13]

Including a transportation analysis as part of the flexitime analysis can be important not only for city governments, but also for organizations. Those firms that take into consideration the impact of flexitime on transportation patterns and congestion can derive public relations benefits. For example, they could, by using flexitime where possible, help the entire city or area run more smoothly. In the future, citizens could associate social responsibility and flex-

---

[13] Nollen, "New Work Schedules in Practice," p. 23.

itime scheduling when considering what an organization is doing for the community.

PART-TIME EMPLOYMENT

Part-time work includes all work demanding less than full time. The U.S. government counts people who work less than 35 hours a week as part-timers. For federal employees, 32 hours a week is the dividing line between full- and part-time work. Today about 30 million workers are considered part-timers, or about 25 percent of the American labor force.[14]

Two thirds of all part-timers are adult women. The next largest component, 25 percent, consists of teenagers. Part-time employment is especially prevalent in the fast-food industry, insurance, and banks. For example, 90 percent of the 250,000 employees of McDonald's fast-food restaurants are part-timers.[15] The median hourly wage was, in 1982, for part-time workers, about $4.50, only slightly more than $1.00 per hour above the minimum wage.[16]

There are several kinds of part-time employees:

Permanent part-time employment. The job and the workers are expected to be part time for a long time on a regular basis.

Job sharing. Two or more part-timers share one job. The workers are part time, but the job is full time.

Work sharing. A temporary reduction in working hours chosen by a group of employees during economic hard times. This is an alternative to being laid off.[17]

Temporary part-time employment. The worker is on a job only a short time (organizations such as Kelly girls).

Phased retirement. Part-time employment selected by employees who are gradually changing from full-time to retired status.

Permanent part-time employment is quite common in wholesale and retail trade industries as well as in service industries. Although it is common, it is still largely unnoticed. Part-time employment works especially well where there are specific jobs to complete, independent projects such as in insurance claims, and where the workload has a predictable cycle such as in banking traffic. On the other hand, part-time employment is not well suited for managerial jobs or where the work flow requires a worker to be continuously available.

An example of staffing an organization with a part-time work force is found

---

[14] Daniel Forbes, "Part-Time Work Force," *Business Month*, October 1987, pp. 45–47.

[15] Judith L. Ennis, "Temporaries," *Personnel Journal*, March 1985, pp. 97–99.

[16] Nancy S. Barrett, "Part-Time Work Increases, Bringing Change to Social Mores and Standards of Compensation," *Personnel Administrator*, December 1983, p. 95.

[17] Fred Best, *Work Sharing: Policy Options and Assessments* (Kalamazoo, Mich.: Upjohn Institute for Employment Research, 1980).

at Control Data Corporation. The company wanted to allow mothers needing supplemental income the opportunity to work. A part-time work schedule was established. Control Data opened a bindery that would collate, bind and mail computer manuals and documents to customers.[18]

The bindery runs from 6 A.M. to 10 P.M. with employees, mostly minority women from an economically depressed area of St. Paul, Minnesota, choosing a three-, four-, or six-hour shift. The choices were designed to fit the workers' needs. The plant employs female heads of households, handicapped people who cannot work full time, and students. Workers are compensated the same hourly rate as full-time workers in comparable jobs at other Control Data plants, and fringe benefits are prorated proportionate to hours worked.

Supervisors work standard eight-hour shifts. However, it should be mentioned that almost all of the supervisors started as part-timers. As their home situations and career plans changed, they expressed interest and converted to full-time work when it was available.

The productivity per capita in this part-time staffed plant is much higher than at other plants of the firm. Profits are up, and employees appear to be committed and dedicated. Management also believes that there is less worker fatigue because of the shorter shifts.

Provident Bank of Cincinnati introduced an interesting solution to the need for part-time help.[19] The bank has time during the week when only two or three tellers, instead of five or six, are needed. The bank created a pay program which would make working part-time on Fridays and other peak times unusually attractive.

At Provident Bank, the average hourly rate earned by tellers eligible for benefits (full-timers) was $5.50, with benefits worth an additional 30 percent. Thus, the average cost to the bank tellers' work was slightly more than $7 per hour. The bank felt that it would take more than $7 per hour to attract and retain individuals for work schedules that called for shorter hours or fewer days.

Provident instituted a peak-time workers program. These employees are those who do not want to work full time, and can afford to be without employer-provided benefit plans. A peak-time teller may be hired to work five hours per day for three days a week. However, his or her schedule may be five hours on Monday, three on Thursday, and seven on Friday. The range paid for peak-timers at Provident is from $6.60 to more than $10. Remember that the bank saves thousands of dollars in fringe benefit costs because peak-time jobs offer high pay but no benefits.

An example of a peak-time schedule for part-time work is shown in Exhibit 19–5. The chart shows that the fewer hours Allan works, the higher the hourly pay rate. Allan's actual pay is determined by multiplying the base pay by the daily index and then by the weekly pay index.

---

[18] A. R. Cohen and H. Gadon, *Alternative Work Schedules: Integrating Individual and Organizational Needs* (Reading, Mass.: Addison-Wesley Publishing, 1979), pp. 100–01.

[19] Stuart J. Maklin and Julie Charles, "Peak-Time Pay for Part-Time Work," *Personnel Journal*, November 1984, pp. 60–65.

EXHIBIT 19-5   Peak-Time Pay for Part-Time Work for an Individual Teller

		Branch: Costa Mesa	Employee: Allan	Base Rate: $5.50 per hour		
		Days Worked per Week	1	2	3	4	5
Hours Worked per Day	**Daily Pay Index**	**Weekly Pay Index**	1.30	1.25	1.20	1.15	1.00
1	1.50		$10.73	$10.31	$9.90	$9.49	$8.25
2	1.45		10.37	9.97	9.57	9.17	7.98
3	1.40		10.01	9.63	9.24	8.86	7.70
4	1.30		9.30	8.94	8.58	8.22	7.15
5	1.20		8.58	8.25	7.92	7.59	6.60
6	1.10		7.87	7.56	7.26	6.96	6.05
7	1.00		7.15	6.88	6.60	6.33	5.50
8	1.00		7.15	6.88	6.60	6.33	5.50

Source: Adapted from PKTmatrix © 1984 CS&A.

One of the objectives of the Provident Bank peak-time pay program is to reduce administrative expense. Also, this type of program assumes that the part-time employees attracted to this type of system value their descretionary time and high take-home pay more than a holiday or permanent job.

Another example of part-time work involves what is being called the flexiforce approach. This is an available pool of people who are paid for working on a scheduled part-time basis.[20] The employees are paid either on a retainer basis or for work actually performed. The flexiforce can fill in the needs and respond to personnel needs on short notice. Retained older, experienced, and knowledgeable employees can serve as a firm's flexiforce.

Some Benefits of Permanent Part-Time Employment and Job Sharing

Permanent part-time employment succeeds when it is used for a specific operating purpose. For example, when Occidental Life Insurance Company's business grew, management decided that it needed more than a single eight-hour day shift of claims examiners, keypunch operators, and record clerks to process business. There was not enough work for a whole eight-hour second shift. The answer was to establish a part-time minishift that worked from 5 P.M. until 10 P.M.[21]

---

[20] Robert C. Ford and Ken Jennings, "The Case for Flexiforce," *Personnel Journal*, December 1984, p. 80.

[21] Nollen, "What is Happening?" p. 14.

When Massachusetts Mutual Life Insurance Company had trouble recruiting full-time office employees, they established job sharing. One employee worked from 9 A.M. to 2 P.M. (usually a mother with children in school) and the other worker came in from 2 P.M. to 5 P.M. (usually a student from a local college).

There may also be a more favorable attitude formed by part-timers toward the organization and its policies than found among full-time employees. One study examined the attitudes of part-time versus full-time employees toward various aspects of organizations: structure, trust, power, and job satisfaction.[22] The researchers found that full-time and part-time employees differed in their attitudes. Part-time employees had more favorable attitudes toward the organization members and the distribution of power in the organization. Part-timers also reported higher levels of overall job satisfaction.

Since this is a study based on employees in only one organization and there are some methodological problems associated with it, such as low reliabilities, the results must be treated cautiously. There is a growing need for more full-time versus part-time employment research to determine empirically the benefits, costs, and problems associated with part-time scheduling.[23]

The main employer benefits of part-time and job-sharing scheduling are reduced labor cost, including less overtime. In addition, productivity is often higher, absenteeism and tardiness are lower, and (except for students), turnover is lower.[24] There is also the possibility that with part-timers there is less job fatigue caused by working on tedious, repetitive jobs. Thus, performance is better because workers complete jobs in shorter time spans.[25]

Some Problems with Part-Time Scheduling

A number of problems are associated with part-time employment. Management in some cases must examine and work out a plan to balance fringe benefits paid to part- and full-time employees. Not all fringe benefits can be prorated to time actually worked. This results in feelings of inequity by both part- and full-timers.

Although most part-timers have paid vacations, only about half get any group health or life insurance or pension plans. A major stumbling block is the health insurance (vacations and pensions can be more easily prorated). Companies are faced with paying $600 to $1,000 annually for health insurance for part-timers. Prorating health insurance premiums payments means that the

---

[22] Bruce J. Eberhardt and Abraham B. Shani, "Full-Time versus Part-Time Employment Status on Attitudes toward Specific Organizational Characteristics and Overall Job Satisfaction," *Academy of Management Journal*, December 1984, pp. 893–900.

[23] Nancy L. Rotchford and Karlene H. Roberts, "Part-Time Workers as Missing Persons in Organizational Research," *Academy of Management Review*, April 1982, pp. 228–34.

[24] Kim Watford, "Shorter Workweeks: An Alternative To Layoff," *Business Week*, April 14, 1986, pp. 77–78.

[25] Ethel B. Jones and James E. Long, "Part-Week Work and Human Capital Investment by Married Women," *Journal of Human Resources*, Fall 1979, p. 18.

insurance company agreement has to fit part- and full-time employees. It is extremely difficult to work out an equitable prorated basis.

One solution to the health insurance problem is to allow employees to select their mix of fringe benefits. As cited earlier in this text, this is called a *cafeteria* benefit program. Full- and part-time employees could choose from among the fringe benefits. The company's contribution to the cafeteria selection could be based on time worked (full or part). Another solution is the one described earlier used by Provident Bank in which peak pay is used to preclude paying any fringe benefits.

Labor unions pose another problem in part-time scheduling. Permanent part-time employment has been referred to as, "Another piece of bread in this dry sandwich of alternative work schedules."[26] Unions are reluctant to support part-time employment because it increases the competition for jobs during periods of high unemployment. The full-time employee more than the part-timer is a union member. Thus, union opposition is largely based on protecting the interests of its members.

There is also the belief that part-time workers are not interested in advancement opportunities. This is a stereotype that comes from part-time employment's association with low-level jobs, and the fact that women and students hold most part-time jobs. There are also some who feel that part-time work is not worthy or masculine. Among all permanent part-time workers, 70 percent are women. These stereotypes are difficult to overcome. The work ethic for decades has encouraged people to work full time. This cultural barrier and the stereotype are slowly being overcome by the positive contributions made by part-time employees. Only through part-time or job-sharing schedules can many people work, earn an income, and make productive inputs into society. This message is slowly beginning to find its way to society.

Managing Part-Time Employment and Job Sharing

A managerial concern of part-time employment and job sharing is their potentially high labor costs. Some labor costs are fixed per employee. Since part-time employees work fewer hours than full-time employees, their hourly cost can be higher. Managers with the aid and guidance of P/HRM specialists must develop a fringe benefit program that is fair to part-time and job-sharing employees. Unless this is done, the stereotypes and negative reactions directed toward part-time employment and job sharing will continue.

Effectively managing various P/HRM activities is also important in controlling costs for part-time and job-sharing work scheduling. Recruitment costs can be high for part-time employment because more people have to be recruited or regular recruitment methods are not suited to finding part-timers

---

[26] John Zalusky, "Alternative Work Schedules: A Labor Union View," *Journal of the College and University Personnel Association*, Summer 1977, p. 42.

and job sharers is attractive enough to retain them as employees. There are also specialized part-time and job-sharing placement companies that may be able to provide services to the organization.

Supervision of part-timers can be costly. The part-time employee is not on the job as much as the full-time employee. Thus, if self-starting, self-motivated part-timers can be attracted, the costs of supervision can be reduced or at least controlled within acceptable limits.

It also makes sense in terms of P/HRM to treat part-time and job-sharing employees as important human resources. Fair treatment, equitable compensation, and opportunities for job-involved decision making are important steps in making part time and job sharing acceptable and attractive types of work schedules.

Job sharing presents a number of special kinds of management problems: (1) matching the workers as partners and then with the job; (2) encouraging and rewarding cooperative work efforts; (3) deciding the specific work schedule; and (4) encouraging communication between partners. If employers initiate job sharing it is very important for the organization to thoroughly analyze the jobs and the prospective partners. The employer's role and involvement are especially important in determining work schedules and creating a supportive atmosphere for the job sharers to work as a team. Even when job-sharing arrangements are initiated by workers there is a distinct need to maintain open communication and cooperation. Instead of balancing the needs and preferences of a single employee and the job, management must balance the needs and preferences of two employees and the job.

COMPRESSED WORKWEEKS

The compressed workweek (CWW) is a work schedule in which a trade is made between the number of hours worked per day, and the number of days worked per week, in order to work the standard number of hours.[27] The CWW can be: (1) four days of 10 hours each—4/40; (2) three-day workweeks often about 12 hours each day—3/36; (3) four-and-one-half-day workweeks with four 9-hour periods and one 4-hour day; and (4) a work weekend of two 12-hour days, paid at premium rates.

In 1980, about 2.7 percent of all full-time, nonfarm wage and salary workers, or about 1.8 million workers, were on CWWs. Exhibit 19–6 indicates that the CWW had leveled off between 1976–79, but 1979–80 witnessed some growth.[28]

---

[27] Simcha Ronen and Sophia B. Primps, "The Compressed Work Week as Organizational Change: Behavioral and Attitudinal Outcomes," *Academy of Management Journal*, January 1981, p. 61.

[28] U.S. Department of Labor, Bureau of Labor Statistics, news release (Washington, D.C.: Office of Information, February 24, 1981).

___

EXHIBIT 19–6   **Growth of Compressed Workweeks**

___

Percent of all nonfarm wage
and salary workers who
work full time

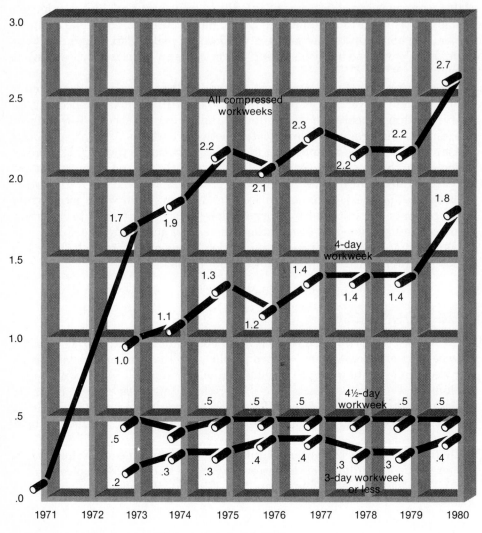

Note: Percent of all nonfarm wage and salary workers who work full time.

Source: Janice Neipert Hedges, "How Many Days Make a Workweek?" *Monthly Labor Review.* April 1975, pp. 29–36. U.S. Department of Labor Statistics, news release, February 24, 1981.

Some Benefits of Compresssed Workweeks

The regular utilization of facilities is a benefit of the CWW. There are fewer start-ups if a four- or three-day schedule is used. However, if a business plant, office, or facility must be open at least five days the CWW cause some job coverage problems.[29] In situations where employers are able to cut utility and overhead costs by closing on the fifth day, the CWW offers cost savings.

There have been a few research studies that indicate that the morale of CWW workers is higher and paid absences lower than workers under standard work schedules.[30] In a quasi-experimental study in a manufacturing facility a 25-month investigation was conducted. The study examined satisfaction, absenteeism, and performance of 4/40 workers versus 5/40 workers. At the 13-month period of the study, workers on the 4/40 work schedule were more satisfied with job conditions, experienced less anxiety-stress, and performed better than did the comparison 5/40 workers. However, these benefits were not found at the 25-month data point.[31] It was concluded that the 4/40 may have a short-term impact, but that long-term benefits, must be questioned and examined more closely.

The Utah State Office of Education undertook an experimental implementation of the compressed workweek,[32] in which the plan was made available at the discretion of employees. Entire divisions elected to remain on standard schedules, while others made a number of optional schedules available on an individual preference basis. The most popular optional schedule was a 4/40. The most improvement among employees in terms of increased morale and productivity were found among those individuals who elected to work the 4/40 schedule. Unfortunately, the productivity improvement were based solely on self-ratings and should be accepted cautiously.

The traditional 5/40 workweek has been under attack in the nursing profession. Because nursing care of hospitalized patients is a seven-day, 24-hour responsibility, nursing has not been one area of CWW popularity. This lack of popularity seems to be changing. The list of hospitals using CWWs is increasing yearly. The CWW schedules for nurses include a 7/70 at Valley Medical Center in Fresno, California, a 7/56 at Baptist Medical Center-Monclair in

---

[29] Richard E. Kopelman, "Alternative Work Schedules and Productivity: A Review of the Evidence," *National Productivity Review*, Spring 1986, pp. 150–65.

[30] L. W. Foster, J. C. Latack, and L. J. Reindl, "Effects and Promises of the Shortened Work Week," paper presented at the 39th annual meeting of Academy of Management, Atlanta, Georgia, 1979.

[31] For the 13-month study, see John M. Ivancevich, "Effects of the Shorter Workweek on Selected Satisfaction and Performance Measures," *Journal of Applied Psychology*, 1974, pp. 717–21; for the 25-month study, see John M. Ivancevich and Herbert L. Lyon, "The Shortened Workweek: A Field Experiment," *Journal of Applied Psychology*, February 1977, pp. 34–37.

[32] David E. Nelson, "Employee Control Is an Important Option in Variable Work Schedules," *Personnel Administrator*, June 1983, pp. 118–23.

Birmingham, Alabama, a 2/16 weekend plan at Women's Hospital in Houston, and a 4/40 at University Hospital in Seattle.[33]

The evaluation of these nurse work-scheduling programs has been conducted by in-house researchers. The results suggest lower staff turnover, reduced overtime, less absenteeism, and improved job satisfaction. There are a number of critics who remain unconvinced about the impact of the CWW. Some feel that nurses on flexitime schedules tend to stand out as an elite group, and this will eventually decrease morale. There is also the issue of fatigue. Nurses working more than eight hours are prone to more errors. An error in nursing can be a life or death matter.[34]

Some Problems with Compressed Workweeks

Labor laws and union contracts often specifically address the issue of working more than eight hours a day. Overtime rates usually have to be paid for a more than eight-hour workday. Collective bargaining has to specifically cover this issue.

One union agreed to a 3/36 plan for 400 full-time employees of the Meredith Corporation printing plant in Des Moines, Iowa. It was decided in labor-management discussions that the printing presses cannot be run on the basis of five-day workweeks. They had to be operated all seven days, but this would be too demanding on employees and their families. The solution was to assign a fourth crew where there were previously three. The company also created two 12-hour shifts per day. This allowed the continuous operation of the presses. One crew works Monday–Wednesday and the other workers Thursday–Saturday. Sunday work is alternatively divided between the crews. The Sunday work is paid at double time. This system is given credit for production improvement, and absenteeism decreases.[35]

A problem with CWWs is that fatigue often affects performance. Working 10-, 11-, or 12-hour days in any job can be very tiring. Not only can performance suffer, but there is the probability of increased accident frequency. A tired worker often inadvertently becomes more lax with regard to health and safety practices. A mistake of a machine operator can cause injury, while an error by a nurse can cause life-threatening problems.

The CWW does not have the flexibility of a flexitime work schedule. The person who must work a compressed schedule may find that his or her life and personal time become more complicated. Those workers with child-rearing

---

[33] Elmina M. Price, "Seven Days On and Seven Days Off," *American Journal of Nursing*, June 1981, pp. 1, 142–43, and "The Demise of the Traditional 5/40 Workweek?" *American Journal of Nursing*, June 1981, pp. 1138–41.

[34] Suzanne LaViolette, "Shortage Spurs Flurry of Flexitime Experiments," *Modern Health Care*, March 1981, p. 42.

[35] "Union Agreement Gives Workers 3-day Week, 4-day Weekends," *Management Review*, January 1981, p. 31.

obligations may have a special set of problems working a 3/36 or 4/40 schedule. They may have to be away from home during times that their children are not in school.

Unlike flexitime and part-time employment, the CWW does not give workers any more freedom of choice. Preferring the CWW schedule in order to stay away from work in larger blocks of time is not a positive vote for this type of schedule. It is more of a job avoidance vote.

Managing Compressed Workweeks

An important part of implementing the CWW is the matching of workers' schedules with the necessary operating schedule. Customers, clients, and others dealing with an organization expect timely service. When a person goes to the store to purchase a product at midday, on say a Friday, she expects the store to be open for business. Management needs to carefully work out a coverage plan when using CWW schedules.

There is also the need to pay close managerial attention to the fatigue associated with longer workdays. Fatigue is a serious problem as each study reporting on the impact of the CWW has shown.[36] Not only can fatigue result in a decrease in effectiveness, it can be harmful to the tired worker, co-workers, and even commuters who will be on the road with the worker. It is management's responsibility to examine more closely the consequences of the longer workday on fatigue. There may well be an increase in legal action brought by workers who claim that the CWW and especially the fatigue caused by it precipitated family, personal, and job-related problems. Certainly management would be implicated in such cases.

QUALITY OF WORK LIFE

Managers are paying increased attention to the quality of work life (QWL) of employees. Specifically, they are concerned with how the QWL affects the productivity of organizations, the morale and well-being of employees, and how it can be improved to help accomplish meaningful organizational and individual goals. The meaning of the QWL is elusive since different interpretations have been offered.[37] To some, QWL refers to industrial democracy or increased worker participation in decision making. To others, QWL refers to a set of interventions intended to improve productivity. There are also some who believe that QWL means the application of methods to humanize the work of employees.

A comprehensive interpretation of the meaning of QWL was developed by

---

[36] Philip J. Hubek and Donald J. Petersen, "Arbitration and the Shortened Work Week: No Easy Answers," *Personnel*, March 1985, pp. 8–10.

[37] John Nirenberg, "The Quality of Work Life Issue: The Corporation as the Next Political Frontier," *International Journal of Manpower* (June 1986), pp. 27–36.

P/HRM Manager Close-Up

Richard W. Hucke
Roy F. Weston, Inc.

Biography

Richard W. Hucke became vice president, Human Resources Division, for Roy F. Weston, Inc. when he joined the firm in 1977. Mr. Hucke has over 15 years experience in all aspects of human resources including both domestic and foreign recruiting, labor relations and negotiations, safety and health management, affirmative action/equal employment opportunities administration, salary administration, relocation (domestic and foreign) and training and development. He is a graduate of Bryant College holding a degree in business administration, a member of the American Society of Personnel Administrators and past officer of the Monmouth/Ocean County, N.J. Industrial Relations Association. Mr. Hucke has taught college courses on OSHA and has developed and conducted management-level seminars on the various aspects of human resources.

Job Description

Mr. Hucke has total responsibility for ensuring the corporation functions from an innovative and progressive human resources vantage by maintaining state-of-the-art knowledge of the various functions of his group.

Specific functions include the maintenance and expansion of a highly professional, technically-oriented staff, development and implementation of corporate policy, identification and method selection of the corporation's training and development needs.

Mr. Hucke reports directly to Mr. Roy F. Weston, president and CEO of the corporation, and has a staff of six including a compensation specialist, services administrator, and a technical recruiter.

(continued)

Views about Human Resources at Weston— Richard W. Hucke

The efficiency with which any organization can be operated will depend to a considerable measure upon how effectively its personnel can be managed and utilized. Since the activities of most organizations today are becoming more and more complex in nature, the managers in these organizations are required to have greater technical competency than was formerly the case. In addition to this greater technical competency, they must possess a better understanding of human behavior and of the processes by which personnel can be managed effectively. Every manager, therefore, must be able to work effectively with people and to resolve satisfactorily the many and varied problems that the management of these people may entail. Effective personnel management requires the development of a program that will permit employees to be selected and trained for those jobs that are most appropriate to their developed abilities. Moreover, it requires that employees be motivated to exert their maximum efforts, that their performances be evaluated properly for results, and that they be remunerated on the basis of their contributions to the organization.

Fortunately, a growing body of knowledge relating to human behavior and to management systems and processes is being accumulated from experience and research that can be of assistance to the manager in developing better relations with subordinates. Human resources management is able to borrow from many of the more basic disciplines and to apply the contributions of these disciplines to the improvement of the personnel program.

There are certain basic processes to be performed, general principles and rules to be observed, as well as tools, techniques, and methods to be utilized in the management of personnel in any organization regardless of its type, purpose, or the qualifications of its personnel. Since all organizations must operate with and through people, the management of such organizations basically is a process of managing people. Any manager or supervisor who is responsible for the work of others in an organization therefore must engage in personnel management and in the various processes, such as training, motivating, and counseling, that this responsibility entails. The primary function of human resources is to provide managers with services and assistance that they may require in managing subordinates more effectively and in accordance with established personnel policies and procedures, to establish and maintain productive application of sound management processes for human resources of the corporation, including sensitivity to the strong input of human considerations to professional capability. Result areas to be considered for such processes are productivity, capability, compliance, cost, dignity, and order.

Walton.[38] He suggested eight categories that when examined in total indicate what is meant by QWL. The categories are:

1. Adequate and fair compensation for hard working, performing employees.
2. A safe and healthy work environment.
3. A job that permits an individual to develop his or her skills and knowledge.
4. Opportunities to grow and develop on the job, while also having job security.
5. A sense of feeling like a team that is helpful and encouraging to one's self-esteem.
6. A work environment that distributes rewards equitably, permits personal privacy, and tolerates dissent.
7. A job that encourages a person to schedule and take personal time for family and leisure activities.
8. An organization that is socially responsible and one that the employee is proud to be working for.

Each interpretation of QWL focuses on the individual employee. Therefore, QWL is defined here as the degree to which employees are able to satisfy their needs, goals, and aspirations while performing their jobs and working with colleagues.

Quality of Work Life and Productivity

Quality of work life and productivity are independent. Management can improve the QWL by reducing the demands made on employees, by slowing down assembly lines, and by increasing the amount of paid time-off given to employees. The result would, in most cases, be reduced productivity.[39]

Why isn't it always possible to improve QWL and productivity at the same time? The answer is that some misunderstandings about work and people exist. First, there is an assumption that improving QWL results in immediate productivity gains. Simply permitting or asking workers to participate in decision making is not always interpreted accurately. An employee who has never participated before is reluctant to change her behavior.[40]

Second, there is an assumption about a simple cause-and-effect linkage. That is, improvements in the QWL lead to higher productivity. Whether improvements occur are contingent on a whole list of factors—the employer's attitudes, how the group perceives the improvements, how the improvements are introduced, and how patient management is in waiting for results.

Third, managers often forget about how the technology, employees, and rituals of a firm interact. Again, the complexities and realities of organizational life result in uncertainty, anxiety, and barriers for the successful introduction of QWL improvements.

---

38 R. W. Walton, "Quality of Working Life: What Is it?," *Sloan Management Review*, Fall 1973, pp. 11–21.

39 J. Lloyd Suttle, "Improving Life at Work—Problems and Prospects," in *Improving Life At Work*, eds. J. Richard Hackman and J. Lloyd Suttle (Santa Monica, Calif.: Goodyear, 1977), p. 9.

40 Barry A. Stein, *Quality of Work Life in Action*, New York: American Management Association, 1983.

Using QWL improvements may take a long time to show productivity gains. The use of QWL improvements should not be viewed as a "quick fix." Any QWL improvements used must be linked to the overall strategic plan of the company and given sufficient time to yield results. It is the patience of managers that is rigidly tested by most QWL programs. Meager productivity gains are often the incentive for discarding or minimizing the QWL effort.

Quality of Work Life Programs

There are a wide array of QWL programs that have been offered, implemented, and evaluated in organizational settings. There are worker participation programs, job design programs, alternative work schedule programs, and employee security programs. The job design approach is covered in Chapter 4, the alternative work schedule programs are covered in the present chapter, and employment security programs are covered in Chapters 11 and 14. Thus, worker participation programs will be developed at this point.

Worker Participation Programs Such prominent behavioralists as Argyris, Bennis, and Likert have encouraged managers to permit more worker participation in decision making.[41] Sashkin claims that employee participation is not only effective but that its use is an ethical imperative.[42] Instead of considering worker participation as an ethical imperative it seems more realistic to examine how it is used and where it is successful.

Joint Union Management QWL efforts have been used with some success. Unions have power to influence various company decisions through contract negotiations and grievance handling. Joint union-management QWL programs can be used to address concerns and problems not spelled out in the collective bargaining agreement. A study in a large midwestern utility examined the impact of a joint union-management QWL program. Three different teams were established.[43] In team A, a steering committee of managers and union representatives was established. In team B, a team of functional managers and the union steward was found. The third, team C, was a problem-solving group of the supervisor and union steward along with volunteers from rank-and-file employees.

All three teams received training in group-process skills and problem-solving skills. Each team addressed problems faced by employees (such as workflow, work schedule, redesign of the job and work area). Each team addressed issues which they considered to be a problem.

Results indicated a significant increase within all three QWL groups in perceptions of the union rank-and-file contribution in improving the job. The

---

[41] Edwin A. Locke, David M. Schweiger, and Gary P. Latham, "Participation in Decision Making: When Should It Be Used?" *Organizational Dynamics*, Winter 1986, pp. 65–79.

[42] Marshall Shaskin, "Participative Management Is an Ethical Imperative," *Organizational Dynamics*, Spring 1984.

[43] James W. Thacker and Mitchell W. Fields, "Union Involvement in Quality-of-Worklife Efforts: A Longitudal Investigation, *Personnel Psychology*, 1987, pp. 97–111.

rank and file believed that they have more influence and say about their jobs. The majority of union members, no matter what team represented them, were favorably predisposed toward union involvement in joint QWL efforts. Whether these same results can be applied to other organizations, unionized and nonunionized, needs to be further examined.

Quality Circles   Quality circles (QC) have been used in QWL programs. A quality circle is a small group of employees and their supervisor from the same work area, who voluntarily meet on a regular basis to study quality control and productivity problems. The group attempts to identify problems, to solve them, and to monitor the implementation of their solutions.[44]

Quality circles are popular in American and Japanese firms. QCs in Japan give specific attention to statistical quality control issues and often meet on their own rather than on company time. A bonus for improvements of QCs in Japan is based on the performance of the entire organization.

QCs in the United States create a parallel organizational structure.[45] They operate independently from the existing organizational structure. Lawler and Mohrman identified six stages in the growth and decline of quality circle. Exhibit 19–7 presents these stages.

Some organizations assign major responsibilities to QCs. Toyota, for example, assigns over 90 percent of customer complaints to its circle for problem-solving solutions. At the Western Electric Plant in Shreveport, Louisiana, suggestions made by one QC about work scheduling is reported to have saved over $500,000.[46]

Lockheed and Honeywell were among the early adopters of QCs in the United States. Lockheed adopted them in the 1970s for use in missile manufacturing projects. Honeywell also adopted them in the 1970s and is still using them as a major example of an organizational change toward embracing participative management.

Critics of quality circles caution managers about simply adopting them without weighing some possible problems.[47] Lawler and Mohrman report that QCs have life cycles that must be understood. The initial enthusiasm carries the group for some time. However, there are issues such as false expectations, cynicism about the QC's impact on the QWL, and burnout about meeting every week that need to be considered. QCs appear to, at least initially, make employees feel better about their job. This, in turn, apparently leads to improved attendance and less turnover for QC participants. However, what about the nonparticipants? Individuals not in QC may resent the fact that participants are meeting four times a month and being paid, while the nonpartici-

44 Philip C. Thompson, *Quality Circles*, New York: American Management Association, 1982.

45 Keith Bradley and Stephan Hill, "Quality Circles and Managerial Interests," *Industrial Relations*, Winter 1987, pp. 68–82.

46 "The Changing American Workplace: Work Alternatives in The 80's," *An AMA Survey Report* (New York: American Management Association, 1985).

47 Edward E. Lawler, III, and Susan A. Mohrman, "Quality Circles: After the Honeymoon," *Organizational Dynamics*, Spring 1987, pp. 42–54.

EXHIBIT 19-7

Phases of a circle's life		
Phase	**Activity**	**Destructive forces**
Start-up	Publicize	Low volunteer rate
	Obtain funds and volunteers	Inadequate funding
	Train	Inability to learn group-process and problem-solving skills
Initial problem solving	Identify and solve problem	Disagreement on problems
		Lack of knowledge of operations
Approval of initial suggestions	Present and have initial suggestions accepted	Resistance by staff groups and middle management
		Poor presentation and suggestions because of limited knowledge
Implementation	Relevant groups act on suggestions	Prohibitive costs
		Resistance by groups that implement
Expansion of problem solving	Form new groups	Member-nonmember conflict
	Old groups continue	Raised aspirations
		Lack of problems
		Expense of parallel organization
		Savings not realized
		Rewards wanted
Decline	Fewer groups meet	Cynicism about program
		Burnout

Source: Edward E. Lawler III and Susan A. Mohrman, "Quality Circles after the Fad," *Harvard Business Review*, January–February 1985, p. 67.

pants are still working. Considering the potential benefits and costs of implementing a QC program is an important consideration for managers.[48]

New Design Plants New design plants have been constructed by such firms as H.J. Heinz, Rockwell, Mead, and Cummins Engine.[49] These plants reflect interest in worker participation in the form of an organizational effort to increase the employees' say about work, rewards, knowledge exchange, and power sharing. In the design and construction of these facilities employees participate in the decisions made about the layout of machinery, equipment, and the recreational areas of the plant. There is also an attempt to have employees help develop jobs that are challenging, motivating, and satisfying. It is because of this type of worker participation that these plants are referred as "new design plants."

The equality of employees is stressed in many new plants. General Motors carefully planned the constitution of a plant in Troy, Michigan.

> At General Motors Corporation's new Saturn headquarters in Troy, Michigan, everybody will be equal. But the office design firm GM hired to furnish the new building didn't quite believe that.
>
> Saturn managers told the firm, which GM won't name, that the furniture and carpeting in every office had to be exactly the same grade and quality—no special treatment for the executives. But the design company ordered special furniture and decoration for Saturn's eight top officials anyway. "More expensive desks, credenzas, lamps, ashtrays, the whole shot," says a GM employee.
>
> Saturn officials stuck to their principles: They cancelled that part of the order. Not taking the "executive" furniture saved the company more than $1 million.[50]

The P/HRM department is usually much more important in new design plants than in traditional ones. Many of the typical P/HRM tasks such as selection and pay administration are assigned to participative work teams. The P/HRM unit doesn't ignore these tasks but works to help the teams accomplish the various activities. Although the P/HRM unit works less on traditional tasks, they are more involved than usual on job design issues.

The benefits of the three worker participation programs just covered—joint union-management committees, quality circles, and new design plants may not only be in terms of dollars and cents. In some cases, improved self-esteem, job satisfaction, and organizational commitment are important results. In general, worker participation programs are initially positively perceived by participants. However, the benefits of such enthusiasm may be short-term, if management holds false expectations and attempts to impose participation on a skeptical, untrained, and under-motivated work force. The worker participa-

---

[48] Edward E. Lawler, III, *High Involvement Management* (San Francisco: Jossey-Bass, 1986).

[49] Ibid, p. 170.

[50] "Saturn's New Plant," *The Wall Street Journal*, August 2, 1985, p. 1.

A RETURN TO THE P/HRM · IN · ACTION

Amanda

Amanda finished her reading on the subject of new work schedules and was interested in flexitime. She believed that it could work in some units, but was still skeptical about the use in other units. For example, in intensive care full-time coverage is important and vital. She also wondered whether providing scheduling alternatives for some nurses and not others would increase the turnover rate even more. Despite these concerns, she was willing to experiment with flexitime on a limited basis. She called Jack Quenton, the P/HRM manager, the supervisor of nursing, and two nursing supervisors to start the process of setting up the experiment.

tion QWL programs like the other attempts at improving the life and experiences of participating employees can be successful in improving productivity and morale. However, there is simply not enough evidence available to declare QWL programs as always being successful.

SUMMARY

A major change occurring in the workplace is the willingness on union leaders, managers, and workers to experiment with various work schedules and to work toward the improvement in the quality of work life. Today, the traditional five-day, 40-hour workweek is followed by most people. However, this chapter shows that P/HRM specialists and managers are becoming more and more involved with nontraditional work schedules. There is also interest in taking steps to help employees satisfy their needs and goals while working on the job.

To summarize the major points covered in this chapter:

1. The work environment, workers' scheduling preferences and expectations, and demographics are changing. Now people are beginning to question the

economic, social, and personal value of working a five-day, 40-hour, Monday–Friday schedule. These questions and many experiments indicate that there are alternatives.

2. Flexitime is the most popular alternative to the traditional work schedule. It allows employees to select their starting and quitting times within limits set by management.

3. Flexitime schedules can differ on many dimensions—for example, variable versus constant length of workday, when the worker must be present, and even the location of where the work takes place.

4. The latest statistics (1980) indicate that 11.9 percent of all full-time wage and salary workers are on flexible schedules. It seems reasonable to predict that by 1993 about 25 percent of these workers will have flexitime schedules.

5. Part-time employment means working less than 35 hours a week in private industry and less than 32 hours a week in the federal government. Twenty-two million Americans, mostly women and teenagers, are part-time employees.

6. Job sharing is a form of part-time employment in which two or more part-timers share a full-time job. This is especially convenient for employees with special personal challenges, such as child rearing or going to school while working.

7. The compressed workweek (CWW) is a schedule in which a trade is made between the number of hours worked per day and the number of days worked per week. Thus, instead of five-day, 40-hour (5/40) schedule, people may work 4/40, 3/36, 7/70, and so forth.

8. There are numerous interpretations of what is the quality of work life. It is defined here as the degree to which employees are able to satisfy their needs, goal, and aspirations while performing their jobs.

9. Quality of work life efforts include job design programs, worker participation programs, alternative work schedule arrangements, and employee security programs.

10. Worker participation programs have appeared in the form of joint union-management teams, quality circles, and new plant designs. Some of the research suggests that these programs can improve morale and productivity.

Questions for Review and Discussion

1. Would job sharing be a solution to problems of layoffs in the steel and automobile industry? Why?

2. Why are quality of work life programs difficult to evaluate?

3. Why would a young worker prefer to work part time?

4. Does working part time pose a threat to the cultural tradition of being employed full time? Explain.

5. What is the value of the compressed workweek to society in times of an energy crunch?

6. Why does the traditional five-day, 40-hour workweek still remain the predominant work schedule in the United States and Canada?
7. Why would managerial support be so important at the start of using flexitime schedule?
8. What are some potential limitations and problems associated with quality circles?
9. It is stated that quality of work life and productivity are interdependent. What does this mean?

GLOSSARY

Compressed Workweek (CWW). A work schedule in which a trade is made between the number of hours worked per day, and the number of days worked per week, in order to work the standard length hours—four days, 10 hours each day or three days, 12 hours each day are examples of the CWW schedule.

Core Work Time. A period of time in a flexitime work schedule in which all employees in a particular unit or group must be at work.

Flexitime Work Schedules. A work schedule in which the employee is able to select his or her starting and quitting time within limits set by management.

Flexible Work Time. A period of time in a flexitime work schedule in which the employee is free to choose whether or not to be on the job.

Job Sharing. A situation in which two or more part-timers share one job. The workers are part time, but the job is full time.

New Design Plants. A plant that is constructed and laid out with inputs made by employees.

Part-Time Employment. A job in which a person works less than 35 hours a week. For federal employees, 32 hours a week is the dividing line between full- and part-time work.

Quality Circles. A 4- to 15-person work group that usually meets once a week to solve work-related problems.

Quality of Work Life. The degree to which employees are able to satisfy their needs, goals, and aspirations while performing their jobs and working with colleagues.

APPLICATION CASE 19–1

Henrico County, Virginia's Police Department Experiment with the Compressed Workweek*

In July, Henrico County, Virginia, implemented a 4/40 workweek for its police division. Under the system, each officer would work four consecutive 10-hour days, as opposed to the seven consecutive 8-hour days he or she had previously worked before receiving any time off. Officers complained that they were physically and mentally fatigued when they had to work seven consecutive days before getting time off. Consequently, the police division suffered from a relatively high turnover and absenteeism rate under the 7/56 schedule.

The chief of police appointed a four-member committee to look at the problems and complaints about the 7/56 schedule. He wanted the committee to develop a plan that would (1) provide more days off and time off on weekends; (2) increase the total officers available during peak hours; (3) decrease the response time to calls; and (4) reduce officer fatigue and absenteeism.

The committee examined a number of alternative work schedules. They found that other police departments around the United States were using variations of a four-day, 10-hour-a-day schedule. These other departments found that a majority of their officers preferred the 4/40 schedule. The Henrico County police committee decided to recommend a four-day, 10-hour-a-day schedule with rotating cycle. Each officer would work four days, then have three days off; four days, three off; and four days, two off. It was necessary to have one cycle of two days in order that the days off would rotate each month. The rotating schedule allowed officers to have up to 33 weekends off per year, as opposed to the 12 allotted under the 7/56 schedule.

Three months after the 4/40 rotating schedule was implemented, an attitude survey was used to acquire officer reactions. Of the officers contacted, 79 percent felt that the 4/40 rotating schedule increased officer safety; 67 percent felt it increased work satisfaction; 96 percent believed it increased the availability of officers during peak hours of call for service; and 57 percent felt it improved their family life.

Six months after implementing the new work schedule, sick leave records indicated a 18.2 percent decline compared to the same period the preceding year. Also, officer productivity increased. Felony arrests increased 42.5 percent, misdemeanor arrests increased 69.5 percent, drunk driving arrests increased 75.4 percent, and other traffic-related arrests increased 38.9 percent. The only noticeable flaws with the new system involved the transfer of information between shifts and the high levels of reported fatigue. The officers

---

* Case is based on Robert H. Crowder, Jr., "The Four-Day, Ten-Hour Workweek," *Personnel Journal*, January 1982, pp. 26–28.

complained that in the 4/40 arrangement less time is taken to trade information. After working for 10 hours the officers are anxious to get away from work as soon as their shift is over. Fatigue is still as nagging a problem as it was with the 7/56 schedule. There is some fear that the fatigue problem may result in tragic consequences for some officers in the future.

The four-person committee is ready to meet again in about four weeks to examine the 4/40 rotating schedule. They are thinking about (1) continuing the schedule as is, (2) making some modifications, or (3) dropping the 4/40 and returning to the 7/56 work schedule. There is some sentiment among officers for each of these options.

Questions for Thought

1. Are the three-month and six-month evaluations sufficient to conclude that the Henrico County 4/40 plan is a success? Why?
2. At this point what option seems to be best for the police officers? Why?
3. Should an employer such as Henrico County be concerned about the family time of its employees? Why?

EVALUATING THE P/HRM FUNCTION

LEARNING OBJECTIVES

After studying this chapter, you should be able to:

- **Define** the evaluation of the P/HRM function.
- **Describe** the difference between functional and dysfunctional turnover.
- **Explain** why P/HRM managers must have diagnostic skills.
- **Discuss** the purposes served by evaluating the activities and programs of the P/HRM unit.

KEY TERMS

Absenteeism
Attitude Survey

CHAPTER OUTLINE

P/HRM ‣ IN ‣ ACTION

Emily   Denton

The setting is a massive conference room. The top managers of General Products, a large manufacturing company in Seattle, are participating in the annual planning meeting. Each functional vice president presents the department's budget for next year, after a review of the past year's accomplishments.

After Emily Park, vice president for marketing, completes her budget request, her advertising budget for the next year is cut, with the explanation that "profits are down at the plant."

Denton Major, vice president for P/HRM and organization planning, speaks next.

Denton: Well, folks, I'm not going to take much of your time. It's been a long day. You know what we do for the company. We hire, train, and pay the employees, provide benefits, counsel, help with discipline, EEO, and so on. P/HRM is not asking for any major in-creases. My budget is simply last year's budget adjusted upward 6 per-cent for inflation. Any questions?

Emily: Wait a minute, Denton. My budget just got cut. Here you come asking for 6 percent more than last year. I suppose we have to have a P/HRM department. But why shouldn't my advertising budget be increased and your budget cut? After all, adver-tising brings in customers and helps us make money. What *specifically* does P/HRM do for our profit and loss state-ment? How *specifically* does P/HRM help us reach our goals of growth and profitability?

Emily has unknowingly pointed out what purpose a personnel audit serves. If Denton had been systematically evaluating the P/HRM department, he would have some answers ready. And it looks like he will need some good ones, or the P/HRM budget and ac-tivities could well be cut.

There is an old motto in P/HRM that, if you can't measure it, forget it. The premise of this saying is that if you can't show what contribution you are making, there is little hope that anyone will pay attention to your requests. Therefore, measurement in terms of evaluation is a high priority need in any P/HRM unit.

Evaluation of the P/HRM function, the Personnel/Human Resource audit, is defined as a systematic, formal experience designed to measure the costs and benefits of the total P/HRM program and to compare its efficiency and effectiveness with the organization's past performance, the performance of comparable effective enterprises, and the enterprise's objective.

Evaluation of the activities and programs of the P/HRM unit is performed for these purposes:

- To justify P/HRM's existence and budget.
- To improve the P/HRM function by providing a means to decide when to drop activities and when to add them.
- To provide feedback from employees and operating managers on P/HRM effectiveness.
- To help P/HRM do its part to achieve the organization's objectives.

Top management's part in the personnel audit is to insist that all aspects of the organization be evaluated and to establish the general philosophy of evaluation. The P/HRM department is often involved in designing the audit. In part the data for the audit arise from the cost/benefit studies of the P/HRM activities as described in Chapters 3–19. A variety of methods can be used to conduct audits, including interviews, questionnaires, observations, or a combination of these.[1] The operating manager's role is to help gather the data and to help evaluate the P/HRM function in the same way it evaluates other functions and users of resources in the organization. An evaluation program can be useful in improving the quality of the programs and services provided by a P/HRM unit.[2]

Evaluation of the P/HRM function is a Stage II activity—many researchers have advocated its implementation, but only a few good empirical studies of effective and ineffective ways of evaluating or auditing P/HRM activity have been done.

In one study, a panel of experts drawn from management, unions, human resource managers, and employees was asked to determine the most important P/HRM department activities.[3] Exhibit 20–1 presents the results of the study.

This study also identified the criteria that were considered to be the best indicator of a P/HRM unit's efforts in an organization. The list of criteria suggest that the satisfaction of the managers and people using P/HRM services and programs is extremely important. See Exhibit 20–2.

The results from this and other studies point to the need for a P/HRM unit to pay attention to the needs and interests of multiple constituents.[4] In fact, Tsui—in conducting the research—refers to her study as a multiple constitu-

---

[1] Wayne F. Cascio, *Costing Human Resources: The Financial Impact of Behavior in Organizations* (Boston: Kent Publishing Co., 1987).

[2] Clay Carr, "Injecting Quality into Personnel Management," *Personnel Journal,* September 1987, pp. 43–51.

[3] Anne S. Tsui, "Personnel Department Effectiveness: A Tripartite Approach," *Industrial Relations,* 1984, pp. 184–97.

[4] Anne S. Tsui, "Activities and Effectiveness of the Human Resource Department: A Multiple Constituency Approach," in *Personnel and Human Resource Management,* ed. R. S. Schuler, S. A. Youngblood, and V. L. Huber (St. Paul: West Publishing), pp. 465–83.

▬▬▬▬▬

EXHIBIT 20–1 Seventeen Most Important P/HRM Department Activities

1. Provide advice and counsel to management on individual employee problem identification and solution (e.g., deal with adverse or difficult personnel situations such as absenteeism).
2. Communicate to management the philosophy, legal implications, and strategy relating to employee relations.
3. Provide advice and counsel to management on employee relations problems.
4. Ensure consistent and equitable treatment of all employees.
5. Administer grievance procedure according to policy (identify and analyze problems, review deviations and exceptions, resolve problems).
6. Provide advice and counsel to management on staffing policy and related problems.
7. Coordinate the hiring procedure (establish starting salaries, send offer letters, follow up to obtain acceptance, administer medical questionnaires).
8. Communicate compensation/benefits programs to management (interpret/explain compensation policies and procedures, inform management of legal implications of compensation practices).
9. Process enrollments and communicate benefits program to employees.
10. Resolve benefits administration problems.
11. Process benefits claims (health, workers' compensation, pension, unusual or unique claims).
12. Assist management in resolving salary problems involving individual employees (salary equity issues).
13. Maintain employee and organization files (keep files orderly and systematic).
14. Ensure compliance with federal and state fair employment practices.
15. Communicate sexual harassment policy and other communications of general EEO philosophy and objectives.
16. Consult with management on the practical implications of corporate human resources programs.
17. Keep up with HR programs developed at the corporate or central personnel departments.

ency approach. Managers, employees, and executives are constituencies that the P/HRM department is serving.

A DIAGNOSTIC APPROACH TO EVALUATION OF THE P/HRM FUNCTION

As emphasized in each chapter, a diagnostic approach to P/HRM practices is considered to be a feasible and informative method. This approach actually encourages the evaluation of the P/HRM unit and its activities. Exhibit 20–3 shows the factors in the diagnostic model that affect evaluation of the P/HRM function in an organization. A major factor in determining whether evaluation takes place is the orientation or attitudes of the controlling interest—the top-level executives—toward evaluation and the organization's style.

Some managers feel that formal evaluations of the function are very useful. Others do not favor them.[5] Formal evaluation programs of the function are

---

[5] Jac Fitz-Enz, "Quantifying the Human Resources Function," *Personnel,* March–April 1980, pp. 41–52.

EXHIBIT 20–2   **Twelve Most Meaningful Criteria for Evaluating the Effectiveness of the P/HRM Department**

Subjective criteria.

1. Level of cooperation from personnel department.
2. Line managers' opinion of personnel department effectiveness.
3. Degree to which the department is open and available to all employees to deal with problems or explain company policies.
4. Employees' trust and confidence in the personnel department.
5. Quickness and effectiveness of responses to each question brought to the personnel department.
6. Rating of quality of service provided by the personnel department to other departments.
7. Rating of quality of information and advice provided to top management.
8. Satisfaction and dissatisfaction of clients—managers and employees.

Objective criteria.

9. Degree to which the department has a strategy to support local management business plans in relation to human resources.
10. Affirmative action goal attainment.
11. Average time taken to fill requisitions.
12. Efficiency—personnel department budget/population served.

---

more likely to be conducted in some types of organizations than others. Larger organizations that are labor intensive and geographically dispersed probably have some type of evaluation for most functional departments, including P/HRM. Such programs are also more likely when economic conditions are bad, particularly for profit-oriented organizations, because they can establish the cost effectiveness of such functions.

It is our contention that evaluation of the effectiveness of P/HRM programs is needed to determine how healthy the overall organization is in accomplishing its mission and goals. Evaluation serves as a unifying force in that it focuses attention on crucial factors such as performance, satisfaction, turnover, and absenteeism. Without an evaluation philosophy and theme, the various P/HRM programs are treated in a fragmented fashion. Staffing experts focus on securing the best new hirees. The compensation specialist's concern is having a competitive pay system. The training expert works to create a learning and development atmosphere. Each of these areas is important for the well-being of the organization, but there is often little effort at integrating the various activities. The attempt to evaluate each of the P/HRM programs separately and together as a collective set of what the P/HRM is doing fosters a unifying spirit. The success or failure of P/HRM is considered in terms of the unit, not as an individual phenomenon.[6]

---

[6] Jac Fitz-Enz, *How to Measure Human Resources Management* (New York: McGraw-Hill, 1984), p. 23.

EXHIBIT 20–3   **Factors Affecting the Evaluation of the P/HRM Function**

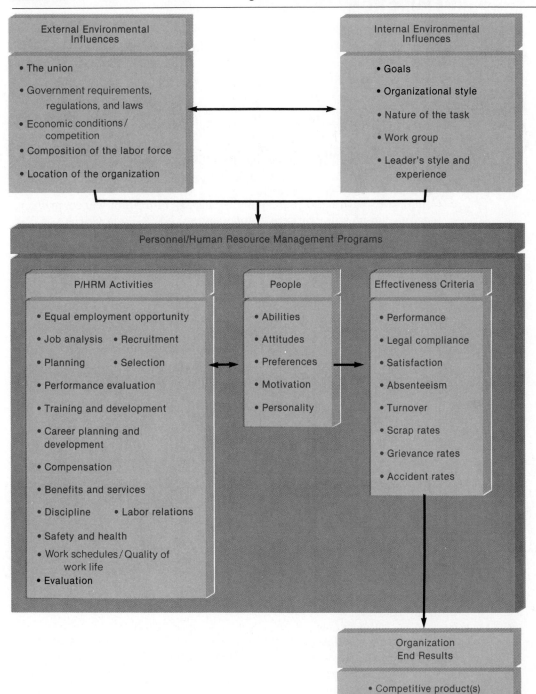

External Environmental Influences

- The union
- Government requirements, regulations, and laws
- Economic conditions/competition
- Composition of the labor force
- Location of the organization

Internal Environmental Influences

- Goals
- Organizational style
- Nature of the task
- Work group
- Leader's style and experience

Personnel/Human Resource Management Programs

P/HRM Activities

- Equal employment opportunity
- Job analysis   • Recruitment
- Planning   • Selection
- Performance evaluation
- Training and development
- Career planning and development
- Compensation
- Benefits and services
- Discipline   • Labor relations
- Safety and health
- Work schedules/Quality of work life
- Evaluation

People

- Abilities
- Attitudes
- Preferences
- Motivation
- Personality

Effectiveness Criteria

- Performance
- Legal compliance
- Satisfaction
- Absenteeism
- Turnover
- Scrap rates
- Grievance rates
- Accident rates

Organization End Results

- Competitive product(s)
- Competitive service(s)

APPROACHES TO EVALUATION
OF THE P/HRM FUNCTION

Once it has been decided that it is useful to evaluate the effectiveness of the P/HRM function and the organization's use of human resources, the next issue is how it should be done and what measures or criteria of effectiveness should be used. The criteria can be grouped as follows:

1. Performance measures.
   a. Overall P/HRM performance. For example, the unit labor costs per unit of output.
   b. P/HRM department costs and performance—the cost per employee of P/HRM programs.
2. Compliance measures.
   a. Compliance with legal requirements such as minimum wages, privacy, termination-at-will, workers' compensation, EEOC, and OSHA.
3. Employee satisfaction measures.
   a. Employees' satisfaction with their jobs.
   b. Employees' satisfaction with P/HRM activities such as training, pay, benefits, and career development.
4. Indirect measures of employee performance.
   a. Employee turnover—rate of quits as a percentage of the labor force and by units over time.
   b. Absenteeism—rate of voluntary absences of the labor force and by units over time.
   c. Scrap rates (poor quality output that must be scrapped).
   d. Other measures of quality.
   e. Rates of employee requests for transfer.
   f. Number of grievances per unit and in total labor force over time.
   g. Safety and accident rates.
   h. Number of improvement suggestions per employee over time.

Each of these measures—or some combination of them—expresses the efficiency and/or effectiveness of the P/HRM effort. To make P/HRM worthwhile, it is necessary for the organization to measure its achievements against specific goals, such as:

Reduce labor costs by 3 percent this year.
Reduce absenteeism by 2 percent this year.
Increase the satisfaction index by 5 percent compared to last year's attitude survey results.

These goals are set relative to past trends, current achievements of other relevant organizations, or higher aspiration level of today's managers.

Once these criteria are set, the next decision is to determine which of the approaches to evaluation is to be used. A BNA survey indicated which ap-

EXHIBIT 20–4   Personnel Evaluation Methods Used

	All Companies	Larger	Smaller
Evaluating department results against goals	33%*	37%	23%
Periodic audit of policies, procedures	25	25	26
Surveys, meetings, discussions, and interviews	20	19	23
Analysis of turnover figures	16	15	19
Analysis of grievances	8	9	10
Analysis of cost of performing various personnel functions	6	7	5
Analysis of training effectiveness	5	5	5
Analysis of accident frequency	5	6	4
Feedback from managers	5	5	5

* Includes 7 percent of companies specifying an MBO program for the personnel department.

Source: *Labor Policy and Practice—Personnel* (Washington, D.C.: Bureau of National Affairs, 1975).

proaches are being most used (see Exhibit 20–4).[7] In this chapter we will examine some of the most frequently used approaches to evaluation of the P/HRM function.

EVALUATION OF CHECKLIST

One approach is to review and analyze the practices of organizations that are considered to be effective in terms of P/HRM policies and practices. This is usually implemented by developing a checklist of the model organization's P/HRM activities. Checklists are also used by consultants to analyze an organization's P/HRM function.

In the checklist approach to evaluation, the P/HRM department or a consultant prepares a list of important P/HRM activities to be performed. The checklist usually requires the analyst to check yes or no columns beside the listed activity. The checklist may also include items designed to determine if existing P/HRM policies are being followed. The items on the checklist are usually grouped by P/HRM activity area, such as employment planning or safety and health. Exhibit 20–5 presents a sample of checklist items that would stimulate discussion and debate among managers about P/HRM activities.

Although a checklist is better than a totally informal approach, it still is a rather simple approach to evaluation. And even though checklists provide a

[7] Bureau of National Affairs, *Employee Absenteeism and Turnover,* Personnel Policies Forum, Survey 106 (Washington, D.C.: U.S. Government Printing Office, May 1974).

format that is relatively easy to record and prepare, scoring interpretation is quite difficult. Three "nos" in one group of items may not equal three others. Some of the policies are more important than others. Ignoring EEOC or OSHA rules is a lot more negative than the absence of a Christmas party, for example.

EXHIBIT 20–5   Personnel Audit: An Illustration (An Interview with the Operating Manager)

1. What would you say are the objectives of your plant?
2. As you see it, what are the major responsibilities of managers?
3. Have there been any important changes in these over the last few years in the plant?
4. Are there any personnel responsibilities on which you think many managers need to do a better job?
5. What are some of the *good* things about employee relations in this plant?
6. Do you feel there are any important problems or difficulties in the plant? Causes? How widespread? Corrective measures?
7. Do you have any personnel goals for the year?
8. Overall, how well do you feel the personnel department does its job? Changes the department should make?

Community relations
9. What are managers expected to do about community relations? Is there plant pressure? Reaction to pressures?
10. What have you done about community relations? Do you encourage subordinates to participate in them? What are your personal activities?

Safety and medical
11. Who is responsible for safety in your area? Role of group leaders and lead men?
12. What things do you do about safety? Regular actions? Results achieved?
13. Do you have any important safety problems in your operation? Causes? Cures? How widespread?
14. What does the specialist do? How helpful are his activities? Other things he should do?
15. Are there any other comments or suggestions about safety you would like to make?
16. Have you any comments about the dispensary? Employee time involved? Types of service offered? Courtesy?

Communication
17. How do you keep your people informed? What are your regular communication activities? Particular problems?
18. How do you go about finding out information from employees? Channels and methods? How regularly are such channels used? How much information is passed on to employee superiors? How much interest do supervisors show? Does personnel provide information?
19. Has the personnel department helped improve communication in the plant? What assistance is needed? Nature of assistance provided?
20. Has the personnel department helped you with your own communication activities?

Communication channels available
21. What improvement is needed in these?
22. Are there any other comments about communication you'd like to make? Any changes or improvements you'd especially like to see?

Manpower planning
23. What kind of plans do you have for meeting the future manpower needs of your own component? Indicate plans for hourly, nonexempt. How far do plans extend into the future?
24. What does your manager do about planning for future manpower needs? How is this planning related to your own planning?
25. What part does the personnel department play in planning for the future manpower needs of your component? Of the plant as a whole?

Personnel development
26. How is the training of employees handled in your group? (on-the-job training) Who does? Procedures followed?

EXHIBIT 20–5   *(concluded)*

27. What changes or improvements do you think should be made in the training of employees? (on-the-job training) Why?
28. What changes or improvements do you feel are needed in the amount or kind of classroom training given here? Why?
29. Have you worked with your subordinates on improving their current job performance? Inside or outside regular appraisal? Procedure? Employee reaction? Results? Improvements needed?
30. Have you worked with subordinates on plans for preparing for future job responsibilities? Inside or outside regular appraisal? Procedure? Employee reaction? Results? Improvements needed?
31. What does personnel do to help you with your training and development problems?
32. Do you have any other comments on personnel development or training?

Personnel practices
33. How are employees added to your work group? New employees for example. (*Probe:* Specify exempt, nonexempt, hourly. Procedure followed? How are decisions made? Contribution of personnel? Changes needed and reasons? Transfers?)
34. How is bumping or downgrading handled? (*Probe:* Specify nonexempt or hourly. Procedure followed? How are decisions made? Contribution of personnel? Changes needed and reasons?)
35. How are promotions into or out of your group handled? (*Probe:* Specify exempt, nonexempt, hourly. Procedure followed? How are decisions made? Contribution of personnel? Changes needed and reasons?)
36. Do you have any problems with layoffs? (*Probe:* Nature of problems? Possible solutions? Contribution of personnel?)
37. How do you handle "probationary" periods? (*Probe:* Specify hourly, nonexempt, exempt. Length of period? Union attitude? How handled?)
38. How are inefficient people handled? (*Probe:* Specify hourly, nonexempt, exempt. How do you handle? How do other supervisors handle? Frequency?)

Salary administration—Exempt
39. What is your responsibility for exempt salary administration? (*Probe:* Position evaluation? Determining increases? Degree of authority?)
40. How do you go about deciding on salary increases? (*Probe:* Procedure? Weight given to merit? Informing employees? Timing?)
41. What are your major problems in salary administration? (*Probe:* Employee-centered? Self-centered? Plan-centered?)
42. Has the personnel department assisted you with your salary administration problems? How? (*Probe:* Administrator's role? Nature of assistance? Additional assistance needed and reasons?)

Salary administration—Nonexempt
43. What is your responsibility for nonexempt salary administration? (*Probe:* Nature of plan? Position evaluation? Changes needed and reasons?)
44. How has the personnel department helped in nonexempt salary administration? (*Probe:* Specify personnel or other salary administrators. Nature of assistance? Additional assistance needed and reasons?)

Source: Reprinted by permission from "Auditing PAIR," by Walter R. Mahler, in *ASPA Handbook of Personnel and Industrial Relations,* ed. D. Yoder and H. Heneman, p. 2–103. Copyright © 1979 by The Bureau of National Affairs, Inc., Washington, D.C. 20037.

STATISTICAL APPROACHES TO EVALUATION

The most frequently used formal evaluation methods are those that examine the work organization's employment statistics and analyze them. The statistical approach can be much more sophisticated than checklists. The statistics

EXHIBIT 20–6 P/HRM Evaluation Ratios

Effectiveness Ratios
Ratio of number of employees to total output—in general.
Sales in dollars per employee for the whole company or by organizational unit (business).
Output in units per employee hour worked for the entire organizational unit.
Scrap loss per unit of the organization.
Payroll costs by unit per employee grade.

Accident Ratios
Frequency of accident rate for the organization as a whole or by unit.
Number of lost-time accidents.
Compensation paid per 1,000 hours worked for accidents.
Accidents by type.
Accidents classified by type of injury to each part of the body.
Average cost of accident by part of the body involved.

Organizational Labor Relations Ratios
Number of grievances filed.
Number of arbitration awards lost.

Turnover and Absenteeism Ratios
Attendance, tardiness, and overtime comparisons by organizational unit as a measure of how
well an operation is handling employees.
Employee turnover by unit and for the organization.

Employment Ratios
Vacations granted as a percentage of employees eligible.
Sick-leave days granted as a percentage of labor-days worked.
Military leaves granted per 100 employees.
Jury duty leaves granted per 100 employees.
Maternity leaves granted per 100 employees.
Educational leaves granted per 100 employees.
Personal leaves granted per 100 employees.
Employment distribution by chronological age.
Employment distribution by length of service with organization.
Employment distribution by sex, race, national origin, religion.
Managerial distribution by chronological age, sex, race, national origin, religion.
Average age of work force.
Average age of managerial work force.

gathered are compared to the unit's own past performance or to some other
yardstick of measurement. Of course, quantitative factors alone never explain
or evaluate anything by themselves. The *reasons* for the statistics are the
important thing; statistics only indicate where to begin to look for evaluation
problems.

The raw data of such reports are interesting themselves, and they can
provide some input to evaluation. Most organizations that perform evaluation,
however, analyze these data by the use of ratios and similar comparative
methods. Exhibit 20-6 provides a list of such ratios and similar analytical
methods. Once these and similar ratios are computed for an organization, they
can be compared to similar organizations' ratios.[8]

The statistical approaches used most frequently consider turnover, absen-

---

[8] Joel Lapointe, "How to Calculate the Cost of Human Resources," *Personnel Journal*, January
1988, pp. 34–45.

teeism, grievances, attitude surveys and other measures of effectiveness, and statistical analysis of the P/HRM department itself. Because of the widespread organizational review of these statistics they were selected for inclusion in this chapter.

Evaluation of Turnover

Turnover is the net result of the exit of some employees and entrance of others to the work organization. Turnover can be quite costly to an employer. One estimate is that it costs American industry $11 billion a year.[9] The costs of turnover include: increased costs for social security and unemployment compensation; terminal vacations; severance pay; underutilized facilities until the replacement is hired; employment costs, such as recruiting ads and expenses, interview time, test costs, computer record costs, and moving expenses; and administration costs of notification and payroll changes. Obviously, there is also a loss of productivity until the new employee reaches the performance level of the one who left the job.

Average monthly turnover rates for the 1985 period presented were 1.1 percent of the work force in the Bureau of National Affairs' survey. The bar graphs in Exhibit 20–7 show turnover averages by size of firm or industry, and region of the country.[10]

All turnover is not a net loss, however. Employees who are not contributing to organizational effectiveness should be retrained or dehired. The employer has no control over some types of turnover: A student's husband or wife, for example, may work until graduation and then move away.

There are several quantitative methods for computing turnover. Some of the traditional formulations are:

$$\text{Separation rate} = \frac{\text{Number of separations during the month}}{\text{Total number of employees at midmonth}} \times 100 \quad (1)$$

$$\text{Quit rate} = \frac{\text{Total quits}}{\text{Average working force}} \times 100 \quad (2)$$

$$\text{Avoidable turnover} = \frac{\text{Total separations—Unavoidables}}{\text{Average work force}} \times 100 \quad (3)$$

Formula 1 is the most general and is the one recommended by the Department of Labor. Formula 2 tries to isolate a difficult type of turnover, and formula 3 is the most refined. It eliminates quits by those groups that can be expected to leave: part-timers and women leaving for maternity reasons. These data can be refined further by computing turnover per 100 employees by length of employment, by job classification, by job category, and by each organizational unit.

---

[9] "Employment Turnover: Measurement and Control," *Compensation and Benefits Review,* June 1987, pp. 64–74.

[10] The BNA data is based on BNA's *Report on Job Absence and Turnover,* 3rd Quarter, 1985.

EXHIBIT   20–7   1983 Turnover Rates: 12-Month Average

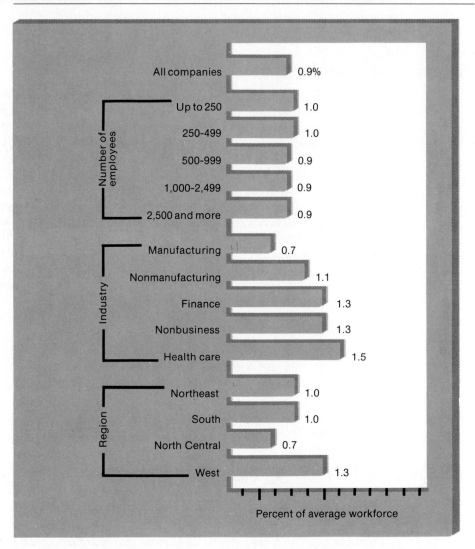

All companies	0.9%
Number of employees	
Up to 250	1.0
250-499	1.0
500-999	0.9
1,000-2,499	0.9
2,500 and more	0.9
Industry	
Manufacturing	0.7
Nonmanufacturing	1.1
Finance	1.3
Nonbusiness	1.3
Health care	1.5
Region	
Northeast	1.0
South	1.0
North Central	0.7
West	1.3

Percent of average workforce

Source: *BNA's Quarterly Report on Job Absence and Turnover, 4th Quarter, 1983* (Bureau of National Affairs, 1984).

One BNA study found that 57 percent of the organizations surveyed computed the data in such a way as to analyze turnover by department or division. This is more likely to be done in large businesses and nonmanufacturing firms than in other types of organizations. Organizations which include all employees in the calculation (67 percent) could determine the differences in turnover by employee groups. In one recent year, the average turnover was 4.2 percent, but the rate in one organization was as high as 38 percent.[11]

---

[11] Bureau of National Affairs, *Employee Absenteeism and Turnover.*

A RETURN TO THE P/HRM · IN · ACTION

Denton applied some quantitative formulas to acquire a better picture of the General Products turnover situation. Here is what he found:

$$\text{Separation rate} = \frac{\text{Average for last six months}}{\text{Total number of employees at mid-month}} \times 100$$

$$= \frac{397}{9{,}000} \times 100$$

$$= \underline{4.4\%}$$

$$\text{Quit rate} = \frac{\text{Total quits}}{\text{Average working force}} \times 100$$

$$= \frac{318}{8{,}750} \times 100$$

$$= \underline{3.6\%}$$

$$\text{Avoidable turnover} = \frac{\text{Total separations—Unavoidables}}{\text{Average work force}} \times 100$$

$$= \frac{397 - 94}{8{,}750} \times 100$$

$$= \underline{3.5\%}$$

He looked at these figures and compared them to figures that he had on two of the main competitors in the Seattle area. He found that General Products' rates were significantly lower than the competitors. This data would help him build a case for P/HRM's contribution to General Products the next time he had to fight for budget dollars.

One way employers analyze the turnover rate is to compare the organization's rate with those of other organizations. Various sources publish average turnover rates quarterly or yearly. These include agencies such as the government labor departments, the Administrative Management Society, and BNA's quarterly reports on turnover and absenteeism. Another approach is to analyze the enterprise's turnover by comparing the differences in rates by employee classifications or departments.

Most theories of turnover maintain that employees leave their jobs when their needs are not being satisfied at their present place of work *and* an alternative job becomes available which the employees believe will satisfy more of their needs. Perhaps the most informative effort at explaining and discussing the turnover process is that offered by Mobley.[12] He suggested, empirically tested, and supported the view that job attitudes are extremely important in the decision to leave an organization. His work indicates that the intention to quit is a significant predictor of actual quitting behavior. Mobley's theory of the importance of job attitudes has been tested and cross-validated with workers in various occupations—clerical, nursing, manufacturing.[13]

---

[12] William Mobley, "Intermediate Linkages in the Relationship between Job Satisfaction and Employee Turnover," *Journal of Applied Psychology,* April 1977, pp. 237–40; and W. Mobley, R. Griffeth, H. Hand, and B. Meglino, "Review and Conceptual Analysis of the Turnover Process", *Psychological Bulletin,* May 1979, pp. 408–14.

[13] Richard T. Mowday, Christine Koberg, and Angeline McArthur, "The Psychology of the Withdrawal Process: A Cross-Validation Test of Mobley's Intermediate Linkages Model of Turnover in Two Samples," *Academy of Management Journal,* March 1984, pp. 79–94.

One organizational researcher has suggested that levels of turnover are often overstated.[14] He suggests that some turnover is beneficial or functional. This is the case when a person wants to leave the organization and the management is unconcerned about the loss. This lack of concern may be due to the poor evaluation of the person's performance or a lack of ability. If researchers add this type of turnover to what is called dysfunctional turnover, the number of leavers is overstated. Dysfunctional turnover occurs when a person leaves an organization and the firm wants to retain the person.

Dalton contends that the traditional analysis of turnover (especially Formulas 1 and 2 in this chapter) disregards the organizational benefits of functional turnover. Even with functional turnover there are some costs—recruitment, training, and a portion of the administrative overhead.[15] Consequently, P/HRM researchers should consider separating dysfunctional and functional turnover.

Analysis of a large number of studies examining the interrelationships between turnover and absenteeism shows that, in general, these factors are intercorrelated.[16] That is, if turnover is high, absenteeism is also likely to be high. These studies also found that both were caused by the same factors. In general, employees first exhibited high absenteeism, which led to high turnover. Thus absenteeism and turnover are not alternative methods of showing dissatisfaction. Rather, high absenteeism is a sign that high turnover is likely in the future.

Overall, organizations try to reduce turnover by a number of methods: better employee selection, orientation, communication, supervisor training, incentive awards, and data analyses. In addition, many organizations have tried to determine why their turnover takes place. One method is to interview employees just before they leave the enterprise to try to determine why they are leaving. This is called an exit interview. Some find exit interviews unreliable and not useful. Others contend that, properly done, they are reliable enough for these purposes. Problems can arise when exiting employees give partial reasons for leaving because they need references from the employer or might want to be reemployed at a future date.

Other methods that have been tried to reduce turnover, besides exit interviews, include telephone or in-person interviews a few weeks after termination. These would seem to have the same flaws as exit interviews, but little data are available on the reliability of these methods. Another approach is to give employees a questionnaire as they are exiting and ask them to complete it and mail it back a month or so later. This gives the employee some protection and would appear to be a much better approach than the others. Organizations

---

[14] D. R. Dalton, "Turnover and Absenteeism: Measures of Personnel Effectiveness," in *Applied Readings in Personnel and Human Resource Management,* ed. R. J. Schuler, J. M. McFillen, and D. R. Dalton (St. Paul, Minn.: West Publishing, 1981).

[15] D. R. Dalton, D. M. Krackhardt, and L. W. Porter, "Functional Turnover: An Empirical Assessment," *Journal of Applied Psychology,* December 1981, pp. 716–21.

[16] R. M. Steers and S. R. Rhodes, "A New Look at Absenteeism," *Personnel,* November–December 1980, pp. 60–65; and Dalton, "Turnover and Absenteeism."

using this method find a rather low percentage of employees complete the questionnaires, however. No reliability data appear to be available on these questionnaires.

In summary, turnover needs to be examined and monitored since it involves the most important resource of an organization. The firm needs to know who is leaving, why they are leaving, and whether any effort on their part can slow turnover. These are questions that can be answered if a thorough evaluation of a turnover program is implemented.[17]

Evaluation of Absences

A second measure used to evaluate the P/HRM function is absenteeism rates.

> Absenteeism is the failure of employees to report for work when they are scheduled to work.
> Tardiness is partial absenteeism, in that employees report late to work.

Absenteeism is undesirable because of its cost and the operating problems it causes.[18] Absenteeism's costs to the organization include the costs of benefits, which continue even when workers are absent, so benefit costs are higher per unit of output. Overtime pay also may be necessary for the worker who is doing the job for the missing worker. Facilities may be underutilized and productivity may drop because of reduced output due to understaffing. There also may be increased costs for replacements, substandard production, the need for more help from supervisors and peers, and increased inspection costs.

It is estimated that 400 million workdays are lost per year in the United States because of absenteeism. This is about 5.1 days per employee.[19] In many industries, absenteeism runs as high as 10 to 20 percent of the work force on any given day. Combining the average number of workdays lost per year with an estimate of the daily cost of nonmanagerial absenteeism per worker, $66 including wages, fringe benefits, and loss in productivity, yields an annual cost of about $26.4 billion.[20]

How is absenteeism computed? The standard formula used by over 70 percent of those who compute absenteeism is:[21]

---

[17] Jeanne M. Carsten and Paul E. Spector, "Unemployment, Job Satisfaction, and Employee Turnover: A Meta-Analytic Test of the Muchinsky Model," *Journal of Applied Psychology*, August 1987, pp. 374–81.

[18] P. M. Muchinsky and P. C. Morrow, "A Multidisciplinary Model of Voluntary Employee Turnover," *Journal of Vocational Behavior*, December 1980, pp. 263–90.

[19] Rick D. Hackett and Robert M. Guion, "A Reevaluation of The Absenteeism-Job Behavior Satisfaction Relationship," *Organizational Behavior and Human Decision Processes*, June 1985, pp. 340–81; and S. F. Yolles, D. A. Carone, and L. W. Krinsky, *Absenteeism in Industry* (Springfield, Ill.: Charles C. Thomas, 1975).

[20] R. M. Steers and S. R. Rhodes, "Major Influences on Attendance: A Process Model," *Journal of Applied Psychology*, August 1978, p. 391.

[21] Bureau of National Affairs, *Employee Absenteeism and Turnover*, p. 15.

$$\frac{\text{Number of employee days lost through job absence in the period}}{\text{Average number of employees} \times \text{Number of work days}} \times 100.$$

Most others use a variation of this formula, such as

$$\frac{\text{Total hours of absence}}{\text{Total hours worked (or scheduled)}} \times 100$$

Of 136 enterprises surveyed by BNA, about 40 percent calculated absenteeism rates, usually for all employees, and most often monthly (54 percent) or annually (40 percent). Of those calculating absenteeism, 70 percent did so by department or division. Most also separated out long-term absences from short-term ones.

Current research raises questions about the use of absence rates, especially aggregate measures of absenteeism, to evaluate the P/HRM function. Some observers suggest abandoning the measure. It appears that it is more useful to pursue research designed to identify absence-prone persons, work groups, working conditions, and communities with a view to designing strategies to reduce absenteeism.

One example is a study by Behrend and Pocock of 1,200 men employed at a General Motors plant in Scotland. One of the major conclusions of this study was that overall absence ratios, although of some use, are open to serious misinterpretation.[22] For example, the "average" employee in their study experienced three absences per year, totaling about 18 days. But the range was from employees who were not absent 1 day in six years to several who were absent 600 days over the six-year period. The authors convincingly demonstrate that it makes much more sense to classify employees into categories of absence proneness. When this approach is used, management can focus on workers with higher absence rates. Remedial action can then be taken to improve health if the cause appears to be illness, or by counseling, discipline, and so on, if health is not a factor.

Evaluation of Complaints and Grievances

A complaint is a statement (in written or oral form) of dissatisfaction or criticism by an employee to a manager.
A grievance is a complaint which has been presented formally and in writing to a management or union official.

Chapter 17 discussed what grievances are and how they are processed. The complaint-grievance rate and the severity of the grievances is another way to evaluate the P/HRM function. Of course, not all complaints or grievances

---

[22] Hilde Behrend and Stuart Pocock, "Absence and the Individual: A Six-Year Study in One Organization," *International Labour Review,* November–December 1976, pp. 311–27.

relate to P/HRM issues. They can be about equipment, machinery, and other matters, too. And the grievance rate can be related to the militancy of the union or the imminence to contract negotiations. Nevertheless, an increase in the rate and severity of complaints and grievances can indicate dissatisfaction, which in turn might lead to increases in absenteeism and turnover. Both factors indicate how successful the P/HRM department is in securing productivity and satisfaction for the employee. Statistical analyses of complaints and grievances have not been done as scientifically as for turnover and absenteeism.

Evaluation Using Attitude and Opinion Surveys

Another indicator of employee and managerial evaluation of the P/HRM program is obtained through the use of attitude or opinion surveys.

> An attitude or opinion survey is a set of written instruments completed by employees (usually anonymously) expressing their reactions to employer policies, practices, and job characteristics.

Effective attitude surveys are designed with precise goals in mind. The questions and items used are designed professionally and are tested on a sample of employees for reliability and validity prior to administration. Several other administrative factors may affect the validity. One is whether the employees feel that the employer is sincerely interested in knowing the truth and will act wherever possible to follow up on their suggestions.

The survey may include many P/HRM activities, job satisfaction, and other aspects of the organization's operations. Usually after the results of the survey are in, they are analyzed and fed back to the employee units. Organizations use attitude surveys to help evaluate the effectiveness of the total P/HRM program, or parts of it, such as pay, benefits, or training.

About 30 percent of organizations (mostly the larger and medium-sized ones) conduct regular attitude surveys. They are usually conducted on a yearly basis.[23] The organization itself can design the surveys, but approaches developed by consultants and similar services are also available. The survey develops a "snapshot view" of employee attitudes by unit and total organization. Typical topics surveyed are given in Exhibit 20–8.

One vital factor in the usefulness of attitude surveys is maintaining confidentiality of the data provided by employees. To assure reliability and validity of the data as far as possible, it has become typical to assure anonymity by questioning groups of employees together. Often the information is gathered by an outside consultant, such as a university professor.

---

[23] "Personnel Policies: Research and Evaluation" (ASPA–BNA Survey No. 37), *Bulletin to Management,* March 22, 1979, p. 6.

EXHIBIT 20–8 **Attitude Covered in Many Surveys**

Attitudes toward Working Conditions on the Job	**Attitudes toward Compensation and Rewards**	**Attitudes toward Supervisor**	**Attitudes toward the Employer**
Physical working conditions	Salaries	Communication abilities	P/HRM policies
Work scheduling and planning	Benefits	Qualifications and abilities	Communications
Work assignments and worker abilities	Promotions	Supervisory style	General reputation in community
Job demands	Status and recognition		Reputation nationally
Job security			Attitudes toward future unionization
Hours of work			
Safety on the job			
Interpersonal relations at work			
Adequacy of training by employer			

A typical survey is handled as follows. The P/HRM department contacts a consultant to administer the survey. The consultant first works with P/HRM in developing the data-gathering approach. Design of these questionnaires or interview schedules is an important technical project. It should be done by professionals in P/HRM or with expertise in surveying. Typically, the consultant works with the P/HRM department and a sample of operating managers and employees in developing the survey. Finally, the consultant gathers the data and processes it or sends it to a computer service center for processing. No one from the employing organization sees the actual data or questionnaires completed by the employees.

In preparation for the attitude survey, employees receive a letter explaining the purpose of the study (such as to improve working conditions). The letter also explains the safeguards for the employees that will be provided, such as the use of consultants. If a questionnaire is used, the employees complete them in homogenous groups (exempt or nonexempt, for example).

The two principle methods used to gather data are interviews and questionnaires. Sometimes both are used by an organization. Surveys indicate that almost two thirds of the employers use questionnaires alone, less than 10 percent use only interviews, and the rest use a combination of both.[24] Studies suggest that information is more reliable and complete if interviews are used. Usually the interviews follow the structured approach. If questionnaires are used, three approaches are followed: yes, no, or don't know answers; open-ended essay questions; or structured questions with multiple-choice answers. An example of the latter is given in Exhibit 20–9.

---

[24] David R. York, "Attitude Surveying," *Personnel Journal*, May 1985, pp. 70–73.

EXHIBIT 20–9   **Attitude Survey (Partial Sample)**

INSTRUCTIONS

This is a survey of the ideas and opinions of Baker Company salaried employees. WHAT YOU SAY IN THIS QUESTIONNAIRE IS COMPLETELY CONFIDENTIAL. We do not want to know who you are. We do want to know, however, how employees with different interests, experience, and doing different kinds of work, feel about their jobs and Baker.

This is not a test. There are no right or wrong answers. Whether the results of this survey give a true picture of the Baker Company depends on whether each of you answers each of the questions in the way you really feel. The usefulness of this survey in making Baker a better place to work depends on the honesty and care with which you answer the questions.

Your answers will be compiled with many others and summarized to prepare a *report* for Baker. Your identity will always be protected. We do not need your name, only your impressions. Your written comments will be put in typewritten form so that your handwriting will not even be seen by anyone at Baker.

Please complete each of the six parts of the survey so that all of your impressions can be recorded. Remember your honest impressions are all that we are asking for.

PART I: THE JOB AND CONDITIONS

The statements below are related to certain aspects of your job at Baker. Please circle the response number that best describes how you feel about the statement.

1 = Strongly disagree   2 = Disagree   3 = Undecided   4 = Agree   5 = Strongly agree

Pay	Strongly Disagree	Disagree	Undecided	Agree	Strongly Agree
My pay is all right for the kind of work I do	1	2	3	4	5
I make as much money as most of my friends	1	2	3	4	5
My pay allows me to keep up with the cost of living	1	2	3	4	5
I am satisfied with the pay I receive for my job	1	2	3	4	5
Most employees at Baker get paid at least what they deserve	1	2	3	4	5
I understand how my salary is determined	1	2	3	4	5
What changes, if any, should be made with the Baker pay system?_____					

Fringe Benefits					
Our major fringe benefit plan provides excellent coverage	1	2	3	4	5
I understand what our fringe benefits at Baker are	1	2	3	4	5
I am satisfied with our fringe benefit plan	1	2	3	4	5
What, if anything, should be done with the Baker fringe benefit plans?_____					

After the data are gathered, they are analyzed. Present responses are compared to past ones to see if the trends are positive or negative. Responses from different subunits are compared to see if some are more favorable than others.

Overall indications lead to management actions of one type or another. Policies are revised, enforced, or created, and the results are communicated to the employees. The attitude survey tends to generate expectations on the part of employees. Thus, management needs to be sure that some feedback and action follow the survey. Failure to do something often results in future resistance to surveys and to a feeling that any survey is ritualistic and not useful, as both managers and researchers have found.[25]

Quality of Work Life Survey For a number of years Graphic Controls Corporation (Buffalo, New York) has worked with the Institute for Social Research (ISR) at the University of Michigan.[26] The ISR serves as an outside research group that surveys the quality of work life in the corporation and prepares a report of its findings. Graphic Controls contacted the ISR seeking help to learn more about the attitudes of its employees.

The first survey was administered in 1975, and the data obtained was used to make a number of decisions. The decisions involved P/HRM policies concerning working conditions, fringe benefits, development of skills, and improvement in the overall quality of work life (environment, supervision, opportunities). In addition to the survey data Graphic Controls reviewed annually safety records, employment, and promotion.

In 1977, Graphic Controls management decided to make the survey and analysis a part of the company's annual report. William Clarkson, the firm's chief executive officer, explains Graphic's interest in surveying and going public like this:

> Psychological research tells us that a key human need is to know where one stands and how one rates. A good manager has measurements for key areas of the business. A quality-of-work life audit provides valid data for one of the cornerstones that make a business successful—the human resources of the organization. For managers and for employees, it provides data about human resources and organization climate and lets them know how they and the corporation are performing in the days ahead.[27]

The ISR researchers and Graphic Controls agreed that the data collected in the survey could be made public. This is a unique agreement. Usually re-

---

[25] R. B. Dunham and F. J. Smith, *Organization Surveys* (Glenview, Ill.: Scott, Foresman, 1979); and Paul R. Lees-Haley and Cheryl E. Lees-Haley, "Attitude Survey Norms: A Dangerous Ally," *Personnel Administrator,* October 1982, pp. 51–56.

[26] Edward E. Lawler, Phillip Mirvis, William M. H. Clarkson, and Lyman Randall, "How Graphic Control Assesses the Human Side of the Corporation," *Management Review,* October 1981, pp. 54–63.

[27] Ibid., p. 56.

searchers turn data over to management. Often, if it doesn't look favorable little is heard about it again. The Graphic Controls audit data was made available to anyone, present or prospective employees, interested in learning about the characteristics of the firm—the quality of work life.

Highlights of the report are presented in Exhibit 20–10. Readers of the report were invited to request a summary document that included information on a more detailed and complete analysis of the audit.

In 1977 the audit measurements occurred in a new context. Following the 1977 audit, the company had been acquired by the Times Mirror and had made a number of major P/HRM policy changes. These major changes are reflected in declines in employee ratings of pay and satisfaction and increases in turnover. On the positive side, there are a number of trends. Employment of women and minorities, identified as a concern in the 1977 survey, increased dramatically in 1979.

EXHIBIT 20–10 **A Report from the Institute for Social Research on the Quality of Work Life in Graphic Controls Corporation**

The health of a corporation is determined not only by its financial results, but also by its relationship with its people. Over the past few years, Graphic Controls has been working with the Institute for Social Research of the University of Michigan to measure wages, working conditions, safety, and other things that make up people's lives at work. This is the first report of the *quality of work* life in the corporation.

This report covers the period from 1975 through 1977. To prepare it, the Institute reviewed corporate records and various employment practices. In addition, employees from all United States locations had the opportunity to complete two confidential surveys about their experiences at work and their satisfaction on the job.

What constitutes a good quality of work life differs from every corporation and or every person. Because it is impossible to measure all of the things that contribute to the quality of work life in a corporation, we have concentrated on the *basic elements* that are common to most of them. Accordingly, we reviewed corporate records and calculated rates for accidents, wage increases, female and minority employment and promotions.

The relationship between a corporation and its people can also be measured in the way working life is satisfying to employees and contributes to their well-being. We, therefore, asked employees to report their *satisfaction* with pay, fringe benefits, job security, their chances to develop their skills and abilities, and other aspects of work life in Graphic Controls. We also recorded their rates of absen-

teeism and turnover. Lastly, we asked employees to report their involvement in community affairs, their satisfaction with their lives, and their outlook toward the future.

On the facing page is a summary of the institute's findings. More complete information on our review of jobs, supervision, and the opportunities employees had to express ideas, air grievances, and participate in decisions is available from Lyman Randall, Human Resources Group, Graphic Controls Corporation.

We hope you find this report interesting and informative. It represents our efforts to provide an accurate and reliable picture of the quality of work life in Graphic Controls. In essence, it is an audit of the human side of the corporation. There is no bottom line in this report. Instead, there are a number of measures that account for some part of people's lives at work. The reader is, therefore, encouraged to weigh each of them when coming to conclusion about the quality of work life in Graphic Controls.

Edward E. Lawler III   Phillip H. Mirvis
Institute for Social Research

The Survey Results

The basic elements of good quality of work life are a safe work environment, equitable wages, equal employment opportunities, and opportunites for advancement.

Highlights:

	1975	1976	1977
OSHA accidents	2.5%	2.0%	1.7%

EXHIBIT 20–10   *(concluded)*

A smaller percentage of the work force suffered serious injuries on the job in 1976 and 1977. The great majority of employees also said they were safe from physical danger at work. Some 8 percent reported that dangerous or unhealthy conditions were a problem for them.

	1975	1976	1977
Wages		*	*

* Increased beyond inflation rate

Wages per hour increased the past two years. Overall, 62 percent of the work force felt that their wages were fair in comparison to those paid by other organizations in the area. 72 percent said their wages were sufficient to meet monthly expenses.

	1975	1976	1977
Female employment	30.5%	32.0%	34.3%
Minority employment	7.5	8.7	8.6

Female employment increased the past two years. Overall, 72% of the female employees reported they were treated fairly on the job. The percentage of minority employees increased in 1976 but not in 1977. Overall, 84 percent of the minority employees said they were treated fairly on the job.

	1975	1976	1977
Promotions	7.0%	11.1%	10.9%

The percentage of employees promoted increased in 1976 but not in 1977. 61 percent of the employees said they were satisfied with their chances for advancement.

The relationship between a corporation and its people can also be measured in the way working life is satisfying to employees and contributes to their well-being on—and off—the job.

Percent Satisfied

Satisfaction	1975	1976–77	Difference
Pay	69.9%	71.0%	1.1%
Fringe benefits	69.0	89.5	20.5
Job security	76.8	76.1	−0.7
Working conditions	71.2	77.2	6.0
Co-worker relations	88.2	89.1	0.9
Accomplishments	80.5	77.7	−2.8
Chances to develop skills	72.4	74.6	2.2
Overall job satisfaction	93.7	90.2	−3.5

Most employees were satisfied with their working lives in both 1976 and 1976–77. During this time, there was a significant increase in satisfaction with fringe benefits and a small increase in satisfaction with working conditions. Other changes were insignificant. Overall job satisfaction is higher than that recorded in Gallup polls and the Institute's own survey of the national work force.

Absenteeism and turnover

Absenteeism went from 3.5 percent to 2.8 percent of the scheduled work hours during the three-year period. Turnover was reduced from 12.7 percent to 9.3 percent of the work force from 1975 to 1976. In 1977, it increased to 12.9 percent. Counting the loss of Business Forms Division employees, 33.3 percent of the work force left in 1977.

Work and the quality of life

Working life contributes, in some measure, to the quality of life. Overall, 95 percent of the employees expressed satisfaction with their lives. 57 percent of the work force were members of community, church, or social organizations, and the vast majority reported voting in local and national elections. 70 percent of the employees said their jobs today were preparing them with the training and experience they need for their jobs in the future. Nationally, fewer workers feel as optimistic about their employment future.

Despite the apparent success of attitude surveys in firms such as Graphic Controls, there are a number of factors for P/HRM specialists in attitude surveys and management to consider. Attitude surveys such as the Graphics Controls audit are costly. There is the expense of administering the survey, auditing P/HRM department records, the fees of researchers or maintaining an in-house survey team, and the productive time lost when managers and employees meet to complete the surveys and interpret the results. In times of inflation, high unemployment, and sluggish productivity, managements often reduce expenditures on such "people programs" as Graphic Controls.

Recall William Clarkson's view about Graphic Controls' reasons for conducting the audit. He makes a lot of sense. Organizations need to monitor continually their human assets. Research indicates that reliable and valid surveys can and often do result in cost savings in reduced absenteeism and turnover. Surveys also can provide an "early warning signal of problem areas."[28]

COMPLIANCE METHODS OF EVALUATION

In the compliance approach to evaluation of the P/HRM function, the main concern is the extent to which personnel procedures reflecting the law or company policy are being followed in the organization. Attempts are then made to determine where changes are needed.

One study describes how First National City Bank (New York), one of America's largest banks, performs this audit. The first step is to identify 18 crucial personnel areas it wishes to audit. Then the bank randomly chooses branch banks (eliminating recently reorganized banks) to be studied. The audit procedure followed is diagrammed in Exhibit 20–11. The review is conducted by the Personnel Practices Review Unit (six personnel reviewers, an operations manager, and clerical support), which reviews all branches every other year.[29] The bank believes that this audit has substantially improved its P/HRM effectiveness.

P/HRM EVALUATION RESEARCH: FINAL COMMENTS

The purposes of P/HRM evaluation research are to find solutions for human resources problems, to aid in evaluation of the P/HRM function, and to extend the knowledge of human resources to all those concerned. This activity is performed by universities, consultants, independent research institutes, and/ or employers. The growing list of employers who perform their own P/HRM research include AT&T, IBM, and General Electric. Sometimes P/HRM research is attached to units other than P/HRM departments, such as research and development groups. One study asked P/HRM researchers to estimate how they spent their time. They reported that they spent 20 percent consulting with line managers, 15 percent running their department, 9 percent on self-development, and 55 percent on research. Of this, 13 percent was spent analyzing P/HRM statistics, 15 percent studying improved means of employment, 16

---

[28] Ibid., p. 63.

[29] Paul Sheibar, "Personnel Practices Review: A Personnel Audit Activity," *Personnel Journal*, March 1974, pp. 211–17.

EXHIBIT 20–11   **Personnel Compliance Audit Process at Citibank**

Source: Paul Sheibar, "Personnel Practices Review: A Personnel Audit Activity." *Personnel Journal*, March 1974, p. 213. Reprinted with permission *Personnel Journal*, Copyright March 1974.

percent on improving the organization climate, and 11 percent studying training and development.[30]

In 1934 Cohen and Nagel suggested that there were four basic ways of knowing. These are tenacity, intuition, authority, and science. Managers and P/HRM researchers use all these techniques. Managers use *tenacity* when they form a belief about a P/HRM issue (such as, if a worker is paid more productivity will increase). This belief continues to be held even if research shows it to be incorrect. Managers use *intuition* on P/HRM matters when they feel an answer to be obvious or when they have a hunch on how to solve a problem. *Authority* is used when managers seek answers or methods or programs from

---

[30] John Hinrichs, "Characteristic of the Personnel Research Functions," *Personnel Journal*, August 1969, pp. 597–604.

an expert or consultant. Asking a performance appraisal expert to implement what he or she feels is best is using authority.

Science in P/HRM as presented in this book is used to solve, diagnose, and evaluate problems. In contrast to tenacity, intuition, and authority, science aims at obtaining answers, charting the way by using information and knowledge that is objective. The meaning of "objectivity" in this sense is that the knowledge about absenteeism, turnover, or safety and health ratios is certifiable, independent of individual opinion. It means that the research data was obtained by the use of the scientific method of inquiry. In other words, the scientific approach to P/HRM evaluation research involves using some rigorous standards of science in an attempt to minimize subjectivity and maximize objectivity.

The use of the scientific approach to P/HRM evaluation research consists of four stages: (1) observation of the situation in the real world; (2) formulation of explanations of the situation using induction; (3) generation of predictions about the situation using deduction; and (4) verification of the predictions using scientific methods. This approach to P/HRM research is shown in Exhibit 20–12. If there is anything that will enhance the prestige and influence of the P/HRM function in organizations, it is the use of more science and rigorous reseach to study and understand the kinds of P/HRM programs covered in Chapters 4–19. By using more P/HRM evaluation research managers can reduce the risks of relying too heavily on opinions or prejudices about people, programs, environmental forces, and the future.

EXHIBIT 20–12   **Four Stages of the Scientific Approach to P/HRM Research**

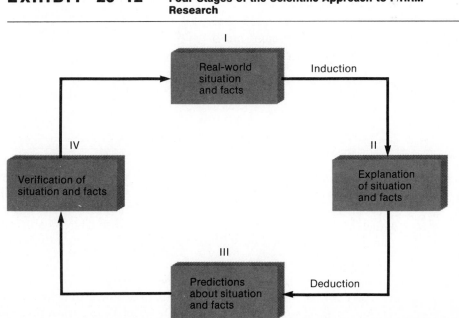

A RETURN TO THE P/HRM ᛫ IN ᛫ ACTION

The setting is again the conference room at General Products. The time is the next annual planning meeting. Last year, because Denton Major was not in a position to justify his budget for P/HRM he was not awarded the 6 percent increase he asked for. In fact, P/HRM was cut by the same percentage figure as the marketing department was. If he could help it, that wouldn't happen again. In the past year, he had examined the P/HRM audit approaches.

In evaluation, use of a checklist or copying other organizations appeared useful and easy. Compliance methods appeared useful, as did attitude surveys. Statistical approaches, especially evaluation of turnover, also appeared to be helpful.

As Denton waited, he was confident of the results of his budget request this year. Eventually, his time came to present his request.

Denton: The P/HRM department has a report that is included in your packet of materials. You'll note that we have the results of our compliance audit. The company is substantially in compliance with government regulations. This was not true a year ago. But we set that as an objective and reached it.

From the checklist, attitude survey, and compliance items, we came up with qualitative and quantitative targets for our P/HRM program. Our major targets were to reduce costly turnover and improve the cost effectiveness of our compensation program.

Next year's objectives are given on page 10 of the report. You'll also note our cost/benefit studies justify the shift of funds among our P/HRM programs and the justification for an 8 percent increase in our budget.

Henry: The budget for P/HRM is well-documented and appears reasonable.

Emily: A big improvement from last year's presentation, Denton.
Denton's budget was approved.

SUMMARY

Any function as important as the effective use of human resources needs to be evaluated. The difficulty in evaluating the results of the P/HRM function is that effectiveness has multiple causes, and it is difficult to separate out how much of the effectiveness results from each cause. Here is a list of some of the major statements in the evaluation section of Chapter 21 to use as a guideline.

1. Evaluation of the P/HRM function is a systematic, formal experience designed to measure the costs and benefits of the total P/HRM program and to compare its efficiency and effectiveness with the enterprise's past performance, the performance of comparable effective organizations, and the firm's objectives.

2. This evaluation is performed to
   a. Justify P/HRM existence and budget.
   b. Improve the P/HRM function by providing a means to decide when to drop activities and when to add them.
   c. Provide feedback from employees and operating managers on P/HRM's effectiveness.
   d. Help P/HRM to do its part to achieve the objectives of the organization.
3. Evaluation of the P/HRM function can be done by one or a combination of the following means:
   a. Checklist.
   b. Statistical approaches, including evaluation of turnover, absenteeism, and complaints and grievances, and the use of attitude and opinion surveys.
   c. Compliance methods of evaluation.

Exhibit 20–13 provides recommendations for the model organizations of P/HRM audits and evaluation and research.

EXHIBIT 20–13 **Recommendations for Model Organizations on Research and Evaluation of the P/HRM Function**

Type of Organization	Check-list	Statis-tical	Compli-ance	Performed by			
				Organiza-tion	Consul-tant	Organiza-tion and Consultant	P/HRM Research Depart-ment
1. Large size, low complexity, high stability			X	X			X
2. Medium size, low complexity, high stability		X	X			X	
3. Small size, low complexity, high stability	X				X		
4. Medium size, moderate complexity, moderate stability		X	X			X	
5. Large size, high complexity, low stability			X	X			X
6. Medium size, high complexity, low stability	X					X	
7. Small size, high complexity, low stability							

P/HRM Manager Close-Up

David A. Miron
Owens-Illinois

Biography

David A. Miron is director of human resource management for Owens-Illinois. He holds a bachelor's degree from St. Joseph's University in Philadelphia, a master's degree in foreign service from Georgetown University, and a doctoral degree in education from Harvard University where he specialized in organizational behavior and human motivation. In addition, he was a fellow in the President's Educational Program in Systematic Analysis sponsored by The White House at the University of Maryland's Graduate School of Economics.

Prior to joining Owens-Illinois in August 1979, David A. Miron was vice president of McBer and Company, a management consulting organization in Boston specializing in human resource development. As part of his consulting at McBer, he worked on

executive development issues at Honeywell, Travelers Insurance Company, Mead Corporation, IBM, General Electric, Wickes, and the U.S. State Department. David Miron speaks Spanish, and he has taught at the Italian government's Institute for Professional Administration. He has also led seminars in Brazil for Promon and in Colombia for Celanese. Prior to joining McBer and Company, he was director of planning for the U.S. Peace Corps with responsibility for developing a five-year planning process in each of the 60 country operations.

Job Description

Mr. Miron is responsible for management development, organization development, and human resource systems at Owens-Illinois.

THE P/HRM MANAGER: A LAST LOOK

This book has been designed to help you view the P/HRM function in action and to see the full range of activities and programs conducted by employees in this function. Some readers may already work in P/HRM or will work in such a department in the future. Certainly most readers will be involved in their careers with human resource issues, problems, and challenges. We have attempted always to be realistic and to show P/HRM in all its glory and power, as well as in a condition of being overworked and even uncertain. There is nothing unique to the P/HRM department being overloaded and uncertain. We all experience these conditions occasionally. In viewing the P/HRM professional and the activities he or she conducts, the book relied on a number of mechanisms.

The Diagnostic Approach

It was shown that the effective P/HRM manager is a diagnostician who observes the various aspects of the organization's environment. She or he considers the size, structure, goals, and style of the organization, and the nature of employees, the tasks, the work groups, and the leaders. The diagnostic manager realizes that the P/HRM policies of the organization must be congruent with all these factors, and others, if P/HRM is to do its part to contribute to organization effectiveness.

The myth that the work of P/HRM units and specialists is too subjective and complex to properly evaluate is not accepted. If this myth is accepted, then P/HRM is set apart from the rest of the organization. The diagnostic approach searches for ways to evaluate the impact, if any, of a specific P/HRM activity or program. It refuses to accept the notion that the effectiveness of the work done by the P/HRM unit and specialists can't be measured. The success of any P/HRM unit depends on management's ability to take measures of performance. There is no escaping the need to measure, evaluate, and monitor P/HRM. Without measures of effectiveness, owners, managers, and employees within the unit itself would have no idea of what contributions P/HRM is making to the organization.

A diagnostic P/HRM manager wants other managers and people to know how well his or her unit is performing. That is, the manager wants to report accomplishments. By using a diagnostic approach and collecting evaluation indicators of performance, the P/HRM manager will not only inform, but will also be able to persuade others about the unit's worth. The need to persuade others is specially important when managers must present their case and attempt to secure limited resources and funds for their unit.

Model Organizations

This mechanism was used in many chapters to focus attention specifically on how P/HRM activities are performed differently in different types of organizations. This is certainly true of the many different kinds of organizations in the private, public, and third sectors.

The Role of the Top Manager and Operating Manager

Top managers and operating managers have important parts to play in the P/HRM process. Successful P/HRM managers know how to relate to these persons and to present P/HRM programs to them in the language and thought processes of operating and top managers. How is this done?

THE P/HRM MANAGER IN ACTION

The P/HRM manager portrayed in this book manages by objectives and works at showing others how P/HRM contributes to organizational goals. Few organizations exist solely to hire and develop people. They exist to reach goals such as producing goods to satisfy customers while achieving a profit, or curing patients at reasonable cost, or improving the education of teenage children in a community.

The P/HRM manager today must not only be a diagnostician, but a researcher and futurist as well. As this chapter and the diagnostic theme of the book illustrates, research of P/HRM programs is essential. Without adequate research important human resource planning, performance evaluation, training and development and industrial relations, P/HRM programs will have to be run on the basis of hunches and intuition.

Many of the measurement and methodological problems associated with P/HRM research still need to be improved.[31] Improvement is likely to be brought about by more thorough and careful research studies being conducted and reported.

As a futurist, the P/HRM manager must develop a profile of the people in society. In the United States and Canada, a wealth of statistics are available to help develop future recruitment, selection, development, and employment growth plans. Some of the statistics that are used and scrutinized are birth rates, changing family patterns, education levels, and age patterns. These statistics need to be consulted so that organizations can better cope with the people available for employment. Today we know that life-styles are changing, and the average U.S. and Canadian citizen is better educated than previous generations of workers. The so-called baby boom generation (25–44 years old) is growing older.

Tomorrow's work force will be more diverse in terms of gender and race, marked by intense competition for jobs and promotions, and less unionized.[32] By 1995, the labor force participation of women is projected to reach 60.3 percent, as compared to 76.1 percent for men. This kind of information will be critical in determining what kind of P/HRM programs will be needed. Most of the decisions made about the programs will emanate from top managers, since they are the strategic decision makers.

---

[31] Marc J. Wallace, Jr., "Methodology, Research Practice, and Progress in Personnel and Industrial Relations," *Academy of Management Review*, January 1983, pp. 6–13.

[32] Fred Best, "The Nature of Work in a Changing Society," *Personnel Journal*, January 1985, pp. 40–41.

The P/HRM manager is part of the team that makes the key decisions, the strategic decisions, such as: What type of person do we need to hire or retain to accomplish our mission? Are we going to grow? In what direction are we going to grow? Are we going to merge with another organization? What type of reward system will be needed to continue being viewed as an attractive firm?

Each of these strategic decisions have important implications for P/HRM managers. And the P/HRM department can provide important counsel about the human resources affecting these decisions. P/HRM can only have the impact it should have if its leadership is well trained to do the job and if it can convey to top management a goal-oriented attitude when seeking additional funds to do its job.

The P/HRM manager who is part of the top-management team will be reporting what programs have been phased out, with appropriate savings, and what programs have been kept, and the savings and improvements resulting from them. Specific budget justifications will be made for proposed additions, and specific measureable results that will help the enterprise reach its goals will be proposed. Further, the P/HRM manager will be able to show how to achieve these results. Managers who are used to making decisions this way will know that this executive team makes the *real* decisions that affect personnel.

In the small organization, the executive responsible for P/HRM and other functions should begin to consider P/HRM decisions in the same hard-nosed way he or she does other decisions. Resources are scarce, and human resources are the most precious to conserve and develop. The failure of small organization owners to pay attention to P/HRM is often a step toward legal suits, loss of key personnel, and lost profits.[33]

Many explanations for economic and productivity woes in the United States and developed Western nations have been advanced. In the United States, the culprits include inadequate investment in new plants, overregulation from the government, and excessive taxation. No doubt these are contributors to many problems. Perhaps a closer look at P/HRM activities and programs also is needed to get to the core of the nation's problems—inflation, lagging productivity, and unfavorable trade balance. P/HRM experts can help attack problems involving human attitudes and behavior. This is the overriding challenge of P/HRM as a field of study and research.

An interesting survey of opinion leaders, corporate officers, consultants, editors, jounalists, and academics in the P/HRM area looked at the future in terms of managing human resources. Several suggestions were offered that seemed worthy of consideration. The P/HRM function was encouraged in the future to:

- Treat employees as important assets.
- Encourage more worker participation in decision making.
- Provide better training for managers and employees.
- Offer better career development opportunities.
- Tie more rewards and recognition to performance.

---

[33] Eric G. Flamholz, Yvonne Randle, and Sonja Sackmann, "Personnel Management: The Tenor of Today," *Personnel Journal*, June 1987, pp. 60–70.

- Develop better labor-management relations.
- Increase the P/HRM input in strategic planning and business decisions.[34]

The implications of changing values in society, an aging population, technological change, the emphasis on equality, and resistance to authority are being recognized by P/HRM practitioners. They are aware that a single plan or program (selection, training, performance appraisal) will not work every time, for all workers, in all organizations. Also, they know that managing workers now requires plans and programs appropriate for today's and tomorrow's work force. The traditional methods to pay workers, schedule work, evaluate performance, select employees, compensate workers, enforce discipline, improve workers' safety and health, and so forth are changing drastically. These and other changes will require proactive P/HRM programs that are difficult to initiate, sustain, and evaluate. Yet, the heart of P/HRM is people: Only in this century have we seen the awakening of organizations to this most important asset. In effect, the P/HRM manager of the future will play an even greater role than is played today in the dynamic, increasingly fast-paced world. Such a set of challenges is not for the faint-hearted. We happen to believe that there are many P/HRM specialists and people interested in P/HRM who are willing to accept such a set of challenges.

Questions for Review and Discussion

1. Since P/HRM evaluation research can be so informative, why isn't it conducted in most firms?
2. What type of information is needed to determine the costs and benefits of a quality of work life program?
3. What kind of research on women in the work force will be needed to help P/HRM managers better utilize their skills, talents, and expertise?
4. Why is it important for a P/HRM unit to clearly display to other units how well it is performing?
5. Why do some experts feel that the level of turnover in organizations has been overstated?
6. Compare and contrast the statistical indicators of P/HRM evaluation. Which are the best indicators? How are they measured?
7. Why must a P/HRM manager be a diagnostician and also look into the future?
8. Why must a P/HRM manager or specialist be proactive in terms of applying his or her skills, knowledge, and ability?
9. Why is perfectly accurate or precise measure of P/HRM activities and programs an ideal that is not likely to be achieved?
10. What changes in demographics should be included in any evaluations of the P/HRM department and its role within an organization?

---

[34] S. William Alper and Russell E. Mandel, "What Policies and Practices Characterize the Most Effective HR Departments?" *Personnel Administrator*, November 1984, p. 124.

GLOSSARY

Absenteeism. The failure of employees to report to work when they are scheduled to do so.

Attitude Survey. A set of written instru-ments completed by employees expressing their reactions to employer policies and practices.

MEASURING THE PERSONNEL/HUMAN RESOURCE ACTIVITIES*

Traditionally, the personnel department has been evaluated in vague, subjective terms. This has occurred for basically two reasons: first, the wrong questions were being asked; second, management bought the claim that it was not possible to apply quantitative methods to a function that was viewed principally from a qualitative standpoint.

The staff and management of what has now come to be called the human resources department allowed that misperception to perpetuate itself. From the inception of the first personnel department until modern times, few people seemed to be concerned about the performance of the department. There was no formal career path into or through personnel, and the few institutions of higher learning that taught personnel administration did not bother to teach measurement techniques. As a result, people did not know how to evaluate their work objectively. For some, the application of cold numbers to a function whose apparent mission was to "help employees with their problems" and to "improve morale" seemed to be a conflict of values. Others did not want to take on the extra work of collecting data and performing the calculations because they saw no use for it. Senior management had not asked for it. In time, a hidden fear developed. The department was often maligned by others within the larger organization. Many personnel people developed the attitude that their job was not too important, and that if they were to go to the trouble of quantitatively measuring and reporting their work the numbers would confirm the perception that they were not doing well. This attitude still exists in the minds of many today.

As a result of not proving their value to the organization in objective terms, the human resources department is not considered part of the mainstream of organizational management. It is viewed as a cost center and a reactive maintenance activity. In order to turn that outmoded attitude around, it is necessary for human resources management to learn to speak the language of business, which is numbers. A mathematical methodology needs to be applied

* By Jac Fitz-enz, Ph.D. President, Saratoga Institute.

as a system that serves both as a day-to-day monitoring instrument and as a model for doing cost justification and cost/benefit analyses of specific projects or programs.

Two of the foremost management authorities of the 1980s, Peter Drucker and W. Edwards Deming, have come out strongly for the development of measurement skill as an indigenous capability of a manager.

BASIC PRINCIPLES

The application of quantitative methods to human resources management has generated a set of basic principles that are critical to the success of the measurement system. These are based on the experience of managers in many types and sizes of organizations.

1. *The productivity and effectiveness of any function can be measured by some combination of cost, time, quantity, or quality indexes.* In some cases, psychological measures of attitudes and morale are also useful and possible.
2. *A measurement system promotes productivity by focusing attention on the important issues, tasks, and objectives.* A quantitative system not only helps to clarify what is to be accomplished, but also how well it should be done.
3. *Professional and knowledge workers are best measured as a group.* In order to be optimally effective, a professional group needs to work together. Measuring the work of individuals in relationship to each other promotes divisiveness and counterproductive competition.
4. *Managers can be measured by the efficiency and effectiveness of the units they manage.* The nature of managerial work is to get things done through other people. Therefore, it follows that the output of the group is an indication of the skill of the manager. There are obvious exceptions to this, but the rule applies nevertheless.
5. *The ultimate measurement is not efficiency, but effectiveness.* The objective of an organization is not only to create the most output with the least input. More important is to create the most appropriate outcome at any given point in time.

BUILDING BLOCKS OF A MEASUREMENT SYSTEM

The first problem that people face when they set out to build a measurement system is the apparent multitude of activities that are taking place and the seemingly impossible task of differentiating, isolating, and labeling of quantifiable variables. It is somewhat analogous to looking at a 1,000-pound steer and wondering how you can get a hamburger out of it. The solution is relatively simple.

There are only four classes of variables that can be subjected to a quantitative measurement system. They are:

1. *People* (as described by their organizational roles, such as receptionist, clerk, recruiter, trainer, compensation analyst, or manager).
2. *Things* (physical objects such as equipment, files, application forms, facilities, and supplies).
3. *Processes* (people doing something with a thing or with another person such as interviewing, filing, training, scheduling, and counseling).
4. *Results* (the outcomes of the interactions of people, things, and processes).

Everything within the department or related to the department's activity, whether it be inside the larger organization or outside it (such as a job applicant), can be classified into one of these four categories.

The next step is to list all the variables within each category that one might want to measure in some way. Then, the variables can be compared one at a time to each other until a relationship that can be expressed in terms of cost, time, quantity (volume or frequency), or quality becomes evident. This outcome is the *dependent variable*.

Examples of some typical dependent variables, often called *measures* by human resource managers, are: interviews per hire, absenteeism rate, hours per trainee, average hire cost, counseling hours per topic, records processed per clerk, or the ratio benefit costs to payroll cost.

Once the dependent variables are chosen for inclusion in the measurement system, an equation must be created to complete the measure. These are often self-evident. Some examples are:

$$\text{Average hire cost} = \frac{\text{Selection costs}}{\text{Number hired}}$$

$$\text{Absenteeism rate} = \frac{\text{Number of absent days}}{\text{Number of work days available}}$$

$$\text{Average health care cost} = \frac{\text{Total cost of health benefits}}{\text{Total number of employees}}$$

$$\text{Cost per trainee hour} = \frac{\text{Total cost of training}}{\text{Number trained} \times \text{Hours trained}}$$

HOW TO QUANTIFY QUALITY

One refuge that opponents of measurement have sought is the issue of quality. They argue that the work of the human resources function is highly qualitative and therefore inherently not susceptible to quantification. The quality issue is not the sole province of the personnel/human resource management department. Products must be manufactured to quality specifications. Salespeople must sell only to accounts that pay their bills. Although it is clear that quality is everyone's criterion, that does not solve the problem of how to quantify it.

The solution lies in the creation of a composite measure. For example, if the issue is recruiter effectiveness, one must first decide what constitutes effectiveness. Clearly, it is a function of more than one measure. If effectiveness could be defined by one objective term, it would not be subjective. A recruiter's effectiveness may be defined as a combination of how fast hires are accomplished, how cheaply they are achieved, how many are completed, and the quality of the people hired. And therein lies another potential problem. Hire quality is a subjective issue itself. In order to use it in the effectiveness measure, it must first be quantified. So, a composite of hire quality needs to be constructed, the quality objectified, and that quantitative value plugged into the recruiter effectiveness formula. The end result might look like this.

Recruiter Effectiveness =

$$\frac{\text{Cost of hire + Time to fill + Quality of hires + (Other chosen indexes)}}{\text{Number of indexes used}}$$

where,

> Cost of hire = \$450 (average)
> Time to fill jobs = 15 days (on average)
> Quality of hires = 90 percent (per quality measure)
> Plus others. . . .

Dollars, days, and percent can be normalized by comparing them to a preset goal and calculating percent of goal achievement for each. Each issue can also be weighted by importance. A simple illustration (omitting "other" undefined variables) is:

Measure	Result	Goal	Goal Achievement Percent × Weighting Factors
Cost of hire	$450	$500	11% × 4 = 444
Time to fill	15	12	80% × 3 = 240
Quality	90%	85%	106% × 5 = 530
			1,214 · 12 = 101%

SUMMARY

In order for the human resources function to take its place as an integral part of the organization, it must learn to use the language of business, which is numbers. This applies whether the organization is profit or not-for-profit. There are a number of personal, departmental, and organizational values to be derived from maintaining a quantitative performance measurement system. Personally, the people in the department are able to see how well they are doing. They are able to identify problems in early stages and find the source of the solution. They have data to build cost justification proposals that will help them obtain needed resources. They will be able to prove their contribution to the productivity and profitability of the larger organization. As a result of all this, they will gain the respect and position they desire.

Bibliography

Cascio, W. F. *Costing Human Resources: The Financial Impact of Behavior in Organizations*. Boston: Kent Publishing Co., 1987.

Kearsley, G. *Costs Benefits and Productivity Training Systems*. Reading, Mass.: Addison Wesley Publishing, 1982.

Phillips, J. J., *Handbook of Training and Evaluation Methods*. Houston: Gulf Publishing Co., 1983.

Fitz-enz, J. *How to Measure Human Resources Management*. New York: McGraw-Hill, 1984.

SOURCES OF PERSONNEL/HUMAN RESOURCE MANAGEMENT INFORMATION: WHERE TO FIND FACTS AND FIGURES

This appendix is divided into three main parts: periodicals, publishers, and organizations specializing in providing information in a variety of areas of P/HRM. While the listings are not intended to be exhaustive, they do provide a good cross section of major sources of facts and figures.

The listings contain the names of national organizations. You might consult your local chamber of commerce, college or university, and personnel association chapter for information and resources as well.

I. Periodicals.

    A. General business journals that often contain P/HRM material.
        Academy of Management Executive
        Advanced Management Journal
        Business Horizons
        California Management Review
        Harvard Business Review
        New Management
        Organizational Dynamics

    B. Specialized journals. The P/HRM specialist can advance his or her knowledge of the field by reading specialized journals. These include:

---

* Paul N. Keaton, University of Wisconsin, La Crosse.

Administrative Management
American Federationist
Arbitration Journal
BNAC Communication (quarterly)
Bulletin on Training (monthly)
Compensation and Benefits Review (quarterly)
Employment Benefit Plan Review
Employee Benefits Journal (quarterly)
Employee Relations Law Journal
Human Resource Planning
Industrial Relations (triannual)
Industrial Relations News (weekly)
Labor Law Journal (monthly)
Monthly Labor Review (monthly)
National Productivity
Personnel (bimonthly)
Personnel Administrator (monthly)
Personnel Journal (monthly)
Personnel Management (monthly)
Personnel Management Abstracts (quarterly)
Public Personnel Management (bimonthly)
Training and Development Journal (monthly)

C. Scholarly journals. The following is a list of publications written primarily for scholars and executives interested in P/HRM management. Reading these requires more technical training than the journals listed above.

Academy of Management Journal
Academy of Management Review
Human Relations
Human Organization
Human Resource Management
Industrial Relations
Industrial and Labor Relations Review
Journal of Applied Behavoral Science
Journal of Applied Psychology
Journal of Human Resources
Journal of Labor Research
Journal of Vocational Behavior
Organizational Behavior and Human Decision Processes
Personnel Psychology
Training: Journal of Human Resource Development

II. Specialized P/HRM Publishers.

Administrative Management Society
2360 Maryland Road
Willow Grove, PA 19090
(215) 659-4300

Bureau of Law and Business, Inc.
64 Wall Street
Madison, CT 06443

Capitol Publications
1300 N. 17th St.
Arlington, VA 22209

Commerce Clearing House, Inc.
4025 W. Peterson Avenue
Chicago, IL 60646
(703) 528-5400

Executive Enterprises Publications Co., Inc.
33 West 60th St.
New York, NY 10023
(212) 489-2680

Federal Publications, Inc.
1120 20th St., N.W.
Washington, DC 20036
(202) 337-7000

National Association for Management
1617 Murray
Wichita, KS 67212
(316) 721-4684

Personnel Policy Service, Inc.
P.O. Box 7715
Louisville, KY 40207
(502) 897-6782

Research Institute of America, Inc.
589 Fifth Avenue
New York, NY 10017

III. Organizations.[1]

A. Private.

American Arbitration Association (AAA)
140 West 51 Street
New York, NY 10020   (212) 484-4000

American Association of School Personnel Administrators (AASPA)
6483 Tanglewood Lane
Seven Hills, OH 44131   (216) 524-3030

American Association for Counseling and Development (AACD)
[formerly American Personnel and Guidance Association (APGA)]
5999 Stevenson Avenue
Alexandria, VA 22304   (703) 823-9800

---

[1] Denise S. Akey, ed., *Encyclopedia of Associations,* 18th ed. (Detroit: Gale Research Company, 1984).

American Compensation Association (ACA)
P.O. Box 1176
Scottsdale, AZ 85252   (602) 951-9191

American Management Associations (AMA)
135 West 50th Street
New York, NY 10020   (212) 586-8100

American Psychological Association (APA)
1200 17th Street, N.W.
Washington, DC 20036   (202) 955-7600

American Society for Hospital Personnel Administration (ASHPA)
840 N. Lake Shore Drive
Chicago, IL 60611   (312) 280-6358

American Society for Personnel Administration (ASPA)
606 N. Washington Street
Alexandria, VA 22314   (703) 548-3440

American Society for Training and Development (ASTD)
600 Maryland Avenue, S.W., Suite 305
Washington DC 20024   (202) 484-2390

Association of Private Pension and Welfare Plans (APPWP)
1725 K Street, N.W., Suite 801
Washington, DC 20006   (202) 659-8274

Bureau of Labor Statistics (BLS) Department of Labor
3rd Street and Constitution Ave., N.W.
Washington, DC 20037

College and University Personnel Association (CUPA)
11 Dupont Circle, Suite 120
Washington, D.C. 20036   (202) 462-1038

Human Resource Planning Society
P.O. Box 2553
Grand Central Station
New York, NY 10163   (617) 837-0630

Industrial Relations Research Association
7226 Social Science Building
University of Wisconsin
Madison, WI 53760   (608) 262-2762

International Association for Personnel Women (IAPW)
5820 Wilshire Boulevard
Suite 500
Los Angeles, CA 90036   (213) 937-9000

International Association of Pupil Personnel Workers (IAPPW)
c/o William E. Myer
P.O. Box 36
Barnesville, MD 20838   (301) 340-7501

International Personnel Management Association (IPMA)
1850 K Street, N.W.
Suite 870
Washington, DC 20006   (202) 833-5860

National Association of Educational Office Personnel (NAEOP)
1902 Association Drive
Reston, VA 22091   (703) 860-2888

National Association of Manufacturers (NAM)
1776 F Street
Washington, DC 20006   (202) 626-3700

National Association of Para-legals Personnel (NAPLP)
c/o Howard W. Ross
9431 N. Leamington
Skokie, IL 60077   (312) 676-9263

National Association of Personnel Consultants (NAPC)
1432 Duke Street
Alexandria, VA 22314   (703) 684-0180

National Association of Pupil Personnel Administrators (NAPPA)
225 N. Washington Street
Alexandria, VA 22314   (703) 549-9117

National Association of Student Personnel Administrators (NASPA)
160 Rightmire Hall
1060 Carmaek Road
Columbus, OH 43210   (614) 422-4445

National Labor-Management Foundation (NLMF)
1901 L. Street, N.W., Suite 711
Washington, DC 20036   (202) 296-8577

Newspaper Personnel Relations Association (NPRA)
11600 Sunrise Valley Drive
Reston, VA 22091   (703) 620-9500

Prentice-Hall Personnel Service
Prentice-Hall, Inc.
Sylvan Avenue
Englewood Cliffs, NJ 07632

Special Interest Group for Computer Personnel Research (SIGCPR)
5776 Stoneridge Mall Road
Atrium, Suite 350
Pleasonton, CA 94566   (415) 463-2800

U.S. Chamber of Commerce
1615 H Street, N.W.
Washington, DC 20062

B. Government.

   1. Federal.

      Bureau of Labor Statistics (BLS)
      Department of Labor
      3rd Street and Constitution Ave., N.W.
      Washington, DC 20210

      Department of Labor
      3rd Street and Constitution Ave., N.W.
      Washington, DC 20210

      Equal Employment Opportunity Commission (EEOC)
      2401 E. Street, N.W.
      Washington, DC 20506

      Federal Mediation and Conciliation Service
      Washington, DC 20427

      Occupational Safety and Health Administration (OSHA)
      200 Constitution Ave., N.W.
      Washington, DC 20210

      Office of Federal Contract Compliance (OFCC)
      200 Constitution Ave., N.W.
      Washington, DC 20210

   2. State Offices of Labor and Industrial Relations

Alabama:	Industrial Relations Office 649 Monroe Street Montgomery, AL 36104
Alaska:	Department of Labor Employment Security Building 416 Harris Street (P.O. Box 1149) Juneau, AK 99811
Arizona:	Labor Department Industrial Commission Commerce Building 1601 W. Jefferson Street Phoenix, AZ 85007
Arkansas:	Department of Labor Capital Hill Building 4th & High Streets Little Rock, AR 72201
California:	Department of Industrial Relations State Building Annex 455 Golden Gate Avenue (P.O. Box 603, 94101) San Francisco, CA 94102

Colorado: Division of Labor
Department of Labor and Employment
1313 Sherman Street
Denver, CO 80203

Connecticut: Department of Labor
200 Folly Brook Blvd.
Withersfield, CT 06109

Delaware: Department of Labor
801 West Street
Wilmington, DE 19801

Florida: Division of Labor
Department of Labor and Employment Security
200 Ashley Building
1321 Executive Center Drive East
Tallahassee, FL 32301

Georgia: Department of Labor
288 Labor Building
254 Washington Street, SW
Atlanta, GA 30334

Hawaii: Department of Labor and Industrial Relations
Keelikolani Building
825 Mililani Street
Honolulu, HI 96813

Idaho: Department of Labor and Industrial Services
400 Industrial Administration Building
317 Main Street
Boise, ID 83702

Illinois: Department of Labor
100 N. 1st Street
Springfield, IL 62702

Indiana: Division of Labor
1013 State Office Building
108 N. Senate Avenue
Indianapolis, IN 46204

Iowa: Bureau of Labor
307 E. 7th Street
Des Moines, IA 50309

Kansas: Employment Division
Department of Human Resources
401 Topeka Avenue
Topeka, KS 66603

Kentucky: Bureau for Manpower Services
Department of Human Services
275 E. Main Street
Frankfort, KY 40601

Louisiana:	Department of Labor 1001 N. 23rd Street Baton Rouge, LA 70802
Maine:	Bureau of Labor Department of Manpower Affairs State Office Building Augusta, ME 04330
Maryland:	Division of Employment Services Department of Human Resources 1100 N. Eutaw Street Baltimore, MD 21201
Massachusetts:	Department of Labor and Industries Leverett Saltonstall State Office Building 100 Cambridge Street Boston, MA 02202
Michigan:	Department of Labor 300 E. Michigan Ave. Lansing, MI 48926
Minnesota:	Department of Labor and Industry Space Center Building 444 Lafayette Road St. Paul, MN 55101
Mississippi:	Employment Security Commission 1520 W. Capitol Street Jackson, MS 39209
Missouri:	Department of Labor and Industrial Relations 421 E. Dunklin Street Jefferson City, MO 65101
Montana:	Department of Labor and Industry 35 S. Last Chance Gulch Helena, MT 59601
Nebraska:	Department of Labor 550 S. 16th Street (P.O. Box 94600) Lincoln, NE 68509
Nevada:	Office of the Labor Commissioner 601 Kinkead Building 505 E. King Street Capitol Complex Carson City, NV 89701
New Hampshire:	Department of Labor 1 Pillsbury Street Concord, NH 03301

New Jersey: Public Employment Relations Commission
                   Labor and Industry Building
                   John Fitch Plaza
                   Trenton, NJ 08625

New Mexico: Labor and Industrial Commission
                   509 Camino de los Marquez
                   Santa Fe, NM 87501

New York: Department of Labor
                   State Campus, Building 12
                   1220 Washington Ave.
                   Albany, NY 12240

North Carolina: Department of Labor
                   Labor Building
                   W. Edenton Street
                   (P.O. Box 27407)
                   Raleigh, NC 27611

North Dakota: Department of Labor
                   State Capitol
                   Bismarck, ND 58505

Ohio: Department of Industrial Relations
                   2323 W. 5th Avenue
                   Columbus, OH 43204

Oklahoma: Department of Labor
                   118 State Capitol
                   Lincoln Blvd.
                   Oklahoma City, OK 73105

Oregon: Bureau of Labor and Industries
                   State Office Building
                   1400 SW 5th Avenue
                   Portland, OR 97201

Pennsylvania: Department of Labor and Industry
                   1700 Labor and Industry Building
                   Harrisburg, PA 17120

Rhode Island: Department of Labor
                   CIC Complex
                   220 Elmwood Ave.
                   Providence, RI 02908

South Carolina: Labor Department
                   Landmark Center
                   3600 Forest Drive
                   (P.O. Box 11329)
                   Columbia, SC 29211

South Dakota: Department of Labor
425 Joe Foss Building
Pierre, SD 57501

Tennessee: Department of Labor
501 Union Street
Nashville, TN 37219

Texas: Department of Labor and Standards
Sam Houston State Office Building
201 E. 14th Street
(P.O. Box 12157, Capitol Station)
Austin, TX 78711

Utah: Division of Labor
Industrial Commission
350 E. 500 Street, South
Salt Lake City, UT 84111

Vermont: Department of Labor and Industry
State Office Building
120 State Street
Montpelier, VT 05602

Virginia: Department of Labor and Industry
4th Street Office Building
205 N. 4th Street
(P.O. Box 12064)
Richmond, VA 23241

Washington: Department of Labor and Industries
334 General Administration Building
Olympia, WA 98504

West Virginia: Department of Labor
B-451 State Office Building 6
1900 Washington Street, E.
Charleston, WV 25305

Wisconsin: Department of Industry, Labor and Human
Relations
401 General Executive Facility 1
201 E. Washington Ave.
(P.O. Box 7398)
Madison, WI 53707

Wyoming: Department of Labor and Statistics
Barrett Building
2301 Central Ave.
Cheyenne, WY 82002

District of
Columbia: Department of Employment Services
600 Employment Security Building
500 C. Street, NW
Washington, DC 20001

C. Addresses of a sample of labor unions in the USA, listed alphabetically by trade with membership figures.

AFL–CIO
815 16th Street, N.W.
Washington, DC 20006   *16,300,000*

Air Line Pilots Association, International (ALPA)
1625 Massachusetts Ave., NW
Washington DC 20036   *33,000*

International Union, United Automobile, Aerospace and Agricultural
   Implement Workers of America (UAW)
8000 W. Jefferson
Detroit, MI 48214   *1,200,000   AFL–CIO*

United Brotherhood of Carpenters and Joiners of America (UBC)
101 Constitution Ave. NW
Washington, DC 20001   *800,000   AFL–CIO*

Amalgamated Clothing and Textile Workers Union (ACTWU)
15 Union Square
New York, NY 10003   *402,000   AFL–CIO, CLC*

Communications Workers of America (CWA)
1925 K St. NW
Washington DC 20006   *650,000   AFL–CIO*

United Food and Commercial Workers International Union
   (UFCWIU)
Suffridge Bldg.
1775 K Street NW
Washington DC 20006   *1,300,000   AFL–CIO*

American Federation of State, County and Municipal Employees
   (AFSCME)
1625 L Street NW
Washington DC 20036   *1,200,000   AFL–CIO*

International Association of Machinists and Aerospace Workers (IAM)
1300 Connecticut Ave.
Washington DC 20036   *900,000   AFL–CIO*

International Union, United Mine Workers of America (UMWA)
900 15th Street
Washington DC 20005   *280,000*

Oil, Chemical and Atomic Workers International Union (OCAW)
P.O. Box 2812
Denver, CO 80201   *140,000   AFL–CIO*

American Postal Workers Union (APWU)
817 14th Street NW
Washington DC 20005   *300,000   AFL–CIO*

United Steel Workers of America (USWA)
Five Gateway Center
Pittsburgh, PA 15222   *1,000,000   AFL–CIO*

American Federation of Teachers (AFT)
11 Dupont Circle NW
Washington DC 20036   *580,000   AFL–CIO*

National Education Association (NEA)
1201 16th Street NW
Washington DC 20036   *1,600,800*

International Brotherhood of Teamsters, Chauffeurs, Warehousemen
    and Helpers of America (IBT)
25 Louisiana Avenue NW
Washington DC 20001   *2,000,000*

CAREER PLANNING

Career planning is an individualized process. Each of us has a unique set of values, interests, and work and personal experiences. Understanding how this unique set of factors blends is an important part of career planning. But it is also necessary to understand the requirements of various jobs so that your own personality and intellectual abilities can be matched with the job. Your career decisions will shape your lifestyle.

College students eventually have to find out how they fit into the spectrum of career choices available. The purpose of this appendix is to provide:

1. A few career basics and hints on self-assessment.
2. Information on the mechanics of getting a job.

CAREER BASICS AND SELF-ANALYSIS

First, before thinking about specific career areas, sit back and spend some time mulling over those things that you want from a career. Here are a few questions to consider:

- Do you want a job or a career? Do you want it to be personally satisfying, or are the financial rewards enough? How important is career advancement?
- Are the status and prestige associated with a career important to you?
- What about financial rewards?
- Do you have geographical preferences? What about living in a large versus a small city?
- What size employer would you prefer? Might this preference change later on?

 Now, think about yourself for a minute.

- What education, experience, and skills do you have to offer?
- Are you quantitatively ("thing") oriented or qualitatively ("people") oriented, or do you enjoy both? There is a place for both types in organizations.
- What are your weak and strong points? How will they relate to your performance on the job?
- What kind of work is interesting?

- What kind of work do you like?
- What kind of work will make you feel worthwhile?

A personal evaluation of these and similar questions is a worthwhile exercise. These questions may help you develop a job or career identity.

Professional Help for Self-Assessment

Professional counselors can help you decide which career path to take. Most high schools and colleges provide free counseling services, where trained professionals help a person perform a realistic self-assessment.

Vocational tests are often used to verify one's self-analysis and to reveal any hidden personal characteristics. This test information is then explained and interpreted by professional counselors. No one test or battery of tests can make a career choice for you. But tests can supplement the information you are reviewing as you mull over career opportunities and personal characteristics. Your college placement office has counselors who can recommend which tests are most appropriate.

In addition, the counselor can help you with your self-assessment by providing publications discussing career opportunities. Some widely publicized and frequently used publications include:

- *College Placement Annual,* College Placement Council, Inc., P.O. Box 2263, Bethlehem, PA 18001—published annually. This annual provides information on current job openings in companies. It also provides suggestions on preparing resumes and interviewing for jobs.
- *Occupational Outlook Handbook,* U.S. Department of Labor, Government Printing Office, Washington, D.C.—published annually. This handbook lists all major companies with a brief description of job requirements, opportunities available, and future job prospects.

Self-assessment, help from a professional counselor, and career publication can provide the necessary background information to properly plan your career. But in the final analysis, you alone must make the career decision and seek appropriate job opportunities. A counselor, parent, or friend cannot make a career decision for you.

THE JOB SEARCH: A PLAN

In school you prepare for examinations by organizing your notes and planning. In searching for a job, you also need to organize and plan. The first job after college can affect your entire career, so a plan is a must. Without a plan, you will lose valuable time and experience unnecessary frustration. There is no single best job-search plan, but there are some basic principles. Because your time is limited, you should use a systematic procedure to narrow the number of job possibilities.

When evaluating any particular career, there are some specific issues that you should consider. As you think back over the broad career options available, examine them with the following areas in mind:

- What are the qualifications for the job? Will you need more education, more experience?
- What is the financial situation? Is the salary reasonable? How are the benefits? What salary is likely in three to five years? Is there going to be a conflict between the value you place on money and your returns from this job?
- What are the opportunities for advancement? Do these appear to jibe with your aspirations?
- What is the present supply and demand status for this field and what might it be in the future?
- Will the job involve much travel? Is that desirable or undesirable? How mobile are you?
- What is the atmosphere associated with the job? Is it pressure-filled, demanding, cooperative, tranquil, or creative?
- Is this job something that you will be proud of? Does it fit your self-image?
- Is it work that you will enjoy? Is it in line with your goals and ethics? Will you be happy?

Within any given career choice, one faces a number of prospective employers. Each company offers different conditions, opportunities, and rewards to its employees. Here are some important questions to ask about the firms you are considering:

- Does the company have opportunities for a person with my skills, aptitudes, and goals?
- What are the promotion opportunities in the company?
- Does the company usually promote from within?
- What type of professional development is available for new employees?
- What kind of working environment exists within the company?
- What is the future growth potential for the company and the industry?

Answers to these kinds of questions will enable you to narrow the available job opportunities. Answers can be found in such sources as company annual reports, *Standard and Poor's Corporation Records,* and *Dun and Bradstreet's Reference Book of Manufacturers.* Another source is the company's employees. If you know some employees, ask them for first-hand information.

Most companies furnish brochures on career opportunities. These sources are impressive, but they often give a totally positive picture of the company. Consult your school's placement officer to learn more about each company and to determine the accuracy of the brochures.

There are two other sources you should consult—newspapers and professional magazines. The classified ads, especially in the Sunday or weekend editions, provide a lot of job information. These advertisements usually provide information about job vacancies, the type of people the company is looking for, and the person or post office box to contact if you are interested. An outstanding listing of job opportunities appears in *The Wall Street Journal*. It lists jobs at the highest level as well as openings at the supervisory level.

Professional magazines, such as *Personnel Journal, Training and Industry, Personnel Administrator,* and *Nation's Business,* often list vacancies. These advertisements are for recent graduates or people with work experience. If you are interested in a particular occupation, consulting the professional magazines in that functional area can be helpful. Specialized trade journals are also good sources for job leads. Even the Yellow Pages in phone directories are a helpful guide to companies operating in a particular area. Talk to family, friends, faculty members, and others who may know of job leads or people with pertinent information.

PERSONALIZING THROUGH A RESUME

After personal and professional self-assessments and a job search via newspapers, professional magazines, and employment agencies, the next step is to personalize your campaign. You must communicate to others who you are. The basic devices used to communicate are the résumé, letters, the telephone, and personal interviews.

A *résumé* is a written summary of who you are. It is a concise picture of you and your credentials for a job. A résumé should highlight your qualifications, achievements, and career objectives. It should be designed to present you as an attractive candidate for a job.

There is no generally accepted format for a résumé. Its purpose is to introduce you to the employer and to get you an interview. Few, if any, employers hire college graduates solely on the contents of a résumé. In most cases, you can attract attention with a one-page résumé. Longer résumés are for people who have had extensive professional experience.

Employees like résumés that read well and look attractive. Résumés read well if they are concise, grammatically correct, and easy to follow. Résumés look more inviting if they are reproduced on an offset press on high-quality paper. There are companies that prepare professional résumés for a fee. The Yellow Pages of the telephone directory can provide names of firms that sell this service.

Other elements found in good résumés are job objectives, educational background, college activities, work experiences, and references. The arrangement of these elements is a personal decision. But keep the résumé uncluttered and neatly blocked, to create an attractive and informative résumé with eye appeal. Exhibit 1 presents an example of an effective résumé.

It may be necessary to prepare a different résumé for each employer, so that your credentials can be slanted for the job openings. Whether you think a different résumé for each company can do the job is a decision that only you can make.

Just as important as the points to include are some points to avoid in preparing your résumé. *Don't:*

EXHIBIT 1   Sample Résumé

JILL M. MURPHY
4896 CRELING DRIVE
NEW YORK, NY 10011

(212) 431-0019

OBJECTIVE   A challenging position in marketing, utilizing analytical and problem-solving skills.

EDUCATION
Sept. 1981   NEW YORK UNIVERSITY
May 1986   School of Business Administration
                    Major: Marketing and Finance
                    G.P.A. 3.9; Dean's List; NYU Tuition scholarship

                    School of Social Sciences
                    G.P.A. 3.9; Dean's List; concentration in mathematics and
                    psychology.

Sept. 1978   NOTRE DAME HIGH SCHOOL
June 1982   G.P.A. 3.9
                    Class Honors; Phi Beta Kappa; National Honor Society; State
                    Champion, Women's Extemporaneous Speaking, 1979; Major
                    Delegation Award at National Model United Nations in Washington,
                    D.C., 1978, 1979.

EXPERIENCE
May 1986   **Assistant Marketing Manager,** PepsiCo.
Present   Responsibilities included the coordination of planning,
                    implementing and evaluating the Pepsi Challenge Program in New
                    York City. This required close liaison with PepsiCo's marketing and
                    sales activities as well as its advertising agency and the media.
                    Achieved increase of over 100% in program participants, totaling
                    over 60,000 people.

                    Planned and implemented a Mountain Dew sampling program.

                    On own initiative, developed a Coordinator's Handbook which
                    PepsiCo plans to distribute nationwide.

Sept. 1985   **Vice President,** Alpha Kappa Gamma Sorority
May 1986   Responsible for housing policies, personnel relations, and
                    discipline.

Sept. 1984   **Assistant Treasurer,** Alpha Kappa Gamma Sorority
Sept. 1985   Responsible for funds to finance all sorority events. Included
                    collection, recording and billing for sixty-five individual accounts.

Summer 1984   **Salesperson,** Revlon, Inc.

Summer 1983   **Information Manager,** Summer Concert Series at New York
                    Universitry.

ACTIVITIES   **Project Director,** Marketing Club at New York University; Seminar for
                    Republican Campaign Coordinators, Washington, D.C.; New York
                    University Campus Orchestra; NYC Symphony Youth Orchestra.

REFERENCES   Available on request.

- State what salary you want.
- Send a résumé with false information.
- Send a résumé that is sloppy and contains typographical or grammatical errors.
- Clutter your résumé with unnecessary information.
- Inform employers that you will accept only a certain kind of position.
- Use fancy colors or gimmicks to sell yourself.

A cover letter should accompany the résumé. The objective of the cover letter is to introduce you. It can also encourage the employer to read your résumé and meet with you. The cover letter should not duplicate the more detailed résumé. Instead, it should add to what is presented in the résumé and show that you are really interested in working for the company. The cover letter also reveals how well you can communicate. This clue is often used by employers to put prospective employees into one of two categories: a good communicator or a poor communicator.

Employers receive cover letters and résumés from many more job applicants than they could ever hire or even interview. Therefore, they screen whatever letters and résumés they receive. Screening is often accomplished rather quickly, so it is better to present your story and objective concisely and neatly.

The number of letters and résumés you send depends on your strategy. Some people narrow down their list of organizations to the ones they really would like to work for and prepare a personal cover letter to accompany the résumé. Other candidates use a "shotgun" approach. They mail numerous letters and résumés to any company with an opening in a particular area of interest. The newspapers, professional magazines, listings in the placement office, telephone directories, directories or organizations, and tips from friends are used to develop a potential list. Then perhaps as many as 200 letters and résumés are sent out.

THE INTERVIEW STRATEGY

An outstanding cover letter, résumé, and job search strategy are not enough to get you the job you want. You must also perform well at the interview. The interview is an oral presentation with a representative of a company. A good recruiter is interested in how a job candidate expresses himself or herself. The interviewer is both an information source and an information prober. As an information source, the interviewer provides you with knowledge about careers in the organization and the company in general. As a prober, the interviewer wants to determine what makes you tick and what kind of person you are.

An Interview Plan

In searching for job openings, it is necessary to have a plan. This is also the case in having a successful interview. In order to do a good job at the interview, you must be thoroughly prepared. Of course, you must know yourself and what type of career you want. The interviewer will probe into the areas you covered in your self-assessment and in developing a career objective. During the interview, you must make it clear why a person with your strengths and objectives should be hired by the company.

The preparation for answering the question "Why you?" involves some homework. You should gather facts about the employer. Annual reports, opinions from employees of the firm, brochures, up-to-date financial data from *The Wall Street Journal,* and recent newspaper articles can be used. Exhibit 2 identifies some of the information that can be used to prepare for the interview. Whether the initial interview is on the campus or in the office of the president of the company, prior preparation will impress the interviewer. This preparedness will allow you to explore other important areas about the company that you don't know about. It will also allow the interviewer to probe into such areas as your grades, motivation, maturity, ability to communicate, and work experience. This information is important for the company in making a decision whether to have you visit for a second, more in-depth interview.

Interview preparation also involves your personal appearance and motivational state. There isn't enough space here to focus extensively on dress, hair, and value codes. The next best advice is to be yourself and to come prepared to meet with a representative of the organization. If you are to work as an accountant for some firm, then you must comply with standards of performance as well as dress and appearance codes. Use your own judgment, but be realistic: employers don't like shoulder-length hair on a salesperson or barefooted production supervisors. These biases will not be corrected in an interview, so don't be a crusader for a cause. The interview is not the best place to project a personal distaste for or discomfort with dress or hair-length standards.

Interviewing makes most people slightly nervous. But if you are well-prepared and really motivated to talk to the representative, the interview will

EXHIBIT 2   Homework Information for the Interview

Location of headquarters, offices, plants

Officers of the organization

Future growth plans of the company

Product lines

Sales, profit, and dividend picture

Price of stock (if available)

Competitors of the company

Organizational structure

Kind of entry-level positions available

Career paths followed by graduates

Union situation

Type of programs available for employees (stock option, medical, educational)

probably go well. Consider the interview as a challenge you can meet because you are interested in succeeding. An alert candidate with modest confidence has a good chance of impressing the interviewer.

The Actual Interview

The interview has been called a conversation with a purpose. During the interview, the company representative and the candidate both attempt to determine if a match exists. Are you the right person for the job? The attempt to match person and job follows a question-and-answer routine. The ability to answer questions quickly, honestly, and intelligently is important. The best way to provide a good set of answers is to be prepared.

Exhibit 3 provides a list of some commonly asked questions. The way you answer these and similar questions is what the interviewer evaluates. Remember that the interviewer is trying to get to know you better by watching and listening.

One effective way to prepare for the interview session is to practice answering the questions in Exhibit 3 before attending the actual interview. This does not mean to develop "pat" or formal answers, but to be ready to intelligently respond. The sincerity of the response and the intelligent organization of an answer must come through in the interview.

Most interviewers eventually get around to asking about your career plans. The purpose of asking these kinds of questions is to determine your reasonableness, maturity, motivation, and goals. The important point is to illustrate by your response that you have given serious thought to your career plans. An unrealistic, disorganized, or unprepared career plan is one way to fail in the interview. Interviewers consider a candidate immature if he or she seems to be still searching and basically confused.

At various points in the interview, it may be appropriate to ask questions. These questions should be important and should not be asked just to appear intelligent. If something is important in evaluating the company, ask the

---

EXHIBIT 3   **Some Questions Frequently Asked by Interviewers**

Why do you want to work for our company?

What kind of career do you have planned?

What have you learned in school to prepare for a career?

What are some of the things you are looking for in a company?

How has your previous job experience prepared you for a career?

What are your strengths? Weaknesses?

Why did you attend this school?

What do you consider to be a worthwhile achievement of yours?

Are you a leader? Explain.

How do you plan to continue developing yourself?

Why did you select your major?

What can I tell you about my company?

question. It is also valuable if you can ask a question that displays meaningfulness. But don't ask so many questions that the interviewer is answering one after the other. Some frequently asked questions are summarized in Exhibit 4.

The majority of interviews last between 20 and 30 minutes. It is best to close on a positive and concise note. Summarize your interests, and express whether you are still interested in the company. Interviewers will close by stating that you will hear from the company. You may want to ask if he or she can give you an approximate idea of how long it will be before you hear from them. Typically, an organization will contact a candidate within four or five weeks after the interview.

One valuable practice to follow after the actual interview is to write down some of the points covered. List the interviewer's name, when the company will contact you, and your overall impression of the company. These notes can be useful if you are called for a later interview. Any person talking to 10 or more companies usually has some trouble recalling the conversation if no notes are available.

One issue that may or may not come up during the interview is salary. Most companies pay a competitive starting wage. Therefore, it is really not that important to ask what your starting salary will be. Individuals with similar education, experience, and background are normally paid the same. Instead of asking about salary in the initial interview, do some checking in the placement office at your school or with friends working in similar jobs.

Should you send a thank you letter after the interview? This seems to be a good way to refresh the interviewer's memory. The follow-up letter should be short. Expressing your appreciation for the interview shows sincerity. It also provides an opportunity to state that you are still interested in the company.

Interviewers are important processors of information for the company, so it is important to impress them at the interview. Unfortunately, not every candidate can win (winning means that the candidate will be asked to visit the company or to undergo further interviewing). "Why was I rejected?" is a

---

EXHIBIT 4   **Some Questions Frequently Asked by Job Candidates**

How is performance evaluated?

How much transfer from one location to another is there?

What is the company's promotion policy?

Does the company have development programs?

How much responsibility is a new employee given? Can you provide me with some examples?

What preferences are given to applicants with graduate degrees?

What type of image does the company have in the community?

What schools provide the bulk of managerial talent in the company?

What are the company's policies for paying for graduate study?

What social obligations would I have?

What community service obligations would I have?

question everyone has to ask at some point. Exhibit 5 lists some of the reasons why candidates are not successful in an interview.

VISITING THE COMPANY AND THE JOB OFFER

If you are fortunate enough to be invited for a company visit, consider yourself successful. The letter of invitation or telephone message will specify some available dates. If you are still interested in the company, you must send a formal acceptance. Even if you are not interested in visiting, a short note thanking the company displays your courtesy.

In some cases, your visit will be coordinated by the interviewer you already met. However, it may be the personnel department or management development officer who handles the details. The important point is not who will be coordinating but that you must again prepare for a series of interviews. During this series, you should be asking specific questions about job duties, performance expectations, salary, fringe benefits, and career paths. It is at this phase of the career and employment decision process that you need this kind of information.

One of the main reasons for inviting candidates to visit the company is to introduce them to managers and the organization. These introductions will be brief, but they are important. It is reasonable to expect to meet five or more individuals during the company visit. In some cases, you will be given a tour of the plant, office, or laboratory. A wide array of people will be asked to comment on your employability after you leave. So consider every interview important, and remember to act alert, organized, and interested. You may be bored because many questions are repeated by different managers, but remember that sincerity and interest are variables that these managers will each be asked to comment on.

During the company visit, you will probably not be given a job offer. In most situations, a week to two weeks may pass before the company contacts you. If

---

EXHIBIT 5   **Some Reasons for Not Winning**

Disorganized and not prepared

Sloppy appearance

Abrasive and overbearing

Unrealistic goals or image of oneself

Inability to communicate effectively

No interest shown in the type of company interviewed

Not alert

Poor grades

Only interested in money

Provided contradictory answers to questions

you are successful, you will receive a formal job offer. After receiving the offer, make an immediate acknowledgment. Thank the employer and indicate an approximate date when you will furnish a decision.

A CONCLUDING NOTE

This appendix has focused on planning. Self-assessment, seeking professional help, the job search, personalizing your job campaign, interviewing, and visiting companies all involve prior planning. The person who plans his or her campaign to find a worthwhile and satisfying job will be more successful than the disorganized person. Thus, the most important principle in finding the best job for you is to work hard at planning each stage. Good luck!

Additional References on Business Careers

Bolles, Richard N. *What Color is Your Parachute?* A Ten Speed Press, 1987.

GLOSSARY

Absenteeism. The failure of employees to report to work when they are scheduled to do so.

Accident Research. The systematic evaluation of the evidence concerning accidents and health hazards.

Adverse Impact. A situation in which a significantly higher percentage of members of a protected group (women, blacks, Hispanics) in the available population are being rejected for employment, placement, or promotion.

Affirmative Action. Giving preferential treatment in hiring, recruitment, promotion, and development to groups that have been discriminated against.

AFL–CIO. A group of union members consisting of individuals that merged membership in 1955 from the American Federation of Labor and the Congress of Industrial Organizations.

Age Discrimination Act of 1967 (Amended 1978). Protects workers between the ages of 40 and 70 from job discrimination.

Agency Shop. A situation in which all employees pay union dues whether or not they are union members.

American Federation of Labor (AFL). A union group devoted to improving economic and working conditions for craft employees.

Apprentice Training. A combination of on-the-job training. The apprentice, while learning the job, is paid less than the master worker. Some of the jobs in which one serves as an apprentice include electrician, barber, tool and die maker, and plumber.

Arbitration. A quasijudicial process in which the parties agree to submit the unresolvable dispute to a neutral third party for binding settlement.

Assessment Center. A selection technique that uses simulations, tests, interviews, and observations to obtain information about candidates.

Attitude Survey. A set of written instruments completed by employees expressing their reactions to employer policies and practices.

Autonomy. The degree to which the job provides substantial freedom, independence, and discretion to the individual in scheduling the work and in determining the procedures to be used in carrying it out.

Behavior Modeling. Participants learn by observing a role model behavior. The fundamental characteristic of modeling is that learning takes place by observation or imagination of another individual's experience.

Behavioral Observation (BOS). A method similar to the BARS that uses the critical incident technique to identify a series of behaviors that describe the job. A 1 (Almost Never) to 5 (Almost Always) format is used to rate behaviors.

Behaviorally Anchored Rating Scale (BARS). A rating scale that uses critical incidents as anchor statements placed along a scale. Typically 6 to 10 performance dimensions, each with 5 to 6 critical incident anchors, are rated per employee.

Boycott. A primary boycott finds union members not patronizing the boycotted firm. In a secondary boycott a supplier of a boycotted firm is threatened with a union strike unless it stops doing business with the firm. This type of boycott is illegal under the Taft-Hartley Act.

Business Representative. The local union's representative who is responsible for negotiating and administering the labor agreement and for settling problems in connection with the contract.

Career. Individually perceived sequences of attitudes and behaviors associated with work-related experiences and activities over the span of an individual's work life.

Career Path. A sequence of positions through which an organization moves an employee.

Career Stages. The distinct stages that individuals go through in their careers, typically: prework, initial work, stable work, and retirement.

Case Method. A training technique in which a description (a case) of a real situation is analyzed by participants. The interaction of the participants and trainer is valuable in improving the degree of learning that occurs.

Central Tendency Error. A rating tendency to give ratees an average rating on each criteria. That is, on a 1 to 7 scale, circling all 4s, or on a 1 to 5 scale, selecting all 3s.

Civil Rights Act, Title VII 1964. An important law that prohibits employers, unions, employment agencies, and joint labor-management committees controlling apprenticeship or training programs from discriminating on the basis of race, color, religion, sex, or national origin.

Classification or Grading System. A job evaluation method that groups jobs together into a grade or classification.

Closed Shop. A situation in which a new employee must be a union member when hired. Popular in the construction, maritime, and printing industries.

COBRA. The Consolidated Omnibus Budget Reconciliation Act of 1985 that requires employers with more than 20 employees to offer continuation of health care coverage for 18 to 36 months after an employee is fired, quits, or is laid-off.

Collective Bargaining. The process by which the representatives of the organization meet and attempt to work out a contract with representatives of the union.

Comparable Worth. An issue that has been raised by women and the courts in recent years. It means that the concept of equal pay for equal jobs should be expanded to the notion of equal pay for comparable jobs. If a job is comparable to other jobs as determined by job content analysis, that job should be paid comparably.

Compressed Workweek (CWW). A work schedule in which a trade is made between the number of hours worked per day, and the number of days worked per week, in order to work the standard length hours—four days, 10 hours each day or three days, 12 hours each day are examples of the CWW schedule.

Congress of Industrial Organizations (CIO). A union formed by John L. Lewis, president of the United Mine Workers. It was formed to organize industrial and mass-production workers and was devoted to improving the economic and working conditions.

Construct Validity. A demonstrated relationship between underlying traits inferred from behavior and a set of test measures related to those traits.

Content Validity. The degree to which a test, interview, or performance evaluation measures skill, knowledge, or ability to perform.

Core Work Time. A period of time in a flexitime work schedule in which all employees in a particular unit or group must be at work.

Craft Union. A group of individuals who belong to one craft or closely related group of occupations, such as carpenters or bricklayers.

Criterion-Related Validity. The extent to which a selection technique is predictive of or correlated with important elements of job behavior.

Critical Incident Rating. The system of selecting very effective and ineffective examples of job behavior and rating whether an employee displays the type of behaviors specified in the critical incidents.

Decertification Election. An election in which employees who are represented by a union vote to drop the union.

Dual-Career Couples. A situation in which a husband and wife have careers.

Employee Assistance Programs. A program designed to help employees with personal, family, and work problems. Although these programs are voluntary, managers are instructed on how to confront problems (e.g., alcoholism, drug abuse) when they occur.

Employee Leasing. Paying a leasing firm to locate and provide the organization with a pool of human resources.

Equal Employment Opportunity Commission (EEOC). The Civil Rights Act, Title VII, 1964 gave the EEOC limited powers of resolving charges of discrimination and interpeting the meaning of Title VII. Later in 1972, Congress gave EEOC the power to bring lawsuits against employers in the federal courts.

Equal Employment Opportunity Programs (EEO). Programs implemented by employers to prevent employment discrimination in the workplace or to take remedial action to offset past employment discrimination.

Exempt Employee. A person working in a job that is not subject to the provisions of the Fair Labor Standards Act (1938) with respect to minimum wage and overtime pay. Most professional, executives, administrators, and outside salespersons are classified as exempt.

External P/HRM Influences. The environmental forces outside the organization, such as unions, government, and economic conditions.

Factor Comparison Method. A job evaluation method that uses a factor-by-factor comparison. A factor comparison scale, instead of a point scale, is used. Five universal job factors used to compare jobs are: responsibilities, skills, physical effort, mental effort, and working conditions.

Feedback. The degree to which carrying out the work activities required by the job results in the individual's obtaining direct and clear information about the effectiveness of his or her performance.

Flexible Work Time. A period of time in a flexitime work schedule in which the employee is free to choose whether or not to be on the job.

Flexitime Work Schedules. A work schedule in which the employee is able to select his or her starting and quitting times within limits set by management.

The 4/5ths Rule. Discrimination is likely to occur if the selection rate for a protected group is less than 4/5ths of the selection rate for a majority group.

Functional Job Analysis (FJA). A job analysis method that attempts to identify what a worker does in performing a job in terms of data, people, and things.

Gainsharing Plans. An organizational-based plan such as the Scanlon Plan designed to permit employer-employee sharing in the benefits resulting from improved productivity, cost reductions, or quality improvements.

Genetic Screening. The use of blood and urine samples to determine whether a job applicant carries genetic traits that could predispose him or her to adverse health effects when exposed to certain chemicals or job-related toxins.

Grid OD. A program that involves six phases that is designed to improve organizational performance. The phases include determining the participants' leadership styles team building, intergroup development, and evaluation.

Grievance. A complaint about a job that creates dissatisfaction or discomfort for the worker.

Guaranteed Annual Wages. An agreement that guarantees regular employees a certain amount of money or hours of work. Its purpose is to provide some degree of economic security.

Halo Error. A rating error that occurs when a rater assigns ratings on the basis of an overall impression (positive or negative) of the person being rated.

Handicapped Person. Any person who has a physical or mental impairment that may limit his/her work or job activities.

Harshness Rating Error. The tendency to rate everyone low on the criteria being evaluated.

Health. The state of physical, mental, and social well-being.

Health Hazards. Those aspects of the work environment which slowly and cumulatively (and often irreversibly) lead to deterioration of an employee's health.

Hot Cargo Agreement. The employer permits union members to avoid working with materials that come from employers who have been struck by a union. This type of boycott is illegal.

Hot Stove Rule. A discipline program that is described in terms of touching a hot stove. There is an immediate burn, a warning system, consistency, and impersonal application of discipline.

Human Resource Information System (HRIS). A method used by an organization to collect, store, analyze, report, and evaluate information and data on people, jobs, and costs.

Human Resource Planning. The process that helps to provide adequate human resources to achieve future organizational objectives. It includes forecasting future needs for employees of various types, accompanying these needs with the present work force, and determining the numbers of types of employees to be recruited or phased out of the organization's employment group.

Immigration Reform and Control Act of 1986. A federal law that requires employers to screen every job applicant's eligibility for lawful employment.

Individual Retirement Account. A plan in which a person is able to save or invest for retirement up to $2,000 which is not subject to taxes. A person can also contribute to an IRA for a nonworking spouse at a rate of $2,250 for both of them.

Internal P/HRM Influences. Those internal (inside the organization) environmental forces, such as goals, organizational style, tasks, work group, and the leader's style of influencing.

Job. A group of positions that are similar in their duties, such as a computer programmer or compensation specialist.

Job Analysis. The process of defining a job in terms of tasks or behaviors and specifying the education, training, and responsibilities needed to perform the job successfully.

Job Analysis Information Format. A questionnaire that provides the core information about a job, job duties, and job requirements.

Job Characteristics Model. A mode of job design that is based on the view that three psychological states toward a job affect a person's motivation and satisfaction level. These states are experienced meaningfulness, experienced responsibility, and knowledge of results. A job's skill variety, identity, and task significance contribute to meaningfulness; autonomy is related to responsibility; and feedback is related to knowledge of results.

Job Description. The job analysis provides information about the job that results in a description of what the job entails.

Job Enrichment. A method of designing a job so that employees can satisfy needs while performing the job. The job characteristics model is used in establishing a job enrichment strategy.

Job Evaluation. The formal process by which the relative worth of various jobs in the organization is determined for pay purposes.

Job Family. A group of two or more jobs that have similar job duties.

Job Layoff. A condition that exists when no work is available and the employee is sent home, management views the no-work situation as temporary, and management intends to recall the employee.

Job Loss. A condition in which there is no work and the individual is sent home permanently.

Job Posting. A listing of job openings that includes job specifications, appearing on a bulletin board or in company publications.

Job Search. The set of activities a person (job candidate) initiates to seek and find a position that will be comfortable and rewarding.

Job Sharing. A situation in which two or more part-timers share one job. The workers are part time, but the job is full time.

Job Specification. The job analysis also results in the specification of what kind of traits and experience are needed to perform the job.

Labor Relations. The continuous relationship between a defined group of employees (e.g., a union or association) and an employer.

Landrum-Griffin Act. A labor law passed in 1959 that is referred to as the bill of rights of union members. It was designed to regulate and audit the internal affairs of unions.

Learning. The act by which a person acquires skills, knowledge, and abilities that result in a relatively permanent change in his or her behavior.

Leniency Rating Error. The tendency to rate everyone on every criteria high or excellent.

Life Events. The dramatic changes in a person's life that can contribute to stress.

Lockout. A management response to union pressures in which a skeleton crew of managerial personnel is used to maintain a workplace and the total plant is basically closed to employees.

Management Development. The process by which managers gain the experience, skills, and attitudes to become or remain successful leaders in their organizations.

Management Position Description Questionnaire (MPDQ). A checklist of 208 items related to concerns and responsibilities of managers.

Mentoring Relationships. A relationship between a junior and senior colleague that is considered by the junior person to be helpful in his or her personal development.

Midcareer Plateau. A point reached during the adult stage of life where a person feels stifled and not progressing as he or she had planned or would like.

Minimum Wage. The Fair Labor Standards Act of 1938, as amended, states that all employers covered by the law must pay an employee at least a minimum wage. In 1988 the minimum wage was $3.35 per hour.

Motivation. The attitudes that predispose a person to act in a specific goal-directed way. It is an internal state that directs a person's behaviors.

National Labor Relations Board. A government regulatory body that administers labor laws and regulations in the private and third sectors.

Nonexempt Employee. A person working

in a job that is subject to the minimum wage and overtime pay provisions of the Fair Labor Standards Act. Blue-collar and clerical workers are two major groups of nonexempt employees.

Occupational Safety and Health Act (1970). An act designed to protect the safety and health of employees. According to this act, employers are responsible for providing workplaces free from hazards to safety and health.

Occupational Safety and Health Administration (OSHA). The government agency responsible for carrying out and administering the Occupational Safety and Health Act.

Open Shop. A work situation in which neither a union is present nor is there a management effort to keep the union out.

Orientation. The P/HRM activity that introduces new employees to the organization and the employee's new tasks, superiors, and work groups.

Outplacement. Services provided by some firms to individuals who are permanently asked to leave. The services may include resume preparation help, counseling, and training.

Part-Time Employment. A job in which a person works less than 35 hours a week. For federal employees, 32 hours a week is the dividing line between full- and part-time work.

Pay Class. A convenient grouping of a variety of jobs that are similar in their work difficulty and responsibility requirements.

Pay Surveys. Surveys of the compensation paid to employees by all employers in a geographic area, an industry, or an occupational group.

Performance Analysis. A systematic procedure that is used to determine if training is needed to correct behavior deficiencies.

Performance Evaluation. The P/HRM activity that is used to determine the extent to which an employee is performing the job effectively.

Personal Bias Rating Error. The bias that a rater has about individual characteristics, attitudes, backgrounds, and so on influence a rating more than performance.

Personality. The characteristic way a person thinks and behaves in adjusting to his or her environment. It includes the person's traits, values, motives, genetic blueprint, attitudes, abilities, and behavior patterns.

Personnel/Human Resource Management (P/HRM). A function performed in organizations which facilitates the most effective use of people (employees) to achieve organizational and individual goals. Terms used interchangeably with P/HRM include *personnel, human resource management,* and *employee development.*

P/HRM Objectives. Objectives are the ends a department such as P/HRM is attempting to accomplish. Some of the specific P/HRM objectives are: (1) to provide the organization with well-trained and well-motivated employees; (2) to communicate P/HRM policies to all employees; and (3) to employ the skills and abilities of the work force efficiently.

P/HRM Policy. A general guide to decision making in important decision areas.

P/HRM Procedure. A procedure is a specific direction to action. It tells a person how to do a particular activity.

Point System. The most widely used job evaluation method. It requires evaluators to quantity the value of the elements of a job. On the basis of the job description or interviews with job occupants, points are assigned to the degree of various factors required to do the job.

Portability. The right of an employee to transfer pension credits accrued from one employer to another.

Position. The responsibilities and duties performed by an individual. There are as many positions as there are employees.

Position Analysis Questionnaire (PAQ). A structured questionnaire of 194 items used to quantitatively assess jobs. It assesses information input, mental processes, work out-put, relationships, job contacts, and various other characteristics.

Preferential Shop. The union is recognized and union members are given preference in some areas. These preferences are in violation of the Taft-Hartley Act.

Pregnancy Discrimination Act of 1978. This law makes it unlawful to discriminate on the basis of pregnancy, childbirth, or related medical conditions in employment-type decisions.

Preventive Programs. A program instituted within an organization to achieve a high level of employee wellness and to decrease health impairment costs. Programs typically involve health screening exams, stress testing, and physician recommendations.

Process Chart. A chart that displays how jobs are linked or related to each other.

Productivity. The output of goods and services per unit of input of resources used in a production process.

Progressive Pattern of Discipline. A discipline program that proceeds from less severe disciplinary actions (a discussion) to a very severe action (being discharged). Each step in the progression becomes more severe.

Ranking of Jobs. A job evaluation method often used in smaller organizations, in which the evaluator ranks jobs from the simplest to the most challenging—for example, clerk to research scientist.

Realistic Job Preview. A briefing that provides a job candidate with accurate and clear information about the attractive and unattractive features of a job. Being realistic so that expectations are accurate is the objective of a realistic job preview.

Recency of Event Rating Error. A rating tendency to use the most recent events to evaluate a ratee's performance instead

of using a longer, more complete time frame.

Recruitment. The set of activities an organization uses to attract job candidates who have the abilities and attitudes needed to help the organization achieve its objectives.

Red Circle Rates. A pay rate above a wage or salary level that is considered maximum for the job class. This means that the job is overpayed and overrated.

Rehabilitation Act of 1973. An act that is enforced by the Office of Federal Contract Compliance Programs (OFCCP), requires that all employers with government contracts of $2,500 or more must set up affirmative action programs for the handicapped.

Reliability. Refers to a selection technique's freedom from systematic errors of measurement or its consistency under different conditions.

Replacement Chart. A display or chart usually of technical, professional, and managerial employees. It includes name, title, age, length of service, and other relevant information on present employees.

Representation Election. A vote to determine if a particular group will represent the workers in collective bargaining.

Restricted Shop. A practice initiated by management to keep a union out without violating labor laws. A restricted shop is an attitude rather than a formal arrangement.

Right-to-Work Laws. A law that specifies that two persons doing the same job must be paid the same wage, whether or not they are union members. Nineteen states have right-to-work laws.

Role Playing. The acting out of a role by participants. Participants play act a role that others in the training session observe. Participants play an active part in role plays.

Safety Hazards. Those aspects of the work environment that have the potential of immediate and sometimes violent harm to an employee.

Selection. The process by which an organization chooses from a list of applicants the person or persons who best meet the selection criteria for the position available, considering current environmental conditions.

Sensitivity Training. A training technique that was first used in 1946. In it small groups of participants focus on emotions and how they feel about themselves and the group. Usually little structure is imposed by the trainer. The group members are encouraged to say or do what they feel.

Sexual Harassment. Unwelcome sexual attention that causes the recipient distress and results in an inability on the part of the recipient to effectively perform the job requirements.

Skill Variety. The degree to which the job requires a variety of different activities in carrying out the work, which involves the use of a number of an individual's skills and talents.

Skills Inventory. A list of the names, certain characteristics, and skills of the people working for the organization. It provides a way to acquire these data and makes them available where needed in an efficient manner.

Strategy. What an organization's key executives hope to accomplish in the long run.

Stress. A person's physical, chemical, and mental reactions to stressors or stimuli in the environment—the boss, co-workers, P/HRM policies, and so on.

Strike. An effort by employees to withhold their services from an employer in order to get greater concessions at the collective bargaining table.

Structured Interview. Interview that follows a prepared pattern of questions that were structured before the interview was conducted.

Taft-Hartley Act. A labor amendment of the Wagner Act, passed in 1947, that guaranteed employees bargaining rights and also specified unfair labor union practices that would not be permitted.

Task. A coordinated and aggregated series of work elements used to produce an output (units of production or service to a client).

Task Identity. The degree to which the job requires completion of a "whole" and identifiable piece of work—that is, doing a job from beginning to end with a visible outcome.

Task Significance. The degree to which the job has a substantial impact on the lives or work of other people—whether in the immediate organization or the external environment.

Team Building. A development method that attempts to improve the cooperation between teams.

Termination-at-Will. A condition under which an employer is free to terminate the employment relationship either for some specific reason or even no reason at all. In a growing number of courts, the employer's right to terminate at will is being challenged.

Training. The systematic process of altering the behavior of employees in a direction to increase organizational goals.

Transactional Analysis. A training technique designed to help the people participating better understand their own ego states and those of others; to understand the principles behind transactions; and to interact with others in a more comfortable way.

Two-Tiered Pay Plans. A pay structure in which the top pay for new employees is substantially lower than that for old (tenure) employees.

Type A Behavior Pattern. An action-emotion complex that can be observed in a person who is aggressive, in a struggle against time, competitive, and chronically impatient.

Unemployment Insurance. Established by the Social Security Act of 1935 to provide a subsistence payment to employees when they are between jobs. The employer and employee contribute to a fund which then pays when the employee is out of work.

Union. A group of employees who have joined together to achieve present and future goals that deal with employment conditions.

Union Shop. A situation in which an employee is required to join a union after being hired.

Union Steward. A union representative who works at the job site to solve disputes that arise in connection with the labor-management labor contract.

Vestibule Training. A trainee learns a job in an environment that closely resembles the actual work environment. For example, pilots at United Airlines train (vestibule) in a jet simulation cockpit.

Vesting. The right of employees to participate in a pension plan.

Wagner Act. A labor law passed in 1935 that was designed to encourage the growth of trade unions and restrain management from interfering with the growth.

Weighted Application Blank. An application form designed to be scored and used in making selection decisions.

Work Group. Two or more people who work together to accomplish a goal and who communicate and interact with each other.

Yellow-Dog Contracts. A contract (now illegal) that required that a person (such as a job applicant) would not join or form a union.

NAME INDEX

COMPANY INDEX

SUBJECT INDEX